A History of the
All-India Muslim League
1906–1947

A History of the
All-India Muslim League
1906–1947

M. Rafique Afzal

OXFORD
UNIVERSITY PRESS

OXFORD
UNIVERSITY PRESS

Oxford University Press is a department of the University of Oxford.
It furthers the University's objective of excellence in research, scholarship,
and education by publishing worldwide in

Oxford New York

Auckland Cape Town Dar es Salaam Hong Kong Karachi
Kuala Lumpur Madrid Melbourne Mexico City Nairobi
New Delhi Shanghai Taipei Toronto

With offices in

Argentina Austria Brazil Chile Czech Republic France Greece
Guatemala Hungary Italy Japan Poland Portugal Singapore
South Korea Switzerland Turkey Ukraine Vietnam

Oxford is a registered trademark of Oxford University Press
in the UK and in certain other countries

Published in Pakistan by Oxford University Press

© Oxford University Press 2013

The moral rights of the author have been asserted

Database right Oxford University Press (maker)

First published 2013

ISBN 978-0-19-906735-0

Typeset in Times
Printed in Pakistan by
Kagzi Printers, Karachi.
Published by
Ameena Saiyid, Oxford University Press
No. 38, Sector 15, Korangi Industrial Area, PO Box 8214,
Karachi-74900, Pakistan.

Dedicated to
those who sacrificed their lives in the struggle
for freedom and Pakistan

Contents

List of Tables

List of Tables

Preface

After the collapse of the Muslim rule in India, the Muslims dispersed into small units, scattered all over the Indian subcontinent with practically no platform for their mutual interaction. In fact, they virtually lost their identity as a community with no direction about their future. The All-India Muslim League provided them a forum at the all-India level where they could deliberate upon their common problems and unite themselves for the protection of their rights and interests. The history of the All-India Muslim League is the story of the Indian Muslims' struggle to define their objectives to protect their rights and interests and to mobilize themselves for their realization. It was through its forum that the Muslim leadership not only united the community but also interacted with the non-Muslim communities of India and the British authorities. The Muslim League in the process passed through several phases. Like the Indian National Congress, it started as an elitist party and was transformed into a mass organization in the final phase (1937–47) of its history. Starting with a fixed number of 400 members for the whole subcontinent including Burma and limiting that membership to those with an income of Rs 500/- per month, besides other strict conditions, it developed into a mass party with membership open to ordinary Muslims, with no other condition except adherence to its ideals, on payment of two annas as annual fee, which was half the subscription fee charged by the Congress from its members. At its inception, it demanded separate electorates, weightage (i.e. more seats than their proportion in population warranted) and reservation of seats in the legislatures and in government jobs for the Muslims, and after passing through different phases, it finally demanded a separate Muslim State in the 'Pakistan Provinces/units' of the north-west (Punjab, Sindh, NWFP and Balochistan) and north-east (Bengal and Assam) of the subcontinent, and 'adequate, effective and mandatory safeguards for the minorities in the partitioned States. Pakistan is a tribute to the subcontinent-wide struggle that it organized under the leadership of Quaid-i-Azam Mohammad Ali Jinnah. Its success was only partial: it secured Pakistan against formidable odds but it was not in the shape that it had demanded; and it could not ensure the 'safeguards' for the minorities that it had visualized.

The record of the All-India Muslim League is preserved primarily in three collections—Archives of the Freedom Movement (AFM), Quaid-i-Azam Papers (QAP) and the Shamsul Hasan Collection (SHC). The first two collections are available in the National Archives, Government of Pakistan, Islamabad, and the third collection has been acquired by the National Documentation Wing (formerly Centre) of the Cabinet Division, Government of Pakistan. SHC is better organized than the other two collections. That part of the AFM which Professor M.H. Siddiqi and his staff sifted when this collection was located at the University of Karachi is properly organized and bound in separate volumes; however, documents in some volumes are paginated and in a few others are numbered but not paginated. Hence some references to the AFM in the present study are to the number(s), and not to the page(s), of the document in a volume. Another part of the AFM lay un-sifted and unlisted in the National Archives in boxes at the time I consulted this collection. QAP are in separate files, most of which bear no table of contents. Two other important primary sources, relevant for the final phase of the AIML (1937–47), are the official collection of documents published by the Government of Great Britain in twelve volumes, edited by Nicholas Mansergh, E.W.R. Lumby, Penderal Moon and others entitled *The Transfer of Power* (London, 1970–82), and the collection of documents published by the Quaid-i-Azam Academy in seven volumes, compiled and edited by Dr Waheed Ahmad, entitled *The Nation's Voice* (Karachi, 1992–2003). I have extensively used these sources and other material listed in the bibliography. There might be more source-material on the AIML and Provincial Muslim Leagues in the private collections in Pakistan but individuals with limited resources cannot search for and use such material. Unlike India, no concerted and sustained effort has ever been made in Pakistan at the official level to collect this source-material and locate it at some central place in the provinces or at the centre.

I am grateful to Professor Ahmad Saeed for promptly responding to my queries. My thanks are due to Mohammad Ramzan, former Director of the National Archives, Government of Pakistan, and his staff, Sajid Mahmud in particular, for the assistance that they extended to me while I was consulting the AFM and QAP. I am thankful to Saleemullah Khan, former Director of the National Documentation Wing (formerly Centre), Government of Pakistan, for helping me in using the material available in the Wing. I am also thankful to the Library staff of the Department of History, Quaid-i-Azam University, for their cooperation and help.

M. Rafique Afzal
Islamabad

Abbreviations

AFM	Archives of the Freedom Movement
AGG	Agent to the governor-general
AICC	All India Congress Committee
AIHM	All-India Hindu Mahasabha
AIMC	All-India Muslim Conference
AIMEC	All-India Muslim Educational Conference
AIML	All-India Muslim League
AIMSF	All-India Muslim Students Federation
AMU	Aligarh Muslim University
CR	Chakravarti Rajagopalachari
DIR	Defence of India Rules
EC	Executive Council
ed.	editor/edited by
F.	File
FCR	Frontier Crimes Regulations
FMA	Freedom Movement Archives
Fs.	Files
HMG	His Majesty's Government
IAR	*Indian Annual Register*
ICS	Indian Civil Service
JUH	Jamiatul Ulama-i-Hind
JUI	Jamiatul Ulama-i-Islam
K.B.	Khan Bahadur
K.S.	Khan Sahib
KPK	Khyber Pakhtunkhwa
MLNG	Muslim League National Guard
MNG	Muslim National Guard
MP(s)	Member(s) of Parliament
MPA	Member of the Provincial Assembly
MSF	Muslim Students Federation
NDC	National Defence Council
NWF	North-West Frontier
NWFP	North-West Frontier Province

PML	Provincial/Presidency Muslim League
Prop.	Proprietor
QAP	Quaid-i-Azam Papers
RTC	Round Table Conference
SHC	Shamsul Hasan Collection
SSI	Secretary of State for India
TP	Transfer of Power
UK	United Kingdom
UP	United Provinces/Uttar Pradesh

Introduction

The failure of the Indian uprising of 1857–58 was the climax of the
decline of Muslim power in the Indian subcontinent. After that, the
British suppressed all the dissenting voices within India; and by the
1870s, they had brought under their jurisdiction directly or indirectly
the whole subcontinent including the remotest parts of Balochistan and
the tribal areas, bordering Afghanistan.[1] They kept under their control
vast landmass inhabited by diverse religious and ethnic communities,
which were out of proportion to their own numerical presence in India,
by using skilful methods of control and administration. They divided
the subcontinent broadly into two parts: British India that consisted of
presidencies, provinces, tribal areas and tribal agencies/territories; and
the princely states that numbered 562 of different sizes. All these units
had different administrative and revenue systems, which contributed to
the development of their distinct personalities and their inhabitants
often came to take pride in their separate identities. New units were
created out of relatively bigger units in British India or the boundaries
of different units were subjected to alteration for administrative and
political convenience, but the boundaries of the princely states once
accepted or created were rarely changed although the British formally
acquired parts of some of these states on lease for fixed periods.
Initially, there was no mechanism for any formal interaction among
these units or their people. The British Crown or its representative, the
viceroy/governor-general, provided them the only common link. While
British India was administered directly, the states were controlled
indirectly through residents and the tribal areas/agencies through
political agents. Institutions like the higher bureaucracy (Indian Civil
Service) and the armed forces ensured internal stability and security
from external threats. A fairly well-developed judicial and administrative
system provided stability at the lower level that had not existed in many
parts of the subcontinent for over a century prior to the British
takeover. The British introduced 'representative' institutions in a
rudimentary form through the Government of India Acts to enable the
Indians to participate in the political system and gain political

experience in the functioning of those institutions. For the Indian states, the British created the Chamber of Princes to provide a forum for their interaction and discussion of common issues but their internal system was left to the will and whims of their rulers.

After 1858, Muslims were divided in their response to the British ascendancy in India. Some Muslims perceived India as *darul harb* (the abode of war) and quite a few of them continued the armed resistance.[2] Gradually, all their isolated pockets of resistance within British India were eliminated, and their remnants were either exiled to the Andaman Islands or they themselves migrated to other Muslim lands or moved to sanctuaries in the North-West Frontier, the tribal areas, or stayed within India but devoting their energies to religious education of the Muslims and avoiding direct contact with the British.[3] The overwhelming majority of the Muslims accepted the British dominance and regarded India as *darul Islam* (the abode of peace) as there were no restrictions on them to practise the basic tenets of Islam. The British had put the blame for the uprising primarily on the Indian Muslims and subsequently looked upon any untoward political move on their part with suspicion. The 'savage British repression' scared many of them and created in them feelings of helplessness.[4] Simultaneously, they faced a challenge to their religious identity and survival from the onslaught of the Christian, and Hindu revivalist, missionaries whose target was often Islam and Prophet Muhammad (PBUH). They published scurrilous literature like Sir William Muir's *The Life of Mahomet* (1858) and Swami Dayanand's (1824–1883) *Satyarth Prakash* (1875) which deeply hurt Muslim sentiments. The *ulama* (Muslim scholars) responded to that challenge by producing polemical literature in the form of books such as Sir Sayyid Ahmad Khan's (1817–1898) *Essays on the Life of Muhammad* (PBUH) (1870) and Sayyid Amir Ali's (1849–1928) *A Critical Examination of the Life and Teachings of Mohammed* (1873) and *The Spirit of Islam* and religious tracts and by holding public debates with the missionaries. Muslim response to the challenge of British ascendancy and the missionaries in turn divided them into new schools of thought/sects like the Deobandis, Barelvis, Ahle Quran, Ahle Hadith and Ahmadis.[5] Each of these schools had its own *darul ulums* (educational institutions) to preserve Muslim religious identity and propagated Islam according to its viewpoint. These institutions proliferated with the passage of time as their alumni established more institutions wherever they settled in India. Leaders and alumni of these schools often indulged in recriminations and denunciation of one another that spoiled harmony among the Muslims at the grassroots and made them vulnerable to exploitation.

Education of the Muslims suffered the most with the British takeover. Loss of political power deprived their education of official patronage, and the diffusion of Muslim *waqfs* (endowments) choked the most important private source of financing Muslim educational institutions. Additionally, due to their own aversion to learn the English language and to acquire modern western knowledge mainly as a result of *fatawa* (sl. *fatwa*—religious injunctions) by religious luminaries, the Muslims as a community with a few exceptions deprived themselves of the educational facilities that the British provided to the Indians under their own auspices.[6] Conversely, non-Muslims had no such reservations to learn the English language or acquire modern education; they not only used the facilities that the British Indian government offered them for education but also benefitted from the institutions that they themselves established for education. Consequently, they rapidly moved far ahead of the Muslims educationally who could not compete with them in any field including the government jobs. Muslims gradually sank into social and economic degeneration and backwardness. At this critical juncture, Muslim social reformers came forward to rejuvenate the community. They exerted to remove Muslim reservations about the acquisition of modern education. The *anjumans* (associations) that they founded for this purpose promoted western education and social reform among the Indian Muslims. These *anjumans* were set up in big and small cities; more notable were those founded in Lahore, Amritsar, Bareilly, Bombay, Madras, Calcutta and Karachi. The schools and colleges that they established rendered invaluable service for the education of Muslims. They raised funds locally and their jurisdiction generally did not extend beyond the limits of their cities. The impact of Sir Sayyid for the promotion of modern education among the Muslims was broader and extensive. During his service as a judicial official under the British, he established schools wherever he was posted; the schools at Moradabad (1859) and Ghazipur (1864) are the notable examples. But his lasting contribution was the establishment of the School (1873) and then College (1877) at Aligarh, which after his death gained the status of a University (1920). The Aligarh College attracted students, and subsequently faculty, from different parts of India. It created an environment that cultivated uniformity of thinking among the Muslims on various issues and played a critical role in removing Muslim qualms about modern education and entry into service under the British. Its alumni who were known as the Aligarhians promoted the cause of education all over India.

The initial experience of the Indian Muslims in matters of organization was in the locally founded *anjumans* in different parts of India. The Mohammadan Literary Society (1865), founded by Nawab Abdul Latif (1828–1893) in Calcutta, had the area of its activities confined to Bengal. The National [from 1883 Central] Mohammadan Association (1877), which Amir Ali set up in Calcutta, had broader objectives and wider range of activity with branches outside Bengal than the Literary Society but it had a short life.[7] The Anglo-Mohammadan [later All-India Muslim] Educational Conference (1886), which Sir Sayyid and his supporters founded, provided the Muslims wider and long-lasting experience in organization. Its annual sessions in different cities of northern India made available to them a useful and convenient forum to interact at the all-India level and deliberate upon common problems. The All-India Muslim Educational Conference (AIMEC), set up a year after the Indian National Congress (1885), kept their attention and energies focused on education and social reform.[8] Sir Sayyid had advised the Muslims to keep themselves aloof from politics and refrain from joining or supporting the Congress demands. Several factors had moved him to give that advice. He believed that Muslim participation in the Congress activities would divert their focus from education to politics and generate in them emotionalism and radicalism which would move them on a path that would necessarily revive the British distrust about their activities. Such a development, he felt, might prove more disastrous for them than the 1857–58 uprising. Other factors were inherent in the Congress demands for competitive examinations and representative system of government. Sir Sayyid believed that Muslims in their prevailing state of education could not get their due share in government jobs through a system of competitive examinations, as they lagged far behind the Hindus in education. The representative system of governance, he argued, was suitable for a homogenous society and such homogeneity did not exist in India.[9] Earlier, he had opposed the Local Self-Government Bill in the Imperial Legislative Council in January 1883 because, in his view, it would induce the larger community to 'override the interests of the smaller community'.[10]

Sir Sayyid and his supporters succeeded in restraining the Muslims from joining the Congress. Some Muslims, however, did associate themselves with the Congress and two Muslim dignitaries, Badruddin

Tayyabji (1844–1906) and Rahimtulla Sayani (1857–1902), presided over its 1887 and 1897 annual sessions but Muslim attendance at the Congress sessions generally depended on the convenience of the place where the session was held. Sir Sayyid tried to provide the Muslims alternative forums for activity although, except for the AIMEC, these failed to develop into viable and durable organizational networks. His first venture was the non-communal United Indian Patriotic Association (1888), which was meant to inform the British people and parliament of the opposition of all the communities to the Congress and its demands. And when the Hindu revivalist activities in the form of the Ganpati festival, the anti-cow killing societies and the cult of Shivaji—to celebrate the exploits of the Maratha Hindu hero Shivaji (1627–80) who ambushed and killed the Mughal general, Afzal Khan—emerged in the 1890s, Sir Sayyid set up a purely Muslim organization, the Mohammadan Anglo-Oriental Defence Association of Upper India on 30 December 1893, to protect the political rights of the Muslims and to prevent them from agitation.[11] Like the Patriotic Association, its method of campaigning was confined to propaganda through newspapers and tracts; and its members were expressly forbidden not to hold public meetings. Unlike the AIMEC, the Patriotic Association failed to create Muslim interest in its objectives and could survive only for a short while. When in 1900, after the death of Sir Sayyid, Sir Anthony MacDonnell (1844–1925), the governor of the United Provinces, passed orders for the use of Hindi written in the Devanagari script as a language of the courts, the Muslims had no platform to protest against this decision.

Written language is an important medium of communication and interaction for the educated individuals and communities. Urdu, written in the Persian/Arabic script was developing into *lingua franca* of both Muslims and Hindus after the British discarded the Persian language. But in 1867, some influential Hindus in Benares (United Provinces) started a movement for the use of Hindi written in the Devanagari script in the courts. Muslims opposed the move and Sir Sayyid foresaw in it Hindu–Muslim conflict and division of the Indians on communal lines. The conflict on the use of language and script continued to simmer till it burst out in the open with the orders of the United Provinces provincial government issued under the instructions of Governor MacDonnell (on 18 April 1900) who had earlier been instrumental in replacing Urdu by Hindi in Bihar. Sir Sayyid's successors at Aligarh, Nawab Mehdi Ali, Mohsinul Mulk (1837–1907) and others, established the Central

Urdu Defence Association to defend the cause of Urdu and its script. The pro-Urdu movement and protest meetings that they organized were so strong that MacDonnell had to come down to Aligarh to threaten its sponsors that if they did not desist from their support of the movement, the British Indian government would discontinue its aid to the Aligarh college. He also warned Nawab Mohsinul Mulk to select either the secretaryship of the Aligarh college or the presidency of the pro-Urdu movement. The threat worked. Mohsinul Mulk did submit his resignation as secretary of the college but withdrew it under pressure from his associates and disengaged himself from the pro-Urdu movement. After his dissociation, the Urdu Defence Association wound up its work. At its last consultative meeting on 21 October 1901, which twenty-six members/representatives from the districts attended, it was decided to organize a 'Political Association', which would endeavour to remove any misunderstanding between the British government and the Muslims, explain the government orders to the Muslims, present the Muslim demands before the government, refrain from offending other communities and oppose the Congress demands for competitive examinations and representative system. Three members, Nawab Mushtaq Husain Wiqarul Mulk (1841–1917), Haji Mohammad Musa Khan (1872–1944) and Shaikh Mohammad Abdullah, were authorized to organize a meeting in Lucknow; and for that purpose, Muslims with an income of at least Rs 500/- per annum were to elect representatives.[12]

It was two years after the consultative meeting that Wiqarul Mulk and Musa Khan undertook to give practical shape to the idea of a political body in 1903. They laid the foundation of a 'Mohammadan Political Association', which was to have branches in the United Provinces and possibly in other provinces with its head office located in Khurja, Bulandshahar District (United Provinces), to protect the cultural and political rights of the Muslims. This association provided a sort of political continuity and served as a precursor of the All-India Muslim League. Wiqarul Mulk himself toured the districts in the United Provinces to establish its 'branches'; and he succeeded in setting up a network of branches in some ten districts which elected representatives for the projected meeting of the Muslim representatives in Lucknow. He also established contacts with prominent Muslims in the Punjab and Bombay for their participation in the activities of the Political Association. The issues that were raised and discussed in the organizational meetings in the districts were: inability of the Muslims to get representation in the legislative councils; protection of the Urdu language; Muslim underrepresentation in government services; promotion of education among the Muslims; and establishment of a Muslim university at Aligarh. However, the heated controversy about the objectives of the Political Association in the press and hurdles created by the government officials in the holding of its meetings killed the initiative.[13] After a spurt of activity for a few months, the Political Association discontinued its organizational work and disappeared from the scene. The next move for a purely Muslim political body was the founding of the All-India Muslim League and the dormant branches of the Political Association were co-opted as its branches.

NOTES

1. P. Hardy, *The Muslims of British India*, New Delhi, 1998, pp. 62–91.
2. For *fatwa* declaring India a *darul harb* issued by Shah Abdul Aziz (1746–1824) and the *ulama* that followed him, see M. Naeem Qureshi, *Pan-Islam in British India: The Politics of the Khilafat Movement, 1918–1924*, Karachi, 2008 (Rev. ed.), pp. 8–9.
3. For an account of one affected, see Mohammad Jafar Thanesari, *Tawarikh-i-Ajib, Ya'ni, Kala Pani*, Karachi, 1962.
4. Hardy, *Muslims of British India*, pp. 61 and 70–71.
5. For details about these schools, see Shaikh Mohammad Ikram, *Mauj-i-Kausar*, Lahore, 1968; and S.M. Ikram, *Modern Muslim India and the Birth of Pakistan (1858–1951)*, Lahore, 1970 (Second rev. ed.), pp. 111–18; Barbara D. Metcalf, *Islamic Revival in British India: Deoband, 1869–1900*, New Jersey, 1982; and Usha Sanyal, *Devotional Islam and Politics in British India: Ahmad Riza Khan Barelwi and his Movement, 1870–1920*, New York, 1996. In 1974, the National Assembly of Pakistan declared the Ahmadis as a non-Muslim minority.
6. Mohammad Noman, *Muslim India: Rise and Growth of the All-India Muslim League*, Allahabad, 1942, pp. 46 and 67.
7. K.K. Aziz, *Amir Ali—His Life and Work*, Lahore, 1968, p. 585.
8. Hardy, *Muslims of British India*, pp. 91–99.
9. Sayyid Ahmad Khan, *Akhiri Mazamin*, Lahore, 1898, p. 46.
10. R. Coupland, *The Indian Problem: Report on the Constitutional Problem of India, 1883–1936*, Part I, London, 1944, pp. 155–56.
11. *Sedition Committee Report*, Calcutta, 1918, p. 1.
12. Archives of the Freedom Movement, National Archives, Government of Pakistan, Islamabad (henceforth cited as AFM), vol. 1. Some documents in the AFM volumes are paginated while other documents bear numbers with no pagination.
13. Ibid.; and Sharif Al Mujahid, *Muslim League Documents, 1900–1947, Volume I (1900–1908)*, Karachi, 1990, pp. 20–40.

PART ONE

1

Formation of the Party, 1906–1910

Three years after the dormancy of the Mohammadan Political Association, the Muslims of India made another move to have a purely Muslim political organization. Several factors influenced their decision. More important among them were the general disillusionment of the educated Muslim youth with the docile policies of their leaders, the inability to get due share in government jobs, the ambition of the politically conscious Muslims to participate in active politics, the unrest caused by the official moves against Urdu and the Bengali Hindu militant agitation against the partition of Bengal (1905) that had benefitted the Bengali Muslims. The immediate and most important reason that activated them into action was the announcement on 20 July 1906 made by the secretary of state for India, Lord Morley (1839–1923), in his speech on the Indian budget in the House of Commons that he would consider any proposal for reform coming from the Government of India. Lord Minto (1845–1914) concurred with his views. This time again, Mohsinul Mulk took the initiative but unlike his reaction to Governor MacDonald's anti-Urdu move, he was now cautious and more calculated than before. Muslims had been dissatisfied particularly with their inadequate representation in the legislative councils and the mode of selection of their representatives; in the United Provinces, where they were 13 per cent, they did not have a single seat by joint electorates.[1] Mohsinul Mulk wanted to articulate and represent the Muslim viewpoint on this and other issues that concerned the Muslim community. Instead of putting pressure on the government in support of the Muslim demands from a public platform, he explored the possibility of presenting the demands directly to the viceroy in a memorial. He approached Lord Minto through W.A.J. Archbold (1865–1929), the principal of the Aligarh college, to get his reaction to the idea of a Muslim deputation presenting a memorandum to the viceroy containing Muslim demands. Minto after consulting the authorities in London agreed to receive the deputation.[2]

After positive response from the viceroy, Mohsinul Mulk, Nawab Imadul Mulk Husain Bilgrami (1844–1926) sat down to draft the memorial and incorporated in it the points that they received from Muslims of different provinces.[3] Then, they drew up a list of thirty-five prominent Muslims; from United Provinces 11, Punjab 8, Bengal 6, Bihar 3, Bombay 3, Madras 1, Sindh 1, Central Provinces 1 and Hyderabad (Deccan) 1, who were to compose the deputation. On 1 October 1906, led by Aga Sir Sultan Mohammad (1877–1957), the young spiritual head of the Ismailis, the deputation met the viceroy in Simla and presented the memorial. The deputation demanded that the Muslims should have representation at all levels of government— legislative councils, municipalities and district boards—through separate electoral colleges in proportion commensurate with not only their numerical strength but also their 'political importance' and their 'contribution to the defence of the Empire'. Besides these demands, they called for the appointment of Muslim judges in the high courts and chief courts, Muslim representation in the senates and syndicates of the Indian universities, Muslim share in the Viceroy's Executive Council whenever Indians were taken on it, and reservation of due share for the Muslims in the gazetted, subordinate and ministerial services of all the provinces. Minto in his reply welcomed the 'representative character' of the deputation and assured its members that the political rights and interests of the Muslims would be safeguarded in any administrative and constitutional reforms.[4]

(A) FOUNDATION

The deputationists realized the need for an all-India Muslim political party to pursue the demands that they had made in the memorial.[5] They resolved to deliberate on this issue in Dhaka, where Muslim leaders from all over the subcontinent were to meet for the annual meeting of the All-India Muslim Educational Conference on 27–29 December 1906.[6] Those Muslims who were educated at the Aligarh college or otherwise associated with it took the initiative. Again, Mohsinul Mulk coordinated their efforts. There was consensus among them about the need for a Muslim political party; minor differences were on its nature and direction. The party was to guide the energies of the 'young restless Muslim radicals' into right channels and prevent them from joining the Congress or adopting a course of action that might damage Muslim interests. Nawab Wiqarul Mulk's 'Mohammadan Political Association', whose organization at the all-India level was still at the embryonic stage provided the political continuity. Aga Khan supported the move from behind the scene and, on Mohsinul Mulk's advice, circulated a letter among the deputationists for transforming themselves into a regular 'committee' to follow up the demands made in the memorial. He tried to tone down the anti-Congress feelings of some of the co-founders. Nawab Sir Salimullah (1871–1915), the host of the Muslim political gathering at Dhaka and an enthusiastic advocate of a Muslim political party, put forward an elaborate proposal.[7] Within the broad objectives of the party he wanted to use it to safeguard the newly created Muslim majority province of Eastern Bengal and Assam and frustrate the Hindu-led militant movement against the partition of Bengal, which bore anti-Muslim overtones. One month before the foundation meeting, he circulated a detailed scheme of an all-India organization, for which he proposed the name of 'All-India Muslim Confederacy'.[8] The British Indian government, contrary to its policy towards the formation of a purely all-India Muslim political party that it had adopted in 1901, did not put any hurdles, perhaps calculating that Muslim emotions would be channelled into chartered territories rather than revolutionary channels like those of the Bengali Hindu revolutionaries. However, there were still apprehensions in some British official quarters that the new party might provide a platform to the 'radical' Muslim youth and encourage them to develop 'pan-Islamism in direct hostility to Christendom'.[9]

Muslim leaders began formal deliberations to form a Muslim political party in Dhaka on 30 December 1906, a day after the conclusion of the All-India Muslim Educational Conference meeting. On Salimullah's motion, Wiqarul Mulk chaired the meeting. The participants, who were drawn from all parts of the subcontinent, included Muslim landed, commercial, educational and professional (retired) elite.[10] Prior to the meeting, in the three-day meeting of the Educational Conference, they had thoroughly debated the issue of a Muslim political party and its possible objectives and reached a consensus. Wiqarul Mulk, in a brief address, urged unity in the Muslim ranks, moderation and tolerance of the sister community, and loyalty to the rulers. Then, he invited Salimullah to move the main resolution that envisaged the formation of the All-India Muslim League (a) to promote among the Muslims of India feelings of loyalty to the British government, and to remove any misconception that may arise as to the intention of government with regard to any of its measures; (b) to protect and advance the political rights and interests of the Muslims of India, and to respectfully represent their needs and aspirations to the government; and (c) to prevent the rise, among the Muslims of India, of any feeling of hostility towards other communities, without prejudice to the other aforementioned objects of the League. This resolution was passed unanimously. Thus, the All-India Muslim League was founded, which was the logical culmination of the developments that had begun with the introduction of 'representative' institutions in India. The party was named 'All-India Muslim League' by consensus. The fact that political organizations bearing the name 'Muslim League' had already been formed and were functioning at least in Bihar and Punjab influenced this decision.[11] Salimullah did not press for naming the new party as 'All-India Muslim Confederacy', the name that he had proposed in his circular letter. The All-India Muslim League witnessed many ups and downs in its history but none ever seriously thought of changing its name. During the Khilafat movement, the Leaguers even rejected a proposal to have an Arabic name—Jamiatul Siyasat al-Hind—for the All-India Muslim League. Again, in 1932–33, they aborted a move to merge the All-India Muslim League into the All-India Muslim Conference and change its name.

At the time of its foundation, the All-India Muslim League appointed an unwieldy sixty-member provisional committee, with powers to co-opt additional members, to frame a constitution within four months; Mohsinul Mulk and Wiqarul Mulk were its members/joint secretaries. The committee members represented different regions of the Indian subcontinent and Burma, which was then part of the British Indian empire.[12] The provisional committee was authorized to convene a meeting of 'representative Indian Muslims' at a suitable place and time to consider and adopt a constitution. One doesn't know the number of co-opted members but a meeting was called at Bankipur when a draft constitution was ready. No decision could be reached at this meeting because the Leaguers in the provinces had sent in, by post, divergent opinions on the draft constitution. The provisional committee decided to refer the draft constitution to its first annual session, which was held in Karachi on 29–30 December 1907. At the Karachi session, the League appointed a more representative 'special committee', consisting of members of the provisional committee and those members of the Simla deputation who were present in Karachi plus three specially invited delegates, to consider the draft.[13] This special committee finalized the draft constitution that was adopted at the first session in

Karachi on 30 December 1907. However, the session adjourned before it could complete all its business. The adjourned session met in Aligarh on 18–19 March 1908, where further corrections and amendments were made in the constitution of the All-India Muslim League.[14]

(B) FORMATION OF THE PARTY

(*i*) *Central League*. The constitution provided an organizational structure that reflected the political experience of its framers and the political needs of the Muslim community at that time according to their perception. It restricted membership exclusively to the Muslim elite by limiting its maximum strength at 400 for the whole subcontinent including Burma, and its strength was raised to 800 in January 1910, and by charging prohibitive registration/admission and annual fees. At the Karachi annual session, it was decided that every member should pay a non-refundable registration fee of Rs 50 and an annual fee of Rs 25 in advance within six weeks of his election as a member. At the Aligarh session, the time for the payment of annual fee was relaxed but even then many quite well-educated and well-off members were unable or unwilling to pay these fees;[15] and in January 1910, the annual subscription was reduced to Rs 20 per annum, payable in advance in four equal instalments. A member was required to pay his dues after his election. One who did not pay two instalments in succession could lose his membership. It was required that a member should be a British Indian Muslim of at least 25 years of age, having spoken and written proficiency in any of the Indian languages. The requirement that a member must be a Muslim was added at the Aligarh session; the rules as approved at the Amritsar session did not have this provision. Another condition was that a candidate for membership must have an income of at least Rs 500 per month; parent's income of that level was acceptable. The central committee, renamed as the council in January 1910, could give exemption under special circumstances and waive any of the conditions for membership. At least 50 and not exceeding 200 members were to be appointed by nomination in the meeting that was to approve the party constitution. The first group of members consisted of thirty-three surviving members of the Simla deputation; the second group was of members of the provisional committee that was appointed at Dhaka in December 1906 to draft the constitution; and the third group comprised the three delegates who had been specially invited to the Karachi session. The total strength of these three groups came to seventy-one. After that, the provincial Leagues or, in their absence, a divisional, district, or town League, if affiliated to the All-India Muslim League, could recommend a person for membership by election. The central committee/council had the final authority to approve membership and could also elect members directly where no such bodies existed in a province.

The framers of the constitution divided the Indian subcontinent and Burma into regions; some regions were designated according to their own conception and termed as 'provinces'. The original constitution distributed the 400 members among them, as shown in Table 1:1.

Table 1.1: Distribution of the AIML members by region

East Bengal and Assam*	70
West Bengal, Bihar and Orissa*	70
United Provinces of Agra (45) and Awadh (25)	70
Punjab	70
Bombay (30) including Sindh (10)	40
Madras	25
NWFP (10) and Balochistan (5)	15
Central Provinces, Berar and Ajmer*	15
Burma	10
British Indians residing in the princely states or elsewhere	15
Total	400

* In these cases, the allocations were not divided among the 'sub-provinces'.

This proportion was maintained when the membership strength was raised to 800. The provincial allocations were made on the basis of proportion of Muslims in the population and their education, financial position and 'social status'. The party was authorized to revise the provincial allocations after every decennial census. A member was elected for a five-year term and was eligible for re-election. No member could in principle exercise his rights unless he had paid his dues. The central committee/council could remove its own member or that of the All-India Muslim League if three-fourth of its members were of the opinion that his presence would damage the party objectives or injure its cause; and this could be done after giving the member an opportunity to explain his position. Such a decision was, however, subject to approval at the annual session. Similarly, the All-India Muslim League could directly remove a member or an office-bearer by a three-fourth majority of its members on the ground that his presence was 'prejudicial to the interests' of the party. Membership enrolment began after the Aligarh session. It was a slow process. It never reached the required strength, whether the limit was 400 or 800. In December 1908, the total membership was 177; at the end of 1909, it was 182; and a year later, it had risen to 270. The number of members who regularly paid their subscription was even less than the total registered members. For instance, in 1911, the total number of members had risen to 700 but only 272 of them had paid their dues; those who had paid their dues were from: (West) Bengal 37, East Bengal and Assam 21; Punjab 59; North-West Frontier Province (NWFP; now Khyber Pakhtunkhwa) 1; United Provinces 85; Bombay 16; Madras 21; Central Provinces and Berar 13; Native States 6; and Burma 13. The non-paying members participated in the activities of the All-India Muslim League although in principle they could not exercise this right unless they had cleared their dues. The honorary secretary used to notify the list of registered members at least eight weeks before the annual session. The quorum for the annual sessions was one-fifth of the total registered members and for the other sessions it was one-eighth. Proxy or written votes by members were not allowed for the annual session. The party could amend its rules and regulations by a two-third majority of its members only at the annual session according to a prescribed procedure.

The central committee/council was the highest executive organ of the All-India Muslim League, designed to promote its aims and objectives, and implement its programme. The party constitution had no provision for a working committee. At first, the central committee consisted of thirty to forty members, who were elected by ballot from amongst the members and included the office-bearers as *ex-officio* members. Its strength was raised to forty at the Aligarh session. The members were apportioned to each province as far as possible on the basis of ratio fixed in the case of members from various provinces [Table 1.2].

Table 1.2: Ratio of the members of the AIML Central Committee/Council according to provincial distribution

East Bengal and Assam	7
West Bengal, Bihar and Orissa	7
UP of Agra and Awadh	7
Punjab	7
Bombay including Sindh	4
Madras	2.5
NWFP and Balochistan	1.5
CP, Berar and Ajmer	1.5
Burma	1
Native States	1.5
Total	40

Fractions in the four cases were settled after a heated discussion. The decision was that Madras should have two members; NWFP and Balochistan one; and Central Provinces, Berar and Ajmer two. As for the remaining one seat, Yaqub Hasan (1875–1940) proposed, and Mian Mohammad Shafi (1869–1932) seconded, that it should go to the NWFP and Balochistan. However, Sayyid Zahur Ahmad (d. 1942) moved an amendment, seconded by Wiqarul Mulk, to the effect that it should be given to United Provinces. Wiqarul Mulk argued that United Provinces was the centre of the All-India Muslim League's 'operations' and the increased strength would help in securing quorum for the meetings of the central committee. Accepting this argument, Mian Shafi pointed out that he and the mover would not press the motion if the house assured that this was a temporary arrangement, specially necessitated by the present needs of the party. After Wiqarul Mulk's assurance that it was a temporary arrangement, Zahur Ahmad's motion was adopted.[16] The All-India Muslim League was to perform functions of the central committee till it was formally constituted. The first central committee was elected at the Aligarh session. At the time of its election, one member proposed that the central committee should be elected for only one year as the process of establishing provincial Muslim Leagues was still incomplete. But this proposal was rejected by twelve to ten votes; after that, members from various provinces were elected. The first central committee, in addition to the office-bearers, consisted of the following members:

Table 1.3: Members of the first central committee of the AIML

United Provinces of Awadh and Agra	Sayyid Nabiullah, Zahur Ahmad, Munshi Ihtesham Ali, Nawab Wiqarul Mulk, Habibur Rahman Khan, Sahibzada Aftab Ahmad Khan (1867–1930), Muzammilullah Khan (1864–1938), and Sayyid Abdur Rauf.
Punjab	Mian Shah Din, Khwaja Yusuf Shah, Mian Mohammad Shafi, Shaikh Abdul Aziz, Shaikh Abdul Qadir, Mian Fazli Husain, and Mian Hissamuddin.
Bombay	Sir Adamji Pirbhai, Rafiuddin Ahmad (1865–1954) and A.M.K. Dehlavi.
Madras	Yaqub Hasan and Ghulam Mohammad Mohajir.
West Bengal, Bihar and Orissa	Nawab Amir Hasan Khan, Nawab Naseer Husain Khan Khayal, Mirza Shujaat Ali Beg (1860–1925), Sayyid Ali Imam, Nawab Sarfraz Husain Khan, Mazharul Haq (1866–1929), and Abdur Rahim.
East Bengal and Assam	Nawab Salimullah Khan, Sayyid Nawab Ali Choudhury, Maulvi Abdul Majid, and Sayyid Mohammad Husain.
NWFP and Balochistan	Mian Abdul Aziz.
Central Provinces, Berar and Ajmer	H.M. Malak.
Burma	A.S. Rafiqi.
Native States	Abdul Majid Khan (1870–1917) (Patiala) and Mohammad Ali (Baroda).

However, members emphasised the need for the formation of League branches at the provincial and district levels.

First constitution of the All-India Muslim League provided for one president, six vice-presidents to represent various provinces, one honorary secretary and two joint secretaries. In January 1910, the party by an amendment raised the number of vice-presidents; now their strength could range from twelve to twenty. All the office-bearers were elected for a three-year term at an all-India session. Any person elected once was eligible for re-election for any number of terms. A candidate for an office was required to send in his nomination, proposed and seconded by two members, at least six weeks before the meeting scheduled for election to the honorary secretary who was to forward these nominations to the members for opinion four weeks before the all-India session. Members present in the session were to vote by ballot. Those members who were unable to attend the session had the right to send in their votes to the honorary secretary in writing. Their votes were counted along with the votes of the members present in the session for the election of office-bearers. The All-India Muslim League held the first election of its office-bearers at the Aligarh session. The Aga Khan was unanimously elected president. Wiqarul Mulk would have been a consensus candidate for the office of honorary secretary but he declined to accept this responsibility because of his ill health and his duties as secretary of the Aligarh college that he had assumed on the death of Mohsinul Mulk on 16 October 1907.[17] On his refusal, Dr Sayyid Hasan Bilgrami (d. 1915) was elected honorary secretary. Hasan was brother of Nawab Husain Bilgrami, and was then member of the secretary of state's council. He had recently retired from the Indian Medical Service and was planning to leave for England. Maulana Mohammad Ali (1878–1931), in his comments on the agenda items, did write that Hasan Bilgrami's election as the honorary secretary would be unfair although he gave no reasons for his comments. Perhaps he had Hasan's planned departure for England in mind, and he proposed the names of Sayyid Ali Imam (1866–1932) as honorary secretary and Sayyid Hasan Imam (1871–1933) as joint secretary. However, he did not press for their election. Haji Mohammad Musa Khan, a trustee of the Aligarh college, was elected joint secretary; the office of second joint secretary remained vacant.[18] Hasan Bilgrami left for England three days after his election as honorary secretary and stayed there till 1913. Musa Khan officiated as honorary secretary with a limited staff till Hasan sent in his resignation in late 1909, and Mohammad Aziz Mirza (1865–1912), who retired from service in the Hyderabad state, was elected to that office in January 1910.

(ii) Provincial Muslim Leagues. The All-India Muslim League needed properly organized and formally affiliated provincial Muslim Leagues, with branches at the district level, for the completion of its organization. The area of a provincial Muslim League normally corresponded with the boundaries of a province as determined by the British Indian government. However, certain All-India Muslim League-designated 'provinces' consisted of several 'sub-provinces'; for example, this was the case with West Bengal, Bihar and Orissa province. In these provinces, the Leagues in the 'sub-provinces' had the status of provincial Leagues. The provincial Muslim Leagues drew up their own constitutions but those had to be in conformity with the constitution of the All-India Muslim League and these constitutions came into force only after their approval by the central League. Except for the fixed number of its representatives on the central committee/council, a provincial Muslim League was free to determine its structure, the

number of its office-bearers and the strength of its executive committee. In fact, the number of office-bearers varied in different provincial Leagues. The formation of provincial Muslim Leagues was an arduous process, which generated political activity that the Indian Muslims had never witnessed in the past. The interaction among the Muslims of various provinces was quite unprecedented, fostering in them communal cohesion and all-India identity. It made them aware of their problems, which they tried to resolve from the platform of the League. Some provincial Muslim Leagues were organized immediately after the adoption of the All-India Muslim League constitution but others took some time; and quite a few others sought help from the central League to organize a branch League. Infighting was a common phenomenon among the Leaguers in the provinces, as holding of its membership and office was indicative of the social status of an individual.

The Punjab and Bihar provincial Muslim Leagues were the first two branches that were organized and affiliated with the All-India Muslim League. In fact, Mian Mohammad Shafi had established a 'Muslim League' in Lahore in June 1906, seven months before the foundation of the All-India Muslim League.[19] This party was merged into the Punjab provincial Muslim League that was formally organized on 5 December 1907, with Mian Mohammad Shah Din (1868–1918) as its president and Mian Shafi as secretary; by that date, it claimed to have branches in ten districts including the district of Lahore.[20] Wiqarul Mulk welcomed its formation. However, a conflict arose in the Punjab when Mian Fazli Husain (1877–1936) asked the All-India Muslim League at the Karachi session to affiliate the Punjab Muslim League that he and his colleagues had established in Lahore in February 1906. The All-India Muslim League deferred a decision on the issue till the Aligarh session. These two rival Leagues divided the Muslim political and educated circles in the Punjab, especially the Anjuman-i-Himayat-i-Islam, and the students and staff of the Islamia college, Lahore.[21] The conflict was taken to the Aligarh session, where Mian Shafi proposed 24 names and Mian Fazli Husain 18 names for election as members on the 24 remaining seats allocated to the Punjab. In total, 35 members had to be elected from the Punjab. Eleven had already been elected— six of group one (those of the Simla deputation), three of group two (those elected in Dhaka) and two of group three (those elected in Karachi).[22] The meeting at Aligarh requested Sahibzada Aftab Ahmad Khan and Shaikh Mohammad Abdullah (1874–1965) to mediate between the two Leagues. Fazli Husain demanded ten members on the executive committee of the Punjab provincial Muslim League, one vice-president, one joint secretary and one assistant secretary. His demands were accepted and the Punjab provincial Muslim League was asked to amend its constitution, where necessary, to accommodate these demands. Following this understanding, on Mian Shafi's motion, seconded by Fazli Husain, the All-India Muslim League unanimously elected members from the Punjab. After that, it was resolved that the Punjab provincial Muslim League 'in its present united form' should be taken as the provincial League established by the All-India Muslim League.[23] If this was the content of the 'understanding' that was arrived at Aligarh between the two leaders, it did not last for long.

Both the leaders, Mian Shafi and Fazli Husain, on their return to the Punjab interpreted the 'understanding' differently. According to Fazli Husain, the All-India Muslim League had decided to establish a provincial League in accordance with its newly framed rules and regulations, and members of two Leagues would be considered members of the Punjab provincial Muslim League. An organizing committee of total 35 members—10 proposed by him and 25 by Mian Shafi—was to organize the provincial Muslim League. He asked Wiqarul Mulk to send him a copy of the resolution that had settled the conflict between the two Punjab Leagues.[24] On the other hand, Mian Shafi believed that at the Aligarh session Fazli Husain's League had been merged into his provincial League and wanted Fazli Husain and his colleagues to accept this merger.[25] He requested Wiqarul Mulk to advise Fazli Husain to accept the Aligarh settlement to this effect.[26] The conflict was not resolved till October 1908. Apparently the central League sided with Mian Shafi's interpretation of the Aligarh settlement. Fazli Husain neither received any response to his letters to Wiqarul Mulk and the central honorary secretary nor did he initially accept Mian Shafi's interpretation of the Aligarh settlement. Meanwhile, the Punjab League led by Mian Shafi continued to function as the recognised branch of the All-India Muslim League. Eventually, Fazli Husain accepted the *fait accompli* and temporarily withdrew from active politics. But he did write to the central honorary secretary that the Punjab League existed without any rules and regulations but he had 'no complaints as he had no desire to play any greater role in political matters'.[27] Soon after, in October 1908, Mian Shah Din was appointed judge of the Punjab chief court and Nawab Fateh Ali Khan Qizilbash (1862–1923) replaced him as president of the provincial Muslim League. The Punjab League gradually broadened its base, which was reflected in its political activities and party elections on 29 March 1910, when Fateh Ali Qizilbash and Mian Shafi were re-elected as its president and secretary, respectively. The party also elected eight vice-presidents—Nawab Mohammad Ali Qizilbash, Nawab Zulfikar Ali Khan, Nawab Rustam Ali Khan, Malik Umar Hayat (1875–1944), Nawab Ibrahim Ali Khan of Kunjpura, Khwaja Yusuf Shah (1849–1926), Seth Adamji Mamoonji, and Ahmad Shah, three joint secretaries—Dr Mohammad Iqbal (1877–1938), Shaikh Abdul Aziz (1867–1941) and Maulvi Mahbub Alam (1863–1933), one assistant secretary—Mirza Jalaluddin—and one financial secretary—Shaikh Gulab Din. The All-India Muslim League acknowledged the Punjab League as its most active branch although some Leaguers in the Punjab questioned this assessment.[28] Fazli Husain's withdrawal from active politics was only temporary. He staged a comeback in the politics of the Punjab provincial Muslim League and All-India Muslim League after consolidating his position in the Punjab.

The Bombay presidency consisted of three parts: northern, central and southern. Deccan comprised its central and southern parts and Gujarat formed the northern part. In April 1907, the process of organizing a League in Deccan began with the appointment of a provisional committee. After fourteen months, in August 1908, the Deccan provincial Muslim League was formally established with branches in the districts. The Aga Khan was elected its president and Rafiuddin Ahmad secretary, with party headquarters in Poona. The party also elected six vice-presidents: Sir Adamji Pirbhai (1845–1913), Sir Karimbhai Ibrahim, Ghulam Mohammad Bhurgari (1878–1924), the Thakore Sahib of Amod, the Nawab of Wai, and Qasim Ali Jairajbhai Pirbhai[29] The following month, it presented an address to the governor in regard to the Muslim demands. Earlier, a League was established in Karachi to facilitate the holding of the first annual session of the All-India Muslim League in that city in December 1907, although the Sindh Muslim League had not yet been established. By March 1909, the Bombay presidency Muslim League had come into existence by extending the League to Gujarat as well.[30] The Bombay League gradually wiped away the influence that pro-Congress Sayyid Badruddin Tayyabji (1844–1906) had exercised on the Muslim youth of the presidency, making the atmosphere in Bombay congenial for Aligarh and the All-India Muslim League.[31] The Aga Khan and Rafiuddin Ahmad continued to hold the offices of president and secretary, respectively. The Bombay presidency Muslim League was the richest provincial branch. At one meeting presided over by the Aga Khan in October 1910, donations and subscriptions amounting to Rs 12,000 were announced, out of which Rs 5000 were collected on the spot.[32] The collection of this much amount was a rare phenomenon at the time even for the All-India Muslim League. The Bombay presidency Muslim League, in a meeting in October 1910 chaired by the Aga Khan, welcomed the appointment of Amir Ali on the Privy Council and of Abbas Ali Beg (1859–1932) on the India Council. It also urged the government to levy cess on the *jagirdars* and *zamindars* of Sindh to fund the secondary and higher education of the Muslims but nothing came out of that resolution.

The formation of the Madras presidency Muslim League was delayed due to differences on the election of party president and secretary although the Muslims of Madras, at a public meeting in February 1908, had decided to establish a League. Nawab Syed Mohammad (1867–1919), a moderate long-time Congressman and chairman of several social organizations of Madras, was a candidate for the office of president. Several Leaguers supported his candidature; among his supporters were Mian Shafi of the Punjab and Abdur Rahim (1863–1947) of Bengal.[33] But one thing went against him. The Congress was holding its annual session in Madras that year and he was chairing its reception committee. Many Leaguers did not like this; Yaqub Hasan wrote to Wiqarul Mulk: 'You may rest assured that even in this corner of India we are too well versed in the teachings of our revered great leader the late Sir Syed to be led astray by any half-hearted new converts to our political creed.'[34] Meanwhile, other aspirants for the office of president came forward. The ensuing controversy blocked immediate decision. Two rival groups emerged in the Madras League that held separate meetings in August and September 1908: one group decided to defer the process of elections till early 1909, i.e. after the Congress session;[35] and the other group established a 'Central Muslim Association of Southern India' to safeguard the interests of the Muslims of Madras and planned to get it recognized as a branch of the All-India Muslim League.[36] However, as a result of mediation by concerned individuals, the two groups agreed to the appointment of a 'representative committee', which, on 17 October 1908, unanimously resolved to establish the Madras presidency Muslim League.[37] Ghulam Mohammad Ali Khan (b. 1882), the Prince of Arcot, was elected president and Mohammad Mahmud Khan (b.

1877) secretary.[38] In 1910, on the latter's resignation, Yaqub Hasan was elected secretary of the Madras presidency Muslim League.

Bengal had two separate provincial Muslim Leagues, one for East Bengal and Assam and the other for West Bengal. The process of their formation was quite slow. In April 1907, a provisional committee was set up, which, in July 1908, formed the East Bengal and Assam provincial Muslim League, with Khwaja Kazimuddin Ahmad Siddiqi (1876–1937) as president and Nawab Salimullah as secretary. It presented a welcome address to the lieutenant governor, demanding a high court in Dhaka, and asked the All-India Muslim League to pass a resolution in support of the partition of Bengal. However, this branch could be recognized only after it had established its organizational structure at the district level. But Salimullah fell ill and could not attend to the party affairs for some time.[39] The formation of the East Bengal provincial Muslim League was completed in October 1909, when Salimullah was elected as president, Raziuddin as secretary, Amiruddin as joint secretary, Sharafatullah as auditor and Khwaja Abdul Aziz as treasurer. The party also elected six vice-presidents. In the party elections of July 1911, Nawab Ali Choudhury (1863–1929) replaced Raziuddin as secretary.[40] The party had its head office in Dhaka. The process of forming a provincial League in West Bengal was much slower than in East Bengal. The decision to this effect was not taken till January 1909, when a representative meeting of the Muslims in Calcutta formed a provincial Muslim League, framed a constitution and elected office-bearers after a heated debate. Two groups competed for party offices: Sayyid Shamsul Huda (1863–1922) led one group and Dr Abdullah al-Mamun Suhrawardy (1881–1935) headed the other group. As a result, most of the offices were filled after a contest. Prince Jahandar Mirza was elected president by defeating Ghulam Husain Arif. The provincial Muslim League constitution provided for three secretaries: two, Shamsul Huda and Naseer Husain Khan Khayal (1880–1934), were elected unanimously while one, Mahbub Ali, was elected by defeating Badruddin Hyder. Four vice-presidents, Prince Ghulam Mohammad of the Mysore family, Serajul Islam, Yusuf Ali Khan and Ahmad Moosaji Salehji, were elected without any opposition while the fifth, Fazle Rabbi, was elected by defeating Maulvi Mohammad Yusuf.[41] The defeated group immediately formed a separate League, and elected Ghulam Husain Arif as president; Abdullah Suhrawardy, Badruddin and Abdul Latif as secretaries; and Sayyid Amir Husain (d. 1910), Prince Bakhtiar Shah of the Mysore family,

Prince Akram Husain (Awadh), Nawab Nasirul Mulk (Persian consul general), Abdul Jabbar, Mohammad Yusuf and Abdul Latif as vice-presidents. [42] Both the Leagues asked the All-India Muslim League for affiliation. The conflict between the two Leagues was finally resolved in June 1910, when Aziz Mirza (honorary secretary) visited Bengal and reorganized a united party.[43] In the elections that followed, Ghulam Mohammad was elected as president, Shamsul Huda as secretary Sultan Ahmad as joint secretary; and Serajul Islam, Mohammad Yusuf Khan, Ahmad Moosaji Salehji and five others as vice-presidents. A new phase began in the Bengal provincial Muslim League after the annulment of the partition of Bengal when one provincial Muslim League was formed for united Bengal.

Bihar had a sizeable number of politically active educated Muslims. They had established a political party by the name of 'Muslim League' even before 1906. They became active after the Aligarh session, and, on 15 March 1908, established the Bihar provincial Muslim League with Sayyid Ali Imam (1869–1932) as president and Mazharul Haq (1866–1929) as secretary, after they had established branches in some districts.[44] Ali Imam chaired the All-India Muslim League annual session at Amritsar in December 1908 and was soon after taken on the Viceroy's Executive Council. Later on, the Bihar League's first secretary, Mazharul Haq, presided over another annual session of the All-India Muslim League. Many Leaguers in Bihar had also been active in the Congress and they continued to participate in its activities even after they had joined the All-India Muslim League. Subsequently, they contributed to the Congress–All-India Muslim League rapprochement that culminated at Lucknow in 1916.

United Provinces (Awadh and Agra), the 'source of the Muslim political movement', did not have a League branch for a long time. Wiqarul Mulk did some preliminary work but due to his duties as secretary of the Aligarh college, he passed on the task of organizing a provincial Muslim League to Musa Khan. In several districts, the branches of the 'Mohammadan Political Association', which Wiqarul Mulk had established, were renamed as the district branches of the provincial Muslim League. When Musa Khan also could not give his full attention to this task, Raja Naushad Ali Khan of Lucknow was appointed 'provisional' secretary. He worked with dedication to organize the party at the district level. During the process of organization, however, differences arose between the Leaguers of Lucknow and Allahabad; the former wanted one provincial Muslim

League for Awadh and Agra with headquarters at Lucknow and the latter wanted two Leagues, one for Awadh and another for Agra with headquarters located at two different places.[45] Even the top leaders including Wiqarul Mulk wavered on this issue. Finally, on 26 June 1909, the Leaguers of the United Provinces of Awadh and Agra held a meeting in Lucknow with Sayyid Nabiullah (d. 1925) in the chair. Wiqarul Mulk moved a resolution in that meeting that there should be only one League for United Provinces; and his motion was unanimously approved. On the following day, the United Provinces provincial League, in a meeting chaired by Sayyid Ihtesham Ali (1869–1943), approved the rules and regulations of the party and elected its office-bearers: Nawab Abdul Majid (1859–1924) of Allahabad as president; Raja Shaban Ali Khan, Ihtesham Ali, Abdur Rauf and Sayyid Aali Nabi (1875–1927) as vice-presidents; Naushad Ali (Lucknow) as secretary, Sayyid Zahur Ahmad and Mohammad Ishaq as joint secretaries, and Azhar Ali and Shaukat Ali as assistant secretaries. It also elected a twenty-member executive committee. Abdul Majid (president) and Naushad Ali (secretary) could not work in harmony for long; as a result, Naushad Ali resigned from his office, complaining that the president was supporting his rivals. The provincial Muslim League began to function smoothly only after its office was shifted from Lucknow to Allahabad in April 1910, and a resident of that city, Ibne Ahmad, was elected its secretary.[46]

The Central Provinces and Berar provincial Muslim League was organized in 1910. Its organization might have been further delayed had H.M. Malak (d. 1923), an affluent businessman and member of the central council, not invited the All-India Muslim League to hold its annual session in Nagpur. The All-India Muslim League accepted his invitation, which necessitated the formation of a League branch in the province before the all-India session. Initially, Malak felt that the twenty members on the central council from Central Provinces and Berar could constitute the provincial Muslim League and its extension to the districts could be deferred to a later date.[47] Aziz Mirza (honorary secretary), however, disagreed with this arrangement and asked him to organize the party at least in six districts. Malak asked Aziz Mirza to assist him in organizing the League at that level. Aziz Mirza deputed Mohammad Yusuf Khan, assistant in the central League office, for this task. Malak personally bore the expenses of Yusuf's organizational tours. Yusuf found the condition of the Muslims in the province quite depressing; according to him, they were either under the control of the provincial and district administrations or the Hindu moneylenders. In a letter to Aziz Mirza on 12 September 1910, he wrote, 'who the devil would have worked in a Province where the very appearance of a Muslim is a personification of contempt. These are Muslims whose lips are the lips of Muslims but their voice the voice of a Hindu'; and in another letter, he wrote, 'Twenty days ago the Chief Commissioner issued a circular prohibiting the Muslims of Central Provinces and Berar from putting on a Turkish Cap or a Fez on the occasion of attending a Darbar. The Muslims of this province felt it very much but could not do anything.'[48] Government officials perceived the organizational work of the League with suspicion. The local Muslims were scared of associating themselves with the League; the CID personnel even trailed Yusuf for some time. The situation slightly changed after the chief commissioner issued a letter urging the officials not to 'disfavour' the League.[49] After a gruelling four-month long campaign, Yusuf was able to establish district Muslim Leagues in all the twenty-two districts of Central Provinces and Berar. On 27 October 1910, Aziz Mirza himself visited Nagpur to formally inaugurate the provincial League, when its office-bearers were elected: Raja Mohammad Azam Shah was elected as president, H.M. Malak as honorary secretary and Asghar Husain Khatib as joint secretary. The party also elected sixteen vice-presidents and thirty members of the provincial Muslim League council. Then, it hosted the annual session in Nagpur, which was preceded by an interesting controversy.[50]

The League that was formed in Ajmer was first recognised as a district Muslim League. The central League accorded this status to the Ajmer League on the plea that it had not sought the 'cooperation of the residents of the Rajputana States' in its formation.[51] According to the central honorary secretary, the party could not have branches in the Indian states but the employees of the states were eligible for membership.[52] The immediate reason behind this pressure perhaps was the situation in the Udaipur state, where Muslims had been prevented from call for prayers in a mosque and those who had defied the order were arrested and then released on the promise that they would not call for prayer or pray in that mosque. This incident attracted the attention of the Muslims in British India who pressurized the All-India Muslim League to take up such issues in the princely states with the Government of India, as it had frequently advocated the causes of the Muslims of Turkey, Iran, Africa and elsewhere.[53] Aziz Mirza toured the Rajputana states to apprise himself of the situation and enrolled members for the League. He met the agent to the governor general and urged him to recruit Muslims on different jobs in the states and provide them facilities for education. When the Ajmer Muslim League—also known as the Rajputana Muslim League—was formally organized on the lines suggested by the central League, its status was raised to that of a provincial Muslim League. Aziz Mirza, who himself attended its inaugural meeting on 18 September 1910, made the announcement to that effect. The provincial Muslim League elected Shaikh Salamuddin as president; Sayyid Abdur Rashid as secretary; Sayyid Mardan Ali and Hakim Mohammad Siddique as vice-presidents; and Imdad Husain as joint secretary.[54] The following year, in October, Sayyid Imamuddin Ali was elected president in place of Salamuddin who along with Mardan Ali was elected vice-president, and Mohammad Siddique as joint secretary.

Burma was then part of the British Indian empire and had a sizeable rich Muslim community engaged in business. On 6 January 1910, at a public meeting in its capital, Rangoon, a Burma provincial Muslim League was founded and a provisional committee was set up to organize the branch. Wiqarul Mulk and Aziz Mirza, who were in Burma in connection with the annual session of the All-India Muslim Educational Conference, also addressed the gathering. The provisional committee, with the help of these two central League leaders, organized the Burma provincial Muslim League and held its elections within four months. A.K. Abdus Shakoor Jamal was elected as president, Ahmad Moolla Dawood as secretary, and M.H.S. Mall as treasurer.[55] It also elected thirteen vice-presidents. The more active Leaguer, Abdus Salaam Rafiqi, was elected as joint secretary. Rafiqi used to edit a monthly newspaper, *Al-Rafiq* (Rangoon), and offered to make it the official organ of the All-India Muslim League in Burma. But the League did not accept his proposal.

During 1906–1910, the All-India Muslim League could not establish its branches in all the provinces and 'sub-provinces' of British India. NWFP, Sindh, Balochistan, Assam and Orissa did not have a branch till a later date. However, the central League itself used to elect members allocated to these regions and they took part in its activities. The League branches that were established in these provinces and sub-provinces at different dates have been discussed in chapters two and seven.

After the foundation of the All-India Muslim League, the Indian Muslims in London—a majority of them were students and Aligarh alumni—felt the need to have a political body of their own in Britain, similar to the British Committee of the Congress, to protect their interests. Amir Ali who had extensively written on the subject and was in contact with the central League leaders in India provided the inspiration and guidance. In 1907, a provisional committee was set up in London under his chairmanship. The All-India Muslim League extended to this committee, and subsequently to the London Muslim League, an annual financial grant of one hundred pounds, equivalent to fifteen hundred rupees.[56] Its nomenclature remained the subject of debate and controversy; the names suggested were the 'British Committee', the 'London Muslim Association', and the 'London Branch'. Hasan Bilgrami objected to its being named as 'London Branch' because its members would then automatically become members of the All-India Muslim League but Amir Ali's argument was that they could not be considered members unless there was an express rule to this effect in the constitution of the central League. Finally, it was named as the 'London Branch of the All-India Muslim League' but it was commonly referred to as the London Muslim League.[57] The branch held its inaugural meeting in London on 6 May 1908, with Amir Ali in the chair. It aimed at protecting the interests of the Muslims, promoting their cooperation with other communities, and bringing them in touch with the thinking of the British leaders. All its office-bearers, except two vice-presidents, were Muslim: Amir Ali was its president; Ibne Ahmad honorary secretary; Sir Henry Seymour King, Sir Raymond West and C.A. Latif vice-presidents; Abdul Ali Anik treasurer; S. Zahur Ahmad joint secretary; and Masudul Hasan (d. 1937) assistant secretary. Dr Mohammad Iqbal was member of its executive committee as well as member of the subcommittee that framed the constitution and rules of the London Muslim League; Hasan Bilgrami, central honorary secretary who was in London, was also taken on these two committees.[58] The London Muslim League had neither any share in the membership of the All-India Muslim League nor did it have any representation on its central committee/council. The All-India Muslim League–London Muslim League relations and their respective authority in the party often evoked controversy and its high mark was reached in 1913, when Sayyid Wazir Hasan (1874–1948) and Maulana Mohammad Ali visited London and differed with Amir Ali on this issue. The resultant crisis would not have been averted had the Aga Khan not intervened and resolved it. The London Muslim League played a crucial role in securing separate electorates for the Muslims of India. It also advocated Muslim causes outside India and extended commendable help to the Muslims suffering in different parts of the world.[59]

(C) LOCATION OF OFFICE

The first office of the All-India Muslim League was understandably located in Aligarh. Some Leaguers were of the view that it should be permanently located in that city because the party could benefit from the services of easily available experienced political workers.[60] But it was soon felt that its location in Aligarh might harm both the Aligarh college and the All-India Muslim League. The reasons for this apprehension were the prevailing student unrest, the tension between the European staff and management of the Aligarh College, and the uncomfortable relations between Wiqarul Mulk and Sir John Hewett (1854–1941), lieutenant governor of the United Provinces. Hewett was of the view that the location of the All-India Muslim League's headquarters in Aligarh and the 'unlimited expansion' of the Aligarh College might contribute to the development of 'Pan-Islamism'.[61] The Leaguers seriously debated the issue of location of the permanent headquarters of their party: whether it should be in Aligarh or at some other place or should it have no permanent office at all. Finally, the All-India Muslim League at its Delhi session in January 1910 decided to have its permanent headquarters in Lucknow and shifted its head office from Aligarh to that city, where it rented a building for this purpose. The head office of the United Provinces Muslim League, which was located in Lucknow, was shifted to Allahabad and remained there for some time.

When the capital of British India was shifted from Calcutta to New Delhi in 1911, the Aga Khan suggested that the All-India Muslim League should also move its head office from Lucknow to Delhi but the party did not take a decision to that effect at that time.[62] The headquarters of the United Provinces Muslim League were, however, moved back to Lucknow. The Leaguers gradually realized that the centre of all-India political activity had shifted from Calcutta to New Delhi and that it was inconvenient to keep the League headquarters in Lucknow. Finally, in December 1926, at the Delhi annual session, the party decided to transfer its head office from Lucknow to New Delhi. The decision was implemented the following month and the head office remained there till Independence.

NOTES

1. Khalid bin Sayeed, *Pakistan: The Formative Phase, 1857–1948*, London, 1968, p. 28.
2. Ikram, *Modern Muslim India*, pp. 80–81; and Hardy, *Muslims of British India*, pp. 153–54.
3. For the initial draft of the memorial prepared by Husain Bilgrami, see Mujahid, *Muslim League Documents*, pp. 90–95.
4. For the text of the memorial, list of members of the deputation and Lord Minto's reply, see ibid., pp. 95–105.
5. In September 1906, they had discussed the need for an all-India Muslim political party. Even earlier, Amir Ali had been impressing upon the Muslims to establish such a political party. 'India and the New Parliament', *Nineteenth Century*, August 1906, pp. 257–58.
6. The conference had decided the venue of its annual meeting in Dhaka on 14 April 1906, long before the Simla deputation.
7. Matiur Rahman reads too much in Aga Khan's absence from the foundation meeting and the proposals that he and Salimullah made about a permanent Muslim organization. *From Consultation to Confrontation: A Study of the Muslim League in British Indian Politics, 1906–1912*, London, n.d. Chapter I.
8. For details of the scheme, see its text in Mujahid, *Muslim League Documents*, pp. 219–25.
9. Hewett to Minto, 3 October 1908, cited in Matiur Rahman, *From Consultation to Confrontation*, p. 49.
10. On taking over the chair, Wiqarul Mulk asked the government servants to withdraw from the meeting.
11. *Report of the Provincial Muslim League Punjab* (Urdu), Lahore, 1907, p. 12; and *Annual Report of the Bihar Provincial Muslim League for the Year 1913*, AFM, vol. 43, no. 80.
12. Mujahid, *Muslim League Documents*, vol. I, pp. 169–70.
13. The three delegates were: Sayyid Hasan Bilgrami, Shaikh Abdul Qadir and Mian Hissamuddin.
14. Rules and Regulations of the All-India Muslim League, adopted by Representative Meeting of Indian Mussalmans, held at Karachi, on 29 and 30 December 1907, in accordance with Resolution No. III, passed at the Dacca meeting of the League of 30 December 1906 and corrected by a meeting of the All-India Muslim League held at Aligarh on 18 and 19 March 1908, Aligarh, 1909.
15. AFM, vol. 37.
16. Mujahid, *Muslim League Documents*, vol. I, pp. 270–71.
17. Wiqarul Mulk to members, 23 February 1908, Mujahid, *Muslim League Documents*, vol. I, pp. 258–59.
18. The second joint secretary, Sayyid Wazir Hasan, was elected in January 1910.
19. Mian Shafi is reported to have suggested the name 'Muslim League' for the proposed Muslim party in his articles in the London *Observer*. Jahanara Shahnawaz, *Father and Daughter*, Lahore, 1971, p. 2.
20. Mohammad Shafi to Wiqarul Mulk, 11 March 1908, AFM, vol. 56.
21. Ghulam Sarwar to Mushtaq Husain, 22 February 1908, ibid.
22. Mohammad Shafi to Wiqarul Mulk, 1 March 1908, ibid.
23. This version was recorded in the report of Haji Musa Khan, officiating honorary secretary, All-India Muslim League, Allahabad, 1908.
24. Fazli Husain to Wiqarul Mulk, 25 March 1908, AFM, vol. 56.

25. Mohammad Shafi to Fazli Husain, 25 March 1908, ibid.
26. Mohammad Shafi to Wiqarul Mulk, 26 March 1908, ibid.
27. Fazli Husain to honorary secretary, All-India Muslim League, 15 September 1908, ibid.
28. *Zamindar* (Lahore), 28 February 1912.
29. AFM, vol. 48.
30. Rafiuddin to Musa Khan, 23 March 1909, ibid.
31. Yaqub Hasan to Musa Khan, 19 January 1909, ibid.
32. Ibid.
33. Musa Khan to Hasan Bilgrami, 21 August 1908, ibid., vol. 82.
34. Yaqub Hasan to Wiqarul Mulk and Musa Khan, 15 July 1908, ibid., vol. 57.
35. On 29 August 1908, Walji Lalji's resolution for the deferment of elections was adopted at a public meeting.
36. Yaqub Hasan to Musa Khan, 24 September 1908, AFM, vol. 57.
37. Yaqub Hasan to Musa Khan, 25 October and 19 November 1908, ibid.
38. Ahmad Mohiuddin and Walji Lalji were elected vice-presidents and Rauf Ahmad joint secretary.
39. Salimullah to Musa Khan, 11 July 1908, AFM, vol. 34.
40. The party elected ten vice-presidents and two joint secretaries; the remaining office-bearers were re-elected including Nawab Salimullah. The provincial Muslim League constitution was amended to allow election of unlimited number of members of the League. Nawab Ali to Aziz Mirza, 25 July 1911, ibid., vol. 35.
41. Naseer Husain Khayal to Musa Khan, 22 January 1909, ibid., vol. 34.
42. *Mussalman*, 29 January 1909.
43. Aziz Mirza to Nawab Salimullah, 16 June 1910, AFM, vol. 35.
44. For details, see ibid., vol. 43.
45. Naushad Ali to Musa Khan, 13 December 1908, and 5 January 1909, and Naushad Ali to Mushtaq Husain, 29 September 1908, and other letters, ibid., vol. 59.
46. Ibid., vol. 113, nos. 8, 17 and 19.
47. Malak to Aziz Mirza, 6 May 1910, ibid., vol. 72.
48. Ibid., vol. 77. The spellings of 'Mohammadan' and 'Musalman' have been changed to Muslim.
49. Yusuf Khan to Aziz Mirza, 7 July 1910, ibid., vol. 72.
50. See Chapter 2.
51. AFM, vol. 110, no. 2.
52. Aziz Mirza to Sayyid Ahmad Sabzwari, 4 February 1912, ibid., vol. 127, no. 52.
53. Ibid., vol. 175, no. 14.
54. Ibid., vol. 110, no. 2
55. Ibid., vol. 58.
56. Musa Khan to Amir Ali, 20 May 1908, ibid., vol. 23.
57. Amir Ali to Musa Khan, 28 May 1908, ibid.; and Hasan Bilgrami to Musa Khan, 15 and 29 May 1908, 26 June, and 10 July, ibid., vol. 82.
58. *Report of the Inaugural Meeting of the London Branch of the All-India Muslim League, London, June 1908*, ibid., vol. 23.
59. For a comprehensive account of the LML, see Muhammad Yusuf Abbasi, *London Muslim League (1908–1928); An Historical Study*, Islamabad, 1988, xiv+426p.
60. Musa Khan to Hasan Bilgrami, 11 June 1908, AFM, vol. 82.
61. Hewett to Minto, 3 October 1908, cited in Matiur Rahman, *From Consultation to Confrontation*, p. 49.
62. The Aga Khan to the Nawab of Dhaka, 3 March 1912, AFM, vol. 64.

2

Organizational Structure and its Working, 1906–1935

During 1906–35, the All-India Muslim League could not develop and maintain itself as a well-knit and broad-based party although it played a vital role in politics whenever it presented a united Muslim front. It was primarily the socio-economic and political underdevelopment of the Muslims that prevented the League to emerge as a cohesive political force. Nevertheless, it took initiative on all important contemporary issues that influenced the Muslims of the Indian subcontinent but showed hesitation in espousing popular Muslim causes that were likely to lead to uncontrolled agitation. Its vacillation to lead them in situations of political confusion and uncertainty often pushed it into short intervals of inactivity. During the periods of its inactivity, the strength of its limited subscription-paying members was further reduced. However, non-payment of dues did not bar any person who had once enrolled himself as a member of the All-India Muslim League from participation in the party meetings and activities. The League did not put any bar on its members from becoming or retaining membership of other political parties including that of the Indian National Congress. This provision encouraged the more enterprising and ambitious members among them to establish, or join, other political parties without breaking their links with the League. Despite all its deficiencies, an overwhelming majority of the Indian Muslims looked to the All-India Muslim League as their sole all-India political party that could address their political problems. No other Muslim political party could gain the confidence of the Muslims or similar status in the politics of India.

(A) THE PARTY CONSTITUTION

The All-India Muslim League frequently amended its constitution to make the party broad-based and efficient or whenever there was a need to do so for other reasons. The constitution could be amended only at an all-India session by a two-third majority of the members present.[1] Except for the changes made at the Nagpur session, the party strictly followed the amendment procedure as laid down in the constitution. Major amendments were made on three occasions, in 1913, 1919 and 1931, besides some minor ones that were introduced on other occasions. The original constitution, as modified in January 1910, remained operative till March 1913. The Leaguers by then found it 'too rigid and exclusive' and then modified it to make it suitable for the changed environment.[2] Wazir Hasan, the honorary secretary, initiated the process and prepared a draft after consulting 'members, non-members and secretaries of several Anjumans'. On 30–31 December 1912, the central council decided to circulate the draft among the provincial Muslim Leagues for comments.[3] The All-India Muslim League approved a revised constitution on the basis of comments received from the provincial Muslim Leagues.[4] Again, after the Lucknow session, the Leaguers felt the need to revise the constitution. The revision process was completed in almost two and a half years. Wazir Hasan started the process on 23 July 1917, when he invited the members to make suggestions in the light of experience gained since 1913.[5] He prepared a draft based on suggestions received from the members.[6] A seven-member committee recast the draft, which the central council approved on 9 July 1918,[7] and the revised draft came before the Delhi session for approval but that session was adjourned before its consideration. The adjourned session convened in Aligarh in March 1919 but dispersed due to lack of quorum. Several other factors—the Khilafat issue, Punjab tragedy and Wazir Hasan's resignation—caused further delay. Finally, Sayyid Zahur Ahmad, Wazir Hasan's successor, brought the revised draft before the All-India Muslim League, which adopted it at the Amritsar session.[8] A few more amendments were made at the Nagpur session.

Some Leaguers were still dissatisfied with the amended constitution. Maulana Hasrat Mohani (1878–1951) voiced their sentiments in his presidential address at the Ahmadabad session, but no further changes were made in the constitution.[9] After the rejuvenation of the All-India Muslim League in 1923–24, the Leaguers occasionally raised the issue but nothing was done till December 1927, when the All-India Muslim

League (Jinnah faction) appointed a committee consisting of president, honorary secretary, Maulana Mohammad Ali and Asif Ali (1888–1953) to amend the constitution. This committee failed to accomplish anything concrete due to its members' engagements elsewhere. The honorary secretary simply stated this fact in his annual report for the year 1928.[10] Attempts made after that also produced no result.[11] The Shafi League also appointed a committee to draft a new constitution but could not do that. Again, in 1929, after the merger of the Jinnah and Shafi Leagues, the united League at its Allahabad session appointed a committee consisting of Nawab Mohammad Ismail Khan (1886–1958), Masud Hasan and Mohammad Yaqub (1879–1942) 'to revise and amend' the constitution. On the basis of its report, the All-India Muslim League revised the constitution at its Delhi session and introduced some basic changes in its structure but the poor state of the party rendered them meaningless.

(B) OBJECTIVES

In 1913, the All-India Muslim League introduced changes in its objectives to reflect the transformation that Muslim thinking had undergone as a result of national and international developments. These changes were meant to strengthen Hindu–Muslim cordiality and bring the party objectives in line with the Muslim aspirations in the changed environment. Clause 2 (a) of the objectives was re-worded as: 'to maintain and promote among the people of this country feelings of loyalty towards the British Crown'. In clause 2 (b), the words 'and to respectfully represent their needs and aspirations to the government' were deleted, which now simply read as 'to protect and advance the political rights and interests of the Muslims of India'. Clause 2 (c) was re-worded as 'to promote friendship and union between the Muslims and other communities of India'. A new clause 2 (d) was added after a heated debate, it called for the 'attainment, under the aegis of the British Crown, of a system of self-government suitable to India, through constitutional means by bringing about, among others, a steady reform of the existing system of administration, by promoting national unity, by fostering public spirit among the people of India and by cooperating with other communities for the said purposes'.[12] The Congress had similar objectives but in a different form. Later on, the League constitution, as amended on 30–31 December 1919, added two more words 'and religious' after 'political' in clause 2 (b) of the aims and objects; M.A. Jinnah (1876–1948) was the mover of this amendment. However, major changes in the objectives were made the following year at the Nagpur session, which reflected the influence of the Khilafat and Non-cooperation movements. Clause 2 (*a*) now called for 'the attainment of *Swaraj* by the people of India by all peaceful and legitimate means', and clause 2 (*d*) was replaced by a new clause that urged the Muslims 'to maintain brotherly relations between the Muslims of India and those of other countries'.[13]

Hasrat Mohani made repeated attempts in the council of the All-India Muslim League and at the Ahmadabad session to bring about more changes in the objectives. The resolution, which he moved in the council, provided that the League should aim at 'complete independence' to put an end to British imperialism, in cooperation with other communities, by 'all possible and proper means', instead of 'all peaceful and legitimate means'. The resolution also recommended reduction of annual subscription from Rs 6 to Re 1; election of office-bearers and members of the central council for one year; and the president of the annual session to assume presidency for the whole year.[14] He acknowledged that such changes could not be made without prior notice to the members but at the Nagpur session, he pleaded, the League had amended the constitution without any prior notice. The president, however, ruled his resolution out of order since the changes involved alteration in the creed of the All-India Muslim League and required sufficient previous notice to the members. Despite this ruling, Hasrat Mohani moved the resolution in the subjects committee where it was rejected. Maulana Azad Sobhani (1882–1957) moved the same resolution in the open session. Hasrat Mohani, who was himself presiding over the open session, permitted discussion on the resolution with the condition that votes would not be taken on it and that the resolution be taken as rejected, as it had already been rejected in the subjects committee. The text of the resolution was, however, printed at the end of the proceedings of the annual session with a factual statement that the resolution had not been passed.[15] The constitution, as revised in 1931, introduced changes in clause 2 (a) of the objectives. The All-India Muslim League now aimed at 'the attainment of full responsible government for India by all peaceful and legitimate means with adequate and effective safeguards for the Musalmans'. The other objectives from 2 (b) to 2 (d) remained the same.[16]

(C) ORGANIZATIONAL STRUCTURE

(i) *Membership*. The party constitution, as amended in 1913, made a major change in the strength of total members. It removed the limit on total membership and abolished provincial quotas. Minimum age for membership was lowered from 25 to 21 years, and now any British Indian Muslim (but not a student who was not a graduate) could apply for membership.[17] The central council could give exemption from all or any of the conditions. A candidate for membership had to have a member to propose and another member to second his candidature, and he had to give a declaration that he would abide by the objects and rules of the All-India Muslim League. A candidate also needed the recommendations of the provincial Muslim League of the area in which he ordinarily resided. The central council had the final authority to approve membership of a candidate by a simple majority. It was empowered to elect directly a member from an area where a recognized provincial Muslim League did not exist. Every member of a provincial Muslim League did not automatically become member of the All-India Muslim League; he had to pass through the same procedure. The admission fee was reduced to Rs 5 and the annual subscription to Rs 6. It was provided that a member would cease to be a member if he had not paid his annual subscription within three months of its due date.[18] The amendments of 1919 elaborated the clause relating to requirements for membership; it now read, 'A Musalman who is a resident of British India or of any of the feudatory States of India or of any other part of the British Empire provided that in the last case he has not been out of India continuously for five years'.[19] A new provision was added that required a candidate to explain the reasons for his not being a member of a provincial Muslim League if his name had not been recommended by any provincial League. The clause regarding defaulting members was recast. Now if a member had not paid his subscription for over a year, the honorary secretary was to give him a notice to make the payment, and if he failed to do that, the central council could remove his name from the list of members but only after passing a formal resolution to that effect. The amendments of 1931 drastically modified the conditions for membership; now a candidate was to become a member simply on payment of annual subscription of Re 1, paid in advance, provided he also declared to abide by the objects and rules of the League. The admission fee was abolished. These relaxations for membership were made at a time when the All-India Muslim League was passing through a critical phase of its history.[20]

Table 2.1: Membership of the AIML

Date	Membership Strength
1 January 1917	586
1 January 1918	712
1 January 1919	707
1 January 1920	843
15 December 1920	953
1 January 1922	1093
1 January 1924	1097
1 January 1925	1284
1 January 1926	1281
15 December 1927	1330

The removal of maximum limit on membership and elimination of provincial quotas did increase the number of members but the total figure was still not very impressive. Its members on the roll in the second decade did not go beyond the three digits and in the third decade it barely touched four digits [Table 2.1].[21] The members of the provincial Muslim Leagues were, however, in addition to this number, besides an undefined number of sympathisers and supporters. One reason for its low membership strength was that the number of Muslims interested in active politics who could afford to pay the dues was very small. Even a large number of those who were members often failed to pay their dues. The central League twice waived the arrears due from members; once in 1910 at the direction of the Aga Khan and then, in August 1920, by a resolution of its central council, which wrote off arrears due from members on 1 January 1920, for the 'past three years or more'. Even after that, the number of defaulters did not diminish; in 1922, only 23 out of 1093 members had paid their dues and the following year, the number was proportionately less than this. Later on, in 1927, 1928, and 1931, the League office repeatedly put up the cases of defaulting members on the agenda of the council meetings but no action was taken against them.[22] Despite low enrolment, the party still claimed that its membership consisted of 'all the intelligentsia of the Muslim community' representing 'every shade of opinion', and did not leave out 'a single prominent man of any town throughout India'. It included the 'Nawabs, nearly all the Ministers, Members of the Legislative Assemblies and Members of the Legislative Councils, leading practitioners, title holders, landowners, merchants, Khilafatists, Tablighis, and *ulama*'.[23] This was not far from the truth. Members could not bring their sectarian differences into the party. In fact, the League provided a platform for the dilution of sectarian tensions among the Muslims. Its members were simply Muslims on its platform and expressed their sectarian or other identities, if needed, outside its forum. On 11 February 1908, following the Sunni-Shia sectarian disturbances in the United Provinces, prominent Leaguers including Wiqarul Mulk and Musa Khan persuaded leading Shia and Sunni dignitaries of Lucknow to sign a declaration, advising members of both the sects to abandon those matters that might endanger sectarian peace. Again, in 1919, the party contributed to the softening of acute Sunni–Shia discord in Lucknow.[24]

(*ii*) *Office-bearers*. The office-bearers and their designations, as defined in the original constitution, were not changed. The amendments and revisions of the constitution simply altered the strength of vice-presidents. The procedure for the election of the office-bearers required that a candidate would send his nomination papers for an office to the central honorary secretary after getting it proposed and seconded by two members. The secretary would then circulate the papers among the members, and elections would be conducted at the annual session by ballot. The absent members could send in their votes by post to the secretary. After December 1931, except for the office of president all the office-bearers were elected from among the members for a term of three years, and they were eligible for re-election. The central council elected the president of the annual session, and it could also fill in any 'casual' vacancy (i.e. an office falling vacant before the expiry of the term) till the next annual session. The All-India Muslim League used to have two kinds of presidents. One was elected at the annual session for a three-year term; and he was better known as the 'permanent' president. He could be re-elected for more than one term. In 1919, the League put a bar on one person holding the office of permanent president for more than two consecutive terms. But in December 1927, the All-India Muslim League (Jinnah faction) removed that condition to facilitate Jinnah's re-election for a third term. The central council elected the other president who simply presided over the annual session and had no authority in the party affairs. The permanent president presided over special and extraordinary sessions. The 1931 amendments introduced a basic change in the office of president. Now, instead of a permanent president, the council elected a president every year, and he held the office until the next annual session.[25] In addition, it continued to have the option to elect someone other than the president to preside over the annual session; after 1934, the council exercised this power only once when Wazir Hasan was asked to preside over the Bombay session. No change was made in the term or mode of election of other office-bearers; the vice-presidents, honorary secretary and joint secretaries were still elected at the annual session for a three-year term.

During 1908–30, five Leaguers served as permanent presidents [Table 2.2]. The Aga Khan was its first permanent president, elected in March 1908, and then for another two years in January 1910. He did not want to be re-elected after the expiry of that term but, on 3 March 1912, the All-India Muslim League unanimously re-elected him as president for another term, appealing to his 'sense of patriotism and love of Islam' to accept his re-election.[26] A few League leaders telegraphically requested him to accept the offer. He agreed to his re-election provided two 'joint presidents' were also elected to share his burden; earlier, at the time of League's inception, he had made a similar proposal, which was not accepted.[27] This time again, the All-India Muslim League did not accept his proposal, as it was not permissible under the 'existing rules' but appealed to him to stay as 'president as before'.[28] He did not press for additional presidents and accepted to stay as the permanent president. In December 1913, he again 'irrevocably' resigned from the presidency, but agreed to be associated with the League as one of its vice-presidents; and on 15 February 1914, the council elected him as a vice-president.[29] Interestingly, he never presided over an all-India session although he was requested to do that on several occasions. He had little time to look after the party affairs on regular basis because of his engagements outside India. The central secretary used to keep him regularly informed about the developments in the party and its position on different issues. He used to give guidelines to the office-bearers and prominent Leaguers whenever he felt the need to do so. The Leaguers in turn respected his views and generally followed his directions. He contributed to the softening of the anti-Congress feelings of some Leaguers and played a significant role in Hindu–Muslim rapprochement. More importantly, donations by him and his disciples contributed to the All-India Muslim League's sustained growth in its early years. Even after he left the presidency, his views on political issues carried weight with the Leaguers.

Table 2.2: Permanent presidents of the AIML, 1908–1930

'Permanent' Presidents	Dates
The Aga Khan	1908–1913
Muhammad Ali Muhammad Khan, Raja Sahib of Mahmudabad	1916–1919
A.K. Fazlul Haq	1919
M.A. Jinnah	1920–1930
Mian Mohammad Shafi (Shafi League)	1927–1929

After the resignation of the Aga Khan, the All-India Muslim League remained without a permanent president for about two years; Mohammad Ali Mohammad, Raja Sahib of Mahmudabad (1877–1931), one of the vice-presidents, looked after the party affairs. At the Bombay session on 1 January 1916, Raja Sahib was formally elected permanent president for a three-year term. During his tenure, the League came closer to the Congress and signed the Joint Reform Scheme that was presented to the British government. His term was to expire on 31 December 1918, but he submitted his resignation two months before that date, effective from 1 November, 'on account of ill-health'. In fact, he resigned before time to enable the party to elect someone else as president and to negate the impression that he would agree to his re-election.[30] On 24 November, the council discussed his resignation but decided to send a 5-member delegation to persuade him to withdraw it.[31] But Raja Sahib refused to withdraw his resignation; even then, the League re-elected him as president for another regular term at the Delhi session. When his re-election was announced, he thanked the members for re-electing him but again submitted his resignation effective from 1 March 1919.[32] Finally, on 20 April, the council accepted his resignation and elected Fazlul Haq (1873–1962) 'provisionally' as president until fresh elections were held at the next annual session. Fazlul Haq wanted to play an active role in the party affairs but the central office did not let him do that; he was informed that so far the presidents had 'very little to do' with the working of the party and that he was 'supposed to watch over the general policy'. The central office, however, conceded that his instructions on any specific issue would be followed.[33]

Before the annual session, there was a move to re-elect the Aga Khan as president; Zahur Ahmad wrote to Yaqub Hasan in London: 'I am anxiously waiting for Aga Khan's reply to my letter. I hope you will get him to agree to be the President of the League'.[34] But Aga

Khan had no 'desire' to become president because he had to stay abroad for long intervals; in addition, his election as president, he felt, would restrict his freedom 'to express freely his views' on various issues. He suggested the name of Raja of Jahangirabad (1851–1921) for the office.[35] However, when the All-India Muslim League met at Amritsar in December 1919, it elected M.A. Jinnah as the permanent president who had recently headed the League delegation that had given evidence before the Joint Parliamentary Committee in London and had resigned from the Imperial Legislative Council in protest against the passage of the Rowlatt Act that had put drastic restrictions on civil liberties.[36] Earlier, he had distinguished himself by his impressive public performance from the platforms of the Congress, the All-India Muslim League and the Imperial Legislative Council. He won public admiration as the champion of civil rights; and the cases that he defended especially that of Bal Gangadhar Tilak (1856–1920) in 1917 became part of the Indian legal history. He joined, and presided over, the Bombay branch of the Home Rule League when its all-India president, Mrs Annie Besant (1847–1933), was interned. Then, in December 1918, he led the Bombay citizens to frustrate a move by some 'loyalists' to present a memorial to Governor Willingdon (1866–1941), on his departure from Bombay; Willingdon had been a die-hard critic of those Indians who had been demanding self-government for India.[37] In 1913, Jinnah had formally joined the All-India Muslim League although he had attended several meetings of its bodies even before that.[38] The most important were the council meetings that had revised the League constitution. He had successfully piloted the Musalman Wakf Validating Bill in cooperation with the All-India Muslim League. Then, he played a crucial role in the All-India Muslim League–Congress rapprochement and chaired the historic session of the League in Lucknow. He was hailed as the 'Ambassador of Hindu–Muslim unity' for his role in uniting the two main political parties. A year before his election as permanent president, he was elected vice-president of the All-India Muslim League. Soon after his election as president, the Khilafat movement pushed the All-India Muslim League into the background. However, he continued to hold the office of permanent president even after his term expired in December 1922. When the issue of expiry of his term was raised, he gave a ruling that the office-bearers would hold office till the next elections. The All-India Muslim League re-elected him for a second term at its Lahore session in May 1924. He could not be elected for a third term because, according to an amendment made in the constitution in 1919, no one could hold a League office for more than two consecutive terms. But by the time his term expired, he was heading the Jinnah League, which could not afford to dispense with his leadership; the party removed the bar on his re-election and elected him president for a third term. The splinter faction, the Shafi League, elected Mian Shafi as the president.[39] Jinnah left for England three months before the expiry of his third term. Like his predecessors, he did not take much interest in the party affairs during his tenure as permanent president. The honorary secretaries and the League office handled these matters. He gave the party office guidance only when it sought his advice and sometimes, when needed, helped it out financially. The Leaguers missed Jinnah when he decided to settle in England after the first Round Table Conference. They were disappointed; one of them asked the central secretary to 'exert all friendly influence' on Jinnah 'to return' and 'lead the community'; he felt that the Round Table Conferences had resulted in the 'misfortune' of the Muslims as they had 'lost one [Maulana] Mohammad Ali dead and another [Mohammad Ali Jinnah] alive'.[40] Another Leaguer wrote to Jinnah: 'I am sure of one thing that in case you decide to leave India . . . the League would immediately succumb to the shock.'[41]

The All-India Muslim League did not conduct the party elections at its Allahabad session because, according to the honorary secretary, that session had been called 'at a very short notice'. After the session, on 15 March 1931, the council discussed the issue, and the honorary secretary proposed that Mian Shafi should be elected the party president till the next session. Husain Imam (1897–1985) did point out that the council had no authority to elect Mian Shafi as president because it was not a case of 'casual' vacancy; in fact, the office of president had fallen vacant on the expiry of Jinnah's three-year regular term. But Mian Abdul Aziz (d. 1946), one of the vice-presidents, who was chairing the meeting, overruled his objection. Then, Hasrat Mohani proposed that instead of electing a new president, one of the vice-presidents should continue to look after the party work till regular elections were held at the next session. However, Mian Abdul Aziz observed that he had already given his ruling and closed any discussion on this issue. The council then unanimously elected Mian Shafi as president till regular elections at the next annual session.[42] Before that session, Mian Shafi was appointed member of the Viceroy's Executive Council. Again, the party had to elect a new president. On 6 December, the council elected Chaudhri Zafrullah Khan (1893–1985) as president although, according to the order of merit based on nominations sent by the provincial Muslim Leagues, he was at number seven of the list.[43] His election as president generated a heated controversy as he was an Ahmadi, and the Ahmadis at that time were under fire from different sections of the Muslim society. His appointment on the Viceroy's Executive Council in June 1932, and resignation from the office of League president averted a crisis. On 3 September, the council accepted his resignation and elected Mian Abdul Aziz as president till the next session.

Now the All-India Muslim League entered the saddest chapter of its history. In addition to a move for its merger into the All-India Muslim Conference, the controversy surrounding its annual session again split the party. On 12 March 1933, the council unanimously decided to hold its session on 29–30 April, and resolved to invite Jinnah from England to preside over it. Jinnah, in response to an invitation from Mian Abdul Aziz, wrote back that he would visit India in December. On receipt of this reply, Mian Abdul Aziz postponed the session till December without consulting the council, on the plea that 'the presence of a personality like that of Mr Jinnah' was essential 'to lead, guide and unite the community' in the 'present chaotic state of Muslim politics'.[44] His ruling as president provoked a heated controversy. When two members raised a point of order in the council meeting against the continuance of Mohammad Yaqub (1879–1942) as the honorary secretary, he ruled that the objection was valid and that the office of honorary secretary was vacant.[45] Shortly after, he gave another ruling that S.M. Abdullah was no longer a joint secretary, as his term had expired on 31 December 1929, and that he had not been re-elected.[46] The other joint secretary, Mirza Ijaz Husain, was saved from removal by death. Mian Abdul Aziz also dismissed the assistant secretary in the League office, Sayyid Shamsul Hasan (1885–1981), who, he alleged, had brought the information about Mohammad Yaqub and S.M. Abdullah to his notice and then, after their removal, had gone in the opposite camp. Henceforth, factionalism intensified.[47] Those Leaguers who disagreed with Mian Abdul Aziz's rulings established a separate League and, on 16 July, elected Hafiz Hidayat Husain (1881–1935) as president and Professor Mirza Mohammad Saeed (1886–1962) as honorary secretary. The split was bridged the following year when presidents of both the Leagues resigned from their offices to facilitate the unanimous election of Jinnah as president.

As for the office of vice-president, the All-India Muslim League changed the number of holders of this office four times. The original constitution had provided for six vice-presidents; and in 1910, their strength was raised to 12–20; in 1919 to 20–50; and in 1931, it was fixed at 15. The office of vice-president was merely a decoratory office, honouring its holder on payment of handsome donations. Many of them made donations regularly, and some made more than was expected of them.[48] The president could delegate his authority to a vice-president or in the absence of the president a vice-president could officiate as president. Once, in 1914–16, Raja of Mahmudabad, a senior vice-president, in the absence of a permanent president, looked after the party affairs till his regular election to that office. The allocated number of vice-presidents was regularly elected partly because they were an important source of the party's finances. Like the vice-presidents, the joint secretaries had no defined duties. The honorary secretary could ask any of them to assist him in the performance of his duties. During 1908–35, the All-India Muslim League in total had ten joint secretaries [Table 2.3]. Except for the period from March 1908 to January 1910, when the League had only one joint secretary (Haji Musa Khan), or in March 1934, when the council appointed three joint secretaries [Nawab Ali, Anwarul Azim (b. 1895) and Shah Masud Ahmad], the party had always two joint secretaries. Two joint secretaries did not complete their terms of office.

Table 2.3: Joint secretaries of the AIML, 1908–1935

Joint Secretaries	Dates
Haji Mohammad Musa Khan	March 1908–December 1919
Sayyid Wazir Hasan	January 1910–February 1913
Sayyid Azhar Ali	March 1913–April 1919
Choudhry Khaliquzzaman	April 1919–December 1926
Masudul Hasan	December 1919–December 1926
Mirza Ijaz Husain	December 1926–May 1933
S.M. Abdullah	December 1926–October 1941
Sayyid Nawab Ali	May 1933–March 1934
Anwarul Aziz	March 1934–1935
Shah Masud Ahmad	March 1934–1935

One, Azhar Ali was appointed as registrar of the cooperative societies of the Bhopal state in April 1919, and the other, Mirza Ijaz Husain, died during his tenure of office. On three occasions, one of the joint secretaries officiated as honorary secretary. In March 1908, Hasan Bilgrami (honorary secretary) nominated Musa Khan to officiate in his place when he himself left for England. Musa Khan held the officiating position for almost two years, practically the whole tenure of Hasan as honorary secretary. Then, in 1919, Musa Khan again officiated as honorary secretary for a little over one month. He performed these duties selflessly and declined to become regular honorary secretary when he was offered to do so. Wazir Hasan was also a joint secretary when he was called upon to act as honorary secretary on the sudden death of Aziz Mirza after an operation in February 1913, till his formal election to that office at the annual session. The office of joint secretary assumed importance after December 1926, when two honorary secretaries, Dr Saifuddin Kitchlew (1884–1963) and Mohammad Yaqub, were not residents of New Delhi where the head office of the All-India Muslim League was then located. The joint secretaries attended to routine party affairs and kept the honorary secretaries regularly informed about important developments.

The honorary secretary was the key office in the party till 1931. The constitution defined only his powers and duties. The amendments made in the constitution at different times did not affect this office. He was responsible for the working of the central office of the League and maintenance of its accounts. He could appoint a subcommittee for any specific purpose. He was empowered to appoint, punish and dismiss the paid employees of the party; in case of dismissal, however, the employee had the right of appeal to the council.[49] He could call an emergency meeting of the members of the council present at the headquarters on matters not affecting the fundamental principles of the constitution. The resolutions passed at such meetings required confirmation at a regular meeting. During his temporary absence, he could nominate one of the joint secretaries as his *locum tenens* and inform the League members of his action by a circular letter.

Table 2.4: Honourary secretaries of the AIML, 1908–1936

Honorary Secretaries*	Dates
Sayyid Hasan Bilgrami	1908–1909
Muhammad Aziz Mirza	1910–1912
Sayyid Wazir Hasan	1913–1919
Sayyid Zahur Ahmad	1919–1926
Dr Saifuddin Kitchlew	1927–1929
Sir Mohammad Yaqub	1929–1933
Mirza Mohammad Saeed (Hafiz Hidayat Group)	1933–1934
Malik Barkat Ali (Mian Aziz Group)	1933–1934
Hafiz Hidayat Husain	1934–1935
Sir Mohammad Yaqub	1935–1936

*At the foundation meeting, Nawab Mohsinul Mulk and Nawab Wiqarul Mulk were elected joint honorary secretaries.

Before the adoption of a constitution, Mohsinul Mulk and Wiqarul Mulk, who had been elected joint honorary secretaries at the foundation meeting, looked after the party work. Both of them played an important role in the framing of the first constitution of the League. However, Mohsinul Mulk could not give sufficient time to the party because of his responsibilities as secretary of the Aligarh college while Wiqarul Mulk did some initial organizational work of the All-India Muslim League along with that of organizing the provincial League in United Provinces; the latter task Wiqarul Mulk handed over to Musa Khan when he himself took over as secretary of the college on Mohsinul Mulk's death. As mentioned elsewhere, Hasan Bilgrami was elected first honorary secretary of the All-India Muslim League at the Aligarh session but he left for England three days after his election [Table 2.4]. Musa Khan performed the duties of honorary secretary in his place with exemplary patience and dedication. He enjoyed the confidence and support of Wiqarul Mulk and used to keep the 'permanent' president (The Aga Khan) and honorary secretary (Hasan Bilgrami) regularly informed about the party affairs and political developments in India. Simultaneously, he attended to organizational matters at the central office and in the provinces. Hasan Bilgrami continued to extend his stay in England for one reason or another and finally sent in his resignation in October 1909.[50] The following year in January, Mohammad Aziz Mirza who had recently retired from the service of the Hyderabad state was elected as honorary secretary. He devoted himself exclusively to the party work and used his administrative skills and experience to complete the process of formation of the provincial Muslim Leagues. He formally established the party office in Lucknow and collected relevant data on various topical issues for use by the party. Funds were available in reasonable amount, which he used for propaganda and publicity. He published literature on the party and its programme, and distributed it widely.[51] None of his successors as honorary secretary did this kind of work till after 1935. The party appreciated his services, and the council even delegated to him the power to accept members into the party as recommended by the provincial Muslim Leagues in anticipation of its approval.[52] In fact, he was the one who established the importance of this office. On his death, Wazir Hasan was elected first as officiating secretary and then as regular secretary at the annual session the following month. He was re-elected for a second term on 1 January 1916.

Wazir Hasan's tenure was quite eventful. Firstly, he was instrumental in revising the party constitution. Secondly, on 4 September 1913, he and Maulana Mohammad Ali paid a 'sudden' visit to England at the party's expense to apprise the British government and public of the 'essential loyalty' of the Indian Muslims and the justice of their demands.[53] Wazir Hasan neither sought the approval of the party for this visit nor did he nominate anyone to look after the party work in his absence. Some members objected to this procedure, but four days after his departure, the council, at an emergency meeting that only the local vice-presidents and council members attended, resolved to authorise Azhar Ali, one of the joint secretaries, to perform the duties of his office and sign cheques and other necessary papers.[54] The council confirmed this decision at a regular meeting on 19 September, in which it thanked the two leaders for undertaking this journey to represent before the British authorities and public the 'views, needs and aspirations' of the Indian Muslims in cooperation with the London branch and other friends in that country, and expressed its 'sincere confidence in them and in their capacity to represent true Muslim interests'.[55] During their stay in London, the two leaders came into conflict with Amir Ali on the status of the London Muslim League, which led to the latter's resignation from the League and created a crisis that was controlled with great difficulty with the help of the Aga Khan. Thirdly, Wazir Hasan played his part in the approval of the League–Congress reform scheme. After the Lucknow Pact, his interest in politics waned. He faced severe criticism for his lack of interest in the 'political movements' and his handling of the party fund. On 28–30 December, the council appointed a three-member (Zahur Ahmad, Nizamuddin and Abdus Salam) committee 'to go through the accounts of the League relating to the expenses' incurred by Wazir Hasan on his tours.[56] Although he was re-elected for a third term but his re-election was not without a dispute.[57] Soon after his re-election, his 'irrevocable' decision to resign as the honorary secretary 'with immediate effect' suppressed any controversy about his performance or his handling of the party fund.[58]

Sayyid Zahur Ahmad, who was asked to officiate as honorary secretary on 20 April 1919, was elected to that office for a three-year term at the annual session. He was re-elected for a second term at the Lahore session in May 1924. As honorary secretary, he lacked Aziz Mirza's tact, experience and resourcefulness and Wazir Hasan's energy and dynamism. During his tenure of office, the All-India Muslim League failed to maintain the scale of its activities. Besides, there was hardly any co-ordination between him and the president partly due to the location of the head office in Lucknow.[59] When the All-India Muslim League decided to shift the head office from Lucknow to New Delhi, Dr Saifuddin Kitchlew was elected its honorary secretary. There was a temporary spurt of organizational activities but the controversies surrounding constitutional issues and the resultant factionalism absorbed the party's attention. Kitchlew lost interest in the League as he gradually became more active in the politics of the Congress.[60] His term expired on 31 December 1929, but the League could not elect his successor, as it failed to hold its annual session that year. On 9 February 1930, the council elected Mohammad Yaqub as the 'casual' honorary secretary till the next annual session but he did not place the issue of election for a regular term before the annual session, according to him, due to short notice at which annual session was called in Allahabad.[61] The following year on 15 March, the council, assuming the powers of the annual session without any authorization, 'unanimously' elected Mohammad Yaqub as honorary secretary. But when, in March 1933, Mian Abdul Aziz ruled his election by the council as invalid, he stayed away from the League. Mirza Mohammad Saeed acted as honorary secretary of one of the two groups of the All-India Muslim League, Hafiz Hidayat group; and on his resignation, this group re-elected Yaqub as honorary secretary in November. When the two Groups merged into a united League, Hafiz Hidayat Husain was elected its honorary secretary. On his death, the council, on 30 December 1935, again elected Yaqub as honorary secretary, and he held that office till the election of Nawabzada Liaquat Ali Khan (1895–1951).[62]

(*iii*) *Council*. The council was the highest executive organ of the party. Originally, its strength was forty elected members plus the office-bearers as *ex-officio* members. No minimum age limit was fixed for its members. They were apportioned to each province as far as possible on the basis of ratio fixed for members from various regions, which was in turn based on the proportion of Muslims in the population of that province and their education, financial position and social status. They were elected for a three-year term and were eligible for re-election. A council member was to complete his term even after the expiry of his term as an ordinary member, provided he had paid his annual fee. The quorum for a council meeting was merely five members including the office-bearers. The council took its decisions by a simple majority. Among its functions were: to fix the date and place of the annual and other all-India sessions; elect president of the annual session; implement its own resolutions and those passed at the all-India sessions; and endeavour to establish a branch League in every province. One-third of the total ordinary members or two-third council members could requisition its meeting. It was required to obtain the opinion of members by correspondence on any matter in hand. It could make by-laws in accord with the basic principles of the party for its efficient working.

The revised constitution of 1913 raised the strength of the council to 150 members; the office-bearers remained its *ex-officio* members. The proportion of representation of various provinces was specified: Delhi 2; United Provinces 25; Punjab 25; Bombay including Sindh 14; Madras 9; NWFP 5; British Balochistan 2; Bengal 30; Bihar and Orissa 15; Assam 6; Central India and Ajmer 2; Central Provinces and Berar 4; Burma 7; and British Indian Muslims residing in the princely states and elsewhere 4 [Table 2.5].[63] The council was empowered to elect members if any provincial Muslim League failed to elect its quota of members within the time limited. Members were elected on or before first March, and every member had to pay Rs 20/- as annual fee in two six-monthly instalments. The council could fill all 'casual' vacancies of office-bearers and council members. Now thirty ordinary members or fifteen council members could requisition a general body meeting. The quorum for the annual session was seventy-five and for other

Table 2.5: Proportional representation of provinces in the AIML Council

Province	1913*	1919*	1931**
Delhi	2	4	10
United Provinces	25	50	50
Punjab	25	50	50
Bombay including Sindh	14	28	Bombay 20 Sindh 10
Madras	9	18	18
NWFP	5	10	10
British Balochistan	2	4	4
Bengal	30	60	60
Bihar and Orissa	15	30	30
Assam	6	12	12
Central India and Ajmer	2	4	6
Central Provinces and Berar	4	Central Provinces (5) Berar (3) 8	10
Burma	7	14	10
British Indian Muslims residing in Princely States and elsewhere	4	8	10

* The office-bearers of the All-India Muslim League were *ex-officio* members of the Council.

** Those members of the central legislature who signed the creed of the League were *ex-officio* members of the council.

all-India sessions thirty. The council was to meet ordinarily once a month. The honorary secretary could call any other meeting if he considered it necessary. Ten members constituted quorum for all the meetings. No resolution was deemed to have been passed or rejected unless 10 per cent of the absent members had expressed their opinions on that resolution. Written opinions were counted as votes. The council was empowered to elect ordinary as well as council members, convene all-India sessions for which it was to select a place, fix a date, and elect a president for the annual session after consulting the League of the province in which the party was to hold that session. It implemented its own resolutions on matters relating to its objects. It regulated and controlled the party fund and could appoint subcommittees to carry out its responsibilities. Besides its powers to affiliate the branch Leagues, it could now give affiliation to any Muslim association and regulate its relations with the central League. The council could delegate any of its powers to the honorary secretary. The remaining provisions about the council were not changed.

The amendments made in 1919 raised the strength of the council from 150 to not more than 300.[64] As a result, the allocations for all the provinces were doubled, with the proviso that the subdivided figures against the Central Provinces and Berar would be: Central Provinces 5, and Berar 3. The annual fee for council membership was reduced from Rs 20 to Rs 12. Another amendment softened the provision about the removal of a council member. It was now provided that if the fee of a member was in arrears for over a year, the honorary secretary would give a notice of payment and if he failed to make the payment within a month after such a notice, the council could remove his name from the list of members. The 1931 revised constitution raised the strength of the council to 310.[65] The members for Delhi were increased from 4 to 10. Now the constitution made a separate provision for Bombay (20) and Sindh (10)—increasing the combined strength by 2 members, added 2 members each for Central Provinces and Berar, Central India and Ajmer, and Indian states and others; and reduced the strength of Burma from 14 to 10. There was one change in the election of council members. Henceforth, every provincial Muslim League elected nine-tenth of the allocated members and the remaining one-tenth of the members were elected at the annual session. It was also provided that every Muslim member of the central legislature would be *ex-officio* member of the council on payment of Rs 12 annually.

The provincial Muslim Leagues elected members of the central council. If they did not elect them on time, which they often did not, the central council was empowered to elect them directly. The councillors were required to pay their annual subscriptions regularly but many of them retained their membership without paying their dues. The party did not take any action against the defaulters. Instead, as in the case of defaulting ordinary members, it waived off the arrears outstanding against the councillors twice: once in 1910 and then in 1920. It did not strictly apply the provision regarding defaulting members till Dr Saifuddin Kitchlew took over as the honorary secretary. Then it removed members from the roll for non-payment of dues, which caused quite a few vacancies in several provinces.[66] Vacancies in the council also occurred when the provincial Muslim Leagues became dormant or otherwise failed to elect their representatives on time partially or in full strength. These vacancies were filled in, often in consultation with the secretaries of the provincial Muslim Leagues,[67] and sometimes, as in 1911, the central honorary secretary himself prepared a list of members for the provinces, which the general body formally approved.[68] And in August 1913, the central council elected members on behalf of the Bengal, Bihar, United Provinces, Central Provinces and Berar, Rajputana, Delhi and Burma provincial Muslim Leagues and for the native states. Except for the Bengal presidency Muslim League, the list of proposed members had been prepared in consultation with the secretaries of the provincial Muslim Leagues. In 1916 also, the central secretary proposed a list of members for all the provinces; some members, however, did object to this procedure.[69] Again, in 1919, the central council elected councillors from the provinces in consultation with the secretaries of the provincial Muslim Leagues, except in the case of the Punjab, Bengal, Madras and Burma provincial Muslim Leagues, which had sent the lists of their representatives.[70] Filling of the vacant seats used to be a 'regular' agenda item for the council meetings after 1927. In March 1929, the total number of vacancies in various provinces was 79;[71] in November 1931, 36; and in May 1932, 58. The interested quarters could manipulate the central League office in such situations to secure the election of members of their choice.[72]

The council held its meetings whenever the party was pursuing any specific political agenda or it was planning to hold its all-India session. But it failed to meet as frequently as was required under the constitution when its organization was dormant or when its leaders were involved in the activities of other organizations.[73] Another reason was that all the members could not afford to attend the council meetings from distant places or at short notice. The party tried to solve this problem by keeping the quorum requirement very low, 5 out of 40 till 1913 and 10 out of 300 after that, or by seeking the opinion of at least 10 per cent absent members on the agenda items by correspondence and counting them as votes. This mechanism, however, did not work successfully. The Leaguers of Lucknow, where the party's head office was located from January 1910 to December 1926, were given unduly large representation on the council for the purpose of securing quorum at the meetings of the council.[74] Even then, the council had often to adjourn meetings due to lack of quorum or for non-receipt of 10 per cent opinions by correspondence. Quorum was not needed for an adjourned meeting, which was considered valid even if the members present were less than the required number. Sometimes the honorary secretary felt frustrated in this kind of situation; once he even threatened to resign. In defence of low attendance at the council meetings, the Leaguers put forward the argument that hardly 'more than a dozen members' attended the meetings of a similar body of the Indian National Congress, which claimed to represent the whole country.[75]

(*iv*) *Working Committee.* The All-India Muslim League constitution had no provision for a working committee till December 1931. The amendments made that year introduced this organ into the organizational structure of the party. The working committee was elected by the central council and consisted of not more than twenty-one members plus the president and honorary secretary as *ex-officio* members. It was required to hold at least one meeting every month. Five members excluding the president and the honorary secretary constituted the quorum for a meeting. The working committee could pass resolutions on any issues but these resolutions were not to be inconsistent with the creed and policy of the All-India Muslim League or any resolution of its council or its all-India session. However, the resolutions passed by the working committee needed approval of the council. The working committee was responsible for implementing the resolutions of the council and the all-India sessions. It controlled and regulated the expenditure under the overall direction of the council and performed such other functions as might be assigned to it by the All-India Muslim League or its council.

On 24 January 1932, the council elected members of the first working committee. Its members were drawn from different provinces without any pre-determined criteria of representation: NWFP 1; Bihar 1; Madras 1; Bombay 1: Sindh 1; Ajmer 1; Bengal 3; United Provinces 4; Punjab 5; and Delhi 3.[76] But soon after this election, the All-India Muslim League went through a factional turmoil that led to a formal split in the party. Therefore, the working committee did not have a chance to function properly and play its role. It became an important executive organ of the party after October 1937, when the All-India Muslim League amended the relevant provisions of the constitution. Its strength remained the same but the president instead of the council was empowered to nominate its members.

(*v*) *Provincial Muslim Leagues.* By 1910, the All-India Muslim League had completed the process of formation of branches in most of the provinces. The provincial Muslim Leagues were free to draw up their own constitutions and draft rules with the approval of the All-India Muslim League; and the party made no attempt to enforce uniformity in their structures.[77] However, the All-India Muslim League did frame rules to regulate the relations between the central League and the provincial Muslim Leagues to prevent any conflict between them.[78] The by-laws that the central council framed provided that the provincial Muslim Leagues would not send anything to the Government of India without consulting the central League; each provincial Muslim League would send its annual report to the central League and vice versa; and the central League would not send any representation to the Government of India relating exclusively to a particular province without consulting the provincial Muslim League concerned.[79] After formation, the provincial Muslim Leagues were simply required to keep the existing members on the roll, elect new members and hold elections of its office-bearers and representatives on the central council after every three years. The provincial Muslim Leagues and the district Muslim Leagues did not enjoy steady growth and went through long spells of inactivity. They became active only when there was any local issue in focus or at the time of party elections or if the All-India Muslim League needed their support on an issue. The Leaguers did espouse emotional issues affecting the Indian Muslims but rarely used the League platform for such objectives. While still retaining the League membership they organized new all-India or provincial and regional platforms or used the platforms of other parties. Two major all-India parties that the Leaguers organized—the Central Khilafat Committee and the All-India Muslim Conference—posed a challenge to the League's survival. The Central Khilafat Committee temporarily pushed it into oblivion and the All-India Muslim Conference at one time threatened its very existence. The First World War, the Khilafat movement, the Simon Commission and fluctuating League–Congress relations influenced its solidarity and factionalised its ranks that often resulted in immobilizing its provincial Muslim Leagues and district Muslim Leagues.

Punjab Provincial Muslim League. After 1911, this branch witnessed renewed factionalism and had strained relations with the central League.[80] The changes in the party constitution especially in its objectives and its unconditional support of Gopal Krishna Gokhale's (1866–1915) Elementary Education Bill, ignoring the Punjab provincial

Muslim League's reservations, were the main reasons for this phenomenon.[81] Mian Shafi tried to avoid an All-India Muslim League–Punjab provincial Muslim League conflict,[82] when he presided over the all-India session that adopted the changes in the constitution; and he addressed a letter to the League members welcoming any League–Congress understanding.[83] But he had to face criticism from within the provincial Muslim League from Nawab Fateh Ali Khan (president, Punjab provincial Muslim League), and others who were opposed to any Hindu–Muslim rapprochement in politics or any change in the creed of the All-India Muslim League.[84] Fazli Husain was not far behind in opposing Mian Shafi.[85] The real threat to Mian Shafi's control of the provincial Muslim League came in 1916, when young dissatisfied 'progressive' Leaguers challenged his 'conservative', and 'unswerving' pro-British, leadership.[86] They declared that the old provincial Muslim League had become defunct, as it had not held its elections that were due in May 1915. Encouraged by some central Leaguers, they formed a new provincial Muslim League at a public meeting in Lahore on 30 January 1916, which elected its office-bearers and its representatives on the central council. The new provincial Muslim League requested the All-India Muslim League for affiliation.[87] Alarmed by this development, Mian Shafi hastily galvanized his supporters; and on 9 February, the old League elected its office-bearers and its representatives on the central council, and sent the information to the central League.[88] Then, a struggle between the two provincial Muslim Leagues ensued. Mian Shafi contended that the new League had no legal standing, and the All-India Muslim League would have to disaffiliate first the old League in order to give affiliation to the new one.[89] The new League, in its request for affiliation, alleged that no constitutionally-constituted League existed in the Punjab; the Shafi-controlled League did not represent the 'sentiments and aspirations' of the Punjab Muslims; it was exploited by a few individuals who had ignored their 'wishes and feelings'; it had thwarted the implementation of the All-India Muslim League's resolutions; and it had remained silent about the disruption of the annual session in Bombay. It asserted that the new League represented the real 'aspirations' of the Punjab Muslims.[90] Wazir Hasan communicated these allegations to Mian Shafi as a formal 'charge sheet' against the old League. Mian Shafi, instead of responding to his letter directly, printed the reply of his League in refutation of the charges and sent one copy to Wazir Hasan.[91] When the All-India Muslim League discussed this issue at its annual session in Lucknow, it disaffiliated the Shafi League and gave affiliation to the new League, which had Nawab Fateh Ali Khan as its patron, Mian Mohammad Din president, Pir Tajuddin (1878–1954) general secretary and Ghulam Rasul Khan (d. 1949) joint as well as finance secretary. In October 1917, Fazli Husain, who had guided the new League from behind the scene, replaced Tajuddin as the general secretary; the latter himself proposed his name.[92]

The new provincial Muslim League did not enjoy smooth sailing. When it wanted to present an address to the viceroy during his visit to the Punjab in March 1917, Lord Hardinge (1858–1944), the private secretary to the viceroy advised Tajuddin to present a 'combined address' on behalf of the Punjab Muslims. Tajuddin tried to do that but failed to work out an agreed mechanism. Eventually, the viceroy accepted a combined address that was presented to him by three organizations: the Shafi League, the Anjuman-i-Himayat-i-Islam, Lahore, and the Anjuman-i-Islamia, Lahore. Tajuddin's representations to the viceroy that his League was the officially affiliated branch of the All-India Muslim League produced no result.[93] This incident dealt a severe blow to the new League. Fazli Husain's views on Muslim representation in the Punjab legislature according to the Lucknow Pact and the rebuffs that he faced in his attempt to preside over an all-India session of the League had a sobering effect on him. He gradually lost interest in the League affairs, came closer to Mian Shafi's viewpoint and patched up his differences with him.[94] During the tumultuous Khilafat days, both Mian Shafi and Fazli Husain associated themselves with the government—the former as a minister in the Punjab government and the latter as a member of the Viceroy's Executive Council at the centre. The Punjab provincial Muslim League was neglected in the process.

Fazli Husain was among those Leaguers who participated in the elections under the Act of 1919 and was elected to the Punjab Legislative Council. He was taken as the minister for education and local self-government; and in that capacity, he reserved seats for the Muslims in the professional and other colleges of Lahore and in government services. He also introduced separate electorates in some municipalities. Muslims of the Punjab appreciated his measures but Hindus perceived them as unfair and a threat to their vested interests. Fazli Husain successfully countered the opposition against his steps in the Punjab council especially after he formed the non-communal Unionist Party that was composed of Muslim, Hindu and Sikh members of the council, but he looked to the All-India Muslim League to combat Hindu opposition at the popular level. He activated the Punjab provincial Muslim League, which invited the All-India Muslim League to hold its adjourned session in Lahore in May 1924.[95] His move generated support for the Punjab League, but it became really active only when Mian Shafi assumed its presidency in February 1927.[96] The enthusiasm that the Lahore session created among the Punjab Muslims was soon spoiled by the controversy surrounding the issue of electorates, which was followed thereafter by differences on the question of boycott of the Simon Commission. The intra-League differences split the All-India Muslim League into two parties: the Jinnah League and the Shafi League. Both parties had separate branches in the Punjab. Malik Barkat Ali (1885–1946) and his friends organized a provincial Muslim League, to which the Jinnah League gave affiliation in February 1928 but interestingly, information about the affiliation did not reach the Punjab League till November that year.[97] Even after the Jinnah League and the Shafi League forged unity in March 1929, it did not energize the Punjab League. It maintained a skeleton structure in Lahore but lost touch with the Leaguers in the districts. The provincial Muslim League became active only after Jinnah assumed the All-India Muslim League's presidency on his return from England.[98]

Bengal Presidency Muslim League. After the annulment of partition of Bengal, the East Bengal and West Bengal presidency Muslim Leagues were united to form one branch, the Bengal presidency Muslim League, at a meeting in Calcutta in March 1912. Nawab Salimullah was elected its president and Nawab Ali Chaudhury and Zahid Suhrawardy (1870–1948) its secretaries.[99] In 1916, Nawab Ali Chaudhury was elected president and Fazlul Haq succeeded him as secretary. All-India Muslim League's acceptance of 40 per cent representation in the legislature for the Bengali Muslims in the Lucknow Pact caused a rift in the presidency Muslim League. Some Bengali Leaguers who disagreed with this formula joined hands with dissident Leaguers from other provinces to form the All-India Muslim Association but failed to get any better deal from the government in the Act of 1919. They were apprehensive about Hindu domination in Bengal and cited the examples of two bodies, the Calcutta University and Calcutta Corporation, which had not returned a single Muslim to the Bengal Legislative Council from the time of their inception to November 1917.[100] The Bengal presidency Muslim League, under pressure from within its ranks, did ask the All-India Muslim League to manage amendment in the Lucknow Pact in order to provide equal representation to Hindus and Muslims from Bengal in the central and provincial legislatures, by reducing the number of seats allocated for other communities.[101] But its efforts did not produce any positive result. The presidency Muslim League was active on other fronts as well. It campaigned for the rescission of internment orders against Mrs Annie Besant, urged the government to cancel the orders against Maulana Abul Kalam Azad (1888–1958) to leave Bengal, to increase his monthly allowance, and to permit him to offer the Asr and Maghreb prayers in the mosque.[102] It protested against the use of the military in communal riots in Noakhali and the resultant 'bloodshed' in a mosque and the censorship imposed on the Muslim press.[103]

After the introduction of the Act of 1919, the Bengal presidency Muslim League again raised the issue of Muslim representation in the Bengal legislature. It did so indirectly and within the party. The Lucknow Pact had provided that no legislation affecting a community would be processed in the legislatures if three-fourth members of that community opposed it. The Act made no such provision. Now, on 30 January 1920, the Bengal presidency Muslim League council called on the All-India Muslim League either to move the Government of India to insert this proviso in the rules framed under the Act or 'to increase Muslim representation in Bengal up to 50 per cent of seats in the Bengal Legislative Council'. Mujibur Rahman Khan (1869–1940), secretary of the Bengal presidency Muslim League, wrote almost apologetically to Zahur Ahmad, the central honorary secretary, in a letter marked 'personal', that 'men like us who are out and out Muslim Leaguers were not inclined to reopen' the question of Muslim representation in the Bengal legislature but a large section of the Muslims in Bengal were pressing for proportionate representation for them in the Bengal legislature. The popularity of the League, he added, depended largely on 'a satisfactory solution' of the issue of Muslim 'representation in the Bengal Council'.[104] However, the All-India Muslim League did not take up the Bengal presidency Muslim League's demand for deliberation. Soon after, many Bengal Leaguers became involved in the Khilafat movement, and several others joined the newly formed Fazlul Haq-led non-communal Proja Party. When the Bengal presidency Muslim League was reactivated in 1927, two parallel Leagues emerged on the political scene. More influential of the two was the one that invited the Jinnah League to hold its annual session in Calcutta. The fortunes of the Bengal presidency Muslim League did not change even after it hosted the session. Like the Madras provincial Muslim League, the Bengal presidency Muslim League also faced a threat of 'extreme action' from the central honorary secretary for supporting the decisions of the Allahabad Unity Conference, but the condition of the All-India Muslim League itself made the threat ineffective.[105]

Sindh Provincial Muslim League. In Sindh, the All-India Muslim League had elected and enrolled a few Muslims as members when it held its first annual session in Karachi. A provincial League was, however, not formed in Sindh till 1920. In 1912, Mir Ayub Khan, the honorary secretary of the Sindh Mohammadan Association, and Hafizulla Shahabuddin, on the suggestion of the Aga Khan, undertook to establish a League branch in Sindh but their move did not result in the formation of a provincial Muslim League.[106] A more serious and determined attempt was made in April 1917. The proposed provincial League was meant to counter the activities of the Sindh Mohammedan Association, which had allegedly fallen into 'the hands of reactionaries' and was planning to present an address to Lord Hardinge to affirm that the Muslims were opposed to home rule. The response of the All-India Muslim League to the formation of the Sindh provincial Muslim League was surprisingly discouraging and inappropriate. On 1 November, a few Muslims met in the Khaliqdina Hall in Karachi to form the Sindh provincial Muslim League and elected Yusuf Ali Alibhai as president, Ghulam Mohammad Bhurgari (1881–1924) vice-president, Ghulam Ali Chagla honorary secretary and Haji Abdullah Haroon (1872–1942) joint secretary. Ghulam Ali Chagla, in a telegram to Wazir Hasan on 3 November 1917, followed by a letter on 7 November, asked for its affiliation with the All-India Muslim League.[107] The central council considered this application as late as 29 February 1919 but still did not take any decision. Interestingly, on 7 May 1919, Abdul Walli, assistant secretary in the central League office, wrote to Ghulam Ali Chagla that he had found an affiliation application on the file but the action taken on it was not there. He requested Chagla to supply him a 'copy of any communication' that he might have received from the central League office! Chagla did not respond to this letter. The issue was again taken up in February 1920, when the Sindh provincial Muslim League elected new office-bearers: Ghulam

Mohammad Bhurgari as president, Abdullah Haroon as vice-president, A.M. Ahmad as honorary secretary and Tayyab Ali Alibhai as joint secretary.[108] On 3 March, A.M. Ahmad asked Zahur Ahmad, central honorary secretary, to place the question of affiliation before the central council to ensure a decision but still no action was taken. On 17 July, A.M. Ahmad again requested the central honorary secretary for affiliation and threatened to go to the press or ask the provincial Muslim League council 'to declare itself an independent body'. Now there was a prompt response; on 18 July, the central council gave the Sindh provincial Muslim League affiliation but the provincial Muslim League had no time to rejoice the decision because its leaders were deeply involved in the Khilafat movement.[109] The Sindh provincial Muslim League revived itself in February 1925, and began its campaign for the separation of Sindh from the Bombay presidency. The Sindh Leaguers widened the base of their campaign when, in 1932, they forged a broader platform, 'the Sindh Separation Conference', in cooperation with leaders of other organizations. The separation conference organized branches at the lower level and observed 16 September as the 'Sindh Day'.[110] It succeeded in its movement for the separation of Sindh from Bombay but the separate identity of the Sindh provincial Muslim League was blurred in the process.

Frontier Provincial Muslim League. The All-India Muslim League could not establish a branch in the NWFP till 1912. The main reason was the British security concerns which kept the atmosphere in the province uncongenial for organized political activity. Some Leaguers expressed their doubts whether or not a provincial Muslim League could ever be organized here.[111] Still, a few courageous souls took the initiative; and in 1912, they founded a provincial Muslim League in Peshawar with Mian Abdul Aziz as president, Sayyid Ali Abbas Bokhari (1887–1926) as general secretary, Qazi Abdul Wali Khan (1880–1959) as vice-president and Kazi Mir Ahmad Khan as joint secretary.[112] Later on, Qazi Abdul Wali Khan was elected its vice-president and Sardar Abdul Hamid Khan, an Afghan prince residing in Peshawar, patron of the provincial Muslim League. Sardar Abdul Hamid was, however, soon removed from that office on discovery that he was an Afghan national and not a British Indian citizen.[113] The Frontier provincial Muslim League functioned in an inhospitable environment, so much so that the government disallowed it to host the annual session of the All-India Muslim Educational Conference in

Peshawar. The provincial Muslim League was perceived 'as a scorpion' that the people avoided, and the attempt to seek its membership was viewed as 'going against the current'.[114] Its members initially came from the Peshawar district but in 1914, a few members were elected from Abbottabad and Dera Ismail Khan following a renewed campaign to increase its members. The provincial Muslim League severely criticized the Frontier Crimes Regulation (FCR), which was used to restrict civil liberties and to control the judicial and police system of the NWFP.[115] The League ran into trouble soon after its formation. In October 1914, Ali Abbas Bokhari, one of the most outspoken critics of the British, was arrested on the charge of making a provocative speech in a Peshawar mosque. Bokhari had alleged that the Islamia College, Peshawar, was 'a political college', which had European civil and military officers including the inspector general of police on its managing committee, designed to stop people from going to Aligarh to prevent the growth of pan-Islamic sentiments, and that the local Muslims on the committee, in his opinion, were running after titles.[116] When the All-India Muslim League made queries from the government about Bokhari's arrest, he was immediately released.[117] After his release, Bokhari moved to the Attock district in the Punjab. The government warned other Frontier Leaguers to desist from organized political activity and removed the active among them from Peshawar to other places.[118] In August 1917, Kazi Mir Ahmad Khan informed the central League that the provincial Muslim League had 'to be broken up' after a warning to every Leaguer from the government, and that currently no League existed in the NWFP. The best course, he advised the central League, was to treat those members who wished 'to keep their connection with the League as mere members' and have no organized body.[119] When Bokhari secretly visited Peshawar, he was again arrested and detained for twenty-six days, after which the chief commissioner, NWFP, ordered him to leave the province and stay in Attock or in any other district of the Punjab. Instead of following that order, he escaped to Kabul via Tirah (Waziristan), where the amir of Afghanistan welcomed him and allowed him to stay in the palace that Amir Abdur Rahman (1844–1901) had built for himself.[120] The provincial Muslim League as an organized political body disappeared after that and was not revived till the mid-1930s. In 1924, when Hindu–Muslim riots broke out in Kohat, it was a Muslim association that defended the Muslim position against the propaganda of the Sanatan Dharam and Hindu Sabha and briefed the All-India Muslim League and other Muslim organizations about the communal situation in the area.[121] Again, it was the Muslim association of Dera Ismail Khan, headed by Nawab Saifullah Khan, which resisted the Hindu Sabha's demand for the re-amalgamation of the NWFP in the Punjab; instead, it demanded the introduction of constitutional reforms in the province, as recommended by the Majority Report of Denys Bray's Frontier Enquiry Committee.[122] Later on, the Muslim association thanked all those who supported Syed Murtaza Bahadur's resolution in the central legislative assembly for the extension of constitutional reforms to the NWFP. In October 1934, an unsuccessful attempt was made in Dera Ismail Khan to revive a League branch in the NWFP.[123]

Bombay Presidency Muslim League. This branch suffered a setback in October 1910, when Lord Hardinge gave a discouraging response to its welcome address that it presented to him on his landing in Bombay.[124] More pressure on its cohesion came around the time of the All-India Muslim League's annual session in Bombay in December 1915. The 'new' Leaguers aggressively asserted themselves and pushed the 'old' Leaguers into the background. Despite these strains, the Aga Khan continued to head the Bombay presidency Muslim League till 1922, though its organization at the lower level went into limbo. After the Lucknow session of 1923, all attempts to organize a new Muslim League or 'reform' the old League produced no result.[125] It was in July 1924, that the Bombay presidency Muslim League was formally revived through the efforts of M.A. Jinnah, with M.C. Chagla as its secretary. This League made arrangements for the annual session in Bombay that year. It did not show much activity after the annual session. In 1927–29, the provincial branch of the Jinnah League was quite active but that was for a very short duration. After that, the League branch remained inactive till Jinnah assumed its presidency after his return from England.

Madras Provincial Muslim League. This branch smoothly functioned till 1920, with Ghulam Mohammad Ali Khan, the Prince of Arcot, as its president and Yaqub Hasan as secretary.[126] That year, Yaqub Hasan was elected its president and Abdul Hamid Khan (1896–1966) its secretary.[127] Soon after this election, the provincial Muslim League was 'swept away' in the Khilafat movement. Yaqub Hasan, who had acted as secretary of the Khilafat delegation to England in 1919, was elected secretary of the Central Khilafat Committee. He and many other

Madras Leaguers plunged themselves into the Khilafat movement and the provincial Muslim League completely disappeared from the political scene. It was not revived till September 1926. In the process of its revival, two parallel Leagues emerged, which participated in the elections to the Madras assembly in December that year. Both the Leagues united after the elections and elected Syed Murtaza Bahadur as president and A.T.M. Ahmad Ibrahim as secretary.[128] Two years later, M. Jamal Mohammad (b. 1889) replaced Syed Murtaza Bahadur as president.[129] In 1932, the Madras provincial Muslim League came into conflict with the central secretary of the All-India Muslim League in regard to the decisions of the Allahabad Unity Conference. The central honorary secretary crudely threatened to disaffiliate the provincial Muslim League for its endorsement of those proposals of the unity conference that the central council had rejected.[130] The provincial Muslim League secretary, communicating the decision of the provincial council in an equally assertive language, dubbed the central honorary secretary's threat as 'unconstitutional' and claimed the right of the provincial Muslim League to express its 'independent opinion' on the issues under reference.[131] The All-India Muslim League could not take any action against the Madras League as the party itself sank into a crisis in 1933.

Bihar Provincial Muslim League. This branch functioned without any controversy, with Sarfraz Husain Khan as president and Fakhruddin (1868–1933) as secretary; and in April 1916, Nurul Hasan replaced the latter as the secretary.[132] Like other provincial Muslim Leagues, it commented on current issues such as Muslim cooperation with the government after the Ottoman entry into the First World War, the controversy regarding the Bombay annual session, and the League–Congress Reform Scheme. Hindu–Muslim relations suffered after Bihar gained the status of a province, which gave the Hindus self-confidence as they enjoyed a comfortable majority. Hindu–Muslim cordiality that had existed since 1912–13, when the Hindus had helped the Muslim victims of the Balkan wars and the Kanpur mosque tragedy, gradually disappeared. In 1917, Bihar witnessed serious communal riots. The provincial Muslim League did relief work for the sufferers but the Khilafat movement pushed it into inactivity. The party was revived in 1925, and re-affiliated with the All-India Muslim League, with Nurul Hasan as its president and Mahmud Shere as secretary.[133] Two years later, in December 1927, Sir Ali Imam was elected its president and

Syed Mohammad its secretary. Soon after, the president got involved in the politics of the 'Nationalist Muslims'; consequently, the activities of the Bihar provincial Muslim League declined. In 1931, a new provincial Muslim League was formed with Masud Ahmad as secretary, which asked the All-India Muslim League for affiliation. The old provincial Muslim League also activated itself in reaction to this move and asked the central League not to affiliate the new League. Thus, two Leagues functioned in Bihar for some time. The central council deputed Syed Murtaza Bahadur to bring about reconciliation between the two Leagues in Bihar. As a result of his efforts, the conflict between the two Leagues was resolved and the united League elected Hasan Jan as its president and Mahmud Shere as secretary. But this unity did not put any new life into the Bihar provincial Muslim League.

United Provinces Provincial Muslim League. The United Provinces branch of the All-India Muslim League could not overcome the conflict between its two principal office-bearers—president and secretary. Nawab Abdul Majid, its president, complained that Ibne Ahmad, the secretary, had often circulated the agenda for the party meetings and offered comments on various issues on behalf of the provincial Muslim League without consulting him. His supporters also challenged Ibne Ahmad's 'exclusive control' of the party funds and demanded their supervision by a finance committee. Ibne Ahmad resented such moves as intrusion into his authority as secretary. He found in the Lucknow Leaguers, who wielded considerable influence in the central party, willing supporters. The Lucknow Leaguers grumbled that the Allahabad Leaguers had more share than them in the executive committee of the United Provinces League, which did not give due weight to the views of Leaguers of other districts.[134] They wanted the district Muslim Leagues and the provincial Muslim League council to participate more effectively in the decision-making process. They also demanded that the headquarters of the United Provinces League should be shifted back to Lucknow. The intra-party conflict persisted despite several attempts at mediation. Meanwhile, the work of the provincial Muslim League stood virtually suspended. Finally, the matter was referred to the Aga Khan for resolution.[135] Consequently, on 9 June 1912, Nawab Abdul Majid was re-elected as president but M.A. Baqi Khan replaced Ibne Ahmad as secretary. However, the pressure for the shifting of provincial Muslim League head office continued till it was moved back to Lucknow.[136] The United Provinces League soon recovered from these conflicts. After the Kanpur Mosque tragedy, it successfully campaigned for the introduction of separate electorates in the municipal and district boards and provided a platform for creating sectarian harmony.[137] The 'concessions' made to the Muslims in the new Municipalities Act provoked strong criticism from the Hindus who raised the slogan of 'Hindus in Danger' and organized conferences to oppose the Act but without any success.[138] The United Provinces League hosted the annual session of the All-India Muslim League in Lucknow in December 1916; and on its leaders' initiative, the principle of weightage for the minorities was incorporated in the Lucknow Pact. It remained quite active at the district level after the Lucknow Pact till it became inactive with the start of the Khilafat movement.[139] Hasrat Mohani tried to activate it in April 1922 but could not do that.[140] The United Provinces League was finally revived in March 1924, with Ehtesham Ali (1869–1943) as president and Raham Ali as secretary; Ehsanur Rahman Kidwai (b. 1887) replaced Raham Ali as secretary in November that year. Its branches in fifteen districts were revived. However, its activities noticeably suffered a decline when the office of the central League was shifted from Lucknow to Delhi and focus moved on issues and places outside the United Provinces.

Central Provinces and Berar Provincial Muslim League. This branch had slowly relapsed into oblivion after the Nagpur session in 1910. H.M. Malak remained its nominal head although, according to his own statement, the party existed at the provincial and district levels for 'namesake'.[141] After December 1916, the Leaguers showed some interest in activating the provincial Muslim League and through the efforts of 'advanced youngsters' or the 'progressives', the Central Provinces and Berar provincial Muslim League was reactivated with Mohammad Yusuf Shareef as its president and Tajuddin, editor of the newspaper *Taj*, and Anisuddin Ahmad as secretaries. H.M. Malak, who was opposed to the Home Rule activities of the 'youngsters', declined to accept the offer of the Leaguers to continue as president of the provincial Muslim League.[142] The 'youngsters' became active in the district Leagues in Central Provinces;[143] and a separate divisional League was organized in Berar with D.K. Soofi as president. But after this spurt of activity for a short while, the Central Provinces and Berar provincial Muslim League again went back into a state of inactivity during and after the Khilafat movement.[144]

Rajputana Provincial Muslim League. This branch continued to be headed by Dewan Imamuddin with Abdur Rashid as its secretary, and it also remained active till the time of the Khilafat movement. It was revived in September 1924, but it actively campaigned for the boycott of the Simon Commission. The 1927 split in the All-India Muslim League divided the Rajputana provincial Muslim League as well; consequently, the two Leagues that emerged ridiculed the representative character of each other by circulating printed leaflets. When the two Leagues were united, the provincial Muslim League then elected Zakaria Allah Rakha as president and Aziz Ahmad Zuberi as secretary.[145]

Delhi Provincial Muslim League. This branch had been accorded the status of a provincial Muslim League in the constitution of the All-India Muslim League. This branch was quite active after the Lucknow Pact especially around 1918 when the central League held its annual session in Delhi. However, except for Dr Mukhtar Ahmad Ansari (1880–1936) and Maulana Mohammad Ali, none who represented the Delhi provincial Muslim League on the central council was resident of Delhi. Once the Delhi provincial Muslim League weakened due to acute factionalism, it could not regain its real strength till after 1935.[146] Orissa still had no recognised provincial Muslim League. In September 1932, the Muslims in the province founded a Muslim association that requested the All-India Muslim League for affiliation but the central League was too involved at that time in its own factional tussles to look into its request. Till that date, no one had been taken from Orissa on the central council.[147]

Burma Provincial Muslim League. It was a peripheral branch, and the All-India Muslim League did not take much interest in its activities after its formation. In 1913, when Ahmad Moolla Dawood undertook to reactivate this branch, he could not find 'a scrap of paper' in its record.[148] No one including the president took interest in its work. Ahmad Dawood when elected president made a fresh start and revived the branch but it failed to sustain its activities for long. It simply commented on the developments in British India rather than on the problems of Muslims in Burma.[149] In the 1920s, the Burma Muslim Leaguers made several unsuccessful attempts to keep the party a live organization.[150] Early in 1931, Dawjee Dadabhai succeeded in making the provincial Muslim League active for a while but after the separation of Burma from British India, the Burma League ceased to function as a branch of the All-India Muslim League.[151] However, the Leaguers especially in south India kept alive their interest in the plight of the Muslims of Burma and rendered them much needed relief and assistance, when they suffered oppression at the hands of the Burmese authorities and began to migrate to British India.

Before 1935, the All-India Muslim League had two affiliated branches outside India: one, the Transvaal Muslim League, which the Indian Muslims living there had organized for their own welfare; and in November 1915, the central council recognized it as its branch in South Africa; and two, the London Muslim League, which remained an active branch during the life-time of Amir Ali. At one time there was a proposal to organize a League branch in Sri Lanka but the idea was not pursued seriously although a few Muslims living there were elected members of the All-India Muslim League.[152]

(*vi*) *Politics of the All-India Sessions.* The constitution required that the All-India Muslim League should hold its annual session at such time and place as its central council would determine. The council could also hold other all-India sessions including those requisitioned by not less than thirty ordinary members or not less than fifteen council members. It was authorized to elect a president who presided over the annual session, while the permanent president presided over extraordinary and special sessions. Seventy-five members constituted a quorum for the annual session and thirty for the other sessions. This quorum requirement was fixed in the constitution in 1913; before that it was at least one-fifth of the registered members for the annual session and one-eighth for other sessions. In 1931, the quorum for the annual sessions was reduced to fifty members. The central council till 1919, and after that a subjects committee, revised and approved the resolutions proposed by members before these were moved in the open session. It was the central council that decided as to who should move, and second, a particular resolution in the open session. Therefore, it would be misleading to conclude that the proposer of a resolution in the printed resolutions was its actual sponsor or author. Two-third members present at an annual session had the power to amend the constitution.

The all-India sessions provided the Indian Muslims the most important platform where they could regularly interact and discuss their political and other problems. The regularity of these sessions fostered in them feelings of affinity and strengthened their all-India Muslim identity. They used the All-India Muslim League to negotiate with the Congress or present their demands to the British/Indian government. During 1906–34, the All-India Muslim League held twenty-three annual sessions, one special session and one extraordinary session, besides the inaugural session. [Table 2.6] Two annual sessions were adjourned: one was then held in Aligarh in March 1908 and the other in Lahore in May 1924. When the All-India Muslim League split up into two parties, first in 1927 and then in 1933, each of the two parties held separate annual sessions. Three presidents-elect did not preside over the annual sessions. Amir Ali, elected twice, could not come from England to preside over the sessions while Abul Kalam Azad, elected once, declined to preside over the session, and Maulana Mohammad Ali could not preside over the fifteenth annual session due to his incarceration. Interestingly, no non-Muslim presided over any of its sessions. There was only once a proposal to invite a retired British lieutenant governor of a province or a former viceroy to preside over the annual session but the party rejected the idea.[153] The dates and venues of the annual sessions were often synchronized with the sessions of the All-India Muslim Educational Conference or the Congress. The annual sessions in this phase (1906–1934) were normally organized in December during the Christmas holidays, except the sessions in 1912 and 1913, which were held during the Easter holidays.

Dhaka was selected as the venue for the inaugural session mainly because the All-India Muslim Educational Conference was holding its annual meeting in that city. Nawab Wiqarul Mulk chaired this session; Nawab Salimullah proposed his name. The All-India Muslim League held its first annual session in Karachi, again because the All-India Muslim Educational Conference was holding its annual meeting in that city. At that time, Sindh neither had the status of a province not did it have a regular organized branch League but none insisted on the formation of a branch League prior to the session that was scheduled on 29–30 December 1907. Ali Mohammad Khan Dehlavi hurriedly formed a local League in Karachi to make arrangements for the annual session. On Wiqarul Mulk's motion, Sir Adamji Pirbhai (1945–1913), a noted Muslim businessman and philanthropist, was elected its president; but because of his old age and ill-health, his son read out his presidential address. The session adjourned before concluding its business. The adjourned session was then convened in Aligarh on

18–19 March 1908. On the motion of Fazli Husain, Shah Din was elected to preside over the adjourned session. The second annual session, and the first after the adoption of the party constitution, was arranged in Amritsar on 30–31 December 1908. On the suggestion of the Aga Khan, the central committee elected Amir Ali to preside over the session but due to the League's inability to fund fully his travel,

Table 2.6: Annual sessions of the AIML, 1906–1933*

President	Place	Year
Nawab Wiqarul Mulk (Inaugural session)	Dhaka	1906
Adamji Pirbhai (1st annual session)	Karachi	1907
Mohammad Shah Din (1st adjourned session)	Aligarh	(Mar) 1908
Sayyid Ali Imam (2nd annual session)	Amritsar	1908
Prince Ghulam Mohammad Ali Khan (3rd annual session)	Delhi	1910
Sayyid Nabiullah (4th annual session)	Nagpur	1910
Nawab Saleemullah Khan (5th annual session)	Calcutta	(Mar) 1912
Mian Mohammad Shafi (6th annual session)	Lucknow	(Mar) 1913
Ibrahim Rahimtullah (7th annual session)	Agra	1913
Mazharul Haq (8th annual session)	Bombay	1915
M.A. Jinnah (9th annual session)	Lucknow	1916
Maulana Mohammad Ali (President-elect) (10th annual session)	Calcutta	1917
Raja of Mahmudabad (Special session)	Bombay	(Aug-Sep) 1918
A.K. Fazlul Haq (11th annual session)	Delhi	1918
Hakim Ajmal Khan (12th annual session)	Amritsar	1919
M.A. Jinnah (Special session)	Calcutta	(Sep) 1920
Dr M.A. Ansari (13th annual session)	Nagpur	1920
Maulana Hasrat Mohani (14th annual session)	Ahmadabad	1921
Mir Ghulam Mohammad Bhurgari (15th annual session)	Lucknow	1923
M.A. Jinnah (15th adjourned session)	Lahore	(May) 1924
Sayyid Raza Ali (16th annual session)	Bombay	1924
Abdur Rahim (17th annual session)	Aligarh	1925

Shaikh Abdul Qadir (18th annual session)	Delhi	1926
Mohammad Yaqub (Jinnah Group) (19th annual session)	Calcutta	1927
Sir Mohammad Shafi (Shafi Group) (19th annual session)	Lahore	1927
Raja of Mahmudabad (20th annual session)	Calcutta	1928
Allama Mohammad Iqbal (21st annual session)	Allahabad	1930
Chaudhri Zafrullah Khan (22nd annual session)	Delhi	1931
Mian Abdul Aziz (Aziz Group) (23rd annual session)	Howrah	1933
Hafiz Hidayat Husain (Hidayat Group) (23rd) annual session)	Delhi	1933

*All sessions were held in December unless otherwise indicated.

he decided not to come and chair the session. On his refusal, the central committee elected Ali Imam as the president who presided over the session. The third session was held in Delhi on 29–30 January 1910. Amir Ali was again proposed for the presidency but a few days before the central committee was to take a decision, he was appointed on the Judicial Committee of the Privy Council; as a result, he decided not to come to India to preside over the session.[154] Sir Ghulam Ali Khan, the Prince of Arcot, was then elected to preside over the session.

The fourth session was held in Nagpur on 28–30 December 1910. The All-India Muslim League selected this venue at the Delhi session on the offer by H.M. Malak, a well-known business figure. It was Malak's persistence that made this session possible in Nagpur. At first, Aziz Mirza, the honorary secretary, insisted that a Central Provinces provincial League must be organized before the session. Earlier, no such condition was laid down for holding the session in Karachi. When the process of establishing the Central Provinces League was near completion, a more serious complication arose. The Aga Khan suggested Allahabad as the venue where the Congress was holding its session and arranging a Grand Exhibition. He promised to give Rs 5000 for the annual session, assuring to raise it to Rs 6000, if it was held in Allahabad.[155] Most of the council members supported his proposal especially as it had come from the permanent president. But Malak refused to accept the change of venue. Sahibzada Aftab Ahmad Khan and several others supported his contention that (i) any change in the venue would set a bad precedent; (ii) the Central Provinces League had established branch Leagues in all the districts; (*iii*) the Allahabad delegates at the Delhi session had refused to host the session, knowing all about the Congress session and the Grand Exhibition; (*iv*) the All-India Muslim Educational Conference, which was meeting in Nagpur, would be effective only if the League session was also held there; (*v*) the change of venue would disappoint Muslims all over India who were looking forward to the session in Nagpur; (vi) and the Nagpur invitation had been accepted at the annual session that the central council was not competent to change. Ignoring Malak's plea, the central council, after debating the issue for two days (24–25 October), decided in favour of Allahabad and appealed to the 'sense of patriotism' of the 'brethren' in Central Provinces to 'cheerfully' accept the decision.[156] But those who were in favour of Nagpur, or opposed the session in Allahabad, refused to accept this decision. They organized public meetings and sent telegrams to the Aga Khan, Aziz Mirza and Amir Ali to put pressure on them to hold the session in Nagpur. Finally, on 6 November, the central council, after discussing Aga Khan's response, resolved not to change the venue from Nagpur to Allahabad. Sayyid Nabiullah was selected to preside over the session because Amir Ali, Aga Khan and Nawab Salimullah declined to accept the presidency; however, Amir Ali promised to preside over the next session if invited by July and offered to bear a part of the expenses.[157]

The All-India Muslim League decided at the Nagpur session to hold its fifth annual session in Delhi during the Coronation Darbar. Amir Ali expected that he would be invited to preside over the session. In March 1911, he inquired from Aziz Mirza about the approximate date of the session if he was to chair it, and suggested that it should be held 'when the echoes of the Darbar' were over. Aziz Mirza informed him that the prospects of inviting him were not 'at all bright' due to shortage of funds and that the session would not be successful, if it was held after the Darbar. Amir Ali still advised that 'controversial matters relating to government measures' should be avoided on the occasion of the coronation.[158] Despite these words of caution, the central council decided to hold the session in Delhi on 13–16 December, a few days before the Darbar, and elected Sayyid Shamsul Huda (1863–1922) as president.[159] The League soon realized the real problem. When the Leaguers approached the Delhi administration for permission to use the All-India Muslim Educational Conference *pandal* for the session, the deputy commissioner informed them that 'it was against the wishes' of the viceroy that any 'communal meetings' should be held during the darbar week in Delhi.[160] Aziz Mirza was not discouraged by this negative response. He was confident that the viceroy would have no objection to the League session, as the Darbar Police Act that the Punjab legislature had recently passed did not apply 'to meetings held under the auspices of associations of recognised standing'.[161] The private secretary of the viceroy accepted Mirza's interpretation of the Police Act but still asked him to hold the League session 'on some other occasion'.[162] When Aziz Mirza approached the Aga Khan for advice, he also directed Mirza to do as suggested by the viceroy.[163] Consequently, the central council decided to postpone the session to 3–4 March 1912 at a place to be decided later on. The reason given out for the postponement was that 13 to 16 December were not public holidays and that a majority of the Leaguers could not attend the session 'without detriment to their ordinary avocations'. Nevertheless the council asked Mirza 'to make a respectful representation of protest' with the viceroy regarding his opinion about the objects of the League and the 'grounds' on which he had decided it 'inadvisable' for it to hold its annual session in Delhi.[164] In reality, the reason for disallowing the session in Delhi was possible Muslim reaction to the announcement that was to be made about the annulment of the partition of Bengal. The president-elect, Shamsul Huda, was also not available due to his appointment as a member of the executive council of the governor of Bengal. New president and venue were selected to restrain any emotional outburst from the Muslims. Calcutta was chosen as the new venue, and the Aga Khan persuaded Nawab Salimullah to accept the presidency although he had earlier repeatedly declined to preside over the session due to 'family engagements'.[165] These changes did not go well with the Muslims.

Meanwhile, factionalism crept into the All-India Muslim League, which divided its members into 'progressives' and 'conservatives'. The intra-party conflict influenced the selection of presidents and venues of the sessions. On 12 August 1912, the central council decided to hold the sixth annual session in Lucknow on 30–31 December and unanimously elected Amir Ali as president.[166] When sufficient funds had been collected to support his travel from London to India and preparations were in full swing, the Aga Khan and Amir Ali, in a joint telegram to the honorary secretary on 29 October, strongly urged him to postpone the session as a 'token mourning' for the 'grave peril' that confronted 'Islam' as a result of the Balkan war. The council, in an emergency meeting of local members on the following day, decided to send a reply to the effect that 'most important questions' were 'awaiting solution' in the next session and all local members viewed postponement 'unjustified and fatal' for the interests of the Indian Muslims. It was much better to hold the League session 'in mourning' than no session at all, and the League asked for a 'reply with reasons'. Amir Ali's secretary responded to this telegram on his behalf, communicating that Amir Ali's Red Crescent work would suffer in his absence and that if the League wanted his presence, the session 'must be postponed'.[167] Despite protests from some members, the central council postponed the session.[168] Instead of an all-India session, the League held a meeting of its council in Bankipur under the chairmanship of the Aga Khan on 31 December, to which 'leaders of the community' including M.A. Jinnah were also invited. After approving amendments in the constitution, the council decided to hold the session in Lucknow on 22–23 March 1913. A few days later, the council elected Mian Shafi, a 'conservative' leader, in place of Amir Ali as president, provided he endorsed the amendments in the constitution, as he had not attended the meeting in Bankipur. This endorsement, it was stated, was needed to allay objections from the 'progressives' to his election as president.[169] The honorary secretary not only obtained assurance from Shafi but also circulated it with his permission among the members that the president-elect was 'in entire agreement with the policy of the League as embodied in the amended constitution and rules'.[170] The sixth session concluded without any conflict.

Before the seventh session, a new element was added to the intra-party conflict. Many Leaguers believed that Hindu–Muslim unity was 'absolutely necessary for the progress of India'; M.A. Jinnah, Maulana Mohammad Ali, Mazharul Haq (1886–1930) and Raja of Mahmudabad were among its active proponents.[171] They felt that the All-India Muslim League and the Congress should meet at the same place and time to evolve common demands for constitutional reform; on 19 May 1913, the Congress secretary made a formal request to the League secretary to that effect.[172] However, the central council's selection of Agra as the venue for the seventh session on 30–31 December, and the election of Sir Ibrahim Rahimtullah (1862–1942) as president, signified a compromise between the 'progressives' and the 'conservatives'. The Agra session convened under the shadow of an imminent clash between the two factions. Shafi appealed to the Leaguers 'to prevent undignified scenes' at the session because that would 'shatter' the League and 'disgrace the [Muslim] community'.[173] Nawab Salimullah felt that postponement of the session was 'extremely desirable' for the interests of the Muslims.[174] However, it was the Aga Khan's resignation as permanent president on 3 November, that had a sobering effect and ensured peace at the Agra session. The session demanded extension of separate electorates to local bodies.[175] Maulana Mohammad Ali and Jinnah asked for deferring the move but on its rejection the latter's comments were, 'Gentlemen, the resolution [for separate electorates] has been passed by the All-India Muslim League. . . . I will abide by it and I bow my head to the verdict of my people'.[176] For the next session, the council selected Rawalpindi as the venue ignoring invitations from Bankipur and Madras, and elected Hasan Bilgrami, who had returned from London, as the president. Again, there was a possibility of an open clash. A proposal was then made to postpone the session on the plea that it did not seem 'expedient' to meet and pass simply a resolution assuring the British crown of 'our loyalty', as the League could not discuss the 'communal question' or the 'Indian administration' during the War. Therefore, the council postponed the session by 20 to 16 votes; again, a clash was averted.[177]

The Muslim Leaguers especially from Bombay and United Provinces did not remain silent for long. Now the initiative came from Jinnah who had been elected member of the central council on 7 February 1915. On his suggestion to Raja of Mahmudabad, Wazir Hasan obtained signatures of Muslim leaders from different provinces to an invitation for a council meeting on 27–28 March.[178] On 20 February, Wazir Hasan informed the Aga Khan about this development. Two days later, Mian Shafi who was one of the signatories of the invitation backed out, observing that any discussion at a 'political meeting' of Muslim rights on the termination of War was 'premature' and would 'excite undesirable feelings' in 'other quarters', meaning thereby the British government.[179] As a result, the proposal was killed and the council meeting was 'indefinitely postponed'. Then, the idea of holding the annual session was floated. Jinnah, Ibrahim Rahimtullah and Fazalbhai Karimbhai (1872–1970) promised to invite the session in Bombay. Invitation for the session was issued under the signatures of twenty-eight Muslims of Bombay but those Leaguers who were opposed to the move including the Aga Khan, Mian Shafi and Suleman Qasim Mitha persuaded a few signatories to withdraw their consent.[180] The council meeting that was scheduled on 6 June, to decide about the session was, therefore, postponed.[181] The issue of calling the annual session was revived in September. Maulana Mohammad Ali exhorted the Leaguers from Lansdowne, where the British had interned him, to hold the annual session in Bombay even if there was no invitation.[182] The opponents did not sit idle. Now Mian Shafi and Nawab Zulfikar Ali Khan (1873–1933) gathered seventeen leading Muslims from Bombay, United Provinces, Madras, Delhi and Punjab in Simla, and in meetings on 8 and 23 September, resolved to oppose the proposal for holding the annual session and requisitioned a council meeting to take a decision to that effect.[183] They were, however, defeated. When the council met on 10 November, it resolved to hold the session in Bombay on 30 December 1915–1 January 1916, by 49 to 13 votes, and elected Mazharul Haq as president. After this decision, tension mounted in Bombay city so much so that government intervention was sought to hold the session peacefully.[184] On 9 December, eight Leaguers representing the two factions including Jinnah, Suleman Qasim Mitha and Rafiuddin Ahmad held a meeting in the Secretariat, with Governor Wellingdon in the chair. It was agreed in this meeting that the All-India Muslim League would hold its session in Bombay, pass a resolution of loyalty to the government, and appoint, if it so desired, a committee to confer with other political parties to frame a scheme of reforms with due safeguards for the Muslims.[185] The first day of the session passed without any untoward incident.[186] On the second day, Suleman Qasim Mitha and his supporters disrupted the proceedings, with the connivance of the police commissioner who stood at the entrance to the *pandal*. The commotion began when Jinnah rose to move the resolution for the appointment of a committee to confer with the committee appointed by the Congress. Hasrat Mohani raised a point of order but the president ruled him out of order. He was allowed to speak following uproar from his supporters in the audience. Mohani asked for the adjournment of the meeting, as members could not express themselves freely. Amidst rowdyism and shouting the session was adjourned to meet at the Taj Mahal Hotel, where the proceedings were then concluded.[187]

For the ninth annual session, Wazir Hasan started the process in August rather than September when it was usually done. There was almost consensus on Jinnah's election as president of the session; except for three members who had suggested Ali Imam's name, everyone else including Ali Imam himself proposed his name.[188] Raja of Mahmudabad, proposing Jinnah's name, paid him rich tribute, observing that among the men 'who have dedicated themselves to the cause of the motherland, no one I believe commands greater admiration—it will be nearer truth if I may say affection and love—than that gifted Mohammedan of the Western Presidency, the Honourable Mr Mohammad Ali Jinnah. Young in years he has shown that in judgement he is ripe; his perseverance, his tact, above all, his single-minded devotion in working for the League in Bombay last year, should entitle him' to be the president.[189] On 11 October 1916, the council elected him president and selected Lucknow as the venue for the session scheduled to be held on 30–31 December because the Congress was holding its annual session in that city. That year, the All-India Muslim Educational Conference decided not to meet in Lucknow because, as Aftab Ahmad Khan informed Wazir Hasan, it would not be 'very wholesome for the quiet work' of an educational body like the Muslim Educational Conference.[190] The All-India Muslim League and the Congress adopted the Joint Reform Scheme at this session.

For the tenth annual session, the central council accepted the invitation of the Bengal presidency Muslim League and decided to hold the session in Calcutta on 30–31 December, and almost unanimously elected Maulana Mohammad Ali as president.[191] Since the president-elect was interned and there was no possibility of his release after the Home Member's reply to Jinnah's question in the Imperial Legislative Council, the Bengal presidency Muslim League had recommended Dr M.A. Ansari as a substitute, but the central council decided to keep the presidential chair vacant, if the British government did not release Mohammad Ali to make him available for the session.[192] The following year, on 28 July, the council resolved to hold a special session in Bombay on 31 August, to consider the Montagu-Chelmsford Report. Bombay was selected as the venue because the Congress was also holding its special session there. The same day, Fazli Husain was elected president of the special session, and in case of his inability, Hakim Ajmal Khan (1863–1927) was to preside over it. Three days after this decision, the council pointed out that according to the constitution it could elect a president for the annual session only and that the permanent president should preside over all other sessions.[193] Accordingly, Raja of Mahmudabad chaired the special session. It is difficult to know the extent to which the negative comments of Dr Mukhtar Ahmad Ansari about the change in Fazli Husain's views on constitutional reforms influenced this revised decision.[194] However, Fazli Husain, in a telegram to Wazir Hasan on 2 August, 'gladly' accepted the decision. But the 'change' in his views affected his prospects to preside over the next annual session. The council meeting that was to elect a president for the annual session was postponed seemingly for lack of quorum but the real reason was that a 'large number of members' had recommended Fazli Husain's name for the presidency. The names of Nawab Ishaq Khan (1860–1918) and Fazlul Haq were added in the new agenda that was issued for the council meeting.[195] A majority of the written opinions received were still in favour of Fazli Husain but the five members present in the meeting in Lucknow on 27 October, elected Nawab Ishaq Khan as president, and decided to hold the eleventh annual session in Delhi during the Christmas holidays.[196] Now Fazli Husain expressed his resentment by adding his voice to those who were opposed to the All-India Muslim League and Congress meeting in the same city.[197] Meanwhile, Nawab Ishaq Khan died a week after his election. The council then elected Fazlul Haq as president. A notable feature of this session was the presence of a large number of *ulama* who spoke on several resolutions but their focus was on the issues of *Khilafat* and protection of Holy Places; among the *ulama* were: Maulana Abdul Bari (1878–1926) and Maulana Salamatullah (d. 1930) of Farangi Mahal, Maulana Azad Sobhani (1882–1957) of Kanpur, Maulana Ibrahim of Sialkot, Maulana Sanaullah (1869–1948) of Amritsar, Maulana Kifayatullah (1875–1952), Maulana Ahmad Saeed (1886–1959) and Maulana Abdul Latif of Delhi. The session adjourned before it could consider amendments in the party constitution; and it was to meet in Aligarh during the Easter holidays on a date to be fixed by the president-elect. But the League could not hold the adjourned session although a date was announced.[198]

The intra-League conflicts intensified at the time of the twelfth annual session. By this time, the number of those who were opposed to the All-India Muslim League and Congress meeting at the same place had increased.[199] Some top League leaders seriously discussed in secrecy a proposal to hold the session in Sukkar (Sindh), away from where the Congress was meeting for its annual session and close to Khairpur Mirs where the All-India Muslim Educational Conference was meeting that year. However, the disclosure of this information and Fazlul Haq's public condemnation of this move finished its prospects.[200] Haji Musa Khan considered it 'suicidal' to hold the sessions of the All-India Muslim League and Congress separately. Even a moderate Leaguer like Sayyid Raza Ali (1882–1949) wrote to the League secretary on 28 October, that he and many other Leaguers believed that it was 'derogatory to Muslim self-respect' for the 'League to follow the Congress from place to place year after year' but keeping in view the 'reign of terror' and 'impartial persecution' of Muslims and non-Muslims in the Punjab by Michael O'Dwyer (1864–1940), it would be 'an act of criminal folly to separate the League from the Congress'. The invitation from the Amritsar Muslim League that had been received earlier in March that year was hurriedly revived and after its endorsement by the Punjab provincial Muslim League, the central council, on 31 October, decided to hold the session in Amritsar on 29–30 December, and elected Hakim Ajmal Khan as president.[201] The Amritsar session did consider Mohammad Yaqub's proposal not to hold the annual session in future where the Congress was meeting.[202] Hakim Ajmal Khan, Malik Barkat Ali and a few others supported the idea. One alternative proposal was to hold the annual sessions during the Easter holidays rather than the Christmas holidays when the Congress used to hold its sessions. Finally, it was decided that the League should discuss this subject next year.[203] The issues of Khilafat and the Punjab tragedy, however, came to dominate politics. The All-India Muslim League deliberated upon them at a special session in Calcutta on 7 September 1920; Jinnah, as permanent president, presided over this session. The central council decided about the thirteenth annual session as late as 1 December 1920, even then at an emergency meeting. It resolved to hold the session in Nagpur on 30–31 December, and elected Dr M.A. Ansari as president out of a list of seven names.[204] The council confirmed these decisions seventeen days later. Thus, the League had to make arrangements for the session in less than a month. It shared the *pandal* with the Congress although the All-India Muslim League secretary himself had felt it 'degrading the League in the eyes of the general public'.[205] On 27 October 1921, the council decided to hold the fourteenth annual session in Ahmadabad on 30–31 December, where the Congress and Central Khilafat Committee were holding their all-India sessions. It elected Maulana Abul Kalam Azad as president; his name was among the six candidates. But Azad declined to accept the presidency 'due to some serious compulsions', which he did not spell out in his letter to the League office. One reason and perhaps the most important one was that the Jamiatul Ulama-i-Hind, at its annual session in Lahore on 18–19 November, under his chairmanship, had decided to appoint an *Amir-i-Shariat* for India and directed a fifteen-member committee to determine the powers and duties of this office. The Jamiatul Ulama-i-Hind was to hold a special session in Badaun on 10–11 December to discuss the report of this committee and formally elect someone as the *Amir-i-Shariat*; Maulana Azad was the most likely candidate for this office. But the All-India Muslim League blocked his ambition to get that office. Ten days before the Jamiatul Ulama-i-Hind special session, the All-India Muslim League council opposed the 'hasty action' of the Jamiatul Ulama-i-Hind to appoint an *Amir-i-Shariat*.[206] This intervention must have upset Azad. Consequently, despite repeated verbal and written requests from the Muslims including one from leading Muslims of Ahmadabad, Azad refused to preside over the annual session. Instead, he suggested the names of Mazharul Haq and Seth Jan Mohammad Chotani (1873–1932).[207] The council did not accept his advice and elected Hasrat Mohani as president.

The All-India Muslim League did not hold its annual session in 1922 although there was an invitation from the Central Khilafat Committee to hold it in Gaya where it was holding its own session but the council did not accept the offer.[208] Early in 1923, the need to hold the session arose amidst a heated debate on 'council entry' at the time of second elections to the Legislatures under the Act of 1919. After informal meetings of the Leaguers in Delhi, Bombay (at the residence of the Aga Khan) and Lucknow, the council decided to hold the fifteenth annual session in Lucknow on 31 March 1923. On Jinnah's advice, the council elected Mir Ghulam Mohammad Bhurgari as president after the Aga Khan declined to preside over the session.[209] Bhurgari accepted the responsibility on Jinnah's insistence despite his serious ill health. He exhorted the Muslims in his presidential address to strengthen the League as it provided a 'common platform' to moderates as well as extremists in them, and that it was the 'best political organization' that could be perfected 'with the least effort'.[210] In an attempt to avoid a conflict between two evenly balanced factions, Bhurgari adjourned the session *sine* die, when a member pointed out absence of quorum in the open session, although, according to Zahur Ahmad, 'sufficient members' were present to maintain the quorum.[211] For the adjourned session, the council accepted the invitation of the Punjab provincial Muslim League to hold it in Lahore on 24–25 May. Because of Bhurgari's death, Jinnah was elected to preside over the adjourned session by a majority of votes.[212] Some Leaguers opposed the decision to hold the session in Lahore and gave two reasons: (*i*) that it would aggravate Hindu–Muslim conflict that was already raging in the Punjab; and (*ii*) that the city was unsafe as it was in the grip of a plague.[213] But by the time the League held its session, the plague had disappeared and the session concluded smoothly with great enthusiasm. The League appointed two committees, a League–Khilafat Distribution of Work Committee and a Reforms Committee to draw up an agreed scheme of reforms in consultation with other political parties. These committees could not meet promptly due to differences between Zahur Ahmad on the one hand and Fazli Husain and Jinnah on the other over the venue of their meetings.[214] For the sixteenth session, Jinnah revived the Bombay presidency Muslim League, and on its invitation, the council decided to hold the session in Bombay on 30–31 December 1924, and elected Raza Ali as president.[215] On Jinnah's advice, the All-India Muslim Educational Conference also held its session in Bombay that year.[216]

The following year, the Aligarh college, which had completed its fifty years on 24 May 1925, decided to celebrate its Jubilee during the Christmas holidays, 25–31 December. Jinnah as permanent president and Sahibzada Aftab Ahmad Khan as secretary of the All-India Muslim Educational Conference informally agreed to hold the annual sessions of the All-India Muslim League and All-India Muslim Educational Conference in Aligarh.[217] Interestingly, the League leaders differed on the venue as well as president of the session. Raja of Mahmudabad and Choudhry Khaliquzzaman (1889–1973), who opposed Aligarh as the venue, were apprehensive that Dr Ziauddin Ahmad (1878–1947) and his associates would 'capture' the League to 'make it pass reactionary resolutions' that might damage Hindu–Muslim relations.[218] United Provinces provincial Muslim League and Jinnah wanted Aligarh as the venue and Hasan Imam as the president while Dr Ziauddin and the Jubilee Committee of the college suggested the names of Fazli Husain and Sir Abdur Rahim to preside over the session. Fazli Husain withdrew his name when he came to know about the controversy. After his withdrawal focus was on Abdur Rahim who was to retire from the executive council of the Bengal governor on 3 January 1926. Abdur Rahim sought permission from the governor to retire earlier, if elected president, and communicated this information to the League secretary.[219] Both sides frantically canvassed in support of their positions. Finally, on 8 November, the council selected Aligarh as the venue for its seventeenth session, and elected Hasan Imam as president.[220] The situation changed when Hasan Imam who had earlier agreed to his candidature and given his consent in writing to Jinnah declined to accept the presidency due to 'unavoidable occupation' of his time during 'the entire Christmas Holidays' and regretted his 'inability' that had 'arisen recently after my letter to Jinnah'.[221] On his refusal, the central council elected Abdur Rahim as president, and he left the executive council on 23 December to preside over the session. For the eighteenth session, the council selected Delhi as the venue and elected Sir Abdur Qadir (1874–1950) out of eight candidates as president of the session that was scheduled on 29–31 December.

Two issues, that of electorates (joint or separate) and all-white Statutory Commission headed by Sir John Simon (1873–1954), influenced the selection of venue and president of the nineteenth annual session. Pressurized by constant Hindu propaganda against separate electorates, thirty Muslim leaders including Jinnah and Mian Shafi, in a meeting in Delhi on 20 March 1927, offered to give up separate electorates provided certain specific Muslim demands were met. But some Leaguers particularly in the Punjab provincial Muslim League opposed the idea of giving up separate electorates. When the council met in Simla on 9–10 September, under Jinnah's chairmanship, to select the venue, dates and president of the session, focus of discussion was on the issue of electorates.[222] While Firoz Khan Noon (1893–1970) led the opposition to joint electorates, Mohammad Yaqub defended the Delhi Muslim Proposals that included joint electorates. A majority of the members were opposed to joint electorates in any form; therefore, there was no formal voting and the president concluded the meeting after giving a summary of the debate. The council deferred a decision on the selection of venue and president to a meeting that was scheduled in Delhi after a Unity Conference.[223] At the Delhi meeting, the council decided to hold the session in Lahore and elected Mian Shafi as president. There was an instant uproar against this decision and the Leaguers from different provinces demanded its reconsideration. On Jinnah's direction, the central office called another meeting of the council on 20 November to reconsider this decision.[224] Simultaneously, Jinnah approached the Aga Khan to preside over the session to keep the All-India Muslim League united. The Aga Khan, in two telegrams to Jinnah on 8 and 9 November, supported the idea of holding the session in Calcutta but promised to preside over it after he had assessed the situation on his arrival in India, to ensure that the League had 'a united national policy'. Jinnah circulated extracts from the telegrams of the Aga Khan among the council members, and argued that the League session in Calcutta would enable the Leaguers to attend the annual meetings of the All-India Muslim Educational Conference and the Congress in Madras, which would not be possible if the League held its session in Lahore.[225]

Meanwhile, the announcement of an all-white Simon Commission on 8 November, complicated the situation. Now focus was more on the Simon Commission than on the issue of electorates. The opposition to the president-elect intensified when Mian Shafi welcomed the Simon Commission and, on 13 November, the Punjab PML resolved to extend cooperation to the Commission despite request from Jinnah to all the Leaguers not to comment on cooperation with the Commission or its boycott before the council had thoroughly examined the issue. Then, Barkat Ali, writing on behalf of the Punjab provincial Muslim League on 15 November, informed the central secretary that 'in view of the council meeting' on 20 November, the 'Lahore invitation may be treated as withdrawn'. However, a day before the council meeting, the Punjab provincial Muslim League secretary authorised Firoz Khan Noon to communicate to the central secretary that the 'invitation was still standing and not withdrawn'.[226] Now the League was clearly divided. Mian Shafi's supporters outmanoeuvred their opponents by their last-minute clumsily conducted moves. His servant brought to Delhi from Lahore sixteen names; one of them was not a council member, saying that they wanted Mian Shafi as president. Eleven telegrams of similar content were addressed to Noon, two to Abdul Halim Ghaznavi (1876–1953), and ten to Nawab Mohammad Yusuf. A few of them had already voted for Calcutta and the Aga Khan. Some of these votes and proxies were invalid, according to the League rules. When the central office informed Noon about the position of votes, he personally inspected the file in the League office two hours before the meeting. The council took decisions by votes, which showed victory for Mian Shafi and his supporters; 23 had voted for Lahore and 17 for Calcutta, and 36 (including 26 from the Punjab) for Mian Shafi and 25 for the Aga Khan. Out of the 13 members who were present in the meeting 9 voted for Shafi and 2 against him, and 2 abstained. Dr Kitchlew dissented from the entire proceedings and submitted his resignation as central secretary in frustration but the members persuaded him to reconsider his decision.[227] Jinnah was abroad (from 5 May to 26 October 1928) and had not attended any of these meetings. The controversy did not end here. Again, telegrams and letters came from Bengal and Madras to Jinnah and Kitchlew, questioning the validity of voting by telegrams and proxy and demanding a revision of the decision. Then, Mian Shafi issued a statement that he was willing to resign in favour of the Aga Khan. Now the central secretary, using powers under section 19 of the constitution and after consulting Jinnah, called a meeting of the council on 11 December, to reconsider the decision about venue and president in the light of these developments. A day before the meeting, the Aga Khan informed Kitchlew that he would not 'accept to replace' Mian Shafi as president and suggested Agra or Delhi as the venue.[228] The council, however, met on the scheduled date at the residence of Hakim Ajmal Khan, one of the vice-presidents, who was to preside over the meeting and had made a request to that effect due to his serious illness. Mian Shafi's supporters did question the legality of holding the meeting but were outvoted. They also participated in the voting on the motion for the selection of Calcutta as the venue but were defeated by 84 to 54 votes. After their defeat, they walked out of the meeting.[229] The council did not discuss the issue of president, as the Aga Khan had declined to replace Mian Shafi. The intra-party conflict now intensified. Hectic efforts at reconciliation could not prevent a break-up into what came to be known as the Jinnah League and Shafi League. All efforts at reconciliation failed; the Jinnah League declined to meet in Lahore and Mian Shafi refused to preside over the session in Calcutta.[230] Consequently, two sessions were held in 1927: one in Calcutta on 30 December–1 January 1928, with Mohammad Yaqub as president; and the other in Lahore on 31 December 1927–1 January 1928, with Mian Shafi as president.[231]

Two sessions—first time in the history of the All-India Muslim League—disturbed the Leaguers. They realized the need for unity but despite that desire, the two Leagues moved in opposite directions.[232] The Jinnah League boycotted the Simon Commission and half-heartedly associated itself with the Congress-sponsored All-Parties Conference while the Shafi League cooperated with the Simon Commission and struggled to maintain its separate identity. The former managed to hold the twentieth session in Calcutta on 26–30 December 1928, and Raja of Mahmudabad agreed to preside over it after great reluctance.[233] While the Shafi League abandoned the idea of holding a session; instead, its leaders organized an All-Muslim Parties Conference in Delhi that the Aga Khan presided. The Jinnah League refused to send any representatives to this Conference, stating that the formation of such 'rival and ad hoc organizations' at 'every crisis in the history of the community' would be 'disastrous' for the Muslim interests.[234] However, it did send a delegation to the National Convention in Calcutta that the Congress had convened to discuss, and adopt, the

Nehru Report. Jinnah's defence of the Shafi League's leaders at the Calcutta session and the rejection of his amendments to the Nehru Report at the National Convention brought the two Leagues closer to each other. The League session in Calcutta was adjourned to meet before the end of May 1929. On 3 March, the council decided to hold the adjourned session in Delhi on 30–31 March.[235] When the council met, there was an uproar and confusion when some Leaguers attempted to get a resolution supporting the Nehru Report passed. Jinnah arrived in the meeting at that moment. When he was apprised of the situation, he briefly addressed the gathering and then adjourned the meeting *sine die*, announcing that the League would meet again to discuss the situation.[236] But the League could not hold any meeting of the council or the annual session in 1929.

In January 1930, Jinnah and Shafi discussed the political situation at an informal meeting in Delhi and agreed to unite the two Leagues to form a 'strong Muslim political organization'. The two Leagues called meetings of their councils in the central office at the Ballimaran Street, Delhi on 23 February; the date was shifted to 28 February, Jumatul Wida, due to Mian Shafi's 'professional engagements'. This joint meeting unanimously adopted a resolution, moved by Jinnah and seconded by Shafi, to the effect that 'the two Leagues do now unite'. Forty-six members signed the document of unity.[237] But this declaration did not produce any spectacular results. The council could not take a decision about the annual session till 13 July. It then resolved to hold the session in Lucknow on 17–18 August, and elected Allama Iqbal as president.[238] Jinnah obtained Iqbal's consent by telegram. But due to the Assembly elections in September and rumours that the Nationalist Muslims might disrupt the meeting in Lucknow, there were demands for a change of venue and dates.[239] Still, on 5 August, Mohammad Yaqub issued invitations for the meetings of the council and the annual session. The League office was temporarily transferred from Delhi to Lucknow for three weeks (2–22 August) for making necessary arrangements. But Nawab Yusuf, Noon and a few others continued to press for the postponement of the session to allow the candidates to organize their campaign peacefully for the Assembly elections. When they found the League office unsympathetic, they approached Jinnah who wired to the honorary secretary, 'I have no objection, consult [the All-India Muslim League] council.' The League office wired back that it was not possible to consult the council at such a short notice. Then, Jinnah on his own authority asked the secretary to postpone the session because he had received 'representations from all the provinces'.[240] Mohammad Yaqub announced the postponement in the press, as he had no time to communicate this information to all the members individually, but he did not postpone the meeting of the council. When the members from Lucknow came to attend the council meeting, they 'strongly condemned' Yaqub for 'arbitrarily' postponing the session and adopted a motion of no confidence in him. Yaqub resigned from his office in protest against this censure and, later on, withdrew his resignation on Jinnah's request.

On 4 October 1930, Jinnah left for London to attend the first Round Table Conference. Before his departure, he again asked the League office to convene a meeting of the council to decide about the venue and date of the session. Lucknow was now out of question. That year, the All-India Muslim Educational Conference and an All-Asia Educational Conference were meeting in Benares. Baba Khalil Ahmad, convenor of the *Salaat* (Prayer) Movement, was hosting the All-India Muslim Educational Conference session in Benares. The League approached him through the *Mutawalli* of the Khwaja Gharib Nawaz's Dargah, and Baba Khalil agreed to host the League session as well. When preparations for the session were under way, it was discovered that the space in the Benares Town Hall where the arrangements had been made would be insufficient for the invitees, and that the League would have to rent tents and chairs to accommodate the delegates and guests for which the League had no funds. Meanwhile, on 8 December, the Tanzim president, Mohammad Husain, invited the League to hold its session in Allahabad where the Tanzim and Jamiatul Ulama-i-Hind were holding their annual conferences. Two days later, the League council accepted this invitation and decided to hold the annual session in Allahabad under presidentship of Iqbal on 29–30 December, rather than shift the date to March 1931, as the League office had suggested. All the arrangements for the Allahabad session were made in less than three weeks.[241]

For the twenty-second session, the council accepted the invitation from Delhi, rejecting the offers from Bombay, Patna and Qadian. The dates fixed were 26–27 December 1931, and these dates were selected to enable the members to attend the All-India Muslim Educational Conference meeting in Patna. Chaudhri Zafrullah Khan, a prominent Ahmadi, was elected president who had hardly ever taken active interest in the League affairs. There was apprehension that Zafrullah's tenure would open a new front for factional conflict and might turn the

All-India Muslim League into a 'tool' of British Imperialism; the honorary secretary, however, defended his election.[242] The anti-Qadiani Muslims and parties including the Jamiatul Ulama-i-Hind and Majlis-i Ahrar-i Islam staged a huge demonstration during the session in Delhi to protest against his presidency.[243] The protest subsided only in June 1932, when Zafrullah Khan was appointed member of the Viceroy's Executive Council. A few weeks after his appointment, he resigned from the League presidency. The Delhi session introduced a more serious conflict. On the Aga Khan's advice, his supporters floated a proposal that the All-India Muslim League and All-India Muslim Conference should be merged into one party because the Muslim community could not afford to run two parties with similar objectives. The League appointed a four-member committee to negotiate with the working committee of the All-India Muslim Conference and submit a report to the council by 1 March 1932. The council was then to merge the two parties and frame 'a constitution of the resulting body'.[244] On 29 May, the council assigned this task to a new five-member committee, as the earlier one had failed to accomplish anything concrete.[245] This committee had also done nothing by 24 December, but the council still proceeded to amalgamate the two parties. On 5 March 1933, it discussed a resolution, moved by Mohammad Yaqub, which proposed merger of the two parties and change of All-India Muslim League's name.[246] The opinions that the council had received from members on the merger resolution had strongly opposed the proposal especially the change in name. The council meeting that discussed this resolution witnessed rowdy scenes. Immediate cause was the presence of journalists whom Mian Abdul Aziz, who chaired the meeting, had invited without taking Mohammad Yaqub (honorary secretary) into confidence. When tension subsided and the resolution was taken up for discussion, one member, Masud Ahmad, raised a fundamental question: whether or not the party constitution authorized the council to decide such a basic issue as merger of the All-India Muslim League into another party and the change in its name? Mian Aziz, quoting the constitution, ruled that the council was not competent to consider such an issue, and that even the time that the Delhi session had given to the committee for drafting a merger proposal had lapsed. Discussion ended when Mohammad Yaqub declared that he had 'no intention' to press his resolution.[247] Now another conflict started. Mian Aziz gave another ruling that Mohammad Yaqub had ceased to be the honorary secretary after 31 December 1931, as he had not been elected regularly, and directed Professor Mirza Mohammad Saeed, one of the joint secretaries, to officiate in his place. The council also decided to hold the twenty-third session in Delhi on 29–30 April 1933, and resolved to request Jinnah to preside over the session. As mentioned elsewhere, Mian Aziz on the receipt of Jinnah's reply postponed the session without consulting the council.

Whatever was left of the All-India Muslim League broke up into two groups: Hafiz Hidayat Group and Mian Aziz Group.[248] Factional tussle started when fourteen members requisitioned an emergency meeting of the council, for which Honorary Secretary Mirza Saeed issued a notice. Mian Aziz reacted immediately and 'dismissed' Mirza Saeed from his office for calling this 'illegal' meeting without his knowledge and removed Shamsul Hasan (1885–1981) from his post for supporting him. His rivals, in an emergency meeting of the council, censured him, removed him from the presidency, restored Mirza Saeed and Shamsul Hasan to their respective positions, and decided to hold the League session. At a 'regular meeting' on 16 July, the council confirmed these decisions and elected Mirza Saeed as honorary secretary and Hafiz Hidayat Husain as president who was to preside over its annual session in Delhi on 25–26 September; later on, the dates were shifted to 25–26 November. The organizers sought police protection to prevent hostile 'demonstrations and picketing'.[249] Mian Aziz convened another 'requisitioned' meeting of the council in Lahore on 9 July, which approved his actions in 'saving' the All-India Muslim League from the 'Delhi clique', elected Malik Barkat Ali as the honorary secretary, located the party's head office at his residence on the Temple Road, Lahore, and decided to hold the annual session at Howrah in Bengal under the presidentship of Mian Aziz.[250] All attempts at a compromise including those by Fazli Husain and Raja of Salempur failed to bridge the gulf between the two groups. Both the groups termed each other's actions as 'unconstitutional' and held separate sessions. However, the news that Jinnah and the Aga Khan would come to India in December 1933 put pressure on both the groups to unite. On his arrival, the Aga Khan advised the All-India Muslim League and the All-India Muslim Conference to keep their 'separate existence' although he revealed that he had been 'anxious' for their merger two years ago.[251] Jinnah on his part expressed his willingness to accept the office of president, provided the two groups desired it and a united council elected him to that office. The council members, at a joint meeting in Delhi on 4 March 1934, united the two groups, and the council of the united Muslim League, after accepting the resignation of office-bearers of the two groups, elected Jinnah as president and Hafiz Hidayat Husain as honorary secretary.[252] But the session scheduled in Lahore was postponed at Jinnah's request. [253]

(D) FINANCES

The All-India Muslim League drew its income from different sources: fees charged from ordinary and council members, office-bearers, delegates and visitors at annual and other sessions and donations by rich individuals. Its council used to approve the annual budget, which was in principle prepared by a finance committee consisting of three members in addition to the president, one vice-president, honorary secretary and one joint secretary. The honorary secretary, or in his absence his *locum tenens*, incurred the expenditure and could draw on the funds within the limits approved in the budget. The finance committee could also incur expenditure on any extraordinary and unforeseen item to the tune of ten per cent of the total budget but it was required to inform the council about the additional expenditure for final approval 'as soon as possible'. The central office of the All-India Muslim League was required to place an audited statement by a chartered accountant before the council.

From the time of its inception to 1920, the All-India Muslim League had reasonable income every year although its flow was quite erratic. The donations by wealthy members and supporters constituted a major component of its funds. The Aga Khan contributed the highest amount; from February 1908 to January 1914, he donated Rs 34,000 to the League fund.[254] However, several ordinary members failed to pay their annual dues regularly or on time. Instead of realizing the unpaid dues from the members, the party often waived off the arrears. The first time it did so was in 1910, on the direction of the Aga Khan. After that, Aziz Mirza introduced a new mechanism to ensure the collection of dues from the members on time. He sent value-payable posts to the members for payment of their dues, which consumed handsome amount on postage, but the outcome was disappointing; by this mechanism, the party simply incurred additional expenditure of substantial amount. Besides, several members refused to receive the value-payable posts and some even resented this method of fee collection as 'insulting'.[255] Similar was the fate of subsequent attempts to collect dues by value-payable posts, which were made by Wazir Hasan in 1914 and by

Mohammad Yaqub in 1931.[256] Waiver of arrears proved an inducement to members not to pay their fees regularly. After December 1916, the number of defaulting members was on the rise. The honorary secretary sent reminders to the defaulting members for payment that produced no positive result. In 1919, the number of members who had not paid their dues was 164 out of a total membership of 777, and in 1920, it increased to 318 out of 953 members. From 1917 onward, the honorary secretary repeatedly placed a list of defaulting members before the council for action under the rules but the council continuously deferred any action. Finally, in 1920, instead of taking action against the defaulting members the party again wrote off the arrears due from members since 1913. Irregular flow of funds had often disturbed the Leaguers. In 1913, the party thought of creating an endowment in the form of a special 'Muslim National Fund' to the tune of Rs 0.5 million, which was to be invested in authorized securities. The council was to have the authority to spend the interest from this amount. The revised constitution of 1913 made provision to that effect, but the idea never reached the stage of implementation, initially due to opposition from the Punjab provincial Muslim League.[257] However, this provision was retained in all the amended and revised constitutions of the party.

After 1920, the All-India Muslim League constantly faced financial crises. Zahur Ahmad's repeated appeals to prominent Leaguers especially the Aga Khan for donations make pathetic reading.[258] The League was forced to reduce its office staff; in April 1922, two *munshis* and two peons who had been working for the League for several years were relieved from service, and another staff member, Abdul Walli, was treated on leave without pay although he was otherwise entitled to paid leave.[259] When the central office was shifted from Lucknow to Delhi, the party's financial 'balance sheet was blank on the credit side'. The donations by some members saved it from 'voluntary liquidation'.[260] Early in 1927, substantial funds were collected through Jinnah's effort but by September, the League had consumed all those funds and was again in debt of about Rs 800.[261] The situation did not improve the following year although annual subscriptions were realized but donations remained shy. Sometimes, Jinnah helped out the office by personal contributions.[262] But after his departure for London, the central office and the party affairs were often maintained by loans from individual Leaguers.[263] In 1930, the annual deficit was Rs 544, in 1931 Rs 417, in 1932 Rs 420, and in 1933 Rs 564.[264] When Jinnah was elected president, the council, in a meeting on 2 April 1934, that he chaired, called for donations to pay up the arrears.[265] Real improvement in finances, however, started after he finally returned from England and assumed the League presidency.

NOTES

1. Sections 27–34 of the Constitution, 1913.
2. Circular letter from Wazir Hasan and the response from members, AFM, vol. 102, nos. 7–19 and 30.
3. Non-members including Jinnah were invited to this meeting. Wazir Hasan to Jinnah, 8 December 1912, ibid., vol. 66.
4. For comments of the provincial Muslim Leagues and individual Leaguers, see ibid., vol. 103, nos. 20A–34.
5. Ibid., vol. 107, no. 2.
6. For the text of the draft, see ibid., vol. 107, no. 33. Two journalists, Ishaq Ali Alvi and Sayyid Jalib Delhavi (1874–1930), of *An-Nazir* (monthly), and the *Hamdam* (daily), respectively, made elaborate comments. *Report of the Honorary Secretary of the All-India Muslim League for the Year ending 31 December 1917*, ibid., vol. 76.
7. Its members were: Mirza Samiullah Beg (b. 1875), Sayyid Alay Nabi, Dr M.A. Ansari, Zafarul Mulk, and Shoaib Qureshi; and All-India Muslim League president and honorary secretary (*ex-officio*).
8. A five-member (Fazli Husain, Maulana Mohammad Ali, Abul Qasim, Dr Ansari and honorary secretary) committee again reviewed the draft. *Proceedings of the All-India Muslim League*, AFM, vol. 88.
9. Ibid., vol. 97, no. 27.
10. Ibid., vol. 146, no. 42.
11. On 28 February 1930, the central council appointed another committee, which also did not do anything. Ibid., vol. 186, no. 30; and vol. 111, nos. 45 and 47; and *Annual Report of the All-India Muslim League for the Year 1930*, ibid., vol. 154, no. 53.
12. Section 2 of the *Constitution of the All-India Muslim League, 1913*, ibid., vol. 107, no. 31; and for the Punjab provincial Muslim League's opposition to the change in objectives, see ibid., vol. 102, no. 41; and vol. 120, no. 23.
13. *Constitution and Rules of the All-India Muslim League as amended up to date*, published by Zahur Ahmad, 1924, p. 1; and resolution passed at the Nagpur annual session on 30–31 December 1920, ibid., vol. 89.
14. Ibid., vol. 126, no. 54.
15. 'Official Text of the Resolutions', compiled by Zahur Ahmad, Lucknow, 1922.
16. *Constitution and Rules of the All-India Muslim League as amended up to date*, published by Mohammad Yaqub, 1932, p. 1.
17. Section 3 of the Constitution, 1913.
18. Section 7 of the Constitution, 1913.
19. In 1931, the condition of five years was removed.
20. Quite a few members left the All-India Muslim League as a result of the 1933 split. Ghulam Bhik Nairang to honorary secretary, 5 August 1933, and Din Mohammad to honorary secretary, 5 August 1933, AFM, vol. 608, nos. 72 and 73, respectively.

21. *Report of the Honorary Secretary for the Year 1920*, AFM, vol. 89; *for the Year 1924*, ibid., vol. 109, no. 14; and *for the Year 1927*, ibid., vol. 125, no. 3; and *Proceedings of the All-India Muslim League 1918–1919*, Amritsar, n. d., ibid., vol. 86.

22. Ibid., vol. 84; vol. 145, no. 14; vol. 177, no. 39; and vol. 178, no. 43.

23. Statement by the joint secretary in March 1929, ibid., 152, no. 10.

24. Haji Mohammad Musa to Zahur Ahmad, 29 April 1919, ibid., vol. 500, p. 4.

25. Dr Ansari made a similar proposal at the time of Raja of Mahmudabad's resignation. Ibid., vol. 139, no. 62.

26. Mian Shafi moved the resolution, which was seconded by Nawab Abdul Majid and supported by Sayyid Nabiullah, Maulana Mohammad Ali, Rafiuddin Ahmad and two others. Ibid., vol. 67.

27. Telegram from the Aga Khan to the president of the session, 3 March 1912, ibid., vol. 64.

28. *Proceedings of the All-India Muslim League, 4 March 1912*, ibid., vol. 65; and Wazir Hasan to the Aga Khan, 24 April 1912, ibid., vol. 482, pp 32–33.

29. Wazir Hasan's circular letter to members, 14 January 1914, ibid., vol. 75; and *Proceedings of the Council of the All-India Muslim League held at Agra*, Lucknow, 1914.

30. Mohammad Ali Mohammad to Wazir Hasan, 29 October 1918, AFM, vol. 139, no. 42.

31. Its members were: Nabiullah, Ihtesham Ali, Wazir Hasan, Zahur Ahmad and Mohammad Waseem (1886–1950).

32. Mohammad Ali Mohammad to Abdul Walli, 28 February 1919, AFM, vol. 143, no. 21. According to one version, Raja Sahib was displeased with the contents of Dr Ansari's speech; and when he was pressed to withdraw his resignation, he expressed his willingness to do that provided Wazir Hasan was retained as the honorary secretary. The Leaguers did not accept that condition. 'Punjab Police Abstract of Intelligence', 1 February 1919, vol. 169, p. 33.

33. Assistant secretary, All-India Muslim League to the president, 29 May 1919, AFM, vol. 80.

34. Zahur Ahmad to Yaqub Hasan, 11 November 1919, ibid., vol. 499, pp. 82–83.

35. Ibid., vol. 483, pp. 15–16.

36. Still, on 6 March 1920, Zahur Ahmad wrote to the Aga Khan, 'I hope the election of Mr Jinnah will meet your approval.' Ibid., vol. 483, pp. 18–21.

37. The citizens of Bombay paid Jinnah tribute by building the 'People's Jinnah (PJ) Memorial Hall'.

38. In a letter to Yusuf Khan (assistant secretary) on 14 August 1910, Aziz Mirza wrote that he had 'succeeded in enrolling Mr Jinnah as a member of our League and he will be a real acquisition to our cause.' AFM, vol. 70.

39. Allama Iqbal was elected its general secretary and Hasrat Mohani its joint secretary.

40. Dawjee Dadabhai, secretary, Burma provincial Muslim League to honorary secretary, All-India Muslim League, 16 February 1931, ibid., vol. 58; and *Report of the Honorary Secretary of the All-India Muslim League for the Year 1931*, ibid., vol. 156, no. 39.

41. Mohammad Yaqub to Jinnah, 8 February 1931, Quaid-i-Azam Papers, National Archives of Pakistan, Government of Pakistan, Islamabad, [henceforth cited as QAP], F. 15, pp. 83–85.

42. The distribution of fifteen written opinions that had been received was: Jinnah 7; Shafi 2; Mohammad Yaqub 1, and no comments 5. AFM, vol. 194, nos. 41 and 71.
43. The order was: 1. The Aga Khan; 2. Jinnah; 3. Sir Sultan Ahmad; 4. Ross Masood; 5. Sir Fazalbhai; 6. Rafiuddin; 7. Chaudhri Zafrullah Khan; 8. Nawab Zulfikar Ali Khan; 9. Sir Mohammad Shafi; and 10. Nawab Ismail Khan. The first two were in London, and the next four declined to accept the office for one reason or the other. Ibid., vol. 197, no. 40.
44. *Statesman* (Delhi), 14 May 1933.
45. *Proceedings of the Meeting of the All-India Muslim League Council held on 12 March 1933*, AFM, vol. 210, no. 30.
46. *Statesman*, 3 June 1933. He conceded that both Yaqub and Abdullah could seek re-election at the next annual session, which was the proper forum for election.
47. Shamsul Hasan who joined the League office as a shorthand writer and typist on 1 July 1916, served the party for the longest duration.
48. Vol. 148 of the AFM exclusively deals with payments made by the vice-presidents.
49. In 1919, the power to appoint an employee carrying a salary of over Rs 50 was vested in the central council.
50. Hasan Bilgrami to Nawab Mushtaq Husain, 9 October 1908, AFM, vol. 82.
51. For instance, see Mohammad Aziz Mirza, *A Talk on Muslim Politics*, Lucknow, All-India Muslim League, 31 July 1910; and also the Aga Khan to Aziz Mirza, 12 July 1910, ibid., vol. 62.
52. Ibid., vol. 53.
53. Notice issued by the joint secretary, 9 September 1913, ibid., vol. 85.
54. For example, see Abdul Majid Khan to Azhar Ali, 9 September 1913, ibid.
55. Some members including Abdul Majid Khan, Mohammad Yaqub and Abdur Rahman Khan criticized the action of the honorary secretary but a majority of them supported the resolution. Ibid., vol. 85; and also see Chapter 3.
56. Ibid., vol. 123, no. 8.
57. Some even challenged his re-election. For handwritten minutes of the meeting of the central council held in December 1919; and Qazi Abdul Ghaffar to honorary secretary, All-India Muslim League, 3 February 1919, see ibid., vol. 80.
58. Wazir Hasan to Abdul Walli, 28 February 1919, ibid., vol. 143, no. 22.
59. This was reflected in their inability to hold the meetings of the subcommittees that were appointed at the all-India session in May 1924.
60. Assistant secretary, All-India Muslim League to Jinnah, 11 September 1929, AFM, vol. 185, no. 31.
61. 'Agenda for the Meeting of the Council' issued by Mohammad Yaqub, 28 February 1931, ibid., vol. 194, no. 41.
62. *Report of the Honorary Secretary of the All-India Muslim League for the Year 1935* [typed], ibid., vol. 168.
63. Text of the Constitution of 1913, AFM, vol. ibid., no. 18.
64. *Constitution and Rules of the All-India Muslim League as amended up to the end of 1919*, published by Zahur Ahmad, Lucknow, 1920.
65. *Constitution and Rules of the All-India Muslim League as amended up to date*, published by Mohammad Yaqub, [Delhi], 1932.
66. AFM, vol. 178, no. 43.
67. Ibid., vol. 123, no 10.
68. Circular letter issued by Aziz Mirza to council members, 21 October 1911, ibid., vol. 203, no. 39.

69. Ibid., vol. 98, nos. 2 and 15. Mian Shafi and Nawab Zulfikar Ali Khan termed this procedure 'as unconstitutional' and detrimental to the interest of the League and the Muslim community. [ibid., vol. 98, nos. 5 and 6.] Jinnah objected to the inclusion of Rafiuddin Ahmad; he wrote: 'I object to the name and propose that some other Sunni name should be substituted. I have not got the list of the members before me. So I cannot say but if Umar Sobhani (d. 1926) is a member of the League, I beg to propose his name.' Ibid., vol. 98, no. 20.

70. Ibid., vol. 297, no. 92; and *Annual Report of the All-India Muslim League for the Year 1926 prefaced by Syed Zahur Ahmad, Honorary Secretary at the Eighteenth sessions of the League held at Delhi*, Delhi, 21 December 1925.

71. Printed notice issued by Honorary Secretary Saifuddin Kitchlew, 12 March 1929, AFM, vol. 577.

72. Zulfikar Ali, Nazar-i-Ala of the Anjuman-i-Ahmadiyya, Qadian to Shamsul Hasan, 19 December 1927, and Dr Mufti Mohammad Sadiq to Shamsul Hasan, 18 February 1929, QAP, F. 606. Zulfikar asked for information about the vacancies in the council from various provinces so that the provincial Muslim Leagues could send the names of Ahmadis for election. Shamsul Hasan informed him about the vacancies in the council for which he wanted nominations of the Ahmadis. [For his 'strictly confidential' letter, see ibid., F. 607.] Dr Sadiq sent six names for election; the names were proposed by him and seconded by Zulfikar. Earlier, Zulfikar had written to Shamsul Hasan on 8 January 1929: 'Hakim Abu Tahir, Rais-i-Calcutta, Member of the All-India Muslim League, is coming to Delhi. Give him the assistance that he needs. We want to enter Ahmadis in the council of the League from every province. Advice and information may be given [to him] about it'. [Ibid., F. 610.] This mechanism perhaps facilitated Chaudhri Zafrullah Khan's election as president for the annual session in December 1931, and Mufti Sadiq's election as member of the working committee in January 1932.

73. *Report of the Honorary Secretary of the All-India Muslim League for the Year 1924*, AFM, vol. 109, no. 14.

74. Aziz Mirza to council members, 21 October 1911, ibid., vol. 203, no. 39; and *Report of the All-India Muslim League for the Year 1920*, ibid., vol. 89.

75. Ibid., vol. 197, no. 21; *Proceedings of the All-India Muslim League for the Year 1918–19*, ibid., vol. 86; *Report of the Honorary Secretary of the All-India Muslim League for the Year 1920*, ibid., vol. 89; ibid., vol. 85, last page; *Report of the Honorary Secretary of the All-India Muslim League for the Year 1928*, ibid., vol. 146, no. 42; Zahur Ahmad to council members, 5 October 1926, ibid., vol. 158, no. 36, 37; and ibid., vol. 140, no. 2; and Zahur Ahmad's letter, ibid., no. 35.

76. Ibid., vol. 208, no. 10.

77. In 1946, the All-India Muslim League adopted a uniform structure for the provincial Muslim Leagues in the model constitution.

78. *Report of the All-India Muslim League for the Year 1911*, ibid., vol. 65. In 1914 and 1927, the Punjab provincial Muslim League and in 1932, the Bengal and Madras provincial Muslim Leagues came into conflict with the central League.

79. Ibid., vol. 84. The same meeting of the council in 1911 also framed by-laws for the conduct of business at the council meetings but when, in 1918, one member, Shoaib Qureshi, asked for such by-laws, the honorary secretary, after two reminders, demonstrated his lack of knowledge by replying that 'there are no rules in existence regarding the conduct of business, as none were ever framed'. Ibid., vol. 139, no. 3.

80. Chaudhri Shahabuddin was the first to criticize the working of the Punjab provincial Muslim League in an open letter to the daily *Zamindar* (Lahore), 28 February 1912. It was in response to the criticism that in May 1912, the Punjab provincial Muslim League organized fresh elections.

81. AFM, vol. 102, no. 41.

82. Aziz Mirza noted 'the sullen attitude of resentment' of the Punjab Leaguers. [Aziz Mirza to Fazli Husain, 15 November 1911, ibid., vol. 203, no. 52.] Mian Shafi complained that 'our Lucknow friends' took decisions about provincial issues without consulting the provincial Muslim Leagues. Shafi to Wazir Hasan, 22 April 1914, ibid., vol. 120, no. 22.

83. Mian Shafi wanted the provincial Muslim Leagues to consider the draft joint scheme before its presentation at the annual session and that they should select members of a committee in proportion to their population that the central League would appoint to review the scheme. Ibid., vol. 93, no. 34.

84. Fateh Ali Khan to Wazir Hasan, 18 May 1913, ibid., vol. 115, no. 18. He wrote that the 'entire' Muslim community of the Punjab resented Mian Shafi's letter, and that he himself was in favour of promoting only social relations between the Muslims and Hindus and for that purpose he had established a 'Hindu–Muslim Association'. Fazli Husain was a member of the association.

85. In 1913, the Punjab provincial Muslim League did not include Fazli Husain in the list of its representatives on the central council; and on query from Wazir Hasan, Mian Shafi informed him that he could not do anything in the matter, as Fazli Husain had not taken any interest in the provincial Muslim League as a member of its executive committee. Shafi to Wazir Hasan, 8 July 1913, ibid., vol. 120, no. 15.

86. A large section of the Leaguers bitterly criticized him for his 'unswerving' pro-British leanings.

87. Chaudhri Abdur Rahman was elected president, Pir Tajuddin general secretary, and Ghulam Rasul Khan joint/financial secretary. [AFM, vol. 120, nos. 28, 30, 31, 34, 36, 38 and 40.] Sardar Sikandar Hayat Khan (1842–1942), in a letter to Wazir Hasan on 8 April, supported the new League as the 'real representative body'. Ibid., vol. 120, no. 50.

88. Nawab Sir Bahram Khan Mazari was elected its president and Mian Shafi general secretary.

89. Shafi to Wazir Hasan, 3 April 1916, AFM, vol. 120, no. 47. He claimed that all the five members elected to the Punjab Legislative Council belonged to his League. Ibid., vol. 120, no. 52.

90. Ibid., vol. 120, no. 60.

91. Ibid., nos. 48, 63, 64, 65 and 68.

92. Ibid., vol. 100, no. 51; and vol. 130, no. 11. Earlier, on 6 May, Wazir Hasan had written to him: 'I think time has arrived now when you should manfully come forward and take the Punjab Provincial Muslim League under your wings. I understand that the . . . League is prepared to accept you as the president.' Ibid., vol. 568, p. 1.

93. Ibid., vol. 130, nos. 3–9. Subsequently, the Shafi League associated itself with an All-India Muslim Association that the dissident Leaguers from Bengal, United Provinces and Madras had organized in opposition to the All-India Muslim League. [*Sitara-i-Subh* (Urdu), Lahore, 5 January 1918.] The Punjab provincial Muslim League dubbed it as an organization of the 'discredited reactionaries'; the

Association had, however, receptivity in some British circles. Habibullah to Wazir Hasan, 9 February 1918, AFM, vol. 130, nos. 15 and 16.

94. Ibid., vol. 117, no. 57.

95. Ibid., vol. 149, no. 5.

96. Shaikh Abdul Qadir was elected vice-president, and Allama Iqbal, Mian Abdul Aziz and Chaudhri Zafrullah Khan secretaries.

97. Honorary secretary to Barkat Ali, 28 February 1928; Mohammad Alam to honorary secretary, 10 November 1928; and honorary secretary to Mohammad Alam, 28 November 1928, AFM, vol. 130, nos. 42, 46 and 47. The Punjab branch of the Shafi League elected Maulana Abdul Qadir (1865–1942) as its president; Malik Barkat Ali, Raja Ghazanfar Ali (1894–1963) and Pir Tajuddin as vice-presidents; and Dr Mohammad Alam as secretary.

98. Shujauddin, Secretary, Punjab provincial Muslim League to assistant secretary, All-India Muslim League, 25 May 1932, ibid., 130, no. 59.

99. S.A. Asghar and Abul Qasim were elected as joint secretaries and A. Rasul (1872–1917) as treasurer, besides the election of fifteen vice-presidents.

100. AFM, vol. 106, no. 37.

101. President, Bengal presidency Muslim League to Raja of Mahmudabad, 10 November 1917, ibid., 106, no. 41.

102. Honorary secretary to A. Rasul, 29 June 1917; Abul Qasim to honorary secretary, All-India Muslim League, 7 August 1917; and Mujibur Rahman to Wazir Hasan, 17 February 1917, ibid., vol. 37.

103. Mujibur Rahman to honorary secretary, All-India Muslim League, 15 September 1918, ibid.

104. Mujibur Rahman sent the resolution to Zahur Ahmad on 31 January 1920. Ibid.

105. Shamsul Hasan Collection (hereafter SHC), Bengal–I: 10, 11, 15 and 18. Fazlul Haq attempted to organize a parallel League with the support of the All-India Muslim League. Shamsul Hasan to honorary secretary, All-India Muslim League, 17 February 1932, AFM, vol. 38.

106. Ayub Khan to honorary secretary, 20 January 1912, ibid., vol. 241, no. 1; and Hafizulla Shahabuddin to honorary secretary, 4 and 21 February 1912, ibid., nos. 3 and 4.

107. Ghulam Ali Chagla to Wazir Hasan, 7 November 1917, ibid., no. 13.

108. Ghulam Ali Chagla, Ayub Khan, Abdul Majid Sindhi, Jan Mohammad Junejo (1886–1921) and ten others were elected members of the council.

109. AFM, vol. 241, nos. 14–18, 22–25; and vol. 144, nos. 4 and 59.

110. Ibid., nos. 33, 34, 36, 39 and 40–43. The conference had Sir Shah Nawaz Bhutto (1888–1957) as chairman, Mohammad Ayub Khuhro as vice-chairman, Abdul Majid Sindhi as secretary and Abdullah Harun as treasurer.

111. Shafi to Wazir Hasan, 31 August 1912, ibid., vol. 148, no. 57; and vol. 206, no. 6.

112. Ibid., vol. 225, no. 60. Mian Abdul Aziz belonged to a business family of Peshawar who did his Bar-at-Law and remained quite active in politics. Bokhari went to Balliol College, Oxford but returned without completing his studies.

113. Abdul Hamid was a grandson of Amir Sher Ali Khan and brother-in-law of the ruling Amir.

114. Kazi Mir Ahmad to Wazir Hasan, 30 May 1913, AFM, vol. 115, no. 41.

115. Abdul Aziz to Wazir Hasan, 22 September 1912, ibid., vol. 206, no 7; and for Jinnah's views on the police administration, see ibid., vol. 27, pp. 1–2.

116. Bokhari to Wazir Hasan, 23 June 1914 and Wazir Hasan to Bokhari, 28 June 1914, ibid., vol. 206, nos. 10 and 11.

117. Ghulam Husain to Wazir Hasan, 16 October 1914, ibid., no. 12; and Wazir Hasan to chief secretary to the chief commissioner, NWFP, 19 October 1914, ibid., no. 13.

118. Kazi Mir Ahmad to Wazir Hasan, 15 April 1916, ibid., no. 14.

119. Kazi Mir Ahmad to Wazir Hasan, 15 August 1917, ibid., vol. 104, no. 63; and his letters of 15 and 18 April 1916, ibid., no. 13.

120. Ali Abbas Bokhari's father to Zahur Ahmad, 20 November 1919, ibid., no. 17.

121. Copies of resolutions of the Muslim association working committee presided over by Nawab Baz Khan to secretary, All-India Muslim League, 4 December 1924, ibid., no. 18.

122. Ibid., no. 14 and 20; *Observer* (Lahore), 7 February 1926; and *Muslim Outlook* (Lahore), 6 February 1926.

123. On 20 October 1934, Nawab Ahmad Nawaz of Dera Ismail Khan wrote to the All-India Muslim League honorary secretary that his son, Allah Nawaz Khan, would promote the establishment of a branch League in the district if he were elected a member of the central council. AFM, vol. 206, no. 22.

124. Ibid., vol. 48.

125. Wazir Hasan to Jinnah, 8 July 1917, ibid., vol. 104, no. 39.

126. There were minor changes in other offices. For instance, in November 1916, the four vice-presidents were: Walji Lalji, Nawab Syed Mohammad, Abdul Quddus Badsha and Rauf Ahmad, and the two joint secretaries were: Abdus Subhan who replaced Asad Ali Khan and Safdar Husain.

127. AFM, vol. 196, no. 40.

128. *The Madras Mail*, 16 September 1926.

129. Syed Murtaza Bahadur and Yaqub Hasan were then elected vice-presidents and B. Poker and Ahmad Ibrahim as secretaries.

130. Mohammad Yaqub to B. Poker, 3 December 1932, AFM, vol. 196, no. 57.

131. The secretary of the Madras provincial Muslim League wrote that 'the function of the All-India Muslim League is to reflect the opinion of the various Provincial Leagues and not to impose upon the Provincial Leagues its own views . . . The Provincial Leagues have at all times the right and the duty to express their own independent opinions on every matter. . . . [The] action of the [Provincial] council . . . is not only proper and unobjectionable but it was the bounden duty of the council to have expressed its independent opinion'. B. Poker to M. Yaqub, 20 December, ibid., vol. 196, 59; and Mohammad Yaqub to Shamsul Hasan, 27 December 1932, ibid., vol. 196, no. 60.

132. In June 1914, Nurul Hasan, Abul Aas (b. 1880), Ismail Ali Khan and Zakaria Hashim were elected as assistant secretaries.

133. Masud Ahmad was elected as joint secretary, and Sarfraz Husain and nine others as vice-presidents.

134. Resolutions of the Lucknow district Muslim League, ibid., vol. 127, no 15.

135. Ibid., vol. 127, nos. 12 and 23. The Aga Khan got a report from Aziz Mirza; and President Abdul Majid sent his version to the Aga Khan. [Aziz Mirza to Ibne Ahmad, 7 January 1912, ibid., vol. 127, no. 40.] The Aga Khan, in a telegram to the Nawab of Dhaka on 3 March 1912, termed 'the present condition of open war between the secretary and president disgrace to Islam'. Ibid., vol. 64.

136. Ibid., vol. 127, nos. 61 and 63.

137. The All-India Muslim League was the only party that provided a common platform to the Shias and Sunnis of Lucknow, and frustrated the Congress attempts to divide the Muslims on sectarian lines. Ibid., vol. 113, no. 93; and vol. 349, no. 102.

138. Ibid., vol. 251, nos. 1–9 and 12. Presidential address of the Raja of Jahangirabad at a public meeting in Lucknow on 11 October 1916, ibid., vol. 251, p. 62.
139. For the Aligarh district Muslim League, see ibid., vol. 349, no. 10; for the Lucknow district Muslim League, see no. 4; for the Pilibhit district Muslim League, see no. 35; and for the Lakhimpur district Muslim League, see no. 9.
140. Ibid., vol. 349, nos. 45, 46, 49 and 50.
141. H.M. Malak to Wazir Hasan, 24 November 1913, ibid., vol. 115, no. 60.
142. Abdul Qadir Siddiqi to honorary secretary, 2 September 1917, ibid., vol. 166, no. 31; and also see nos. 33–35, 38 and 41.
143. *Report of the Honorary Secretary of the All-India Muslim League for the Year ending 31 December 1917*, ibid., vol. 76.
144. Ibid., vol. 166, no. 43.
145. Ibid., vol. 110.
146. Ibid., vol. 216, nos. 3 and 5.
147. A.S. Khan to honorary secretary, All-India Muslim League, 14 September 1932, ibid., vol. 174, no. 31; and see also nos. 32 and 33.
148. Ahmad Moolla Dawood to Wazir Hasan, 9 June 1913, ibid., vol. 58.
149. For instance, see minutes of the meeting held on 21 September 1913, ibid.
150. Ibid.
151. Dawjee Dadabhai to Wazir Hasan, 16 February 1931, ibid., vol. 58.
152. *Report of the All-India Muslim League for the Year 1915*, ibid., vol. 69.
153. Circular letter from Wazir Hasan, honorary secretary, All-India Muslim League, 30 June 1914, ibid., vol. 75.
154. Ibid., vol. 21, no. 37.
155. For his letter to Aziz Mirza, 31 August 1910, see ibid., vol. 52; and Ibne Ahmad to Aziz Mirza, 4 September 1910, Aziz Mirza to M. Ishak, 3 October 1910, and Aziz Mirza to Yusuf Khan, 7 October 1910, ibid., vol. 45.
156. For his telegram to Aziz Mirza, 11 October 1910, see ibid., vol. 53.
157. Aga Khan to Aziz Mirza, 26 October 1910, Amir Ali to Aziz Mirza, 3 November 1910, Fazli Husain to Aziz Mirza, 4 November 1910, Habibur Rahman to Aziz Mirza, 8 November 1910, and Nawab of Dhaka to Aziz Mirza, 10 November 1910, ibid., vol. 54.
158. Amir Ali to Aziz Mirza, 3 March 1911, Aziz Mirza to Amir Ali, 27 March 1911, and Amir Ali to Aziz Mirza, 21 April 1911, ibid., vol. 60.
159. On 23 July, the council decided the dates of the session and, on 18 August, elected the president. It rejected Nawab Ali Choudhury's two proposals: one, that the president should not be from the province in which the All-India Muslim League was holding its session; and two, that the president-elect should get his speech approved by the council. For a discussion on these issues, see ibid., vols. 83 and 84.
160. Those who met the Deputy Commissioner were Wiqarul Mulk, Ajmal Khan, Abdullah Jan and Aziz Mirza.
161. Aziz Mirza to Ajmal Khan, 12 October 1911, AFM, vol. 60.
162. For his letter of 17 October 1911, see ibid.
163. On 23 October, Aziz Mirza had wired to the Aga Khan: 'Viceroy replies holding League sessions during Darbar undesirable. Would now suggest presenting address to King if Your Highness can arrange.' On 28 October, the Aga Khan wired back: 'Naturally as Viceroy desires. Better hold meeting Easter. Do not conceive idea of address to His Majesty being accepted.' Ibid.

164. For resolutions passed at the council meeting on 5 November 1911, see ibid., vol. 84.

165. Salimullah's son had died a few days before the session. [Ibid., vol. 103, no. 33.] The Aga Khan's telegram read: 'Owing special reasons Nawab Dacca proposed if he refuses then Shafi'. The Aga Khan to Aziz Mirza, 10 February 1912, ibid., vol. 64.

166. League office to the Aga Khan, 15 August 1912, ibid., vol. 66. Peshawar and Lahore were also considered as the venues for the session. Abdur Rahman to Wazir Hasan, 6 June 1912, ibid., vol. 447, p. 5.

167. Wazir Hasan to editors of newspapers, 2 and 3 December 1912, ibid., vol. 66.

168. Ibid., vol. 91, no. 86. For instance, on 11 December, Mazharul Haq sent a telegram to Aziz Mirza about the threat of a 'great split' in the Muslim ranks; and two days later, Haji Musa Khan asked for an extraordinary session to 'save' the League. Ibid., vol. 66.

169. For comments by Mujibur Rahman, editor of the *Mussalman*, see ibid., vol. 64; and Wazir Hasan to Shafi, 6 February, ibid., vol. 68.

170. Circular letter of 13 February 1913, ibid., vol. 68.

171. Jinnah to Wazir Hasan, 21 May 1913, ibid., 115, no. 17.

172. Satyendra Bose to Wazir Hasan, 19 May 1913, ibid., vol. 115, no. 21.

173. Mohammad Shafi to Azhar Ali, ibid., 10 December 1913, vol. 85.

174. Nawab of Dhaka to joint secretary, All-India Muslim League, 13 December 1913, ibid., vol. 85; and Ghulam Husain, sub-editor of the *Comrade*, to Azhar Ali, ibid., vol. 68.

175. Interestingly, this session passed a resolution moved by Nawab Zulfikar Ali Khan, appreciating the 'heroic struggle carried on by Mohandas Karamchand Gandhi [1869–1948] and his co-workers and called upon 'the people of all classes and creeds to continue to supply them with funds'. Ibid.

176. QAP, F. 784, p. 330.

177. Wazir Hasan to Mohammad Ali, 5 September 1914, AFM, vol. 75.

178. On 15 February 1915, Wazir Hasan wrote to Jinnah, 'I received a great stimulus from the letter which you wrote to the Raja of Mahmudabad urging upon him the necessity of holding a meeting of the League'. Ibid., vol. 92, no. 60.

179. Earlier, on 27 January, Mian Shafi was 'in complete accord with the proposal' and had authorized Wazir Hasan 'to subscribe' his name 'to the circular letter'. Shafi to Wazir Hasan, 22 February 1915; and Wazir Hasan to Aga Khan, 20 February 1915, ibid., vol. 92.

180. For details, see Wazir Hasan to Jinnah, 20 March 1915, ibid., vol. 92, no. 68; and Ibrahim Rahimtullah to Wazir Hasan, 4 May 1915 and other letters, ibid., vol. 95.

181. Letters of Suleman Qasim Mitha and Gul Mohammad to Jinnah, 2 June 1915, ibid., vol. 69.

182. His letter of 26 September 1915, ibid., vol. 93, no. 1. He sent resolutions proposing political status for India after the War similar to that of the self-governing British colonies, and suggested a joint League-Congress conference.

183. The participants included Ibrahim Rahimtullah, Fazalbhai Karimbhai, Raza Ali, Asad Ali Khan, Nawab Mohammad Ishaq, Dr Ziauddin Ahmad, Hakim Ajmal Khan and Shaikh Ghulam Sadiq (1853–1921). Mian Shafi and Zulfikar Ali Khan, in a joint confidential letter to Wazir Hasan in October, proposed that instead of the annual session, the All-India Muslim League members should meet during the Easter Holidays and that no constitutional and administrative reforms should be put forward during the War. Zulfikar Ali Khan, in a separate telegram to Wazir

Hasan on 22 October, warned that 'persistence in holding public session may lead to disruption'. Ibid., vol. 69.

184. There was a massive campaign of fresh enrolment of members especially from Bombay; Jinnah proposed quite a few names. [For the enrolment forms, see ibid., vols. 94 and 270.] The government intervention was sought on Mitha's suggestion. *Bombay Chronicle*, 6 December 1915.

185. Other members were: Faiz Tayyabji, Fazalbhai Karimbhai, Mohammad Daim, Hakim Abdullah Shah, and Sharif Devji Kanji. The League was also to pass a resolution requesting the British government to extend the term of office of Lord Hardinge.

186. Among them were S. Banerjea (1848–1925), B.N. Basu, Mrs Annie Besant, Hormsji A. Wadia, Madan Mohan Malaviya and M.K. Gandhi.

187. Suleman Qasim Mitha was heard saying, 'This is Congress'. 'They want to join the Congress'. 'Why should they speak in English?' One member shouted that those sitting on the stage were not Muslims because they had shaved their beards and wore English dress. Another objection was that the resolution of loyalty to the British had been passed on the second, and not the first, day. AFM, vol. 69.

188. Those who opposed his candidature were critical of his pro-Congress leanings. One was Fazli Husain who wrote, 'Jinnah's name came to my mind but then he won't do, for it would mean that the League has lost its individuality.' Fazli Husain to Wazir Hasan, 16 August 1916, ibid., vol. 564, pp. 37–38.

189. His letter to Wazir Hasan, 19 August 1916, ibid., vol. 70.

190. His letter to Wazir Hasan, 15 August 1916, ibid.

191. Mohammad Ali got 34 out of 35 votes. Amir Ali, Sahibzada Abdul Qayyum (1866–1937) and Abdullah Yusuf Ali were the other candidates.

192. Ibid., vol. 114, no. 17, and vols. 76 and 105.

193. Just five local members were present when the central council took this decision. Ibid., vol. 123, no. 3.

194. For Dr Ansari's comments, see ibid., vol. 117, no 69. The Associated Press had published Fazli Husain's views on the Reforms along with those of Mian Shafi and others. [Ibid., no. 57; and *The Tribune*, 29–31 July 1918.] The dates of the special session were shifted to 30 December 1918–1 January 1919.

195. AFM, vol. 139, nos. 9 and 21. Fazli Husain was conscious of the real reason behind the postponement, and he informed Wazir Hasan in a telegram on 11 October that he would not like to preside over the session unless the council was 'fairly unanimous about it'.

196. Six members had expressed their opinion votes in favour of Fazli Husain, 5 for Ishaq Khan and 2 for Fazlul Haq. The five members present were: Mohammad Waseem, Abid Husain, Ishaq Ali, Naziruddin and Wazir Hasan. Ibid., vol. 123, no. 5.

197. For his strong comments, see ibid., vol. 139, no. 66. Mohammad Yaqub had started this opposition in 1917.

198. Yaqub Hasan to Abdul Wali, 26 April 1919, ibid., vol. 499, no. 10.

199. Malik Barkat Ali to Zahur Ahmad, 14 August 1919, ibid., vol. 87.

200. For his statement, see the *Independent* (Allahabad), 17 October 1919; and AFM, vol. 87.

201. The opinions received were: Hakim Ajmal Khan 8, Dr M.A. Ansari 8, Yaqub Hasan 6 and G.M. Bhurgari 1. Fazli Husain had withdrawn his name because the League was meeting in the Punjab.

202. For Mohammad Yaqub's comments on the agenda items, see AFM, vol. 145, no. 3. Jinnah who had arrived in the meeting wearing Turkish cap was specially allowed to speak in English; and Urdu translation was given after his speech.
203. Ibid., vol. 145, no. 28.
204. Ibid., nos. 26, 45, and 50. Fazli Husain's name was among the seven names but he declined to be a candidate.
205. Honorary secretary to secretary, reception committee, Nagpur session, 12 December 1920, ibid., vol. 89.
206. For the council resolution, see ibid., vol. 126, no 30; and Parvin Rozina, *Jamiatul Ulama-i-Hind: Dastawezat-i-Markazi Ijlas hai Aam 1919–1945*, Islamabad, 1980, pp. 131–32.
207. AFM, vol. 97, nos. 7–9; and vol. 126, p. 38.
208. For printed letters of Zahur Ahmad, dated 4 December 1922, see ibid., vol. 126, no. 71; and dated 27 January 1923, see ibid., vol. 147, no.5.
209. Ibid., vol. 101, nos. 1–6, 14–25 and 33; and vol. 147, 12, 13, 16 and 18.
210. For his address, see ibid., vol. 101, no. 81.
211. For Zahur Ahmad's circular letter of 4 July 1923, see ibid., vol. 101, no. 83.
212. Ibid., vol. 149, nos. 5 and 17. The council rejected Mohammad Yaqub's proposal to elect Raza Ali as president.
213. Ajmal Khan to Zahur Ahmad, 18 July 1923, ibid., vol. 101, no. 88.
214. For their correspondence, see ibid., vol. 573.
215. Jinnah proposed three names: Iqbal, Hasan Imam and Raza Ali.
216. Jinnah to Zahur Ahmad, 20 October 1924, AFM, vol. 116, no. 2.
217. Aftab Ahmad to Zahur Ahmad, 23 June 1925, ibid., vol. 135, no. 3.
218. Zahur Ahmad to Jinnah, 30 October 1925, ibid., no. 27.
219. Aftab Ahmad to Zahur Ahmad, 27 October 1925, ibid., no. 34.
220. The opinion votes for various candidates were: Hasan Imam 12; Abdur Rahim 4; Fazli Husain 6: Saifuddin Kitchlew 6; the Aga Khan 3. After Hasan Imam's withdrawal, Kitchlew's name was also considered.
221. Hasan Imam to Zahur Ahmad, 10 November 1925, AFM, vol. 135, no. 51; and Zahur Ahmad to Jinnah, AFM, vol. 135, no. 71.
222. Jinnah to Mirza Ijaz Husain, ibid., vol. 163, no. 53. The League also invited the Central Khilfat Committee, Jamiatul Ulama-i-Hind and Tabligh leaders to this meeting.
223. For the printed notice by Saifuddin Kitchlew and proceedings of the council meeting, see ibid., vols. 110 and 163.
224. Ibid., 171, no. 30.
225. Jinnah quoted the Aga Khan's telegram in his press statement of 10 November 1927. Ibid., vol. 167, no. 8; and *Muslim Outlook*, 12 November 1927.
226. Mohammad Iqbal to honorary secretary, All-India Muslim League, 19 November 1927; and Firoz Khan Noon to honorary secretary, 19 November, AFM, vol. 124.
227. Saifuddin Kitchlew to Jinnah, 21 November 1927, ibid., vol. 167, no. 56. For assistant secretary's letter to Jinnah, 21 November 1927, see ibid., no. 53. For the votes and proxies, see the same volume.
228. For his telegram of 10 December, see ibid., vol. 171, no. 62.
229. Ibid., vol. 125, p. 1.
230. For the correspondence, see ibid., vol. 176.
231. Jinnah declined to preside over the Calcutta session as the permanent president, as was suggested by the League office. Assistant secretary to Jinnah, 12 December 1927, ibid., vol. 171, no. 85.

232. Mohammad Shafi to Mohammad Yaqub, 17 February 1928, ibid., vol. 130, no. 44; and Jinnah's statement of 26 February 1928, ibid., vol. 177, no. 13.

233. Raja of Mahmudabad to Saifuddin Kitchlew, 16 November 1928, ibid., vol. 178, no. 21.

234. Ibid., vol. 146, no. 40. Some members of the Jinnah League did attend the conference in their individual capacity.

235. For circular letter of Saifuddin Kitchlew, see ibid., vol. 577; and Shamsul Hasan to Saifuddin Kitchlew, 10 February 1929, ibid., vol. 185, no. 1.

236. Ibid., vol. 151, no. 2; vol. 152, nos. 4 and 10.

237. Ibid., vol. 186, nos. 17, 23, 24, 28 and 32; and *Annual Report of the All-India Muslim League for the Year 1930*, ibid., 154, no. 53.

238. Sir Sultan Ahmad, Fazlul Haq and Sahibzada Abdul Qayyum were the other candidates.

239. Mohammad Iqbal to Mohammad Yaqub, 1 and 4 August 1930, ibid., vol. 153, nos. 23 and 25.

240. Jinnah to Mohammad Yaqub, 12 August 1930, ibid., vol. 154, no. 4; see also ibid., nos. 7 and 10.

241. For the correspondence, see ibid., vol. 154.

242. Ahmad Saeed to Sir Mohammad Yaqub, 23 December 1931, ibid., vol. 156, no. 20; and Mohammad Sulaiman Qadri Chishti (Phulwari Sharif) to secretary, 24 December 1931, ibid., no. 24.

243. One Leaguer expressed his apprehension that if the Qadianis were thrown out of the pale of Islam today, tomorrow it would the Shias and then the other sects. Ibid., no. 40.

244. Obaidur Rahman to Sir Mohammad Yaqub, 19 December 1931, ibid., no. 14. The members were: Zafrullah Khan, Mohammad Yaqub, S.M. Abdullah and Mirza Ijaz Husain.

245. Its members were: president of the League, Mohammad Yaqub, S.M. Abdullah, Mirza Ijaz Husain and Haji Rashid Ahmad. Ibid., vol. 208, no. 31.

246. Earlier that day, the All-India Muslim Conference Executive Board had approved the merger proposal and proposed the appointment of a joint committee to draft a constitution.

247. AFM, vol. 210, nos. 1, 11, 12, 30 and 31. Before the conclusion of the meeting, Mian Aziz was physically removed from the chair. He and his supporters then walked out of the meeting. On this, one member remarked that this 'meeting definitely marks the death of the League. Hitherto the League . . . [had] . . . proceeded on parliamentary method of debate and discussion. But today I was pained to see abuse and assault as the only effective arguments in place of civilized debate'.

248. On 12 May, several Leaguers from different provinces had, in a joint manifesto, called on members of all the parties that had objectives similar to the League to join the All-India Muslim League to broaden its base.

249. Honorary secretary, reception committee, to A.H. Layard, district magistrate; and deputy superintendent of police to honorary secretary, 23 November 1933, AFM, 161, no. 9 and 12, respectively.

250. Ibid., vol. 210, no. 41; vol. 160, no. 30; and the *Statesman*, 12, 14, 30 May 1933. Prominent Leaguers from Bengal, Punjab, United Provinces, Madras and Bihar signed the requisition.

251. *The Statesman*, 10 December 1933 and 16 February 1934.

252. For the proceedings of the meeting, see AFM, vol. 219, no. 7.

253. For details, see Chapter 4.

254. AFM, vol. 482, p. 46.

255. Aziz Mirza to Ghulam Mohammad Munshi, 5 May 1910, Adamji Pirbhai to honorary secretary, 21 May 1910, Umar Hayat Tiwana to Aziz Mirza, 22 May 1910, and Mohammad Yaqub to Aziz Mirza, 23 May 1910, ibid., vol. 202, nos. 16, 36, 44 and 57.

256. Ibid., vols. 244 and 597.

257. For the Punjab provincial Muslim League's opposition, see Mohammad Shafi to Wazir Hasan, 12 May 1914, ibid., vol. 75; and Wazir Hasan to Mohammad Ali, 16 May 1914, ibid., vol. 75.

258. For instance, see ibid., vol. 126, no. 70; vol. 483, pp. 28, 32, 33, and 34; and vol. 593, p. 20.

259. Ibid., vol. 522, pp. 17, 19, 20, and 34. In March 1912, the League had five staff members in the office, and by May 1920, their number had risen to eight.

260. *Report of the Honorary Secretary for the Year 1927*, ibid., vol. 125, no. 3.

261. Gul Mohammad to honorary secretary, 25 February 1927, ibid., vol. 130, no. 36; and minutes of the council meeting held on 9–10 September 1927, ibid., vol. 110.

262. In September 1929, Jinnah donated Rs 1000 when the assistant secretary wrote to him that it would be impossible for him 'to keep the [League] office open' without funds. Assistant secretary to Jinnah, 11 September 1929, ibid., vol. 185, no. 31; and *Annual Report of the All- India Muslim League for the Year 1930*, ibid., vol. 154, no. 53.

263. For instance, see Zahur Ahmad to Jinnah, 3 April 1924, ibid., vol. 108, no. 2; and Shamsul Hasan to Mohammad Yaqub, 26 January 1930, ibid., no. 39.

264. *Annual Report of the All-India Muslim League for the Year 1931*, Delhi, [1931]; and *Annual Report of the All-India Muslim League for the Years 1932 & 1933 up to 15th November*, Delhi, [1933].

265. In that meeting, Jinnah donated Rs 500, Liaquat Ali, Haji Rashid Ahmad and Maulana Obaidur Rahman Rs 100 each, and eight others Rs 50 or less. Ibid., vol. 219, no. 36.

3
Recognition by Performance, 1906–1921

All-India Muslim League provided the Muslims of different regions of India a common platform to articulate their demands. No other political party ever enjoyed Muslim confidence to the extent similar to that of the All-India Muslim League. The League aimed at securing for the Muslims due share in the political set-up of the future. It contributed to their political and social development in the process. Immediately after its formation, it struggled to safeguard their interests in the Act of 1909, besides taking interest in other topical issues. It put pressure on the British government and subsequently negotiated with the Congress to achieve its objectives. In addition, it endeavoured to secure fair share for the Muslims in government services without which it was difficult to safeguard their interests. It also strove to protect their religious and cultural rights whenever there was an occasion to do so. It provided a platform for the promotion of modern education, sectarian harmony and social interaction and actively campaigned to defend the Urdu language, Muslim *waqfs* (endowments) and mosques. It extended all possible assistance to the Muslims outside India, sometimes even ignoring the state of their own servitude.

(A) CONSTITUTIONAL REFORMS

At the time of its inception, the primary concern of the All-India Muslim League was to protect Muslim interests in the proposed constitutional reforms that Lord Morley (secretary of state for India), had announced in his speech. Before its formation, Muslim representation by election in the institutions of legislative councils and local self-government had been highly inadequate, which the government had tried to rectify by nominations. But the Muslims did not perceive those nominated on these legislative and local bodies as their true representatives. Therefore, they demanded separate electorates and weightage, i.e. more representation than their proportion in population warranted, in view of their 'historical and political importance'. It appeared from the positive response of Lord Minto, the viceroy, to the memorial presented by the Simla deputation and its endorsement by the secretary of state for India that the British government would accept their demands. That was, however, not the case. The League had to maintain a steady pressure on the governments in India and London in support of its demands. Its struggle eventually produced mixed result.

The Government of India initiated the process of formulation of constitutional reforms in October 1907, when after yearlong deliberations and with Morley's approval, it published a scheme of reforms and invited comments on its contents by 31 March 1908. This scheme reserved four seats for the Muslims in the Imperial Legislative Council: two filled by nomination and two by elections through Muslim electorates. Some Hindus realized 'the expediency of giving special representation' to the Muslims while others criticized the scheme as a device to divide the Indians on religious grounds.[1] The issue of reservation of seats in the provincial councils was not dealt with at this time; it was deferred till the total strength of each council had been determined. The All-India Muslim League appointed a committee consisting of Wiqarul Mulk, Nabiullah, Zahur Ahmad, Yaqub Hasan (1875–1940), Rafiuddin Ahmad, Fazli Husain and Khwaja Yusuf Shah at its Aligarh annual session to consider the scheme. This committee prepared a report after taking into consideration the suggestions that had been sent to the Government of India by the Punjab provincial Muslim League and the trustees of the Aligarh college, and those mailed by individual Leaguers to the central honorary secretary. It also commented on the proposal of an advisory council for the viceroy but the idea of that council was dropped before the finalization of reforms. On the basis of this report, the All-India Muslim League demanded ten seats for the Muslims in the Imperial Legislative Council, one for each province and one for the trustees of the Aligarh college, and also asked for a fixed number of seats in each provincial council, providing at least one seat for the Muslims in each division. In addition, it wanted reservation of seats for them in all the local bodies—municipalities and district boards. It hoped that exclusively Muslim electorates would fill all the Muslim seats and that there would be no nomination at all.[2] The Government of India's despatch of 1 October 1908, to the secretary of state for India incorporated some of the League's demands. It provided five seats for the Muslims in the Imperial Legislative Council—all elected by separate electorates—and reserved a fixed number of seats in all the provincial councils, elected on the basis of separate electorates except those in the Punjab council where these were to be filled in by nomination.[3]

On the receipt of Government of India's despatch, Morley drew up his own scheme of reforms that he sent to the Government of India on 27 November 1908. Some prominent Hindu leaders and a few British liberal politicians had opposed the Muslim demand for separate electorates and weightage. Morley's scheme reflected their influence and that of the Congress leaders who had gone to England to represent before the secretary of state for India and British politicians their viewpoint on the proposed reforms.[4] His scheme recognised the principle of representation of important communities like the Muslims in the legislative councils; however, the proposal of joint electoral colleges in the scheme, composed of a fixed number of Muslims and Hindus in proportion to their population who were to elect jointly their representatives in like proportion, negated the principles of separate electorates and weightage. The League rejected the scheme and observed that, if implemented, it would return 'mandatories' of the majorities rather than 'members' representing the Muslims.[5] The pressure that the provincial Muslim Leagues, Muslim press and non-League Muslim bodies built up in India and London against the scheme of a joint electoral college was 'simply phenomenal'. The All-India Muslim League passed resolutions on this subject at its Amritsar session and appointed a special committee, headed by Ali Imam, which presented a memorial to the viceroy based on these resolutions.[6] The London Muslim League passed resolutions of similar content; in addition, Amir Ali and his young co-workers in London put forward their viewpoint in the press. They approached members of the parliament, exerting to persuade them to oppose the Indian Councils Bill if it did not include the Muslim demands. On 27 January 1909, a nine-member deputation of the London Muslim League, led by Amir Ali, presented a memorial to Morley on behalf of the All-India Muslim League, demanding 'unadulterated' system of separate electorates. The League pressure worked. Morley soon acknowledged that the joint electoral college scheme had been merely a suggestion and that it was 'practically dead' due to the Muslim opposition. Interestingly, an invisible pressure on Morley was his concern about the 'very severe and injurious reaction in Constantinople' if any injustice was done to the Indian Muslims.[7] Minto on his part realized that if separate electorates were not given to the Muslims, the British would have 'an infinitely worse trouble than anything that can arise from Hindu opposition'.[8] Morley assured the Aga Khan that Muslim demands would be fulfilled. But the Indian Councils Bill, as moved in the House of Commons, reserved a few seats for the Muslims on the basis of separate electorates, in addition to those they might win through joint electorates. The number of seats was less than that demanded by the Muslims, filled in partly by elections and partly by nomination.[9]

The All-India Muslim League had gradually gained confidence. Now it began to press the Muslim demands as a matter of right, and not as a concession. Its pressure climaxed in a meeting of representatives of all the provincial Muslim Leagues, except those of Madras and Burma, at Lucknow on 23 May 1909, with Wiqarul Mulk in the chair, where the Leaguers reiterated their demands: separate electorates, weightage at all levels and representation by election and not by nomination. The intensity of the Muslim campaign for separate electorates persuaded some moderate Congress leaders like Gopal Krishna Gokhale to drop their opposition to the system.[10] In England, the Aga Khan, speaking at the annual meeting of the London Muslim League on 24 June, warned that the constitutional reforms were 'doomed to failure' if these did not carry out to the full the pledges made to the Muslims. The central committee of the All-India Muslim League reaffirmed his statement.[11] While the London Muslim League rigidly stuck to these demands, the All-India Muslim League showed signs of disunity. Ali Imam, president of the Amritsar annual session, indicated his agreement to the relaxation of separate electorates in areas where the Muslims could successfully compete with the non-Muslims. He made this suggestion to the viceroy on 4 February 1909, and repeated it at the Bihar provincial conference on 10 April and in a letter to the press on 2 May.[12] He supported the Government of India's proposal to fill some seats by separate electorates and some by joint electorates at a meeting of five Muslim leaders that Minto had invited in Simla on 26 June; the latter had modified his views on the electorates issue because of opposition from the Hindus. Ali Imam and Mian Abdul Aziz (of Peshawar), two of the five Muslims, went straight from Simla to Aligarh and unsuccessfully tried to get this proposal approved by the general body of the All-India Muslim League. On 10 July, a meeting of the general body was hastily convened but it dispersed without transacting any business due to absence of a quorum. On the following day, when there was a quorum, another controversy cropped up. Now it was pointed out that according to clause (d) of rule 23 of the constitution, the meeting had not been lawfully convened, as the League office had neither obtained comments of the members on the agenda items nor the central committee had taken a formal decision about the meeting that had been convened. Wiqarul Mulk and Musa Khan acknowledged these 'irregularities' and amidst heated discussion the meeting was adjourned till the afternoon. When the Leaguers met in the afternoon, none was willing to preside over the meeting because the opposing sides were evenly balanced, and then four members staged a walkout to break the quorum. Musa Khan informed the private secretary to the viceroy that the League's comments could not be sent in time due to the abortive meeting.[13] Despite the absence of endorsement from the All-India Muslim League, the Government of India's despatch of 22 July, provided eight seats for the Muslims, six to be filled by separate electorates and two by nomination if they failed to get the specified number of seats through joint electorates. Nevertheless, on 12 September, the central committee of the All-India Muslim League reiterated Muslim demands—separate electorates at all levels and weightage.[14] Finally, Morley worked out a compromise with the help of the Aga Khan that was incorporated in the rules and regulations framed under the Indian Councils Act that had been passed on 25 May. Muslim seats in the Imperial Legislative Council were raised from 6 to 8 out of total 28 elected seats—all elected on the basis of separate electorates.[15] Similarly, seats were reserved for the Muslims in the provincial legislative councils; Muslim proportion in the elected seats was: Madras 2 out of 20; Bombay 4 out of 21; (West) Bengal 4 out of 25; United Provinces 4 out of 21; and East Bengal and Assam 4 out of 17. The seats reserved for the Muslims in the Punjab council were to be filled by nomination. The Aga Khan undertook to obtain the acceptance of the All-India Muslim League to this 'settlement'. The Government of India and the provincial governments were to decide the issue of electorates in the municipal and district boards; at this time, the League did not press for separate electorates in these institutions.[16] The All-India Muslim League, at its Delhi annual session in January 1910, after the Aga Khan's inaugural address, appreciated the constitutional reforms and assured cooperation for their success; however, members expressed their disappointment at the denial of elections by separate electorates to the Punjab for its legislative council.[17] The provision of separate electorates was in a way expression of nebulous collective all-India Muslim identity and their implementation deepened that identity.

The constitutional reforms brought into focus the relative numerical strength of various communities in the Indian population, Muslims as a minority and Hindus as a majority. The All-India Muslim League disputed the Hindu majority, questioning the listing of 'depressed communities' as part of the Hindu community, citing Sir Bampfylde Fuller's (1854–1935) work and Lala Lajpat Rai's (1865–1928) endorsement.[18] Its leaders twice attempted to get the depressed communities listed in the decennial census as a separate class. Once, they did in 1910–1911, arguing that the inclusion of 'depressed communities' under the head 'Hindus' gave the Caste Hindus a 'fictitious' majority, placed other communities especially the Muslims in an 'abiding' disadvantage, and deprived the depressed communities themselves of the facilities of education and government jobs. The Madras provincial Muslim League did point out to Aziz Mirza that the caste Hindus would not like this idea because it would reduce their numerical strength and provide the depressed communities 'government jobs that the Brahmans would not like' to give them.[19] Another attempt was made in 1940–1941, when Liaquat Ali Khan, as general secretary of the All-India Muslim League, requested the census commissioner to enlist only such persons as Hindus who came within the four Vernas as established by Manu in his Smruti.[20] Abdur Rahman Siddiqi (1887–1953) and his uncle, Ali Mohammad Khan Dehlavi, provided the material in support of this demand.[21] The latter contended that only such people should be categorized as Hindus who came within the four 'varnas' of the 'Manusmriti', i.e. Brahman, Kshetria, Vysia and Sudra; the rest should be classed under a separate head as 'Panchama' or Scheduled Castes or whatever they preferred to call themselves.[22] But on both the occasions, the British Indian government declined to accept the viewpoint of the All-India Muslim League.

(B) SOCIAL AND OTHER ISSUES

The All-India Muslim League did not ignore to take up those issues that indirectly related to politics or topical issues that seriously engaged Muslim attention. Next to constitutional reforms its focus was on securing a fair share for the Muslims in high offices and public services proportionate to their population and importance. The Simla deputation had made this demand in its memorial and the All-India Muslim League reiterated it in its resolutions. Whenever the British planned to appoint a Hindu to any high office, the League would demand the appointment of one Muslim as well. For instance, in March 1909, when the government announced the appointment of a Hindu, Satyendra P. Sinha (1864–1928), on the Viceroy's Executive Council, the League pressed for the appointment of one Muslim, threatening that it would not 'welcome' the constitutional reforms if that was not done.[23] Consequently, Ali Imam was appointed on the Executive Council in response to this pressure. Later on, the All-India Muslim League and the provincial Muslim Leagues organized similar pressure for the appointment of Muslims wherever provincial governors were provided with executive councils.[24] The secretary of state for India had one Hindu (K.G. Gupta [1851–1926]) and one Muslim (Husain Bilgrami) on his council; and when a Hindu was proposed to succeed Husain Bilgrami, the All-India Muslim League's campaign against that proposal secured the appointment of Mirza Abbas Ali Beg (1859–1932) to that office.[25] The All-India Muslim League also demanded the appointment of Muslim judges on all the high/chief courts in the provinces and put pressure, where needed, to secure this objective.[26] Thus, Sayyid Karamat Husain (1852–1917) was appointed as judge of the high court of judicature of the United Provinces, Abdur Rahim as judge of the Madras high court, Sharfuddin (1856–1921) as judge of the Calcutta high court, and Mian Shah Din as judge of the Punjab chief court.[27] Likewise Amir Ali (president, London Muslim League), was appointed on the Privy Council.

Muslims had emphasized their inadequate share in government services since the time they had accepted the British ascendancy in India. The All-India Muslim League raised this issue at its inception but took it up more seriously after the acceptance of its demand for separate electorates. It repeated the demand at its annual sessions and council meetings. The Government of India, in response to a letter from Aziz Mirza (honorary secretary) informed him that the government wanted the Muslims to have a share in public services proportionate to their 'number and importance' and educational and other qualifications but it had no information to suggest that any provincial government was against this policy. Aziz Mirza was advised to represent any Muslim grievances on this count to the provincial governments.[28] The League did some solid work. Its central office collected statistics about the proportion of Muslims in various government services and professions through the provincial Muslim Leagues, individual Leaguers and Muslim employees.[29] These statistics showed that, except for a few 'executive branches' in the United Provinces and Punjab, Muslims had totally inadequate representation in other departments of these provinces, and that their representation in all the services in other provinces was disappointing. Aziz Mirza cited this information in his speech at the Nagpur annual session and formally communicated it to the heads of various government departments, requesting them to keep it in view at the time of fresh recruitments.[30] Simultaneously, he forwarded this information to the secretaries of the provincial Muslim Leagues urging them to take up this issue with the relevant departments of the provincial governments and report to him about the progress.[31] The central League established a 'Muslim Employment Bureau' at its head office in Lucknow to facilitate employment of Muslim candidates.[32] The provincial Muslim Leagues in the Punjab, Bengal, Bombay and United Provinces worked on similar lines.[33] This campaign did increase recruitment of Muslims but could not eliminate completely their paucity in various services. Again, in the 1920s, the All-India Muslim League raised this issue with similar intensity when Fazli Husain's policies as minister of education and local self-government in the Punjab came under fire from the Hindus.[34] After 1935, Muslim employees in various services and departments formed associations to advocate employment issues and the League supported their demands.

The All-India Muslim League took up matters that were likely to affect Muslim recruitment in services. When the British government reduced the age-limit for the candidates in the Indian Civil Service examination from twenty-three to twenty-two years with a corresponding increase in the period of probation in England, it made representations to the government for reconsideration of this decision. It was argued that one-year training should not be necessary for the Indian probationers and that if this was done, it would reduce the possibility of Indians entering the covenanted services whose number in the higher ranks was already very small.[35] Similarly, the League raised its voice against the new regulations of the Council of Legal Education in London for the admission of Indian students into the Inns of Court. It considered one regulation particularly harsh that required every Indian candidate to provide a certificate of good character from the district magistrate of the district of his residence on the ground of his personal acquaintance of the candidate extending over a period of one year. As a result of its protest, this regulation was not strictly enforced.[36] The

All-India Muslim League also asked for a greater share for the Indians in higher ranks of the British army to which till then persons of only British birth were eligible.[37] This demand was met during the First World War in 1917, when the Indians were allowed in principle to enter the commissioned ranks of the British army. The League hoped that the rules framed to implement this decision would meet the wishes of the people, and that training colleges would be established in India, and Muslim claims would receive 'full consideration'.[38]

Muslim politics and education were closely interlinked. The Aligarh alumni and like-minded individuals from all over India had played a vital role in establishing the All-India Muslim League. Its foundation was laid at the venue of an educational association, the All-India Muslim Educational Conference. These organizations, All-India Muslim League and All-India Muslim Educational Conference, shared common platform for several years and often had common leadership. Prominent Leaguers were associated with the Anjumans and educational institutions that were established in various provinces. The close association of the All-India Muslim League and its leaders with the Aligarh college and then university that began at the time of its inception lasted till independence. The Leaguers made useful contribution to the Muslim university movement. On Sir Sayyid's death, his followers had started a movement to realize his dream of a Muslim university.[39] They set up a 'Sir Syed Memorial Fund Committee', chaired by Mohsinul Mulk, to collect funds for this purpose. The target fixed was to collect one million rupees. The All-India Muslim Educational Conference endorsed the proposal at its twelfth session in Lahore. When the campaign for the collection of funds was under way, Lord Curzon (1859–1925) and the Education Commission (1902) opposed the establishment of 'denominational' universities. Consequently, the Muslim university movement slowed down. The Simla deputationists had again raised the issue in their memorial but their primary interest was in the constitutional reforms. After the introduction of reforms under the Act of 1909, the All-India Muslim League focused its attention on raising the status of the Aligarh college to that of a university. It passed a resolution to this effect at its Delhi annual session and accelerated the pace of the university movement.[40] The Aga Khan had now estimated the initial cost of the university at two million rupees.[41] Two committees, a Muslim University Foundation Committee, headed by the Aga Khan with Wiqarul Mulk as its secretary, and a Constitution Committee, chaired by Raja of

Mahmudabad with Sayyid Ali Bilgrami (1851–1911) as its secretary and Dr Ziauddin Ahmad as its joint secretary, were set up to work for the proposed university.[42] The All-India Muslim League, the provincial Muslim Leagues and prominent Leaguers spent the whole year of 1911 in the collection of 'subscriptions for the University'.[43] The League organized a systematic campaign and widely circulated propaganda literature on the issue. Aziz Mirza himself wrote a 14-page pamphlet entitled *Muslim University aur Uske Maqasid* ('Muslim University and its Objectives'), which was published by the Neval Kishore Press, Lucknow. This campaign was meant to persuade maximum number of Muslims, rich and poor, from Peshawar to Rangoon to contribute to the university fund. The idea was to give them a 'feeling of ownership' and make the institution really a 'Muslim National University'. Some rich Muslims made handsome donations: the Nizam of Hyderabad donated Rs 5 lakhs; the Aga Khan Rs 1.25 lakhs; Nawab of Rampur Rs 1.50 lakhs; and Begum of Bhopal, Raja of Mahmudabad and Raja of Jahangirabad each one lakh rupees. Muslims of Bombay gave three lakh rupees and those of Rangoon contributed more than one lakh rupees. The Islamic character of the proposed university was emphasised to attract wider support for the movement. Sir Sayyid's observation that the students of the proposed university would have philosophy in their right hand, science in their left hand and the crown of the first *kalima* on their heads was highlighted.[44] Personalities belonging to different religious schools of thought either personally contributed to the university fund or participated in the fund-raising campaign; among them were Maulana Abdul Bari Farangi Mahalli (1878–1926); Syed Ali al-Hairi and Syed Mohammad Husain, the Shia dignitaries; Pir Sayyid Jamaat Ali Shah (1841–1951), a prominent Brelvi figure; and Maulana Abu Saeed Mohammad Husain and Nuruddin, the Ahle Hadith scholars.[45] The amount that was finally collected exceeded the estimated target; the total collection stood at Rs 2,970,000.[46] The Constitution Committee drafted a constitution of the Muslim university, providing for a fully autonomous university controlled by the Muslims and giving affiliation to Muslim educational institutions throughout India.[47]

The government response reflected a desire on its part to control the university directly and restrict its jurisdiction in those times of rising pan-Islamic fervour and emerging all-India Muslim identity.[48] The government wanted that the governor general should be the chancellor of the university whose advice, if repeated a second time, should be binding on the governing body, and who was to give final approval to the appointment of professors. The power of affiliation was to be restricted to the city of its location![49] Even otherwise, the government was making moves to restrict the influence of the Aligarh college by encouraging the foundation of colleges at different places such as the Islamia colleges in Peshawar and Lahore whose objective partly was to keep Muslim students away from the Aligarh college.[50] This policy did disillusion the Muslims but they still adopted a course of negotiation for the realization of their objectives. In December 1912, the All-India Muslim Educational Conference demanded that the university should be named 'Muslim University'; the power of control should vest in the chancellor and not in the governor-general-in-council; the university should have powers similar to those enjoyed by the Aligarh college; the statutes regarding affiliation should remain as proposed; and the powers of the court, the council and the senate should not be modified.[51] After prolonged negotiations, a compromise was worked out, which was incorporated in the university bill that Mian Mohammad Shafi, a Muslim Leaguer and Aligarh alumni, moved as education member in the Imperial Legislative Council. On 9 September 1920, the bill was finally passed; and the All-India Muslim League welcomed the establishment of the Muslim university in a resolution moved by Maulana Azad at the Nagpur annual session.[52] The university was named as the Aligarh Muslim University. The court, the highest governing body, was elected by the Muslims and was empowered to elect the chancellor, the pro-chancellor and the vice-chancellor—the last office required approval of the governor-general-in-council.[53] The university's power of affiliation was, however, restricted to the Aligarh district. Later on, in 1940, the All-India Muslim League again made an attempt to empower the Aligarh Muslim University to affiliate Muslim educational institutions from all over India but it was then perceived as a 'reflection of the "Pakistan" attitude of the Muslims' and the move did not succeed.[54]

Primary education was another area that engaged the attention of the All-India Muslim League. At the Nagpur annual session, the League called for making 'primary education free and gradually compulsory' throughout India and suggested its experimentation in a few selected areas.[55] When the moderate Congress leader, Gopal Krishna Gokhale, introduced the Elementary Education Bill in the Imperial Legislative Council to introduce gradually the principle of compulsion into the elementary education system, the All-India Muslim League and its provincial branches, except the Punjab provincial Muslim League, welcomed the bill. In August and October 1911, the All-India Muslim League council heatedly debated the provisions of the bill, and drafted a resolution for the annual session that accepted its principles but asked for 'due safeguards' for the religious education of the Muslims, Urdu as a 'sole medium of instruction' and equal representation of Muslims and Hindus on the controlling boards.[56] The opposition of the Punjab provincial Muslim League to the element of compulsion in the bill raised a serious controversy within the ranks of the All-India Muslim League.[57] As a result, the central council passed a resolution in support of the bill by 20 to 5 votes. At the annual session in Calcutta, Maulana Azad's remarks that only the title-holders were opposed to the bill provoked an unpleasant scene and disturbed the proceedings; but when peace was restored, the president ruled him out of order. Still, the atmosphere was so charged that the members had to go into an anteroom to vote on the bill. A resolution was passed by a majority of votes; and the opponents of the bill abstained from voting. The final resolution accepted the principles of the bill and simply asked for adequate safeguards for the interests of the Muslims.[58]

The All-India Muslim League viewed the Urdu language after religion as a uniting bond for the Indian Muslims and wanted it to be the *lingua franca* and 'sole medium of education' for them, except for the Muslims in East Bengal and Madras.[59] Muslims in the Punjab supported the Urdu language for an additional reason; they were opposed to the Punjabi language, its Gurmukhi script and the Punjabi-medium schools, which at that time the Sikhs had started to establish in the Punjab. Mian Shafi considered even the translation of a pamphlet into Punjabi 'suicidal to the position' that the Punjab provincial Muslim League had taken on the Urdu–Punjabi controversy.[60] However, the All-India Muslim League rarely organised any concerted pro-Urdu campaign directly although it reacted to any move that was likely to harm the Urdu language or its script. The only time that it did campaign in support of Urdu was during the preparation of the census in 1911, when the Hindus were campaigning for Hindi; and later on, in 1941, when it urged the Muslims to register Urdu as their mother tongue during the preparation of the census even if they knew a little bit of it.[61] It passed resolutions to oppose any anti-Urdu activities especially the moves by non-Muslims to establish Hindi in the United Provinces and Bombay, and Punjabi and Hindi in the Punjab as the vernacular languages and made representations to the government.[62] Later on, in

1923, it protested against the decision of the Bihar and Orissa legislative councils prohibiting the use of Urdu characters in the courts.[63] There were often demands for using the Urdu language in conducting the meetings of the All-India Muslim League to which the central office would respond that it could not do that because the Muslims of Bengal, Madras, Bombay and far-flung areas did not know the Urdu language.[64]

Another issue that engaged the Leaguers' attention was that of *waqfs*. Before the advent of the British, the Indian Muslims used to institute two kinds of *waqfs*: one, the *waqf-alal-aulad* (endowment for the descendants), for the welfare of the endower's family and descendants, and the other *waqf* was meant for public welfare. The chaos following the decline of the Mughal empire and the British ascendancy disrupted the *waqfs* and their administration.[65] Disruption and mismanagement of the *waqfs* resulted in the ruination of the Muslim families and destroyed many institutions of public welfare and education. Muslims began to show their concern about the state of the *waqfs* when the courts after the abolition of the posts of *qazis* gave conflicting verdicts in several cases. The climax was a ruling by the judicial committee of the Privy Council in the *Fata Mahomed Ishak v. Russomaya* case in 1894 to the effect that the creation of *waqf-alal-aulad* was not lawful according to the Muslim law. This judgement agitated the Muslims; and a consensus emerged among the Sunni and Shia jurists that the Privy Council had misinterpreted the Muslim law.[66] The problem was that they could not approach the Privy Council for a review of its ruling, as the council had never revised its judgements. The effect of this decision could be rectified only by fresh legislation. Therefore, the All-India Muslim League at its Amritsar annual session called for legislation to validate the Muslim *waqf* law with safeguards against any fraud and reiterated it at its Delhi and Nagpur annual sessions.[67] It was left to M.A. Jinnah to initiate the process of legislation on this issue. In 1906, he had supported a resolution in the Calcutta Congress on this issue and, in February 1910, had asked a question in the Imperial Legislative Council. Three months after the Nagpur session, he moved the Musalman Waqf Validating Bill in the Imperial Legislative Council to enable the Muslims to create *waqfs* for their families and descendants, which, after its processing through the select committee, was passed in April 1913.[68] Simultaneously, the All-India Muslim League urged the Government of India to institute a survey of Muslim *waqfs* 'designed mainly for the public benefit' to ensure their better administration.[69] The All-India Muslim League failed to induce the Government of India to undertake such an exercise; and the League honorary secretary was informed that the government could inquire only into any specific case of mismanaged *waqf* that was referred to it. The League itself could not investigate all the cases of mismanaged *waqfs* with its own limited resources; therefore, it simply resolved to repeat its earlier request to the Government of India.[70] The Leaguers' struggle met with success in 1923, when the Mussalman Waqf Act was passed, which was amended in 1935. This Act required all the *waqfs* to file an audited statement of accounts with the district magistrate.[71] Any defaulting *mutawallis* or those falsifying the accounts could be prosecuted in a court of law. All the provincial governments under the pressure of the Leaguers gradually enforced the Act.[72] Many Leaguers, including Jinnah, were associated with the *waqf* boards that various provincial governments set up to assist in the administration of *waqfs*.

The All-India Muslim League never initiated any legislation for the enforcement of Muslim personal law but did oppose any proposal that was likely to affect negatively any Muslim religious practice. In October 1911, when the League was asked to comment on B.N. Basu's Special Marriages Bill that would have legalised marriages prohibited by the *Shariat*, it asked the government not to apply its provisions to the Muslims, if the bill was passed, because it would amount to undue interference in Muslim personal law.[73] The bill, however, did not reach the enactment stage. The All-India Muslim League also endeavoured to get for the Muslims employees in government offices short leave for offering prayers especially the Friday prayer during working hours. The issue came to its notice in March 1910, when the resident engineer in the East India Railways at Dhanbad disallowed three Muslim employees time for the Friday prayer and, on their refusal to comply with these orders, suspended them and forfeited their pay. When these employees approached Aziz Mirza, he advised them to appeal to the chief engineer in Calcutta. On appeal, they were restored in their positions but their pay for the period of suspension and all kinds of leave were forfeited.[74] The issue did not end here. In August 1911, the All-India Muslim League council unanimously adopted the proposal of Hakim Nuruddin, head of the Ahmadi community, for two hours' leave for the Friday prayer and that of Wiqarul Mulk for half-an-hour leave every day for *zohar* (midday) prayer.[75] The council reiterated this resolution in November 1912.[76] Later on, in December 1918, the All-India Muslim League at its Delhi annual session asked the government to declare Friday a half-holiday for the Muslim employees.[77] Perhaps, as a result of this pressure, the Muslims were allowed half-holiday on Friday in government institutions before independence. Similarly, the All-India Muslim League represented Muslim feelings whenever any mosque was desecrated, dishonoured or affected in any way. Besides the well-known Kanpur mosque tragedy, the League firmly raised the cases of the Jamia masjid (Delhi) and Badshahi masjid (Lahore), when Muslims were denied access to these mosques.[78] Sometimes, it took up minor issues that agitated Muslim sensitivities; for example, the Government of India, on its representation, issued a circular that Muslims should be addressed as 'Muslims', and not as 'Mohammadans'.[79]

During Aziz Mirza's tenure as honorary secretary, the Leaguers embraced the idea floated by Amir Ali of establishing 'clubs' in the cities for the social and economic development of the Muslims. The Leaguers organized social activities in the clubs that were established in major cities. Aziz Mirza himself was elected permanent president of the club in Lucknow, which had a debating society, a library and a reading room; this club also contributed to the promotion of sectarian harmony in the city. Similar clubs were founded in Bombay, Lahore, Calcutta, Dhaka and several other district headquarters in the provinces.[80] Some of these clubs survived till independence.

(C) MUSLIM DISCONTENT

In 1911–13, several events in and outside India agitated the Muslims of India and shook their confidence in British fairness and promises. Major events within India were the annulment of the partition of Bengal, refusal of a charter of a Muslim university in accordance with the Muslim wishes and the Kanpur mosque tragedy, and those outside India were the Italian invasion of Tripoli, the Balkan wars and the Russian aggression against Iran. These events agitated every section of the Muslim society. The All-India Muslim League attempted to provide leadership and a political platform to the disillusioned Muslims to express their feelings in those calamitous circumstances.[81]

The annulment of the partition of Bengal was one such event within India. During their rule, the British had created presidencies, provinces and administrative areas, and marked or changed the boundaries of these units without regard to racial, ethnic or linguistic homogeneity of their inhabitants. The primary motive behind such changes was administrative convenience or security consideration. The partition of

Bengal apparently came in that category. Announced on 3 December 1903, and implemented on 16 October 1905, it created a new province of Eastern Bengal and Assam where the Muslims found themselves in a large majority. No community had demanded these changes in the administrative setup. The Bengali Muslims saw in these changes benefits and opportunities for their social, economic and political advancement. The policies of Sir Bampfylde Fuller, the lieutenant governor of the new province, benefited the Muslims who now had facilities of education and openings for government jobs. Muslim peasantry looked forward to some relief from the oppression of the Hindu landlords; however, the government was careful to prevent the transformation of any pre-existing peasant discontent into an uprising against the landlords.[82] On the other hand, the Bengali Hindus perceived in the partition of Bengal a British design to divide the Bengalis in order to damage the emerging Indian nationalism. Lieutenant Governor Fuller's moves including his crude methods to prevent students' participation in the anti-partition agitation fuelled their anger. When the anti-partition movement intensified, the militants among the Bengali Hindus resorted to violent tactics. The boycott of foreign goods including the British goods and promotion of indigenously manufactured goods, or the swadeshi movement, found popular support with the Hindus, which inflicted considerable financial loss to the British manufacturers. The anti-partition movement spread to areas outside Bengal.

The Congress and Bengali Hindus displayed unprecedented determination in their anti-partition movement while the All-India Muslim League and the Bengali Muslims, except for a few personalities like Nawab Salimullah and Nawab Ali Chaudhry, demonstrated complacency, indecisiveness and indifference on the issue. Muslims were lulled into immobility by Morley's categorical statement in the House of Commons on 26 February 1906, that the partition of Bengal was a 'settled fact', a statement that was repeatedly reaffirmed by the two viceroys, Minto and Hardinge. They remained loyal and dependent on the government assurances and never felt the need to counter the anti-partition movement by anything similar to the agitation organized by the Hindus. They simply passed a few resolutions at public meetings in different provinces in support of partition. One explanation for this indifference was given by Musa Khan; in a letter to Hasan Bilgrami, honorary secretary of the All-India Muslim League, in June 1908, he wrote that 'no one knew that there were so many Muslims in Bengal and because of lack of such knowledge there was no sympathy for them'.[83] They failed to keep track of the changes in British official thinking, even after the prompt acceptance of resignation of the pro-Muslim Lieutenant Governor Fuller—he had banned anti-partition meetings and singing of *Bande Mataram*—and other signs of British willingness to reconsider partition.[84] Those few Leaguers who came to know of its possible reversal did not firmly raise their voice from the League platform. The Bengali Muslim masses in vain waited for someone to lead them.[85] The Simla deputation, despite Nawab Salimullah's insistence, had not even mentioned the issue of partition in its memorial 'to avoid' unnecessary controversy.[86] After its foundation, the All-India Muslim League simply passed resolutions on two occasions: once, at its inaugural session in Dhaka, the capital of the new province, when it resolved that the partition would prove beneficial to the Muslims and condemned all 'methods of agitation' against it; and the second time, when the Madras Congress passed a highly provocative anti-partition resolution, the League in response adopted an equally strong pro-partition resolution at its Amritsar annual session to 'inform the Government and the public' of the Muslim standpoint.[87] Interestingly, three months before the Amritsar session, Hasan Bilgrami, after an hour-long meeting with Morley in London, had insisted on moving a resolution in this session for the reversal of partition but desisted from doing so on the advice of Wiqarul Mulk and Musa Khan.[88] Earlier, he had opposed any motion in the League meetings for the maintenance of partition because it might be considered 'an aggressive policy'![89] The Aga Khan, the League president, himself never spoke in public for the preservation and stability of partition. Before the Simla deputation, he had confided to Morley and Minto his opposition to the partition; however, he felt that its undoing would be 'full of very serious risk'.[90] Even the Bengali Leaguers did not come out to voice firmly their sentiments in support of partition. When Aziz Mirza passed on to them information about the Hindu moves against the partition and indicated the option of agitation to preserve it, the East Bengal presidency Muslim League executive committee decided to send simply 'a telegram through the Viceroy to His Majesty the King-Emperor on the occasion of his coronation' and resolved not to take any active steps 'in the matter at present'.[91] By then it was too late. The annulment of partition was announced at a time when the All-India Muslim League was asking for a separate high court and a university in Dhaka.[92]

Although the League leaders had displayed vacillation and confusion in supporting the partition of Bengal but Muslim disillusionment and shock over its annulment was widespread. They were apprehensive of an angry outburst from the Muslims against the annulment; therefore, they convened a 'consultative' meeting in Delhi to prevent that possibility and present a united response. Nawab Salimullah who was suffering from carbuncle and was unable even 'to stand on his legs properly' came from Dhaka to attend the meeting.[93] The joint response was contained in Wiqarul Mulk's article in the *Aligarh Institute Gazette* (10 January 1912), in which the annulment decision was criticized but accepted and the Muslims were urged to rely, after God, on their own strength rather than on the government for the protection of their rights.[94] The Bengali Muslims, at a League-sponsored 'representative meeting' in Dhaka on 30 December 1911, and the All-India Muslim League, in a resolution moved by Maulana Mohammad Ali at the Calcutta annual session, recorded 'deep sense of regret and disappointment' at the annulment in 'utter disregard of Muslim feelings' but expressed the hope that the government would 'safeguard Muslim interests' in Bengal.[95] The announcement of a university in Dhaka and special education officer for the eastern districts of Bengal was perceived a poor compensation for the annulment and even these proposals took time to mature.[96] The Leaguers were now quite sensitive about their all-India Muslim identity. When Edwin Samuel Montagu (1879–1924), then under secretary of state for India, justified the annulment decision in the House of Commons on 26 April 1912, and observed that the Muslims of India were not a 'homogenous nationality' and that the Muslims of East Bengal had 'no relation with those outside Bengal', they instantly reacted to these remarks. The Punjab and Madras provincial Muslim Leagues passed strongly worded resolutions against these remarks, followed by similar resolutions passed by other provincial Muslim Leagues.[97] Wazir Hasan observed that it was adding 'injury to insult' by indulging in 'gratuitous flings at our nationality', and the All-India Muslim League expressed its anguish that the Muslims had started 'the painful task of healing the wounds' inflicted by the annulment when Montagu 'thought it fit to rip open the sores' by the 'most unwarranted and inopportune thrust on them'.[98] Montagu was so cornered that he publicly regretted his remarks and recognised the 'unity of the Indian Muslims'.[99]

The Kanpur Mosque tragedy was another shocking event. It was a horrific example of the brutish use of the State security forces against unarmed civilians struggling to preserve the sanctity of their religious site. On 11 November 1909, the United Provinces government had notified the acquisition of land for the expansion of a road in Kanpur— A.B. Road—that included a portion of a masjid in the Machhli Bazaar (Fish Market), which abutted on the road, and a Hindu temple (mandir). Both the communities, Muslims and Hindus, made representations to the government. No acceptable solution could be found and the dispute lingered on. When Lieutenant Governor Sir James S. Meston (1865– 1943) visited Kanpur in November 1912, he announced that the masjid and the mandir would not be disturbed. The Kanpur district administration, however, accepted the plea of the local Hindu Mahasabha and its leader Madan Mohan Malaviya (1861–1946) not to demolish the mandir but insisted on acquiring the portion of the Machhli Bazaar mosque, arguing that the place used for *wuzu* (ablutions) was not part of the mosque, and offered proportionate land in return elsewhere. The *mutawallis* of the mosque, supported by the Kanpur district Muslim League and the municipal board, contended that the relevant portion, used for *wuzu*, was part of the Mosque and its sale or acquisition of land in exchange was not permissible according to the *Shariat*; and they obtained *fatawa* from the *ulama* to that effect.[100] When the district administration refused to accept their plea, the Muslims of Kanpur, in a memorial signed by 1200 Muslims, appealed to Lieutenant Governor Meston that the acquisition and demolition of the relevant portion was 'a direct encroachment' on their religious rights and appealed to him to 'save the mosque from being partially demolished'. But Meston supported the district administration and asked the memorialists to accept another site in return for the surrendered portion of the Mosque.[101] After Meston's negative response, the Kanpur district Muslim League approached the All-India Muslim League to take steps to protect the Mosque. Raja of Mahmudabad personally visited Kanpur and brought another memorial for submission to the viceroy.[102] However, on 1 July 1913, before the All-India Muslim League could do anything, armed police surrounded the mosque and H.G.G. Tyler, the district magistrate, accompanied by a large force of armed police, carried out the demolition. A press communiqué justified the action. The demolition disturbed the Muslims throughout India but they were initially 'lulled into inaction' because of the correspondence that went on between the government and Maulana Mohammad Ali, and the verbal assurances of the government to Raja of Mahmudabad.[103] The All-India Muslim League and the provincial Muslim Leagues regretted the 'Kanpur sacrilege' and in telegrams to the viceroy demanded restoration of the demolished portion of the mosque to the Muslims.[104] Muslim press gave wide coverage to the meetings that were organized to protest against the demolition. The climax was reached on 3 August 1913, when thousands of Muslims gathered in the Kanpur Idgah Ground. A few hundred of them including women and children went to see the demolished site. Armed and mounted police surrounded them, and District Magistrate Tyler ordered the police to open fire and, according to his own statement, shooting continued for fifteen minutes in which 500 cartridges were used. Indiscriminate firing even on those who took refuge inside the mosque left evidence of 'awful butchery of innocent men' on the walls.[105] Twenty-five persons were killed, 50 injured, and 105 arrested who were put on trial for 'rioting'![106]

The Kanpur mosque tragedy evoked Muslim sympathies for the victims. Lieutenant Governor Meston's observations, justifying the action and the use of force, further inflamed Muslim sentiments.[107] The Leaguers demanded an impartial inquiry by a committee of official and non-official members because the lieutenant governor himself had assumed a partisan role.[108] They urged the viceroy to transfer the cases of the under-trial prisoners from the Allahabad high court to Calcutta; and Mian Shafi prepared a memorial for that purpose.[109] Two Leaguers (Wazir Hasan and Mohammad Ali) secretly left for London to present Muslim grievances before the British government and public.[110] They dodged the British Indian intelligence by obtaining passports under unfamiliar names of W. Hasan and M. Ali. Their mission was perceived as 'unsuccessful' because the secretary of state for India and the British cabinet ministers, on receipt of negative reports about them from the viceroy and Lieutenant Governor Meston, had even declined to meet them. But they were warmly received on their return; and on 20 December 1913, Jinnah presided over the function that the Anjuman Ziaul Islam organized for their reception in Bombay. The British Indian government soon realized the gravity of the situation and withdrew from the hard stance of the local administration. The viceroy personally visited Kanpur and, on 14 October, rescinded the orders of the lieutenant governor and directed the restoration of the demolished portion to the Muslims at government expense.[111] All the 105 prisoners were released unconditionally and the cases registered against them were withdrawn. The construction of the demolished portion, however, took quite some time to reach completion. The government gave Rs 5000 for the construction of the demolished portion of the mosque.[112]

The Leaguers collected funds to help the affected families. The total collections reached more than Rs 80,000.[113] Strangely enough, all the funds were not disbursed, and later on, the un-used funds were utilized for the sufferers of the Bihar riots in 1917.[114] These developments on the domestic scene strengthened feelings of all-India Muslim solidarity.

The woes of the Muslims outside India coincided with the problems that they faced within India. They naively looked to Britain as the 'greatest Muslim power' for the alleviation of Muslim sufferings outside India.[115] The failure of Britain to come up to their expectations aggravated their frustration and discontent. The tragic events began in September 1911, when the Italian forces, with British and French connivance, invaded Ottoman Tripoli and ruthlessly swept away Muslim resistance. The escalating aggressive Italian actions including the blockade and bombardment of the Arabian ports posed a threat to Muslim holy cities of Makkah and Madina, which distressed the Indian Muslims.[116] Some League enthusiasts who were worried about the safety of the holy places established the Anjuman-i-Khuddam-i-Ka'ba to campaign for their protection.[117] The emotional writings of Muslim poets, writers and journalists and the extensive coverage of the events in the newspapers like the *Comrade*, *Zamindar*, *al-Hilal*, *Hamdard*, and *Muslim Gazette* inflamed Muslim sentiments. Those who wrote about or organized support for the sufferers were all associated with the All-India Muslim League. Some Leaguers were ready to ignore their own problems to pursue the cause of the Muslims outside India and a few were anxious to go to Turkey as volunteers to fight against the Italian forces while others wanted to address their own and outside Muslims' problems simultaneously.[118] Initially, the Leaguers hesitated to organize public meetings to protest against the Italian invasion when the London Muslim League urged them to do so, because the issue was linked with foreign affairs, and the government, in a communiqué, had directed the public to observe neutrality on the issue.[119] The Leaguers in the provinces, however, pressed the All-India Muslim League for guidance and a unified policy.[120] Finally, on 15 October 1911, the All-India Muslim League council adopted a policy resolution, in which it sympathized with Turkey, condemned the Italian invasion as breach of 'international morality', asked for British intervention to put an end to 'an unjust and unconscionable war', appealed to the Muslims to collect funds for the sufferers and called for a complete boycott of Italian goods by the Indian Muslims.[121] In November, the council reiterated this resolution, which was endorsed in a slightly modified form at the annual session in March 1912.[122] On the instructions of the All-India Muslim League, various provincial and district Muslim Leagues organized protest meetings, in which they passed resolutions of similar content, and sent the copies to the British authorities. The Punjabi Muslims organized an effective boycott of the Italian goods, and Muslims in Bombay, Bengal, United Provinces and Madras followed their example.[123] The British response was, however, not very encouraging; and the League was informed that 'the present moment' was not 'opportune for intervention'.[124]

The Russian bombardment of the Imam Raza shrine in Meshed (Iran), and the looting of valuable historic artefacts from the Imam's Shrine followed the Italian invasion. It highlighted Russia's continued occupation of northern Iran and the repression of the Iranians.[125] The All-India Muslim League council, in a resolution passed in December 1911, expressed its resentment at Russia's aggressive policy towards Iran, with whose people the Indian Muslims had 'strong ties of common religion and culture', and appealed to the British government 'to secure and maintain the independence and integrity' of Iran. It conveyed its gratitude to Earl Curzon, Lord Lamington, and Professor E.G. Browne (1862–1926) of the Cambridge University for advocating the cause of Iran, hoping that their advice would result in the emancipation of Iran from the Russian occupation.[126] The provincial and district Muslim Leagues, on a directive of the All-India Muslim League, held meetings in major Indian cities to pass resolutions on the lines of the central council's resolution; the Sunnis and Shias in Lucknow and other cities in United Provinces demonstrated unprecedented unity in holding joint meetings.[127] The British government, in response to appeals from the All-India Muslim League, did invite the attention of the Russian government through its ambassador in St. Petersburg and Russian ambassador in London to the issue.[128] But the situation in Iran continued to deteriorate, and two years later, the All-India Muslim League again urged the British government to persuade Russia to evacuate northern Iran to enable the Iranians to work for their 'regeneration' without foreign intervention.[129]

These events were followed by developments in the Balkans. In October 1912, the Balkan states formed an alliance to launch a combined attack on the Ottoman Turkey in the Balkans that resulted in immense Muslim suffering especially in Macedonia. The British press suppressed the news about the atrocities; instead, there was propaganda against Islam and the Muslims so much so that even the US government thought of legislation to stop Muslims from entering the US.[130] The Indian Muslims again held protest meetings and sent letters/telegrams to the British authorities for intercession; the *Pall Mall Gazette* (31 January 1913) asked the British authorities not to attach too much importance to the resolutions passed by the Indian Muslims.[131] The All-India Muslim League council criticized the proposal to partition the Turkish provinces in Europe, and postponed its annual session that year to express solidarity with Turkey.[132] In addition, the central League, the provincial Muslim Leagues and individual Leaguers organized a campaign to collect funds to help the Muslim sufferers in Tripoli and the Balkans. They established a Red Crescent Society in Calcutta and another in London to render assistance to the victims. The All-India Muslim League collected about Rs 7 million, which were in addition to the funds collected by the provincial Muslim Leagues and individual Leaguers.[133] These funds were sent to the Turkish prime minister through the British ambassador in Turkey to help the destitute. The All-India Muslim League and the Red Crescent Society of the London Muslim League sent several medical missions to Turkey including the more famous one led by Dr M.A. Ansari for the treatment of victims.[134] The Leaguers resented the statements made by some British ministers in support of the Balkan states, and expressed their disappointment when the British foreign office termed the All-India Muslim League's demand for 'an independent international inquiry into the atrocities' as impracticable 'in the present circumstances'.[135] These events strengthened the pan-Islamic sentiments of the Indian Muslims and shook their trust in, and unwavering dependence on, the British government. The Leaguers were now quite emotional about even insignificant sympathetic gestures and began to look for new options in politics.[136]

(D) THE LUCKNOW PACT

The All-India Muslim League initiated moves to recast its policies. It gradually came closer to the Congress to devise a common platform. In fact, since its very inception the League had deliberately avoided unnecessary criticism of the Congress policies. Its struggle was focussed primarily on protecting Muslim interests in the constitutional reforms. Once that objective was achieved, its leaders began to cultivate the Congress. For instance, Wiqarul Mulk appreciated the Congress achievements in the past, some of which he gratefully acknowledged had benefited the Muslims as well, and explained Muslim loyalty to the British in terms of Muslim 'self-interest' and 'communal consideration'.[137] Consequently, the Leaguers responded positively to a move by the Aga Khan and Sir William Wedderburn (1838–1918) for a joint conference of the All-India Muslim League and Congress leaders that was held in Allahabad on new year's day in 1911. Among the forty Muslim and sixty Hindu participants were Nawab Sayyid Mohammad, Shamsul Huda, Gopal Krishna Gokhale, Sir Pherozeshah Mehta (1845–1915), Pandit Madan Mohan Malaviya, Pandit Motilal Nehru (1861–1931), Ibrahim Rahimatullah, Fazalbhai Karimbhai, Mazharul Haq and M.A. Jinnah.[138] However, the committee that the conference appointed to bring about Hindu–Muslim understanding could not achieve anything tangible partly because of the conflicting viewpoints of its members on the system of separate electorates; some Congress leaders strongly criticized acceptance of this system by the British government while the All-India Muslim League pressed for its extension to the provincial councils and all the self-governing public bodies like the district and municipal boards.[139] After a temporary halt, the All-India Muslim League resumed the revision of its policies although it was a slow and interrupted process. Events in and outside India strengthened its resolve to pursue this course.[140] The change was not very smooth. It divided the Leaguers into two loosely defined factions that were referred to as the 'progressives' and 'conservatives' or the 'young party' and the 'old party'. The 'progressives' were led by young self-confident Leaguers who were keen to amend the party constitution to meet the new situation, ready to take decisions even if these displeased the British government, and prepared to ignore Muslim interests in pursuit of rapprochement with the Congress while the conservatives consisted of the old guard who were opposed to, or hesitant about, amending the League constitution and were unwilling to support any move that might displease the government and were against, or cautious about, any united action in cooperation with the Congress. The progressives gradually came to dominate the League policies and the conservatives were either sidelined or temporarily dissociated themselves from the party.[141]

In March 1913, the All-India Muslim League at its annual session amended its objectives to bring these in line with those of the Congress and expressed the hope that the Hindu and Muslim leaders would periodically meet 'to find a *modus operandi* for joint and concerted action'.[142] Mian Shafi, who presided over this session, circulated a printed letter, urging joint work on issues where League-Congress agreement existed without waiting for complete unanimity.[143] Another printed letter followed his letter from Wazir Hasan to prominent Muslim and Hindu leaders, suggesting that four members of each community from every province should meet in Lucknow in September to determine the preliminaries for future organised action.[144] The Leaguers and Congressmen generally welcomed the proposal; and Jinnah, in a letter on 21 May, appreciated the idea and offered his cooperation in this 'noble work'.[145] Mian Shafi informed the Leaguers that he had already invited three non-Muslim organizations of the Punjab (Indian Association of Lahore, Punjab Hindu Sabha and Chief Khalsa Diwan) to prepare a joint representation to the Government of India for raising the status of the Punjab to a regulation province with an executive council and a high court.[146] The Congress supported the proposal for joint action, and its secretary suggested that the two parties should hold their annual sessions at the same time and place.[147] The intra-League conflict and the outbreak of the First World War, however, obstructed any progress on this proposal but those supporting it persisted in their efforts. Finally, the two parties succeeded in holding their annual sessions in Bombay in December 1915. While the Congress in Bombay bridged the gulf between its 'moderate' and 'extremist' factions that had occurred at its Surat session in 1907, the All-India Muslim League witnessed ugly scenes of a rift that had been brewing in its ranks. Nevertheless, both the parties resolved to appoint committees to draw up a joint scheme of reforms for implementation after the war. The League reform committee, consisting of seventy-one members (United Provinces 15; Punjab 10; Bengal 11; Bombay and Sindh 15; Madras 4; Bihar and Orissa 9; Central Provinces 1; NWFP 1; Delhi 3 and Burma 3) with the League president and secretary as its *ex-officio* president and secretary was asked to draft a scheme of reforms after conferring with different organizations and submit its report to the council for presentation at the next annual session.

The Congress reform committee prepared a draft reforms scheme in an atmosphere of harmony, which the All India Congress Committee approved on 22–24 April 1916. That was not the case with the All-India Muslim League. The intra-party bitterness of the Bombay session had lingered on after its conclusion. As a result, neither the All-India Muslim League nor the provincial Muslim Leagues could seriously deliberate upon constitutional issues especially the proportion of Muslim representation in various legislatures. Its reform committee started its work as late as 7 May, when.Wazir Hasan circulated a letter, asking its members to give 'a brief statement of their views' about the reforms, but the response was disappointing.[148] Then, he obtained a copy of the Congress reforms scheme and, on 26 July, sent his own draft scheme to the members that, he wrote, was 'purely tentative', intended 'to serve as a basis for discussion', suggesting that the secretaries of the provincial Muslim Leagues might obtain the opinions of their councils on it. The draft provided 65 elected members in a central legislature of 100 members; and 15 of them were to be elected through separate electorates by the Muslims; interestingly, there was a proviso that members elected by the Muslims 'need not necessarily' be Muslim. For the provincial legislatures, the draft proposed 75 elected members out of total 100 members. Twenty members out of the elected members were to be elected by separate electorates but the draft did not indicate Muslim proportion in various provinces.[149] The League reform committee discussed this draft in Lucknow in a meeting on 21 August, that only eight local members including the president and the honorary secretary attended. After this meeting, on 12 October, nineteen Indian members of the Imperial Legislative Council sent a memorandum to the viceroy for post-war reforms, embodying the principles of a scheme of self-government. The League reform committee again discussed the draft scheme in Calcutta in a meeting chaired by Nawab Ali Choudhry on 16 November, a day before it conferred with the Congress reform committee. It decided to propose that not less than one-third Muslims out of the total elected members in the central legislature should be Muslim and that only Muslims should elect them. The proposal for Muslim proportion in every provincial legislature was that it should be one-third of the total elected members in all the provinces![150] This proportion was altered at the All-India Muslim League–Congress joint conference on 17–18 November, when the conference worked out an agreement on Muslim proportion in all the provinces except United Provinces and Bengal. The Congress was unwilling to give to the Muslims more than 25 per cent in United Provinces and more than one-third in Bengal in view of Hindu opposition in these two provinces. Jinnah, the main advocate of All-India Muslim League–Congress rapprochement, was at this time more interested in 'swaraj' than communal proportions; his observation was, 'I am willing to agree to any scheme whatever proportion may be fixed if it leads to something by which we can not only secure swaraj but keep it.'[151] Finally, the joint conference decided to settle the disputed points in December, a day before the Congress session. The League committee, meeting two days after the joint conference, resolved not to accept less than one-third in United Provinces and less than 40 per cent, possibly more, in Bengal.[152] The voices for constitutional reforms for Sindh and NWFP were too weak to be heard. The Punjabi Leaguers of conflicting viewpoints were united on Muslim proportion in the province, and were able to secure 50 per cent representation for the Muslims of the Punjab. In December, the Bengali Leaguers could secure only 40 per cent although they did press for more till the last moment. The arguments used against them were that they would not get even this percentage in an open contest because of their poverty and socio-economic backwardness, which would reduce the strength of their qualified voters, and that their percentage had been adjusted 'in consideration of the Muslim interests of all the provinces'.[153] The United Provinces Muslims were able to get 30 per cent representation at the joint conference. The draft was finalized after these modifications.

At their historic sessions in Lucknow, the Congress and the All-India Muslim League adopted the joint reforms scheme on 29 December 1916; and on 31 December, respectively. Several Congress leaders attended the League session and many Leaguers in return were present at the Congress session.[154] The joint scheme was known as the Lucknow Pact although the parties did not formally sign any document. The scheme was meant to be the first step towards the establishment of 'complete self-government' in India. It provided for the following percentage of Muslims in various provincial legislatures; and they were to be elected on the basis of separate electorates. The total strength of the legislative councils was not to be less than 125 in major provinces and 50–75 in minor provinces:[155]

Table 3.1: Percentage of Muslims in various provincial legislatures according to the Lucknow Pact

Provinces	Muslim percentage	Muslim percentage in Population
Bengal	40	53
United Provinces	30	14
Punjab	One-half	55
Bombay	One-third	20
Madras	15	6
Bihar and Orissa	25	10
Central Provinces	15	6

Muslims were not to contest elections on any other seats except those representing special interests. No bill or a resolution affecting a particular community was to be taken up for legislation if three-fourth of its members opposed it. The provinces were to have partial autonomy with financial powers. Four-fifth members of the 150-member central legislative council were to consist of elected members, and one-third of the elected members were to be Muslims elected from the provinces with the same percentage as provided for the provincial legislatures by separate electorates. Its powers with regard to legislation and money bills were to be enhanced. Half of the governor general's council was to consist of Indians elected by the elected members of the legislative council. The council of the secretary of state for India was to be abolished; henceforth his salary was to come from the British exchequer. His position was to be the same as that of the secretary of state for self-governing British colonies. The Indian citizens were to have the same rights as enjoyed by other citizens of the empire. The scheme called for Indian representation in commissioned and non-commissioned ranks of the armed forces, and provided for the separation of executive from the judiciary. Jinnah was one of those few political leaders who played a crucial role in drafting the joint reforms scheme and in persuading the Congress and the League to accept it; for his services, he was hailed as the 'Ambassador of Hindu–Muslim unity'.

(E) THE STRUGGLE FOR REFORMS

Both the parties struggled for the acceptance of the Joint Reforms Scheme by the British government. The All-India Muslim League empowered its council to appoint a fifteen-member committee to undertake all the necessary work in this connection; its members were drawn from: United Provinces 3 (Al-i-Nabi, Abdul Majid and Nabiullah); Bengal 2 [Fazlul Haq and Abul Qasim (1871–1936)]; Bombay 2 (Ibrahim Rahimatullah and M.A. Jinnah); Bihar and Orissa 2 [Mazharul Haq and Hasan Imam (1871–1933)]; Madras 2 [Mir Asad Ali (1879–1933) and Yaqub Hasan]; Punjab 2 (Fazli Husain and Barkat Ali); Central Provinces and Berar 1 (Seth Bisrambhai); and Burma 1 (Ahmad Moolla Dawood); the president and secretary were its *ex-officio* members. Another three-member (Raja of Mahmudabad, M.A. Jinnah and Mazharul Haq) committee, in cooperation with a similar committee of the Congress, was to go to England after the war to persuade the British government and public to accept the demands made in the joint reforms scheme. On 6 May 1917, the All-India Muslim League council selected members of the two committees.[156] Meanwhile, several developments agitated the two parties and moved their leaders to assume an aggressive posture. The Leaguers were disturbed by the continued detention of the Ali brothers (Shaukat Ali and Mohammad Ali) and other Muslim leaders; and the All-India Muslim League organized public meetings all over India, demanding the release of all the interned Muslim leaders especially the Ali brothers.[157] On 15 June, the Madras government ordered the internment of Mrs Annie Besant, leader of the All-India Home Rule League, along with her colleagues G.S. Arundale and B.P Wadia, for campaigning in support of self-government.[158] A number of provocative statements from high British officials had preceded the internment order. Lord Sydenham had denounced the Memorandum as 'revolutionary', linking it with 'German intrigue';[159] Michael O'Dwyer (1864–1940), the Punjab governor, and Lord Pentland, the Madras governor, had made observations of a similar nature; and Lord Chelmsford (1868–1933), the viceroy, in a speech in Calcutta, had described the demands in the Memorandum as 'catastrophic', and the Government of India had sent a circular laying down the official policy towards the movement for self-government.[160] Mrs Besant's internment proved the last straw and brought in a spontaneous reaction. The All-India Muslim League Council recorded its 'most emphatic protest' on her internment and vowed to campaign constitutionally for the Joint Reforms Scheme.[161] Its members began to join the two Home Rule Leagues in the provinces. Jinnah joined Mrs Besant's Home Rule League and led its Bombay branch as its president, making it the most well-organized and effective branch.

On 27–28 July 1917, Bombay hosted a joint conference of the All-India Muslim League council and the All India Congress Committee; Jinnah was one of its main organizers.[162] The conference demanded: an 'authoritative' policy statement from the British government for making India a self-governing member of the British empire; acceptance of the joint reforms scheme for post-war implementation; publication of the proposals that the Government of India might frame for public discussion; and immediate release of Mrs Besant and her colleagues. It also reiterated the demand for the release of the Ali brothers. It called upon the All-India Muslim League council and the provincial Congress committees to consider the 'advisability' of adopting a policy of 'passive resistance' to carry out the political work; Mian Shafi opposed the idea of passive resistance and in cooperation with the dissenters from other provinces established the All-India Muslim Association with the Prince of Arcot as its president and himself as secretary.[163] Another joint conference in Allahabad in the first week of October was to deliberate upon the opinions that might be received from the two parties about starting a 'passive resistance' movement. The Bombay conference decided to send a four-member [M.A. Jinnah, Wazir Hasan, V.S. Srinavasa Sastri (1869–1946) alternately C.P. Ramaswami Aiyer, and Tej Bahadur Sapru (1875–1949)] delegation to England in September to promote the joint reforms scheme; its departure was, however, contingent upon the advice of William Wedderburn who was in contact with the secretary of state for India in London.[164] Meanwhile, Wazir Hasan circulated the 'passive resistance' resolution among the League members, requesting them to send their opinions by 15 September. So did the Congress secretary. This kind of 'pressure' worked and there was an immediate response from the British government. After a meeting with the secretary of state for India, Wedderburn advised by wire the secretaries of the All-India Muslim League and the Congress to have 'patience' and promised to 'telegraph further' when the situation became 'clearer'.[165] The situation cleared on 20 August, when the new Liberal secretary of state for India, Edwin Montagu (1879–1924), made the announcement in the House of Commons that the British policy was to increase 'the association of Indians' in the administration and develop gradually 'self-governing institutions with a view to the progressive realization of responsible government in India as an integral part of the British Empire', and that he himself would visit India in the coming winter to consult the viceroy and 'representative bodies' there. The British were, however, to be the 'judges of the time and measure' of every stage of this policy. On 16 September, Mrs Besant and her colleagues were released; and the removal of bar on the Indians' entry into the commissioned ranks of the army was announced. The Ali brothers and other Muslim internees, however, remained incarcerated.

The All-India Muslim League council and the All India Congress Committee, at a second joint conference in Allahabad on 5–6 October 1917, welcomed the announcement by the secretary of state for India and postponed a decision on 'passive resistance' *sine die*.[166] Even otherwise, the idea of 'passive resistance' had not evinced a very encouraging response; an overwhelming majority of League councillors had opposed it.[167] The joint conference appointed a 37-member deputation including ten Leaguers to present an address to the secretary of state for India during his visit to India, and set up a twelve-member committee including one Leaguer to prepare the address together with a memorandum in support of the joint reforms scheme. The conference asked the provincial Muslim Leagues, provincial Congress Committees, and other political organizations to make their own presentations to the secretary of state for India and the viceroy in support of the joint reforms scheme.[168] Some unfortunate tragic events intervened to disrupt the League–Congress struggle. Before the arrival of secretary of state for India, violent wide-scale riots broke out in Bihar and eastern United Provinces, affecting about 124 villages in the districts of Arrah, Gaya, Patna and Jaunpur; at some places violence lasted for four weeks, from Idul Azha to the month of Moharram. The enormity of Muslim loss with hardly a word of sympathy from the Hindu leaders aroused Muslim suspicions about some prior planning of the violence.[169] Many Leaguers now felt that the joint reforms scheme was insufficient to protect the Muslims and proposed amendments in its contents. The proposed amendments covered a wide spectrum including: (*i*) constitutional protection of Muslim majorities in Bengal and Punjab; (*ii*) introduction of reforms in the NWFP; (*iii*) formation of Sindh into a separate province; (*iv*) extension of separate electorates to district and municipal bodies; (*v*) reservation of seats for the Muslims in government services in every province; (*vi*) Muslim representation on the governing bodies of the public universities; (*vii*) maintenance of Urdu with its Persian script as the *lingua franca* in those provinces where it was in use; and (*viii*) freedom to practise religion and its ceremonies on Idul Azha and Moharram without any interference.[170] Some Muslims in Bihar even started a signature campaign against the joint reforms scheme, in opposition to the pro-scheme signature campaign. These developments bruised the League–Congress concord but Muslim anger was soon directed against the government. On 14 November 1917, influential Muslim leaders representing various parts of India met in Lucknow and, after supporting the joint reforms scheme, decided to send an All-India Muslim deputation to the secretary of state for India to make a presentation based on proposals mentioned at (v) to (viii) above; the release of the Ali brothers topped the list, and the League demand for a commission to inquire into the anti-Muslim movement in Bihar was shelved.[171] The following day, the All-India Muslim League, at an emergency meeting, supported the idea of a Muslim deputation and its demands, and put the blame for the communal violence mainly on the failure of the CID, for its failure to forewarn about the riots, and on the security authorities, for the delay in controlling the situation. The emergency meeting appointed a committee to look into the memorandum that the twelve-member joint committee had prepared to ensure its conformity with the joint reforms scheme and directed its members to dissociate themselves from the deputation if it did not do so. The Congress agreed to modify the memorandum after some reluctance to incorporate only the inconsequential alterations suggested by the All-India Muslim League. On 26 November, the joint League–Congress deputation presented it to the secretary of state for India.[172] The All-India Muslim League, at its Calcutta annual session in December, endorsed the resolutions passed at the emergency session and urged the British government to implement the joint reforms scheme. The Government of India, however, refused to allow the all-India Muslim deputation to present its address to the secretary of state for India unless it deleted the paragraph relating to the release of the Ali brothers who had qualified their undertaking to the government that on release they would not resort to unconstitutional and violent methods by words 'without prejudice to our allegiance to Islam'.[173] Instead of deleting the relevant paragraph, the deputation preferred not to present the address to the secretary of state for India. The League deplored the Government of India's condition for the presentation of the address.[174]

When the 'Report on Indian Constitutional Reforms', or the Montagu–Chelmsford Report, was published on 8 July 1918, the All-India Muslim League and the Congress called special sessions in Bombay on 31 August–1 September, to consider its proposals. Before the sessions, a twelve-member committee of the All-India Muslim League council discussed the report and made its recommendations.[175] Then the All-India Muslim League council and the Congress subjects committee jointly drafted, and adopted, 'unanimous resolutions', which the two parties reiterated subsequently at their annual sessions in Delhi in December. Both the parties protested against the insinuation in the Report that the Indians were unfit for responsible government, and demanded a 'Declaration of Rights' for the Indians as British citizens. The declarations of the Allied statesmen including Woodrow Wilson (1856–1924), the US president, regarding every nation's right of self-determination and the Indians' sacrifices in the War were cited in support of India's claim to self-government. It was demanded that the two representative political organizations—the All-India Muslim League and the Congress—should represent the Indians at the peace conference, and Amir Ali or some other prominent persons like Maulana Mahmud Hasan (1851–1920) and Maulana Mohammad Ali should represent the Muslims at the conference.[176] It welcomed the idea of forming a League of Nations for settling international disputes by arbitration and demanded a proper place in its deliberations for India. Its main resolution termed the Montagu–Chelmsford Report as 'unsatisfactory' and called for a system of responsible government both at the centre and in the provinces, including fiscal autonomy as enjoyed by self-governing British colonies, reservation of a limited number of subjects with the centre, and complete provincial autonomy. The Muslim proportion of representation should be the same as provided in the joint reforms scheme. The League resolved to send a deputation to England during the second reading of the Government of India Bill to work with a similar committee of the Congress for constitutional reforms according to the principles embodied in the resolutions of the special sessions.[177] The Katarpur communal riots in September, in which Muslims suffered heavy losses at the hands of Hindus, and the Calcutta riots, which originated with objectionable remarks about Prophet Mohammad (PBUH) in an article in the *Indian Daily News* of Calcutta (27 July 1918), and cost more than five hundred Muslim lives, intervened but did not block the struggle for constitutional reforms.[178] The All-India Muslim League did criticise negative comments by the Hindu leaders about the prevalence of pan-Islamic feelings among the Muslims but did not let them come in the way of the League–Congress joint struggle for reforms.[179] The real stumbling block was the post-war British policy towards Turkey and the response of the Indian Muslims.

On 9 March 1919, the council of the All-India Muslim League elected a 34-member (United Provinces 10; Bengal 4; Punjab 4; Bombay 4; Delhi 3; Madras 1; Bihar 3; Sindh 3; and Central Provinces and Berar 2) deputation to represent its views on constitutional reforms, safety of Turkey and Khilafat; and one member (Abdul Wali Khan of Peshawar) was added on the suggestion of Maulana Shaukat Ali (1873–1938). Fazli Husain's request that representation of the provinces on the deputation should be the same as on the All-India Muslim League council was not accepted.[180] The council elected an eight-member 'advance party', or the first batch, consisting of Hasrat Mohani, G.M. Bhurgari, Dr M.A. Ansari, Yaqub Hasan, Maulana Abdul Bari (1878–1926), Maulana Mohammad Ali, Shoaib Qureshi (1904–

1962) and Abdur Rahman Siddiqi. The members were to bear their own expenses but the League provided the deputation funds for incidental expenditure in London. They were themselves to obtain passports while the League office obtained eight priority certificates from the government without which no passenger could be booked because of limited number of passages available.[181] The advance party could not proceed immediately with its full strength mainly because the government suspected that its members would be more involved in the Turkish affairs than the constitutional reforms for India.[182] The United Provinces government declined to issue a passport to Hasrat Mohani despite repeated protests of the League.[183] Dr Ansari and Mohammad Ali decided not to go. Shoaib Qureshi was given the passport after considerable delay; and he and Abdur Rahman Siddiqi reached England in September. Maulana Bari was willing to bear his own expenses but refused to be photographed for the passport. Jinnah who had earlier declined to be a member of the advance party although he was on the larger deputation now expressed his desire to go in the advance party; he was given one priority certificate. On this, Zahur Ahmad wrote to Dr Ansari on 20 May, that whatever might be his personal views, Jinnah would advocate in England 'the views that prevail among Indian Musalmans upon all important questions of the day', and Ansari in his reply on 22 May, endorsed his opinion with the remarks that 'Jinnah is a great acquisition to the deputation'.[184] Yaqub was the first to leave for England on 17 May, followed by Jinnah and Bhurgari who sailed on the same ship on 7 June. These three Leaguers, Jinnah, Yaqub and Bhurgari, constituted the All-India Muslim League deputation. Shoaib Qureshi, Abdur Rahman Siddiqi and Hasan Imam, who joined the deputation later, did not take 'any practical part' in its activities for constitutional reforms. Jinnah was selected to act as the spokesman of the deputation while Yaqub Hasan functioned as its secretary who used to send regular reports to the League office in Lucknow.[185] Malik Barkat Ali was prepared to go in the advance party at his own expense and had obtained his passport but the League office did not respond to his request.[186] The deputation submitted written answers to the joint parliamentary committee. On 13 August, Jinnah and Yaqub appeared before the parliamentary committee to give evidence; they could not appear on a date fixed earlier because Jinnah 'contracted cold and was laid up in bed with fever'.[187] Jinnah in his evidence advocated dyarchy both at the centre and in the provinces, which was in line with the joint reforms scheme but not in accord with the resolutions that the All-India Muslim League had passed after the Lucknow session.

The League–Congress struggle had limited impact on the final shape of the constitutional reforms as incorporated in the Act of 1919. The All-India Muslim League considered these reforms as 'inadequate and unsatisfactory', and deeply regretted the denial of full responsible government both at the centre and in the provinces. Still, it recognized the reforms as 'a definite step towards the goal of full responsible government' and called on the Indians to work the reforms 'to demonstrate their capacity for complete self-government'. It also demanded the application of the principle of separate electorates to the local bodies, and the acceptance of all the demands made by the abortive all-India Muslim deputation. The League asked the Congress to appoint a committee to confer with a committee of the All-India Muslim League to arrive at an understanding on issues arising out of the Act of 1919 and the demand for complete responsible government.[188] With the All-India Muslim League and Congress gradually shifting their focus on issues other than the reforms, the government framed the rules and regulations under the Act of 1919, without consulting them. The rules and regulations naturally did not come up to the League's expectations, which its central council termed as 'retrograde' and against the spirit of the promised 'substantial first step in responsible government'.[189] By this time, the Khilafat issue and the Punjab tragedy had come to dominate the political scene, and constitutional issues were relegated into the background.

(F) THE KHILAFAT MOVEMENT

The simmering pan-Islamic sentiments of the Indian Muslims had flickered in 1911–13. The First World War and Turkey's decision to join it against the allied powers fostered them and increased the number of pan-Islamists; some of them were associated with the revolutionary movements like the Ghadr Party and Raishmi Rumal (Silk Letter) Movement.[190] A major war aim of the allied powers including that of Britain vis-à-vis Turkey was to break up the Ottoman empire and bury permanently the threat of pan-Islam. These powers signed bilateral and multilateral agreements to put that aim into effect, and the agreements included the promise of a Jewish state in Palestine. The British, therefore, saw in the pan-Islamists in India an obstacle to the achievement of that aim. The Indian government used restrictive laws, including the Defence of India Act and the Press Act, against them and interned some of their more vocal and effective leaders like the Ali brothers, Maulana Zafar Ali Khan (1873–1956) and Maulana Abul Kalam Azad, who had the skills to stir up pan-Islamic emotions and closed down their newspapers, the *Comrade*, *Hamdard*, *Zamindar*, *al-Hilal* and *al-Balagh*, to prevent the propagation of their ideas. Simultaneously, it appealed to the traditional loyalty of the Indian Muslims by publicizing itself as the 'greatest Muslim power' and a friend of the Muslims and Turkey, expecting unqualified Muslim support in men and material for the war without demur; Muslims constituted a major portion of the 1,215,338 military personnel that was sent abroad and suffered 101,439 casualties.[191] It encouraged some *ulama* to issue a *fatwa*, declaring the war a political war and not a *jihad*.[192] The All-India Muslim League repeatedly assured the British crown before and after Turkey's entry into the war of the 'deep-rooted loyalty' of the Indian Muslims. In return, the British promised that the navy and army of the allied powers would not attack the holy places of Islam in Arabia and Iraq although the integrity of the Ottoman empire was never promised.[193] When Sharif Husain of Makkah declared independence from the Ottoman empire, the All-India Muslim League and its branches expressed 'deep abhorrence' of his action. The British government held out an assurance to the Muslims that after the war, Hejaz would be ruled by 'an independent Muslim power', and that the Muslims of India and other countries would settle the issue of *Khilafat* without non-Muslim interference. Wazir Hasan sent out this assurance to the provincial Muslim Leagues, requesting their secretaries, however, to communicate it to only 'representative and responsible' Muslim leaders.[194] Subsequently, on 5 January 1918, the British prime minister promised not to deprive Turkey of its capital Istanbul and the fertile Turk-inhabited lands of Asia Minor and Thrace.[195] The All-India Muslim League's continual demands for the release of Muslim internees particularly the Ali brothers were in a way expression of pan-Islamic feelings.[196] Its resentment increased when, after the release of Mrs Annie Besant and her colleagues, Maulana Mohammad Ali was not set free to preside over the annual session of the All-India Muslim League in December 1917.[197] The whole Indian Muslim community, the League declared, shared the views of Mohammad Ali as these were 'based on purely religious grounds'; thus, every Muslim was guilty of a 'similar crime'. It expressed anguish over the home member's reply in the negative to Jinnah's question in the Imperial Legislative Council for the release of the Ali brothers, and urged that the sympathy of the Indian Muslims for their co-religionists outside India was not incompatible with their loyalty to the British crown.[198] The All-India Muslim League resolved at an emergency meeting in Lucknow to agitate both in India and Britain to secure the release of the Ali brothers but desisted from doing that on the advice of M.K. Gandhi (1869–1948).[199]

After the signing of the armistice on 11 November 1918, the British Indian government became apprehensive about the reaction of the Indian Muslims, in case the peace terms with Turkey were against their expectations. The Indian Muslims on their part were worried about the fate of Turkey, the Khalifa and the holy places due to continuous anti-Turk propaganda in the British media by journalists, politicians and Christian clergy.[200] Their non-representation at the Imperial War Conference in London that had discussed issues affecting Muslim states and holy places, and the nomination of two non-Muslims, Sir S.P. Sinha (1864–1928) and the Maharaja of Bikaner (1880–1943), to represent India at the Paris Peace Conference, ignoring All-India Muslim League's request for Muslim representation, added to their concerns.[201] The Muslim mood was reflected at the League's annual session in Calcutta. Dr Ansari's reception address, Fazlul Haq's presidential address, and the session's resolutions voiced Muslim emotions and grievances in an aggressive anti-British tone.[202] The presence of 'respected and revered *ulama*' in large number at the session added strength to the pan-Islamists but enhanced the British government's anxiety. Among the *ulama* present were: Abdul Bari and Salamatullah representing Farangi Mahal; Abul Wafa Sanaullah Amritsari (1869–1948) and Mir Ibrahim Sialkoti (1874–1956), representing the Ahle Hadith; Azad Sobhani (1882–1957) of Kanpur; and Kifayatullah (1875–1952), Ahmad Saeed (1886–1959) and Abdul Latif representing Anjuman-i-Ulama of Delhi; Hafiz Mohammad Ahmad of Deoband.[203] The League protested against the occupation of Hejaz, Jerusalem, Najaf-i-Ashraf, Karbala and other holy places by the British forces, and asked for their immediate restoration to the Muslims. It requested the British government to dissuade the allied powers from taking any step that might change the status of the holy places [Resolution no. 7]; and called for the solution of the issue of *Khilafat* according to Muslim wishes, requesting the British government to prevent interference by the allied powers in its resolution [Resolution no. 8].[204] Soon after, sixty-six *ulama* in a signed *fatwa* emphasized the need, according to the *Shariat*, of a *Khalifa* or *Imam*; the defining of boundaries of the *Jaziratul Arab* and expulsion of Jews, Christians and idolaters from its limits; and the duty of all Muslims to help a Muslim state under attack from non-Muslims.[205] The British government, in its response to Resolutions 7 and 8, affirmed that the issue of *Khilafat* 'must be decided by the Muslims themselves without [outside] interference' but declined to take any further action as requested in the resolutions; the All-India Muslim League considered the response as 'unconvincing'.[206] The official nervousness about possible Muslim reaction was reflected in the forfeiture of Dr Ansari's reception address of the Calcutta annual session by the governments of the Punjab, United Provinces and Burma on the charge that it contained material that was likely to incite acts of violence, disloyalty and class hatred. The League denounced the forfeiture of Dr Ansari's address as 'an unwarranted and unjustifiable attack on the legitimate constitutional rights of the people', and demanded the withdrawal of these orders.[207]

Now the British Indian government wanted to equip itself with wartime powers to deal with any post-war adverse situation that might arise principally out of British policy towards Turkey. In February–March 1919, it rushed through the Imperial Legislative Council the Rowlatt bills, which were based on the Sedition Committee Report.[208] One bill, the Criminal Law (Emergency Powers) Bill, was introduced on 9 February; and the other, the Indian Criminal Law (Amendment) Bill, was moved on 10 February. There was a spontaneous reaction, demonstrated in well-attended protest meetings throughout India in which the bills were denounced as 'Black Laws'.[209] Jinnah resigned from the Imperial Legislative Council in protest. The protest meeting in the Jallianwala Bagh in Amritsar developed into a monumental tragedy, a magnified version of the Kanpur mosque tragedy, when Brigadier-General R.E.H. Dyer (1863–1927) ordered firing without adequate warning to disperse a prohibited but peaceful gathering, which resulted in, according to official estimates, 379 deaths and 1,200 wounded. Both Sir Michael O'Dwyer (governor) and Lord Chelmsford (viceroy) approved Dyer's action. Martial law was imposed to control reaction in the Punjab, a province that had provided 360,000 men and about Rs 100 million for the war.[210] It was administered with unprecedented brutality, inflicting indiscriminately on the Punjabis humiliation, torture, public flogging and imprisonment by summary trials. There was even aerial bombing in Gujranwala to disperse a peaceful demonstration. If the Rowlatt Act and the repressive policy was devised to deflect the force of the Khilafat issue, it only partially succeeded by dividing the energies of the Indian leaders. The 'Punjab tragedy' became a hot issue but the British government treated it lightly. After a great deal of pressure from the All-India Muslim League and the Congress, in July 1919, the government appointed the Hunter Committee to inquire into the 'Punjab troubles'. Its proceedings, however, lacked seriousness, and its conclusions were insulting to the Indians.

After the war, the British government dealt with Muslim appeals on the issues of *Khilafat* and Turkey with indifference. The Jewish secretary of state for India, Edwin Montagu, led the Indian delegation to the peace conference in Paris with two non-Muslim members, Sir S.P. Sinha and the Maharaja of Bikaner. Three Muslims—the Aga Khan, Aftab Ahmad Khan and Abdullah Yusuf Ali (1872–1953)— accompanied the delegation as mere appendage to assist the delegation. The 'passionate' case that this delegation made out for lenient treatment of Turkey had understandably no impact at all on the peace conference. The All-India Muslim League still naively hoped that it might be able to save the integrity of Turkey, the institution of *Khilafat* and the holy places by public pressure and appeals to the British sense of justice and wartime promises. Its central council and branch Leagues passed resolutions at public meetings throughout India and sent them to the viceroy, the secretary of state for India and the prime minister.[211] It also tried to make direct representations to the viceroy and the British government in London, but its representatives faced insults and denial of common courtesies. The viceroy declined to meet a Muslim deputation, dismissing its request with the remarks that he was aware of the Muslim views and had conveyed these to the authorities in London.[212] The League leaders in London made out a case on *Khilafat* and wanted to submit a memorial to the prime minister but he refused to receive the deputation or even give a private interview to its head, M.A. Jinnah. Nevertheless, on 27 August, the deputation sent a representation to the prime minister, signed by Jinnah, Yaqub, Bhurgari and Hasan Imam.[213] The League deputation returned from London disillusioned. The funds that the All-India Muslim League and individual Muslims like Abdullah Haroon (Karachi) and Mohammad Jamal (Rangoon) had sent from India for the deputation were spent on establishing an Islamic Information Bureau in London, which after Yaqub Hasan's return to India was looked after by Mirza Hashim Ispahani, and on bringing out the short-lived *Muslim Outlook* (London), edited by Marmaduke Pickthall (1875–1936).[214] At this time, the London Muslim League also activated itself to represent the Indian Muslim viewpoint before the British government. The Aga Khan and Amir Ali led the campaign with great zeal; Mushir Husain Kidwai (1877–1937), Mirza Hashim Ispahani and a few others assisted them.[215] Since January 1919, they had been expressing their concerns to the prime minister about the future of Turkey. On 14 June, they submitted a detailed memorial to him on the subject, which was signed by thirty-eight Muslims.[216] The All-India Muslim League directed its provincial and district branches to pass resolutions in support of this memorial to urge the prime minister to secure acceptance of the Muslim demands by the allied powers.[217] Numerous memorials on the lines of this memorial were sent to the secretary of state for India, the foreign secretary and the prime minister from India and London.[218] But all these appeals had no effect on the British government. It was reported in the press in August that the British government had approved the internationalisation of Istanbul and cession of Thrace to Greece.[219]

The Leaguers were disturbed by these reports. They realized that their campaign had failed to have any impact, and that the All-India Muslim League alone could not handle the issue. Therefore, the central council, at an emergency meeting on 29 August 1919, resolved to convene an All-India Muslim Conference in Lucknow on 21 September, instead of a special session of the League as some Leaguers had suggested, to voice the demands 'more effectively' from a broader platform, and to invite non-League Muslims to the conference whether they had participated in politics in the past or not.[220] Zahur Ahmad, the honorary secretary, issued the invitations under the names of thirty-five convenors belonging to different regions of India and sent letters to the provincial Muslim Leagues to bring Muslims in large numbers to the conference.[221] Emissaries also went around persuading the Muslims to attend the conference. The League printed and distributed ten thousand copies of a pamphlet in Urdu and English, containing literature that had so far accumulated on the Turkish question. The result was a historic gathering; about 1000 Muslims came from outstation including 400 from outside the United Provinces.[222] The conference appealed for maintaining the unity of Sultan-Caliph's spiritual position and temporal power as a ruler and protested against the break-up of Turkey into separate states with Christian powers as their mandatories. The Ahmadis were not allowed to present dissenting views at the conference on the Khilafat and other issues.[223] The conference opposed the internationalisation of Istanbul and cession of Thrace to Greece, and denounced the occupation of Smyrna by the Greek forces, calling upon the allied powers to secure its immediate evacuation. At the end, the conference approved the establishment of a Khilafat committee of Bombay that had been set up in March 1919, and recommended the formation of branch committees. As a result, the Central Khilafat Committee emerged on the political scene that the Leaguers rushed to join throughout India. The conference called on the Muslims to observe 17 October, Friday, as *Yaum-ud-Dua wal-Ihtejaj* (Day of Prayer and Protest) to pray for 'the integrity of the Khilafat'. The League members provided the necessary network to make the day, also known as the 'Khilafat Day', a success.[224] The prime minister's response displayed arrogance and insensitivity to the intensity of Muslim feelings. His public speech in Sheffield that coincided with the prayer day was highly provocative. He regarded it England's 'divine mission' to restore 'order and good government' in Muslim lands through Christian mandatory powers. Then, speaking in the House of Commons, he called General Edmund Allenby (1861–1936) 'the hero of the last crusade' for conquering Palestine. Referring to Salonika as 'the gateway' to Christianity's first entry into Europe, he declared in another speech that the victors could not be 'robbed of the fruits which cost them so dear'. The council of the All-India Muslim League expressed 'alarm and indignation' over these remarks, reminding the prime minister of wartime promises, and warned of a 'widespread agitation' resulting from 'absolute loss' of 'Muslim faith in British fairness and justice'.[225]

The threat to Turkey's integrity depressed the Indian Muslims, and the signing of the 'unfair and unjust' Anglo–Persian Convention at this time added to their depression.[226] The All-India Muslim League along with the Central Khilafat Committee and the newly founded Jamiatul Ulama-i-Hind provided them leadership. The League still played the lead role. Zahur Ahmad, ignoring the fate of the Jinnah-led deputation in London, sought the Aga Khan's advice about the utility of new deputations to London and Washington to represent the Indian Muslim viewpoint on the Turkish issue. Bhurgari, Kidwai and Ispahani in a joint reply from London on the Aga Khan's behalf advised that Muslim deputations should be immediately sent to London but not to Washington, as the US statesmen had 'entirely washed their hands off commitments in any part of Europe or the Middle East'.[227] The option of 'progressive boycott' of selective British goods and non-participation of Muslims in the peace celebrations, in the event of adverse settlement of the Khilafat issue, were considered a possibility. Zahur Ahmad was on the committee that prepared the list of British goods selected for boycott.[228] The All-India Muslim League at its Amritsar session, which the newly released Muslim internees including the Ali brothers attended, endorsed these decisions. This session justified 'all possible methods of constitutional agitation', including the boycott of the British army, 'if it was likely to be used outside India for Imperial and anti-Islamic purposes'.[229] It was decided to send a Muslim delegation to England and the US. Muslims largely abstained from the peace celebrations. Another development was the increasing participation of Hindus in the meetings on the Khilafat issue. The League reciprocated this gesture by calling upon Muslims to sacrifice animals other than cows on Idul Azha.[230] The Congress, and the Hindu community, 'gratefully' welcomed it 'as one of the greatest steps' on the part of the Muslims towards Hindu–Muslim unity.[231] Earlier, in April, during the *Satyagraha* against the Rowlatt bills, Mahatma Gandhi and Maulana Abdul Bari had worked out an understanding on Muslims abandoning cow-sacrifice in return for Hindu support on the Khilafat issue.[232] Now there were demands in Central Provinces and Bombay that the All-India Muslim League and the Congress should jointly demand an official ban on cow-sacrifice. Muslims were, however, not ready to go to that extent; therefore, when a bill to this effect came before the Bengal Legislature, they opposed it.[233] Later on, the League reaffirmed the resolution relating to cow-sacrifice at its Nagpur session but appealed to the 'Hindu brethren to refrain from securing legislation or other compulsory measures' to enforce it.[234]

The release of Muslim internees who joined the Central Khilafat Committee gave a fresh impetus to the Khilafat movement. They raised its tempo. The idea of a Muslim delegation to England took a practical shape. The viceroy was now sympathetic, and received a joint Muslim-Hindu deputation. He not only gave the Maulana Mohammad Ali-led delegation permission to leave for England but also promised to facilitate its visit.[235] Gandhi's non-cooperation programme gathered support after the *ulama* gave it their approval in a *fatwa*. The Central Khilafat Committee discussed the programme thoroughly at its all-India conference in Bombay on 15–17 February 1920, with G.M. Bhurgari in the chair, but deferred a decision till the British response to the delegation's demands was known. The prime minister did meet the delegation briefly and heard its representation but there was no change in the official stance. The delegation failed to get a hearing at the peace conference and abandoned the idea of a visit to the US.[236] The delegation's meetings with the French and Italian prime ministers and the pope were merely ceremonial and had no impact on the peace settlement. Now the Khilafatists accepted Gandhi's non-violent non-cooperation programme, and on 11–14 April 1920, the Central Khilafat Committee decided to implement it in stages after the publication of the peace terms. Since the issue at this time was that of *Khilafat*, the programme applied only to the Muslims. On 11 May, the peace terms were announced. These terms were worse than what the Indian Muslims had feared. Turkey was eliminated as an independent entity, and the Sultan-Caliph was left with almost nothing. Separate states were carved out of the Ottoman empire and Muslim states among them were given to the allied powers as mandates. Muslims without exception were heart-broken. The Central Khilafat Committee wanted to go ahead immediately with the non-cooperation programme; the return to India of Maulana Mahmud Hasan, former head of the Darul Ulum at Deoband, and others from their internment in Malta in June added force and emotionalism to the issue. But the Congress put a temporary check; instead of taking a decision it referred the issue to its special session in Calcutta in September. The Central Khilafat Committee went ahead with its preparation; it issued a manifesto, presented a memorial to the viceroy for the revision of the peace terms with Turkey and observed an all-India *hartal* (strike) on 1 August. Some Central Khilafat Committee members promoted the idea of *hijrat* (migration) to Afghanistan, and the Afghan ruler announced that he would welcome the immigrants. The *hijrat* frenzy captivated the Muslims especially of Sindh and NWFP for some months. Thousands of Muslim families were uprooted and immensely suffered in the process. This fanciful scheme was abandoned only when Afghanistan's doors were closed to the immigrants and the Central Khilafat Committee refused to embrace it formally. Gandhi added the issues of *swaraj* (self-government) and the Punjab tragedy to that of *Khilafat* to draw in non-Muslims into the movement. The publication of the Hunter Committee Report on the Punjab tragedy provided the excuse; the Majority Report of the Hunter Committee had exonerated the guilty officials and whitewashed their excesses by such epithets as 'error of judgment', 'unnecessary acts' and 'mistakes', which infuriated the Indians without exception.

The All-India Muslim League faced a serious dilemma. A majority of its leaders and workers were supportive of the non-cooperation programme but a dwindling minority was either hesitant to support the programme or was opposed to it. The All-India Muslim League had not yet discussed the programme at any level. Meanwhile, the Central Khilafat Committee leaders began to pressurize the League to pronounce its official position. One leading Central Khilafat Committee–League leader reminded Zahur Ahmad that the Khilafat committees had done the work of the All-India Muslim League, and those Muslims who placed 'confidence' in the judgment of the 'experienced politicians and intellectuals' of the League would be disappointed if it still maintained its 'habitual dumbness and lethargy', holding out the warning that the League would 'become extinct' as a Muslim organization if it did not break its 'Ostrich-like silence'.[237] Zahur Ahmad's explanation was that the Central Khilafat Committee was running 'at breakneck speed', which made it 'difficult for the League to keep pace with it', but agreed that the League could not 'keep silent' for 'very long' and 'must tackle the question of non-cooperation'.[238] On 18 July 1920, the council of the All-India Muslim League discussed the political situation and endorsed its resolution of 29 February, which had expressed 'indignation' at the 'frenzied outbursts of Christian bigotry' in the media by the clergy in England, holding out a warning that such activities would embitter Muslim–Christian relations. It appealed to the Government of India to desist from sending Muslim or other Indian troops to the Middle East against the Muslims to repress their 'patriotic and religious movements' and demanded withdrawal of troops already stationed there. It protested against the 'grossly harsh and unjust' peace terms offered to Turkey, which were against the wartime promises made to the Indian Muslims and detrimental to the institution of *Khilafat*. These terms were used, it observed, as a device to deny the Muslims the right to choose their own *Khalifa* but the Muslims would not rest till the restoration of integrity of the *Khilafat* and sanctity of the Jaziratul Arab and the Holy Places according to the dictates of Islam. It also criticized the Majority Report of the Hunter Committee and called on the government to punish those who were involved in the Punjab tragedy. The July meeting of the council did not touch upon the non-cooperation programme, but it decided to hold a special session in Calcutta on 7 September, where the Congress and Central Khilafat Committee were meeting to discuss: (*i*) the Turkish peace treaty, the *Khilafat* and Holy Places; (*ii*) the government action on the Hunter Committee Report; and (*iii*) rules and regulations under the Act of 1919.[239]

Many League leaders had expressed doubts about the utility of the non-cooperation programme. For Zahur Ahmad the boycott of government services and legislative councils amounted to 'political suicide' for the Muslims.[240] Fazli Husain wrote to Zahur that 'Muslim politics are running amuck . . . [and are] likely to cause incalculable harm in the future. What should the League do? Raise a voice of protest . . . or go with the current and later bewail its bad luck. . . . What do you say? And what is the position of our president [M.A. Jinnah]?' Zahur agreed with his views and informed him that the president had not yet expressed 'his views on the present situation'.[241] Jinnah on his part realized that any 'conflict of opinions' at that juncture would be 'most injurious' for the League and, to avoid it 'at any cost', suggested that the council should meet on 5–6 September 1920, before the special session, to formulate a policy.[242] The council met on the scheduled dates and besides drafting resolutions for the special session, it demanded that (*i*) Lord Chelmsford should be recalled; (*ii*) Sir Michael O'Dwyer should be impeached; and (*iii*) General Dyer, Colonel Doveton, Rai Sahib Sri Ram Sud and other officers who were guilty of 'gross cruelty and injustice' should be 'rigorously dealt with under the law'; but the government, instead of punishing them, exonerated General Dyer, retiring him with a handsome pension out of the Indian revenues and simply 'warned' the other culprits.[243] Jinnah, in his brief presidential address to the special session, pithily expressed his feelings, 'First came the Rowlatt Bills — accompanied by the Punjab atrocities — and then came the spoilation of the Ottoman Empire and the Khilafat. The one attacks our liberty, the other our faith. . . . One degrading measure upon another, disappointment upon disappointment, and injury upon injury, can lead a people to only one end. It led Russia to Bolshevism. It has led Ireland to Sinn Feinism. May it lead India to freedom.'[244] He advised the Leaguers 'to weigh pros and cons' before taking a decision. After adopting two resolutions on the *Khilafat* and Punjab issues, the special session observed that 'the establishment of full responsible government in India' could vindicate 'national and religious honour' and prevent 'a repetition of similar wrongs in future'. At the end, the League resolved that it had no other option but to adopt the Central Khilafat Committee-inaugurated policy of 'progressive non-violent non-cooperation' to get the wrongs righted and responsible government established. It advised: (*a*) surrender of titles and honorary offices and resignations from nominated seats in local bodies; (*b*) refusal to attend the government levees, durbars, and other official and semi-official functions held by government officials or held in their honour; (c) withdrawal of children from schools and colleges owned, aided or controlled by the government and in place of such schools and colleges establishment of national schools and colleges in various provinces; (d) boycott of British courts by lawyers and litigants and establishment of private arbitration courts for the settlement of disputes; (e) refusal on the part of the military, clerical and labouring classes to offer themselves as recruits for service in Mesopotamia; (f) withdrawal of candidates of their candidatures for election to the legislative councils and refusal on the part of the voters to vote for the candidates; (g) progressive boycott of foreign goods; and (h) social boycott, in accordance with *Shariat*, of those Muslims who would act against the advice given in this resolution in spite of their being able to afford to act upon the same and of being personally asked and required to do so, provided that the local Khilafat committees also would have the authority to proclaim such social boycott. Clause (i) was an amendment that Maulana Azad had moved to the main resolution.[245] The League reiterated these resolutions at its Nagpur annual session and expressed satisfaction at the progress of non-cooperation. Jinnah along with several others opposed the non-cooperation programme at the special session of the Congress, despite threat of physical violence from Maulana Shaukat Ali, and alone at the Nagpur Congress. He resigned from the Congress on this issue; earlier, he had left the Home Rule League when that party changed its name to Swarajya Sabha and adopted the non-cooperation programme. He warned Gandhi, who controlled and led the non-cooperation movement, that it would 'lead to disaster'.[246]

The Leaguers were clearly divided into three groups: the first group actively participated in the Central Khilafat Committee-run non-cooperation movement; the second group cooperated with the government to work the reforms under the Act of 1919; and the third group opposed non-cooperation but did not cooperate with the government in the working of reforms due to its unresponsive attitude. Prominent Leaguers were in all the three groups; Jinnah was in the third group. The Central Khilafat Committee gained precedence over all the other parties including the All-India Muslim League. The Jamiatul Ulama-i-Hind and the Congress were its active partners in the movement. The Khilafat committees developed an efficient and effective organizational network to provide support to the non-cooperators right from the all-India level to the grassroots. The League directed its members to cooperate with the Khilafat committees.[247] Funds were available to the Central Khilafat Committee in abundance, which no other political organization so far had at its disposal for political work. In the absence of any credible system of accounting and auditing, there were allegations of misuse and embezzlement of funds.[248] The Khilafat movement generated unprecedented enthusiasm in the Muslim masses including Muslim women throughout India, but it produced mixed results. The All-India Muslim League did not participate in the elections to the newly constituted legislatures. Voters generally stayed away from polling and a number of Leaguers withdrew their candidatures from the elections. The League did call upon those of its members who had been elected in different provinces to resign from their seats but none of them listened to such appeals. The number of persons who surrendered their medals and titles or left honorary offices was not very impressive. A few lawyers suspended their practice but most of them returned to the courts after a short while. Even fewer litigants boycotted the courts or went to the alternate Khilafatist-established arbitration courts, which soon disappeared from the scene.[249] The movement put up an impressive popular show in pressuring the trustees of the Muslim educational institutions to reject government aid or disaffiliate themselves from government universities, but the outcome in concrete terms was disappointing. The Aligarh Muslim college and the educational institutions run by the Anjuman-i-Himayat-i-Islam of Lahore presented the most glaring examples of resistance to this pressure. The All-India Muslim League expressed its dislike of the action of the trustees of those educational institutions, without naming them, which had not refused government aid or had not disaffiliated themselves from the public universities, and appreciated Nadwatul Ulama's refusal to accept the government aid.[250] The number of teachers leaving government or government-aided educational institutions was negligible but that of students was quite large and they swelled the ranks of the volunteer organizations that the political parties established. The Khilafatists provided a singular example of an alternative educational institution in the form of the newly founded Jamia Millia Islamia, with Hakim Ajmal Khan as *Amir-i Jamia* and Maulana Mohammad Ali as *Shaikhul Jamia*. They organized a successful boycott of the Prince of Wales' visit. The swadeshi movement, or the use of locally manufactured goods, received great impetus, and the All-India Muslim League called on all the Muslim educational institutions, religious and otherwise, to immediately start technical classes with a view to encourage home industries.[251]

The Khilafat movement could not maintain its high tempo for long. Several developments broke up its force. The British raised the bogey of an Afghan invasion with the support of the Indian Muslims to scare the Hindu nationalists. Maulana Mohammad Ali's explanation to the effect that he would oppose any invasion from Afghanistan meant to subjugate India but would support one if its objective was *jihad* against the British did not remove their suspicions about pan-Islam.[252] In Turkey, Mustafa Kamal (1881–1938) had successfully led the Turkish nationalists against the Greeks to restore sovereignty over Turkish territories, and established a government in Angora. The Indian Muslims eulogized his victories and sent him funds to support his campaign. The news about possible British military assistance to the Greeks against the Turkish Nationalists provoked the Khilafatists and induced them to make aggressive speeches against the British. Amidst heightened emotions, Lord Reading, the new viceroy, manoeuvred an 'apology' from the Ali brothers through Gandhi by using the threat of prosecution against them, which hurt their popular image and sowed the seeds of Gandhi–Mohammad Ali rift, which meant Hindu–Muslim split. Public criticism of the 'apology' and conflicting interpretation put on it by the viceroy and Mohammad Ali spurred the latter to repudiate it and assume a more aggressive posture than before. On 9 July 1921, the All-India Khilafat conference in Karachi, on Mohammad Ali's motion, adopted a resolution that declared it *haram* (unlawful) for a Muslim to serve in the British Indian army or help in its recruitment process. The Conference held out a warning that if the British government would fight, directly or indirectly, against the Angora government, the Indian Muslims would start civil disobedience and establish complete independence at the next session of the Congress in Ahmadabad.

The government was alarmed by the positive response in the military circles to the Karachi conference resolution and the *mutafiqqah* (agreed) *fatwa* that about 500 *ulama* had signed, declaring enlistment or service in the British Indian army as *haram*.[253] The Ali brothers along with five others including one Hindu [Dr Saifuddin Kitchlew (1888–1963), Pir Ghulam Mujaddid (1881–1958), Maulana Husain Ahmad, Nisar Ahmad and Shri Shankar Acharya] were prosecuted on the charge of 'criminal conspiracy to seduce' Muslim officers and soldiers in the army from their duty. The court sentenced all the accused Muslims to two years' rigorous imprisonment but acquitted the accused Hindu.[254] The trial and punishment of the Muslim leaders were symbolic, meant to remove the most effective speakers and organizers of the Khilafat movement from the political scene, as numerous other Congress and Jamiatul Ulama-i-Hind leaders who had expressed similar sentiments were not touched. The adoption of complete independence as the objective and civil disobedience as the strategy by the Congress and All-India Muslim League at the Ahmadabad sessions was deflected after great effort on technical grounds. The government banned all the volunteer organizations that the political parties had started to use for political mobilization. The Mappila 'uprising' in the Malabar district of the Madras presidency to establish '*Khilafat*' in India and reports of forcible conversion of some Hindus also hurt the movement. The government repression with the cooperation of the Hindu moneylenders had provoked this uprising. The Mappilas turned their anger against the government officials and the Hindus. The recently disbanded Mappila military personnel joined the Khilafatists and turned the struggle into guerrilla warfare. Martial law was imposed and administered with extreme severity to control the situation. The loss of human life was enormous, which contributed to embitter Hindu–Muslim relations. The death of seventy Mappilas on a railway wagon by suffocation highlighted the enormity of repression. In all, 2,239 Mappilas were killed, 1,652 wounded, 79,900 imprisoned and an indefinite number of them deported to the Andamans. The All-India Muslim League, at its annual session in Ahmadabad in December 1921, appointed a five-member committee to inquire into the causes and incidents of Mappila troubles including the reported forcible conversion of Hindus.[255] Later on, in 1925, the League vehemently opposed the deportation and rehabilitation of the Mappila prisoners in the Andamans.[256] After the Ahmadabad sessions of the Central Khilafat Committee, Congress and All-India Muslim League, pressure on Mahatma Gandhi for immediate action mounted; therefore, on 1 February 1922, he finally gave an ultimatum to the viceroy for civil disobedience that was to start on 12 February. But eight days before the scheduled date, a clash between the police and the mob at Chauri Chaura in the Gorakhpur district (United Provinces) resulted in the death of twenty-two security personnel. Consequently, Gandhi was forced to call off the whole movement. The issue of *Khilafat* itself was removed from practical politics after the Angora government first, in November 1922, divested the Khalifa of his temporal authority, and then, on 3 March 1924, the Turkish national assembly abolished the very institution of *Khilafat*. The focus of the Indian Muslims also shifted from the *Khilafat* to other political issues.

The Khilafat movement temporarily eclipsed the All-India Muslim League although the Muslims gained experience in organizational and propaganda techniques. It generated in them unique political consciousness and communal affinity at the grassroots. But its failure dispersed the Muslim political forces, which proliferated into small insignificant political parties, advocating issues of topical and local importance. The eclipse of the All-India Muslim League and the identity of its objectives with those of the Congress raised doubts about the utility of its very existence as a separate political entity. In September 1921, one councillor gave notice of a resolution for the dissolution of the All-India Muslim League, as the Central Khilafat Committee and the Congress, it was argued, were doing its work more efficiently.[257] These views were forcefully presented by the chairman of the reception committee of the Ahmadabad annual session, Abbas Tayyabji (1853–1936), who suggested that the League should either be dissolved or merged into the Congress.[258] However, Hasrat Mohani, who was presiding over the session, opposed the proposal and stressed the need to retain the League by recounting its services for the Muslim community, arguing that it was on the League platform that 'all sections of political opinion among the Muslims, extremist or moderates, have so far been, and in future too will probably be, brought together'.[259] After his observation, nobody pressed for the acceptance of the merger proposal although this was partly the reason for not holding the next annual session of the All-India Muslim League in Gaya. The Central Khilafat Committee continued to function as a political body for some time in view of the non-resolution of the issue of *Khilafat*, but once the Turkish national assembly abolished the very institution of *Khilafat*, the Central Khilafat Committee itself lost any relevance and gradually disappeared from the political scene.

NOTES

1. Syed Razi Wasti, *Lord Minto and the Indian Nationalist Movement, 1905 to 1910*, Oxford, 1964, pp. 168–69.
2. 'Suggestions on the Council Reform Scheme of the Government of India by the All-India Muslim League', AFM, vol. 10.
3. Francis Robinson, *Separatism among Indian Muslims: The Politics of the United Provinces' Muslims, 1860–1923*, London, 1974, pp. 153–54.

4. *The Indian Mirror*, 18 June 1908, cited in Matiur Rahman, *From Consultation to Confrontation*, p. 91n.

5. Resolution passed at the Amritsar annual session, Pirzada, *Foundations*, vol. I, p. 59.

6. *The Statesman*, 10 February 1909.

7. *The Times* (London) 28 January 1909; and Morley to Minto, 28 January 1909, cited in Matiur Rahman, *From Consultation to Confrontation*, p. 108.

8. Minto to Morley, 7 April 1909, cited in Wasti, *Lord Minto*, p. 179.

9. *Hansard*, Fifth Series (Commons), vol. III, 1 April 1909, col. 500–2, cited in Robinson, *Separatism*, pp. 156–57.

10. *Proceedings of an Extraordinary General Meeting of the All-India Muslim League held at Lucknow on the 23rd of May 1909*, Aligarh, 18 September 1909, AFM, vol. 18.

11. 'An Abortive Meeting of the All-India Muslim League', ibid., vol. 19, no. 55; and also see ibid., vol. 20, no. 43.

12. Amir Ali to Musa Khan, 4 June 1909, ibid., vol. 26.

13. *A Brief Account of an Abortive Meeting of the All-India Muslim League held at Lucknow on 10 and 11 July 1909*, Aligarh, 1909, AFM, vol. 19.

14. Musa Khan to private secretary to the viceroy, 13 September 1909, and Robinson, *Separatism*, p. 160n

15. Matiur Rahman, *From Consultation to Confrontation*, p. 148; and Robinson, *Separatism*, p. 161.

16. *Report of the All-India Muslim League for the Year 1911*, AFM, vol. 65.

17. Pirzada, *Foundations*, vol. I, pp. 120–22.

18. Mohammad Shafi to the Aga Khan, 28 February 1910, AFM, vol. 456, p. 3; Aziz Mirza to Fazalbhai Karimbhai, 26 April 1910, ibid., vol. 456, p. 4; resolution passed by the All-India Muslim League council, ibid., vol. 52; Aziz Mirza to Ibne Ahmad, 22 July 1910, ibid., vol. 456, pp. 6–8; and Aziz Mirza to secretary (home department), Government of India, Simla, 12 October 1910, ibid., vol. 456, no. 9. Aziz Mirza cited Sir B. Fuller (*Studies of Indian Life and Sentiments*, pp. 42–44) and Lajpat Rai's acknowledgement in the *Indian Review* (May 1910) in support of this position.

19. M.A. Kuddus Badsha to Aziz Mirza, 24 October 1910, AFM, vol. 456, pp. 15–16.

20. Liaquat to census commissioner, Government of India, 12 September 1940, and census commissioner to honorary secretary, All-India Muslim League, 19 February 1941, ibid., vol. 458, pp. 25, 28–30, and 43; and also see ibid., vol. 456, pp. 18, 40 and 44.

21. A.R. Siddiqi to Jinnah, 10 February 1940, A.M.K. Dehlavi to Liaquat, 12 July 1940, and Liaquat to A.R. Siddiqi, 15 August 1940, ibid., vol. 458, pp. 1, 3, 4A and 9.

22. A.M.K. Dehlavi to Jinnah, 4 May 1940, QAP, F. 256, pp. 87–88.

23. Resolution passed by the central council, AFM., vol. 16; and representation of the All-India Muslim League, London branch to the secretary of state, 25 January 1909, ibid., vol. 25.

24. For Madras, see ibid., vol. 196, no. 21; for Bengal, see ibid., vol. 545, p. 5; and for the executive councils in the Punjab and United Provinces, see resolution passed by the central council on 22 November 1911, ibid., vol. 61.

25. Ibid., vol. 52. Aziz Mirza, in a letter to the secretary of state for India on 28 April 1910, hoped that the appointment of a Muslim on this position would become 'a

permanent feature'. Ibid., vol. 545, p. 6; and Aziz Mirza to secretary (home department), Government of India, ibid., vol. 545, p. 7.

26. Resolution passed at the Aligarh session in March 1908; and Musa Khan to Aga Khan, 17 June 1908, ibid., 482, pp. 9–10.

27. Mohammad Shafi to Wiqarul Mulk, 10 April 1908; Shah Din to Wiqarul Mulk, 11 April; Amir Ali to lieutenant governor, Punjab, ibid., vol. 56; and Yaqub Hasan to Musa Khan, 17 September 1908, ibid., vol. 57.

28. H.G. Stokes, deputy secretary, Government of India to honorary secretary, All-India Muslim League, 2 June 1910, AFM, vol. 545, p. 10; for League memorandum to the Government of India, see Aziz Mirza to secretary (home department), Government of India, 7 March 1910, ibid., p. 1; and also see secretary (home department), to Aziz Mirza, 30 September 1911, ibid., p. 61.

29. For province-wise statistics preserved in the All-India Muslim League record, see ibid., vols. 524–525; and Aziz Mirza to secretaries of the provincial Muslim Leagues, 23 April 1910, ibid., vol. 545, pp. 2–3. Aziz Mirza covered the princely states in this exercise. Ibid., vol. 110, and vol. 175, nos. 7, 9, 10, 49, 50 and 51.

30. For the text of his speech, see Pirzada, *Foundations*, vol. I, pp. 210–13.

31. Aziz Mirza to secretaries of the provincial Muslim Leagues, 13 July 1910, AFM, vol. 545, p. 15. Mian Shafi met personally, or led League deputations to, the heads of government departments, requesting them to give due representation to the Muslims. The Punjab provincial Muslim League also maintained a register of candidates seeking employment. Mohammad Shafi to Aziz Mirza, 6 July 1910, ibid., vol. 56.

32. For some record of the bureau including applications and dossiers of candidates, see ibid., vols. 526–531, and 541.

33. For the Punjab provincial Muslim League's deputations that met heads of various departments, see ibid., vol. 56.

34. Resolutions passed at the adjourned session in Lahore and at the Aligarh annual session.

35. *Report of the All-India Muslim League for the Year 1911*, ibid., vol. 65; and resolution of the council, AFM, vol. 84.

36. Resolutions passed by the central council on 15 October 1911, ibid., vol. 84; and *Report of the All-India Muslim League for the Year 1911*, ibid., vol. 65.

37. Resolution passed at the Nagpur session.

38. Resolution passed at the Calcutta session.

39. Shan Muhammad, *The All-India Muslim Educational Conference (Select Presidential Addresses) 1886–1947*, New Delhi, 2003, p. 166. For four articles on the Muslim university, written by Sir Sayyid's admirers in English journals in 1898–99, see K.K. Aziz (comp.), *Modern Muslim India in British Periodical Literature*, vol. 1, Islamabad, 1998, pp. 319–47.

40. Aziz Mirza to Trustees of the Mohammadan Anglo Oriental College, Aligarh, 30 January 1911, enclosing resolution passed at the Delhi annual session, AFM, vol. 432.

41. For statement by the Aga Khan, see ibid., 432, p. 28. Earlier, in his presidential address to the All-India Muslim Educational Conference in December 1902, he had estimated the total cost of the university at Rs 10 million.

42. Chapter entitled 'The Aligarh Muslim University', *History of the Freedom Movement*, vol. IV, Karachi, 1970, p. 254.

43. *Report of the All-India Muslim League for the Year 1911*, AFM, vol. 65.

44. Presidential address of Nawab Sir Mohammad Hamidullah Khan (1894–1960) at the Muslim University Foundation Committee session on 8 April 1917, at Aligarh, Bhopal, 1917, p. 2.

45. AFM, vol. 432.

46. Ibid., p. 63.

47. Ibid., pp. 18–21; and Gail Minault and David Lelyveld, 'The Campaign for a Muslim University, 1898–1920', *Modern Asian Studies*, 1974.

48. *The Comrade*, 9 December 1911, pp. 448–49.

49. The reply was conveyed through Sir Harcourt Butler (1869–1938), the governor of United Provinces, on 9 August 1912. Wazir Hasan's printed circular letter dated 22 April 1912, AFM, 102, no. 30.

50. Abdul Rashid Khan, *The All-India Muslim Educational Conference: Its Contribution to the Cultural Development of Indian Muslims, 1886–1947*, Karachi, 2001, p. 97; and correspondence between Lord Hardinge, Harcourt Butler, the education member, and George Roos-Keppel (1866–1921), chief commissioner of the NWFP, in the Butler Papers, vol. 85, cited in Lal Baha, *N.-W.F.P. Administration under British Rule, 1901–1919*, Islamabad, 1978, pp. 212–14.

51. AFM, vol. 432, p. 60; and Shan, *Muslim Educational Conference*, p. 199.

52. AFM, vol. 89.

53. Begum Sultan Jahan (1858–1930) of Bhopal was elected first chancellor of the university, the Aga Khan pro-chancellor, Raja of Mahmudabad vice-chancellor and Dr Ziauddin pro-vice-chancellor.

54. For opinions on the Aligarh Muslim University (Amendment) Bill, moved in the central assembly by Ziauddin Ahmad, see QAP, F. 1114, pp. 221–270; and a resolution moved by Qazi Isa in the All-India Muslim League council on 19 September 1940, AFM, vol. 262, p. 62.

55. Resolution passed at the Nagpur annual session.

56. AFM, vol. 127, no. 1; and resolution drafted by the central council on 15 October 1911, ibid., vol. 84. The United Provinces Muslim League had suggested most of these safeguards. Ibne Ahmad, secretary, United Provinces League to L. Stuart, secretary to government, United Provinces, 9 June 1911, ibid., 74.

57. For its impact on factionalism in the Punjab, see a letter by Chaudhry Shahabuddin, in the Urdu daily *Zamindar* (Lahore), 28 February 1912.

58. AFM, vol. 84; and *Proceedings of the All-India Muslim League Session, 3–4 March 1912*, ibid., vol. 67.

59. For a discussion in the All-India Muslim League council on 5 October 1911, see ibid., vol. 74. Burma was mentioned along with East Bengal and Assam. *Report of the All-India Muslim League for the Year 1911*, ibid., vol. 65.

60. For his letter to Aziz Mirza, 10 October 1910, see ibid., vol. 63.

61. Aziz Mirza to Ibne Ahmad, 22 July 1910, ibid., vol. 456, pp. 6–8; for a few public meetings held on this issue, see ibid., vols. 458 and 459. After the revival of the All-India Muslim League, the Leaguers including Jinnah extended support to the movement that the Majlis-i-Taraqqi-i Urdu, headed by Maulvi Abdul Haq, started for the promotion of Urdu.

62. For instance, see resolution passed by the central council on 15 October 1911; another resolution passed by the All-India Muslim League at its Lucknow session on 31 December 1916; and still another passed at its Calcutta session on 31 December 1917, ibid., vols. 84, 71, and 76.

63. Ibid., vol. 101, no. 77.

64. Ibid., vol. 108, no. 16; vol. 194, nos. 23 and 24.

65. Ibid., vol. 121, no. 13.
66. The jurists included Justice Amir Ali and Justice Mahmud, and the Nadwatul Ulama under the guidance of Allama Shibli Nomani (1957–1914) sent a memorial to the government signed by thousands of Muslims.
67. Pirzada, *Foundations*, vol. I, pp. 82, 136–37, and 178–93. Shibli Nomani spoke at the Delhi session.
68. M. Rafique Afzal, *Selected Speeches and Statements of the Quaid-i-Azam Mohammad Ali Jinnah, 1911–34 and 1947–48*, Lahore, 1966, pp. 1–11 and 20–25.
69. Resolution passed at the Delhi session, Pirzada, *Foundations*, vol. I, p. 134.
70. *Report of the All-India Muslim League for the Year 1911*, AFM, vol. 65; and Pirzada, *Foundations*, vol. I. pp. 251–52.
71. Resolution passed at the Lucknow session on 31 March 1923, AFM, vol. 101, no. 79.
72. Resolution passed at the Lahore session on 24–25 May 1924, and resolution passed at the Bombay session on 30–31 December 1924, *Resolutions of the All-India Muslim League from May 1924 to December 1936*, published by (Nawabzada) Liaquat Ali Khan. For the implementation of the Act, see AFM, vol. 121, nos. 13, 14–16, 19 and 23; and QAP, F. 1118, pp. 126–34; and for the controversy about its application to the Dawoodi Bohras, see AFM, vol. 121, nos. 12, 13, and 22.
73. For opinion of the All-India Muslim League council, see AFM, vols. 74 and 84.
74. Ibid., vol. 593, pp. 1–13.
75. All the provincial Muslim Leagues had supported the proposals. On 17 July 1911, Khwaja Kamaluddin (1870–1923) had sent a memorial based on Hakim Nuruddin's proposal to the Government of India. Ibid., vol. 83.
76. Ibid., vol. 91, no. 86.
77. Ibid., vol. 134, no. 10.
78. Resolution of the All-India Muslim League council passed on 27 July 1919, ibid., vol. 140, no. 36; Zahur Ahmad to the commanding officer, Civil Area, Lahore, 10 May 1919, ibid., no. 5; resolution passed at the Delhi annual session in December 1918, ibid., vol. 80; and *Report of the Honorary Secretary of the All-India Muslim League for the Year 1919*, ibid., vol. 86. During their rule, the Sikhs took over the Badshahi Masjid for military purposes. The British continued this occupation till 1856 when it was handed over to the Muslims with certain conditions; one condition was that the army commandant could deny access to the mosque whenever he thought it necessary. Muslims availed this conditional permission ten years later.
79. Hafiz Haq Nawaz Khan to honorary secretary, 19 October 1935, ibid., vol. 206, no. 24.
80. Records of some of these clubs are preserved in ibid., vols. 504–9.
81. For a moving editorial in the *Zamindar*, see its 28 December 1911 issue.
82. M.N. Das, *India under Morley and Minto: Politics behind Revolution, Repression and Reforms*, London, 1964, p. 33.
83. AFM, vol. 82.
84. Wasti, *Lord Minto*, pp. 11, 35–38, 49; and Das, *India under Morley and Minto*, pp. 34–44. He resigned in August 1906.
85. Das, *India under Morley and Minto*, p. 44.
86. Noman, *Muslim India*, pp. 74–75.
87. Pirzada, *Foundations*, vol. I, pp. 12 and 83–85.
88. Hasan Bilgrami to Wiqarul Mulk, 9 October 1908; and Hasan Bilgrami to Musa Khan, 16 October 1908, AFM, vol. 82.

89. Hasan Bilgrami to Musa Khan, 29 May 1908; and Musa Khan to Hasan Bilgrami, June 1908, ibid.
90. Minto to Morley, vol. III, 4 October 1906, Morley Papers, cited in Das, *India under Morley and Minto*, p. 44.
91. AFM, vol. 35.
92. For resolutions drafted by the central council for the annual session, 15 October 1911, see ibid., vol. 84.
93. Salimullah to Aziz Mirza, 7 December 1911, ibid., vol. 35.
94. 'The Fate of Muslims in India', *Aligarh Institute Gazette*, 20 December 1911. Aziz Mirza informed the joint secretary of the United Provinces Muslim League that Wiqarul Mulk's article reflected the result of 'collective consultation' held in Delhi and not his own views. Abdul Wadud to Aziz Mirza, 19 December 1911; and Aziz Mirza to Abdul Wadud, 21 and 30 December 1911, AFM, vol. 127, nos. 26, 27 and 34.
95. *Proceedings of the All-India Muslim League, 4 March 1912*, AFM, vol. 65; and Nawab Ali to Aziz Mirza, 18 January 1912, ibid., vol. 36.
96. Nawab Ali to Aziz Mirza, 17 February 1912, ibid., vol. 36.
97. Ibid., vol. 91, nos. 33 and 36.
98. For Wazir Hasan's comments on 14 May 1912, see ibid., vol. 91, no. 37.
99. For a resolution of the All-India Muslim League council, see ibid., no. 46; and resolutions of the Burma provincial Muslim League council on 18 July 1912, ibid., vol. 58.
100. Ibid., vol. 119, nos. 3, 5 and 70.
101. For the memorial dated 12 April 1913, and the government response, see ibid., vol. 119, nos. 4 and 5.
102. For letters by Fazlur Rahman, secretary of the Kanpur district Muslim League to the honorary secretary, All-India Muslim League, 13 and 19 May, and 1 and 24 June 1913, see ibid., vol. 119, nos. 5, 6, 8 and 9.
103. Wazir Hasan to Mohammad Ali, 10 July 1913, and Mohammad Ali to Wazir Hasan, 13 July 1913, ibid., vol. 119, nos. 12 and 13.
104. Wazir Hasan to council members, 23 July 1913; and Yaqub Hasan to Wazir Hasan, 23 July 1913, ibid., nos. 15, 16, and 18; and resolution passed at the emergency meeting of the All-India Muslim League council on 20 July 1913, which was confirmed at a regular meeting on 31 August, ibid., vol. 85.
105. A.M. Khwaja's account after his visit to the Mosque in Musa Khan to Wazir Hasan, 16 August 1913, ibid., vol. 119, no 33.
106. Besides those who were put on trial, about fifty children were released after one night's detention.
107. For a moving letter by Raza Ali, 14 August 1913, see AFM, vol. 119, no. 30.
108. Aftab Ahmad Khan to Wazir Hasan, 10 August 1913; Fazalbhai Karimbhai to Wazir Hasan, 11 August 1913; Sarfraz Husain Khan to Wazir Hasan, 12 August 1913; and Fazli Husain to Wazir Hasan, 13 August 1913, ibid., nos. 21, 23, 24, 26, and 28; and also see Wazir Hasan's circular letter of 7 August 1913, ibid., vol. 85. For legislation to protect religious places, see Mohammad Ismail Khan to Wazir Hasan, 23 August 1913, ibid., vol. 85.
109. Mohammad Shafi to H. Wheeler, home secretary, Government of India, 22 and 26 August 1913, ibid., vol. 119, nos. 38 and 40.
110. Afzal Iqbal, *Life and Times of Mohamed Ali*, Lahore, 1979, pp. 99–100.
111. Allah Bakhsh Yusufi, *Maulana Mohamed Ali: The Khilafat Movement*, Karachi, 1980, pp. 242–43.

152   A HISTORY OF THE ALL-INDIA MUSLIM LEAGUE

112. AFM, vol. 119, no. 64; and vol. 134, no. 10.

113. Ibid., vol. 119, no. 17.

114. The balance of over Rs 25,000 remained with Mazharul Haq till November 1917, when, on a request from the Muslims of Calcutta, the All-India Muslim League formally directed him to hand it over to Raja of Mahmudabad, the permanent president, for the Bihar Relief Fund. Ibid., nos. 59–63.

115. For a resolution of the All-India Muslim League council, 27 November 1912, see ibid., vol. 91, no. 86.

116. Aziz Mirza to home secretary, Government of India, 15 February 1912, ibid., vol. 62.

117. For details, see M. Naeem Qureshi, *Pan-Islam in British Indian Politics: A Study of the Khilafat Movement, 1918–1924*, Leiden, 1999, pp. 60–61.

118. Ibne Ahmad to Aziz Mirza, 28 December 1911, ibid., vol. 62; Sayyid Mohammad Fakhir to secretary, All-India Muslim League, 23 October 1911, ibid., vol. 61; and Maulana Shaukat Ali's letter in the *Aligarh Institute Gazette*, 30 October 1912.

119. For telegrams from the London Muslim League to League leaders, and a moving letter by Ross Masud to Aziz Mirza, 17 November 1911, urging solidarity with the Muslims of Turkey, see AFM, vol. 61.

120. For telegrams from the president, Eastern Bengal and Assam provincial Muslim League to Aziz Mirza, 3 October 1911; Yaqub Hasan to honorary secretary, All-India Muslim League, 2 October 1911; and Central Provinces League to Aziz Mirza, 2 October 1911, ibid., vol. 61.

121. For a resolution of the All-India Muslim League council, see ibid.

122. For a resolution of the All-India Muslim League council passed on 2 November 1911, see ibid.

123. Mohammad Ikramul Haq to honorary secretary, All-India Muslim League, 6 October 1911, ibid.

124. H.S. Crosthwaite, under secretary to the Government of United Provinces, 22 November 1911, ibid.

125. Maulana Mohammad Ali's presidential address to the Congress, 28 December 1923, in the *Indian Annual Register (IAR)*, vol. II, p. 35.

126. For the text of the resolution, see *Proceedings of the Meeting of the Council of the All-India Muslim League held on 24 December 1911*, AFM, vol. 84. On 4 March 1912, the All-India Muslim League at its Calcutta session endorsed this resolution.

127. For telegrams to all the provincial Muslim Leagues, 15 December 1911, see ibid., vol. 61.

128. For copies of the correspondence, see ibid., vol. 62.

129. For resolutions passed by the central council on 7 March 1913, and the annual session on 23 March, see ibid., vol. 85; and Pirzada, *Foundations*, vol. I, p. 28.

130. Khwaja Kamaluddin to members of the All-India Muslim League, 18 February 1913, AFM, vol. 62.

131. For resolution of the Calcutta annual session passed in March 1913, see Pirzada, *Foundations*, vol. I, p. 280.

132. AFM, vol. 91, no. 86; remarks by Herbert H. Asquith (1852–1928), *The Times*, 11 November 1912; and Qureshi, *Pan-Islam*, p. 64.

133. Maulana Zafar Ali Khan, editor of the *Zamindar*, personally handed over to the Turkish authorities the funds that he had collected through his newspaper.

134. For correspondence regarding the medical missions, see AFM, vol. 62; and Raza Ali's letter, ibid., vol. 119, no. 30. The central council urged Amir Ali 'to take steps for the establishment of the British Red Crescent Society as a permanent institution

to ensure its recognition at The Hague'. Aziz Mirza to newspaper editors, 25 April 1912, ibid., vol. 62.

135. Eyre A. Crowe's letter, ibid., vol. 62.

136. The central council passed a resolution thanking those Hindus who had attended a protest meeting in Calcutta. [Aziz Mirza to Nawab Ali Chaudhury, secretary, Bengal PML, 23 April 1912; and Aziz Mirza to newspaper editors, 25 April 1912, ibid.] Khwaja Hasan Nizami (1878–1957), in a circular letter on 13 November 1913, urged the Muslim leaders to benefit from this situation by forging Hindu–Muslim unity. Ibid., vol. 61.

137. Wiqarul Mulk's speech at a public meeting in Rangoon on 6 February 1910, ibid., vol. 58; Mirza, *Muslim Politics*, pp. 22–24; and Muhammad Aziz Mirza, *Muslim League aur uske Usul*, Lucknow, 1910, p. 9.

138. *Paisa Akhbar* (Lahore), 3 and 16 January 1911.

139. *Report of the All-India Muslim League for the Year 1911*, AFM, vol. 65.

140. For instance, see Hasan Nizami to Aziz Mirza, 13 November 1913; and Aziz Mirza to Hasan Nizami, 15 November, ibid., vol. 61.

141. For an informed account of the sharp divisions in the All-India Muslim League, see Mohammad Yaqub to Zahur Ahmad, 12 July 1919, ibid., vol. 111; and Nawab Abdul Majid to Zahur Ahmad, 25 July 1919, ibid., vol. 111, no. 25.

142. Resolution passed at the Lucknow annual session in March 1913.

143. For his printed letter of 11 April 1913, see AFM, vol. 115, no. 2.

144. For the printed letter of 28 April 1913, see ibid., vol. 115, no. 4.

145. For numerous other letters from the League and Congress leaders, see ibid., vol. 115.

146. Mohammad Shafi to Wazir Hasan, 5 July 1913, ibid., no. 14.

147. Satyendra Bose to Wazir Hasan, 19 May 1913, ibid., no 21; and C.Y. Chintamani to Wazir Hasan, 8 July 1913, ibid., no. 60.

148. For Wazir Hasan's printed letter to members, and replies of some members, see ibid., vol. 564, pp. 3–8, and 16.

149. For Wazir Hasan's printed letter to members, 26 July 1916, along with the draft proposals, and comments of some members on the draft, see ibid., pp. 14, 15, 18, 22–28, 30–38, and 42–44.

150. Ibid., vol. 565, p. 27.

151. Ibid., pp 30–31.

152. Twenty-nine members (Punjab 2, United Provinces 10, Bihar and Orissa 4, Bombay 5 and Bengal 8) attended this meeting. Nawab Ali Chaudhury, A. Rasul, Fazlul Haq, Mohammad Akram Khan (1868–1968) and Mujibur Rahman (editor of the *Mussalman*) were among the Muslim Leaguers from Bengal who attended the joint conference. Ibid., p. 36.

153. Nawab Sarfraz Husain to honorary secretary, All-India Muslim League, 16 February 1919, ibid., vol. 144, no. 5. Muslim population of Bengal had increased rapidly. In 1872, Muslims were 16,681,836 as compared to 17,258,304 Hindus and by 1911 their number had risen to 23,989,719 as compared to 20,380,771 Hindus. This transformation of a socially and economically backward minority to a majority was not acceptable to the Bengali Hindus who were far ahead of the Bengali Muslims in every respect. The Bengali Hindus used this argument to deny the Bengali Muslims their majority. Musa Khan to the editor of the *Pioneer* (Allahabad), 23 June 1909 [unpublished], ibid., vol. 18; and *The Bengal Weekly* (Calcutta), 24 February 1941, QAP, vol. 5, pp. 9–9A; and *Proceedings of the 9th Session of the All-India Muslim League, Lucknow 1916*, Lucknow, 1917.

154. AFM, vol. 71.

155. For the text of the joint reforms scheme, see ibid., vol. 565, pp. 65–69. Major and minor provinces were not identified.

156. Ibid., vol. 104, no. 3.

157. Ibid., vol. 494, pp. 5–9, and 35–36.

158. In 1916, two Home Rule Leagues had been launched: one by Bal Gangadhar Tilak in April and the other by Mrs Annie Besant in September.

159. 'The Danger in India', *Nineteenth Century and After*, December 1916.

160. *Report of the Honorary Secretary of the All-India Muslim League for the Year ending 31 December 1917*, ibid., vol. 76; and B. Pattabhi Sitaramayya, *The History of the Indian National Congress (1885–1935)*, Allahabad, 1935, pp. 223–24.

161. The resolution was passed at an emergency meeting on 27 June 1917, and its copies were sent to the prime minister, secretary of state for India, the viceroy and the press. AFM, vol. 114, no. 10.

162. The delay in convening the joint conference was due to the month of Ramazan. G.M. Bhurgari to honorary secretary, All-India Muslim League, 26 June 1917; Subharao to Wazir Hasan, 2 July 1917; Jinnah to Wazir Hasan, 2 July, 1917: and telegrams from Wazir Hasan to Jinnah and others, 3 July 1917, ibid., vol. 104, nos. 26, 28–31.

163. Mian Shafi's telegram to Wazir Hasan, 11 August 1913, ibid., vol. 274, no. 53.

164. *Report of the Honorary Secretary of the All-India Muslim League for the Year ending 31 December 1917*, ibid., vol. 76; and vol. 114, no. 12.

165. For his telegram, see ibid., vol. 104, no. 64.

166. Ibid., vol. 114, no. 14; and vol. 104, nos. 1 and 62.

167. Ibid., vol. 104, nos. 67–87.

168. Ibid., vol. 566, nos. 7 and 8; and vol. 114, no. 18.

169. For an account of the riots, see a note by Raza Ali in ibid., vol. 112, no. 16.

170. For a printed letter signed by Raja of Mahmudabad and Wazir Hasan, 10 October 1917, and some replies and comments communicated to Wazir Hasan including those from Niaz Mohammad, honorary secretary, Anjuman-i-Islamia, Saharanpur, 15 October; Khwaja Mohammad of Gaya, 29 October; Abdul Anik, Delhi, 28 October; Rafiullah, 31 October; K.B. Kuddus Badsha, 2 November; Sayyid Nurul Hasan, 29 October; Fazlul Haq, 12 November; Mujibur Rahman, 12 November; and others, see ibid., vol. 106, nos. 9–17, 33, 37, 41, 52; and vol. 112, nos. 14, 17 and 18; and vol. 571. See also Mohammad Yaqub's printed note, 'Appeal to Indian Muslims', ibid., vol. 112, no 15; and Raza Ali's note, '*Musalmanon ka Tahuffuz kiyun kar ho*? [How do (we) protect the Muslims?]', ibid., vol. 112, no. 16. For constitutional reforms in the NWFP and formation of Sindh as a separate province, see ibid., vol. 112, no. 14; and vol. 92, no. 19.

171. Ibid., vol. 112.

172. Ibid., no. 26; and Wazir Hasan to C.Y. Chintamani, 16 November 1917, ibid., vol. 566, p. 46, and honorary secretary to Nabiullah and others, 18 November 1917, ibid., vol. 566, p. 64; and vol. 567, no. 1; Zahur Ahmad, *The Task Before us*, ibid., vol. 89; and *Report of the Honorary Secretary of the All-India Muslim League for the Year ending 31 December 1917*, ibid., vol. 76.

173. Afzal Iqbal, *Mohamed Ali*, pp. 130–31.

174. For its resolutions, AFM, vol. 76; and a message from Ali brothers' mother, *Bi Amman* Abadi Bano Begum (1851–1924), see ibid., vol. 73.

175. For membership of the committee and its report with a note of dissent by Zahur Ahmad and Samiullah Beg, see ibid., vol. 567, pp. 30–34.

176. Dr M.A. Ansari to assistant secretary, All-India Muslim League, 16 December 1918, ibid., vol. 134, nos. 2 and 3.

177. For resolutions passed at the special session of the All-India Muslim League held in Bombay on 1 September 1918, see ibid., vol. 79, no. 33; vol. 123, no. 4; vol. 134, no. 10; vol. 139, no. 5; and Pirzada, *Foundations*, vol. I, pp. 467–70. The council, in view of the decision to send a deputation to England, did not consider the proposal by Vallabhbhai J. Patel (1875–1950), president of the Gujarat Political Conference, to convene a special joint All-India Muslim League–Congress session in London. Ibid., vol. 139, no. 88.

178. Ibid., vol. 123, no. 6; vol. 139, nos. 26, 33, 34; and Pirzada, *Foundations*, vol. I, pp. 495–96, and resolution adopted about the Katarpur riots at the Delhi session in December, AFM, vol. 80. The central council demanded a commission to inquire into the firing in Calcutta by the military and the police but on the government's refusal, a non-official commission conducted an inquiry.

179. For instance, see B.C. Pal's comments, AFM, 130, no. 19; vol. 117, no. 36; and V.J. Patel's views in I.K. Yajnik, *Gandhi as I knew him*, Bombay, 1933, pp. 105–6.

180. For his letter to the League Office, 3 March 1919, see AFM, vol. 143, no 28.

181. For correspondence between the League office and secretary, Government of India, see ibid., vol. 369, p. 13; vol. 568, pp. 25–26; and vol. 143, no. 13. The Congress had obtained fifteen priority certificates while the All-India Muslim League asked for 16 and got 8.

182. Yaqub Hasan to Abdul Walli, 28 April 1919, ibid., vol. 499, pp. 11, 15.

183. P. O'Donnell, chief secretary, Government of United Provinces to honorary secretary, All-India Muslim League, 24 February 1919, ibid., vol. 369, p. 13.

184. Ibid., vol. 569, pp. 25, 27, 51 and 53.

185. *Proceedings of the All-India Muslim League for 1918–19, presented by Maulvi Zahur Ahmad, Honorary Secretary at the annual session of the All-India Muslim League at Amritsar on 29 December 1919*, Amritsar, n. d.

186. Barkat Ali to Abdul Walli, 22 March 1919, AFM, vol. 143, no. 49; and also see ibid., vol. 568, pp. 52 and 53.

187. Yaqub Hasan to Zahur Ahmad, 7 and 13 August 1919, ibid., vol. 499, p. 38.

188. Ibid., vol. 86.

189. Ibid., vol. 144, no. 59.

190. For details, see P.C. Bamford, *The Histories of the Non-co-operation and Khilafat Movements*, Delhi, 1925; T.R. Sareen, *Indian Revolutionary Movement Abroad, 1905–1921*, New Delhi, 1979; S.S. Josh, *Hindustani Gadar Party: A Short History*, New Delhi, 1977; and Zafar Hasan Aibak, *Aap Biti*, Lahore, 1964.

191. S.M. Burke and Salim al Din Qureshi, *The British Raj in India*, Karachi, 1997, p. 150.

192. Husain Ahmad Madni, *Naqsh-i-Hayat*, Deoband, 1953, vol. 2, pp. 211–12; Robinson, *Separatism*, pp. 270–71; and Qureshi, *Pan-Islam*, 76–77.

193. For instance, see *Report of the All-India Muslim League for the Year 1915*, AFM, vol. 69; and resolution passed at the Lucknow annual session, ibid., vol. 71.

194. Ibid., vol. 99, nos. 8 and 9; and letter from the deputy commissioner, Lucknow to Wazir Hasan, 19 July 1916, and Wazir Hasan to secretaries of the provincial Muslim Leagues, 24 July 1916, ibid., vol. 62.

195. Ibid., vol. 501, pp. 16–19; and *The Times*, 7 January 1918.

196. For some of the resolutions of the League bodies, see AFM, vols. 69, 95 and 114.

197. For the text of conditional undertaking that the Ali brothers were willing to give for their release, and the account of two forged letters that were used to continue their internment, see Afzal Iqbal, *Mohamed Ali*, pp. 125–42.

198. For Jinnah's question and the Home Member's reply, see *Proceedings of the Indian Legislative Council, April 1917 to March 1918*, vol. LVI, Calcutta, 1918, p. 433.

199. For the text of the resolution passed at the All-India Muslim League emergency meeting in Lucknow, see AFM, vol. 76.

200. Ibid., vol. 37.

201. Dr Ansari to Wazir Hasan, 27 May 1918, ibid., vol. 117, no. 9; and resolutions of the central council passed on 9 July 1918, ibid., vol. 134, no. 13, and on 24 November 1918, ibid., vol. 123, no. 7.

202. For the text of the resolutions, see ibid., vol. 134, no. 10.

203. Ibid., vol. 37 and 80.

204. The League in another resolution opposed the demand for additional war expenditure of £45 million from the Indian revenues because of acute famine and extreme poverty in India, arguing that India had already contributed £100 million for the cost of war, besides large 'voluntary' private contributions. It also demanded that the Arms Act, Press Act and the Defence of India Act should be repealed, and criticized the 'Report of the Sedition Committee' chaired by Sir Sidney Rowlatt. Ibid., vol. 134, no 10.

205. Cited in Qureshi, *Pan-Islam*, pp. 101–2.

206. Honorary secretary to home secretary, Government of India, 1 January 1919, and his reply of 15 February, ibid., vol. 568, pp. 55–56 and 57. Ibid., vol. 123, no. 9.

207. For a resolution of the central council, 30 March 1919, ibid., vol. 123, no. 9.

208. Afzal, *Speeches and Statements*, pp. 84–113.

209. For the All-India Muslim League's call to the provincial Muslim Leagues to pass resolutions against the bills at protest meetings, see ibid., vol. 143, no. 48.

210. M.S. Leigh, *The Punjab and the War*, Lahore, 1922, pp. 284–85; *The Punjab Administration Report, 1917–18*, Lahore, 1919, pp. 1–3; and S. Qalb-i-Abid, *Muslim Politics in the Punjab, 1921–47*, Lahore, 1992, pp. 31–32.

211. For reports about the meetings and the resolutions, see AFM, vol. 500.

212. Jan Mohammad Chotani to Zahur Ahmad, 18 June 1919, and Zahur Ahmad to Jan Mohammad Chotani, 7 July 1919, ibid., vol. 501, p. 5 and 6; and *Hamdam*, 16 July 1919. See also AFM, vol. 503, pp. 32–33.

213. For the text of the representation, see AFM, vol. 499, pp. 50–54. There was some misunderstanding about Jinnah not signing the Memorial but it was soon removed. For details, see ibid., vol. 499, pp, 20–22; vol. 569, pp. 31, 32; and Yaqub Hasan to Zahur Ahmad, 24 July 1919; and 16 January 1920, ibid., vol. 499, pp. 31–32 and 90.

214. For the accounts of these funds, see ibid., vol. 499, pp. 92–116.

215. For the Aga Khan's advice to the Muslim Leaguers in India to invite Hindus in their meetings, see ibid., vol. 501, p. 15; and vol. 503, p. 70.

216. For the text of the memorial, see ibid., vol. 140, no. 19.

217. Ibid., 123, no. 11; and Fazli Husain to Zahur Ahmad, 13 August 1919, ibid., vol. 500, p. 13.

218. For instance, see (*i*) memorandum by Yaqub Hasan, a member of the All-India Muslim League delegation, the Khilafat committee and the Southern Indian Chamber of Commerce to the prime minister, 1 July 1919, ibid., vol. 499, 36A; (*ii*) The Aga Khan, A.S.M. Anik, Abbas Ali Beg, M.H. Ispahani, Amir Ali, Abdullah Yusuf Ali, Kamaluddin, Mushir Husain Kidwai, and twenty-seven others

to secretary of state for foreign affairs, 1 January 1919, ibid., vol. 499, p. 36A and vol. 503, p. 4; (*iii*) The Aga Khan, Amir Ali, and twenty-nine others to A.J. Balfour, secretary of state for foreign affairs, 3 March 1919, ibid., vol. 499, p. 36B, and vol. 503, p. 5; (*iv*) The Aga Khan and others, 3 April 1919, ibid., vol. 503, p. 6; (*v*) Aga Khan, Amir Ali, Abbas Ali Beg, Aftab Ahmad Khan, Yaqub Hasan, Mushir Husain Kidwai, and several others to the prime minister, 14 June 1919, ibid., vol. 499, p. 36D.

219. Ibid., vol. 140, no. 49 and 50; and *Pioneer*, 17, 18 August 1919.

220. Ibid., vol. 123, no 12.

221. Ibid., vol. 495, pp. 17, and 19.

222. *Report of the Honorary Secretary of the All-India Muslim League for the Year 1919*, ibid., vol. 86.

223. For details, see statement by Sher Ali of Qadian, ibid., vol. 497, pp. 73–74.

224. For the text of the resolutions passed at the Conference, and Zahur Ahmad's letter of 30 September to members, see ibid., vol. 497, no. 269. Earlier, the central council had appointed a six-member Khilafat committee, with powers to co-opt three other Muslims (or Maulvis) 'to carry out the duties and exercise the powers of the council'.

225. For resolutions passed by the All-India Muslim League council on 31 October and 29 November, see ibid., vol. 141, no. 15 and 38.

226. For a resolution passed by the All-India Muslim League council on 29 November, see ibid., vol. 141, no. 20.

227. For a telegram and a letter from them to Zahur Ahmad on this issue, 13 November 1919, see ibid., vol. 499, pp. 84–85; and for Yaqub Hasan's views, see his letters to Zahur Ahmad, ibid., vol. 499, pp. 86 and 90.

228. For Zahur Ahmad's printed circular of 30 November 1919, and resolution of the central council of 7 December 1919, see ibid., vol. 86 and vol. 123; and for a pamphlet on 'Progressive Boycott' by Zahur Ahmad, see Noormahomed's letter, ibid., vol. 87.

229. For resolution moved by Pir Sayyid Fazal Shah (of Jalalpur Sharif, Jhelum), seconded by Maulana Mohammad Fakhir and supported by Hasrat Mohani, see ibid., vol. 86.

230. Resolution moved by Dr Ansari and seconded by Tassaduq Ahmad Khan Sherwani (1884–1935) at the Amritsar session.

231. For letters and telegrams from the Hindus welcoming the step, see ibid., vol. 519.

232. Punjab Police Abstract of Intelligence, 41/14, 15 April 1919, para. 504.

233. AFM, vol. 519. Gujranwala (Punjab) was perhaps the only place where the municipal committee decided to ban the slaughter of a milk-giving cow or a calf. Ibid., vol. 130, no. 33.

234. Ibid., AFM, vol. 89.

235. The delegation members were: Sayyid Sulaiman Nadvi (1884–1953), Syed Husain and Hasan Mohammad (1882–1955); and later on, Abul Qasim and Mushir Husain Kidwai joined them.

236. For an account of the delegation, see M. Naeem Qureshi, *Mahomed Ali's Khilafat Delegation to Europe (February–October 1920)*, Karachi, 1980.

237. Ajmal Khan to Zahur Ahmad, 30 June 1920, AFM, vol. 96, no. 7

238. Zahur Ahmad to Hakim Ajmal Khan, 3 July 1920, ibid., vol. 96, no. 8.

239. Ibid., vol. 123, nos. 14, 15; vol. 144, no. 59; and vol. 500, pp. 8–9.

240. Ibid., vol. 501, p. 40.

241. Fazli Husain to Zahur Ahmad, 27 July 1920, and Zahur Ahmad to Fazli Husain, 31 July, ibid., vol. 144, nos. 39 and 40.
242. Jinnah to Zahur Ahmad, 7 August 1920, ibid., 144, no. 41.
243. Resolutions nos. XII–XV passed on these issues at the Amritsar session, Pirzada, *Foundations*, vol. I, p. 537; and AFM, vol. 145, nos. 14 and 24.
244. Noman, *Muslim India*, p. 190; and Pirzada, *Foundations*, vol. I, pp. 542–43.
245. AFM, vol. 96, no. 37; and *Report of the Honorary Secretary of the All-India Muslim League for the Year 1920*, ibid., vol. 89, Appendix V.
246. For his letter, see M.H. Saiyid, *Mohammead Ali Jinnah (A Political Study)*, Lahore, 1962, p. 92; and M. R. Jayakar, *The Story of my Life*, vol. I, Bombay, 1958, pp. 404–6.
247. For a resolution of the council, see AFM, vol. 126, no. 30.
248. David Page, *Prelude to Partition: The Indian Muslims and the Imperial System of Control, 1920–32*, Karachi, 1987, pp. 96–97.
249. *Report of the All-India Muslim League for the Year 1920*, AFM, vol. 89, and resolution moved by Hakim Ajmal Khan, seconded by Tassaduq Ahmad Khan Sherwani and supported by Azad Sobhani (1882–1957) and Shamsuddin Ahmad.
250. For a resolution passed at the Nagpur session on this issue, see ibid., vol. 89.
251. Hasrat Mohani moved the resolution at the Nagpur annual session and Moazzam Ali seconded it.
252. *Zamindar*, 29 April 1921.
253. *Mutafiqqah Fatwa*, published by Maulvi Mushtaq Ahmad, Meerut, 1921.
254. For details, see AFM, vol. 502; and R.V. Thadani (ed.), *The Historical State Trial of the Ali Brothers and Five Others*, Karachi, 1921.
255. For the council resolution, see AFM, vol. 126, no. 30; and C.G. Nair, *The Moplah Rebellion, 1921*, Calicut, 1923.
256. Resolution passed at the Aligarh annual session.
257. AFM, vol. 126.
258. For the text of his address, see ibid., vol. 97, no. 26.
259. Pirzada, *Foundations*, vol. I, p. 557.

4

Fumbling in the Dark, 1922–1934

The All-India Muslim League activated its organization after a short interval of political inactivity. It attempted to unite the scattered Muslim political forces on its platform to evolve uniformity in Muslim political thinking. It articulated and advocated Muslim demands that were raised from different quarters. Jinnah as its 'permanent' president (1919–1930) put them forward from its platform; and his 'Fourteen Points' reflected Muslim political consensus. He kept himself regularly in touch with the Congress leaders to arrive at a Hindu–Muslim settlement to replace the Lucknow Pact in order to press the British government to establish responsible government in India. At this time, the initiative for communal rapprochement generally came from the Muslim leaders particularly Jinnah rather than the Congress leaders. However, the All-India Muslim League could not prevent its leaders from dissipating their energies by creating and using new political platforms to advocate topical issues. Instead of forming League parties in the legislatures, the Leaguers themselves founded non-communal parties in some assemblies: Jinnah founded the Independent Party in the central legislative assembly, Fazlul Haq formed the Krishak Praja Samity in the Bengal council and Mian Fazli Husain set up the Unionist Party in the Punjab council. Besides these and other existing platforms, Muslims formed a few new popular platforms like the Majlis-i-Ahrar-i-Islam, the Khaksar movement and the Khudai Khidmatgar movement to voice diverse issues. The All-India Muslim Conference formed after the holding of the Aga Khan-chaired All-Muslim Parties Conference in Delhi was the high point of this trend; and at one time, the All-India Muslim Conference threatened the very existence of the All-India Muslim League as a separate entity. However, Muslims maintained the League platform to voice their all-India political demands.

(A) PARTY IN LIMBO

The All-India Muslim League survived the threat posed to its existence during the Khilafat movement although it was battered in the process. The Central Khilafat Committee and Jamiatul Ulama-i-Hind, the two by-products of the Khilafat movement, temporarily overshadowed the League. Even after the collapse of the Khilafat movement and the abolition of the very institution of *Khilafat*, these two parties maintained their separate existence. During the Khilafat movement, the Indian National Congress under Gandhi's leadership had temporarily provided the political parties an overall umbrella, which subsequently inspired its leaders particularly the Nehrus, Motilal (1861–1931) and Jawaharlal (1889–1964), to perceive the Congress as the 'sole national party'. For about two years, the All-India Muslim League had remained dormant, which strengthened this perception. In 1922, the All-India Muslim League did not hold its annual session. Even its council could meet only twice in that year. In September, the council was to hold an emergency meeting, which could not be convened on the scheduled time because only two members turned up for the meeting. When the required quorum was complete, the council simply passed two resolutions: (*i*) it congratulated Mustafa Kamal for the victories of the Turkish forces; and (*ii*) it appealed to the Indian Muslims to extend financial assistance to the Turkish leader 'as a religious duty'.[1] In December, the second council meeting merely decided not to accept the Central Khilafat Committee invitation to hold the annual session of the League in Gaya where the Congress, Central Khilafat Committee and other political parties were meeting for their annual sessions.[2] Its financial condition was dismal. That year, only 23 out of its 1,093 members had paid their annual dues, donations were non-existent, and its appeals for funds elicited no response. The following year, though the membership stood at 1,097, the subscriptions had declined to Rs 264 as against 826 in 1922.[3] As a result, it had to lay off some members of its paid regular staff who had served the League for several years. The party could not fully recover from its recurring financial crises till after 1935.

Meanwhile, several developments within India worried the Muslims. Communal harmony had gradually disappeared after the Mappila 'uprising' and circulation of exaggerated accounts of forcible conversion of some Hindus.[4] The Hindu nationalists believed in the authenticity of these accounts. The Arya Samaj became active and so did the All-India Hindu Mahasabha whose leaders began to make aggressive statements against the Muslims. The All-India Hindu Mahasabha president, at the Gaya session in December 1922, urged the Hindus to establish volunteer organizations whose object should be to create 'awe and fear' in the hearts of Muslims.[5] Soon after, the Shudhi (lit. purification) and Sangathan (lit. solidarity) movements, led by Pandit Madan Mohan Malaviya, Lala Lajpat Rai and Swami Shradhanand (1856–1926), were founded to do missionary work and to strengthen Hinduism. Some Hindu leaders campaigned for the conversion of Muslims to Hinduism or their expulsion from India 'on the pattern of Moors of Spain'. A few Muslims had expressed similar fears if they were not properly organized.[6] The incident that alarmed the Muslims was the conversion of thousands of Muslim Malkana Rajputs to Hinduism in central India. They responded immediately and organized the Tabligh (lit. propagation) and Tanzim (lit. solidarity) movements to counterbalance the Hindu missionary activities and prevent recurrence of any cases of apostasy. These four organizations— Shudhi, Sangathan, Tabligh and Tanzim—came to wield significant influence among the Hindus and Muslims. Their members were also active from the platforms of the All-India Muslim League and the Congress; both these political parties consulted their leaders on all important communal and political issues. The All-India Muslim League formally appreciated the programme of the Tanzim, and elected its president, Dr Saifuddin Kitchlew, as its own honorary secretary, and the Congress sought All-India Hindu Mahasabha's support in the general elections of 1926 and many of its members including Pandit Motilal Nehru owed their victory to that party. Communal riots became a recurring phenomenon that widened the gulf between the two communities. The reasons for riots were often cow-sacrifice especially at the time of Idul Azha, playing of music in Hindu religious processions in front of mosques particularly at the time of prayers and on the occasion of Moharram, and the publication of sacrilegious literature such as the *Rangila Rasul* and *Risala Vartman* against Islam and Prophet Mohammad (PBUH). Riots occurred throughout India and left hardly any significant city or town unaffected by this 'infection'. Their severity did not diminish till after 1927. The riots in Kohat (NWFP), which started after the publication of an anti-Islam poem by Jivan Das, secretary of the Kohat Sanatan Dharma Sabha, and resulted in the temporary evacuation of almost the entire Hindu population from that city, caused rift between Gandhi and the Ali brothers who gave conflicting interpretations to these events. The All-India Muslim

League defended the Kohat Muslims, stating that they had been provoked into this action and had suffered more losses than the Hindus but appealed to their co-religionists to welcome the Hindus back into the city.[7]

Hindu–Muslim conflict in the Punjab was of a different nature, which absorbed the attention of the leaders of both the communities. Here, besides other reasons, the policies of Mian Fazli Husain as minister for education and local self-government added to communal tensions. Three major communities inhabiting Punjab were Muslims, Hindus and Sikhs. Muslims in comparison to Hindus were backward educationally and economically, and underrepresented in elective institutions and public services. Fazli Husain planned to give them their due share in education, local self-government and public services in accordance with the spirit of the Lucknow Pact. He allocated 40 per cent seats for the Muslim candidates in the colleges of Lahore — medical college, engineering college and government college — and raised Muslim representation in local self-government from 44 to 49 per cent. The reservations on communal basis were also extended to the newly opened intermediate colleges in the province. The Punjab government under Fazli Husain's influence made reservations in all the public services. These steps benefited the Muslims but hurt the vested interests of the Hindus who turned against him with vengeance and missed no opportunity to discredit him.[8] The press especially the vernacular newspapers intensified communal bitterness: the Hindu newspapers attacked him and his policies while their Muslim counterparts came to his defence. Communal hostility in the Punjab also affected Hindu–Muslim relations in other provinces. All attempts to resolve the conflict in the Punjab failed and the province was dubbed in frustration as the 'Ulster' of India.[9] Muslims had grievances in other provinces as well. For instance, in the United Provinces, the legislative council reduced Muslim representation in the district boards from 30 to 25 per cent despite unanimous opposition from the Muslim members.[10] Muslim under-representation in every aspect of life was more conspicuous in Bengal than anywhere else. They joined hands with the Hindus in the legislative council in the hope of getting due share but the Congress rejection of the Bengal Pact disappointed them.[11]

Muslims turned to the All-India Muslim League for support and guidance. The issue that moved them into action was the second elections to the legislatures under the Act of 1919. They made an abortive attempt to reactivate the party. The All-India Muslim League along with the Congress and other parties had boycotted the first elections. The issue of 'council entry' at the time of second elections became the subject of heated debate in all the political parties and caused sharp divisions in their ranks. The Congress and Central Khilafat Committee split up into two factions: (*i*) 'pro-changers' who called for entry into the councils by participating in the elections; and (*ii*) 'no-changers' who advocated continuation of the policy of boycott of the elections and non-cooperation outside the Legislatures. On 1 January 1923, Motilal Nehru and C.R. Das (1887–1925), who led the 'pro-changers', after their defeat at the Congress annual session in Gaya, established the 'Congress-Khilafat-Swaraj Party', which decided to participate in the elections and wreck the constitutional reforms from within the Legislatures. Later on, in September, the 'pro-changers' scored a victory when the Congress passed a permissive resolution, allowing its members to participate in the elections. The Swaraj Party took part in the elections and formed parties in various Legislatures, which eventually developed into parliamentary wings of the Congress. The All-India Muslim League as a party deprived itself of this electoral and legislative experience. In March 1923, it discussed a resolution on 'council entry' at its Lucknow session. The Central Khilafat Committee 'no-changers' who had retained their League membership attended the session with full force and prevented its adoption. Before the open session, the subjects committee adopted one resolution, moved by Dr M.A. Ansari, which called for the appointment of a committee to prepare a 'national pact' on specified lines in cooperation with the Congress, Central Khilafat Committee, Jamiatul Ulama-i-Hind, All-India Hindu Mahasabha and other representative bodies of various communities but rejected the main resolution, moved by Jinnah, which after a five-hour heated discussion recommended entry into the legislatures and demanded dominion status for India. The fate of Jinnah's resolution in the open session was quite uncertain and a conflict between pro-changers and no-changers seemed imminent, as the two groups were evenly balanced on the issue of council entry. The Leaguers wanted to avoid a clash. Therefore, when a member pointed out lack of quorum in the open session, the president adjourned the session *sine die*.[12] The indecision on the issue of council entry denied the League an opportunity to contest the elections and function in the legislatures as a party because unlike the Congress it faced no pressure to revise its decision. The Leaguers participated in these and subsequent elections as independent candidates. After the elections, many of them formed, or joined, non-communal parties in various legislatures, which was not compatible with the spirit of separate electorates. Among these parties were the Independent Party in the central assembly, the Krishak Praja Samity in the Bengal council and the Unionist Party in the Punjab council. Nobody thought of organizing League parties in the legislatures till the late 1930s.

(B) DEMANDS OF THE ALL-INDIA MUSLIM LEAGUE

The All-India Muslim League was reactivated at the Lahore annual session in May 1924. A majority of the Leaguers desired to coordinate its activities with the Central Khilafat Committee and Jamiatul Ulama-i-Hind to avoid a conflict in the objectives and working of these parties. It was suggested that the All-India Muslim League should focus on the political rights of the Indian Muslims, the Jamiatul Ulama-i-Hind on social issues and *tabligh*, and the Central Khilafat Committee on the issues of *Khilafat* and relations with the Muslim world.[13] The League discussed these issues at its Lahore session and appointed an eighteen-member committee to confer with the working committee of the Central Khilafat Committee to prepare a scheme for the organization of public activities of the community and present it before the council and, if necessary, at the next annual session.[14] Despite frantic efforts of Fazli Husain, who was one of its members, no meeting of the committee could be arranged. Zahur Ahmad, the honorary secretary, was blamed for not holding the meeting. At the Bombay annual session, the League re-emphasized the need to coordinate the activities of various Muslim associations and parties that represented 'different shades of political thought' in different parts of the country. The honorary secretary was directed to invite them to a meeting and fix 'a proper time and place' for a conference in consultation with them.[15] Now the honorary secretary did call a meeting of the Muslim associations in Delhi in February 1925, but nothing tangible could be worked out.[16] Members of the Central Khilafat Committee and other Muslim parties continued to participate in the League activities till the Nehru Report divided the Muslims. However, the League generally left the issues relating to *Khilafat* and the Muslim world to the Central Khilafat Committee and Jamiatul Ulama-i-Hind and rarely commented on them directly.[17]

(*i*) *The Demands*. Muslim thinking on constitutional issues had moved beyond the provisions of the Lucknow Pact. Those demands that the All-India Muslim League had been reluctant to advocate before 1920 now found receptive ears. Initially, it adopted them haphazardly but subsequently presented them in a consolidated form. The process began at the Lahore annual session (May 1924) and continued at the Bombay (December 1924), Aligarh (December 1925) and Delhi (December 1926) annual sessions. The first demand was for a federal system of government with limited powers vested in the Hindu-controlled majority at the centre. The Lucknow Pact had simply asked for the transfer of partial authority at the centre to the Indians as a first step towards self-government. By the time of the Amritsar annual session (December 1919), both the All-India Muslim League and the Congress were asking for 'full responsible government' or 'Swaraj', as enjoyed by other self-governing British colonies. The All-India Muslim League did not comment on the system of government although some Leaguers had put forward a few suggestions on this subject. Hasrat Mohani's proposals are quite well known. At the Ahmadabad annual session, he had asked the All-India Muslim League to adopt not only complete independence as its political goal but also to demand the formation of an Indian republic 'on the lines of the United States of America', where the Muslims would have authority in the Muslim majority provinces and the Hindus in the Hindu majority provinces in order to remove Hindu apprehensions about pan-Islam and Muslim fear of Hindu majority rule at the all-India centre.[18] At the Lahore session (May 1924), the All-India Muslim League formally demanded a federal system at the centre with the provinces having 'full and complete' autonomy and the authority of the federation confined to matters of 'general and common concern'. Then, at the Bombay annual session, the subjects committee reiterated this demand but the modified resolution adopted in the open session did not mention it.[19] The federal principle was, however, implied in the resolutions passed at the Aligarh and Delhi annual sessions that asked for fully autonomous provinces.

The second demand was to preserve Muslim majorities in the Muslim majority provinces. The All-India Muslim League had surrendered these majorities in Bengal and Punjab in the Lucknow Pact, accepting 40 per cent in Bengal and 50 per cent in the Punjab. This percentage was further reduced during the process of enactment and implementation of reforms under the Act of 1919. The working of the reforms made the Muslims realize its implications, when the Hindus opposed the extension of this percentage to other spheres. At that time, Bengal, Punjab and NWFP were the only three Muslim majority provinces; NWFP did not have constitutional reforms and British Balochistan was not a separate province. The All-India Muslim League aimed at protecting Muslim majorities in these provinces.[20] Attached to this issue was the principle of weightage for the minorities in the Hindu majority provinces. The League demanded 'adequate and effective' representation for the minorities in every province, ensuring, however, that the majority in any province would not be reduced to a minority or even to equality. It also emphasized that any territorial redistribution should not disturb Muslim majorities in Bengal, Punjab, and NWFP.[21] The subjects committee at the Bombay annual session did include Balochistan in this list as well but it was dropped in the open session perhaps because it did not have the status of a full-fledged province.[22] The reason for the reduction of slim Muslim majorities in Bengal and Punjab was partly the principle of weightage for the Hindu minorities in these provinces. It was now suggested that instead of these two provinces, the Hindus should be given weightage in NWFP, Sindh and Balochistan, where the Muslim proportion in the population was quite large.[23]

The third demand was for constitutional reforms in the NWFP. This issue remained in the limelight in the 1920s. The Afghan War, the Khilafat and Hijrat movements, military expedition in Waziristan and underground revolutionary activities in the NWFP made the British sensitive to even a minor development in this region. Muslims advocated constitutional reforms in the NWFP but Hindus demanded its re-merger with the Punjab. While the daily *Zamindar* (Lahore), in a series of articles entitled *Sar-zamin-i Be-A'in* ('Land without Constitutional Reforms'), analyzed the conditions in the NWFP and called for constitutional reforms but, on 21 July 1921, a Hindu member moved a resolution in the central assembly for a judicial merger of NWFP with the Punjab and for a review of its creation as a province. In February 1922, the government appointed an eight-member (3 Muslims, 2 Hindus and 3 British officials) committee to inquire into the issue of reforms.[24] This Frontier Enquiry Committee headed by Denys Bray, in its Majority Report, refuted the arguments against the reforms and made out a case for their introduction in the NWFP, as enjoyed by other provinces.[25] While the Muslim members of the Bray Committee unanimously called for reforms, the Hindu members dissented and demanded its re-merger with the Punjab. The All-India

Hindu Mahasabha and its ancillary bodies launched a systematic campaign and blocked the implementation of the Majority Report. The All-India Muslim League planned to raise this issue at its Lucknow annual session (1923) but it could not do that because the session was adjourned without completing its business.[26] When the adjourned session met in Lahore, the All-India Muslim League emphasized 'the immediate and the paramount necessity' of reforms in the NWFP to place it 'in a position of equality with the other major provinces'. The Bombay annual session reiterated this resolution.[27] But the government did not take any notice of these resolutions. Then, the Aligarh annual session asked the members of the central assembly and the Punjab council to press the government to implement the recommendations of the Majority Report of the Frontier Enquiry Committee.[28] On the suggestion of the All-India Muslim League, Syed Murtaza Bahadur, president of the Madras provincial Muslim League and a member of the Jinnah-led Independent Party, brought in the central assembly a resolution recommending extension of reforms to the NWFP. Muslims outside the assembly campaigned for its acceptance and Hindus held meetings demanding its rejection. Jinnah and his colleagues in the Independent Party supported the resolution but the Swarajists including Motilal Nehru opposed it.[29] As a result of Jinnah's strategy, the resolution was passed without a division. The government, however, did not take any steps to implement it. The All-India Muslim League reiterated this demand at the Delhi annual session, calling on the government to remove the apprehensions of the Muslims, not only of the NWFP but of the whole of India, in this matter.[30]

The fourth demand related to the separation of Sindh from the Bombay presidency and its formation into a separate province. Harchandrai Vishandas, a prominent Sindhi Hindu leader, was the first to raise the issue of separation of Sindh from the Congress platform; but after him, the Congress consistently opposed the demand when the Sindhi Muslims began to voice it from 1920 onward.[31] The All-India Muslim League took notice of the demand at its Lahore session in May 1924, when a resolution was drafted but it was not moved in the open session. At the Bombay annual session, the party formally took up the issue of separation of Sindh from Bombay in a resolution that Rafiuddin Ahmad moved and Gul Mohammad Khan seconded. It was argued that there was no ethnological, geographical or any other basis to keep Sindh with the Bombay presidency and that this arrangement had proved detrimental not only to the best interests of the Sindhis but had also affected the development of that area. It was demanded that Sindh should be separated from Bombay and constituted into a separate province.[32] This resolution was passed at the Bombay annual session and reiterated at the subsequent annual sessions of the All-India Muslim League.

Another demand was about the protection of religious rights, laws and ceremonies of the Muslims, which recurrent communal riots had brought to spotlight. It was suggested that Hindu–Muslim conciliation boards should be set up at the district level with a central board in the capital of every province to settle communal disputes; as a result, some boards were established but these could not develop into regular institutions.[33] The All-India Muslim League demanded full religious liberty, i.e. liberty of belief, worship, observances, propaganda, association and education, for all the communities. A resolution of similar content was passed at every session. Another protection that the League sought for the Muslims was that no bill or resolution should be passed in any legislature or in any elected body, if three-fourth members of any community in that body opposed it on the ground that it would be injurious to the interests of that community.[34] Again, this resolution was reiterated at every session. On the issue of electorates, the All-India Muslim League slightly modified its inflexible stance. It called for the representation of communal groups by separate electorates, with the proviso that any community at any time could abandon separate electorates in favour of joint electorates.[35] The Punjab experience moved the All-India Muslim League to press for adequate Muslim representation in public services. The Lahore session asked the central council to appoint a committee to investigate Muslim grievances regarding their inadequate representation in public services and submit a report with suggestions for remedial measures. When the central council did not take any action on this resolution, the Bombay session asked the 34-member committee, which had been appointed to consider the proportion of Muslim representation in various legislatures, to formulate proposals to determine Muslim share in public services. Again, this committee failed to do any work, and the Aligarh session simply urged the Government of India and the provincial governments to take suitable steps to secure adequate jobs for the Muslims in various services. The Delhi session reiterated a resolution of almost similar content.[36] Following the actions taken by the Punjab government, other provinces also fixed quotas for the Muslims in public services. Later on, in 1934, when Fazli Husain was member of the Viceroy's Executive

Council, the Government of India reserved 25 per cent of all vacancies for the Muslims, laying down the procedure to ensure that, and they could also be considered for additional vacancies out of the quota reserved for other minorities.[37]

The All-India Muslim League took interest in several other issues of a topical nature. The violent revolutionary movement in Bengal was such an issue. The governor general had promulgated an ordinance that gave the government arbitrary powers to curb civil liberties to control violence. The All-India Muslim League discussed this issue at its Bombay session. It disapproved the violence but asked the government to withdraw the ordinance because it did not have the approval of the legislature. It called for trial according to ordinary law of all those who had been detained under its provisions. It also demanded the withdrawal of Regulation III of 1818, which empowered the government to arrest and confine persons suspected of public crimes without warrant, without trial and without giving them the reasons for such arrests or confinement.[38] The League asked the government to release the detainees in Bengal or to put them on trial without delay.[39] It also took notice of the situation in the state of Jammu and Kashmir. At the Lahore session, it pointed out the socio-economic and political backwardness of the 95 per cent 'poor and down-trodden' Muslims of the state, and called upon the Kashmir durbar to provide them special facilities for education and give them the 'rightful place in the public services' to ameliorate their 'present hopeless condition'.[40] The maharaja, in response to these moves, enacted the Agricultural Relief Act to give relief to the agriculturists in the state. Some of the other issues on which the All-India Muslim League passed resolutions were: elementary education, female education, adult education, boy scouts movement, use of swadeshi goods, establishment of Muslim banks, and formation of cooperative societies, cooperative stores and mortgage banks.[41] It also took keen interest in the affairs of the Indians in South Africa particularly the Muslims.[42]

(ii) *Delhi Muslim Proposals.* In 1926, communalism intensified and the frequency of riots increased. The casualty figures that year, according to official estimates, were 176 dead and 2,207 injured, which was the highest in that decade; the riots in Calcutta and Rawalpindi in particular were brutal.[43] The Hindu nationalists in and out of the Congress had all along erroneously put the blame for the Hindu–Muslim conflict solely on the system of separate electorates, which they regarded harmful for the development of a united democratic Indian polity. From 1922 onward, the All-India Hindu Mahasabha and its ancillary bodies had launched a concerted campaign against the system of separate electorates. In April 1926, the Mahasabha at its ninth annual session appealed to the Hindus of 'all shades of opinion' for a 'determined stand' against separate electorates. It built up steady pressure that deeply influenced Hindu thinking. Its propaganda influenced even Lord Olivier, a former secretary of state for India, and Lord Irwin (1881– 1959), the viceroy, who publicly spoke against separate electorates, and opposed their extension to other spheres. The Muslims, however, stuck to the system, believing that such observations showed ignorance about the real reasons behind the introduction of separate electorates.[44] Fazli Husain emphasized the need for a response to the All-India Hindu Mahasabha's propaganda campaign, and Sir Abdur Rahim went through all the judgments of the higher courts in cases of communal riots to show that there was no connection between riots and separate electorates.[45] Nonetheless, the All-India Hindu Mahasabha accelerated its anti-separate electorate campaign in the general elections of November 1926. Besides the victory of its own candidates in these elections, several Congressmen owed their success to its support.[46] This factor enhanced its influence with the Congress whose leaders actively participated in the anti-separate electorate campaign. The turning point was the assassination of the Sangathan leader, Swami Shradhanand, a few days before the annual session of the All-India Muslim League in Delhi. The League expressed its profound regret at this 'horrible outrage' but simultaneously condemned the assault on Muslims by the Hindus in retaliation, in which one Muslim lost his life, and hoped that such incidents would move the leaders to work for Hindu–Muslim unity.[47]

The anti-separate electorates campaign disturbed those Leaguers who believed in Hindu–Muslim unity as a prerequisite for responsible government in India. Jinnah was one of them. He took the initiative; and on 17 March 1927, as permanent president of the All-India Muslim League, he invited under his own signatures seventy-two prominent Muslims from different parts of India including members of the central legislative assembly and council of state to meet in Delhi on 20 March 'to discuss Hindu–Muslim settlement'. Telegraphic messages were sent to those who were out of Delhi. Several invitees expressed their inability to attend this consultative meeting at such a short notice.[48] Nevertheless, thirty leading Indian Muslims including Leaguers and

Khilafatists turned up. After intense deliberations, they consolidated some Muslim demands that had been put forward since the Lahore session (May 1924). The formula formally signed by them laid down that the Muslims were prepared to accept joint electorates provided: (*i*) Muslim representation in the central legislature was not less than one-third; (*ii*) proportion of Muslim representation in Bengal and the Punjab was in accordance with their population; (*iii*) Sindh was separated from Bombay and constituted into a separate province; (*iv*) reforms were introduced in the NWFP and Balochistan on the same footing as in any other province; and (*v*) Muslims would make to the Hindu minorities in Sindh, NWFP and Balochistan the same concessions that the Hindu majorities in other provinces would make to the Muslim minorities.[49] The final shape of the Delhi Proposals, as this formula was commonly referred to, was subject to ratification by the All-India Muslim League, the Congress and other Hindu and Muslim parties. It was hoped that they would ratify the proposals. Jinnah issued a clarification on 29 March, that the Delhi Proposals were inter-dependent and could be accepted or rejected in toto without any modification.[50] The Muslims who took the radical decision of abandoning separate electorates included some of its staunch supporters. But the response from the Hindus was neither immediate nor in the same spirit in which the Muslims had made the Proposals. The Hindu nationalists denounced them as 'petty bargaining', terming, for instance, the separation of Sindh as partitioning the Indian subcontinent into Hindu India and Muslim India.[51] The All-India Hindu Mahasabha, at its tenth session in April 1927, opposed the creation of new provinces and directed its working committee to prepare its own proposals on the basis of joint electorates. It called on the All India Congress Committee that any decision on the Delhi Proposals on its part would be 'premature and harmful'.[52] As a result, the All India Congress Committee did not accept the Delhi Proposals till May, and its open session ratified that decision in December. By that time new elements had been introduced into the debate. The Delhi Proposals, a landmark in communal relations, were, however, not the first move to form a united Hindu–Muslim stand for the political advancement of India.

(C) ATTEMPTS AT RAPPROCHEMENT

In the 1920s, quite a few attempts were made to work out a new joint Hindu–Muslim scheme to replace the Lucknow Pact. The Congress, at its Gaya session in December 1922, appointed a committee to prepare a 'national pact'; Dr M.A. Ansari, Lala Lajpat Rai and one Sikh were its members. Similarly, the All-India Muslim League on Dr Ansari's motion appointed its own committee at its Lucknow session. The League committee did not accomplish anything concrete. But before the Congress committee could finalize its report, C.R. Das, leader of the Swaraj Party in the Bengal council, negotiated with three Muslim leaders of Bengal—Sir Abdur Rahim, Dr Abdullah al-Mamun Suhrawardy (1875–1935) and Huseyn Shaheed Suhrawardy (1893–1963)—, and signed an agreement, commonly known as the Bengal Pact, which the Bengal provincial Congress committee ratified on 16 December 1923. This pact made some liberal concessions to the Bengali Muslims; it provided that Muslim representation in the Bengal legislature should be on the basis of population and by separate electorates. Muslim–Hindu ratio in the local self-government should be 60:40 in the districts where the Muslims were in the majority and vice versa. Muslim share in services should be 55 per cent and they be given 80 per cent share in fresh recruitments till that ratio was reached. In addition, it was agreed that music before mosques would be stopped and Muslims would have the right to sacrifice cow.[53] In return, Muslim members pledged to support the Swaraj Party in the Bengal council. The support of the twenty Muslim members in the Bengal council enabled the Swarajists to make the reforms unworkable in Bengal. The only other province where the Swarajists could score such a victory was Central Provinces. Muslim members in the Bengal legislature so loyally stuck to the Bengal Pact that they even voted against the demand for the much-needed grant for the Dhaka university.[54] But the Congress at its Cocanada annual session rejected the Bengal Pact and referred the national pact that its own committee had prepared to a new committee for reconsideration. Nobody heard of the national pact after that, and the Bengal provincial Congress committee could not revive the Bengal Pact even after its re-endorsement in May 1925.[55]

The All-India Muslim League made the next attempt. At its Lahore session (May 1924), it appointed a sixteen-member committee to draft a constitution in consultation with the committee(s) that might be appointed by other political parties.[56] Zahur Ahmad (honorary secretary), approached the office-bearers of four political parties: Pandit Jawaharlal Nehru (secretary, Indian National Congress); C.R. Das (president, Swaraj Party), C.Y. Chintamani (1880–1941; secretary, Indian Liberal Federation), and secretary of the Home Rule League, requesting them to appoint similar committees. The response was disappointing. Chintamani supported the idea but promised a reply after the annual session of the Liberal Federation. The Home Rule League expressed its inability to respond as Mrs Annie Besant, its president, was in London and there was no reply at all from the Swaraj Party. The Congress response reflected the perception of the Congress leaders about the nature of Congress–League relations that had developed during the Khilafat movement. Jawaharlal Nehru, in a letter to Zahur Ahmad, informed him that the Congress was engaged in an intensive constructive programme and had paid 'little attention' to draft 'a model constitution for India' but promised to place his letter before the Congress working committee.[57] When the working committee discussed Zahur Ahmad's letter on 3 October, the committee considered it inadvisable 'to appoint a committee at present to go into this matter'. Jawaharlal Nehru, however, invited the League committee to attend the forthcoming session of the Congress at Belgaum and raise the issue there. On Zahur Ahmad's query, as to the capacity in which the members of the League committee would attend the Congress session, Jawaharlal responded that the Lucknow district Congress committee or the United Provinces provincial Congress committee could elect members of the League committee as delegates and asked Zahur Ahmad to approach the provincial committee for this purpose. Enclosing a copy of the constitution and rules of the United Provinces provincial Congress committee, Jawaharlal added: 'No particular discussion is contemplated, so far as I am aware, but it is open to any member of the Subjects Committee to bring any subject, and it is highly likely that the subject you mention will be brought up. There is no intention at present to appoint a Committee.'[58] In view of this response, the All-India Muslim League dropped the whole idea of drafting a constitution.

After Gandhi's fast and an unfruitful unity conference in September 1924, the Congress took its own initiative and sponsored an All Parties Conference in Bombay on 21 November. The All Parties Conference appointed a large unwieldy committee representing different political parties with Pandit Motilal Nehru as its secretary (*i*) to prepare an agreed scheme of *Swaraj*, (*ii*) to recommend the proportion of representation of different communities in various legislatures and services, and (*iii*) to suggest steps to enable all the political parties to join the Congress.[59] The committee asked the secretary to invite suggestions from the political parties and associations to find a basis for the 'union of all parties within the Congress'. When Motilal corresponded with Zahur Ahmad on this proposal, the latter referred him to the 'independent nature' of the League organization, observing that its cooperation with the Congress in the past had been 'in the best interests of the country'. Its members had been free to join the Congress and one of its founder members, Maulana Mohammad Ali, was currently its all-India president. He referred to the League initiative taken earlier, which the Congress working committee had rejected on 3 October. The League, he wrote, could not merge itself into the Congress or become a branch of the Congress because its objective was to synthesize 'opinions of all shades of political thought among the Indian Muslims'. He informed Motilal that the League committee appointed at the Bombay session was ready to confer with any committee that might be appointed by the Congress, and circulated his correspondence with Motilal among the members of the League council. On this, Motilal complained that his letters had been misunderstood, expressing the hope that the League would take a 'more reasonable view' of the correspondence.[60] Zahur Ahmad replied that he had never meant 'to cast aspersions on any one' and believed that Motilal would regret the 'strictures' that he had passed when he would read the 'correspondence again in calmer moments'. The Congress proceeded with the All Parties Conference under its umbrella. Jinnah was among those Leaguers who responded to the Congress initiative, and was optimistic about a Hindu–Muslim settlement.[61] Mian Shafi, Maulana Mohammad Ali, Abul Kalam Azad, Saifuddin Kitchlew, Mushir Husain Kidwai, and Sahibzada Abdul Qayyum were among the other Muslim participants. When the All Parties Conference committee met in Delhi on 23 January 1925, Jinnah remarked at the outset, 'we have come to sit with you as co-workers. Let us put our heads together not as Hindus and Muslims but as Indians. Do you want to discuss or do you want to wait? The choice is yours'.[62] He asked for the revision of the Lucknow Pact to incorporate the Muslim demands that the All-India Muslim League had put forward at the Bombay annual session. Lala Lajpat Rai, who spoke after Jinnah, opposed the Muslim demands particularly the demand for separate electorates and demanded weightage for the Sikhs in the Punjab. The All Parties Conference committee then appointed a forty-member subcommittee with the same mandate as that of the larger committee. But the Hindus and Muslims stuck to their respective positions. Then, Lajpat Rai dissociated himself from the subcommittee, stating that there was no 'hurry for a fresh pact' and declined to accept the view that a Hindu majority in some provinces and a Muslim majority in others was 'the only remedy' of the communal problem. Jinnah firmly stuck to the Muslim demands for which the Hindu leaders and press criticized him for advocating 'special Muslim interests'. Jinnah in defence argued that he had done that as a representative of the Muslims and called for a 'representative government as a first step' before the ideal of 'establishing a democratic government' in India. On 5 March, after the All Parties Conference subcommittee had failed to evolve a 'united scheme', Gandhi and Motilal jointly announced its adjournment *sine die*.[63]

Lord Birkenhead's (1872–1930) challenge to his Indian critics to frame a constitution for India acceptable to different communities prompted the next move. The Delhi Proposals were meant to meet this challenge and facilitate the framing of an agreed constitution. But the apathetic Hindu response to these proposals started a debate among the Leaguers about the advisability of abandoning separate electorates.[64] On 2 May 1927, the Punjab provincial Muslim League reaffirmed its faith in the principle of separate electorates.[65] Before the all-India session, the All-India Muslim League council tried to evolve a broad Muslim consensus on the Delhi Proposals. The council convened a consultative meeting in Simla on 9–10 September, to which representatives of the Central Khilafat Committee, Jamiatul Ulama-i-Hind, Tabligh and other Muslim associations were invited. Jinnah advised the central League office not to 'leave out anyone who may afterwards feel aggrieved. I would be rather on the side of inviting more than less.'[66] The League office issued about four hundred invitations. Jinnah presided over the meeting. The discussion centred on the issue of separate electorates. Firoz Khan Noon (1893–1970) led the opposition to joint electorates while Mohammad Yaqub put up the defence. A majority of those present were against the acceptance of joint electorates in any form, although there was no voting and the debate was closed after a summary by the president, M.A. Jinnah. It was decided to hold another consultative meeting in Delhi after the results of the multiparty unity conference were known. The issue of electorates was now mixed up with the Simon Commission, which divided the All-India Muslim League into two parties, the Jinnah League and the Shafi League. The Jinnah League adopted the Delhi Proposals at its Calcutta session in a slightly modified form. Resolution number four of this session called for the acceptance of joint electorates only after Sindh had been actually constituted into a separate province and reforms were introduced in the NWFP and Balochistan. The resolution required that no bill or resolution on inter-communal matters would be moved, discussed or passed in any legislature or in any other elected body, if three-fourth members of the community affected thereby opposed the motion. It also called for guarantees in the future constitution of liberty of conscience, i.e. liberty of belief and worship, freedom of religious observances and association, and freedom to carry on religious education and propaganda with due regard to the feelings of others, and without interfering with similar rights of others. Clauses (*i*) and (*iv*) of the Delhi Proposals were not changed. The Jinnah League authorized its council to confer with the Congress working committee or with such other organizations as it might consider proper.[67]

The Delhi Proposals were shelved for three reasons: the opposition of the All-India Hindu Mahasabha; lukewarm support of the Congress; and fissures in the All-India Muslim League. While the Shafi League cooperated with the Simon Commission, the Jinnah League initially engaged itself with the Congress on the basis of resolution four of its Calcutta session. The Congress working committee convened an All Parties Conference in Delhi on 12–22 February 1928, which the All-India Hindu Mahasabha, Liberal Federation, Sikh League, and other associations attended. The Jinnah League appointed a committee to represent its viewpoint at the Conference. The All Parties Conference decided to frame a constitution on the basis of joint electorates; full responsible government with reservation of seats for the present (the All-India Hindu Mahasabha opposed reservations of seats for majorities in any province); re-distribution of provinces on linguistic basis; introduction of an administrative system in the new provinces similar to the one prevalent in the old provinces; and reciprocal concessions for the minorities in the provinces.[68] The Jinnah League immediately responded to the All Parties Conference's decision and the All-India Hindu Mahasabha's stance on its demands. Its council resolved to hold a meeting of representatives of the Central Khilafat Committee, Jamiatul Ulama-i-Hind, Tabligh Conference, Ahle Hadith, and Jamaat-i-Ahmadiyya of Qadian and Lahore 'to define the Muslim attitude'; and the League secretary issued about five hundred invitation letters.[69] The council in this meeting resolved that the Congress-sponsored All Parties Conference's decisions were not 'in conformity' with resolution four of its Calcutta session, and regretted that the All-India Hindu Mahasabha had practically rejected its proposals. It appointed a thirteen-member committee to confer with various organizations to apprise them of the viability of resolution four.[70] But it failed to achieve anything positive because the Congress did not wait for an agreement with its committee. On 19 May, the Congress-sponsored All Parties Conference appointed a committee to frame a constitution for India; Motilal Nehru was its president and Jawaharlal, his son, its secretary. Two members of the Jinnah League, Ali Imam and Shoaib Qureshi, without the approval of the party, were included in this committee. But even they did not participate in its proceedings. Ali Imam fell ill and Shoaib Qureshi withdrew from its deliberations at an early stage because the committee had not accepted resolution four in its entirety.[71] Both of them did not sign the final report. The All Parties Conference committee drafted a scheme, better known as the Nehru Report, which another All Parties Conference approved in Lucknow. The Jinnah League was invited to this conference but it did not send any delegate. A few Leaguers, however, attended this conference in their individual capacity. The Nehru Report recommended dominion status for India; a unitary form of government with residuary powers vested in the centre; no weightage for the Muslim minorities in the Hindu majority provinces; no reservation of seats for the Muslims at the centre; formation of Sindh as a separate province if financial consideration allowed; and introduction of constitutional reforms in the NWFP after the promulgation of a constitution based on the Nehru Report.

The Nehru Report divided the Muslims into three groups. One group, which included the Shafi League, vehemently opposed the Report and unsuccessfully tried to unite the Leagues on this basis.[72] It organized an All-Muslim Parties conference in Delhi in December to formulate Muslim demands; the Aga Khan presided over this conference. The second group supported the report unreservedly.[73] The third group that included the Jinnah League neither accepted the report nor rejected it but wanted a few major changes in its contents. The Jinnah League at its Calcutta session decided to send a 23-member delegation to attend the All-India National Convention that the Congress convened to approve the Nehru Report. Jinnah who led this delegation raised four demands at the convention that:

1. Muslim representation in the central legislature should not be less than one-third of its total membership;

2. Bengal and Punjab should have seats in the provincial legislatures on the basis of population in case adult franchise was introduced, subject to its re-examination after ten years;
3. residuary powers should vest in the provinces and not in the centre; and
4. separation of Sindh from Bombay and its formation into a separate province and introduction of reforms in the NWFP should not be contingent upon the introduction of a constitution based on the Nehru Report.[74]

He placed these demands first before a committee that the All-India National Convention appointed to examine the proposed amendments in the Nehru Report but the committee turned them down. Jinnah did not give up and raised the amendments in the open session. Sir Tej Bahadur Sapru (1875–1949), leader of the Indian Liberal Federation, supported him and asked the delegates to accept his demands but M.R. Jayakar (1873–1959), leader of the All-India Hindu Mahasabha, vehemently opposed their acceptance. Jinnah passionately appealed, 'We are sons of this land, [and] we have to live together. We have to work together and whatever our differences may be let us not arouse bad blood'.[75] But his arguments and pleas did not convince the convention to change its position. Instead, he had to hear strictures on his representative credentials. His proposals regarding one-third Muslim representation in the central legislature, vesting of residuary powers in the provinces and an alternative to adult franchise were all rejected one by one.[76] His delegation went back to the Jinnah League that was in session disillusioned. The League session was adjourned, and the central council was directed to summon the adjourned session at a suitable place and time in future.

On 3 March 1929, the council of the Jinnah League decided to hold the adjourned session in Delhi during the Easter holidays on 30–31 March to formulate united demands of the Muslims. It authorized Jinnah to work out an agreed formula in consultation with leaders of various 'schools of thought'.[77] Jinnah met with Mian Shafi who agreed to send delegates of his party to the adjourned session. The Shafi League sent a ten-member delegation that included Mian Shafi himself, Allama Iqbal, Shaikh Abdul Qadir (1874–1950) and Firoz Khan Noon.[78] The pro-Nehru Report Leaguers were not sitting idle. They were desperate to get the League's endorsement to their viewpoint. On the meeting day, while Jinnah who was to preside over the session was busy negotiating with one group at the residence of the ailing Hakim Ajmal Khan, they started the proceedings in his absence. Dr Mohammad Alam (1887–1947), a Leaguer from the Punjab, occupied the presidential chair and hurriedly declared amidst confusion and uproar that Abdur Rahman Ghazi's (1889–1976) resolution supporting the Nehru Report had been adopted. Jinnah arrived right at that moment. On his arrival, silence prevailed. When he was apprised of the situation, he briefly addressed the gathering and then adjourned the meeting *sine die*, announcing that the League would meet again to discuss the situation.[79] Jinnah had prepared a formula in accordance with the direction of the central council after consulting Muslims of different schools of thought. This formula, called Jinnah's Fourteen Points, articulated all the Muslim demands that had been made since the introduction of constitutional reforms including those made at the All Muslim Parties Conference in Delhi. It was moved at the session in the form of a resolution; and it laid down that no future constitution would be acceptable to the Muslims unless it was based on the following principles:

1. Federal form of government with the residuary powers vested in the provinces;
2. Uniform measure of autonomy to all the provinces;
3. Adequate and effective representation of the minorities in every legislature and elected bodies of the country without reducing the majority in any province to a minority or even equality;
4. Muslim representation in the central legislature not to be less than one-third;
5. Separate electorates for the communal groups, provided any community could abandon its separate electorates in favour of joint electorates;
6. Any territorial redistribution would not affect the Muslim majority in Punjab, Bengal and NWFP;
7. Full religious liberty, i.e. liberty of belief, worship and observance, propaganda, association and education, would be guaranteed to all communities;
8. No bill, or resolution or any part thereof should be passed in any legislature or elected body if three-fourth members of any community in that body opposed it on the ground that it would be injurious to the interests of that community or an alternative would be devised;

9. Sindh should be separated from the Bombay presidency;
10. Reforms should be introduced in the NWFP and Balochistan as in other provinces;
11. Adequate representation of the Muslims in the state services and in local self-government with due regard to the requirements of efficiency;
12. Adequate safeguards for the protection of Muslim culture and for the promotion of Muslim education, language, religion, personal laws and Muslim charitable institutions;
13. At least one-third share for the Muslims in the central and all the provincial cabinets;
14. Changes in the constitution would be made with the concurrence of the States constituting the Indian federation.

The Fourteen Points maintained that Muslim representation by separate electorates in the legislative bodies was inevitable, which could not be taken away from them without their consent, and that they would not accept joint electorates unless their rights and interests in the preceding points were safeguarded.[80]

The acceptance of the Nehru Report at the Calcutta National Convention bridged the gulf between the Jinnah League and the Shafi League and united them into one party in March 1930. This decision, however, did not stop the transformation of the All-Muslim Parties Conference into a regular party, the All-India Muslim Conference. Even otherwise, the unified League did not produce any notable results. Although Allama Iqbal's idea of a separate Muslim state in northwest India from its platform in his Allahabad address momentarily attracted public attention but it was neither adopted by the party as its goal nor did it transform the League into a broad-based party. His address, however, inspired Muslim writers, intellectuals, youth and politicians who wrote about, or organized a movement for, a separate Muslim state before and after 23 March 1940. The League continued to comment on issues of a topical nature. For instance, it strongly protested against the refusal of the Punjab and NWFP governments to grant passports to the Punjab Medical and Afghan Red Crescent missions that wanted to go to Afghanistan for humanitarian assistance. Earlier, in December 1928, it had appreciated King Amanullah Khan's (1890–1939) efforts to make Afghanistan a 'great and progressive country'.[81] The League recorded its protest against the Balochistan government, which had refused the passage of Abdul Ghaffar Khan and Mian Jafar Shah (b. 1903) to

Qandhar.[82] The Muslim political forces were otherwise dispersed into several minor political parties in the post-Nehru Report era; some were supportive of the League position and others hostile or indifferent to its stance. More significant among these parties were the All-India Muslim Conference, All-India Nationalist Muslims Conference, Majlis-i-Ahrar-i-Islam, Khudai Khidmatgars and Khaksar movement. Meanwhile, Jinnah interacted with the British and Hindu leaders to bring about responsible government through constitutional reforms. His attempts were in continuation of the struggle that had begun after the introduction of the Act of 1919.

The Congress had declared at the Calcutta National Convention that if the British government did not accept the Nehru Report by 31 December 1929, it would declare complete independence of India and launch a civil disobedience movement to achieve that objective. Attempts were made to prevent a clash. Jinnah made his own efforts. Early in 1930, he supported Sir Tej Bahadur Sapru's move to convene another All Parties Conference to bring about communal harmony. There were a couple of preliminary meetings but the idea did not draw any broad support. Then, Jinnah himself took the initiative. He wrote to the newly elected Labour Prime Minister, Ramsey MacDonald (1866–1937), whom he knew from the time he had worked with him on a commission in 1913, asking him to hold a round table conference to find a solution of the constitutional problem of India. This was not the first initiative on this issue. Several others had preceded it.

(D) BRITISH INITIATIVES, ALL-INDIA MUSLIM LEAGUE AND THE REFORMS

Section 84A of the Act of 1919 stipulated the appointment of a statutory commission within ten years of its introduction to examine the working of the reforms. However, as early as September 1921, the central legislative assembly had demanded a review of the reforms but the secretary of state for India declined to do that as, according to him, sufficient time had not elapsed to test them. In January 1922, Jinnah and Pandit Madan Mohan Malaviya made an unsuccessful attempt to organize a government–Congress–All-India Muslim League round table conference to settle, among other issues, the issue of 'Swaraj'.[83] The following year, during the budget session, the central assembly twice emphasized the need for immediate constitutional advance but there was no response from the British government. Then, in the second assembly in February 1924, Motilal Nehru moved an amendment to T. Rangachariar's (1868–1945) resolution that demanded a representative round table conference to recommend, with due regard to the protection of different minorities, a scheme of constitution for India and to submit it to the parliament for enactment after its approval by a newly elected central assembly. Jinnah as the leader of the independents in the central assembly supported Motilal's amendment and facilitated its adoption by a large majority.[84] Major political parties at their all-India sessions that year adopted resolutions to endorse this amendment. The All-India Muslim League, at its Lahore session, demanded a 'complete overhaul' of the Act of 1919 to establish full responsible government and spelt out the safeguards that it required for the Muslims. On 24 June 1924, the government appointed an eight-member committee of official and non-official members, chaired by Sir Alexander Muddiman, to investigate the working of the reforms in order to recommend any amendments in the Act to remove its 'imperfections'. The Muddiman Committee included two Muslims: M.A. Jinnah and Mian Shafi, then Law Member in the Government of India.[85]

The All-India Muslim League did not submit any proposals to the Muddiman Committee. The League council, when pressed by its members to do that, sent the resolutions adopted at the Lahore session to the committee; in addition, it demanded the abolition of the system of dyarchy, restriction on the powers of the governors and those of the central government on the provincial governments, and adequate and effective Muslim representation in all the elected bodies and public services.[86] The Punjab provincial Muslim League was the only branch of the All-India Muslim League that submitted a Memorandum to the Muddiman Committee; Malik Barkat Ali, one of its vice-presidents, also gave evidence on its behalf.[87] The Muddiman Committee submitted two reports, a majority report and a minority report: the majority report observed that the Indians had gained valuable experience in responsible government under the reforms but the terms of reference of the committee prevented it from making any recommendations inconsistent with the Act; and the minority report concluded that the system of dyarchy had failed and a new constitution should be framed on a permanent basis. The minority was transformed into a majority when Mian Shafi supported the minority report after he left the portfolio of law member. In May 1925, the council of the All-India Muslim League supported the minority report and, at its Aligarh annual session, demanded the appointment of a royal commission to prepare a constitution to establish responsible government in India, with safeguards for the Muslims.[88] The League reiterated this resolution at its Delhi annual session. Jinnah-led Independents and the Swarajists missed no opportunity in the central assembly to press for the appointment of a royal commission to revise the Act. Finally, on 18 November 1927, the British government appointed a statutory commission under the chairmanship of Sir John Simon (1873–1954), but it had no Indian as its member. The non-representation of Indians caused widespread disappointment. Jinnah who had urged the viceroy to secure the inclusion of at least two Indians commanding 'the confidence of political-minded' Hindus and Muslims in the commission felt deeply hurt; for him the exclusion of Indians from the commission was the 'butchery of the soul' of India.[89]

The Simon Commission caused a split in the All-India Muslim League: the Shafi League cooperated with the commission and its members served on the Indian central committee composed of members of the central assembly and the council of state that toured India along with the commission, while the Jinnah League boycotted the commission and many of its members actively cooperated with those parties that organized the boycott. The Congress adoption of the Nehru Report, its ultimatum to the government for its acceptance, and the successful boycott of the commission contrary to the viceroy's calculations, killed any positive effect that the commission and its report might have had on the constitutional developments. The All-India Muslim League council considered the report as the 'most unsatisfactory and inadequate' document, as its authors had refused to accept 'vital' Muslim demands including the one for separate electorates.[90] There was a deadlock. Now Jinnah promoted the idea of a round table conference. On 19 June 1929, in a letter to Prime Minister MacDonald, he asked for steps to break the 'serious deadlock'. Political India, he wrote, had boycotted the statutory commission and similar fate awaited its recommendations and those of the Government of India, which he assumed would be 'reactionary'. India, he felt, had lost faith in Britain, which needed to be restored. Britain should declare unequivocally that it was pledged to give dominion status to India. He suggested that the prime minister should invite a round table conference of about fifteen representative Indian political leaders before the constitutional proposals were finalized for enactment by parliament. The prime minister must have discussed Jinnah's proposal with Lord Irwin, the viceroy, who was at that time in England on a four-month leave. He responded to Jinnah's letter on 14 August, communicating that the recommendations of the commission would not be more than an 'advice' to the government, and that Britain intended to give dominion status to India as Lord Irwin had announced in the central assembly on 29 January 1929.[91] Jinnah's influence was reflected in Irwin's announcement which he made on his return from England on 31 October, that Britain's intention, implicit in the Declaration of August 1917 was to give dominion status to India and that the British government intended to invite representatives of different parties and interests in British India and the states to prepare proposals for the parliament that might 'command a wide measure of general assent'.[92]

The Congress laid down pre-conditions for its participation in the round table conference, that: the discussions at the round table conference should be based on full dominion status; the Congress be given 'predominant representation' at the round table conference; amnesty be announced for all political prisoners; and the Government of India should be run immediately as far as possible on the lines of a dominion government.[93] There was a possibility of an open conflict. Jinnah was keen to prevent that. He corresponded with the viceroy and the Congress leaders, and also held a meeting with Gandhi where Vithalbhai J. Patel (1873–1933) and his brother Vallabhbhai (1875–1950) were also present. It was agreed that five leaders (Gandhi, Jinnah, Vithalbhai Patel, Motilal Nehru and Tej Bahadur Sapru) should meet the viceroy.[94] As agreed, the viceroy invited them to a meeting by telephonic messages. However, their discussions failed to produce any agreement but Sapru still believed that it was 'impossible to get a settlement' without Jinnah's 'cooperation and guidance'.[95] Then, the Congress opted for complete independence, which was declared on 26 January 1930, and called on the All India Congress Committee to start civil disobedience including non-payment of taxes where it deemed fit. Since the All-India Muslim League did not hold any all-India session that year, its council, in February 1930, welcomed the announcement about the round table conference. Muslims generally held aloof from the Congress-sponsored civil disobedience movement except the Khudai Khidmatgars under the leadership of Abdul Ghaffar Khan. The government crushed the movement in the NWFP with unusual severity, before as well as after Gandhi's participation in the second Round Table Conference. The All-India Muslim League council asked the Congress to call off the civil disobedience movement and urged the government to withdraw all repressive measures to create a proper atmosphere for the round table conference. It also drew the attention of the government to the 'serious situation' in the NWFP and asked for 'proper steps in consultation with the leaders to restore tranquillity and harmonious normal conditions'.[96] It asked for the announcement of a schedule of the round table conference at an early date to avoid any further aggravation of the situation.[97]

The first Round Table Conference was held in London on 12 November 1930. The British government selected the 89 delegates; 58 of them represented various communities and interests of British India including 16 Muslims; and the remaining were taken from the States. The Congress boycotted the first Round Table Conference, which concluded on 19 January 1931, and Gandhi was its sole representative at the second Round Table Conference, which was held from 7 September to 1 December 1931, after the signing of the Gandhi–Irwin Pact. The All-India Hindu Mahasabha and the Liberal delegates represented the viewpoint of the Hindus. The discussion of communal issues created repeated deadlocks at the second Round Table Conference. Consequently, the prime minister intervened and promised to announce his own decision if there was no agreement among the delegates. As the delegates failed to arrive at an agreement, on 2 August 1932, a communal award was issued in an official announcement. The third Round Table Conference sat in the winter of 1932–33, and simply dealt with minor and technical issues.

The All-India Muslim League as a party had no role in the selection of Muslim delegates to the round table conferences although Jinnah was perhaps consulted in the selection of a few delegates to the first Round Table Conference and Fazli Husain, then member of the Viceroy's Executive Council, for the second and third Round Table Conferences.[98] All the delegates were selected for their eminence in public life at the provincial and all-India levels. Most of the Muslim delegates were, or had been, members of the All-India Muslim League. Therefore, they were often referred to as the League delegates. Later on, the All-India Muslim League expressed its confidence in them, and its council formally acknowledged the services of the Aga Khan, Jinnah and Shafi at the round table conferences and congratulated them for the 'unanimity and solidarity' of their stance.[99] Muslim delegates came from different backgrounds who had advocated opposite viewpoints on political issues in the recent past. They were not expected to show unanimity of thought but surprisingly they developed remarkable understanding on Muslim demands and put up a united front in the face of Hindu opposition. Muslim demands had been consolidated in Jinnah's fourteen points. The Aga Khan acted as head of the Muslim delegation, Jinnah provided the delegates with clarity of thought and Mian Shafi presented some of the crucial Muslim proposals. For instance, at the second Round Table Conference, Mian Shafi put forward Jinnah's proposal for conditional acceptance of joint electorates with the Aga Khan's endorsement. However, Muslim politics within India presented a chaotic picture.[100] There was no unity of organization and thought. Their energies were dissipated in several small organizations that advocated conflicting viewpoints. The All-India Muslim League itself was afflicted with acute disunity. Its all-India sessions of 1931 and 1933, instead of presenting a united Muslim stand at that critical juncture, demonstrated serious rifts in its ranks. The council was more active than the all-India sessions and tried to represent its viewpoint. Despite this state of the party and the community in India, Muslim unity at the round table conference produced some useful results.

One positive outcome was the introduction of constitutional reforms in the NWFP; however, the weightage that was provided for the minorities in the assembly was unprecedented. Earlier, the Nehru Report had made the constitutional reforms in the NWFP contingent upon the approval of an all-India constitution based on its recommendations, and the Simon Commission had even refrained from recommending their introduction although it recognized the right and need for constitutional reforms in the province. At the first Round Table Conference, the NWFP committee recommended that the province should be elevated to a status similar to other provinces with modifications to suit the local conditions and final adjustment with the central government.[101] Jinnah and other Muslim delegates tried to soften the Hindu opposition to constitutional reforms in the NWFP. While the All-India Muslim League welcomed the reforms and urged the British government to give them immediate effect, the Congress denounced the proposed reforms, arguing that these were not conducive for good governance and, if introduced, asked for adequate safeguards for the minorities.[102] The council of the All-India Muslim League condemned all attempts to dilute the reforms, warning that if NWFP was given a differential treatment there would be a great upheaval and demanded that the report of the NWF Crimes Regulations Enquiry Committee should be published and all repressive laws be withdrawn from the province.[103] Prime Minister MacDonald formally announced the decision for raising the status of the NWFP to a governor's province with an elected legislature at the second Round Table Conference on 1 December 1931, after a report by a committee chaired by Henry Graham Haig on the distribution of subjects between the centre and the province and on financial matters. The following year in April, NWFP had a governor and an elected assembly. The high weightage for the minorities in the provincial assembly was the cost that the NWFP Muslims paid for the introduction of constitutional reforms.

The round table conferences also moved forward the case of separation of Sindh from the Bombay presidency. The Sindh subcommittee of the first Round Table Conference had recommended formation of Sindh into a separate province subject to an inquiry about its financial viability. The council of the All-India Muslim League supported the round table conference decision with the hope that the requisite finances would be found to separate Sindh from Bombay before or simultaneous to the inauguration of the new constitution.[104] It passed quite a few resolutions to keep up the pressure.[105] The Miles Irving Committee conducted an inquiry into the financial resources and concluded that the separated Sindh would start with a deficit of about ten million rupees.[106] The Hindu delegates at the round table conference continued to oppose separation of Sindh from Bombay while the Muslim delegates pressed for it. The communal award broke the deadlock and accepted the formation of Sindh into a separate province provided satisfactory means to finance it were ensured.[107] Now the Sindhi Muslims, supported by the all-India Muslim leaders, organized a sustained campaign in support of separation.[108] They established a new body, the Sindh Azad Conference, to organize the pro-separation propaganda campaign.[109] They observed 16 September 1932, as the 'Sindh Separation Day', followed by a similar Day on 15 November. The Sindhi Hindus set up the Sindh Hindu Conference in retaliation to campaign against separation because it would reduce them into a minority in the new province. The process of separation progressed slowly. Ayub Khuhro (1901–1980) as representative of the Sindh Azad Conference made out a well-argued case in his evidence before the joint parliamentary committee in London. The decision to constitute Sindh into an autonomous province was made simultaneous to the enactment of the Act of 1935. Sindh became a separate province on 1 April 1936. The round table conference totally ignored the question of reforms in Balochistan. The council of the All-India Muslim League criticized this attitude, and the Balochs expressed their concerns at an

All-India Baloch Conference where they demanded extension of reforms with provincial autonomy to Balochistan. They also demanded that Dera Ghazi Khan and Upper Sindh districts, in which Balochs were in the majority, should be merged into Balochistan. This conference elected office-bearers and passed forty-seven other resolutions, which its vice-president, Nawabzada Mohammad Yusuf Ali Khan, sent to the All-India Muslim League.[110]

The round table conference delegates failed to reach an agreement on the mode and quantum of Muslim representation in the Punjab and Bengal. Muslim delegates wanted to preserve the slim Muslim majority in the Punjab, but the Hindus aspired to retain their dominant position by denying them a majority in the legislature. The Sikhs whom the British had replaced as rulers of the Punjab but who constituted only 13 per cent of the total population came up with a demand for 30 per cent representation in the Punjab legislature on the analogy of Muslim weightage in the United Provinces where Muslims with similar proportion in the population had the same weightage.[111] The Hindu leaders encouraged them to stick to their demands. Similarly, Muslims wanted to protect their small majority in Bengal but the Hindu delegates at the round table conference were unwilling to concede that. In addition, Muslims wanted one-third representation in the central legislature but the Hindus were not ready to give them more than their proportion in population warranted. Initially, Muslim delegates linked all these demands with separate electorates, and offered weightage to non-Muslim minorities in Sindh and NWFP instead of Bengal and the Punjab.[112] They made several proposals but none found acceptance. Finally, Mian Shafi made an offer on behalf of the Muslim delegates to Dr B.S. Moonje (1872–1948) in the minorities committee of the second Round Table Conference for a communal accord on the basis of joint electorates if it provided one-third representation to the Muslims in the federal legislature; Muslim representation in Bengal and Punjab on the basis of population; weightage for the Muslims in the Muslim minority provinces and for the Hindus in Sindh and NWFP; and reservation of seats for the two communities but no candidate was to be declared elected unless he had received at least 40 per cent votes of his community, and at least 5 per cent of the votes cast by the other communities wherever they were a minority of 10 per cent, and 10 per cent where they constituted a larger minority.[113] Hindu and Sikh delegates rejected the offer.[114] The All-India Muslim League supported this offer of conditional acceptance of joint electorates; but after its rejection by the Hindu delegates, the League decided not to make any new proposal although it expressed its willingness to consider any proposal that might be made by the non-Muslims.[115] When the second Round Table Conference adjourned without a settlement of the communal issue, the prime minister announced that the British government would give its decision if various communities failed to reach an agreement. There was a deadlock in negotiations on the issue of communal representation.

The All-India Muslim League simply pressed for the acceptance of its demands and made no further move to end the deadlock.[116] It urged the provincial Muslim Leagues not to suggest, or accept, any new proposals out of line with its policy. For example, when the Bengal presidency Muslim League proposed adult franchise and joint electorates, with no reservation of seats for the Muslims in Bengal to reach a communal settlement, its council demanded an explanation from the presidency Muslim League for making a proposal against the policy of the All-India Muslim League.[117] It also killed a similar move by the Madras provincial Muslim League. Meanwhile, the government proceeded with the issue of franchise. The League sent replies to the questionnaire that was circulated by the Indian franchise committee and gave its comments on its final report.[118] It questioned the utility of special constituencies, separate seats for labour and differential qualifications for women. It wanted equality of women with men and opposed their enfranchisement on the basis of qualifications of their husbands. It emphasized that any representation of special interests should not reduce communal percentage.[119] In August 1932 came the provisional scheme of minority representation, commonly known as 'communal award', which allocated seats to different communities in various provincial legislatures. The award provided for Muslims 29 seats (including 1 seat for women) out of 215 seats in Madras; 63 (including 1 for women) out of 200 seats in Bombay; 119 (including 2 for women) out of 250 seats in Bengal; 66 (including 2 for women) out of 228 seats in the United Provinces; 86 (including 2 for women) out of 175 seats in the Punjab; 42 (including 1 for women) out of 175 seats in Bihar and Orissa; 14 out of 112 seats in the Central Provinces (including Berar); 34 out of 108 seats in Assam; 36 out of 50 seats in NWFP; 30 (including 1 for women) out of 175 seats in Bombay; and 34 (including 1 for women) out of 60 seats in Sindh. In addition, Muslims could participate in the elections on special seats reserved for labour, landholders, universities and commerce and industry. The award deferred the allocation of seats in the federal legislature to a later date. The All-India Muslim League council reiterated its demand for allocation of one-third seats in the central legislature. During the third Round Table Conference, the British government, in a supplementary communal award on 24 December 1932, accepted the Muslim demand and agreed to allocate 33.3 per cent seats for the Muslims in the central legislature.[120]

At first, the All-India Muslim League hesitated to give the communal award its endorsement. On 4 September 1932, its council declared that the award did not fulfil the minimum demands of the Muslims and denied them in particular their statutory majorities in Bengal and the Punjab. The League, therefore, did not commit itself that the constitution, if framed on its basis, would be 'acceptable to the Muslim community or not'.[121] But when there were moves to modify the communal award to whittle down its provisions that were beneficial for the Muslims, the League then came out in its defence. It opposed any move to bring it 'into the orbit of controversy' unless there was an alternative proposal that improved the Muslim position. It was willing to consider any 'definite proposal' based on separate electorates that might be made by the 'accredited agencies' of the majority community.[122] The most notable attempt was made at the Allahabad Unity Conference on 3 November 1932, which was attended by Hindu, Muslim, Sikh and Christian representatives. The suggestions made at the unity conference were based on joint electorates and reservation of seats. However, the All-India Muslim League council and the working committees of the All-India Muslim Conference and the Jamiatul Ulama (Kanpur), at a joint meeting chaired by Abdullah al-Mamun Suhrawardy, declared that the Allahabad proposals fell short of the Muslim demands. In addition to Jinnah's fourteen points, it called for reservation of 40 per cent seats for the Muslims in Assam, the same weightage for the Muslims in Madras as allowed to the Hindus in the NWFP, one seat each by separate electorates for the Muslims of the Delhi and Ajmer provinces in the federal legislature, and at least 27 per cent representation for the Muslims in Bihar and Orissa. This three-party meeting did not give any final verdict, as it was pointed out that the Allahabad proposals were yet 'tentative'.[123] On 27 November, the League council endorsed the All-India Muslim League–All-India Muslim Conference–Jamiatul Ulama (Kanpur) decisions and emphatically declared that the Allahabad proposals were not acceptable to the Muslims. When the All-India Muslim League was invited to the follow-up conferences in Lucknow and Allahabad to finalize the proposals of the first Allahabad Unity Conference, the All-India Muslim League declined to attend these conferences.[124] The decisions of these conferences, the council observed on 24 December, did not mark any 'substantial improvement on the proposals' of the first unity conference. The council also opposed a proposal made by some delegates at the round table conference to empower the legislatures to amend the constitution of the provinces, and in case such powers were conferred on the legislatures, these should be valid only if at least three-fourth Muslim members of the legislature concerned supported them.[125]

On 17 March 1933, the British government issued the White Paper, which incorporated its decisions in the light of the round table conferences and, in April, appointed a joint parliamentary committee to consider the future government of India. As mentioned elsewhere, the All-India Muslim League at that time was undergoing acute intra-party conflicts. Five days before the issuance of the White Paper, its council, by a vote of 10 to 7, had decided to hold a joint All-India Muslim League–All-India Muslim Conference–Jamiatul Ulama (Kanpur) meeting to discuss the White Paper, rejecting a proposal by Abdul Matin Choudhry (1895–1948) for inviting other parties on the ground that their objectives were not similar to those of the All-India Muslim League.[126] The League could not hold the scheduled joint meeting due to intra-party rift; but twelve days later, its working committee observed that the White Paper had shattered the hopes for a responsible government in India, and that the postponement of the all-India federation had made its emergence doubtful. It criticized the vagueness of the phrase 'special responsibility' of the governor general that bestowed upon him enormous powers, besides his other powers including those to govern by ordinances. Even the ministers in charge of the transferred subjects at the centre would be responsible to him rather than the federal legislature. There would hardly be any improvement in governance at the centre, and the proposals relating to the provincial governments would also bear similar results. The exclusion of British Balochistan from the constitutional reforms and their introduction in Orissa was 'a direct hit' on the 'legitimate expectations of the Indian Muslims'. The White Paper, the working committee resolved, required major changes to make it acceptable to the Muslims.[127] Later on, the Hafiz Hidayat group appointed a two-member (Mohammad Yaqub and Abdur Rashid) committee to give evidence before the joint parliamentary committee while the Aziz group called on the parliamentary committee not to allow these members to appear as witnesses on behalf of the All-India Muslim League; the two members, however, did give evidence before the parliamentary committee.[128] Both the groups were in favour of retaining the communal award. Therefore, in December 1933, the Leaguers opposed a move to convene an All-Parties Muslim Conference to resume the Allahabad unity talks to find a formula based on joint electorates to replace the communal award.[129] The council of the Hafiz Hidayat group, in an emergency meeting on 12 December, warned that any revision or reconsideration of the communal award would be 'extremely detrimental' to Muslim interests and urged the convenors of the proposed conference to postpone it.[130]

In March 1934, the two groups of the All-India Muslim League forged unity and elected Jinnah as president who provided the Leaguers the much-needed clarity of thought. On 2 April, the central council under his chairmanship accepted the communal award until different communities agreed upon an alternate formula and expressed its readiness to negotiate with other political parties to find an acceptable constitution on its basis. Jinnah himself drafted the resolution.[131] He was then on a short visit to India and went back to England the same month. During his absence, the council twice at emergency meetings on 10 May and 24 June, reiterated the 2 April resolution when there was pressure for changing the communal award.[132] It also passed resolutions on Palestine. At this time, Fazli Husain and Nawab Ahmad Said Khan Chhatari (1888–1982) proposed the creation of a new political body—Parliamentary Majlis; the League secretary tagged along with them.[133] On 13 August, the council, with Raza Ali in the chair, approved the proposal. The Parliamentary Majlis was to put up candidates in the elections to the central assembly that were scheduled in October–November. The formation of a new political organization to contest the elections generated opposition, which gathered strength in the League circles when it was proposed that the All-India Muslim League should be merged into this body. The merger proposal killed the whole idea of a Parliamentary Majlis.[134] Although the League itself did not participate in the elections to the central assembly but individual Leaguers were elected as its members. The Muslims of Bombay elected Jinnah in his absence; and in December 1934, he again visited India for a little longer duration than the earlier one in April 1932.

During Jinnah's stay, on 27–28 January 1935, the council discussed the report of the joint parliamentary committee and resolved that its recommendations were more reactionary than those of the White Paper. However, as far as the communal award was concerned, it reiterated its position as reflected in its resolution of 2 April 1934, i.e. it accepted the award provisionally and conveyed its willingness to negotiate with any community or political party to secure an acceptable constitution for India.[135] At a subsequent meeting on 16 February, it demanded reforms in Balochistan immediately or its amalgamation with Sindh. Some of the other steps, which it suggested for Balochistan, were the introduction of the system of elections in the local bodies, codification of customary law and reforms in the Jirga system. It also demanded the release of Abdus Samad Khan Achakzai (1907–1973) and Abdul Aziz.[136] In pursuance of the resolution on communal award, Jinnah negotiated with Dr Rajendra Prasad (1884–1963), then Congress president, and discussed an alternative constitutional formula to replace the communal award; the formula was, however, subject to approval by the All-India Muslim League and the Congress.[137] They broke off negotiations when a section of the Congress and the Hindu Mahasabha leaders opposed the formula.[138] Meanwhile, Jinnah took oath of membership of the central assembly and revived the Independent Party under his leadership. When the joint parliamentary committee report came up before the central assembly for discussion in February 1935, Jinnah presented the All-India Muslim League position on the report and displayed his parliamentary skills. He moved a three-part amendment to the main resolution asking for the acceptance of the report; his amendment called on the members: to reject the all-India federation consisting of British India and the princely states; to accept the provincial part after certain specified modifications in those sections that placed restrictions on provincial autonomy; and to accept the communal award until various communities agreed upon an alternative formula.[139] The central assembly adopted his three-part amendment. The Congress members voted along with the Independent Party for the first two parts but abstained from voting on the third part, which was adopted with the support of the official bloc and European members. A bill drafted on the lines of the joint parliamentary committee report had been introduced in the parliament in December 1934, which after its passage in the two Houses with minor amendments received the royal assent in the following August. The Government of India Act of 1935, as the new legislation was referred to, separated

Burma from India and put Sindh and Orissa, along with the NWFP, on an equal footing with the older provinces. The Act visualized an all-India federation, which was to become a reality only if rulers representing 50 per cent of the total population of all the States signed the instrument of accession to fill 52 of the 104 seats allocated to the states in the upper house of the legislature. Its most important feature was the separate legal personality that it conferred on the provinces. The governor was responsible to the provincial legislature in all matters except when he was acting 'in his discretion' or exercising 'his individual judgement' in the discharge of his 'special responsibilities'. The seven responsibilities that were listed included safeguarding the legitimate interests of the minorities, the prevention of any grave menace to the peace and tranquillity of the province, the protection of the rights of the civil servants and the prevention of administrative discrimination against British commercial interests.[140]

On 16 February 1935, the council of the All-India Muslim League had decided to hold its twenty-fourth annual session in Lahore on 20–21 April in the Easter holidays, and elected Jinnah as the president.[141] The Leaguers in the Punjab were quite enthusiastic about the decision. This reminded them of their role in the 'revival' of the All-India Muslim League in May 1924, when they had hosted the fifteenth adjourned session in Lahore. Now they felt that they could play the same role. They constituted a reception committee that included among its members Allama Iqbal, Ahmad Yar Daultana (1896–1940) and Khalifa Shujauddin (1887–1955); and the committee issued an appeal to the Muslims to participate in the session. When the preparations for the session were halfway through, suggestions came in for its postponement for some time. Two viewpoints emerged: one pressed for holding the session on the scheduled dates; and the other asked for its indefinite postponement. Jinnah had planned to leave for England on 23 April. He did not want to leave behind any unnecessary controversy. Therefore, he advised the Leaguers to postpone the annual session altogether till the next year. He hoped that the secretaries of the reception committee would agree with his advice and, if necessary, seek the approval of the council.[142] The reception committee accepted Jinnah's advice subject to approval by the council, which, in a meeting in Lahore on 21 April, endorsed it in deference to the wishes of the president.[143] During Jinnah's absence, the council met twice in Delhi. On 22 June 1935, it expressed sympathy for the sufferers of the Quetta earthquake, and opposed any move to modify the communal award in a way that might damage Muslim interests.[144] In the second meeting on 21 July, it sympathized with the sufferers of the fire that destroyed parts of Abbottabad and Peshawar cities. It appreciated the assurances given by the secretary of state for India and the British cabinet for the protection of Muslim rights under the communal award and emphasized that these rights should not be taken away without Muslim consent and without an agreed settlement between the communities. It viewed with abhorrence the demolition of the Shahidganj mosque by the Sikhs under official protection, and the discriminatory policies followed by the Punjab government towards the Muslims. It called upon the government to restore the site of the mosque to the Muslims and demanded funds for its rebuilding. It urged the Muslim leaders to consider the usefulness of sending a deputation to the viceroy for this purpose. The first major task that Jinnah undertook on his return from England was to attempt to bring about Muslim–Sikh reconciliation on the issue of the Shahidganj mosque. Then, the All-India Muslim League started its new phase and held its long-awaited annual session in Bombay. Soon thereafter, Jinnah embarked upon his mission to revive and reorganize the All-India Muslim League.

NOTES

1. AFM, vol. 126, nos. 66–67 and 69.
2. Ibid., no. 71.
3. Zahur Ahmad's letters to council members issued on 23 January, 5 and 9 April 1922, ibid., vol. 595; and *Report of the All-India Muslim League for the Year 1922*, Lucknow, 1922, pp. 1–2.
4. Circulation of pamphlets like the *Dastan-i-Zulm* (Amritsar, 1922) and *Malabar ki Khuni Dastan* (Saharanpur, 1922) spoiled the communal atmosphere.
5. AFM, vol. 101, no. 79.
6. Masudul Hasan to Zahur Ahmad, 5 September 1924, ibid., vol. 573.
7. For information, see the resolution on this issue, moved by Zafar Ali Khan and seconded by Barkat Ali, *Resolutions of the All-India Muslim League from May 1924 to December 1936*, published by (Nawabzada) Liaquat Ali Khan; K.M. Seethi, 'Aligarh and the Muslim Nation', *The Awakening*, vol. II, no. 3, November 1940, p. 13; Allah Bakhsh Yusufi, *Sarhad aur Jiddo Juhd-i-Azadi*, Lahore, 1968, pp. 371–73; and AFM, vol. 206, no. 18.
8. For Fazli Husain's views on the Hindus' response to his policies, see his letter to Zahur Ahmad, 21 March 1923, AFM, vol. 101, no. 40.
9. One Swarajist Hindu, Duni Chand, published a book on this subject entitled *The Ulster of India* (Lahore, 1936).
10. Zahur Ahmad's printed letter to the council members, 27 January 1923, AFM, vol. 147, no. 5.
11. For the Bengal Pact, see section (c) of this chapter.

12. Pirzada, *Foundations*, vol. I, pp. 572–73; and AFM, vol. 101, no. 79; and vol. 147, no. 29.

13. Aqeelur Rahman Nadvi to Zahur Ahmad, 28 March 1823; and Abdul Hamid to Zahur Ahmad, AFM, vol. 101; and Shoaib Qureshi to Zahur Ahmad, 26 July 1924, ibid., vol. 573.

14. Its members included Jinnah, Fazli Husain, Fazlul Haq, Agha Safdar (b. 1935), Murtaza Bahadur, Zahur Ahmad and Mohammad Yaqub.

15. Resolution to this effect was passed at the Bombay annual session that was proposed by Shaukat Ali, seconded by Zafar Ali and supported by Jinnah and Aftab Ahmad Khan.

16. AFM, vol. 109, no. 37.

17. For instance, see resolution passed at the Aligarh session regarding Iraq, and the one passed at the Bombay session about Egypt. [Zahur Ahmad's letter to Mohammad Yaqub in reply to his of 13 August 1926, ibid., vol. 158, nos. 13 and 14.] It did comment on Sultan Abdul Aziz Ibne Saud's activities vis-à-vis Muslim Holy Places. Ibid., vol. 157, nos. 31, 34, 36, 37, and 44; and vol. 150, no. 25.

18. Hasrat Mohani's presidential address at the Ahmadabad annual session, 31 December 1921, ibid., vol. 97, no. 27.

19. Ibid., vol. 121, no. 5.

20. For strong comments on the surrender of Muslim majorities in Bengal and Punjab, see Amir Hasan Naz to honorary secretary, All-India Muslim League, 25 February 1923, ibid., vol. 147, p. 23; and for Fazli Husain's views, see ibid., vol. 109, no. 12.

21. For the evolution of this demand, see the resolutions passed at the Lahore, Bombay, and Aligarh annual sessions.

22. Resolutions adopted by the subjects committee of the All-India Muslim League on 31 December 1924, ibid., vol. 121, no. 5.

23. Pirzada, *Foundations*, vol. II, p. 22.

24. Its members were: Raza Ali, Shahabuddin, Abdur Rahim, T. Rangachariar, N.M. Samarath, H. Bolton, A.H. Parker and Denys Bray.

25. *Report of the North-West Frontier Enquiry Committee and the Minutes of Dissent*, Delhi, 1924, pp. 22–23.

26. Printed letter from Zahur Ahmad to members, 27 January 1923, AFM, vol. 147, no. 5.

27. Resolution passed at the Lahore annual session, moved by Mian Abdul Aziz and seconded by Abdul Majid Qureshi; and the resolution adopted at the Bombay annual session, moved by Aftab Ahmad Khan, seconded by Abdul Aziz and supported by Maulana Mohammad Ali.

28. Resolution passed at the Aligarh annual session, moved by Mian Abdul Aziz, seconded by Ali Imam and supported by Maulana Mohammad Ali, Qazi Mohammad Aslam, Noor Bux and Dr L.K. Hyder.

29. For instance, see resolutions of the Hindu Sabha and the Muslim Association of Dera Ismail Khan, AFM, vol. 206, no. 14; *Muslim Outlook*, 6 February 1926, and *Observer* (Lahore), 7 February 1926. For further details, see *Legislative Assembly Debates*, Delhi, 1926, vol. VIII, no. 9; Afzal, *Speeches and Statements*, pp. 238–46; and Shan Muhammad, *The Indian Mussalmans: A Documentary Record*, Delhi, 1985, p. 165.

30. Resolution passed at the Delhi annual session.

31. Afzal, *Speeches and Statements*, pp. 381–83.

32. Resolution passed at the Aligarh annual session.

33. Resolutions passed at the Lahore and Aligarh annual sessions.
34. Resolution passed at the Aligarh annual session.
35. Resolution passed at the Bombay annual session.
36. Resolutions passed at the Aligarh and Delhi annual sessions.
37. S. M. Ikram, *Modern Muslim India and the Birth of Pakistan (1858–1951)*, Lahore, 1970, pp. 216–17 and 224–25.
38. Resolution passed at the Bombay annual session.
39. Resolution passed at the Delhi annual session.
40. Resolution moved by Pir Tajuddin and seconded by Mohammad Sadiq.
41. Resolutions passed at the Lahore session.
42. AFM, vol. 122, nos. 5 and 11; and vol. 150, no. 30; and resolutions passed at the Lahore, Aligarh and Delhi annual sessions.
43. Memoranda submitted by the Government of India and the India Office, cited in Page, *Prelude to Partition*, p. 74, Table 7; and see also AFM, vol. 158, nos. 1–5.
44. Aftab Ahmad Khan to Zahur Ahmad, 25 September 1926, AFM, vol. 157, no. 24; and Mohammad Yaqub to Zahur Ahmad, 15 August 1926, ibid., vol. 158, nos. 13–14.
45. Fazli Husain to Zahur Ahmad, 2 May 1926, ibid., vol. 157, no. 5; and Dr Ghulam Umar to Zahur Ahmad, 21 May 1926, ibid., vol. 158, no. 6.
46. C.S. Ranga Iyer, *India: Peace or War*, London, 1930, pp. 116–17.
47. Resolution passed at the Delhi annual session.
48. AFM, vol. 163, nos. 20–28.
49. Cited in Matlubul Hasan Saiyid, *Mohammad Ali Jinnah (A Political Study)*, Lahore, 1945, pp. 368–69. As for constitutional reforms in Balochistan, the Aga Khan had expressed his disappointment as early as 1910, although the All-India Muslim League did not formally make the demand till 1927. Pirzada, *Foundations*, vol. I, p. 105.
50. *IAR*, 1927, vol. 1, p. 37.
51. Ibid., p. 426; and *Inqilab* (Lahore), 7 June 1928.
52. On 27 April 1927, Deva Ratna Sharma, general secretary of the Mahasabha, communicated this resolution to the All-India Muslim League. AFM, vol. 469, pp. 6–8.
53. Maulvi Abdul Karim, *Letter on Hindu–Muslim Pact*, Calcutta, 1924; and Page, *Prelude to Partition*, pp. 42–44.
54. Pirzada, *Foundations*, vol. II, p. 56.
55. *IAR*, 1925, vol. I, p. 406.
56. Its members included Jinnah, Fazli Husain, Fazlul Haq, Agha Safdar, Zahur Ahmad, Raza Ali, Khaliquzzaman (1889–1973), Asif Ali, Mian Abdul Aziz, Sayyid Murtaza Bahadur and Shoaib Qureshi.
57. Zahur Ahmad's letters to office-bearers of other parties, 8 July 1924; C.Y. Chintamani to Zahur Ahmad, 14 July; and Zahur Ahmad to Jinnah, 31 July, AFM, vol. 573.
58. Jawaharlal to Zahur Ahmad, 17 October 1924, ibid., vol. 573, no. 64.
59. *IAR*, 1925, vol. 1, pp. 67–73.
60. Motilal–Zahur correspondence, AFM, vol. 573.
61. Zahur Ahmad to Jinnah, 14 December 1924, ibid.
62. *IAR*, 1925, vol. I, p. 68.
63. Ibid., p. 77; and Saiyid, *Jinnah*, pp. 344–45. Duni Chand, published a book on this subject entitled *The Ulster of India* (Lahore, 1936).
64. AFM, vol. 163, no. 49.

65. *Inqilab*, 4 May 1927.
66. For a printed letter of invitation, see AFM, vol. 163, no. 56; and no. 53 for Jinnah's advice.
67. Pirzada, *Foundations*, vol. II, pp. 119–21.
68. AFM, vol. 177, no. 14.
69. Assistant secretary to council members, 1 March 1928, ibid., vol. 177, no. 23.
70. Its members were: Jinnah, Raja of Mahmudabad, Sahibzada Abdul Qayyum, Raja Nawab Ali, Nawab Ismail Khan, Shah Mohammad Zubair, Raja Ghazanfar Ali, Mohammad Yaqub, Fazal Ibrahim Rahimatullah, Maulvi Tufail Ahmad, Abdul Matin Choudhry, Abdul Jabbar, and Saifuddin Kitchlew.
71. *All-Parties Conference, Report of the Committee*, Allahabad, 1928, pp. 19–22.
72. Shamsul Hasan to honorary secretary, 19 August 1928, and S. Abdullah to Saifuddin Kitchlew, 3 October 1928, AFM, 146, nos. 2 and 7; and *Inqilab*, 23 November 1928.
73. Among them were: Dr Ansari, Maulana Azad, Dr Kitchlew, Dr Alam and M.C. Chagla.
74. *The Proceedings of the All-Parties National Convention, Calcutta, 1928*, Allahabad, 1929, p. 78.
75. *IAR*, 1928, vol. II, p. 131.
76. For details of the proceedings, see ibid., vol. I, pp. 117–31.
77. For circular letter by Saifuddin Kitchlew, honorary secretary, All-India Muslim League, see AFM, vol. 577.
78. Those Leaguers who issued an appeal for participation in the session were: Jinnah, Abdullah Haroon, Mohammad Yaqub, Nawab Ismail Khan, Sayyid Murtaza, Mohammad Ali, Abul Kalam Azad, Maulana Abdul Qadir Qasuri, Maulana Habibur Rahman (1867–1950), Shaikh Hissamuddin, Maulana Mohiyyuddin, and Maulana Abdur Rahman Ghazi.
79. For relevant details about the session, see AFM, vols. 151, 152, 185, 368, 371 and 372.
80. M.A. Jinnah, *History of the Origin of "Fourteen Points"*, Bombay, 1929.
81. AFM, vol. 146, no. 40.
82. Ibid., vol. 152, no. 1.
83. Ibid., vol. 126, nos. 56, 57 and 61; and *IAR*, 1921–22, pp. 353–74.
84. L.F. Rushbrook Williams, *India in 1924–25*, Calcutta, 1925, pp. 55–56, and Afzal, *Speeches and Statements*, pp. 114–21.
85. Other members were: the Maharaja of Burdwan, Tej Bahadur Sapru, Sivaswami Iyer, Arthur Froom, Henry Moncrieff Smith and Dr R.P. Paranjpye (1876–1966).
86. Honorary secretary, All-India Muslim League to secretary, Reforms Enquiry Committee, 23 November 1924, AFM, vol. 573, no. 70; see also nos. 62 and 65; and vol. 149, no. 40.
87. M. Rafique Afzal, *Malik Barkat Ali: His Life and Writings*, Lahore, 1969, pp. 31–34.
88. Jinnah to Zahur Ahmad, 29 April 1925, AFM, vol. 157, no. 14; and see also no. 20.
89. For Jinnah's remarks at the All-India Muslim League session in Calcutta, see ibid., vol. 125; and see also Jinnah to Lord Irwin, 31 October 1927, Pirzada, *Quaid's Correspondence*, Lahore, 1987, p. 152.
90. For a resolution passed on 13 July 1930, see AFM, vol. 186, no. 49.
91. B.L. Miller to Jinnah, 2 June 1929; C.P. Duff to Jinnah, 8 July 1929; Ramsey MacDonald to Jinnah, 14 August 1929; and Jinnah to Ramsey MacDonald, 7 September 1929, QAP, F. 15, pp. 1–8.

92. *Gazette of India Extraordinary*, 31 October 1929, pp. 163–65. Irwin informed Jinnah about the announcement in advance. Irwin to Jinnah, 31 October 1929, QAP, F. 15, pp. 17–18.
93. Saiyid, *Jinnah*, pp. 464–65.
94. Jinnah to Irwin, 3 December 1929, Pirzada, *Quaid's Correspondence*, p. 154; V.J. Patel to Jinnah, 10 December 1929; and Sapru to Jinnah, 13 December 1929, QAP, F. 15, pp. 25, 27–29.
95. QAP, F. 15, pp. 53–58; and Sapru to Jinnah, ibid., F. 15, pp. 46–47.
96. For a resolution passed by the council on 13 July 1930, see AFM, vol. 186, no. 49. According to Yusufi (*Jiddo Jamiatul Ulama-i-Hindd-i-Azadi*, p. 515.), about 325 persons were killed in this civil unrest.
97. Resolution passed by the All-India Muslim League council on 3 February 1930.
98. Jinnah to Irwin, 6 August 1930, and Irwin to Jinnah, 11 August 1930, QAP, F. 1088, pp. 35–40; and Ikram, *Modern Muslim India*, pp. 223–24.
99. AFM, vol. 197, nos. 15 and 41.
100. The Aga Khan to Jinnah, 29 March 1931, QAP, F. 15, pp. 117–18; and Khalid Shamsul Hasan, *The Punjab Muslim League and the Unionists: An Account Based on the Documents in the Shamsul Hasan Collection*, Karachi, 2005, pp. 57–58.
101. Diwan Chand Obhrai, *The Evolution of the North West Frontier Province*, Peshawar, 1938, pp. 129 and 188.
102. Ibid., p. 129; and for resolutions of the All-India Muslim League council passed on 15 March 1931 and 6 December, see AFM, vol. 194, no. 71; vol. 197, no. 43; and for a resolution of the open session, see Pirzada, *Foundations*, vol. II, p. 190.
103. AFM, vol. 197, no. 15.
104. For a resolution passed by the All-India Muslim League council on 15 March 1931, ibid., vol. 194, no. 71.
105. For instance, see resolutions of the All-India Muslim League council passed on 3–4 September and 27 October 1932, ibid., vol. 209, nos. 16 and 38.
106. On 15 November 1931, the central council expressed its deep disappointment on the Irving Report, re-emphasizing that separation of Sindh constituted 'one of the most important Muslim demands of a fundamental character'. Ibid., vol. 197, no. 15.
107. Hamida Khuhro, *Mohammed Ayub Khuhro: A Life of Courage in Politics*, Lahore, 1998, pp. 94–105.
108. Shahnawaz Bhutto, in a letter to Mohammad Yaqub on 6 June 1932, thanked the all-India Muslim leaders for their 'strong and unstinted support'. AFM, vol. 208, no. 41.
109. Shahnawaz Bhutto was elected president, Ayub Khuhro vice-president and Miran Shah general secretary, Abdul Majid Sindhi joint secretary and Abdullah Haroon treasurer. Ibid., vol. 241, pp. 40–43.
110. For the text of the resolutions, see ibid., vol. 462, no. 62.
111. Ujjal Singh and Sampuran Singh, 'Sikhs and the New Constitution for India', London, 1931.
112. For a resolution of the All-India Muslim League council passed on 15 March 1931, see AFM, vol. 194, no. 71.
113. Khalid, *Punjab Muslim League*, pp. 57–58. For a resolution of similar content passed by the All-India Muslim League council on 6 December, see AFM, vol. 197, no. 43.
114. The Aga Khan to Jinnah, 24 December 1930, QAP, F. 15, pp. 70–71.

115. For a resolution passed by the All-India Muslim League council on 6 December 1931, see AFM, vol. 197, no. 41; and also see QAP, F. 1122, pp. 121–22.
116. For a resolution passed by the All-India Muslim League council on 24 January 1932, see AFM, vol. 208, nos. 10 and 31.
117. Ibid., no. 12; Suhrawardy to Mohammad Yaqub, 14 June 1932, ibid., vol. 38; and resolution passed by the All-India Muslim League council on 3–4 September 1932, ibid., vol. 209, no. 16.
118. Ibid., vol. 122, no. 6, 9; and vol. 208, no. 10.
119. Ibid., vol. 122, no. 18; and J.A. Shahnawaz to honorary secretary, 25 May 1932, ibid., vol. 208, no. 27.
120. For a resolution passed by the All-India Muslim League council on 3–4 September 1932, see ibid., vol. 209, no. 16. On 25 September 1932, the Poona Pact reserved seats for the Depressed Classes out of the general seats in the provincial legislatures.
121. Ibid., vol. 209, no. 16. The IAR (vol. II, pp. 335–36) does not mention this part of the League council's resolution.
122. For a resolution passed by the All-India Muslim League council on 23 October 1932, see AFM, vol. 209, no. 16.
123. Ibid., vol. 209, no. 31; and IAR, 1932, vol. II, pp. 281–301; and for the All-India Muslim League–Madras PML controversy over the Allahabad proposals, see AFM, vol. 196, no. 57 and 58.
124. For a resolution passed by the All-India Muslim League working committee and council, see AFM, vol. 122, nos. 19 and 20.
125. Ibid., vol. 209, nos. 39, 41 and 43.
126. Ibid., vol. 210, no. 30; and the Statesman, 13 March 1933.
127. AFM, vol. 122, no. 25.
128. Statesman, 11 July 1933; and AFM, vol. 210, no. 41; and vol. 211, no. 43.
129. For a press statement by the Muslim Leaguers, see Statesman, 10 December 1933.
130. AFM, vol. 211, no. 59.
131. For the draft resolution in his handwriting, see ibid., vol. 219, no. 32 and 36.
132. Ibid., vol. 219, nos. 52 and 64.
133. The council passed resolutions to this effect in its meetings held on 30 June and 12–13 August 1934.
134. Syed Shamsul Hasan, Plain Mr. Jinnah, Karachi, 1976, pp. 61–62.
135. AFM, vol. 220, no. 7 and 8.
136. For resolutions passed by the central council on 16 February 1935, see ibid., vol. 220, pp. 18–19.
137. For the text of the proposed Jinnah–Rajendra Formula, see Uma Kaura, Muslims and Indian Nationalism: The Emergence of the Demand for India's Partition, 1928–40, New Delhi, 1977, pp. 102–3.
138. After the 1937 elections, the Rajendra–Jinnah Formula became the subject of a controversy between Jinnah and the Congress leaders.
139. Jamil-ud-Din Ahmad (ed.), Some Recent Speeches and Writings of Mr. Jinnah, Lahore, 1946, pp. 1–20.
140. Reginald Coupland, The Indian Problem, 1833–1935, Oxford, 1968, pp. 132–48.
141. The central council took this decision in its meeting held on 16 February 1935.
142. Jinnah to S.M. Abdullah, 7 April 1935, AFM, vol. 168, no. 9.
143. For the resolutions passed by the reception committee on 12 April 1935, see ibid., no. 12; and by the council on 21 April 1935, see ibid., vol. 220, no. 17.
144. Ibid., vol. 220, pp. 30–31.

PART TWO

5

Revival of the All-India Muslim League, 1935–1937

The All-India Muslim League existed in a very bad shape when M.A. Jinnah finally returned from England to assume the office of president. Similar was the condition of the League branches at the provincial, district and lower levels, wherever these had survived from extinction. The surviving branches functioned ineffectively in the capitals of the provinces with little contact with the members and supporters at the grassroots. Personal rivalries and factional conflicts with no sense of direction had sapped the energies of the League leaders. The central League had a hollow structure, which was maintained by a few dedicated individuals who tried to organize regularly party meetings with great difficulty. It had faced budget deficits for several years past and its activities were sustained on meagre donations from rich Muslims or borrowed money. The disillusioned League workers had gone into local and other newly organized political parties which were more active than the All-India Muslim League and its branches. The Leaguers had joined, and some of them led, these political parties. Muslims generally felt dismayed by this state of Muslim politics and the League. Jinnah took over the leadership of the All-India Muslim League in such a dismal state of the party organization.[1]

(A) BOMBAY ANNUAL SESSION

On Jinnah's return from England, the All-India Muslim League council met on 30 December 1935, in which it re-elected him as president for a one-year term, 'ending in April 1937, or till the next annual session at the end of 1937'. The council decided to hold the twenty-fourth annual session in Bombay during the Easter holidays on 11–12 April 1936, and authorized Jinnah to select a president for the session from among four Leaguers: Mian Fazli Husain, Begum Jahan Ara Shahnawaz

(1896–1979), Sir Sultan Ahmad (1880–1963) and Nawabzada Liaquat Ali Khan.[2] Before the selection of a president, Jinnah accepted an invitation from the Punjab to mediate between the Muslims and Sikhs on the Shahidganj mosque dispute in Lahore. The Shahidganj dispute originated in the middle of the eighteenth century, when the Sikhs took over the Shahidganj mosque and the adjacent tomb; and in 1924, it was declared a *gurdwara* under the Sikh Gurdwara Act.[3] The Muslims disputed its declaration as a *gurdwara*. The dispute went before a tribunal that decided the case against the Muslims in 1930. The Anjuman-i-Islamia, Lahore and the *Mutawalli* of the adjacent tomb who had represented the Muslim case did not go into appeal against this decision. When the Sikhs were about to demolish the Shahidganj mosque, the Muslims of Lahore gathered at the site to prevent its demolition. The Punjab government called in police and a military contingent to avert a communal clash. The Sikhs promised that they would not demolish the mosque until the Shromani Gurdwara Parbandhak Committee had decided the issue on 8 July 1935. But on the night before that date, they demolished the mosque virtually under official supervision.[4] This incident inflamed Muslim sentiments throughout the country. Mobs including volunteers of the *Neeli Posh* (Blue Shirt), a short-lived organization that Maulana Zafar Ali Khan had established for the Shahidganj cause, daily took out processions to protest against the demolition. On 20 July, the security forces indiscriminately fired on a peaceful demonstration, killing and injuring several persons. Section 144, curfew and arrest of Muslim leaders could not restore calm in the city. The Punjab provincial Muslim League, the All-India Muslim League and the All-India Muslim Conference passed resolutions condemning the demolition ȯf the Mosque and firing on the peaceful demonstrators.[5] The Government of India approved the actions of the Punjab government and refused to appoint any committee to investigate these events.[6]

While the Muslims started a civil disobedience movement in Lahore, the Sikhs and Hindus began to organize themselves to counter that movement. No all-India leader was willing to come forward to mediate and ease the tension between the two communities, Muslims and Sikhs.[7] Therefore, both the communities looked on Jinnah's acceptance to play the role of 'conciliator and peacemaker' with admiration. He visited Lahore and stayed there from 21 February to 7 March 1936, and only once went to Delhi for one day to preside over a meeting of the All-India Muslim League council on 29 February. During his busy schedule in Lahore, he interacted with members of all the communities of Lahore—Muslims, Sikhs, Hindus and Christians. He addressed several exclusively Muslim as well as mixed gatherings arranged by different organizations including two large meetings in the Badshahi mosque, Lahore. On his appeal, the Muslims first suspended and then abandoned altogether the civil disobedience movement and agreed to resolve the dispute by constitutional and peaceful means. The Punjab government in response granted amnesty to the Shahidganj prisoners, withdrew the orders against Maulana Zafar Ali Khan and Sayyid Habib (1891–1952) under the Indian Press Act, and restored the forfeited securities of the newspapers to facilitate the negotiations.[8] The Sikh leaders welcomed the intercession of Jinnah whom they remembered for his selfless role in their difficult days in the early 1920s when he had described them as 'one of the flowers of India'.[9] So did the Hindus who nostalgically referred to his 'nationalist days' with the Congress. The Punjabi youth was inspired by his voluntary gesture of mediation and his expression of nationalistic sentiments in his speeches. Muslim youth felt proud that the All-India Muslim League president had come to resolve a problem on which the Muslim community felt so strongly. His relatively long stay in Lahore and his talks with the leaders softened communal tension and bitterness in the Punjab and helped in restoring communal harmony. Before his departure from Lahore, he appointed a Shahidganj Conciliation Committee consisting of Muslim, Sikh and Hindu leaders to work out a settlement of the dispute; and its members were: Allama Iqbal, Mian Abdul Aziz Malvada, Maulana Abdul Qadir Qasuri (1863–1942), Sardars Sampuran Singh, Ujjal Singh and Buta Singh, and Pandit Nanak Chand and Raja Narendra Nath. The conciliation committee, however, was unable to arrive at a solution. Jinnah again visited Lahore in April but could not find a way out. On his advice, however, the Punjab Muslims, instead of resorting to agitation, sought legal recourse and took the dispute to the court of the district judge, Lahore.[10]

During his stay in Lahore, Jinnah tried to persuade Fazli Husain to preside over the All-India Muslim League's annual session in Bombay but the latter firmly declined to accept the offer.[11] The real reasons for his refusal are not known. Maybe he perceived Jinnah's mediation efforts between the Muslims and the Sikhs in Lahore and his association with his harshest critics in the Punjab especially the Majlis-i-Ahrar-i-Islam intrusion into his arena of politics;[12] or it might have been at the behest of the British authorities who were then opposed to communally organized and Jinnah-led Muslim League in the provinces; or it might be simply due to his general introversion not to play any overt public role from an all-India platform. Other personalities in the list that the council had suggested to preside over the annual session either declined to accept the offer or were not available. Then the League searched for a Muslim personality from outside the list. Sahibzada Abdul Qayyum (1863–1937) was among those approached but he did not feel confident enough to shoulder the responsibility.[13] Finally, Jinnah approached Wazir Hasan, former honorary secretary of the All-India Muslim League who had recently retired as chief judge of the Awadh high court, and he accepted the offer. On 29 February, the council formally elected him to preside over the Bombay session.[14] The preparations for the session were already under way. The Bombay Muslim Leaguers had constituted a reception committee chaired by Sir Karimbhai Ibrahim that enrolled more than 300 members of the committee on payment of Rs 10 each. The visitors to the session were to pay an entry fee of Rs 5, and the fee for a reserved seat was Rs 2 and for unreserved Re 1.[15] Thus, sufficient funds were collected to meet the expenditure for the session. The office of the All-India Muslim League provided advice on organizational matters and party literature for circulation.

The Bombay session was convened on schedule. The All-India Muslim League, in a resolution moved by Jinnah on 12 April 1936, protested against the imposition of the constitution under the Act of 1935 against the will of the Indian people. Similar had been the reaction of the Congress. The League rejected the proposed federation of British India and the princely states, terming it as the 'most reactionary, retrograde' and 'fundamentally bad' step, which would delay indefinitely the goal of full responsible government for India and called for its review by the parliament before its inauguration. The party, however, decided to work the provincial part, despite its most objectionable features, for what it was 'worth'. It also resolved to take part in the provincial elections under the Act although it had practically no organization at the provincial level or in the districts. Besides, it had never participated in electoral politics and its constitution provided no machinery for participation in the elections. Therefore, the Bombay session authorized Jinnah to constitute a central election (parliamentary) board under his presidentship, consisting of not less than thirty-five members, with powers to form and affiliate provincial election boards in various provinces, giving due consideration to conditions in each province. Jinnah accepted the responsibility, promising that he would struggle like the proverbial 'spider which endeavoured to go up [the wall] and fell, and again and again moved up' and that for him 'there was no despair'.[16] He urged the Muslims to organize themselves 'to deserve recognition' and not to depend on any one.[17] Henceforth, he acted exactly on these lines. The Bombay session elected Nawabzada Liaquat Ali Khan as the honorary secretary for a three-year term, and authorized the central council to elect two joint secretaries; on 26 April, the council elected S.M. Abdullah (1888–1951) and Husain M. Malik (1910–1987) to these offices.

(B) ELECTIONS, 1937

During 1929–34, the weakening of the All-India Muslim League had seen dispersion of Muslim politics and political parties. Several new Muslim political parties emerged in the provinces, advocating local and topical issues. Some of them were more active than the provincial Leagues. Jinnah wanted these Muslim parties in the provinces to participate in the 1937 elections from the platform of the All-India Muslim League. The Muslims could negotiate, he argued, a settlement with the Congress and the British after the elections with one united voice. Before announcing the personnel of a central parliamentary board, he toured the provinces where elections had to be organized to persuade local Muslim parties and their leaders to accept his viewpoint, i.e. to forge unity on the platform of the All-India Muslim League. His mission was practically that of an individual, as the All-India Muslim League and its branches had virtually no functional organizational structure in any province. After his tour, the council discussed the composition of the central parliamentary board at a meeting in Delhi that leaders of different Muslim parties attended. On 21 May 1936, after his further four-day talks with the Punjab leaders, he announced a 56-member central parliamentary board, on which Bengal had 8, Madras 4, United Provinces 9, Bihar 5, Central Provinces 2, Assam 2, Sindh 4, NWFP 4, Punjab 11, Delhi 1 and Bombay 6 members. The central parliamentary board had representatives of religious as well as regional and provincial parties: for example, Maulana Husain Ahmad Madni (1879–1957), Maulana Kifayatullah (1872–1952) and Maulana Ahmad Saeed (1888–1959) of the Jamiatul Ulama-i-Hind; Shaikh Hussamuddin (1897–1967), Chaudhri Afzal Haq (1895–1942), Chaudhri Abdul Aziz Begowal (d. 1943) and Khwaja Ghulam Husain of the Majlis-i-Ahrar-i-Islam; Maulana Zafar Ali Khan, Maulana Ishaq

Mansehravi (1856–1962), Sayyid Zainul Abidin Gilani (1885–1960) and Abdur Rahman Ghazi of the Majlis-i-Ittehad-i-Millat; A.K. Fazlul Haq of the Krishak Praja Party; Sayyid Abdul Aziz (1885–1949) of the United Party of Bihar; Shaikh Abdul Majid Sindhi (1889–1978) of the Sindh Azad Party; and Nawab Ahmad Said Khan Chhatari and Nawab Mohammad Yusuf of the National Agriculturalist Party of the United Provinces were members of the board. No member was taken from Orissa on the central parliamentary board, as Jinnah did not have 'proper information' about that province. On 19 September, the central parliamentary board co-opted fifteen more members from Bengal, Bombay, Madras, Bihar, United Provinces and Assam, and in June, the central board approved its rules and regulations and a manifesto.

Jinnah had to keep a balance between Muslims with pro-Congress and pro-British proclivities in a situation of individual and factional rivalries. The British officials in some provinces exerted their own pressure to dissuade Muslim leaders from serving on the Jinnah-led central parliamentary board, as they were interested in promoting non-communal parties.[18] Jinnah could neither consult all the members whom he nominated on the central parliamentary board nor could he include in it all the prominent Muslim politicians of India. He had based his selection on the eminence of the nominees in politics at the provincial and all-India levels. Consequently, a few nominees resigned from the central parliamentary board; some believed that a board composed of members with incompatible and opposite viewpoints could not function with harmony and others criticized its composition for the exclusion of their favourites.[19] Some Leaguers were under the impression that the central parliamentary board would act 'autocratically' and dictate terms to the provincial boards leaving them little autonomy. There were still others who resented the ban on holding simultaneously the tickets of two parties, those of the League and a local party, in the provincial elections.[20] A few even doubted Jinnah's organizational abilities because he had never been directly involved in the organization of a political party at the grassroots except his less known work as president of the Bombay branch of the Home Rule League during Mrs Annie Besant's internment. One scholar-politician even observed that Jinnah had not done 'a day's solid political work' and organization was 'foreign to him'.[21] Some Muslims propagated that he would take the League into the Congress camp and others asserted that he would side with the British government.[22] Such responses were expressions of feelings of jealousy, intolerance and ignorance. Jinnah silenced his critics by asking for suggestions to improve the composition of the central parliamentary board and by declaring that the alterations could be made in its composition without amending its rules. Besides, the central parliamentary board empowered him to take disciplinary action against 'any member who might be found guilty of insubordination, disloyalty or defiance of the policies' as laid down by the central board. Jinnah on his part demonstrated extreme patience in dealing with his detractors and in handling personal rivalries and factional tussles.

The central parliamentary board developed an organization of its own, completely separate from that of the All-India Muslim League. It provided for a president, a secretary and a treasurer. The board formally elected M.A. Jinnah as its president, Abdul Matin Choudhry as secretary and Amir Ahmad Khan, the Raja of Mahmudabad (1914–1973), as treasurer.[23] It was authorized to have a working committee and could appoint subcommittees to perform its functions. It was empowered to raise funds for the elections and disburse these for propaganda and publicity. The procedure for the central parliamentary board meetings was elaborately laid down. Members from various provinces on the central parliamentary board were responsible for constituting provincial election (parliamentary) boards, and get them affiliated with the central board. If they were unable to do so within a reasonable time, the central parliamentary board had the authority to establish and affiliate any provincial parliamentary board. These provincial parliamentary boards were to select candidates for the elections and provide a list of the candidates to the central parliamentary board two months before the polling dates. The candidates for the elections were to sign a pledge that they had accepted the programmes of the central parliamentary board and the provincial parliamentary board. They had to abide by this pledge and were barred from signing the pledge of any other party. A provincial parliamentary board could cooperate with any group(s) after the elections by votes of a two-third majority provided the aims and objects of the group(s) were in line with those of the central parliamentary board and the provincial parliamentary board. The central parliamentary board had the power to suspend or disaffiliate any provincial parliamentary board; and in September 1936, it authorized Jinnah to take disciplinary action against any of its members who might be guilty of 'insubordination, disloyalty or defiance' of its principles and policies. It could amend its rules by a two-third majority. The council or any other party organ, except the all-India session, had no authority over the central board.[24] The central parliamentary board issued a programme on 11 June, in which the All-India Muslim League declared to protect the religious rights of the Muslims—the opinions of the Jamiatul Ulama-i-Hind and the Shia *Mujtahids* in this regard were to receive due weight; to secure the repeal of all repressive laws; to resist those that encroached upon fundamental liberties of the people and led to their economic exploitation; to divert funds from the administration to the development expenditure; to nationalize the Indian army and reduce its expenditure; to encourage the development of industries including the cottage industries; to regulate currency, exchange and prices; to take steps for the uplift of the rural population; to sponsor measures to alleviate rural indebtedness; to make elementary education free and compulsory; to promote Urdu language and script; to reduce the burden of taxation; to create healthy public opinion and general political consciousness; and to take other steps for the amelioration of the general condition of the Muslims. The All-India Muslim League was, however, opposed to any movement that aimed at the 'expropriation of private property'. The provincial parliamentary boards, when constituted, issued their own manifestoes that were in line with that of the central parliamentary board.

The provincial parliamentary boards were formed after a strenuous process. Jinnah had practically little to offer except his own past record and appeal to the Indian Muslims to unite on the all-India platform of the Muslim League. It was quite difficult to persuade the provincial leaders to eschew personal and factional rivalries and rise above provincial loyalties. After extensive tours and protracted negotiations, Jinnah was able to form provincial parliamentary boards in Bombay, Punjab, United Provinces, Bengal, Madras and Assam, which were affiliated with the central parliamentary board. The provincial parliamentary board that he set up in the province of Central Provinces and Berar broke up into two groups. Jinnah's efforts to establish provincial parliamentary boards in Sindh and Bihar did not succeed and as for Orissa, he was neither familiar with its Muslim leaders nor had the time to approach them. The process of forming central parliamentary board-recognised provincial parliamentary boards began with Bombay. Here the provincial parliamentary board was constituted without any difficulty. Jinnah himself was elected its president and Husainbhai Lalji (b. 1886) its secretary; and later on, M.M.S. Ispahani and then T.T. Barodwala followed Husainbhai Lalji as secretary of the board. The Bombay provincial parliamentary board functioned smoothly without any intra-party conflict. In July 1936, it issued a manifesto and selected its candidates for the elections. There were only two appeals against the selected candidates, which the central parliamentary board settled amicably.[25]

The formation of a Punjab provincial parliamentary board was not so smooth. Jinnah's frequent visits to Lahore produced limited success. At first, he talked to Fazli Husain, the leader and mentor of the non-communal Unionist Party, the largest party in the provincial assembly since 1923. He tried to persuade Fazli Husain to use the all-India platform of the League for the elections and coalesce with any non-Muslim group or party in the Punjab assembly after the elections. But Fazli Husain declined to accept his proposal, as he had already decided to participate in the elections from the Unionist platform, believing it injurious to the interests of the Punjab Muslims to use the platform of the League. Besides, he could not sit on the Punjab provincial parliamentary board with his unrelenting critics, the Ahrar, who had been denouncing his pro-Ahmadi sympathies; and his emissaries failed to convince Jinnah that the Ahrar would simply exploit the League platform for their own propaganda.[26] He tried to use his influence to damage the central parliamentary board in the Punjab and elsewhere.[27] Jinnah's unreserved support came from Allama Iqbal and his followers. The Majlis-i-Ahrar-i-Islam and the short-lived Majlis-i-Ittehad-i-Millat were reluctant to join the Punjab provincial parliamentary board unless the All-India Muslim League had 'complete independence' as its objective and banned the entry of the Ahmadis into the League.[28] They were told that it was only the All-India Muslim League annual session that could take decisions on both these issues. The differences were eventually resolved and both the parties agreed to become part of the provincial parliamentary board.[29] The Punjab provincial Muslim League was revived in the process which formally barred the Ahmadis from enrolling as its members to meet the Ahrar demand and recommended to the All-India Muslim League to adopt 'complete independence' as the party objective.[30] However, the Majlis-i-Ahrar and Ittehad-i-Millat did not stay in the Punjab provincial parliamentary board for long. Soon after, they left the Board: the former in June 1936; and the latter in September, using their differences with the League over the dues of a candidate's subscription and fee for the party ticket.[31] They were perhaps expecting funds from the League for fighting the elections rather than themselves spending handsome amounts just to obtain the party tickets. This was in contrast to those *ulama* attached to the Congress who got funds from that party for the election campaign.[32] After their exit, some of their members stayed with the League. The Punjab provincial parliamentary board was then restricted to the provincial Muslim League whose members came essentially from the cities and whom the Unionist leader ridiculed as 'miscellaneous urbanites'.[33] The death of Fazli Husain on 9 July, did not bring about any change in the situation, except that one prominent Unionist, Malik Zaman Mehdi (1879–1941), joined the Punjab provincial parliamentary board and Maulana Zafar Ali Khan returned to the League fold.[34] The new Unionist leader, Sardar Sikandar Hayat Khan (1892–1942), stuck to Fazli Husain's policies for the time being. The Punjab provincial parliamentary board issued a manifesto in line with that of the central parliamentary board and in October, Jinnah visited Lahore to inaugurate its election campaign. The Punjab provincial parliamentary board could, however, field only seven candidates in the elections.

Factionalism in the United Provinces Muslims that hurt the unity of the provincial parliamentary board was partly the result of their grouping as 'nationalists' and 'conservatives'. The attempts by the British and the Congress to mould Muslim thinking particularly in that province to serve their interests caused further complications. At that time, Muslims had two main political parties in the United Provinces: Muslim Unity Board led by Choudhry Khaliquzzaman and Raja of Salempur; and the National Agriculturist Party led by Nawab Mohammad Yusuf and Nawab Ahmad Said Khan Chhatari.[35] The United Provinces Muslim League had been revived on 26 October 1935, after eight years of inactivity, but the Leaguers still preferred to use the platforms of the unity board and the Agriculturist Party. Earlier, in November 1934, the pro-Congress Leaguers, the Khilafatists and some Jamiatul Ulama-i-Hind *ulama* had formed the Muslim Unity Board to participate in the elections to the central assembly while the primarily pro-British Muslims had recently founded the National Agriculturalist Party. Jinnah had included members of both these parties and leading Jamiatul Ulama-i-Hind *ulama* in the central parliamentary board after consulting most of them individually. The representatives of these parties carried their mutual differences into the United Provinces parliamentary board when the provincial parliamentary board was formed in the presence of Jinnah on 15 August 1936, with Raja of Salempur as its chairman. They wanted to control the provincial parliamentary board and looked to Jinnah for endorsement. Their leaders travelled to Lahore and then to Bombay to seek his guidance and direction.[36] Khaliquzzaman outmanoeuvred his rivals in this tussle. Nawab Yusuf and Nawab Chhatari left the provincial parliamentary board because they wanted to contest the elections on the tickets of both the parties, the League as well as the National Agriculturist Party, but the central parliamentary board rules did not allow such an arrangement. Therefore, they decided to participate in the elections on the tickets of the National Agriculturalist Party. Liaquat Ali Khan was among those who resigned from the United Provinces parliamentary board but contested the elections as an independent candidate, and kept Jinnah regularly informed about his moves.[37] Unlike the Majlis-i-Ahrar-i-Islam and Ittehad-i-Millat, which left the Punjab provincial parliamentary board before the elections, the Jamiatul Ulama-i-Hind in the United Provinces stayed with the United Provinces parliamentary board and did not break away till after the elections. The United Provinces parliamentary board put up thirty-five candidates in the elections.

Muslim politics in Bengal at the time of elections revolved around four political parties: (*i*) the United Muslim Party, founded by Nawab Khwaja Habibullah (1895–1958), Huseyn Shaheed Suhrawardy (1893–1963), and Khwaja Nazimuddin (1894–1964) and his brother Khwaja Shahabuddin in May 1936; (*ii*) the Krishak Praja Samity, reorganized by its founder-president Fazlul Haq, which retained its non-communal character although its Hindu component was negligible but it had a strong group of Muslims with pro-Congress leanings; (*iii*) the New Muslim Majlis, founded by Abdur Rahman Siddiqi, M.A.H. Ispahani (1902–1981) and others; and (*iv*) the Bengal presidency Muslim League. The competition among these parties created a serious conflict that they were all anxious to resolve. On their joint invitation, Jinnah visited Bengal in August 1936 in order to mediate among them to create unity in the Muslim ranks and bring them along with Muslims of other provinces on the platform of the All-India Muslim League.[38] Jinnah visited Bengal for a week (17–23 August) and successfully persuaded all of them to join a 48-member provincial parliamentary board, on which United Muslim Party and Krishak Praja Samity had fifteen members each, New Muslim Majlis and provincial Muslim League seven members each; and Jinnah was empowered to nominate four members to give representation to those elements that might not be otherwise represented on the board.[39] The agreement was based on three points: (*i*) the creed of the Bengal provincial parliamentary board would be the same as laid down in the central parliamentary board;

(*ii*) the provincial programme would depend entirely on the Bengal provincial parliamentary board; and (*iii*) there would be nothing in the provincial programme inconsistent with the policy and programme of the central parliamentary board.[40] All the parties accepted the All-India Muslim League as the only representative party of the Muslims and agreed to work under the banner of the central parliamentary board in accordance with its policy and programme. But soon after the formation of the provincial parliamentary board, Fazlul Haq realized that he had been outmanoeuvred by his rivals, as he found the members of his party in a minority on the parliamentary board. His frustration increased when the provincial parliamentary board refused to incorporate the economic programme of his party especially the abolition of Permanent Settlement in its manifesto. The ensuing conflict generated bitterness and acrimony which eventually led to the exit of Fazlul Haq and his party from the provincial parliamentary board before the elections.[41] The contest on the Muslim seats in Bengal remained confined to the candidates of the provincial parliamentary board and the Krishak Praja Samity. On the request of the provincial parliamentary board, Jinnah again visited Bengal and toured the districts of Calcutta, Dhaka, Mymensingh and Comilla for nine days (3–11 January 1937) in support of the candidates put up by the provincial board.[42]

In Madras, the Leaguers had revived the district Muslim Leagues before the formation of the provincial parliamentary board. The central parliamentary board had four members from Madras: three (M. Jamal Mohammad, Sayyid Murtaza Sahib and Abdul Hamid Khan) from the Tamil region, one (B. Poker) from Kerala but none from the Andhra region.[43] Although those nominated had been quite well-known in the politics of the Madras PML and the All-India Muslim League yet the imbalanced representation from various regions invited criticism against the nominations.[44] Jamal Mohammad chaired the Madras provincial parliamentary board, with three secretaries (B. Poker, Abdul Hamid Khan and Ahmad Ibrahim), and the board selected thirteen candidates for the Madras legislative assembly and one for its legislative council.[45] The leadership of Jamal Mohammad, a rich businessman and a philanthropist who was widely respected in the Madras presidency, softened the criticism of the dissenting members. Jamal provided funds and his personal staff to assist in the election campaign; and all the League candidates except one were elected.[46] In the province of Central Provinces and Berar, two League leaders, Sayyid Rauf Shah (1896–1954) and Mohammad Yusuf Shareef, had been nominated on the central parliamentary board. Jinnah visited Nagpur and constituted a provincial parliamentary board, but as soon as he left, differences arose between them in the process of selection of candidates for the elections. Jinnah invited them to Bombay to resolve their differences. On 22 December, they had a meeting with him along with their supporters. At the end of discussions, they signed a pact and finalized a list of candidates on the fourteen Muslim seats. But the conflict resurfaced as soon as they returned to their province.[47] They set up two separate provincial parliamentary boards whose members blamed each other for wriggling out of the Bombay Pact. On 1 January 1937, Jinnah again visited Nagpur to resolve their differences but failed to bring about an understanding between the two groups, as they had already selected and fielded their candidates. The two provincial parliamentary boards, however, accepted the policy and programme of the central parliamentary board and approached the electorate in the name of the League.[48]

In Sindh, three Muslim parties were in the field to contest the elections. The Sindh Azad Party that had been established in September 1935, by combining three parties: the Karachi Khilafat Committee, the Sindh Hari Association and the Sindh branch of the Jamiatul Ulama-i-Hind.[49] It was headed by the veteran politician Shaikh Abdul Majid Sindhi with Mazhar Ali Alavi as secretary. It claimed to have forty-eight branches in the districts. On the day Sindh became a separate province, it issued its manifesto. Jinnah nominated four members from Sindh on the central parliamentary board; Abdul Majid Sindhi, Hakim Fateh Mohammad Sehwani, Mohammad Siddiq Khadda and Hashim Gazdar. All the four nominees hailed from Karachi, which had only two electoral constituencies, and they held mutually conflicting views.[50] Abdul Majid Sindhi wanted to affiliate the Sindh Azad Party with the All-India Muslim League as its branch without changing its name but that could not be done under the constitution of the League. This factor partly hindered the formation of a Sindh provincial parliamentary board. Even Jinnah's visit to Karachi in December 1936, could not bring about any positive results.[51] The second party, the Sindh United Party, was founded by Haji Abdullah Haroon, as a non-communal party on the pattern of the Punjab Unionist Party although it had practically no significant non-Muslim component. It was formally launched on 9 June 1936, when it issued its rules and a manifesto. It counted Sir Shahnawaz Bhutto (1888–1957) and Sir Ghulam Husain Hidayatullah (1879–1948) among its leaders who otherwise had been rivals in provincial politics. The optimism generated by this demonstration of unity soon disappeared when the Sindh United Party split up on the election of office-bearers. On 1 November 1936, the party elected a president (Abdullah Haroon), three vice-presidents [Shahnawaz Bhutto, Hidayatullah and Miran Mohammad Shah (1898–1963)], two secretaries (Ayub Khuhro and Hashim Gazdar), and two joint secretaries [Hatim Alavi (1898–1976) and Meharali Shah].[52] Hidayatullah left the party along with his supporters that included Ayub Khuhro, Mir Bandeh Ali Talpur (d. 1975) and Noor Mohammad, alleging that the Sindh United Party had broken a pledge by electing Miran Mohammad Shah as the third vice president.[53] He formed a new party, the Sindh Muslim Party, which issued a manifesto on the eve of elections and fielded its own candidates.

In the NWFP, one Muslim group enjoying popular support for their recent struggle against the British was the Khudai Khidmatgars, which was aligned with the Congress. Jinnah and other Leaguers had made their contribution for the introduction of constitutional reforms in the NWFP before and during the round table conferences. In February 1935, they had joined other members in the central legislative assembly to demand that the ban on the Khudai Khidmatgar organization should be lifted.[54] Jinnah had spoken on issues relating to the NWFP but perhaps had never visited the region. After the Bombay session, the Frontier Muslim Leaguers revived the provincial Muslim League, and Jinnah nominated four of them, Malik Khuda Bakhsh (1889–1951), Peer Bakhsh (1904–1975), Allah Bakhsh Yusufi (1900–1968) and Rahim Bakhsh Ghaznavi (1903–1979), on the central parliamentary board. In August 1936, they set up a provincial parliamentary board on their own initiative but subsequently most of them joined the Muslim Independent Party that Sahibzada Abdul Qayyum had established with himself as president and Peer Bakhsh as secretary to contest the elections. After the revival of the provincial Muslim League, the Leaguers had made several requests to Jinnah to visit the province. After they joined the Muslim Independent Party, a formal invitation was sent to him on its behalf.[55] Finally, in October, Jinnah visited the NWFP for one week (18–24 October), held talks with the leaders of different parties, spoke to the students of the Islamia college and Edwardes college and addressed a few public meetings. The only other place, besides Peshawar, that he visited was Landi Kotal.[56] Jinnah's Frontier visit was more of an educational tour. After assessing the political situation in the province, he did not insist that the Leaguers should maintain a completely separate platform in the elections. Therefore, the Leaguers participated in the elections on the tickets of the Muslim Independent Party or as independent candidates.

In Bihar, the provincial Muslim League was revived soon after the Bombay session but initially it could not draw much public support.[57] The province had three other parties. There was the Muslim Unity Board, which was similar to the one that existed in the neighbouring United Provinces; the unity board enjoyed wide popular support.[58] Before the elections, in September 1936, a new party, Muslim Independent Party, was formed with Maulana Abul Mahasin Mohammad Sajjad (1882–1940), the *Naib-i-Amir* of the influential religious body the *Amarat-i-Shariat*, as its president. The third party was the Majlis-i-Ahrar-i-Islam that had considerable support throughout Bihar. Jinnah included members of these parties in the central parliamentary board but he could not muster enough support in the province to form a separate provincial parliamentary board. In the absence of a League platform, the Leaguers participated in the elections on the tickets of other political parties. In Assam, two provincial Muslim Leagues had nominally survived since the days of the Simon Commission, one led by Faiz Noor Ali and Serajuddin; and the other headed by Maulvi Mohammad Abdullah. These Leagues were reactivated after the Bombay session. Abdul Matin Choudhry was in the League that Faiz Noor Ali headed. Jinnah nominated Abdul Matin along with M.A. Razzaque on the central parliamentary board from Assam. This League established a few sub-divisional and district Leagues and asked the All-India Muslim League for affiliation. The other League continued to have its separate existence. Because of the divisions in the Leaguers, Jinnah did not form a provincial parliamentary board in Assam. The two Leagues participated in the elections separately but forged unity after the elections.[59]

The central parliamentary board and provincial parliamentary boards organized the election campaign on the basis of their manifestoes. Jinnah assisted them by coordinating their activities in his frequent visits to the provinces. He repetitively advised the Muslims to unite on the League platform and cooperate with any group or party with objectives similar to those of the League party after the elections. His arguments with Pandit Jawaharlal Nehru, the Congress president, during his election tour of Bengal (3–11 January), warmed the hearts of the Muslims of India and rallied them round him and the League candidates. Nehru's observations were a mixture of the Congress self-perception as the only majority political party in India and his own dogmatic socialist and idealistic worldview, expressed in a pompous, dismissive and flippant style and language. Jinnah's tone in his speeches changed after Nehru's observations. He responded to Nehru's assertions in an equally spirited, confident and cutting language. Nehru, in the course of a speech, had observed: 'there are only two parties in India—the [British] Government and the Congress—and others must line up.' Jinnah's reply on 3 January, was: 'I refuse to line up with the Congress. I refuse to accept this proposition. There is a third party in this country and that is Muslim India. . . . We are not going to be the camp followers of any party. . . . We are willing as equal partners to come to a settlement with our sister communities in the interest of India.'[60] Nehru reacted and said on 11 January: 'I am totally unable to think on . . . communal lines . . . Such ideas are medieval and out of date . . . Religion is a . . . personal matter . . . [To] stress religion in political and economic [matters] is obscurantism. . . . What does the Muslim League stand for? Does it stand for the independence of India—for anti-Imperialism? I believe not. It represents . . . the upper middle classes. I come into greater touch with the Muslim masses than most of the members of the Muslim League.'[61] Jinnah responded on 19 January:

> Pandit Jawaharlal Nehru is torn between Benares and Moscow . . . his claim that he has got a large body of Muslim followers cannot be accepted by any intelligent man . . . [Like the Muslim League, the Congress is also composed of] estimable persons of the upper middle class . . . What is the total number of members of the Congress? . . . I would ask him also to define how he wants us to fight Imperialism. At one time he says we must wipe off all the Princes . . . capitalists, confiscate their property . . . [and at] another time he says we must present a united front for the achievement of freedom first and . . . decide everything else through a constituent assembly at some unknown date. . . . The Congress [is not] the sole custodian of Indian nationalism. . . . We are not prepared to merge ourselves into any organization, however great it may be. . . . The urgent question facing every nationalist in India today is how to create unity out of diversity. . . . I would request him to come to earth . . . and give up his fantastic programme. Is he going to rise or remain as Peter Pan, who never grew up?[62]

This was just the beginning. More was to come after the elections.

The All-India Muslim League demonstrated its presence in electoral politics although its success was not spectacular in numerical terms. It had come into the field from almost non-existence in the middle of 1936 and completed its preparations with practically no experience in collective electoral politics in a short period of six months. Even then, its performance in the elections was commendable as compared to the number of Muslim seats that the Congress won in the elections, as shown below:[63]

Table 5.1: Election results, 1937

Province	Total Muslim seats (including special constituencies)	All-India Muslim League	Congress	Total Seats
Bombay	30	20	3	175
Punjab	89	2	2	175
United Provinces	64	29	3	228
Bengal	119	40	-	250
Madras	29	11	4	215
Central Provinces and Berar	14	-	-	112
Sindh	35	-	-	60
NWFP	38	-	15	50
Bihar	40	-	-	152
Assam	34	10	-	108
Orissa	4	-	-	60
Total	496	110*	27	1585
Bombay	30	20	3	175

* These seats do not include those Leaguers who won the seats as independent candidates in provinces where the provincial parliamentary boards could not be constituted or in the Central Provinces and Berar where the board broke up into two groups.

Jinnah claimed that the All-India Muslim League had won 60 to 70 per cent of the seats that its members had contested in the elections. The strength of the League in the provincial assemblies in the following years fluctuated; therefore, various contemporary sources give different number of seats in the provinces, depending on the time of the citation. The number of the League members of the provincial assembly gradually increased, as the number of those who joined the League was much higher than those who left the party. By the time of the Calcutta special session, the League had formed assembly parties in Bengal, Punjab, NWFP, Bombay, United Provinces, Bihar, Assam, Madras and Central Provinces; soon after that in the Sindh assembly.

(C) FORMATION OF MINISTRIES

The Congress won 716 out of 1,585 seats in the provincial assemblies, which included only twenty-seven Muslim seats out of which fifteen were in the NWFP assembly. It had secured majorities in six out of eleven provinces. After its initial reluctance to accept offices because of the special powers and responsibilities of the governors in the Act of 1935, concerning the protection of minorities, services and other matters, the Congress accepted to form ministries in these provinces on getting assurances to its satisfaction. Later on, it also formed a coalition government in the NWFP as well. For the interim period, i.e. between the declaration of results and assumption of power by the Congress, interim ministries were sworn in to look after the administration. The Congress philosophy, as vaguely hinted at by Pandit Jawaharlal Nehru in 1924 and put forth by him as its president with more clarity in the 1937 election campaign, that the Congress provided the Indians a 'national forum' within which political parties like the All-India Muslim League, Jamiatul Ulama-i-Hind, All-India Hindu Mahasabha and others should function as social and religious groups was relentlessly pursued after the elections.[64] The Congress implemented this philosophy first in the formation of ministries in the Hindu majority provinces, and then in its Muslim mass contact movement. Conversely, Jinnah on his assumption of the League presidency and in the election campaign had repeatedly offered to cooperate with the Congress or any party which had objectives similar to those of the All-India Muslim League. After the elections, he reiterated this offer of forming coalitions/alliances 'if the basic principles are determined by common consent'.[65] But the League had limited options, as it was neither a majority party nor the largest party in any province although it had reasonable number of seats in the assemblies of Bengal, Bombay, Madras, United Provinces and Assam. The Congress had the initiative in the Hindu majority provinces where it had clear majorities and could easily form ministries.

After the elections, in March 1937, the Congress working committee appointed a three-member [Maulana Azad, Babu Rajendra Prasad

(1884–1963) and Sardar Vallabhbhai Patel] parliamentary subcommittee to keep itself in touch with the work of the Congress parties in the provincial assemblies to 'advise them in their activities'. Then, in July, each member of the subcommittee was assigned to look after the party affairs in different provinces: Azad dealt with matters relating to Bengal, United Provinces, Punjab and NWFP; Rajendra Prasad had Bihar, Orissa and Assam in his purview; and Patel oversaw matters in Sindh, Central Provinces and Berar, Madras and Bombay.[66] Members of this subcommittee and the Congress president, Nehru, played a crucial role in determining the Congress–League relations in the provincial assemblies. Rajendra Prasad spelt out the party policy without any ambiguity. Commenting on the chances of Congress–League cooperation in the assemblies, he declared in Patna on 4 March, that the two parties were fundamentally different in their objectives — the former was in favour of working the constitution while the latter was for wrecking it — and that there could be no cooperation between them until individual Leaguers joined the Congress.[67] This was precisely the policy that the Congress leaders followed in their negotiations with the League leaders in the formation of ministries. In Bombay, Bal Gangadhar Kher (1888–1957), the chief minister-designate, wanted to coalesce with the twenty-member Bombay League assembly party, which had also added to its strength ten Independent Muslim members of the provincial assembly.[68] He asked Jinnah as president of the Bombay provincial parliamentary board to give him two League members to join his ministry. Jinnah readily agreed, and offered Kher his party's fullest cooperation to the Congress ministry in Bombay. When Patel came to know of this development, he immediately rushed to Bombay to prevent Kher from doing that. Kher was directed to ask those Leaguers who would join his ministry to resign from the League and join the Congress. The League summarily rejected the suggestion.[69]

The Congress–League talks for coalition-formation in the United Provinces further embittered relations between the two parties. Many pro-Congress Leaguers, who had worked on the Congress parliamentary board in the 1934 elections to the central assembly, had keenly looked forward to a new chapter in the League–Congress relations. The United Provinces parliamentary board had won twenty-nine seats in the provincial assembly while the remaining Muslim seats had been shared by the National Agriculturalist Party and Independents. After the elections, some Independents had formed a Democratic Party.[70] Jinnah visited Lucknow in March 1937, when both these groups, the National Agriculturists and Independents, joined the United Provinces League assembly party. All the League members of the provincial assembly including the new ones then signed the League pledge and elected Khaliquzzaman as their leader in the assembly.[71] At this stage, the members of the provincial assembly of the Jamiatul Ulama-i-Hind left the League provincial parliamentary board and joined the Congress; their number, however, was negligible. Before the formation of the United Provinces ministry, Govind Ballabh Pant (1887–1961), leader of the Congress assembly party, Azad and Nehru negotiated with Khaliquzzaman to associate the United Provinces League with the Congress ministry. During these talks, Khaliquzzaman failed to keep his colleagues in the provincial parliamentary board or Jinnah regularly informed about the progress of his talks with the Congress amidst rumours about his abandoning of separate electorates, which caused misunderstanding about his moves. When he did not respond to Jinnah's written queries for three weeks, Jinnah stated the factual position in a press statement to prevent anything happening out of line with the League policy.[72] Finally, on 7 May, the United Provinces board met in Lucknow with Jinnah in the chair to appraise the whole situation. After thorough discussion, the misunderstandings were removed and Jinnah expressed his confidence in the provincial Muslim League leadership, describing United Provinces as 'the heart of Muslim India'.[73] The United Provinces board unanimously authorized Khaliquzzaman to continue his negotiations with the Congress leaders. When Khaliquzzaman resumed the talks with Pant and Azad in middle of July, they asked him to sign a document detailing amazingly bizarre Congress terms for coalition.[74] The terms provided that the League assembly party would cease to function as a separate group in the United Provinces legislature and its members of the provincial assembly would become part of the Congress assembly party. They would then have the same privileges and obligations as the Congress members, and be subject to the discipline of the Congress and implement the policy laid down by its working committee. The League provincial parliamentary board would also stand dissolved, and the Leaguers in future would be bound to support the candidates put up by the Congress in the bye-elections. In return, the League members would have representation in the United Provinces ministry.[75] No self-respecting leader of a political party could accept such humiliating terms. This was the end of Khaliquzzaman's talks with the Congress leaders.[76]

The Congress then began to approach individual Leaguers who had been 'overwhelmed' by its victory at the polls and were willing to cooperate on its terms.[77] A few Leaguers were tempted by offers of ministries or just opted to support the Congress without any condition. The long-time Leaguer Yaqub Hasan in Madras, Hafiz Mohammad Ibrahim (1889–1968), a close relative of Maulana Hifzur Rahman Seoharvi (1901–1962), in United Provinces, Yusuf Shareef in Central Provinces and Berar, and Dr Yasin Noori (1895–1971) in Bombay who had been elected on the League ticket became ministers in the Congress governments in their respective provinces.[78] The pro-Congress statements of Wazir Hasan, former honorary secretary of the All-India Muslim League and president of its Bombay session (1936), urging the Leaguers to abjure the political role of their party, were equally embarrassing for the League leadership.[79] The All-India Muslim League could not tolerate these desertions. It gradually enforced discipline in the party to put a stop to this trend and took disciplinary action against those who had deviated from its policy and programme.[80] Initially, it had not visualized any breach of discipline at that level. Before the elections, when a resolution was proposed in the central council that if it was proved against a member that he had opposed a candidate put up by a League provincial parliamentary board, his name should be removed from the membership of the League. Jinnah had disallowed this resolution to be moved in the council.[81] Now the League took disciplinary action against those who had joined the Congress ministries or had worked against its policy and programme; Jinnah himself wrote and signed the show cause notices to some of them. Consequently, membership of a few prominent long-time Leaguers was cancelled; among them were such political figures as Yaqub Hasan, Wazir Hasan and Yusuf Shareef.[82] Following this example, the names of several Leaguers in the provinces were also removed from the League membership.[83] These disciplinary actions dispelled the impression that anyone could stay in the All-India Muslim League by violating its policy and programme or could easily stage a comeback into the party. Hafiz Mohammad Ibrahim left his seat in the United Provinces assembly but did not resign from the ministership. He was re-elected in a bye-election in Bijnor, allegedly by using official pressure, unlimited financial resources of the Congress and other unfair methods. Earlier, the League had won the hotly contested bye-election in Jhansi (United Provinces) and that bye-election had generated so much enthusiasm that Haji Abdussattar Haji Essak Sait (1896–1968) sent one thousand copies of an appeal on behalf of 1.5 million Mappilas in support of the League candidate for distribution in the constituency.[84] Ibrahim's victory did not do much damage to the League's image because of its victory in the Jhansi and four other bye-elections.[85] Later on, in July 1939, when Azad renewed his efforts to wean away Leaguers in the Central Provinces, the All-India Muslim League working committee laid down the policy that no provincial Muslim League should negotiate with the Congress on the Hindu–Muslim question and if it received any such proposal, it should ask the Congress leaders to approach the president or the working committee.[86]

(D) MUSLIM MASS CONTACT MOVEMENT

After an analysis and assessment of the election results and its poor performance in the Muslim constituencies, the Congress concluded that the lack of Muslim support to its candidates in the elections had been due to the absence of its interaction with the Muslim masses. Therefore, it decided to launch a Muslim mass contact campaign rather than interact with any intermediary Muslim political party. The 'terms of coalition' that it had offered to the Bombay and United Provinces League assembly parties were a reflection of this policy. The Congress president, in pursuance of this policy, issued a circular letter to the provincial Congress committees, asking them to work among the Muslim masses. He proposed the formation of provincial mass contact committees to arouse Muslim interest in the Congress affairs and to enrol them as members. He advised the provincial Congress committees to publish the information about the party meetings in Urdu as well, at a time when the provincial Congress assembly parties were exerting to make Hindi as the official language.[87] For this Muslim mass contact campaign, the Congress could use only a couple of liberal Hindus; Pandit Nehru was the most prominent among them. It had to depend largely on the Muslims, initially the nationalist Muslims in its ranks who shared its philosophy and saw in Jinnah's ambition to unite all the Muslims under the banner of one Muslim political organization 'too optimistic a view of the situation'.[88] Then, it won over the religious leaders, comprising a section of the Jamiatul Ulama-i-Hind and the Majlis-i-Ahrar-i-Islam, who were disillusioned with the working of the central parliamentary board and provincial parliamentary boards of the League.[89] In addition, these Muslims were attracted by the anti-imperialist and pro-complete Independence slogans of the Congress.

Azad played a crucial role in winning them over to the Congress. At his instance, the Jamiatul Ulama-i-Hind leaders at a Muslim conference in Allahabad on 17 May 1937, chaired by Maulana Hifzur Rahman, pronounced their 'unanimous opinion' that 'the only right policy and correct attitude for the Muslims to act upon and adopt is to unconditionally join the Indian National Congress and participate in the *satyagraha* for the freedom of the country'.[90] The Majlis-i-Ahrar-i-Islam in the Punjab, after its separation from the provincial parliamentary board, turned its propaganda guns against the League. The Congress leaders exploited the oratorical gifts of its leaders for their benefit. Then, there were the Khudai Khidmatgars who were ready to pay back manifold the Congress support that they had received in their difficult days in the struggle against the British.

The Congress Muslim mass contact campaign had two aspects. One aspect was to give a positive projection to the party, its leadership and its programme among the Muslims. The party's organizational machine, its vast financial resources and the network of the pro-Congress print media, some of which its members owned and administered, were employed in this campaign. Moreover, wherever the Congress ministries were in office the official resources were also available to fund and run the mass contact campaign and engage paid workers for the organizational work at the district and grassroots level. The Congress propagated that it was the only non-communal 'national' party in India that gave equal space and treatment to members of all the communities. Its all-India leaders like Gandhi, Nehru, Subhas Chandra Bose (1897–1945) and Azad who actively participated in this campaign were painted as non-communal, anti-imperialist and revolutionary personalities who had made great sacrifices for the Indian national cause. The Congress programme was to wreck the constitution under the Act of 1935, and to have a constituent assembly on the basis of adult franchise to frame a new constitution. Its focus was on its anti-imperialist struggle for the freedom of India. The party emphasized its social and economic reform plans to ameliorate the condition of the common person without any discrimination. Its leaders bluntly denied the existence of any Hindu–Muslim question or the minorities' problem.[91] The second aspect of the Congress mass contact campaign was the negative depiction and vilification especially of its main rival, the All-India Muslim League, its leadership particularly Jinnah, and its programme. The All-India Muslim League was depicted as a religious group whose objectives were based on a medieval concept. It was composed of Muslims of upper middle class, and was controlled and run by them for their vested interests. Its membership was less than the Muslim membership of the Congress.[92] It was a communal body, and if it wanted any settlement with the Hindus, Nehru advised the League, it must negotiate with the Hindu communal party, the All-India Hindu Mahasabha. Interestingly, the Congress working committee, in its meeting on 11–16 December 1938, formally listed these two parties as communal organizations.[93] Jinnah was maligned by all kinds of negative epithets, a 'reactionary', a 'rank communalist', a 'fanatic', 'unpatriotic', pro-British and 'ally of the Imperialists'. The League was denounced as a 'reactionary force' that did not have the freedom of the country as its ideal.[94] Despite the availability of all kinds of resources at its disposal, the Congress Muslim mass contact movement failed to produce the desired results and was soon abandoned.

The Muslim League on its part had begun its own mass contact campaign; Jinnah wanted to make the All-India Muslim League a 'really representative Parliament of Muslim India'.[95] The Congress indirectly helped the All-India Muslim League to broaden its support-base. Its target had not been just the All-India Muslim League; it included any Muslim group or Muslim-dominated party that was allied with the League or was not in line with the Congress policy. For example, it denounced the Krishak Praja Party and dubbed its leader, Fazlul Haq, as 'orthodox' and 'die-hard communalist' and derided the Punjab Unionist Party and its leaders, Sikandar Hayat Khan, as 'reactionaries', 'toadies', and 'pro-Imperialists'. These Muslim-dominated parties resented this policy, which gradually brought them closer to the All-India Muslim League without much persuasion.[96] The Congress in its campaign had won over those groups that were willing to support its policy and programme. Its initial focus was on the Jamiatul Ulama-i-Hind, which created a rift in that party's ranks.[97] The Jamiatul Ulama-i-Hind's splinter groups, the Markazi Jamiatul Ulama, Kanpur (United Provinces) and Delhi, and the Sarhad Jamiatul Ulama in the NWFP, moved towards the All-India Muslim League, and their leaders came to hold offices in the League. Subsequently, the widely respected Deobandi *alim*, Maulana Ashraf Ali Thanvi (1863–1943), when approached by some Muslims, gave a *fatwa* that countered the one issued by his younger Deobandi colleagues in favour of the Congress, that according to Islamic injunctions it was the religious duty of the Muslims to join the League.[98] The rift in the Deobandi *ulama* on this issue gradually widened, which reduced the capacity of the pro-Congress Jamiatul Ulama-i-Hind to play any effective role in all-India politics, except in a couple of constituencies in the United Provinces and Assam. In Bihar, the Majlis-i-Ahrar-i-Islam and its three members of the provincial assembly joined the provincial League *en bloc*. The *ulama* of Farangi Mahal, led by Maulana Abdul Bari's son Jamal Mian (b. 1920), sided with the All-India Muslim League right from the beginning. Some Brelvi *ulama* and *pirs* like Maulana Abdul Hamid Badauni (1898–1970) and Pir Jamaat Ali Shah, though had no strong organization like the Jamiatul Ulama-i-Hind but had a large following, were already active in the All-India Muslim League from the time of its revival. Jinnah welcomed these groups into the All-India Muslim League. Instead of 'fighting for the distant ideal' when the Hindus and Muslims would 'cease to be Hindus and Muslims, politically', Jinnah urged that the Congress leaders should first solve the problem of the minorities. He asked them to face the realities, and not to believe in the principle of 'acquisition first and distribution afterwards' or in the dictum 'possession first and partition afterwards'. No fully democratic responsible government, he observed, could be constructed in any country unless a 'sense of security and confidence' was created in the minorities. The Muslims needed the League till they felt secure. Jinnah advised the Muslims to unite, organize and consolidate themselves on its platform to have self-respect, self-confidence and self-reliance, and stop 'waiting at other's doors'. He denied that the All-India Muslim League was a religious party, explaining that it was a political party, which aimed at protecting the rights of the Indian Muslims. Jinnah conceded that Nehru personally might not think 'on communal lines' but 99 per cent of the people who surrounded him 'not only think on communal lines but their words and their deeds speak eloquently'.[99] He asserted that like the Congress, the League's ideal was freedom of the country. It was as anti-imperialist as the Congress or any other party, and it had campaigned in the elections to send 'patriotic nationalists and independents' to the provincial assemblies. Freedom should not mean freedom for the majority because, Jinnah asserted, even an ordinary majority could be 'extremely oppressive and tyrannical', and it was reasonable to assume that a 'majority, with a fundamentally different culture, traditions, social life and outlook' would try to force its ideals on the minorities.[100] Citing the example of Germans in Czechoslovakia, he wanted the 'religion, culture, language and political existence in national life' of the Muslims 'adequately and effectively' safeguarded.[101] He believed that the Muslims and the Hindus could not merge their identities into each other 'because of the fundamentally different heritage and culture of the two communities', but they could join hands to 'march together to the goal of freedom'.[102]

The All-India Muslim League did not attend to the organization of the party due to its involvement in the provincial elections. The initiative for the emergence of a few party branches in the districts and provinces came primarily from the Leaguers at that level without any direction from the central League. Jinnah's focus remained on the central parliamentary board, the provincial parliamentary boards and the election process, which provided the Leaguers more activities than the formal organs of the party. The League constitution, as amended in 1931, had provided for a working committee but Jinnah did not nominate the first one till 16 May 1938, and the central council met only twice after the formation of the central parliamentary board to discuss inconsequential matters.[103] Another reason for not focusing on the party organization was that the All-India Muslim League had been engaged in amending the constitution in a way that it would suit the new political environment. Meanwhile, the All-India Muslim League and the Muslims in general felt agitated by the Congress policy to bypass or to absorb Muslim parties, which somewhat softened the intensity of factional tussles in the Muslim groups and leaders. The rival groups in the provinces patched up their differences and were willing to associate themselves with the All-India Muslim League or to merge themselves into its ranks.[104] The Leaguers now enthusiastically revived the party branches or formed new ones in the provinces, districts and cities that eagerly sought affiliation with the All-India Muslim League.[105] The honorary joint secretary reported in October 1937, that Jinnah had awakened 'a new spirit in the people' that had resulted in the formation of about 600 ward, district and provincial Leagues throughout India, in the NWFP, Punjab, Delhi, United Provinces, Central Provinces Bengal and Madras.[106] The Leaguers urged the All-India Muslim League to adopt 'complete Independence' as the party objective to counter the Congress propaganda.[107] Invitations poured in from different corners of the Indian subcontinent for Jinnah to visit himself or send his representatives to the invited regions.[108] At first, Jinnah handled the party matters practically alone, as Liaquat Ali Khan, the honorary secretary, had gotten busy in his own election as an independent candidate in the United Provinces. He did not resume his work as the honorary secretary till March 1937; and soon after that, he left for Europe, appointing with Jinnah's approval Husain M. Malik, one of the joint secretaries, as his *locum tenens* to look after his work. He did not return to take charge of his office till after the Lucknow session.[109]

(E) LUCKNOW SESSION: THE TURNING POINT

The Lucknow session provided the climax of the All-India Muslim League's response to the Congress initiatives. Jinnah had received several suggestions from the Leaguers including one from Allama Iqbal to hold a Muslim convention to respond to the Congress policies. He reflected on all these suggestions and planned his strategy with caution and calculation. He wanted to use the League platform to make its annual session a historic one, a turning point in the history of the party, which would not only give its response to the Congress moves but also lay down the strategy to organize the party on sound footing. The selection of Lucknow as the venue for the session was not a smooth affair. On 21 March 1937, the council of the All-India Muslim League had decided to hold the session in Lucknow on 17–19 April, and elected Jinnah as the president.[110] But the dates were first shifted to August at the request of the United Provinces Muslim League, due to the League–Congress talks for the formation of a coalition ministry. In addition, the city of Lucknow itself at this time was feeling the heat of other activities. It had become the scene of controversies generated especially by the Shia–Sunni conflict, mixed with social and factional tussles among the Muslim leaders. Keeping these factors in view, some League leaders advised that the League should not hold its annual session in Lucknow.[111] One leading figure wrote from Allahabad that United Provinces 'is a bed of thorns' and that he was 'nervous' about holding the League session in the province.[112] Another Leaguer wrote that Lucknow, 'a hotbed of intrigue and factionalism', was 'the most undesirable place' for the annual session of the All-India Muslim League.[113]

Jinnah had to take these reports seriously. He was then receptive to the idea of changing the venue from Lucknow to Calcutta or Darjeeling.[114] He even broached the subject with Huseyn Shaheed Suhrawardy who welcomed the idea. Jinnah had another reason in mind; he felt that if the annual session was held in Calcutta, it would smooth out the affairs of the Bengal presidency Muslim League.[115] On 29 July, a representative meeting of the Muslims of Calcutta formally invited the All-India Muslim League to hold its session in that city.[116] Jinnah discussed even its tentative dates with Suhrawardy.[117] But when those Leaguers in United Provinces, who had built up an atmosphere for the session, learnt about a possible change of venue they panicked. They did realize the 'serious difficulties' of holding the session in Lucknow but suggested Allahabad as an alternative venue where there was 'absolutely no danger of any interference' from anywhere, assuring an unparalleled popular reception. The 'prestige of the League', they pointed out, would receive a 'great shock' and 'spell disaster' for its movement in the United Provinces if it did not hold its session there. The Congress Muslims, they felt, would propagate that they had 'scared' the Leaguers away from United Provinces. They desperately beseeched Jinnah not to change the venue, as it was timed with their rejection of the humiliating terms offered by the Congress for 'coalition', the desertion of prominent Leaguers, and the bye-elections on the five seats that had fallen vacant as a result of election petitions. One of them wrote that the United Provinces League needed 'outside help and encouragement to get sufficient strength to crush the internal foes and that strength can come only if the annual session is held here and in no other way'.[118] Nawab Mohammad Ismail Khan put forward the arguments in a more forceful manner.[119] Jinnah saw the strength of these arguments but he did not want to disappoint the Leaguers in Bengal also. Therefore, it was finally decided that the All-India Muslim League should hold its annual session in Lucknow on 15–18 October 1937, and a special session in Calcutta the following year in April.[120]

The Lucknow session witnessed convergence of Muslims from all over the subcontinent. Jinnah sent invitations to prominent Muslims under his own signatures, in addition to a general circular letter sent by the League office.[121] Several Muslim leaders responded to his invitation and attended the League session. Sahibzada Abdul Qayyum (NWFP) who could not attend the session due to illness sent a contingent of his supporters.[122] One delegate, Mohammad Hashim Khan Ghilzai, came from Balochistan for the first time.[123] The Bombay presidency Muslim League sent a contingent of thirty Muslim National Guards, along with the delegates, which became the 'nucleus' of the projected all-India National Guards' organization.[124] In total, about 1200 delegates attended the session. Those who could not attend the session were elated simply by the presence of diverse Muslim groups from all over India on the All-India Muslim League platform. The Muslim press representatives from different regions requested for passes to attend the session, and several Muslim associations sought affiliation.[125] Muslim chief ministers of Bengal, Punjab and Assam along with several ministers were present among the delegates. After the 1937 elections, Fazlul Haq, the Krishak Praja leader, had entered into a coalition with the Bengal presidency Muslim League to form the ministry in Bengal.[126] Harassed by the Congress he had gradually moved closer to the League. The Bengali Leaguers had been reporting to Jinnah that Fazlul Haq was ready to 'embrace' him, as he had accepted the League as the 'exponent of Muslim political opinion' both in provincial and all-India matters and wanted to organize the Praja Samity as a party for the good of the ryot.[127] Similarly, Ahmad Yar Khan Daultana was keeping Jinnah regularly informed about the Unionists' gradual shift towards the League and their keenness to join the party. After consulting Jinnah in late September, Sardar Sikandar Hayat Khan along with a contingent of his supporters attended the League session in Lucknow.[128] He along with Fazlul Haq and Sir Mohammad Saadulla (1886–1955), chief minister of Assam, formally re-joined the League.[129] There was elation and celebration in the League circles. Jinnah, in his presidential address, recounting the difficulties that the League had faced in contesting the provincial elections, lashed out at the Congress for its post-election policies, which had demonstrated as if 'Hindustan is for the Hindus', and at the British for their failure to protect the minorities according to the provisions of the Act of 1935. He asked the Muslims to devote their energies on self-organization and self-development, and not to look to the British or the Congress for assistance. They should not be discouraged by taunts such as 'communalists', 'toadies' and 'reactionaries'. Instead of the Leaguers, he observed, these appellations really fitted those Muslims who had unconditionally surrendered themselves to the Congress and abused their community; and as soon as they did so the Congress hailed them as the 'nationalists of the nationalists'. The Muslims should believe in themselves and take their destiny in their own hands. All the constitutional safeguards, he warned, would prove fruitless if these were not backed by power. Organization, he advised, would generate power that would ensure for them 'justice, fairplay and goodwill'. The Congress mass contact movement, he said, was a device to divide the Muslims, and its demand for a constituent assembly on the basis of adult franchise before the settlement of the communal problem was like 'putting the cart before the horse'. He reiterated his offer to cooperate with any party to settle the problems.[130]

At the Lucknow session, the All-India Muslim League changed its creed from full responsible government to full independence of India 'in the form of a federation of free democratic states'. The party unfurled a green flag with crescent and a star in white, which was formally adopted as the party flag at the special session in Calcutta. This flag became a party symbol and the League leaders used to hoist it in public ceremonies, terming it as the 'flag of Islam'.[131] Unfurling the League flag in Bombay on 6 June 1938, Jinnah observed that this flag had been given to the Muslims by Prophet Mohammad (PBUH) several centuries ago.[132] The party opposed the all-India federation as detrimental to the interests of the Indians particularly the Muslims. It regarded the introduction of joint electorates in the local bodies as inconsistent with the spirit of the communal award and called on its members in the assemblies to oppose any move to introduce that system in the local bodies. It criticized the British policy in Waziristan, which was meant to deprive the tribes of their freedom that they 'loved more than their lives', and condemned the demolition of the Shahidganj mosque, demanding its restoration to its original condition. It demanded immediate steps for the introduction of democratic reforms in Balochistan similar to those of other provinces. It called for the abolition of the Line System in Assam, which interfered with inter-provincial migration and inflicted hardships on the migrants. The issue of language also came up for discussion; and Jinnah got a briefing from Maulvi Abdul Haq (1870–1961) on the Urdu–Hindi question before the session. In a lengthy resolution, it was simply demanded that efforts should be made to make Urdu 'the universal language of India'.[133] Again, in December 1938, when the issue of language came up before the party, Jinnah, in deference to the sentiments of the Bengali members, observed that the All-India Muslim League had no official language as yet but as far as possible the proceedings of its meetings should be conducted in Urdu; and a resolution was passed to the effect that it 'shall make efforts to make Urdu the universal language of India'.[134] The Lucknow session also deprecated the recommendations of the Royal Palestine Commission, and appealed to the rulers of the Muslim countries to use their influence to save the holy places in Palestine from non-Muslim domination and asked the British government to change its pro-Jewish policy.[135] The working committee was asked to prepare and implement a programme of social, educational and economic reform.

On 17–18 April 1938, the All-India Muslim League held a special session in Calcutta, which was devoted to the Shahidganj mosque issue. Earlier, in January that year, a division bench of the Punjab high court had dismissed the appeal filed on behalf of the Muslims against the judgment of the district judge, Lahore, and on an appeal of the party council, the Muslims observed Friday, 22 February, as the Shahidganj Day all over India.[136] The All-India Muslim League adopted a revised constitution for its organizational structure at the Lucknow session that came into effect on 1 February 1938. The president was authorized to appoint organizing committees in every province from among the members of the council of the All-India Muslim League to form primary, district and provincial Leagues. The last date for the completion of the process of membership enrolment and party elections was 20 February; a few days later, this date was extended to 31 March. The organization process was, however, not completed on schedule. Most of the provincial Muslim Leagues were organized by the time of the next annual session in Patna, but in a few cases due to factional tussles the process of organization went on beyond the scheduled dates.

NOTES

1. QAP, F. 147, pp. 6–7.
2. AFM, vol. 220, pp. 71–72.
3. 'The Shahidganj Gurdwara: Origin and History of the Movement', *IAR*, 1935, vol. I, pp. 327–40.
4. Firoz Khan Noon to honorary secretary, All-India Muslim League, 24 July 1935, AFM, vol. 521; and *IAR*, 1935, vol. II, pp. 195–96.
5. For resolutions passed by the Punjab provincial Muslim League on 25 July 1935, and those of the All-India Muslim League council adopted on 21 July and 30 December, see AFM, vol. 521, pp. 44–46, and vol. 220, no. 43, and vol. 512, p. 53; and Firoz Khan Noon to Hafiz Hidayat Husain, 24 July 1935, ibid., vol. 521.
6. H.G. Hallet, secretary to the Government of India, to Sir Mohammad Yaqub, honorary secretary, All-India Muslim League, 29 January 1936, ibid., vol. 512, p. 53.
7. For Shamsul Hasan's comments on a letter from Zafar Ali Khan, see ibid., vol. 521, p. 36.
8. *IAR*, 1936, vol. I, p. 9.
9. Jinnah's concluding speech at the Lahore session of the All-India Muslim League on 25 May 1924, AFM, vol. 109.
10. Waheed Ahmad (ed.), *Quaid-i-Azam Muhammad Ali Jinnah: The Nation's Voice: Towards Consolidation, Speeches and Statements, March 1935–March 1940*, Karachi, 1992, pp. 12–34; *Punjab Police Abstract of Intelligence for the Year ending 31 December 1936*, Lahore, pp. 95, 105, 125, 126, 190, and 203; and Janbaz Mirza, *Tehrik-i-Masjid-i-Shahidganj* (Urdu), Lahore, 1988.
11. Azim Husain, *Fazl-i-Husain: A Political Biography*, London, 1946, pp. 306–7.

12. The Ahrar did not hide their happiness on Jinnah's visit. QAP, F. 320, p. 1.
13. Mohammad Yaqub to Sahibzada Abdul Qayyum, 18 February 1936, AFM, vol. 168, nos. 26 and 29.
14. Raja of Salempur canvassed for his own election but did not succeed. Mohammad Yaqub to Wazir Hasan, 1 March 1936, ibid., no. 30.
15. Mohammad Ali Chaiwala to Shamsul Hasan, 25 March 1936, ibid., vol. 168, no. 38.
16. Ibid., vol. 167, no. 67.
17. *Hindustan Times*, 28 April 1936. Ed.
18. Raja of Mahmudabad's observations, C.H. Philips and Mary Doreen Wainwright (ed.), *The Partition of India: Policies and Perspectives, 1935–1947*, London, 1970, p. 384; and Khalid, *Punjab Muslim League*, p. 81.
19. Mazhar Ali Azhar wanted Ghulam Husain replaced by Daud Ghaznavi. QAP, F. 514, p. 8.
20. For instance, see Abdul Aziz to Jinnah, 28 May 1936, ibid., 1090, p. 1; and Abul Aas to Jinnah, 30 May 1936, ibid., F. 821, pp. 14–15; Raghib Ahsan to Jinnah, 31 May 1936, ibid., F. 204, pp. 3–4; and Waheed, *Nation's Voice: Towards Consolidation,* pp. 57–58.
21. Shafaat Ahmad Khan to Fazli Husain, 15 June 1936, Khalid, *Punjab Muslim League,* p. 80.
22. *Statesman,* 20 August 1936.
23. Abdul Matin was elected secretary of the central parliamentary board, a few days after Liaquat's election as honorary secretary of the All-India Muslim League.
24. For Jinnah's ruling in the council meeting to this effect on 21 March 1937, see AFM, vol. 222, pp. 74–77.
25. Mohammad Ali Chaiwala to Jinnah, 10 December 1936, QAP, F. 1089, pp. 50–52.
26. Ahmad Yar Daultana to Fazli Husain, 13 April 1936, Khalid, *Punjab Muslim League,* pp. 72–73.
27. Fazli Husain to the Aga Khan, 22 June 1936, ibid., pp. 78–79.
28. Maulana Zafar Ali Khan and his supporters had formed the Ittehad-i-Millat to campaign for the restoration of the Shahidganj mosque to the Muslims. For the Ahrar demand for barring the entry of the Qadianis into the Muslim League, see Maulana Habibur Rahman's statement in the *Civil & Military Gazette,* 28 April 1936.
29. The central parliamentary board included leaders of the Jamiatul Ulama-i-Hind, Majlis-i-Ahrar-i-Islam and Majlis-i-Ittehad-i-Millat.
30. Ashiq Husain Batalvi, *Iqbal ke Akhiri do Saal,* Lahore, 1978, pp. 326; and Ghulam Rasul to honorary secretary, All-India Muslim League, 27 April 1937, AFM, vol. 187, no.1.
31. The Ahrar wanted an applicant for the ticket to deposit Rs 25/- and the selected candidate to pay Rs 100 while the Board decided for Rs 50 deposit and Rs 500 from selected candidates plus he had to pay for organizing any propaganda. *Punjab Police Abstract of Intelligence for the Year ending 31 December 1936,* p. 274.
32. Printed leaflet issued by Mohammad Abdul Latif Yazdani, general secretary of the Raipur (Central Provinces) district Muslim League, quoting Nehru's letter to Rafi Ahmad Kidwai, published in the *Wahdat* (Delhi), 12 August 1937; QAP, F. 26, p. 82.
33. Fazli Husain's observation, Khalid, *Punjab Muslim League,* p. 73; and also see *Punjab Police Abstract of Intelligence for the Year ending 31 December 1936,* pp. 202–3 and 212–13.

34. Barkat Ali to Jinnah, 31 July 1936, QAP, F. 215, p. 3. By June, Zafar Ali Khan had left the central parliamentary board because its objective was not complete independence.
35. *IAR*, 1935, vol. II, p. 313.
36. Ahmad Said Chhatari to Jinnah, and to Liaquat, 29 April 1936, QAP, F. 605, pp. 1 and 3.
37. Ibid., F. 514, p. 13; and for a detailed account of Liaquat's participation in the provincial elections, see Muhammad Reza Kazimi, *Liaquat Ali Khan and the Freedom Movement*, Karachi, 1997, Chapter III.
38. QAP, F. 311, pp. 1–3; F. 993, pp. 3–4; and *Star of India*, 21 August 1936.
39. Z.H. Zaidi (ed.), *M A. Jinnah-Ispahani Correspondence, 1936–1948*, Karachi, 1997, pp. 21–22; and *Star of India*, 5 October 1936.
40. QAP, F. 1089.
41. *Star of India*, 5 October 1936.
42. Suhrawardy to Jinnah, 4 and 18 December 1936, QAP, F. 458, pp. 1–2 and 4.
43. For instance, see secretary, South Arcot DML to honorary secretary, All-India Muslim League, AFM, vol. 205, no. 3; and QAP, F. 864.
44. *Madras Mail*, 22 and 26 May 1936. It was alleged that they had supported joint electorates and opposed the Communal Award.
45. AFM, vol. 205, nos. 5 and 6.
46. *Report of the President of the Annual Meeting of the Madras Presidency Muslim League held on 10th November 1940*, ibid., vol. 265, pp. 73–74; and report presented at the party meeting on 18 June 1939, ibid., vol. 215, no. 18.
47. QAP, F. 514, pp. 34 and 53–58; and F. 1089, pp. 45–49 and 64.
48. Ibid., F. 651, pp. 1–3 and 8–9; and F. 865, pp. 17–18; and *Tribune*, 6 January 1937.
49. Allen Keith Jones, *Politics in Sindh, 1907–1940: Muslim Identity and the Demand for Pakistan*, Karachi, 2002, pp. 38–56.
50. Hatim Alavi to Jinnah, 2 June 1936, QAP, 208, pp. 1–2.
51. Abdul Majid to Jinnah, 7, 8, 12 and 17 December 1936, ibid., F. 514, pp. 35–40 and 46–47; and Mazhar Ali Alavi to Jinnah, 18 November 1936, ibid., F. 897, pp. 20–22; and Jinnah to M.A. Alavi, 18 December 1936, Ahmad Saeed, *Quaid-i-Azam Mohammad Ali Jinnah: A Bunch of Rare Letters*, Lahore, 1999, p. 26; and Jones, *Politics in Sindh*, pp. 46–47.
52. *Daily Gazette*, 2 November 1936.
53. Hamida Khuhro, *Mohammed Ayub Khuhro: A Life of Courage in Politics*, Lahore, 1998, pp. 138–39.
54. Waheed Ahmad (ed.), *Quaid-i-Azam Mohammad Ali Jinnah: Speeches, Indian Legislative Assembly, 1935–1947*, Karachi, 1991, pp. 55–57.
55. Malik Khuda Bakhsh to Jinnah, 30 April and 19 September 1936; and Peer Bakhsh to Jinnah, 14 September and 14 October 1936, QAP, F. 233, pp. 1–9; and Peer Bakhsh to Jinnah, 21 January 1937, ibid., F. 515, p. 6.
56. Ibid., F. 514, pp. 18, 20 and 23; and Waqar Ali Shah, *Muslim League in N.W.F.P.*, Karachi, 1992, pp. 26–28.
57. Tajammul Husain to Jinnah, 22 April 1936, QAP, F. 565, p. 1.
58. S. Moinullah to honorary secretary, All-India Muslim League, 7 May 1936, AFM, vol. 579.
59. For organization of the provincial Muslim League, see *Sylhet Chronicle*, 9 August 1936; Abdul Matin to Jinnah, 31 October and 10 November 1936, and 13 April and 8 May 1937, QAP, F. 244, pp. 8–10 and 15; M. Tayyabulla, general secretary, Assam provincial Muslim League, to Jinnah, camp, Srinagar, 10 April 1936, ibid.,

F. 821, p. 55; and a document signed by Fakhruddin Ahmad, vice-president, M. Tayyabulla, and Wajid Ali and Nurul Haque, secretaries, ibid., F. 1018, p. 3.

60. Ibid., F. 811, p. 1; and *Star of India*, 4 January 1937.

61. QAP, F. 811, p. 2.

62. Ibid., p. 22; and Waheed, *Nation's Voice: Towards Consolidation*, pp. 116–20.

63. OIOC/L/PO/99, Elections 1937, 'The Results of the Indian Provincial Elections, Memorandum by the Secretary of State for India'.

64. QAP, F. 811, p. 70; and also see Chapter 3.

65. *Star of India*, 2 March 1937.

66. A.M. Zaidi and S.G. Zaidi (eds.), *The Encyclopaedia of the Indian National Congress*, New Delhi, 1981, vol. 11, pp. 271–72, and 285–86.

67. QAP, F. 811, p. 70; and resolution of the United Provinces Muslim League parliamentary board passed on 25 April 1937, ibid., F. 1119, p. 218.

68. News report, 28 February 1937, QAP, F. 139, pp. 21–22.

69. Kanji Dwarkadas, *India's Fight for Freedom, 1913–1945*, Bombay, 1966, pp. 466–67.

70. Liaquat to Jinnah, 11 March 1937, AFM, vol. 449, p. 2.

71. *Statesman*, 20 March 1937, Batalvi, *Iqbal ke Akhiri do Saal*, pp. 373–74; and Liaquat to MLAs, 11 March 1937, AFM, vol. 449, p. 2.

72. Jinnah's statement, *Star of India*, 27 April 1937; and QAP, F. 515, p. 56.

73. Press interview on 10 May 1937.

74. For the text of the terms, see Choudhry Khaliquzzaman, *Pathway to Pakistan*, Lahore, 1961, p. 161. The Congress did not listen to any friendly advice. For Maulana Shaukat Ali's appeal to Nehru, see *Sentinel* (Bombay), 22 April 1937.

75. Khaliquzzaman, *Pathway to Pakistan*, pp. 160–62.

76. For Nawab Ismail's role in the rejection of the Congress offer, see Nawab of Chhattari to Jinnah, 12 August 1937, QAP, F. 242, pp. 2–5.

77. Nawab Chhatari's observation in his letter to Jinnah, 17 May 1937, ibid., F. 24, pp. 223–24.

78. Raja Ghazanfar Ali, one of the two members who won elections on the League ticket in the Punjab, joined the Unionist Party and was subsequently inducted in the government as parliamentary secretary.

79. For instance, addressing a meeting in Bareilly, Wazir Hasan observed that no 'other organization except the Indian National Congress can speak on behalf of eight crore Muslims'. *IAR*, 1937, II, p. 3; and Haji Abdussattar Haji Essak to Jinnah, 22 June 1937, QAP, F. 648, p. 1.

80. A.M.K. Dehlavi wanted the League to purge all the 'shaky elements' whom he termed '*Kachraa*' (waste). Dehlavi to Jinnah, QAP, F. 256, p. 35.

81. For Jinnah not allowing this resolution to be moved on 9 June 1936, see AFM, vol. 222, no. 45.

82. Abdul Razzak to Jinnah, 5 September 1937, QAP, F. 25, pp. 2–4; and Jinnah to Yusuf Shareef, 10 October 1937, ibid., p. 92; and honorary secretary to Wazir Hasan, 15 October 1937, honorary secretary to Yaqub Hasan, 15 October 1937, A.R. Siddiqi and M.A.H. Ispahani to honorary secretary, 15 October 1937, Wazir Hasan to honorary secretary, 15 October 1937, AFM, vol. 222, nos. 61, 62, 64, and 66–67. By 1940, Wazir Hasan was disillusioned with his Congress friends and was talking 'very appreciatively and affectionately' of Jinnah. K. Wade to Jinnah, 22 June 1940, QAP, F. 181, pp. 1–2.

83. For instance, see QAP, F. 25, p. 15; F. 568, pp. 16 and 25; and AFM, vol. 222, no. 68.

84. For his letter to Jinnah, 11 July 1937, see QAP, F. 988, pp. 13–14.

85. Hafiz Ahsan to Jinnah, 5 January 1938, ibid., F. 1093, pp. 67–70; and also see Zakir Ali to Jinnah, 29 October 1937, ibid., F 223, p. 17; Hasan Erteza to Jinnah, 25 July 1937, ibid., F. 26, pp. 300–303; and Haji Abdussattar Haji Essak Sait to Jinnah, 11 July 1937, ibid., F. 988, pp. 13–14; Maulana Mazharuddin to Jinnah, n.d., ibid., F. 909, p. 146; and S.M. Habibullah to Jinnah, 6 October 1937, ibid., F. 270, p. 1. For the type of propaganda against the League candidate in the Bijnor bye-election, see 'The Bijnor Bye-election in Retrospect', ibid., F. 1006, p. 98.

86. Resolution passed by the All-India Muslim League working committee on 2–3 July 1939, AFM, vol. 128, no. 29.

87. *Times of India*, 20 April 1937; and Waheed, *Nation's Voice: Towards Consolidation*, pp. 137–39.

88. Asaf Ali's statement, *Hindustan Times*, 15 May 1937; and his two letters to Jinnah, 28 May and 4 June 1937, and Jinnah's response, 28 May 1937, QAP, F. 24.

89. Zafar Ali Khan to Jinnah, 6 May 1937, ibid., F. 357, p. 1.

90. Ibid., F. 24, p. 209.

91. Nehru's statement on 25 April 1937.

92. QAP, F. 865, pp. 137–38.

93. For minutes of the working committee, see A.M. Zaidi and S.G. Zaidi, *Encyclopedia of the Indian National Congress*, vol. 11, pp. 491–500.

94. Jinnah's press statement of 29 April 1937, *Star of India*, 3 May 1937; and that of 2 July, ibid., 7 July 1937; and Hatim Alavi to Jinnah, 15 October 1937, AFM, vol. 179, no. 53.

95. He made these remarks in a speech on the death anniversary of Maulana Mohammad Ali in the Mohammad Ali Park in Calcutta. *Star of India*, 4 January 1937.

96. Suhrawardy to Jinnah, 23 July 1937, QAP, 458, pp. 11–12; and Habibullah to Jinnah, 30 July 1937, ibid., F. 26, pp. 287–88; and Tufail Haider to Jinnah, 16 April 1937, ibid., F. 24, pp. 50–51; and Press statement by Ahmad Yar Daultana, chief secretary of the Unionist Party, 19 April 1937, ibid., F. 24, p. 159; Barkat Ali to Jinnah, 28 April 1937, ibid., F. 24, p. 43; and S.M. Habib to Jinnah, 13 August 1937, ibid., F. 26, pp. 80–81.

97. Nawab Ismail to Jinnah, 4 October 1937, ibid., F. 339, pp. 23–26.

98. On 4 December 1938, the All-India Muslim League council had resolved to get *fatwa* from the *ulama* against Muslims joining the Congress, and published them under the authority of the All-India Muslim League through the agency of the local Leagues in the language of each province or district.

99. Jinnah's statement, 29 April 1937, QAP, F. 811, p. 108; and ibid., F. 811, p. 112.

100. Later on, he argued that 'freedom should not be monopoly of a few, like the Whites in America to the exclusion of the Red Indians and Negroes'. *Civil & Military Gazette*, 10 May 1938.

101. Ibid., 6 May and 21 September 1937; *Tribune*, 18 May 1937; and Waheed, *Nation's Voice: Towards Consolidation*, p. 172.

102. *Star of India*, 22 March 1937.

103. The council met on 9 June 1936, and 21 March 1937, and after that it met in 1938.

104. M.M.S. Ispahani to Noor Mohammad, 23 November 1937, QAP, F. 568, p. 39.

105. For the formation of Leagues in the districts and cities and their activities, see ibid., F. 24, pp. 4–5, 6–7, 59, 160–61; F. 458, p. 7, 10; F. 648, pp. 2, 5–6; F. 834, p. 152; F. 900, pp. 88–89; AFM, vol. 174, pp. 40, 41; vol. 205, no. 7, 9, 13, 14, 15, 16; and Iqbal to Jinnah, 13 August 1937, QAP, F. 26, p. 206.

106. *Honorary Joint Secretary's Report for the Years 1936–1937*, AFM, vol. 187; and also ibid., vol. 170, no. 68.

107. Barkat Ali to Jinnah, 28 April 1937, QAP, F. 24, p. 43; Zafar Ali Khan to Jinnah, 6 May 1937, ibid., F. 357, p. 1; and Abdur Rab Nishtar's observations in the meeting of the All-India Muslim League council on 21 March 1937, ibid., F. 394, pp. 1–4.

108. Ibid., F. 25, pp. 6–8; and F. 458, pp. 6 and 7.

109. Husain M. Malik to Jinnah, 21 May 1937, ibid., 387, p. 1; and Husain M. Malik to Shamsul Hasan, 2 October 1937, AFM, vol. 170, no. 35.

110. AFM, vol. 222, no. 50.

111. For instance, see Abdul Matin to Jinnah, 15 July 1937, QAP, F. 244, p. 18.

112. S.M. Husain to Jinnah, 7 June 1937, ibid., F. 24, pp. 153–54.

113. Shafaat Ahmad Khan to Jinnah, 26 May and 4 and 8 June 1937, ibid., F. 24, pp. 126–27 229–30, and 143.

114. S.M. Husain to Jinnah, 7 June 1937, ibid., F. 24, pp. 153–54.

115. Jinnah to Suhrawardy, 3 July 1937, and Suhrawardy to Jinnah, 23 July 1937, ibid., F. 458, pp. 8 and 12.

116. Suhrawardy to Jinnah, 3, 10 and 21 August 1937, and Raghib Ahsan to Jinnah, 6 August 1937, ibid., F. 26, pp. 149, 168, 240 and 258.

117. Jinnah to Suhrawardy, n.d., ibid., F. 26, p. 307.

118. Zakir Ali to Jinnah, 2, 7 and 8 August 1937; Raja Mahmudabad to Jinnah, 10 August 1937; Nawab Ismail to Jinnah, 11 August 1937; and S.M. Husain to Jinnah, 11 August 1937, ibid., F. 26, pp. 151–52, 167, 174–75, 182, 237, 246, and 299.

119. Nawab Ismail to Jinnah, 11 August 1937, ibid., F. 26, pp. 184–85.

120. Ibid., F. 26, p. 149. On 6 August, Raghib Ahsan was the first to make a proposal to this effect in his letter to Jinnah. [Ibid., F. 26, p. 154.] For the change in dates to October, see assistant secretary, All-India Muslim League, to secretary, reception committee, 27 July 1937, AFM, vol. 170, no. 1, 2, 7 and 8.

121. Jinnah to Shamsul Hasan, 21 September 1937, AFM, vol. 170, no. 9.

122. Abdul Qayyum to Jinnah, 10 October 1937, QAP, F. 25, p. 60.

123. Mohammad Hashim Khan Ghilzai to honorary secretary, All-India Muslim League, 1 October 1937, AFM, vol. 170, no. 27; and Haji Abdussattar Haji Essak Sait to Shamsul Hasan, 29 September 1937, ibid., vol. 170, no. 21 and 22.

124. M.M.S. Ispahani to secretary, reception committee, 2 October 1937, ibid., vol. 170, no. 37.

125. Ibid., vol. 179, nos. 1 and 3.

126. Nawab of Dhaka to Jinnah, 13 March 1937, QAP, F. 566, pp. 1–3.

127. Raghib Ahsan to Jinnah, 6 August 1937, ibid., F. 26, p 149; and PS to Fazlul Haq to Raja Mahmudabad, 10 October 1937, AFM, vol. 172, no. 17.

128. Ahmad Yar Daultana to Jinnah, 8 and 22 May, and 10 June 1937, QAP, F. 24, p. 157, and F. 255, pp. 1–3; Zakir Ali to Jinnah, 8 August 1937, ibid., F. 26, pp. 166–67; and Afzal Hasnie to honorary secretary, All-India Muslim League, 28 September 1937, AFM, vol. 170, no. 15.

129. Sikandar Hayat had joined the Muslim League in 1913; and Fazlul Haq was one of its founder-members.

130. Pirzada, *Foundations*, vol. II, pp. 264–73.

131. For instance, see Jinnah's speech in Gaya, Bihar, *Star of India*, 11 January 1938.

132. For the adoption of a white flag, see Hafiz Sabihuddin to secretary, All-India Muslim League, 15 October 1937, AFM, vol. 187, no. 12.

133. Abdul Haq to Jinnah, 5 October 1937, QAP, F. 25, p. 25.

134. Waheed, *Nation's Voice: Towards Consolidation*, p. 324; and AFM, vol. 187, nos. 38, 54 and 55.

135. For earlier resolutions of the League council on Palestine and observance of 19 June 1936, as the Palestine Day, see AFM, vol. 219, no. 36 and vol. 222, no. 48; and Pirzada, *Foundations*, vol. II, pp. 274–80.

136. In May 1940, the Privy Council in London also dismissed an appeal filed against the decision of the Lahore High Court.

6

Search for a Goal, 1940

The failure of the Indian leaders to work out an agreement on the Hindu–Muslim question at the round table conferences brought in the British-formulated communal award that was incorporated in the Act of 1935. The Act provided for a Federation of British India and princely states and gave autonomy to the provinces in British India but left the people of the states at the whims of their rulers. While the representatives of British India in the federal legislature were to be elected directly the rulers were to nominate those of the states. The All-India Muslim League rejected the all-India federation but decided to work the provincial part of the Act for what it was 'worth' till an acceptable alternative was evolved in consultation with the other political parties. The Congress rejected the whole constitutional framework provided in the Act and demanded a constituent assembly elected on the basis of adult franchise to frame a new constitution for a free India. Nevertheless, it participated in the provincial elections under the Act to wreck the constitutional reforms from within the legislatures but it practically worked the provincial part by assuming power in the provinces after some initial reluctance. Its leaders struggled for the acceptance of their party as the sole representative party of the Indians, denying any role in politics to other political parties, which it desired to function merely as social and religious groups. On the contrary, the All-India Muslim League under Jinnah's leadership aimed at its acceptance as the sole representative party of the Muslims of India before it negotiated a settlement of the Hindu–Muslim problem. The Congress rule in the Hindu majority provinces, the League–Congress intermittent unfruitful talks and the League–British–Congress interaction helped the All-India Muslim League to determine the inherent aspirations of the Muslims of India and to spell out their goal.

(A) CONGRESS RULE AND THE ALL-INDIA MUSLIM LEAGUE

The Congress rule in the Hindu majority provinces had an ominous start for the Muslims. Its refusal to associate the League as a party in the formation of provincial ministries—a decision that the Congressmen later regretted—and the induction of Muslim ministers by questionable methods alienated the Leaguers, who then resolutely resisted its Muslim mass contact movement.[1] The Congress leaders in their exuberance of overwhelming victory callously overlooked Muslim sensitivities while the Leaguers closely and minutely observed their actions. Muslims perceived in the Congress policies an arrogance of power and a desire to establish the *raj* of the Hindu majority in place of the British Raj.[2] Many Hindus at the grassroots emulated the attitude of their leaders. Jinnah once alleged that the Congress committees especially in the countryside and 'even some Hindu officials were behaving as if the Hindu Raj had already been established'.[3] The Congress ministries in the Hindu majority provinces revived and advocated those issues that had caused Hindu–Muslim tension in the past and added new ones of similar nature with an obsessive fervour. They adopted the party and Hindu communal symbols as official and 'national' symbols that provoked and agitated the Muslims. The League missed no opportunity to use such moves to its advantage. For the Congress, it was simply a matter of implementing its policy and programme, for which it had obtained a mandate in the provincial elections and did not feel obligated to consult the League at any level. Muslims perceived in the Congress attitude and policies a reflection of the 'Hindu mind' and a demonstration of a picture as if 'Hindustan is for the Hindus'.[4] The Congress and Hindu Mahasabha leaders made statements that strengthened this perception. Veer Savarkar's (1883–1966) presidential address to the nineteenth session of the All-India Hindu Mahasabha in Allahabad became a symbol of Hindu revivalism, which Bhai Parmanand (1874–1947), in his foreword to its printed version, termed as the 'National Bible' of the Hindus. Even Gandhi began to start his daily work, Jinnah once observed, by prayer and recital of the *Bhagavad Gita* and believed in '*ashrams* and *samities*, *ahimsa*, spinning wheel, *khaddar*, *Bande Mataram*, *Sanskitized* Hindi, *Vidya Mandir*, and Wardha scheme.'[5] For the League, it was 'a replica and a foretaste' of Hindu revivalism. Feelings of hostility ran so high that C. Rajagopalachari (1878–1972), the moderate chief minister of

Madras, opposed even the admission of a condolence motion in the assembly on the death of Maulana Shaukat Ali, the well-known leader of the Khilafat and Non-cooperation movements.[6] And Savarkar repeatedly made the observation that the Indian Muslims were like the German Jews who should be treated like them.[7]

One old issue, revived with great passion, was the playing of music in processions of Hindu festivals before the mosques at the time of prayers, which used to cause tension and sometimes resulted in riots and loss of mostly Muslim lives and property.[8] There was a sharp increase in the desecration of mosques in the Hindu majority provinces.[9] At some places, Muslims were prevented from repairing the mosques, and at a few others, they were even stopped from calling the *azan* (call for prayer).[10] Secondly, the sacrilegious literature on Islam and Prophet Muhammad (PBUH) that the Hindu nationalists published frequently exacerbated communal feelings that often led to violence.[11] Thirdly, cow-sacrifice by the Muslims especially at the time of Idul Azha was another source of dispute.[12] Hindus felt that with the Congress in power in the Hindu majority provinces, there should be an end to this practice. More sophisticated and educated among them attempted to seek legislative sanction on the plea of shortage of healthy livestock and those at the lower rungs of the society crudely employed violent means to stop cow-sacrifice.[13] The Congress rule added some new issues that aggravated Hindu–Muslim conflict. One, the Congress ministries in the Hindu majority provinces adopted the tricolour Congress flag as the official flag of the provincial governments, which was hoisted at public buildings including those of the government, municipalities, local boards, public schools and libraries. The Congress ministers and party officials used to unfurl the flag at officially arranged functions, expecting the public including the Muslims and in the case of schools the Muslim students to salute it as the 'national' flag. Sometimes the flag-hoisting ceremonies led to disturbances and riots. Muslims resented the hoisting of the Congress tricolour flag at public functions; and the Leaguers began to hold their own League flag-hoisting ceremonies at their functions, which occasionally resulted in communal trouble. For instance, a flag-hoisting ceremony in Gaya led to riots, in which thirteen Muslims were killed and forty injured, besides the loss of property. The military had to be called in to control the situation. The Gaya League rejected the official explanation about the riots and demanded an impartial inquiry.[14] Secondly, the Congress introduced the thirty-six line (twenty-nine lines in Sanskrit and seven in Bengali) song, the *Bande Mataram* (Hail to the Motherland), as the 'national' song in the Hindu majority provinces. This song had appeared in Bankim Chandra Chatterji's (1838–1894) novel, the *Anandamath* (1882), which had clear anti-Muslim overtones and depicted a Hindu Sanyasi rebellion of a century earlier. The Bengali Hindus had used it as the 'national' song in their movement against the partition of Bengal. After 1937, the provincial Congress assembly parties adopted it as the 'national' song and used it to start proceedings of the legislative assemblies and other public functions outside the assemblies.[15] Its singing was made compulsory in public schools.[16] Muslims including the pro-Congress among them unanimously opposed the singing of this song. The Congress working committee did respond to their criticism and dropped all except the first two stanzas of the song.[17] Even then, the context remained there which did not assuage Muslim sentiments. Jinnah perceived in the Congress response a display of 'arrogance and a patronizing spirit'.[18] Thirdly, the Congress-controlled provincial and local governments discriminated against the Muslims in the recruitment of services. There was also discrimination in the application of law and deployment of security forces; for example, the Muslims, and not the Hindus, were inflicted collective fines in the disturbances on the occasion of Moharram in Badaun.[19] The Congress governments did not hesitate to close down Muslim presses and newspapers that were critical of their policies.[20] They opposed the extension of separate electorates to local bodies without which it was impossible for the Muslims to get due representation in these bodies. The council of the All-India Muslim League once adopted a resolution authorizing the local Leagues to devise means to achieve that objective but deleted the words 'by any possible means according to the local conditions and if necessary by launching civil disobedience' from that resolution.[21]

Muslims were agitated the most seriously by the Wardha Scheme of basic education, or the Vidya Mandir Scheme, which was inspired by the spirit of *ahimsa* (non-violence) and unity of the 'Indian nation'. It was meant to inculcate these values in the Indians from their childhood. It visualized uniform syllabi of education and development of one language, Hindustani. It engaged pro-Congress authors to write the textbooks. The publication of the Vidya Mandir Scheme and its planned introduction by stages in the Hindu majority provinces stirred up reaction among the Muslims. The branch Leagues and individual Leaguers flooded the All-India Muslim League office with complaints in the form of resolutions passed at meetings and letters calling for action against the scheme. On 4 December 1938, the central council appointed an eight-member committee to examine this scheme to find out its impact on the Urdu language and its script and on the 'separate national identity' of the Muslims.[22] The committee was also asked to submit an educational scheme that would create in Muslim boys and girls 'Islamic mentality, strengthen the Islamic characteristics and, at the same time, fully equip them to meet the exigencies of the present age'.[23] It prepared a report that the central council circulated among its members for comments and empowered the central working committee to formulate definite proposals.[24] The working committee, after evaluating the comments, concluded that (i) the Wardha Scheme of education was calculated to destroy gradually Muslim culture to secure the domination of Hindu culture; (ii) it imposed the Congress ideology that aimed at inculcating, among others, the doctrine of *ahimsa*; (iii) its object was to infuse the political creed, policy and programme of the Congress in the minds of children; (iv) it ignored to provide facilities for religious instruction; (v) it was meant to suppress Urdu, the *lingua franca* of India, under the guise of Hindustani that was highly Sanskritized Hindi; and (vi) the books that some provincial governments had prescribed and provisionally sanctioned were offensive to Muslim sentiments and were devoted to the praise of the Hindu religion, philosophy and heroes, minimizing the Islamic contribution to the world in general and India in particular, disregarding Muslim culture, history and heroes and speaking of them with scant courtesy.[25] This committee, however, did not propose any alternative scheme of education, but Professor Mohammad Afzaal Qadri (1904–1975) of the Aligarh Muslim University, a member of the committee, prepared on his own initiative a 27-page preliminary report about primary and secondary education to serve as a basis for Muslim education in the light of Islamic ideals.[26] The All-India Muslim League sent a copy of this report to the All-India Muslim Educational Conference for consideration.

These issues and the general attitude of the Hindus in the Congress-governed Hindu majority provinces deeply worried the Muslims. The number of communal riots increased with the passage of time.[27] The provincial Muslim Leagues on the direction of the All-India Muslim League made representations to the governors requesting them to take steps to protect their rights under the Act of 1935, but the governors' inaction to redress their grievances fuelled their frustration. All-India

Muslim League's policy decision was to keep its struggle within constitutional limits.[28] Therefore, it simply condemned the governors for their failure to use their 'special powers' to protect the interests of the Muslims and the minorities. Jinnah believed that the British government would give the Congress a free hand as long as its 'interests imperial or otherwise' were not touched and defence remained intact.[29] When the provincial Muslim Leagues particularly those in Central Provinces and Bihar sought permission from the All-India Muslim League to launch civil disobedience against the Congress governments, it advised them not to adopt such a course of action.[30] When these provincial Muslim Leagues increased pressure, the All-India Muslim League at its Patna session authorized the working committee to take a decision for 'direct action', if and when necessary. The Leaguers including those in Bihar strictly followed the party policy except in Central Provinces where the Vidya Mandir Scheme was first implemented. The eleven-member Central Provinces and Berar League assembly party staged a walkout from the assembly on 17 September 1938, when the speaker disallowed M.M. Haq's adjournment motion to discuss the official communiqué about Muslim agitation against the Vidya Mandir Scheme,[31] and the Nagpur and Jabbalpur district Muslim Leagues and city Muslim Leagues constantly protested against the pro-Hindi, pro-Vidya Mandir and anti-Urdu moves of the Congress ministry.[32] Once, the provincial Muslim League started civil disobedience without waiting for the approval of the central working committee.[33] Nawab Siddiq Ali Khan (1900–1974) who led the agitation was arrested along with several other protestors. The military had to be called in Jabbalpur to control the situation. The central working committee appreciated 'the brave fight' that the provincial Muslim League and district Muslim Leagues had put up in Central Provinces but called on them not to 'resort to any direct action or unlawful activity' without its approval and deputed Liaquat to visit the province to mediate between the Congress ministry and the provincial Muslim League.[34] The civil disobedience movement was called off following an agreement, which Pandit Ravi Shanker Shukla (1877–1969), the chief minister, signed on behalf of the Congress ministry and Liaquat on behalf of the provincial Muslim League assembly party.[35] Still, there were often communal eruptions in Central Provinces when the Congress government failed to implement the terms of the Shukla–Liaquat agreement.[36] The compulsory teaching of Hindi in Madras had to be withdrawn under pressure from various groups including non-Brahmans and Muslims.[37] But Oriya was introduced as the medium of instruction in Orissa without any protection to Urdu.[38]

The All-India Muslim League employed different tactics to publicize Muslim grievances and effectively used this campaign to unite the Muslims on its platform. A committee consisting of politicians and *ulama* of the Muslim-minority provinces toured Sindh, Punjab, and NWFP, and another committee went to Bengal and Assam to assess the situation. A similar committee of the Muslim majority provinces toured the Muslim-minority provinces to apprize itself of the nature of Muslim grievances.[39] The Congress governments soon felt the heat of this campaign; and in July 1939, the provincial home ministers at a conference in Simla, without directly referring to it, asked the provincial governments to 'undertake a concerted campaign against propaganda of a communal nature'.[40] The All-India Muslim League, its branches and individual Leaguers profusely documented the Muslim grievances. They sent memoranda on the grievances to the governors for action, with copies endorsed to the provincial Muslim Leagues and the All-India Muslim League.[41] Three detailed reports are better known than the others: one by S.M. Shareef (1880–1972), the second by A.K. Fazlul Haq and the third by an All-India Muslim League committee, known as the Pirpur Report. These reports were meant to prove that the provincial part of the Act of 1935 had failed, as the governors had been unable to protect the minorities in the Hindu majority provinces according to its provisions. S.M. Shareef, vice-president of the Bihar provincial Muslim League and president of its publicity committee, prepared a report on Muslim grievances in Bihar, which is known as the *Shareef Report*.[42] On Jinnah's advice, he sent its copies to members of the All-India Muslim League working committee, Muslim members of the central legislature, members of the British cabinet and parliament and editors of important Indian and British newspapers.[43] When Rajendra Prasad asked Jinnah about the Muslim grievances in Bihar, S.M. Shareef on his instructions sent copies of this report to him as well as to Jawaharlal Nehru and Subhas Chandra Bose (1897–1945).[44] But Rajendra Prasad, who sent his reply on 12 November 1939, informed that the Muslim grievances could not be investigated because after the resignation of the Congress ministry, the former ministers did not have access to the official record.[45] The second report was prepared by Fazlul Haq, chief minister of Bengal. After a bitter public altercation between him and Nehru, the two leaders had agreed to tour the Hindu majority provinces to investigate the Muslim grievances. Although the proposed tour did not materialize partly due to resignation of the Congress ministries but Fazlul Haq himself visited Central Provinces and Bihar and published a report based on cases from these provinces.[46] The Bengal residency Muslim League sent 400 copies of this report to the All-India Muslim League for distribution.[47] The third report was prepared by a committee, chaired by Syed Mohammad Mehdi (b. 1896) of Pirpur, which the council of the All-India Muslim League appointed on 20 March 1938.[48] A year later, Jinnah sent copies of the *Pirpur Report* to Viceroy Linlithgow (1887–1952), and eight other British officials, demanding an inquiry into the Muslim grievances by a royal commission.[49] His demand was supported by the president of the All-India Depressed Classes Association, M.C. Raja.[50] One thousand copies of the *Pirpur Report* were sent to England for distribution among the British officials, politicians and press.[51] In mid-July, the Congress did respond to reports about Muslim grievances to disparage them as mere propaganda. Its provincial governments, at Vallabhbhai Patel's suggestion, 'investigated' the charges and contradicted them in official communiqués as 'unfounded'. The provincial Muslim Leagues, however, issued rejoinders to these communiqués to counter these assertions.[52] Rajendra Prasad offered to hold a judicial inquiry into the Muslim grievances by Sir Maurice L. Gwyer (1878–1952; chief justice of the federal court), but by then it was too late, as Jinnah had already requested the viceroy for an inquiry by a royal commission because the viceroy and the governors were responsible for the protection of rights and interests of the minorities under the Act.[53] A royal commission composed of purely judicial personnel was expected to be 'completely detached from the poisoned atmosphere' of India.[54] The British government, however, did not accept the League demand on the plea that it was 'not in the interest of either party [All-India Muslim League or Congress] or of India as a whole', and that it would embitter communal relations.[55] The League expressed its 'sense of bitter resentment' at the rejection of its demand, which, it felt, was due to the 'colossal ignorance of the conditions prevailing in India'.[56]

Muslim grievances under the Congress rule contributed to strengthen the 'national identity' of the Indian Muslims and shook the Leaguers' confidence in the usefulness of western democracy for the protection of their rights in India. The intensity of Muslim resentment was demonstrated in the way they observed Friday 22 December, as the 'Day of Deliverance and Thanksgiving' on Jinnah's call when the Congress ministries resigned in the provinces. Before the announcement,

Jinnah conferred with prominent League leaders, and Liaquat consulted the *ulama* 'on the form of Thanksgiving prayer'.[57] Jinnah swept aside all objections against the Day of Deliverance; and its observance influenced millions of people.[58] Besides arousing Muslim masses in the remotest parts of the subcontinent, the country-wide observance of the Day confirmed Muslim apprehensions that the Hindu-dominated Congress rule in a democratic parliamentary system of government would mean the *raj* of the permanent Hindu majority that would suppress their religion and culture and deprive them of their social, economic and political rights.[59] Some Muslims were apprehensive that if the Hindu majority was perpetually in power at the centre, the fate of the Muslims would not be dissimilar to that of their co-religionists in Spain a few centuries ago.[60] This perception was further reinforced by the 'talks' that the League and Congress leaders held for the settlement of the Hindu–Muslim problem. Henceforth, the League firmly opposed any move to revive the Congress ministries in the provinces. Once, Jinnah even threatened the possibility of a civil war if the British government re-installed the Congress ministries.[61]

(B) LEAGUE–CONGRESS TALKS

During 1935–39, Jinnah interacted with Gandhi and the Congress presidents to resolve the Hindu–Muslim problem. After 1937, the All-India Muslim League authorized Jinnah to hold these talks and discouraged other Leaguers including Nawab Ismail, Sikandar, Fazlul Haq and G.M. Sayed (1904–1995) from negotiating with the Congress leaders or the British authorities on its behalf on the Hindu–Muslim question. However, all the League–Congress 'talks' remained enmeshed in deciding the 'conditions precedent' and proved a fruitless exercise. In fact, the two sides endeavoured to consolidate their respective position in the Muslim community. While the All-India Muslim League used the time to broaden its support-base, the Congress utilized it to win over different Muslim groups to use them in their talks with the League. In January–February 1935, Jinnah and Dr Rajendra Prasad, then Congress president, had held the first round of talks in Delhi. On the initiative of some Congress leaders these talks were started on a draft formula that was to replace the communal award, subject to its approval by the League and the Congress. Before the two parties could formally take up the draft formula, the All-India Hindu Mahasabha, some Bengali Congressmen and Sikh leaders from the Punjab came out to oppose it. Therefore, the draft formula was dropped; and in February 1935, Jinnah simply informed the League council about the nature of his talks with Rajendra Prasad. Nevertheless, he did appeal to the Hindu Mahasabha leaders not to set 'complete supremacy and ascendancy of the Hindus' as their 'ideal' and 'to treat the Muslims as their equals'. There could be no joint Hindu–Muslim struggle, he cautioned, unless the Hindu 'mentality underwent a complete change'. He hoped that the Congress with its 'wider experience' and 'good training' would 'overcome that section [of the Hindus] and assure the Muslims' that the future government of India would not be 'a Hindu government but an Indian government', in which the Muslims would not only be treated fairly but also 'as the equals of the Hindus'.[62] But Nehru upset Jinnah's expectations by his supercilious and dismissive attitude in the election campaign for the Provincial Assemblies. Then, Jinnah denounced the 'ostrich-like' attitude of the Congress for not facing the real problem.

After the elections, Jinnah again tried to open the door for talks with the Congress via Gandhi whom he considered the 'decisive' person in the decision-making process of the Congress although the latter was not even its paid member. He approached Gandhi through Bal Gangadhar Kher, the Bombay Congress leader. Gandhi's response was disappointing; he declined to intervene. His reply from Teethal to Jinnah's overture was, 'Kher has given me your message. I wish I could do something but I am utterly helpless. My faith in [Hindu–Muslim] unity is as bright as ever; only I see no daylight out of the impenetrable darkness, and in such distress I cry out to God for light.'[63] Instead of anything positive resulting from this contact, the Congress and Hindu Mahasabha leaders accelerated their tirade against Jinnah. Nehru, who succeeded Rajendra Prasad as the Congress president, contemptuously advised Jinnah to approach the Hindu Mahasabha to arrive at a Hindu–Muslim settlement! After that, Nehru and Rajendra Prasad joined hands in an anti-Jinnah campaign, insinuating that he was responsible for the failure of the Jinnah–Rajendra talks in 1935, and that the Congress would have endorsed the draft formula, if it had been approached.[64] Nehru castigated Jinnah that the Congress had more Muslims within its fold than the League. Both the Congress leaders, Nehru and Rajendra Prasad, offered to restart talks on the basis of Jinnah–Rajendra formula and get it approved by the Congress; simultaneously, they held out a threat that if Jinnah did not accept their offer the All-India Muslim League would face desertions in the United Provinces League.[65] Jinnah rebutted their allegations, observing that he found no difference between the Congress and Hindu Mahasabha leaders, and dismissed Nehru's comments derisively.[66] He gave his version of the Jinnah–Rajendra talks, maintaining that he never agreed to the draft formula that had emanated from Rajendra Prasad and his friends and that the talks were terminated when the Hindu Mahasabha and a section of the Congress opposed the formula. He promised to place any formula approved by the Congress and sent to him before the All-India Muslim League annual session at Lucknow.[67] The controversy ended only after the Congress leaders from Bengal refuted the position taken by Rajendra Prasad and Nehru and endorsed Jinnah's version regarding the Jinnah–Rajendra talks.[68] Jinnah made another attempt to approach Gandhi through Diwan Chamanlal but again failed to get a positive response.[69] This was a few days before the Lucknow annual session on 15–18 October 1937.

The success of the Lucknow session surprised the Congress leaders. Now there was a slight change in their attitude. They realized that the Congress could not ignore the All-India Muslim League any more and had to talk to its leaders but without giving up, as Nehru put it, 'its principles'.[70] Both Gandhi and Nehru corresponded with Jinnah.[71] The Jinnah–Gandhi correspondence (19 October 1937–20 April 1938) makes interesting reading although it is devoid of any substance as to the terms for a Hindu–Muslim settlement.[72] At the end of this correspondence they agreed to hold a formal meeting, as it was not possible to draft proposals for settlement by correspondence. Interestingly, Gandhi suggested that Jinnah should first negotiate with Azad whom, he wrote to Jinnah, he had accepted as his 'guide' after the death of Dr M.A. Ansari. But Jinnah did not accept this line of negotiations. He stated his position unambiguously and with clarity: he wrote that the All-India Muslim League should be accepted as the 'one authoritative and representative organization' of the Muslims and that Gandhi should represent 'the Congress and other Hindus throughout the country'. Prior to his meeting with Gandhi, Jinnah was willing to meet Nehru or Subhas Chandra Bose, who had succeeded Nehru as the Congress president, but not Azad. However, he wrote to Gandhi that the question of a Hindu–Muslim settlement would not 'be clinched without reference again to you by either of them. Therefore, I will prefer to see you first.' Gandhi reluctantly agreed to meet Jinnah, not as the representative of the 'Congress or other Hindus' but promised 'to exert all the moral influence' that he had with the Congress 'to secure an honourable settlement'. The meeting was scheduled to take place at Jinnah's residence in Bombay on 28 April 1938.

Meanwhile, Jinnah and Nehru corresponded to find a solution of the Hindu–Muslim problem.[73] Although the League council vested Jinnah with full powers to hold talks with Nehru but he used to discuss every letter and its possible reply in meetings with his colleagues. The Jinnah–Nehru correspondence (18 January–16 April 1938) had an inauspicious start; the two leaders expressed in public their conflicting standpoints on various issues including the 'atrocities' committed on the Muslims in the Congress-governed Muslim-minority provinces.[74] The high point was Nehru's sarcastic remarks at the Haripura Congress in February 1938. While moving a resolution assuring the minorities protection of their religious and cultural rights, he ridiculed: 'I have examined the so-called communal question through the telescope and, if there is nothing, what can you see.'[75] Jinnah's response to such observations was, 'you cannot solve the problem by ignoring it, but [can do it] by tackling it'.[76] The Jinnah–Nehru correspondence highlights the difference in the approach of the two leaders to the problem. Nehru did not consider it desirable to carry on arguments in the press. Jinnah agreed with him but regarded any discussion by correspondence 'equally undesirable' and suggested that they should hold a meeting to discuss the problem. But Nehru disagreed with him and insisted that Jinnah should identify 'the points of difference' and discuss them by means of correspondence. Jinnah wrote back that such a method was 'highly undesirable and most inappropriate' and would 'lead us nowhere'. But on Nehru's insistence he pointed out some issues that had been identified in the press, and sent him extracts from write-ups of two newspapers: one extract was from the *Statesman* (New Delhi edition, 12 February 1938); and the other from the *New Times* (Lahore, 1 March 1938, from an article by Ain-el-Mulk, 'Through Muslim Eyes'). But he firmly declined to send him any suggestions of his own for consideration by Nehru and his colleagues or to carry on further correspondence with him. He requested Nehru, who by then had been replaced by Subhas Chandra Bose as the Congress president, to ask the Congress to communicate with him officially to that effect so that he could place the matter before the League council. But Nehru did not give up. He himself identified and listed fourteen points of difference that included the communal award, Muslim personal law, religious ceremonies, cow-slaughter, *Bande Mataram*, tricolour flag, Urdu language and its script, and Muslim representation in services and local bodies. He discussed every issue in detail, defending the position that the Congress and its provincial ministries had taken on these issues. Jinnah perceived in the tone and language of Nehru's letter 'arrogance and militant spirit' as if the Congress was already the 'sovereign power'. According to him, Nehru had pronounced his judgment on the points that he had himself raised. One interesting comment on the Jinnah–Nehru correspondence was by G. Venkata Subha Rao, president of the Andhra Swarajya Party, Bezwada, who wrote:

> Pandit Nehru insists beyond the limits of decorum in some places — that correspondence is to be preferred to personal talks, and in spite of repeated protests of Mr Jinnah. . . . And, at the end of it, while Mr Jinnah has given not a whit of his own mind, Pandit Nehru has poured forth lecture after lecture of his none-too-inscrutable politico-economic fancy . . . in contrast to the deep diplomacy and high statesmanship of Mr Mohammad Ali Jinnah, who, in the face of deep provocation, did not reveal even an iota of [his] political mind, which is still a mystery to many.[77]

Now Jinnah refused to negotiate with the Congress unless it recognized the All-India Muslim League 'on a footing of complete equality'. After his unsuccessful talks with Jinnah, Nehru went to England to befriend the British leaders. During his more than three-month long stay in England, he met with Lord Zetland (1876–1956) and Lord Halifax to press the British government to accept the Congress demands. In addition, he solidified his bonds with senior members of the Labour Party during this visit. His talks with the Labour leaders — Clement Attlee (1883–1967), Sir Stafford Cripps (1889–1952), and a few others — at Filkins, Cripps's country house, were meant to prepare a new constitutional scheme that the Labour Party would implement when it came to power.[78] Cripps brought this draft scheme with him when he came to India on a private visit in 1939–40 and showed that scheme only to Gandhi and Nehru.

After the Jinnah–Nehru talks, Gandhi took over the thread of talks. On 28 April 1938, he had a short meeting with Jinnah at his Bombay residence but the next day he left for the NWFP to negotiate with the Khudai Khidmatgars.[79] Gandhi and Nehru demonstrated by their actions that they were hardly serious in their talks with the League. Gandhi was interested more in strengthening his bonds with the Khudai Khidmatgars than his talks with Jinnah. His primary concern was to refute Jinnah's claim that the League was 'the only authoritative and representative' party of the Muslims of India. During his tour of the NWFP, he stayed with Dr Khan Sahib (1882–1958), the chief minister, to show the Congress–Khudai Khidmatgars solidarity. Although at this stage the Khudai Khidmatgars did not merge their party into the Congress but they agreed to stay in alliance with it.[80] On his return from the NWFP, Gandhi refrained from holding direct negotiations with Jinnah, using the excuse that 'orthodox Hinduism' would 'most assuredly repudiate' him if he attempted to do that; and, on 29 May, as if to prove the correctness of his statement, the working committee of the All-India Hindu Mahasabha deprecated any attempt by the Congress 'to enter into negotiations with the Muslims on behalf of the Hindus' without its 'sanction'.[81] But, in a letter to Jinnah on 22 May, Gandhi asked his reaction to the inclusion of a Muslim in the committee that would negotiate with the League on behalf of the Congress. On 5 June, Jinnah gave his response on this issue in his letter to Subhas Chandra Bose, the new president of the Congress, after he had discussed Gandhi's proposal in the council of the All-India Muslim League.

After this momentary contact with Gandhi, Jinnah and Subhas Chandra Bose held formal protracted 'talks' by correspondence from 15 May to 16 December 1938.[82] Unlike the Jinnah–Nehru correspondence, the Congress now began to discuss formally Jinnah's letters to Subhas Chandra Bose and his replies to Jinnah in its working committee, which was in a way indication of lack of confidence in the Congress president and brewing intra-Congress tussle for the control of the party. Jinnah on his part had discussed every letter sent to, or received from, the Congress leaders with the working committee and/ or the central council right from the beginning of his talks with them.[83] The Jinnah–Bose talks began when they held discussions in May; and the latter gave him a note for finding an agreement on the basis that: 'The Congress and the All-India Muslim League as the authoritative and representative organization of the Muslims of India have hereby agreed to the following terms of a Hindu–Muslim settlement by way of a pact.' Jinnah wanted to qualify the position of the Congress, 'as the authoritative and representative organization of the solid body of Hindu opinion', which in fact had been indicated in a note by Bose prior to this note, but when Bose declined to accept this qualification, he did not insist on it.[84] The League working committee discussed Bose's note; and on 5 June, Jinnah communicated to him the conditions that the central council laid down for talks with the Congress in three resolutions, that: (*i*) the Congress should accept the All-India Muslim

League as 'the authoritative and representative' party of the Muslims; (*ii*) it was 'not desirable to include any Muslim' in the Congress negotiating committee as suggested by Gandhi; and (*iii*) the League would consult the representatives of other minorities and interests, when necessary, to create in them a sense of security.[85] The Congress working committee, Bose wrote in reply on 25 July, could not agree to the League demand as defined in resolution number one because the Congress had the support of other Muslim parties, several Muslims were its members and the overwhelmingly Muslim NWFP was on its side. The working committee did not agree to the second condition; and so was the case with the third condition because, the Congress asserted, the All-India Muslim League was a 'communal' party and the Congress a 'non-communal' party; and as if to endorse this assertion, on 11–16 December 1938, it formally declared the League a 'communal organization'.

Jinnah and Bose argued in defence of their party positions. The League, Jinnah wrote to Bose on 2 August, was convinced of its representative position that the Congress had recognized from the Lucknow Pact (1916) to Jinnah–Rajendra Prasad talks (1935); but now it needed its reiteration because Nehru had denied even the existence of the League in his statement that there were only two parties in India, the British government and the Congress. The very fact that the Congress had approached the League to settle the Hindu–Muslim problem proved its 'authoritative and representative' character. The League council was aware, he wrote, that there was a Congress coalition ministry in the NWFP and there were some Muslims in the Congress ranks but their number was insignificant and in addition, as members of the Congress they had forfeited their right to speak on behalf of the Muslim community. Moreover, no other Muslim political party had ever claimed to speak, or negotiate, on behalf of all the Muslims of India. As for the inclusion of a Muslim in the Congress negotiating committee, Jinnah argued, the position of that Muslim would be most embarrassing for that person because the negotiating committee was meant to solve the Hindu–Muslim problem and such a Muslim would have neither the confidence of the Hindus nor that of the Muslims. The consultation with the other minorities, Jinnah informed, was required in view of the Congress note. The Congress, Bose replied, was willing to appoint a negotiating committee only if the All-India Muslim League did not insist on its recognition as the authoritative organization of the Muslims of India. Jinnah reaffirmed that the working committee would negotiate only on the basis that he had mentioned in his letters of 5 June and 2 August.[86] The working committee, Bose wrote back on 16 December, was not willing to start negotiations with the League on the basis that he had stated in his letters under reference.[87] This letter brought to an end the League–Congress talks by correspondence. The Congress did not feel any pressure or urgency to renew the talks with the All-India Muslim League for a settlement of the Hindu–Muslim problem as its ministries in the provinces were working smoothly without any pressure from any quarter.

(C) FEDERATION, WAR, AND THE RENEWAL OF TALKS

The All-India Muslim League had opposed the all-India federation under the Act of 1935. It struggled to prevent its implementation. The Congress held views on the federation similar to those of the League. However, some British and Hindu politicians advised its leaders that if it abandoned the federal scheme, the Muslims would break the unity of India and establish 'Pakistan'; on the other hand, Jinnah exerted to ensure that the Congress did not change its position on the federation.[88] He also exercised his influence on some rulers of the princely states in determining their attitude towards the federation. The states constituted an indispensable component of the federation, which could not come into existence unless the rulers representing 50 per cent of the total population of all the states signed the instrument of accession. The Act empowered the rulers to nominate the representatives of their states in the federal legislature. The Congress policy towards the states facilitated Jinnah's task. Before 1937, it had refrained from directly interfering in the affairs of the states. Now it started to pressurize the rulers to make their nominations at its bidding or to secure a more 'representative' system to ensure its majority in the federal legislature in case federation came into being.[89] Patel was in charge of these operations. The targets were the Hindu majority, and not the Muslim majority, States. Instead of direct intervention, the Congress used the reform movements that were active in these states.[90] It supported the All-India States People's Congress to promote its objectives. At first, it tried to keep distance from its organization but without hiding its ambition 'to replace the Paramount Power' in the near future.[91] Its Satyagraha movement and the activities of the Arya Samaj and the Hindu Mahasabha, particularly in the Rajkot and Hyderabad states, agitated the Muslims who organized their own movements to counter these activities and sought help from the All-India Muslim League.[92] Like the Congress, the All-India Muslim League did not intervene in the affairs of the states but once it did hold out a threat that if the Congress and Hindu organizations did not desist from their activities, which were, it accused, actuated by ulterior motives, it would be forced to take steps to safeguard the interests of the Muslims.[93] The League supported the organizations that the Muslims of the states established to protect their rights and Jinnah helped them in the formation of the All-India States Muslim League.[94] It expressed its concern over the pro-Congress activities in the states, as these had aggravated communal tension and made riots a recurring phenomenon.[95] Because of these activities, the already indifferent rulers of the states became lukewarm in their support of the idea of an all-India federation. In January, the British government gave them six months' time, which was extended up to 1 September, to intimate their final decision about accession. The future of the federation was put in doubt in July 1939, when they formally communicated their reservation about the federation in a joint memorandum to the viceroy.[96] The All-India Muslim League council congratulated them for their stand against the federal scheme.[97]

All-India federation under the Act of 1935 was virtually buried with the outbreak of the Second World War when the viceroy announced its suspension. Now the Congress was again willing to hold talks with the All-India Muslim League on the Hindu–Muslim question but these talks, like the earlier ones, did not go beyond the preliminary stage. On 3 September 1939, before the League–Congress talks, Linlithgow announced Britain's entry into the war without taking the Indian political parties into confidence and asked for their cooperation in the prosecution of the war. The next day, he held separate meetings with Gandhi, Jinnah and chairman of the Chamber of Princes; and a couple of weeks later, he met with fifty Indian leaders representing different shades of opinion and interests. The Congress in return for its cooperation demanded a declaration from the British government of its war aims to the effect that: India would be an 'independent nation' after the war; a constituent assembly would be appointed to frame a constitution; and India would be accorded independent status immediately 'to the largest possible extent'. Furthermore, the Congress demanded that Indian freedom must be based 'on democracy and unity [of India]'.[98] The All-India Muslim League spelt out its position in the meetings of its working committee on 18 September and 22 October that Jinnah communicated to the viceroy.[99] The working committee observed that the scheme of federation should have been 'abandoned completely' rather than merely 'suspended' and that the Muslims wanted to work for 'free India with Free and Independent Islam' as equal partners with the majority community. It asked the viceroy and the governors to exercise their special powers under the Act to protect the minorities, which they had not done so far. It opposed any 'federal objective' which must 'necessarily result in majority community rule under the guise of democracy and parliamentary system of government'. It demanded a declaration from the British government that (*i*) as soon as circumstances permitted or immediately after the War, it would examine *de novo* the entire problem of India's future constitution, apart from the Act of 1935; (*ii*) it would not adopt any constitution without the consent and approval of the two major communities, Muslims and Hindus; (*iii*) it would meet all the reasonable demands of the Arabs in Palestine; and (*iv*) Indian troops would not be used outside India against any Muslim country. Jinnah was authorized to seek clarifications from the viceroy on these points.[100] The viceroy after consulting the government in London about the conflicting demands made by the Congress and the All-India Muslim League announced the British policy on 18 October, that: dominion status remained its goal for India; the British government would review the constitution at the end of the war in consultation with the leaders of public opinion in India; and that the viceroy planned to form a 'consultative group' representing the Indian political parties and the states for the prosecution of the war. The League appreciated the viceroy's statement but reiterated its demand that the future constitution should be wholly examined and revised *de novo* after the war and that it would not accept any constitution unless it met with its 'full approval'; however, it refrained from expressing its opinion on the 'consultative group' until its scope, functions and powers were 'fully known', and authorized Jinnah to seek clarification from the viceroy about his statement for the removal of its doubts.[101] The Congress reaction was unexpectedly abrupt and harsh; on 22 October, its working committee called on its ministries in the provinces to tender their resignations in protest against the viceroy's statement, a decision that its leaders later regretted.[102] Keeping in view these irreconcilable positions of the two parties, Linlithgow again had a meeting with Jinnah, Gandhi and the Congress president, Rajendra Prasad, on 1 November; but Jinnah and the Congress leaders stuck to the demands of their parties.[103] Linlithgow asked them to hold a separate meeting among themselves to reach an agreement in the provincial field, followed by their participation in the central government as members of the Viceroy's Executive Council.[104]

Even before the viceroy's proposal, Jinnah and the Congress leaders had tried to establish contact with one another. Rajendra Prasad had invited Jinnah to Wardha to seek his views in shaping the policy of the Congress by its working committee in the prevailing political situation but the latter had expressed his inability to come because the League working committee was holding its own meeting in Delhi.[105] Azad, in a telegram to Jinnah on 16 October 1939, had expressed his 'wish' to meet him, but Jinnah reiterated the All-India Muslim League's policy about a Leaguer's meeting with a Congress Muslim leader, and refused to discuss with him anything relating to the Hindu–Muslim question although he was otherwise prepared to see him.[106] Meanwhile, Jinnah and Nehru established contact through Raghunandan and, after a preliminary meeting, agreed to meet again.[107] However, formal talks were first held between Jinnah and Gandhi on 1 and 2 November, as the viceroy had suggested. Jinnah recorded the gist of these talks. The first point that the two leaders deliberated upon was the question of Hindu–Muslim unity. After a 'great deal of discussion', Gandhi categorically told Jinnah that the Congress could neither accept the All-India Muslim League as 'the authoritative representative' organization of the Muslims, as there were other Muslim organizations, nor the Congress itself could represent only Hindu India or speak on its behalf. If that was the position, Jinnah argued, then any agreement reached between the All-India Muslim League and the Congress would be binding neither on the Muslims nor on the Hindus. The second point that they discussed was the viceroy's proposal, formally communicated to Jinnah, Gandhi and Rajendra Prasad on 2 November, to the effect that the Congress and the All-India Muslim League should first reach an agreement in the provincial field and then work out proposals for their representation in the central government as members of his executive council.[108] This 'make-shift arrangement' was meant for the duration of hostilities, pending a review of the whole constitution after the war. Gandhi insisted that before they reached an agreement on these issues, the British government should make a declaration that it had accepted the Congress demands. On Jinnah's insistence, Gandhi dictated the nature of the declaration that he wanted from the British government, it was to the effect that: 'His Majesty's Government [was] to declare that at the end of the War, British power will accept any chartered freedom framed by a duly elected [Constituent] Assembly on a franchise to be agreed upon between parties. The Constitution should safeguard the rights and privileges of the accepted minorities to their satisfaction.' Jinnah pointed out that his formula was vague and impractical; two of its points, a 'franchise to be agreed upon between parties' and safeguards for the minorities 'to their satisfaction', would raise insoluble controversies. On a query about the representation of the princes, Gandhi maintained that they were the creation of the feudal system crafted by the British, and their representatives could be included in the constituent assembly at a later date. He insisted that his formula was 'clear' and the constituent assembly that it proposed would 'automatically and finally' solve the 'general Hindu–Muslim question'. He was unwilling to discuss with Jinnah any agreement between the Congress and the All-India Muslim League in the provincial field or/ and at the centre; but before they dispersed, he asked Jinnah to discuss the viceroy's proposal with Nehru.[109]

A formal Jinnah–Nehru meeting, as had been agreed upon earlier, did not materialize but the two leaders did exchange letters following All-India Muslim League's announcement to observe 22 December, as the 'Day of Deliverance and Thanksgiving' to express its relief that the Congress ministries had at last ceased to function. Both of them stuck to their respective party positions. Jinnah insisted that the Congress should accept the All-India Muslim League as 'the authoritative and representative organization' of the Muslims of India and refused to endorse the Congress demand for a British declaration on the war aims as it had proposed, while Nehru was willing to accept the All-India Muslim League as 'an influential' but not as 'the sole' organization of the Muslims 'to the exclusion of all others' or to modify the declaration that the Congress had demanded from the British government.[110] They did not proceed any further, as they saw no common ground or common objective for discussion.[111] An unpleasant incident at this time was the exchange of scathing criticism between Gandhi and Jinnah on the failure of the League–Congress–British talks. Gandhi wrote in an article in the *Harijan*, 'Janab Jinnah Sahib looks to the British power to safeguard the Muslim rights. Nothing that the Congress can do or concede will satisfy him. . . . There can be no limits to the Muslim League demands.' Jinnah expressed shock on these remarks, observing that Gandhi's comment 'is far from the truth and is a libel on the whole Muslim community of India. . . . We are determined to fight and fight to the last ditch for rights to which we are entitled in spite of the British or the Congress. We do not depend on anyone'.[112] Earlier, Jinnah's response to such allegations was that the League had only one ally, 'the Muslim nation', and 'one and the only one' to whom they looked 'for help is God'.[113] On 3 November, the Congress wrote to the viceroy about the failure of the Congress–League talks and communicated its decision about the resignation of its ministries in protest against the rejection of its demands.[114] Jinnah also informed the viceroy about the failure of talks because the Congress had refused to discuss anything until the British government had accepted its demands. He sought clarifications from the viceroy, as directed by the working committee, on the four points in his letter of 5 November. The British response was evasive and non-committal. Linlithgow, in his letter to Jinnah on 23 December, simply conveyed that his earlier announcement, which had been made with the approval of the British government, did not exclude examination of any part either of the Act of 1935 or of the policy on which it was based and that the British government realized the 'importance of the contentment of the Muslim community' and the weight that it attached to its views would not be underrated. On the two points relating to the Arab demands in Palestine and the use of the Indian troops against the Muslim countries, the British response was that it had framed its policies keeping in view the 'reasonable' demands of the Arabs in Palestine and that the second point was too hypothetical to warrant a response.[115] The League working committee appreciated the British reply on the first point but considered it unsatisfactory on the second point because it vested the 'final decision' about the 'fate and future' of the Muslims of India in the hands of Britain; and the working committee asked Jinnah to place its views before the viceroy for reconsideration to 'remove all doubts and apprehensions from the mind of Muslim India'.[116]

The British government was still hopeful about an all-India federation. It tried to pursue that objective through Sikandar Hayat Khan (chief minister of the Punjab). At this critical juncture, when the Congress was pressing for complete independence and a constituent assembly elected on the basis of adult franchise to frame a constitution without settling the Hindu–Muslim question and the British were non-committal, posturing virtually neutrality and indifference on the basic issues affecting the Muslims, the All-India Muslim League decided to define what was in the hearts of Muslims of India. The decision was not taken in haste. The League leaders had been in touch with the contemporary Indian Muslim political thinking but had observed complete silence about the party's final goal after it began the process of its reorganization. Jinnah was often criticized for keeping all the cards close to his chest. Of course, there were occasional indications about the possible goal but the All-India Muslim League as a party deliberately avoided any formal definition or declaration. Since the beginning of the process of its reorganization, the League had simply expressed its response on topical issues and attempted to resolve them on a short-term basis. Its focus had remained on broadening its support-base, consolidating its strength and solidifying its organization into a well-knit party. The Congress rule and that party's refusal to hold any serious meaningful talks with the All-India Muslim League helped the League to crystallize its goal that would reflect the aspirations of the Muslim community. After witnessing the working of 'democratic institutions' in the Congress-governed Hindu majority provinces, Jinnah was convinced about the unsuitability of the western democratic institutions in the communally charged environment of India because, in his view, the introduction of these institutions would result in the rule by a permanent unchangeable religious majority.[117]

(D) THE GOAL

(*i*) *Lahore Resolution.* After the collapse of Muslim rule in India and with British ascendancy, many individuals had expressed their views about the political future of India. They suggested several possibilities. One possibility that occasionally came to light particularly at the time of Hindu–Muslim tensions was the division of the Indian subcontinent into Hindu India and Muslim India, or creation of a separate Muslim state in the Muslim majority areas. Before the All-India Muslim League formally embraced this idea as its ideal, a number of proposals were floated by Muslim, Hindu and British personalities. Several factors motivated them to put forward these ideas. One was the diverse racial, religious, linguistic and cultural composition of the population of India, which had never been administered as one unified entity before the British rule and concentration of Muslims in certain areas especially in the north-west and north-east of the subcontinent. Secondly, the creation of a Muslim state was expected to resolve the persistent Hindu–Muslim problem and stop the recurring communal riots. Thirdly, it would settle the issue of pan-Islam, i.e. it would allay Hindu apprehensions about possible Muslim aggression from the north-west of the subcontinent, as Hindu India and Muslim India would have sizeable minorities of their co-religionists in each other's territories, and simultaneously fulfil the Indian Muslim aspirations to have direct spiritual and cultural links with the Muslims in west Asia. Lastly, it would enable the Muslims to develop freely their political, economic and cultural life according to their own ethos and values without any outside interference.

One scholar has identified more than 170 direct and indirect references to the idea of a separate Muslim state in India, which were presented before 23 March 1940. There might still be several others that lie buried in old files of newspapers, magazines and pamphlets. All the proposals before that of Allama Iqbal were of a transitory nature, in the sense that no one took any serious notice contemporaneously. These proposals were subsequently discovered by research scholars.[118] Iqbal used the All-India Muslim League platform for the first time to put forward his ideas in his presidential address at its Allahabad annual session, which received immediate attention in India and England, where the British and Indian leaders were meeting at the round table conferences in London. He had deeply reflected on the contents of his address and took one thousand copies of its printed version to Allahabad for free distribution. He preferred to forego participation in the first Round Table Conference rather than miss the annual session whose venue and dates were changed many a time. Whether or not he discussed his ideas with Jinnah who had played a significant role in his election as president of the session, one does not know, but the two had developed, according to Jinnah's statement, 'communion of views' since 1929, and whom he regarded his 'friend, guide and philosopher'.[119] Besides, Jinnah had himself a 'vision' of a separate Muslim state in 1930.[120] And during his stay in London, Chaudhri Rahmat Ali (1897–1951) and his fellow students in England, who coined the name 'Pakistan' by taking letters from the names of the regions in the north-western Muslim majority areas [*P*unjab, *A*fghania (NWFP), *K*ashmir, *S*indh and Balochis*tan*], often had discussions with him to enlist his support.[121] Iqbal put across his nebulous ideas about a Muslim state in his Allahabad address but refrained from doing that in public the rest of his life, except hinting at it indirectly in his presidential address to the All-India Muslim Conference in 1932.[122] In 1937, he wrote letters to Jinnah, urging him to make a formal declaration to that effect from the platform of the All-India Muslim League but left the timing of such a declaration to Jinnah's discretion. Iqbal's presidential address inspired students, writers and politicians, and so did Chaudhri Rahmat Ali's 'Pakistan National Movement' that had a number of adherents in different parts of India including the 'Pakistan provinces'[123] and the Aligarh Muslim University.[124] Henceforth, any scheme suggesting even remotely or vaguely the division of India and establishment of a Muslim state was labelled as 'Pakistan': the Hindus dubbed any such scheme with derision and the Muslims embraced it with exhilaration. The name 'Pakistan' became more popular than its author himself.

The idea of a separate Muslim state, however, needed a political party and a leader on the ground to transform it into reality.[125] All-India Muslim League and Jinnah filled that need. Jinnah on his part did not openly advocate it till March 1940, and disclosed his vision of 1930 about a separate Muslim state a few years later. But he did reveal his mind in private on more than one occasion in 1938–39.[126] All-India Muslim League's movement for a Muslim state was gradual. After the League's revival, Jinnah had begun to make references to 'Muslim nation' and 'Muslim nationalism', stating his views consistently and with clarity. He denounced the British fixation with the unity of India and their attempts to introduce federalism as the basis of its polity, and the Congress self-perception as the only 'national forum' totally ignoring the diversity in India. He vowed to resist by 'constitutional agitation' all the British moves to impose an all-India federation and dismissed the Congress assertions as self-deception. His focus was on Muslim unity without which, he believed, Muslims might be 'reduced to a class of Shudras and Pariahs of the future' or to a status similar to the African Americans; he urged them, as early as 12 April 1936, to unite under the banner of the All-India Muslim League to 'arrive at a settlement with the Hindus as two nations, if not as partners'.[127] Perceiving intolerance and hostility in the attitude of the Hindus and the Congress policies, he emphasized that the Muslims should 'unite as a nation' and then 'live or die as a united nation'.[128] When pressurized from within the party ranks to change the party creed from 'responsible government' to 'complete independence', the All-India Muslim League meaningfully changed it at the Lucknow annual session to establishment of 'full independence in the form of a federation of free democratic states'.[129] The frequency of the Leaguers' observations on Muslim nationalism gradually increased. In October 1938, the Sindh provincial Muslim League conference in Karachi made a clearer statement about the 'political self-determination of the two nations known as the Hindus and Muslims', recommending that the All-India

Muslim League should 'devise a scheme of Constitution' so that the Muslims might 'attain full independence'.[130] One press comment was: 'The rally of Muslims [in Sindh] . . . has once more brought the dream of Pakistan to the fore. . . . This was bound to be the reaction among the Muslims to the policy of pan-Hinduism which the majority community, even the Congress . . . has been following for years past. . . . The idea of a Muslim India or Pakistan . . . was but a perfectly natural and intelligible reaction to the dream of a Hindu India'.[131] Then, at the Patna annual session in December Professor Abdus Sattar Kheiri (d. 1945), of the Aligarh Muslim University, proposed a resolution, which was seconded by his colleague, Dr Abid Ahmad Ali (1903–1974), that the Indian Muslims were not a minority but a nation who should have 'the right of self-determination'.[132] Though the League did not formally adopt this resolution, it authorized Jinnah to explore the possibility of a 'suitable alternative' to the scheme of federation embodied in the Act of 1935, which would 'safeguard the interests of the Muslims and other minorities'.[133] On 26 March 1939, the League working committee met at the residence of Nawab Ismail Khan (1886–1958), in Meerut and further deliberated upon this issue, where Liaquat observed, 'If Hindus and Muslims could not now live together amicably in India . . . then they might be able to do so by dividing the country on a religious and cultural basis.'[134] Jinnah made 'no secret of the fact that Muslims and Hindus are two nations' and that the Muslims could not maintain their status as such unless they had 'national self-consciousness and national self-determination'.[135] At Meerut, he appointed a constitution subcommittee with the concurrence of the working committee to examine various schemes that had already been propounded by those who were 'fully versed in the constitutional development of India and other countries' and those that might be submitted hereafter to the League president and report its conclusions to the working committee at an early date. The subcommittee consisted of M.A. Jinnah (president), Sikandar Hayat Khan, Nawab Ismail Khan, Sayyid Abdul Aziz, Haji Abdullah Haroon, Khwaja Nazimuddin, Abdul Matin Choudhry, Sardar Aurangzeb Khan (b. 1892) and Nawabzada Liaquat Ali Khan (convener); and on 3 February 1940, Khaliquzzaman replaced Abdul Aziz who had accepted the prime ministership of the Hyderabad state.[136]

Meanwhile, there were attempts to modify the federal scheme as provided in the Act of 1935, to make it acceptable to the Congress. As mentioned elsewhere, in mid–1938, Nehru held discussions with the

British authorities in London for its possible modification but the League's opposition killed that possibility. Then, in January 1939, the British government asked the princes to decide about the accession of their states to the proposed federation by 1 September 1939. Keeping this background in view, Sikandar presented a scheme of federation 'based on regional or zonal grouping of units' and pressed the League for its acceptance. He had Linlithgow's blessings in the promotion of his scheme and positive signals from the Congress, which had communicated to him a 'genuine desire' for a League–Congress rapprochement; but without revealing this information to Jinnah, he tried to get his support for his zonal federation scheme. Jinnah did not oblige him with his approval.[137] Again, when he wanted to bring out his scheme in print-form, he asked for Jinnah's endorsement to the effect that his scheme was an 'improvement over the scheme embodied in the Act [of 1935]'.[138] Jinnah politely declined to give his comments, stating that he could not give his opinion as he had not studied any of the schemes. The issue was, he wrote to Sikandar, 'what will be acceptable to the Muslims of India. I hope you will appreciate my position that as president [of the All-India Muslim League] I cannot anticipate the views of the [Constitution] Subcommittee or the working committee and certainly above all [those of] the All-India Muslim League' on any alternative scheme.[139] Despite this response from Jinnah, Sikandar persisted in promoting his scheme and met with the Congress leaders including Gandhi, Nehru and Azad without the knowledge of the All-India Muslim League executive committee or its president, which caused tension between him and the League.[140] Jinnah publicly negated any impression that the League had anything 'directly or indirectly' to do with Sikandar's scheme or any other schemes that were in circulation.[141] The real hurdle in the way of an all-India federation came from the princes who blocked its implementation by expressing their reservations to the viceroy. Soon after, the outbreak of the Second World War resulted in its suspension. However, Sikandar did not give up the advocacy of his scheme.

Jinnah and the central office of the All-India Muslim League received several proposals, in addition to those that were already available in print, suggesting schemes of federation, confederation or partition of India.[142] The Majlis-i-Kabir-i-Pakistan and others sent their schemes for consideration.[143] All-India Muslim League's constitution subcommittee and the foreign committee along with the authors reviewed the schemes. The foreign committee and the authors jointly discussed the schemes twice: once in September 1939, when they sent a joint report to the League committee;[144] and the second time in January–February 1940, when Abdullah Haroon forwarded the five-point recommendations to the central working committee.[145] The constitution subcommittee discussed nine schemes including the detailed ones by Dr Abdul Latif (1893–1972), a former Professor of English at the Osmania University in the Hyderabad state and honorary secretary of the Muslim Culture Society, Hyderabad (Deccan),[146] Mian Kifayat Ali (1902–1994), a distant cousin of Mian Fazli Husain, who wrote under the pseudonym of 'A Punjabi' and his book was published by Nawab Shahnawaz Khan of Mamdot (1883–1942; president of the Punjab provincial Muslim League),[147] and Professor Syed Zafrul Hasan (1979–1949) and Professor Muhammad Afzaal Husain Qadri,[148] of the Aligarh Muslim University.[149] However, the League committees and the authors could not agree on any of the existing schemes and did not evolve any new scheme.[150] At this time, Chaudhri Rahmat Ali also paid a visit to India after his long stay abroad. The purpose of his visit was in connection with the annual session of the All-India Muslim League in Lahore and possible adoption of a separate homeland for the Muslims as the goal. He corresponded with Jinnah from New Delhi, where he had an appointment with Jinnah but could not keep it due to indisposition, and from Karachi, where he stayed in hotels but did not come to Lahore to attend the historic session.[151]

Jinnah was now ready to show his cards. He wanted the All-India Muslim League to declare, what had been 'stirring the heart of Muslim India', a separate state for the Muslims as its final goal with statutory provisions for the protection of minorities in the partitioned states as its objective without spelling out the details.[152] Earlier, on 5 September 1939, he had told Linlithgow that the Indian Muslims would demand partition of India in the event of a Hindu-dominated centre.[153] On 3–6 February 1940, the working committee met to deliberate upon the party demand and the future constitution of India. Before the meeting, Linlithgow used every device first to know Jinnah's mind and when he did not get any clue, he unsuccessfully tried to talk him out of the possibility of partition.[154] Then, Sikandar promised Linlithgow a day before the meeting that he would force the working committee and Jinnah to produce 'a constructive scheme'. Linlithgow asked him to get support of the League for the federal scheme and 'make it acceptable to the Muslims'.[155] Similar 'pressure' was used on some other members as well. When the working committee met on

3 February, Sikandar advocated his zonal federation scheme. The working committee endorsed neither his scheme nor any other scheme.[156] A few days later, the League also ignored to consider the scheme that Sir Zafrullah Khan propounded as an alternative.[157] Instead, it simply approved five constitutional principles or 'broad outline' that should form the basis of the future constitution. This 'broad outline' provided that:

1. Muslims are not a minority in the ordinary sense of the word. They are a nation.
2. British system of democratic parliamentary party system of government is not suited to the genius and condition of the people of India.
3. Those zones which were composed of majority of Muslims in the physical map of India should be constituted into independent dominions in direct relationship with Great Britain.
4. In those zones where Muslims were in minority their interests and those of other minorities must be adequately and effectively safeguarded and similar safeguards shall be provided for the Hindu and other minorities in the Muslim zones.
5. The various units in each zone shall form component parts of the federation in that zone as autonomous units.[158]

Jinnah communicated this 'broad outline' to the viceroy and demanded firmer assurances from the British government about the future constitution, refusing to leave 'the final decision' about 'the fate and future of Muslim India' in the hands of Britain.[159] The League waited for a response from the British government to its working committee's resolution.[160]

On 22–24 March 1940, the All-India Muslim League held its session in Lahore to pass the resolution that called for the creation of a separate Muslim state.[161] This session was preceded by a tragic incident; the police firing on the Khaksars on 19 March, which left thirty persons dead and several injured. The League amicably reconciled the conflicting positions on the principles embodied in the main resolution. The draft that was discussed on 22 March, was the one that Sikandar had prepared on the basis of the 'broad outline', and which incorporated his own ideas as well.[162] Besides providing for the creation of regions (dominions) in the north-western and eastern zones of India in which units were to be 'completely autonomous and sovereign', it called for a weak all-India structure, or a central agency, designated as the grand council of the united dominions of India, whose decisions could be effective only if approved by at least a two-third majority. A four-member (Jinnah, Nawab Ismail, Sikandar and Barkat Ali) subcommittee drastically modified this draft; Jinnah who was opposed to retaining any link at the all-India level himself made the corrections.[163] There is no evidence to suggest that Sikandar opposed or objected to the amended draft; and later on, he revealed in the Punjab assembly that the subcommittee amended his draft out of its original shape.[164] An agreed resolution was finally produced that Fazlul Haq moved in the open session on 23 March, after its approval by the working committee and adopted the following day.[165] The Lahore Resolution demanded that:

> no constitutional plan would be workable in this country or acceptable to the Muslims unless it is designed on the following basic principles, viz., that geographically contiguous units are demarcated into regions which should be so constituted, with such territorial readjustments as may be necessary, that the areas in which the Muslims are numerically in a majority, as in the North-Western and Eastern zones of India, should be grouped to constitute 'Independent States' in which the constituent units shall be autonomous and sovereign.
>
> That adequate, effective and mandatory safeguards should be specifically provided in the constitution for minorities in these units and in the regions for the protection of their religious, cultural, economic, political, administrative and other rights and interests in consultation with them; and in other parts of India where the Mussalmans are in a minority, adequate, effective and mandatory safeguards shall be specifically provided in the constitution, for them and other minorities, for the protection of their religious, cultural, economic, political, administrative and other rights and interests in consultation with them.
>
> This session further authorizes the working committee to frame a scheme of constitution in accordance with these principles, providing for the assumption finally, by the respective regions, of all powers, such as defence, external affairs, communications, customs and such other matters as may be necessary.[166]

According to Jinnah, the resolution was passed after 'mature consideration';[167] and he regarded it as the 'soul' of Muslim India—'a matter of life and death' for the Muslims, and 'not a counter for bargaining'.[168]

(*ii*) *Post-Lahore Resolution Stance*. At the Madras session (April 1941), the All-India Muslim League slightly modified the Lahore Resolution and incorporated its 3-point revised version in the aims and objects of the party.[169] The first point modified the first paragraph of the resolution, which now read:

> The establishment of completely Independent States formed by demarcating geographically contiguous units into regions which shall be so constituted, with such territorial adjustments as may be necessary, that the areas in which the Musalmans are numerically in a majority, as in the North-Western and Eastern zones of India, shall be grouped together to constitute Independent States as Muslim Free National Homelands in which the constituent units shall be autonomous and sovereign.

The other two points related to 'adequate, effective and mandatory safeguards' for the protection of 'religious, cultural, economic, political, administrative and other rights and interests' of the minorities in the Muslim and non-Muslim regions 'in consultation with them'.[170] This modified version of the Lahore Resolution was made part of the membership form of the All-India Muslim League'.[171]

The Lahore Resolution did not give a name to the Muslim state(s) that it had resolved to establish in the subcontinent. In fact, the word 'Pakistan' was mentioned neither in its text nor in the speeches on it by the League leaders. After its adoption, its opponents contemptuously dubbed, and its supporters passionately hailed, the state that it envisaged as Pakistan. The All-India Muslim League took almost a year to embrace the name. Its reluctance to adopt this name was partly due to the difference between Rahmat Ali's detailed scheme, which was associated with the name of Pakistan, and the principles enunciated in the Lahore Resolution.[172] But the name 'Pakistan' had come to have a special fascination for the Indian Muslims who began to use it synonymously with the Lahore Resolution. Its use gained currency in the League meetings and in the speeches of the Leaguers especially those of its young political workers. At first, Jinnah reluctantly agreed that it could be referred to as the 'Lahore Resolution, popularly known as the Pakistan Resolution'.[173] It was Sikandar's tirade against the Lahore Resolution and his opposition to its naming as the Pakistan Resolution that led to the removal of the 'bar' against its formal use by the League and the Leaguers. When Sikandar's criticism of the Lahore Resolution in his speeches particularly the one in the Punjab assembly was reported in the press in February 1941, Jinnah asked for his explanation. He responded that he had been misreported but requested Jinnah 'to eschew the word Pakistan'.[174] The issue came up before the central working committee on 22 February 1941, when it was decided to observe 23 March, every year all over India to explain 'the principles of the Lahore Resolution popularly known as the Pakistan Resolution as the only permanent and peaceful solution of India's constitutional problem'. Sikandar moved an amendment to the resolution that the words 'popularly known as Pakistan Resolution' should be deleted; his amendment was lost, every member of the working committee except him voted against it. Then, he moved a resolution to differentiate the Lahore Resolution from Rahmat Ali's scheme or any other scheme put forward under that name. That resolution was also defeated when put to vote; Sikandar was alone to vote for it.[175] Henceforth, the All-India Muslim League began to use the name 'Pakistan' officially and observed 23 March, every year as the Pakistan (Resolution) Day.[176]

The 'sovereign status' of the Muslim state, completely separate from the rest of India, and its territorial limits came under consideration after the Lahore Resolution. This was partly because the All-India Muslim League did not work out the details of its Pakistan scheme. Jinnah's stance was that the British government and the Congress should first accept the principles of the Lahore Resolution and then the League would work out the details; and he cited the examples of Burma and Ireland where the principle of separation and independence was accepted first and the details were worked out subsequently. He discouraged any discussion in public of such issues, which might cause intra-League fissures.[177] He frequently asked the Leaguers that if they had any scheme or proposal to explain or to elaborate the Lahore Resolution, they should send it privately to the League, which would consider it at the proper time and urged them to stick to its principles.[178] There were quite a few proposals about the limits of the two parts of the Muslim state. One Leaguer suggested that the boundary of the north-western part should be up to Agra; and another proposed that certain areas be excluded from the two parts to raise the proportion of Muslim population in the state.[179] Jinnah himself proposed that a corridor should be provided to link the two parts that was to run via Delhi, Lucknow, Allahabad and Patna.[180] But he vehemently opposed any suggestion that called for the retention of even the semblance of an all-India centre. For example, the main reason for the tension between him and Sikandar after March 1940, was the latter's repetitiously public advocacy of his zonal scheme and retention of an all-India centre. The cordiality in their relations developed only after the former submitted to the will of the Muslim majority.[181] Again, when the Abdullah Haroon-chaired Foreign Committee prepared a scheme based on the Lahore Resolution, which kept a link at the centre, he totally dissociated the League from its work.[182] This scheme was a revised version of Dr Abdul Latif's scheme of a federation of culturally homogenous States 'in the light of the Lahore Resolution' which sought to preserve 'the unity of India'.[183] The Foreign Committee published this scheme on 17 February 1941. Jinnah issued a statement the next day, in which he contradicted that it was a League-sponsored scheme.[184] When Dr Latif continued to insist on its linkage with the League committee, Jinnah angrily reacted, 'I have repeatedly made it clear . . . that the Muslim League had appointed no such committee as you keep hopping upon. . . . Please let me make it clear once for all that neither Sir Abdullah Haroon nor you should go on talking of this committee or that committee and involving the Muslim League or its authority behind the proposals that may be formulated by individuals and groups'.[185] When Dr Latif continued to insist on his scheme, G.M. Sayed wrote to him, 'Partition of India is the only lasting solution of the problem. . . . It is idle to hope for any satisfactory result from attempts at rapprochement between elements that are in their very nature poles apart. . . . Such attempts, however genuine, are . . . likely to be interpreted as signs of weakness and affect our cause.'[186] And Abdullah Haroon wrote to Latif that all the proposals were coming from the Muslims, and the Hindus had not reciprocated these feelings and they wanted 'complete unity of India under their domination'. Since there was no reciprocity, Abdullah Haroon wrote, such proposals were 'detrimental to the Muslim Nation and its cause'.[187] Soon after, on 24 August 1942, Firoz Khan Noon, then Defence Member, GoI, in an address to the AMU Students Union, made a proposal out of line with the Lahore Resolution; he proposed the division of India into five—two Muslim and three Hindu—dominions.[188] These dominions were to be 'completely independent' but were to have a central authority consisting of nominees of the five dominions to administer subjects like defence, customs, foreign relations and currency; simultaneously, he remarked that he followed 'the same policy inside the cabinet (sic) as Mr Jinnah did outside'.[189] When Jinnah read his observations, he wrote to Noon that the latter had not really appreciated 'the fundamental principles underlying the policy and programme' of the League, and impressed upon him to leave the constitutional problem and its solution to the League and that he should not commit himself 'in any way individually'.[190] When Dr Saeeduddin Ahmad of the AMU approvingly wrote about Noon's proposal, suggesting that the League should join the central authority, 'if any good can accrue from it', Jinnah responded that in his 'judgment', it would be 'fatal to the Lahore Resolution' to talk of 'any centre whatsoever'.[191] Noon assured Jinnah that he would be 'behind the Muslim League' whenever there was 'anything for serious consideration'.[192]

The Leaguers presented quite a few proposals about the geographical limits, and the number, of the Muslim State(s), and the League leadership promised to give any proposals that were sent to the party 'due consideration'. The Madras Resolution (April 1941) did not clearly demand one State; it visualized 'Independent States as Muslim Free National Homelands' with 'autonomous and sovereign' constituent units in the Muslim majority areas of the north-west and north-east of India. The Leaguers often referred to two Muslim States/Federations, one in the north-west and the other in the north-east; and contrary to Jinnah's and Leaguers' reaction against the proposals for retaining an all-India centre, none raised any objection to proposals about the number of states.[193] The Bengal famine and the debate on this calamity in the British parliament in November 1943, brought about clarity in the League thinking. The inability of the north-eastern part to handle a crisis situation came into focus and its viability and survival as a separate sovereign state came to be questioned. The League looked for an alternative to offset possible pressure from the British policy makers about its viability. Jinnah invited proposals from the Bengal presidency Muslim League, and in response received quite a few schemes.[194] After deliberations, it was decided to have Pakistan as one state based on provinces as its constituent units; Jinnah expressed his views in his speeches and interviews with foreign journalists; more notable is his interview in December 1943, with Beverley Nichols, the author of the *Verdict on India*.[195] He spelt out the League's position on Pakistan with more precision in his talks with Gandhi in September 1944; that the six provinces/units—Punjab, Sindh, the NWFP, Balochistan, Bengal and Assam—in the two Muslim majority zones would form constituent units of one state.[196] The All-India Muslim League formally adopted Pakistan as its goal at the convention of newly elected Muslim League legislators on 9–10 April 1946, when the Cabinet Mission was visiting India.[197]

(*iii*) *Nature of the State*. After the Lahore Resolution, All-India Muslim League's focus was on the struggle to achieve Pakistan. It deliberately avoided issues that were likely to generate unnecessary debate, cause divisions in its ranks, and deflect its attention from its goal, i.e. Pakistan. It was conscious of the condition of the Muslim society and the degree to which it had declined socially over the past centuries. It wanted to take steps to reform and regenerate the Muslim society. Appointment of committees like the G.M. Sayed-chaired committee and bodies like the Majlis Ta'mir-i-Milli (Reconstruction Committee of the Community) and Islamic Baitul Mal committee with Maulana Husain Mian of Bhulwari Sharif as convener indicated realization of the need for social and religious reform.[198] The task of regeneration was not that easy. Muslim intellectual and political leadership had to reconcile the concepts about the state and society as these had evolved in Muslim history with the needs of the modern times. The development of any synthesis had to take into consideration the sensitivities of mutually antagonistic sections/sects of the Muslim society, which Jinnah's charismatic leadership and the force of the Pakistan ideal had united or silenced. Such a task required, besides sound scholarship and wisdom, deep reflection, patience, tolerance and hard work over a long period. The League had neither the time nor the degree of requisite expertise for that task. Immediately it had to organize the Muslims to achieve Pakistan. Its leaders in their campaign to mobilize the Muslim masses referred to Islam and Islamic symbols and terminology in order to unite them on its platform. They had popular declarations for Muslim unity like 'One God, One Book, One Prophet', 'Islam is a complete code of life, polity and social order', Islam 'is a complete code of human existence', '*Pakistan ka Matlab kia, La Ilaha Illalla*', etc.[199] The creation of synthesis of the different strands of Muslim and modern thought was left to the elected leadership of the Pakistan state.

Similar was the case of framing a constitution for Pakistan before independence. The Lahore Resolution authorized the All-India Muslim League working committee to frame a constitution in accordance with its principles. Neither the working committee nor any other statutory body took steps to appoint a committee to frame a constitution. If the League had embarked upon doing that, it would have squandered away its energies in hypothetical debates and distracted the attention of its leaders and workers from the struggle for Pakistan. The post-independence constitutional debates on determining the place of Islam in the constitution amply prove the usefulness of the policy that the

League under Jinnah's guidance followed. However, the League leadership tried to allay any apprehension that the constitution might not be Islamic in content; Jinnah himself gave assurances in his statements and in communications to the Leaguers that the constitution of Pakistan would be based on Islamic ideals.[200] In a letter to Pir Aminul Hasnat of Manki Sharif who played a critical role in the final phase of the Pakistan movement, he wrote that:

> when the preliminary question of Pakistan being established is settled it will not be the League that will frame the constitution of Pakistan but the inhabitants of Pakistan in which 75% will be Mussalmans and therefore you will understand that it will be a Muslim government and it will be for the people of Pakistan to frame the constitution under which the Pakistan government will come into being and function. Therefore there need be no apprehension that the constitution-making body which will be composed of overwhelming majority of Muslims can ever establish any constitution for Pakistan other than one based on Islamic ideals, nor can the Government of Pakistan when it comes into being act contrary to Islamic ideals and principles.[201]

Again, on 21 September 1945, he wrote to one M. Abdullah of Peshawar:

> As regards the constitution of Pakistan, it is not for any individual or any one body, even for the matter of that, for the All-India Muslim League to frame a constitution for Pakistan, and . . . the constitution can only be framed by the *Millat*, through its chosen representatives, which in modern language is called the constitution-making body and that body can only be formed when the boundaries of Pakistan have been defined. Once it has been done the chosen representatives of the people would form the constitution-making body and they will as a sovereign body deal with the question of framing of the constitution.[202]

NOTES

1. For C. Rajagopalachari's observations, see the Annual Number of the *Amrita Bazar Patrika*, cited in *TP*, vol. IV, p. 370; and for Nihchaldas Vazirani's views, see his letter to Jinnah, 29 October 1942, QAP, F. 191, p. 17.
2. For example, see Sayyid Abdul Aziz's remarks in his reception address at the Patna annual session, *IAR*, 1938, vol. II, pp. 343–44.
3. *Star of India*, 10 January 1938; and Jinnah's presidential address at the Sindh PML Conference in Karachi, 8 October 1938, *IAR*, 1938, p. 353.
4. Jinnah's remarks in his presidential address at the Lucknow annual session, Pirzada, *Foundations*, vol. II, p. 268.

5. Waheed, *Nation's Voice*, vol. II, p. 9.
6. AFM, vol. 188, no. 58.
7. QAP, F. 1098, p. 317.
8. Resolution passed by the central council on 27–28 August 1939, AFM, vol. 253, p. 75.
9. For instance, see an 8-page pamphlet by Abul Hasan, 15 April 1939, QAP, F. 1097, pp. 64–69; for police firing on a peaceful Muslim gathering near the Moulganj mosque in Kanpur, see AFM, vol. 253, p. 77; and vol. 291, pp. 45–46; and see also a report by Tajuddin, vice president of the Central Provinces and Berar provincial Muslim League, ibid., vol. 118, no. 66; and a resolution of the central council passed on 27–28 August 1939.
10. Mohammad Abbas Vidyarthi, *Dastan-i-Bihar*, Patna, [1939]; and Jinnah to Nehru, 17 March 1938, *Re: Hindu–Muslim Settlement, Correspondence between Mr Gandhi & Mr Jinnah and between Pandit Jawaharlal Nehru & Mr Jinnah*, Bombay, 1938, citing an extract from the *New Times* (Lahore), 1 March 1938, p. 14.
11. For riots resulting in loss of Muslim lives following the murder of a Hindu, Jagdev Rao Patel, who wrote pamphlets critical of the Quran and Prophet Mohammad (PBUH), see QAP, F. 1097, pp. 23–24 and 100–101.
12. For the Bihar government's ban on cow-sacrifice and the provincial Muslim League's reaction, see AFM, vol. 190, no. 1; vol. 191, no. 3 vol. 557, pp. 15–16 and 17–24; and vol. 558.
13. For an amendment, moved by M.G. Chitnavis on 9 December 1937, seeking ban on the slaughter of milch and agricultural cattle especially cows in view of 'appalling fall of cattle wealth' of the Central Provinces, see QAP, F. 16, pp. 137–39.
14. Dr S. Qamaruddin Qadri, secretary, town Muslim League, Gaya, AFM, vol. 557, pp. 9–13; and QAP, F. 1097, pp. 248–51; and 193–96; and for a conflict over flag-hoisting in Jabbalpur (Central Provinces) in March 1939, see ibid., F. 1332, pp. 2–24.
15. On 27 January 1937, the Madras League assembly party staged a walkout against the singing of this song. *IAR*, 1937, vol. I, p. 167.
16. AFM, vol. 561, pp. 17–18.
17. For a resolution of the Congress working committee passed on 26 October–1 November 1937, see *IAR*, 1937, vol. II, p. 326.
18. *Star of India*, 4 November 1937.
19. Muzaffar Ahmad, secretary, Badaun district Muslim League to Liaquat, 13 August 1939, AFM, vol. 559, p. 10; for Muslim grievances in the districts of Badaun and Barielly, see an 8-page pamphlet, ibid., vol. 559; resolutions of the Badaun district Muslim League working committee denouncing the police tax imposed by the provincial government on Muslims; and resolution of the central council passed on 27–28 August 1939, ibid., vol. 77; and letters to president and secretary, All-India Muslim League, from Muslims in the Benares and Kanpur riots, ibid., vols. 77 and 559. See also Haithwaite to Jinnah, 24 June 1940, QAP, F. 21, p. 8.
20. AFM, vol. 118, no. 61.
21. Ibid., vol. 253, p. 76.
22. Maulvi Abdul Haq was especially invited to the Lucknow annual session to brief the participants about the Urdu–Hindi question. For his letter to Jinnah, 5 October 1937, see QAP, F. 25, p. 25.

23. The final report was signed by Raja of Pirpur, Afzaal Qadri, Karimur Rahman and Sayyid Nawab Ali.
24. *Report of the Committee appointed by the Council of the All-India Muslim League to examine the Wardha Scheme,* convener, Raja Syed Mohammad Mehdi of Pirpur, Lucknow, n.d. For comments on the draft report, see AFM, vol. 560; and for a resolution of the central council passed on 8 April 1939, see ibid., vol. 252, p. 55.
25. For a resolution of the League working committee passed on 2–3 July 1939, see ibid., vol. 128, no. 30.
26. Afzaal Qadri to Liaquat, n.d., and Liaquat to Afzaal Qadri, 24 May 1939, ibid., vol. 560.
27. For a resolution passed at the special session of the All-India Muslim League in Calcutta on 17–18 April 1938, see ibid., vol. 198, no. 67, in which the provincial Muslim Leagues were asked to collect information about all the incidents and send reports to the central council. See also Ansar Ahmad to honorary secretary, All-India Muslim League, 23 February 1940, ibid., vol. 199, no. 51.
28. For Jinnah's press interview, see *Tribune,* 21 October 1938.
29. For his observations, see Pirzada, *Foundations,* vol. II, pp. 268 and 278–88.
30. For moves by the All-India Muslim League to prevent civil disobedience in Bihar and Central Provinces, see AFM, vol. 122, nos. 49 and 68; and vol. 128, nos. 11 and 30; and for Jinnah's interview to the Associated Press, see *Times of India,* 21 October 1938. Jinnah disallowed a resolution by Rizwanullah in the central council that called on the Muslim Leaguers to boycott the meetings convened by the Congress or its allied parties unless permitted by the working committee or the president. Ibid., vol. 246, p. 17.
31. *IAR,* 1938, vol. II, p. 205.
32. AFM, vol. 558, pp. 62–63, 66–67, and 71–72. In April 1939, the League assembly party again staged a walkout to protest against the government policy. Abid Husain to Jinnah, 10 April 1939, QAP, F. 1097, pp. 23–24.
33. Abdur Rauf to Jinnah, 24 and 26 January 1939, ibid., 1130, pp. 10 and 14.
34. Liaquat to Jinnah, 24 April 1939, ibid., F. 48, pp. 16–19; and resolution of the All-India Muslim League working committee passed on 5 December 1938.
35. Ibid., vol. 558, pp. 16–43. For resolutions passed by the All-India Muslim League working committee on 8–10 October 1938, and 26 March 1939, see ibid., vol. 122, p. 47 and vol. 128, p. 12; and for letters of Liaquat, Rauf Shah and Chief Minister Shukla, 23-point provincial Muslim League demands, and chief minister–provincial Muslim League agreement, see ibid., vol. 561, pp. 1–14 and 33–34; *Hitavada* (Nagpur), 22 December 1939; and Liaquat to Jinnah, 10 February 1939, QAP, F. 1130, p. 37.
36. For a resolution passed by the All-India Muslim League working committee on 3–6 February 1940, deploring the police firing on the Muslims on 15 January, see AFM, vol. 129, p. 15.
37. E.V. Ramaswami to Jinnah, 27 February 1940, QAP, F. 531, pp. 4–5; secretary, Muslim League, Salem, to Jinnah, 26 June 1938, ibid., F. 823, p. 94; resolution of the Muslim Mahajana Sabha passed on 18 July 1938, ibid., F. 1095, p. 171 and pp. 78–79; and for cases filed under the Criminal Law Amendment Act against anti-Hindi demonstrators, see AFM, vol. 205, no. 50.
38. Kamaruddin, president of the Cuttack Muslim League to Jinnah, 3 June 1938, QAP, F. 566, p. 10.

39. AFM, vol. 246; honorary secretary to Abdur Rauf, 3 March 1939, and Mohammad Asghar to Liaquat, 17 October 1939, ibid., vol. 51 and 58; and *Star of India*, 20 November 1939.

40. Resolution passed by the All-India Muslim League working committee on 2–3 July 1939, AFM, vol. 128, no. 30.

41. For some material listing Muslim grievances, see *Memorial of Grievances of Muslims presented by the Ahmadabad District Muslim League*, Ahmadabad, 22 December 1939, 10 p.; and Mohammad Abbas Vidyarthi, *Dastan-i-Bihar*, Patna, [1939]; secretary, Nagpur Muslim League to honorary secretary, All-India Muslim League, 26 July 1939, AFM, vol. 558, pp. 66–67; secretary, Jabbalpur Muslim League to honorary secretary, All-India Muslim League, 27 September 1939, ibid., vol. 558, pp. 71–72; and Altaf Husain to Jinnah, 9 December 1939, (enclosing a collection of papers from the *Star of India* relating to the oppression in Bihar), QAP, F. 119, pp. 5 and 14–188. In 1939, the Jabbalpur Muslim League issued a 'Muslim Bulletin' about the communal situation but its publication was discontinued after four issues at the request of the chief minister [Ibid., vol. 558, pp. 78–82], and the Bombay presidency Muslim League issued a 49-page report on the Hindu–Muslim riots in Bombay. [QAP, F. 117] QAP, Fs 114–16 contain documents relating to Muslim grievances against the Congress ministries and its officials that Jinnah received from July 1939 to February 1940. See also *It Shall Never Happen Again*, with a foreword by Qazi Isa, Delhi, 1946; and *What Muslims Suffered When Congress Ruled—The Tragic Story of 1937–39* [Delhi?], 1946.

42. *Report of the Bihar Muslim Grievances Enquiry Committee*, prepared and written by S.M. Shareef, Patna, 2 December 1938, 73 p.

43. QAP, F. 565, p. 11; and F. 1098, p. 174. For a documentary survey of the Congress rule, see two-volume work by K.K. Aziz, *Muslims under Congress Rule, 1937–1939: A Documentary Record*, Islamabad, 1978–9.

44. S.M. Shareef to Rajendra Prasad, 29 October and 9 November 1939, QAP, F. 17, pp. 47–48.

45. Ibid., F. 17, 49–50.

46. *Muslim Sufferings under Congress Rule*, issued by the Bengal Provincial Muslim League, December 1939.

47. Huseyn Shaheed Suhrawardy to Abdullah Haroon, 3 November 1939, QAP, 458, p. 17; Fazlul Haq to Liaquat, 14 November 1939, AFM, vol. 39; Fazlul Haq to Jinnah, 22 November 1939, QAP, F. 281, pp. 1–4; and Altaf Husain to Jinnah, 15 January 1940, ibid., F. 772, p. 43.

48. *Report of the Inquiry Committee appointed by the All-India Muslim League to inquire into Muslim Grievances in Congress Provinces*, President, Raja Syed Mohammad Mehdi of Pirpur, [and] published by the secretary, All-India Muslim League, Lucknow, 1939 [*Pirpur Report*], 81 p.

49. Linlithgow to Jinnah, 18 March 1939, QAP, F. 50, p. 2; and also see ibid., pp. 6–11.

50. *IAR*, 1939, vol. II, p. 40.

51. Shamsul Hasan to Firoz Khan Noon, high commissioner for India, 23 May 1940, AFM, vol. 218, no. 57.

52. *IAR*, 1940, vol. I, p. 269; and Abdussattar Sait to Jinnah, 30 July 1939, QAP, F. 447, pp. 16–22.

53. For the correspondence, see *Statesman*, 14 October 1938; and QAP, F. 1090, pp. 135–36; and for the basis of Jinnah's rejection, see Waheed, *Nation's Voice: Towards Consolidation*, pp. 420–21 and 465.

54. Jamiluddin Ahmad, *Some Recent Speeches and Writings of Mr. Jinnah*, Lahore, 1946, p. 151.

55. For reply by Sir Hugh O'Neill to a debate on India in the House of Commons on 24 January 1940, see *IAR*, 1940, vol. I, pp. 4 and 34; and for Linlithgow's assessment of Muslim grievances, see Linlithgow to Amery, 8 January 1942, *TP*, vol. I, p. 17.

56. Resolution passed by the All-India Muslim League council on 25 February 1940, AFM, vol. 284, p. 60.

57. QAP, F. 335, pp. 40–43.

58. For Abdur Rahman Siddiqi's criticism of this decision and his highly disparaging remarks about Jinnah that he subsequently regretted, see AFM, vol. 284, p. 8.

59. R.N. Rustomji to Jinnah, 14 August 1944, QAP, F. 1072, pp. 271–72.

60. Raza Ali to Jinnah, 18 March 1942, ibid., F. 141, p. 12.

61. Linlithgow to secretary of state for India, 6 February 1940, cited in Ikram Ali Malik (comp.), *Muslim League Session 1940 & the Lahore Resolution (Documents)*, Islamabad, 1990, pp. 252–53.

62. *Times of India*, 23 April 1935; and QAP, F. 1006, p. 63.

63. Gandhi to Jinnah, 22 May 1937, Syed Sharifuddin Pirzada, *Quaid's Correspondence*, Rawalpindi, 1987, p. 95.

64. For statements of the leaders, see *IAR*, 1937, vol. II, pp. 231–32; and for Jinnah–Rajendra joint signed statement, see *IAR*, 1935, vol. I, p. 295.

65. For several letters and telegrams from Muslim Leaguers asking Jinnah to arrive at a settlement on the basis of this formula, see QAP, F. 26, pp. 69–70; F. 458, p. 11; F. 515, pp. 48 and 51; and the *Tribune*, 22 July 1937.

66. *Tribune*, 6 July 1937; and for Jinnah's strongly worded comments, see ibid., 22 July 1937.

67. Jinnah's statement, ibid., 28 July 1937.

68. *Amrita Bazar Patrika*, 11 July 1937; and for a statement by Akhil Chandra Dutta of 12 January 1938, stating that the Bengali Hindu leaders did not accept the formula, see QAP, F. 1093, p. 167.

69. D. Madhava Rao to Jinnah (personal and confidential), 11 October 1937, QAP, F. 25, p. 68.

70. For Nehru's statement, see the *Statesman*, 12 February 1938.

71. For Jinnah's refutation of Azad's assertion that he was responsible for his talks with Gandhi, see the *Civil & Military Gazette*, 4 May 1938.

72. For Jinnah–Gandhi correspondence, see *IAR*, 1938, vol. I, 359–62; *Re: Hindu–Muslim Settlement, Correspondence between Mr Gandhi & Mr Jinnah and between Pandit Jawaharlal Nehru & Mr Jinnah*, pp. 1–4; and Pirzada, *Quaid's Correspondence*, pp. 95–101.

73. For Jinnah–Nehru correspondence, see *IAR*, 1938, vol. I, pp. 562–76; *Re: Hindu–Muslim Settlement, Correspondence between Mr Gandhi & Mr Jinnah and between Pandit Jawaharlal Nehru & Mr Jinnah*, pp. 5–24; and Pirzada, *Quaid's Correspondence*, pp. 260–88.

74. For Nehru to Jinnah, 4 January 1938; and Nehru's press statement of 3 January, see QAP, F. 17, pp. 1 and 4; and *Pioneer*, 3 January 1938.

75. *New Times* (Lahore), 1 March 1938.

76. *Tribune*, 10 February 1938.

77. 'The Jinnah–Congress Talks: A Review', 26 June 1938, QAP, F. 1095, pp. 9–17.

78. For the League council's resolution on this subject passed on 30–31 July 1938, see ibid., vol. 247. See also Raza Ali to Jinnah, 19 July 1938, QAP, F. 1095, p. 177;

Abdullah Haroon's speech at Hyderabad, *Daily Gazette*, 3 July 1938; and R.J. Moore, *Churchill, Cripps and India, 1939–1945*, Oxford, 1979, p. vi.

79. For the preliminary points raised in the Jinnah–Gandhi meeting, see QAP, F. 40, pp. 10–12.

80. Abdur Rab Nishtar to Jinnah, 18 May 1938, ibid., F. 394, pp. 6–8.

81. For the text of the resolution, see AFM, vol. 469, pp. 13–15; and *IAR*, 1938, vol. I, p. 18.

82. Before Jinnah negotiated with Bose by correspondence, he had four meetings with him on 11, 12, 14 and 15 May [QAP, F. 40, pp. 13–19], and one meeting with Gandhi on 20 May. Ibid., pp. 20–24.

83. *Statesman*, 1 February 1938.

84. For a copy of the note that Bose handed over to Jinnah, see *Re: Hindu–Muslim Settlement*, pp. 79–81.

85. For eleven-point demands that the All-India Muslim League council sent to the Congress dealing with cultural, administrative and political matters, see *IAR*, 1938, vol. I, pp. 59–60.

86. For Jinnah–Bose correspondence, see Pirzada, *Quaid's Correspondence*, pp. 51–58.

87. Bose to Jinnah, 16 December 1938, QAP, F. 16, p. 179.

88. For instance, see his correspondence with C.P. Shukla, editor of the *Harijan*, in the *Civil & Military Gazette*, 10 August 1939; his statement in the *Star of India*, 31 July 1939; Jinnah to Shukla, 9 August 1939, QAP, F. 49, p. 186; Liaquat to Jinnah, 2 August 1939, ibid., p. 187; and Waheed, *Nation's Voice: Towards Consolidation*, pp. 380–84.

89. U. Phadnis, *Towards the Integration of the Indian States, 1919–47*, London, 1968, pp. 121–22. See also resolution passed by the All-India Muslim League working committee on 4 December 1938.

90. For resolution on the States passed in the Haripur (Gujarat) Congress on 19–21 February 1938, see A.M. Zaidi and S.G. Zaidi (eds.), *Encyclopaedia of the Congress*, pp. 424–40. On 15–19 May 1938, the Congress working committee even advised that the use of the word 'Congress' for the organization of the States be avoided.

91. Gandhi's warning to the princes in December 1938, cited in R.J. Moore, *The Crisis of Indian Unity, 1917–1940*, Oxford, 1974, p. 308. For the Congress attempt to keep its organization aloof from the party in the princely states, see resolution passed by the Congress working committee on 15–19 May 1938.

92. For details, see Sardar Patel's statement in the *Hindustan Times*, 22 November 1938; for the Rajkot affair, see QAP, F. 33 and F. 1139, and for Jinnah's correspondence with Fazlullah, see ibid., F. 568, p. 48 and F. 1130, pp. 11 and 13; for an account by the Bombay residency Muslim League, see ibid., F. 568, p. 56; and F. 1097, p. 44; for resolution of the All-India Muslim League council in support of the Hyderabad State, see AFM, vol. 252, pp. 57–58; and for a resolution passed at the Patna annual session, see Pirzada, *Foundations*, vol. II, pp. 319–20.

93. Resolution passed at the Patna annual session.

94. For the condition of the Muslims of Jaipur and refugees from there, see QAP, F. 252, p. 57; and also see Muslim League, Patiala to Quaid-i-Azam, ibid., F. 1097, pp. 237–41.

95. Resolution passed by the All-India Muslim League working committee on 26 March 1939.

96. Sikandar to Jinnah, 21 June 1939, QAP, F. 16, pp. 6 and 198. By 1 September 1939, only one-fourth of the princes had signed the instrument of accession.

97. Resolution passed by the All-India Muslim League council on 27–28 August 1939, AFM, vol. 253, p. 80.

98. Resolutions passed by the Congress working committee on 15 September 1939, and by the All India Congress Committee on 10 October 1939.

99. Linlithgow to Jinnah (secret), 17 and 24 October 1939, and Jinnah to Linlithgow, 23 October 1939, QAP, F. 95, pp. 2, 21 and 24.

100. Resolutions passed by the working committee on 17–18 September and 22 October 1939, Sharifuddin Pirzada, *Foundations of Pakistan: All-India Muslim League Documents, 1906–1947*, Karachi, 1989, pp. 309–313; Jinnah to Linlithgow, 5 November 1939, Pirzada, *Quaid's Correspondence*, pp. 207; and amendments moved by the League parties to the Congress resolutions in the provincial assemblies, *IAR*, 1939, vol. II, pp. 243–46; and Hasan Ispahani to Jinnah, 1 October 1939, QAP, F. 18, p. 3.

101. Resolution passed by the All-India Muslim League working committee on 22 October 1939.

102. V.P. Menon, *The Transfer of Power in India*, New Delhi, 1981, p. 10.

103. For Linlithgow-Jinnah correspondence before the meeting, see QAP, F. 95, pp. 25–27.

104. For Muslim Leaguers' perception of these meetings, see Abdul Hamid Khan, Secretary of the Madras provincial Muslim League to Jinnah, 29 September 1939, QAP, F. 321, p. 5; and Dr S.M. Haider to Jinnah, 28 December 1939, ibid., F. 872, pp. 165–66; and also see Laithwaite to Jinnah, 7 October 1939, ibid., F. 18, p. 5.

105. For the correspondence, see the *Star of India*, 14 September 1939.

106. QAP, F. 17, pp. 33, 34, 35–36 and 37.

107. Raghunandan to Jinnah, 19 October 1939, Jinnah to Nehru, 24 October 1939, and Nehru to Jinnah, 1 November 1939, ibid., F. 17, pp. 26, and 27–28, 43.

108. Letters from Linlithgow to Jinnah, Congress president and Gandhi, 2 November 1939, ibid., F. 95, pp. 28–32; and *IAR*, 1939, vol. II, 242–44.

109. For a typed script of the Jinnah–Gandhi talks, QAP, F. 18, pp. 36–40; and also see AFM, vol. 237, pp. 6–7.

110. *IAR*, 1940, vol. I, p. 27. Nehru mentioned the Jamiatul Ulama-i-Hind, Majlis-i-Ahrar, All-India Shia Conference, All-India Momin Conference, etc, apart from trade unions and peasant unions that had Muslim members.

111. Nehru to Jinnah, 9 and 14 December 1939, and Jinnah to Nehru, 13 and 15 December 1939, QAP, F. 17, pp. 80, 90–93.

112. AFM, vol. 227, pp. 60–61, 63; QAP, F. 266, p. 9; *Star of India*, 6 November 1939; and *IAR*, 1939, vol. II, pp. 39–60.

113. For his views, see his presidential address at the Patna annual session on 26 December 1938.

114. Rajendra Prasad to Linlithgow, 3 November 1939, QAP, F. 95, pp. 43–44.

115. Jinnah to Linlithgow, 4 November 1939, Linlithgow to Jinnah, 6 February 1940, QAP, F. 95, pp. 56–47; and Linlithgow to Jinnah, 23 December 1939, Pirzada, *Quaid's Correspondence*, pp. 207–210.

116. Resolution passed by the All-India Muslim League working committee on 3–6 February 1940, AFM, vol. 129, no. 15.

117. For his views on this subject, see his article in the *Time and Tide* (London), 19 January 1940, Jamiluddin, *Some Recent Speeches and Writings of Mr. Jinnah*, pp. 128–38.

118. K.K. Aziz has dealt with this subject in a four-volume work, *A History of the Idea of Pakistan*, Lahore, 1987. For a list of 170 proposals/reports, see volume 3, pp.

671–94; and for some earlier 'discoveries', see Sharifuddin Pirzada, *Evolution of Pakistan*, Karachi, 1963, and *Pakistan Resolution and the Historic Lahore Session*, Karachi, 1968; and M. Rafique Afzal, 'Origin of the Idea of a Separate Muslim State', *Journal of the Research Society of Pakistan*, January/April 1966; and 'Introduction' to M. Rafique Afzal (ed.), *The Case for Pakistan*, Islamabad, 1988.

119. Jinnah to Inamullah Khan, 16 May 1944, QAP, F. 1092, p. 250.

120. His reply to a questionnaire, ibid., F. 1067, pp. 7 and 10.

121. Abdur Rahim to Quaid-i-Azam, 2 July 1943, ibid., F. 1101, p. 143.

122. Latif Ahmad Sherwani (ed.), *Speeches, Writings and Statements of Iqbal*, Lahore, 1977, p. 28.

123. Although Balochistan was not a province yet it was invariably referred to as a 'province' or a 'unit' of Pakistan.

124. Sarfaraz Husain Mirza (comp.), *Tehrik-i-Pakistan aur Majlis-i-Kabir-i-Pakistan ka Qalmi Jihad*, Islamabad, 1998; and Ahmad Bashir to Jawaharlal Nehru, 6 December 1939, QAP, F. 900, pp. 157–63. Maulana Abdul Wadud (president, Jamiatul Ulama, Sarhad) organized the Sarhad provincial Pakistan Majlis.

125. Chaudhri Rahmat Ali's Pakistan National Movement did have some unspecified number of 'branches' and adherents in India but even these disappeared after the adoption of the Lahore Resolution.

126. For instance, see Sir Francis Low, 'Memories of the Quaid-i-Azam', *The Pakistan Society Bulletin*, London, Autumn 1962, pp. 17–18, cited in Aziz, *Idea of Pakistan*, vol. 3, pp. 627–28.

127. For his speech on a resolution that he moved in the twenty-fourth session of the All-India Muslim League on 11–12 April 1936, see AFM, vol. 168, no. 67; and for his public speeches in Patna on 27 October 1937 and in Calcutta on 28 December, see *Star of India*, 1 November and 29 December 1937.

128. His remarks in a speech in the All-India Muslim League council on 21 March 1937, AFM, vol. 222.

129. Resolution passed at the Lucknow annual session in October 1937. Earlier, on 26 September 1937, the Calcutta Muslim League conference had demanded a change in the All-India Muslim League's creed to 'complete independence and the creation of free Islam within a free India.' [Aziz, *Idea of Pakistan*, vol. 3, p. 626.] For Sardar Nishtar's proposal in the All-India Muslim League council on 21 March 1937, in support of 'complete independence' to attract the Muslim youth away from the Congress, see AFM, vol. 222, no. 58.

130. *Resolutions of the All-India Muslim League from October to December 1938*, Delhi, n.d., pp. 65–68.

131. 'Pakistan—I', *The Light*, 16 October 1938; and comments of the *Bombay Chronicle*, 13 October 1938.

132. AFM, vol. 188, no. 66; and also see Mohammad Yaqub to Sayyid Abdul Aziz, president of the reception committee, All-India Muslim League, Patna annual session, 24 December 1938, ibid., vol. 188, no. 79.

133. Resolution passed at the Patna annual session in December 1938.

134. On 25 March 1939, Liaquat expressed similar views in his presidential address to the Divisional ML Conference at Meerut. AFM, vol. 351, p. 21; and also see *Star of India*, 27 March 1939. Later on, in December, Liaquat told Sir Stafford Cripps during the latter's visit to India that 'recently the Muslim opinion had become very strong for partition of India into Muslim India and Hindu India'. For this information, see Liaquat to Jinnah, 13 December 1939, QAP, F. 335, pp. 50–60.

135. *Star of India*, 12 April 1939.

136. AFM, vol. 128, no. 12; and vol. 129, no. 15.

137. Sikandar to Jinnah, 30 May and 21 June 1939, QAP, F. 16, pp. 6, 192–93 and 198; and statement by Khurshid Ali Khan, one of the secretaries of the Punjab Unionist Party, ibid., F. 353, pp. 3–5.

138. The printed work was entitled *The Outlines of a Scheme of Indian Federation*, Lahore, 1939.

139. Sikandar to Jinnah, 19 July 1939, and Jinnah to Sikandar, 30 July 1939, QAP, F. 353, p. 10.

140. V. Patel to Nehru, 3 July 1939, in Jawaharlal Nehru, *A Bunch of Old Letters*, Bombay, 1960, pp. 386–87.

141. *Civil & Military Gazette*, 26 October 1939.

142. Besides the detailed schemes, there were recurring references to partition into Muslim India and Hindu India in the speeches and writings of Muslim leaders and writers. Aziz, *Idea of Pakistan*, vol. 3, pp. 641–45. For some more schemes, see QAP, F. 96.

143. For the Majlis-i-Kabir-i-Pakistan, which was in contact with Rahmat Ali, see Ahmad Bashir to Jinnah, 21 October 1939; and 8 November, QAP, F. 96, pp. 57–59 and F. 1097, pp. 294–95, respectively; and for Ahmad Bashir's opposition to Latif's scheme, see his letter to Jinnah, 22 March 1939, ibid., F. 96, pp. 63–65 and 69A. The Punjab Muslim Students Federation's scheme was named as the 'Pakistan Caliphate Scheme', which, on 15 February 1940, Moharram Ali Chishti sent to Jinnah. See also Abdus Sattar Khan Niazi ('Yaghistan', Railway Road Lahore) to Liaquat, 17 October 1939, AFM, vol. 230.

144. The authors, in a printed letter in September 1939, communicated their proposals, that: (1) the Muslims constituted a distinct nation and must have the right of self-determination; (2) the Muslim majority provinces were the embodiment of the hope and future of Muslims of India, and as such could not be permitted to be enslaved in an all-India Federation under the perpetual domination of a Hindu majority at the centre; (3) the future of Muslims of the minority provinces lay in their own determination to guard their separate political and cultural entity and the support they received from their brethren in the majority provinces; and (4) the Hyderabad State was the symbol of a thousand years old empire of the Muslims in India. The Muslims could not tolerate any attempt to undermine the sovereignty of the Nizam. QAP, F. 96, pp. 73–75.

145. The five 'fundamental principles' were: '(1) the Muslims of India are a separate nation entitled to the right of self-determination; (2) they would not agree to be reduced to a position of minority for any reason; (3) they shall have a separate National Home in the shape of an autonomous state; (3) the Muslims in the rest of India shall be treated as the nationals of the aforesaid Muslim state; and (5) the Indian Muslim nation shall stoutly resist any interference in these basic principles.' Abdullah Haroon, chairman, foreign committee to honorary secretary, All-India Muslim League, 2 February 1940, ibid., F. 96, pp. 70–72.

146. *The Muslim Problem in India*, Karachi, 1939 (with an Introduction by Haji Sir Abdullah Haroon); an earlier version was published from Bombay in 1939, entitled *The Cultural Future of India*. His scheme proposed four Muslim cultural zones, two in the north-west and north-east and two in north India and Hyderabad, and eleven Hindu cultural zones in the rest of India; the zones linked at the centre in a loose federation. His scheme visualized full exchange of population. For more information, see Latif–Abdullah Haroon–Jinnah correspondence, in QAP, F. 26,

pp. 311–13; F. 48, pp. 12, 25–26 and 35–37; F. 96, p. 69; F. 370, pp. 1–37; and F. 823, pp. 48–52.

147. *The Confederacy of India*, Lahore, 1939. He proposed division into five 'countries' each with a federal structure: Indus region; Rajasthan and the central India states; Deccan states including Hyderabad and Mysore; Hindu India including the rest of India; and Bengal excluding the Hindu districts but including parts of Assam and other states. These 'countries' were to form a confederation with only one common subject of defence for which each one had to make equal contribution.

148. *The Problem of Indian Muslims and its Solution*, Aligarh, 1939. This scheme, also known as the Aligarh Scheme, proposed three independent and sovereign states: the Muslim state in the north-west to be called Pakistan federation; another state in the north-east to constitute a separate Muslim federation; and the Hindu state in the rest of India to be called Hindustan. See also QAP, F. 135, pp. 2–10.

149. The other schemes discussed were those by Mamdot, Rizwanullah, K.B. Kifaitullah, Asadullah, Punjab Muslim Students Federation and the Majlis-i-Kabir-i-Pakistan. Aziz, *Idea of Pakistan*, vol. 3, p. 648.

150. 'Confidential Note for the President', QAP, F. 96, pp. 55–56.

151. Ahmad Bashir, secretary, Majlis-i-Kabir-i-Pakistan to Jinnah, 30 January, and 7 March 1940, ibid., F. 901, pp. 10 and 22; Jinnah to Rahmat Ali, 8 February 1940, ibid., F. 518, p. 48A; Rahmat Ali to Jinnah, 3 and 11 March 1940, ibid., F. 873, pp. 204; F. 518, p. 58; and Mohammad Mahmood Ahmad (philosophy department, Aligarh Muslim University) to Jinnah, 8 March 1940, ibid., F. 873, p. 203.

152. Jinnah made these remarks in his presidential address, Aligarh Muslim University students' union, on 10 March 1941. The Muslim League had given a shape, he said on another occasion, to the idea of Pakistan that the Muslim community had been nourishing since long. Speech at a meeting organized by the Balochistan Muslim Students Federation on 7 July 1943, Waheed, *Nation's Voice*, vol. III, p. 247.

153. R.J. Moore, 'British Policy and the Indian Problem, 1936–40', C.H. Philips and Mary Doreen Wainwright (eds.), *The Partition of India: Policies and Perspectives, 1935–1947*, London, 1970, p. 84.

154. Linlithgow to Zetland, 4 January 1940, Mss Eur D 609 21b–22, p. 4, IOL, cited in Aslam Malik, *The Making of the Pakistan Resolution*, Karachi, 2001, p. 120; and Laithwaite to Jinnah, 9 January 1940, QAP, F. 95, pp. 58–59; and John Glendevon, *The Viceroy at Bay*, London, 1971, p. 138.

155. Text of the telegram from viceroy to secretary of state, 1 February 1940, Linlithgow Papers, Mss Eur F/125/19, cited in Malik (comp.), *Muslim League Session*, pp. 247–48; and Linlithgow to Zetland, 31 August 1939, IOL, Mss. Eur. 609, cited in Hamida Khuhro, *Ayub Khuhro*, pp. 193–94.

156. Sikandar Hayat was not present when the working committee adopted a resolution on the subject. Later, he obtained its copy from the general secretary. Liaquat to Sikandar, 13 March 1940, AFM, vol. 207, p. 18.

157. For the text entitled 'Zafrullah Khan's Note on Dominion Status', see Ikram Ali Malik, *Truth is Truth: A Rejoinder to Abdul Wali Khan*, Lahore, 1990, Appendix I, pp. 75–113.

158. AFM, vol. 129, no. 15. On 25 February, the All-India Muslim League council confirmed the resolution adopted by the working committee.

159. Telegram from viceroy to secretary of state for India, 26 February 1940, Malik (comp.), *Muslim League Session*, pp. 258–59.

160. Linlithgow to Jinnah, 28 February and 10 April 1940, Sir John Gilbert Laithwaite to Jinnah, 8 March 1940, and Jinnah to Linlithgow, 8 April 1940, QAP, F. 95, pp. 69–72.

161. For a list of delegates from different provinces, see AFM, vol. 213.

162. Ashiq Husain Batalvi's version [Hamari Qaumi Jiddo Juhd: January 1940, se December 1942 tak, Lahore, 1975, pp. 24–25.] about the drafting of the Lahore Resolution is more credible than those of other contemporary writers and politicians.

163. For draft resolution with corrections in Jinnah's handwriting, see AFM, vol. 214, pp. 70–73; and for amendments proposed by Abdullah Haroon, Husain Imam, Ahmad Said Chhatari, Ali Mohammad Rashidi, Aziz Ahmad Khan, Mushtaq Ahmad Gurmani (1905–1981), Abdul Hamid Khan (Madras), Zahiruddin, Rizwanullah, Mohammad Noman and Z.H. Lari (1906–1972), see ibid., vol. 214, nos. 40–44 and 51.

164. For Sikandar's statement, see IAR, 1941, vol. I, p. 47.

165. Fazlul Haq was slightly indisposed but he attended the session on Liaquat's persistence. Telegram from Bengal premier to secretary, All-India Muslim League, 20 March 1940, and secretary to premier, 20 March, AFM, vol. 213, nos. 5 and 8.

166. Ibid., vol. 214, pp. 99–100.

167. Jinnah's address to the Aligarh Muslim University students' union on 10 March 1941, AFM, vol. 237, p. 7.

168. Ibid. Jinnah quoted the Dutch proverb, when 'soul is lost all is lost', in his presidential address to the Punjab Muslim Students Federation Pakistan session in Lahore on 1–2 March 1941, ibid., F. 230.

169. For details, see '(a) Objectives' Chapter 7.

170. Pirzada, Foundations, vol. II, p. 372.

171. See Section '(a) Objectives' in Chapter 7.

172. That year, Rahmat Ali had published his Pakistan (Cambridge, 1940).

173. For example, see his response to the Punjab Muslim Students Federation, which was holding a 'Pakistan Conference' on 15–16 February 1941, in Jinnah to Abdul Hamid Mirza, 20 January 1941, QAP, F. 957, p. 52.

174. Jinnah to Sikandar, 3 February 1941; and Sikandar to Jinnah 7 February, ibid., F. 353, pp. 43–45.

175. AFM, vol. 133, no. 9.

176. IAR, 1941, vol. I, p. 53; and QAP, F. 561, p. 66; F. 519, pp. 18–19; and Jinnah's telegrams, ibid., F. 998, p. 1; and AFM, vol. 335, pp. 2–93.

177. For Jinnah's views against retaining an all-India centre, see his extempore address at the Madras session, Pirzada, Foundations, vol. II, pp. 359–71.

178. For instance, see Jinnah to Tamizuddin Khan, 29 May 1941, QAP, F. 355, p. 2; Jinnah to Nawab S.M. Ismail, 15 and 25 November 1941, ibid., F. 304, p. 120, and F. 1092, p. 143; A.M.K. Dehlavi to Jinnah, n. d., ibid, F. 256, pp. 144–45; Jinnah to Faruq Rahimtullah, 5 August 1941, ibid., F. 424, p. 1; Jinnah to Hasrat Mohani, 20 July 1940, ibid., F. 378, p. 15; Jinnah to Fakhre Alam, 25 March 1941; and Jinnah to Fazlur Rahman, 4 April 1941, ibid, F. 874, pp. 88 and 93–94; IAR, 1941, vol. I, p. 61; Jinnah to K.P. Mallikharjanudu, 12 February 1943, Shamsul Hasan Collection (hereafter SHC), Non-Muslims-I: 19; and Jinnah to A. Lehuraux, 19 January 1944, Jinnah Papers, Second Series, vol. X, p. 128.

179. AFM, vol. 256, pp. 41–42; and vol. 342, no. 45. It was proposed that the exclusion of the Ambala division from the north-western part would raise the Muslim population from 56.7 to 62.7 per cent; and the exclusion of the Burdwan

division from the north-eastern part would raise the proportion of Muslim population of Bengal from 54.8 per cent to 63.3 per cent. For details, see QAP, F. 1099, pp. 18–24.

180. Linlithgow to Amery, 24 May 1943, *TP*, vol. III, p. 941.

181. Jinnah to Hamid Nizami, 4 June 1942, QAP, 1116, p. 121; *IAR*, 1942, vol. II, p. 108; and AFM, vol. 138, no. 7; and also see 'Punjab Provincial Muslim League' in Chapter 8.

182. Abdullah Haroon to president, All-India Muslim League, 23 December 1940, QAP, F. 274, pp. 141–55.

183. Latif to Abdullah Haroon, 23 April 1940, ibid., F. 370, pp. 39–49; and Latif to Jinnah, 30 May 1940, ibid., p. 50; and SHC, Hd-II: 141–44.

184. For his statement, see Waheed, *Nation's Voice*, vol. II, p. 145; and *IAR*, 1941, vol. II, p. 41.

185. Jinnah to Latif, 15 March 1941, QAP, F. 370, p. 65.

186. Sayed to Latif, 28 May 1941, SHC, Hd-II: 150.

187. For the reaction of Dr Afzaal Husain Qadri, Abdullah Haroon and others, see SHC, Hd-II.

188. Five dominions were: (1) Bengal and Assam; (2) Central Provinces, United Provinces and Bihar: (3) Madras; (4) Bombay; and (5) Punjab, Sindh, the NWFP and Balochistan.

189. *Dawn*, 30 August 1942; QAP, F. 399, pp. 89–90; and Jamiluddin Ahmad to Jinnah, 3 September 1942, ibid., F. 67, p. 38.

190. QAP, F. 399, pp. 60–61.

191. SHC, Misc. I: 38–39.

192. Noon to Jinnah, 5 September 1942, QAP, F. 399, p. 62. Despite this assurance, on 12 June 1944, Noon proposed to Amery the division of British India into five states with a government at the centre nominated by the viceroy. For details, see Amery to Wavell, 13 June 1944, *TP*, vol. IV, p. 1028.

193. For a two-state proposal by S.M. Shareef, see *Dawn*, 22 February 1941; and Mujibur Rahman Khan, *Pakistan* (1942), cited in Haroon-or-Rashid, *Bangladesh*, pp. 183–84.

194. For a sixteen-page note in support of the economic and military viability of Eastern Pakistan, see QAP, F. 337, 4–22; for Raghib Ahsan's eleven-page proposal for a 'Confederacy of East Pakistan and Adibasistan', see QAP, F. 5, pp. 1–35 and F. 204, pp. 320–22 and 324–29; and SHC, Bengal-IV; and for Nazimuddin's proposal of Eastern Pakistan consisting of Bengal minus Burdwan division, Assam and Muslim majority part of Purnea district of Bihar, see Casey to Wavell, 11 September 1944, *TP*, vol. V, p. 29. Also see *Huseyn Shaheed Suhrawardy and the Inner History of the United Bengal Scheme*, Karachi, 1951, pp. 4–7.

195. Beverley Nichols to Jinnah, 11 January 1944 (enclosing copy of the interview taken on 18 December 1943), QAP, F. 785, pp. 98–104.

196. For details, see Section 'CR Formula and Jinnah–Gandhi Talks' in Chapter 9.

197. See Section 'Legislators' Convention' in Chapter 11.

198. Resolution no. 8 of the All-India Muslim League council moved by Maulana Jamal Mian and passed on 26–27 October 1941, AFM, vol. 277, p. 120; for a committee to promote Muslim interests according to the Shariat, see *Dawn*, 2 November 1941; for the Majlis, sponsored by Khairul Anam (editor, *Mohammadi* and manager Bengali daily *Azad* [Calcutta]); Habibullah Bahar (editor *Bulbul* [Calcutta]); Abdul Jabbar Wahidi (editor, *Asre Jadid* [Calcutta]), and S.M. Usman (secretary, Calcutta

Muslim League), see QAP, F. 1115, pp. 374–75; and also see Section on 'Ulama and Mashaikh' in Chapter 7.

199. Liaquat, 30 March 1940, AFM, vol. 422, p. 4; Raghib Ahsan to Jinnah, 8 January 1941, QAP, F. 204, p. 122; and also see Chapters 7 and 10.

200. M. Hamidullah of the Osmania University, Hyderabad to Jinnah, 9 Jamadus Sani, 1365 H, QAP, F. 895, pp. 159–60; Nazar Fatima, 81-Railway Road, Lahore to Quaid-i-Azam, 21 October 1944; and Jinnah to Nazar Fatima, 25 October 1944, SHC, Pb-I: 14; Saida Zuberi to Jinnah, 2 August 1943, QAP, F. 877, p. 122; M.A. Faruque to Jinnah, 24 March 1943, and Jinnah to M.A. Faruque, 9 April 1943, ibid., F. 876, pp. 84 and 123; Mohammad Shamsul Haq Shams (editor, Ihlan [Jalandhar]) to Quaid-i-Azam, 24 July 1942, ibid., F. 827, pp. 69–71; Jinnah to Hameed Kalanjiam, 29 October 1940, ibid., F. 873, p. 584; for Jinnah's response to K.M. Munshi's speech in Lahore, see Dawn, 9 November 1941; and for Amir Ahmad Khan, Raja of Mahmudabad's two speeches advocating an Islamic state, see AFM, vols. 49 and 164, no. 21.

201. Jinnah to Sajjada Nashin Sahib of Manki Sharif, the NWFP, 18 November 1945, Ahmad Saeed, Quaid-i-Azam: Rare Letters, pp. 175–76.

202. SHC, APMO-40.

7

Reorganization and Mobilization, 1937–1947

The All-India Muslim League built up a subcontinent-wide network of its organization that led the movement for Pakistan. Under the gifted and inspiring leadership of Quaid-i-Azam Mohammed Ali Jinnah, it united a disparate, internally divided and dispersed crowd of socially, economically and politically backward Muslims into a 'nation' and achieved for them a separate homeland within a short span of seven years against formidable odds. Jinnah played a pivotal role in the whole process. He inspired the Muslim elites and masses without the distinction of age, gender, profession and creed and gave coherence to the League thinking. The All-India Muslim League established not only its own organizational structure with an uninterrupted process of regular membership enrolment and party elections of its different tiers from the primary to the all-India level but also encouraged different sections of the Indian Muslim society like women, students, *ulama* and *mashaikh*, professionals, workers and businessmen to organize their own separate pro-League platforms and then mobilized them to achieve its goal of the separate Muslim state of Pakistan. The process of organizing the League was gradual, and every step was taken carefully and timed well.

Immediately after Jinnah's return from England, the League could not focus its attention on its organization. Its decision to participate in the provincial elections under the Act of 1935 consumed the time and energies of the Leaguers. The focus was on the creation of an election machinery, collection of funds, an election campaign and post-election issues. Jinnah had created new bodies, the central parliamentary board and provincial parliamentary boards, as directed by the Bombay annual session because neither the League had ever contested any elections nor the party constitution provided for an election machinery. During 1934–37, the party frequently amended and revised its constitution. On

2 April 1934, the central council appointed an eleven-member constitution committee for its review, and after two years, on 25 April, it adopted some minor amendments on its recommendations.[1] The following year, on 21 March, the central council again felt the need for changes and appointed an eight-member committee headed by Nawab Ismail Khan. This committee submitted its report after two meetings in Delhi (30 March) and Meerut (7 April), and the All-India Muslim League revised the constitution on its recommendations at its Lucknow annual session that came into force on 1 February 1938.[2] The League organized itself at the primary, city, district, provincial and all-India levels in accordance with this constitution.[3] From the Patna session (December 1938) onward, it introduced further amendments at every annual session in the light of the experience that it gained, as it moved forward in its struggle.[4] Again, in 1943, it felt the need for a thorough revision of the constitution when, on 23 April, its working committee appointed a two-member (Nawab Ismail and Liaquat) 'Revision of the Constitution Subcommittee', which submitted its report at the Karachi annual session after getting feedback from the provincial Muslim Leagues. It amended the constitution in the light of this report.[5] The League constitution provided several statutory bodies: besides the office-bearers, it had a working committee, a council, (after December 1943) a central parliamentary board, provincial Muslim Leagues and all-India annual and special sessions.[6] These statutory bodies established new bodies such as Muslim [League] National Guard, all-India women's subcommittee, foreign committee, central civil defence committee, and committee of action. These statutory and non-statutory bodies were meant to broaden, consolidate and strengthen the support-base of the All-India Muslim League.

(A) OBJECTIVES

The 1937 constitution radically changed the aims and objects of the All-India Muslim League. Now it aimed at 'the establishment in India of full Independence in the form of a federation of free democratic States' in which the rights and interests of the Muslims and the minorities were adequately and effectively protected.[7] This remained its objective till the Madras annual session in April 1941, when it amended its creed to bring it in line with 'the Lahore Resolution, popularly known as Pakistan'. Liaquat moved the amendment to refute the hostile propaganda that the Pakistan demand was 'merely a counter for bargaining', stating that henceforth every Leaguer 'would have to take an oath of allegiance to Pakistan'. According to Section 2 (a), the All-India Muslim League now aimed at:

1. The establishment of completely independent states formed by demarcating geographically contiguous units into regions which shall be so constituted, with such territorial readjustments as may be necessary, that the areas in which the Mussalmans are numerically in a majority, as in the north-western and eastern zones of India, shall be grouped together to constitute independent states as Muslim free national homelands in which the constituent units shall be autonomous and sovereign;
2. That adequate, effective and mandatory safeguards shall be specifically provided in the constitution for minorities in the above mentioned units and regions for the protection of their religious, cultural, economic, political, administrative and other rights and interests in consultation with them;
3. That in other parts of India where the Mussalmans are in minority, adequate, effective, and mandatory safeguards shall be specifically provided in the constitution for them and other minorities for the protection of their religious, cultural, economic, political, administrative and other rights and interests in consultation with them.

The remaining part of Section 2 was retained without any change; that party still aimed: (b) to protect and advance the political, religious and other rights and interests of the Indian Muslims; (c) to promote friendly relations and unity between the Muslims and other communities of India; and (d) to maintain and strengthen brotherly relations between the Muslims of India and those of other countries.[8] The objectives in Section 2 (a) to (d) were made part of the League membership form, which every candidate for membership was required to sign at the time of enrolment.[9] Later on, these objectives were incorporated in the model constitution that the central committee of action framed for the provincial Muslim Leagues on the direction of the central working committee and implemented it with effect from 1 July 1946.[10]

Meanwhile, on 7–9 April 1946, all the newly elected League members of the central and provincial legislatures met as representatives of the Muslim nation at a legislators' convention in Delhi. As the 'Parliament of Muslim India', they adopted a resolution drafted by a subjects committee consisting of 10 per cent of legislators from each province as their goal;[11] the resolution demanded

1. That the zones comprising Bengal and Assam in the north-east and the Punjab, North West Frontier Province, Sindh and Balochistan in the north-west of India, namely Pakistan zones where the Muslims are a dominant majority, be constituted into a sovereign independent state and that an unequivocal undertaking be given to implement the establishment of Pakistan without delay;
2. That two separate constitution-making bodies be set up by the people of Pakistan and Hindustan for the purpose of framing their respective constitutions;
3. That the minorities in Pakistan and Hindustan be provided with safeguards on the lines of the All-India Muslim League Resolution passed on 23 March 1940, at Lahore.

Every legislator signed a pledge to support the Pakistan demand and carry out the directions of the All-India Muslim League to attain this 'national goal'. The All-India Muslim League introduced several other organizational changes to equip the party for its struggle.

(B) ORGANIZATIONAL STRUCTURE

(i) *Membership.* The party constitution now restricted membership to Muslims who were residents of British India.[12] Contrary to pre-1937 position, the Muslims of the princely states and other parts of the British empire could not become its members. When the Muslims of the states approached Jinnah, he advised them to organize themselves separately, observing that the 'children of Islam are all one and no geographical or political partitions shall stand between them from sympathizing with one another'.[13] The age-limit for membership was lowered from 21 years to 18, and annual fee for membership, paid in advance, was reduced to two annas. Membership expired on 31 December, every year. A member ceased to be a member unless he renewed his membership by paying his subscription for the next year within two months; in April 1941, this period was extended to three months. The 1946 model constitution for the provincial Muslim Leagues attempted to bring about uniformity in membership enrolment (from 1 January to 28 February); preparation of electoral rolls and elections of primary Leagues (by 20 March); elections of city Muslim Leagues, district Muslim Leagues and provincial Muslim Leagues (by April), followed by the All-India Muslim League elections. No member who had not been a member of a primary League for at least one year was eligible for any office in the League at any level.[14] Adherence to party objectives continued to be a condition for membership. A candidate for membership could become a member if he fulfilled all the conditions and paid the annual fee. Now membership did not require approval of any party organ. The provincial Muslim Leagues were, however, empowered to exempt a candidate for membership from any of the conditions. A non-Muslim could not become a member.[15] The party otherwise welcomed support to its cause from any quarter including that from the non-Muslims.[16] Before 1938, there was no bar on a League member becoming member of another political party including the Congress. Although the constitution remained silent on this issue yet there was a gradual change. The demand for barring its members from retaining membership of other parties came from Bihar. On 3 April, Jinnah gave a ruling on a point raised in a council meeting that anyone who was a member of another party could not become member of the League unless he resigned from that party.[17] The League office could not communicate this ruling to the provincial Muslim Leagues; therefore, the demand was again raised from the same quarter.[18] On 4 December, the council formally resolved that a member who was associated with any other party whose general policy was opposed to the Muslims should not become, or remain, a member of the League. Every provincial Muslim League council was empowered to enforce this decision subject to right of appeal before the central working committee.[19] The demand for a foolproof bar still persisted especially from Bihar but the council did not take any decision.[20]

The constitution had a simple provision for membership, that a candidate for membership must be a Muslim and felt no need to define, explain or qualify it.[21] The eligibility of Ahmadis to become members was now questioned. Before 1936, no one had objected to their enrolment as members or their holding offices in the party.[22] Some Ahmadis had held party offices at all levels including the office of all-India president. Problem arose when the Indian Muslims organized support for the Kashmiri Muslims against the oppressive rule of the Dogra Hindu ruler. The Majlis-i-Ahrar-i-Islam, founded in 1929, opposed the activities of the Ahmadis in Kashmir particularly their *tabligh* (missionary) work. Some prominent Punjabi Muslims organized an All-India Kashmir Committee to help the Kashmiri Muslims; the Kashmir committee was chaired by the spiritual head of the Ahmadis, Mirza Bashiruddin Mahmud (1889–1965). Allama Iqbal was one of its members for some time. After his resignation from the Kashmir committee, he denounced the Ahmadis and their beliefs, regarding them outside the pale of Islam. In 1936, when the Punjab provincial Muslim League was revived under his patronage, the party barred the Ahmadis from its membership.[23] The opposition to their enrolment as members came from other provinces as well where the Majlis-i-Ahrar-i-Islam had influence.[24] Instead of enrolling themselves individually as members, the Ahmadis raised the issue with Jinnah for 'collective' membership. Maulvi Farzand Ali wrote to Jinnah on 10 February 1938, that the 'headquarters of the Ahmadi Movement' were seriously considering whether to join the Congress or the All-India Muslim League, pointing out the ban on their entry into the Punjab provincial Muslim League. The Ahmadis, he indicated, would be 'reluctantly driven to negotiate with the Congress' unless they were treated like the other Muslims to enrol as members and hold offices in the League. When Jinnah did not respond to his letter, he sent a reminder on 17 March, asking for a ruling from him that the Ahmadis 'as a class will be eligible for all the privileges which are open to the Muslim community including nomination as candidates for all Legislatures on the Muslim League ticket'. Jinnah, acknowledging his letter on 18 March, simply sent him the party literature including the constitution and asked him 'to adopt such course as you may consider proper'.[25] After this, whenever the issue was raised, Jinnah and the central League office simply pointed out the conditions for membership as laid down in the constitution.[26] The controversy resurfaced in May–June 1944, when Jinnah, in an interview with an Ahmadi member of the legislative assembly, Akbar Ali, reiterated the provision of the party constitution for enrolment of members. S. Zainulabidin (Nazir, Amoor-i-Aama, Ahmadiyya Movement), in a press note, gave his own interpretation to the interview, to which Jinnah wrote back to him on 5 May, that in his interview with Akbar Ali he had simply hinted at clause 4 of the League constitution.[27] Soon after, Jinnah went to Srinagar, where on his arrival, in response to a question as to who could become a member of the Muslim conference, he stated the conditions laid down in the League constitution for its membership, and appealed to the Kashmiri Muslims 'not to raise any sectarian issues but to organize the Muslims and bring them on one platform and under one flag'.[28] The Congress and Ahrar leaders propagated that Jinnah had permitted the Ahmadis to enrol as League members. Jinnah's supporters were disturbed by this propaganda,[29] and were satisfied only when he sent to Hamid Nizami (1915–1962) copies of his correspondence with Zainulabidin and issued a press statement on 10 June, observing that he had not agreed to anything nor he had 'the power to do so' under the party constitution.[30] The issue was then transformed into a demand for the declaration of Ahmadis as non-Muslims, and the Ahrar pressed the League to propose legislation on this issue.[31] Jinnah avoided to be dragged into a divisive religious issue. The pressure in this regard increased during the general elections but then Maulana Shabbir Ahmad Usmani (1885–1949), at one time Shaikhul Hadis at the Darul Ulum, Deoband, defended the League position in his interaction with the *ulama*.[32] Now the Ahmadis began to enrol themselves individually as members and the spiritual head of the Ahmadis was ready to extend support to the All-India Muslim League on different issues.[33]

(*ii*) *Office-bearers*. The October 1937 constitution of the All-India Muslim League provided for a president, an honorary secretary, a treasurer, and two joint secretaries; the office of vice-president was dropped. The terms of all the offices were now reduced to one year. The central council elected the president from among those who were nominated by the provincial Muslim Leagues while the other office-bearers were still elected at the annual sessions. The role of the treasurer and two joint secretaries was not very significant. In 1936, Amir Ahmad Khan Raja of Mahmudabad (1914–1973) was elected treasurer; and he was re-elected to that office every year. Early in the process of reorganization, he was instrumental in persuading a few rich individuals to make donations to the League, besides making personally liberal contributions especially for organizing the annual session in Lucknow. The scope of his role as treasurer diminished when there was a regular flow of funds and Jinnah on behalf of the League developed a system of accounting and auditing. However, he continued to play an important role in the League politics in other capacities, in particular as president of the All-India Muslim Students Federation. Husain M. Malik and S.M. Abdullah were elected joint secretaries every year till 1941, when in October that year M.A. Momin (Calcutta) and Mahbub Ahmad (Lahore) succeeded them; and in April 1943, Mahbub Ahmad and Maulana Jamal Mian were elected to these offices. The joint secretaries normally performed their duties, if assigned, under the guidance and supervision of the central honorary secretary. After 1936, Husain Malik was the only joint secretary who officiated as honorary secretary for a few months when Liaquat was busy elsewhere.

Before 1936, the central honorary secretary had been the key office-bearer. His authority was now considerably reduced. The constitution, however, still listed separately his powers but these were gradually hedged in by constitutional provisions and resolutions of the statutory bodies of the All-India Muslim League. He exercised those powers that were delegated to him by the central council or the working committee or the president and those that were incidental to his office. Otherwise, he could only appoint, punish and dismiss the paid employees in the central League office. He could convene an emergency meeting of the council members present at the headquarters on matters not affecting the fundamental principles of the constitution. However, the decisions of an emergency meeting needed confirmation at a regular meeting of the council. During his whole tenure as honorary secretary, Liaquat who was elected honorary secretary at the Bombay annual session chaired only one emergency meeting on 9 January 1940. Soon after his election in 1936, he was engaged in his election campaign as an independent candidate to the United Provinces legislative assembly and resumed his duties after the election. Then, in May 1937, he asked Husain Malik to officiate as honorary secretary 'during his absence in England for a few months', after he obtained Jinnah's approval for this decision.[34] Liaquat was re-elected as honorary secretary every year. There was criticism on his re-election only once in December 1943, when Jinnah himself defended him, eulogizing his services to the League and the Muslim community. He described him as his 'right hand' man who though a nawab behaved like a thorough proletarian, and called on the other nawabs to follow his example.[35] He held the office of honorary secretary without interruption till December 1947. There was once a suggestion, after Liaquat joined the interim government (1946–47), to have someone else as the honorary secretary but the idea was not pursued seriously.[36]

The central office of the All-India Muslim League was in a shambles when Liaquat was elected its general secretary. Sayyid Shamsul Hasan (assistant secretary) was the only experienced worker available. Jinnah himself had attended to the office work during Liaquat's absence, at a time when he had no regular staff of his own.[37] He recorded minutes of some meetings in his own handwriting. After Liaquat resumed the duties of his office, Jinnah continued to provide guidance in the office matters. In fact, his advice was sought even on minor changes in the office. Liaquat ensured efficient functioning of the office as the party expanded its activities. In 1938, Sayyid Hasan Riaz (1894–1972) was engaged as the special publicity officer; and the information bureau that had been established the previous year was attached to the central office. Hasan Riaz began to edit the party's official Urdu newspaper, *Manshoor*, which the party launched that year.[38] As funds became available, the party engaged regular, instead of part-time, staff. By 1944, its central office had expanded with a remarkable increase in its activities. Then, it divided its work into three sections or groups. Each section was looked after by an assistant secretary: M.A. Aziz administered Section A; Zafar Ahmad Ansari (1908–1991) Section B; and Shamsul Hasan Section C. Liaquat and Nawab Ismail along with the three assistant secretaries signed the document that spelt out the division of work.[39] Separate office staff was assigned for each section while Badrul Hasan (office superintendent) maintained the record of all the three sections. The head of each section—an assistant secretary—was responsible for the publicity relating to his section. Later on, there was further allocation of work: Nawab Siddiq Ali Khan looked after the work of the Muslim (League) National Guards; Nawab Mohammad Yamin Khan (1886–1966), secretary of the central League assembly party, dealt with matters relating to the Muslims in government services; and Zafar Ahmad Ansari was given the additional duty of looking after matters relating to the central committee of action.[40] Qazi Isa was made in charge of the propaganda and publicity cell that was created in the central office for the general elections, and separate staff was hired for that purpose.[41]

Liaquat, in addition to looking after the party organization, served on all the important committees and subcommittees that the League statutory bodies appointed on different occasions. His important but less known contribution was as the director of the English newspaper, the *Dawn* (Delhi), which Jinnah acknowledged, would not have 'attained the success' in 'a short period' without his 'supervision'.[42] Jinnah urged Liaquat to work 'constantly' and guide 'the selfless and sincere workers' who had done 'wonderful work all over India'.[43] By hard work, honesty, dedication, sincerity of purpose and a non-partisan balanced approach Liaquat came to hold a position in the party hierarchy next to Jinnah. He outshone his more experienced and resourceful political colleagues by his performance, his devotion to Jinnah and his dedication to the League and its ideal.[44] In March 1945, when Jinnah fell seriously ill and could not directly attend to the party work, he entrusted the task of looking after the party affairs to Liaquat and Nawab Ismail, chairman of the central committee of action, for three months. In 1946, he was called upon to lead the League team in the interim government and was subsequently elected to become the first prime minister of Pakistan. He earned all these honours by his commitment to the All-India Muslim League as its honorary secretary.

The constitution provided for a president whom the central council elected from among those nominated by the provincial Muslim Leagues for one year, and he held office till the next annual session. After Jinnah's election as president for a one-year term on 4 March 1934, the central council continued to re-elect him every year. The League scrupulously maintained the ritual of elections. Every year, all the provincial Muslim Leagues would propose his name for the presidency, and the central council formally elected him to that office. There was never any rival candidate, which demonstrated that the All-India Muslim League owed its revival and strength to his organizational skills and expressed the Leaguers' confidence in his leadership. In fact, there was twice a proposal to make him life-president of the All-India Muslim League: once, in 1938, Premier Sikandar Hayat, paying tribute to his 'unswerving faith' in the League and his 'unremitting and energetic work' in the provinces despite 'heavy physical strain', made this suggestion but Jinnah did not accept the honour; and later on, in February 1941, Nawab Sayyid Mohammad Ismail, president of the Bihar provincial Muslim League, proposed a resolution to the same effect.[45] When Ismail raised the issue in the council, Liaquat responded that such a proposal would require amendment in the constitution. While Jinnah himself appreciated the Leaguers' confidence in his leadership, he advised them never to elect any person as the life-president of the party 'whosoever he might be'. As far as his own case was concerned, he observed, 'Let me come to you at the end of every year and seek your vote and your confidence. Let your president be on his good behaviour. I am definitely opposed to your [ever] electing a life-president'.[46] The council, in addition to electing him president every year, unanimously chose him to preside over all the annual and special sessions of the All-India Muslim League, with the exception of the Bombay annual session, which, on his suggestion, Wazir Hasan presided.[47]

The constitution did not list separately the powers and duties of the president till December 1943; he used to exercise the powers delegated to him by the statutory bodies—all-India session, central council and working committee—and their committees and subcommittees. For instance, the Bombay annual session empowered him to appoint central parliamentary board and provincial parliamentary boards to participate in the provincial elections under the Act of 1935. Once these boards were constituted, he operated through them. Later on, whenever he corresponded or negotiated with the Congress leaders or the British authorities, he would regularly consult the working committee whose decisions were formally confirmed by the council. The statutory bodies often gave him powers that he could exercise in case of emergency. For example, on 31 January 1938, the council vested him with full powers to hold talks with Nehru 'on any lines which he thought fit'; and on 22 October 1939, the working committee authorized him to advise and guide the provincial Muslim League assembly parties in case of an emergency. Then, the Madras annual session unanimously gave him wider authority; it empowered him to take all necessary steps for the promotion of the League cause till the next session, provided these steps were consistent with the policy and goal of the All-India Muslim League and resolutions of its annual sessions. The Allahabad annual session again empowered him with similar authority; but at that time there was one dissenting voice.[48] Even after such authorization, Jinnah would always go back to the working committee or the council for consultation and approval. It was in December 1943, that the All-India Muslim League formally designated the president by an amendment in its constitution as the 'principal head of the whole organization', and he was to exercise 'all the powers inherent in his office'. He was to ensure that all the authorities worked in consonance with the constitution and rules of the All-India Muslim League. Another amendment made at that time, perhaps keeping in view the state of his health, empowered the president to nominate a member of the council 'to act for him during his absence due to illness or any other cause'.[49] Throughout his tenure as the League president, Jinnah never took action against anyone who was critical of his person but he did not let the party forgive anyone who went against its policy and decisions or colluded with the 'enemy' unless that person openly regretted his actions. He tried to bring the League leaders from the 'Pakistan zones' to play a role at the all-India level but did not succeed in many a case. Two glaring examples are those of G.M. Sayed (1904–1995) and Nawab Iftikhar Husain Mamdot (1906–1969). He liked both of them: Sayed for his frank opinions and fresh ideas and Mamdot for his simple and sincere nature and his and his family's dedicated work for the League and its ideal. He encouraged both of them to participate in the League's politics at the all-India level but they would often revert back to provincial politics.

On his return from England, Jinnah had undertaken to organize the Muslims on the League platform as a mission. His declining health and personal comfort did not come in his way. After 1935, he stopped taking his normal annual vacations, abandoning his annual trips to England that he used to undertake before the first Round Table Conference. After that, he visited London only once, in December 1946. Henceforth, he would go to different places within India primarily for rest and health reasons. His visits were to the Nandi Hills, Matheran, Srinagar, Mastung and Ziarat. If one looks at his frequent physical breakdowns, it seems almost a miracle that he survived the strain of the freedom struggle; considering the general condition of the Indian Muslims, some perceived him as 'a gift [to them] from Heaven'.[50] His serious indisposition started after the Lucknow annual session when he had to shun political activity on medical advice for a few days in November 1937.[51] The following year, he was taken ill in February and March; and towards the end of the year, he suffered a breakdown around the time of his daughter's marriage to a Parsi.[52] There were then rumours about his retirement from active politics but he personally refuted the press reports to that effect.[53] It was on 30 May 1939, that he wrote down his will during another spell of illness, followed by a codicil thereto on 25 October 1940, which remained sealed till a week after his death. After that, he frequently fell ill but. did not have a serious physical breakdown till April 1941. That month he fell unconscious *en route* to Madras for the annual session of the All-India Muslim League; he could not attend to several social and political engagements in that city and had to postpone his scheduled extensive tour of South India.[54] On return, he rested at Matheran to recover; the doctors advised him complete rest but he did not listen to their advice.[55] Immediately before the arrival of Sir Stafford Cripps in March 1942, he was taken ill for a while.[56] Then, in May–June 1943, he was again unwell but did not cancel his long-awaited visit to Balochistan in July.[57] On his return from Quetta, he faced an assault on his life by a Khaksar worker, Rafiq Sabir, and seriously sprained the right side of his hip in the struggle; and he had to avoid political activity for a few weeks to recover.[58] Again, in April–June the following year, he was unwell and visited Srinagar to recuperate. On his return from Kashmir he again fell ill in August.[59] The following year, in March–April, he had the most serious physical breakdown of his life; Dr Albert Beatty and Dr A. Rahman attended to him and strictly advised him 'not even to see visitors' and take 'complete rest' for a few months.[60] This time he had no choice; and he had to listen to medical advice. He cancelled his meeting with the viceroy, scheduled on 7 March. He handed over the charge of the party affairs to Liaquat and Nawab Ismail for three months. But his response to queries from his devotees and admirers during this illness was typical, i.e. 'there was nothing serious the matter with me constitutionally except a complete breakdown due to pressure of work, anxiety and over-work for the last seven or eight years without a holiday'.[61] Even after this, he often fell ill but there was no major breakdown till the Punjab holocaust attending partition.[62] Apparently, his illness did not affect his political work, as he would continue to attend to party matters without interruption. This was, and is, the popular perception. In reality, he could not directly attend to several important affairs of the party that had expanded beyond the capacity of one individual and missed many a public function; the most conspicuous example is the cancellation of the thirty-second annual session of the All-India Muslim League that had been scheduled in Lahore on 30 March 1945.[63] He worked through committees that the statutory bodies appointed to do the party work. The chairmen or/and the convenors of these committees regularly reported to him verbally as well as in writing and he advised them when he felt it necessary. The lack of direct public interaction was compensated by the information that he received from different quarters through correspondence. He encouraged the Leaguers and friendly non-Leaguers to write to him; consequently, he would often be more informed even on local issues than the local leaders.[64] His perseverance to work even during illness inspired his colleagues and political workers to work with extraordinary dedication for the League and its cause.

Jinnah was conscious of the disruptive effects of sectarian and ethnic conflicts on Muslim solidarity; therefore, he warned the Muslims especially the youth about 'the lurking danger of tribalism and sectarianism' and exhorted them 'to speak with one voice—that of Islam'.[65] He never allowed the All-India Muslim League to involve itself in sectarian, linguistic and ethnic conflicts.[66] He steered the party clear of the Shia–Sunni conflict that raged in the United Provinces particularly in Lucknow in the 1930s, ignoring the immense pressure for intervention from within the League. However, he extended assistance to Allama Inayatullah Khan Mashriqi, head of the Khaksar Movement, who thoughtlessly plunged himself into the conflict that resulted in the arrest of Khaksar workers who had gone there from the NWFP, Punjab and Sindh. His policy to keep the All-India Muslim League scrupulously aloof from sectarianism persuaded him not to commit himself either way on the Ahmadi issue. He firmly stuck to the provisions of the All-India Muslim League constitution. He urged the Muslims to project themselves only as Muslims. His advice to the Muslims during the preparation of the 1941 census was that every Muslim should give simply one answer to questions about 'race, tribe or caste' that 'he is a Muslim' and that his answer about religion 'should be Islam'. The answer to questions about mother tongue should be 'Urdu', but if anyone was totally ignorant of Urdu, he should mention the language that he knew.[67] He used religious symbols and festivals to unite the Muslims on the League platform. When he had almost single-handedly embarked upon the task of party reorganization, he cited the example of Prophet Mohammad (PBUH) who was, he stated, a 'minority of one in the world' when he started his mission and 'wrought the greatest revolution in the shortest time' by the power of 'faith, organization, discipline and sacrifice'; and he urged the Muslims to follow his example.[68] This was the source of the motto that he gave to the Muslims especially to the Muslim youth: faith, unity and discipline. He advised them to 'go step by step' and not 'to get excited all of a sudden'; and they should 'take one step and stand solidly rather than take ten steps and then go back'.[69] He urged the Leaguers to organize the Muslims, 'train them, drill them and make of them the most wonderful political army that India has ever seen' and then the League would 'soon reach the goal of our freedom'.[70] His moving speech to the council of the All-India Muslim League in July 1939, is a specimen of his personal commitment to the Muslim cause. He did not feel shy of being branded as a 'communalist' by his opponents for doing his 'duty to the Muslims'.[71] His speeches and writings are replete with references to Islam and Muslim regeneration but this did not generate in him any feelings of hostility towards the non-Muslims because, as he once said, 'when we fight for Pakistan, we are fighting against the British and not against the Hindus' to get 'our freedom and establish Pakistan'.[72] A conspicuous example is his refusal even to autograph for an admirer his photo on the title page of the weekly *Time* magazine (22 April 1946) that carried the description, 'Mohamed Ali

Jinnah. His Moslem tiger wants to eat the Hindu cow', because, he wrote, it was 'offensive to the sentiments of the Hindu community'.[73] His moving exhortation to the Allahabad journalists' association on 5 April 1942, was: 'I agree that there is a wide difference today between the Hindus and the Musalmans. Whether you are here Hindus, Muslims, Parsis or Christians, all I can say to you is this that however much I am criticized, however much I am attacked—and today I am King Charles' head in some quarters, let me tell you—and this I tell you most sincerely—that I believe, and I honestly believe, that the day will come when not only Musalmans but this great community of Hindus will also bless, if not during my lifetime, after I am dead, the memory of my name.' Unlike the Congress, which missed no opportunity to woo and exploit those Muslims and Muslim parties that were critical of, or opposed to, Jinnah, All-India Muslim League and the Pakistan scheme, he did not indulge in negative politics when he was advised to encourage the formation of a new congress to divert the energies of the Congress 'from the offensive to the defensive side'.[74] He discouraged reactive campaigning against any party that denounced the League or its demands.[75] Again, he could have done a lot of damage to the Congress and Hindu solidarity by using these tactics, as the non-Muslim minorities especially the non-Brahmans of South India and the Adibasis of Bihar were even ready to come under the League banner, if the party opened its doors to the non-Muslims.[76] But he did not adopt those tactics and constantly urged the Leaguers to follow the constitutional path and skilfully restrained them from resorting to civil disobedience on the issues of Palestine (1938), Shahidganj mosque (1936, 1938), unrest in the princely states (1939) and other similar emotional issues.[77] However, the All-India Muslim League did use these tactics in the Punjab, NWFP and Assam in 1947, when it saw all the doors for constitutional struggle to achieve Pakistan closed.

Jinnah discouraged factionalism in the provincial Muslim Leagues that increased with the growth and expansion of the party. He demonstrated exemplary patience and neutrality in dealing with factional tussles, as he once wrote to Makhdum Murid Husain Qureshi of Multan, 'Let me inform you that I am not influenced by any person or persons nor am I actuated by any feeling of ill-will against anybody.'[78] The party under his guidance did not discriminate among the members on the basis of 'old' and 'new' Leaguers. He advised the Leaguers not to create 'unnecessary bitterness' even against the opponents of the Lahore Resolution because, he believed, they would soon realize that Pakistan was 'the best solution' of India's 'most complex problem' for which there was 'no parallel in the world'. This strategy proved successful, as the League slowly began to absorb local leaders and workers of other Muslim political parties, which eventually left behind merely skeletons of those parties. Jinnah advised the Leaguers not to be arrogant or be carried away by sentiments but to reflect on the means to revive the fallen nation. That objective, he advised the Muslim youth, could be achieved by focusing on 'at least three main pillars which go to make a nation worthy of possessing a territory and running a government': (*i*) education; (*ii*) powerful economy through commerce, trade and industry; and (*iii*) defence— defence against external aggression and for internal security; his emphasis was on the development of an air force that was a 'decisive weapon of modern war'.[79]

Jinnah's efforts to unite the Muslims showed signs of success within one year of his assumption of the League presidency. The yearnings of a Muslim that Jinnah should have 'the same sway over the Muslim masses' as Pandit Nehru had over the Hindus were soon more than fulfilled.[80] Jinnah's followers and supporters expressed their devotion by addressing him with different appellations; they began to address him with titles such as *Amirul Mulk, Uncrowned King of Muslim India, Mujahid-i-Millat, Count of Pakistan, Messiah of Muslim India, Mohibb-i-Millat, Sher-i-Islam, Ghazi, Saviour of the Muslims, Fakhr-i-Islam, Mohafiz-i-Islam, Quaid-i-Muslimin, Khalifa of Islam* and *Quaid-i-Azam*.[81] The last title stuck to his name.[82] He did not arrogate to himself any superior position in the party; he once wrote to a League leader in Bihar, 'We are both servants of the Muslim League and Muslim India and there is no question of one being a subordinate and the other a superior, except in the constitutional sense when we have to exercise our rights and perform our duty as laid down by our constitution and rules'.[83] In October 1941, one member wanted to move a resolution in the council of the All-India Muslim League to confer on him formally the title of '*Quaid-i-Azam*' to which Liaquat responded that such matters were 'best suited for the annual session'.[84] No such resolution ever came again before the annual session but on the eve of independence, on 12 August 1947, the Constituent Assembly of Pakistan, on Liaquat's motion, adopted a resolution that he should be addressed as Quaid-i-Azam Mohammad Ali Jinnah in all official Acts, documents and correspondence with effect from 15 August 1947.

(*iii*) *Working Committee*. Like the Congress, the League constitution provided for a president-nominated 21-member working committee; the president and honorary secretary were its *ex-officio* members. It met as frequently as the president desired. Five members excluding the office-bearers constituted quorum of a meeting. It could take decisions for the realization of its objectives, which had to be consistent with the policy and creed of the party and resolutions of the central council and all-India sessions. Its decisions were subject to confirmation by the council. It implemented the resolutions of the council and the all-India sessions; prepared annual budgets and authorised expenditure; sanctioned all payments above Rs 50 that were not included in the budget; employed and dismissed the office staff; appointed subcommittees to fulfil its duties; and performed all other functions assigned by the all-India sessions and the council.

Those nominated on the working committee were generally the office-holders of the provincial Muslim Leagues, leaders of the provincial Muslim League assembly parties or prominent Leaguers.[85] Its membership carried prestige and political importance. The League leaders keenly looked for nomination on the working committee. When Jinnah announced its personnel for the first time in May 1938, there was criticism for the exclusion of well-known Leaguers from its membership. Several names were mentioned that had been omitted, in particular those of Zafar Ali Khan (Punjab), Maulana Akram Khan (Bengal), Hasrat Mohani (United Provinces), Jamal Mohammad (Madras), Maulana Abdul Hamid Badauni (United Provinces), Maulana Qutbuddin (United Provinces), Maulana Mazharuddin (1888–1939) (Delhi), and Maulana Shakirullah (NWFP).[86] Ahmad Yar Daultana wanted two more nominations from the Punjab.[87] Jinnah defended his decision, arguing that everyone suggested could not be included in the working committee because its total strength was limited to twenty-one members and that it was in a way his 'cabinet' which the constitution authorized him to select.[88] The Leaguers accepted his decision, and in the subsequent years, Jinnah made only a few essential changes in its composition. There was a reason for every change.[89] For example, new members were included on the death of Maulana Shaukat Ali, Ashiq Warsi, Shahnawaz Khan Mamdot (1884–1942), Abdullah Haroon and Barkat Ali. Two others were added when two members (Fazlul Haq and G.M. Sayed) were expelled from the All-India Muslim League. Membership of one member (Abdur Rahman Siddiqi) was discontinued after his opposition to the observance of the 'Day of Deliverance' and his use of highly impolite language about Jinnah in a press statement.[90] One member (Sayyid Abdul Aziz) resigned his membership on his appointment as prime minister of the Hyderabad state and another member [A.M.K. Dehlavi (1875–1952)] moved to London. During 1938–47, in total, twenty-seven Leaguers, besides Jinnah and Liaquat as *ex-officio* members, served on the working committee [see Table 7.1].

Table 7.1: Working Committee of the AIML, 1938–47

	1938	1939	1940	1941	1942	1943	1944	1945	1946	1947
Ex-officio										
M.A. Jinnah (President)	√	√	√	√	√	√	√	√	√	√
Liaquat Ali Khan (Secretary)	√	√	√	√	√	√	√	√	√	√
Member										
Assam—Abdul Matin Choudhry	√	√	√	√	√	√	√	√	√	√
Assam—Mohammad Saadullah	√	√	-	-	-	-	-	-	-	-
Balochistan—Qazi Mohammad Isa	-	-	√	√	√	√	√	√	√	√
Bengal—A.R. Siddiqi	√	√	-	-	-	-	-	-	-	-
Bengal—A.K. Fazlul Haq	√	√	√	√	-	-	-	-	-	-
Bengal—Khwaja Nazimuddin	√	√	√	√	√	√	√	√	√	√
Bengal—M.A.H. Ispahani	—	-	-	-	√	√	√	√	√	√
Bengal—Maulana Akram Khan	-	-	√	√	√	√	√	√	√	√
Bihar—Husain Imam	-	-	-	√	√	√	√	√	√	√
Bihar—Latifur Rahman	-	-	√	√	√	√	√	√	√	√

Bihar—Mohammad Ashiq Warsi	√	√	-	-	-	-	-	-	-	-
Bihar—S.M. Shareef	-	-	√	-	-	-	-	-	-	-
Bihar—Sayyid Abdul Aziz	√	√	-	-	-	-	-	-	-	-
Bombay—A.M.K. Dehlavi	√	√	√	-	-	-	-	-	-	-
Bombay—I.I. Chundrigar	-	-	-	-	-	√	√	√	√	√
Bombay—Karimbhai Ibrahim	√	√	√	√	√	-	-	-	-	-
Central Provinces & Berar—Abdur Rauf Shah	√	√	√	√	√	√	√	√	√	√
Delhi—Begum Mohammad Ali	-	√	√	√	√	√	√	√	√	√
Madras—Haji A.S.H. Essak Sait	√	√	√	√	√	√	√	√	√	√
NWFP—Abdur Rab Nishtar	-	-	-	√	-	√	-	√	√	√
NWFP—Aurangzeb Khan	√	√	√	√	√	√	√	√	√	√
NWFP—Bakht Jamal	-	-	-	√	√	-	√	-	-	-
NWFP—Khan Sadullah Khan	√	√	√	-	-	-	-	-	-	-
Punjab—Iftikhar Husain Mamdot	-	-	-	-	√	√	√	√	√	√
Punjab—Malik Barkat Ali	√	√	√	√	-	-	-	-	-	-
Punjab—Mian Bashir Ahmad	-	-	-	-	√	√	√	√	√	√
Punjab—Shahnawaz Mamdot	-	-	√	√	-	-	-	-	-	-
Punjab—Sh. Karamat Ali	-	-	-	-	√	√	√	√	√	√

Punjab—Sikandar Hayat	√	√	√	√	-	-	-	-	-	-
Sindh—Ayub Khuhro	-	-	-	-	√	√	√	√	√	√
Sindh—G.M. Sayed	-	-	-/	√	√	√	√	√	-*	-
Sindh—Haji Abdullah Haroon	√	√	√	√	-	-	-	-	-	-
Sindh—Sh. Abdul Majid	√	√	-	-	-	-	-	-	-	-
United Provinces— Khaliquzzaman	√	√	√	√	√	√	√	√	√	√
United Provinces— Maulana Shaukat Ali	√	-	-	-	-	-	-	-	-	
United Provinces— Nawab Ismail Khan	√	√	√	√	√	√	√	√	√	√
United Provinces—Raja of Mahmudabad	√	√	√	√	√	√	√	√	√	√

* G.M. Sayed's name was struck off after his expulsion from the party.

Jinnah consulted the working committee as often as he needed its decision for any action. Even otherwise, he would seek its advice on every important issue, especially when he was negotiating with the Congress leaders or the British authorities. On important occasions, members of the working committee would be invited to stay in Delhi or Simla and remain accessible for the duration of the talks/negotiations. For example, they remained available to Jinnah for consultation when he held talks with Lord Linlithgow (October 1939) and Sir Stafford Cripps (March–April 1942), or when he negotiated with Lord Wavell (June–July 1945), the Cabinet Mission (1946), and Lord Mountbatten (April–August 1947).[91] Members freely expressed their opinions in the meetings and thoroughly debated the issues without any reservation. Jinnah would listen to the views of the members, give his own opinion and finally bring out consensus on the issue under discussion. Some decisions were taken by voting. Early in the life of the working committee, its members used to express publicly their views on important issues or on issues that had been discussed in its meetings. The party gradually put a stop to this tendency because the opponents of the League often used such statements against the party. At some meetings, oath of secrecy was administered to ensure secrecy. On 25 December 1938, the central council called upon prominent Leaguers particularly members of the working committee not to make any statement on 'a vital matter without the authority of the working committee or in a case of emergency in consultation with the president'.[92] Abdur Rahman Siddiqi's statement about the 'Day of Deliverance' further strengthened the working committee's position. The working committee then resolved that its members should not express publicly their views against its decision or that of the president, while still remaining its members.[93] After the Muslim premiers' talks with Azad on 13 June 1940, it forbade its members from holding talks with the Congress leaders that involved Hindu–Muslim settlement. The working committee gradually assumed wide powers; it was authorized to control, direct and regulate the activities of the All-India Muslim League in consonance with its constitution and rules. It could take disciplinary action against those members of the council who acted against its decisions or its aims and objects. Similar action could be taken against any office-bearer of a provincial Muslim League for failing in his duties or for ignoring the decisions of the central working committee. In both cases, there was a right of appeal to the central council. The working committee could dissolve or disaffiliate any provincial Muslim League for ignoring the decisions of the All-India Muslim League, again subject to a right of appeal to the central council.[94] It was authorized to delegate any of its powers to any committee of its members or the president or the honorary secretary with such conditions as it might deem fit. It held its last meeting at the governor-general's house on 13 December 1947, a few days before the formal dissolution of the All-India Muslim League.

(*iv*) *Council.* The October 1937 constitution provided for a 465-member council; and its membership was apportioned to different provinces as given in Table 7.2.

Table 7.2: Provincial distribution of the council members according to the October 1937 constitution

Province	Seats
Ajmer	5
Assam	25
Bengal	100
Bihar	30
Bombay	30
British Balochistan	5
CP and Berar	20
Delhi	15
Madras	20
NWFP	20
Orissa	10
Punjab	90
Sindh	25
UP	70
Total	465

In April 1942, the strength of its members from Balochistan was raised from five to ten. The following year, in April, an amendment in the constitution provided for a provincial league in Coorg with five representatives on the central council; and in December, this League was designated as the Bangalore–Coorg provincial Muslim League, which brought the total strength of the central council to 475. The central office-bearers were its *ex-officio* members.[95] In addition, all the elected members of the central legislature were deemed to be its *ex-officio* members, provided they were members of some branch League and had paid their annual subscriptions. Similarly, the secretaries and, after December 1938, the presidents of every provincial Muslim League were made its *ex-officio* members. Furthermore, in April 1941, the all-India president was empowered to nominate up to twenty members from such province(s) and in such proportion as he might consider necessary which otherwise had not been represented on the council. The provincial Muslim Leagues elected their quota of members one month before the annual session for a one-year term; in December

1938, the period was raised from one to two months; and from April 1941, they were to elect them before 15 November, every year.[96] The central council had the power to elect members if any provincial Muslim League failed to elect them within the prescribed time. Every member was required to pay in advance an annual subscription of Rs 6; an amendment in December 1938, required that he had to pay his subscription within two months from the date of the notice by the central office in order to remain a member of the council.[97]

The council could decide to convene the annual session and any special session at suitable time and place. Fifty members could also requisition a special session. Quorum at all the sessions was 100. Members of the council and delegates of the provincial Muslim Leagues could participate and vote at these sessions on payment of the delegate's fee of Rs 2; the number of such delegates was not to exceed three times the number fixed for the council from a province. The council functioned as the subjects committee to finalize the resolutions for the all-India session. It was required to hold at least four, and after April 1941, two meetings every year at the discretion of the central honorary secretary but with the approval of the president. Fifteen councillors could also requisition a special meeting of the council. The quorum for the council meetings was fifteen but this requirement did not apply to the adjourned meetings. The honorary secretary was required to send the notice along with the agenda to the members at least fifteen days before an ordinary meeting and seven days before a special meeting. Written opinions were counted as votes at all meetings; but this provision was subsequently deleted. The council was to elect a president for the annual session, collect information useful for the party objectives, pass resolutions on matters relating to its objectives, implement the decisions, control the party expenditure and appoint Auditors. It could affiliate and disaffiliate the Leagues under the rules. It could frame by-laws for the conduct of meetings, provided these did not conflict with the basic principles of the constitution. It was empowered to take disciplinary action against its members who violated the decisions of the League and acted in contravention of its objectives. It could delegate any of its powers to the honorary secretary with such limitations as it deemed fit. As its membership was quite large, it could not hold meetings frequently and at short notice; besides, it involved handsome expenditure. Therefore, it delegated some of its powers initially to subcommittees on case to case basis and then to the president for one year or/and the working committee.[98]

The central council was regularly constituted without interruption, as it was the highest party organ after the all-India session. The council itself used to fill the seats if any provincial Muslim League failed to send its representatives on the central council or if there was a vacancy.[99] It often constituted a small committee in such cases with authority to select the representatives. For instance, in April 1941, it appointed a three-member (Liaquat, Raja Mahmudabad and Hasan Ispahani) committee, and in 1942, a two-member (Liaquat and Nawab Ismail) committee to elect members on the vacant seats.[100] It directed the provincial Muslim Leagues not to re-elect any member who had failed to pay the dues in the previous year, and if any provincial Muslim League failed to remit the proportion of its contribution to the central League, it was not entitled to elect any representative on the central council. It would hold meetings even if the party did not have sufficient number of agenda items to meet the constitutional requirement, as was once the case in 1943.[101] Its importance increased after December 1943, when the All-India Muslim League was unable to hold any all-India session. Then, it would take the final decisions on vital matters. It was this body that accepted the Cabinet Mission Plan in June 1946, and the following year the 3 June Plan. Its last session was held after Independence in Karachi on 14–15 December 1947, when it was bifurcated into two parties, one was to function in Pakistan and the other in Bharat.

(v) *Central Parliamentary Board*. The central parliamentary board and provincial parliamentary boards that had been constituted for the 1937 elections were allowed to function for some time. At its Patna annual session, the All-India Muslim League decided that the provincial parliamentary boards would continue to function till the reorganized provincial Muslim Leagues established alternative machinery for the selection of candidates for the provincial assemblies. The right of appeal against the decisions of the provincial parliamentary boards was vested in the central working committee, which was empowered to constitute machinery to select candidates for any bye-election to the central legislature. Till April 1941, the working committee was empowered to appoint subcommittees for the selection of a candidate in a bye-election. For instance, it formed a three-member (Abdullah Haroon, Nawab Ismail and Raja Mahmudabad) subcommittee to select a candidate on the central Assembly seat that had fallen vacant on the death of Maulana Shaukat Ali.[102] After that, the working committee authorized the president to appoint a parliamentary committee for this purpose; consequently, Jinnah appointed a five-member committee consisting of Nawab Ismail, Husain Imam, Nazimuddin, Qazi Isa and Liaquat (convenor). The provincial parliamentary boards were dissolved as soon as the reorganized provincial Muslim Leagues constituted alternative machinery for the selection of candidates for the provincial assemblies. Later on, in December 1943, the constitution made separate provision for the formation of central parliamentary board and provincial parliamentary boards. The central working committee framed rules of these Boards, which provided that it would appoint a central parliamentary board every year to select candidates in a bye-election to the central legislature. The central parliamentary board was required to ensure that a provincial parliamentary board was properly constituted in every province and functioned under its supervision, and that the League parties were established in the central and provincial legislatures.[103] It heard and took decisions on appeals filed against the decisions of the provincial parliamentary boards and resolved any dispute between a provincial parliamentary board and a provincial Muslim League or its assembly party. On 27 December 1944, the working committee appointed a three-member central parliamentary board consisting of Liaquat (convenor), Khaliquzzaman and Husain Imam. The following year, in July, it revised the rules and regulations of the central parliamentary board and provincial parliamentary boards, and re-appointed them on the central parliamentary board that functioned during the general elections.[104] On 26 July–2 August 1946, its strength was raised to five; and the two additional members were Nazimuddin and Ismail Ibrahim Chundrigar (1897–1960).[105] Jinnah never interfered with the functioning of the central parliamentary board and provincial parliamentary boards. The CPB, however, kept him regularly informed about its activities and sought his advice, when needed. Any appeal or representation that Jinnah received from any quarter against the award of party ticket or any other election matter he used to forward it without any comment to the relevant body, the central parliamentary board or the provincial parliamentary board, for consideration and decision.

After the 1934 elections to the central legislative assembly, the Leaguers had worked in the assembly under the umbrella of the non-communal Independent Party, which Jinnah had founded in the central assembly in 1924. It was on 20 March 1938, that the council of the All-India Muslim League decided to form a League Assembly Party, with Jinnah as its leader and Dr Ziauddin Ahmad as its secretary. Six months later, Sir Mohammad Yamin Khan who joined the League Assembly Party along with four other Democratic Party members succeeded Dr Ziauddin as its secretary when the latter was elected vice-chancellor of the Aligarh Muslim University.[106] Early in 1939, its strength in the assembly rose to twenty-six and in the council of state to seven.[107] In 1940, Liaquat, after his election as member of the legislative assembly in a bye-election, was elected deputy leader of the League Assembly Party; and with Jinnah's increasing involvement in party matters elsewhere, he practically assumed its leadership. After the expulsion of one member, Sir Abdul Halim Ghaznavi, for four years effective from 3 July 1939, the League Party in the assembly emerged as a cohesive and active force.[108] In September that year, it staged a walkout in protest against the inability of the governors and the governor-general to protect the Muslims and minorities in the provinces under the Act of 1935. After the amendments in the constitution in December 1943, the central parliamentary board came to exercise general control on the League party in the assembly. Similarly, the central parliamentary board oversaw the formation and working of the League parties in various provincial legislatures.[109]

(vi) *All-India Sessions*. The annual and special sessions of the All-India Muslim League constituted an important forum. These sessions provided the League leaders and workers an opportunity to interact at the all-India level. During 1936–45, the League held eight annual sessions and one special session: six in the Easter holidays, two in the Christmas holidays, and one in October [see Table 7.3]. The Bombay (April 1936) and Lucknow (October 1937) sessions have already been discussed.[110] Every successive session was a display of increasing Muslim solidarity and the League's popularity. At the Lucknow annual session, Sikandar Hayat had offered the League to hold a special session on the Shahidganj issue in Lahore. But when he assessed the situation on his return, he felt that a special League session in Lahore might spoil the communal atmosphere in Lahore. Therefore, he requested Jinnah through Ahmad Yar Khan Daultana for a change of venue.[111] After observing 22 February, as the Shahidganj Day, on 20 March, the central council reiterated the decision to hold the special session in Calcutta on 18–19 April.

Table 7.3: Annual sessions of the AIML

President	Place	Date
Sir Wazir Hasan (24th annual session)	Bombay	April 1936
M.A. Jinnah (25th annual session)	Lucknow	October 1937
M.A. Jinnah (Special session)	Calcutta	April 1938
M.A. Jinnah (26th annual session)	Patna	December 1938
M.A. Jinnah (27th annual session)	Lahore	March 1940
M.A. Jinnah (28th annual session)	Madras	April 1941
M.A. Jinnah (29th annual session)	Allahabad	April 1942
M.A. Jinnah (30th annual session)	Delhi	April 1943
M.A. Jinnah (31st annual session)	Karachi	December 1943

The All-India Muslim League held its twenty-sixth annual session at Patna on 26–29 December 1938, on the invitation of the Bihar provincial Muslim League; it was viewed as 'the most successful session that the League ever held'.[112] On 2–3 July 1939, the council decided to hold the twenty-seventh annual session in Lahore on 28–30 December; Liaquat wrote to Sikandar, president of the Punjab provincial Muslim League organizing committee, and Shahnawaz Mamdot, chairman of the reception committee, for making the necessary arrangements. The session, however, could not be held on the scheduled dates perhaps due to the League–Congress–British parleys after the outbreak of the world war. Jinnah did not agree to any change of venue when there was suggestion to that effect. On 9 January 1940, the council members present at the headquarters in Delhi at an emergency meeting of the working committee, chaired by Liaquat, decided to hold the session on 22–24 March; the council confirmed this decision on 25 February. Some Leaguers still asked for postponement because elections to the Calcutta corporation were scheduled in the last week of March. But Jinnah overruled these objections. Again there were demands for postponement in view of the tragic police-Khaksar clash in Lahore on 19 March, that had resulted in the loss of more than thirty human lives. Sikandar, apprehensive of any further untoward incident, used all kinds of pressure tactics even that of the governor to persuade Jinnah to agree to the postponement.[113] But the dates were not changed. The session was held on schedule and passed off peacefully.

After the Lahore session, the council normally left the selection of venue and fixing of dates of the sessions to Jinnah although it would formally take a decision before every session. For example, on 29 September, the council authorized Jinnah to select the venue and fix the dates for the twenty-eighth annual session. After consultation with various provincial leaders, he selected Madras as the venue on the invitation of the Madras provincial Muslim League and fixed 12–15 April 1941, as its dates.[114] On 26–27 October 1941, the council again authorized him to fix the place and date for the twenty-ninth session. He selected Allahabad as the venue and 3–6 April 1942 as the dates for the session. For the thirtieth annual session, he selected Delhi as the venue and the dates were 24–26 April 1943. The Sindhi leaders had requested Jinnah before the Delhi session to hold one League session in Karachi.[115] On 26 April, the Sindh provincial Muslim League president along with six party members invited him to hold the next annual session in Karachi.[116] Jinnah accepted that invitation, and the thirty-first session was held there on 24–26 December. He wanted to hold the thirty-second annual session in Peshawar in November 1944, for which the Frontier provincial Muslim League council had formally decided in May 1944, but subsequently he could not persuade the provincial leadership to stick to this decision.[117] It was then decided to hold this session in Lahore on 30 March, the following year on the invitation of the Punjab provincial Muslim League.[118] When all the arrangements had been finalized, Jinnah himself fell seriously ill and the session was indefinitely postponed. No fresh dates could be fixed for the session although some Leaguers had suggested that 'first week of November will be most suitable'.[119] Thus, the Karachi session proved to be the last annual session of the All-India Muslim League.

(vii) *Muslim (League) National Guards*. The statutory bodies of the All-India Muslim League—all-India sessions, council and working committee—appointed committees and subcommittees to create new bodies to undertake specific tasks. Like other Indian political parties in the 1930s, it also decided to have its own body of volunteers and named it 'The Muslim National Guards of India'. The uniform initially approved for the Muslim National Guard was green shirt or coat with a badge of crescent and star in white.[120] The Bombay presidency Muslim League was the first branch to organize Muslim National Guards to inculcate 'discipline of thought, speech and action' among its members who were to undertake social and relief work. A small contingent of the Bombay Muslim National Guards, the nucleus of the projected all-India organization, attended the Lucknow annual session.[121] After this session, M.M.S. Ispahani, secretary of the Bombay presidency Muslim League, prepared a detailed scheme of Muslim National Guards, which an eight-member subcommittee of the central council examined.[122] The council as a first step, on 7 April 1939, authorized the presidents of the provincial Muslim Leagues to organize Muslim National Guards in the provinces and then appointed a four-member committee to bring about uniformity in their organizational structures; and the committee was to report to the central working committee.[123] Consequently, several provincial Muslim Leagues organized Muslim National Guards and some of them sent their contingents to the Lahore session. On 15 June 1940, the central working committee approved an elaborate structure of the Muslim National Guards to train and discipline Muslims for their social and physical uplift and to maintain peace, tranquillity and order in the country.[124] It provided for an active (*mustaid*) corps, a reservist (*mahfooz*) corps, whose members could not assume active duties due to age, occupation or physical disability, and a juvenile corps, consisting of boys below the age of sixteen. The all-India organization was headed by a *salar-i-azam*, later renamed *salar-i-ala*, and every province had a *salar-i-suba* with an organization going down to the grassroots. Every guardsman had to swear a pledge to Allah and the Holy Quran to serve the organization. His uniform was now khaki or green coat or shirt, khaki trousers and khaki cap or turban; and every province was directed to select and maintain just one colour. The working committees of the provincial Muslim Leagues were responsible for organizing the Muslim National Guards to enable them to discharge their duties of maintaining 'peace, tranquillity and order in the country worthy of the best traditions of Islam'. The training of the guardsmen was not for 'any military purpose' but aimed at creating 'in them a spirit of service and sacrifice' to make them 'a disciplined body of enthusiastic selfless workers for the social, economic and political uplift of the masses'. The ultimate responsibility for the organization and supervision of the Muslim National Guards was vested in the central working committee.[125]

The provincial Muslim Leagues, district Muslim Leagues and city Muslim Leagues organized Muslim National Guards in pursuance of the direction of the central working committee. The government restrictions on volunteer organizations during the Second World War hindered their smooth development; and their real strength varied from province to province. The Muslim National Guards in principle had autonomous existence within the provincial Muslim Leagues whose office-bearers normally could not hold offices in its organization although there were deviations from this principle in some provinces.[126] The situation changed when the central committee of action approved a constitution and rules for the Muslim National Guards, linking its organization at different levels with that of the League and, on 13 May 1944, appointed Nawab Siddiq Ali Khan, a League activist from Central Provinces, as the *salar-i-ala*, and four *Nazims*—S.M.A. Ashraf (1900–1955) (Meerut); Khalilur Rahman (1904–1972) (Lahore); Agha Ghulam Nabi Khan (b. 1912) (Kot Sultan, Sindh); and Benazir Ahmad (Bengal)—to assist Siddiq.[127] Nawab Siddiq toured the provinces, often in the company of the central committee of action members, and appointed *salar*s in the provinces in consultation with the presidents of the provincial Muslim Leagues, where none had been appointed or the provincial presidents were simultaneously holding the additional charge of *salars*.[128] The Muslim National Guard bodies, male as well as female, rendered useful service to the League candidates in the bye-elections and the general elections.[129] The central League formally rectified the impression, whenever and wherever it was created, that the autonomous existence of the Muslim National Guards meant their total independence from the provincial Muslim Leagues. Following the 'direct action' resolution of July 1946, the Muslim National Guards were further augmented and consolidated when Mian Khurshid Enver (d. 1948), who resigned from government service to serve the League cause, was appointed its chief organizer.[130] He also organized Muslim Women National Guards. Meanwhile, the central committee of action revised the rules of the 'All-India Muslim League National Guard', as the organization was renamed, and, on 8 September, reappointed Siddiq Ali Khan as the *salar-i-ala* for one year. Khurshid Enver was appointed *naib salar-i-ala* for the 'Pakistan provinces' and Mirza Itemaduddin Ahmad of Loharu was given the charge of the remaining provinces. The male and female members of the Muslim National Guards rendered valuable assistance in the civil disobedience movements in early 1947 and helped those who were affected in the riots before and during partition.

(*viii*) *Women's Subcommittee.* 'No nation', Jinnah exhorted the Muslims, 'can ever be worthy of its existence that cannot take with them their women', and that no struggle could ever succeed without their participation.[131] The All-India Muslim League established an

All-India Muslim women's subcommittee at its Patna annual session, which was meant to organize Muslim women at the all-India level under its banner to create in them political consciousness and enable them to participate in the struggle for the social, economic and political emancipation of the Muslim nation.[132] Earlier, Jinnah had appreciated the presence of women in *purdah* (veil) at a meeting in Gaya and referred to Muslim history when women had taken active part in the political, economic, social and educational life of the community. He appealed to the Muslims at the Aligarh Muslim University 'to free their women from the shackles of seclusion' and permit them to participate in the social and political uplift of their community.[133] In March 1939, he nominated Begum Maulana Mohammad Ali (1885–1947) on the working committee, observing that the time had come 'to have one who could represent the views of the women of India, and their wants and requirements in the national life of the Muslims'. The provincial Muslim Leagues elected women on the central and provincial councils. The All-India women's subcommittee consisted of thirty-two members drawn primarily from the politically conscious women or relatives of prominent Muslim families and had the power to co-opt more members. The subcommittee was reconstituted at the Madras and Delhi sessions. It established provincial and district committees under the auspices of the provincial Muslim Leagues and district Muslim Leagues, enrolled Muslim females as members of the League, adopted means to create political consciousness among the Muslim females, and guided them in all matters for the uplift of the Muslim society. The Patna session overruled the issue of *purdah* and other objections that were raised in organizing them on the League platform.[134] Begum Habibullah, Begum Aizaz Rasul (1909–1972), and Lady Abdullah Haroon led the organization at the central level. Miss Fatima (1898–1967), Jinnah's sister, was an active member of various bodies of the Bombay presidency Muslim League and the All-India Muslim League; and her presence at public platforms along with Jinnah inspired the Muslim women to participate in politics.

The process of organizing Muslim females on the League platform was a slow process in view of their general social and economic condition. The central subcommittee co-opted the existing Muslim women organizations in some provinces as its branches or established new ones where there were none in existence. However, the centre of activities of the women's committees was essentially the urban areas. Membership was drawn from the socially active Muslim women or those who were involved in educational activities. The first demonstration of their strength was their participation in the Lahore session (1940) in large number not only from the Punjab but also from other provinces. The provincial women's committees organized activities on various ceremonial occasions. Muslim female students especially of the Islamia colleges in different cities were a source of their membership and strength. In 1941, they organized themselves on the pattern of the Muslim male students as the All-India Muslim Girl Students' Federation, which had branches in all the provinces. Two years later, the provincial women's committees organized the Muslim Women National Guards on the instructions of the central subcommittee. Muslim women and female students participated in the 'Pakistan Conferences', observed 'Muslim League weeks' and organized other activities in support of the All-India Muslim League and the Pakistan demand.[135] Jinnah himself did not miss an opportunity to address the Muslim females especially the female students and advised them to work for Muslim regeneration. The central subcommittee held its all-India moots essentially at the time of the All-India Muslim League's annual sessions. Although the activities of the women's committees were on a limited scale because of their general condition and social restrictions yet these committees played an important role in the awakening of the Muslim females in the urban areas. The central committee of action oversaw their organizational work.[136] The silent work that the women's committees performed was demonstrated in the Muslim constituencies in the general elections. After the elections, they played a remarkable role in the civil disobedience movements that the provincial Muslim Leagues organized against the Unionist ministry in the Punjab and against the Congress–Khudai Khidmatgar ministry in the NWFP.

(ix) *Foreign Committee*. The All-India Muslim League appointed a foreign and inland deputations subcommittee, commonly known as the foreign committee, to implement its council's resolution of 4 December 1938, which called for the appointment of League deputations to visit the Muslim majority and minority provinces to apprise the Muslims of the condition of their brethren in the Congress-governed Muslim minority provinces, and to send deputations to Muslim and other countries to counter the Congress propaganda against the All-India Muslim League. Haji Abdullah Haroon was its chairman, Nawab Shahnawaz Khan Mamdot, Raja of Mahmudabad and Sardar Aurangzeb

Khan its members; Pir Ali Mohammad Rashidi (1915–1987) was selected as its secretary.[137] Its head office was in Karachi and subsequently, it established a sub-office in Lahore. In May–June 1939, a twelve-member deputation from the Muslim minority provinces headed by Nawab Siddiq Ali visited five major cities in the Punjab, five in the NWFP and eight in Sindh.[138] Abdullah Haroon personally bore the expenses of these tours. A similar deputation from the Muslim majority provinces toured the Congress-governed Muslim minority provinces. The foreign committee functioned because of Abdullah Haroon's passionate attachment to its work and the funds that he put at its disposal.[139] It sent pro-League literature outside India especially to Muslim countries. Abdullah Haroon sent greetings to the heads of Muslim states on Eid and other occasions but no deputation is known to have gone to foreign countries under its auspices.[140] It co-opted members and invited them to its meetings.[141] Before the Lahore session, it co-opted Ghulam Rasul Mehr (1894–1971), Akhtar Husain, Professor Abdus Sattar Kheiri (d. 1945) and Dr Abdul Latif as members and evaluated the partition schemes in cooperation with their authors and sent the recommendations to the central working committee.[142] But the central council had neither authorized the foreign committee to co-opt additional members nor had it asked its comments on the partition schemes.[143] Besides, the council had not fixed any time-limit for this committee. Perhaps, for these reasons, the Lahore session authorized the working committee to select its new personnel.[144] Neither the working committee nor the president made any fresh nominations for the foreign committee, and when the old committee co-opted new members and began to work out the details of the Lahore Resolution, Jinnah himself put a stop to its work. The foreign committee disappeared after that.

(*x*) *Civil Defence Committee*. The All-India Muslim League began its systematic organization after the Lucknow session.[145] Before that, it had made no concerted effort to organize itself at the grassroots although after Jinnah's return from England a few branches had emerged in the provinces on local initiative. During 1938–40, it completed the process of its reorganization and affiliation of the provincial Muslim Leagues with the All-India Muslim League in accordance with its new constitution.[146] Every provincial Muslim League was free to draft and approve its constitution and rules; the only condition was that these should not be in conflict with the constitution and rules of the All-India Muslim League. There was no mechanism to ensure organizational uniformity in the provincial Muslim Leagues. The only time that the central League could scrutinize the provincial Muslim League constitution and its working was at the time of its affiliation; after that, it simply asked for its 10 per cent share in the income of the provincial Muslim Leagues or nomination of its representatives on the central council. The All-India Muslim League leadership was conscious of this loophole, and took steps for its rectification.[147] At first, Jinnah had thought of monthly conferences of at least two leaders from every province to coordinate the working of the provincial Muslim Leagues but this idea was not pursued. On 27 August 1939, the central council decided to appoint a committee, with Maulana Akram Khan as its convener, to survey the working of the provincial Muslim Leagues and make recommendations for any improvement, but nothing tangible came out of it.[148] Then, on 28 October 1941, the All-India Muslim League convened a consultative meeting of the presidents and secretaries of all the provincial Muslim Leagues in Delhi, which Jinnah chaired.[149] The working of every provincial Muslim League was reviewed in the light of formal presentations made by the office-bearers. At the end, detailed instructions were formulated for the maintenance of office record, collection of funds, auditing of accounts, propaganda and other organizational matters.[150] On 4 November, Liaquat communicated these instructions to the provincial Muslim Leagues for implementation.[151] Another conference of similar nature was held in Delhi in February 1942.

The party still needed to do more concentrated work to consolidate its organization. The process began with the appointment of an all-India civil defence committee, which was a by-product of the international situation resulting from the Second World War and the grave dangers it posed to the security of India. The All-India Muslim League at its Allahabad session authorized Jinnah to appoint a committee 'to take steps for the protection of life, honour and property of Muslims in consultation with the Provincial Leagues'. In pursuance of this resolution, on 12 April 1942, Jinnah appointed a central civil defence committee with Nawab Ismail as its chairman and Nazimuddin, Khaliquzzaman and Qazi Isa as its members. Sayyid Zakir Ali, a member of the central council from United Provinces, was engaged as its secretary and a separate section was created in the All-India Muslim League office to look after its work.[152] Jinnah attended its first meeting in Delhi. The central civil defence committee decided to tour all the provinces to acquaint itself with the conditions on the ground and establish provincial civil defence committees with tiers at the district and city levels.[153] The civil defence committees were to assist the public 'in case of air-raids, or invasion, or provocation leading to disorder and lawlessness'. Later on, when rationing was introduced due to food shortages, the civil defence committees assisted in the distribution of food items.[154] The League authorized these committees to cooperate on equal terms with similar bodies set up by the government or the political parties.[155] These committees cooperated with similar bodies of other political parties including those of the Congress and the Communist Party of India that were engaged in relief activities.[156] The central civil defence committee conducted extensive tours of the provinces, starting from the United Provinces in April 1942 and going on to Bihar, Bengal, Assam, Orissa, Madras, Bombay, Delhi, Punjab, NWFP, Sindh and Balochistan, completing its first tour in July 1942, at an expense of Rs 4,893.[157] During this tour, in which it covered fourteen thousand miles in two months, it established civil defence committees in every province and directed them to set up defence committees at the lower level and send monthly reports of their work to the central office.[158] During the tour, Nawab Ismail used to send interim reports to Jinnah, and gave a comprehensive written report on his return. After that, he frequently discussed the working of the defence committees with Jinnah and gave him written reports every month and a detailed report after every three months, based on the reports that he received from the provincial civil defence committees.[159] After a review of the working of the civil defence committees on 10 November, the central civil defence committee divided itself into two teams to supervise separately the civil defence activities in the Muslim majority and minority provinces. In mid-1943, these teams again toured all the provinces; but their more frequent visits were to the war-affected regions of Bengal and Assam.[160] The central civil defence committee and provincial civil defence committees also sent regularly the reports of their activities to the press.[161]

During the discussions on the civil defence committees in November 1942, Jinnah asked Nawab Ismail to inspect the offices of the provincial Muslim Leagues and their working in four provinces: United Provinces, Bihar, Bengal and Assam. While submitting his reports on these branch Leagues, Nawab Ismail observed that periodic inspection of the provincial Muslim Leagues would make them 'more efficient' and enable the central League to plan better for the future.[162] The issue of efficient party organization was also raised in the central council but on Jinnah's advice, its consideration was deferred till the annual session.[163] Meanwhile, Jinnah formally instructed the central civil defence committee to supervise and inspect the working of all the provincial Muslim Leagues.[164] Zakir Ali collected information from the provincial Muslim Leagues about matters relating to the organization of the provincial Muslim Leagues by circulating a questionnaire.[165] By August 1943, Jinnah and Nawab Ismail had agreed to combine the organization of the provincial Muslim Leagues with the civil defence work and rename the central civil defence committee with redefined terms of reference.[166] Consequently, the tenure of the central civil defence committee was not renewed. At the Karachi annual session, it was decided to entrust functions of the central civil defence committee to a committee of action. The provincial civil defence committees were, however, allowed to function to assist the local authorities in food distribution in view of the paucity of licensed Muslim shops and inadequate representation of Muslims on the rationing staff. They were asked to send monthly reports and a comprehensive report of their work from the time of their inception to 10 May 1944, to Zafar Ahmad Ansari, in the central office.[167] On 10 January 1945, the central committee of action formally decided to wind up the provincial civil defence committees and their branches in the districts, as their continuance was not needed any more. Those in charge of these committees were directed to send in their final reports to the central committee of action and hand over the record and accounts with balance if any to the provincial Muslim Leagues.[168] They did as instructed.

(*xi*) *Committee of Action*. The All-India Muslim League at its Karachi annual session authorized Jinnah to appoint a committee of action consisting of five to seven members to organize the Muslims to resist the imposition of an all-India federation or any other constitution for a united India and prepare them for the struggle for Pakistan. On 27 December 1943, after consulting the working committee, Jinnah appointed a committee of six members—Nawab Ismail (chairman), G.M. Sayed, Haji Abdussattar Haji Essak Sait, Nawab Iftikhar Husain Mamdot (1906–1969), Qazi Isa, and Liaquat (convener)—to organize, coordinate and unify various League branches according to the constitution, rules, policy and programme of the All-India Muslim

League. The working committee delegated to the committee of action its powers (*i*) to appoint subcommittees, (*ii*) to control, direct and regulate the activities of the provincial Muslim Leagues, and (*iii*) to take disciplinary action against any League member who acted against the party decisions, and against any office-bearer of a provincial Muslim League who failed in his duties or ignored the decisions of the central working committee, and (*iv*) to suspend, dissolve or disaffiliate any provincial Muslim League.[169] Later on, in August 1946, following the 29 July resolutions, Jinnah reconstituted the central committee of action with minor changes in its membership. Nawab Ismail was still the chairman and Liaquat its convener, but now its members, besides Haji Abdussattar, were Nazimuddin, Abdur Rab Nishtar (1899–1958), Abdul Matin Choudhry, and Mian Mumtaz Mohammad Daultana (1916–1995).[170] It decided to organize committees of action at the provincial and lower levels. These committees were empowered to exercise all the functions normally performed by the provincial Muslim League working committees and councils and functioned under its supervision and control.[171] Zakir Ali was engaged as supervisor on monthly payment of Rs 100 plus travel expenses 'to examine and scrutinize the work of the provincial offices and to submit periodical reports' to the central committee of action about the working of these offices and general condition of the provincial Muslim Leagues, with powers to issue instructions to them to bring about uniformity in their system and efficiency in their working.[172] At first, the central committee of action engaged M.A. Aziz, and then Zafar Ahmad Ansari, as its secretary, and separate staff was hired to look after its work; and the central office was given Rs 10,000 per annum to meet the additional expenditure.[173] Funds were placed at its disposal for the general elections.[174]

The central committee of action held eight meetings in 1944, six in 1945, four in 1946, and six in 1947. Its focus was on the consolidation of the party organization and mobilization. During 1944–45, like the central civil defence committee members, its members toured all the British Indian provinces, often accompanied by Zakir Ali, Zafar Ahmad Ansari, and Siddiq Ali Khan. Besides looking into the party organization, it deputed its members to participate in meetings and conferences organized by the provincial Muslim Leagues and the district Muslim Leagues; and its chairman and convener gave regular reports of its activities to Jinnah.[175] The inspection reports that Zakir Ali prepared after his visits to the offices of the provincial Muslim

Leagues were also submitted to the committee of action chairman as well as Jinnah.[176] On the basis of these reports, instructions were formulated and issued to the provincial Muslim Leagues for implementation.[177] The points raised in them related to uniform dates of membership enrolment, election of office-bearers, and proper maintenance of office record, library, press clippings and the party propaganda.[178] The central committee of action held regular meetings of presidents and secretaries of the provincial Muslim Leagues in the 'Pakistan' and other zones.[179] Its work increased the efficiency of the provincial Muslim Leagues and brought about uniformity in their working. Then, it prepared a model constitution for the provincial Muslim Leagues in consultation with them and the central working committee to ensure complete uniformity in their organizational structures.[180] This constitution was implemented after the general elections and made effective from 1 July 1946; the NWFP and Bihar provincial Muslim Leagues were allowed to adopt it even before that date.[181] The process of reorganization of other provincial Muslim Leagues in accordance with the model constitution was completed in a period of turmoil by July 1947. The central committee of action also dealt with factional disputes in the provincial Muslim Leagues as well. It successfully resolved the disputes in the Delhi, Balochistan and Assam provincial Muslim Leagues, but it was unable to settle the conflict in the Punjab and Sindh provincial Muslim Leagues, which led to the expulsion of Sardar Khizr Hayat Khan Tiwana (1900–1975) and G.M. Sayed from the party. Similarly, its attempt to reorganize the Frontier provincial Muslim League by deputing one of its members, Qazi Isa, did not produce the desired results.

The central committee of action attended to several other organizational matters. One of its subcommittees finalized the constitution of the All-India Muslim League National Guard, which it adopted and implemented.[182] Another subcommittee effectively resolved the issues hindering the organization of women under its banner and streamlined the working of the women's committees.[183] The presidents of the provincial Muslim Leagues appointed women's subcommittees to do social and educational work.[184] A planning committee worked on an economic plan. Haji Abdussattar Haji Essak Sait collected the initial data about trade and industry, and labour and occupational unions in response to a questionnaire.[185] Still, the dearth of requisite data about Muslims and Muslim majority areas, shortage of Muslim personnel in various fields of economy and unrelenting opposition to the Pakistan demand limited the League's capacity to prepare a comprehensive economic plan.[186] A committee of writers with Jamiluddin Ahmad (1914–70), Lecturer in English at the Aligarh Muslim University, as convenor was appointed to publish literature under its supervision to promote the League cause.[187] Another committee, the central vigilance committee with Mohammad Yamin Khan as convenor, was appointed to watch over the rights and interests of the Muslims in government services and take appropriate steps to get their legitimate grievances redressed and to secure for them their due share in all the government services.[188] Other subcommittees included the education subcommittee with Dr Afzaal Husain Qadri as convenor and the socio-religious reforms subcommittee with G.M. Sayed as convenor to suggest appropriate measures to infuse true Islamic spirit among the Muslims to remove un-Islamic customs and ideas that had crept into the Muslim society of India.[189] The work done by the central committee of action largely contributed to the League's success in the general elections.

Muslim Students. Jinnah encouraged different segments of the Muslim society to organize their own separate platforms and mobilized them, when needed, to explain and support the Pakistan demand. Muslim students of the educational institutions, established by the Muslim Anjumans, government and Christian missionaries, constituted an important section of the politically conscious society. More important were the male and female educational institutions that the Muslim Anjumans had founded in Lahore, Peshawar, Karachi, Quetta, Calcutta, Dhaka, Bombay and Madras, as they catered to the needs of almost exclusively Muslim students. All the Anjumans had administrative and governing bodies on which Muslim notables were adequately represented. During 1937–47, the Leaguers or Muslims with pro-League leanings came to control the administrative and governing bodies of these institutions. Even in the NWFP, a stronghold of the pro-Congress Khudai Khidmatgars, as early as 1938, a League candidate defeated the Congress–Khudai Khidmatgars candidate in the elections to the office of secretary of the Islamia college, Peshawar. Although the faculty members of these educational institutions did not take active part in politics like those of the Aligarh Muslim University, they had deep sympathies for the All-India Muslim League and the Pakistan demand. However, the students of these institutions had freedom to organize local bodies of students or to associate themselves with the all-India Muslim students' organizations. The Aligarh Muslim University had a unique character among the Muslim educational institutions of India and occupied a pivotal position among the educated Muslims.[190]

The Aligarh Muslim University, which Jinnah described as the 'arsenal of Muslim India', used to attract Muslim students and faculty members from all over India. It was a melting pot for the Indian Muslims; and fostered in them uniform cultural identity. It put no restrictions on its faculty members or students on their association with the political parties. The All-India Muslim League, 'nationalist' Muslims, Ahrar, Ahmadis, socialists and communists competed with one another to gain influence in the Aligarh Muslim University.[191] The university atmosphere was more congenial for the League supporters than the others. The Leaguers gradually came to dominate its administrative and academic bodies. As mentioned elsewhere, the Aligarh Muslim University court, the highest administrative organ that gave representation to different categories of Indian Muslims, used to elect the chancellor, vice-chancellor, pro-vice-chancellor, treasurer and members of the executive council. The court had five life members— the Aga Khan, Sayyid Subhanullah and rulers of the states of Hyderabad, Bhopal and Bahawalpur—and the rest were elected members. An overwhelming majority of the Leaguers were elected members. For example, in 1939, pro-League graduates were elected on all the twelve seats reserved for the registered graduates that had fallen vacant, defeating the pro-Congress candidates including a former minister, Hafiz Mohammad Ibrahim. Important League leaders including Jinnah, Liaquat, Nawab Ismail, Sikandar Hayat and Raja of Mahmudabad, and pro-League graduates and professionals were its elected members. The non-League forces were unable to re-establish their influence through such non-party bodies like the 'Academic Internationale'.[192] Consequently, the Leaguers played a critical role in the decision-making process of the university. Even otherwise, Jinnah after the League's revival came to enjoy unrivalled influence on the decision-making process of the Aligarh Muslim University as the leader of Muslim India. Interestingly, even in 1938, he played a mediatory role in the election of Sir Shah Sulaiman (1886–1941) as the vice-chancellor, when he persuaded Nawab Ismail and Dr Ziauddin to withdraw from the contest to facilitate his election for a three-year term.[193] When Shah Sulaiman's (1886–1941) term expired, the Leaguers had acquired dominant position in the court, and their candidate, Dr Ziauddin, was easily elected vice-chancellor for two consecutive terms.[194] He held this office till 1946 when he resigned as a result of student protest but then he was elected rector of the Aligarh Muslim University and died soon afterwards.[195] The students' union was another important institution of the Aligarh Muslim University whose president used to be a professor but the vice-president, secretary and other office-bearers were elected by, and from, the students. In the union elections of 1937, pro-League candidates won all the offices against the pro-Congress candidates, and after that they continuously repeated this performance every year.[196] While in these elections, they had 'Free Islam in a Free India' as their motto; in 1941, they adopted 'Pakistan' as their ideal.[197] Jinnah presided over the installation ceremony of the union in 1937, and after that he regularly visited Aligarh on similar occasions.[198] Another institution that some teachers and students created was the Aligarh Muslim University League. They enrolled League members from among the teachers and students and, after formal elections, constituted a branch League: Dr Abid Ahmad Ali was elected its first president and Abdul Wahab Kheiri its secretary.[199] The United Provinces League on its request recognized its status as that of a city Muslim League on the condition that its enrolment would never be less than one thousand; besides the president, at least two staff members would be members of its working committee; and it would not participate in the University politics.[200] Still another body that was created at the Aligarh Muslim University was the Bachha (Juvenile) Muslim League in 1939; and Muslim juveniles in other parts of India followed this example and established similar Leagues.[201] The All-India Muslim League used all these institutions for the expansion of its support-base and for its campaign in the general elections.

In the 1930s, Indian students who were influenced by different ideologies—nationalism, communism and socialism—set up various bodies to promote them. When Muslim students experienced discrimination in these bodies, which the Hindu students monopolized, they formed purely Muslim organizations. The discrimination against the Muslim students had disturbed Jinnah who personally witnessed its demonstration in Lucknow in August 1936, when he presided over the first all-India conference of the United Provinces Unity Students' Federation that Pandit Nehru had inaugurated; the conference did not elect a single Muslim student as an office-bearer.[202] Even otherwise, Muslim students were inspired by Jinnah's fervent defence of Muslim position in politics; according to one account, they now looked to him as 'our guide, our philosopher, our leader and our father' who had infused 'a new life in the [Muslim] nation'.[203] In 1936–37, Muslim students' unions and associations all over India, from Peshawar to Chittagong, invited him to address them.[204] Jinnah advised the Muslim students to unite on one all-India platform. On his advice, at a preliminary meeting in Lucknow on 17 January 1937, they set up a committee to organize themselves, with Mohammad Waseque as general secretary and Mohmmad Noman (1914–1972) as organizing secretary.[205] After a heated debate on the merits of a purely Muslim organization, the organizing committee drafted a constitution under Jinnah's guidance.[206] The new organization, the All-India Muslim Students Federation, held its first conference in Calcutta on 27–28 December 1937, under Jinnah's chairmanship, where its constitution was formally approved. The constitution was revised in 1940, and further amended in 1941 and 1944.[207] Any *bona fide* male or female student of not less than thirteen years of age or any person who had left studies and was unemployed for one year could become its member on payment of two annas fee. Every member of an affiliated provincial organization was recognized as a member of the All-India Muslim Students Federation. In addition, any person who was not a student but was interested in its activities could become an associate member on payment of fifteen rupees per year. The All-India Muslim Students Federation had branches all over British India and, unlike the All-India Muslim League, in the princely states. It created solidarity in the ranks of the Muslim students by holding conferences, establishing study circles, organizing propaganda tours and by publishing and distributing literature including its magazines, the *Awakening* (English) and the *Bedari* (Urdu).

The All-India Muslim League and the provincial Muslim Leagues had no direct control on the All-India Muslim Students Federation or provincial Muslim Students Federations but the League leaders on Jinnah's direction used to advise and guide the All-India Muslim Students Federation and its branches, where needed. Some leaders enrolled themselves as associate members and were formally elected presidents.[208] For example, Raja of Mahmudabad was elected president of the All-India Muslim Students Federation; Mian Bashir Ahmad (1893–1971) and Hamid Nizami (1915–1962), when he was not a student, president of the Punjab Muslim Students Federation; Professor A.B.A. Haleem president of the United Provinces Muslim Students Federation; Qazi Isa president of the Balochistan Muslim Students

Federation; and Liaquat president of the Delhi Muslim Students Federation. Normally Jinnah himself or a leading Leaguer presided over the annual and other conferences of the All-India Muslim Students Federation and its branches. He would readily send messages to students' conferences and magazines, when asked to do so, and would exhort them to focus on their studies to prepare themselves for the struggle in future. His message to the Sindh Muslim Students Federation organ, the *Moslem Voice*, was typical: 'Remember that the work that is being done today by the All-India Muslim League is to fall on your shoulders tomorrow. Have you therefore equipped yourselves, trained yourselves and disciplined yourselves enough to prove worthy of the responsibility? If not, go ahead.'[209] He urged the Muslim students to 'maintain complete unity and solidarity' in their ranks, otherwise 'nobody can help you if you quarrel among yourselves and [then] you will go under'.[210] On another occasion, he advised: 'organize yourself and learn to work in a team. Let us go step by step. Do not be impatient. Time is coming when we are really ready . . . to achieve our goal'.[211] It was at one of the students' functions at the Aligarh Muslim University that Jinnah gave the famous watchwords of 'Faith, Unity and Discipline' which became not only the motto of the students but also of the Leaguers. The letter head of the All-India Muslim Students Federation and All Bengal Muslim Students League bore these words in this order although Jinnah used these words in this and a different order in his speeches and correspondence. Jinnah repeatedly advised them 'to keep themselves abreast of the political, social and economic developments' of India as well as the world at large but not to 'take active part' in politics because their primary duty to themselves, their parents and the 'nation' was to devote their energies to their studies.[212] The Muslim Students Federation, he exhorted the Punjab branch, was not 'a political organization' and the students should devote their time to their studies, and work for the League cause only during vacations and holidays.[213] 'Don't depend upon anybody', he wrote in his message to its Rawalpindi Conference, '[we] will emerge out of [this] ordeal purer, better, [and] stronger than we have ever been.'[214] He felt that 'the responsibility of achieving our national goal and maintaining our national prestige and national glory' rested on 'the shoulders of the coming generation alone'.[215] The Muslim Students Federations assisted the provincial Muslim Leagues in their organizational work, especially in provinces like the Punjab, Assam and Bihar where the League leaders were either too involved in factional tussles or were otherwise inactive. The Muslim Students Federation branches in the provinces of the north-west and Jammu and Kashmir State coordinated their activities to work for the League cause.[216] The students were trained and employed more methodically in different provinces to campaign for the League candidates in the general elections.[217]

Ulama and Mashaikh. Ulama and *mashaikh* constituted another important segment of the Muslim society. Jinnah recognized their potential for organized propaganda and mass mobilization, as he had witnessed it in the Khilafat movement and after that. When he formed the central parliamentary board in 1936, he nominated representatives of the Jamiatul Ulama-i-Hind and Majlis-i-Ahrar-i-Islam on it after consulting their leaders. Both the parties accepted the nomination of their members on the central parliamentary board and provincial parliamentary boards. The All-India Muslim League in return pledged in its manifesto to give 'due weight' to the opinions of the Jamiatul Ulama-i-Hind and Shia *Mujtahids* for the protection of religious rights of the Muslims. However, this 'alliance' did not last for long: the Majlis-i-Ahrar-i-Islam left it before and the Jamiatul Ulama-i-Hind after the elections without clearly spelling out the reasons for their break-up with the League. The Jamiatul Ulama-i-Hind–All-India Muslim League break-up and the Congress policies in the Hindu majority provinces divided the Deobandi *ulama*. Maulana Husain Ahmad Madni led the main faction of the Jamiatul Ulama-i-Hind that began to support the Congress; his position as head of the Darul Ulum, Deoband enhanced the importance of this faction. But many leading Deobandi *ulama* disagreed with this policy and remained supportive of the All-India Muslim League; among them were Mazharuddin, Midrarullah (1913–1994) and Mohammad Shoaib (1901–1981) who led the Jamiatul Ulama-i-Hind factions in Kanpur and NWFP; and Shoaib was once elected president of the Frontier provincial Muslim League.[218] After the Cripps Mission, the Sarhad Jamiatul Ulama, made 'Pakistan' as its creed and campaigned in its support.[219] Jamal Mian, son of Maulana Abdul Bari and leading *alim* of Farangi Mahal, formally joined the League to negate the impression that the *ulama* as a whole were with the Congress.[220] Maulana Ashraf Ali Thanvi, the well-known Deobandi *alim* with a large following, after ascertaining the views of the political parties on a questionnaire, issued a *fatwa* entitled *Tanzimul Muslimin* (Organization of the Muslims) that enjoined upon the Muslims to join the League rather than the Congress. Many Muslims including quite a few Deobandi *ulama* followed his advice. Another prominent pro-League Deobandi *alim*, Maulana Shabbir Ahmad Usmani, at one time *Shaikhul Hadis* at the Darul Ulum, Deoband attempted to bring about reconciliation between the All-India Muslim League and the Jamiatul Ulama-i-Hind but the Jinnah–*ulama* meeting that he arranged in Delhi in 1940 could not bridge their differences.[221] The Brelvis who claimed to represent the *sawad-i-azam* (the grand majority) of the Sunni Muslims had comparatively fewer *ulama* and *mashaikh* interested in politics and their two ineffective and usually dormant organizations, the All-India Sunni Conference and the Jamiatul Asfiya, had been confined to purely religious and spiritual matters. Several Brelvi *ulama* and *mashaikh* who were active in politics like Abdul Hamid Badauni and Burhanul Haq participated in politics from the League platform.[222] Some of them held offices in the provincial Muslim Leagues, and others served on its committees. After the general elections of 1945–46, they activated their organizations, All-India Sunni Conference and Jamiatul Asfiya, in support of the All-India Muslim League. The Jamiat Ahle Hadith which constituted a much smaller body of Sunni Muslims supported the League and its leaders particularly Maulana Mohammad Ibrahim of Sialkot despite his old age and ill health conducted extensive tours to promote the Pakistan demand.[223] The Shias were adequately represented in the top slot of the League and were assured of protection of their religious rights in Pakistan although the Shia *ulama* generally refrained from active politics.[224] When some of them felt insecure as a result of the Shia-Sunni conflict in the United Provinces, they established the All-India Shia Political Conference to protect their interests. But whenever there was an anti-League and pro-Congress move from any Shia group, they would set up rival bodies to offset its impact. The spiritual head of the Bohras also issued instructions to his followers to support the League candidates in the Sindh elections where their number was quite substantial.[225]

After the failure of its 'alliance' with the Jamiatul Ulama-i-Hind and MAI, the All-India Muslim League permanently dropped the idea of forming a similar all-India alliance with any political party in future. However, it allowed its members to retain membership of a political party whose policy was in line with its policy and welcomed the support of such parties to its cause. Jinnah occasionally issued appeals to the Muslims and members of the Muslim parties including the

Jamiatul Ulama-i-Hind, Majlis-i-Ahrar-i-Islam and Khaksars to join the League but refused to negotiate with any group or party for its support to the League cause.[226] Those Muslim parties that refused to join or to support the League gradually lost popular backing, and were eventually left with hollow organizational structures with highly depleted membership. The All-India Muslim League placated the *ulama* in its ranks by taking them on its committees and used their services for the propagation of its message. They served on committees that toured the provinces to apprise the Muslims about the plight of their co-religionists in the Congress-governed Muslim minority provinces and which reviewed the Muslim Dissolution of Marriage Bill. But the League did not constitute any exclusively *ulama*-composed committee to advise on 'such matters as concerned the Shariat', as suggested by Jamal Mian at the Patna session.[227] They were associated with the G.M. Sayed-chaired subcommittee that the central committee of action appointed 'to find ways and means to infuse true Islamic spirit and eradicate un-Islamic ideas and customs'.[228] Sayed invited 'scholars of Islamic culture' to send proposals to cast off 'the yoke of foreign political or religious ideas',[229] and Zafar Ahmad Ansari interacted with the *ulama* on behalf of this subcommittee, which, however, could not accomplish anything concrete partly due to G.M. Sayed's involvement in the politics of Sindh.[230] The *ulama* who were invited to meet the subcommittee in Lahore included Sulaiman Nadvi (1884–1955), Shabbir Ahmad Usmani, Shabbir Ali, Zafar Ahmad Usmani, Kifayatullah, Abul Ala Maududi, Mohammad Ilyas and Mohammad Zakariyya.[231] *Ulama* and *mashaikh* on their part wanted to make their contribution to the Pakistan movement partly to secure a position of influence in the new Muslim state. They realized that they could effectively counterbalance the impact of the pro-Congress Jamiatul Ulama-i-Hind only through a pro-League *ulama* party.[232] The result was the foundation of the All-India Jamiatul Ulama-i-Islam in October 1945, which mobilized the pro-League *ulama* and *mashaikh* throughout India and successfully neutralized the impact of the shrinking number of the pro-Congress *ulama*. The Brelvis who were initially active from the Jamiatul Ulama-i-Islam platform subsequently activated their own dormant bodies, which organized the well-known conference in Benares to support the League.[233] The All-India Muslim League coordinated the resources of the religious forces in support of its candidates in the general elections.

Muslim Workers and Businessmen. Muslim employees and workers organized separate pro-League platforms, either on Jinnah's advice or on their own initiative. The All-India Muslim League had a long history of interaction with Muslim employees/workers and with those Muslims seeking employment. Its contribution in their recruitment and its role in advocating their demands had been quite significant since its inception. Now it encouraged them to organize themselves to protect their interests and mobilized them in support of the League cause. Muslim employees in the railways were the pioneers. As early as March 1932, they had founded the All-India Railway Muslim Employees Association at a conference in Lucknow, with Dr Ziauddin Ahmad as president, which put forward their demands including the demand for the reservation of due share in jobs for the Muslims.[234] Muslim employees in the post and telegraph department followed their lead and organized the All-India Postal Muslim Employees Union. The government offered to recognize these bodies provided they dropped the word 'Muslim' from their names. The postal union accepted, but the All-India Railway Muslim Employees Association rejected, the offer.[235] Nevertheless the government reserved 25 per cent jobs for the Muslims in various departments. The reservations were, however, subverted by promotions of employees resulting in Muslims getting fewer jobs than their due share and even those at lower positions. Other grievances including those relating to promotions, training and scholarships for higher studies abroad were added to this issue. The League supported these demands; and in March 1939, Jinnah moved a cut motion during the debate on the budget in the central assembly to highlight Muslim under-representation in the services.[236] The government assured investigation into the Muslim grievances.[237] After March 1940, the All-India Railway Muslim Employees Association's renewed pressure for recognition resulted in the addition of a rule in the railway code empowering the railway officers to take disciplinary action against those employees who were enrolling themselves as its members; and the railway member himself moved in the Viceroy's Executive Council against the recognition of communal associations or unions.[238] After the rejection of a League's resolution in the central assembly for the recognition of communal unions, there was a sharp rise in cases of discrimination and victimization of Muslim employees.[239] On 1 April 1941, the League Assembly Party staged a walkout from the central assembly to protest against this policy, and Jinnah, in a memorandum to the viceroy on its behalf, represented the

Muslim case in the railway services.[240] The All-India Railway Muslim Employees Association emerged as a well-organized body with active branches in Lahore, Lucknow and Calcutta, and a widely circulated organ, the fortnightly *Railwayman* (Lucknow).[241] Its annual conferences were presided over by prominent Leaguers including Jinnah, Liaquat, Fazlul Haq and Suhrawardy, and the one in December 1943, was held in the League pandal at the Karachi annual session.[242] Despite official restrictions the trend to form Muslim employees' associations did not stop; members of an All-India Muslim Employees Association were quite active around the time of the general elections.[243] Later on, in June 1946, seven different unions united to form an All Muslim Employees Federation with Sayyid Ali Imam 'Dara' as its organizer.[244] Muslim workers in Malabar initiated the move to organize Muslim labour in 1942, when some of them including a large number of Beri workers separated themselves from the All-Kerala Trade Union Congress and formed a Muslim labour union. They broadened their base in May 1944, on Haji Abdussattar Haji Essak Sait's advice, by forming the Malabar district Muslim labour union, which along with other locally organized unions urged the All-India Muslim League to organize an All-India Muslim Labour Union to safeguard effectively the interests of the Muslim labour.[245] The central committee of action seriously took up the proposal, which a majority of the provincial Muslim Leagues formally supported, but the Trade Union Act that disallowed registration and recognition of communal unions blocked its implementation.[246] The Muslim labour unions continued to function in the provinces and mobilized support for the League candidates in the general elections.

Jinnah had always been in contact with Muslim businessmen and industrialists.[247] They had looked to him and the All-India Muslim League for the protection of their interests. This was amply demonstrated during the enactment of the Indian Income Tax Amendment Bill (1938). Muslim businessmen flooded the League office with requests for the modification of those provisions of the Bill that adversely affected them.[248] Jinnah's role in this legislation provided relief to the Muslims engaged in business abroad.[249] Henceforth, he constantly advised them to unite in chambers in every province and form a broader all-India platform to protect their interests. Initially, there were only two Muslim chambers: one in Calcutta and another in Bombay; even these two were often engaged in personality-oriented petty rivalries. Jinnah's proposal and his continuous persuasion for an all-India federation, composed of provincial chambers, took some time to materialize. Several young and energetic businessmen particularly M.A.H. Ispahani of the Calcutta chamber and Habib I. Rahimatullah (1912–1991), president of the Bombay chamber, came forward to realize his objective, and by March 1944, Muslim chambers had been constituted in most of the provinces.[250] The Punjab chamber had Sir Sayyid Maratab Ali (1883–1961) as president and Naseer A. Shaikh as secretary, which presented Jinnah an address on his visit to Lahore in March, and on his advice requested the all-India federation for affiliation.[251] He persuaded Sir Adamjee Haji Dawood to accept the presidency of the federation.[252] In April, the federation of chambers of commerce and industries held its inaugural meeting in Delhi with Sir Adamjee in the chair, and approved a constitution and elected its office-bearers. Representatives of the chambers in Calcutta, Bombay, Madras, Karachi, Patna, Kanpur, Lahore, Peshawar, Delhi and Amritsar participated in its deliberations; the Central Provinces and Berar did not have a chamber and the Balochistan chamber expressed its inability to participate 'this time'.[253] Sir Adamjee was elected as its president, Habib I. Rahimatullah as senior vice-president and M.A.H. Ispahani as junior vice-president, and members were taken from different affiliated chambers.[254] This became the third federation; the other two federations were the British federation and the Indian federation. This federation not only provided a forum to the Muslim business community to represent their viewpoint but also inspired them to support the All-India Muslim League and its cause.

Communists/Socialists. According to the All-India Muslim League constitution, any Muslim could enrol himself as a member of the League. His/her religious or political persuasion was not questioned as long as he accepted the aims and objects of the League. The objectives of the League and the Communist Party of India were totally different from each other; and in the 1930s, no communist could think of becoming member of a communally organized party like the League. Similarly, some Leaguers perceived communism as an irreligious ideology that was incompatible with the League's ideology and they wanted its elimination in all its forms.[255] There was a slight change in their mutual perception during the Second World War after the Communist Party of India central committee in September 1942, and the Communist Party of India first congress in May 1943, conceded the Muslims' right to autonomous state existence and of secession, i.e.

the party indirectly recognised the Pakistan demand, although its concept of nationalism remained diametrically opposed to that of the League. Consequently, special correspondents of the communist newspapers like the *Peoples' War* [ed. Dr K.M. Ashraf (1903–1962)] and its Urdu version, the *Qaumi Jang* [ed. Sajjad Zaheer (1905–1973)] and other communists attended the Delhi and Karachi annual sessions and other League functions.[256] Quite a few communists attended the Karachi annual session; four on behalf of these two newspapers and one correspondent, Mahmudali Daniyal Latifi, came on behalf of the Gujerati version of the *Peoples' War*, the weekly *Lokyuda*.[257] The pro-Pakistan stance of the Communist Party of India and increased social interaction between the communists and the Leaguers created an atmosphere in which Nawab Ismail, the central civil defence committee chairman, allowed the League food committees to cooperate with the committees of other parties with similar objectives; among them were the Communist Party of India-organized food committees.[258] The food committees of the two parties especially in Bengal jointly did some commendable relief work.[259] The resultant congeniality persuaded many a communist to join the League as members.[260] They felt that they could capture the League organization at different levels and influence its programme according to their viewpoint.[261] The election manifestoes of the Punjab and Bengal provincial Muslim Leagues for the general elections partially reflected that influence.[262]

A League-communist closer cooperation, however, could not be worked out on a durable basis mainly because of opposition from within the League.[263] In fact, it caused intra-League tension and aggravated factionalism in the Punjab provincial Muslim League and more so in the Bengal presidency Muslim League.[264] Jinnah's and Liaquat's strong observations against the communists/socialists neutralized their influence within the League. Addressing the Punjab Muslim Students Federation conference in Lahore on 19 April 1944, Jinnah observed that the Leaguers could not be duped by the 'flattery' of the League that the communists had 'indulged in', and declared: 'Hands off! Hands off!! I say Communists, Hands off!!! If you try the same game [of winning over by flattery], it will hit back like a boomerang. We do not want any flag except the League flag of Crescent and Star. Islam is our guide and a complete code of our life. . . . We don't want any isms, socialism, communism or national socialism'.[265] Similarly, in 1945, Liaquat in his tour of southern India refused to be garlanded by the communists, making it clear that the

League would not allow its platform to be used by any other political party.[266] He rationalized his stance in his tour of Bengal; addressing the students in Calcutta, he observed, 'how can a communist or any other leader be allowed to use the League platform and if anybody has been doing that, let me tell you he is doing the greatest disservice to the cause of Islam . . . and to the cause of the Muslim League. My young friends who believe in that communism or through communism they will secure Pakistan are greatly mistaken. They may secure Pakistan of the conception of communism but they will not secure the Pakistan of the Islamic conception. Pakistan has no meaning for me, if it is not of Islamic conception. . . . I warn you against this danger of communism to Islam'.[267] No communist, socialist or progressive was formally thrown out of the League for his views. However, quite a few communists — including Daniyal Latifi, at one time office secretary of the Punjab provincial Muslim League — left the League on their own accord or they decreased their visibility from the League platform. Nevertheless, they continued to support the League demand for Pakistan.

(C) PRESS, PUBLICITY, AND PROPAGANDA

Before Independence, the means of propaganda were extremely limited. The electronic media was confined to the All-India Radio, which was controlled by the pro-Congress Hindus. One out of the six news editors was a Muslim who was in charge of the Middle East section but even he was merely a figure head as the non-Muslim chief news editor supervised all the Middle East and Pushto bulletins. The Associated Press of India, United Press of India and Orient Press of India were the three news agencies that catered to the needs of the All-India Radio. The first two agencies were Hindu in composition and outlook and the third, much smaller than the other two, was the only agency that gave coverage to the news about the League. The Leaguers complained that the news coverage on the All-India Radio bore anti-Muslim and anti-League slant; in April 1943, Liaquat formally moved a cut motion in the central assembly to criticize the All-India Radio for promoting sectarianism among the Muslims. The allegation was that the All-India Radio aired a programme on the Madhe Sahaba without caring for its effect on the Shias and then cancelled it without regard to the feelings of the Sunnis.[268] When Patel took over charge of Information in the interim government, verbal orders were given against the use of Orient

Press of India messages without clearance from the chief news editor or the director of news; subsequent transformation of the All-India Radio, the League alleged, turned it into a propaganda machine of the Congress.[269] Gandhi's articles in the *Harijan* and his prayer meetings were given wide coverage while Jinnah's statements were either ignored or given in brief and sometimes misleading summaries were broadcast. Again, verbal instructions were issued to the All-India Radio to refer to Nehru as the prime minister of India and subsequently it was directed to address him as the vice-president. Mehr Chand Khanna virtually controlled news coverage about the NWFP; consequently, in October 1946, the All-India Radio gave a favourable coverage of Nehru's 'receptions' in the Tribal Areas. Comparatively, the reporting about the Bihar and Bengal tragedies was biased against the Muslims. The League did complain about the misuse of a public organ but no action was taken on its complaints.[270]

Press was the primary medium of propaganda available to a political party at that time. The All-India Muslim League had no newspaper of its own at the time of its revival in 1935–37, as it had never thought of organized propaganda prior to that, except during the time of Aziz Mirza (honorary secretary, 1910–1913) who established a propaganda network that included circulation of pro-League printed literature but this network did not survive after him.[271] Then, in 1927–28, Dr Saifuddin Kitchlew (honorary secretary) had plans to create an 'Information and Publicity Bureau' with branches at the district level but he could not accomplish anything concrete due to lack of funds and intra-League conflicts. However, after 1935, the League desperately needed a supportive press to meet the needs of a growing party to explain the viability of its programme and to counter the propaganda of its far more resourceful opponents. Initially, it had to depend on the existing newspapers. A few Anglo-Indian newspapers gave it coverage but only when there was any newsworthy event.[272] The powerful Hindu-owned press, whose control rested with the Congress and Hindu Mahasabha leaders backed by the Hindu financiers, was highly critical of Jinnah and the Pakistan scheme. Its denunciation mounted as the League expanded its activities so much so that even Nehru felt obliged to apologise to Jinnah.[273] Muslim press lacked resources—finances as well as experienced Muslim journalists.[274] It consisted of three categories. One category was of newspapers that were controlled and edited by pro-Congress 'nationalist' Muslims, and their criticism was more or less similar to that of the Hindu-controlled press.[275] The second category was of newspapers supporting the pro-British Muslim politicians and political parties; and they gave the All-India Muslim League coverage except when their loyalty to their patrons was on the line.[276] The third category was of newspapers including the newly founded pro-League newspapers that championed its cause. Most of these newspapers were in Urdu, a few in the regional languages and much fewer in the English language. The Leaguers were usually their proprietors as well as editors; joint ventures were quite rare. Some newspapers were named as 'Pakistan' and 'Muslim League'. Jinnah sent messages to every pro-League newspaper without any reservation whenever a proprietor or an editor would make a request. Most of these newspapers were launched by the League enthusiasts including the students with little experience and without estimating the long-term cost of their ventures. As a result, many a newspaper had a very short life, extending over a period of a few months to a couple of years due to lack of sufficient funds, dearth of professional journalists, limited circulation and shortage of newsprint due to the world war. Despite the shortcomings, Muslim press played a remarkable role in the broadening of the League's support-base and in popularizing the Pakistan demand in the Muslim masses. But it was no match to the Hindu press and its reach was highly limited. Some pro-League and League newspapers that were published in British India are mentioned here.

Punjab had quite a few well-known Urdu newspapers; among them were the dailies *Ihsan* (ed. S.M. Sohail), *Zamindar* (ed. Maulana Zafar Ali Khan), *Shahbaz* [ed. Murtaza Ahmad Khan (1899–1959)], *Inqilab* (eds. Ghulam Rasul Mihr and Abdul Majid Salik), *Paisa Akhbar* and *Seyasat* (ed. Sayyid Habib). The first two were totally committed to the League cause but the others were often influenced by the fluctuations in the League–Unionist relations. Jinnah was especially delighted by the pro-League stance of the daily *Ihsan* and once, on the invitation of its proprietor, Malik Noor Ilahi, paid a visit to its office as a mark of his appreciation for its pro-League work; and later on, the Punjab Leaguers praised the publicity that the daily *Ihsan* along with the dailies *Zamindar* and *Nawa-i-Waqt* gave to the League campaign in the general elections.[277] Malik Barkat Ali, at one time the only League member of provincial assembly in the Punjab assembly, launched a quality English weekly, the *New Times*, to defend the League and its policies, but due to financial constraints the weekly survived only for a few months. The English newspaper *Eastern Times* (ed. Abdul Hamid Khan) was started as a daily (10 September 1931) and turned into a weekly for lack of funds (1936) but was again transformed into a daily (1 July 1942). It appeared without interruption, and gave the League sympathetic coverage especially after the *Paisa Akhbar* management took it over in 1940.[278] When Jinnah was planning to start a League-owned newspaper from Lahore to serve the 'western Pakistan zone', its owner offered its takeover by the party but the proposal did not materialize.[279] Prof. Malik Mohammad Inayatullah edited and published a daily, the *Muslim League* (Urdu), to propagate the League cause but it survived for a short while.[280] The Punjab provincial Muslim League itself brought out an Urdu weekly *Pakistan* in June 1944, which helped it in the general elections.[281] The Urdu fortnightly *Nawa-i-Waqt* [ed. Hameed Nizami (1915–1962)] was originally a non-commercial venture; launched by the former Punjab Muslim Students Federation members a week after the adoption of the Lahore Resolution (29 March 1940), and ran it with exemplary dedication on honorary basis.[282] It was converted into a weekly on 1 June 1942, and daily on 22 July 1944. It became virtually a League paper although it never hesitated to offer constructive criticism. Mian Iftikharuddin (1907–1962), who resigned from the Punjab Congress presidency before the general elections to join the League, established the Progressive Papers Limited and brought out the English daily *Pakistan Times* on 4 February 1947, in which he gathered some gifted 'leftist' journalists; Faiz Ahmed Faiz was engaged as its editor and Jinnah consented to associate his name with the paper.[283] All these newspapers were issued from Lahore. In 1937, Qutab Din, a pleader, founded an Urdu weekly *Rahnuma* and *Mujahid* (ed. Abdus Salam Hakeem) in Rawalpindi, and the same year, Imam Bakhsh Nasikh founded the *Saadat* that appeared as a weekly from Kamalia in 1937 and as a daily from Lyallpur (Faisalabad) in 1945. Some of the Punjab newspapers also catered to the needs of other provinces of 'western Pakistan zone', but these provinces had their own newspapers as well. The Sindhi daily *Al-Wahid* (ed. Maulvi Abdul Ghafur) was the most influential newspaper of Sindh, and prominent Leaguers served on its board of directors; in October 1941, it was transformed into a limited company in which the Haroons (Haji Abdullah and his two sons, Yusuf and Mahmud) had the largest shares; other shareholders were Hasan Bakhsh Shah, Ayub Khuhro, G.M. Sayed and Abdul Majid Sindhi.[284] The weekly *Muslim Voice* (ed. Pir Ali Mohammad Rashidi) projected the League policies in Sindh. When Rashidi was expelled from the League and turned it against the party in the general elections, A. Aziz brought out the weekly *The Sind Times* to counter the impact of its campaign. Then, there were the English dailies *Sind Observer* and the *Daily Gazette*. In 1944, Sayyid Sarwar Shah Gilani founded and edited the bilingual weekly *Al-Jamaat* (Urdu and Sindhi) to advocate an Islamic government in Pakistan. Khalifa Mohammad Ismail Baloch edited the Urdu weekly *Ittehad-e-Balochan*. Then, there were the Urdu dailies *Hayat* (ed. Haji Naziruddin) and Sindhi daily *Hilal-i-Pakistan* (ed. Abdul Shakoor Munshi) and weeklies *Millat* (ed. Hakim Sher Husain Qadir), and *Nusrat* (ed. Maulvi Abdul Haye Haqqani). On 1 October 1942, the Sindh Muslim Students Federation launched the monthly *The Moslem Voice*. NWFP had the Urdu dailies *Sarhad* (ed. Allah Bakhsh Yusufi), *Millat* (ed. Rashid Akhtar Nadvi), *Mazlum Dunya* (prop. and ed. Abdur Rahman Riya) and *Sada-e-Pakistan* (ed. Ghulam Mustafa) and weeklies *Al-Falah* and *Hamdam* in Peshawar, *Pakistan* (ed. Ghulam Husain Shah) in Abbottabad, *Naujawan Sarhad* (ed. Taj Mohammad Taherkheli) in Haripur and *Mujahid* (ed. Shahzada Fazal Dad, president of the district Muslim League) in Dera Ismail Khan. The only English weekly was the *Khyber Mail* (ed. Zakaullah Khan). In Balochistan, Qazi Isa established the weekly *Al-Islam* (ed. Maulana Abdul Karim) in 1939, which was converted into a daily in March 1943; and Mir Jafar Khan Jamali founded the daily *Tanzeem* (ed. Nasim Hijazi) to propagate the League's activities. The weekly *Zamana* (ed. Barkat Ali Azad) aimed at projecting 'progressive views' to the Muslim youth. Maulana Ubaidullah Khan edited the *Kalimatul Haq* and subsequently the daily *Al-Farooq* in 1941. The Balochistan Muslim Students Federation issued the *Khurshid* and weekly *Jamhur* (prop. Malik Azam Khan and eds. Masud Ghaznavi and Rafiq Piracha). The daily *Balochistan-e-Jadid* (ed. Mohammad Nasim Talvi), founded in Karachi in 1933, had circulation both in Balochistan and Sindh.

Bengal had the Bengali dailies *Azad* (ed. Nazir Ahmad Choudhry), *Muhammadi* (ed. Maulana Akram Khan), founded by Haji Abdullah, and *Ittehad*, (ed. Abul Mansur Ahmad); and the Bengali weekly *Aman* and Urdu weekly *Ittehad* (both edited by Najmul Huda), the Bengali weekly *Madeena* (ed. Nazir Ahmad Chowdhury); the Urdu daily *Asre Jadid* (ed. Maulana Shaiq Ahmad/Ali Karim Siddiqi),[285] founded in 1921, and weekly *Jihad* (Y.K. Taufiq); and the English dailies *Star of India* (ed. Pothan Joseph/L.A. Atkinson/Usman Ahmad Ansari)[286] and *Morning News* (ed. Syed Mohsin Ali), founded by Abdur Rahman Siddiqi and Khwaja Nuruddin, and weeklies *New Life* (ed. S.M. Jameel), *Comrade* (ed. Mujeebur Rahman Khan) and *Spokesman* (ed.

Dr Sayyid Jilani); all these newspapers projected the League and its activities. The daily *Mussalman*, founded in 1906, supported the League policy as long as it lived. In 1941, the Dhaka university students brought out the fortnightly *Pakistan* to familiarize the students with the League demand. On 18 November 1945, the provincial Muslim League launched the weekly *Millat* (ed. Abul Hashim). Assam had the English weekly *Assam Herald*, founded by Abdul Matin Choudhry, and the Bengali weekly *Jugabheri* (both edited by Mohammad Raziuddin) to project the League and its policies. The Assam Muslim Students Federation had its own organ, the *Provati* (ed. Raziur Rahman), issued from Sylhet. In the United Provinces, the Lucknow Urdu dailies *Haque* (ed. M.A. Rauf Abbasi) and *Haqiqat*, and the weeklies *Mashriq* (ed. Waris Khan and Ahmad Khan Warsi), *Hamdam* (ed. Habib Ansari), and *Pakistan* (ed. S. Rais Ahmad Fatimi) projected the League and its demand. The pro-League Allahabad English weekly turned daily *Star* (ed. Hasan Moiuddin Abbasi) was launched on 1 May 1938; its editor claimed it to be the only Muslim daily in north India but it survived for just two years. In June 1942, Dr S.N.A. Jafri founded and edited the English weekly *Onward* in Allahabad. Then, there were the Urdu weeklies *Al-Wahid* (ed. Abdul Wahid) in Bijnor, *Bedar* in Gorakhpur, *Khidmat* and *Qaumi Akhbar* (ed. Maulana Ismail Zabih) in Kanpur, *Mukhbar-i-Alam* (ed. Qazi Abid Ali Rizvi), founded in January 1938, and bi-weekly *Jiddat* (ed. Sultan Ahmad Khan) in Moradabad, and the Urdu daily *Dabdabai Sikandari* in Rampur that did pro-League propaganda. The Muslim Youth Study Circle brought out the English weekly *Spirit of Youth* (Mahmudul Haq Usmani). Abdus Sattar Kheiri of the Aligarh Muslim University issued the monthly *Spirit of the Time*, which his wife, Fatima, edited before the two were incarcerated during the war for alleged Nazi connections. Khaliquzzaman started the Urdu daily *Tanvir* (ed. Mushaffiquzzaman) in 1945, and Fasihuddin Ahmad the *Pakistan Times* (Aligarh) before the general elections. The pro-League newspapers in Patna were the Urdu daily *Sada-e-Aam* (prop. and ed. Sayyid Nazir Hyder), founded in 1942, and the bi-weeklies *Muslim League* (prop. Abdul Aziz/ Manzoor Husain) and *Ittehad* (ed. Sultan Ahmad). The *Ranchi Sentinel* did propaganda work in Chotanagpur. Two weeklies, the *Muslim Times* and *Al-Farooq* (ed. A.S. Farooqi), of Nagpur, *Al-Burhan* (ed. S.Z.H. Ali) of Akola (Berar) and *Jowher* were the main newspapers explaining the League policy in the Central Provinces and Berar province. Ajmer had the Urdu weekly *Aadil*.

Madras had a variety of Muslim newspapers in different languages, all supporting the All-India Muslim League, Jinnah and the Pakistan scheme. Besides the weekly turned daily *Deccan Times* (ed. Abdul Hameed Khan/A.A. Raoof), founded in 1933,[287] it had the Urdu daily *Hamdard* (prop. Sultan Mohiuddin), the English weekly *Musalman* (ed. Mohammad Husain) and the *Sunday Observer*, the Tamil biweekly turned daily *Saiful Islam* (ed. Maulvi Ahmad Sayeed), and the Tamil weekly turned daily (in March 1941) *Darul Islam* (ed. Badshah Daud Shah) to project the League policies. After the closure of the *Darul Islam*, the Coimbatore city Muslim League started the weekly *Pakistan* (ed. M.A. Rahman), on Jinnah's birthday in 1942. The Madras provincial Muslim League started the bilingual (Urdu and Tamil) weekly *Muslim* (ed. S.M. Abdul Majeed), Abdullah Khan brought out the *Muslim Youth* and Muhammad Reza Khan, secretary of the Madras district Muslim League, edited the English weekly *The Muslim India* to propagate the League ideal. A few Muslim youth published the Urdu weekly *Pakistan* to popularize the League demand. The Tinnevelly district Muslim League issued the Tamil monthly *Munnetram* (Advance) to campaign for the League. The Malayalam daily *Chandrika* (Tellicherry; ed. Abdur Rahman)), founded by Haji Abdussattar Haji Essak Sait, played a significant role in bringing the Mappillas into the League. Mohammad Ali Kamal published the Urdu daily *Azad* from Banglore. Bombay had the Urdu dailies *Khilafat* (ed. Riazuddin Faridi), *Inquilab*, *Ittehad* (ed. Zille Abbas), *Iqbal* (ed. Irshad Beg Chughtai) and *Al-Hilal* (ed. Mohammad Ihsan), and the weekly *Mujahid* (ed. Sattar Jhavri); the Gujarati dailies *Rozegar* (ed. M.H. Qureshi) and *Muslim Times* (ed. M. Sadiq), and weeklies *Paigham* (ed. Maulana Fazlullah), *Insaf*, *Muslim-Gujrat* (ed. Azimuddin F. Mundai), *Deen* (ed. N.N. Qureshi), *Pakistan* (ed. Husen Khan J. Babroo), *Millat* (ed. Fakhre Matri) and *Vakil*; and the English weeklies *Muslim* (ed. Hamid Qazi), *Star Weekly* (ed. Aziz Beg) and *Morning Herald* (ed. Yusuf Afghan), founded by Hasan A. Shaikh, secretary of the Bombay presidency Muslim League, to explain the League's policies. The Kanarese weekly *Desh-Mitra* (Hubli) was meant to guide the Muslim masses about the League and its policies. The Surat MSF issued the *Crescent* in English, Urdu and Gujarati. Bangalore had the Urdu daily *Pasban* (eds. H.M. Ismail Tabish, secretary of the Bangalore–Coorg provincial Muslim League, and Maulana Hasan Mosanna). Delhi had two well-known Urdu newspapers, the daily *Wahdat* and the biweekly *Al-Aman*, both owned and edited by Maulana Mazharuddin, at the time of the League's revival, passionately advocating its cause and survived after his assassination on 14 March 1939.[288] Then, there were the pro-League *Delhi Times* (ed. Mohammad Qasim Shauq), which lived only for five months, the daily *Payam* (ed. Abdul Hamid Shimlavi), the *Muslim Opinion* (ed. Hifazat Husain Zaidi), and the monthly *Tegh* (ed. Abul Bayan Azad). The Delhi Muslim Students Federation circulated the English monthly, the *Pakistan Herald* (from 22 March 1942), and one Urdu monthly, the *Raheel*, to create religious and political consciousness among the students. During the Second World War, Mir Khaiilur Rahman started the *Jang*, initially as an eveninger, which was subsequently turned into a daily. The weekly turned daily *Anjam* (ed. Iqbal Ahmad Siddiqi/S.A. Sabiri/Fahimuddin Noori) supported the League policy.[289] The Orient Press of India was the main source of feeding news to the Muslim press; earlier in January 1938, the idea of a Muslim information service that Khwaja Hasan Nizami (1878–1957) floated did not materialize.[290]

Jinnah was directly associated with the founding of three newspapers. When he was president of the Bombay presidency Muslim League, the party decided to publish two newspapers—one in Gujarati and the other in English—to project its stand and counter the antagonistic propaganda. It appointed a press and propaganda committee chaired by Jinnah to collect funds for this purpose; Mohammad Ali Chaiwala was its secretary and Karimbhai Ibrahim, Abu Bakr Beg Mohammad, Noor Mohammad Chinoy and Fateh Mohammad Haji Yusuf Khandwani its treasurers.[291] A Jinnah-led deputation toured the presidency and collected a handsome amount but due to non-availability of experienced journalists in the English language, it decided to start first a Gujarati weekly, the *Vatan*;[292] and in March 1945, it was converted into a daily when the government refused the provincial Muslim League permission to publish a new Gujarati or English daily.[293] The All-India Muslim League also had plans to publish two newspapers from Delhi: one in Urdu and the other in English.[294] Jinnah was keen to implement this plan. When sufficient funds had been collected, it was decided to start with an Urdu weekly. It was argued that an English newspaper should be launched carefully because of the fate of some popular Muslim-controlled English newspapers like the *Mussalman* (Calcutta) and *Muslim Outlook* (Lahore).[295] Thus, the All-India Muslim League started the Urdu weekly *Manshoor* with Hasan Reyaz as its editor. It used to publish, besides other material, documents of the League organs, and was converted into a daily on 25 December 1944.[296] Although it gave due publicity to the League and the Pakistan scheme but it could not develop into a quality newspaper. Even after its regular publication, the pressure for a newspaper in English continued to build up from within the League. Jinnah himself was quite enthusiastic about it. A few rich Muslims from the United Provinces who did not want their names to be disclosed had placed Rs 50,000 at his disposal for this purpose.[297] After making necessary arrangements and engaging Hasan Ahmad of the Orient Press of India as editor, Jinnah launched the English weekly *Dawn*; and Liaquat agreed to supervise its production.[298] Its first issue appeared on 26 October 1941, which carried Jinnah's message, making it clear that it was 'an entirely independent venture' by a few individuals and its funding had no link with the Bombay Press Fund or the All-India Muslim League fund and that the weekly would 'advocate and champion' the Muslim cause and the policy and programme of the All-India Muslim League and would not 'neglect the cause and welfare of the peoples' of India.[299] The *Dawn* weekly under Liaquat's supervision and Jinnah's guidance met with unprecedented success.[300] Jinnah then decided to bring out an English daily. After flirting with the idea of taking over the *Star of India*, or acquiring the *Statesman* from Lady Yule, the sole proprietor, or launching a completely new daily and naming it the 'Star of Asia', as suggested by M.A.H. Ispahani, he agreed with Liaquat's proposal to convert the weekly *Dawn* into a daily. Pothan Joseph, an Indian Christian, who was with the *Star of India*, was engaged to edit the daily. Jinnah was so impatient to bring it out that when Joseph's joining was delayed, he wrote to Liaquat on 3 September 1942, 'we must go ahead—Joseph or no Joseph'. Pothan Joseph joined the *Dawn* on 1 October; and its first issue appeared on 12 October, the Eidul Fitr day.[301] Jinnah asked Liaquat to continue to work as director to supervise its publication and business side, and in June 1943, requested him to look after the *Manshoor* as well. Liaquat was offered Rs 2,000 per month as remuneration for this work with effect from 1 October 1943, which he formally accepted.[302] On 4 November 1946, Waheeduddin Ahmad filed a 'Deed of Declaration of Trust' about the *Dawn* on Jinnah's behalf, in which he was declared the sole Mutawalli having the power to nominate his successor(s) who would act as mutawalli(s) and had the power to change such nominee(s).[303] Jinnah's ambition to start another daily in the English language from Lahore, however, remained unfulfilled although he had collected sufficient funds for that venture.[304] In January 1946, the All-

India Muslim League created a department of publicity and information headed by Qazi Isa, which published and widely circulated pamphlets, advertisements and posters during the general elections in 1945–46.[305]

Like other Muslim professionals, Muslim journalists struggled to form a separate platform to work for their welfare. The problem was that the volume of Muslim press and the number of Muslim journalists were too small to sustain such an organization on a long-lasting basis.[306] In addition, Muslim journalists had limited opportunities for employment. Still, in 1939, they formed the All-India Muslim Journalists Association with Maulana Zafar Ali Khan as its president and Hasan Moiuddin Abbasi as its organizing secretary. But this Association did not survive for long perhaps because Abbasi's paper, the *Star*, ceased publication. After that, Muslim journalists attempted to organize themselves locally. In 1942, Dr Jafri of the weekly *Onward* formed a journalist association in Lucknow, the journalists in Delhi founded the Muslim Journalists Federation with S.A. Sabiri of the *Anjam* as its president, and some journalists in Bombay established the Muslim Gujarati Journalists Association with Nizamuddin Quraishi as its president. They asked for representation on the press advisory board and newsprint advisory committee.[307] Soon after, Maulana Akram Khan of the *Azad* floated the idea of an all-India journalist organization. He convened with Jinnah's approval the first conference of the pro-League journalists at Delhi where the All-India Muslim Journalists' Association was founded, with Akram Khan as president and Z.A. Suleri (1913–99) of the *Dawn* as secretary. The association aimed at working for the interest of Muslim newspapers in regard to newsprint quota, advertisements, etc. and of the Muslim working journalists regarding their employment, security of service, salaries and other related matters. It also aspired to speak with one voice on 'fundamental political issues'. The federation called on the Muslim associations already in existence to affiliate themselves with this body and appointed provincial organizers to set up branches in the provinces where none existed.[308] It functioned as a loosely organized body of Muslim journalists. Later, on 9 May 1947, editors of about fifty-four Muslim newspapers and magazines, at a convention in the Anglo-Arabic college hall in Delhi on 9 May 1947, founded the All-India Muslim Newspaper Editors' Association, with Altaf Husain (*Dawn*) as its president and Hamid Nizami (*Nawa-i-Waqt*) as secretary, and revitalized the Muslim Journalists' Association.

The Leaguers also produced modest volume of literature to project the party, its leader and the Pakistan ideal. Among the few book-length studies were the works by Mohammad Noman,[309] A.A. Raoof,[310] Matlubul Hasan Saiyid (1915–84),[311] and Z.A. Suleri.[312] The collections of Jinnah's speeches, statements and correspondence provided inspiration and guidance to his followers.[313] Pothan Joseph planned to write Jinnah's memoirs but the idea did not mature.[314] Likewise, the enormity of party work and ill-health prevented Jinnah from fulfilling his own ambition to write. He did write prefaces to a few works including the ones based on a collection of articles by M.R.T. [Mohammad Sharif Toosi (1900–1983)][315] and a couple of articles including the more noted one entitled 'The Constitutional Future of India' in the *Time and Tide* (London, 9 March 1940). But he could not write the article for the *Foreign Affairs* (New York) or the weekly articles for the *Statesman* (Delhi), which their editors were keen to publish,[316] nor could he do the book-length study on the 'Moslems of India', for the American audience, for which he planned to sign a contract with Doubleday Doran and Company Inc., New York.[317] However, he established a Home Study Circle with the help of 'a few well-wishers' in his office at Mount Pleasant Road, Malabar Hill, Bombay to provide the public all the literature, pamphlets and books, and information about the activities, policy and programme of the All-India Muslim League. Matlub H. Saiyid, his private secretary, was in charge of the Home Study Circle, and any person could become its member by paying Rs 5 refundable deposit money. A member would get all the League literature free of cost except that not meant for free distribution.[318] Started in July 1941, the Home Study Circle was wound up in May 1943. The provincial Muslim Leagues and the Muslim students federations in the provinces set up their own study circles and libraries.[319] Later on, the committee of writers selected authors who wrote articles in the press;[320] Shaikh Muhammad Ashraf (1902–1980), a publisher from Lahore, published separately thirteen articles in the 'Pakistan Literature Series'.[321] The Leaguers also used poetry to inspire the Muslims to get their support; poems were regularly sung at the party functions. The poem sung at the Patna session [*Agar Muslim hai to Muslim League mein Aa* (If [you are a] Muslim come into the Muslim League)] gained considerable popularity, and so did many other songs.[322] At Jinnah's suggestion, Mian Bashir Ahmad composed a song [*Ley ke rahin ge Pakistan* (we will surely get Pakistan)] for the Delhi annual session (April 1943).[323]

The all-India sessions of the All-India Muslim League used to be grand gala events not only for the city and the province in which these were organized but also for the participants from outside that province who would take back memories of the sessions. These sessions and several other functions were filmed and shown in the cinema houses and at especially arranged gatherings.[324] The historic Lahore session was filmed, and its 2,000-feet long film was distributed all over India; J. Mandal was especially sent to Calcutta to obtain certificate from the board of censors.[325] Newspapers brought out special numbers/supplements on the Pakistan Resolution, Allama Iqbal, Quaid-i-Azam's birthday and Muslim League. The provincial Muslim Leagues and their branches, the Muslim students federations and the women's committees used to organize workers' camps and 'Pakistan conferences', which had similar impact on the Muslims at the grassroots.[326] The party formally decided to celebrate religious functions like Eidul Fitr, Eidul Azha, Shabe Bara'at and Eid-i-Milad to promote 'political unity and social solidarity' among the Muslims; the League-organized Seerat conferences had similar objective.[327] When the Punjab government banned Pakistan conferences on the plea of communal harmony, the Multan district Muslim League transformed the conference and procession of the Miraj Sharif into a 'Pakistan conference'.[328] The All-India Muslim League often directed its branches to observe different days to popularize the League and its ideal; some of the days were: Jinnah's birthday, Sir Syed Day, Iqbal Day, (Maulana) Muhammad Ali Day, Muhammad bin Qasim Day, [Mustafa] Kamal Day, Shahidganj Day, Manzilgah Day, Palestine Day, Muslim Countries Day, Pakistan (Resolution) Day,[329] Thanksgiving Day (13 August 1943), and Direct Action Day.[330] When a day was observed, the Leaguers at different levels would organize public meetings, bring out processions and hold prayer ceremonies. On the directive of the All-India Muslim League, its branches observed one week in every three months as the 'Muslim League/Pakistan Week', which was meant to increase membership enrolment and to explain the party policy and programme.[331] Similarly, on its direction, the provincial Muslim Leagues set up 'rural propaganda committees' and engaged paid *moballighin* (propagandists) to convey the League's message in the rural areas. They would send regularly reports of their activities to the central office and Jinnah.

Publicity Abroad. The All-India Muslim League recognized the value of propaganda in foreign countries; but unlike the Congress, it had extremely limited resources in manpower and finances that Jinnah used with extreme care and circumspection.[332] The League's passionate advocacy of Muslim issues especially the Palestine issue generated support for the League not only within India but in the Muslim world as well. This policy blunted the hostile propaganda by the Congress and its allies that had equated the Pakistan scheme with the Jewish demand for a homeland in Palestine; and the pro-Jewish stance of the Congress-allied Hindu party, the All-India Hindu Mahasabha, which had formally demanded recognition of Palestine 'as the Jewish homeland', damaged the Congress.[333] All the Muslim political forces in India appreciated the League's policy, which contributed to the broadening of its base. The Abdullah Haroon-chaired foreign committee had this item as part of its agenda, and it extensively distributed party literature in the Muslim world.[334] The All-India Muslim League warned the British government that the Indian Muslims and rest of the Islamic world would regard Britain 'as the enemy of Islam' if it persisted 'in its pro-Jewish policy in Palestine' and that the Jewish 'national home' in Palestine would lead 'to a state of perpetual unrest and conflict'.[335] When the Arabs in Palestine were repressed, evicted forcibly from their lands and deported on a massive scale to Seychelles, South Africa and other places, the All-India Muslim League and its branches observed Friday, 26 August 1938, as the 'Palestine Day' to protest against this policy and the proposed partition of Palestine.[336] It deputed a delegation to participate in the Inter-Parliamentary Muslim and Arab Congress for the defence of Palestine that was held in Cairo.[337] And when the British government convened a Palestine conference in London to find an agreed solution, it demanded representation on it because Jerusalem was the first *Qibla* of the Muslims; Jews from countries other than Palestine had been invited to the conference; and Britain had made promises to the Arabs and the Indian Muslims during the First World War.[338] On the rejection of its demand, the League Assembly Party moved an adjournment motion in the central assembly, which the governor-general disallowed; and then on Jinnah's call it observed 8 February 1939 as the 'All-India Palestine Day'. The League delegation, however, went to England, presented a memorandum on the Palestine issue to the prime minister and assisted the Arab delegates at the London conference.[339] After the conference, the prime minister issued a White Paper, ending British commitment to the Jews under the Balfour Declaration, calling for conditional independence for a unitary Palestinian state after ten years; and admission of 15,000 Jewish immigrants annually into Palestine for five years, with immigration after that subject to 'Arab consent'. On the All-India Muslim League's representation in support of the Arab demands, Linlithgow assured Jinnah that the British government would not go against these demands; and Jinnah communicated this letter to the Supreme Arab Council of Palestine in Baghdad through the consul general of Iraq in Bombay.[340] It was in this background that on the League's invitation several delegates from the Muslim countries attended its historic annual session in Lahore.[341] The only resolution besides the 'Pakistan Resolution' that Jinnah allowed to be moved at this session was on Palestine. During the war, the All-India Muslim League observed 1 November 1940, the last Friday of Ramzan, as the 'Muslim Countries Day' to demonstrate its solidarity with the Muslim countries.[342] Towards the close of the war, the British government under the American–Zionist pressure changed its policy on immigration. The League protested against this change, and denounced the Joint Anglo-American Commission of Inquiry into Palestine and its report that renewed immigration of 100,000 Jews into Palestine—according to the White Paper immigration had to end on 31 March 1944, and called for the creation of a Jewish homeland there.[343] Jinnah was the first leader in the Muslim world to raise his voice against this policy, and on his appeal, 26 October 1945, was observed as 'Palestine Day' all over India. His emotional expressions warmed Muslim hearts but caused concern in pro-Jewish circles in England and the US; and he sent a strongly worded telegram to the US President, Harry S. Truman, asking him to desist from this policy.[344] Henceforth, the movement for the partition of Palestine and creation of Israel was concurrent with the final phase of the Pakistan movement; and some of the hurdles in the acceptance of the Pakistan demand were the result of the League's policy on Palestine.[345] The League's advocacy of the Palestine issue enhanced its image in the Muslim world, and the Arabs in response supported the Pakistan demand. For example, King Ibn-i-Saud of Arabia rejected an offer by some Jewish agency of £25 million 'for remaining silent' on the Pakistan issue.[346]

After March 1940, the Leaguers had keenly felt the need to explain the Pakistan scheme in England and the US.[347] It was proposed that the All-India Muslim League should have its own newspaper published from London.[348] Another proposal was to appoint a new foreign relations committee to disseminate correct information abroad to counter the Congress propaganda and to educate public opinion there about the justice of the Muslim demand for self-determination and Pakistan.[349] Still another one was that India's representative in the US should be a Muslim, as all the Indians who had been appointed till then were Hindus.[350] But none of these proposals could be implemented. On 28 March 1944, the central committee of action discussed Qazi Isa's proposal to establish some agency in England to project the League demand and suggested that someone should be sent to England to do the groundwork.[351] Nothing came out of this proposal. The League did request the Government of India for passage and travel facilities for a deputation of principal League leaders including Jinnah to England and the US but the government response was not positive.[352] In May 1944, Jinnah asked Firoz Khan Noon to suggest someone to organize propaganda for the League in England but the latter could not find a 'dependable Muslim' in London.[353] However, Jinnah ignored to take up immediately a detailed plan for a Muslim Information Centre with an estimated cost of £1500 per annum that Iqbal Ali Shah sent to him from London.[354] Then, in February 1946, Nazimuddin stressed the need for propaganda in England 'on behalf of the League' because the British public had 'very little knowledge of the Muslim demand' and proposed that the League should send 'a person of status' who should be a good speaker and writer with some funds at his disposal to 'get the English papers publish Muslim League news'. But his proposal also could not be given practical shape.[355] Meanwhile, the Indian Muslims and students in England established a 'Muslim League Branch' in November 1944 that carried on pro-Pakistan propaganda. This 'League Branch' published pamphlets and a monthly *Rahnuma* to explain the Pakistan demand. The monthly was soon converted into a fortnightly *Pakistan*; and Z.A. Suleri, foreign correspondent of the daily *Dawn* in London, was engaged as its editor.[356] It was after the withdrawal of the League's acceptance of the Cabinet Mission Plan that Jinnah cautiously sponsored a move to establish a 'Muslim India Information Centre' with Z.A. Suleri as its secretary to project directly the League's viewpoint in England. The agents of M.M. Ispahani Ltd in London, Messrs R.E. Wilcox & Co, initially provided the centre accommodation for a month. Later the centre hired its own two-room space at Grosvenor Gardens, Victoria. Jinnah remitted £1000 to Messrs R.E. Wilcox & Co for the expenses and asked them to keep an eye on the work of the centre and the secretary and refer to him any expenditure that the secretary might ask beyond the office requirement.[357] In September 1946, Altaf Husain (1900–1968), editor of the *Dawn*, was sent to England who wrote pamphlets for distribution by the centre.[358] On his suggestion, it brought out a monthly 'Muslim India Information Bulletin'; its first issue appeared on the day of centre's inauguration, i.e. 13 January 1947. Although these activities made little noticeable impact on the British policies but these did influence the Indian Muslim community in England.

The least expensive and easiest way to communicate news abroad was to establish contact with the foreign correspondents and representatives of news agencies based in India. This is what Jinnah did after 1940, especially with the correspondents and representatives of news agencies from England and the US.[359] The All-India Muslim League made no serious attempt to have even a rudimentary infra structure in the US although Jinnah's desire to explain the Pakistan scheme to the American people is reflected in his unfulfilled ambition to write a book for them on the Indian Muslims. Two organizations, India League of America and the India Welfare League Inc., deliberated upon issues relating to India's freedom. Dr Mobarak Ali Khan was secretary of the first and president of the second League.[360] The India League used to organize lectures which usually had an 'anti-Pakistan' slant.[361] One Indian Muslim, S. Muzaffar Ahmad, an 'Investment Economist and India Trade Consultant', who lived on 120-Broadway, Room 2807, New York City, was among those who wrote in defence of the League and used to send copies of pro and anti-Pakistan writings published in the American press including the *New York Times* to Abdullah Haroon and Jinnah. Abdullah Haroon sent to him as well as the office-bearers of the India League literature about the All-India Muslim League.[362] However, Jinnah did not encourage Muzaffar Ahmad when he wanted to organize an American branch of the All-India Muslim League and asked through Abdullah Haroon for financial assistance.[363] The India Welfare League Inc. extended 'full support' to the All-India Muslim League but in return sought its assistance for the enactment of a bill to allow the Indians to become US citizens.[364] Early in 1943, Begum Jahan Ara Shahnawaz who was lady-in-charge of the women's section of the information department of the Government of India visited the US and delivered a series of lectures on the Pakistan scheme to dispel the Congress propaganda although she had not yet rejoined the League after her expulsion from the party on the issue of national defence council; Sir Zafrullah Khan was with her during this visit and he also informed the League leadership about this situation. Both of them participated in the Herald Tribune Forum in New York on 'Islam and Democracy', which was organized on 8–10 November 1942. On her return to India, she conveyed to Jinnah through her cousin, Mian Bashir Ahmad, that the League should send a deputation consisting of Khaliquzzaman, M.A.H. Ispahani and a student to the US to explain the Pakistan scheme because the US representatives would have a 'powerful voice' at the peace conference.[365] But before the general elections in India, the All-India Muslim League simply sent the party literature for distribution in the US.[366] Americans' knowledge of the Pakistan demand remained dismal, as pointed out at the time by an American scholar sympathetic to the Muslim cause.[367] It was during the deadlock following the League's withdrawal of acceptance of the Cabinet Mission Plan that Jinnah received an invitation from the New York Herald Tribune Forum to explain the Muslim case for independence to the American public. Instead of himself participating in the forum, Jinnah sent Begum Shahnawaz, who had by then rejoined the League, and M.A.H. Ispahani. After attending the forum, they toured several cities in the US for two weeks to explain the Pakistan demand. The acquaintances that Ispahani made in this visit were of great help to him when he was sent to the US as Pakistan's first ambassador after Independence. The few Muslim students then studying in the US played a useful role. They wrote in the press in defence of the Pakistan demand; and Mohammad Amin Khan Tarin as editor of the *Muslim News Bulletin* of the association of Muslim students in America brought out a special Pakistan issue in July 1947.[368]

The Indian Muslims living in countries like South Africa and Sri Lanka supported the Pakistan demand and occasionally contributed to the League fund but their number was too small to make much impact.[369] The Chinese did not take active interest in political developments in India but a few Chinese delegations did come to India and met with leaders of the Indian political parties. In mid-1938, a Chinese Near East Goodwill Mission came to India, and the League was among those parties that entertained its members.[370] During the Second World War, in February 1942, Marshal Chiang Kai-Shek visited India, and met with the Congress and League leaders. Generalissimo displayed lack of knowledge of the Indian situation—and he did not hide this fact from Jinnah—but he was visibly closer to the Congress than the League and at the end of his visit extended support to the Congress position, by calling on Britain to 'transfer real power' to India, without making any reference to the Pakistan demand. Jinnah was obviously disappointed and criticised his observations.[371] It is, however, interesting to note that the Communist Party of China was the only party of China that 'openly sided with the Muslims of India' and supported their demand for Pakistan; Professor Ahmad Ali, author of the *Twilight in India* and professor of English at the Presidency College, Calcutta, who was then visiting professor at the National Central university, Nanking (China), communicated this information to Jinnah in a detailed 'confidential' note entitled 'China, Muslims and Pakistan: A Brief Survey of the Chinese Attitude to Muslims in China and India'.[372]

(D) FINANCES

No political party can function efficiently and successfully without sufficient funds at its disposal to support its activities. Before 1936, the All-India Muslim League had an erratic flow of funds; and like the other Indian political parties, it had a loose system of accounting and auditing. The tendency to economize was absent when the party had plenty of funds which forced it to borrow in times of financial constraints. Jinnah had once advised the Muslims to handle the party funds carefully to negate the impression that the Indians generally mismanaged public funds.[373] He had kept himself totally aloof from the management of party finances during his tenure as its 'permanent' president; the honorary secretary or the party office used to handle the funds. After the Khilafat movement, the All-India Muslim League had frequently faced financial crises and borrowed money even for routine expenses. On its revival in 1935–36, it inherited debt rather than funds. After that, Jinnah played a key role in establishing the League on reasonably sound financial footing. The party had an elected treasurer, Raja of Mahmudabad, and two auditors, Haji Abdullah Haroon—Husain Imam succeeded him on his death—and Haji Abdussattar Haji Essak Sait; and they were all re-elected to these offices every year.[374] Still, Jinnah used to get the party funds regularly audited by a chartered firm—as he did his personal financial assets—and the annual audited statements were made public.[375] No funds could be disbursed or advanced without his authorization for which the party formally gave him the authority. Funds were given to individual Leaguers or branch Leagues in advance for a specific purpose but whoever was the recipient he had to give a detailed statement of expenditure along with necessary receipts. The sources of the League's finances were the same as before its revival: subscription fees from ordinary members, council members, delegates and visitors to the all-India sessions, direct donations/contribution from individuals, and 10 per cent of the provincial Muslim Leagues' collections other than those that they received in the form of donations.[376] The scale of annual fees was drastically reduced: an ordinary member now paid on his/her enrolment only two annas—one-eighth of a rupee that was half of the Congress membership fee—and a central councillor paid Rs 6. Expulsion of some top Leaguers on different charges made warnings from the central office for non-payment of dues look credible; and unlike the pre-1936 phase, when arrears were often waived, now there were no lapses or arrears on this count. A person could not be registered as an ordinary member unless he had paid his dues. The central honorary secretary formally communicated to the provincial Muslim Leagues that if they failed to send their required 10 per cent contributions, they would not be entitled to elect their representatives on the central council for the following year.[377] In addition, the phenomenal rise in the popularity of the All-India Muslim League prompted the Leaguers to pay on time all the requisite dues. After 1936, the party never faced any financial crisis due to judicious management of funds under Jinnah's supervision although these funds in real terms and in comparison to the Congress were very small.

During 1937–47, Jinnah issued formal appeals for funds for the All-India Muslim League thrice and one time each for the State of Pakistan (1947), the Palestine and the victims of calamities like the Bengal famine (1943) and Bihar massacre (1946).[378] He did not give a call for donations for the League immediately on his return from England. Funds for the Bombay session had been raised locally; and in the provincial elections of 1937, the party candidates had themselves supported their election campaigns. The first appeal that Jinnah made was after the elections when he embarked upon the reorganization of the All-India Muslim League. On 7 June 1937, he appealed to the Muslims to send him directly their donations at his postal address— Little Gibbs Road, Malabar Hill, Bombay—to enable him to establish a central fund.[379] On 30–31 July, the working committee appointed a 24-member fund committee with powers to co-opt more members. All its members were prominent Muslims hailing from different provinces. Raja of Mahmudabad was elected its convenor who along with Sir Karimbhai Ibrahim functioned as its treasurers and held in trust the funds that the fund committee collected.[380] The members themselves gave donations and persuaded others to do the same; the response was quite encouraging.[381] The idea was to collect money from only rich Muslims, as one person was required to donate at least Rs 100.[382] Jinnah made the second appeal on 21 March 1942, when the All-India Muslim League needed funds for its expanded political activities and propaganda.[383] Then, his appeal was to every rich and poor Muslim 'to contribute his mite' to the League fund, called the 'Muslim National Fund', so that the party could organize the struggle for Pakistan. The appeal was the first of its kind; in the sense that it was meant to make every Muslim feel that he was a participant in the Pakistan movement.[384] After considering different ways of collecting funds, Jinnah concluded that the best way for those who wished 'to help was to send their contributions direct' to him to avoid any misrepresentation or scandal.[385] The Muslims, one Leaguer observed, had 'blind faith' in Jinnah and would 'flood [him] with money'; and he wrote to Jinnah, 'We know our generation will not get a leader like you'.[386] His observations were not far from reality. Rich Muslims contributed in thousands of rupees and the poor in a couple of rupees.[387] Even small children saved their pocket money to give their share in paisas.[388] The contributors were from every part of India, from Chittagong to the tribal areas in the north-west. The contributions were sent through cheques, drafts, postal orders, money orders and currency notes by registered insured parcels. Initially, Jinnah himself signed the receipts for the donations when their number was small.[389] And when the number of money orders ran into thousands Jinnah thanked those who were sending money by this mechanism and asked them to retain the receipts issued by the post office as acknowledgement in order to save a considerable amount of expense on postage.[390] His acknowledgement letter carried the motto: 'Love of one's country is of all human instincts the most enduring. It is in every child and it persists till death.' When the number of contributors became unmanageable, the *Dawn* began to publish at short intervals up-to-date information about province-wise contributions, which generated a spirit of competition:[391] On 19 April 1942, United Provinces was at the top of the list with total contributions of Rs 16,100,[392] but the following month, on 12 July, Bombay and Punjab with Rs 38,600 each topped the list of contributors and United Provinces had fallen to number five in the list.[393]

The third appeal that Jinnah made was on the eve of the general elections, two days after the conclusion of the Simla conference. The All-India Muslim League, he observed in a statement from Simla on 16 July 1945, needed funds to fight the general elections and appealed to the Muslims to contribute funds for the All-India Muslim League and the provincial Muslim Leagues. He disagreed with the suggestion that the central League should first collect all the funds and then distribute them among the provincial Muslim Leagues.[394] His advice was that the central League and the provincial Muslim Leagues should separately collect and manage the election funds. He asked those who wished to contribute to the central election fund to send their contributions directly to him, and repeatedly emphasized that he had not, and would not, authorize anyone to collect funds for the central League on his behalf.[395] There were still a few deviations from his direction; a glaring example was that of the Delhi provincial Muslim League which led to allegations of misuse of funds against its general secretary, Anis Hashmi (1920–1991); the central committee of action appointed Haji Abdussattar Haji Essak Sait to conduct an inquiry; and in his report, he absolved Hashmi of any responsibility.[396] The response to Jinnah's call for funds was spontaneous. There was a regular flow of funds from all parts of India. Muslims outside India in South Africa, Bahrain, Gulf, Saudi Arabia, Iran and Sri Lanka mailed their donations to Jinnah for elections and victims of riots.[397] Various League and non-League Muslim organizations including Muslim/Memon Chambers of Commerce presented him 'purses' at formal functions.[398] At one of these functions on 12 August, he asked the Muslims to give him 'silver bullets' and the League would 'finish the job'. The response from Kadayanallur to this suggestion was quite interesting: the Camalia Muslim Women Association sent him eighty tolas of silver in the shape of 'Silver Bullets' and Batlul Islam Sangam gave him a silver sword weighing eighty tolas.[399] The total amount collected for the central election fund is not available but according to a statement of receipts and payments issued by the All-India Muslim League for the period from 27 May 1942, to 30 November 1945, the total collection less bank charges was Rs 1,951,577; and this amount was in addition to the investments that the League had made out of the election fund.[400]

Among the other appeals that Jinnah made was one for donations to the Bengal Relief Fund to help the victims of the Bengal famine and cyclone. The Calcutta Muslim Chamber of Commerce managed this fund. Donations came not only from within India but also from abroad, from Saudi Arabia, South Africa and Palestine; King Ibne Saud personally contributed Rs 10,000 to the relief fund.[401] Jinnah used to forward to the Calcutta chamber all the cheques that he received for the Bengali victims. The chamber closed the Bengal Relief Fund on

31 December 1943, with a total collection of Rs 677,662: Rs 512,169 in cash and Rs 165,500 in kind. But even after the closure, the fund continued to receive contributions; and the total collections as on 4 January 1944 were Rs 692,910; the help in kind was in addition to this amount.[402] Then, after the Bihar tragedy in October–November 1946, Jinnah appealed for contributions to help the victims and established a 'Quaid-i-Azam Mohammad Ali Jinnah Bihar Relief Fund'. The response to his appeal was 'remarkable indeed and the subscriptions poured in with rapidity, which necessitated special staff to be engaged by the Habib Bank, Delhi'.[403] The central League maintained these funds and audited its accounts separately.[404] The last appeal that Jinnah made was for the 'Pakistan Fund' after the 3 June Plan in order to support and build the new state of Pakistan.[405] At the time of Independence, the League transferred this fund to the Government of Pakistan.

NOTES

1. Three members, Sir Mohammad Yaqub, Husain Imam and Abdul Matin Choudhry, signed the report. For minutes of the committee, see AFM, vol. 111, no. 54.
2. Its members were: Sayyid Mohammad Ashraf (convener/secretary), Masudul Hasan, S.M. Husain, Maulana Shaukat Ali, Sayyid Murtaza Bahadur, Husain Imam, and Mian Ghiasuddin; and the last two members did not attend any meeting. QAP, F. 25, pp. 102–9.
3. *Constitution and Rules of the All- India Muslim League (As amended up-to-date)* [Typed], AFM, vol. 111, no. 58.
4. Pirzada, *Foundations*, vol. II, pp. 320–21, 372–73 and 393.
5. AFM, vol. 142, no. 4; vol. 269, pp. 51–52 and 55.
6. For the provincial Muslim Leagues, see Chapter 8.
7. Resolution passed at the Lucknow annual session.
8. *Constitution and Rules of the Al- India Muslim League*, Delhi, May 1941, pp. 1–3.
9. For instance, see membership form (Urdu) signed by Jinnah on 2 March 1946, QAP, F. 568, pp. 173–74.
10. *Model Constitution & Rules for Provincial Muslim Leagues*, published by (Nawabzada) Liaquat Ali Khan, Delhi, n.d., pp. 1–2.
11. The subjects committee had members from: Assam 4; Bengal 14; Bihar 4; Bombay 4; Central Provinces and Berar 1; Madras 4; NWFP 4; Orissa 1; Punjab 9; Sindh 3; United Provinces 8; Central Assembly 10; and Council of State 3.
12. However, according to the constitution of the All-India Muslim League assembly party, a non-Muslim could also become a member of the central League assembly party. Z.H. Zaidi (ed.), *Jinnah Papers, Quest for Political Settlement in India, 1 October 1943–31 July 1944*, Islamabad, 2004, second series, vol. X, p. 297.
13. *The Evening News*, Bombay, 19 September 1938; and *The Light*, 24 September 1938.
14. AFM, vol. 192, no. 4.
15. Liaquat to Azmat Ali Wasti, n.d., ibid., vol. 131, no. 48.

16. Jinnah to S.K. Ghosh, 10 September 1946, SHC, Assam—I: 67.
17. Abdul Ghani (member of the legislative assembly from Bihar) to general secretary, All-India Muslim League, 24 June 1938, AFM, vol. 610.
18. For a letter to the general secretary, All-India Muslim League, 4 October 1938, see ibid., vol. 188, no. 14.
19. Resolutions proposed by Husain Mian of Phulwari Sharif and Mahmud Hasan, joint editor, the *Deccan Times*, ibid., vol. 291, p. 46; and vol. 188, no. 58a; and resolution passed by the council, ibid., vol. 247, p. 89; and QAP, F. 204, p. 121.
20. Abdul Aziz to Liaquat, 6 March 1939, AFM, vol. 128, no. 5.
21. Once, there was a proposal that any Muslim who was eligible to pay *zakat* could not become a member unless he had paid the *zakat* but it was not accepted. Mohammad Faruq to Jinnah, 13 October 1937, ibid., vol. 187, no. 9.
22. In fact, they had been invited to attend the Bombay annual session. Nazir, Amoor-i-Amma, Qadian to Shamsul Hasan, 15 April 1936, ibid., vol. 168, no. 45.
23. Ghulam Rasul (honorary secretary, Punjab provincial Muslim League) to Jinnah, 28 November 1937, QAP, F. 1091, p. 163. He requested Jinnah on behalf of Iqbal that the latter should be consulted on the issue in case Mirza Bashiruddin Mahmud, the spiritual head of the Ahmadis, contacted him.
24. 'A Leaguer' to Jinnah, 7 November 1937, ibid., F. 898, p. 79; M. Nasim, bar-at-law, Allahabad to Jinnah, 9 January 1938, ibid., F. 1093, pp. 105–7; and Ch. Mohammad Fazl (Kharagpur) to Jinnah, 9 May 1939, ibid., F. 870, pp. 11–12.
25. Ibid., F. 654, pp. 38–41.
26. Jinnah to J.R. Deen, 23 May 1940, ibid., F. 873, p. 328. When Liaquat asked Shamsul Hasan about possible further 'definition' of the word 'Muslim' by a constitutional amendment, he responded that such an amendment would 'cause havoc and create religious and sectional controversies in the League'. He pointed out that it was the *fatwa* of the founder of the Ahmadi community himself, regarding Muslims other than Ahmadis as *kafirs*, which had 'dug a wide gulf' between the Muslims and Ahmadis. Shamsul Hasan to honorary secretary, All-India Muslim League, 9 August 1940, AFM, vol. 467, pp. 17–19.
27. Zainulabidin's note and Jinnah's letter, *Jinnah Papers*, second series, vol. X, pp. 329 and 338–39.
28. For the text of his press conference, see QAP, F. 1117, pp. 3–4.
29. For instance, see Ghulam Hasan Butt to Jinnah, 4 May 1944, AFM, vol. 162, no. 42; Chaudhri Mohammad Siddique to Jinnah, 6 June 1944, QAP, F. 878, pp. 148–51; Mohammad Shafi to Jinnah, n.d., ibid., F. 652, pp. 1–2; and Hamid Nizami to Jinnah, 5 June 1944; and *Nawa-i-Waqt* (Lahore), 25 February 2006.
30. Jinnah to Abdul Hamid Nizami, 13 June 1944, QAP, F. 1102, p. 284; and *Dawn*, 11 June 1944. For notice of a resolution by Maulana Abdul Hamid Badauni against the admission of Ahmadis into the League, see agenda for the central council meeting, 30 July 1944, AFM, vol. 287, no. 50.
31. Izzuddin Pal to Quaid-i-Azam, 1 August 1944, QAP, F. 878, pp. 242–43. The following year, on 31 May, the general secretary of the Majlis-i-Ahrar-i-Islam, in a letter to general secretary, All-India Muslim League, called upon the Muslim members of the central assembly including Jinnah, Liaquat, M.A. Kazmi, Zafar Ali Khan, Abdul Ghani and Ghulam Bhik Nairang to introduce a bill in the central assembly to declare the Ahmadis as a non-Muslim community. AFM, vol. 464, pp. 35–36.
32. For letters from Habibur Rahman to Shabbir Ahmad Usmani, see Muhammad Anwarul Hasan (comp.), *Anwar-i-Usmani*, Karachi, 1966, pp. 155–64. One

Ahmadi, Fateh Mohammad Siyal, who was elected as an independent candidate, joined the League after the elections. QAP, F. 1136, p. 312.

33. For his letter to Jinnah, 2 March 1947, see QAP, F. 290, p. 1. He informed Jinnah that Sir Zafrullah Khan had persuaded Khizr Hayat and Muzaffar Ali Qizilbash to resign from the chief ministership and ministership, respectively.

34. Liaquat to Jinnah, ibid., F. 335, pp. 5–8; and Husain Malik to Jinnah, 21 May 1937, ibid., F. 387, p. 1.

35. Pirzada, *Foundations*, vol. II, pp. 480–81.

36. At one time, Jinnah had seriously thought of engaging Malik Ghulam Mohammad (1895–1956) or Mian Mumtaz Daultana as the 'general organizing secretary'. QAP, F. 132, p. 73; and F. 846, p. 31.

37. It was in July 1944, that Jinnah engaged Khurshid Hasan Khurshid as his personal secretary on regular basis. Earlier, he had employed individuals on part-time basis. Naimul Haq to Jinnah, 8 February 1940, ibid., F. 1098, p. 174; and Khurshid Hasan to the director BBC, New Delhi, 28 August 1944, ibid., F. 921, pp. 10–11.

38. Honorary joint secretary to provincial Muslim League, 22 August 1938, AFM, vol. 131, no. 20; and Hasan Reyaz to Jinnah, 11 January 1940, QAP, F. 833, p. 15.

39. The three sections were: Section A — *Organization*: Framing of model constitution, Women's Subcommittee, Complaints and disciplinary action against any Muslim Leaguer, office-bearer or individual and allied matters; Economic Uplift: Education, National Guards, and [Press] Cuttings Bureau; Section B — *Socio-religious Reforms*: Civil Defence Committees, Parliamentary Board, and Library; Miscellaneous A: General Correspondence incidental to the office of the Honorary Secretary and allied matters; and Section C — *Establishment*: Accounts, Printing and Purchases, Miscellaneous B: General management in connection with holding of meetings and allied matters of miscellaneous nature. [AFM, vol. 539, pp. 13–14.]

40. Zafar Ahmad Ansari to Dewan Abdul Basit (secretary, Assam provincial Muslim League), 13 September 1944, ibid., vol. 417.

41. Ibid., vol. 540, p. 6.

42. Jinnah's observation, Pirzada, *Foundations*, vol. II, p. 481.

43. QAP, F. 335, p. 206.

44. Perhaps, as a mark of respect, he wrote almost all his letters to Jinnah in his own handwriting.

45. *Hindustan Times*, 5 December 1938; and Liaquat to S.M. Ismail, 4 February 1941, AFM, vol. 243, p. 24.

46. *Civil & Military Gazette*, 25 February 1941.

47. AFM, vol. 174, no. 63; vol. 199, no. 9; vol. 263, no. 1; vol. 285, no. 40; vol. 286, no. 60; and vol. 288, p. 45.

48. Hasrat Mohani voted against the motion; and the participants allowed him to speak on it only after Jinnah's intervention. *Dawn*, 12 April 1942.

49. Section 33 of the *Constitution and Rules of the All-India Muslim League*, published by (Nawabzada) Liaquat Ali Khan, Delhi, January 1944.

50. Abdus Sami, president, Bijnor district Muslim League, 20 October 1939, QAP, F. 578, 28–33.

51. Jinnah to Shamsul Hasan, 6 November 1937, AFM, vol. 179, no. 105; Liaquat to Jinnah, 10 November 1938, QAP, F. 335, p. 11; Ibrahim Husain to Jinnah, 16 November 1937, ibid., F. 994, p. 6; Huseyn Shaheed Suhrawardy to Jinnah, 16 November 1937, ibid., F. 458, p. 13; Shamsul Hasan to Jinnah, 23 November 1937,

AFM, vol. 179, nos. 108 and 111; and Barkat Ali to Jinnah, 3 December 1937, QAP, F. 215, p. 8.

52. Ziauddin to Jinnah, 9 and 15 November 1938, QAP, F. 203, pp. 5 and 8.

53. Ahmad Yar [Daultana] to Quaid-i-Azam, 12 November 1938, ibid., F. 760, p. 316; and Amir Ahmad Khan to Jinnah, 17 December 1938, ibid., F. 1129, p. 256; and for rumours about his retirement from active politics, see the *Bombay Sentinel*, 24 September 1938.

54. He conducted an extensive tour of South India after his recovery in June 1941.

55. Jinnah to Abdul Hameed Khan, 3 May and 30 July 1941, QAP, F. 321, pp. 50 and 51; Jinnah to Ikhlas, 8 April 1941, ibid., 293, p. 1; Ziauddin to Jinnah, 12 April 1941, ibid., F. 519, p. 28; Mohammad Ashraf to Jinnah, 12 April 1941, ibid., F. 519, p. 24; Jinnah to Begum Aizaz Rasul, 24 April 1941, ibid., F. 428, p. 6; Jinnah to Qazi Isa, 5 May 1941, ibid., F. 302, p. 67; Abdul Aziz to Jinnah, 8 May 1941, ibid., F. 29, p. 3; and M.O.A.K. (Nizam) to Jinnah, 29 May 1941, ibid., F. 29, p. 20. See also letters in ibid., F. 149.

56. Yusuf and Mahmud Haroon to Jinnah, 18 December 1941, ibid., F. 1130, p. 180; and Abdul Hamid Khan to Liaquat, 4 December 1941, AFM, vol. 266, p. 53.

57. Liaquat to Jinnah, 18 and 29 June 1943, AFM, vol. 481, nos. 24 and 25; and Abdur Rauf Shah to Jinnah, 24 June 1943, ibid., vol. 443, no. 65.

58. Ahmad Said to Jinnah, 19 June 1943, SHC, Hd-II: 77; Hameed Nizami to Jinnah, 30 July 1943, QAP, F. 1099, p. 181; Liaquat to Jinnah, 6 and 19 August 1943, AFM, vol. 481, pp. 27–29 and 32; Chundrigar to Liaquat, 7 August 1943, ibid., vol. 286, 31; and resolutions of the central working committee (on 13 November 1943) and central council (on 14 and 15 November), ibid., vol. 142, no 15 and vol. 286, no. 60.

59. Jinnah to Ahmad Ispahani, 20 May 1944, SHC, Bengal-III: 28; Jinnah to Mohammad Ali Chaiwala, 18 April, 4 and 19 May, 1944, QAP, F. 80, pp. 4, 11 and 13; Jinnah to Abdul Hamid Khan, 24 June 1944, ibid., F. 321, p. 55; Liaquat to Jinnah, 18 August 1944, and Jinnah to Liaquat, 19 August, AFM, vol. 481, pp. 54, 55 and 61.

60. Jinnah to Iftikhar Husain Mamdot, 25 March 1945, SHC, Pb-III: 8; QAP, F. 784, p. 80; K.H. Khurshid, *Memories of Jinnah* (ed. Khalid Hasan) Lahore, 1999, pp. 90–91 and Shamsul Hasan, *Plain Mr. Jinnah*, pp. 89, 92–93.

61. Jinnah to Mumtaz Daultana, 7 June 1945, SHC, Pb-III: 34. Jinnah wrote letters of similar content to Nazimuddin, Maulana Bhashani and others. [SHC, Bengal-III: 7; and SHC, Assam-I: 55.].

62. Jinnah to Dr Jal Patel, 31 December 1945, QAP, F. 185, p. 5.

63. For instance, see ibid., F. 228, pp. 7–8. The Assam and NWFP provincial Muslim Leagues might have overcome the crises that they faced in March 1945, had Jinnah not been seriously ill.

64. The most prolific correspondent was Mrs Rallia Ram of Lahore who would send him press cuttings along with her lengthy reports.

65. *Civil & Military Gazette*, 26 March and 2 April 1940.

66. For his dislike of intolerance, see Jinnah to Zafarul Mulk, 15 September 1944, SHC, MISC-I: 61.

67. AFM, vol. 458, p. 80.

68. *Star of India*, 7 January 1937.

69. See his address to the Aligarh Muslim University students' union on 1 April 1939, ibid., 8 April 1939.

70. Waheed, *Nation's Voice: Towards Consolidation*, p. 472.

71. *Star of India*, 7 August 1939.
72. Speech in Bombay, *Dawn*, 28 December 1945.
73. The *Time* magazine of 22 April 1946 carried his photograph on its cover page. Also see his letter of 24 June [1946], QAP, F. 199, p. 107.
74. Khwaja Hasan Nizami to Jinnah, 3 May 1937, ibid., F. 24, pp. 60–61.
75. M.M.S. Ispahani to Jinnah, 21 May 1939, ibid., F. 33, p. 27. In May 1939, Jinnah did not allow the Bombay Muslim Leaguers to organize a 'League week' to counter the Ahrar propaganda.
76. When Jinnah was to meet the viceroy, leaders of the Scheduled Castes including Dr B.R. Ambedkar, asked Jinnah to speak on their behalf as well [ibid., F. 175, p. 4; F. 192, p. 14; and F. 923, pp. 5, 11, 12 and 67]. See also secretary, Dravidian committee of Conjeeveram to Jinnah, 31 August 1942; and Jinnah to secretary, Dravidian committee, ibid., F. 27, pp. 94 and 96; Jinnah to E.V. Ramaswami, 17 August 1944, SHC, Non-Muslims-I: 34; Mrs K.L. Rallia Ram to Jinnah, 3 November [1946], ibid., F. 1057, pp. 104–6.
77. Jinnah to Azad Samdani, 22 May 1941, ibid., F. 874, p. 113.
78. For his letter of 21 June 1944, see ibid., F. 1092, p. 254.
79. Presidential address at the special Pakistan session of the Punjab Muslim Students Federation, 2 March 1941, and presidential address at the Aligarh Muslim University students' union on 10 March, Jamil-ud-Din Ahmad (ed.), *Speeches and Writings of Mr. Jinnah*, vol. I, Lahore, 1960, pp. 221–37 and 237–44.
80. QAP, F. 24, p. 52.
81. One, Amir Hasan Mirza believed him to be the 'Khalifa of Islam to lead the Muslim world to be free from the subjugation of the West through Pakistan'. Mirza's letter to Jinnah, 5 May 1946, ibid., 1107, p. 218; also see telegram of the Muslim Navajavan League, Calcutta, to Jinnah, AFM, vol. 198, no. 40; Hatim Alavi to Quaid-i-Azam, 23 December 1945, SHC, Sindh-VII: 25; Shamim Faruqi to Jinnah, 10 June 1938, QAP, F. 976, p. 7; Sharifur Rahman to Quaid-i-Azam, 17 July 1938, ibid., F. 1095, pp. 206–8; Abdul Wali Khan to general secretary, All-India Muslim League, 10 March 1940, AFM, vol. 214, no. 8; Hasan Murtaza to Jinnah, 25 July 1937, QAP, F. 26, pp 300–303; Abdul Hamid Shamim, secretary, Iqbal Association, Vaniyambadi (North Arcot) to Jinnah, 30 December 1938, ibid., F, 899, pp. 161–62, and Hasrat Mohani in *Dawn*, 28 December 1945.
82. For a note on the title 'Quaid-i-Azam', see Sharif al Mujahid, *Quaid-i-Azam Jinnah: Studies in Interpretation*, Karachi, 1981. Appendix 1.
83. QAP, F. 304, p. 136.
84. Liaquat to Bahauddin Ahmad Gilani, 9 October 1941, AFM, vol. 277, p. 10.
85. QAP, F. 1015, p. 31.
86. *Zamindar*, 22 May 1938; Mohammad N. Ahmad to Jinnah, 31 May 1938, QAP, F. 1056, pp. 45–46; Farmuzal Haq to Jinnah, 17 May 1938, ibid., F. 867, pp. 162–63; and Abdul Matin to Jinnah, 21 August 1938, ibid., F. 244, p. 27.
87. Ahmad Yar Daultana to Jinnah, 18 and 21 May 1938, ibid., F. 255, pp. 10–11 and 20–21.
88. Ibid., F. 823, pp. 83–85, 95.
89. Liaquat to Jinnah, 10 May 1940, ibid., F. 335, pp. 199–200.
90. Statement by A.R. Siddiqi and the editorial, *Star of India*, 8 December 1939; and Fazlul Haq's statement and comments by others, QAP, F. 119, pp. 2, 4–5 and 8–9; and AFM, vol. 118, no. 69; and vol. 129, nos. 1, 2 and 5.
91. Liaquat to members of the working committee, 7 and 17 October 1939, AFM, vol. 128, no. 43 and 46.

92. Ibid., vol. 247, p. 115.

93. Resolution passed by the working committee on 3–6 February 1940, ibid., vol. 129, no. 15.

94. These amendments regarding disciplinary action and disaffiliation were made at the Lahore and Madras annual sessions.

95. In December 1938, they were also made *ex-officio* members of all the provincial councils and working committees.

96. According to an amendment made in the constitution in April 1943, the honorary secretary, in special cases and for good reasons, could extend with the approval of the president the time for election by a provincial Muslim League.

97. In April 1941, another amendment extended the period to three months.

98. Jinnah to Williams, 18 March 1942, QAP, F. 107, pp. 18–22.

99. AFM, vol. 253, pp. 69–70.

100. Ibid., vol. 263, p. 90; and vol. 285, p. 106.

101. Liaquat to Jinnah, 29 June 1943, ibid., vol. 481, pp. 25, 26.

102. Ibid., vol. 122, no. 53; and vol. 133, no. 9.

103. *Constitution and Rules of the All-India Muslim League*, published by Liaquat Ali Khan, Honorary Secretary of the All-India Muslim League, January 1944, Delhi, n. d., pp. 13, 15–16.

104. AFM, vol. 269, p. 52; Liaquat to Jinnah, 31 January 1944, ibid., vol. 481, p. 47; and vol. 142, no. 27; and also see Chapter 10.

105. Ibid., vol. 142, no. 56.

106. *Times of India* 28 October 1938.

107. *IAR*, 1939, vol. I, p. XXIII; and QAP, F. 203, pp. 6–7.

108. A.H. Ghaznavi was the one expelled for his public criticism of the League policy. Liaquat to Abdul Halim Ghaznavi, 18 April 1939, AFM, vol. 252, pp. 61–62; *Statesman*, 19 April 1939; and working committee's resolution passed in its meeting on 2–3 July 1939, AFM, vol. 168, no. 30.

109. AFM, vol. 190, no. 12; QAP, F. 812, p. 2; and F. 1097, p. 118.

110. See Chapter 5.

111. Maqbool Mahmood to Jinnah, 21 February 1938, QAP, F. 134, p. 20; and Ahmad Yar Daultana to Jinnah, 16 February 1938, ibid., F. 671, pp. 4–5.

112. Ahmad Yar Daultana to Jinnah, 13 January 1939, ibid., F. 255, p. 24.

113. Mian Amiruddin, *Yaad-i-Ayyam*, Lahore, 1983, p. 64; and Ikram Ali Malik (comp.), *Muslim League Session 1940 & the Lahore Resolution (Documents)*, Islamabad, 1990, p. xii.

114. QAP, F. 321, p. 46.

115. Jinnah to Khuhro, 9 December 1942, ibid., F. 365, p. 104.

116. Those who signed the invitation were: Hashim Gazdar, G.M. Sayed, Yusuf Haroon, Fazlullah, G. Allana, Ayub Khuhro and Abdul Majid Sindhi.

117. Jinnah to Aurangzeb, 4 May and 12 July 1944, *Jinnah Papers*, second series, vol. X, pp. 335 and 559; and Ziauddin to Liaquat, 4 May 1944, AFM, vol. 342, no. 90.

118. AFM, vol. 345, no. 11.

119. Jinnah to Mumtaz Daultana, 7 June 1945, SHC, Pb-III: 34.

120. Resolution passed by the All-India Muslim League council at its Delhi meeting on 20 March 1938, AFM, vol. 246, p. 55.

121. M.M.S. Ispahani to Jinnah, 4 December 1937, QAP, F. 762, pp. 3–4 and 4–17, enclosing draft rules of the Muslim National Guards prepared by him and revised by M.A. Chaiwala; M.M.S. Ispahani to secretary, reception committee,

All-India Muslim League, AFM, vol. 170, no. 37; and for opposition to the scheme, see Ahmad Saeed (Chhatari) to Jinnah, 23 September 1938, QAP, F. 160-A, pp. 561–62.

122. M.M.S. Ispahani sent 50 copies of a scheme entitled 'Plea for Muslim National Guards' by F.K. Khan Durrani to the central League. See his letter to Jinnah, 1 December 1938, QAP, F. 1094, p. 300; and F. 1095, p. 149. M.M.S. Ispahani was convener of the subcommittee headed by Nawab of Chhatari.

123. Its members were Raja of Mahmudabad (convener), Mian Ziauddin (NWFP), Yusuf Haroon (Sindh) and Sayyid Amjad Ali (Punjab). For Unionist opposition to the idea, see Ziauddin to M.A. Jinnah, ibid., F. 49, p. 13.

124. Ibid., F. 335, pp. 58 and 71 and 302, p. 40. On the approval of the Muslim National Guard scheme, M.M.S. Ispahani handed over the record and funds to the provincial Muslim League president. Ibid., 312, p. 39.

125. For details, see resolution of the central working committee passed on 15–17 June 1940, AFM, vol. 129, no. 28; draft 'Muslim National Guard' with corrections, QAP, F. 111, pp. 40–60; honorary secretary, All-India Muslim League to presidents and secretaries of the provincial Muslim Leagues, 4 November 1941, AFM, vol. 325; and constitution and rules of the Muslim National Guard, as approved by the Central Committee of Action, 8 September 1946, Waheed, *Nation's Voice*, vol. V, pp. 398–604.

126. AFM, vol. 129, no. 28; vol. 137, no. 3; and vol. 264, nos. 30 and 42; and QAP, F. 352, pp. 9–12; F. 828, p. 24; and F. 1098, pp. 292–93; and *IAR*, 1942, vol. I, p. 84.

127. AFM, vol. 192, nos. 4 and 10.

128. Nawab Ismail to general secretaries of the provincial Muslim Leagues, 18 May 1944, ibid., vol. 155, no. 62.

129. Ibid., vol. 180, nos. 27, 31, 66–68. The Punjab Muslim National Guards brought out a weekly *Saadat*. For Quaid's message of 24 April 1945, to the weekly, see QAP, F. 579, pp. 102–4.

130. Khurshid Enver to Quaid-i-Azam, 26 March [1946], QAP, F. 1331, pp. 1–2; and chairman, committee of action to chief organizer, 14 August 1946, AFM, vol. 182, no. 8.

131. Waheed, *Nation's Voice: Towards Consolidation*, p. 500.

132. For an account of their role, see Sarfaraz Hussain Mirza, *Muslim Women's Role in the Pakistan Movement*, Lahore, 1969.

133. Speech on 7 February, *Pioneer*, 9 February 1938.

134. *Resolutions of the All-India Muslim League from October 1937, to December 1938*, Delhi, n. d., pp. 58–60; and QAP, F. 813, p. 13.

135. For an account of the 'Muslim League Week' observed in Lahore and Bombay in 1939, see Fatima Begum to Fatima Jinnah, 12 May 1939, QAP, F. 1097, p. 150, and also pp. 156–58.

136. AFM, vol. 155, no. 29; an vol. 263, pp. 14–15, 33.

137. QAP, F. 561, p. 46.

138. Ibid., F.48, pp. 11, 14–15.

139. Abdullah Haroon to Hasrat Mohani, 23 May 1939, ibid., F. 48, p. 38.

140. Ibid., F. 274, pp. 56–61.

141. For a complete list of invitees to its first meeting in Lahore on 29 January 1939, and second meeting on 12 June 1939, see ibid., F. 48, p. 40; and F. 824, p 54. The invitees included Khaliquzzaman, Abdur Rahman Siddiqi, Liaquat Ali Khan, Sikandar Hayat, Muhammad Irfan, Akhtar Husain, Dr Abdul Latif, Abdus Sattar Kheiri, Sajjad Hyder Yaldrum, Ghulam Rasul Mehr and Abdul Majid Salik.

142. Ibid., F. 427, pp. 1–2.

143. Press note, ibid., F.48, pp. 14–15.

144. Ali Mohammad Rashidi to Jinnah, 5 June 1940, ibid., F. 427, pp. 1–2.

145. Liaquat's letter to the provincial Muslim Leagues, 16 November 1937, AFM, vol. 187, no. 70.

146. The council itself gave affiliation to some provincial Muslim Leagues and where further scrutiny was required, it appointed subcommittee(s) to decide the issue of affiliation. Ibid., vol. 129, no. 15.

147. Jinnah to Liaquat, 6 July 1938, ibid., vol. 246.

148. Naimul Haq to Liaquat, 17 January 1940, ibid., vol. 184, no. 45; assistant secretary, All-India Muslim League, to Naimul Haq, secretary, publicity committee, Bihar provincial Muslim League, 29 January 1940, ibid., vol. 184, no. 46; and resolution on the agenda of the central council meeting held on 23 February 1941, ibid., vol. 263, p. 32A.

149. Liaquat to Jinnah, 1 October 1941, and circular notice by Liaquat, 24 September 1941, ibid., vol. 480, pp. 5–6.

150. The provincial Muslim Leagues were urged to enrol at least 10 per cent of the Muslim population as primary members and 1 per cent as Muslim National Guard volunteers. *Dawn*, 2 November 1941.

151. Minutes of the meeting held on 28 October 1941, and general letter from the honorary secretary, All-India Muslim League, to presidents and honorary secretaries of all the provincial Muslim Leagues dated 4 November, AFM, vols. 159 and 325.

152. *Dawn*, 19 April 1942.

153. For details about the process of organization of the civil defence committees, see AFM, vols. 314–16 and 318–19.

154. For duties of the provincial civil defence committees as defined by the central civil defence committee, see ibid., vol. 303, pp. 4–5.

155. Jinnah to Abdul Hamid Khan, 28 February 1942, QAP, F. 875, p. 29. The party allowed this cooperation because, Jinnah said, 'the work of civil defence . . . is to help the suffering and helpless'. Statement by Nawab Ismail of 29 April 1942, AFM, vol. 304, pp. 9–10; and Maghfoor A. Ijazi to civil defence committee members, 22 April 1942, ibid., vol. 306, pp. 4–6.

156. For some members' objection to cooperation of the League committees with the 'Peoples Food Committees' of the Communist Party of India, see Haji Abdussattar H. Essak Sait to Liaquat, 6 August 1943, ibid., vol. 142, no. 9; and Shamsul Hasan to secretary, central civil defence committee, ibid., vol. 142, no. 13.

157. Three-monthly reports in Nawab Ismail to Jinnah, 14 July 1942, QAP, F. 761, pp. 53–83; Nawab Ismail to Jinnah, 1 and 29 May 1942, ibid., F. 761, pp. 2–7 and 31–39; and Zakir Ali to Quaid-i-Azam, 11 June 1942, ibid., p. 52. See also Hamidul Haq to Zakir Ali, 29 May 1942, and Zakir Ali to Hamidul Haq, 19 September, AFM, vol. 304, pp. 18, 19 and 53; Zakir Ali to Mayeenuddin, 30 July 1942, and Mayeenuddin to Zakir Ali, 12 August 1942, ibid., vol. 303, pp. 17 and 31; Abdos Sobhan to Nawab Ismail, 30 April 1942, and Nawab Ismail to Abdos Sobhan, 4 May 1942, ibid., vol. 312, 1–2.

158. For the names of the office-bearers of the provincial civil defence committees, see ibid., vol. 307, pp. 62–63.

159. For instance, see Nawab Ismail to Quaid-i-Azam, 10 August 1942; and 23 December 1942, QAP, F. 761, pp. 94–100 and 129; and Nawab Ismail to Jinnah, 2 April 1943, ibid., F. 761, pp. 165–72.

160. Nawab Ismail to Jinnah, 27 May 1943, ibid., F. 339, p. 15; and 15 June 1943, ibid., F. 761, pp. 178–192A.

161. Ibid., F. 761, pp. 122–23; and AFM, vol. 316, pp. 104–110.

162. Nawab Ismail to Jinnah, 2 April 1943, QAP, F. 761, pp. 165–172, and 172A.

163. For instance, see resolutions proposed by Afzaal Husain Qadri, Maulana Hamid Badauni and Wajid Bakhsh Kadri, AFM, vol. 264, pp 18 and 23, and vol. 286, no. 6; and also see Liaquat to Abdul Hamid Khan, [5] March 1943, ibid., vol. 264, p. 51.

164. Zakir Ali to Karimbhai Ibrahim, 29 March 1943, ibid., vol. 308, p. 78.

165. QAP, F. 761, pp. 141–42.

166. SHC, OM-I: 68 (2).

167. Nawab Ismail to presidents and secretaries of the provincial Muslim Leagues, AFM, vol. 155, no. 58.

168. Ibid., vol. 201, no. 1. For text of the civil defence committee's resolution and Nawab Ismail's letter to heads of the provincial civil defence committees, see ibid., vol. 165, nos. 33 and 34; and for record and accounts of the central civil defence committee handed over to the All-India Muslim League, see ibid., vol. 320, pp. 1 and 9–12.

169. Ibid., vol. 269, pp. 51–52.

170. *Dawn*, 26 August 1946.

171. AFM, vol. 182, no. 81; and vol. 193, pp. 51–52.

172. Ibid., vol. 155, no 62; vol. 417, p. 23; and vol. 159, no. 18.

173. Ibid., vol. 417, p. 44; and vol. 192, no. 4

174. It incurred an expenditure of Rs 134,166 from June 1945 to March 1946, and had a balance of Rs 1,269 in its account.

175. For details of the tours and other activities, see AFM, vol. 155, no. 1, 4; vol. 159, nos. 22, 25, 44, 45, 46, 50, 51, 59, 60–62, 65, 68; vol. 165, nos. 6, 7, 26, 48, 49, 54; vol. 192, no. 4; Jinnah to Liaquat, 5 February 1944, ibid., 481, p. 48; Liaquat to Jinnah, 6 February 1944, ibid., vol. 481, p. 49; and Liaquat to Nazimuddin, ibid., vol. 165, no. 91.

176. For list of Inspection Reports, see ibid., vol. 201, no. 19.

177. Ibid., vol. 165, no. 47, 59; and Zafar Ahmad Ansari to Shamsul Hasan, 29 April 1945, ibid., vol. 165, no. 88.

178. For 'Uniform Procedure for Provincial Leagues', see ibid., vol. 155, no. 39; and also see four-page printed letter issued by Zafar Ahmad Ansari to honorary secretaries of the provincial Muslim Leagues, 8 December 1944, ibid., vol. 159.

179. Ibid., vol. 155, nos. 27, 28, and 38.

180. For the process of drafting the model constitution, see ibid., vol. 155, no. 62; and vol. 159, no. 9. G.M. Sayed prepared the initial draft.

181. Statement of the chairman, central Committee of Action, ibid., 181, no. 49; and his letter to the presidents/secretaries, provincial Muslim Leagues, 20 April 1945, ibid., vol. 165, no. 86; his letters of 15 and 27 June 1946, ibid., vol. 181, no. 45; and ibid., vol. 417, p. 52. See also minutes of the central working committee, ibid., vol. 142, no. 52.

182. Ibid., vol. 192, no. 3. The subcommittee consisted of Qazi Isa (convener), Siddiq Ali Khan and Yusuf Haroon.

183. For more information, see ibid., vol. 192, nos. 4 and 10.

184. Minutes of the meetings of the Women's Subcommittee with the committee of action on 26–27 March 1944, ibid., vol. 192, pp. 18–20.

185. Ibid., vol. 192, no. 3.

186. For a detailed account, see Ian Talbot, 'Planning for Pakistan: The Planning Committee of the All-India Muslim League, 1943–46', *Modern Asian Studies*, October 1994, pp. 875–89; and Dr Noreen Talha, 'Economic Planning and Committee of Action (1943–47)', *Pakistan Journal of Social Sciences*, Islamabad, December 2010, pp. 93–114.

187. Ibid., nos. 4 and 10.

188. Nawab Ismail to general secretaries of the provincial Muslim Leagues, 18 May 1944, ibid., vol. 155, no. 62. Yamin Khan was given Rs 500 per annum for secretarial and allied expenditure; and Dr Ziauddin, Haji Abdussattar and Maulvi Abdul Ghani were its members. Ibid., vol. 417, p. 40; and vol. 192, no. 10.

189. For details, see ibid., vol. 155, no 31; vol. 192, no. 4. Besides Sayed, Maulana Hamid Badauni, Maulana Ghulam Murshid, Maulana Jamal Mian, Khaliquzzaman, Raja Mahmudabad, Allama I.I. Qazi and Ali Akbar Shah were its members.

190. For the role of the Dhaka university, see M.N. Safa, 'Dacca University—Its Role in the Freedom Movement', in *A History of the Freedom Movement*, vol. IV (1936–1947), Part I & II, Karachi, 1970, pp. 300–330; and for an account of some schools and colleges, see 'Off-shoots of the Aligarh Movement', see ibid., vol. III (1906–1936) Part II, Karachi, 1963, pp. 415–444.

191. For the influence of the Ahmadis, see petition by Abdul Jabbar Kheiri to members of the University Court, AFM, vol. 433.

192. Jamiluddin Ahmad to Jinnah, 4 June and 15 August 1940, QAP, F. 199, pp. 14–15 and 30–31.

193. Wahab Kheiri to Jinnah, 27 March 1938, ibid., F. 769, pp. 16–18.

194. Ghulam Bhik Nairang after consulting Jinnah had proposed his name; and Dr Abdus Sattar Kheiri had supported his candidature from the Dehra Dun district jail. Dr Zakir Husain, the rival candidate, who had been elected to the executive council and was supported by the Congress, staged a walk-out when a motion for the postponement of the meeting was rejected. Sir Abdul Qadir and Abdullah Yusuf Ali were the other candidates; the latter might have withdrawn his name but he was in London at the time of elections. As for Abdul Qadir, even the four members who attended the meeting from the Punjab voted for Ziauddin. The court did not accept the proposal of the Hyderabad State for the election of Nawab of Chhatari as a compromise candidate. Ziauddin to Jinnah, 24 April 1941, ibid., F. 203, pp. 35–36; Abdus Sattar Kheiri to Jinnah, 27 February; and 16 August 1941, ibid., F. 362, pp. 1–3 and F. 1099, pp. 140–43; and Nazimuddin to Jinnah, 25 February 1941, ibid., F. 39, pp. 41–42.

195. After the general elections, the students' union, the Muslim League and the Muslim students' federation competed to gain influence in the university, which adversely affected its discipline. Dr Ziauddin's impatience to wind up, or control, these bodies landed him in trouble. According to one version, he virtually forced the Aligarh Muslim University League president, Manzare Alam, to leave the university, and put a ban on the *Aligarh Magazine* for writing a note on the 'Bihar martyrs'. Amidst a student protest, he was forced to resign. Dr Ziauddin, however, blamed 'a few communist students' who exploited the name of the League. The executive council did ask him to withdraw his resignation but he left the decision to Jinnah, as his term even otherwise was about to expire. For details, see Dr Ziauddin to Liaquat, 1 May 1946, AFM, vol. 435, p. 71; Abid Ahmad Ali to Quaid-i-Azam (confidential), 20 February 1947, QAP, F. 210, pp. 8–13; Dr Ziauddin to Quaid-i-Azam, 2 January 1947, ibid., F. 591, p. 3; M.M.A. Khan to Quaid-i-Azam, 18 November 1946, 27 January 1947, SHC, D-141 and 148; and Tariq Hasan, *The*

Aligarh Movement and the Making of the Indian Muslim Mind, 1857–2002, New Delhi, 2006, pp. 240–41.

196. Mohammad Yusuf, 'Students and Politics: A Student's View', *The Awakening*, vol. II, no. 3, November 1940, AFM, vol. 227, no. 41.

197. Manifesto of the pro-League candidate, QAP, F. 1115, pp. 361–64; Mohammad Noman to Jinnah, 13 January 1938, ibid., F. 1093, pp. 162–64; Shakir Hasan Khan to Liaquat, 13 February 1941, AFM, vol. 237, p. 14; and Jamiluddin Ahmad to Jinnah, 21 December 1941, ibid., F. 1092, p. 148. The students' magazine, *The Muslim University Magazine*, played an important role in inspiring the Muslim students.

198. QAP, F. 769, p. 9.

199. Ibid., F. 210, pp. 2, 5 and 7. Jamiluddin Ahmad was secretary of its publicity committee.

200. *Ittelaat* (Fortnightly), 10 January 1945; and secretary, Aligarh Muslim University League to president, United Provinces League, 7 January 1944, AFM, vol. 356, no. 1.

201. Referring to the role of children in early Islamic history, Jinnah appreciated the novelty of the idea. AFM, vol. 352.

202. For Jinnah's comments, see his presidential address to the All-India Muslim Students Federation, 27 December 1937, *IAR*, 1937, vol. II, p. 467.

203. Mohammad Noman to Quaid-i-Azam, 28 March 1939, QAP, F. 398, pp. 6–9.

204. For invitations from various students Unions and Associations from all over India, see ibid., F. 956.

205. For controversies surrounding its formation, see Mohammad Noman, *Report of the Preliminary Session, All-India Muslim Students Conference*, Aligarh, [1938] and other documents, see AFM, vol. 227.

206. For a twelve-page handwritten draft scheme of All-India Muslim Students Federation and a manifesto that Mohammad Noman sent to Jinnah, see QAP, F. 1080, pp. 1–12 and 13–17.

207. For details, see AFM, vol. 227, no. 5; and vol. 228, nos. 1 and 7.

208. QAP, F. 197.

209. Abdul Alim Darshani to Quaid-i-Azam, 18 September 1942; and Jinnah to Abdul Alim Darshani, 26 September 1942, ibid., F. 957, pp. 135–38 and 140.

210. Jinnah to Syed Sajjad Husain, Editor, Salimullah Muslim Hall Union Magazine, 20 January 1942, ibid., F. 1100, p. 21.

211. Jinnah's address to the AMU Union on 10 March 1941, AFM, vol. 227, p. 8.

212. Waheed, *Nation's Voice: United We Win*, vol. II, p. 339; and Jinnah to Anwar Husain, 22 May 1944, *Jinnah Papers*, vol. X, pp. 390–91.

213. Hameed Nizami to Jinnah, 7 and 19 May 1943, Jinnah to Hameed Nizami, 14 May 1943, QAP, F. 396, pp. 10, 11 and 12; and Jinnah to Manzoor Ilahi Rabbani, 15 November 1941, Saeed, *Quaid-i-Azam: Rare Letters*, pp. 89–90; and *Civil & Military Gazette*, 23 November 1941.

214. For his message to the Punjab Muslim Students Federation conference in Rawalpindi, see Jinnah to Manzurul Haq, 27 February 1942, QAP, F. 769, pp. 419–21.

215. Jinnah to A. Kunhabdullah, Government Muslim High School, Malappuram, 16 January 1943, ibid., F. 27, p. 251.

216. Hameed Nizami to Jinnah, 16 February 1943, ibid., F. 396, p. 6.

217. For an account of the All-India Muslim Students Federation, see Mukhtar Zaman, *Students' Role in the Pakistan Movement*, Karachi, 1978; and Muslim students'

correspondence compiled and edited in three volumes by Sarfaraz Hussain Mirza, *Muslim Students and Pakistan Movement: Selected Documents (1937–1947)*, published by the Pakistan Study Centre, University of the Punjab, 1988–89; and for an account of the Punjab branch, see Sarfaraz Hussain Mirza, *The Punjab Muslim Students Federation (1937–1947)*, Islamabad, 1991.

218. Mazharuddin to Jinnah, n. d., QAP, F. 909, p. 146; and secretary, Jamiatul Ulama-i-Hind to Jinnah, 14 January 1938, ibid., F. 1129, pp. 74–75. The Jamiatul Ulama-i-Hind propaganda against Mazharuddin allegedly contributed to his murder in his office by an unknown person. *Din-Dunia*, Delhi, 28 August 1938.

219. QAP, F. 672, pp. 12 and 13.

220. For his statement, see the *Times of India*, 9 October 1938; and for a resolution of the central council seeking *fatwas* from the *ulama*, supportive of the League position, see Waheed, *Nation's Voice: Towards Consolidation*, p. 615.

221. Shabbir Ahmad Usmani to Jinnah, 6 February 1940, QAP, 1092, pp. 50–51; and also F. 1096, p. 482.

222. For instance, see SHC, Hd-II: 54 and 55.

223. AFM, vol. 464, pp. 58–59; and Ibrahim Mir Sialkoti to Zafar Ahmad, 15 February 1946, ibid., vol. 438, p. 57.

224. Jinnah to Raja Mahmudabad, 25 February 1940, *Dawn*, 27 February 1946.

225. QAP, F. 274, p. 297.

226. For the two viewpoints, see correspondence between Jinnah and Maulana Ahmad Saeed, secretary, Jamiatul Ulama-i-Hind, in May–July 1944, following Jinnah's appeal at the Muslim Students Federation conference in Sialkot on 30 April, SHC, APMO-3–6; Raghib Ahsan to Jinnah, 13 June 1944, QAP, F. 1102, pp. 285–86; and Jinnah to Abul Wafa, president, provincial Jamiat conference, Kolhapur, 20 May 1944, ibid., F. 1102, p. 190.

227. AFM, vol. 191, no. 3.

228. The *ulama* on the subcommittee included Jamal Mian, Hamid Badauni and Ghulam Murshid.

229. For his printed circular letter of 14 March 1944, see AFM, vol. 382, pp. 16 and 39.

230. Zafar Ahmad, secretary, central committee of action to G.M. Sayed, 2 September 1944, ibid., vol. 159, no. 15; Zafar Ahmad's letter to the *ulama*, ibid., no. 77; and G.M. Sayed to Nawab Ismail, 7 September 1944, ibid., vol. 393, p. 54.

231. For a response from Mohammad Zakir, Nazim, Darul Ulum Mohammadi, to Ghulam Murtaza Shah, president Sindh, 7 May 1944, provincial Muslim League, AFM, vol. 471, p. 42.

232. After the British prime minister's announcement of 20 February 1947, the Jamiatul Ulama-i-Hind invited Jinnah to forge a united stand of all the Muslim parties for the protection of religious and political rights of the Muslims; he agreed with the proposition but appealed to Jamiatul Ulama-i-Hind members to join the League and make their 'contribution to Muslim national cause for the achievement' of Pakistan. For details, see Jinnah–Maulana Hifzur Rahman correspondence in QAP, F. 667, pp. 4–5 and F. 672, pp. 5–9.

233. After Independence, the Brelvis founded the Jamiatul Ulama-i-Pakistan.

234. QAP, F. 1118, pp. 49–51. The reservations were made vide secretary of state for India's notification No. F/14/17/B/33—Communal Representation in Services (Imperial and Provincial) Establishment Section 1—General dated 4 July 1934.

235. However, after 1940, the Union renamed itself as the All-India Post and Telegraph Muslim Employees Union with a membership of seventy thousand and had once Jinnah as its president.
236. *Eastern Times*, 31 March 1939.
237. Liaquat to H.C. Smith, secretary to the Government of India, Home Department, 12 August 1943, AFM, vol. 546, p. 90.
238. M. Inayat, secretary, All-India Railway Muslim Employees Association, to Quaid-i-Azam, 1 October 1940, ibid., vol. 552, pp. 23–24. The association also demanded representation on the railway bodies and increase in the proportion of Muslim representation from 25 to 33 per cent in view of the fact that the proportion of Muslims had gone up to about 30 per cent after the separation of Burma from India. Ibid., vol. 544, pp. 6–8.
239. In March 1941, the central assembly rejected the resolution by 48 to 17 votes. For numerous cases alleging discrimination and victimization, see Liaquat to C.E. Jones, finance department, Government of India, 29 March 1943, ibid., vol. 546; and also vols. 547–51.
240. For details, see ibid., vol. 544, and QAP, F. 203, pp. 34, 41 and 44, and F. 1118, pp. 49–51, 92–99 and 115–22. See also Liaquat's presidential address at the All-India Railway Muslim Employees Association conference in Lucknow on 29 November 1941, *Dawn*, 7 December 1941.
241. M.H. Usmani was its editor-in-chief and Firoz Ahmad its editor.
242. The All-India Post and Telegraph Muslim Employees Union also held its conference in the League pandal. For Jinnah's addresses at the All-India Railway Muslim Employees Association functions, see *Eastern Times*, 10 and 30 March 1944.
243. AFM, vol. 552, pp. 43–44 and 71.
244. Ali Imam to Jinnah, 2 July 1946, QAP, F. 254, pp. 1–2.
245. K.K. Aboo to Liaquat, 16 January 1945, AFM, vol. 552, pp. 33–35.
246. For views of the provincial Muslim Leagues, see ibid., vol. 552.
247. For his address to the Memon Chamber of Commerce and Memon Merchants' Association, see the *Star of India*, 6 June 1938.
248. For copies of these representations, see AFM, vol. 899. The Calcutta Muslim Chamber of Commerce sought his assistance to get Muslim representation on the Reserve Bank of India. A. Rahman, secretary of the Chamber to Jinnah, 7 November, QAP, F. 899, pp. 101–110.
249. For his speech and interpolations in the debate on the Bill, see Waheed Ahmad (ed.), *Quaid-i-Azam Mohammad Ali Jinnah: Speeches (in the) Indian Legislative Assembly, 1935–1947*, Karachi, 1991, pp. 336–67.
250. For the text of some of the correspondence relating to the formation of the federation, see M.A.H. Ispahani, *Quaid-e-Azam Jinnah as I Knew Him*, Karachi, 1976, pp. 113–23.
251. *Dawn*, 25 March 1944; and Jinnah to M.A.H. Ispahani, 8 April 1944, *Jinnah Papers*, Second Series, vol. X, p. 269.
252. The expenditure of thirty thousand on the Federation's office was shared by the Ispahanis (one-third), Sir Adamjee (one-third) and the rest (one-third). Ibid., F. 584, p. 5.
253. Hassan Ispahani to Jinnah, 24 April 1945, *Quaid-e-Azam Jinnah as I Knew Him*, pp. 120–21.

254. Members were from Madras 2; Sindh 2; Bombay 2; Calcutta 3; Punjab 4; Bihar 1; United Provinces 2; Delhi 2; Chittagong 1 and NWFP 1. QAP. F. 1118, pp. 24–25.

255. For instance, see resolution to this effect proposed by Abdus Sattar Kheiri and seconded by Dr Abid Ahmad Ali for the Patna annual session to be held in December 1938 although it was not moved. AFM, vol. 188, no. 68.

256. Sajjad Zaheer and one other attended the Delhi session. Sajjad Zaheer to Liaquat, 30 March 1943, and Liaquat to Sajjad Zaheer, 7 April 1943, AFM, vol. 260, pp. 3–4.

257. AFM, vol. 257. The four communists were: K.M. Ashraf, Ali Sardar Jafri, Sajjad Zaheer and A.S. Basra. In addition to them, others began to cover meetings of the League council; among them were Sayyid Shahidullah of the Bengali weekly *Janyuddha*, Romesh Chandra of the *Peoples' War* and Sohan Singh Josh, editor of the Punjabi weekly *Jang-i-Azadi*. Ibid., vol. 287, pp. 52, 56 and 67; and see also Sajjad Zaheer to Jinnah, 12 August 1944, QAP, F. 905, p. 66.

258. Sajjad Zaheer to Nawab Ismail, 10 May 1943; and Nawab Ismail to Sajjad Zaheer, 27 May 1943, AFM, vol. 309, pp. 34–35 and 56.

259. Secretary, district peoples' defence committee to Jinnah, 31 August 1943, SHC, Bengal-1: 28.

260. See a press clipping of a statement by G.M. Sayed, 17 December 1943, QAP, F. 208, p. 9.

261. Some like Hatim Alavi, Hamza Alavi's uncle, believed that deception was the modus operandi of the communists. QAP, F. 208, p. 9.

262. Abul Hashim, *In Retrospection*, Dacca, 1974, p. 79; and section on the Punjab provincial Muslim League in Chapter 8. Among the advocates for closer cooperation with the communists were G.M. Sayed and Mian Bashir Ahmad. [AFM, vol. 258; and QAP, F. 208, p. 9.] For complaints of communist influence in the Bengal presidency Muslim League, see Shahid Ahmad to Liaquat Ali Khan, 17 May 1945, AFM, vol. 42, pp. 21–25; and for Nazimuddin's views that the provincial Muslim League had been 'invaded by the communists', see Casey to Wavell, 12 January 1945, GFR, L/P&J/5/151, pp. 3–4, cited in Harun-or-Rashid, *Foreshadowing of Bangladesh*, p. 176.

263. For some editorials critical of the communists, see *Nawa-i-Waqt* (Lahore), 25 October, 1 November 1944, and 12 and 23 May 1946, in Sarfraz Husain Mirza, *Tehrik-i-Pakistan, 1944–1947*, Lahore, 1947, pp. 933–42.

264. For several resolutions moved on this issue in the central council on 25 February 1945, see AFM, vol. 288, no. 28. For instance, Qazi Isa was worried about the communist influence on the Lahore students [Qazi Isa to Jinnah, 21 January 1944, *Jinnah Papers*, Second Series, vol. X, p. 130.], and Nazimuddin was convinced that the Bengal presidency Muslim League had been 'invaded by the communists'. Casey to Wavell, 12 January 1945, GFR, L/P&J/5/151, pp. 3–4, cited in Harun-or-Rashid, *Foreshadowing of Bangladesh*, p. 176.

265. *IAR*, 1944, vol. I, p. 212.

266. AFM, vol. 232, no. 54.

267. *Star of India*, 12 May 1945, p. 6, cited in Harun-or-Rashid, *Bangladesh*, p. 177. See also Shahid Ahmad to Liaquat Ali Khan, 17 May 1945, AFM, vol. 42, pp. 21–25.

268. *Payam*, 12 April 1943; and SHC, P & P-III: 58.

269. Statements by Mohammad Ali Hoti and Faqira Khan, *Dawn*, 7 and 9 February 1947.

270. QAP, F. 1015, pp. 93–100.
271. *Report of the Honorary Secretary of the All-India Muslim League for the Year 1927*, AFM, vol. 125, no. 3; and *Annual Report of the All-India Muslim League for the Year 1928*, ibid., vol. 146, no. 42.
272. Among these newspapers were the *Civil & Military Gazette, Statesman, Times of India, Evening News of India*, and *Bombay Chronicle*.
273. Pandit Nehru stated that 'no Congress leader approves of . . . unseemly attacks against Mr Jinnah and other Muslim League leaders . . . . I apologize to Mr Jinnah, on my own as well as my colleagues' behalf'. [For his statement of 15 July 1937, see the *Muslim-Gujrat*, QAP, F. 1084, p. 21.] He made a similar statement in 1939. Jinnah on his part discouraged negative slogans against the Congress leaders. For instance, see Comrade Mohammad Husain to Quaid-i-Azam, AFM, vol. 132.
274. Jinnah had once commented that it was difficult to find 'really capable men' who would be willing 'to devote their whole time and if I can secure that body of men, we can really revolutionize our people and their activities in every department of life'. AFM, vol. 318, p. 11.
275. Among these newspapers were the *Madina* (Bijnor), *Al-Jamiat* (Delhi), *Ansari* (Delhi) and *Millat* (Delhi).
276. Newspapers like the *Inqilab* of Lahore.
277. The Montgomery (Sahiwal) district Muslim League resolved to present gold medals to these dailies for this work. Nasim Hasan to Quaid-i-Azam, 28 February 1946, QAP, F. 579, p. 114.
278. Ahmad Saeed (ed.), *The Eastern Times on Quaid-i-Azam*, Islamabad, 1983, pp. xv–xvii. After its takeover, Mian Abdul Hamid became its editor.
279. For details, see QAP, F. 1101, pp. 11–14, 41–42, 105–9 and 311.
280. For his letter to Liaquat, 21 May 1942, see AFM, vol. 138, p. 91. Jinnah discouraged the use of 'Muslim League' as the name of any newspaper because that would convey the impression that it represented the official views of the All-India Muslim League. For his letter to S.M. Shareef, who had asked him to give 'a few words of appreciation' for the weekly *Muslim League* (Urdu) issued from Bihar, see QAP, F. 445, pp. 8 and 11.
281. Iftikhar Husain Mamdot to Quaid-i-Azam, 7 June 1944, QAP, F. 372, p. 14. A.H. Khalil was its manager.
282. Hameed Nizami placed the services of the *Nawa-i-Waqt* and its staff at Jinnah's disposal. [His letter to Jinnah, 22 April 1944, ibid., F. 1102, pp. 104–5] When requested, Jinnah used to send messages to the newspaper on important occasions.
283. Iftikharuddin to Quaid-i-Azam, 28 January 1947, AFM, vol. 142, p. 2.
284. Ibid., vol. 326, p. 89.
285. More than one name indicates joint editors or editors at different times.
286. On Jinnah's appeal, Ahmad Ispahani and Sir Adamjee Dawood supported the *Star of India*, when it faced financial crisis in 1941. QAP, F. 258, pp. 1–2; and F. 1009, p. 75.
287. Jamal Mohammad, Abdul Hakim and Jalal Ibrahim constituted its Board of Directors.
288. For the League's advocacy of its case when the government demanded one thousand rupees security from the paper, see resolution No. 12 passed by the All-India Muslim League working committee, Pirzada, *Foundations*, vol. III, p. 320.
289. For a resolution of the All-India Muslim League council, criticizing the conviction of its editor, Maulana Usman Azad, in February 1941, for publishing a poem

criticizing the ideology of the Congress, see Waheed, *Nation's Voice*, vol. I, pp. 478–79.

290. Hasan Nizami to Jinnah, 21 January 1938, QAP, F. 1093, p. 146; and Jinnah to Hasan Nizami, 7 March 1938, ibid., F. 397, p. 2.

291. Jinnah to Motiwalla, 30 April 1940, ibid., F. 148, p. 9.

292. Five influential businessmen acted as the trustees of its Fund so that the capital was not exhausted, and its first issue appeared on 22 March 1942.

293. *Jinnah Papers*, Second Series, vol. X, pp. 318–19.

294. S.A. Latif was ready to get early retirement from the Osmania university to edit the English newspaper of the League but the idea was not pursued subsequently. For his letter to Jinnah, 10 June 1937, see QAP, F. 24, pp. 124–45.

295. Founded by Abdur Rasul in 1906, the *Mussalman* wound up its publication in 1935, and survived after that with the support of the New Muslim Majlis. [Abdur Rahman to Jinnah, 9 November 1936, ibid., F. 1006, p. 14.] The *Muslim Outlook* had already ceased publication. For proposals by Hasan Reyaz, see ibid., F. 1015, pp. 140–47.

296. During the War, the refusal of the government to extend it sufficient newsprint quota reduced its volume from 16 to 6 pages, which also delayed its conversion into a daily. Liaquat to Jinnah, 28 August 1944, AFM, vol. 481, p. 56; and Hasan Reyaz to Quaid-i-Azam, 1 and 25 October 1945, *Plain Mr. Jinnah*, pp. 225 and 232.

297. Ibid., F. 811, p. 190.

298. Jinnah to Liaquat, 24 July 1941, QAP, F. 335, p. 207.

299. According to Liaquat, the daily was meant 'to tell the British Government of the Muslim attitude on the current problems, to make our views known abroad against the well-organized publicity methods of our critics and also to educate the Muslims into an alert understanding of the policy upon which we should stand united'. For his printed letter dated 31 October 1942, see ibid., F. 27, p. 168.

300. On 2 September 1943, Liaquat wrote to Jinnah that the daily *Dawn* was making about 'ten thousand a month far in excess of our expectations'. [AFM, vol. 481, p. 33.] For a statement of income and expenditure of the *Dawn* for the period from 7 October 1942 to 31 March 1943, see QAP, F. 77, p. 48.

301. For the Jinnah-Liaquat correspondence, see AFM, vol. 480, pp. 62–77; Ispahani to Jinnah, 28 May 1942, QAP, F. 307, p. 168; Altaf Husain to Jinnah, 18 April [1942], ibid., F. 289, p. 1; and for the money advanced to Liaquat for this purpose, see ibid., F. 335, p. 223. Altaf Husain took over as editor in October 1946.

302. Jinnah to Liaquat, 2 August 1944, and Liaquat to Jinnah, 2 August, AFM, vol. 481, pp. 51–53. The same day, Jinnah gave Liaquat the power of attorney. Its funds were deposited in the Imperial Bank of India, Delhi; and S. Rasool & Co. Registered Accountants, the firm that used to audit the All-India Muslim League funds, audited its accounts. For instance, see QAP, F. 77, p 30; and F. 78, p. 39.

303. Waheeduddin to Jinnah, 4 November 1946, ibid., F. 1012, pp. 136–37 and 140.

304. Maratab Ali, Rafi Butt and Naseer A. Shaikh had contributed Rs 25,000 each and so did a fourth Muslim who did not want his name to be revealed. SHC, Pb-II: 14 and 19; and ibid., Pb-IV: 86.

305. The Department issued pamphlets like 'Why I Joined Muslim League?', 'It shall Never Happen Again' and 'A Nation Betrayed'.

306. Jinnah was conscious of the dearth of 'really capable and competent' Muslim journalists. [Jinnah to M.A. Husain, 16 May 1944, *Jinnah Papers*, Second Series, vol. X, p. 369.] Once, Hatim Alavi proposed that the League governments in the

provinces should institute foreign scholarships for the education of journalists in the UK, US and Australia to meet the deficiency in trained journalists but the proposal did not materialize. Hatim Alavi to Quaid-i-Azam, 13 November 1944, SHC, Sindh-II: 63.

307. QAP, F. 907, pp. 183–86; F. 1101, pp. 83–84; SHC, P & P-III: 55; and *Dawn*, 16 August 1942.

308. The provincial organizers were: Assam—M.A. Samad (*Assam Herald*, Shillong); Balochistan—Maulana Abdul Hai (*Al-Islam*, Quetta); Bengal—Habibullah Bahar (*Azad*, Calcutta); Bihar—S. Sultan Ahmad (*Ittehad*, Patna); Bombay—Dr A.H.Kazi and Sadiq (*Watan*, Bombay); Delhi—Mohammad Usman Azad (*Anjam*); Hyderabad (Deccan)—Maulana Hamid Moinuddin (*Rahbar-i-Deccan*); Madras—Abdul Latif Farooqi; NWFP—Allah Bakhsh Yusufi (*Sarhad*, Peshawar); Punjab—Maulana Abdul Majid Salik (*Inqilab*, Lahore) and Hameed Nizami (*Nawa-i-Waqt*, Lahore); Sindh—Din Mohammad (*Al-Wahid*, Karachi); and United Provinces—Dr S.N.A. Jafri (*Onward*, Lucknow) and Abdur Rauf Shah (*Haque*, Lucknow).

309. *Muslim India*, Allahabad, 1942. The All-India Muslim League funded its publication, after evaluation by a three-member (Nawab Ismail, A.M.K. Dehlavi and S.M. Shareef) committee, and Noman donated its royalty to the All-India Muslim League fund. Later on, the League provided him funds to update it but that job he could not do.

310. *Meet Mr. Jinnah*, Madras, 1944.

311. *Muhammad Ali Jinnah: A Political Biography*, Lahore, 1945. Saiyid and Noman also used the material that the All-India Muslim League and Jinnah provided them. Shaikh Mohammad Ashraf published Saiyid's work after the approval of its manuscript by Liaquat. [QAP, F. pp. 25–28; and AFM, vol. 133, no. 9; and vol. 129, no. 28.]

312. *My Leader*, Lahore, n. d.

313. More known is the collection of his speeches that Jamiluddin Ahmad compiled and Shaikh Muhammad Ashraf (Lahore) published in January 1942; by April 1946, this collection had run into fourth edition. Sharifuddin Peerzada compiled his correspondence as *Leaders' Correspondence with Mr. Jinnah*, Bombay, 1944; he continued to expand its volume by including new letters. Similarly the publication of *Letters of Iqbal to Jinnah* (Lahore, 1944) with a foreword by Jinnah himself had the same influence.

314. Pothan Joseph to Shaikh Ashraf, 16 May 1944, AFM, vol. 450, p. 10B.

315. Mohammad Sharif Toosy was headmaster of the M.B. High School, Wazirabad and in May 1943, he moved to the D.B. High School, Chawinda (Sialkot District). When, in January 1943, the secretary (Lampton Berry), office of the Representative of the President of the USA, New Delhi wanted to know the identity of M.R.T., Liaquat after consulting Jinnah declined to reveal it.

316. SHC, P & P-III: 28 and 29.

317. For details, see QAP, F. 132, pp. 9–12; F. 874, p. 146; F. 955, pp. 1–2; F. 1008, p. 12; F. 1101, p. 169; and F. 1120, 53–60; and SHC, P & P-III, 2, 4 and 15. The publisher wrote to Jinnah, 'I am most anxious to see your book appear in the USA, in order to balance Hindu propaganda . . . and give your side of the position. I am sure that it will be very widely read, both in England and America.' But due to ill health and pressing engagements in politics, Jinnah indefinitely postponed its writing and did not sign the new contract that the publisher had drawn up.

318. The literature included *History of the Origin of the Fourteen Points, India's Problem of her Future Constitution, Nationalism in Conflict in India* and *Pakistan*

and Muslim India, Jinnah-Gandhi Correspondence, Jinnah-Nehru Correspondence, Jamiluddin Ahmad's *Muslim India and its Goal,* Fazlul Haq's *Muslim Sufferings,* and *Pirpur Report.* For a longer list, see AFM, vol. 236, no. 31.

319. The Punjab Muslim Students Federation established 'study circles' in every college of the province and a Pakistan library in Lahore. M. Ilyas, secretary, Punjab Muslim Students Federation to Quaid-i-Azam, QAP, F. 1101, p. 13.

320. In May 1945, the committee consisted of Jamiluddin Ahmad (convenor), Mian Bashir Ahmad (Lahore), Abdus Sattar Kheiri (Aligarh), Dr Qazi Saeeduddin (Lahore) and Hasan Reyaz. Zafar Ahmad (Ansari), secretary, committee of action to Jamiluddin Ahmad, 6 May 1945, AFM, vol. 180, no. 1.

321. The present author edited these articles in book-form, *The Case for Pakistan,* which the National Institute of Historical and Cultural Research, Islamabad published in 1979.

322. A.M.K. Dehlavi to Liaquat, 14 January 1940, AFM, vol. 199, no. 37.

323. For his letter to Jinnah and Liaquat, 15 April 1943, see QAP, F. 197, pp. 74–75, and AFM, vol. 282, no. 29. For a compilation of poems on this subject, see Nasir Zaidi and Mahmudur Rahman (comp.), *Woh Rahbar Hamara woh Quaid Hamara,* Karachi, 1976.

324. QAP, F. 27, p. 172. See also Proprietor, Regal Talkies, Dharwar, 11 January 1939, ibid., F. 1008, p. 4; and Recording Department of the Gramophone Company Ltd to Jinnah, 6 August 1938, ibid., F. 1095, p. 334. For filming the Lahore annual session, see AFM, vol. 218, no, 2, 6, 7, 13 and 15; and for Jinnah's Frontier visit in November 1945, see *Star of India,* 3 December 1945.

325. For the distribution of the film, see QAP, F. 312, p. 35; and F. 335, pp. 62–69; and AFM, vol. 218, nos. 17–19, 23–35, 50, 59 and 64. For his reception in Calcutta at the time of the All-India Muslim League's special session in April 1938, see the *Statesman,* 17 April 1938; and for his reception on the occasion of Sindh provincial Muslim League conference in October 1938, see the *Times of India,* 9 October 1938; and for the Patna session, see QAP, F. 49, pp. 214–17; F. 1129, pp. 260–62 and AFM, vol. 188.

326. M.A. Aziz, secretary, CA to secretaries provincial Muslim Leagues, 26 April 1944, AFM, vol. 155, no. 52.

327. H. Ahmad to Jinnah, 23 May 1938, QAP, F. 867, pp. 215–16; Hasan Nizami to Jinnah, June 1939, ibid., F. 49, pp. 11–12; Maulvi Mahmud to the editor, *Manshoor,* 9 March 1942, AFM, vol. 249; and for a resolution moved by Maulana Sibghatullah of Farangi Mahal and passed by the central council in Delhi on 27–28 August 1939. Earlier, on 30–31 July 1938, the working committee in pursuance of a resolution of the council had appointed a three-member [Maulana Shaukat Ali, Col. Rahman and Liaquat Ali Khan (convener)] propaganda and publicity committee; the name of a fourth member, Prof. Mirza Mohammad Saeed, was added in October.

328. Sayyid Zainul Abidin, president, Multan district Muslim League to Liaquat, 7 June 1942, AFM, vol. 138, no. 93; and his letter to Quaid-i-Azam, 15 July 1942, QAP, F. 827, p. 46.

329. AFM, vol. 333 contains reports about the observance of the 'Pakistan Day'.

330. Jinnah himself fixed 1 September 1940, the last Friday of Ramzan, as a day to demonstrate the deep feeling of sympathy and concern of Muslim India with the Muslim countries.

331. QAP, F. 346, p. 28; AFM, vol. 51; and *Dawn,* 21 December 1941.

332. M.L. Geoffrey to Jinnah, 17 August 1937, QAP, F. 26, p. 30; and Jinnah to S.M. Ahmad, 14 July 1941, ibid., F. 874, p. 146. The Congress had a well-established and active network in London, headed by Krishna Menon, which regularly issued a weekly news bulletin and organized meetings.

333. *The Light*, 16 February 1939.

334. For instance, it published a book on the 'All-India Muslim League and the Indian Problem' and distributed ten thousand copies in Arabic in the Muslim world. It also distributed 3000 copies in Urdu, 5000 in Persian and 5000 in French. Ali Mohammad Rashidi to Jinnah, 3 November 1939, QAP, F. 561, p. 46.

335. Resolutions passed at the annual sessions in Lucknow and Patna. Even earlier, the All-India Muslim League had opposed the creation of a Jewish state in Palestine. Telegram from Hafiz Hidayat Husain to the viceroy, *National Call* (Bombay), 11 November 1933, AFM, vol. 221.

336. Earlier, the All-India Muslim League had observed 19 June 1936, as the 'Palestine Day' to protest against the British policy based on the Balfour Declaration. [Jinnah's presidential address at the Sindh provincial Muslim League conference held on 8–9 October 1938, AFM, vol. 242, pp. 13–14.] Some documents relating to the Palestine issue and the All-India Muslim League have been compiled and published in book-form; for instance, see Atique Zafar Shaikh and Mohammad Riaz Malik (comp. and ed.), *Quaid-e-Azam and the Muslim World: Selected Documents, 1937–1948*, Karachi, 1990.

337. The League delegation consisted of Khaliquzzaman, A.R. Siddiqi, Hasrat Mohani and Maulana Mazharuddin. Maulana Mohammad Irfan represented the All-India Khilafat Committee and Maulana Kifayatullah and Maulana Mohammad Ishaq the Jamiatul Ulama-i-Hind at the Cairo congress.

338. For Jinnah's telegram to the SSI, 6 February 1939, see QAP, F. 1025, p. 212.

339. The delegation also submitted a representation on behalf of the Indian Muslims to the British government through the SSI. Ibid., F. 49, pp. 81–88 and 117–32.

340. Ibid., F. 498, p. 29 and F. 479, p. 14.

341. Abdullah Haroon to Jinnah, 17 July 1939, and resolutions proposed by Maulana Burhanul Haq and Sir Karimbhai Ibrahimbhai for the central council meeting to be held on 27–28 August 1939, ibid., F. 274, p. 26; and AFM, vol. 253; and vol. 291, p. 48.

342. QAP, F. 274, p. 156; F. 902, p. 22; and F. 1023, pp. 5–6; and AFM, vol. 262, p. 78; vol. 277, p. 119; and vol. 286, no. 60.

343. Resolution moved from the chair at the Delhi annual session, Waheed, *Nation's Voice*, vol. III, p. 213.

344. Sayyid Amin Al-Husaini to Jinnah, 12 October 1945, *Plain Mr. Jinnah*, pp. 216–17.

345. See Chapter 11.

346. Jinnah revealed this information in a speech in the Habibia Hall, Lahore, on 17 January 1946. See also Chapter 11.

347. Jinnah to Lord Lothian, 29 May 1940, and Lothian to Jinnah, 13 July 1940, cited in Waheed, *Nation's Voice*, vol. II, pp. 158–59.

348. QAP, F. 392, p. 32; and AFM, vol. 285, p. 112.

349. Resolution proposed by I. Khan on 5 April 1943 for the central council, ibid., vol. 286, no. 3.

350. *TP*, vol. II, p. 266.

351. AFM, vol. 155, nos. 34; and vol. 192, no. 4; M. Rafi Butt to Quaid-i-Azam, 9 March 1944, QAP, F. 829, p. 2; Liaquat's letter of 11 January 1945, AFM, vol.

165, no. 30; and Hasan Suhrawardy's tentative scheme to project the League viewpoint in Britain, QAP, F. 457, pp. 9–15.

352. *Hindustan Times*, 11 July 1945; Waheed, *Nation's Voice*, vol. IV, p. 175.

353. Firoz Khan Noon to Jinnah, 12 May 1944, *Jinnah Papers*, vol. X, p. 350.

354. Iqbal Ali Shah to Firoz Khan Noon, 7 July 1944 (including his memorandum for a Muslim information centre), QAP, F. 399, pp. 148–52.

355. Nazimuddin to Jinnah, 24 February 1946, ibid., F. 392, pp. 83–84.

356. The first issue was edited by S.Z. Ahmad (joint editor) because of Suleri's illness. On 8 February 1946, Ali Mohammad Khan, in response to Jinnah's letter of 14 December 1945, sent him two issues of the fortnightly *Pakistan*. Ibid., F. 939, p. 14; and ibid., F. 575, pp. 3–6.

357. R.E.B. Wilcox to Jinnah, 21 April 1947, and Jinnah to Wilcox & Co, 8 June 1947, ibid., F. 156, pp. 142–45; and for a negative view of Suleri's performance, see Hasan Ispahani to Jinnah, 29 May 1947, ibid., F. 68, p. 41.

358. These were: 'India: the last 10 Years', 'Why Pakistan?' and 'Fifty Facts about Pakistan'. See also Liaquat to Jinnah, 3 September 1946, ibid., F. 335, pp. 264–67.

359. SHC, P & P-III: 6, 20.

360. QAP, F. 955, p. 8.

361. The research bureau of the India League of America published a paper entitled 'Birthday Present to Nehru', in the *India Today*, vol. 1, no. 8 (November 1940), which articulated the Congress position.

362. Abdullah Haroon sent the All-India Muslim League literature to Ahmad as well as to those who had written in the *New York Times*. Abdullah Haroon to S.M. Ahmad, 30 December 1940, QAP, F. 274, pp. 158–58; and also ibid., pp. 160–61.

363. On 3 May 1941, Abdullah Haroon forwarded Ahmad's letter on this subject to Jinnah. [SHC, Sindh-I: 1–2.] S.M. Ahmad sent to Jinnah through Begum Shahnawaz his proposals for the propagation of the League and its message in the US. S.M. Ahmad to Jinnah, 4 January; and 30 March 1943, QAP, F. 1101, pp. 1–3, 38 and 55–62.

364. QAP, F. 1099, pp. 60–61 and 66–67.

365. Jahan Ara Shahnawaz, *Father and Daughter: A Political Autobiography*, Lahore, 1971, pp. 179–86; Bashir Ahmad to Jinnah, 14 February, QAP, F. 1092, pp. 156–57; and Qazi Isa to Jinnah, 6 April 1943, ibid., F. 302, p. 123. On her return from the US, Begum Shahnawaz, in a letter to Jinnah on 30 March 1943, wrote that she was gifting ten squares of land in the Muzaffargarh district to the All-India Muslim League. Ibid., F. 1092, p. 174.

366. Chief controller of exports, commerce department, Government of India to assistant secretary, All-India Muslim League, 20 June 1945, AFM, vol. 556, p. 15, permitting the export by post to the US one parcel weighing about ten seers containing literature of the All-India Muslim League.

367. J. Clark, associate professor of geology and vertebrate palaeontology, contributed an article in the June 1946, issue of the Carnegie magazine in which he gave a 'fair exposition' of the Muslim viewpoint. He wrote to Jinnah, 'Frankly, most of the publicity regarding Indian social and political affairs which had been released in this country has been by the Congress party itself or by the Brahman students who occasionally infest our universities. Most Americans know nothing about Muslim people except what they gain from exceedingly biased stories and movies of the ancient Crusades'. QAP, F. 1122, p. 73.

368. Ibid., F. 1108, pp. 96–101.

369. O.L.M. Shamsuddeen to Jinnah, 24 July 1946, ibid., F. 936, p. 28.

370. Statement by M.M. Ispahani who was convener of the committee that arranged a reception in honour of the Chinese Delegation on 27 July 1938, ibid., F. 1095, p. 295.

371. *Civil & Military Gazette*, 22 February 1942; for text of Jinnah's statement, see *Dawn*, 1 March 1942; and also see Nehru to Gandhi, 27 February 1942, S. Gopal (ed.), *Selected Works of Jawaharlal Nehru*, Second Series, vol. III, New Delhi, 1985, p. 475.

372. QAP, F. 1120, p. 190.

373. Jinnah's concluding speech at the Lahore session of the All-India Muslim League on 25 May 1924, AFM, vol. 109; and for loose handling of public funds by the Khilafat leaders that led to criticism and allegations, see Riazul Islam, 'Maulana Mohammad Ali aur Khilafat Fund', *Jang* (Karachi), 25 August 1970; and Qureshi, *Pan-Islam*, p. 373.

374. For one year after Abdullah Haroon's death, Haji Abdussattar Haji Essak Sait alone had audited the accounts.

375. When Jinnah was president of the Bombay presidency Muslim League, the Habib & Co used to audit the accounts of the Bombay League.

376. According to Jinnah, the annual income from 'gate money' and membership fees amounted to about Rs 14,000. Waheed, *Nation's Voice*, vol. II, p. 384.

377. For resolution passed by the central council on 27–28 August 1939, and Liaquat's letters to the secretaries of the provincial Muslim Leagues, see AFM, vol. 184.

378. For the Palestine Relief Fund, see QAP, F. 148, p. 11.

379. Ibid., F. 160-A, p. 532.

380. Resolution of the All-India Muslim League working committee passed on 9–10 October 1938.

381. For instance, see Alhaj Ebrahim Motiwalla (Rangoon) to Jinnah, 14 June 1937; and 12 December 1939, QAP, 561, p. 9 and ibid., F. 380, pp. 4–5; Ahmad Saeed (Chattari) to Jinnah, 31 July 1937, ibid., F. 26, p. 249; Nazimuddin to Jinnah, 6 February 1940, ibid., F. 392, pp. 6–7; and Jinnah to Nawab Musharraf Husain, 16 January 1938, and Jinnah to Nawab of Jahangirabad, 16 January 1938, ibid., F. 148, pp. 1 and 9; and F. 160, pp. 5–6.

382. Statement by the Raja of Mahmudabad in the *Indian Nation*, 29 December 1938; and QAP, F. 813, p. 13.

383. For the text of his appeal, see QAP, F. 107, pp. 16–17; and for his reluctance to make a general appeal to the Muslims for funds earlier, see A.M.K. Dehlavi to Jinnah, 11 May 1940, ibid., F. 256, pp. 90–91.

384. Ghulam Bhik Nairang offered to distribute leaflets containing information about the fund through the Tabligh organization. Ibid., F. 1134, pp. 30–31.

385. Ibid., F. 761, p. 145; and *Dawn*, 22 March 1942. He repeatedly made announcements to this effect and wrote to those who made queries about the mode of sending him their contributions. For instance, see Jinnah to secretary, Muslim Youth League, Bangalore cantonment., 12 June 1942, QAP, F. 903, pp. 11–12; secretary to Quaid-i-Azam to Mohammad Jamil Kashmiri, 28 August 1942, ibid., F. 588, p. 462; and Jinnah to Mushtaq M. Khan, 3 October 1942, ibid., F. 27, p. 108.

386. Kh. Rahim Bux (Lahore) to Quaid-i-Azam, 25 March 1942, ibid., F. 582, pp. 21–22.

387. Jinnah's letter to the Muslims of Unchegaon (15 May 1942) who had sent him ten rupees, in which he wrote, 'I value it more as it comes from their heart . . . I accept this little sum with gratitude and hope that it will help create a feeling of greater

organization, greater solidarity and greater cooperation among ourselves'. SHC, II: 1.

388. Azizur Rahman (student of class 5, Chamba High School, Amritsar) to Quaid-i-Azam, 29 April 1942, QAP, F. 52, p. 174; and Javed Ahmad (student of class 2), ibid., F. 857, pp. 21–22; and 'Muslim India Speaks', speech by Quaid-i-Azam M.A. Jinnah, president, All-India Muslim League at a meeting held under the auspices of the Muslim university union on 2 November 1942, AFM, vol. 237. Files 150–55 of the QAP relate to various funds.

389. *Dawn*, 19 April 1942.

390. SHC, OM-II: 119.

391. For such sentiments, see Ismail H. Omer to Quaid-i-Azam, 19 July 1942, QAP, F. 903, p. 22; and for donations and contributions made in March-April 1942, see ibid., F. 63.

392. The contributions in rupees from other regions were: Punjab 10,700; Hyderabad 6,200; Delhi 5,700; Madras 5,200; Bombay 4,200; Sindh 3,900; Bengal 3,500; Central Provinces 3,400; Bihar 2200; NWFP 1,500; Balochistan 1,200; Assam 1,200; and Misc. 1,200, ibid., F. 1134, p. 23.

393. The contributions in rupees from other regions were: Hyderabad (Deccan) 25,800; Bengal 24,800; United Provinces 23,400; Delhi 15,300; Madras 6,900; Sindh 6,400; Bihar 5,500; Central Provinces 5,300; NWFP 4,700; Balochistan 1,700; Assam 1,700; and Misc. 52,100. Ibid., F. 834, p. 84.

394. Mumtaz Mohammad Khan to Jinnah, 23 July 1945, and Jinnah to Mumtaz, 31 July, 1945, SHC, Pb-III: 36.

395. Jamil-ud-Din Ahmad (ed.), *Speeches and Writings of Mr. Jinnah*, vol. II, Lahore, 1964, pp. 190–91; Jinnah to Shafqat Ali Khan, 6 August 1945, SHC, OM-II: 66; and Jinnah to Khan Bashir Bakhsh, 24 April 1942, and Jinnah to Maulana Burhanul Haq, 5 May 1942, QAP, F. 150, pp. 310 and 321.

396. For details, see SHC, OM-II: 117; and AFM, vol. 410, pp. 58–60 and 74; and vol. 413, p. 1.

397. QAP, F. 27, pp. 88–89; F. 64, p. 29; F. 65, pp. 9, 123 and 126.

398. The SHC, OM-II volume contains letters and acknowledgements of contributions. Abul Hasan Sayyid Ali, president of the Majlis Ittehadul Millat, sent him a handsome amount including one lakh rupees from one K.B. Abdul Karim Baboo Khan. See also SHC, OM-II: 83 (1–2); and QAP, F. 311, p. 16; and F. 830, p. 63.

399. Jinnah to secretary, Camalia Muslim Women Association, Kadayanallur, 19 September 1945, SHC, OM-II: 76.

400. QAP, F. 61, pp. 8–9. For annual statements of accounts and expenditure, see AFM, vol. 128, no. 12 vol. 417, pp. 12, 14, 18, 19, and 34, and vol. 460; SHC, OM-I: 38–39; and QAP, 587, pp. 142 and 143, F. 835, p. 94, F. 857, p. 132.

401. Jinnah disallowed the *Dawn* to start a Bengal Relief Fund to avoid unnecessary duplication. Jinnah to Mahmood Hasan, QAP, F. 581, p. 253.

402. These figures were given by secretary, Muslim Chamber of Commerce, on 5 January 1944. See ibid., F. 583, p. 6; and F. 584, pp. 110, 131, 139 and 144.

403. Jinnah's statement ibid., F. 156, p. 85; and press account, ibid., F. 680, p. 122. Files 680–83 of the QAP deal with the Bihar Relief Fund.

404. Ibid., F. 860; and SHC, OM-II: 152. The tribes of the Khyber Agency donated Rs 10,003 to the Bihar Relief Fund.

405. Waheed Akhtar Mian to Quaid-i-Azam, 24 June 1947, QAP, F. 1108, pp. 78–79. Volume 1134 also contains information about the Pakistan Fund.

8

Muslim League Branches, 1937–1947

The strength of the All-India Muslim League rested with the state of its provincial Muslim Leagues, which were responsible for organizing the party at the primary, town/village, city, tehsil/subdivision, and district levels. According to the 1937 party constitution, the council of the All-India Muslim League had the authority to give affiliation to a provincial Muslim League; and by this mechanism, the party could indirectly control and oversee the formation and organization of a provincial Muslim League at its different tiers. At the Lahore annual session, the working committee was empowered 'to control, direct and regulate' the organization of the provincial Muslim Leagues. It could 'suspend, dissolve or disaffiliate' any provincial Muslim League which failed in its duties or ignored the decisions of the All-India Muslim League subject to a right of appeal to the central council; and in December 1943, the working committee delegated these powers to a central committee of action. Every provincial Muslim League was responsible for the collection of membership fees, and had to pay 10 per cent of its income other than the donations to the All-India Muslim League. It elected its quota of members for the central council; and in case of its failure to do so, the council itself could fill the vacancies. A provincial Muslim League organized branch Leagues at district and lower levels, which were deemed to have been affiliated with the All-India Muslim League if these were affiliated with the provincial Muslim League. The meetings of the presidents and secretaries of all the provincial Muslim Leagues in November 1941, followed by regular tours of the provinces by members of the central civil defence committee and then the central committee of action contributed to the consolidation of the party organization. The central committee of action by regular inspections kept the provincial Muslim Leagues active and brought about in them organizational uniformity. The model constitution that it framed for the provincial Muslim Leagues was meant to achieve that objective but it was implemented piecemeal due to the turbulent political environment of 1946–47. Every primary League was required to enrol at least 75 per cent of the Muslim voters in their area of jurisdiction.[1]

Emergence of factionalism was a natural phenomenon for a rapidly growing and expanding political party, as control on its organs at any level signified influence and power. It was manifested in personal and factional rivalries especially in the provinces where the League formed ministries. The political forces outside the party contributed to its intensification. It was non-existent at the central level due to Jinnah's charismatic leadership and his skilful handling of crises and partly because it assumed power at the centre towards the end of the freedom struggle. Two elements, Jinnah's leadership and the popularity of the Pakistan ideal at the grassroots, kept the fissiparous tendencies in the provincial Muslim Leagues in check. There were a few cases of defection and expulsion from the League, but those who went out of the party put the blame on the local leadership and did not abandon allegiance to the ideal. The strength of the League varied from province to province. When the All-India Muslim League was revived in 1935–37, it had in all fourteen provincial Muslim Leagues: in the Punjab, Sindh, NWFP, Balochistan, Bengal, Assam, United Provinces, Bombay, Madras, Bihar, Central Provinces and Berar, Orissa, Ajmer-Merwara and Delhi; and a fifteenth League—Coorg–Bangalore provincial Muslim League—was created and affiliated in 1943. The party constitution did not make any distinction among the provinces. After 1940, however, there were informal references to the Muslim majority provinces as units of the 'Pakistan Zones'. The Sindh provincial Muslim League at G.M. Sayed's initiative made a move to coordinate the party activities in the 'Pakistan provinces' of the north-west and the state of Jammu and Kashmir but his move was not pursued seriously.[2] Till December 1943, the constitution had a provision, 'London Branch of the All-India Muslim League, if any', which was then amended as 'branches of the All India Muslim League, if any, outside India'. The party after its revival did not initiate any move on its own to organize a branch outside British India but it gave affiliation to the Leagues organized by the Indian Muslims outside India. After 1937, the constitution had no provision to have branch Leagues in the princely states, but almost every state had a League or a Muslim party organized on its pattern that had contacts with the League leaders particularly Jinnah.

(A) THE PROVINCIAL MUSLIM LEAGUES

(*i*) *Punjab Provincial Muslim League*. The Punjab provincial Muslim League was revived on 30 May 1936, when Allama Iqbal was elected its patron, Mian Abdul Aziz Malvada (1872–1971) president, and Ghulam Rasul Khan (d. 1949) general secretary.[3] Two of its seven candidates in the 1937 provincial elections, Malik Barkat Ali and Raja Ghazanfar Ali, won their seats but after the elections the latter defected to the Unionists. The Unionist Party won 88 out of total 175 seats in the Punjab assembly, elected Sardar Sikandar Hayat Khan as its leader, and in cooperation with the Hindu and Sikh parties formed a ministry with the support of 120 members of the provincial assembly. Once in power, the Unionist Muslims were receptive to the idea of joining the League to counter the Congress propaganda against them. The League–Unionist unity talks climaxed at the Lucknow annual session where Sikandar made a complicated four-point statement, which provided that (*i*) Sikandar on his return to the Punjab would advise Muslim Unionists to join the League and sign its creed; the signatories would be subject to the rules and regulations of the central parliamentary board and provincial parliamentary board but this would not affect the Unionist-led coalition; (*ii*) the groups constituting the Unionist Party would in the future elections and bye-elections jointly support the candidates put up by their respective groups; (*iii*) the Muslim members of the provincial assembly, elected on or accepting the League ticket, would constitute the League party in the Punjab assembly, the League party would be free to maintain or enter into coalition or alliance with any other party consistently with the fundamental principles, policy and programme of the League, such alliances might be formed before or after the elections, and the existing combination should maintain its present name, the 'Unionist Party'; and (*iv*) in view of this agreement the Punjab provincial parliamentary board should be reconstituted.[4] Although the document incorporating this statement was neither signed by the League president or any other of its office-bearers nor formally approved by any of its statutory bodies yet it was commonly referred to as the 'Sikandar–Jinnah Pact'.

Muslim unity displayed at Lucknow inspired the Punjabi Muslims but the conflicting interpretations put on the 'Pact' marred the political atmosphere. The 'old' Leaguers felt that they had stood by Jinnah in difficult times; therefore, they had the right to maintain their hold on the party. Their apprehension was that the 'new' Leaguers (the Unionists) merely wanted to control the provincial Muslim League.

Therefore, they pressed the Unionists to join the League without giving them any party office(s).[5] Conversely, the Unionists aspired to control the provincial Muslim League by their majority and refused to be left 'at the mercy' of the 'old' Leaguers who simply wanted them to join the League.[6] They demanded two offices—that of general secretary and finance secretary—for their nominees.[7] Besides, some of them were swayed by multiple loyalties, their loyalty to the British authorities, the non-Muslim partners, and the League. Sikandar himself faced a dilemma: his non-Muslim colleagues Chaudhri Chhuto Ram (1881–1945) in particular termed the 'Pact' as his 'surrender' to Jinnah while the Punjab Leaguers pressurized him to join the League unconditionally.[8] Both the 'old' and 'new' Leaguers made representations to Jinnah against each other. Jinnah who was unwell at the time advised them to have patience, stressing that there was no difference between old and new Leaguers and that their differences could be patched up.[9] The two groups, however, set out on separate courses. The 'old' Leaguers started the process of party organization, opening and affiliating new branches mainly in the urban areas. They claimed to have established branches in 26 out of 29 districts, adopted a constitution and, in March 1938, elected office-bearers: Iqbal as patron, Nawab Shahnawaz Mamdot as president and Ghulam Rasul as general secretary, and ninety representatives on the central council. No Unionist was elected to any office.[10] This provincial Muslim League requested the All-India Muslim League for affiliation. On the other hand, Sikandar sponsored a non-communal Zamindara League that began to establish branches in the districts to allay the apprehensions of his non-Muslim colleagues. His break-up with the League seemed imminent but the adverse decision of the Punjab high court in the Shahidganj case, the country-wide observance of a Shahidganj Day and his emotional declarations including his offer to resign as chief minister prevented such a development.[11] The decisions of the All-India Muslim League not only released the pressure on the Unionists in regard to the Shahidganj issue but also gave them control of the provincial Muslim League.[12]

Before the Calcutta special session, the central council refused affiliation to the provincial Muslim League because its constitution was in conflict with that of the All-India Muslim League on two counts: (*i*) it empowered the provincial Muslim League to affiliate any Muslim association; and (*ii*) it allowed direct membership of the provincial Muslim League while the All-India Muslim League constitution required every member to be a member of some primary League.[13] The provincial Muslim League amended its constitution to meet these objections but it was still denied affiliation. Seventy Muslim Unionist members of the provincial assembly had signed the League creed; and Sikandar made an announcement to that effect at the Calcutta session.[14] Jinnah was authorized to resolve the conflict. With the consent of the two groups, he appointed a committee of 35 members, out of which 22 were Unionists, with powers to co-opt more members to organize the provincial Muslim League; and Sikandar was its chairman[15] Factional tussle did not subside partly because both the groups were unwilling to modify their standpoints. Iqbal's death (21 April 1938), three days after the Calcutta special session, weakened the 'old' Leaguers. Nevertheless, Ghulam Rasul, an 'impulsive' and 'strong-headed' person according to his own friends, did not hesitate to assert his authority as secretary of the provincial Muslim League and provincial parliamentary board, which was not 'reconstituted' as the 'Sikandar–Jinnah Pact' had visualized. An embarrassing situation arose when the provincial parliamentary board could not give the party ticket to Shaikh Mohammad Sadiq in a bye-election, which became a point of inquiry in an election petition against him in which Jinnah gave evidence in his defence before the election tribunal.[16] Again, a split was averted because focus was on the Unionists' performance. Sikandar's popularity graph rose when his ministry passed four agrarian bills, which benefited the agriculturists in general.[17] But his offer of unconditional Muslim support to Britain in the event of war in a speech at Simla evoked strong criticism against him in the central council.[18]

Factionalism was revived when the Unionists pushed Nawabzada Khurshid Ali Khan's name as general secretary in opposition to Ghulam Rasul.[19] The two groups carried on separate organizational activities in the districts which confused the Leaguers who pressed for one united League.[20] There was a temporary respite when, in March 1939, the organizing committee unanimously elected Mian Ramzan Ali (1881–1964), who had recently retired as postmaster general of the Punjab, as general secretary.[21] But factional tussle restarted when Sikandar denounced Ashiq Husain Batalvi, an 'old' Leaguer and his staunch critic, as a 'political adventurer', alleging that he had joined hands with Dr K.M. Ashraf, a leftist leader who was then secretary in the Congress office, to establish a rival 'Punjab Muslim League Radical Party'.[22] When Jinnah came to know about the new party, he directed Batalvi to work in accordance with the provincial Muslim League constitution.[23] In retaliation to Sikandar's attack, Batalvi moved two resolutions against him in the central council on 27 August: one was about his speech on the Indo–British trade agreement in April that was against the policy of the All-India Muslim League; and the second was about the circulation of his 'zonal federation scheme' which was again not in line with the party policy.[24] The council referred both these resolutions to the working committee for necessary action, and simultaneously directed the organizing committee to complete its task by 15 November 1939, otherwise it would be 'deemed to have been dissolved'.[25] On Sikandar's motion, the organizing committee condemned the activities of Batalvi, Malik Zaman Mehdi and Ghulam Rasul in the name of the provincial Muslim League, and asked the All-India Muslim League to take disciplinary action against them.[26] The All-India Muslim League, however, did not consider their activities actionable. Now the provincial Muslim League was organized without the association of Sikandar's opponents.[27] On 10 January 1940, its council elected the office-bearers—Nawab Shahnawaz Mamdot as its president and Mian Ramzan Ali as general secretary—and requested the All-India Muslim League for affiliation.[28] Its opponents questioned the validity of the organization process and appealed to the All-India Muslim League not to give it affiliation because it had failed to organize itself within the stipulated time, i.e. 15 November 1939.[29] The working committee appointed an inquiry committee; and on 25 February 1940, the council empowered it to decide the issue of affiliation. After hearing the two sides, the inquiry committee accorded the provincial Muslim League affiliation.[30] This decision signalled Sikandar's victory in the factional tussle.

The provincial Muslim League seemingly came under the Unionist control.[31] But the situation rapidly changed. The Lahore annual session did not bring any credit to Sikandar. The police firing on the Khaksars on 19 March, and banning of their party tarnished his image and the ambiguity of his stand on the Lahore Resolution damaged his influence among the Muslims. The participation of some Unionists in the war committees despite the ban imposed by the All-India Muslim League, and Sikandar's parleys with Azad without taking Jinnah into confidence seriously affected his standing in the League.[32] In addition, the response of the Speaker to Barkat Ali's queries about the existence of the League party in the Punjab assembly and the allocation of a seat to him on the back benches further impaired Sikandar's image.[33] On 2 September 1940, the ban on the Khaksars was lifted, but now the Muslim youth was not willing to submit. It was in an assertive mood. On 1 December, the provincial Muslim League council passed a resolution under their pressure, requiring every Leaguer to take an oath of allegiance to the Pakistan scheme. And when the provincial Muslim League held the party elections through the old rather than the new council and dropped Barkat Ali's name from the list of Punjab's representatives on the central council, they lodged protest with the All-India Muslim League, questioning the validity of the election process.[34] Consequently, Barkat Ali was taken on the council in the re-elections.[35] Shahnawaz Mamdot was elected as president, Shaikh Sadiq Hasan as vice-president, Ramzan Ali as general secretary; and Khalilur Rahman (1904–1972) and Prof. Malik Inayatullah (1900–1966) as secretaries. Muslim youth developed direct contact with Jinnah who encouraged them to 'work steadily, patiently, and with determination and all humility' for the League.[36] In 1941, Jinnah himself or some prominent Leaguers presided over the 'Pakistan conferences' that the League organized in Lahore, Rawalpindi, Lyallpur (Faisalabad), Sialkot, Montgomery (Sahiwal) and other cities, which reflected the changing popular mood. The student-led rural propaganda committee organized tours in the summer vacations and sent regular reports to Jinnah.[37]

Henceforth, every move that Sikandar made undermined his position in the League. The pro-Pakistan propaganda agitated his Hindu and Sikh cabinet colleagues. He tried to keep a balance, and in doing that unnecessarily distanced himself from the Lahore Resolution and even opposed its terming as the 'Pakistan Resolution'.[38] His derision of the resolution in the Punjab assembly in March 1941, and at a students' conference in Faisalabad in July was rebutted by Jinnah himself. The acrimony and heated controversy over Sikandar's observations and his association with the government-sponsored national defence council were temporarily settled when Sikandar acknowledged Jinnah as his 'Quaid-i-Azam', stating in the working committee, 'I have nothing to say in my defence, and I am willing to abide by the orders of our President, whom I have acknowledged as my Quaid-i-Azam, and follow his instructions whatever he decides, right or wrong'.[39] The prevalence of Jinnah's viewpoint, however, made the young Leaguers more confident and less restrained in their criticism of Sikandar. The party elections on 7 December 1941, were conducted in a relatively smooth atmosphere when Shahnawaz Mamdot and Sadiq Hasan were re-elected to their respective offices, but Khalilur Rahman replaced Ramzan Ali as the general secretary.[40] On 22 February 1942, when Sikandar pleaded for 'unconditional and wholehearted' support in the war effort in the working committee, he had to face strong criticism from the members. Now he was not prepared to face this criticism; and when the working committee rejected the Cripps' offer, he submitted his resignation from its membership. Following an understanding between him and Jinnah, he did not press for the acceptance of his resignation and Jinnah did not nominate him on the working committee for the next year.[41] The death of Shahnawaz Mamdot on 8 March, that year was another bad news for Sikandar, as Shahnawaz had kept some balance among the diverse groups in the provincial Muslim League. A further setback for him was a 'revolt' that month of about a dozen Unionist members of the provincial assembly who asked the speaker to allot them a separate bloc of seats in the assembly.[42]

Sikandar was shrewd enough to realize the mood of his community. On 29 March 1942, when the provincial Muslim League council met to fill the vacancy of the party president, he himself proposed the name of Iftikhar Husain (1906–1969), son of Shahnawaz Mamdot, for that office. Sikandar suppressed the desire, if he had any, to have someone else as the president.[43] Iftikhar Mamdot who was supported by the Muslim youth was elected president unopposed. Jinnah welcomed his election, hoping that he would follow in the footsteps of his 'noble father whose heart and soul was with Muslim India and the Muslim League'.[44] With the young Mamdot as president surrounded by Muslim youth particularly those of the Muslim Students Federation, there was a change in the Leaguers' mood. They aggressively launched a pro-Pakistan campaign, organizing conferences to counter the impact of the anti-Pakistan conferences that the Hindus, Sikhs and pro-Congress Muslims were holding in the Punjab.[45] Apprehensive of a clash between pro- and anti-Pakistan forces, the Punjab government empowered the district magistrates to restrict or ban any conference that was likely 'to exacerbate communal feelings'. When the district magistrate of Jalandhar using this power banned a 'Pakistan conference' in Phillaur that Zafar Ali Khan was to preside, the Leaguers protested against this ban, threatening to defy the order by civil disobedience. Jinnah restrained them and settled the matter peacefully.[46] On 18 November, the reorganized provincial Muslim League held its first conference in Faisalabad that Jinnah inaugurated and Nazimuddin presided over that conference. Earlier, on 7 November, Iftikhar Mamdot had been re-elected president unopposed; Sikandar congratulated him on his re-election and denied the existence of any 'Sikandar formula'[47] that was in circulation as an alternative to the Lahore Resolution, emphasizing his loyalty to the League and Jinnah and his submission to the 'will of the majority'.[48] Still, Sikandar had to face criticism in the council for not organizing the League party in the Punjab assembly. But he did not live long enough to see the changed environment, as he died of a heart attack on 26 December, after participating in the wedding ceremonies of his two sons and a daughter.

Sikandar's death ended a phase in the politics of the Punjab provincial Muslim League. Before the Muslim members of the provincial assembly could elect his successor, Governor Sir Bertrand Glancy (7 April 1940–7 April 1946) arbitrarily selected Sardar Khizr Hayat Khan Tiwana (1900–1975), a member of Sikandar's cabinet and one of the several aspirants for the office of chief minister; and on 31 December, he was sworn in as the chief minister. Neither Glancy nor Khizr consulted the League leadership; in fact, the former refused to see Iftikhar Mamdot when he made a request for an interview.[49] Still, the Punjab provincial Muslim League welcomed Khizr's selection to avoid intra-League conflict. On 6 February, Shaukat (1915–1998), Sikandar's eldest son, joined his cabinet after his resignation from the army; and, in May, he was returned to the Punjab assembly in a bye-election. At first, Jinnah did not like the way Shaukat was brought into the cabinet,[50] but the latter earned his acceptance by his enthusiastic work for the League.[51] The British would have preferred the more experienced Malik Firoz Khan Noon as chief minister but he declined to come in the way of Khizr's ambitions.[52] Like Sikandar, Khizr had to cater to his multiple loyalties under unfavourable circumstances and with lesser personal qualities than those of his predecessor.[53] He had little interest in popular politics and his capabilities were questioned even by Wavell (1883–1950) who expected Glancy to make up for his deficiencies.[54] Immediate threat to the provincial Muslim League solidarity came from a group of Leaguers who established a 'Muslim League Workers' Board of the Punjab' to enrol half a million members and form a League Party in the assembly. Nawabzada Rashid Ali Khan (1904–1974), the Lahore city Muslim League president, was its prime mover and financer who was elected secretary of the board and some senior Leaguers were elected its office-bearers.[55] But Jinnah discouraged this breach of party discipline and directed Rashid to wind up immediately the workers' board.[56] The board disappeared before it could take off the ground. More serious challenge to Khizr was the issue of formation of a League party in the assembly; pressure for this had begun to build up in the last days of Sikandar.[57] Several Punjab members of the legislative assembly had approached Jinnah for this purpose.[58] Khizr faced sharp criticism in the central council when he asserted in its meeting in Delhi on 7 March 1943, that the League party existed in the Punjab assembly under the Sikandar–Jinnah Pact, which, he admitted, had not functioned efficiently and promised to take concrete steps to make it active. But a League assembly party with an independent policy did not suit the British who were keen to preserve the non-communal character of the Punjab ministry. Besides, Glancy backed by Wavell was opposed to any move that might increase Jinnah's influence in the Punjab and broaden the support for the Pakistan scheme. He disliked the Sikandar–Jinnah Pact because its terms, in his opinion, favoured Jinnah's position. Whenever Khizr showed signs of weakness both Glancy and Wavell were there to prevent him from succumbing to the League pressure. Khizr's Hindu and Sikh colleagues also opposed the All-India Muslim League-controlled provincial Muslim League, which Jinnah could use to promote the Pakistan scheme.[59] The Hindu charismatic leader and senior minister in the Unionist cabinet, Sir Chhuto Ram, assumed the role of Khizr's mentor who, in April 1943, prevented a move by the League members of the legislative assembly to adopt a resolution in the Punjab assembly on 'Pakistan' similar to the one that the Sindh assembly had passed in March by suddenly proroguing the assembly session.[60]

Now Jinnah's focus was on the Punjab, which he frequently described as 'the cornerstone of Pakistan'. Early in 1943, he decided to shift his regular residence to Lahore to look after the party work in the Punjab and other areas of '[western] Pakistan'.[61] He planned to purchase his own accommodation because he did not like to stay with anyone for a long duration. His search for residential property in Lahore matured in October when he purchased a house, but unfortunately it was taken over by the army apparently for its war-time needs.[62] It is not unlikely that Glancy and Wavell might have used their influence to prevent any possibility of Jinnah's prolonged stay in the Punjab because the general impression was that if 'the Punjab fell to Jinnah', it 'would be hard to avoid Pakistan'.[63] Despite Jinnah's political influence and frantic efforts the army did not vacate his house even after the termination of the War till eight days before Independence! This setback did not diminish his interest in the Punjab affairs. He continued to guide the Muslim youth in organizing tours of the rural areas for pro-Pakistan propaganda, and the provincial Muslim

League opened a political training centre, the 'Summer School of Politics', to train political workers whom he once addressed; Iftikhar Mamdot was closely associated with these ventures.[64] Jinnah established direct contact with the Punjab Leaguers at the district level.[65] The tussle for the provincial Muslim League leadership intensified factionalism. Khizr, Shaukat and Mamdot led the main factions that tried to control the provincial Muslim League; Mumtaz Daultana soon joined them in the race. There were quite a few aspirants for the offices of the provincial Muslim League president and chief minister; Khizr and Shaukat were the main contenders for the latter office.[66] Jinnah tried to mediate, exhorting them that 'in solidarity and unity of the Muslims lay their salvation'.[67] Consequently, broad unanimity was temporarily worked out that was reflected in the party elections on 5 December 1943; the council unanimously elected Mamdot as president; Khizr proposed and Barkat Ali seconded his name. Karamat Ali was elected unopposed as the general secretary; soon after, Daultana replaced him in that office.[68] The council empowered Mamdot to select the provincial Muslim League representatives on the central council. Khizr was to stay as the chief minister.

Now the provincial Muslim League faced two problems. One, a few councillors challenged the legality of the elections, alleging that the council meeting had been convened without proper notice; the district Muslim Leagues had not been asked to send their nominations for the office of president; non-members had participated in the voting; and the president had been unlawfully authorized to nominate representatives on the central council.[69] After a formal inquiry, the central working committee upheld the elections as 'perfectly valid' but declared the selection of members by the president on the central council as 'invalid' and called for fresh elections of members that the party held on 28 May 1944.[70] The second and more serious problem was the state of the League assembly party. Jinnah had closely watched the controversy about the naming of the Punjab ministry as the League coalition ministry and formation of a League assembly party.[71] In November 1943, the central working committee approved the constitution of the Punjab League assembly party after its scrutiny by a subcommittee.[72] The snags appeared when the time came for concrete steps. Khizr might have gone along with the process of formation of the assembly party had he been free to do that. But Glancy, supported by Wavell, and his non-Muslim partners in power stood in the way, which aggravated the intra-provincial Muslim League tensions; the death of Khizr's father, Sir Umar Hayat Khan, on 25 March, shook his confidence and made him vulnerable to their pressure.[73] Goaded by these forces, he insisted on the maintenance of a status quo, i.e. continuance of the Unionist ministry without any change in its nomenclature and invoked the Sikandar–Jinnah Pact as if it were an unalterable permanent arrangement. However, the All-India Muslim League emphasized that a Leaguer's primary loyalty was to his own party rather than to any other party, and that the League assembly party could form a coalition under its auspices with the other assembly parties. Jinnah stayed in Lahore for six weeks and held unfruitful talks with Khizr trying to persuade him to accept the League's viewpoint. On the breakdown of these talks, Khizr's cabinet colleague, Shaukat, who had been publicly urging him to accept Jinnah's advice, tendered his resignation in protest.[74] Glancy demonstrated his partiality when instead of accepting his resignation dismissed him from his office on the charge of displaying communal bias as minister;[75] this extreme step was meant to prevent 'a general stampede' from the Unionist ranks.[76] Two Leaguers from south Punjab, Sardar Jamal Khan Leghari (Dera Ghazi Khan) and Nawab Ashiq Husain Qureshi (Multan), were lured into the ministry. Khizr indulged in a tirade against the League and Jinnah, which provided a basis for a charge-sheet against him. On 27 May, the central committee of action after protracted negotiations and an unsatisfactory explanation from Khizr expelled him from the party, a decision that the central council endorsed in Lahore on 30 July.[77]

Khizr realized the futility of forestalling the growth of the provincial Muslim League and popularity of the Pakistan scheme.[78] Nevertheless, he did not give up easily, as he had control of the civil administration, blessings of Glancy and Wavell, and support of his non-Muslim partners. With this kind of backing, his government restrained the defection of the members of the provincial assembly to the provincial Muslim League in any large number, and advised the Muslims not to organize themselves outside the assembly on communal lines.[79] Under his leadership, the Unionists propped up the ineffective non-communal bodies like the Zamindara League and the Jat Sabha under official patronage.[80] They used administrative machinery and restrictive laws to control the League and pro-Pakistan propaganda.[81] The provincial Muslim League used every device to expand its support-base; and the central committee of action opened a branch office in Lahore to provide it guidance.[82] However, its campaign to win over members of the provincial assembly had limited success.[83] It could enlist only twenty-six members of the provincial assembly by the end of 1944, when on Jinnah's advice it elected Mamdot as its leader, who accepted this role after a lot of persuasion, and Shaukat as its deputy leader.[84] Those who joined the League assembly party were prepared to stand up against the Glancy–Khizr administration.[85] More successful and quite effective were the extensive tours that the provincial Muslim League organized in the districts in the summer of 1944 and in December 1944–February 1945, for which all-India League leaders assisted the party.[86] It was due to its rising popularity that the Punjab government refused to allow it to host the All-India Muslim League's annual session in Lahore in March 1945.[87] Its membership reached half a million; and in February–March, its elections at all levels were conducted in a peaceful atmosphere; Mamdot was elected president and Mumtaz Daultana general secretary. However, the defeat of Abdullah Malik, a leftist political worker, as the propaganda secretary developed into a communist–non-communist tussle in the Lahore city Muslim League that climaxed in the suspension of the city League in October 1945.[88] An uneasy truce was maintained till June 1946, when the central committee of action restored the city Muslim League.[89] The party manifesto in English advocating radical economic reforms was translated into Urdu and given wide publicity; in total, 30,000 copies of the manifesto were distributed.[90] Pressures and restrictions including the arrest of party workers could not hinder its growth.[91] By the time of the general elections, the provincial Muslim League had firmly established itself at the grassroots, and several prominent Muslims who had sat on the sidelines rushed to join the party. The election results surprised everyone: the League emerged as the largest party in the assembly. After the elections, a few newly elected members of the provincial assembly including president of the Punjab Congress, Maulana Daud Ghaznavi, joined the League raising its strength to eighty. On 27 February 1946, the League assembly party elected Mamdot as its leader, Shaukat as deputy leader and Mian Nurullah as secretary; Firoz Khan Noon who aspired for its leadership could not muster the requisite support.[92]

Glancy performed his last anti-League act after the elections. Mamdot who claimed the support of 87 members of the provincial assembly, which included 2 Hindus, 4 Scheduled Caste members, 2 Indian Christians and 1 Sikh, called on Glancy to invite him to form the ministry. Instead of accepting his request, Glancy helped in clobbering a Khizr-headed Unionist–Congress–Sikh coalition with the connivance of Azad, who asserted that henceforth Khizr would 'live in the Congress world'.[93] The Glancy–Congress manoeuvring was designed to damage the League's case in support of the Pakistan scheme before the Cabinet Mission.[94] The uncertainties following the All-India Muslim League's withdrawal of acceptance of the Mission's plan generated intra-League tensions. Two factions—one led by Mamdot and Daultana and the other led by Noon and supported by Shaukat and Iftikharuddin—competed for the party leadership.[95] Noon who aspired to be the leader of the assembly party had promised support to Shaukat for the presidency of the provincial Muslim League while Iftikharuddin who did not want any office was against Mamdot because the latter had opposed his nomination for membership of the constituent assembly in the central parliamentary board. Before factionalism could aggravate, the central committee of action postponed the forthcoming party elections and appointed a Mamdot-headed nine-member committee of action, which exercised all the powers of the provincial council and working committee.[96] This decision diverted the energies of the provincial leaders from possible infighting to moves against the Khizr ministry. The movement that the provincial Muslim League launched against the Khizr ministry in January 1947, following the ban on the Muslim League National Guards, was soon transformed into a popular upsurge, in which every section of the Muslim society participated, and ended only after Khizr resigned. Soon after, Punjab was partitioned in pursuance of the 3 June Plan. Mamdot was elected leader of the West Punjab assembly, and sworn in as the first chief minister of the post-Independence Punjab.[97]

(ii) *Sindh Provincial Muslim League*. The provincial Muslim League had lost its identity in the struggle for the separation of Sindh from the Bombay presidency. On 1 April 1936, Sindh emerged as a separate province, and elections were held for its first assembly. Jinnah tried to form a united platform of the local Muslim parties but failed to establish a provincial parliamentary board. The Leaguers participated in the elections as independents or on the tickets of other parties. Thirty-five Muslim seats out of total 60 seats in the assembly were secured by various parties: Sindh Azad Party 3, Sindh United Party 21, Sindh Muslim Party 3, Congress 1 and Independents 7. The Sindh Azad Party was closer to the League than the other parties.[98] The Sindh Congress and the Hindu Independent Party shared the non-Muslim seats. The strength of the Muslim parties remained fluid throughout the life of the assembly due to lack of discipline among their members. On 22 March 1937, Shaikh Ghulam Husain Hidayatullah, leader of the Sindh Muslim Party, formed the first coalition ministry consisting of his party, some Sindh United Party members, the Sindh Congress and the Hindu Independent Party; and named it as the Democratic Coalition Party. He was its leader, Gobindram and Mir Bandeh Ali Talpur its deputy leaders, Ayub Khuhro and Nihchaldas Vazirani its secretaries and Mir Ghulam Ali Talpur its joint secretary.[99] The excuse not inviting the Sindh United Party, the largest party in the assembly, to form the ministry was that its two top leaders had been defeated in the elections, Haji Abdullah Haroon by K.B. Allah Bakhsh Gabol and Sir Shahnawaz Khan Bhutto by Abdul Majid Sindhi.

Early in February 1938, the Leaguers reorganized the provincial Muslim League and elected Shaikh Abdul Majid Sindhi as president who merged his Sindh Azad Party into the League.[100] On 21 March, the Hidayatullah ministry lost the support of its coalition partners for its stand on land alienation, money-lending and rates of interests and resigned when the assembly passed a cut motion supported by the Congress, Hindu Independent Party and Sindh United Party. Then, Hidayatullah formed the Democratic Party, which merged itself into the provincial Muslim League.[101] Two days after the exit of his ministry, Allah Bakhsh Mohammad Omar Soomro (1897–1943), the Sindh United Party leader, formed the next ministry by coalescing with the Sindh Congress and Hindu Independent Party. Some members of the provincial assembly of the Sindh United Party, who disagreed with him, joined the provincial Muslim League. When he was in trouble by June, Abdul Majid Sindhi and Hidayatullah jointly offered to support him provided he along with his group joined the League, signed its pledge and followed its policy and programme inside and outside the assembly.[102] Although he did not accept their proposal immediately but the situation changed within two months when his ministry faced a no-confidence motion partly for its acceptance of the enhanced assessment rates to pay off the Sukkur barrage debt. Then, Abdullah Haroon optimistically informed Jinnah that 27 out of 34 members of the provincial assembly were ready to sign the League pledge and if Muslim mass opinion was mobilized by holding a provincial conference all the Muslim members of the provincial assembly might do so.[103] Abdul Majid Sindhi provided Jinnah a similar analysis and a detailed break-up of a possible League-led coalition, he wrote: the opposition party in the assembly that he was heading had 17 members, out of whom 12 had signed the League pledge; the G.M. Sayed group of five members of the provincial assembly and five others were also willing to join the League. If this coalition assumed power, two other members of the provincial assembly and Pir Ilahi Bakhsh, if he was offered a ministership, would join in; this would raise the strength of the League supporters to thirty. Jinnah's visit, Sindhi wrote, might bring Allah Bakhsh's followers into the League if not Allah Bakhsh himself. But he did point out the real snag in the Muslim politics of Sindh: he lamented, 'our misfortune is that every one of us wants to become a minister or a minister-maker.'[104] Henceforth, this phenomenon was to haunt the ministerial stability in Sindh.

The Sindh provincial Muslim League held a conference in Karachi on 8–12 October 1938, which proved a landmark in the Muslim struggle for freedom. Jinnah's reception was historic and the main resolution of the conference was a prelude to the Lahore Resolution.[105] He proudly proclaimed his Sindhi origin and urged the Sindhi Muslims to forge unity in their ranks. For once it appeared as if all the Sindhi Muslim leaders would respond to his call and unite on the League platform. On 9 October, he chaired a meeting of six leaders of different groups (Allah Bakhsh, Ilahi Bakhsh, Ghulam Husain Hidayatullah, Mir Bandeh Ali, G.M. Sayed and Abdul Majid Sindhi); chief ministers Sikandar Hayat and Fazlul Haq were also present in that meeting. After prolonged talks, they signed a five-point agreement that called for the formation of a League party in the Sindh assembly; submission of resignation of the ministers to the governor simultaneously with a proposal from the leader of the League assembly party for the formation of a new ministry; a meeting of those members of the provincial assembly who had joined or agreed to join the League assembly party on 12 October; election of leader of the assembly party by a unanimous vote or otherwise Jinnah would have the authority to make the nomination; and selection of ministers by a similar procedure. Sikandar was asked to advise the Sindh ministry on the enhanced revenue assessment and his advice was to be accepted 'as final'.[106] Meanwhile, the Congress leaders were not sitting idle. Earlier, in August, when there was a possibility of a vote of no-confidence against the ministry, Vallabhbhai Patel, Azad and Acharya Kripalani had rushed to Sindh and then flown to Wardha for consultation with Gandhi on a draft 'secret pact' with Allah Bakhsh. While the Congress was still considering that pact, the five-point agreement among the Sindh

Muslim leaders seriously raised 'the danger' of a League ministry in Sindh.[107] Now the Congress moved fast to prevent that possibility, renewing its unconditional support to the Allah Bakhsh ministry. J.H. Garret (acting governor) helped them by not accepting Jinnah's proposal for convening the assembly session because he was apprehensive that a League ministry might reject the enhanced revenue assessment. Consequently, in the leaders' meeting on 12 October, Allah Bakhsh backed out of his commitment and refused to join the League unless he was given a prior assurance that he would be elected leader of the League assembly party and allowed to continue as chief minister. He left the meeting when his demand was not accepted. The Leaguers then relented from their position for the sake of unity in Muslim ranks and consented to accept his demand provided he joined the League. But he did not consider the League offer because by that time he had accepted the Congress offer for support. Despite this setback, the League made some gains in Sindh. Twenty-seven members of the provincial assembly joined its assembly party and elected office-bearers: Ghulam Husain Hidayatullah as its leader, Mir Bandeh Ali as deputy leader, Hashim Gazdar as chief whip, Ghulam Ali Talpur and Noor Mohammad Shah as assistant whips and Ayub Khuhro as general secretary. Hidayatullah on his election as the leader promised that he would not be a candidate for any cabinet position.[108] After the Sindh provincial Muslim League conference, Jinnah toured interior Sindh, visiting Jacobabad, Shikarpur, Larkana and other cities, where he was given warm reception by the people whom he exhorted 'to awake from slumber and agitate for their rights'.[109] The provincial Muslim League was reorganized, with Abdullah Haroon as president and Abdul Majid Sindhi as secretary; and the All-India Muslim League gave it affiliation in December.[110] The Leaguers now eagerly waited for the assembly session that was to meet in February 1939, and hoped to defeat the Allah Bakhsh ministry. But a painful shock awaited them. One day before their no-confidence motion, Allah Bakhsh disrupted their ranks by luring Hidayatullah and Bandeh Ali out of the League with offers of ministerships. The no-confidence motion was lost by thirty-two to seven votes. The League assembly party with its much reduced strength elected Ayub Khuhro as its leader and Hashim Gazdar as general secretary.[111] The League leaders in frustration and anger tried to make up the loss of face and strength by denouncing the defectors especially Hidayatullah and the Hindus who had facilitated the defection.[112] Soon after, the Manzilgah (camping ground) mosque issue provided them an unexpected opportunity to earn the sympathy and support of the Muslim masses.

The Manzilgah mosque, comprising a mosque and a *serai* (inn), had been built during the time of Emperor Akbar, by his governor, Sayyid Masum Shah. Like several other mosques in India, the British had taken over this mosque along with the attached *waqf* property in Sukkur for use by the military. The Sindh administration retained its control even after the army vacated it. Around 1920, the Muslims began to demand its possession but the rich and influential Hindus who had built temples in its proximity stood in the way; they felt that Muslim control of the Manzilgah mosque might hamper their access to their religious site.[113] The Sukkur district Muslim League supported by local Muslim parties renewed the demand after the 1937 elections but the elected governments failed to hand over the mosque to the Muslims. While the Hidayatullah ministry skilfully shelved the issue but the Allah Bakhsh ministry used it for its survival, promising the Muslims including his Jamiatul Ulama-i-Hind supporters that the mosque would be restored to them within a short time. But Allah Bakhsh, who realized the divided opinion in his coalition ministry on this issue, simply made promises but took no action, hoping that the demand would wither away. When there was no progress for the restoration of the Mosque, the Sukkur district Muslim League approached the provincial Muslim League, which at its October 1938, provincial conference demanded its restoration to the Muslims. Allah Bakhsh's promises kept the movement simmering till it started to heat up in the middle of 1939. The provincial Muslim League after an unsuccessful meeting with Allah Bakhsh appointed a Manzilgah restoration committee headed by Abdullah Haroon to organize the movement; Ayub Khuhro, G.M. Sayed (secretary) and Hashim Gazdar were among its active members. On its call, the Sindhi Muslims observed 18 August, as the Manzilgah Day. It threatened to launch passive resistance with effect from 1 October, for which a Khuhro-headed committee started to recruit volunteers and collect funds. The response was 'spontaneous and bewilderingly unexpected', demonstrating 'complete' unity in the ranks of the Sindhi Muslims.[114] The provincial Muslim League and All-India Muslim League leaders desperately approached the governor and the governor-general for action under the Act of 1935, but nothing positive resulted from their attempts.[115] When volunteers began to gather in the Idgah Ground in Sukkur, the district administration initially imposed section 144 to control the situation. The provincial Muslim League launched the movement on the scheduled date without formal authorization of the central League. The Sindh government mishandled the whole affair. On 1 October, Muslim volunteers occupied the mosque and began to court arrest. Within three days more than one thousand volunteers had been arrested. On the third day, the government suddenly without any explanation released all the detainees who returned in larger number along with new volunteers to reoccupy the mosque. The government was worried that the unrest in Sindh might spill over to other parts of India. Meetings had been held outside Sindh on this issue; the largest one was in Lahore organized by Maulana Zafar Ali Khan. The Balochistan government had stopped publication of all material about the Sukkur riots and the telegraph office withheld even a telegram from the Balochistan provincial Muslim League to Jinnah because it was perceived as 'objectionable'.[116] The Hindu leaders, on whose support the Allah Bakhsh ministry survived, pressed him for firm action to, get the mosque vacated. The governor, on the advice of the ministry, promulgated a special ordinance empowering the government outside the ordinary law to deal with the situation. The provincial Muslim League and the All-India Muslim League demanded immediate withdrawal of the special ordinance and peaceful settlement of the issue.[117] After hectic negotiations, it was agreed that the volunteers would vacate the mosque and the government would announce its decision about the mosque within six weeks; Abdullah Haroon persuaded the Muslims to withdraw their demand for limiting the time to four weeks.

The pressure on the Allah Bakhsh ministry mounted when the All-India Hindu Mahasabha held a conference in Sukkur on 12–14 November 1939, which Dr B.S. Moonje presided. The Hindu Mahasabha urged the Sindh government to abandon its 'weak and vacillating policy' and get the mosque vacated. A sitting Hindu minister revealed that even if the mosque was returned to the Muslims its present condition and surroundings would be drastically changed: the doors and ventilators opening on the main road would be closed; the entrance to the mosque would be given from the back side; and the compound walls would be so raised that the mosque would become invisible. The Muslims of Sukkur perceived in these conditions an addition of 'insult to injury' and demanded 'a promise in writing' from Allah Bakhsh that his government would hand over the mosque to the League without any alterations. Abdullah Haroon was willing to accompany Allah Bakhsh to Sukkur to persuade the Muslims of that city to accept even these conditions but the latter refused 'point blank' to promise anything in writing, and declined 'to give even an oral understanding'. Abandoning a peaceful settlement, he vowed 'to teach a lesson to the fellows' in Sukkur who wanted 'to get the upper hand in the matter'. Repression followed the failure of talks. The government removed the volunteers from the mosque by using teargas and baton-charge. Prominent League leaders and thousands of political workers were imprisoned or interned. Muslim press was gagged, strictly prohibited from publishing reports of daily developments, while no such restrictions were imposed on the Hindu-controlled press. The events relating to the Manzilgah mosque evoked sympathies of the Muslims outside Sindh.[118] Communal clashes that started in Sukkur, where the Muslims who constituted a minority in the city suffered more losses than the Hindus, spread to the cities of Shikarpur, Rohri, Larkana and Jacobabad and the villages in their vicinity, where the Hindu losses were equally enormous. Military was called in to assist the police to restore order; and additional troops had to be requisitioned from Quetta when the troops stationed in Sindh proved insufficient. The affected areas witnessed arson, looting, killing and destruction of property on an unprecedented scale. No authentic estimate of losses was ever made; according to one report, over one hundred persons were killed and more than that number injured. After the riots, the provincial Muslim League helped those wrongly implicated or convicted for involvement in the riots; Ali Mohammad Rashidi was secretary of the provincial Muslim League public grievances bureau that was set up for this purpose.[119] A two-member (Nawab Shahnawaz Mamdot and Sir Karimbhai Ibrahim) committee of the All-India Muslim League inquired into these tragic incidents,[120] and so did Khan Abdul Qayyum Khan (1901–1981) on behalf of the Congress.[121] Justice Weston, who conducted the official inquiry, supported the Muslim position. In February 1941, the government handed over the mosque and the adjacent building to a board of trustees, and the ground was reserved for Muslim education. On receiving this information, Jinnah wrote to Sindhi: 'There only remains my deep sorrow for those who suffered and sacrificed for what obviously was a just . . . demand of the Muslims which the Sindh Government . . . bungled so badly. I also sympathize with those Hindus who suffered but it was entirely due to the machinations of their leaders who were responsible for putting up the most arrogant and unjustifiable opposition to the Muslim demand with which they had nothing to do'.[122] The Manzilgah mosque issue created durable Muslim support for the League at the grassroots.

After the Sukkur riots, the Hindu and Muslim leaders agreed to cooperate and, on 7 March 1940, voted out the Allah Bakhsh ministry.[123] The Leaguers were, however, outmanoeuvred in the process of forming a coalition. On 18 March, the ministry that was sworn in had three League ministers (Sindhi, Khuhro and Sayed) and two Hindu ministers (Nihchaldas Vazirani and Rai Sahib Gokaldas) but was headed by the amiable and unassuming non-League Muslim, Mir Bandeh Ali. More serious was the pressure on the League from its coalition partners to introduce joint electorates in the local bodies, which was against the All-India Muslim League policy as laid down at the Patna session.[124] Immediately, the ouster of Allah Bakhsh from power, assumption of ministerial offices by the Leaguers and their presence at the Lahore session with fanfare generated great enthusiasm for the League in Sindh. But on their return from Lahore, the Sindh assembly passed a bill introducing joint electorates in the municipal boroughs, and discussed a similar bill for other local bodies. It faced more serious trouble after Allah Bakhsh recovered from the Manzilgah setback. Again, he caused disruption in its ranks with the help of Azad and Nihchaldas Vazirani, a shrewd and ambitious Hindu politician from upper Sindh. Muslim Leaguers' desire for broader Muslim unity was skilfully exploited to reconcile the Allah Bakhsh group with other Muslim groups and bring them all close to the Congress. On 20 November, Khuhro, Sayed, Sindhi, Bandeh Ali and Allah Bakhsh held 'unity talks' in the presence of Azad and Vazirani. Allah Bakhsh wanted chief ministership for himself and a ministry for Hidayatullah. It was agreed that: Sindhi would resign as minister to make room for Allah Bakhsh or Hidayatullah, and Bandeh Ali would resign as chief minister by 15 February 1941, to enable Allah Bakhsh to assume that office, and Hidayatullah was to take his place as minister. If at that stage Bandeh Ali decided to stay in the ministry, Khuhro was to resign to make room for him, which would leave only two League ministers.[125] The League assembly party had been dissolved before the talks started while the Hindu assembly parties, the Sindh Congress and Hindu Independent Party, were not touched. A 21-point programme that included introduction of joint electorates in all the local bodies was adopted, and a joint advisory committee with Bandeh Ali as its chairman and Sayed as its secretary was appointed to oversee its implementation. Bandeh Ali declined to give anything in writing but

Khuhro and Sayed, in a letter to Vazirani on 20 November, accepted this arrangement, asking him on Azad's advice to keep it 'secret'.[126] Azad signed no document but since he had manoeuvred this 'reconciliation', the arrangement was known as the 'Azad Pact'. Neither the provincial Muslim League council and its assembly party nor the All-India Muslim League were taken into confidence. Abdullah Haroon, the provincial Muslim League president, was out of Karachi and on his return he categorically stated that those who had negotiated with the Congress president had no authority from the party to do so, and the Sindh provincial Muslim League stood 'committed to nothing unless a specific decision' was taken by its council.[127] The 'Pact' had a bad start. Sindhi on Abdullah Haroon's direction refused to resign; instead, Sayed resigned as minister to make room for Allah Bakhsh.[128] The following month Jinnah visited Karachi for a professional engagement. Bandeh Ali joined the League during his stay. On 20 December, the Sindh provincial Muslim League council, in three policy resolutions, (i) vowed to oppose the introduction of joint electorates in the local bodies; (ii) directed Bandeh Ali, Khuhro and Sindhi to constitute a League party in the Sindh assembly by 31 January 1941, and hold its meeting on 12 February; and (iii) appointed an eight-member committee with Sayed as chairman and Gazdar as secretary to organize the party in the towns and villages of Sindh. The committee was to function under the general supervision of the provincial Muslim League council and working committee and submit a report to the working committee after every three months.[129] Due to opposition from the League, the Sindh government withdrew the joint electorates bill that had been moved in the assembly and, in February, even deferred the implementation of joint electorates in the municipalities till an agreement was reached on the all-India basis.[130]

Jinnah was aware of Azad's activities in Sindh but had no information about the 'secret pact', which came to light in January 1941, when Azad and Vazirani pressed the Sindh provincial Muslim League leaders to implement its 'terms' and the Congress used it for anti-League propaganda. When Jinnah came to know of its details, he concluded that it was not a 'pact' between two political parties but an arrangement arrived at among individuals that was not binding on the provincial Muslim League. It was a 'manoeuvre', in his view, that burdened the League with responsibilities but gave it no power. He was in favour of maintaining status quo in the composition of the ministry, advised Bandeh Ali not to resign and did not insist on Allah Bakhsh's resignation. Sayed and Khuhro who were party to the 'secret pact' did press him to accept it for the sake of 'unity' of Muslim groups in the assembly. Jinnah considered it 'absurd' for the three Leaguers 'to resign in order to make room' for Hidayatullah, and disliked their emphasis '*ad nauseam* upon the peculiar conditions' of Sindh. He counselled the Leaguers to 'stand by the resolutions' of the Sindh provincial Muslim League council passed in Karachi in his presence on 20 December 1940, because any departure from them would be disastrous for the League and Muslims of Sindh.[131] He asked Sayed to concentrate on organizing the party at the grassroots and urged Khuhro to establish the League party in the assembly as it was 'the only way' for the League to survive in Sindh. He also wrote to Vazirani 'not to exert his influence' to bring about a change in the personnel of the ministry but Vazirani did not follow Jinnah's advice.[132] The Leaguers accepted Jinnah's advice after some reluctance; for instance, G.M. Sayed assured Jinnah of his 'implicit obedience' to him despite his own 'views and judgment' because, he wrote, 'I have accepted you as my leader'.[133] However, the League assembly party, which was formed on 12 February, with Khuhro as its leader, failed to keep the Bandeh Ali ministry in office.[134] On 4 March, Bandeh Ali left office after Allah Bakhsh along with Vazirani and Gokaldas resigned as ministers, and three days later, Allah Bakhsh formed a ministry by taking these two Hindu leaders as well as Hidayatullah and Ilahi Bakhsh as ministers. The Leaguers then withdrew from the advisory committee that had been appointed to implement the 21-point coalition agenda.[135]

Once the Leaguers were out of power, they turned to organize the party, as the provincial Muslim League had decided and as desired by Jinnah who encouraged them to focus their energies on the party organization; he wrote to Sayed (18 March 1941) that if they did this work for some time, 'no power on earth' could stop their progress, and urged Khuhro (25 March) to organize the party outside the Assembly and 'its results would appear soon'.[136] In addition to the League workers, the Sayed-chaired organizing committee engaged paid *moballigh*s (propagandists) and trained them to carry the League message to the rural areas. Jinnah provided them party literature for free distribution. Sayed translated some of the League tracts into Sindhi and also himself wrote pamphlets to make the workers 'fully conversant with the whole idea of Pakistan'.[137] Like other provincial Leagues, the Sindh provincial Muslim League organized 'Pakistan conferences' in the districts. On Jinnah's advice, the Leaguers did not succumb to the temptation of ministerships in September 1941, when Allah Bakhsh made them offers with the approval of the Congress.[138] Jinnah encouraged them in moments of frustration, emphasizing the need for 'patience, steadiness and silent work' and assured them eventual victory.[139] In March 1942, the provincial Muslim League elected Abdullah Haroon as president as well as treasurer, Khuhro and Hashim Gazdar as vice-presidents, Sindhi as general secretary and Agha Ghulam Nabi Pathan and Yusuf Haroon as joint secretaries. It raised issues which had worried the Sindhi Muslims.[140] At that time, Sindh was attracting agricultural labour for its vast cultivable land from outside Sindh; some Leaguers wanted Muslim labour from south Punjab while the Hindu leaders were in favour of getting Hindu labour from Rajputana.[141] The provincial Muslim League council, however, laid down a policy guideline that agricultural land should not be given in perpetuity or sold to non-Sindhis whatever the circumstances; and the government jobs in Sindh should be reserved for Sindhis and domiciled Sindhis—the term 'domiciled' was to include only those persons who had permanently settled in Sindh for more than twenty-five years. It also called for permanent and inalienable tenancy rights for the *haris* (cultivators) and for reservation of seats for them in the assembly in the future constitution.[142] Before it could pursue this agenda, the sudden death of Abdullah Haroon (27 April 1942) absorbed its attention. His death caused two vacancies, that of the party president and a seat in the central assembly, which became a source of infighting in the provincial Muslim League. Ali Mohammad Rashidi aspired for the assembly seat; and when he could not get the League ticket, he in collusion with Allah Bakhsh coaxed Yusuf Haroon to stand for the League presidency to cause factional tussle in the party to facilitate the smooth election of Maula Bakhsh, Allah Bakhsh's brother, on the assembly seat. On the other hand, Khuhro, Sindhi and Sayed wanted to see Yusuf nominated on the central assembly seat and a senior Leaguer elected as the party president. When the provincial Muslim League working committee and council met on 17 May, Sayed proposed Khuhro's name for the presidency and Rashidi suggested Yusuf's name. Simultaneously, he was asking Nawab Ismail (chairman of the central civil defence committee) for Khuhro's nomination on the central working committee to satisfy his 'vanity'; but in reality he was trying to keep him out of the race for the presidency.[143] The party prevented a conflict by postponing the election of president. Meanwhile, Khuhro as the senior vice-president was asked to officiate as president.[144] The All-India Muslim League on the recommendation of the provincial Muslim League adopted Yusuf as its candidate for the assembly seat. The bye-election was, however, not held till 1 February 1943, because Yusuf's name was not listed in the electoral roll, and which could be included on the order of the governor-general. The League made a request to that effect and this process delayed the bye-election.[145] Prominent Sindhi leaders and Mir Jafar Khan Jamali (1908–1967) who had influence in the constituency campaigned for him, and he won the seat.[146]

During the war, unrest and lawlessness prevailed in rural Sindh, for which the government blamed the Hurs (lit. free persons), followers of Sayyid Sibghatullah Shah, Pir Sahib of Pagaro; some Hindus put the blame on the formation of Sindh as a separate province.[147] The arrest of Pir Pagaro on 24 October 1941, and his 'deportation' first to Karachi and then to Nagpur aggravated the tense situation. On 20 March 1942, the Allah Bakhsh ministry passed the Hur Outrages Act to 'control' the Hurs but failed to do that, and on 1 June, martial law was imposed in more than half of Sindh. The ministry endorsed the decision to stay in office. Pir Pagaro and the Hurs underwent inhuman treatment under martial law. A military tribunal tried Pir Pagaro in secrecy in the Hyderabad central jail and convicted him. On 23 March 1943, he was hanged but the information about that was not disclosed for a fortnight and his dead body was buried at an unknown site. Military courts hanged or sent into exile a large unspecified number of Hurs after summary trials. Pir Pagaro's palatial residence at Pir Jo Goth was raised to the ground by aerial bombing; and by a martial law order his moveable and immoveable property worth millions of rupees was forfeited to the crown; even the female members of his family were deprived of their valuable jewellery. His two young sons, after studies at Aligarh till 1946, were taken to a tutorial establishment in London, and his followers, declared as 'criminal tribes' under the Sindh Criminal Tribes Act, were detained in 'concentration' camps in the open fields surrounded by barbed wires. An atmosphere of terror prevailed in Sindh during martial law; and even after that, any 'undesirable' person could be declared a Hur and convicted.[148] Muslims resented the discrimination shown by the British in the treatment of the Hurs and the 1942 Congress Satyagrahi revolutionaries although they were guilty of crimes of a similar nature.[149] The League could not do much in the situation; it could prevent neither the convictions nor block the prolongation of martial law. However, it did whatever it could possibly do. On 15 June, a four-member (Khuhro, Sindhi, Gazdar and Sayed) Sindh provincial Muslim League delegation met the governor and discussed with him the situation, criticizing the ministers' incompetence and imposition of martial law in the presence of the Act of 1935 and the Defence of India Rules. It asked for a court of inquiry to investigate the circumstances leading to the proclamation of martial law and a provincial assembly session to discuss the political situation but the governor did not accept any of these demands.[150] On the motion of the League members, both the houses of the central legislature protested against the imposition of martial law and its unnecessary continuation. The All-India Muslim League at its Delhi annual session deplored the trial and execution of Pir Sahib of Pagaro by a martial law court rather than a judicial tribunal for offences allegedly committed before the introduction of martial law. It demanded the immediate lifting of martial law, the restoration of Pir Pagaro's properties and treasures to a representative committee of the Muslims and provision of adequate maintenance allowance for his heirs.[151] Besides the martial law, in July–August, devastating floods inundated vast areas of land in Sindh and displaced about 75,000 people. The provincial Muslim League conducted relief work within its limited resources.[152]

Martial law, floods and Allah Bakhsh's renunciation of the British titles in support of the Quit India movement led to the removal of his ministry.[153] Governor Sir Lancelot Graham, instead of inviting Ayub Khuhro, leader of the largest party in the assembly, asked Ghulam Husain Hidayatullah in his discretion to form the ministry and, in case of his failure, threatened to impose governor's rule in Sindh. Now the League leaders could not resist the temptation of ministerial offices. Ignoring the League policy not to coalesce with Muslim individuals and groups in the assembly, the Sindh League assembly party by a vote of fourteen to one (Abdul Majid Sindhi) joined the Hidayatullah ministry, bypassing Jinnah's telegram not to do so; and the provincial Muslim League working committee and council endorsed this decision.[154] Two Leaguers, Khuhro and Gazdar, were sworn in as ministers.[155] Khuhro and Sayed then pleaded with Jinnah that they had tried to contact him on the telephone for five days but failed to do so because of faulty lines; Jinnah did not accept their explanation as, he wrote, he had been 'receiving calls in perfect order'. Meanwhile, they persuaded Hidayatullah to join the League by showing him Jinnah's telegram; interestingly, they then argued with Jinnah in his defence.[156] But they panicked when Jinnah told them that the governor should either invite Khuhro to form the ministry or the League should sit in the opposition.[157] Then, with their blessing, the Sindh Leaguers flooded Jinnah with resolutions, passed at public meetings, and telegrams urging him to allow the League to stay in the ministry.[158] In view of these appeals and a joint personal representation by Khuhro, Sayed and Yusuf, Jinnah took the matter to the working committee, which appointed a subcommittee headed by Nawab Ismail to investigate and decide the issue.[159] The subcommittee interviewed Khuhro and Gazdar in the presence of Sayed, Yusuf and twenty central councillors from Sindh. Except for Abdul Majid Sindhi, all others expressed the opinion that the League ministers should stay in office. Finally, the subcommittee decided that: Pir Ilahi Bakhsh, the non-League Muslim minister, should sign the League pledge and if he did not, another Leaguer should replace him; and Hidayatullah should assure Jinnah in writing that he would carry out the League policy and his instruction, and his five followers should join the League.[160] After the requisite assurance from Hidayatullah and the entry of Ilahi Bakhsh along with nine others into the League, the subcommittee allowed the ministers to continue in office.[161] The Sindh provincial Muslim League washed away the stains of this crisis and earned a unique distinction when, on 3 March 1943, the Sindh assembly on Sayed's motion passed a resolution by 24 to 3 votes that endorsed the principles embodied in the Lahore Resolution.[162]

The election of the party president revived factionalism. Khuhro and Sayed who aspired for this office endeavoured to strengthen their position by recruiting supporters in the process of membership enrolment and party elections in the districts. There were complaints that Sayed was planting his own men in the district Muslim Leagues; and in one case, he even nominated all the office-bearers of a district Muslim League and its representatives on the provincial council; Faqir Mohammad Mangrio, who belonged to that district, on Khuhro's advice, filed a complaint against this procedure and an inquiry proved his contention.[163] The 'progressives' in the party, inspired by G.M. Sayed, moved that the provincial Muslim League executive—working committee and council—should oversee the working of the ministry and that ministers should not hold offices in the party.[164] They supported the *mukaddims* and hereditary *haris* in their struggle against the *jagirdars* who were supported by the 'conservatives'.[165] The conflict was resolved only when Jinnah brought about reconciliation between them. On 13 June 1943, he presided over a meeting of the provincial council which, on his advice, unanimously elected G.M. Sayed as president, Yusuf Haroon as general secretary, and G.A. Allana and Mohammad Amin Khoso as joint secretaries.[166] This unanimity among the Leaguers steeply increased the League's popularity; Jinnah himself observed after a tour of Sindh and Balochistan that 99 per cent Muslims were with the League.[167] That year its membership rose to 177,218 with 547 branches; and the strength of its assembly party went up to thirty members.[168] The provincial Muslim League established a civil defence committee with G.M. Sayed as its chairman and Mahmud Haroon as secretary, and its activities consolidated its support at the grassroots. The League won two bye-elections; in one case, its candidate, Ahmad Khan Sadhayo, defeated Allah Bakhsh's brother, Maula Bakhsh, by securing 6,191 against 4,195 votes.[169] The provincial Muslim League hosted the last annual session of the All-India Muslim League in Karachi, and made elaborate arrangements for a warm reception of Jinnah and the visiting dignitaries. The success of this session was a tribute to the unity in the Sindh League leadership.[170]

The League faced no threat from the Congress or any Muslim party in Sindh. But its own leaders, Khuhro, Sayed and Hidayatullah, brought down its prestige in their pursuit to exercise absolute control on the party and power in Sindh. At first, the conflict was between Khuhro and Sayed; and Hidayatullah ostensibly sat on the sidelines. It was manifested in the process of membership enrolment and party elections; Faqir Mohammad Mangrio was now joined by Mir Ghulam Ali Talpur and several others who questioned the election process in Mirpurkhas, Tharparkar, Hyderabad and Karachi.[171] The conflict spilled over to the mayoral contest in Karachi: Khuhro supported Yusuf, and Sayed endorsed Gazdar.[172] Yusuf was elected Mayor but mutual bitterness intensified. Khuhro supported by Yusuf ousted Sayed from the board of directors of the daily *Al-Wahid*.[173] Jinnah constantly advised them all 'to work in harmony' and rise above 'petty disputes'.[174] He wrote to a Leaguer, 'it is mystery to me why some of these leading men in Sindh cannot see how unwise it is for them and for the Muslim League organization to quarrel among themselves and bring down the prestige of the League and their own'.[175] G.M. Sayed, after his re-election as president on 14 May 1944, made moves with more confidence.[176] For some time, however, focus was on the party organization. M.A. Sayyid was elected as secretary and the party was revamped and popularized at the grassroots by such steps as 'Buy from Muslims only' campaign and observance of a 'Muslim Trade Day'.[177] But G.M. Sayed's ambition to control the ministry through the party executive that he had packed with his supporters brought him into conflict with his rivals. The party on his initiative launched a systematic campaign against the ministers charging them with corruption and nepotism, demanding their resignation.[178] Earlier, Sayed's target had been Khuhro, and not Hidayatullah; in fact, the latter had consulted Sayed in his moves against Khuhro.[179] Jinnah's conciliatory moves provided only temporary respite.[180] The conflict cost Khuhro his freedom; as minister, he had made enemies in influential quarters. He was capable, energetic and courageous with a touch of arrogance but was crudely dismissive of administrative niceties and procedures, passionately attached to the League, blamed the Hindu leaders for the aggravation of divisions among the Sindhi Muslims, and was 'notoriously' pro-Muslim in his attitude and policies; thus, he alienated the British governor, members of the higher bureaucracy, the Hindus and many of his League colleagues.[181] His implication in the murder of Chief Minister Allah Bakhsh Soomro, and arrest on 26 September 1944, temporarily removed him from the political scene.[182] Both Sayed and Hidayatullah contributed to his incarceration.

After Khuhro, the Sayed–Hidayatullah conflict burst out in its worst form. A vicious circle set in. Hidayatullah refused to take Sayed's nominee (Mohammad Ali Shah) as Khuhro's replacement in the ministry.[183] Sayed soon avenged this 'insult'. In a bye-election on the seat that had fallen vacant on the death of the newly elected Ahmad Khan Sadhayo, Hidayatullah's son, Anwar, was a candidate for the League ticket. Sayed ensured that the provincial parliamentary board and the central parliamentary board did not award him the party ticket. The central parliamentary board did depute Husain Imam to Sindh who reported in Anwar's favour but due to Sayed's opposition, the central board ignored his report as well as appeals from several Sindhi leaders in his support.[184] Sayed's last-minute moves resulted in the election of Maula Bakhsh; his opponents suspected that he was doing all that at the behest of Nihchaldas Vazirani.[185] He also displeased the Talpurs by opposing their candidate and by campaigning for his rival in the Tando Mohammad Khan bye-election.[186] Hidayatullah outdid Sayed; he issued orders for his internment in his hometown, Sann, under the Hur Outrages Act but public protest restrained him from implementing the orders or even making these public.[187] Meanwhile, he brought in Ghulam Ali Talpur, one of Sayed's critics, as minister and removed Gazdar from the ministry, who was close to Sayed and critical of

Hidayatullah.[188] The central parliamentary board, the central committee of action and even Jinnah could not stop the infighting.[189] Sayed who had personally seen his internment orders was furious and desperate to take revenge. He manoeuvred to bring down the Hidayatullah ministry on 23 February 1945, despite the fact that the provincial Muslim League assembly party had twice expressed confidence in his ministry; one confidence vote was taken on the night prior to the no-confidence vote and Sayed himself had dinner with Hidayatullah after that meeting.[190] Hidayatullah easily constituted a new ministry, by bringing in Maula Bakhsh as minister. Again, this was not in line with the party discipline. Jinnah directed Hidayatullah to ask Maula Bakhsh to join the League and remove him if he declined to do so; in case Hidayatullah was unable to reconstitute a new ministry without him, he should sit in the opposition.[191] Now twelve members of the provincial assembly including Sayed and Gazdar who had voted against the ministry were willing to support Hidayatullah; and on 14 March, he reconstituted the ministry.[192] Jinnah's serious illness and his handing over the charge of the All-India Muslim League to Liaquat and Nawab Ismail counted in this last-minute reconciliation. In the absence of Khuhro, Sayed had no competitors in the party, as Hidayatullah operated primarily at the level of the assembly party.[193] He easily filled the provincial Muslim League council with his supporters, which passed a resolution empowering the party executive to control the assembly party.[194] The scene changed before the general elections, when Khuhro after his honourable acquittal in the murder case re-appeared on the political scene.[195] The intra-party conflict arose on the distribution of tickets for the elections, which climaxed in Sayed's expulsion from the party.[196] Sayed continued to function under the umbrella of a Sindh League, claiming it to be the genuine League in Sindh, and supported the Pakistan demand.

After the elections, thirty prominent Leaguers, meeting at Yusuf Haroon's residence with Liaquat in the chair, decided to set up a 'Sindh Provincial Organizing Committee'; Gazdar was its chairman and Yusuf its convener to organize League branches in Sindh. This committee had the powers of the provincial council and other statutory committees; Yusuf extended it a loan for office expenses, as G.M. Sayed had refused to hand over the party fund amounting to Rs 10,000 to the committee; the reorganized provincial Muslim League elected Gazdar as its president.[197] A Leaguer, Sayyid Miran Mohammad Shah, was elected speaker of the assembly; the central League restrained Gazdar from contesting this office.[198] The League members of the provincial assembly formed the assembly party and elected Hidayatullah as its leader and Ayub Khuhro as deputy leader.[199] The Sayed group, Maula Bakhsh-led nationalist Muslims and Vazirani-led Congress formed a coalition party in the Sindh assembly, with Sayed as its leader. Even after forming this party, Sayed still wanted to stage a comeback in the League. Both Hidayatullah and Khuhro supported his re-entry; Jinnah, however, wanted Sayed to regret his past acts in which he had violated the party discipline and dissociate himself from the 'enemy camp', i.e. the Congress. But these initiatives and those of others failed to mature although, according to one report, Sayed was willing to 'surrender unconditionally'.[200] Simultaneously, the Congress was trying to get an invitation for Sayed from the governor to form the ministry but the British did not like to be seen so blatantly unfair to the League here as well, as they had been in the Punjab. Besides, Hidayatullah was a more skilful tactician and diplomat than Iftikhar Mamdot. His ministry survived by a narrow margin of one vote, securing 30 votes against 29. Sayed started an anti-League campaign through his Sindhi daily, the *Qurbani*; and by July, he had weaned away two League members of the provincial assembly. Now Hidayatullah, instead of intriguing to secure a majority and have an unstable ministry, advised Governor Francis Mudie to dissolve the assembly and hold fresh elections. Amidst controversy and Congress opposition, the assembly was dissolved and fresh elections were held on 9 December. The League improved upon its strength in the elections, securing 33 out of 35 Muslim seats; the nationalist Muslims elected on the remaining two seats also joined the League. Sayed's defeat in the elections removed the threat to the stability of its ministry from that quarter; and he stopped his manoeuvring because the Congress refused to extend him patronage.[201] Jinnah prevented a possible Khuhro–Hidayatullah tussle for power; in fact, on his advice, Khuhro who felt that he deserved to be the chief minister more than Hidayatullah again proposed his name for the leadership of the League assembly party, and he himself was elected its deputy leader.[202] The Hidayatullah ministry began to implement the eight-point constructive programme that included imparting of free and compulsory primary education, introduction of the Sindh university bill and appointment of a committee of impartial experts to examine the condition of *haris* (peasants). The Sindh League assembly party adopted this programme in Jinnah's presence and took steps to look after the refugees.[203] When the All-India Muslim League assumed power in Pakistan, Hidayatullah took over as governor and Khuhro formed the first post-independence ministry.

(*iii*) *Frontier Provincial Muslim League*. In the NWFP, Sahibzada Abdul Qayyum Khan formed the first ministry after the elections that lasted for about five months (1 April to 3 September 1937). When the Congress decided to accept offices, his ministry suffered a defeat by 27 to 22 votes. On 7 September 1937, Dr Khan Sahib (1882–1958), the Khudai Khidmatgar–Congress leader in the assembly, formed the next ministry. The Leaguers had not been disillusioned by the absence of a separate election platform or by the results of the elections. They began to establish League branches around the time of the Lucknow annual session. Several branches emerged in the six districts, some requesting the All-India Muslim League for direct affiliation.[204] On 3 September, they held a conference in Abbottabad that a noted Khudai Khidmatgar Abdul Khaliq Khaleeq presided, where a provincial Muslim League was set up with Maulana Mohammad Shoaib (1901–1981), *nazim* of the Jamiatul Ulama, NWFP, as president and Mohammad Ismail Ghaznavi (1897–1988) as general secretary; the object was to get it affiliated with the All-India Muslim League at the Lucknow session.[205] This conference passed resolutions on issues that were then engaging Muslim attention: Shahidganj mosque; British military operation in Waziristan; relief in land revenue; opposition to the partition of Palestine; and expression of confidence in Jinnah's leadership.[206] A Frontier provincial Muslim League delegation attended the Lucknow session and three of its members (Mohammad Kuli Khan, Sajjad Ahmad Jan and Abdul Wahid Khan) served on the subjects committee.[207] On their return, the Leaguers reactivated the organizational drive with greater fervour. By March 1938, they had organized the party in all the six districts.[208] That month, the provincial Muslim League council re-elected Maulana Shoaib as president, Mian Ziauddin (1901–1987) as vice-president, Ismail Ghaznavi as general secretary, and Sajjad Ahmad Jan and Abdul Wahid Khan as joint secretaries, Qazi Abdul Halim as propaganda secretary, and Arbab Shamsuddin as treasurer; and also elected twenty representatives on the central council.[209] A provincial Muslim League delegation attended the Calcutta special session, even before the party's formal affiliation with the All-India Muslim League, which was given in June, and the organizers made proper arrangements for their reception and stay.[210] The Calcutta session called on the Muslims 'to take special steps to combat' the anti-Muslim activities of the Congress in the NWFP; Jinnah, however, restrained them and advised that the time was not yet ripe to counter the Congress propaganda.[211]

The NWFP was the only Muslim majority province where the Congress could form its ministry.[212] The Congress–Khudai Khidmatgar relations were, however, still tenuous. Therefore, top Congress leaders—Gandhi, Nehru, Rajendra Prasad, Vallabhbhai Patel, Subhas Chandra Bose and Maulana Azad—paid frequent visits to solidify these relations; the resourceful Mehr Chand Khanna, the finance minister, and Khudai Khidmatgars coordinated their activities.[213] During May 1938–March 1939, Gandhi paid three visits; the first was of an exploratory nature during which, according to Sardar Nishtar, Abdul Ghaffar Khan (1890–1988) 'definitely refused' the provincial Congress committee's demand 'to either merge the Khudai Khidmatgars into the Congress or make them subordinate to the provincial Congress'.[214] His second visit was for a longer duration (5 October–9 November 1938) and proved more fruitful than the first one; its object, according to Gandhi, was 'to study minutely the Red Shirt organization' and find out ways to utilize it 'for the service of the country at large'.[215] Now the Congress working committee, on Frontier provincial Congress committee's proposal, recommended the addition of a proviso to article IV of the Congress constitution that recognized the Khudai Khidmatgars as its 'volunteer organization' in the NWFP under Ghaffar Khan's leadership; the volunteer organization was free to adopt its own pledge keeping in view the Congress policy.[216] The third visit was in March the following year to open a training centre and a workers' home for the Red Shirts in the NWFP. There is no evidence of any direct Jinnah–Ghaffar contact although Mohammad Yunus, then a student at the Islamia college, Peshawar was keen to arrange a meeting between them. Both the leaders agreed to meet in Delhi but it is not known whether that meeting took place or not.[217] Gandhi's visits consolidated the Congress–Khudai Khidmatgar bonds but caused discontent in a section of the Frontier Muslims including the Khudai Khidmatgars.[218] Simultaneously, the Congress was conducting its Muslim mass contact movement, which was as unpopular among the Muslims here as elsewhere. Some steps of the Congress ministry itself damaged its popularity; these were: cancellation of the 'Islamic textbooks' in the district board schools, dismissal of 400 Muslim employees in the hydro-electric department on the complaint of a Hindu engineer, recruitment on vacant posts by competition and reduction in the government grant to the Islamia college, Peshawar in retaliation to the defeat of its candidate for the secretaryship of the college. The provincial Muslim League, of course, protested against these actions.[219] As a result, several prominent Khudai Khidmatgars felt so strongly that they left the Congress and joined the League; the most important defections were of Khan Samin Jan (1893–1956), a member of the provincial assembly, Bakht Jamal (1900–1975), Rahim Bakhsh Ghaznavi (1903–1979) and Malik Taj Ali Khan.

The Frontier provincial Muslim League benefited from this atmosphere in the Haripur bye-election in Hazara. The League as well as the Congress launched intense election campaigns. The climax of the Congress campaign was a conference in Abbottabad, in which its leaders denounced the League and its policies. In response, on the All-India Muslim League's request, several Leaguers including Zafar Ali Khan, Jamal Mian Farangi Mahalli, Maulana Abdul Hamid Badauni, Raja of Mahmudabad, Hasrat Mohani, Haji Abdullah Haroon, Abdul Majid Sindhi and Syed Mohammad Mehdi of Pirpur visited the province to counteract the Congress propaganda.[220] The All-India Muslim League especially deputed Maulana Shaukat Ali who had considerable influence in the NWFP since the Khilafat days to campaign for its candidate; and he toured the province for three weeks.[221] The League candidate, Abdur Rashid Taherkheli, won the bye-election against Mehdi Zaman Khan. After this victory, Khaliquzzaman presided over an impressive provincial Muslim League conference in Abbottabad on 10–11 September. During this campaign, Sardar Nishtar resigned from the ministerial party.[222] Then, Sardar Bahadur Khan defeated the Congress candidate, Aslam Khan, in another bye-election. Jinnah quite optimistically looked forward to the day when the NWFP would have a League ministry and felt confident that it would come 'perhaps sooner than many people think'.[223] The League made gains not only in Hazara and southern districts of Bannu, Kohat and Dera Ismail Khan but also in Peshawar and Mardan.[224] It built a memorial for the martyrs of the Qissa Khani Bazaar firing while the Khudai Khidmatgars erected a separate memorial.[225] The strength of the League assembly party increased; and, in November 1938, it was reported at 24 members of the provincial assembly against 25 of the Congress.[226] However, the possibility of a League ministry was still not that close. A Frontier provincial Muslim League contingent participated in the Patna annual session, where the All-India Muslim League condemned the British policy at 'the forcible subjugation of the independent tribal belt' and the Congress move to make the tribal areas part of the settled districts.[227] The following year, the All-India Muslim League sent a delegation of Muslim-minority provinces to the NWFP to apprise the Frontier Muslims of the plight of the Muslims in the Hindu-majority provinces.[228] Simultaneously, the Frontier provincial Muslim League organized meetings to protest against the policies of the Congress ministry.[229] On 25 September 1939, the ministry, finding the existing laws insufficient to deal with the law and order situation, introduced a goonda bill in the assembly to control the unrest resulting from the League protest and the Waziristan operations.[230] The bill was highly restrictive of fundamental rights. It defined a 'goonda' to include a person using abusive and improper language in public or otherwise and also one who associated himself with such a person. The accused could not appear in the court in person nor could he seek legal aid, and the witnesses against him whose names could not be disclosed were to give evidence *in camera*. Anyone convicted could be fined, imprisoned, or expelled from the province. The NWFP assembly passed the bill amidst a demonstration organized by the Peshawar city Muslim League outside its building.[231] The Frontier provincial Muslim League set up a 'war council' to plan civil disobedience against this legislation and sought approval from Jinnah who raised the issue with the viceroy. Consequently, the governor, on the viceroy's advice, withheld assent to the bill.[232] Dr Khan Sahib was saved from any further embarrassment when, on 7 November, his ministry resigned on the direction of the Congress. The decline of the Congress continued and when it launched the Quit India movement it failed to muster popular support in the NWFP.[233]

Meanwhile, on 29 October 1939, the Frontier provincial Muslim League elected its new office-bearers: Sadullah as president and Ziauddin as general secretary.[234] Its support-base was also broadened; more than fifteen hundred Leaguers from the Frontier districts attended the Lahore session where Aurangzeb spoke on the main resolution.[235] On 17 November 1940, the party again changed its leadership; now Bakht Jamal replaced Sadullah as president.[236] This change was partly a reflection of the growing Aurangzeb–Sadullah rivalry.[237] Earlier, the two had jointly manoeuvred Maulana Shoaib's ouster from the presidency, which gave credence to a malicious anti-League propaganda that the big Khans had come to dominate the provincial Muslim League. Their personal conflict gradually worsened and hindered the development of local leadership that could work for the League although there was gradual rise in membership enrolment.[238] A capable and dedicated political worker, Bakht Jamal failed to assert his authority as president, and when he did that by urging control of the League executive on the ministry, he lost the presidency to Taj Ali Khan; Ziauddin was continuously re-elected as the general secretary.[239] Bakht Jamal served on the central working committee for two years (1941 and 1942). Jinnah wanted to nominate him again but could not do that because Aurangzeb manoeuvred to drop his name from the list of provincial Muslim League representatives on the central council; and membership of the council was a requirement for nomination on the working committee.[240] Due to intra-party conflicts, the Frontier provincial Muslim League was unable to consolidate the support that the Pakistan scheme had generated for the League at the grassroots. Jinnah sent a central League delegation to assist the party and began to encourage Muslim youth to work for the party.[241] But the reports about the low state of the party did not diminish.[242] The central civil defence committee toured NWFP in June 1942, and its members individually as well as collectively reported to that effect.[243] One member found a 'very genuine enthusiasm among the masses at large' for the 'Muslim League and the ideal of Pakistan' but lamented 'a real dearth of workers'.[244] Another member praised 'the quiet work' done by Bakht Jamal but complained about others not taking advantage of the 'League mindedness of the general public', and suggested the appointment of a committee to organize the League.[245] On the receipt of the central civil defence committee report, Jinnah advised the Frontier Leaguers, 'some of you [League leaders] should take off your coats now and organize, harness and consolidate the Muslims of your province'.[246] Apparently, the Leaguers did not follow his advice. The following year, the central civil defence committee supervisor in his report listed in detail the organizational defects in the Frontier provincial Muslim League.[247] Then, Jinnah summoned Bakht Jamal and Darwesh Mohammad Khan to Delhi and gave them necessary instructions.[248] During this period, the Leaguers provided relief to the Kazakh refugees before their eventual settlement in the Hyderabad state; the Kazakhs had come after the Soviet occupation of their land.[249]

Aurangzeb's focus had been on the chief ministership rather than the party organization. He cultivated the governor and higher bureaucracy in that pursuit, and kept away from the League workers. The British government, however, did not want to alienate completely the Congress and the Khudai Khidmatgars. In addition, they were not sure whether Aurangzeb would be able to muster and maintain a majority or not. The Quit India movement proved a turning point. Then, all the hurdles in Aurangzeb's way were removed.[250] Finally, Aurangzeb, after he had provided Governor Cunningham a signed list of requisite number of members of the provincial assembly, was invited to form the ministry; and on 25 May 1943, the first League ministry in the NWFP was sworn in.[251] A few Leaguers still opposed their party assuming power under Aurangzeb's leadership. They were apprehensive that his leadership 'might damage the Muslim League'.[252] The League, one supporter warned, might temporarily retain its influence due to its own prestige and the 'charm' of Jinnah's name but there was bound to be a 'terrible reaction'.[253] His assessment eventually proved correct. But immediately, the League scored victory. Bye-elections were due on four Muslim seats on 6–7 August: the constituencies were spread over the whole province: (i) Peshawar city (Urban), (ii) Khalil (Rural), (iii) Mardan (Rural), and (iv) Cities of Dera Ismail Khan, Kohat, Bannu and Abbottabad (Urban). The provincial Muslim League constituted a selection board, which selected Ghulam Husain, Arbab Sher Ali Khan, Ayub Khan and Nawab Nasrullah Khan as its candidates. The Congress also decided to field its candidates; Mehr Chand Khanna was behind this decision who wanted to show to 'the world at large' that the Frontier Province was not for Pakistan.[254] The Frontier provincial Muslim League pooled in its local and all-India resources and won all the four seats;[255] the constituency in Mardan used to be a stronghold of the Khudai Khidmatgars.[256] Commenting on the results, V.D. Savarkar, the Hindu Mahasabha president, admitted that the Muslims of the Frontier Province were the followers of the League.[257] Jinnah was elated by this 'decisive victory', which had raised 'the honour, prestige and reputation of the League', but appealed to the Frontier Muslims 'to give up internecine quarrel' and stand united under its banner.[258] But they failed to do that.

The Aurangzeb ministry could neither provide good governance nor was it able to unite and strengthen the provincial Muslim League. Aurangzeb himself failed to rise above personal biases. Instead of conciliating his rivals in the party, he not only hardened their animosity by his attitude but also created new opponents. Besides, his critics levelled charges of corruption, nepotism and maladministration against him and his ministers.[259] Although no inquiry was ever made into the veracity of these charges but the persons he associated with strengthened the negative perception about him even in friendly quarters; the Congress–Khudai Khidmatgars, of course, missed no opportunity to use any negative material for anti-League propaganda.[260] The scarcity of commodities of daily use and their high prices added to the unpopularity of his ministry; and he was blamed for giving the hoarders a free hand.[261] His support to Governor Cunningham's move to revise the constitution of the Islamia college, Peshawar added to his unpopularity, which, if implemented, would have brought it completely under bureaucratic control. The protest by the college alumni and timely intervention of the All-India Muslim League prevented that eventuality. The amendments that were finally adopted in the college constitution were based on consensus. This incident further spoiled Aurangzeb's relations with Sadullah, secretary of the Islamia college, whose house he had subjected to police search for 'hoarding unlicensed weapons'.[262] The intra-party dissensions crept into the party ranks and the ministry; as early as October 1943, Arbab Ayub Khan wanted to move a no-confidence motion against the ministry but, on Sadullah's suggestion, agreed to seek Jinnah's advice. [263] Jinnah's intervention, when he invited prominent Frontier Leaguers including the ministers to Delhi, provided only a temporary relief.[264] The party organization was ignored. The central committee of action, after an intensive tour (13–29 June 1944) of the six districts and interviews with various delegations, decided to intervene directly.[265] Liaquat wrote to the central committee of action chairman that the Frontier provincial Muslim League was 'in a terrible mess' and unless immediate steps were taken it would 'suffer a setback from which it will be difficult to recover'.[266] But instead of appointing a local committee and supervising its work as had earlier been suggested by the central civil defence committee in its report, the central committee of action entrusted the task to one of its members, Qazi Isa, who was empowered to supervise the enrolment process and elections from the primary to the provincial levels. The existing office-bearers were, however, allowed to look after the routine work till the election of new office-bearers.[267] Qazi Isa started his work in an impressive manner but then left it to the *ad hoc* committees that he appointed and failed to do any direct supervision.[268] His alleged partiality, arrogance and close association with Aurangzeb damaged the whole reorganization process, which had not been completed even by April 1945; some dissident League workers in frustration organized a new body, the Khuddam-i-Muslim League, to keep the party on the right track.[269]

The Congress–Khudai Khidmatgars fully exploited the intra-Frontier provincial Muslim League conflict. They weaned away five League members of the provincial assembly (Raja Manochehr, Abdur Rashid Taherkheli, Sadullah Khan, Faizullah Khan and Mohammad Afzal Khan); and, on 12 March 1945, with their help defeated the Aurangzeb ministry by 24 to 18 votes; four days later, Dr Khan Sahib formed the Congress ministry.[270] Aurangzeb put all the blame for the defeat of his ministry on Mehr Chand Khanna and Iskandar Mirza who, he alleged, used the Kasturia Memorial Fund and intrigue to bring about the defections.[271] The malaise, of course, lay within the Frontier provincial Muslim League, which was displayed in ugly scenes on 25 March, when it met to elect delegates for the annual session that had been scheduled in Lahore on 30 March; Sadullah and his supporters violently disrupted that meeting.[272] The Leaguers from the Hazara district had their own grievances and those of southern districts, Kohat, Bannu and Dera Ismail Khan supported them.[273] Now the central committee of action took another drastic action; it dissolved the Frontier provincial Muslim League and its branches to facilitate fresh elections but still authorized Qazi Isa to supervise the elections, and placed all the party funds, registers, books and other relevant papers at his disposal.[274] Nothing tangible was accomplished. The Frontier Leaguers went into the general elections in this state of disarray. The central parliamentary board hastily made last minute arrangements to contest the elections; and its performance in the prevailing circumstances was quite satisfactory. The organizational work was taken up seriously after the elections. The central committee of action appointed an organizing committee with Samin Jan Khan as chairman, Mohammad Ali Khan Hoti secretary and Arbab Noor Mohammad Khan treasurer to organize the party; and authorized the president and treasurer to operate the party funds.[275] The committee had representatives from the district Muslim Leagues: Hazara 6; Mardan 7; Kohat 3; Bannu 4; Dera Ismail Khan 6; and Peshawar district 11; and Peshawar city had 3 representatives.[276] Henceforth, the Frontier provincial Muslim League functioned smoothly and cohesively with hardly any sign of factionalism. None raised any dissenting voice. Even Aurangzeb quietly served on the organizing committee as an ordinary member. The reorganized party displayed unprecedented unity and skilfully used the political developments in 1946, especially the Muslim massacre in Bihar and elsewhere, to broaden its support-base at the grassroots. The pro-League *ulama* and *mashaikh* held 'Pakistan conferences' in major cities. There was regular inflow of Congressmen and Khudai Khidmatgars into the League. Consequently, in February 1947, the League candidate, Mohammad Ishaq Khan, defeated Mian Shakirullah Khan, a Congress–Khudai Khidmatgar candidate, in the Kamalzai constituency bye-election in Mardan by a margin of 588 votes; and this was despite liberal distribution of oil, sugar and cloth by the Congress ministry.[277] Before the bye-election, Dr Khan Sahib had confidently challenged the League that the Kamalzai bye-election would conclusively prove whether Pathans wanted Pakistan or Hindustan.[278] Apprehensive of another defeat, he declined to hold bye-election in the Abbottabad East constituency. The provincial committee of action-led civil disobedience movement in February–June 1947, further solidified the support-base of the League. By the time of the referendum, the political scenario had completely changed.

(iv) *Balochistan Provincial Muslim League*. Balochistan was broadly divided into British Balochistan including the leased areas, princely states and tribal areas. The formation of a provincial Muslim League in British Balochistan was delayed because no all-India party was allowed to establish a branch here till late 1930s. Even otherwise, the British administration here arbitrarily put restrictions on civil liberties; for example, on 29 January 1934, Abdus Samad Khan Achakzai was imprisoned for three years under the Frontier Crimes Regulations for advocating constitutional reforms and remained incarcerated beyond the period of his sentence, and a Baloch sardar, Abdur Rahman Khan Bugti, was detained first in Balochistan for three years and then in Ranchi (Bihar) for another period of more than three years without any charge; in addition, he was deprived of his assets.[279] Surprisingly, during the Second World War in 1941, the administration prohibited entry into Quetta without passport, which caused immense hardship to those Balochistanis who were residing outside Balochistan. Besides these restrictions, the All-India Muslim League did not need a parliamentary board here, as Balochistan had no elected legislature. The Anjuman-i-Watan, led by Abdus Samad Khan Achakzai, with hardly fifty members and the Qalat State National Party, consisting of mostly Qalat state employees, were the only active local political parties. The Congress had declined to give affiliation to the Anjuman-i-Watan, even as late as September 1940, and decided to maintain with it only 'friendly contacts'. In August 1939, the Jamiatul Ulama-i-Hind opened a branch but initially its orientation was completely religious.[280]

Earlier, in 1926, an Anjuman Naujawanan-i-Baloch was established, which, in 1931, was transformed into Anjuman-i-Ittehad-i-Balochan wa Balochistan, and was led by Yusuf Magsi and Abdul Aziz Kurd. Jinnah and the All-India Muslim League had been advocating constitutional reforms in British Balochistan since 1927; and the leaders here had kept him informed about their demands. Before the revival of the All-India Muslim League, its council had demanded that Balochistan should either be given the status of a province or be amalgamated with Sindh. It also advocated: representation of British Balochistan in the central legislature; freedom of speech, association and press; introduction of the system of elections in the local bodies; codification of the customary law; and reforms in the jirga system.[281] The revival of the All-India Muslim League was seen in Balochistan with positive expectations.[282] At its Lucknow annual session, the All-India Muslim League demanded 'a democratic system' in British Balochistan similar to the other provinces 'to replace the present arbitrary' form of governance; and at the Sindh provincial Muslim League conference in October 1938, a Baloch deputation led by K.B. Allah Bakhsh Gabol, deputy speaker of the Sindh assembly, had requested Jinnah to raise the issues of constitutional reforms in Balochistan and lifting of the ban on recruitment of the Balochs in the army that had been imposed since 1925.[283] The Sindh conference itself passed a resolution, demanding constitutional reforms in Balochistan.[284] Then, at its Patna annual session, the All-India Muslim League reiterated the demand for immediate steps to give British Balochistan the status of a full-fledged province. The following year, Jinnah asked Qazi Isa, who had just returned from England after his bar-at-law, to organize a provincial Muslim League in Balochistan. Qazi Isa established League branches in different districts including one in his hometown, Pishin.[285] The branch in Quetta had Mir Mohammad Ismail Nausherwani as its president and Maulvi Ubaidullah Baloch, editor of the *Kalimatul Haq*, as its secretary.[286] On 10–11 June, the Balochistan provincial Muslim League was formally established at a meeting in Quetta; Qazi Isa was elected its president, Ghulam Mohammad Khan Tareen its general secretary, Sardar Mohammad Usman Khan Jogezai, Mir Qadir Bakhsh Zehri and Malik Shah Jahan its vice-presidents, and Malik Mohammad Usman its joint secretary.[287] It demanded: educational facilities, representation in government services and constitutional reforms. Following its formation, the All-India Muslim League council condemned the British policy and demanded the status of a full-fledged province for Balochistan along with a 'first-rate college'.[288] Qazi Isa drafted a constitution that the provincial Muslim League adopted. On the provincial Muslim League's invitation, Maulana Zafar Ali Khan and Maulana Abdul Hamid Badauni toured Balochistan to counter the pro-Congress propaganda.[289]

The All-India Muslim League promptly responded to requests from the Balochistan provincial Muslim League. It gave the provincial Muslim League affiliation without much scrutiny and endorsed its socio-political demands.[290] Jinnah nominated Qazi Isa on the central working committee in response to a resolution of the provincial Muslim League, and Isa served on the committee till 1947.[291] When the provincial Muslim League demanded that its seats in the central council should be raised from five to ten, the All-India Muslim League immediately accepted the demand at the Allahabad annual session.[292] Its delegates regularly participated in its all-India sessions; Qazi Isa led its contingent to the Lahore session where he spoke on the main resolution.[293] The provincial Muslim League kept itself active by holding frequent meetings in different parts of the province, but its annual conferences during summer usually marked the height of its activities when all-India League figures would come to preside over its functions. Jinnah was to inaugurate its first annual conference on 26–28 August 1940, but due to his illness Liaquat came to preside over it.[294] The provincial Muslim League could not hold its annual conference in 1941, but the following year, Nawab Iftikhar Husain Mamdot presided over the second annual conference on 4–5 July, which two central civil defence committee members (Nawab Ismail and Khaliquzzaman) and Nawab Bahadur Yar Jang (1905–44) addressed.[295] Jinnah inaugurated the third annual conference in July 1943, where the party demanded female educational institutions, elected municipality for Quetta and the status of a full-fledged province for Balochistan. He felt that the Balochistan administration was 'political and semi-military', which was incapable of appreciating peoples' feelings and civil rights.[296] He advised the Baloch leaders to 'adapt yourself to the times in which you are living and the time that is coming hereafter. Muslim League has no desire nor is it the policy of the Muslim League that we should do anything to harm the Sardars, Nawabs and Chiefs. We ask you to realize your responsibilities, realize your own duties and come in line with your people. . . . Give up your jealousies . . . [and] . . . don't quarrel over small matters. Observe one rule that you are prepared to give up your individual conveniences and interests for the collective good of your Nation. . . . If you organize yourself on these lines, Balochistan I tell you is going to play a very important part in the Pakistan Scheme'. When Jinnah was presented a 'historical sword', he observed, 'it will only be unsheathed in our defence and not for any aggressive purpose'.[297] After the conference, he visited Qalat on the invitation of the Khan of Qalat, Ahmad Yar Khan, who arranged two camps at Chapar Garden and Harboi Hills for his three-day stay.

The Balochistan provincial Muslim League and the All-India Muslim League focussed on the introduction of reforms in British Balochistan.[298] On 18 September 1939, a League member, Mir Ghulam Bhik Nairang (1876–1952), moved a resolution in the central assembly asking for immediate steps to establish provincial autonomy in Balochistan on the same footing as in other provinces. The government response reflected a strange logic; that British Balochistan was already administered by its own people under the customary law; its people would not part with the Jirga system; and the Arms Act had not been enforced here. The resolution was defeated by 40 to 11 votes.[299] Two years later, in March 1941, the League again demanded reforms in Balochistan in the central assembly by moving a cut motion in the budget session. The government again opposed the demand, arguing that British Balochistan could not have reforms because according to the size of its population it was not 'bigger than a tehsil of the Punjab and United Provinces'. But it ignored to mention the examples of three other chief commissioner's provinces—Delhi, Ajmer–Marwara and Coorg—which were much smaller in area, population and political influence than Balochistan; the first two had representation in the central assembly and the third had a legislative council since 1924. The motion was again lost by 40 to 18 votes.[300] When every attempt at reforms was blocked, the Balochistan provincial Muslim League in frustration proposed Balochistan's merger into any of the contiguous full-fledged Muslim provinces, the NWFP, Punjab and Sindh. Abdul Majid Sindhi even formally proposed a resolution at the Allahabad annual session for its amalgamation with Sindh, spelling out the reasons for his proposal; the All-India Muslim League, however, ignored his resolution and simply reiterated the demand that 'the Province of British Balochistan be forthwith elevated to the same constitutional level as other Indian provinces'.[301] Qazi Isa again gave notice of a resolution for the Karachi annual session, asking for the merger of Balochistan into Sindh but it was not moved in the open session.[302] After the Karachi annual session, Jinnah himself sent a memorandum to the agent to the governor-general raising various reform issues; and in March 1944, Liaquat, as deputy leader of the League assembly party, moved a resolution in the assembly for the appointment of a committee to inquire into issues of provincial autonomy for Balochistan, its representation at the centre, introduction of elective system in the Quetta municipality and increase in the educational grant. The central assembly unanimously passed this resolution. But the government failed to appoint any committee, using the pretext of war, but it did provide for one representative for Balochistan in the central legislature, introduced elective system in the Quetta municipality but on the basis of joint electorates and increased the educational grant for Balochistan.[303] The League continued to press its demand for reforms. Sardar Mohammad Khan Jogezai who had been president of the Zhob district Muslim League (1939–43) was nominated on the one seat allocated for Balochistan in the council of state.[304] The Balochistan provincial Muslim League secured all the Muslim seats in the first elections of the Quetta municipality; in one ward, a Congress candidate not only withdrew in favour of the League candidate but also joined the League.[305]

The Balochistan provincial Muslim League was not free from intra-party conflicts, which was often reflected in the Qazi Isa–Jafar Jamali tussle for leadership. Qazi Isa was frequently out of Balochistan for long durations but retained the presidency of the League.[306] Sometimes the provincial Muslim League had to wait for his return for months. After his election as chairman of the provincial civil defence committee in June 1942, Mir Jafar Khan Jamali, who was also vice-president of the provincial Muslim League, began to criticize Qazi Isa for the way he had led the provincial League.[307] His criticism and the activities of the civil defence committee under his leadership provoked Qazi Isa and his supporters.[308] Jamali sponsored a newspaper, the *Tanzeem*, which competed with *Al-Islam*, the newspaper controlled by Qazi Isa, for pro-League propaganda. When Jinnah visited Balochistan for about three weeks in 1943 (26 June–18 July), he brought about reconciliation between them that facilitated smooth re-election of Qazi Isa as the provincial Muslim League president.[309] But mutual recrimination re-started soon after Jinnah left the province. Abdul Ghafur Durrani, joint secretary of the provincial Muslim League and secretary of the civil defence committee, sided with Qazi Isa and refused to work with Jamali on the Balochistan civil defence committee, alleging that the latter was working against the interests of the Balochistan provincial Muslim League.[310] Jamali had his own list of grievances against Qazi Isa and the provincial Muslim League office concerning the provincial Muslim League organization, which he communicated in the form of a petition to Nawab Ismail and Liaquat.[311] Qazi Isa in his reply refuted the charges and counter-charged Jamali for inaction as chairman of the civil defence committee and for supporting anti-Balochistan provincial Muslim League propaganda.[312] The central committee of action inquired into Jamali's complaints but without any positive outcome; the conflict continued to simmer.[313] Qazi Isa kept his hold on the Balochistan provincial Muslim League presidency.[314] The intra-party conflict belittled the role that the party could have played in the social and political development of Balochistan.[315] Qazi Isa damaged himself by his work in other areas. His opponents were critical of his role in the NWFP where the central committee of action had deputed him to supervise the process of party organization. It was alleged that he was partisan, unduly sided with Aurangzeb, and misinformed the central committee of action and Jinnah about his work. The results of the general elections in the NWFP strengthened that perception although Qazi Isa refuted all these allegations.[316] The withholding of funds by Qazi Isa that had been collected for the Anjuman-i-Islamia, Quetta for educational purposes after the defeat of his candidate for its secretaryship further harmed his position. He handed over the funds to the Anjuman on Jinnah's intervention but it hurt his public image.[317] He aspired to represent Balochistan on the seat provided in the constituent assembly under the Cabinet Mission Plan and desperately tried to get the League's nomination. But this became a bone of contention between him and his opponents who doubted his potential to win the seat. His opponents in the provincial Muslim League promoted the candidature of Nawab Mohammad Khan Jogezai in protest against his attitude. After Jinnah's discussions with the Balochistan provincial Muslim League leaders, the League decided not to put up any official candidate on the seat to avoid an intra-party rift and supported Jogezai who defeated the Congress candidate, Abdus Samad Achakzai, by 61 to 13 votes.[318] Qazi Isa in frustration launched a tirade against the *sardars* and the *sardari* system, which further weakened his standing in the party. Jinnah expressed his displeasure by distancing himself from Qazi Isa whom he otherwise liked and at one time had thought of nominating him on the viceroy's Executive Council, if Cripps' proposals had materialized.[319] Jogezai proved the veracity of the League's decision when he decided not to attend the inaugural session of the constituent assembly on 9 December 1946, and voted for Pakistan under the 3 June Plan.[320]

Meanwhile, the Balochistan provincial Muslim League had focused on its organization. Jinnah's visit to Balochistan (14 September–20 October 1945) for his much-needed rest, and his stay at Mastung and Quetta helped to strengthen the provincial Muslim League and inspired the Leaguers to work for its cause.[321] After his departure, the provincial Muslim League prepared an elaborate programme to organize its branches. It enrolled new members and set up branches in several towns and villages.[322] The Balochistan provincial Muslim League and Muslim Students Federation sent their contingents to Sindh to campaign for the League candidates in the general elections.[323] On 30 March 1946, after the elections of the district Muslim Leagues and city Muslim Leagues, the reorganized provincial Muslim League re-elected Qazi Isa as its president in his absence, Ghulam Mohammad Khan as general secretary, Shah Jahan and Haji Rahmatullah as vice-presidents and Malik Jan Mohammad as salar of the Muslim League National Guards. Some district Muslim Leagues and city Muslim Leagues were not represented at the election meeting, which revived factionalism but it was overshadowed by other issues like the status of British Balochistan, the leased areas and the princely states and election of a representative from British Balochistan to the constituent assembly of Pakistan.[324] The simmering factionalism reappeared at the time of fresh enrolment of members and party elections that climaxed in a firing incident at Usta Mohammad.[325] Qazi Isa sent a report of the incident to the central League and urged the central committee of action to take it up 'at the first available opportunity' but the central committee of action 'decided to take up the case after 15 August 1947'.[326]

(v) *Bengal Presidency Muslim League.* After the 1937 elections, the party position in the Bengal assembly necessitated the formation of a coalition ministry.[327] The Bengal presidency Muslim League and Krishak Proja Samity worked out a coalition that other parties and Independents joined. Its terms were: Fazlul Haq would be leader of the coalition party and chief minister; Muslim-non-Muslim ratio in the cabinet would be 6:3, with Krishak Proja Samity two ministers including the chief minister and one deputy minister; and the provincial Muslim League three ministers plus the offices of speaker and chief whip.[328] The proportion of Hindu ministers was soon raised from 3 to

5 (3 Caste Hindus and 2 Scheduled Castes).[329] The pro-Congress Muslims in the Krishak Proja Samity might have persuaded their leaders to coalesce with the Congress but that party had not yet decided about acceptance of offices. The fourteen-point programme of the coalition toned down the radical items of the Krishak Proja Samity manifesto. The provincial Muslim League–Krishak Proja Samity association brought Fazlul Haq and his colleagues closer to the Leaguers that eventually led to their rejoining the League. Fazlul Haq made a formal announcement to that effect at the Lucknow annual session. After the formation of the coalition ministry, the Krishak Proja Samity ineffectively maintained its separate identity as a social organization that worked for the uplift of the rural poor. A small dissident group that disagreed with the terms of the provincial Muslim League–Krishak Proja Samity coalition especially the toning down of its economic programme left the Krishak Proja Samity to form the 'Independent Proja Samity'.[330]

After the Lucknow annual session, Jinnah appointed a committee to reorganize the provincial Muslim League in Bengal in accordance with the All-India Muslim League constitution.[331] The process of framing a provincial Muslim League constitution, enrolment of members and party elections from the primary to the provincial levels was completed by 8–9 April 1939, when Fazlul Haq was elected president, Huseyn Shaheed Suhrawardy general secretary, and M.A.H. Ispahani treasurer.[332] Fazlul Haq's passionate advocacy of Muslim issues including Muslim grievances in the Congress-governed Hindu majority provinces provoked the Bengali Hindus who denounced his policies and, in August 1938, brought no-confidence motions against his ministry. The League solidly stood behind him in and outside the assembly. The rejection of all the no-confidence motions, legislation of tenancy and money-lending laws and introduction of new recruitment rules that benefited the educated Muslims created a favourable atmosphere for the League to broaden its support-base.[333] Besides winning the bye-elections to the Bengal legislature, it won eighteen out of twenty-two Muslim seats in the elections to the Calcutta municipal corporation. Its performance in the elections of the union boards was equally remarkable. It actively participated in the annual sessions of the All-India Muslim League, hosted its special session in Calcutta and sent a large contingent to the Lahore annual session where Nazimuddin served on the committee that finalized the Lahore Resolution and Fazlul Haq moved it in the open session. Muslim parties other than the

League almost disappeared from the political scene in Bengal. The absence of any challenge had a negative effect; the Leaguers ignored the party organization although the ritual of membership enrolment and party elections was scrupulously observed.

The solidarity of the Bengal presidency Muslim League was put to test during the war. The British and the Congress began to cultivate the League premiers: the former desired their unqualified support for the war and the latter wanted settlement of the communal issue on provincial basis in order to dilute the Pakistan demand. On 13 June 1940, Maulana Azad, the new Congress president, held parleys with the premiers, Fazlul Haq and Sikandar. When the issue came up before the central working committee, it formally prohibited its members from discussing any issue involving Hindu–Muslim settlement with the Congress leaders without the permission of the president to avoid 'any misunderstanding or misconstruction in future'.[334] This was simply a matter of party discipline but both the premiers disliked the restriction. Fazlul Haq urged its review by the working committee but did not do anything beyond that.[335] His relations with the League started to deteriorate when his cabinet colleagues and Jinnah opposed his advocacy of a national government, and the Bengal presidency Muslim League celebrated '23 March 1941', as the 'Pakistan Day' against his wishes.[336] The turning point came in July, when Fazlul Haq accepted membership of the national defence council. At first, he was willing to resign his membership of the national defence council on the advice of Suhrawardy, Maulana Akram Khan and Manzur Murshid, his nephew/son-in-law and private secretary, but he backed out due to pressure from the British, put through Sir Zafrullah Khan and the Hindu members.[337] Then, he perceived in Jinnah's direction a threat to his person. Although he reluctantly resigned from the national defence council but, in a letter to Liaquat on 8 September, tendered his resignation from the central council as well as the working committee, accusing Jinnah of behaving 'arbitrarily' and the League leaders from the Muslim minority provinces of acting without understanding the problems of the Muslims of Bengal and Punjab.[338] The strong reaction that his response generated among the Leaguers particularly the youth in Bengal and elsewhere compelled him to tender an apology for his remarks, which the working committee accepted by 7 to 6 votes with one abstention.[339] Now his supporters moved him in another direction; they formed a Progressive Party with his approval, which, on 28 November, transformed itself into Progressive Coalition Party

A HISTORY OF THE ALL-INDIA MUSLIM LEAGUE

consisting of six small groups in the Bengal assembly including the Hindu Mahasabha and the Congress (Forward Bloc). On 1 December, his cabinet colleagues, Nazimuddin, Suhrawardy, Tamizuddin and Nawab of Dhaka, resigned, which led to the fall of his ministry; but four days later, he assumed the leadership of the Progressive Coalition Party. The League members of the provincial assembly re-formed an assembly party and elected Nazimuddin as their leader. The governor who had earlier promised to invite Nazimuddin to form the ministry backed out of his commitment.[340] On 11 December, Fazlul Haq formed a new ministry after an unsuccessful attempt to retain his link with the League by putting the entire blame for the crisis on intra-provincial Muslim League conflicts.[341] On his refusal to leave the Progressive Coalition Party, Jinnah expelled him from the League, declaring him ineligible for its membership at any level; the central working committee, the Bengal presidency Muslim League and the All-India Muslim League annual session confirmed his expulsion.[342] Fazlul Haq's new coalition ministry had a small group of Muslims whose number rapidly dwindled; among the reasons were his induction of Dr Shyama Prasad Mukerji into the cabinet and the rapid rise of the League in Bengal. The provincial Muslim League turned down the governor's proposal to associate it with the Haq ministry.[343]

The Leaguers focused on the party organization and anti-Haq campaign, which climaxed in the provincial Muslim League conference at Serajganj on 14–15 February 1942;[344] Jinnah was given a royal reception on his arrival in the city. Here the provincial Muslim League elected its office-bearers: Maulana Akram Khan replaced Fazlul Haq as president, and Huseyn Shaheed Suhrawardy was re-elected as general secretary and M.A.H. Ispahani as treasurer.[345] After the conference, Jinnah toured the province for ten days.[346] The League workers and students including those of the Dhaka university who had been punished following two communal clashes caused by the singing of *Bande Mataram* on the campus campaigned against the Haq ministry, which tried to control the situation by using restrictive laws including the Defence of India Rules. The Dhaka university suspended the students' union and banned the entry of convicted students in the university halls.[347] The provincial Muslim League observed an 'Anti-Repression Day' to protest against this policy and represented to Governor Sir J.A. Herbert for intervention.[348] It used various tactics to broaden its support-base. On Suhrawardy's direction, it organized a 'League Fortnight' to increase its membership and that of the Muslim

League National Guards.[349] It worked more methodically on the advice of central civil defence committee whose members especially its chairman, Nawab Ismail, paid several visits and toured the districts particularly those directly affected by the war.[350] The central civil defence committee appointed a provincial civil defence committee that functioned quite successfully when Suhrawardy was its chairman. Later on, it constituted a separate East Bengal zone Muslim League civil defence committee and engaged a paid chief organizer, Benazir Ahmad, who established a network of district defence committees to coordinate its work mainly in the war-affected districts.[351] The central civil defence committee chairman lauded the work done by Suhrawardy, Benazir Ahmad and the students.[352] Zakir Ali prepared inspection reports that helped in maintaining efficiently the party office and organization.[353] Suhrawardy's successor as general secretary, Abul Hashim (1943–46), effectively carried on the organizational work; and Jinnah provided him guidance and received regular progress reports from him.[354] In April 1944, the party opened a branch office in Dhaka that had jurisdiction in seven eastern districts; that year, its strength rose to some 0.55 million.[355] Abul Hashim drafted a manifesto that proposed radical reforms and circulated it among the Leaguers.[356] Spelling out the reasons for the League's popularity, Abul Hashim wrote in a 'strictly confidential' report to the central party that it was 'not so much to the fact that a League ministry is in office as to the phenomenal growth in popularity, esteem and influence of the League as a whole among Muslims all over India'.[357]

By March 1943, Fazlul Haq's ministry had lost its majority in the assembly; and he was desperately trying to rejoin the League.[358] That month, the League candidates had won all the six Muslim seats in the triennial elections to the Bengal council—upper house—and defeated ministerial candidates in two bye-elections (Natore and Balurghat) to the Bengal assembly.[359] On the fall of the Haq ministry, the Bengal presidency Muslim League after intense deliberations and much reluctance decided to assume office in a situation when the Japanese were bombing the eastern districts and the whole province was engulfed in famine. Nazimuddin formed the ministry amidst this crisis. His ministry's primary task was to provide relief to those affected by the famine and the resultant diseases. Acute food shortages and lack of medical facilities aggravated the catastrophe.[360] Some three million lives were lost and numerous Bengalis migrated to neighbouring provinces, more than half a million moved into Assam. The opposition censured the Nazimuddin ministry; and Jinnah held the central government responsible. Others put the blame on the corrupt officials and the greed of rich Hindus who controlled the grain trade.[361] The ministry did whatever was humanly possible. Suhrawardy as minister for civil supplies and as chairman of the Muslim League relief committee with Moazzem Husain (Lalmia) as its secretary used the provincial Muslim League and Bengal civil defence committee network for the relief operations.[362] The ministry made arrangements for directly feeding about 0.3 million people.[363] The united Punjab–Bengal relief committee headed by Nawab Mamdot sent food grains and other relief items from the Punjab, so did Sindh and other provinces.[364] With the approval of the central civil defence committee chairman, the provincial Muslim League and Bengal civil defence committee coordinated the relief work with the food committees of the Communist Party of India that some Leaguers resented.[365] The Hindu-controlled press used the tragedy for anti-League propaganda.[366] The League was maligned not only in India but also in England despite the fact that the Woodhead Commission absolved it of any responsibility for lapses in the relief work.[367] The anti-League propaganda influenced some quarters to question even the economic and strategic viability of 'East Pakistan'.[368] Although the relief work that the League bodies did at the grassroots strengthened the party but the hostile propaganda weakened the ministry. In addition, Nazimuddin's inability to control nepotism and favouritism and to take firm action against the hoarders contributed to the unpopularity of his ministry.[369] His majority started to thin out after July 1944, partly because of delayed action against the hoarders and profiteers; and nine months later, he felt that he could avert a defeat of his ministry either by winning over the 'corrupt elements' or by aligning with the Hindu group.[370] Jinnah's advice to him was: 'I would not, under any circumstances, have anything to do with the corrupt elements and as regards coalition with the Hindu group, yes, but on honourable terms. I would rather be in opposition with honour than run a precarious ministry'.[371] His ministry fell on 28 March 1945; after that, the governor administered Bengal under section 93 till after the general elections. Before the elections, a tussle had started between Nazimuddin and Suhrawardy for post-election leadership of the party, which could be observed in the composition of the provincial parliamentary board and selection of candidates but it did not develop into an open rift.[372] Nazimuddin's defeat in the elections further removed that possibility.

After the elections, Suhrawardy who was elected leader of the Bengal presidency Muslim League assembly party formed the ministry. The 'Pakistan Resolution' that the League legislators' convention adopted on his motion raised his stature in the League circles. Nazimuddin could have posed a threat to Suhrawardy but he was thinking of retiring from politics and planning to establish industries in Bengal.[373] Jinnah tried to dissuade him from doing that by suggesting his name first as prime minister of the Hyderabad state and then as the high commissioner of Pakistan in England.[374] Meanwhile the party organization did not receive due attention. Floods in the 1946 summer blocked the process of membership enrolment and party elections according to the model constitution. Soon after, the central committee of action temporarily shelved the whole process of organization; instead, it appointed a provincial committee of action with network going down to the primary level to look after the party affairs.[375] By March 1947, the party was still asking for extension in time for holding elections.[376] Suhrawardy's authority began to erode after the Calcutta and Noakhali riots although he successfully faced a no-confidence motion in September 1946.[377] Instead of getting credit for preventing the riots from spreading on a wider scale, as these did in Bihar, he was wrongly blamed for the violence in Calcutta.[378] His declining influence encouraged his rivals to assert themselves. At first, they gathered around Fazlul Haq who had rejoined the League and was in search of a place in politics for himself.[379] On 20 March 1947, seventy-four members of the provincial assembly and members of the legislative council represented in a memorandum to the central League for a change in the composition of the ministry because, they asserted, its continuation would 'endanger the interests of the party, community and the country'.[380] But Jinnah restrained them and advised them to maintain unity in their ranks 'at this critical moment'.[381] Then, the controversy surrounding the proposal of 'Free United Bengal' further weakened Suhrawardy's position in the League. The partition of Bengal according to the 3 June Plan and the emergence of East Pakistan damaged his prospects to stay as chief minister and paved the way for Nazimuddin to stage a comeback in politics.

(*vi*) *Assam Provincial Muslim League*. The results of the 1937 elections showed that no party had secured a majority in the Assam assembly. The League members of the provincial assembly who constituted themselves into an assembly party and elected Sir Mohammad Saadulla

(1885–1955) as their leader in due course gathered the strength of 32 out of total 34 Muslim members of the provincial assembly while the Congress enjoyed the support of 30 to 34 members during the life of the assembly.[382] Twenty-three assembly seats were shared by three groups—Tribals, Scheduled Castes and Europeans—who could swing the balance in favour of any of the two major parties. This distribution of seats was a manifestation of the population of Assam, 'a province of minorities' where no community had a clear majority.[383] Regular inflow of Bengali Muslims into Assam was, however, rapidly raising the proportion of the Muslim population.[384] During 1937–47, Saadulla and Pandit Gopinath Bardoloi, leader of the Congress assembly party, alternately formed coalition ministries. Saadulla formed the first ministry on 1 April, leading a coalition party, called the Assam United Party. When his ministry resigned on 18 September 1938, Bardoloi headed the next coalition ministry but he could not find a Muslim member of the provincial assembly to induct as minister. His ministry survived only because the speaker adjourned the assembly session to save it from a no-confidence motion that 60 out of 107 members of the provincial assembly had signed.[385] When the Congress ministry resigned on 17 November 1939, Saadulla again formed the ministry. Except for a short period (25 December 1941–25 August 1942), when the governor directly administered Assam under section 93, Saadulla retained power till the 1945–46 general elections; however, on 23 March 1945, he transformed his ministry into an all-party ministry and inducted Congress and Hindu Nationalist Party ministers without the required authorization from the central parliamentary board.[386] After the general elections, on 11 February 1946, Bardoloi formed the ministry, which stayed in office till independence.

Maulana Abdul Hamid Khan Bhashani (1880–1976), a charismatic Bengali migrant activist, who had the knack to mobilize the masses, was convenor of the committee that Jinnah appointed to organize the provincial Muslim League; Abdul Matin Choudhry and Sir Saadulla were its members.[387] When the provincial Muslim League was reorganized, Bhashani was elected its first president. The All-India Muslim League might have held its twenty-ninth annual session in Assam instead of Allahabad but the provincial Muslim League could not make its arrangements during the Easter holidays due to rains.[388] Bhashani stayed its president till 1941, when Saadulla, who was then chief minister, replaced him as president and Modabbir Husain, a minister in his cabinet, was elected general secretary. The ministers, however, could neither attend to party affairs properly nor could they hold the party elections on time.[389] The declining state of the party activated the young Leaguers and Muslim Students Federation workers who demanded that the ministers should not hold offices in the party. The central civil defence committee chairman reported this development to Jinnah after his first visit to Assam in May 1942, when a provincial civil defence committee was set up with Abdul Haye as chairman and Mayeenuddin Ahmad as secretary.[390] The demand for the separation of party and ministerial offices caused intra-party tension that deepened with the passage of time. On the central civil defence committee's second visit in June 1943, the Leaguers agreed to hold a meeting of the provincial Muslim League council to appoint a committee to reorganize the party. When Saadulla did not convene the meeting, they requisitioned its meeting, which was held on 20 August, even then under pressure from the central civil defence committee chairman.[391] The council appointed an organizing committee with Bhashani as chairman and Mayeenuddin as secretary. The provincial Muslim League that this committee reorganized with the help of Muslim youth held a conference at Barpeta on 11–12 April 1944, chaired by Khaliquzzaman; the central committee of action deputed Iftikhar Mamdot and Qazi Isa to attend this conference.[392] At Barpeta, the provincial Muslim League elected Bhashani as president and Dewan Abdul Basit (1911–1996) as general secretary, and shifted its head office from Shillong to Sylhet.[393] Some Leaguers in the ministerial camp alleged that the Barpeta conference had been illegally convened; their contention was that the organizing committee should have submitted its report to the provincial Muslim League council and had no authority to convene a conference on its own initiative.[394] But the success of the Barpeta conference, public response to Bhashani's extensive tours, and Saadulla's unauthorized agreement with the Congress for an all-party coalition silenced the critics.[395] The central civil defence committee temporarily resolved the intra-party conflict, which reappeared in November, when the provincial Muslim League's nominee, Dewan Basit won in a bye-election and the provincial Muslim League expelled Majduddin and Abdul Khaleque from the party who had contested the election against him with the tacit support of some ministers.[396] On 28 January 1945, the Gauhati provincial Muslim League conference smoothly re-elected Bhashani as president and Dewan Basit as general secretary;[397] subsequently, Mahmud Ali (1919–2006), an Muslim Students Federation activist, replaced Basit in that office. The discriminatory 'line system' in Assam accentuated the intra-provincial Muslim League conflict.

Migrants had come into the thinly-populated Assam as 'coolies' for the tea gardens or as cultivators, clearing the jungles and cultivating the land. While the indigenous inhabitants and non-Muslim migrants, mostly Nepalese and non-Bengalis, could acquire land anywhere in Assam, the Bengali Muslim migrants who inhabited mainly the plain districts of the Assam/Brahmaputra Valley (Goalpara, Kamrup, Darrang, Nowgong and a small part of Lakhimpur) could not settle beyond certain demarcated areas—an arrangement that was better known as the 'line system'. The migration of Bengali Muslims had started around the turn of the twentieth century, and there was an influx of migrants during the Second World War as a result of the Bengal famine and official 'grow more food' policy. The issue of migration assumed communal dimensions with the rise in the number of Bengali Muslim migrants. The All-India Muslim League at its Lucknow annual session had demanded the abolition of the line system because it interfered with inter-province migration, infringed fundamental rights of the citizens and created a landless class.[398] The first Saadulla ministry on Abdul Matin Choudhry's motion appointed a seven-member committee which in its report recommended modifications in the line system; its Congress members opposed and its Muslim members supported the abolition of this system.[399] The ministry resigned before it could implement the report. The first Bardoloi ministry ignored to implement the report; instead, before its resignation it tightened the line system. The second Saadulla ministry adopted a development scheme in 1940, which reserved 30 per cent land for future expansion and divided the remaining 70 per cent land into blocks for the settlement of indigenous Assamese (Hindus and Muslims), tribal people, scheduled castes and migrants. But this scheme was shelved when the governor took over the administration under section 93. The influx of Bengali migrants, 'grow more food' campaign and pressure from the provincial Muslim League again brought the issue into focus.[400] In August 1943, the Assam government issued a resolution to regularise the unauthorised occupation by the migrants who had reclaimed government land up to January 1943, and to de-reserve the surplus professional grazing reserves for settlement.[401] The Leaguers saw in this decision rapid transformation of Assam into a Muslim majority province, and supported it by citing the resolution on fundamental rights that the Indian National Congress had passed at its

Karachi session (1930) and Nehru's observation who had termed the line system as 'certainly undesirable' and had advised Bardoloi not to give it 'communal colour'.[402] On the other hand, the Hindu Mahasabha and the Congress vehemently opposed the new policy because migration of Bengali Muslims up to the proposed date would transform them into a majority in Assam. They invoked the slogan of 'Assam for the Assamese', which influenced many indigenous Muslims including Chief Minister Saadulla himself, who was under pressure due to the Surma Valley procurement scandal, and supported non-Muslim migration into Assam.[403] These conflicting positions blocked the implementation of the August 1943 resolution.

On 15 January 1945, the Saadulla ministry changed its policy and reversed the August 1943 resolution by a more comprehensive policy statement, which legalized allotment of land only to those migrants who had come to Assam before 31 December 1937.[404] It fixed the same date for the legalization of occupation of land on surplus professional grazing reserves, and called for the eviction of occupants of land after that date; those occupants who could prove that the government land they had been allotted had eroded or had been requisitioned by the army were exempted and allowed to stay till they were given alternate land.[405] This policy was applicable in districts which had Bengali Muslim migrant population (Nowgong, Kamrup, and Darrang) and not in those districts (Sibsagar and Lakhimpur) where non-Muslim migrants had settled.[406] The provincial Muslim League at its Gauhati conference denounced this policy and demanded settlement of the Bengali migrants anywhere without any restrictions.[407] Saadulla's refusal to modify this policy aggravated intra-provincial Muslim League tension.[408] He then negotiated with leaders of the opposition parties—Bardoloi, (Congress) and Rodini Kumar Choudhry (Hindu Nationalist Party)—and broadened his coalition ministry into an all-party ministry and gave the portfolio of revenue to Rodini Kumar to implement the new policy.[409] Forcible eviction and police firing on the migrants in the Koimari reserve in Barpeta precipitated a crisis. Bhashani urged the All-India Muslim League to intervene.[410] Jinnah was not available for advice as due to his serious illness he had handed over the charge of the party to Liaquat and Nawab Ismail for three months. Two central parliamentary board members, Liaquat and Khaliquzzaman, twice visited Assam to resolve the conflict but Saadulla refused to accept their suggestions including one for the transfer of revenue portfolio to a Muslim minister because it was part of his agreement with the opposition.[411] The League ministry, Liaquat wrote to Saadulla on 27 May 1945, should resign if the evictions were not stopped because the League could not be in coalition with those whose object was 'to harm the interests' of the Muslims.[412] As a result of this pressure, evictions were temporarily halted. In July, the All-India Muslim League working committee discussed the land settlement policy in a meeting at Simla with Jinnah in the chair, and instructed Saadulla to amend the Policy so that: 'Persons who have sown one crop should not be evicted.'[413] Saadulla did not press the Congress leadership for the acceptance of this amendment but simply conveyed it to that party, and the Congress communicated its rejection as late as December. The Saadulla ministry, however, formally endorsed the proposed amendment on 1 February 1946, a day before it resigned.[414]

Bardoloi formed the post-election ministry, which relentlessly pursued evictions to frustrate the mounting pressure from the All-India Muslim League for the inclusion of whole of Assam in eastern Pakistan. On Jinnah's advice, the provincial Muslim League decided to challenge the line system in the courts and advised the evictees to spread out and cultivate government wasteland for their subsistence.[415] When evictions did not stop, the provincial Muslim League decided to launch a civil disobedience movement on 28 April 1946, subject to approval by the central committee of action; and Bhashani went on a fast unto death for over a week.[416] Faced with this pressure, the Bardoloi ministry temporarily suspended the eviction operation, which continued during the monsoon season except for isolated cases of eviction. It resumed systematic evictions in October. After an unsuccessful attempt to involve Nehru and Liaquat for mediation, the provincial Muslim League renewed its pressure on the central committee of action for permission to launch a civil disobedience movement.[417] When the evictions intensified in January 1947, after another temporary suspension in December, the provincial Muslim League established a nine-member Bhashani-headed committee of action to counteract this policy by civil disobedience, which it started on 9 March.[418] The central committee of action deputed Khaliquzzaman to Assam who chaired a provincial Muslim League meeting in Sylhet that endorsed the decision for civil disobedience.[419] The Congress government, perceiving in it a plan to bring forcibly the whole of Assam into the eastern Pakistan zone, used the security forces to suppress the movement. The security forces in Assam consisted of the Assam Regiment, the Assam Rifles and the Rail Force; the first two were maintained by the central government and the third one had been raised by the provincial government during the Quit India movement. There was not a single Muslim in any of these forces.[420] In addition to the arrest of leaders and workers, 44 persons were killed and 300 injured in the civil disobedience movement, which was withdrawn on 11 June, only after the announcement of the 3 June Plan.[421] The League renewed its conditional offer of assistance to the government for the implementation of the settlement policy but without any positive result.[422]

(*vii*) *Bombay Presidency Muslim League.* After the 1937 provincial elections, on 28 February, twenty League members of the provincial assembly along with ten Muslim independents, at a meeting chaired by Jinnah, formed the League assembly party and elected Ali Mohammad Khan Dehlavi as leader, S.M. Hasan as secretary and K.B. Jan Mohammad as the party whip.[423] The assembly party resolved that no League member of the provincial assembly should negotiate with any party or group or the governor except through his leader; and the negotiation should be subject to confirmation by the party. When a League member of the provincial assembly, M. Yasin Nurie, was taken as a minister, the assembly party staged a walkout from the assembly.[424] The following year, in May, a 25-member organizing committee, which Jinnah had appointed, framed a constitution of the provincial Muslim League and established a permanent party office in Bombay to 'claim the Muslims back' into the League.[425] The committee systematically organized primary Leagues and district Muslim Leagues; and on 10 July 1938, the reorganized provincial Muslim League elected Jinnah as president and M.M.S. Ispahani as honorary secretary.[426] The provincial Muslim League dissolved the provincial parliamentary board in January 1939, after it had set up alternative machinery.[427] Jinnah and Ispahani were continuously re-elected to their offices till 1940. During their tenure, the Bombay branch emerged as the most dynamic branch, enjoying a sound financial position with its funds audited annually by a chartered firm. It organized impressive annual conferences; the first one in Ahmadabad, the second in Sholapur and the third in Hubli; and Ali Mohammad Khan Dehlavi, Sardar Sikandar Hayat and Raja of Mahmudabad presided over these conferences, respectively. It was the first branch to sponsor Muslim National Guards; and by 1944, it had 4,440 guards of different categories.[428] It took keen interest in issues of Muslim interest: it demanded prohibition in Bombay; opposed 10 per cent tax on immovable property; termed the textbooks prepared by the Jamia Millia for official use in the primary Urdu schools of Bombay as unsuitable for the Muslim children; urged the central League to press for legislation to have a central organization for the administration of Muslim *waqfs*, and pioneered a resolution against Abdur Rahman Siddiqi for criticising Jinnah on his call for the observance of the Day of Deliverance.[429]

Ismail Ibrahim Chundrigar succeeded Jinnah as the provincial Muslim League president; the latter, however, continued to serve on its working committee till November 1941, and after that gave the party advice, whenever it needed.[430] During 1941–47, five Leaguers served as its general secretaries: Haji Noor Mohammad Ahmad (1941–42) replaced M.M.S. Ispahani,[431] followed by Aziz Ghafur Qazi (1942–44), Yusuf Moledina (1945–46), Hasan A. Shaikh (1946–47), and Abdul Kader Hafizka (1947). During the war, it appointed an emergency committee to help the war-affected people even before the central civil defence committee visited Bombay. When the central civil defence committee appointed a provincial civil defence committee with Karimbhai Ibrahim as its chairman and Aziz Ghafur Qazi as its general secretary in May 1942, the provincial Muslim League transferred the funds and record of the emergency committee to the new body. The Bombay civil defence committee organized defence committees at the district level, a provincial volunteer corps and subcommittees including a food subcommittee, which cooperated with similar committees of other parties including that of the Communist Party of India and did useful relief work. The provincial Muslim League played a key role in keeping the textile mills of Ahmadabad open that the pro-Congress mill owners had shut down during the Quit India movement, and which had affected thousands of Muslim workers.[432] They also helped those Leaguers who were affected by the collective fines that the government had imposed indiscriminately on the citizens during the Quit India movement. Abdul Qadir Shaikh succeeded Karimbhai Ibrahim as the civil defence committee chairman when the latter resigned due to illness and partly because of his differences with Aziz Ghafur Qazi.[433] Factionalism crept into the Bombay presidency Muslim League in 1944, when dissident Leaguers formed a 'progressive group' that made repeated unsuccessful attempts to dislodge Chundrigar from the provincial Muslim League presidency.[434] However, this did not diminish in any way the League's influence and it won all the seats in the general elections. Chundrigar left the presidency only when he joined the interim government. Hasanally P. Ebrahim was then elected as its president and Abdul Kader Hafizka as general secretary.[435] During November 1946–January 1947, Bombay and Ahmadabad witnessed communal riots; the provincial Muslim League did relief work and its president sent daily reports to Jinnah and Chundrigar.[436]

(*viii*) *Madras Presidency Muslim League.* Before the revival of the provincial Muslim League, the Leaguers had set up branch Leagues in different regions of the Madras presidency: in Tamilnadu, Andhra Desa and Malabar/Kerala. On 23 April 1937, the Andhra Muslim League had been established in Vizagapatam with Mahbub Ali Beg as president and Rasul Khan Ghaznavi as secretary; and Nawab Bahadur Yar Jang presided over its first regional conference in June.[437] The Malabar Muslim League, after its formation, organized a conference in Tellicherry in December, and its moving spirit was Haji Abdussattar Haji Essak Sait, who served on the central working committee from 1938 to 1947.[438] In January 1938, twelve Muslim organizations of Madras united to form the Tamilnadu Muslim League at a conference that P. Khalifulla chaired.[439] The process of organizing the League at the presidency level, however, was completed on 18 June 1939, with the help of Haji Abdussattar Haji Essak Sait, when a constitution was approved and office-bearers were elected with M. Jamal Mohammad as president. On 2–3 July, the All-India Muslim League gave it affiliation, and an assembly party was formed with Jamal Mohammad as leader and Dr Abdur Rawoof as secretary.[440] In November 1940, Jamal was re-elected as president; and the next November, Syed Mahmud Padsha replaced him in that office.[441] Its membership was 42,811 in 1939, which rose to 46,092 in 1940, and 112,078 in 1941. Jinnah felt 'pride and pleasure' at the way the League was organized from the bottom to the top in Madras. The provincial Muslim League barred its members from holding simultaneously membership of any other party; consequently, three members of the provincial assembly resigned their membership of the Justice Party to retain the League membership.[442] It won the two Muslim seats in the Madras legislative council: one unopposed and the other by eighty votes against nine.[443] It raised Muslim issues including the demand for the inclusion of accounts of Muslim heroes in the vernacular textbooks used in the primary and secondary schools, broadcasting of Urdu programmes on the All India Radio, legislation against playing of music before mosques following communal riots in Nellore as a result of the activities of the All-India Hindu Mahasabha, and expression of confidence in Jinnah as the accredited leader of the Muslims and the All-India Muslim League as their representative body and the establishment of Pakistan with safeguards for the minorities as their creed.[444]

During the war, the Madras presidency Muslim League did useful relief work especially for the Muslim refugees who came from Burma and other places in the Far East, and protested against the collective fines that the government imposed and realized from the Muslims during the Quit India movement.[445] By the end of 1944, it had a solid organization, with about 2,000 Muslim League National Guards, and elected Mohammad Ismail (1896–1972) as president and his brother, Ahmad Ibrahim, one of its secretaries; both of them were re-elected to these offices in March 1946.[446] The visit of central committee of action members followed by Liaquat's extensive tour of the Madras districts for two weeks in the company of Haji Abdussattar Haji Essak Sait and Siddiq Ali Khan further broadened the influence of the League in southern India.[447] However, the Madras presidency Muslim League was not devoid of factionalism; and the resignation of Allapichai, one of its secretaries, in 1943 was symptomatic of this phenomenon.[448] Factional tussle reappeared during the general elections on the issue of distribution of party tickets. It was alleged that Jamal Mohammad and his relatives had controlled the provincial Muslim League for several years and still dominated the provincial parliamentary board, which under their influence had given party tickets in the elections to their favourites. The dissidents made an unsuccessful attempt to establish a rival body, the Muslim League workers' conference, but the sweeping victory of the League in the general elections silenced the dissenters.[449] There were demands for the division of the Madras presidency Muslim League into separate provincial Leagues for Tamilnadu, Andhra and Kerala, but the party did not take any decision on this issue.[450] In May 1947, the provincial Muslim League that was reorganized according to the central committee of action-framed model constitution re-elected Mohammad Ismail as president and Ahmad Ibrahim as one of the three secretaries, and demanded a separate state to be called Moplastan, consisting of 'those parts wherein the majority of the population or the whole of it is Muslim'.[451] Later on, in July, the provincial Muslim League working committee spelt out the safeguards that it urged the All-India Muslim League to secure for the Muslims of the Hindustan provinces.[452] But none of these demands could be seriously pursued in those turbulent days.

(*ix*) *United Provinces Provincial Muslim League*. The coalition-formation controversy in the United Provinces after the 1937 elections had one positive aspect; the Leaguers resolved to focus their energies on the party organization. Nawab Ismail as president and Khaliquzzaman as leader of its assembly party provided the leadership.[453] Both of them were continuously re-elected to these offices till independence. The Leaguers from United Provinces not only focused on strengthening the provincial Muslim League but also played an invaluable role in consolidating the League at the all-India level.[454] One issue that dissipated their energies was the Shia–Sunni sectarian conflict that raged in the province in the 1930s. United Provinces was the seat of principal Sunni *darul ulums*, and its capital, Lucknow, was 'the very centre of Shia religion and culture in India'.[455] The conflict had first surfaced in the city on the issue of *madhe sahaba* [praise of the Companions of Prophet Mohammad (PBUH)] in 1907–8, but harmony returned after the leaders of the two sects signed an agreement.[456] It was agreed that the *madhe sahaba* processions would not be brought out on three days: *Yaum-i-Ashur*, *Chehlum* and 21 Ramzan, the day of martyrdom of Hazrat Ali, the fourth pious caliph. The sectarian conflict continued to simmer; and in 1935, it reappeared on the issue of *madhe sahaba*. Two years later, one candidate allegedly used sectarian slogans in his election to the United Provinces assembly.[457] The situation deteriorated further after the Congress assumed power in United Provinces so much so that several Leaguers asked Jinnah not to hold the All-India Muslim League's twenty-fifth annual session in Lucknow.[458] The League was not discouraged; the session was held in Lucknow and passed off peacefully. But when the Congress launched its Muslim mass contact campaign with the help of Jamiatul Ulama-i-Hind *ulama* and Majlis-i-Ahrar-i-Islam workers, it allowed the Sunnis to take out *madhe sahaba* processions. That provoked the Shias who reacted by bringing out *tabarra* [curses (on the first three pious caliphs)] processions.[459] Lucknow witnessed painful ugly scenes of sectarian divide; the Sunni and Shia processionists competed in chanting '*madhe sahaba*' and '*tabarra*' on the streets of the city.[460] The Hindus participated in the processions of both the sects; a section of the Shias in return for their participation declared to abandon cow slaughter and a Sunni organization, the Anjuman-i-Namoos-i-Sahaba, funded *sabil*s to provide drinks to the Hindus participating in the Hindu festivals.[461] No appeal could stop the sectarian conflict that intermittently resulted in violence.[462] The Congress government, which initially might have instigated sectarianism to manipulate Muslim support, now wanted intervention from any quarter to restore peace. It was at first at Nehru's initiative that Allama Inayatullah Mashriqi (1888–1963), leader of the Khaksar Movement, intervened to stop by force the sectarian conflict in the United Provinces. The arrival of Khaksars from Sindh, Punjab and NWFP on the roads of Lucknow and their aggressive posture created a new security problem for the provincial government, culminating in police–Khaksar clashes. Several United Provinces League leaders and workers, Sunni as well as Shia, were individually involved in these activities; but the All-India Muslim League as a party scrupulously kept itself aloof from the sectarian controversies.[463] Jinnah faced immense pressure for intervention but he refused to intervene unless both sides jointly invited him to mediate.[464] Initially, he encouraged others to attempt at the resolution of the conflict. But when there was a deadlock in negotiations between the United Provinces government and the Khaksars, the United Provinces government, Nehru and leading Muslims asked Jinnah to intervene, and on their request, he tried to arrange reconciliation between them.[465] The intensity of the conflict lasted throughout the Congress rule in the United Provinces, and was reflected in the selection of a candidate in the bye-election from the Bulandshehr constituency.[466] Peace returned with the resignation of the Congress ministry. Even after that, sectarianism did often manifest itself but there was no major incident of violence.[467]

The League displeased a large section of the Sunnis and Shias in the United Provinces and elsewhere by its policy of neutrality in the sectarian conflict. Some parties like the Jamiatul Ulama-i-Hind, the Majlis-i-Ahrar-i-Islam and the All-India Shia Political Conference, a bye-product of the Shia–Sunni conflict in the United Provinces, disliked the League for not supporting their respective viewpoints. The Congress and the British often used them to question the All-India Muslim League's claim as the sole representative party of the Indian Muslims.[468] The League temporarily suffered but ultimately it benefited when the Muslims realized the wisdom of this policy.[469] Then, several workers of these parties defected to join the League, leaving them with highly limited popular support. The United Provinces Muslim League slowly recovered from the shock of sectarianism and reactivated itself especially after the visit by the central civil defence committee and its inspection report.[470] The provincial civil defence committee with Sayyid Rizwanullah (1904–1964) as its president—he was also general secretary of the United Provinces League—and Nawab Shamsul Hasan as secretary formed defence committees in 39 districts and 17 cities.[471] Their formation was timed with the resurgence of branch Leagues and increase in membership enrolment. The Gorakhpur civil defence committee did more useful work than the other district defence committees.[472] The United Provinces Muslim Students Federation built up a separate structure similar to the provincial civil defence committee to train volunteers and do relief work.[473] The provincial Muslim League also issued a weekly news bulletin, the *Ittelaat* (Lucknow), to project its activities. By the time of the party elections in 1943, it had validly constituted branches in 48 districts and 25 towns (with a population of 15,000 or more) with 271,817 members. Though this number of its members was less than the ideal of 10 per cent of the total Muslim population that the League had fixed but the inspection report recorded that almost the 'entire Muslim population' of the United Provinces was with the League and its 'ideal of Pakistan'.[474] In June 1943, the provincial Muslim League leadership flirted with the idea of forming a coalition ministry in the absence of the Congress but it did not mature. The following year, the provincial Muslim League witnessed acute factionalism when Nawab Ismail, after informing Jinnah, wanted to go on four-month leave, and the provincial council elected Rizwanullah to officiate in his place as president. Rizwanullah's impatience to assert his new authority provoked resentment, leading to the resignation of senior members of the working committee that he immediately accepted.[475] Despite this infighting, the League won more than 90 per cent of the Muslim seats in the municipal elections in the United Provinces; in many cases, the nationalist Muslims and Independent candidates forfeited their securities.[476] After the municipal elections, Nawab Ismail resumed the presidency to avert the threat of a split in the party.[477] The provincial Muslim League, with Nawab Ismail as president and Aizaz Rasul as general secretary, who was elected to that office in April 1944, soon regained its strength and cohesion.[478] But subsequently the provincial Muslim League could not be properly reorganized according to the model constitution on time due to Nawab Ismail's involvement in the party affairs outside United Provinces and communal riots in several districts of the province.[479]

(x) *Bihar Provincial Muslim League.* The Bihar provincial Muslim
League was reorganized in March 1938, when its council approved a
constitution and elected its office-bearers: Sayyid Abdul Aziz as
president, Sayyid Jafar Imam as general secretary, and Nawab Sayyid
Mohammad Ismail, S.M. Shareef and three others as vice-presidents.[480]
Sayyid Hasan and then Badruddin Ahmad succeeded Jafar Imam as
general secretary; Abdul Aziz was re-elected as president. After the
Lucknow annual session, Jinnah toured Bihar and was overwhelmed
by the warm reception that he received in the cities that he visited.
During his tour, two political parties, Majlis-i-Ahrar-i-Islam and United
Party, including their members of the provincial assembly, merged
themselves into the provincial Muslim League; the third party,
Independent Party, continued to maintain its separate existence. By
December 1938, the provincial Muslim League had formed a thirteen-
member party in the Bihar assembly. Jinnah was again given a historic
reception when he came to preside over the twenty-sixth annual session
in Patna; the processionists covered him with 'flowers and bathed [him]
in rose water and perfume'; and he addressed them 'in broken Urdu'.
Abdul Aziz was initially supportive of the Leaguers retaining
simultaneously their membership of the Congress, and even accepted
to chair the 'corruption committee' appointed by the Congress ministry
and endorsed its mass literacy campaign which some Leaguers
considered 'a suicidal mistake'.[481] But he was gradually disillusioned
by the Congress policies. The Bihar provincial Muslim League fully
participated in the campaign that the League launched in and outside
Bihar to project the Muslim grievances in the Congress-governed
Muslim minority provinces.[482] Muslim grievances in Bihar were
profusely documented not only by the Bihari Muslims themselves but
also by Muslims from outside the province.[483] Abdul Aziz left the Bihar
provincial Muslim League presidency in December 1939, when he
accepted the office of prime minister in the Hyderabad state. The
provincial Muslim League then elected Nawab Sayyid Mohammad
Ismail as president and Badruddin Ahmad as general secretary.[484] The
'Pakistan Resolution' evoked emotional responses from its supporters
and opponents in Bihar, a province with 13 per cent Muslim population
and known as Gandhi's province. Bihar Sharif, an important Muslim
city, saw horrible expression of these emotions in April 1941, when
communal riots broke out following an 'anti-Pakistan conference'.[485]
Twenty-seven Muslims were killed and 109 injured; the brutality of the
murders moved everyone.[486] A five-member provincial Muslim League

deputation led by its president met the governor, Sir Thomas Hewart, and presented a memorandum on Muslim grievances in Bihar including those relating to Bihar Sharif riots.[487] There was, however, no positive outcome. When a Bihar provincial Muslim League enquiry committee prepared a report on these riots, the Bihar government confiscated all its copies. The League then announced to observe 15 August as the 'Bihar Sharif Day'; again, the government put a ban on all meetings and processions in connection with these riots.[488] All-India Muslim League demanded an inquiry into these discriminatory actions.[489] Still, no official inquiry was conducted into these riots. But the Bihar government tried to demonstrate fairness by prohibiting the All-India Hindu Mahasabha from holding its annual session in Bhagalpur and six other districts of Bihar under the Defence of India Rules. When the All-India Hindu Mahasabha held its annual session that year, V.D. Savarkar, in his presidential address, aggressively declared, 'Militarization and industrialization of our Hindu nation ought to be the first two immediate objectives . . . if we want to utilize the war situation in the world as effectively as possible to defend the Hindu interests.'[490] There was a positive response from the Hindus and their proportion in the army rose during the war.

The activities of the Bihar provincial Muslim League had slowed down after the resignation of the Congress ministries in December 1939, but in April 1942, when a provincial civil defence committee was appointed, with Latifur Rahman as its chairman and Mazhar Imam as secretary, the party began to expand its activities.[491] The Bihar civil defence committee established branches in all the sixteen districts and organized social and relief work in cooperation with the provincial Muslim Students Federation.[492] Factionalism then crept into the party. Sayyid Ismail and Badruddin Ahmad had been continuously re-elected its president and secretary, respectively; but their re-election in April 1944, for a fifth term invited serious objections. Their opponents alleged that the 'Ismail group' had contrived to control the party by unfair means.[493] The expulsion of Maulana Abdul Quddus, a Gaya district Muslim League leader, for three years added to the intensity of the intra-party tussle. Instead of quietly accepting his expulsion, Maulana Quddus made a representation to the All-India Muslim League against his expulsion. The central committee of action deputed Qazi Isa to inquire into his case and report about the general state of the. Bihar provincial Muslim League.[494] Qazi Isa concluded in his report that the provincial Muslim League was functioning according to its constitution, recommended fairness and justice to Abdul Quddus, demanded action against those involved in recriminatory propaganda against him, and blamed the communists for the general unrest in the party.[495] The expulsion case of Abdul Quddus continued to shuttle between the central committee of action and the provincial Muslim League till 26 April 1946, when Badruddin informed Zafar Ahmad Ansari that 'all proceedings against Maulana Quddus [had been] dropped.'[496] When one of the factions had refused to accept Qazi Isa's report, it was then suggested that Abdul Aziz, who was bedridden due to illness after his return from the Hyderabad state, should be elected president as a compromise. Abdul Aziz's refusal to accept the office did not deter them to insist on his election as president.[497] They requisitioned a meeting of the council to remove the technical hurdles in the way of his election. The provincial Muslim League council met on 10 June, with Sayyid Ismail in the chair, but the meeting adjourned without taking any decision after a ruling by the chairman that the representatives of the Shahabad district Muslim League on the council had not been properly elected.[498] After another two months' delay and on the intervention of central committee of action, the council again met on 5 August, and elected its office-bearers. Now Husain Imam was elected president by securing 41 votes against Sayyid Ismail who secured 36 votes; and Badruddin was unanimously re-elected general secretary.[499] The provincial Muslim League then forged broader unity, and participated in the general elections with relatively more cohesion, mobilizing different sections of the society particularly the Muslim Students Federation. After the general elections, Sayyid Ismail was elected leader of the League assembly party, Latifur Rahman deputy leader, Mazhar Imam chief whip and Abdul Ghani secretary. In October–November 1946, Bihar witnessed Muslim massacre on a scale that India had never seen before.[500] The provincial Muslim League was not equipped to meet that kind of challenge. Muslims of other provinces rushed to render assistance. Husain Imam resigned from the Bihar provincial Muslim League presidency due to his engagements outside the province; Jafar Imam then succeeded him as president by securing twenty-six votes against eight of his rival, Amin Ahmad. Muslims emigrated from Bihar on a large scale but the provincial Muslim League on Jinnah's advice prevented a wholesale migration of the Muslim population. In April 1947, the provincial Muslim League at a conference in Gaya suggested partition of Bihar into Hindu and non-Hindu provinces but no one took any serious notice of that suggestion.[501]

(*xi*) *Central Provinces and Berar Provincial Muslim League.* In April 1938, Jinnah appointed a committee, with Sayyid Abdur Rauf Shah (1878–1954) of Berar, a former Khilafatist, as convener, which reorganized the Central Provinces and Berar provincial Muslim League. Rauf Shah was elected its president and Nawab Siddiq Ali Khan its general secretary. Rauf Shah was continuously re-elected to that office till 1947; but in October 1939, Mohammad Asghar[502] succeeded Siddiq Ali Khan as general secretary and, in January 1946, followed by Abdul Majid Khan. Seven members of the provincial assembly who had been elected on the Rauf-led provincial parliamentary board's tickets and two Independents formed the League assembly party.[503] The Yusuf Shareef-led rival League dispersed when two of its members of the provincial assembly joined the Congress ministry. Maulana Azad tried to entice the provincial Muslim League into the ministry on terms more or less similar to the ones that the Congress had offered to the United Provinces League in 1937, but failed in that mission.[504] The provincial Muslim League denounced the Congress policies in regard to the Vidya Mandir Scheme, hoisting of Congress flag on public buildings, singing of *Bande Mataram* at official functions, and replacement of Urdu by Hindustani/Hindi as the *lingua franca*.[505] This campaign ensured the League's popularity among the Muslims; and as early as November 1937, a League candidate won a bye-election by securing 90 per cent votes.[506] Factionalism on regional lines was reflected in the demand for two separate Leagues: one for Central Provinces and the other for Berar.[507] At first, Tajuddin from Jabbalpur (Central Provinces) supported by Nawab Siddiq and Maulana Burhanul Haq (1892–1984) pressed this demand, arguing that the Leaguers from Berar with fewer members than the Central Provinces dominated the provincial Muslim League. When, in October 1939, the provincial Muslim League council voted against this demand, they asked for equitable representation of the two regions on the provincial council.[508] Nawab Bahadur Yar Jang, on Jinnah's request, visited the province and worked out a formula of representation for the two regions on the council: Central Provinces was allocated 80 seats and Berar 60;[509] in addition, a specified number of seats were given to each region on the basis of the strength of its party members.[510] But the provincial Muslim League working committee, instead of its council, adopted a modified version of this formula, i.e. allocated seats simply on the basis of population and gave no weightage to membership strength in a region. The conflict, therefore, lingered on. Meanwhile, Nawab Siddiq's protest demonstrations against a provincial Muslim League-organized conference in Nagpur invited disciplinary action against him. The provincial Muslim League expelled him from the party for two years, but did not make the decision public because of Siddiq's prosecution and imprisonment for four months in the Shatrangipura mosque (Nagpur) affair; in that case, the police had desecrated the mosque and lathi-charged Muslims during prayers. Siddiq was tried for making a fiery speech following the police action that had prompted ten Muslims to beat up the Hindu superintendent of police who had led the action.[511] The civil disobedience movement that followed called for an impartial inquiry, leading to more arrests. Haji Abdussattar Haji Essak Sait, on Jinnah's instructions, went to Nagpur and negotiated an agreement between the government and the provincial Muslim League that resulted in the release of Nawab Siddiq and other detenus. The agreement, which was smoothly implemented, stipulated that the government would express regret on the mosque incident; Nawab Siddiq would be released without expressing regret or putting his signatures on any paper; and a League deputation would assure the government that it was never Siddiq's intention to suggest attack on the superintendent of police.[512]

Nawab Siddiq faced the order of expulsion from the League on his release. The provincial Muslim League disaffiliated the Nagpur district Muslim League and city Muslim League when these branches did not implement the expulsion order.[513] Jinnah sympathized with Siddiq but expressed his inability to intervene as he had no constitutional authority in the matter; however, he pointed out that Siddiq under the party constitution could appeal to the central working committee against his expulsion, if he so desired.[514] Siddiq filed an appeal and so did the Nagpur district Muslim League and city Muslim League.[515] On 22 February 1941, the central working committee appointed a three-member (Liaquat, Khaliquzzaman and Haji Abdussattar Haji Essak Sait) subcommittee to inquire into these appeals and resolved to hold in abeyance the decisions of the provincial Muslim League till the submission of its report. The subcommittee could not conduct the inquiry immediately because of its members' engagements elsewhere. Among other factors for the delay were the police firing on a *tazia* procession in Jabbalpur, desecration of a mosque in Gotegaon, and communal riots in Amraoti in which seven Muslims were killed and eighty-four injured.[516] When the members of the subcommittee visited Nagpur in October, they proposed that the concerned parties should first make an attempt to resolve their differences on their own. This proposal was accepted and the subcommittee gave one-month's time to the parties to arrive at a settlement.[517] But before they could reach an agreement, Siddiq was again arrested and convicted on the charge of fomenting communalism; now Rauf Shah was among those who came to his defence. The central working committee also intervened, urging the government to release him as it had released the Satyagrahi and other political prisoners.[518] On his release, Siddiq settled his differences with the provincial Muslim League; and soon after, the All-India Muslim League practically removed him from the provincial political scene by assigning him the task of organizing the all-India Muslim League National Guards. Maulana Burhanul Haq, president of the Jabbalpur district Muslim League, then took up the issue of regional representation on the provincial Muslim League council, which started a new factional tussle.[519] The provincial Muslim League tried to dislodge Burhanul Haq from the district Muslim League presidency by promoting his rival, Iftikhar Ali, and by negative campaigning against him but all its attempts failed; and Burhanul Haq managed his re-election as president.[520] Finally, the central committee of action settled the issue of regional representation on the council in the model constitution that gave due weight to both the viewpoints.[521] The provincial Muslim League participated in the general elections with more unity, but its electoral victory aggravated Muslims' sense of insecurity, as the whole outlook of the Hindu community drastically changed after the elections.[522] Responsible Hindu leaders began to talk of revenge against the Muslims for supporting the Pakistan demand; and even Chief Minister Shukla once asked the Muslims 'to adopt a common political ideology with the Hindus or pack up their beddings and migrate to Jinnah's Pakistan'.[523] On the eve of independence, the provincial Muslim League called on Nawab Ismail, chairman of the central committee of action, to hold a meeting of the presidents and secretaries of the provincial Muslim Leagues to devise ways and means to protect the rights and interests of the Muslims of the Hindustan zone but that meeting could not be organized in those unsettling circumstances.[524]

(*xii*) *Orissa Provincial Muslim League*. Muslims were about 2.5 per cent in the population of Orissa. Due to their backwardness and limited resources, they had not participated in the politics of the All-India Muslim League. The League and its leaders were equally ignorant about the condition of Muslims in Orissa. An organizing committee, appointed in November 1937, after forming the district Muslim Leagues, established an Orissa provincial Muslim League in December 1938, with Cuttack as its headquarters, and elected Latifur Rahman as its president and K.B. Ahmad Bakhsh as general secretary.[525] Both of them were sitting members of the provincial assembly. On 16 December, Ahmad Bakhsh as general secretary requested the All-India Muslim League for affiliation and corresponded with the central League office. Meanwhile, M.A. Jalil, a rich hide merchant, organized a rival League with himself as president and Yaqub Ali Beg as general secretary. Jalil also requested the All-India Muslim League for affiliation of his League and corresponded with the central League office as president of the Orissa provincial Muslim League. The All-India Muslim League demonstrated its ignorance of the party affairs in Orissa by giving recognition to both the Leagues, accepting secretary of one League and president of the other, and elected members of the central council from Orissa.[526] When the central working committee came to know of its mistake, it did not send anyone from the central League to Cuttack to investigate the matter but asked the Bengal presidency Muslim League honorary secretary to depute someone to Orissa for inquiry and report.[527] The delay in settling the dispute fuelled factional rivalry and disillusioned the League workers.[528] A League member of the provincial assembly, M.S. Khan, joined the Orissa coalition ministry in this state of confusion without obtaining the required authorization from the League bodies. The provincial civil defence committee that Syed Wajid Ali formed under his chairmanship in Cuttack kept the League functioning with the enthusiastic support of the All-Orissa Muslim Students Federation.[529] It criticised the adoption of Oriya as the medium of instruction in Orissa, demanded Urdu as the medium of instruction for the Muslim students, and asked for permission to any Muslim school to affiliate itself with any university outside Orissa. The government did not care to respond to these demands.[530]

In 1943–44, top five leaders of the Orissa provincial Muslim League died, one after another, within a short span of time, which relegated the party into immobility.[531] It reactivated itself when it had to fight a bye-election on a provincial assembly seat that had fallen vacant on the death of Ahmad Bakhsh. The central committee of action sent Zakir Ali to assist the provincial Muslim League to organize itself. Almost every Muslim in Orissa, Zakir Ali wrote after a visit in July 1944, was a Leaguer. The League candidate in that bye-election, Mohammad Yusuf, won the seat, securing 658 votes against 617 scored by all the three candidates opposing him.[532] Before Zakir left Cuttack, he set up an *ad hoc* committee to organize the provincial Muslim League, which the central committee of action subsequently approved. The process of party organization in the districts and at the provincial level that started in August was completed during Zakir's second visit in March–April 1945.[533] K.S. Fazle Haq was elected president of the reorganized provincial Muslim League and Maulana Qadir Bakhsh its general secretary; the following year, M.A. Amin replaced Qadir Bakhsh in that office. The provincial Muslim League won all the seats in the general elections, and elected Mohammad Yusuf as leader of the League Assembly party and Latifur Rahman as its deputy leader. The Bihar massacre of the Muslims created a deep sense of insecurity in the Muslims of Orissa. The provincial Muslim League advised the Muslims scattered 'in the towns and suburbs' to concentrate themselves in the 'more populated Muslim localities'. The affluent among them on their own moved to such localities, and the provincial Muslim League assisted those who could not afford to make their own arrangements.[534] However, no figures of such movements are available.

(*xiii*) *Ajmer–Merwara Provincial Muslim League.* Ajmer was the centre of political activities in the Ajmer–Merwara province because Khwaja (Moinuddin) Sahib's *dargah* (shrine), which the Indian Muslims held in high esteem, was located here. There were three mutually hostile groups around the Dargah: one group headed by the Dewan (Sajjadanashin), the second group led by the Mutawalli and the third group consisted of the Khadims. The Dewan–Mutawalli conflict influenced provincial politics.[535] The provincial Muslim League that was reorganized in 1938, after the formation of the district Muslim Leagues, elected Mirza Abdul Qadir Beg, a former Khilafatist and nephew of Hakim Ajmal Khan, as the president and Mohammad Khalil Khan as its general secretary.[536] Qadir Beg who had supported the Dewan on the Dargah Act enjoyed the support of his group but the Khadims disliked the Act, and once even assaulted him for his role in its enactment.[537] He managed to stay as president till independence but often faced criticism from the supporters of the Mutawalli especially at the time of his re-election as the president. On his first election, several Leaguers alleged that he had manoeuvred his election by unfair means and urged the central League not to give the reorganized provincial Muslim League affiliation.[538] Then, at the time of his re-election, Sayyid Asrar Ahmad, who represented the Mutawalli group, levelled the same charges, demanding an inquiry into the elections.[539] Quite a few Leaguers joined him in this campaign.[540] Finally, in 1940, the All-India Muslim League deputed Zakir Ali to hold an investigation on the spot and submit a report. Zakir supervised the elections and recommended the affiliation of the provincial Muslim League that the central League formally accorded.[541] Now Qadir Beg's opponents propagated that Zakir had lived in Ajmer in the 1920s, and that his friendship with Beg had influenced his recommendation for affiliation. But now no one took notice of their protest. The following year, Ghazi Mohyuddin alias Piarai Mian, the Sajjadanashin, was elected general secretary along with Qadir Beg's re-election as president.

Now S.M. Zauqi, a senior journalist and a Leaguer of long standing, started a campaign against the office-bearers.[542] As a result, in April 1944, the central committee of action again sent Zakir to look into the working of the provincial Muslim League. When Zakir visited Ajmer, Qadir Beg and Mohyuddin offered to resign from their offices but none of their opponents came forward to assume the responsibility of leading the party. The dissenting Leaguers wanted them to stay in their offices but asked them to devote more time for the party work. The provincial Muslim League reactivated itself with the help of the Muslim youth and Muslim Students Federation workers, and also assumed the responsibilities of the civil defence committee. In addition, it looked after the functioning of the Anjuman-i-Taalim Dehat (Rural Education Committee) and Anjuman-i-Tablighul Islam (Committee for the Propagation of Islam), and campaigned for the recruitment of Muslims in government and railway services in accordance with the quota fixed by the Government of India in 1934.[543] Its critics did not disappear because the provincial Muslim League did not strictly follow the instructions that Zakir had left for the party in his inspection report. In April 1945, eight out of fifteen members of its working committee resigned; the young Leaguers protested that the provincial Muslim League had again reverted to a state of inactivity except in the Ajmer district.[544] The central committee of action took notice of these complaints but the steps it took could not stop the propaganda that the two factions launched against each other through posters and other means.[545] Qadir Beg's election as member of the chief commissioner's advisory council despite the opposition of the rival faction negated all the propaganda against him that he was unpopular among the Muslims.[546] Soon after, the party started the process of membership enrolment and elections from the primary to the provincial level in accordance with the model constitution; the central committee of action closely monitored this process. In July 1947, the provincial Muslim League elected its office-bearers, Qadir Beg was again elected as president and Dr Ishrat Husain as general secretary.[547] The two factions finally reconciled and shared the party offices; Qadir Beg's faction still had the dominant share in the party offices.[548]

(*xiv*) *Coorg–Bangalore Provincial Muslim League*. When Coorg was raised to the status of a chief commissioner's province, its 16 per cent Muslims had demanded proportionate representation in its legislative council on the basis of separate electorates but the government did not accept their demand.[549] The result was that not a single Muslim was returned to the Coorg legislative council when its first elections were held on the basis of joint electorates.[550] The Leaguers had party organizations both in Coorg and Bangalore but the All-India Muslim League did not recognize them as separate branches. Coorg had quite an active League which, in 1942, had Abdur Rahman Khan as its secretary. Similarly, Bangalore had a separate League with Abdur Razzaq Khan Husaini as its president, Abdul Aziz Siddiqi as secretary and Mahmud Khan Niazi as treasurer; however, the Bangalore civil defence committee and Muslim Students Federation were more active than the League.[551] The two Leagues, in Coorg and Bangalore, had the status of district Muslim Leagues; they requested the All-India Muslim League for affiliation. The problem was that the total Muslim population of Coorg was then about 15,000 and that of Bangalore around 50,000.[552] Keeping in view the proximity of the two areas and their modest population, the council of the All-India Muslim League joined the two applications and with the consent of the two Leagues gave the combined Coorg–Bangalore Muslim League the status of a provincial League and allocated five seats for its representatives on the council. On 6 February 1944, the Coorg–Bangalore provincial Muslim League council elected its office-bearers with Modi Abdul Ghafur as its president and H.M. Ismail Tabish as the general secretary, and held a conference, when the central civil defence committee members visited the province.[553] The following year, in February, Liaquat presided over its annual conference during his tour of southern India.[554] Despite its persistent pressure, the government did not accept its demand for reservation of seats for the Muslims on the basis of separate electorates in the provincial legislative council.[555] The provincial Muslim League did not give up its demand and reiterated it when it was reorganized according to the model constitution.[556]

(*xv*) *Delhi Provincial Muslim League.* The Delhi provincial Muslim League, as organized under the 1937 party constitution, dominated Muslim politics of the capital of India. Location of the All-India Muslim League headquarters in Delhi added to its importance and made the central leadership sensitive to developments in this branch. Factional tussle in the provincial Muslim League remained a constant source of concern for the League leadership. It began with the first elections, when Shujaul Haq was elected president and Mian Abdul Ghani general secretary. The tussle continued after the next elections, when Shaikh Waheeduddin Ahmad was elected president and Sayyid Saghir Ali Qadri general secretary.[557] At first, the conflict was reflected in the 'Fatehpur Mosque Pushta Agitation': one faction was led by Maulana Mazharuddin, proprietor-editor of the daily *Wahdat* and the biweekly *Al-Aman*, and the other was headed by Haji Rashid Ahmad (1883–1952). Factional leaders blamed one another for links with the Congress, urging the All-India Muslim League for disciplinary action. The central working committee took notice of these complaints and authorized Liaquat to deal with the matter.[558] The assassination of Mazharuddin in March 1939, by an unknown gunman had a sobering effect on both the factions. Then, the provincial Muslim League elected Begum Mohammad Ali as its president. However, a peaceful atmosphere remained only for a short while.[559] Allegations of irregularities in the enrolment process and party elections again aggravated factionalism; the infighting resulted in the defeat of the League candidates in the municipal elections.[560] The central working committee appointed a two-member (Liaquat and Begum Mohammad Ali) committee to conduct an inquiry.[561] On the basis of the inquiry report, the working committee dissolved the Delhi provincial Muslim League and authorized Liaquat to arrange fresh elections.[562] The reconstituted provincial Muslim League elected Shaikh Abdus Salam as president and Abdul Ghani as general secretary, whom Abdul Wahid Qureshi replaced in that office the following year. In 1942, Abdul

Salam and Qureshi were also elected chairman and secretary of the Delhi civil defence committee, respectively. The civil defence committee organized its own branches, where needed, and exerted pressure to ensure regular supply of food grains and price control of commodities of daily use.[563]

In 1944, there were again reports of factional tussle for the control of the provincial Muslim League. The central committee of action, to which the working committee had delegated its powers in such matters, on a request from the provincial Muslim League itself, appointed a three-member (Nawab Ismail, Liaquat and Haji Abdussattar) subcommittee to conduct the party elections.[564] The enrolment process was completed according to a schedule announced by this subcommittee. The central committee of action appointed Yamin Khan, secretary of the central League assembly party, as election officer, who supervised the election process from the primary to the provincial level. On 9 June, the reconstituted provincial Muslim League elected its office-bearers: Professor Mirza Mohammad Saeed as president and Anis Ahmad Hashmi as general secretary.[565] Early in 1945, the central committee of action again made arrangements for the party elections, and Yamin Khan supervised the process; both the principal office-bearers, Mirza Saeed and Anis Hashmi, were re-elected.[566] Before the next party elections, Anis Hashmi resigned when it was alleged that he had collected funds for the party without any authorization and mismanaged the same; the inquiry into the case lingered on till independence.[567] Qadiruddin Ahmad and Hamid Ali Qureshi were then elected president and general secretary, respectively. For the supervision of the 1946 party elections, the central committee of action appointed Aslam Saifi as the election officer but in October, the elections were postponed due to the law and order situation in Delhi. Instead of conducting the party elections, in April 1947, the central committee of action appointed a twelve-member *ad hoc* committee, with D.M. Malik as chairman and Mian Abdur Rahman as its convenor, and empowered it with all the powers of a provincial branch till such time that the party had constituted a provincial Muslim League in accordance with the model constitution. The deteriorating communal situation in Delhi, however, did not allow the League to reconstitute the provincial Muslim League.

(B) MUSLIM LEAGUE ABROAD

Before Independence, almost every Indian Muslim living in a foreign country was an advocate of the All-India Muslim League and its demand for Pakistan, as every Hindu was the spokesperson of the Congress and its demands. Wherever they were in substantial number they tended to organize Muslim Leagues. The Indian Muslims in South Africa and Sri Lanka had such Leagues, which kept themselves in touch with the All-India Muslim League, but none of these Leagues had the status of an affiliated branch till December 1943, when an amendment in the constitution allowed the formation of League branches 'outside India'.[568] The Indian Muslims in England had always been keen to work for the All-India Muslim League; but unlike the early decades of the twentieth century, they had no distinguished personality like Amir Ali who could organise them and influence the government policy and public opinion in that country. Haji Abdullah Haroon tried to have a set-up in London with the help of Waris, Amir Ali's son, and a few young Muslims, to give publicity to the activities of the League in England but his proposal did not go beyond the preliminary stage.[569] Nevertheless, in November 1944, some Muslims founded a Muslim League and elected Ali Mohammad Khan of Coventry as its president.[570] Named as the 'Muslim League Branch, Great Britain', it claimed to have 9 branches and 718 members. Its president requested for affiliation but his request did not mature although Jinnah showed interest in its work and its linkage with the All-India Muslim League.[571] The London League was quite active and published first the monthly *Rahnuma* and then the fortnightly *Pakistan*. But it was not devoid of factionalism; Abbas Ali claimed the presidency of a rival party which he dissolved at the time of Jinnah's London visit in December 1946. At the time of independence the London League, headed by S.D. Khan with Nazir Ahmad as secretary, hosted a dinner at the birth of Pakistan.[572]

(C) ALL-INDIA MUSLIM LEAGUE AND THE STATES

The 1937 constitution of the All-India Muslim League had no provision for League branches in the princely states. After its revival on Jinnah's return from England, some old branches in the states were revived but the All-India Muslim League declined to give them affiliation due to absence of any provision in the constitution.[573] Before 1937, the All-India Muslim League as well as the Congress had refrained from interfering in the affairs of the states but after that, the Congress changed its policy. Its object then was to secure pro-Congress nominees for the federal legislature under the Act of 1935. Its intervention was selective and indirect; it was in those states where it suspected that the rulers might not nominate pro-Congress members to the legislature, and it began to press for reforms more vigorously in these states than the others. Its movement started in the Kathiawar states and the Hyderabad state. It marshalled the support of the Arya Samaj and Hindu Mahasabha workers and their *jathas* came to these states from all over India. The promotion of the All-India States Peoples' Congress, which had been founded in 1927, was a by-product of this movement. The Congress campaign created unrest in the states and embittered Hindu–Muslim relations particularly in the states of Rajkot, Jaipur, Jodhpur, Patiala and Bhavnagar.[574] Communal riots in Jaipur and arrival of Muslim refugees from there in Delhi gave the conflict greater visibility.[575] Muslims of the affected states looked to the All-India Muslim League for support. At first, Muslim students from these states at the Aligarh Muslim University attempted to elicit that support.[576] All-India Muslim League extended them support without amending its constitution or changing its policy of non-interference.[577] Jinnah encouraged them to organize their own platforms to 'resist tyranny', promising them every assistance 'wherever they may be' because, he declared, no 'geographical limits' could 'divide the children of Islam'.[578]

Quite a few Muslims wanted the League to have its branches in the states but the All-India Muslim League did not amend its constitution to make a provision to that effect.[579] However, Jinnah personally interacted with the Muslim leaders of the states, encouraging them to develop their own political platforms. Consequently, Muslim Leagues or Muslim organizations under different names emerged in the states to protect the rights of the Muslims. In October 1939, on his advice, Nawab Bahadur Yar Jung, a firebrand orator and a passionate advocate of Islam and Muslim rights, established an All India States Muslim League with its headquarters at Nagpur. The All India States Muslim League adopted a constitution and elected Bahadur Yar Jung as its president.[580] Earlier, in December 1938, he had been elected president of the Majlis-i-Ittehadul Muslimin, an organization founded by the Muslims of the Hyderabad state in 1927. His passionate and aggressive campaign for the protection of Muslim rights in the prospective reforms in the Hyderabad state and his criticism of Sir Akbar Ali Hydari

(1869–1942), the prime minister, brought him into conflict with the Nizam, Mir Sir Usman Ali Khan (1886–1967), and his administration; the Nizam in retaliation divested him of his honorific title and cancelled his *jagir*.[581] He was prepared to adjust himself with his changed status but Jinnah intervened and brought about reconciliation between him and the Nizam who then restored his title as well as the jagir. Even after that, his relations with the Nizam often remained uncomfortable and strained, which disabled him to concentrate fully on the organization of the All India States Muslim League.[582] The All India States Muslim League held its first meeting in Nagpur on 4 March 1940, followed by a session in Lahore along with the annual session of the All-India Muslim League. Although Bahadur Yar Jung addressed several meetings of the All-India Muslim League on Jinnah's suggestion—his speech at the Karachi annual session was memorable for its oratory and contents—but he never enrolled himself as a member of the All-India Muslim League. In fact, Jinnah did not want to mix up the two bodies, All-India Muslim League and All India States Muslim League.[583]

Muslim organizations existed in the major states but their existence and independence of action depended upon the whims of the rulers whenever they actively involved themselves in politics. Bhopal, Mysore, Indore, Alwar, Gwalior and Rajputana states had quite active Muslim Leagues while Hyderabad had Majlis-i-Ittehadul Muslimin, Jammu and Kashmir had All Jammu and Kashmir Muslim Conference, and Bahawalpur had All Bahawalpur State Muslim Board and Jamiatul Muslimin. These organizations loosely associated or affiliated themselves with the All India States Muslim League. However, unlike the Congress-backed All-India States Peoples' Congress, the All India States Muslim League could not build itself up on sound, well-knit and effective footing. Besides the lack of financial resources, it did not have the support of any ancillary bodies like the well-organized Arya Samaj and All-India Hindu Mahasabha. While Nehru was elected president of the All-India States Peoples' Congress quite a few times, Jinnah avoided to preside over its functions but directed prominent Leaguers to do that.[584] He wanted the All India States Muslim League to maintain its separate identity although it held its annual sessions regularly at places where the All-India Muslim League met for its annual sessions. Bahadur Yar Jung could not really focus his attention on the All India States Muslim League due to his continuous conflict with the Nizam's administration, lack of financial resources and multiplicity of the systems of the Princely States. Jinnah expressed his dissatisfaction on the state of its organization in a letter to Bahadur Yar Jung on 10 December 1942, he wrote: 'Please don't think I feel angry with you in any way. That is not possible. But I do feel this that the States Muslim League under your leadership . . . [has] . . . not worked systematically. . . . Yours is a great responsibility as president of the All India States Muslim League and I find there is no systematic and methodical working of the organization either administratively or otherwise.'[585] Despite all its shortcomings, the All India States Muslim League under Bahadur Yar Jung's leadership had quite an impressive visibility in his lifetime.[586] However, his activities were negatively affected by the whimsical actions of the rulers. For example, in September 1943, when he went to Kashmir to preside over a conference in Srinagar organized by the All Jammu and Kashmir Muslim Conference, the ruler not only banned the conference but also put a ban on his stay in the state; he and his wife were taken out of Srinagar and left stranded on the road.[587] After Bahadur Yar Jung, the leaderless All India States Muslim League went into oblivion. An attempt was made to revive it in February 1947, when its council decided to reorganize the All India States Muslim League and hold its annual session 'to take stock of the present position of the Muslims in the States'. Manzare Alam, a former Aligarh Muslim University student leader, who was actively behind this move, wrote to Jinnah who advised him 'to keep in touch with Mr Nishtar, who, I see, is taking interest in the All India States Muslim League. It is not possible for me to attend to each and every problem, as you see I am already pressed with matters which leave me no time.'[588]

NOTES

1. AFM, vol. 159, no. 80; vol. 181, no. 12; vol. 182, no. 20; vol. 193, no. 13; and vol. 417, pp. 52, and 102–3.
2. For G.M. Sayed's report of his NWFP tour to Jinnah dated 9 June 1942, see QAP, F. 460, pp. 8–10.
3. Malik Barkat Ali and Khalifa Shujauddin were its vice-presidents and Mian Abdul Majid and Ashiq Husain Batalvi joint secretaries. Its office was located at 12-Temple Road, Lahore, which was the residence of Barkat Ali.
4. For the text entitled 'Terms of Sikandar–Jinnah Pact', see QAP, F. 1049, p. 2.
5. Barkat Ali to Jinnah (Private and Confidential), 10 November 1937, ibid., F. 865, p. 342; and Mohammad Iqbal to Jinnah, 10 November 1937, cited in Khalid, *Punjab Muslim League*, pp. 109–110.
6. Ahmad Yar Khan Daultana to Jinnah, 15 November 1937, QAP, F. 255, pp. 6–7.

7. Sikandar to Jinnah, 15 November 1937, ibid., F. 353. Sikandar wrote to Jinnah that no 'Muslim Unionist had refused to join the provincial Muslim League but they have no confidence in Ghulam Rasul and consequently hesitate to collect or pay subscription so long he is there'.

8. Chhuto Ram made the observation in a statement on 21 October 1937.

9. Jinnah to Barkat Ali, 20 November 1937, Khalid, *Punjab Muslim League*, pp. 110–11; and Barkat Ali to Jinnah, 4 February 1938, QAP, F. 215, pp. 11–14.

10. Malik Mehdi Zaman Khan was elected deputy president, Barkat Ali and Shujauddin vice-presidents, Mian Abdul Majid finance secretary, and Sh. Mohammad Hasan, Mian Bashir Ahmad and Ashiq Husain joint secretaries.

11. AFM, vols. 198 (nos. 67 and 69), 246 and 521 deal with the Shahidganj issue.

12. Zafar Ali Khan to president/secretary, All-India Muslim League, 18 April 1938, ibid., vol. 198, no. 51.

13. Honorary secretary, All-India Muslim League to Ghulam Rasul, 4 April 1938, ibid., vol. 131, no. 11. The central council appointed a 5-member affiliation committee with Nawab Ismail as its chairman to consider the applications of various provincial Muslim Leagues for affiliation.

14. Jinnah's statement in the conference of the Punjab members of the legislative assembly, *Dawn*, 12 March 1944.

15. AFM, vol. 131, nos. 12, 15 and 16.

16. Ahmad Yar [Daultana] to Jinnah, 13 May 1938, QAP, F. 995, p. 3; and Jinnah to Ahmad Yar, n.d., ibid., F. 995, p. 4; Jinnah's message in his support, ibid., F. 579, p. 2; *Tribune*, 9 February 1939; and Waheed, *Nation's Voice: Towards Consolidation*, p. 350.

17. Ian Talbot, *Khizr Tiwana, Punjab Unionist Party and the Partition of India*, Surrey, 1996, pp. 71–73.

18. Z.H. Lari moved a resolution in the central council that criticized his offer of unconditional support to the British in the event of war. Sikandar argued that he had made that speech as the Punjab premier and not on behalf of the League or the Muslims. The resolution was withdrawn on the intervention of Jinnah who, refuting Sikandar's arguments, observed that one could not divide one's soul into two and that Sikandar's primary allegiance was to the League. He suggested that if the house desired it might be laid down that no prominent Muslim Leaguer particularly a member of the working committee should make a pronouncement on a vital issue without the permission of the working committee or the president. But this was not laid down as a policy and Lari withdrew his resolution. AFM, vol. 247; *Hindustan Times*, 5 December 1938; and Waheed, *Nation's Voice: Towards Consolidation*, pp. 311–16.

19. AFM, vol. 131, no. 29.

20. For Barkat Ali's resolution seeking dissolution of the existing organizing committee and appointment of a new one, which was not moved in the working committee, see AFM, vol. 122, no. 54 and 68; and for proceedings of a public meeting in the Barkat Ali Mohammedan Hall on 25 February 1939, urging immediate steps to organize the provincial Muslim League, see ibid., vol. 131, nos. 32, 33 and 36.

21. Ramzan Ali to Liaquat, 16 March 1939, ibid., vol. 131, no. 35. In February, Ghulam Rasul refused 'to run the Muslim League as a department of the Unionist Party' and resigned. *C&MG*, 24 June 1939; and QAP, F, 49, p. 114.

22. For Batalvi's letter to Jinnah and a copy of the new party's manifesto, see QAP, F. 870, p. 29 and F. 1137, pp. 332–62, respectively; and Sikandar to Jinnah, 19 August and 5 September 1939, ibid., F. 353, pp. 16 and 17.

23. Jinnah to Batalvi, 4 May 1939, Ashiq Husain Batalvi, *Hamari Qaumi Jiddo Juhd*, Lahore, 1995, Part One, p. 364, and Ashiq's (private and confidential) letter to Jinnah, 24 August 1939, QAP, F. 16, pp. 199–200.

24. For resolutions of the central council, see AFM, vol. 253, p. 74.

25. Ibid., vol. 253, pp. 71–72. For the Batalvi-Jinnah correspondence on this issue, see QAP, F. 48, pp. 33–34.

26. On 14 September, the organizing committee demanded Batalvi's expulsion from the League for his alleged links with the enemies of the League. AFM, vol. 131, nos. 40–41.

27. Nasrullah to Jinnah, 2 December 1939, QAP, F. 342, pp. 1–9.

28. Sardar Sir Mohammad Nawaz Khan was elected deputy president, Mian Amiruddin financial secretary, Mohammad Ali Jafari organizing secretary, and Sikandar president of the League assembly party and chairman of the provincial parliamentary board.

29. While Sikandar pleaded for its affiliation in the meeting of the working committee on 4 February 1940, arguing that if it was not affiliated the League would cease to exist in the Punjab, Barkat Ali argued against its affiliation.

30. For depositions by Barkat Ali and Nawab Mamdot before the Punjab inquiry committee consisting of Nawab Ismail Khan, Raja of Mahmudabad and Khaliquzzaman, see AFM, vol. 132, nos. 7–8.

31. QAP, F. 236, pp. 7–8.

32. Barkat Ali to Jinnah, 14, 18 and 23 June 1940, ibid., F. 215, pp. 33, 34 and 38; and Barkat Ali to Liaquat, 18 February 1941, AFM, vol. 133, no. 8.

33. Hakim Ahmad Shuja to Barkat Ali, 15 November 1940, Barkat Ali to Hakim Ahmad Shuja, 18 November and 2 December 1940; and Barkat Ali to Jinnah, 25 December 1940, QAP, F. 796, pp. 5–17.

34. Abu Saeed Anwar to Sikandar, 13 December 1940, AFM, vol. 138, no. 11; and his letter to Jinnah about the provincial Muslim League council meeting of 1 December 1940, ibid., vol. 132; and also see ibid., vol. 129, no. 28; vol. 132, no. 58; and vol. 491, pp. 3–7; and QAP, F. 215, pp. 60–61.

35. Barkat Ali to Jinnah, 15 February and 26 June 1941, and QAP, F. 215, pp. 67 and 69.

36. Jinnah to Zafrullah Khan, 24 July 1941, ibid., F. 388, p. 1.

37. For reports of some of these tours, see ibid., F. 1099, pp. 31–37, 41, and 45.

38. *IAR*, 1940, vol. II, p. 29; and 1941, vol. I, p. 47.

39. Jinnah to Sikandar, 29 August 1941, QAP, F. 353, p. 38; and for Sikandar's speech and the bitterness that it generated, see the *Tribune* and *Civil & Military Gazette*, 6 July 1941; and Barkat Ali to Quaid-i-Azam, 6 July 1941, QAP, F. 1092, pp. 71–74; Abdul Hamid Qadri to Quaid-i-Azam, 21 July 1941, ibid., F. 1099, p. 71; and Ataullah Wakeel to Liaquat Ali Khan, 29 July 1941, AFM, vol. 138, no. 23.

40. Prof. Inayatullah was re-elected as secretary while Mohammad Ali Jafari was elected secretary on the seat vacated by Khalilur Rahman. Rab Nawaz Khan was elected organizing secretary and Mian Firozuddin as *salar-i-azam*. For the proceedings, see AFM, vol. 491, pp. 10–12.

41. Sikandar to Jinnah, 6 and 28 March 1942; and Jinnah to Sikandar, 9 March 1942, QAP, F. 353, pp. 55–57, 58 and 59.

42. Statement by Sir Mohammad Jamal Khan, QAP, F. 353, pp. 14–15; and for Jamal Khan's contact with Jinnah, see Barkat Ali to Jinnah, 18 April 1942, and Jinnah to Jamal Khan, 24 April 1942, ibid., F. 215, pp. 82–83 and 84.

43. For minutes of the meeting of the provincial Muslim League council held in the Barkat Ali Mohammedan Hall on 29 March 1942, see AFM, vol. 491, pp. 13–15. Various district Muslim Leagues had recommended the names of Sikandar, Zafar Ali Khan, Barkat Ali, Nawab Nizam Ali Khan, Sadiq Hasan and Raja Ghazanfar Ali for the office of president.

44. Jinnah to Iftikhar Husain Mamdot, 15 May 1942, QAP, F. 372, p. 4.

45. QAP, F. 396, p. 3; and AFM, vol. 326, pp. 77–84.

46. For details, see Rab Nawaz Khan to Liaquat, 18 May 1942, QAP, F. 347, p. 1; Khalilur Rahman to Liaquat, 18 May 1942, AFM, vol. 138, no. 86; Prof. Malik Inayatullah to Nawabzada Liaquat Ali Khan, 21 May 1942, ibid., vol. 139, no. 91; Hamid Nizami to Quaid-i-Azam, 23 May 1942, QAP, F. 520, p. 13; Z.H. Lari and 25 other All-India Muslim League council members to Liaquat, n.d., AFM, vol. 292, p. 6; Jinnah to Sikandar, QAP, F. 520, p. 13; Sikandar to Jinnah, 28 May 1942, ibid., F. 353, p. 61; Barkat Ali to Jinnah, 30 May 1942, ibid., F. 215, pp. 83–86; Jinnah to Iftikhar Husain Mamdot, ibid., F. 1363, p. 21; and Jinnah to Liaquat, 10 July 1942, AFM, vol. 480, p. 61.

47. For his formula, see Glancy to Linlithgow, 10 July 1942, TP, vol. II, pp. 359–62.

48. The content of his speech in a Sikh gathering was totally different [Tribune, 28 November 1942; and Bashir Ahmad to Quaid-i-Azam, QAP, F. 701, p. 10.]. Sadiq Hasan was elected vice-president, Khalilur Rahman general secretary, Abbas Kirmani organizing secretary by defeating Rab Nawaz Khan, Mian Amiruddin financial secretary, Abdus Sattar Khan Niazi (1915–2000) propaganda secretary, Hameed Nizami publicity secretary and Wilayat Ali Khan salar-i-azam by defeating Mian Firozuddin. AFM, vol. 491, pp. 17–19.

49. In a letter to Linlithgow on 2 January 1943, Governor Glancy recounted the intrigue that had gone into the selection of Khizr as chief minister. MSS. EUR. F. 125/92.

50. Jinnah is reported to have advised Shaukat, when he first met him, to go back to the army and that his appointment was 'an insult to democracy'. Glancy to Linlithgow, 17 April 1943, TP, vol. III, p. 898.

51. For his aggressive speeches in support of the League, Jinnah and the Pakistan scheme for which the governor formally reprimanded him, see Glancy to Linlithgow, 20 July and 6 August 1943, ibid., vol. IV, pp. 110–11 and 161–62.

52. Amery to Linlithgow, 29 December 1942, ibid., vol. III, p. 434.

53. Khizr had lived under the shadow of his father and reluctantly entered politics to fulfill his wishes.

54. TP, III, 17 April 1943; and also see Glancy to Linlithgow, 23 April 1943, cited in Khalid, Punjab Muslim League, p. 136; and Glancy to Wavell, 20 October 1943, ibid., pp. 137–38.

55. Zafar Ali Khan was elected its president, Barkat Ali senior vice-president, Mian Nurullah junior vice-president, Sayyid Mustafa Shah Gilani joint secretary, Rab Nawaz Khan propaganda secretary and Mian Abdul Karim finance secretary.

56. For details, see AFM, vol. 162, nos. 4, 5, 9 and 10; and QAP, F. 344, pp. 63, 93, and 99–101; F. 828, p. 1; F. 701, pp. 28–31; F. 1092, 156–57; and F. 1101, pp. 15–18.

57. For the Punjab League assembly party and the 'Sikandar–Jinnah Pact', see resolutions proposed by Maulana Abdul Hamid Badauni and S. Naimul Haq in the central council on 7 March 1943, AFM, vol. 264, pp. 25 and 17, respectively.

58. Among them were Sir Mohammad Jamal Khan, Sir Mohammad Nawaz Khan and Makhdum Mohammad Raza Khan. Jamaal Khan to Jinnah, 13 April 1943, QAP, F. 1092, p. 176; Jinnah to Jamaal Khan, 15 April 1943, ibid., p. 15; and Jinnah to Nawaz Khan (Kot Fateh Khan, Attock district), 9 April 1943, ibid., F. 340, p. 5.

59. *Civil & Military Gazette*, 2 July 1943.

60. Mohammad Raza (Gilani) to Quaid-i-Azam, 23 April 1943, QAP, F. 1101, pp. 97–101. A similar move by Sadullah Khan was deflected by Chief Minister Aurangzeb for fear of losing non-Muslim support. Cunningham to Linlithgow, 13 September 1943, *TP*, vol. IV, pp. 245–46.

61. Shaikh Niaz Ali to Jinnah, 27 July 1943, QAP, F. 877, p. 66.

62. *The Leader*, 12 October 1943; and AFM, vol. 305, p. 84. Nawab Iftikhar Mamdot had helped in the purchase of this 'newly built spacious bungalow' and he revealed this information at a public function organized in Jinnah's honour in Lahore.

63. Wavell to Amery, 8 November 1944, *TP*, vol. V, p.187. For Glancy's unhappiness at Jinnah's Punjab tour in November 1942, see his letter to Linlithgow, 28 November 1942, ibid., vol. III, p. 319; and for Khizr's desire that the central government should 'keep Jinnah . . . out of the Punjab', see Wavell to Amery, 20 June 1944, ibid., vol. IV, p. 1035.

64. Hameed Nizami to Quaid-i-Azam, 7 and 19 May 1943, QAP, F. 396, pp.10–12; and Mian Bashir Ahmad to Jinnah, 27 March 1943, ibid., F. 197, pp. 64–65; and also see AFM, vol. 230, nos. 12–15.

65. Hameed Ahmad, Secretary, Sargodha district Muslim League to Quaid-i-Azam, 18 July 1943, QAP, F. 1101, pp. 156–60; and S. Nasir Mahmud, Secretary, Sialkot city Muslim League to Quaid-i-Azam, 27 November 1943, ibid., F. 828, p. 107.

66. Mohammad Sharif Toosi to Quaid-i-Azam, 2 July 1943, QAP, F. 877, pp. 3–12; Hamid Nizami to Quaid-i-Azam, 30 August, 17 September and 2 December 1943, Jinnah to Hamid Nizami, 10 September 1943, ibid., F. 638, pp. 2–5, 6, 7–8 and 9; and Chaudhri Faqir Chand to Jinnah, 17 July 1943, ibid., F. 1101, pp. 154–55; and Liaquat to Quaid-i-Azam, 6 February 1944, AFM, vol. 481, p. 49.

67. Rab Nawaz Khan to Quaid-i-Azam, 25 August 1943, in QAP, F. 851, p. 39; and Mohammad Sharif Toosi to Quaid-i-Azam, 2 July 1943, ibid., F. 877, pp. 3–12; also see Iftikhar Mamdot to Quaid-i-Azam, 10 September 1943, ibid., F. 372, p. 12; and Jinnah to Iftikhar Mamdot, 11 September 1943, ibid., F. 1363, pp. 19–20.

68. The council elected Sahibzada Abbas Shah as organizing secretary, Rab Nawaz Khan as propaganda secretary, Ch. Abdul Karim as publicity secretary, Amiruddin as finance secretary, and Wilayat Ali Khan as *salar-i-azam*.

69. Mohammad Alam, Zafar Ali Khan, Mohammad Ali Jafari and others to secretary, All-India Muslim League, 15 December 1943, AFM, vol. 162.

70. On 23–27 December 1943, the central working committee appointed a three-member (Nawab Ismail, Khaliquzzaman and Qazi Isa) committee, which submitted a report on 1 March 1944. QAP, F. 579, pp. 68–76.

71. Jinnah to Khizr, 4 October and 5 November 1943, and Khizr to Jinnah, 24 October 1943, ibid., F. 334, pp. 1–4; and also see ibid., F.197, pp. 68–71.

72. The committee consisted of Nawab Ismail, Khaliquzzaman and Nazimuddin. AFM, vol. 142, no. 15; and vol. 162, nos. 33 and 34.

73. Glancy to Wavell, 14 and 21 April 1944; Wavell to Glancy, 15 April 1944; and Wavell to Amery, 18 April and 16 May 1944, *TP*, vol. IV, pp. 880, 882, 898, 906 and 968–69.

74. For the statement by Shaukat Hayat, 28 April 1928, see SHC, Pb-III: 46.

75. Shaukat denied the charge that he had shown any bias in sacking Mrs Durga Das, inspectress of schools of the Lahore corporation, and asked for the publication of the facts of the case. Shaukat to Khizr, 28 April 1944, SHC, Pb-III: 47; Shaukat to the governor, 6 August 1944, ibid., p. 48; office of the secretary to the governor to Shaukat, 16 August 1944, and Shaukat's reply, ibid., pp. 49–50.

76. Glancy to Wavell, 24 April 1944; Wavell to Amery, 1 May 1944; and Glancy to Wavell, 8 May 1944, *TP*, vol. IV, pp. 923 and 941.

77. For the Liaquat–Khizr correspondence that led to Khizr's expulsion, see AFM, vols. 159 and 162.

78. Linlithgow to Amery, 2–4 May 1943, *TP*, vol. III, p. 940.

79. For a resolution passed by the Punjab provincial Muslim League working committee on 16 July 1944, calling on the Muslims to reject the advice, AFM, vol. 162, no. 57.

80. Wavell had asked Glancy to advise Khizr to organize a party and not to expect everything from the British government. Wavell to Amery, 20 September 1944, *TP*, vol. V, pp. 44–45.

81. AFM, vol. 162, nos. 41, 46.

82. Liaquat's statement, 5 May 1944, ibid., vol. 155, no. 59.

83. Iftikhar Mamdot to Jinnah, 7 June 1944, QAP, F. 372, pp. 14–15; and also see Liaquat to Jinnah, 5 June 1945, and Jinnah to Liaquat, 1 and 9 June 1945, AFM, vol. 481, pp. 80, 82 and 84.

84. Habib to K. Hasan, 5 and 15 November and 4 December 1944, QAP, F. 921, pp. 41–42, 45–46 and 57–58; Mumtaz Daultana to Quaid-i-Azam, 19 November 1944, SHC, Pb-III: 28; for appeals to elect Shaukat as the leader, see Mohammad Husain to Quaid-i-Azam, 22 November 1944, and Abu Saeed Enver to Quaid-i-Azam, 25 November 1944, ibid.-I: 25 and 26; and for Jinnah's advice, see his letter to Mamdot, 28 November 1944, ibid.-III: 5.

85. QAP, F. 921, pp. 62–65.

86. For details about the tours in the districts, see AFM, 159, nos. 94, 95, 96; vol. 162, nos. 19, 59, 60, 71; vol. 165, nos. 2, 3, 12; QAP, F. 579, p. 90; SHC, Pb-I: 30; SHC, Pb-III: 1, 2 and 11; Report by Nazir Ahmad Khan, advocate, Montgomery, 10 January 1945, AFM, 345, no. 1; and Report by general secretary, Mumtaz Daultana, SHC, Pb-I: 6.

87. SHC, Pb-I: 38 and 39.

88. For an exaggerated account of the 'communist' influence in the Punjab, see AFM, vol. 345, nos. 32–33.

89. The leftist Daniyal Latifi had to leave his position as office secretary of the provincial Muslim League. See correspondence of the president (Abdul Karim) and secretary (Sh. Zafar Hasan) of the Lahore city Muslim League and others, ibid., vols. 181 and 183.

90. Daniyal Latifi published its English version and Mian Bashir Ahmad translated it into Urdu. Bashir Ahmad to Jinnah, 3 January 1945, SHC, Pb-III: 14

91. AFM, vol. 288, p. 51; and Inspection Report No. 10 dated 26 February 1945, of the general administration of the provincial Muslim League and its central office by Zakir Ali, ibid., vol. 201, no. 7. The central working committee appointed a

committee (Husain Imam, Raza Kazmi and Abdur Rauf Shah) to investigate the complaints. Ibid., vol. 159, no. 39.

92. Mahmudali Daniyal Latifi to Quaid-i-Azam, 22 February 1946, QAP, F. 1003, pp. 6–7.

93. Ibid., F. 1116, p. 32. Khizr had Manohar Lal, Jamal Khan Leghari, Ashiq Husain Qureshi and Muzaffar Ali Qizilbash in his cabinet. This proved the correctness of Jinnah's remarks made in a lighter mood at a gathering of students that Khizr could form a ministry even with one Muslim MLA. *Dawn*, 20 January 1946.

94. Nishtar to Jinnah, 7 March 1946, QAP, F. 394, pp. 13–16.

95. Iftikhar Husain to Quaid-i-Azam, 31 October 1946, ibid., F. 372, p. 20; and Vicky Noon to Jinnah, 1 September 1946; and 9 November, SHC, Pb-IV: 43.

96. Other members of the committee were: Noon, Ghazanfar Ali, Shaukat, Karamat Ali, Iftikharuddin, Mian Abdul Bari, Maulana Daud Ghaznavi, and Maulana Ghulam Mohyuddin. For the notice issued by the office of the All-India Muslim League, Delhi, 14 October 1946, see AFM, vol. 182, no. 33.

97. There was opposition to his election as leader of the assembly party; the argument used against him was that he belonged to East Punjab and had been elected to the Punjab assembly from there. Although the conflict did not assume any serious proportion at the time but it was indicative of factional tussle in future. Iftikhar Husain to Quaid-i-Azam, 25 June 1947, ibid., F. 636, pp. 1–4; and Noon to Jinnah, 22 March; and 3 April 1947, ibid., F. 159, pp. 159 and 161.

98. For relative strength of the parties given in different sources, see Jones, *Politics in Sindh*, Table 3.4.

99. G.M. Sayed, *Struggle for New Sind: A Brief Narrative of the Working of Provincial Autonomy in Sind during the Decade of 1937–47*, Karachi, 1949, p. 13.

100. *Statesman*, 18 April 1938. Abdul Majid Sindhi, who promised to enrol fifty thousand members and establish four hundred branches, called on the Muslim members of the legislative assembly to sign the League pledge.

101. Abdul Majid to Jinnah, 17 May 1938, QAP, F. 16, pp. 109–110; and also see AFM, vol. 241, pp. 50–56.

102. For the document signed by Sindhi and Hidayatullah on 7 June 1938, see QAP, F. 16, p. 129. The central League asked A.M.K. Dehlavi to study the situation in Sindh and submit a report to the president. For a resolution to this effect passed by the central working committee in Bombay on 4–5 June 1938, see AFM, vol. 122, no. 31.

103. Abdullah Haroon to Jinnah, 2 August 1938, QAP, F. 1090, p. 57; and M.A. Khuhro to Kadermia, 3 August 1938, ibid., F. 1095, pp. 320–21.

104. Abdul Majid to Jinnah, 26 August 1938, ibid., F. 1095, pp. 511–13. Abdul Majid was willing to make way for Abdullah Haroon whose presidency, he believed, would bring in funds to support the expansion of the League.

105. For Jinnah's reception, see a note by Ali Mohammad Rashidi, general secretary of the reception committee of the Sindh provincial Muslim League conference dated 23 October 1938, in AFM, vol. 242, no. 9.

106. QAP, F. 134; and *Times of India*, 14 October 1938. After the failure of unity talks, the proposed reference of revenue assessment to Sikandar was withdrawn.

107. Abdul Majid to Jinnah, 25 August 1938, QAP, F. 1095, pp. 513–14; Hatim Alavi to Jinnah (confidential), 12 October 1938, ibid., F. 599, p. 1; and *Times of India*, 30 August 1938.

108. *Times of India*, 15 October 1938; and Ali Mohammad Rashidi, 'Political Situation in Sindh' (cyclostyled), AFM, vol. 248, p. 18.

109. *Times of India*, 17 and 19 October 1938.
110. For details, see AFM, vol. 241.
111. For a list of the members of the legislative assembly who remained with the League, see ibid., vol. 381.
112. For proceedings of the meetings held in and outside Sindh and the resolutions passed, see ibid., vol. 248.
113. The account that follows is primarily based on material relating to the Manzilgah mosque in QAP, F. 274, pp. 64–97; Hamida Khuhro, *Ayub Khuhro*, Chapter 10, pp. 169–92; and *Report of the Inquiry Committee appointed under Section 3 of the Sind Public Inquiries Act to enquire into the riots which occurred at Sukkur in 1939*, Karachi, 1939.
114. G.M. Sayed to Jinnah, 1 September 1939, QAP, F. 460, pp. 1–3.
115. Abdullah Haroon to governor, Sindh, 25 September 1939, governor's secretary to Abdullah Haroon, 26 September 1945, Abdullah Haroon to governor's secretary, 27 October 1945; and J.M. Corin to Abdullah Haroon, 27 October 1945, QAP, F. 274, pp. 37–43; Ayub Khuhro to Jinnah, 2 October 1939, ibid., F. 776, p. 58; Pir Sirhindi to Jinnah, ibid., F. 776, p. 94; for formulas presented by Jinnah and the government, see ibid., F. 274, pp. 46–48; and *Daily Gazette*, 29 October 1939.
116. Qazi Isa to Jinnah, 8 December 1939, QAP, F. 302, p. 25.
117. For a resolution passed by the All-India Muslim League working committee on 22 October 1939, see AFM, vol. 128, no. 65.
118. For instance, see ibid., vol. 118, p. 67; and Hamida Khuhro, *Ayub Khuhro*, p. 178.
119. Abdul Majid to Jinnah, 24 January 1941, QAP, F. 454, pp. 2–3; and Ali Mohammad Rashidi to ministers, 22 April 1940, ibid., F. 917, pp. 28–30.
120. Ayub Khuhro to Jinnah, 28 December 1939, ibid., F. 365, p. 2.
121. For an incomplete copy of his 'Report about the Communal Riots in Sukkur Town and the surrounding villages submitted to the Congress Working Committee by Abdul Qayyum, B.S. (Economics, London, Barrister-at-Law MLA (Central)', Peshawar, dated 18 January 1940, see ibid., F. 965, pp. 28–30 and 161–79.
122. Jinnah to Abdul Majid, 30 January 1941, ibid., F. 454, p. 4; and resolution passed by the Sindh provincial Muslim League council on 26 January 1941, ibid., p. 186.
123. For instance, see Ayub Khuhro to Jinnah, 3 February 1940, ibid., F. 518, p. 21.
124. On 21 April 1940, the provincial Muslim League working committee opposed any proposal to introduce joint electorates in the local bodies.
125. QAP, F. 365, p. 8; and F. 873, p. 600; and Jinnah's statement on 7 February 1941, Waheed Ahmad, *Nation's Voice*, vol. II, pp. 142–46.
126. Sayed and Khuhro to Nihchaldas, 20 November 1940, S.K. Chandio (ed.), *Jinnah–Khuhro Correspondence, 1938–1946*, Rawalpindi, 1996, p. 49.
127. For full text of his press statement on 21 November, see QAP, F. 274, p. 132.
128. For Abdullah Haroon's position on the 'pact', see his letter to G.M. Sayed, 15 January 1941, ibid., F. 274, p. 176.
129. Ibid., F. 835, p. 145; and for Sayed's note in which he proposed the organizing committee, see ibid., F. 460, pp. 66–68.
130. *Star of India*, 26 December 1940; and Ayub Khuhro to Jinnah, 30 January 1941, ibid., F. 365, pp. 4–5; Jinnah to Ayub Khuhro, 8 February 1941, ibid., vol. 365, p. 6; and for resolution of the All-India Muslim League council passed on 23 February 1941, see Pirzada, *Foundations*, vol. III, p. 345.
131. Jinnah to Abdullah Haroon, 20 January 1941, QAP, F. 274, p. 184; and for the Sindh provincial Muslim League council's resolution against joint electorates passed on 26 January 1941, ibid., F. 274, p. 185.

132. For details, see correspondence, ibid., F. 365 and 460; Jinnah's statement on the issue, ibid., F. 1060, pp. 13; his letter to Abdul Majid, 29 January 1941, ibid., F. 874, p. 30; Abdul Majid to Jinnah, 4 February 1941; and Jinnah to Abdul Majid, 8 February 1941, ibid., F. 454, pp. 5–9; Bandeh Ali to Jinnah, 3 February 1941, ibid., F. 218, pp. 2 and 2A; Nihchaldas Vazirani to Jinnah, 9 February 1941, ibid., F. 1085, pp. 12–20; and *IAR*, 1941, vol. I, pp. 26, 37, 39 and 41.

133. Sayed to Jinnah, 24 January 1941, QAP, F. 460, p. 32; and Jinnah–Haroon correspondence, ibid., F. 274, pp. 191–94, 199 and 217.

134. For details, see Jinnah–Bande Ali correspondence, ibid., F. 218, pp. 5–12 and 17–20.

135. M.A. Khuhro to Sidhwa, leader of the Sindh Congress assembly party, 18 March 1941, ibid., F. 365, p. 17.

136. Ibid., F. 365, pp. 17 and 18.

137. Sayed to Jinnah, 15 March 1941, ibid., F. 460, p. 71; Sayed to manager, Dar-ul-Isha'at, Majlis-e-Ittehad-e-Muslimin, Hyderabad Deccan, 14 March 1941, ibid., p. 73; Abdullah Haroon to Jinnah, 3 May 1941, ibid., F. 274, pp. 213–14; Jinnah to Sayed, ibid., F. 460, p. 78; and SHC, Hd—II: 147 and 149; and a report on the state of the party, AFM, vol. 326, pp. 88.

138. *IAR*, 1941, vol. I, p. 67, and vol. II, pp. 3 and 21; and QAP, F. 274, p. 226.

139. For his letters to G.M. Sayed (14 June 1941) and M.A. Khuhro (1 October), see QAP, F. 460, p. 78 and F. 365, p. 33, respectively.

140. For Abdullah Haroon's memorandum regarding remission of the barrage debt and Muslim under-representation in government services submitted to the viceroy on his visit to Sindh, ibid., F. 274, p. 249.

141. Makhdum Murid Husain to Jinnah, 22 April 1943, ibid., F. 531, p. 34; and F. 579, pp. 95–96.

142. Resolutions passed by the provincial Muslim League council on 8 March 1942, AFM (vol. 248, pp. 41–43), which Abdullah Haroon sent to Liaquat the following day.

143. Nawab Ismail to Jinnah, 20 July 1942, QAP, F. 339, p. 13; and Yusuf Haroon to Jinnah, 23 July 1942, ibid., F. 274, pp. 259–61.

144. For a note by Khuhro to Jinnah, AFM, vol. 381, pp. 1–4; and Sayed to Jinnah, 8 and 16 June 1942, see QAP, F. 460, pp 5–7 and 11–12. Jinnah's response to various proposals by the provincial Muslim League leaders was: 'I hope that you will settle everything with regard to the executive and the office-bearers of the Provincial Muslim League amicably and in cooperation with others and you are the best judges as to who should be the president and general secretary.' Jinnah to Sayed, 24 June 1942, ibid., F. 460

145. Abdul Majid to Liaquat, 20 May 1942, Liaquat to Yusuf Haroon, 5 June 1942, Yusuf Haroon to Liaquat, 31 December 1942, Liaquat to Yusuf Haroon and Khuhro, 5 January 1943, AFM, vol. 381.

146. Khuhro to Jinnah, 5 June 1942, QAP, F. 365, pp. 46–47; Jinnah to Khuhro, 10 June 1942, ibid., F. 365, p. 48; and Jinnah to Jafar Khan, 17 June 1942, appreciating his services in the campaign, ibid., F. 314, p. 1.

147. For instance, see a letter from the honorary secretary of the Bhaibund Shewa Mandal to Gandhi, 26 May 1942, AFM, vol. 248, p. 56.

148. I.A. Shaikh to honorary secretary, All-India Muslim League, 5 August 1942, ibid., vol. 137, p. 17; and *Dawn*, 23 August 1942.

149. For resolution passed at the Delhi annual session, see Pirzada, *Foundations*, vol. II, pp. 431–32.

150. Khuhro to Jinnah, 16 June 1942, QAP, F. 365, pp. 49–57; and for a seven-page resolution of the Sindh provincial Muslim League working committee, see AFM, vol. 248, pp. 59–65. Ayub Khuhro, leader of the League assembly party, in a letter to Governor Hugh Dow on 4 July, asked him to summon a session of the assembly at an early date preferably before 15 August 1942 under Section 62 (2) of the Government of India Act of 1935; and he recounted the reasons for that. For a copy of the letter, see ibid., vol. 248, pp. 66–67.

151. Pirzada, *Foundations*, vol. II, p. 432. In February 1947, the property of Pir Sahib Pagaro was transferred to the government of Sindh, and a trust was created to support the family. *Dawn*, 10 February 1947.

152. AFM, vol. 248, pp. 74–79; and QAP, F. 274, p. 262; and F. 365, pp. 61–63 and 73.

153. Allah Bakhsh to Linlithgow, 31 August 1942, *TP*, vol. II, pp. 856–59.

154. Khuhro and Sayed to Jinnah, 13 and October 1942, and Jinnah to Khuhro and Sayed, 12 October, QAP, F. 365, pp. 77–80. Sindhi resigned from the general secretaryship of the provincial Muslim League in protest.

155. *Daily Gazette*, 23 October 1942. Hidayatullah also weaned away two members of the legislative assembly of the Hindu Independent Party, Rai Gokaldas and Dr G.H. Hemandas, who joined his ministry. For Nihchaldas Vazirani's comments on the situation, see his detailed letter to Jinnah, QAP, F. 191, pp. 17–24.

156. Khuhro and Sayed to Jinnah, 16 October 1942, Chandio, *Jinnah–Khuhro Correspondence*, p. 99; Sayed to Jinnah, 18 October 1942, QAP, F. 875, pp. 409–410; Yusuf Haroon to Jinnah, 4 October 1942, and Jinnah to Yusuf Haroon, ibid., F. 274, p. 268; and Sayed's ten-page note to Jinnah, detailing the reasons and events that influenced the members of the legislative assembly to join the Hidayatullah ministry, ibid., F. 854, pp. 33–42. Sayed wrote at the end of the note that they had not 'lost sight of' Jinnah's instructions and that 'if at all it is thought that we have erred, it may be due to error of judgment, but never with a view to ignore the advice of the Quaid-i-Azam or to lower the prestige of the Muslim League'. For Jinnah's statement, see *Civil & Military Gazette*, 21 October 1942.

157. Jinnah to Khuhro, 14 October 1942, QAP, F. 365, p. 76. Jinnah telegraphed to Yusuf Haroon on 4 October, that 'If Governor suspends [the Assembly] it is his responsibility. We cannot regulate our policy according to bogey cry and Allah Bakhsh would get more powerful'. Ibid., F. 274, 268 and 273.

158. For instance, see resolutions passed by the Sukkur municipality and Jacobabad municipality, and telegrams by Pir Mujaddid, Sardar Hidayatullah, and Ali Mohammad Marri, general secretary, All-India Baloch Conference, and others, ibid., F. 999, pp. 24–38, and 42. See also Jafar Khan Jamali to Jinnah, 2 October 1942, ibid., F. 1005, pp. 46–47; Zakir Ali to Nawab Ismail, 18 September 1942, AFM, vol. 310, p. 68; Sadik Ali Shah, general secretary, Shikarpur district Muslim League to Jinnah, 3 January 1943, QAP, F. 27, pp. 216–18; Shamsuddin, president, Dadu city Muslim League to Jinnah, 23 October 1943, ibid., F. 27, p. 188; Abdul Hayee Haqqani, editor, the weekly *Nusrat* to Quaid-i-Azam, 23 October 1942, ibid., F. 1010, p. 37. Allama I.I. Kazi wrote to Jinnah [QAP, F. 875, pp. 413–14] that the Sindhi Hindus wanted the 'eradication of Muslims' to secure 'dominance' and that the Muslim Leaguers 'with power in their hands' could enroll 99 per cent Sindhi Muslims as members.

159. Khuhro to Jinnah, 19 and 23 October 1942, and Sayed and Khuhro to Jinnah, 22 October, ibid., F. 365, pp. 88–90.

160. For report of the five-member (Nawab Ismail, Khaliquzzaman, Nazimuddin, Qazi Isa and Husain Imam) subcommittee, see ibid., F. 138, pp. 12–13; and Hidayatullah–Jinnah correspondence, ibid., F. 286, pp. 1–5.

161. Khuhro to Nawab Ismail, 23 November 1942, and Khuhro to Jinnah, 4 December, ibid., F. 365, pp. 101 and 74–75; and note signed by Nawab Ismail, 11 December 1942, ibid., F. 827, pp. 118–20. Those who joined included Makhdum Ghulam Haider of Hala, Ghulam Ali Talpur, Ghulamullah Talpur, Suhrab Khan Sarki, Mir Mohammad Khan Chandio and A.K. Gabol.

162. *Sindh Assembly Debates*, vol. 17, no. 6, cited in D.A. Pirzada, *Growth of Muslim Nationalism in Sind*, Karachi, 1995, pp. 172–73.

163. AFM, vol. 381, no. 34. The three-member (Nawab Ismail, Qazi Isa and Khaliquzzaman) committee that the central working committee had appointed about the Punjab elections was asked to inquire into the complaints in the Sindh elections as well; the committee found the allegations correct and directed the Sindh provincial Muslim League to hold elections rather than make nominations. For a report of the inquiry committee and other relevant details, see ibid., vols. 381 and 382.

164. The Sindh example was soon followed in Bengal where Suhrawardy, a minister, left the office of general secretary and in Assam where Chief Minister Saadulla left the party presidency.

165. QAP, F. 531, p. 27; Mukaddims of Sindh to Jinnah, and Sayed's ten-page memorandum, AFM, vol. 381, pp. 34–43; and SHC, Sindh-I: 3–5.

166. G.A. Allana and Mohammad Amin Khoso were elected joint secretaries. During this visit, Jinnah performed the opening ceremony of the Sindh Islamia College and personally donated Rs 5,000. AFM, vol. 236, pp. 59–62 and 64–65.

167. Jinnah to Nawab Ismail, 18 July 1943, QAP, F. 761, p. 218.

168. *Annual Report of the Sindh Provincial Muslim League for the Year 1943–44*, SHC, Sindh-I: 24; and Inspection Report no. 11, 18 August 1944, AFM, vol. 200, no. 13; and for a list of members of the legislative assembly, see Hidayatullah to Liaquat, 20 January 1944, ibid., vol. 382, p. 7.

169. The Jamiatul Ulama-i-Hind, Majlis-i-Ahrar-i-Islam and Khaksars had supported Maula Bakhsh in this bye-election. In the second bye-election, Sardar Ali Gohar was elected on another seat that had fallen vacant on the death of K.S. Rasul Bakhsh.

170. *Annual Report of the Sindh Provincial Muslim League for the Year 1943–44*, AFM, vol. 200, pp. 37–47.

171. Ghulam Ali to Jinnah, 5 and 7 April 1944, ibid., vol. 382, pp. 53–61; and Mir Allah Dad, Arbab Togachi, Ghulam Mohammad Wassan, Darya Khan Rajpar and Faqir Mohammad Mangrio to Liaquat, 5 and 17 April 1944, ibid., pp. 66–69 and 73; Kazi Mohammad Alam, general secretary, Hyderabad district Muslim League, 8 January 1944, ibid., p. 1; A. Aziz, general secretary, Karachi city Muslim League, to Nawab Ismail, ibid., vol. 383, pp. 71–73; Liaquat to Sayed, 30 December 1944, ibid., pp. 88–89; and also see several other letters, AFM, vol. 383.

172. K.B. Gabol to Jinnah, 7 April, ibid., vol. 382, p. 64; Dr A.A. Khan to president, Sindh provincial Muslim League, 14 April 1944, ibid., pp. 76–77; and Yusuf Haroon to Jinnah, 27 May 1944, ibid., vol. 383, p. 36.

173. Hashim Gazdar to Quaid-i-Azam, 30 June 1944, SHC, Sindh-I: 37. Ghulam Mohammad Wassan was elected director in place of Sayed.

174. Hashim Gazdar to Quaid-i-Azam, 8 April 1944, SHC, Sindh-I: 10; Jinnah to Gazdar, 15 April 1944, AFM, vol. 382, p. 79; and Jinnah to Sayed, 13 June 1944, SHC, Sindh-I: 25.

175. Jinnah to Mir Jafar Khan Jamali, 26 December 1944, ibid., Sindh-IV: 9.

176. The council elected Ghulam Nabi Pathan and Ghulam Ali Talpur as vice-presidents, Ghulam Hyder Shah as general secretary who defeated Yusuf Haroon, and M.A. Hafiz and G. Allana as joint secretary. It also elected a provincial parliamentary board consisting of the party president, the Premier, Ghulam Ali Talpur, Mohammad Ali Shah and Ghulam Nabi Pathan.

177. QAP, F. 192, p. 13.

178. *The Sindh Observer*, 27 July 1944. See resolution of the Sindh provincial Muslim League working committee passed on 7 July 1944, *IAR*, 1944, vol. II, p. 194; and resolution of the central working committee passed on 29–31 July 1944, AFM, vol. 159, no. 39. Sayed had reportedly planned to install Gazdar as chief minister. Hatim Alavi to Quaid-i-Azam (confidential), 6 August 1944, SHC, Sindh-I: 56.

179. Ghulam Husain to Quaid-i-Azam, 11 and 14 March 1944, *Jinnah Papers*, Second Series, vol. X, pp. 203 and 206.

180. For Jinnah's attempts, see SHC, Sindh-I: 47–50 and 53. Jinnah wrote to Hidayatullah (16 August), 'My repeated and earnest request to you and others is that for the sake of our cause and welfare of our people you should put an end to these private controversies and bickering . . . [None] of you is going to benefit by it, except a momentary victory of one against the other . . . which can give no satisfaction to any decent man, let alone Muslim leaders of Sindh. I wish you would show this letter to every one of them—call them together and put matters right.' Ibid., p. 62 and also Yusuf Haroon to Jinnah, 20 September 1943, QAP, F. 1092, p. 187.

181. Hidayatullah to Quaid-i-Azam, 11 and 14 March 1944, SHC, Sindh-I: 7 and 9, complaining about his colleagues' infighting and Khuhro's involvement in the murder case. For several letters to Jinnah in support of Khuhro, see AFM, vol. 382, nos. 40–49; and also see SHC, Sindh-I: 7, 12, 14, 20, 21, 25 and 68.

182. The government banned public meetings in Sindh and lifted the ban only after an assurance that Khuhro's case would not be discussed. SHC, Sindh-II: 43; and III: 31 and 33.

183. Hidayatullah to Jinnah, 24 and 31 October and 1 November 1944, ibid.: 44 and 45; and Waheed, *Nation's Voice*, vol. IV, pp. 16–19. Another point of dispute was the induction of Roger Thomas as minister, but soon after, he resigned from that office and was reappointed as Adviser to the government.

184. For details about various moves for the award of the League ticket, see the correspondence, AFM, vols. 383 and 384; and SHC, Sindh-III: 15 and IV: 4, 5, 27, 28, 40, 47 and 50.

185. Jinnah's response to a request from Hidayatullah for intervention was, 'It is for you people in Sindh to build in cooperation and unity or destroy in disunity, by pulling each other down. To me the whole affair is painful reading indeed. It is very difficult to help when the leading men who are expected to know better and guide the people are quarrelling among themselves like children.' For his letter, 26 December 1944, see SHC, Sindh-IV: 5; and also see Ilahi Bakhsh to Quaid-i-Azam, 28 January 1945, ibid.-V: 26; and Jinnah to Jafar Khan Jamali, 26 December 1944, ibid.-IV: 9.

186. AFM, vol. 385, pp. 3–4, 8–9, 12, 18 and 20; and SHC, Sindh-IV: 59 and 61.

187. SHC, Sindh-IV: 62–64; and Iftikhar Husain to Liaquat, 22 January 1945, AFM, vol. 385, p. 22; and Aminuddin to honorary secretary, All-India Muslim League, 22 January 1945, ibid., vol. 288, p. 25.

188. For letters of Hidayatullah, Ghulam Ali Talpur and Sayed to Jinnah and vice versa in November 1944, see SHC, Sindh-II, III and IV; and AFM, vol. 385, p. 2.

189. For details, see correspondence and reports, AFM, vol. 385; and SHC, Sindh-IV and V.

190. For resolution of the League assembly party expelling Sayed and Gazdar from the assembly party, see AFM, vol. 385, p. 21. For further details, see 'Report in Brief, 28 February 1945', SHC, Sindh-V: 27.

191. Jinnah's statement of 30 January 1945, AFM, vol. 385, p. 24.

192. At first, they had laid down the condition that either Sayed or Gazdar be taken in the ministry but Jinnah opposed the proposal and they extended support without any condition. Sayed to Liaquat, 14 March 1945, SHC, Sindh-VI: 24 and Gazdar to Liaquat, 14 March 1945, AFM, vol. 385, p. 54.

193. Some of Sayed's opponents, however, did establish a parallel Muslim League, alleging that he had manipulated the removal of the ban on the publication of chapter 14 of the *Satyarath Prakash*, which had been imposed after protests from the Muslims. Pir Ghulam Mujaddid Sirhindi to Quaid-i-Azam, 5 July 1945, QAP, F. 538, p. 841; Ali Akbar Shah to Quaid-i-Azam, 22 August 1945, ibid., F. 830, pp. 80–82; Abdul Aziz to Quaid-i-Azam, 30 May 1945, SHC, Sindh-VI: 1 and 12; and for Jinnah's views on the ban, see Ibid.-II: 53.

194. *Annual Report of the Sindh Provincial Muslim League for the Year 1944–45, 3 June 1946*, AFM, vol. 385, pp. 66–67; and for resolution of the Sindh provincial Muslim League council, see AFM, vol. 385, pp. 58–59; and for Jinnah's attempt to soften Sayed's attitude in the meeting with him on 14 July 1945, see ibid., p. 73.

195. SHC, Sindh-VI: 15 and 16.

196. See also Chapter 10.

197. For proceedings of the meeting held on 7 February 1946, see AFM (vol. 386, pp. 11, and 12–14), which were subsequently approved by the committee of action. See also QAP, F. 580, pp. 54–56; and AFM, vol. 181, no. 28 and vol. 193, no. 13.

198. Miran Mohammad Shah to Liaquat, 22 February 1946, Hidayatullah to Liaquat, 23 February, Liaquat to Gazdar, and Gazdar to Liaquat, 11 March, AFM, vol. 386, pp. 24, 27, 31, and 43; and also see Miran Mohammad Shah to Quaid-i-Azam, 14 March 1946, QAP, F. 556, p. 100, and Gazdar to Quaid-i-Azam, 17 March 1946, ibid., F. 848, pp. 8–10.

199. Khuhro and Yusuf to Quaid-i-Azam, February 1946, ibid., F. 1133, p. 12.

200. Ghulam Husain and Khuhro to Quaid-i-Azam, n.d., and Jinnah to Ghulam Husain and Khuhro, n.d., ibid., p. 18. Iftikhar Mamdot, Begum and Mian Bashir Ahmad and others in the Punjab actively supported his re-joining the League. According to Begum Bashir, Sayed was willing to 'surrender unconditionally'. Geti to Mian Bashir Ahmad, 23 March 1946, ibid., p. 175.

201. Patel to Vazirani, 28 December 1946, Sardar *Patel's Correspondence*, vol. 3, pp. 137 and 140–41, cited in Waheed, *Nation's Voice*, vol. V, pp. 510. Qazi Akbar defeated Sayed who filed an election petition but the tribunal gave its verdict after independence.

202. Khuhro to Quaid-i-Azam, 14 and 20 December 1946, QAP, F. 852, pp. 27–28 and 29–30. The pro-Hidayatullah and pro-Khuhro campaign stopped when twenty-two members of the legislative assembly entrusted the task of ministry-formation to Jinnah in whose decision they expressed 'full faith'. Ibid., F. 576, pp. 32–33.

203. *Dawn*, 4 January 1947.
204. For instance, see Abdul Wahid, secretary, Nowshehra Muslim League to president, All-India Muslim League, 16 May 1937, QAP, F. 865, pp. 64–65; Muhammad Anwar Khan, *The Role of N.W.F.P. in the Freedom Struggle*, Lahore, 2000, pp. 98–102 and 111–13; and Sayed Wiqar Ali Shah, *Ethnicity, Islam, and Nationalism: Muslim Politics in the North-West Frontier Province, 1937–1947*, Oxford, 1999, pp. 100–101.
205. Maulana Shakirullah and Sajjad Ahmad Jan were elected vice-presidents, Maulana Ishaq Mansehravi joint secretary and Qazi Abdul Hakim treasurer. Abdul Hakim to honorary secretary, All-India Muslim League, 3 October 1937, AFM, vol. 170, no. 41; and Sajjad Ahmad Jan to honorary secretary, reception committee, All-India Muslim League, 7 October 1937, ibid., vol. 170, no. 68.
206. The All-India Muslim League condemned the British policy in Waziristan at its Lucknow session and demanded a change in this policy.
207. Abdul Qaiyum to Jinnah, 10 October 1937, QAP, F. 25, p. 60; M. Ismail Ghaznavi to Liaquat, 8 April 1938, AFM, vol. 198, no. 10; and also ibid., vol. 179, no. 64.
208. The six district Muslim Leagues elected the following as presidents and general secretaries:

District	President	General Secretary
Peshawar	Ghulam Husain	Mohammad Ismail Ghaznavi
Hazara	Sajjad Ahmad Jan	Basiruddin Qureshi
Kohat	Pir Saeed Shah	Mian Ghulam Hyder Akhtar
Bannu	Ghulam Hyder Khan	Nasrullah Khan
Mardan	Khan Behram Khan	Fida Mohammad Khan
Dera Ismail Khan	Haq Nawaz Khan	Maula Dad Khan

209. AFM, vol. 206, nos. 29 and 49. Maulana Shoaib defeated Mian Ziauddin who was supported by Aurangzeb and Sadullah.
210. Liaquat to Shamsul Hasan, 11 April 1938, ibid., vol. 198, no. 9.
211. Another resolution for which notice had been given but was not moved stated that the All-India Muslim League 'condemns the policy of the Frontier government in the matter of victimization of the Muslims in the interest of non-Muslims, which it has been carrying on ever since it has come to power'. Ibid., no. 65.
212. Jinnah, in his presidential address to the Sindh provincial Muslim League conference on 8 October 1938, had observed that NWFP for which the All-India Muslim League had struggled for constitutional reforms against every machination including that of the Congress was now 'under the heel of Wardha' and hoped that soon the Frontier Muslims would 'come home' in the fold of the All-India Muslim League.
213. NWFP Police Abstracts Int., vol. XXXIV, 21, 24 and 31 January 1938; 3 and 24 May 1938, and vol. XXXV, 21 February 1939.
214. Nishtar to Jinnah, 18 May 1938, QAP, F. 394, p. 7; and *IAR*, p. 20.
215. *Times of India*, 24 October 1938. Gandhi wrote in the *Harijan* ('Khudai Khidmatgars and Badshah Khan', 19 November 1938): 'The Frontier Province must remain a place of pilgrimage for me. For though the rest of India may fail to

show true non-violence, there seems to be good ground for hoping that the Frontier Province will pass through the fiery ordeal'. *Statesman*, 20 November 1938.

216. According to the *IAR* (1939, vol. II, pp. 232–33), this proviso was added in October 1939.

217. Yunus to Jinnah, 23 March 1937, 5 October 1938, and 4 March 1939, QAP, F. 672, p. 16; F. 468, pp. 1–2; and F. 160-A, pp. 388–90. For Ghaffar Khan's attempt at rapprochement with the League, see Aurangzeb to Jinnah, ibid., F. 329, pp. 142–43.

218. Muslims disliked a press photograph that showed Abdul Ghaffar Khan having lunch with the Hindu leaders.

219. NWFP Police Abstracts of Int., vol. XXXIV, 10 January 1938, 8 March 1938; and vol. XXXV, 21 and 28 March 1939; and 25 April 1939. The League protest against the reduction in funds for the Islamia college resulted in the withdrawal of the orders.

220. AFM, vol. 206, no. 26; vol. 274, p. 12; QAP, F. 823, p. 10; F. 1129, p. 76; and Sadullah to Jinnah, 23 September 1938, ibid., F 160A, pp. 553–56.

221. For the funds collected to support his tour, see AFM, vol. 122, no. 31. The funds were handed over to Sadullah and Aurangzeb with the request that they would submit a detailed account of the expenditure.

222. Ghulam Husain to Jinnah, 30 July 1938, QAP, F. 1129, p. 141.

223. Jinnah to Ziauddin, August 1938, ibid., F. 1090, p. 59.

224. Mohammad Mehdi of Pirpur to Jinnah, 27 September 1938, ibid., F. 160, pp. 475–76.

225. NWFP Police Abstracts of Int., vol. XXXV, 2 May 1939; and also see Sadullah to Liaquat, 25 August 1938, AFM, vol. 206, nos. 41 and 42.

226. For a detailed analysis of the two sides, the government and the opposition, see Aurangzeb to Jinnah, 24 November 1938, QAP, F. 1094; and also see ibid., F. 329, pp. 4–8 and 10.

227. Pirzada, *Foundations*, vol. II, pp. 323–24.

228. It consisted of Nawab Siddiq Ali Khan, Maulana Burhanul Haq, Mohammad Asghar, Zakir Ali and Mazhar Imam.

229. For a report, see Aurangzeb to Jinnah, 28 June 1939, QAP, F. 49, pp. 112–13.

230. Peshawar archives, F. 815, pp. 101–111, cited in Anwar Khan, *Freedom Struggle*, pp. 125–27. In just one week in May, the League had held twenty-three meetings.

231. For demonstration and conviction of ten Leaguers, see QAP, F. 329, pp. 223; and AFM, vol. 206, nos. 54 and 56.

232. Ziauddin to Jinnah, 30 September 1939, QAP, F. 472, pp. 1–3; Wiqar Ali, *Muslim Politics in the North-West Frontier Province*, pp. 77–80; and Anwar Khan, *Freedom Struggle*, p. 129.

233. Cunningham to Linlithgow, 28 September 1942, *TP*, vol. III, p. 55.

234. Agha Lal Badshah was elected vice-president, Malik Shad Mohammad joint secretary and Mian Ghulam Husain treasurer. The provincial Muslim League also elected twenty-one members on the All-India Muslim League council.

235. During his student days at Aligarh, Aurangzeb had been president of the Aligarh Muslim University students' union.

236. Sadullah was elected vice president, Malik Shad Mohammad re-elected joint secretary, Zaman Khan assistant secretary and Ghulam Husain treasurer. For a list of names of the presidents and secretaries, see AFM, vol. 342, no. 10.

237. Qazi Isa to Jinnah, 30 January 1941, QAP, F. 302, pp. 62–63.

474   A HISTORY OF THE ALL-INDIA MUSLIM LEAGUE

238. In 1939, it was 10,700 members; in 1940, 26,400 members; in 1941, 32,780 members. Peshawar archives, F. 753, p. 27, cited in Anwar Khan, *Freedom Struggle*, p. 163.
239. AFM, vol. 343, no. 1. According to Bakht Jamal, 'his position' as the Frontier provincial Muslim League president had been 'just like Mr Abul Kalam Azad . . . [that of] a nominal figure-head'. Ibid., vol. 342, no. 58.
240. Jinnah to Bakht Jamal, 22 February 1944, QAP, F. 878, p. 25.
241. In January 1941, a delegation consisting of Nawab Bahadur Yar Jang, Maulana Hamid Badauni and Qazi Isa came to explain the Lahore Resolution. Jinnah to Sadullah, 20 January 1941, ibid., F. 348, p. 1; and also see Hameed Nizami to Jinnah, 16 February 1943, ibid., F. 396, p. 6.
242. Ziauddin to Liaquat, 30 September 1941, AFM, vol. 326, pp. 65–67; also see ibid., vol. 343, pp. 20 and 25.
243. *Report of the Central Civil Defence Committee*, QAP, F. 761, pp. 53–83.
244. G.M. Sayed to Jinnah, 9 June 1942, ibid., F. 460, pp. 8–9. The League membership had risen from 10,700 in 1939 to 32,780 in 1941.
245. Nawab Ismail to Jinnah, ibid., F. 761, pp. 18–19.
246. Jinnah to Ziauddin, 23 August 1942, ibid., F. 472, p. 14. The marriage of Dr Khan Sahib's daughter at this time to an Indian Christian had damaged the Khudai Khidmatgars' public image. 'Diary of Firoz Khan Noon's tour of the north-west India', October 1942, ibid., F. 399, p. 110.
247. Zakir Ali to general secretary, Frontier provincial Muslim League, 30 March 1943, AFM, vol. 310, p. 42; and Ziauddin to Liaquat, 23 January 1943, ibid., vol. 326, p. 68.
248. Darwesh Khan, secretary, Mardan district Muslim League to Liaquat, 3 March 1943, ibid., vol. 264, p. 44; and Jinnah to Bakht Jamal Khan, 13 March 1941, QAP, F. 300, p. 1; and Jinnah to Darwesh Khan, 13 March 1941, ibid., F. 332, p. 1.
249. For a resolution passed by the All-India Muslim League council on 22 February 1942, see AFM, vol. 285, no. 107 and 108; Aurangzeb to Jinnah, 28 May 1942, QAP, F. 329, p. 163; and Khaliquzzaman to Zakir Ali, AFM, vol. 317.
250. Aurangzeb Khan to Firoz Khan Noon, 27 and 29 January 1943, QAP, F. 399, pp. 119–21 and 124–25; and Aurangzeb to governor, 1 May 1943, ibid., F. 329, pp. 204–8.
251. Besides Chief Minister Aurangzeb, Muslim ministers were: Samin Jan Khan, Sardar Abdur Rab Nishtar and Abdur Rahman. Sardar Ajit Singh, an Akali leader, was another minister.
252. Nawab Ismail to Jinnah, 23 July 1943, AFM, vol. 310, p. 60; and Abdur Rashid to Jinnah, 28 May 1943, and Amin Tareen to Quaid-i-Azam, 15 August 1943, QAP, vol. 1101, pp. 134–35 and 172.
253. Abdur Rahim to Quaid-i-Azam, 2 July 1943, ibid., F. 1101, p. 144.
254. Nawab Ismail, Khaliquzzaman and Qazi Isa to Jinnah, 23 July 1943, ibid., F. 761, p. 223.
255. On Jinnah's direction, Jamal Mian, Maulana Badauni, Raja of Mahmudabad and Nawab Mamdot and all the central civil defence committee members stayed in the NWFP during the election campaign. Ibid., F. 761, pp. 196–201; and AFM, vol. 318, p. 32.
256. Cunningham to Linlithgow, 24 August 1943, *TP*, vol. IV, p. 186.
257. Annual report of the honorary secretary, All-India Muslim League, December 1943, AFM, vol. 268, p. 10.
258. Jinnah to Aurangzeb, 13 August 1943, QAP, F. 531, p. 76.

259. AFM, vol. 344, no. 37.

260. Dr A.A. Khan to Quaid-i-Azam, 30 July 1944, QAP, F. 829, p. 53.

261. QAP, F. 1117, pp. 143–44; and AFM, vol. 236, nos. 38 and 39.

262. For more information on this move about the Islamia college, see Sadullah to Cunningham, 8 July 1944, AFM, vol. 485, pp. 6–7; Cunningham to Sadullah, 15 June, p. 4; statement by S. Qaim Shah, a trustee of the college, on 12 July, p. 19; resolution of the old boys of the Islamia college on 20 July, p. 12; resolution passed by the Jamiatul Ulama, Sarhad, in the Mahabat Khan mosque on 20 July, p. 13; Sadullah to Nawab Ismail, 30 July, p. 3; resolution of the committee of action passed on 1–2 August, pp. 16–17 but withheld by Liaquat from the press; Sadullah to Liaquat, 11 August, p. 19; Jinnah to Liaquat, 15 August, p. 20, asking him to release the resolution; and amended constitution adopted by the board of trustees of the college by consensus on 4 September, *Dawn*, 13 September 1944. See also Sadullah to Jinnah, 21 July 1944, and Aurangzeb to Jinnah, 16 August and 6 September 1944, in Z.H. Zaidi (ed.), *Jinnah Papers*, Second Series, vol. XIII, pp. 547–49, 552–53 and 561–62; Sadullah to Jinnah, 1 September 1945, SHC, NWFP, 1: 59.

263. Ziauddin to Quaid-i-Azam, 26 October 1943, *Jinnah Papers*, Second Series, vol. X, p. 34; and also see *TP*, vol. IV, p. 245.

264. K.H. Khurshid, *Memories of Jinnah*, (ed. Khalid Hasan), Lahore, 1999, p. 85; and Bakht Jamal to Jinnah, 17 December 1943, *Jinnah Papers*, Second Series, vol. X, p. 87. Jinnah simply advised, 'there should be only one watchword for us all: *Forget and Forgive*. Stand united and work for our cause, then alone we shall be in a position to achieve our goal of Pakistan'. *Jinnah Papers*, vol. X, p. 169.

265. AFM, vol. 155, nos. 70 and 72; vol. 192, p. 13; and vol. 342, nos. 94, 95, 97, 98 and 108–111. For complaints against the ministry, see allegations of the Anjuman Tahaffuz-i-Haquq-i-Ghuraba (Society for the Protection of the Rights of the Poor), 22 June 1944; Jamiatul Ulama, Dera Ismail Khan; Faqira Khan to Qazi Isa, 28 June 1944, Qazi Abdul Hakim to Liaquat, 28 June 1944, ibid., vol. 343, nos. 38–40, 48, 51 and 52; and for an account of the central civil defence committee's tour and its interviews with various delegations, see ibid., nos. 75–77 and 80–85, 95–98.

266. For his letter of 17 June 1944, see ibid., vol. 155, no. 28.

267. Zafar Ahmad Ansari, secretary, committee of action to president and secretary, Frontier provincial Muslim League, 15 August 1944, ibid., vol. 344.

268. Zakir Ali to Zafar Ahmad Ansari, 26 October 1944, ibid., vol. 159, no. 43; and for his tour of Bannu, Lakki, Dera Ismail Khan, Teri and Peshawar and distribution of League literature, see ibid., vol. 344, nos. 16, 19–21, 24 and 28.

269. For Qazi Isa allegedly giving misleading reports to the committee of action and Jinnah, see Habib to Khurshid Hasan, 1 and 24 May 1945, QAP, F. 782, pp. 11–12 and 48; and also see AFM, 344, nos. 38, 40, 43, 44, 47 and 48, for Aurangzeb seeking extension in the enrolment process.

270. For details of the relative strength of the parties, see AFM, vol. 165, no. 89.

271. Since December 1944, Governor Cunningham had been predicting the fall of the Aurangzeb ministry. Wavell to Amery, 12 December 1944, *TP*, vol. V, p. 302.

272. For an account of the meeting and other details, see Ziauddin to Liaquat, 25 March 1945, and Abdur Rahman Riya to Liaquat, 25 March 1945, Karim Bakhsh to Liaquat, 26 March 1945, AFM, vol. 344, nos. 51–53; and vol. 193, no. 2.

273. For a detailed note by the Hazara leaders to Quaid-i-Azam in November 1945, see QAP, F. 830, pp. 164–67.

274. Liaquat to Ziauddin, 18 April 1945, ibid., vol. 165, no. 83, enclosing a copy of the central committee of action's resolution.
275. Zafar Ahmad Ansari to Ziauddin, 22 April 1944, AFM, vol. 181, no. 16 and 17, asking him to hand over the papers and funds of the Frontier provincial Muslim League in his possession to office-bearers of the committee. Two members, Nawab Akbar Khan and Mian Ziauddin, were added after the initial announcement.
276. Zafar Ahmad Ansari to Samin Jan, Mohammad Ali Hoti and Arbab Noor Mohammad, 19 April 1946, ibid., vol. 366, no. 15.
277. *Pakistan Times* (Lahore), 8 and 15 February 1947.
278. Ibid., 16 February 1947.
279. For Achakzai's incarceration, see resolution passed by the All-India Muslim League council on 16 February 1935, with Jinnah in the chair, demanding his release and that of Abdul Aziz, ibid., vol. 220, no. 15.
280. *IAR*, 1940, vol. II, p. 221.
281. On 16 February 1935, Jinnah presided over the meeting of the central council that passed resolutions on these issues.
282. Jafar Khan to Jinnah, 26 October 1938, QAP, F. 1094, pp. 159–60.
283. Abdul Wadud Khan to Liaquat, 2 August 1944, AFM, vol. 293, pp. 79–80; and *Daily Gazette*, 9 October 1938.
284. The resolution was moved by Maulvi Sanaullah and seconded by M.A. Khalique.
285. For entry of the Jamalis in the League, see Qazi Isa to Jinnah, 1 November 1939, QAP, F. 302, pp. 19–20.
286. Mohammad Ali Khan Ghilzai was its vice-president; Abdus Samad Khan Yasinzai joint secretary; Malik Usman Kansi treasurer and Comrade Abdul Khaliq Kansi propaganda secretary. Earlier, in 1938, a League had been established in Quetta with Seth Mohammad Azam as president.
287. For an account of an earlier meeting, see a letter from Arbab Karam Khan and twenty-one others, 8 May 1939, and Qazi Isa to Jinnah, 12 May 1939, QAP, F. 302, pp. 1–2 and 4–11. The central council elected five members on its recommendation: Nawab Mehrab Khan Bugti, Arbab Karam Khan, Sardar Ghulam Mohammad Khan Tareen, Abdullah Jan Panezai and Abdul Ghaffar Khan Achakzai. In February 1940, Malik Jan Mohammad replaced Ghulam Mohammad Tareen on the central council.
288. Resolution passed by the central council in its meeting in Delhi on 27–28 August 1939. For discrimination against the local people in jobs, see Qazi Isa to Jinnah, 25 September 1939, ibid., F. 302, pp. 16–18.
289. Balochistan Weekly Intelligence Bureau Summary, 15 July 1939, Acc No. 1679, F. No. L/PS/12/3219, pp. 198, 481and 502.
290. AFM, vol. 253, pp. 12–14 and 81; and vol. 293, p. 1. On 27 August 1939, it was given affiliation; and by that time, it had enrolled twenty thousand members.
291. For a resolution passed by the Balochistan provincial Muslim League on 30 October 1939, see ibid., vol. 293, pp. 14–15.
292. Qazi Isa moved the resolution at the Allahabad annual session and Mir Jafar Khan Jamali seconded it. The five new members were: Malik Usman Khan, Mir Din Mohammad Khan, Malik Amir Jan Khan, Mian Abdul Karim and Begum Isa.
293. For instance, see the list of delegates for the Delhi annual session, AFM, vol. 259.
294. Jinnah's message to the conference, 21 July 1940, QAP, F. 302; and also see Jinnah to Liaquat, 19 July 1940, ibid., F. 335, p. 86.
295. At that time the Balochistan provincial Muslim League had 44 primary Leagues (Quetta-Pishin-16; Fort Sandeman-8; LoraLai-6; Sibi-4; Nasirabad-8; and

Nushki-2), about 16,000 regular members, with 495 Muslim National Guards in the districts. Qazi Isa's signed statement of 28 October 1941, AFM, Vol. 326, no. 4.

296. For Jinnah's public address in Quetta, see *Dawn*, 18 October 1945.

297. *Dawn*, 13 July 1943; and Qazi Mohammad Isa, *Balochistan: Case and Demand*, Daily Gazette Press, Karachi, 1944, AFM, vol. 293, pp. 34–47.

298. As early as 16 February 1935, the All-India Muslim League council, with Jinnah in the chair, demanded Balochistan's representation in the central legislature, elected local bodies, codification of customary law and reform in the Jirga system. AFM, vol. 220, no. 15.

299. *IAR*, 1939, vol. II, p. 104.

300. Ibid., p. 48; and Qazi Isa, *Balochistan*, pp. 10–11.

301. AFM, vol. 255, p. 34; and Pirzada, *Foundations*, vol. II, 393. The tribal sardars, in a representation to Linlithgow on 22 October 1942, asked for representation at least at the centre, if immediate provincial autonomy was not possible. Qazi Isa, *Balochistan*, p. 12.

302. AFM, vol. 269, p. 38.

303. For the Balochistan provincial Muslim League's protest against joint electorates and its demand for separate electorates, see ibid., vol. 371, pp. 46–47; and also see ibid., vol. 293, p. 80; and vol. 371, p. 3; and *Dawn*, 10 June 1944. Before the introduction of elective system, the vice-chairmanship of the Quetta municipality was held for a one-year term by rotation by nominees of the Muslim, Hindu, Sikh, Parsi and European communities.

304. He had left the Zhob provincial Muslim League presidency due to his differences with Qazi Isa.

305. All the Sikh voters came to the polling station with Pakistan badges and voted for the League candidates. Even on the one seat reserved for the minority communities, one Independent candidate (a Parsi) defeated the Congress candidate. *Dawn*, 13 September 1946.

306. For instance, see Abdul Ghafur Durrani to Zakir Ali, 27 October 1942, AFM, vol. 302, no. 23.

307. Abdul Ghafur Durrani was elected secretary of the Balochistan civil defence committee with Jan Mohammad Khan Kansi, *salar-i-azam* of the MNGs, Akhundzada Abdul Ali and Amin Jan Khan as its members.

308. For list of donors and other activities of the Balochistan civil defence committee, see AFM, vol. 302.

309. Jafar Khan to Quaid-i-Azam, QAP, F. 531, pp. 55–56.

310. Abdul Ghafur Durrani to secretary, central civil defence committee, 21 October 1943, AFM, vol. 302, no. 32.

311. Jafar Khan to Liaquat, 31 March 1944, ibid., vol. 293, pp. 50–52, and Jafar Khan to Nawab Ismail, ibid., vol. 155, no. 48.

312. For Qazi Isa's reply, see ibid., vol. 155, no. 18.

313. Liaquat to Qazi Isa, 19 April 1944, and notes by Zafar Ahmad Ansari (14 May) and Nawab Ismail (19 May), ibid., vol. 155; Zafar Ahmad Ansari to Jafar Khan, 7 September 1944, ibid., vol. 159, no. 20; and Jafar Khan to Nawab Ismail, 18 October 1944, ibid., vol. 293, pp. 69–71.

314. For criticism of the elections, see Abdus Sattar 'Pakistani' to Quaid-i-Azam, 4 April 1946, QAP, F. 883, pp. 272–74; Abdul Karim to Qazi Isa, 4 April 1946, AFM, vol. 371, pp. 17–20; Sibi Muslim League to Qazi Isa, 6 April 1946, ibid., vol. 371, p 21; and Qazi Isa to secretary, Balochistan provincial Muslim League, 8 April 1946, ibid., vol. 371, p. 22.

315. For instance, the party established a hospital in Quetta, the Jinnah Hospital for Women, which was run by a board elected by the city Muslim League. AFM, vol. 371, pp. 33 and 38.

316. Questions were also raised about his role on behalf of the central committee of action in the factional disputes of the Bihar and Sindh PMLs.

317. The donations were given by: Nizam of Hyderabad Rs 20,000; Nawab of Bhopal Rs 12,000; Jinnah Rs 10,000; and Anjuman-i-Afaghina Rs 750. For details of the dispute, see Qazi Isa to Ghulam Rasul, 3 December 1945, QAP, F. 610, pp. 7–8; Jinnah to Qazi Isa, 5 December 1945, ibid., F. 610, p. 4; and Ghulam Rasul to Qazi Isa, 13 December 1945, AFM, vol. 371, p. 2; and for a resolution of the Anjuman on this issue, see QAP, F. 908, p. 34. The funds were returned through Mir Shahbaz Khan Nausherwani and Ghulam Rasul. The management of the Anjuman named the hall of the Islamia high school, Quetta as 'Jinnah Hall'.

318. For Jinnah's advice, see his letter to Malik Mohammad Azam, 24 June 1946, and Mohammad Azam to Quaid-i-Azam, 22 June 1946, QAP, F. 564, pp. 9 and 10; for Yahya Bakhtiar's proposal to Jinnah (6 July 1946) 'not to issue official League ticket to any person', see ibid., F. 548, p. 856; and for League's decision not to put up any candidate, see Liaquat's statement in *Dawn*, 9 and 14 July 1946, and *TP*, vol. VIII, p. 66.

319. Qazi Isa to Quaid-i-Azam, 21 June 1948, QAP, F. 614, pp. 7–10. For Jinnah's displeasure, see the note by A.S.B. Shah, secretary to the governor-general, 18 June 1948, ibid., F. 888, p. 98.

320. Mohammad Khan Jogezai's interview to the Orient Press, *Dawn*, 15 December 1946.

321. For an account of Jinnah's visit, see Inamul Haq Kausar, 'Glimpses of Quaid-i-Azam's Two Visits to Balochistan', *Journal of the Pakistan Historical Society*, Karachi, July-October 1976; and *Dawn*, 18, 19 October 1945.

322. For a list, see *Dawn*, 6 January 1946; and press statement by Abdul Hamid Khan, joint secretary Balochistan provincial Muslim League, 2 February 1947, AFM, vol. 371, pp. 49–50.

323. Ibid., vol. 371, p. 27.

324. QAP, F. 34, pp. 4–5; and *Dawn*, 13, 24 and 28 June 1946.

325. Zafar Ahmad Ansari to Qazi Isa, 26 March 1947; Mohammad Akbar Khan to office secretary, All-India Muslim League, 21 April 1947; resolution of the Balochistan provincial Muslim League, 29 April 1947; Abdul Hamid Khan to chairman of the committee of action, Quaid-i-Azam, Liaquat and Altaf Husain, 18 May 1947; and Zafar Ahmad Ansari to president, Balochistan provincial Muslim League, 21 May 1947, AFM, vol. 371.

326. Ibid., vol. 371, pp. 83–84.

327. Soon after the elections, the party position was: Bengal provincial Muslim League 39; Independents (Muslim) 43; Krishak Proja Samity 36; Tippera Krishak Samity 3; Congress 52; Independents (Hindu) 39; Hindu Nationalists 3; Hindu Mahasabha 2; European Group 25; Anglo-Indians 4; and Indian Christians 2. On the 17 elected seats in the Upper House (Legislative Council), Bengal presidency parliamentary board won 7 seats, Independents 9 and Krishak Proja Samity 1.

328. Fazlul Haq had defeated Nazimuddin in the elections; and the latter was subsequently elected in a bye-election on a seat vacated by Suhrawardy by 5,147 against 719 votes; and his opponent lost his security deposit.

329. Jinnah to Nawab of Dhaka, 13 March 1937, QAP, F. 566, pp. 1–3; and *Star of India*, 1 April 1937.

330. *Star of India*, 15 March 1938.
331. The Bengal provincial Muslim League that existed before its reorganization had elected K.G.M. Faroqui as president on 22 August 1937.
332. The provincial Muslim League elected five vice-presidents: Maulana Akram Khan, M.A.H. Ispahani, Adamji Dawood, Khwaja Habibullah and Ruhul Amin; and five assistant secretaries: Farmozul Haq, Abdul Hakim, Abdus Sobur, Abdul Bari and Zahur Ahmad Choudhry [AFM, vol. 39]. In August 1939, the All-India Muslim League council gave the party affiliation.
333. The relevant laws were: the Bengal Tenancy (Amendment) Act, the Agricultural Debtors' Act, the Money-Lenders Act and the Bengal Services Recruitment Rules.
334. For resolution passed by the working committee on 15–17 June 1940, see AFM, vol. 129, no. 28.
335. QAP, F. 289, p. 8.
336. Herbert to Linlithgow, 23 November 1940, GFP, L/P&J/5/147, cited in Harun-or-Rashid, *The Foreshadowing of Bangladesh: Bengal Muslim League and Muslim Politics, 1936–1947*, Dhaka, 1987, pp. 128, 130 and 192; and for details, see QAP, F. 204, pp. 1–2, 109, 120, 147 and 149; and F. 281, pp. 27 and 27 A.
337. Raghib Ahsan to Quaid-i-Azam, 12 and 20 August 1941, QAP, F. 1099, pp. 147–48 and 205–6; Mohammad Noman to Jinnah, 11 August 1941, ibid., F. 1092, pp. 81–82
338. Manzur Murshid, Altaf Husain, director of publicity in Bengal, and Fazlul Haq's cabinet colleagues desperately tried to mediate. He might have resigned from the national defence council even earlier than he did had there been no official pressure on him. At Sir Zafrullah's instance, he even flirted with the idea of forming an 'Independent Muslim League' but Suhrawardy with whom he broached the subject discouraged him from initiating any such move. Jinnah to Akram Khan, 1 August 1941, and Akram Khan to Jinnah, 7 August 1941, ibid., F. 337, pp. 1 and 3; and Raghib Ahsan to Quaid-i-Azam, 12 and 20 August 1941, ibid., F. 1099, pp. 147–48 and 205–6; Jinnah to Liaquat, 18 September, 5 and 7 October 1941, and Liaquat to Jinnah, 1 and 3 October 1941, ibid., F. 480; and Liaquat's statement, ibid., F. 1092, pp. 118–19.
339. For instance, see resolutions passed by the Hoogly district Muslim League, Chittagong district Muslim League, and Calcutta district Muslim League, AFM, vol. 233, no. 5; QAP, F. 1100, pp. 6–7; and F. 834, pp. 145–47. The Muslim Leaguers in Delhi and Simla organized demonstrations against him when he visited those cities [QAP, F. 470, pp. 1–8; and F. 1092, pp. 135 and 136]. The Bengal Muslim students organized a conference, to which Jinnah's message was: 'Let our motto be faith, unity and discipline. Pakistan is our sacred goal and stands for equality of manhood, justice, freedom and peace. To achieve this ideal we should not be deterred by opposition or obstacles. Caravan must march on'. Jinnah to Huseyn Shaheed Suhrawardy, 17 September 1941, ibid., 458, p. 28; and *IAR*, 1941, vol. II, pp. 20 and 21; for Fazlul Haq's explanation and the working committee's decision, see Fazlul Haq to Liaquat, 13 October 1941, Liaquat to Jinnah, 15 October 1941, and Jinnah to Liaquat, 16 and 18 October 1941, and Nazimuddin to Jinnah, 22 October 1941, ibid., F. 480; and resolutions of the central working committee passed on 27 October 1941; and 16 November, AFM, vol. 133, no. 36 and vol. 136, no. 17.
340. Nazimuddin to M.A. Jinnah, QAP, F. 392, pp. 76–78.
341. Fazlul Haq to Liaquat, 8 December 1941, and Liaquat to Fazlul Haq, 9 December, ibid., F. 107, p. 29; and F. 785, pp. 85–86. Nawab of Dhaka defected from the

League to join the Haq ministry. For Fazlul Haq's statement in the high court, alleging that Nazimuddin, Suhrawardy and Tamizuddin had conspired against him, see ibid., F. 109, p. 7; and his letter to Liaquat, ibid., F. 107, p. 12.

342. Ibid., F. 335, PP. 210–11; AFM, vol. 136, no. 41; vol. 285, p. 107; and *IAR*, 1942, vol. I, p. 67. Fazlul Haq unsuccessfully attempted to form a rival Muslim political party: in February 1942, he set up a Muslim Majlis with himself as its president and Humayun Kabir as secretary; and in June, he tried to form a Progressive All-India Muslim League by addressing a letter to prominent Muslim Leaguers.

343. QAP, F. 392, pp. 61–62 and 69–70.

344. Hasan Ispahani to Jinnah, 8 January 1942, ibid., F. 307, pp. 130–31.

345. The presidency Muslim League also elected five assistant secretaries including Farmozul Haq and Fazlur Rahman and five vice-presidents. *Dawn*, 22 February 1942.

346. Fazlul Haq filed a civil suit against Jinnah for expelling him from the League. The case stayed in the court till 23 July 1947, when it was dismissed, each party paying its own cost. Jinnah's notes to Williams, 8 and 13 March 1942, QAP, F. 107, pp. 8–15; Orr Dignam to Jinnah, 19 June 1943, ibid., F. 1092, p. 179; and Orr Dignam & Co to M.A.H. Ispahani, 23 July 1947, and Ispahani to Jinnah, 26 July 1947, ibid., F. 110, pp. 1–2.

347. *IAR*, 1942, vol. I, p. 40. The Dhaka university students included Serajul Haq, Khondkar Mushtaq Ahmad, Shamsul Haq and Zahurul Haq; Fazlul Quader Choudhry was arrested in Calcutta. AFM, vol. 305, pp. 10–12; and QAP, F. 392, pp. 51–53.

348. Herbert to Linlithgow, 11 February 1942, cited in Harun-or-Rashid, *Foreshadowing of Bangladesh*, p. 147. On 25 April 1942, Suhrawardy wrote to Jinnah that the Bengali Muslims had realized that 'Pakistan means everything to them and they are not prepared to support anyone whose activities may cause it damage'. QAP, F. 458, p. 37.

349. Ibid., F. 458, p. 40; and *Dawn*, 31 May 1942.

350. AFM, vol. 304, pp. 10–11; vol. 159, nos. 8 and 13.

351. The districts were: Mymensing, Tipperah, Noakhali, Chittagong, Barisal and Dhaka. For tour report by Nawab Ismail to Jinnah, 5 July 1943, see ibid., vol. 303, p. 68; memo issued by the central civil defence committee on 23 September 1943, ibid., vol. 305, p. 69; and also see Benazir Ahmad to the central civil defence committee chairman, ibid., p. 144; and Benazir's reports, ibid., vol. 320, pp. 17–31.

352. In his tour report to Jinnah on 5 July 1943, Nawab Ismail wrote: 'In Bengal besides Mr Suhrawardy there is no other public man who exercises such influence in the Districts of Bengal as he does. Moreover, he has direct contact with the masses and the students. . . . I have no hesitation in saying that the popularity of the League in Bengal is in great measure due to the untiring and selfless efforts of the student community who have carried on unceasing propaganda among the Muslim masses.' Ibid., vol. 320.

353. Inspection Report, 6 February 1943, QAP, F. 761, pp. 275–77. Abdul Momin was its first chairman and Hamidul Haq Chowdhury its secretary but they could not accomplish much, and after Suhrawardy, Maulana Akram Khan, the presidency Muslim League president, functioned as the civil defence committee chairman and Abdul Majid as secretary.

354. In November 1943, Maulana Akram Khan was elected president and Abul Hashim secretary of the Bengal presidency Muslim League. They were re-elected to these offices the following year in November.

355. A.Z.M. Razai Karim to Jinnah, 15 April 1944, QAP, 1092, p. 229; and Jinnah to Razai Karim, 22 May 1944, ibid., F. 1102, p. 211; and Inspection Report no. 12 of 12 March 1945, on the general administration of the Bengal presidency Muslim League and its central office, AFM, vol. 201, no. 14.

356. 'Report presented by Mr Abul Hashim, secretary, Bengal Presidency Muslim League to the Council of the Bengal Presidency Muslim League annual meeting 1944, Calcutta, 17th November 1944', pp. 12–13.

357. 'Review of the Muslim League Organization in Bengal', submitted by the secretary of the Bengal presidency Muslim League to the secretary, All-India Muslim League, 30 July 1944', SHC, Bengal-1: 42.

358. For an unsuccessful attempt by Fazlul Haq to rejoin the League, see his correspondence with Jinnah, Waheed, *Nation's Voice*, vol. III, pp. 156–61.

359. *Star of India*, 25 March 1943; and *Memoirs of H.S. Suhrawardy*, p. 14.

360. A lot of literature has appeared on the Bengal famine depicting different viewpoints. For instance, see Paul R. Greenough, *Prosperity and Misery in Modern Bengal: The Famine of 1943–44*, New York, 1982; Amartya Sen, *Poverty and Famines: An Essay on Entitlements and Deprivation*, Oxford, 1981; Dipak R. Basu, 'Sen's Analysis of Famine: A Critic', *Journal of Development Studies*, 22 (1962); Peter Bowbrick, 'The Causes of Famine: A Refutation of Professor Sen's Theory', *Food Policy*, 11, no. 2; and M.M. Islam, 'The Great Bengal Famine and the Question of FAD Yet Again', *Modern Asian Studies*, 41, no. 2 (2007).

361. Amery to Wavell, 1 October and 19 November 1943, *TP*, vol. IV, pp. 354, 358 and 486.

362. AFM, vol. 391, no. 22; vol. 305, pp. 114–15; vol. 286, no. 60; vol. 264, p. 78.

363. *Azad*, 30 November 1943; and QAP, F. 359, pp. 1–3.

364. For a letter of thanks from H.S. Suhrawardy to Nawab Iftikhar Husain, 25 March 1944, see QAP, F. 1092, p. 224; and also see 'An Appeal to the Muslims of India', issued by Moazzem Husain, and another appeal in Urdu signed by Nazimuddin, Suhrawardy, Akram Khan, Abul Hashim and Moazzem Husain, AFM, vol. 269. File 365 of the QAP is full of relief activities of the All-India Muslim League.

365. For an appeal of the Communist Party of India to the All-India Muslim League, see AFM, vol. 269, pp. 84–84; and also see ibid., vol. 305, pp. 26, 28–29 and 32; and vol. 391, no. 3.

366. Pothan Joseph to Jinnah, 4 October 1943, SHC, P & P-II: 17.

367. The famine was the result of: shortage of total supply of rice due to low yield that was assembled by January 1943, and dearth of stock of old rice carried forward from 1942–43, besides the export of rice, shortage of wheat supply, cyclone of October 1942, influx of refugees from Burma and military deployment; absence of control on distribution; hoarding and the hoarders' demand against price control that was supported by Dr Shyama Prasad Mukerji who represented the big business; and the failure of the central government to come to Bengal's assistance on time. For a detailed account, see 'Muslim League and the Bengal Famine', AFM, vol. 391, pp. 10–21.

368. Ibid., vol. 286, no. 79; and *Star of India*, 15 November 1943; and also see a note on the economic and military viability of East Pakistan, QAP, F. 337, pp. 4–22.

369. Shahabuddin, Nazimuddin's brother, was generally blamed for this phenomenon. Raghib Ahsan to Quaid-i-Azam, 14 May 1943, QAP, F. 1101, pp. 128–30.

370. Nazimuddin to Liaquat, 7 July 1944, AFM, vol. 142, no. 20; Badi Ahmad to Quaid-i-Azam, 11 October 1944, SHC, Bengal-1: 32; Jinnah to Badi Ahmad, 26 October

1944, SHC, ibid., p. 33; and Nazimuddin to Jinnah, 31 March 1945, ibid.-III, pp. 5 and 8.

371. Ibid.-III, p. 9. Nazimuddin alleged that his majority had been diluted by funds provided by the Marwaris and the Hindu Mahasabha. Nazimuddin to Jinnah, 31 March 1945, AFM, vol. 392, pp. 29–30, with copies to Nawab Ismail and Liaquat.

372. While Abul Hashim promoted Suhrawardy as the prospective chief minister of Bengal, his opponents alleged that he was 'hobnobbing with the communists' and wanted to replace him by A.M. Malik, a trade union leader, as the presidency Muslim League secretary. Khaliquzzaman on Jinnah's direction visited Bengal and patched up their differences. Liaquat to Jinnah, 5 June 1945, AFM, vol. 481, p. 82; and also see ibid., vol. 232, no. 54.

373. Nazimuddin to Jinnah, 6 July 1946, QAP, F. 392, p. 86.

374. Ibid., and Nazimuddin to Jinnah, 14 April 1947, ibid., F. 392, pp. 86 and 87–88.

375. Akram Khan to Nawab Ismail, 26 July 1946, AFM, vol. 182, no. 2; and Akram Khan to Nawab Ismail, 24 September 1946, Nawab Ismail to Maulana Akram Khan, 28 September 1946, and Farmozul Haq to chairman, committee of action, 4 October 1946, ibid., vol. 192, nos. 24, 25 and 27.

376. Habibullah Bahar, acting secretary of the Bengal presidency Muslim League to honorary secretary, All-India Muslim League, 24 March 1947, and Zafar Ahmad Ansari to general secretary, Bengal presidency Muslim League, 29 March 1947, ibid., vol. 394. Extension was given till 15 June.

377. TP, vol. VIII, p. 587.

378. Suhrawardy to Jinnah, QAP, F. 458, pp. 51–52. See also Chapter 11.

379. He aspired to be the president of the Bengal presidency Muslim League and cultivated the students by criticizing the ministry. His supporters included Nurul Amin, Hamidul Haq, Mohan Mia and Abdullah al-Mahmood. Suhrawardy to Jinnah, 20 February 1947, ibid., F. 458, pp. 54–56.

380. AFM, vol. 394, pp. 24–25. Fazlul Haq was one of the signatories.

381. Jinnah to Habibullah Bahar, 1 April 1947, QAP, F. 566, p. 45. Jinnah reiterated his advice when a six-member (Nurul Amin, Habibullah Bahar, Yusuf Ali Choudhury, Wahiduzzaman, Sharfuddin Ahmad and Yusuf Husain Choudhury) delegation of dissenters met him in Delhi.

382. On the election day, the League had nine members but before Saadulla formed the ministry its strength had risen to thirty-two.

383. According to the 1941 census, its population was mainly composed of Caste Hindus (3.5 million), Muslims (3.4 million), Tribals (2.4 million) and Scheduled Castes (0.6 million).

384. Ten to fifteen thousand Bengali Muslims had been migrating into Assam every year. Muslim population in the Assam valley districts excluding Garo Hills had risen from 355,320 in 1911 to 1,303,902 in 1941. During the Bengal famine, in one go more than half a million Muslim immigrants came into Assam that transformed the Muslims as the largest single group. QAP, F. 1122, p. 25.

385. Star of India, 10 October 1938; Abdul Matin to Jinnah, 22 and 26 September 1938, QAP, F. 160-A, pp. 511–13; and resolution passed by the All-India Muslim League working committee in Karachi on 8–10 October 1938, AFM, vol. 122, no. 47.

386. IAR, 1941, vol. II, p. 45.

387. For an Assam provincial Muslim League headed by Maulana Bhashani organized before the Lucknow session and its affiliation with the All-India Muslim League, see Sakhawatul Ambia (1894–1969) to honorary secretary, All-India Muslim

League, 1 October 1937, and honorary secretary to Sakhawat, 4 November 1937, AFM, vol. 164, nos. 17 and 18; and also QAP, F. 24, pp. 1–2.

388. Abdul Hamid to Jinnah, n.d., SHC, Assam-1: 1; and Abdul Matin to Jinnah, 11 October 1940, QAP, F. 244, p. 34.

389. Mayeenuddin to Quaid-i-Azam, 20 November 1942, AFM, vol. 303, pp. 33–40; and Nawab Ismail to Quaid-i-Azam, ibid., vol. 303, p. 60.

390. For a report on the activities of the Assam civil defence committee and Muslim Students Federation, see AFM, vol. 303, pp. 11–16.

391. For a requisition signed by several Muslim Leaguers on 9 June 1943, see SHC-Assam, 1:13; and AFM, vol. 303, p. 53–55. For the delay in holding the requisitioned meeting, see Nawab Ismail to Mayeenuddin, 10 July 1943, and Mayeenuddin to Nawab Ismail, 12 August 1943, and Nawab Ismail to Ajmal Ali Choudhry, president of the Assam Muslim Students Federation, 10 July 1943, Ajmal Ali to Nawab Ismail, 16 July and 4 August 1943, and Nawab Ismail to Sir Saadulla, 9 August and 10 September 1943, ibid., vol. 303, pp. 25–28 and 30–31. Saadulla informed Nawab Ismail that the delay in holding the meeting had been due to his illness to which he responded that there would not have been any misunderstanding if he had informed the Muslim Leaguers about the reasons for the delay.

392. Liaquat to Abdul Matin Choudhry, 26 March 1944, ibid., vol. 169, no. 10; and also see ibid., vol. 155.

393. The conference also elected Dewan Mohammad Ahbab and Amjad Ali as vice-presidents; Mumtazuddin Ahmad and Fazlul Haque Selbarsi assistant secretaries; and G.A. Khan treasurer. It expressed confidence in Jinnah's leadership and faith in Pakistan, demanding that Bengal and Assam should be formed into 'an independent sovereign state to be known as Eastern Pakistan'. For resolution adopted at the conference, see ibid., vol. 169, nos. 18–21.

394. For the correctness of the party elections, see Maulana Bhashani's lengthy letter to the secretary, committee of action, 8 July 1944, ibid., vol. 169, pp. 56–60.

395. Ibid., vol. 169, no. 31. The Muslim Leaguers from the Surma Valley termed it as a 'grand immigrants conference', not a League conference. Modabbir Husain to Liaquat, 13 April 1943, Zafar Ahmad to Modabbir Husain, 29 April 1943, Zafar Ahmad to Abdul Hamid Khan, 10 May 1943, Liaquat to Saadulla and Abdul Hamid Khan, 25 July 1943, and Mahmud Ali to Liaquat, 1 August 1943, ibid., vol. 169, nos. 23–25 and 41–42.

396. For this issue, see the correspondence, ibid., vol. 298; and for Jinnah's endorsement of Basit, see his letter to Abdul Hamid Khan, 13 November 1944, QAP, F. 851, p. 5.

397. Abdul Matin to Liaquat, 6 January 1945; and Liaquat to Abdul Matin and Abdul Hamid Khan, 10 January 1945, AFM, vol. 299, pp. 6 and 9. Abdul Bari and K.B. Mohammad Rafique were re-elected as vice-presidents; Mumtazuddin as joint secretary; and Mohammad Akram and Mahmud Ali as assistant secretaries.

398. For resolution passed at the Lucknow session in October 1937, see Pirzada, *Foundations*, vol. II, p. 280.

399. Maulana Abdul Hamid Khan, *Line System or 'The Pegging Act' in Assam*, Calcutta, 1945, Appendix C, pp. 6–16. Chaired by F.W. Hockenhull, the committee had three Congress members and three Muslim members.

400. Ismail Khan to Quaid-i-Azam, 15 June 1943, AFM, vol. 303, p. 60.

401. The decision was based on Matin's note to the cabinet. See his letters to Nawab Ismail, 1 and 14 July 1943, ibid., pp. 24 and 89.

402. Amar to Quaid-i-Azam, 4 July 1943, QAP, F. 1101, pp. 146–48. The Karachi Congress resolution had provided: 'Every citizen is free to move throughout India and to stay and settle in any part thereof to acquire property and to follow any trade or calling and to be treated equally with regard to legal prosecution or protection in all parts of India.' Nehru's observation in his letter to Bardoloi, Abdul Hamid, *Line System*, pp. 2–4 and 18–19.

403. At the Barpeta conference, Saadulla 'compared the situation in Assam to Palestine where the Arabs resented the import of Jews' [M.A. Rashid to president, All-India Muslim League, 21 April 1944, QAP, F. 1102, pp. 94–99]. For the pressure on Saadulla, see *Whither Assam? Drifting to Civil War?*, published by Assam provincial organizing committee, Gauhati, 1944, pp. 22–23.

404. For a conference in December 1944, prior to the change in policy, which Saadulla, Bardoloi, Bhashani and others addressed, see *Whither Assam?* pp. 40–41.

405. For a printed copy of the government resolution on land settlement in Assam, see AFM, vol. 300, pp. 33–35.

406. Liaquat to Saadulla, 24 May 1945, ibid., vol. 300, p. 107.

407. Ibid., vol. 299, pp. 17–18.

408. For Jinnah's telegram for intervention, see Jinnah to Saadulla, 21 February 1945, and Saadulla's response, 24 February, SHC, Assam-I: 48 and 50.

409. Bhashani, two League members of the legislative assembly and leader of the Bengali migrants opposed the formation of coalition with the Congress; and the decision about coalition-formation did not have the approval of the central parliamentary board.

410. Jinnah could not intervene due to illness. Emphasizing the need for organization, Jinnah wrote to Bhashani: 'Out of ashes the true followers of Islam in Assam will rise with the noble spirit of Islam that will sweep away the traitors, hirelings and quislings among us. Face your opponents with power and organization which will be irresistible.' SHC, Assam-I: 53, 54 and 55 [Atful Hye Shibly (*Abdul Matin Chaudhury: Trusted Lieutenant of Mohammad Ali Jinnah*, Dhaka, 2011, p. 9) incorrectly attributes its addressee to be Matin]; secretary, central committee of action to Saadulla, 27 April 1945, AFM, vol. 299, p. 44; and Liaquat's statement on 28 May 1945, ibid., vol. 301, p. 3.

411. Abdul Matin to Liaquat, 16 February 1945, Abdul Hamid Khan to Liaquat, 19 March 1945; and other correspondence, ibid., vol. 300, pp. 20–22 and 35. For Rodini Kumar's inclusion as revenue minister being part of Saadulla's agreement with the opposition, see Liaquat to Saadulla, 16 and 18 May 1945, and Saadulla to Liaquat (confidential), 19 and 24 May 1945, ibid., vol. 300, pp. 84, 88–91 and 104–8.

412. Ibid., vol. 301, pp. 1–2; and Liaquat to Jinnah, 5 June 1945, ibid., vol. 481, pp. 81–83.

413. Resolution of the All-India Muslim League working committee, ibid., vol. 142, no. 56.

414. Saadulla's statement, ibid., vol. 301, p. 58; and Abdul Matin, 'Immigrants in Assam', ibid., p. 87.

415. For a resolution passed by the provincial Muslim League working committee on 8 March 1946, see ibid., vol. 299, p. 100; and for Jinnah's advice, see Ghiyasuddin Pathan to secretary, All-India Muslim League, 17 March 1947, ibid., p. 101. On 10 April, the All-India Muslim League council demanded the withdrawal of the system and protested against evictions. Ibid., vol. 278, p. 25.

416. For resolution of the provincial Muslim League working committee and protest meetings, see ibid., vol. 301, pp. 34–40; and also see Mahmud Ali to Quaid-i-Azam, 7 November 1946, QAP, F. 563, pp. 1–5.

417. For resolution of the Assam provincial Muslim League, 18 November 1946; and Mahmud Ali, general secretary, Assam provincial Muslim League, to secretary, committee of action, 24 December 1946, see AFM, vol. 301, pp. 44–45, 48 and 57.

418. Mahmud Ali to secretary, committee of action, 26 February, ibid., vol. 299, p. 98; and Saadulla to Jinnah, 16 April 1947, QAP, F. 455, p. 1. Saadulla and Basit were members of the committee.

419. For the committee of action's response, see Zafar Ahmad to Maulana Abdul Hamid, 2 and 7 January 1947, and Zafar Ahmad to general secretary, Assam provincial Muslim League, 7 January 1946, AFM, vol. 299, pp. 92–93; and also see ibid., vol. 142, no. 64.

420. Dewan Abdul Basit to chairman, committee of action, 21 May 1947, ibid., vol. 182, no. 73.

421. The central League provided funds to the provincial Muslim League for relief work.

422. Among the conditions were that all those migrants who had sown at least one crop on the government land or professional grazing reserves would be entitled to settlement of land irrespective of the time of their arrival in Assam. For details, see Liaquat to Saadulla, 11 July 1947, ibid., vol. 301, p. 4.

423. Four out of five Muslim members in the Bombay council of state belonged to the Muslim League.

424. QAP, F. 312, p. 12; and F. 139, pp. 21–23.

425. For resolution passed by the Bombay presidency Muslim League on 17 May 1938, and Jinnah's speech, see ibid., F. 811, p. 176.

426. This provincial Muslim League also elected Abdul Hamid, Editor of the *Khatoon*, joint secretary and M.A. Chaiwala and Husain Beg treasurers, and thirty representatives on the central League council. Ibid., F. 1094, pp. 290–91; and F. 1095, p. 151; and AFM, vol. 49.

427. For letter signed by T.T. Barodwala, honorary secretary, Bombay presidency parliamentary board, 23 April 1939, see QAP, F. 1016, p. 81.

428. 'Inspection Report No. 9 dated 28 January 1945, on the working of the Bombay presidency Muslim League and its office', AFM, vol. 201, no. 1.

429. For resolutions passed by the party, see AFM, vols. 49 and 51; and QAP, F. 824, p. 102. The wording of the resolution on prohibition passed at a meeting chaired by Jinnah was checked by I.I. Chundrigar and Mohammad Ali Chaiwala.

430. Jinnah to secretary, Bombay presidency Muslim League, n.d., QAP, F. 568, p. 121.

431. Mohammad Omer Kokil was elected as joint secretary, and Sir Karimbhai Ibrahim and M.A. Chaiwala treasurers. *Dawn*, 16 November 1941.

432. For the state of the provincial Muslim League and its accounts up to 31 July 1943, see AFM, vol. 51.

433. For details, see the correspondence and reports, ibid., vols. 307 and 308.

434. For details, see ibid., vol. 51; and vol. 400, pp. 65–70, 72 and 85; and QAP, F. 1137, p. 8.

435. It also elected three vice-presidents—A.A. Kittur, Noor Ahmad and Dr A. Patel; two joint secretaries—Nuruddin Bandukwala and Khwaja Ghulam Jilani; and one treasurer—Aziz Ghafur Qazi.

436. For resolutions passed by the provincial Muslim League on 17 November 1846, see AFM, vol. 402, pp. 42–45; and QAP, F. 1128.

437. QAP, F. 24, pp. 63–64 and 140–41. For a demand to recognize the Andhra Muslim League as a separate branch, see secretary, Andhra Muslim League to Jinnah, 13 August 1937, AFM, vol. 205, no. 10.

438. Abdussattar Sait to Shamsul Hasan, 8 June 1937, AFM, vol. 205, no. 10, 11 and 13; Abdussattar to Jinnah, QAP, F. 1119, p. 22; and for another conference at 'Jinnahabad' in Calicut on 29–30 April 1940, presided over by Fazlul Haq, see AFM, vol. 265, p. 26–29 and 42.

439. P. Khalifulla, president of the Tamilnadu Muslim League to Jinnah, 22 February 1938, QAP, F. 823, p. 25.

440. The provincial Muslim League elected five vice-presidents and three secretaries (B. Poker, Abdul Hamid Khan and K.T.M. Ahmad Ibrahim), and one treasurer (Abdul Karim). AFM, vol. 215, nos. 9, 10, 15 and 17.

441. In November 1941, the party elected six vice-presidents, besides electing Ahmad Ibrahim, Abdul Latif Faruqi and A.M. Allapichai as secretaries and Abdul Karim as treasurer.

442. *Report of the President to the Annual Meeting of the Madras Presidency Muslim League held on 10 November 1940*, AFM, vol. 265, pp. 70–72; and Haji Abdussattar Haji Essak Sait to Jinnah, 10 January 1940, QAP, F. 1092, p. 31.

443. Jamal Mohammad to Jinnah, 20 March 1940, AFM, vol. 207, no. 28.

444. For the provincial Muslim League's stance on various issues, see ibid., vol. 214, no. 34; vol. 266, pp. 3, 25, 43, 46–49; vol. 267, pp. 12 and 35; vol. 277, pp. 120–21; and vol. 336, pp. 14–22.

445. Ibid., vol. 137, nos. 3, 22, 31 and 42; vol. 215, no. 16; and vol. 285, no. 32; and QAP, F. 904, pp. 8–22.

446. For the organization and accounts of the Madras presidency Muslim League, see the Inspection Report No. 7 dated 11–13 January 1945, AFM, vol. 200, no. 18.

447. Liaquat to secretary, Madras presidency Muslim League, 19 December 1944, ibid., vol. 159, no. 82; also see vol. 165, nos. 8, 10, 11, 13, 18, 22, and 25; and vol. 159, nos. 88, 91–93; and Liaquat to Jinnah, 31 January 1945, ibid., vol. 481, p. 67. For Liaquat's tour of the districts, see ibid., vol. 416.

448. Ahmad Ibrahim, honorary secretary, Madras presidency Muslim League to honorary secretary, All-India Muslim League, 3 August 1943, ibid., vol. 286, no. 25; and resolution passed by the central working committee on 17 and 15 November 1943, ibid., 142, p. 15.

449. Syed Murtaza Bahadur to Jinnah and Liaquat, 15 October 1945, QAP, F. 1235, pp. 1–3; and also see AFM, vol. 536, pp. 13, 16, 22–23, 37, 38, and 42–45.

450. For instance, see honorary secretary, Ramnad district Muslim League to secretary, central committee of action, 23 February 1945, AFM, vol. 338, p. 8.

451. For resolution passed by the Madras presidency Muslim League on 27 May 1947, see ibid., vol. 538, p. 56.

452. For details of the safeguards demanded by the provincial Muslim League, see ibid., vol. 182, no. 79.

453. Ihsanur Rahman Kidwai was elected general secretary of the United Provinces League; subsequently, Sayyid Rizwanullah succeeded him in that office. Aizaz Rasul and Abdul Wahid were elected as joint secretaries and Raja of Mahmudabad as treasurer.

454. For details of its organizational activities, see AFM, vol. 353, nos. 1–6, 10, 13 and 14; and vol. 355, p. 21.

455. Jafar Husain to Jinnah, [October] 1939, QAP, F. 900, pp. 139–40.

456. Maulana Zafarul Mulk, 'The Case of Madhe Sahaba', *Pioneer*, 13 July 1939; and also see Chapter 2, Section (*a*) Organizational Structure (*i*) *Membership*

457. Shafaat Ahmad Khan to Jinnah (secret), 18 May 1939, QAP, F. 161, pp. 89–92. Raja of Mahmudabad's suggestion that Khaliquzzaman's removal from the leadership of the League assembly party would strengthen the party was a reflection of the sectarian bias. Amir Ahmad Khan to Jinnah, 8 August 1937, ibid., F. 26, pp. 195–96.

458. Shafaat Ahmad Khan to Jinnah, n.d., ibid., F. 26, pp. 65–66; Amir Ahmad Khan to Jinnah, 7 June 1937, ibid., F. 24, pp. 130–31; and 8 August 1937, ibid., F. 26, p. 196; and S.M. Husain to Jinnah, 7 June 1937, ibid., F. 24, pp. 153–54; and for S.M. Abdullah's resolution that was not allowed to be moved, see AFM, vol. 187, no. 27.

459. J.J. Allsop and H.S. Ross, 'Report of the Madhe Sahaba Committee', 15 June 1937, *Government Gazette of the United Provinces Extraordinary*, Lucknow, 28 March 1938, pp. 1–23; and *Moonlight* (weekly), Lucknow, 10 April 1939, pp. 1–4.

460. Mohammad Salman to Jinnah, 8 March 1938, QAP, F. 995, pp. 8–9; Nawab Ismail to Jinnah, 6 May 1939, ibid., F. 48, p. 30; Khaliquzzaman to Jinnah, 17 June 1939, ibid., F. 49, p. 25; and Khaliquzzaman, *Pathway to Pakistan*, pp. 212–15.

461. Faiyaz to Jinnah, 22 March 1939, 'Thinker' to Jinnah, 8 April 1939, Kujhwa Shias, Bihar to Jinnah, 8 April 1939; Hasan Ispahani to Jinnah, 8 April 1939; Anjuman-i-Faruqia to Jinnah, 8 April 1939, QAP, F. 161, pp. 25, 29–33; and S. Daud, president, CP and Berar Bohra League to Jinnah, 17 May 1939, ibid., F. 1220, pp. 1–2.

462. For instance, see an appeal made by twenty-two influential Muslims including Sikandar Hayat, Fazlul Haq, Syedna Tahir Saifuddin, Khizr Hayat, Sir Mirza Ismail, Sir Sultan Ahmad and Nawab Nisar Ali Qizilbash, Abdullah Haroon and Raza Ali on 2 June 1939, *Statesman*, 3 June 1939. For the number of Shias and Sunnis arrested and fined, see *IAR*, 1939, vol. II, pp. 6, 19 and 160.

463. Jinnah to Sir Raza Ali (private and confidential), 8 July 1939, QAP, F. 161, p. 126. Following the All-India Muslim League's example, the United Provinces League also kept itself aloof from the controversy. S. M. Ismail to Jinnah, 10 April 1939, ibid., F. 161, pp. 38–40; and statement by Khaliquzzaman, *Hindustan Times*, 14 June 1939.

464. Ziauddin to Jinnah, 11 May 1938, QAP, F. 203, p. 2. For instance, see his telegram to Raja of Mahmudabad on 25 April 1939, 'Your conversation phone Muslim League willing help solution Shia–Sunni internecine quarrel. Those who are leading them call truce, refer matters to us' [Handwritten draft, ibid., F. 161, p. 65]. Jinnah also received several telegrams from the Shias and Sunnis from different parts of India for intervention. M.A.H. Ispahani wrote (11 April 1939): 'I appeal to you to assist in ending the Madhe Sahaba row in Lucknow; otherwise I fear a very serious rupture in the very ranks of the Muslim League—God help us!' [QAP, F. 305, p. 35.] In a joint telegram on 1 May 1939, Ismail Khan, [Raja of] Pirpur and [Raja of] Mahmudabad urged Jinnah, 'For God's sake come [to Lucknow] critical moment for Muslims'. His response (3 May) was, 'My opinion my coming [to] Lucknow inadvisable. Your telegram discloses no ground or object nor have I any definite information [of the] situation'. Ibid., F. 161, pp. 73–74.

465. For agreement signed by Dr Sir Ziauddin and acting premier of United Provinces, and Jinnah–Mashriqi correspondence, see ibid., F. 101, pp. 38–40. This period witnessed perhaps the high point of Jinnah–Nehru cordiality.

466. For details of the controversy, see AFM, vol. 361, pp. 1–7, 31, 37; vol. 362, pp. 92–93, 100, 102–3, 120, 121, 138, 143–48, 155, 170, 172–74, 181 and 182.

467. For instance, see Iqtedaruddin Hasan to Quaid-i-Azam, 21 July 1942, Iqtedaruddin Hasan to Liaquat, 21 July 1942, and Liaquat to Iqtedaruddin, 7 August 1942, ibid., vol. 354, pp. 54–66 and 68–72; and Aminuddin Mian to Nawab Ismail, 18 January 1943, ibid., vol. 314, p. 17. In 1946 also, there were complaints of Congress exploitation of Shia–Sunni differences. Raza Ali to Jinnah, 5 July 1946, QAP, F. 220, pp. 15–17.

468. IAR, 1939, vol. II, p. 355.

469. Inspection Report of Zakir Ali, 3 February 1943, QAP, F. 761, pp. 154–59. See also Khaliquzzaman to Jinnah, 4 November 1940, QAP, F. 1092, p. 61; resolution passed by the central working committee on 22 February 1941, AFM, vol. 133, no. 9; and Hasan Reyaz to Jinnah, 30 June 1941, QAP, F. 561, p. 56.

470. For details, see QAP, F. 761, pp. 154–59; and AFM, vol. 326, pp. 95–98, 99–104 and 110–15.

471. It established branches in 39 districts and 17 cities. For details, see a press clipping, AFM, vol. 302.

472. Ibid., vol. 313, pp. 34, 43–47 and 58; and reports by Shamsul Hasan, secretary of the UP civil defence committee to secretary, central civil defence committee, ibid., vol. 314, pp. 4–7, 20–21, 31–32 and 46–49; and vol. 315, pp. 11–13 and 14–16.

473. Mohammad Zunnurain to provincial Muslim League office, 21 April 1942, ibid., vol., 313, p. 4.

474. For the provincial Muslim League's activities, see 'Inspection Report No. 3 dated 23 July 1944, on the Working of the United Provinces Muslim League', 24 July 1944, ibid., vol. 200, no. 6. Copies of this report were sent to all the provincial Muslim Leagues.

475. Earlier, Rizwanullah had been charged with mismanaging party funds, and after an inquiry, he had to return Rs 1,148 to the party. For details, see Jamal Mian to Jinnah, 12 July 1944, JP, second series, vol. X, p. 560; AFM, vol. 357, p. 29; and QAP, F. 335, pp. 224–25.

476. AFM, vol. 356, pp. 89 and 100; and vol. 357, p. 26; vol. 417; and vol. 165, no. 62; and for the formation of a provincial parliamentary board, see ibid., pp. 23–24.

477. For details of the intra-party conflict, see Ittelaat, 25 July and 10 September 1944; and AFM, vol. 356, pp. 59, 63, 64 69–72; vol. 357, pp. 25, 58; vol. 358, no. 1, 3, 22, 41 and 65. On Nawab Ismail's resumption of the presidency, which Rizwanullah also welcomed, Liaquat wrote to Jinnah (28 August 1944): 'You must have been glad to read in the papers that things were amicably settled in the United Provinces. It should have never happened. However, all is well that ends well.' Ibid., vol. 481, p. 57.

478. Zahid Ali Khan, Mustansarullah and Ch. M. Rafi were elected as secretaries and Raja Mahmudabad as treasurer. Ibid., vol. 356, pp. 28–29.

479. Ibid., vol. 360, pp. 9, 10 and 25.

480. Three others were: Ashique Warsi, Mohammad Shafie and M. Fazlul Rahman. For details of its organization, see ibid., vol. 184, no. 14; and QAP, F. 565, p. 1; and F. 865, pp. 132 and 108–9.

481. M. Ashique to Jinnah, 25 June 1938, QAP, F. 565, pp. 5–7; and Amrita Bazar Patrika, 22 June 1938.

482. For instance, see QAP, F. 1095, pp. 138–43; and AFM, vol. 174, no. 52

483. See Chapter 6.

484. The party elected six vice-presidents (Latifur Rahman, S.M. Shareef, Badrul Hasan, Abu Jafar, Sayyid Hasan, and Qadir Bakhsh Khan), two joint secretaries (Moinuddin Ahmad and Azizur Rahman), one treasurer (Sharfuddin Hasan) and one publicity officer (Shah Husain Mian). Badruddin Ahmad to general secretary, All-India Muslim League, 26 November 1940, AFM, vol. 184, no. 71.

485. The conference was held in a charged atmosphere, following provocative and aggressive speeches by Savarkar and Dr Shyama Prasad Mukerji; and in the third week of April, Sardar Mohan Singh along with a Frontier Hindu deputation had visited Patna showing photographs of alleged Muslim excesses in Sindh and NWFP [Ibid., vol. 518, pp. 70–78]. The newspaper, *Muslim League*, was confiscated for publishing news about the riots. Taqi Rahim, *Tehrik-i-Azadi mein Bihar ke Mussalmanon ka Hissa*, Patna, 1998, pp. 402 and 422.

486. The rioters desecrated 12 mosques, damaged 4 madrassas and burnt 185 houses of the Muslims.

487. For the memorandum, see QAP, F. 565, pp. 34–46; and a report by Badruddin to Jinnah, 10 May 1941, ibid., F. 565.

488. Ibid., F. 304, p. 107; and *IAR*, 1941, vol. II, pp. 10 and 236–37.

489. For resolutions passed by the All-India Muslim League working committee on 24–26 August, see AFM, vol. 133, no. 30.

490. The Indian Liberal Federation condemned the ban on the All-India Hindu Mahasabha session in Bhagalpur, and Gandhi demanded the lifting of ban. *IAR*, 1941, vol. II, pp. 22, 38, 46 and 47.

491. Jafar Imam and Maulana Qamruddin were the two other members. Latifur Rahman who served on the central working committee for seven years (1940–1947) was president of the All-India Momin Conference, which effectively countered the pro-Congress stance of its splinter group led by Abdul Qayyum Ansari.

492. For the activities of the civil defence committee, see Latifur Rahman to Quaid-i-Azam, 30 April 1942, QAP, F. 570, p. 107; and a document signed by Zakir Ali and secretary, Bihar civil defence committee, 27 April 1942, and Mazhar Imam's letters to Zakir Ali, 21 May, 18 July and 8 August 1942, AFM, vol. 306, pp. 8–10, 25, 28, 32 and 33–38.

493. For the allegations, see A. Rahim Khan to Quaid-i-Azam, 12 April 1944, QAP, F. 1102, p. 54; and 'Summary of the Urdu Memorandum on the affairs of the Bihar Provincial Muslim League', 12 December 1944, AFM, vol. 395, pp. 8–10. That year S.M. Shareef had contested the elections for the office of president against Sayyid Ismail.

494. Naimul Haq and five others and the Gaya district Muslim League were the complainants.

495. 'Report submitted by Qazi Mohammad Isa regarding the affairs of the Bihar Muslim League', 8 August 1945, AFM, vol. 395, pp. 29–33. Qazi Isa stayed with Sayyid Ismail and interviewed some of the complainants at his residence.

496. For details of the case, see ibid., vol. 332.

497. Abdul Aziz, in a letter on 10 April, had written, 'I cannot place my feet on the ground. Because of the intensity of my ailment I am completely laid up. I cannot move. I cannot participate even in consultation'. Even after this letter, the provincial Muslim League, by a vote of 55 to 24, sent a 5-member deputation to persuade him to accept the presidency but he declined to agree [Ibid., vol. 396, pp. 22–23]. In addition to illness, he did not fulfill another constitutional requirement: that an office-bearer should have been a member of some primary League for at least one year.

498. S.M. Ismail to Dr Abdul Ahad, 18 June 1945, ibid., vol. 396, p. 76.
499. The council also elected Sharfuddin as treasurer, Latifur Rahman, Jafar Imam, Habibur Rahman and Shafiqul Haq as vice-presidents, and four joint secretaries.
500. See Chapter 11.
501. M.A. Warsi to Zafar Ahmad, 19 April 1947, AFM, vol. 397, p. 66.
502. During the 1946 elections, Mohammad Asghar was expelled from the League for three years for contesting the elections against the League candidate after he was refused the party ticket. He was the only non-League Muslim elected from this province. In July 1947, the League took him back on his 'unconditional apology'. Ibid., vol. 443, pp. 24 and 84.
503. Abdur Rauf Shah to Jinnah, 8 January 1937, QAP, F. 443, p. 3. In 1940, the provincial Muslim League shifted its headquarters from Nagpur to Akola.
504. Abul Kalam Azad to Abdur Rauf Shah, 27 May; and 17 June 1939, Abdur Rauf to Jinnah, 20 June 1939, and Jinnah to Abdur Rauf Shah, 22 June 1939, ibid., F. 49, pp. 42–47 and 58.
505. See Chapter 6.
506. AFM, vol. 118, nos. 25 and 59. Its membership was 24,033 in 1938 to 28,852 in 1939, 33,703 in 1940, 22,000 in 1944 and 890,110 in 1945. Ibid., vol. 442, pp. 1–3.
507. QAP, F. 824, pp. 152 and 235–36; and F. 443, pp. 13–19; and AFM, vol. 423, pp. 3, 4, 12 and 26.
508. AFM, vol. 423, pp. 82–84.
509. This was the proportion of Muslim representation from these regions in the provincial assembly.
510. For details of the formula, see Bahadur Yar Jang to president, provincial Muslim League, 5 March 1940, QAP, F. 570, pp. 56–57.
511. For the Shatrangipura mosque affair, see AFM, vols. 423, 424 and 425.
512. Haji Abdussattar to Liaquat, 8 December 1940 (cc to president, All-India Muslim League), QAP, F. 561, pp. 50–55; and AFM, vol. 425, pp. 30, 133–37, 140 and 144.
513. For the provincial Muslim League–Jabbalpur district Muslim League conflict, see AFM, vol. 431, which exclusively deals with this issue.
514. Jinnah's advice to Siddiq was in response to his telegram of 28 December 1940: 'Ten weeks' imprisonment shattered health wife ill lost child. Top it Provincial Muslim League expelled me two years seek protection. Pray grant permission retire.' QAP, F. 352, p. 7.
515. For his seventeen-page appeal, see ibid., F. 352, pp. 14–30.
516. AFM, vol. 429 deals with these incidents. For withholding the publication of the inquiry report on the Amraoti riots by the sessions judge, because of involvement of important Hindu leaders, see Mohammad Asghar to Liaquat, 22 August 1943, ibid., vol. 440, no. 20.
517. This decision was written on a document that was signed by Rauf Shah, Mohammad Asghar, Abdur Rahman (publicity secretary) and Siddiq Ali Khan. Ibid., vol. 428, p. 99–100.
518. Ibid., vol. 136, p. 41.
519. For the provincial Muslim League's stand on the allocation of seats on the council on the basis of population, see Rauf Shah to Liaquat, 11 August 1943, ibid., vol. 440, pp. 23–26.
520. For details of the provincial Muslim League–Jabbalpur district Muslim League conflict, see ibid., vol. 431. It was propagated that Burhanul Mulk advocated

seclusion of women; and for that reason, the Zenana (Women) Muslim League had been disaffiliated.

521. *Model Constitution & Rules for Provincial Muslim Leagues (Framed by the Committee of Action under the direction of the Working Committee of the All India Muslim League)*, Delhi [1946], Sections 10–14.

522. For instance, see AFM, vol. 443, pp. 3, 5, 13, 24, 32 and 84.

523. 'Open Letter to Mr Shukla, Premier, CP & Berar', 18 November 1946, ibid., vol. 442, p. 36; and Burhanul Haq to D.P. Misra, minister for local self-government, 21 October 1946, QAP, F. 1107, p. 33.

524. A.G. Kazi, general secretary, Central Provinces and Berar provincial Muslim League to chairman, committee of action, 7 July 1947, AFM, vol. 182, no. 77.

525. For the district Muslim Leagues in Cuttak, Bhadrak, Puri and Balasore, see QAP, F. 867, p. 82; and for the provincial Muslim League, see AFM, vol. 534, pp. 2–5; Ahmad Bakhsh to general secretary, All-India Muslim League, 16 December 1938, AFM, vol. 584, p. 6; and also QAP, F. 160, pp. 197–98; F. 823, p. 58, and F. 865, p. 130.

526. For details, see Liaquat to Ahmad Bakhsh, 16 January, 2 May 1940, Ahmad Bakhsh to Liaquat, 24 January, 5 March 1940, M.A. Jalil to Liaquat, 28 February 1940, and Shamsul Hasan to Ahmad Bakhsh, 1 April 1940, AFM, vol. 534; Ahmad Bakhsh to Jinnah, 2 February 1942, QAP, F. 1098, pp. 152–53; and resolution no. 5 of the central working committee of 25 February 1940, Pirzada, *Foundations*, vol. III, p. 324.

527. For a resolution passed on 15–17 June 1940, see AFM, vol. 129, no. 28; and Liaquat to Huseyn Shaheed Suhrawardy, 25 June 1940, ibid., vol. 534.

528. Ibid., vol. 312, p. 6; and vol. 535, p. 1.

529. For activities of the Orissa provincial Muslim League and civil defence committee, see ibid., vol. 312, pp. 11, 17, 23–26, 31, 34–35, 51 and 54–65; and vol. 535, pp. 24–25; and QAP, F. 761, pp. 136 and 137.

530. AFM, vol. 312, pp. 40–50 and 80; and vol. 535, pp. 13–14.

531. 'A Muslim' to Jinnah, 4 October 1945, ibid., vol. 535, pp. 53–66.

532. Zakir Ali to chairman, committee of action, 31 July 1944, ibid., vol. 535, pp. 18–20.

533. Ibid., vol. 535, pp. 36–50.

534. M.A. Amin, secretary, Orissa provincial Muslim League, 13 December 1946, ibid., vol. 535, p. 89; and 'Plan for Rehabilitation' by secretary, Orissa provincial Muslim League to secretary, central committee of action, 4 January 1947, ibid., pp. 90–91.

535. For the conflict, see M. Khalil Khan, *Judgment of the Judicial Committee of the Privy Council*, Ajmer, 1946.

536. For the office-bearers and members of the Leagues in three districts (Ajmer, Merwara and Nasirabad), see Khalil Khan to general secretary, All-India Muslim League, 7 March 1938, AFM, vol. 404, pp. 20–22. Its membership was 4,694 out of a total population of 97,000 Muslims. About 50 per cent of the 50,000 population of district Nasirabad consisted of railway employees who could not become members of the League.

537. Mohammad Khalil Khan to general secretary, All-India Muslim League, 25 January 1938, ibid., pp. 9–10.

538. For objections raised by Abdul Jabbar, Syed M. Husain Chishti, Abdul Aziz Khan and others, see ibid., vol. 404.

539. Qadir Beg had counter-charged that Asrar had supported the Congress in the municipality. Asrar Ahmad to Liaquat, 27 June 1940, ibid., pp. 77–80.

540. Abdul Jabbar to Liaquat, 12 October 1940, ibid., pp. 81–82.

541. Ibid., pp. 86 and 88.

542. For instance, see S.M. Zauqi to Quaid-i-Azam, 12 and 26 November 1941, Jinnah to Zauqi, 3 December 1941, and Zauqi to Liaquat, 7 June 1943, ibid., vol. 405. The All-India Muslim League council adopted a resolution about the working of the Dargah Act in its meeting held on 14–15 November 1943, and sent its copy to secretary of the League Assembly Party for consideration. Ibid., vol. 286, no. 28.

543. 'Inspection Report No. 2 dated 30 April 1944 on the working of the Provincial Muslim League, Ajmer–Merwara', ibid., vol. 200, no.2; and also QAP, F. 237, pp. 1–4.

544. For example, see K. Ahmad Naim Siddiqi, Ahmad Saleem Siddiqi, M. Yasin Khan, Sh. Abdul Qadir and M. Ahmad Siddiqi to convener, central committee of action, 25 September 1945, AFM, vol. 405, pp. 80–81.

545. Ibid., vol. 406. Qadir Beg expelled from the provincial Muslim League five of his critics, who were also active in the Muslim Students Federation.

546. Adil (Ajmer), 14 March 1947.

547. AFM, vols. 406 and 407.

548. Ishrat Husain to Zafar Ahmad, secretary, central committee of action, 15 July 1947, AFM, vol. 407, pp. 60 and 64. Other office-bearers were: Shaikh Rahman Bakhsh and Abdul Hamid as vice-presidents; Ashraf Ali Fazil, Abdul Ghani and Abdul Karim as joint secretaries; and Munshi M. Ramzan as treasurer.

549. For resolution making these demands that Abdur Rahman Khan, general secretary, Anjuman-i-Ittehad-i-Islam, sent to the GoI with a copy to Jinnah, 19 May 1938, see QAP, F. 899, pp. 163–64. The Congress had pressed the demand by the Coorg Congressmen for the formation of Coorg into a separate province and held in abeyance the resolution of its own working committee passed at Haripura recommending its amalgamation with Madras.

550. Abdul Majid Khan to Quaid-i-Azam, 12 August 1942, ibid., F. 569, pp. 1–2.

551. For details, see Aziz Siddiqi to Zakir Ali, 18 August 1942, AFM, vol. 302, nos. 35, 36, 39 and 40. Bangalore was a cantonment directly under the crown through the governor-general.

552. Hasan Mosanna to Zakir Ali, n.d., ibid., no. 58; and also see ibid., vol. 341.

553. The council also elected two vice-presidents (M.M. Siddiq and Abdul Hamid Cassim), two joint secretaries (Modi Abdul Sobhan and Abdul Majid Khan), and one treasurer (Abdus Salam). Ismail Tabish to Nawab Ismail, 7 February 1944, ibid., vol. 417, pp. 62–63; and see also vol. 341, nos. 32 and 33.

554. For his presidential address on 21 February 1945, see ibid., vol. 341, no. 62.

555. For a resolution of the provincial Muslim League to this effect and response of the Government of India, see ibid., pp. 77 and 79.

556. For details, see H.M. Ismail Tabish to secretary, committee of action, All-India Muslim League, 12 November 1946, ibid., vol. 182, no. 38.

557. For other office-bearers, see QAP, F 561, p. 33; and AFM, vol. 216, no 56.

558. Mazharuddin to Jinnah, 23 June 1938, QAP, F. 375, pp. 1–2; Shujaul Haq to Liaquat, 24 July 1938, AFM, vol. 216, no. 26; and also see nos. 24, 25, 31–33 and 46–51; and press clipping from the Ansari, 23 June 1938, ibid., vol. 375, p. 3. The British had taken over the Fatehpuri mosque and the Bangash serai, a building on the western side of the mosque, during the 1857 uprising. In 1862, the mosque and the Sarai were handed over to a ten-member management committee. The Sarai was auctioned and purchased by Chunnamall and Saligram; and when, in 1935, Seth L.N. Gadodia purchased it, the Muslims started an agitation for the Pushta,

a passage between the mosque and the Sarai. The management committee filed a lawsuit, and then arrived at a compromise with Gadodia who agreed to provide a space of four feet between the two buildings. The Delhi provincial Muslim League revived the agitation and campaigned against Rashid Ahmad, a municipal commissioner of Delhi and member of the management committee of the mosque, for reaching an agreement on the Pushta.

559. For other office-bearers, see ibid., no 65.

560. For factionalism and defeat in the municipal elections, see ibid., vol. 223, nos. 40–43.

561. For a resolution of the working committee, see ibid., vol. 122, no. 47; and for 'Report of the Enquiry Committee', 14 May 1940, see ibid., vol. 223, no. 19.

562. Volumes 367–69 of the AFM contain documents relating to these elections.

563. For the activities of the civil defence committee, see ibid., vol. 310, pp. 1–2, 9–12 and 28.

564. Ibid., 408, pp. 11, 18–19 and 27.

565. The party elected four vice-presidents (Waheeduddin, Abdul Wahid Usmani, Ghazi Anwarul Haq, and Mian M. Bashir), four joint secretaries (Sikandar Mirza, Rafi Kalia, Abdul Baqi and Idris Ahmad Qadri), one office secretary (M. Jamilur Rahman) and one treasurer (Nawab Qadeeruddin Ahmad).

566. AFM, vol. 410, pp. 1, 2, 9, and 56.

567. Ibid., vol. 408, pp. 85–89 and 92–93; vol. 410, pp. 58–60; and vol. 413, p. 1.

568. For an invitation from the Sri Lanka Muslim League to Jinnah to visit that country, see QAP, F. 936, p. 28; and for the amendment, see Waheed, *Nation's Voice*, vol. III, p. 682.

569. For his letter to Jinnah, 22 April 1939, QAP, F. 48, p. 12.

570. On 10 January 1945, the central committee of action deferred consideration of a proposal to establish a League branch in London.

571. Ahmad Saeed, *Quaid-i-Azam: Rare Letters*, p. 167. On 26 September 1946, Ali Mohammad wrote to Jinnah, 'I understand you want to help the League branch here so that it may be able to convert more efficiently and quickly the public opinion in favour of Muslim India. Moreover, I think it will become an indispensable and most important branch of the League in case the All-India Muslim League is outlawed.' Ibid., F. 575, pp. 3–6.

572. Ibid., F. 575, p. 9.

573. For Jinnah's response to a request to this effect from Bhopal, see *Civil & Military Gazette*, 20 September 1938.

574. QAP, F. 900, pp. 16–18; and AFM, vol. 128, no. 30.

575. QAP, F. 812, p. 169.

576. Ibid., F. 74, pp. 5–11.

577. Resolution of the All-India Muslim League working committee passed on 2–3 1939, AFM, vol. 128, no. 30.

578. *The Light*, 24 September 1938; *Evening News* (Bombay), 19 September 1938; and *Star of India*, 8 April 1939. For a resolution of the All-India Muslim League council passed on 5 December 1939, see AFM, vol. 122, p. 53.

579. Malik Barkat Ali to Jinnah, 7 August 1938, QAP, F. 1095, p. 348; and Manzare Alam Ansari, general secretary, All-India Muslim Students Federation to Liaquat, 26 March 1939, AFM, vol. 227, no. 14.

580. Bahadur Yar Jung to Jinnah, 19 July 1942, SHC, Hd-II: 43.

581. *IAR*, 1941, vol. I, pp. 42–43; SHC, Hd-II: 37–38: and QAP, F. 319, pp. 31, 38 and 45–46.

582. For Bahadur Yar Jung–Nizam conflict, see QAP, F. 29, pp. 10–21, 26–31 and 45–49; F. 30, pp. 1–16; F. 319, pp. 31 and 45–46; and F. 395, p. 8.
583. Nawab Siddiq Ali Khan, *Be Taigh Sipahi*, Karachi, 1971, p. 106; and also see Qazi Isa to Jinnah, 21 January 1944, *Jinnah Papers*, Second Series, vol. X, p. 130.
584. Bahadur Yar Jung to Jinnah, 7 March 1940, QAP, F. 1092, pp. 59–60; and Jinnah to Syed Maqbool Ahmad (Mysore state), 25 October 1944, ibid., F. 982, p. 6.
585. SHC, Hd-II: 47.
586. For its demands during Jinnah–Linlithgow talks and Cripps Mission, see *IAR*, 1942, vol. I, pp. 67–68.
587. Jinnah to Bahadur Yar Jung, 6 September 1943, SHC, Hd-II: 59.
588. Manzare Alam to Jinnah, 9 and 19 March 1947; and Jinnah to Manzare Alam, 24 March 1947, QAP, F. 227, pp. 23–24. Earlier, following the Bihar massacre, he had given a similar answer to Ghulam Bhik Nairang who had drawn his attention to the condition of the Muslims in the Alwar State. Nairang to Jinnah, 18 October 1947; and Jinnah to Nairang, 8 November 1947, SHC, Pb-III: 68–69.

PART THREE

9

Reluctance at Recognition, 1940–1945

The Lahore Resolution embodied basically three principles: one, establishment of a Muslim homeland in the Muslim majority regions in the north-west and north-east of the Indian subcontinent; two, 'adequate, effective and mandatory' safeguards for the minorities in the partitioned states; and three, the initiation of a constitution-making process based on these principles for the Pakistan regions. The second and third principles were dependent upon the acceptance of the first principle. The Leaguers tentatively expressed their views on both these principles but the League did not address them because its struggle was focused on the acceptance of the first principle. The tripartite British–All-India Muslim League–Congress negotiations were held in two phases: the first phase began soon after the adoption of the Lahore Resolution and ended with the Simla conference in June–July 1945; and the second phase started after the general elections of 1945–46 and concluded with the creation of Pakistan. The premise of the Pakistan demand was that the Muslims of India constituted a 'nation' by any definition of that term and had the right to have a separate homeland in the two Muslim majority regions of the subcontinent. The British as well as the Congress leadership never accepted that premise. But despite almost insurmountable odds, the All-India Muslim League under Jinnah's leadership did not relent from its position on fully sovereign Pakistan with its own Armed Forces because, it upheld, the principles of the Lahore Resolution provided the only long-lasting basis for the settlement of the Hindu–Muslim problem. It perceived and interpreted even the minutest sign from any quarter of a possible division of India as a step towards its goal. When the British and Congress leaders reluctantly conceded the Pakistan demand and agreed to partition India, it was, according to them, a territorially-based division while the All-India Muslim League believed it otherwise.

(A) BRITISH GOVERNMENT AND THE DEMAND FOR PAKISTAN

The British had viewed India as a 'jewel' in the crown and considered themselves as the unifiers of its socially, ethnically and religiously divided communities into one entity and had provided them political stability, after over a century of anarchy, and a political system based on strong institutions of civil bureaucracy and Armed Forces. They could not visualize its partition that, they believed, would destroy its unity and institutions and looked forward to leaving India, if they had to, united and did not care whether it had a unitary, federal or a confederal system.[1] Their will to keep it under their control by force had gradually waned, as their youth had been fast losing interest even before the Second World War in serving the traditionally peaceful and lucrative positions in the higher bureaucracy and the armed forces in India partly because of the rising and competing aspirations for freedom and self-rule of the politically conscious Indians and the increasing communal tensions that often led to violence.[2] The war had accelerated that process. Henceforth, their focus was on protecting their commercial and strategic interests for the future. In addition to these factors, some British politicians were apprehensive of the possible impact of a Muslim state particularly in the north-west of India and its proximity with the West Asian and Central Asian Muslim states on pan-Islamic sentiments and the proposed partition of Palestine and the creation of a state for the Jews. However, immediately the British devoted their energies on the mobilization of the Indian resources for the war. Like the British, the Hindus, the caste Hindus in particular, and the Congress believed in the indivisibility of India, the Bharat Mata, and visualized a unitary democratic parliamentary system of government after independence.

Before 23 March 1940, the All-India Muslim League had considered the British policy about the future constitution, as conveyed by the viceroy in his announcement of 18 October 1939, and in his letter to Jinnah on 23 December, unsatisfactory because it did not meet its demand for 'a definite assurance' that 'no declaration should, either in principle or otherwise, be made or any constitution be enforced' by the British government or enacted by the parliament 'without the approval and consent' of the Muslims of India, and that the League did not want to leave the 'final decision' about the 'fate and future of Muslim India' in the hands of Britain. The League working committee asked Jinnah to get assurances from the viceroy to 'remove all doubts and apprehensions from the mind of Muslim India'.[3] Jinnah did that in his meeting with Linlithgow on 6 February 1940, and waited for his response.[4] Soon after, the All-India Muslim League adopted the Lahore Resolution as its goal and observed Friday, 19 April, as the 'Muslim Independence Day' to confirm popular support for its demand for 'Muslim self-determination'.[5] Its branches all over India, from the primary to the provincial level, organized over 10,000 meetings throughout India on that day in support of the Lahore Resolution.[6] But this did not have much effect on the British thinking; and as a forewarning to the League, on 18 April, several members of parliament commented on the Lahore Resolution in the parliament. None of them, whether Conservative, Labour or Liberal, spoke a word in its support. Wedgwood Benn (Labour) plainly stated that the division of India on the basis of race and religion was a 'perfectly hopeless' proposition and would 'not find any support' in Britain, and Lord Zetland (secretary of state for India) called it a 'counsel of despair', as he believed in the 'vision of a united India'.[7] Linlithgow termed it 'as no more than a bargaining counter'; his response, therefore, was similar to the one that he had given earlier and so was the case of the new secretary of state for India, L.S. Amery (1873–1955) who spoke on similar lines in the House of Commons on 23 May.[8] The Congress denunciation of the Lahore Resolution was equally forthright and vehement. Its proposal for a united stand of the political parties and the 'conference' of Azad, its newly elected president, with the Muslim premiers on 13 June, was meant to subvert the League solidarity and the Pakistan scheme.

The All-India Muslim League planned its strategy in this unfriendly and hostile environment. It was not deterred by the negative reaction that the Lahore Resolution generated; Jinnah vowed, 'Whether they [British and Hindus] agree or whether they do not, we shall fight for it [Pakistan] to the last ditch'.[9] He kept the line of communication with the viceroy, promising Linlithgow that he would place his letter of 19 April, before the central working committee for consideration and communicate its views to him 'as soon as possible'.[10] The League expressed its unwillingness to extend all-out support in the war effort until the British government had given it satisfactory assurances about the future constitution and a fair share in governance at the centre and in the provinces.

(*i*) *War Committees, Intra-League Tension and the August Offer*. The British government was keen to mobilize every element of the Indian society in the war effort and formulated its policy keeping in view the conflicting standpoints of the League and the Congress on the future constitution. During the war, it did that by conciliatory, persuasive and coercive techniques. After India's entry into the war, some governors constituted war boards or committees; and on 5 June 1940, the viceroy announced a uniform policy of forming war committees in every district of India primarily to disseminate information about recruitment and for the collection of funds for the war. This policy divided the Leaguers: some of them particularly the pro-British and those in power in the provinces were in favour of unconditional support to Britain in the war effort, ready to ignore any assurances about the future constitution—the British Indian administration naturally encouraged such elements, while the others were also willing to extend support but after they had received firm assurances about the future constitution and had a fair share in governance. The delay in the British response caused an intra-League rift.[11] Jinnah handled the situation with tact and patience. He asked the Leaguers not to join the war committees because the British government had not consulted the League in formulating this scheme, and convened a meeting of the working committee to take a policy decision.[12] On 15–17 June, the working committee discussed the political situation and the viceroy's letter of 19 April. It was pointed out that even as early as November 1939, the League was willing to consider the viceroy's proposal of joining the provincial governments followed by appointment of its representatives on his executive council and had left the provinces where it was in power free to cooperate with the government, pending satisfactory assurances about its demands, but the Congress had rejected that proposal. And the viceroy showed 'no real trust' in Muslim leadership and his attitude conveyed the impression as if the British government were waiting for a positive response from the Congress. The League working committee was of the view that no useful purpose would be served by joining the executive council and provincial governments or the war committees unless close cooperation was agreed on an all-India basis, and not province-wise, between the Government of India and the All-India Muslim League and such other parties as were willing to cooperate, and authorized Jinnah to communicate with the viceroy in this regard. It called on the Leaguers not to serve on the war committees and wait for instructions from the president, pending the result of his talks with the viceroy.[13]

Jinnah placed 'tentative proposals' of the All-India Muslim League, which had been confidentially discussed in its working committee, before the viceroy in his interview with him on 27 June 1940, and, four days later, on 1 July, sent a 'private and personal' memorandum to his private secretary, Gilbert J. Laithwaite. It was represented in the memorandum that (i) the Lahore Resolution had become 'the universal faith of Muslim India', and the British government should not make any announcement that would in any way militate against its 'basic and fundamental principles' and assure the Muslims that no interim or final scheme of constitution would be adopted without their prior approval; (ii) for the duration of the war, the government should expand the executive council within the framework of the present constitution and the Muslims should have equal representation with the Hindus on the executive council if the Congress came in, otherwise they should have a majority, as the main burden and responsibility would then be borne by them; (iii) a majority of non-official advisers should be Muslims in the (former Congress-governed Hindu majority) provinces where section 93 was in operation and adjustments by agreement could be made in the provinces where governments were run by coalitions; (iv) a war council, and not a war advisory council, with equal representation of Muslims and Hindus if the Congress came in, otherwise with a Muslim majority, should advise the government on defence and related matters; the rulers of the princely states could join such a council; and (v) the League should have the right to nominate all the Muslim representatives on the executive council, the war council and the non-official advisers of the governors in the provinces under section 93.[14] The League did not make the acceptance of the Pakistan demand, the 'sheet anchor' of Muslim India, a 'condition precedent' because it did not want 'to embarrass' the British government when it was engaged 'in a struggle of life and death' and decided to wait for its acceptance after the end of hostilities.[15] The viceroy, in his reply on 6 July, noted the League's proposals but disputed its position on various points and declined to accept its right to nominate all the Muslim representatives.[16] However, he promised Jinnah that the British government would give the League's proposals 'full consideration'. Jinnah, in his reply on 17 July, upheld that there was nothing in the memorandum that could not be implemented by way of convention, and if the viceroy and secretary of state for India showed a 'spirit of trust and cooperation' in the

Muslims the legal and constitutional bottlenecks could be overcome. The League waited for the British response. Conversely, the Congress working committee, at a meeting in Delhi on 3–7 July, and the All India Congress Committee at its Poona session on 28 July, demanded acknowledgement of complete independence of India and as an immediate step formation of a provisional national government commanding 'the confidence of all the elected elements in the central legislature' and enjoying 'the closest cooperation of the responsible governments in the provinces'.[17] Gandhi communicated the Congress demands to the viceroy.

Meanwhile, the intra-League conflict intensified, not without encouragement from the official quarters and the Congress, which posed a threat to its internal cohesion.[18] Some Leaguers including premiers Fazlul Haq and Sikandar, who had met Azad on 13 June, advocated that the Leaguers should join the war committees without any reservation and pressed Jinnah to forge a united stand of all the political parties on the issue. They stuck to their position even after the decision of the central working committee not to join the war committees. Sikandar publicly asserted that the working committee had allowed the Punjab and Bengal Leaguers to serve on the war committees; consequently, some Leaguers including the Punjab provincial Muslim League president, Nawab Shahnawaz Mamdot, joined the war committees.[19] Jinnah immediately contradicted Sikandar's interpretation and prohibited the Leaguers from joining the war committees.[20] Shahnawaz not only complied with his directive and resigned from the war committee but several Leaguers on the direction of the Punjab provincial Muslim League working committee refrained from serving on the war committees; and similar was the response of the Leaguers in other provinces.[21] While Fazlul Haq wrote to Jinnah on 24 June, that the prohibitory decision was 'impolitic and inadvisable in the present circumstances' and asked for its review by the working committee; otherwise, the 'most ardent Leaguers', he warned, might leave the League.[22] Then, both Fazlul Haq and Sikandar jointly urged Jinnah to cooperate with the British government and accept power at the centre, suggesting that the League would unanimously insist on the viceroy to include Jinnah in the central cabinet.[23] Jinnah was neither deterred nor tempted by these tactics; he considered it 'incompatible' with Muslim 'self-respect' to cooperate with a government that was not prepared 'to show trust' in them and share with them 'the authority and control at the centre and in the provinces' whether the Congress came in or not; the Muslims could not, he wrote to a Leaguer, 'be reduced to the position of hangers on of the system'.[24] Sikandar encouraged some Punjab Leaguers to raise the standard of revolt. On 16 July, thirty-five, and on 23 July, fifteen members of the central council from the Punjab requisitioned a meeting of the council; the requisitionists in both the notices wanted consideration of three resolutions, that: (i) instructions should be issued to the Leaguers all over India to participate in the war committees; (ii) if the reply of the British government to the League demands was to the satisfaction of the working committee, the League should not break negotiations merely on the question of personalities so long as the appointments on the executive council and in the provincial governments were made from among the Leaguers; and (iii) the working committee should select five Leaguers to confer with representatives of other political parties if they showed a desire to negotiate with the All-India Muslim League for the settlement of political and communal issues.[25] Sikandar actively promoted this move and sent emissaries to other provinces to get proxy votes in support of these resolutions.[26] Jinnah was 'disappointed' by Sikandar's attitude and activities and felt 'sad' for him.[27] The Leaguers who were opposed to this move launched their own campaign to counter it.[28]

The delay in the British response hurt the League because the contents of its 1 July memorandum had not been made public.[29] Jinnah was conscious of this fact but Linlithgow had asked him not to reveal its contents.[30] Finally, on 2 August 1940, he wrote to Linlithgow, 'how long do you expect me to wait and not give any idea to the general Muslim public as to what are the [the League's] proposals?' The publication of the League's proposals that it had made to the British government, he wrote, could not create 'any misunderstanding with regard to your position'.[31] Two days later, on 4 August, the viceroy was keen to meet Jinnah during his visit to Bombay;[32] and the next day, the Punjab councillors withdrew both the requisition notices for the council meeting, which even otherwise Jinnah as the League president had disallowed.[33] Then, the Punjab provincial Muslim League sent a three-member (Nawab Shahnawaz Mamdot, Ghazanfar Ali and Mohammad Ali Jafri) deputation to Jinnah in Bombay 'to explain the peculiar conditions' of the Punjab but Jinnah was not convinced and declined to exempt the Punjab Leaguers from the ban.[34] Before Jinnah's meeting with Linlithgow on 12 August, the viceroy had made the momentous two-part announcement of the British policy on 8 August, better known as the August Offer. The first part of the offer went beyond reiterating the October 1939 British assurances, promising dominion status for India after the war and giving 'full weight' to the views of the minorities in any revision of the Act of 1935, or the policy on which it was based; the August Offer provided that the British government 'could not contemplate the transfer of their present responsibilities for the peace and welfare of India to any system of government whose authority is directly denied by large and powerful elements in India's national life. Nor could they be parties to the coercion of such elements into submission to such a government'.[35] Amery (secretary of state for India), clarifying this announcement in the parliament on 14 August, made an important observation that 'India cannot be unitary in the sense that we are in this island . . . India's future house of freedom has room for many mansions'.[36] The All-India Muslim League perceived in the viceroy's announcement and Amery's clarification a positive sign in support of its demand; therefore, it expressed satisfaction that the British government had met its demand for a clear assurance that 'no future constitution, interim or final, will be adopted by the British government without the Muslim League's approval and consent'.[37] Henceforth, the League considered this part of the August Offer sacrosanct, regarding it as a British pledge to the Muslims, the minorities and the princes, and strongly opposed any move at its revision or replacement. However, it criticized the comments in the viceroy's announcement and secretary of state for India's clarification about 'the theory of unity of national life', which it regarded 'historically inaccurate and self-contradictory', and reiterated its faith in the Lahore Resolution, which, it believed, was the only solution of the 'complex problem of India's future constitution'.[38] On the other hand, the Congress denounced the August Offer and missed no opportunity to get it quashed. Its leaders never forgave Linlithgow whom they considered instrumental in its promulgation.

The second part of the August Offer authorized the viceroy to expand his executive council to include representative Indians and establish a war advisory council, which would have representatives of the princely states as well, but deferred a decision on the appointment of advisers to governors in the provinces under section 93 to a later date.[39] When Jinnah met Linlithgow on 12 August, he did not get 'a complete picture' of the executive council or the war advisory council, as the latter himself did not yet have the details. Subsequently, it was tentatively suggested that the League would have two out of possibly eleven members of the executive council for which it was to give a panel of four names; Sir Mohammad Zafrullah Khan was not to be counted in the League quota if he remained in the executive council, and five out twenty on the war advisory council.[40] The League considered the British offer regarding the executive council and the war advisory council as 'unsatisfactory', and authorized Jinnah to seek 'further information and clarification' from the viceroy. Jinnah met Linlithgow again on 24 September, but failed to get exact information about either the executive council or the war advisory council or any satisfactory answer on the point that if any party decided to join the executive council at a later stage it would be allowed to do so on terms that had the approval of the All-India Muslim League; and the government also refused to associate non-official advisers to governors in the provinces under section 93.[41] The only concession was on a minor point that the nominees of the League, and for that matter of any other party if it so desired, would be selected by confidential discussion between the leader of that party and the viceroy.[42] Since the demand about the future constitution had been met in the first part of the August Offer, the League working committee allowed those of its members who felt that they could serve 'any useful purpose' by associating themselves with the war committees to do so. Simultaneously, it appointed a subcommittee to take disciplinary action against those Leaguers who had earlier acted against the working committee's resolution regarding the war committees; consequently, six members, three from the Punjab and three from Bengal, were expelled from the League.[43]

On 28 September 1940, the All-India Muslim League working committee, and the next day its council, rejected the British offer in regard to the executive council and the war advisory council, despite its 'desire to help in the prosecution of war'. It gave four reasons for the rejection, that (*i*) the inclusion of only two League members in the executive council whose portfolios as well as total strength of the executive council had not yet been finally determined did not give the League real share in governance at the centre; (*ii*) no indication had been given as to the position of the League members in case any other party decided to join the executive council at a later stage, which might require its reshuffling; (*iii*) real and effective cooperation of the Muslims could not be secured in the provinces under section 93 unless nonofficial advisers were associated with the governors which the government had refused to appoint; and (*iv*) the war advisory council was still in embryo, except that its strength would probably be twenty, and its formation would be taken up after the expansion of the executive council was complete.[44] Jinnah denounced the British policy which did not care for the Muslim support on 'an honourable basis' but he and the Leaguers did not indulge in any anti-war rhetoric; in fact, he clarified that the League's rejection did not mean non-cooperation in the war effort.[45] The League tactfully preserved its internal unity that had been under severe strain since the viceroy's announcement about the war committees. On the other hand, the Congress cohesion remained under constant strain. Subhas Chandra Bose's forward bloc that he had formed to unite the left wing and anti-imperialist elements within the Congress after his resignation from its presidency on 1 May 1939, followed by his exit from the party; and the supporters of his viewpoint after his self-imposed exile kept up the pressure and deeply influenced the Congress policies. Several of the Congress moves—its demand for the declaration of war aims, its decision to launch individual Satyagraha for the sake of 'liberty of speech' and its Quit India movement—were partially influenced by this pressure; these moves also displayed its desire to sidetrack the Pakistan scheme. After the rejection of the British offer, the All-India Muslim League and the Congress expressed their resentment against the government during the debate on the supplementary finance bill in the central assembly in November 1940. As a result, the finance bill was rejected by 55 to 53 votes; the Congress voted for the motion and the League assembly party abstained from voting.

A deadlock followed after that. Linlithgow announced that he would keep the expansion of the executive council and formation of the war advisory council on hold till sufficient representative support was available. Now Gandhi assumed active leadership of the Congress, which decided at Wardha to launch 'individual Satyagraha' to force the British government to accept its demands. The individual Satyagraha led to the incarceration of top Congress leaders and workers. The All-India Muslim League did not opt for this kind of strategy although Jinnah did warn the British government, 'We [the Muslims] may be less in numbers and we are; but we could give you . . . hundred times more trouble than the Congress . . . if we desire or determine; but we do not want to [do so].'[46] The League used the period that followed the stalemate to strengthen its organization, consolidate its support-base and popularize the Pakistan scheme at the grassroots. Jinnah declared that Pakistan, which had been 'an article' of his faith, was now the goal for which the Muslims would 'live for and, if necessary, die for' because it was a struggle for the very 'soul of the Muslim nation', and refuted Linlithgow's assertion and the Congress propaganda that it was 'a counter for bargaining'.[47] He repeatedly made similar observations in his speeches and in private correspondence. Whenever a statement about the unity of India emanated from any responsible British quarter, the League did not let it go unchallenged. When Amery (secretary of state for India), in his speeches in December 1940, made remarks about the unity of India and against its division, the League's working committee and council strongly criticized him, terming his pronouncements against the British promises to the Muslims, and reaffirmed its adherence to the Lahore Resolution.[48] Another issue on which the League turned its attention during the war was aggression against the Muslim countries and their occupation by the allied powers.[49] The League branches all over India observed 1 November 1940, the last Friday of the month of Ramzan, as the 'Muslim Countries Day' to express the Indian Muslims' sympathy and support for the Muslim countries and to put across their dissatisfaction with the British policy in Palestine. Jinnah's interview on that day to the representative of the *News Chronicle* was censored and not allowed to reach London; in that interview, he had simply asked the Indian Muslims to help their 'Muslim brethren wherever they are, from China to Peru,' because Islam enjoined them to do so and to organize themselves in various fields—social, economic and political.[50]

(*ii*) *National Defence Council.* The British government was keen to break the deadlock and associate with the official bodies those Indian political parties and personalities that were not pursuing a policy of non-cooperation. The All-India Muslim League was one such party but it opposed association of its members with the official bodies because the government had not trusted it with any real share in governance.[51] Jinnah strictly followed this policy. In March 1941, when the defence secretary of the Government of India invited him to nominate two Leaguers on a team of the central legislature that was to visit military installations and institutions in the country, he declined to do that because it was against the League policy.[52] And when the government included a League member of the council of state (Husain Imam) in the defence consultative committee, he immediately asked him to resign and that member followed his directive.[53] Early in July, Linlithgow and Amery, after a lull of about ten months, worked out a

A HISTORY OF THE ALL-INDIA MUSLIM LEAGUE

scheme for the expansion of the executive council from seven to twelve members with the strength of the Indian members raised from three to eight and formation of a thirty-member national defence council ostensibly in pursuance of the August Offer. Linlithgow disregarded the League policy in the formulation of this scheme, and successfully persuaded three League premiers—Sikandar Hayat (Punjab), Fazlul Haq (Bengal) and Saadulla (Assam)—and prominent Leaguers— Nawab Ahmad Saeed Chhatari, Sir Sultan Ahmad and Begum Jahan Ara Shahnawaz—to accept membership of the national defence council and executive council. The whole scheme was prepared in secrecy: neither the viceroy took the League into confidence in its preparation nor did the League premiers and prominent Leaguers inform Jinnah when they accepted membership of these bodies.[54]

On 20 July 1941, when the scheme had been finalized, Linlithgow thought of informing Jinnah 'in advance'. He asked Sir Roger Lumley (governor of Bombay), to apprise Jinnah orally of its details. But Lumley was not 'entirely fit' to deliver Linlithgow's message to Jinnah in person. He had to communicate the message through a letter that he sent to Jinnah by a special messenger. Jinnah received the letter on the morning of 21 July. The viceroy in his message conveyed that he had decided to expand the executive council due to 'pressure of work' in connection with the war and to constitute a national defence council to associate 'non-official Indian opinion' with the prosecution of the war; and that Muslim premiers and 'persons of the highest eminence' had been invited to serve on the executive council as representatives of 'the great Muslim community'. Jinnah responded the same day; he deeply regretted the decision and disapproved the tactics that had been used to secure the consent of the League premiers and prominent Leaguers because it would embarrass the League and hoped that the viceroy would 'avoid such a contingency'. It was 'hardly fair or proper', Jinnah wrote, that the viceroy should have approached members of the League over the head of its president and executive, knowing fully well the policy of the All-India Muslim League. It would neither be creditable for a Leaguer to accept membership of any of these bodies contrary to the policy of his party nor would it do any credit to the government if it succeeded in alluring that member, thus creating a breach in the League. Persistence in this action, he wrote, would cause bitterness in the League-government relations that had so far been non-existent, however emphatically the League had disapproved the official policy.[55] Jinnah's protest could not block the scheme; and on 21 July, it was issued in a communiqué. His public comments on the scheme were the same that he had communicated to the viceroy in private, maintaining that the scheme was similar to the one that the All-India Muslim League had rejected on 28 September 1940, and that it would not secure the 'wholehearted, willing and genuine support' of Muslim India.[56]

The scheme was likely to break the solidarity of the All-India Muslim League and undermine the legitimate authority of its president. Premiers Sikandar and Fazlul Haq believed that they had been taken on the national defence council in their official capacity and not as representatives of the Muslim community or the League; therefore, they publicly asserted that they had not violated the party discipline.[57] Quite a few Leaguers thought on similar lines.[58] But Jinnah who was privy to the background of the scheme through the viceroy's message viewed it otherwise; he felt that those who had accepted the executive council and national defence council membership had gone against the party policy and called on them to resign or face disciplinary action.[59] Amery's remarks in the house of commons confirmed Jinnah's viewpoint: then, on 22 July, in reply to a question from Reginald W. Sorensen, the prime minister himself boasted that 'in spite of the Muslim League, the viceroy had succeeded in securing the cooperation of many representative men, some of whom were members of the Muslim League'; and on 1 August, he made the provocative remarks, 'I am glad to think that regardless of party leaders and in defiance of party discipline patriotic Indians have come forward to work for India's defence.'[60] The All-India Muslim League could not accept this attack on the integrity of its leadership. Jinnah had the authority, according to a resolution of the Madras annual session, to take disciplinary action against those who had accepted the scheme but he preferred to decide the issue in a meeting of the working committee on 24 August; the item of disciplinary action against the three premiers and prominent Leaguers was at the top of its 'confidential' agenda. There was widespread popular support for the disciplinary action. The district Muslim Leagues, city Muslim Leagues and Muslim Students Federations appreciated Jinnah's statement of 22 July, and urged him to expel those who had accepted executive council and national defence council memberships.[61] Some Punjab Leaguers sent a four-member [Nawab Shahnawaz Mamdot, Sir Mehr Shah, Raja Ghazanfar Ali and Mir Maqbool Mahmud (1897–1948)] deputation on behalf of the Muslim members of the legislative assembly of the Punjab to Bombay to represent their viewpoint before the League president to ward off any disciplinary action. Jinnah held Linlithgow responsible for the dissensions in the League ranks.[62] His meeting with him on 16 August, was not very comfortable; Linlithgow tried to convince him that the Muslim premiers had been taken in their official capacity. But the viceroy must have been embarrassed when Jinnah pointed out that none had made any assertion to that effect so far and that it was contrary to the message that he had received through Governor Lumley. Jinnah asked Linlithgow to send for a copy of the message that he had sent to verify the veracity of his statement but the viceroy saved himself from embarrassment by saying that he would look up the message. On 28 August, Jinnah released the viceroy's message, his own reply and an account of his meeting with the viceroy to the press.

The controversy surrounding the Leaguers' acceptance of the executive council and national defence council membership momentarily overshadowed the League's response to the viceroy's scheme. On 24–26 August, when the working committee met in Bombay to discuss the issue, Jinnah read out the viceroy's message that he had received through Lumley. Sikandar who was present in the meeting after listening to the message immediately decided to resign from the national defence council; subsequently, he explained his resignation in a press statement and Jinnah then advised him not to entertain and accept any fresh proposal without consulting him.[63] Saadulla who had not attended the meeting asked for a copy of the viceroy's message and resigned on its receipt. The working committee decided to serve the other Leaguers with ten days' notice to resign or face disciplinary action, and authorized Jinnah to take necessary action. Fazlul Haq submitted his resignation very reluctantly and after a bitter controversy.[64] All the others except Sir Sultan Ahmad and Begum Shahnawaz resigned. Jinnah expelled Sultan Ahmad from the party for five years 'to maintain and secure discipline and correct standard of public life'.[65] Begum Shahnawaz put up the plea that she had been taken 'as a representative of the women and the Punjab'; but Jinnah did not accept her explanation, communicating to her telegraphically, 'cannot cut yourself up [into] different capacities to flout [the League's] mandate. Please comply [with the] working committee's resolution without delay. Clear ten days' notice expires [on] 10 September.' On her refusal to resign, Jinnah expelled her from the party for five years.[66] The working committee also passed a resolution on the scheme. It deplored that the viceroy had gone out of his way to canvass members of the League to secure their association with the scheme behind the back of the League president, knowing that the All-India Muslim League had rejected a similar scheme and Jinnah had communicated that decision to him. The scheme, the working committee recorded, had been resuscitated as a concession to the Hindus and in utter disregard of the wishes of the Muslims of India and the solemn promises made to them by the British government. It condemned Amery's remarks in the house of commons made in his speech on 1 August, and expressed its alarm that the British government would permit the secretary of state for India and 'a responsible minister of the Crown' to make pronouncements which amounted to 'breach of faith with Muslim India'. Quoting from the viceroy's announcement of 8 August, and secretary of state for India's speeches, it expressed the belief that the British government would not prejudge the constitutional issue and resolve it by 'agreement between the principal parties'.[67]

On 26–27 October 1941, the All-India Muslim League council endorsed the decisions of the working committee and appointed a five-member (Jinnah, Liaquat, Nawab Ismail and G.M. Sayed and Maulana Akram Khan) committee to decide, in consultation with the League assembly party, the course of action that the League should adopt in the central legislature to show its resentment against the attitude of the viceroy and the British government in the way the scheme was devised and carried out.[68] The working committee decided that the League should withdraw from the central legislature for the remaining period of the autumn session to register its protest, after the League leaders in the central assembly and the council of state had made a statement about the boycott. On 28 October, when the central assembly opened its proceedings, Jinnah made a brief hard-hitting statement about the way Muslim offer of cooperation had been treated, and appealed to the government and the press not to misrepresent the League because it was 'the government, and government alone' that was responsible for the deadlock. The British government talked of cooperation, he said, on such terms that 'no self-respecting man could accept'. After making the statement, he along with other members of his party walked out of the central assembly. Two weeks later, on 11 November, the League members in the council of state staged a similar walk-out, following a brief statement by their leader, Husain Imam.[69] Jinnah, addressing the Aligarh Muslim University students' union on 2 November, declared that Pakistan was not 'a mere slogan or a counter for bargaining',— denouncing such propaganda as the 'most reprehensible lie'—but like the Atlantic Charter, it was a charter for the Indian Muslims for which they would 'sacrifice anything and everything'.[70] Two weeks later, the working committee urged the British government not to take any further step or make any adjustment in future 'even within the framework of the present constitution' without the approval and consent of the All-India Muslim League and warned that any action taken without its approval would be 'deeply resented' and the responsibility for the consequences would be entirely that of the government.[71] The British response came on 15 December, when Linlithgow, in a speech in Calcutta, reaffirmed the policy enunciated in the August Offer. The stalemate, however, continued till March 1942, when the war cabinet devised fresh proposals and sent Sir Stafford Cripps (1889–1952) to India to talk to the viceroy and the Indian political leaders to work out an agreement.[72]

(*iii*) *Cripps 'Proposals'*. Several factors influenced the British war cabinet to put forward fresh proposals to break the deadlock and attempt to associate the Indian political parties with the war effort. Firstly, the Atlantic Charter of August 1941, that Franklin D. Roosevelt (1882–1945), the US president, and Winston S. Churchill (1874–1965), the British prime minister, had signed advocated the principles of democracy and the right of self-determination; and India could not be denied indefinitely the application of these principles.[73] Roosevelt frequently advised Churchill, especially after the bombing of Pearl harbour on 7 December, to respond to the Indian aspirations.[74] Secondly, there was pressure from the British politicians and the press on the war cabinet for a change in policy towards India.[75] Thirdly, the Congress leaders now seemed amenable to cooperation in the war effort after the failure of the individual Satyagraha.[76] The amnesty given to the Satyagraha prisoners, which came as a great relief to the Congress, resulted in the release of its top leaders including Nehru and Azad.[77] At Bardoli on 23 December, Gandhi admitting failure of the individual Satyagraha had tendered his resignation from the party leadership. The working committee passed resolutions, endorsed by the All India Congress Committee at Wardha, which were perceived to show its readiness to cooperate in the war effort.[78] However, it vehemently opposed the August 1940 declaration, which Nehru wanted 'consigned to the dustbin', and insisted on a new policy.[79] It called for a constitution-making body after the war, elected on the basis of adult franchise, to frame a constitution of free India providing due protection to the minorities. As an interim measure, it wanted a provisional national government functioning as a cabinet responsible to the elected legislature. Fourthly, on 2 January 1942, Sir Tej Bahadur Sapru sent a cable to the British prime minister with copies to the viceroy and the secretary of state for India on behalf of a non-party leaders' conference, signed by him and eleven others, demanding: immediate declaration of India as a unit equal to other units of the British Commonwealth and transformation of the Viceroy's Executive Council into a truly 'national government' representing all the recognized political parties and communities.[80] The Congress supported these demands that were almost similar to its own demands. Fifthly, the allied reverses in the war and rapid advance of the Japanese army in the Far East after the bombing of Pearl Harbour (Singapore fell on 15 February 1942, Rangoon on 8 March, and the Andaman Islands on 23 March), reaching the borders of Assam and eastern Bengal, worried the British government, moving it to seek support of the Indian political parties. Sixthly, the strident anti-Imperialist tone of the speeches by Nehru, whom Gandhi had described at Bardoli as his successor, had an impact on the British and allied leaders. Lastly, the British allies used 'friendly pressure' on the British government to conciliate the Congress to get its wholehearted support in the war. Early in 1942, Marshal Chiang Kai-shek, the Chinese leader and a friend of Nehru, visited India essentially to bring about British–Congress reconciliation. His meetings with Jinnah were meant to cover up the real object of his visit.[81] But he could not hide his pro-Congress proclivities, when he was confronted with Muslim apprehension that his Congress friends had brought him to influence the British to make peace with the Congress.[82] An indirect outcome of Chiang Kai-shek's overt pro-Congress posture was that the Chinese communists began to sympathize with the All-India Muslim League and its ideal.[83]

The All-India Muslim League functioned in an environment that favoured a change in the British policy primarily to win over the Congress. On 27 December 1941, and 22 February 1942, its working committee asked the British government to stick to its August 1940 Declaration, opposed any change that would treat India as 'a single national unit' or 'prejudge and rule out Pakistan', and hoped that the League would not be coerced into accepting a system of government with which it did not agree.[84] Jinnah warned the British government not to force Muslim India to fill the Indian jails 'to convince them' that 'Pakistan is now our sacred creed and article of faith.'[85] The League was then assured that the British would stand by the August 1940 declaration.[86] As a war-time arrangement, Jinnah repeatedly offered to join any government at the centre if the League had 50 per cent seats in, what he preferred to call, 'a co-national or a coalition government, rather than a national government'.[87] At first, Prime Minister Churchill was against putting 'the Congress in charge' because, in his view, its rule and that of the 'Hindoo Priesthood machine would never be tolerated by a fighting race'.[88] And Linlithgow and Amery were in agreement that any 'fresh constitutional advance' would complicate the already difficult war situation and wanted to secure cooperation of the Indian political parties in the war effort within the ambit of the existing policy.[89] The 'war paper' that Amery put up to the war cabinet on 28 January 1942, concluded that 'there was no immediate further interim constitutional advance that we can make. We have in the [August] 1940 Declaration a long-term policy which . . . can achieve a settlement. We cannot go back on pledges which it embodies: our business is to stand by it and expound it confidently and with conviction and not apologetically'.[90] But even after these firm assertions, there was a sudden change after Churchill's visit to Washington (22 December 1941–14 January 1942); and the return of Sir Stafford Cripps, a friend of Nehru and labelled by a critic as the 'English Gandhi' for his pro-Congress sympathies, from his eighteen-month-long diplomatic assignment in Moscow.[91] Attlee and Cripps, who joined the cabinet as the Lord Privy Seal and became leader of the House of Commons, advocated a change in British policy towards India to cultivate the Congress.[92] On 9 February, Churchill after consulting Cripps presented a scheme before the war cabinet that envisaged a defence of India council, elected on the basis of proportional representation by the existing members of the lower houses of the provincial assemblies with due proportion of representatives of the princely states, to help in the war effort; and after the war, this council was to frame a constitution that the British government would accept.[93] His primary aim was to satisfy Roosevelt and his own coalition partners. When Linlithgow received this scheme through the secretary of state for India, he raised quite a few objections; eventually, he was asked to prepare an alternative draft. And Amery endorsed the draft declaration that he produced.[94]

On 28 February 1942, the war cabinet constituted a six-member committee on India to finalize the draft declaration; Attlee was its chairman and Cripps one of its members. The India committee amended the draft in the light of suggestions that it received from different quarters.[95] The final draft provided that the object of the British government was to create a new Indian union that would constitute a dominion after the war equal to other dominions of the British Commonwealth and owing allegiance to the crown. After the war, elections would be held to the provincial assemblies that would elect, unless the Indian leaders of the principal communities agreed upon some other form before the end of hostilities, a constitution-making body to frame a new constitution for India; and the government would accept and implement that constitution forthwith. This constitution-making body would be one-tenth of the electoral college and have representatives of the states as well. Paragraph (c) (i) of the draft gave a province 'that is not prepared to accept the new constitution to retain its present constitutional position, provision being made for its subsequent accession if it so decides'. With such non-acceding provinces, the British government would be prepared to agree upon new constitutional arrangements 'on lines analogous to those here laid down'. The British government was 'to bear full responsibility for the defence of India' till the framing of the constitution and it invited the immediate and effective participation of the leaders of the principal sections of the Indian people in the counsels of India, the Commonwealth and the United Nations.[96] When information about the Hindu pressure for the acceptance of the Congress demands leaked out, Jinnah wrote to Churchill that if the British government intended to make such a move, it should accept the Pakistan demand.[97] Firoz Khan Noon, then member of the executive council, also urged the secretary of state for India through the viceroy that if the British government wanted to declare India a dominion immediately, it must simultaneously concede the Pakistan demand; and if India was to become a dominion after the war, it should be ensured that Muslims would have Pakistan if the Hindus failed to reach an agreement with them, otherwise Muslim India, Noon cautioned, would be up in arms.[98] Endorsing Noon's demand, Amery wrote to Churchill the same day that the non-acceding provinces should have 'an equally good prospect of Dominion status' and proposed an amendment in the draft to make it 'explicit'.[99] Two days later, Jinnah telegraphed a message to Churchill on behalf of the League assembly party that no declaration should be made that would 'prejudice, prejudge or militate in any way against the Muslim demand for Pakistan'.[100] He also wrote to British members of parliament, impressing upon them the need for the acceptance of the Pakistan demand.[101] Although Churchill used Noon's and Jinnah's communications about Pakistan to soften the pressure from Roosevelt, and the 'Memorandum by the SSI', which the India committee approved on 6 March, clearly mentioned two unions that the princely states could join, 'the main [Indian] Union' and the 'Pakistan Union', but the draft that the Attlee-chaired India committee finalized made no explicit provision to that effect.[102] The war cabinet, however, could not ignore the concerns raised by several knowledgeable circles that it would strengthen the League and the Pakistan demand in the Punjab, affect adversely the unity of the armed forces, which had a sizable Muslim component, and spoil Muslim–Sikh relations.[103] Linlithgow's threat of resignation, if the draft did not incorporate his suggestions, was an additional factor.[104] Earlier, Attlee and Cripps were eager to remove Linlithgow from the viceroyalty but that idea was dropped to avoid any impression that he had been 'sacked to please the Congress'.[105] Therefore, on 9 March, the war cabinet deferred the publication of the draft declaration; instead, it accepted Cripps' offer to go to India to have discussions with the viceroy and the Indian political elements to reach an agreement on the draft; and on 11 March, Churchill made an announcement in the house of commons to that effect.[106] The draft declaration was given to Cripps 'as his general instructions'. One point of anxiety for the war cabinet in the selection of Cripps was his pro-Congress past that was likely to generate negative reaction from the League.[107]

Sir Stafford Cripps arrived in Delhi on 23 March 1942 and began his preliminary meetings with the leaders of the political parties. His meeting with Jinnah unexpectedly went off smoothly, as Cripps disarmed the League president 'by apologizing in advance' for his anti-League articles in the *Tribune* of May 1940, saying that they 'represented his views at that time, and if they were wrong he was sorry'.[108] Jinnah tried to allay the apprehensions of the Leaguers about Cripps' partiality, observing that he had come to India as a representative of the British government and not in his personal capacity. We do not know exactly the amendments that Jinnah suggested in the draft but according to Cripps, he wanted the closing words of its paragraph (c) (i) changed to make the possibility of a second dominion 'clearer'. Cripps wrote to the secretary of state for India without taking Jinnah into confidence for the amendment of this paragraph, proposing omission of all words after 'prepared' and their substitution by the words 'to agree upon a new constitution, giving them the same full status as Indian union, and arrived at by a procedure analogous to that here laid down'; the India committee approved the amendment as he proposed.[109] The draft still made no mention of the procedure by which non-accession of a province would be determined. Cripps suggested orally to Jinnah and then at his press conference that after the framing of the constitution the legislative assembly of a province could decide by voting, and that if the vote for accession in a province was less than 60 per cent, then there could be a plebiscite of 'the adult male population' of that province. But his suggestion, Jinnah contended, gave the right of self-determination to the territorial units rather than to the two nations, Hindus and Muslims.[110] Maulana Azad, the Congress president, focused his discussion primarily on defence although he did object to the option of non-accession provided for the provinces. Cripps got the draft amended to accommodate the Congress viewpoint on defence; the relevant part of the amended draft provided that the responsibility for defence was of the British government 'as part of their world war effort', whereas 'the task of organizing to the full the military, moral and material resources of India must be the responsibility of the Government of India with the cooperation of the peoples of India'.[111] On 29 March, Cripps released the draft declaration at a press conference., and tried to please the Congress in his responses to questions; to a question whether the declaration had conceded Pakistan, his answer was 'certainly not', and the possibility of a second union, he insisted, was not Pakistan and that the executive council would function as a cabinet and the viceroy's role would be that of a British monarch.[112]

The All-India Muslim League devised its strategy in this situation. Its working committee remained in session from 27 March to 11 April. Jinnah assured the worried Leaguers at the Allahabad annual session on 4 April, 'our aim is Pakistan and whatever the proposals might be, if they are such that we cannot achieve Pakistan we will never accept them. . . . Our firm determination is and our only goal is one— Pakistan—Pakistan—Pakistan.'[113] Meanwhile, Cripps negotiated exclusively with the Congress leaders, in particular with Nehru and Azad, as if complete power had to be transferred to the Congress. The Congress leaders demonstrated a strange logic on the non-accession provision: they admitted 'the principle of self-determination' for the Muslims but disputed the way it had been incorporated in the draft declaration.[114] The League patiently waited for the conclusion of the Cripps–Congress talks and raised no serious objection to their partisan nature. Cripps evolved a formula for the division of authority in defence matters between an Indian member, in charge of the department of defence, and the commander-in-chief as the war member, looking after the operations of war, to satisfy the Congress although he had no authorization from the war cabinet to assume this responsibility.[115] The Congress rejected the formula that he prepared. Then, Colonel Louis Johnson, President Roosevelt's personal envoy and head of the US Technical Mission in India, who had arrived in Delhi on 3 April, intervened to assist in the revision of the formula on defence which was amended and approved by the Congress working committee.[116] Cripps sent the revised formula to London for approval. But Lord Linlithgow and Lord Wavell, the commander-in-chief, who disagreed with the contents of the revised formula, wrote separately to Churchill against its acceptance, as any final arrangement was subject to approval by the war cabinet. Cripps had to terminate the negotiations when the war cabinet disagreed with any change in policy during the war and rejected the revised formula.[117] Jinnah's assessment was that if the Congress demand had been accepted, it would have transformed the executive council into 'a Grand Fascist Council', and would have left the Muslims and the minorities 'entirely at the mercy of the Congress raj'.[118]

The All-India Muslim League perceived that the British government had indirectly recognized the 'principle of Pakistan' in the Cripps proposals for the first time since the adoption of the Lahore Resolution. Therefore, in its discussions immediately after Jinnah's meeting with Cripps, it gave the impression that it might accept the British offer; and Sikandar conveyed that 'confidential information' to Cripps but the developments that followed moved the League to reject the offer.[119] Its rejection was conveyed in a mildly-worded lengthy resolution of the working committee passed on 11 April, in which it resolved that the August 1940 declaration, which promised the Muslims that neither the constitution-making machinery would be set up nor the constitution itself be enforced without the approval and consent of Muslim India, was still valid because the draft declaration embodied 'proposals' and not 'decisions' of the war cabinet. It expressed gratification that 'the possibility of Pakistan' had been 'recognized by implication' but regretted the rigidity of the offer, i.e. it could 'be accepted *in toto*' and 'not in parts'. It listed the reasons for its refusal to accept the offer, that: (*i*) it was meant to constitute one Indian dominion and relegated the proposal of more than one union to 'the realm of remote possibility';

(*ii*) the League could not enter the constitution-making body because its primary object was to create one Indian union while the League stood for partitioning India. Besides, its members would be elected by means of proportional representation and not by separate electorates which would place the Muslims at the mercy of Hindu majority; (*iii*) no procedure had been laid down for the provinces to exercise the option of non-accession. Cripps' explanatory proposal of a plebiscite, which was not part of the draft declaration, ignored the fact that the Muslims under the prevailing system were in a minority in the assemblies of the Muslim majority provinces of the Punjab and Bengal, and the weightage in the NWFP was so heavy that its majority could be easily manipulated. Reference to the whole 'adult male' population and not to the Muslims in the case of plebiscite in a province if a majority of the votes in the assembly was less than 60 per cent would deny them 'the inherent right of self-determination';[120] (*iv* & *v*) the provisions relating to the states lacked clarity if there was disagreement between the contracting parties, i.e. the successor authority and the states; and (*vi*) the interim arrangements were neither definite nor open to modification. In conclusion, the working committee reiterated that unless the Pakistan demand, which was now its creed, was 'unequivocally accepted', the League could not accept any scheme about the future.[121] The Congress working committee rejected the British offer because it did not transfer defence to the Indians, empowered the rulers to nominate the states' representatives on the constitution-making body and accepted the principle of secession of provinces 'to meet a communal demand'.[122]

On 11 April, Cripps announced the failure of his mission and withdrew the British offer.[123] Whatever were the reasons for the failure—whether it was due to the absence of the Congress–Cripps agreement on defence or non-accession option for the provinces, Linlithgow's opposition, or Churchill's devious tactics or absence of the war cabinet's approval—it temporarily spoiled Cripps–Congress relations.[124] Both sides blamed each other for the failure. Cripps believed that the Congress had missed an opportunity to capture real power of a united India and held Gandhi responsible for wrecking the negotiations at the last moment, by his two-hour long telephonic conversation from Wardha with the Congress leaders. He alleged that the Congress had approached Colonel Johnson who functioned in his individual capacity, rather than as representative of President Roosevelt, to arrive at a settlement. He used Jinnah's 1939 arguments to defend his position that in the prevailing atmosphere, transfer of power would mean 'dictatorship of the majority' because the legislature would be composed of inflexible communal majority and minority.[125] The Congress leaders were demanding transfer of power to such a majority; Cripps ridiculed that they wanted 'all or nothing'; they 'could not have all, so they got nothing'.[126] For him, the Congress was now 'fundamentally reactionary—a merging of mill owner capitalism, reactionary Hinduism and a democratic façade'.[127] Gandhi in retaliation termed the British offer a 'blank cheque on a crashing bank', deploring it as 'a misfortune' that its bearer was Cripps, who was 'acclaimed as a radical among Radicals and a friend of India'.[128] Nehru refuted Cripps' allegations that the Congress had approached Colonel Johnson to act as a mediator, and reproached him for thinking on every matter in communal terms, 'which even Mr Jinnah does not do'.[129] In fact, the Congress was worried about possible fissures within its own ranks on the Pakistan issue. Voices had been raised from within its ranks, pressing the leadership to negotiate with the League on this issue. While Azad upheld that the negotiations with Cripps broke down on defence alone, Chakravarti Rajagopalachari revealed that the Congress had rejected the offer due to the non-accession option provided for the provinces.[130] Rajagopalachari attempted to organize pressure on the Congress to talk to the League on the Pakistan issue.

(B) CONGRESS AND THE DEMAND FOR PAKISTAN

(i) *Anti-Pakistan Scheme Drive.* The Congress led the opposition to the Pakistan scheme. Some of its leaders denounced it in religious terms: Gandhi called it 'vivisection of India' and its acceptance for him 'amounted to a sin'; Rajagopalachari described it as 'cutting the cow into two halves'; and Azad viewed it against 'the spirit of Islam'.[131] Nehru characterized it 'foolish', 'anti-national' and 'pro-Imperialist' scheme.[132] Several Hindu leaders including Gandhi and Sir Rama Swami Iyer (1864–1946) saw the possibility of 'civil war' on this issue.[133] The League–Congress interaction after the Lahore Resolution was minimal and the few contacts that did take place were mostly indirect.[134] At first, the Congress leaders tried to ignore the Pakistan scheme, dismissing it for its 'nebulous' nature and pressing the British government to accept its own demands for complete independence, democratically framed constitution and provisional 'national' government.[135] If the Congress demands were accepted before a Hindu–Muslim settlement, the League argued, it would result in a permanent Hindu majority rule; even the system of separate electorates was now looked at with reservation because it meant three Hindu votes against one Muslim vote.[136] Jinnah repeatedly called on the Congress to give one-fourth of India to the Muslims and keep the remaining three-fourth for the Hindus. In July 1940, Jinnah and Gandhi held talks separately with the viceroy and presented him the demands of their respective parties; the result was the 1940 August Offer. There was no League–Congress contact at all during these 'talks', except for Rajagopalachari's 'sporting offer' that he would persuade the Congress to invite Jinnah or any other Leaguer to form the 'national government' but none took him seriously.[137] After the August Offer, Jinnah asked the Congress leaders in the central assembly during the debate on the supplementary finance bill, 'why not you and I meet and put our heads together? If you make a practical proposition, we present a common united demand to Mr Amery or for the matter of that to the British Parliament or the British nation if you like?'[138] Nothing came out of his appeal. The Congress leaders believed that the August Offer gave the League a veto that it might use for the creation of Pakistan; therefore, after September 1940, its energies were focused on getting the offer repealed or replaced by a new British policy. Instead of facing the Pakistan demand squarely, it virtually found escape in the 'individual Satyagraha' to secure what it called 'liberty of speech'. Started with great fanfare on 17 October, this policy landed some 23,000 Congress political workers in jail including 40 members of the All India Congress Committee. The League kept itself aloof, as it perceived in this movement 'a weapon of coercion and blackmail' to force the British government to accept the Congress demands and reject the Pakistan scheme.[139] Its policy proved beneficial to its cause although some Leaguers initially doubted its efficacy.[140] The Congress was soon bogged down and desperately awaited for an opportunity to wriggle out of the impasse.

The Congress encouraged the anti-League forces in its drive against the Pakistan scheme and activated them especially whenever the British and Indian political parties were holding talks on constitutional issues. The opponents of the Pakistan scheme included Hindus, Sikhs and 'nationalist' Muslims. Firstly, the Hindu 'nationalists' and their parties, which, in Jinnah's words, 'masqueraded under different names' but 'patrolled and reconnoitered' on behalf of the Congress, like the All-India Hindu Mahasabha and All India Hindu League, did not need much encouragement. Their leaders like V.D. Savarkar, the ideologue of the Hindutwa, Dr B.S. Moonje, Dr Shyama Prasad Mukerjee and Dr J.P. Srivastava believed in the unity of 'the Hindu nation' and condemned the Pakistan scheme, terming it as anti-Hindu, 'anti-national' and 'a mere fad and a dream'.[141] They organized anti-Pakistan conferences to oppose the scheme. In March 1941, they held a Punjab, Sindh and NWFP Hindu conference in Lahore, presided over by Dr Mukerjee, in which they called on every Hindu to save India from 'the proposed vivisection'.[142] Then, in June–July, they convened a series of anti-Pakistan conferences and rallies in different parts of India; addressing a Tamilnadu Hindu Mahasabha conference, Dr Moonje declared that 'the only nationalism, which existed in the world, was the nationalism of the dominant community in a country'![143] K.M. Munshi with Gandhi's blessings launched a new body, the Akhand Hindustan Front, to oppose the Pakistan scheme. Jinnah noted the intensity of such campaigns: Pakistan demand, he wrote to Liaquat, was 'a crime, nay high treason' according to the Hindu nationalists, whereas preaching 'Akhand Bharat' was 'national and patriotic'; and if the Leaguers talked of Pakistan, they were dubbed as 'fanatics' and when the Hindus talked of 'Hindudom' and Hindu *raj* for the whole of India they claimed to be 'liberals' and 'nationalists'.[144] The Hindu nationalists affirmed their stand at the famous All-India Hindu Mahasabha annual conference at Bhagalpur (Bihar) on 24 December 1941; Savarkar's plan of 'militarization and industrialization' of the Hindus was meant 'to establish Hindu raj'; and if that happened, he believed, Pakistan would 'evaporate into the air'; and that if the Muslims did not 'behave', the Hindus would 'annex Afghanistan'.[145] Their hostile propaganda with religious connotation diminished the acceptability of Pakistan by the Hindus, which naturally pushed numerous pro-Congress Muslims to join the All-India Muslim League. They did not confine their opposition to themselves; they participated in conferences organized by the Sikhs and instigated them to establish 'Sikhistan'; Savarkar's inflammatory message to one Akali conference was: 'when the Sikhs were but a handful they ruled the Muslim majority in the Punjab and right up to Kabul. Now that they have grown into millions, they can never be, and need not be, overawed by the reduced Muslim majority'.[146] The resultant bitterness harmed the prospects of communal harmony.

Secondly, the 'moderate' Hindu leaders, who had been active members of the Congress in the past, were equally opposed to the partition of India. Although they had much less popular support than the Hindu nationalists but they enjoyed greater influence with the British administrators, politicians and press. Their moves were more subtle than those of the Hindu nationalists but their real object was to 'torpedo the Pakistan demand'. They became active in politics when Gandhi-inspired individual Satyagraha faced an impasse. Sir Tej Bahadur Sapru, the veteran Liberal politician who termed the Pakistan scheme as 'black treachery', took the initiative and, on 14 March 1941, convened a conference of Non-Party Leaders in Bombay, which the All-India Hindu Mahasabha leaders (including Savarkar and Moonje) attended but to which not a single Muslim leader was invited, to help the Congress to give up individual Satyagraha and return to normal politics 'without appearing to lose face'.[147] Earlier, he had made an unsuccessful bid to arrange a Jinnah–Gandhi meeting. Jinnah was ready to meet Gandhi or any other Hindu leader on behalf of the Hindu community but the idea was dropped when Gandhi refused to meet him as a Hindu leader.[148] The non-party conference demanded that India should not be treated as 'a dependency'; henceforth its constitutional position should be similar to any other self-governing unit of the British Commonwealth.; and the Viceroy's Executive Council should be reconstituted to function as a truly 'national government' responsible to the crown during the war and thereafter assuming the role of a dominion government—similar were the Congress demands.[149] The conference appointed a standing committee to pursue its demands but its memorandum to the British prime minister made little impact as it was regarded contrary to the August 1940 declaration.[150] Jinnah equated the non-party leaders' conference with 'the Dutch Army, all Generals and no privates', an 'appendage to the Congress', and alleged that the Congress and All-India Hindu Mahasabha leaders had engineered this move to sabotage the Pakistan scheme.[151] In December 1941, when a possible change in British policy was in the air, Sapru convened another non-party leaders' conference, at which earlier resolutions were reiterated. His cable to Prime Minister Churchill on 2 January 1942, which eleven other Indian leaders including two less known Muslims— Rahimatullah Chinoy (Bombay) and Mohammad Yunus (Patna)—had signed, assumed great importance due to Sapru's own persistence, President Roosevelt's involvement and British keenness to respond to his overtures. The League was not aware of Sapru's cable to the prime minister but when, on 21 February, the non-party leaders met again to restate their demands, its working committee denounced them and directed its branch Leagues to pass a resolution at public meetings, saying that the League 'treats with contempt' the proposals of the non-party conference, 'considers them as harmful to the peace and tranquillity of India', and 'emphatically and wholeheartedly supports the resolution' that the All-India Muslim League had passed on 22 February. The provincial Muslim Leagues, district Muslim Leagues and city Muslim Leagues formally adopted this resolution at public meetings and sent its copies to the viceroy.[152] The League campaign went a long way in neutralizing the pressure in support of the Sapru proposals. However, the standing committee of the non-party leaders' conference survived after that to put pressure on the British government whenever constitutional issues came under consideration.

Lastly, the Congress tried to win over anti-League Muslims and Muslim parties and groups. Its policy was to woo prominent Leaguers, whenever it was possible, and create platforms of anti-League parties to refute the League's claim that it was the sole representative party of the Indian Muslims.[153] The opposition of the anti-League Muslims and their parties was based on the assertion that: the Congress stood for independence while the League followed a pro-Imperialist policy to destroy the unity of India; the League was dominated by Muslims with vested interests and advocated a narrow reactionary ideology; the League would not protect the interests of all the Muslims in the proposed state; Pakistan would be economically unviable and its establishment would hurt the united strength of the Indian Muslims. Maulana Azad, the ideologue of the Khilafat movement who was respected in religious circles for his scholarship, was instrumental in implementing the Congress strategy. From early 1938 onward, Gandhi had repeatedly suggested to Jinnah that Azad should first hold talks with the League leaders on behalf of the Congress to settle the Hindu–Muslim question. But Jinnah and the League had consistently refused to accept this proposition because, it was argued, the conflict in India was between Hindus and Muslims, which could not be settled by a (Congress) Muslim holding talks with a (League) Muslim. Whenever Azad had himself approached Jinnah for talks before 23 March 1940, the latter had politely declined to discuss with him any political issues. Instead of respecting the League's viewpoint, on 15 February 1940, about a month before the adoption of the Lahore/Pakistan Resolution, the Congress at Gandhi's behest elected Azad as its all-India president by an overwhelming majority, by 1861 votes against 183 of his rival M.N. Roy (1886–1954), and continued to have him in that office till July 1946. Azad's election as the Congress president was meant to give the party a non-communal and 'national' face to the outside world. The Congress used his influence to win over Muslims and attempted to induce the League to hold talks with him but this policy only embittered the Leaguers' relations with pro-Azad Muslims.[154] The Leaguers appreciated, and Azad's supporters resented, Jinnah's well-known comments when Azad, a few days after his assumption of the Congress presidency and after his talks with the Muslim premiers on 13 June 1940, raised a political issue with Jinnah;[155] the latter was annoyed and wrote back, 'I refuse to discuss with you, by correspondence or otherwise, as you have completely forfeited the confidence of Muslim India. Can't you realize you are made a Muslim "show-boy" Congress president to give it colour that it is national and deceive foreign countries?'[156] Gandhi himself indirectly confirmed the Congress strategy in his article in the *Harijan* entitled 'My Reply to Qaid-e-Azam' by posing the question, 'Can a Hindu organization have a Muslim divine as President?'[157] Except for its anti-League strategy, Azad as president was of little value to the Congress in its negotiations with the British partly because of his limited knowledge of the English language.[158] Unlike the leaders of all the other political parties, he never met the British negotiators alone. Asaf Ali (1888–1953) and then Nehru accompanied him in his talks with Sir Stafford Cripps; and Pandit Govind Ballabh Pant and then Nehru went with him in his meetings with Wavell during the Simla conference as his interpreters.[159] Surprisingly, he merely used to sign the letters in English from the Congress to the British negotiators that Nehru drafted for him. These facts in the eyes of the Leaguers substantiated Jinnah's denunciation of Azad.

After the 1937 elections, Azad had helped the Congress in its Muslim mass contact movement and then as a member of its three-member parliamentary committee had endeavoured to win over Muslim members of the provincial assembly particularly in the United Provinces, Sindh and Central Provinces, with mixed results.[160] His attempt to wean away League members of the provincial assembly in Central Provinces and Berar through a former Khilafatist, Abdur Rauf Shah, by an offer of ministership, makes interesting reading; he wrote to him in a touching letter, 'I had decided last year to retire from active and responsible occupation in the Congress, as my health does not permit me to carry on my literary pursuits along with heavy Congress work. . . . But I could not do so as I had to finish some work. . . . One of the unfinished works related to the Muslim ministership of your province'.[161] But here he did not succeed. Then, on 13 June 1940, he met with Muslim Premiers including Sikandar and Fazlul Haq in Delhi to settle the Hindu–Muslim question at the provincial level bypassing the All-India Muslim League and its president. The Aga Khan was expected to bless this move; and it was hoped that a 'Gandhi–Aga Khan–Sikandar–Fazlul Haq understanding would have a more far-reaching effect than the Lucknow Pact of 1916.' Jinnah, it was calculated, would then either have 'to toe the line or stand in haughty aloofness unable to change the course of history'.[162] The Leaguers felt agitated but the proposal, if it had any substance, eventually failed to materialize.[163] When the League working committee took it up for discussion, it accepted Sikandar's plea that the Muslim premiers had met Azad purely in their 'individual' capacity at the latter's invitation; however, the working committee resolved that henceforth none of its members should negotiate with the Congress leaders any Hindu–Muslim question or any other matter requiring a League–Congress settlement without the permission of the League president to avoid any misunderstanding.[164] Azad did not give up. In December 1940, he succeeded in creating a rift in the League by encouraging Fazlul Haq to pressure Jinnah to talk to the Congress for a Hindu–Muslim settlement and by persuading the League leaders in Sindh to sign a 21-point agreement.[165] The following year, in December, he won over Fazlul Haq who decided to join and lead the Progressive Coalition Party. Still later, he disrupted the League ranks in Sindh when he won over G.M. Sayed and persuaded him to fight the general elections from the platform of a dissident provincial Muslim League. Then, he was partially responsible for the post-election instability in Sindh that did not end till fresh elections were held in that province in December 1946. After the general elections, he manoeuvred the formation of a Khizr-led coalition ministry in the Punjab with the connivance of Governor Glancy under the patronage of the Congress.[166]

The anti-League Muslim elements generally used their own platforms to oppose the Pakistan scheme. Except for the Khudai Khidmatgars (NWFP), who merged their organization into the Congress, the others maintained their separate identities but none of them had any meaningful representation in the legislative assemblies. The Congress encouraged them to form common platforms to make their voice effective. Their first attempt was the convening of an Azad Muslim Conference in Delhi on 27–30 April 1940, nine days after the All-India Muslim League had observed a successful country-wide

'Muslim Independence Day'. The Jamiatul Ulama-i-Hind, Majlis-i-Ahrar-i-Islam, All-India Momin Conference, Independent Party (Bihar), Anjuman-i-Watan (Balochistan) and All-India Shia Political Conference participated in this conference, which was presided over by Allah Bakhsh Soomro whom the Sindh League had recently ousted from the chief ministership. The Congress extended full support to the Conference and Azad served as one of its conveners; its main resolution termed the Pakistan scheme as 'impractical and harmful' to the country in general and to the Muslims in particular.[167] It set up an Azad (Independent) Muslim Board to promote its objectives. Before the August Offer, on 20 July, the board organized another Azad Muslim Conference in Lucknow to support the Congress viewpoint.[168] The anti-League parties showed more hectic activity separately as well as collectively before and during the Cripps Mission to disprove the representative character of the All-India Muslim League.[169] Some of their leaders including Allah Bakhsh Soomro sent telegrams to the British prime minister, disparaging the Pakistan scheme; and the Leaguers tried to defuse their impact.[170] The exaggerated claim of the pro-Congress Momins that they represented 45 million Muslims found mention in the house of commons; on investigation, the figures were discovered to be totally incorrect.[171] Azad in his address to the Jamiatul Ulama-i-Hind annual session in 1942 supported the Congress demand.[172] Immediately before Cripps' arrival in India, on 28 February–1 March 1942, the Congress-sponsored nine-party Azad Muslim Parties Board organized another political conference in Delhi, presided over by Allah Bakhsh, which nine anti-League Muslim parties included Jamiatul Ulama-i-Hind, Majlis-i-Ahrar-i-Islam, Shia Political Conference, Momin Conference,[173] Ittehad-i-Millat, and Khudai Khidmatgars attended. Asaf Ali, a member of the Congress working committee, stage-managed this conference on behalf of the Congress, drafted its resolutions that were in line with the Congress demands and arranged for their publicity.[174] The activities of these Muslim parties had significant propaganda value which hurt the negotiating position of the All-India Muslim League although their linkage with the Congress and rapidly growing popularity of the Pakistan scheme among the Muslims gradually diluted their strength.

(*ii*) *Quit India Movement and the Aftermath*. The Congress remained in a state of constant denial on the Pakistan issue, even when there were stirrings within its ranks urging its leaders to see the ground realities. In November–December 1940, some 'enlightened' Hindus in Madras had pressed the Congress 'to accept Pakistan'; and Rajagopalachari's 'sporting offer' was to deflect that pressure.[175] Early in 1942, when the Cripps Mission was underway, Rajagopalachari unsuccessfully advised the Congress to talk to the League for a Hindu–Muslim settlement; and after this failure, he revealed that the primary reason for the Congress rejection was the non-accession option, which was partially reflected in the All India Congress Committee's resolution.[176] He then actively campaigned for Congress–League talks on the Pakistan issue although his object, as he defined it in his formula, was to preserve the broader unity of India. On 22 April, the Madras Congress assembly party, with Rajagopalachari in the chair, passed two resolutions in which it: (*i*) urged the All India Congress Committee 'to acknowledge the Muslim League's claim for separation should the same be persisted in' at the time of framing the constitution of India and invited the League for consultation to form a national government at the centre; and (*ii*) called for the formation of coalition governments in the provinces and asked permission from the All India Congress Committee to form one in Madras.[177] But, on 2 May, the All India Congress Committee rejected his resolution by 120 to 15 votes that sought recognition of the League's claim for separation; instead, it adopted Jagat Narain Lal's counter resolution by 92 to 17 votes, which provided that the Congress would not accept any proposal to disintegrate India.[178] After that, Rajagopalachari resigned his membership of the Congress working committee to campaign in Madras in support of his proposal, appealing to Nehru to meet Jinnah to settle the Pakistan issue. The Congress and All-India Hindu Mahasabha leaders denounced Rajagopalachari and launched an offensive against him for advocating that proposal. Nehru was willing to meet Jinnah to discuss India's freedom but not the Pakistan issue, vowing to fight it 'with all the power he could command'.[179] Gandhi came to Rajagopalachari's rescue, writing in the *Harijan* that he was 'entitled to a respectful hearing' as his motive was 'lofty' and not 'selfish'.[180] When the Madras Congress assembly party met again on 15 July, it rescinded its earlier resolution on Pakistan and endorsed Jagat Narain Lal's resolution. Now Rajagopalachari resigned his membership of the Congress as well as the Madras assembly to canvass support for his proposal. None approached Jinnah and the League for talks on the Pakistan issue.

The Congress leaders had seen in the unexpectedly abrupt termination of the Cripps Mission a betrayal of their British friends. They were angry and in a revengeful mood, and so were their British friends. Added to their anger was their perception that the British were weak and vulnerable at that point of time because of continuous Allied reverses on the war front in North Africa and the Far East. Their calculation was that the British forces in India could not withstand a Japanese invasion, a miscalculation on the part of the Congress leaders.[181] Gandhi had started writing articles in the *Harijan*, asking the British to leave India to save its unity and deprive the Japanese an excuse for invasion; now, in his view, the British withdrawal from India and its Independence was a 'condition precedent' for Hindu–Muslim unity. Nehru after a meeting with Gandhi at Wardha was in full agreement with him.[182] Jinnah's rebuttal of Gandhi's thesis about Hindu–Muslim unity was 'blacklisted' in the Hindu press; his response came in an interview with a correspondent of the Associated Press of America, in which he demanded that Britain should in fairness 'hand over the Muslim homelands to the Muslims and the Hindu homelands to the Hindus' otherwise 'terrible chaos and disaster' would follow if it took steps 'even with the help of America' against the Pakistan scheme.[183] Both the British and the Congress paid no heed to his advice. News had also been filtering into India about the Indian National Army that Subhas Chandra Bose had raised in the Far East with the help of the Japanese army to free India, using mostly Indian prisoners of war. Early in July, the Indian National Army at a conference in Bangkok called for Indian independence, affirming the Congress as the only representative party of India that believed in its unity and indivisibility and recognized its tricolour flag as the national flag.[184] The Congress leaders must have been elated by this unforeseen support and concluded that the only way to free India and avoid partition was the end of British rule. On 6 July, its working committee passed the 'quit India' resolution, asking the British to leave India, a decision which the All India Congress Committee endorsed on 8 August. Its copies were dispatched to Churchill, Roosevelt, the Russian ambassador in London and other members of the United Nations. It did not feel obligated to consult the All-India Muslim League in this desperate solo venture.

The Congress miscalculated the severity of the British response. The British government knew the Congress plans through the secret documents that it had seized in their search operations of Congress offices or intercepted and moved with alacrity to meet the 'Quit India' challenge.[185] On 9 August, it arrested top Congress leaders including Gandhi and members of the working committee, declared the provincial Congress committees and All India Congress Committee as unlawful bodies and suppressed the ensuing violent civil disobedience movement by ruthless tactics including use of large-scale arrests, whipping in jails and collective fines.[186] The League working committee, in a lengthy resolution on 20 August, which its council endorsed on 9 November, deplored the Congress decision to insist on the British government 'to hand over power to the Hindu oligarchy' and force the Muslims to submit to its 'dictation'. The Congress had persistently opposed, the League resolved, 'the right of self-determination for the Muslim nation' while claiming the right of self-determination for 'India', which was 'a mere euphuism for a Hindu majority' rule. It had put forward a new 'fantastic theory' that Hindu–Muslim settlement would 'only follow the withdrawal of British power from India'. In fact, it wanted to establish 'Hindu raj' and 'deal a death-blow' to the Pakistan scheme. The League demanded a declaration from the British government that it would abide by 'a verdict of a plebiscite of the Muslims' on Pakistan, and offered to 'negotiate with any party on a footing of equality to set up a provisional government in India' to help in the war. It directed the Muslims to abstain from the Congress movement.[187] Jinnah was uncompromising on the Pakistan issue; at a press conference on 13 September, he offered to join a 'provisional and composite Government', provided the League had 50 per cent seats in such a government and all the parties including the British accepted the Pakistan scheme.[188] To a question about his influence on the Indian soldiers, he observed, 'If the Muslim League were to decide—mind you, I am not in touch with anybody—but I have little doubt in my mind that a very large body in the army will fall out . . . I think you will find the entire [North-West] frontier ablaze'; and 'the entire Middle East' would 'support the Muslim demand'.[189] Liaquat forwarded copies of the League resolution of 20 August, to the provincial Muslim Leagues, and on their direction, the district Muslim Leagues and city Muslim Leagues held public meetings to explain its contents.[190] Following the pattern of the Congress, Jinnah forwarded copies of the resolution to the viceroy, secretary of state for India, Prime Minister Churchill and members of the United Nations. The government exempted the League members from collective fines, wherever they were fined, as it had kept itself aloof from the Congress movement.[191]

Jinnah's comment on 'Quit India' that the British should first 'divide' India and then 'quit' became the Leaguers' slogan.

The British government remained non-committal on the Pakistan issue and made no declaration, as the League desired.[192] None of its 'signals' indicated support of the League demand: Churchill simply wanted to maintain status quo, i.e. adherence to the August 1940 declaration; Linlithgow spoke of the 'geographical unity' of India in his presidential address to the annual meeting of the associated chamber of commerce in Calcutta on 17 December 1942, and Amery (secretary of state for India) eulogized Emperor Akbar at a function in London that was organized to celebrate that emperor's centenary to prove that 'historically India was united'. But the League remained firm on the Pakistan issue; Jinnah insisted that the Congress leaders should settle the Hindu–Muslim problem 'as friends' to ensure justice to both the nations, Hindu and Muslim. 'Pakistan presupposes freedom and independence of India', he exhorted, and repeatedly urged the Hindus to have three-fourth of India and allow the Muslims to have one-fourth of its territory. 'Let me live', he said on 2 November, 'according to my history in the light of Islam, my tradition, culture and language, and you do the same in your zones'.[193] The Congress did not respond to the League's resolution of 20 August, or Jinnah's appeal partly because its leaders were incarcerated. In November 1942, Rajagopalachari offered to operate as a mediator between Jinnah and Gandhi, and the former did not discourage him from playing that role provided the Pakistan scheme was the basis of negotiations.[194] But when Rajagopalachari approached Linlithgow for permission to meet Gandhi in jail, he was denied access; an official communiqué explained that the government could not provide special facilities for discussion with persons who had been detained on the charge of revolutionary activities. Soon after, Gandhi saw a positive sign in Linlithgow's remarks of 17 December, and directly approached him, threatening to go on fast if he was not informed about any error that he had committed.[195] Linlithgow who saw no change in Gandhi's attitude asked him to give any suggestion to bring about a change in the British policy. Gandhi responded that he could do so only after he had met with members of the working committee, a condition that the viceroy was not ready to fulfil. On 10 February, he went on a 21-day (10 February–3 March) fast and declined to accept the government offer of release for the duration of the fast. An all-party conference in Delhi on 18 February, with Sir Tej Bahadur Sapru in the chair, demanded his

unconditional release, but Churchill refused to accede to the request on
the pretext that there could be no discrimination between Gandhi and
other Congress leaders.[196] The League kept itself aloof from these
negotiations, and Jinnah declined to associate himself with the Sapru-
organized all-party conference because the situation emanating from
Gandhi's fast was 'a matter for the Hindu leaders to consider and
advise him accordingly'.[197] The all-party conference met again after
Gandhi's fast and submitted a memorandum to the viceroy for his
release but Linlithgow declined even to receive its deputation as he had
seen no change in the attitude of Gandhi and the Congress leaders.[198]

Before Gandhi's fast, it was suggested that Jinnah should make a
move to get the Congress leaders released from jail. He took such
suggestions quite 'flattering' and 'complimentary' but frankly admitted
that he had neither 'the power to put them in jail' nor 'the power to
open the jail gates'. The Congress had launched the Quit India
movement, he said, without settling the Hindu–Muslim problem but
freedom would come only after its settlement and the initiative for that
had to come from Gandhi and the Congress.[199] Some Congress leaders
and Rajagopalachari impressed upon Jinnah that Gandhi would be
willing to come to an agreement with the League on the basis of
Pakistan but the British government was preventing him from
establishing contact with him for this purpose.[200] Keeping these signals
in view, Jinnah, in his presidential address at the All-India Muslim
League's Delhi annual session on 24 April 1943, observed, 'Nobody
would welcome it more than myself, if Mr Gandhi is even now really
willing to come to a settlement with the Muslim League on the basis
of Pakistan. Let me tell you that it will be the greatest day for both
Hindus and Musalmans. If he has made up his mind, what is there to
prevent Mr Gandhi from writing direct to me? . . . What is the use of
going to the Viceroy and leading deputations? I cannot believe that . . .
[the government] will have the daring to stop such a letter if it is sent
to me. . . . If there is any change of heart on his [Gandhi's] part he has
only to drop me a few lines, when I assure you, the Muslim League
will not fail whatever may have been our controversies in the past.'[201]
Gandhi did write a letter to Jinnah but in that he simply expressed a
wish to meet him face to face without indicating any change of his
views on the Pakistan scheme. The government, apparently as a matter
of 'its policy in regard to correspondence or interviews' with Gandhi,
did not forward his letter in original to Jinnah but communicated the
gist of its contents to him and, on 24 May, issued a communiqué on

this issue. Among the reasons that influenced the government decision not to forward Gandhi's letter were: the threatening tone of Jinnah's speech and the earlier decision of the government not to allow Rajagopalachari, the US envoy Phillips, and the all-party deputation to meet Gandhi.[202] Immediately after that, Jinnah issued a statement on the letter; and, on 4 June, responding to a question at a press conference, he stated that he had no reason to doubt the official information. A deadlock followed after that, except for a call from Allama Inayatullah Mashriqi, leader of the Khaksar Movement, to his followers to send telegrams, letters and resolutions to Jinnah from 15 June to 25 July 1943, asking him to meet Gandhi to resolve the Pakistan issue. Nothing could come out of such a naive move.[203] Its unfortunate by-product was a physical attack on Jinnah in his office in Bombay by a Khaksar worker.

(*iii*) *CR Formula and Jinnah–Gandhi Talks.* The All-India Muslim League firmly stood by its demand that 'the principle of Pakistan' should be accepted before any negotiations.[204] Early in 1944, Chakravarti Rajagopalachari (CR) made an attempt to break the deadlock. On 11 February, he advised the Hindus that they should not be scared of the Pakistan scheme and accept the division of India even into ten different states if they could get independence, but the states that he visualized were those of the Soviet Union.[205] He drafted a six-point formula, better known as the CR Formula, apparently on the basis of Pakistan but in a way that it would dilute the League demand and, on 8 April, sent it to Jinnah; according to him, Gandhi had approved this formula during his fast in February–March 1943. But neither had Rajagopalachari mentioned the formula or its approval by Gandhi to Jinnah at that time nor had Gandhi referred to it in his 'undelivered' letter of 4 May 1943. The CR Formula provided terms for a Congress–League settlement to which Jinnah and Gandhi would agree and endeavour to get them approved by their respective parties. It stipulated that: (*i*) subject to the terms set out as regards the constitution of free India, the League would endorse the demand for independence and cooperate with the Congress in the formation of a 'provisional interim government' for the transitional period; (*ii*) at the end of war, a commission would demarcate those contiguous districts in the north-west and north-east in which Muslims were in an 'absolute majority', and in those areas a plebiscite on the basis of adult franchise or other practicable franchise of 'all the inhabitants' would decide whether or not they should be separated from Hindustan, the districts on the border would have the right to join either of the two states; (*iii*) all the parties would be free to campaign in support of their viewpoints during the plebiscite; (*iv*) in the event of separation, mutual agreement would be entered into for safeguarding defence, commerce, communications and for other essential purposes; (*v*) any transfer of population would be on an absolutely voluntary basis; and (*vi*) these terms would be binding only in case of transfer by Britain of full power and responsibility for the governance of India.[206] Rajagopalachari insisted that Jinnah should immediately accept the formula without any modification. Jinnah refused to 'take the responsibility of accepting or rejecting it' but promised to place it before the League working committee. But this procedure was not acceptable to Rajagopalachari, and Jinnah left the matter at that.

Meanwhile, on 6 May 1944, Gandhi was released from jail on medical grounds, following an attack of malaria although he was not released earlier in February, when his wife who was on her own volition sharing his incarceration died. He requested Wavell to release the members of the Congress working committee or to permit him to meet them in jail. But, on 22 June, Wavell declined to accede to his request and the government published the correspondence that had passed between Gandhi and the two viceroys, Linlithgow and Wavell, during his detention.[207] It was after Wavell's rejection of Gandhi's request that on 30 June, Rajagopalachari again wrote to Jinnah that Gandhi was still supportive of his Formula and wanted to publish its text and Jinnah's rejection. Jinnah immediately telegraphed to Rajagopalachari that he had not rejected his formula but simply wanted to place it before the working committee to which the latter had not agreed. He expressed his willingness to do that if Gandhi was to send him direct his proposal. Nothing came out of this correspondence which, on 9 July, Rajagopalachari released to the press. Then, on 17 July, Gandhi himself sent a touching letter to Jinnah in Gujrati along with a translation that the latter received in Srinagar on 22 July, where he was resting after a long spell of work, in which he expressed his desire to meet Jinnah. The League working committee and council discussed this letter in Lahore in their meetings on 29–30 July, where Jinnah gave his analysis of the CR Formula, which, in his view, offered 'a shadow and a husk, maimed, mutilated, and moth-eaten Pakistan', and the procedure suggested to implement it was 'hardly conducive to friendly negotiations' and its form was 'pure dictation', as it was 'not open to any modification'.[208] Still, he welcomed that 'at last' Gandhi had accepted 'the principle of partition'. The council vested Jinnah with full powers to negotiate on its behalf. Simultaneous to his correspondence with Jinnah, Gandhi was corresponding with Wavell, after the publication of his interview with Stuart Gelder of the *News Chronicle*, in which he had reiterated the Congress demand for the formation of a 'national government' responsible to the elected members of the central assembly, where the Hindus would have a clear majority. But that proposal was shot down at the initial stage. Interestingly, the anti-League Muslim parties at Azad's instance again activated themselves and established an All-India Muslim Majlis, which convened a joint conference in Delhi on 17–18 August to put pressure on the All-India Muslim League to forge a united Muslim stand on the CR Formula; the All-India Muslim League declined to attend the conference.[209] Gandhi used the standpoint of the Muslim Majlis in his talks with Jinnah.

The Jinnah–Gandhi talks were to start on 19 August, but due to Jinnah's illness these talks were held from 9 to 26 September.[210] The record of the talks was preserved through letters that the two leaders exchanged during this period.[211] If Gandhi's object, as he confided to Rajagopalachari, was to prove from Jinnah's 'own mouth' the 'absurdity' of the Pakistan scheme, he did not succeed in that; the talks further strengthened the Leaguers' resolve in the justice of their demand.[212] Three documents came under discussion in these talks: the CR Formula, the Lahore Resolution and Gandhi's proposals. At the outset, when Gandhi informed that he had come to talk in his individual capacity and not in any representative capacity, Jinnah pointed out that he would have preferred to negotiate and, if possible, settle the Hindu–Muslim question with someone who had 'a representative status'. Nevertheless, he explained the Lahore Resolution and tried to persuade Gandhi to accept its principles but the latter was opposed to its very basis. Instead, he suggested the CR Formula as an alternative for discussion. Jinnah regarded that formula 'vague and nebulous' and, on Gandhi's request, communicated the points on which he sought clarifications. (Point 1) Jinnah wanted to know formally the capacity in which Gandhi would be a consenting party if an agreement was reached. (Point 2) Who would frame 'the constitution for a free India', which was referred to in clause 1, and when would it come into force? Was the League's endorsement required for the Congress demand as embodied in the August 1942 resolution? If that was so, that would be against the League's resolutions and its creed. He wanted to know the basis or the lines on which the 'provisional interim government' would be formed for the transitional period. (Point 3) He raised several queries about the commission that was to organize the plebiscite and the nature of the franchise.[213] Who would appoint the commission, determine the franchise and give effect to the verdict of the plebiscite? (Point 4) Who were meant by 'all parties' in clause 3? (Point 5) He wanted to know the parties and the machinery through which they would enter into 'mutual agreement', as mentioned in clause 4. What was meant by safeguarding defence, commerce and communications and other essential purposes, and safeguarding against whom? (Point 6) He wanted to know the agency and machinery through which, and to whom, Britain would transfer power. Gandhi had not expected such a minute scrutiny of the CR Formula as Jinnah had done,[214] therefore, he was vague and evasive in his response. His position on some of these points was diametrically opposed to that of Jinnah. On point 1, he informed that he was approaching Jinnah in his individual capacity but promised to use his influence to 'persuade' the Congress to ratify any agreement that they would reach. Point 2, the Congress and the League would form by agreement the provisional interim government that would frame a constitution for the whole of India after the withdrawal of British power. Point 3, the provisional government would appoint the commission; determine the form of plebiscite in areas where the Muslims were not in 'absolute majority' but the franchise would be a matter for discussion; and 'absolute majority' meant a clear majority as in Sindh, NWFP and Balochistan.[215] Point 4, 'all parties' meant 'all parties interested'. Point 5, 'mutual agreement' meant agreement between the contracting parties. A 'central or joint board of control' would be constituted for 'safeguarding defence, etc,' against all who might put 'the common interests in jeopardy'. Point 6, power would be transferred to the provisional government as early as possible. Jinnah again raised the points that had not been answered and picked up new ones resulting from Gandhi's response. He was especially keen to know Gandhi's views on the composition and powers of the provisional government, and to whom it would be responsible. Gandhi was apparently bogged down and then 'shunted off' the CR Formula and tried to put Jinnah on the defensive by seeking clarifications from him to understand the Lahore Resolution, which he termed 'indefinite'.

Gandhi disputed the two-nation theory to which the Lahore Resolution itself, he wrote, had made no reference, arguing that 'a body of converts and their descendants' could not claim to be a nation 'apart from the parent stock'. Mere acceptance of Islam did not make the Muslims a separate nation. Then, he raised fifteen points, some arising out of the Lahore Resolution and others not directly related to it. Jinnah in his response stated that he could not explain the two-nation theory by correspondence and referred Gandhi to two works, one by Dr B.R. Ambedkar[216] and the other by M.R.T.,[217] which the latter considered inadequate for understanding the two-nation theory. He replied in brief to the questions that arose out of the Lahore Resolution. That Pakistan was not mentioned in the Lahore Resolution and did not bear its original meaning; but it had become synonymous with it. Its goal was not pan-Islam and any question to that effect was 'a mere bogey'. The word 'Muslim' did not require any explanation and that the Muslims 'are a nation'. The constituents, i.e. the six provinces—Punjab, Sindh, the NWFP, Balochistan, Bengal and Assam—, in the two Muslim majority zones would form units of one state, Pakistan. The demarcation of boundaries of the units would be undertaken as soon as the principles of the Lahore Resolution were accepted; and the application of the resolution was confined to British India. Adequate, effective and mandatory safeguards for minorities, Jinnah wrote, would be a matter of negotiation with the minorities in the two states, Pakistan and Hindustan. The Lahore Resolution provided, Jinnah wrote, basic principles and the details would be worked out by the contracting parties after its acceptance. Both leaders argued for and against the principles embodied in the resolution and stuck to their respective standpoints. On 22 September, Gandhi suggested 'a way out. Let it be a Partition as between two brothers, if a division there must be.' Jinnah asked him to elaborate his proposals and provide him the 'rough outlines'.

On 24 September, Gandhi put forward the details of his proposals in a patronizing way. Assuming that India was not 'two or more nations' but one family consisting of many members of whom Muslims in the north-west and north-east zones where they were in 'absolute majority' desired to live in separation from the rest of India, he was prepared to 'recommend to the Congress and the country' to accept the claim contained in the Lahore Resolution 'on my [Gandhi's] terms'. A commission approved by the Congress and the League should demarcate the areas of absolute Muslim majority, and then the wishes of the inhabitants of the demarcated areas should be ascertained through the votes of the adult population of the areas or through some equivalent method. If the vote was for separation, these areas would form a separate state as soon as possible after India was free from foreign domination. A treaty of separation should provide 'for the efficient and satisfactory administration of foreign affairs, defence, internal communications, customs, commerce and the like, which must necessarily continue to be matters of common interest between the contracting parties.' The treaty would contain terms to safeguard the rights of minorities. After the acceptance of these terms, the Congress and the League would decide common course of action for the attainment of independence; and the League would be free to remain out of any Congress-sponsored direct action. And independence meant as envisaged in the August 1942 Quit India resolution. Jinnah's comments were that the August 1942 resolution, Jagat Narain Lal's resolution and Gandhi's proposals were opposed to the principles of the Lahore Resolution. If implemented, these would maim and mutilate the boundaries of the Pakistan provinces, and even in such mutilated provinces, the right of self-determination would be exercised not by the Muslims but by all the inhabitants. Besides, the League wanted a complete settlement immediately on the basis of Pakistan and Hindustan by a united struggle, and not after the withdrawal of British power. The Lahore Resolution did not envisage, he wrote to Gandhi, any central authority and all matters of security arising out of geographical contiguity would be decided by the constitution-making bodies of the two countries. On the other hand, Gandhi believed that the CR Formula and his own proposals had provided 'the substance and essence' of the Lahore Resolution. Perhaps, keeping in view British keenness to see India united, he suggested that 'a third party or parties' could be invited 'to guide or even arbitrate [between] us'. He advised Jinnah 'to think fifty times before throwing away' his 'offer' and asked him to provide him an opportunity to address the League council or its open session, if the offer was not acceptable to him. Jinnah was of the view that the CR Formula and Gandhi's proposals had 'a very close family resemblance' and both were calculated to 'torpedo the Pakistan demand'. The question of third party or parties, Jinnah wrote, did not arise as Gandhi had repeatedly made it clear that he was having these talks 'as an individual seeker'. As to Gandhi's request to address the League council or its open session, Jinnah informed him that under the League constitution, only a member or a delegate was allowed to participate in the deliberations of these bodies. No agreement in his opinion could be reached unless 'fully accredited' representatives of the League and the Congress were involved in the negotiations. On 26 September, the talks ended in failure: Jinnah hoped that it was not 'the end of our efforts'; and Gandhi called it 'an adjournment *sine die*'. But these were mere pious wishes. After this, the issue of partition did not come under discussion between the League and Congress leaders till after the general elections.

Jinnah in his last letter had expressed his apprehension that many in Gandhi's circle were waiting 'to pillory' him when a word would go out about the failure of the talks. That is what happened; the Hindu politicians and press denounced and caricatured him for sticking to the Pakistan scheme. Even Gandhi himself joined the campaign, accusing Jinnah of suffering from 'hallucination'. He conceded that the Muslims could have 'a separate state' where they had 'obvious majority' but if they claimed 'utterly independent sovereignty' for that state, that was 'an impossible proposition'; and that would mean 'a fight to the knife'.[218] The Leaguers were disturbed by the hostile propaganda and tried to counter it by distributing thousands of printed copies of the Jinnah–Gandhi talks and related documents throughout India. On 1 October, the Bombay presidency Muslim League passed a comprehensive resolution on the political situation, spelling out that the CR Formula and Gandhi's proposals did not provide 'the substance or essence of the Lahore Resolution'; the Muslims were entitled 'to exercise their inherent right' of self-determination as a Muslim nation and 'not as inhabitants of a territorial unit'; and real Hindu–Muslim unity would be achieved only if the 'basic and fundamental principles' of the Lahore Resolution were accepted 'freely, frankly and honestly'.[219] On Jinnah's advice and in response to Liaquat's communication, all the provincial Muslim Leagues organized public meetings at which they adopted resolutions on the lines of the Bombay presidency Muslim League's resolution.[220] The next serious attempt to break the deadlock was made at the Simla conference where the Wavell plan was discussed.

(C) THE WAVELL PLAN

After the failure of the Cripps Mission, the British government had maintained status quo in regard to constitutional advancement of India. Still, quite a few proposals were floated to break the deadlock. These proposals essentially focused on interim arrangements. Their British and Hindu sponsors and advocates believed that working together of the Congress and League representatives in an interim government would generate communal harmony that would pave the way for one constituent assembly of a united India. The object was to shelve and eventually eliminate the Pakistan scheme. Lord Wavell as the viceroy-designate had submitted a memorandum to the war cabinet in September 1943, before his departure for India, which proposed a coalition government at the centre in which all the executive council members would be Indians, except the commander-in-chief and the viceroy. For this purpose, he wanted permission of the war cabinet to invite the Indian political leaders 'to a secret round-table conference' in the viceroy's house in Delhi for discussion. On 7 October, the war cabinet, due to opposition from Churchill and Attlee, declined to accede to his request but asked him to make his recommendations for further steps at any time in future.[221] Wavell waited for a year before he made his next proposals. Meanwhile, he in vain attempted to soften the Congress attitude: on 17 February 1944, in his address to the central assembly, he emphasized the 'geographical unity of India' for economic and security reasons and sent a copy of his address to Gandhi as a statement of his 'point of view'; at that time, the latter was himself trying to win over Wavell by his softly worded letters to him.[222] But the League resented Wavell's anti-Pakistan scheme remarks in his address: Jinnah considered them 'provocative and thoughtless', demonstrating as if the viceroy was throwing a 'bait to the Congress' to secure its 'good behaviour during his tenure'; and the *Dawn*, the semi-official organ of the All-India Muslim League, produced a cartoon in which Wavell was shown extracting a dead mouse from his mental hand bag.[223] The pro-League writers wrote in the press to disprove his thesis; more known is the article by Qazi Saeeduddin Ahmad a professor at the Aligarh Muslim University, 'Is India Geographically One?'[224] The League expressed its annoyance against the viceroy's remarks by manoeuvring the defeat of several government motions during the Budget session in the central assembly, so much so that Wavell was apprehensive that he might have to certify the finance bill.[225] Wavell released Gandhi on his own initiative, a decision that Churchill did not like. He seriously pursued a plan for a transitional or provisional government during, and more persistently after the failure of, the Jinnah–Gandhi talks.

Wavell wanted to put in office a government composed of representatives of the main political parties before the end of the war without touching on the long-term settlement or the Pakistan scheme.[226] His plan was similar to the one that he had submitted to the war cabinet in September 1943, at the time of his departure for India. He sent his plan to Amery (secretary of state for India) on 20 September 1944, after consulting the governors, the commander-in-chief and his European advisers. The plan visualized a provisional government consisting of six Hindus, six Muslims, one Sikh and one member of the Depressed Classes, in addition to the commander-in-chief and the governor-general and functioning according to the existing constitution. This government would remain in office until the new constitution came into force. It would appoint representatives of British India to the peace conference and other international conferences; consider the composition of the constituent assembly that would draft a constitution; and negotiate the treaty with Britain. Wavell felt the need to hold talks with Gandhi and Jinnah about his plan. If they were agreeable, he looked forward to convening a conference of principal leaders, which would propose names of a provisional government for the approval of the British government through regular channels; and in a subsequent communication, he suggested possible names of the invitees to the conference. The new government would then take office and governments in the provinces under section 93 would be formed simultaneously or soon afterwards. If the conference found it necessary or desirable to hold fresh elections, these would be organized after the new central and provincial governments had assumed office. The princely states would be brought in at the time of framing the constitution.[227] He abandoned the idea of talking to the two leaders after the failure of the Jinnah–Gandhi talks but stressed the need for a fresh move by the British government to break the deadlock because the two main parties in his view were 'incapable of finding a solution'.[228] He limited the proposed conference to ten members: Gandhi (Congress), and one other; Jinnah (Muslim League), and one other; Ambedkar (Depressed Classes); Tara Singh (Sikhs); M.S. Aney (non-Congress Hindus); Khizr Hayat (non-League Muslims); and M.N. Roy (Labour).[229] Doubts were expressed about the acceptability of his plan. The sceptics were worried that the Congress might reject it as it was essentially on the lines of the short-term proposals of the Cripps offer; and the League would not commit itself to any plan that did not provide for Pakistan and Jinnah would claim the right to nominate all the

Muslim members of the provisional government.[230] Wavell also realized possible opposition to his plan in the war cabinet and approached Prime Minister Churchill directly to secure his support.[231] He was keen to visit London to explain and defend his plan.[232] Before his plan came up before the war cabinet for discussion two other proposals with more or less similar objectives were put forward: one by the Sapru Committee and the other by Bhulabhai Desai (1877–1946), leader of the Congress party in the central assembly. When the war cabinet formally discussed the Wavell plan, it decided to wait for two to three months for the recommendations of the Sapru Committee and then invite Wavell to London to defend his plan if the cabinet was not in its favour.[233]

(i) *Sapru Committee*. Both the proposals, one by the Sapru Committee and the other by Bhulabhai Desai, were made at Gandhi's behest and with Wavell's tacit endorsement. Gandhi's primary aim was to get the Congress leaders released from jails in order to move on with the struggle for freedom. When his repeated attempts for their release had met with failure, he thought of a joint Congress–League pressure. This had been one of the aims of his talks with Jinnah, but the talks failed due to his unwillingness to pay the price that Jinnah demanded for such a venture. However, he persisted in exploring fresh avenues. Conversely, Wavell believed that if the proposals for an interim government originated with the Indian leaders, these would have more acceptability with the British government and the Indian people than his own plan; and Desai's proposals, he naively estimated, could break the Congress solidarity as well and weaken its opposition to the war efforts. At first, Sir Tej Bahadur Sapru on Gandhi's advice advocated these proposals from the platform of the non-party conference.[234] Sapru and his 'Liberal' colleagues still wielded considerable influence with the British government but not to the extent that they had enjoyed at the time of the Cripps Mission. At that time, they were so influential that, according to Amery (secretary of state for India), the 'whole genesis of the Cripps offer was in fact a telegram from Sapru & Company to Winston'.[235] Interestingly, the twelve-volume British government-sponsored project (*The Transfer of Power, 1942–47*) starts with a cable from Sapru and his friends. But, early in April 1944, the British government had rejected the demands that Sapru had made on behalf of the non-party conference for coalition or representative ministries in provinces under section 93, a 'truly national government' at the centre and release of the Congress leaders.[236] Now in late October and early November 1944, Sapru after several meetings with Gandhi agreed to hold a meeting of the standing committee of the non-party leaders and discussed with him the resolution that it was to adopt. Wavell agreed to provide Sapru all 'reasonable assistance'.[237] The Standing Committee, in a meeting on 18–19 November, decided to appoint a conciliation committee to examine the communal question from a constitutional and political viewpoint and approach different parties and their leaders to find a solution within two months and secure its acceptance by all the parties concerned. On 3 December, Sapru who was authorized to constitute the conciliation committee announced its twenty-two members that included three Muslims who at that time had hardly any political influence.[238]

Sapru sent a copy of the resolution of the standing committee and a summary of his statement in its explanation to Jinnah. He communicated to Jinnah the ambitious agenda of the conciliation committee in detail, that: it would study the views of the main political parties about the future constitution; analyze full implications of the Pakistan scheme; and evaluate the full import of the CR Formula, Gandhi's proposals and the demands of the All-India Hindu Mahasabha, the Sikhs, the Scheduled Castes and other important bodies. It would then make 'concrete suggestions' to resolve the prevailing controversies in politics. Sapru expressed his desire for a meeting with Jinnah along with one or two members of the conciliation committee 'to obtain clarification' from him 'on the practical aspects of the problem'. But Jinnah emphatically declined to see him because, he wrote, he could not recognize the non-party conference or its standing committee or the conciliation committee and the way Sapru proposed to deal with the political situation. He was otherwise willing to meet Sapru and did not mean to show him any discourtesy.[239] He published his correspondence with Sapru to avoid any misunderstanding. Despite his publicly expressed views about the Sapru Committee and the general impression that its deliberations would be 'worthless' without Jinnah's participation, Sapru continued to pursue the agenda of the standing committee. The British government in London put undue weight on its deliberations and, surprisingly, deferred consideration of the Wavell plan. The war cabinet communicated to Wavell that his plan was not materially different from the proposals that he had discussed in September 1943, and that the most suitable time for his visit to London to discuss his plan would be after the outcome of the Sapru Committee's deliberations was known, which presumably would be in two to three months.[240] It was after the receipt of this communication that Wavell lost interest in the Sapru Committee and its possible findings, and began to push Desai's proposals, even at the cost of his own plan.[241]

The Sapru Committee did send interim proposals in a cable to Wavell in London in April 1945, when the war cabinet was discussing plans for provisional arrangements in India. The standing committee in its interim recommendations opposed the division of India into 'two or more separate, independent and sovereign states or the non-accession of provinces', and provided for a union assembly, with 10 per cent seats reserved for special interests such as commerce and industry, landholders, labour and women, and the remaining seats distributed among various communities; Muslims would have equal number of seats with the Hindus other than Scheduled Castes, provided they agreed to the substitution of separate electorates by joint electorates. It recommended a national government at the centre with similar parity between the Hindus and Muslims.[242] Jinnah denounced the Sapru Committee and termed the 'pompous and pious profession' of its members that they were a detached and independent body as 'utterly false'. Its proposals, he commented in a press statement, were meant to torpedo the Pakistan scheme and Muslim India would not accept any constitutional change on the basis of united India. He hoped that the British government would honour its pledges to the Muslims and not impose a constitution on them without their 'approval and consent'. He concluded, 'I should be failing in my duty, having regard to the temper, determination, and deep feelings of Muslim India regarding this issue, if I did not draw the attention of Britain to the disastrous consequences it might lead to, for which the British Government alone would be responsible'.[243] The final report of the Sapru Committee appeared in May but no one took notice of its recommendations.

(ii) *Liaquat–Desai Pact.* Bhulabhai Desai's scheme, better known as the so-called 'Liaquat–Desai Pact', originated in dubious circumstances.[244] On 15 November 1944, Wavell had a meeting with Desai who sounded the viceroy about his proposal of a national government at the centre composed of members of the existing legislature and coalition governments in section 93 provinces, provided the members of the Congress working committee and others were released. Wavell welcomed his proposals but opposed the release of the Congress leaders.[245] Then, he approached Jinnah, through Francis Mudie, to know his views on the political situation. Mudie after a meeting with Jinnah on 24 November, reported that the League president was not interested in the Sapru Committee and opposed the procedure that in March 1942, Cripps had suggested for framing a new constitution but was willing to cooperate in the formation of a coalition government representing the political parties at the centre without hinting at the proportion of their representatives. Wavell was not satisfied with the Mudie–Jinnah talks and his impression was that Jinnah might have extracted 'more out of Mudie than he gave away himself'.[246] Two weeks later, on 6 December, Wavell himself had his first meeting with Jinnah after his assumption of viceroyalty. In that meeting, Jinnah argued that united India was a British creation and 'an impracticable proposition', while Wavell who was personally opposed to the Pakistan scheme insisted on a united India and a coalition government at the centre which might create communal harmony and facilitate 'a solution of the constitutional problem by consent'. Jinnah expressed his willingness to consider any proposal that the British government might put forward for the formation of a provisional government under the existing constitution but reiterated at the end his conviction that 'Pakistan was eventually both necessary and desirable'.[247] This interaction demonstrated that Wavell could not easily manipulate Jinnah to accept any proposal out of line with the policy of the All-India Muslim League. And when Wavell, in his address to the associated chamber of commerce in Calcutta on 14 December 1944, spoke of the need for a united India and opposed any 'major surgical operation such as Pakistan', Jinnah countered his arguments in his speeches during his tour of Ahmadabad (Gujarat) in January 1945.[248]

Bhulabhai Desai drafted his proposals after the war cabinet linked Wavell's plan and his visit to London with the final report of the Sapru Committee, which was likely to take two to three months. On 3–5 January 1945, Desai held meetings with Gandhi who gave him guidelines for the formation of a Congress-League interim government at the centre, advised him to get 'the previous approval of Jinnah' and promised to inform the Congress working committee at 'the proper moment' to the effect that 'Bhulabhai had acted with his approval'.[249] On the basis of these discussions, Desai drafted his 'Proposals for the Formation of an Interim Government at the Centre', which stipulated a Congress–League agreement to form an interim government at the centre that would have (*a*) equal number of nominees of the Congress and the League; the nominees could be from outside the central legislature; (*b*) representatives of the minorities, in particular the

Scheduled Castes and the Sikhs; and (c) the commander-in-chief.[250] The government thus formed would function under the existing constitution but would not invoke the 'reserve powers' of the governor-general, if any measure was not passed by the legislative assembly. Its first step would be to release the members of the Congress working committee. The governor-general would be approached to propose that he desired a Congress–League interim government at the centre and invite Jinnah and Desai, either jointly or separately, to form the government 'on the basis of this understanding'. After that, coalition governments would be formed in the provinces that were under section 93.[251] Liaquat came into the picture after Desai had finalized the draft of the proposals. According to Liaquat, Desai had informally discussed with him after the 1944 autumn session of the central assembly the possibility of some interim arrangements at the centre. But it was on 11 January 1945, when Liaquat was to leave on a tour of the Madras presidency that Desai showed him his proposals; and he had with him two copies of the draft; he himself initialled one copy and gave it to Liaquat and took Liaquat's initials on the other. The proposals were 'to be treated as strictly private and confidential'. Liaquat told him that its contents could be 'the basis for discussion' but these would need the support of Gandhi and approval of Jinnah 'who was the proper authority to entertain any proposals on behalf of the Muslim League'. Desai had Gandhi's endorsement and informed Liaquat that he had plans to meet Wavell and Jinnah.[252] When the information about the 'pact' leaked to the press, on 15 January 1945, Liaquat issued a denial of any 'pact'. A week later, on 22 January, Jinnah who was on a tour of Ahmadabad categorically disclaimed his approval of the Liaquat–Desai negotiations.[253] Strangely enough, neither Desai nor Wavell, who became an advocate of Desai's proposals, thought of contacting Jinnah who was supposed to be a partner in the proposed coalition government at the centre. Similar was the posture of the India committee when Wavell approached the secretary of state for India. In fact, Jinnah's denial was not taken seriously![254]

On 13 January 1945, Desai met with Evan Jenkins (private secretary to the viceroy), and, on 20 January, had an interview with Wavell and explained to both of them main features of his scheme.[255] Interestingly, none of them asked Desai for an authentic copy of his scheme; and even Wavell simply took notes of the main points of the conversation![256] Wavell then sought authorization from the war cabinet to talk to Jinnah and if his attitude was favourable to see him and Desai together.[257] But the India committee of the war cabinet thought it 'undesirable' for Wavell to see Jinnah 'at this stage', raising several queries, and asked Wavell that his private secretary should see Liaquat to ascertain whether Desai's scheme had been prepared with Jinnah's approval.[258] Wavell himself answered some queries but insisted on the course of action that he had suggested, opposing any discussion between his private secretary and Liaquat. He expressed his preference for Desai's scheme, which bore similarity with his own plan, because it had been prepared by 'influential Indians' and had the support of the right wing of the Congress; and he planned to deal with the Leader of the Congress assembly party in the selection of members of the provisional government rather than with the official Congress, i.e. the Congress working committee.[259] Wavell's naïve insistence was 'tantamount to accepting the Desai proposals in principle' without knowing its implications; and the India committee was unwilling to accept that. The India committee, however, agreed to his meeting with Jinnah and Desai without committing himself 'in any way' as to the 'acceptability or otherwise' of the scheme; the object was to ascertain the extent of Hindu and Muslim support that it enjoyed.[260] Wavell accepted this suggestion and proposed to meet Jinnah first and, in case he reacted favourably, to meet him and Desai together. If an acceptable solution resulted from these talks, he planned to visit London by early March, stressing that any delay would decrease chances of success.[261] He was hesitant to face Jinnah directly because, according to him, his 'reputation' was not 'very encouraging'; and Jinnah tended to be 'extremely reasonable in general conversation' but was too technical when it came to a decision. He approached John Colville (governor of Bombay), provided him the background of the Desai scheme and his own interaction with the war cabinet and sent him the queries on which elucidation was required from Jinnah. He requested Colville to meet Jinnah and telegraph the result of his talk with him.[262] On 24 February, Colville talked to Jinnah for two hours. Jinnah emphatically denied that there had ever been any authorized discussion between Desai and Liaquat and that the former had no authority to make any suggestion about the attitude of the League. He informed Colville that he was reaching Delhi on 6 March, and would meet Wavell soon after his arrival in the city, if the date and time were fixed. He refused to go to Delhi earlier for health reasons and the meeting was fixed on 7 March.[263]

On his arrival in Delhi on 7 March, Jinnah suddenly fell seriously ill and postponed his meeting with Wavell. Amery expressed his apprehension that Jinnah's illness might delay Wavell's London visit as Attlee, chairman of the India committee, had a busy schedule after 4 April; he had to participate in the Commonwealth World Organization conference and then attend the San Francisco conference. Wavell was seemingly shaken by this information and could not accept the indefinite postponement of his visit to London. Now Desai's scheme, which he had so far passionately advocated, was for him 'only [an] incidental development' and 'a side issue'; and he was unwilling to wait indefinitely for Jinnah's recovery and did not care for Desai who, he alleged, was 'talking rather loosely' with his friends, offering some of them portfolios in the new government. He was keen to know, he wrote to Amery, the mind of His Majesty's Government about his own plan than 'the mind of Desai and Jinnah'.[264] Attlee's suggestion in view of his own engagements was that the right time for Wavell's visit would be in the beginning of June. When Wavell got this information, he protested in the 'strongest possible terms' against any postponement of his visit, insisting that he should know His Majesty's Government's mind regarding its future policy in India before the end of war in Germany. His Majesty's Government, in view of his strong feelings for immediate consultation, agreed to his visit 'as soon as possible'.[265] Wavell arrived in London on 23 March, along with Jenkins, his private secretary, and V.P. Menon, who had succeeded H.V. Hodson as the reforms commissioner to the Government of India in 1942. Any long-term constitutional settlement was not discussed because Jinnah would then insist 'on Pakistan as a pre-requisite' for that; and the British government was not 'prepared either to impose a united India on the Muslims or a divided India on the Hindus. Progress under the existing constitution, leaving the ultimate solution in abeyance', was seen as 'the only practical course.'[266] After intensive talks on various proposals for about two months the war cabinet approved a plan that basically included interim arrangements.[267] On 14 June, ten days after his return from London, Wavell announced the plan, and a simultaneous announcement about it was made by Amery (secretary of state for India) in the house of commons.

(iii) The Simla Conference. The Wavell plan authorized the viceroy to reconstitute his executive council in a way that it would represent the main communities and include equal proportion of caste Hindus and

Muslims. All the executive council members would be Indians except the viceroy and the commander-in-chief, who would be in charge of the war portfolio. The executive council would function under the existing constitution but the governor-general would not exercise his constitutional powers to override unreasonably the executive council in certain circumstances. Wavell was to convene a conference of twenty-one leaders in Simla on 25 June, to discuss the formation of a politically representative executive council. The invitees would include Jinnah, Gandhi, Leader of the Congress and deputy leader of the League in the central legislative assembly, leaders of the League and Congress in the council of state, chief ministers and last chief ministers of section 93 provinces, leaders of the Nationalist Party and European group in the central assembly and one representative each of the Sikhs and the Scheduled Castes. The members of the Congress working committee who were still in jail would be released. After the formation of the executive council, coalition ministries would be formed in provinces under section 93. For Jinnah and the League, the composition of the executive council was of vital interest because, in addition to its power to prosecute the war against Japan and run the government in British India including the post-war development, the executive council was to evolve agreement on the future constitution. Wavell issued invitations for the conference that was to meet on 25 June; originally, Azad was not invited obviously not to offend Jinnah. Jinnah and Gandhi were asked to meet the viceroy one day before the conference. On Gandhi's response that he represented no institution and that the Congress president should be invited to represent that party, invitation was also issued to Azad who agreed to attend the conference subject to approval by the Congress working committee. Gandhi offered to remain available in Simla for 'advice', provided the viceroy and the Congress working committee so wished. He objected to the use of the term 'caste Hindus' because it was derogatory and conveyed an erroneous impression that the Congress was only their representative while its claim was that it represented all the communities. On 21 June, the Congress working committee, ignoring its Quit India resolution for complete independence, decided to participate in the conference at Simla in the hope of assuming power.

Jinnah and the League had not been involved directly or indirectly in the evolution of the Wavell plan except for the so-called Liaquat–Desai pact, which was used against the League.[268] At the Simla conference, its representatives were six out of twenty-one invitees.

When Jinnah met Wavell on 24 June, a day before the conference, he raised three points: (*i*) the League should have the right to nominate all the Muslim members of the executive council; (*ii*) if a majority of the Muslims were opposed to any issue in the executive council that issue should not be decided by voting because they would be in a minority and the smaller minorities would vote with the Hindus due to the identity of their long-term goals; and (*iii*) the Muslims should have a fair share of the key portfolios such as home, finance, foreign affairs and war transport. Wavell rejected all the three demands. Despite this negative response, the League participated in the conference to find a way out of the impasse.[269] On 25 June, Wavell opened the conference and after his opening remarks, he clarified that the expression 'caste Hindus' simply meant Hindus other than the Scheduled Castes, and gave clarifications about other matters particularly those relating to foreign affairs. When he assured Azad that the plan had not branded the Congress as a communal party, Jinnah interjected that it represented the Hindus to which Dr Khan Sahib objected; Wavell saved the situation by his observation that the Congress represented its members; both Jinnah and the Congress leaders accepted that explanation. Jinnah made it clear that the Wavell plan was a stop-gap arrangement and would not affect in any way the League demand for Pakistan or the Congress stand for independence. The future constitution would be framed by agreement and it would not be imposed on the country, as the British government had clarified its position. The League would accept a constitution, he said, only if it was framed on the basis of Pakistan, a position that was fundamentally different from the Congress demand for a united India and common central government. It would be wrong, he stated, to question the representative character of each other; the Congress represented 90 per cent of the Hindus and the League represented 90 per cent or more of the Muslims.[270]

On the second day, Wavell on Jenkins's advice placed a two-part agenda before the conference: Part A covered general points about the qualities of members, nature of portfolios, and so on; and Part B related to the strength and composition of the executive council and the method by which the names of the panels would be submitted to the viceroy.[271] There was agreement on Part A but the political parties disagreed on Part B. The conference adjourned to give time to the parties, essentially the League and the Congress, to resolve their differences. Jinnah and Pandit Govind Ballabh Pant, former chief minister of the United Provinces, on behalf of the Congress, held negotiations, as the former refused to talk to Azad.[272] Pant proposed an executive council of 16 members, while Jinnah suggested an executive council of 14 members that would include 5 Hindus, 5 Muslims, one Sikh and one Scheduled Caste, besides the viceroy and the commander-in-chief. Pant asked two seats for the pro-Congress Muslims from the Muslim quota that Jinnah refused to accept, insisting that the League should have the right to nominate all the Muslim members. On 27 June, the conference again adjourned after a brief session to provide the Congress and the League more time to bridge their differences. Pant stuck to his position and Jinnah reiterated the League's right to nominate all the Muslims. They failed to reach an agreement. When Jinnah saw Wavell the same day; the latter suggested allocation of one seat from the Muslim quota for a Unionist Muslim in view of the importance of the Punjab 'both to the Army and the food supply'.[273] Wavell was under pressure from Glancy and Khizr who were apprehensive that if the League assumed power at the centre, it would be difficult for the Unionists to survive in power unless there was a Unionist Muslim on the executive council.[274] Jinnah refused to accept Wavell's suggestion. He was willing to compromise on the five seats provided Wavell promised to make a declaration conceding self-determination for the Muslims before the announcement of names for the executive council but Wavell had neither the intention nor the mandate to do that.[275] Now Wavell came up with a new proposal, which could be used to bypass Jinnah's demand. When the conference reassembled on 29 June, and was informed about the failure of Jinnah–Pant talks, he first suggested five points, to which the participants agreed, that the new executive council would agree: (*i*) to prosecute effectively the war against Japan; (*ii*) to recommend men of ability and influence for the new executive council; (*iii*) to take steps as soon as the executive council was established to solve the long-term problem — the future constitutional structure of India; (*iv*) to work under the existing constitution until the new constitution came into force; and (*v*) to accept the explanation given by the viceroy and the secretary of state for India in their speeches on the exercise of veto by the viceroy.[276] Then, he proposed that all the parties should send him panels of names whom they would like to be on the executive council; the lists should contain more names than the number of seats available to them; and they could suggest names of others also but a distinction had to be made between people whom they regarded as their party members and others. He would consider these names, and possibly add some names of his own, and prepare a panel acceptable to all concerned. The League and the Congress each were asked to send him lists of not less than eight and not more than twelve names; and the remaining delegates were to send three names each. The nominations and consultation with the party leaders would be kept secret. The representatives of the Congress and the League promised to give their responses after consulting their working committees; the remaining delegates straight away accepted the procedure.[277]

From 3 to 6 July, the Congress working committee held its meetings, which Dr Khan Sahib and Maulana Husain Ahmad Madni attended by special invitation, and finalized a list of names that was submitted to the viceroy.[278] The League working committee remained in session from 6 to 14 July and took decisions on issues that came up for its consideration. On 6 July, it raised three points: (i) it proposed that instead of submitting a panel, the procedure suggested by Linlithgow at the time of the August Offer and accepted by the League should be followed, i.e. its representatives should be selected in confidential discussions between Wavell and Jinnah; (ii) the League should select all the Muslim members after consultation with the viceroy before they were recommended by him to the British government for appointment; and (iii) some effective safeguards other than the governor-general's veto as announced by the secretary of state for India should be provided to protect Muslim interests from majority decisions of the executive council.[279] On 7 July, Jinnah communicated these points to Wavell and had an interview with him on the following day for one and half hour. Focus of discussion was on the second point. Wavell refused to give any guarantee that all Muslim members would be League nominees but was prepared to accept five names if Jinnah did not wish to send him more names.[280] Jinnah refused to do that unless Wavell promised in advance to accept the League's nominations on all the Muslim seats.[281] There was difference of opinion in the League ranks on the acceptance of the Wavell plan and submission of a panel, which was used to spread rumours about its solidarity, but the absence of any defections disproved these rumours.[282] Jinnah dispelled such rumours by his public statement, declaring at a reception organized in his honour by the Simla district Muslim League, 'Nothing will make me accept any proposal or scheme which I think is likely to prejudge, prejudice or militate against our goal of Pakistan', and warded off possible pressure from within and outside the League by adding that the delegates at the conference were 'in the position of advisers to Lord Wavell' and the services of the League working committee members had been 'requisitioned' for that purpose, but 'do not forget we are only advisers, when the true picture emerges it cannot be binding upon the All India Muslim League until it has been ratified by our organization.'[283] The League working committee approved the stand that Jinnah had taken at the conference.[284]

Even after Jinnah's categorical refusal to submit a panel, Wavell made a provisional list of names for the executive council and sent it to London for approval. He used his own judgment in selecting four Leaguers (Liaquat, Khaliquzzaman, Nazimuddin and Haji Abdussattar Haji Essak Sait) and one Khizr-nominee (Sir Mohammad Nawaz Khan), for the five Muslim seats. Interestingly, he did not include any nationalist Muslim in the provisional list perhaps on Gandhi's advice who had publicly stated that the Congress would not insist on one Muslim seat for a nationalist Muslim provided the Unionists were given 'one seat on the basis of independent Muslim representation outside the Muslim League'.[285] The war cabinet discussed this list on 10 July; the general sense in the meeting was that Wavell should, in the first instance, communicate to Jinnah privately the Muslim names and 'endeavour to persuade him to put these names forward, or at least accept them, as his list'. While communicating this information to Wavell, Amery asked him to show Jinnah the names of the remaining members in the list only to 'let him know' that it did not 'contain a Congress Muslim'. If Jinnah was 'obdurate', he wrote, it would be his 'funeral' and advised the viceroy to 'rub the point into him as strongly as you can'.[286] Wavell had a meeting with Jinnah on 10 July, and informed him about the five Muslim nominees. Jinnah 'absolutely refused even to discuss the names' with Wavell unless he agreed that (a) all Muslim members were taken from the League, and (b) no decision objected to by the Muslims should be taken in the executive council 'except by clear two-thirds majority or something of that kind'. These conditions, he told Wavell, were fundamental and he could do no more unless the viceroy accepted them.[287] According to Wavell, after Jinnah's negative response, he did not show the remaining part of the provisional list to Jinnah or any other delegate.[288] He saw Gandhi after Jinnah left. When he verbally informed him about the latest developments, Gandhi calmly observed that the British government would have 'to decide sooner or later to come down on the side of the Congress or the League, or of Hindu or Muslim, since they could not resolve their differences by themselves'.[289] Wavell consulted the governors by telegram on the advisability of going ahead without the League but they were evenly divided in their opinions; the governors of two key provinces, Bengal and Punjab, were against the formation of the executive council without the League.[290]

On 14 July, the conference held its last session where Wavell himself accepted the responsibility for its failure. Azad tried to put the blame on the League because it had demanded the right to nominate Leaguers on all the Muslim seats. Jinnah defended the League stance, observing that the Congress stood for a united India while the League wanted Pakistan and these two positions were 'entirely incompatible'. The League had asked the British government to guarantee two conditions: the first was the acceptance of Pakistan which Wavell's broadcast and Amery's speech in the house of commons on 14 June, had put in cold storage indefinitely; and the second was that the Muslims should have equality of representation in any interim arrangement but the British government had accepted none of these conditions. It suited the Congress, he said, to accept the Wavell plan for it stood for a united India but it was not in the interest of the League to accept the plan.[291] The conference dispersed without any positive outcome. The Congress leaders including Gandhi wanted Wavell to implement his plan without the League's cooperation and participation but he was not prepared to take that risk, apprehensive of a Muslim backlash.[292] Soon after, the Labour Party after its landslide victory in the general elections formed the government with Clement Attlee as prime minister; and on 15 August, the war came to an end with the surrender of Japan; Germany had already capitulated on 6 May. One reason for the rejection of the League stance at the Simla conference was that its representative status was contested. Therefore, the League demanded fresh elections to the central and provincial legislatures to determine the representative status of the political parties.[293] And Jinnah declared on 6 August, 'Let us go ahead with measures for a permanent constitutional settlement. Pakistan must be decided if the issue of freedom and independence of India is to be decided. We will never surrender on the issue of Pakistan to anybody as our claim is just and righteous one and is the only solution for India.'[294]

NOTES

1. Statement of Sir Hugh O'Neill, under-secretary of state for India, in the House of Commons, in 359 H.C. Deb. 5s., 18 April 1940, column 1170; views of P.J. Griffiths, leader of the European group in the central legislative assembly, *TP*, vol. VII, p. 242; Wavell's statement, ibid., vol. VII, p. 332; Hasan Suhrawardy to Jinnah, 11 November 1942, QAP, F. 457, p. 76; and passionate speeches of the members of parliament when Prime Minister Attlee made the announcement about the Cabinet Mission on 15 March 1946.
2. For a declining number of British youth going to India, see Amery to Linlithgow, 5 January 1942, and Linlithgow to Amery, 21 February 1942, *TP*, vol. I, pp. 10–11 and 216.
3. Linlithgow to Jinnah, 23 December 1939, and Jinnah to Linlithgow, 23 February 1940, Pirzada, *Quaid's Correspondence*, pp. 209–213; draft communiqué, QAP, F. 95. p. 63; and resolution No. 1 passed by the working committee on 3–6 February 1940, Pirzada, *Foundations*, vol. III, p. 282.
4. Jinnah to Linlithgow, 8 April 1940, Waheed, *Nation's Voice*, vol. II, p. 58.
5. On 30 March 1940, Liaquat asked all the provincial Muslim Leagues to direct their branches to observe the day by holding public meetings in support of the Lahore resolution; and on 14 April, Jinnah called on the Leaguers for the observance of the day.
6. Liaquat gave this figure in the central assembly. For meetings held in Bengal and Assam, see vols. 327–30; Balochistan vols. 418 and 421; Punjab and Delhi vols. 372–73; Madras vols. 374–78, and 420; United Provinces vols. 347 and 379–80; Bihar vol. 339; NWFP, Orissa, Sindh, Indian States, Burma and Sri Lanka vol. 421; Bombay vol. 418; Central Provinces and Berar vol. 419; and various organizations including women's branches vol. 422 of the AFM.
7. 359 H.C. Deb. 5s., 18 April 1940, column 1174; and 116 H.L. Deb, 5s., 18 April 1940, column 173. Such 'irresponsible pronouncements', Jinnah observed, showed 'complete ignorance' of the Indian situation and were 'calculated to shake the faith of the Muslims of India' in the Lahore Resolution. Waheed, *Nation's Voice*, vol. II, pp. 17–18.
8. Linlithgow to Jinnah, 19 April 1940, Pirzada, *Quaid's Correspondence*, pp. 213–14; and *Civil & Military Gazette*, 24 May 1940.
9. Jamil-ud-din Ahmad, *Some Recent Speeches and Writings of Mr. Jinnah*, vol. II, Lahore, 1946, p. 188.
10. Jinnah to Linlithgow, 18 May 1940, Pirzada, *Quaid's Correspondence*, pp. 214–15.
11. Sikandar to Jinnah (telegram), 24 May 1940, Jinnah to Sikandar, 27 May 1940, QAP, F. 353, pp. 20 and 24; Sikandar to Jinnah, 31 May 1940, ibid., F. 21, pp. 1–3; and Jinnah to Khaliquzzaman, 4 June 1940, ibid., F. 364, p. 11.
12. Jinnah to Linlithgow, 18 May 1940, SHC, Misc. I: 2; and for Jinnah's refusal to attend a meeting of the defence ministry unless the All-India Muslim League had received the required assurances, see the *Star of India*, 9 April 1940.
13. For resolutions passed by the working committee, see AFM, vol. 129, no. 28.
14. Jinnah to Laithwaite, 1 July 1940, Pirzada, *Quaid's Correspondence*, pp. 217–18.
15. Waheed, *Nation's Voice*, vol. II, pp. 85 and 221; and *IAR*, 1941, vol. II, p. 295. Hasrat Mohani was one of those Leaguers who advised Jinnah to insist on the viceroy to accept the Pakistan scheme after the war. For his telegram to Jinnah, see QAP, F. 95, p. 95.

16. On 29 June, Linlithgow had met Gandhi but could make 'no material progress' in his talks.

17. For the resolution of the Congress working committee passed in its meeting in Delhi on 3–7 July 1940, and ratified at a meeting of the All India Congress Committee in Poona on 27–28 July, see Menon, *Transfer of Power*, p. 91.

18. For pressure from the bureaucracy and some 'seasoned loyalists' on the Leaguers 'not to carry out the instructions' of the working committee', see Jinnah's press interview, *Star of India*, 11 July 1940.

19. For views critical of Sikandar's position, see AFM, vol. 262, p. 51; and QAP, F. 825, pp. 53 and 79.

20. *IAR*, 1940, vol. I, p. 80; and *Star of India*, 18 June 1940.

21. Jinnah to Shahnawaz Mamdot, 21 June and 3 July 1940, QAP, F. 373, pp. 3 and 5; for the provincial Muslim League working committee's resolution, see AFM, vol. 132, no. 34; and for resignations in Bihar, see *IAR*, 1941, vol. II, p. 21; for resignations of Aurangzeb and Sadullah, see QAP, F. 215, p. 36; and for other documents relevant to this issue, see ibid., F. 97, pp. 11, 13–14, 16, 18–19 and 20–31, and F. 331, pp. 2–3.

22. For his telegram to Jinnah, 24 June 1940, see QAP, F. 281, p. 8; and for an account of Bengal presidency Muslim League working committee meeting on this issue, see ibid., F. 204, pp. 1–2.

23. Jinnah to Fazlul Haq and Sikandar, 5 July 1940, Sikandar to Jinnah, 5 and 8 July 1940, and Jinnah to Sikandar, 1 August, ibid., F. 97, pp. 3–10; and F. 353, pp. 32–36.

24. Jinnah to Nawab Mohammad Yusuf, 22 June 1940, ibid., F. 469, p. 19.

25. For the text of the resolutions, see ibid., F. 568, p. 103; and AFM, vol. 262, p. 9; and for a list of the signatories, see ibid., vol. 132, p. 40.

26. Jinnah to Liaquat, 13 August 1940, QAP, F. 335, pp. 130–31; Nazimuddin to Jinnah, 7 August 1940, ibid., F. 392, pp. 24–29; and Ghulam Bhik Nairang to Jinnah, 16 August 1940, ibid., F. 1098, pp. 308–9.

27. Jinnah–Aurangzeb correspondence, QAP, F. 329, pp. 95, 97 and 115; Barkat Ali to Jinnah, 16 July and 5 August 1940, and Jinnah to Barkat Ali, 9 August 1940, ibid., F. 215, pp. 47–48 and 54–55.

28. Shamsul Hasan to Nawabzada Khurshid Ali Khan, 25 July 1940, AFM, vol. 262, p. 12; Barkat Ali to Liaquat, 5 August 1940; Liaquat to Barkat Ali, 7 August 1940, ibid., vol. 132, nos. 39–40; and vol. 262, pp. 21–50.

29. For apprehensions about a split, see Ali Mohammad Rashidi to Jinnah, 25 July 1940, QAP, F. 427, p. 3.

30. Jinnah to Linlithgow, 17 July 1940 and Linlithgow to Jinnah, 24 July 1940, ibid., F. 95, pp. 107–8.

31. Jinnah to Linlithgow, 2 August 1940, ibid., F. 95, p. 109.

32. J.B. Irwin to Jinnah, 4 August 1940; and Jinnah to Irwin, 5 August 1940, ibid., F. 95, pp. 110 and 111.

33. For Jinnah's reasons disallowing special meeting of the council, see his letter to Liaquat, 9 August 1940, AFM, vol. 262, p. 20; and for further details, see the Jinnah–Liaquat correspondence, QAP, F. 335, pp. 5–6, 82–86 and 108–115.

34. For minutes of the Punjab provincial Muslim League meeting held in Lahore on 14 July 1940, see ibid., F. 579, pp. 20–21; and Jinnah's statement, *Star of India*, 12 August 1940.

35. The viceroy sent advance copies of the announcement to the League, Congress and All-India Hindu Mahasabha.

36. Amery's speech in the parliament, 14 August 1940, Waheed, *Nation's Voice*, vol. II, pp. 727–39. The viceroy himself told Dr B.S. Moonje, the Mahasabha leader, that 'the Pakistan scheme could not be ruled out when the future constitution for India was being considered'. *Leader*, 26 September 1940.

37. Resolution passed by the working committee in its meeting on 31 August–2 September 1940.

38. For a strongly worded resolution of the League working committee on Amery's speech on the Lahore Resolution in the house of commons, passed at its meeting on 31 August–2 September 1940, see AFM, vol. 129, no. 40.

39. *IAR*, 1940, vol. II, pp. 372–73.

40. Linlithgow to Jinnah, 14 August 1940, Pirzada, *Quaid's Correspondence*, pp. 221–22.

41. Linlithgow rejected Jinnah's suggestion for representation on 50:50 basis. Menon, *Transfer of Power*, p. 98.

42. Linlithgow to Jinnah, 25 September 1940; and Jinnah to Linlithgow, 26 September, Pirzada, *Quaid's Correspondence*, pp. 222–25.

43. AFM, vol. 262, p. 57; and *IAR*, 1941, vol. I, pp. 22–23 and 32. Members expelled from the Punjab were: Nawabzada Khurshid Ali Khan, Nawab Muzaffar Khan and Sardar Ahmad Khan of Fatehkot.

44. Resolution passed by the working committee on 28 September 1940, AFM, vol. 129, no. 59.

45. For his speech in the All-India Muslim League council on 29 September 1940, see Waheed, *Nation's Voice*, vol. II, p. 51. Jinnah released to the press his correspondence with the Viceroy.

46. Speech in the central assembly, Ahmad, *Some Recent Speeches and Writings*, pp. 220–21.

47. For Jinnah's address to the Delhi MSF on 24 November 1940; his address to the Punjab Muslim Students Federation on 2 March 1941; and his interview with a London newspaper, see Waheed, *Nation's Voice*, vol. II, pp. 87, 174 and 118, respectively.

48. *IAR*, 1941, vol. I, p. 42; Menon, *Transfer of Power*, p. 104; and Waheed, *Nation's Voice*, vol. II, p. 118; and resolution passed by the All-India Muslim League working committee on 22 February 1941; and by the council on 23 February.

49. Resolutions passed by the All-India Muslim League working committee regarding Muslim countries particularly Iran in its meeting on 24–26 August 1941, AFM, vol. 133, no. 30; and vol. 136, no. 21.

50. Its text appeared only in the *Times of India* (Bombay). Nazimuddin to Jinnah, 9 November 1940 and Jinnah to Nazimuddin, 12 November 1940, in QAP, F. 392, pp. 35–37; and for further details about the League and the Muslim world, see Chapter 7.

51. For Jinnah's insistence on association of the League with real authority in government, see his telegram to Secretary of State for India Amery and Prime Minister Churchill, 31 December 1940, QAP, 490, p. 7.

52. Jinnah to C.M.G. Ogilvie, 27 March 1941, ibid., F. 501, p. 3.

53. Jinnah to Husain Imam, 25 May and 14 June 1941, and Husain Imam to Jinnah, 19 June 1940, ibid., F. 296, pp. 20, 23 and 41.

54. The viceroy had asked the premiers to keep their nomination secret.

55. On 28 August 1941, Jinnah released this correspondence to the press. *IAR*, 1941, vol. II, pp. 300–302 and 318–19.

56. File 770 of the QAP includes telegrams to this effect.

57. Ibid., F. 1122, pp. 231–32; and *IAR*, 1941, vol. II, p. 7.
58. For instance, see Ayub Khuhro to Jinnah, 23 August 1941, QAP, F. 365, pp. 25–26; and Ahmad Yar Daultana to Jinnah, 6 August 1941, ibid., F. 255, pp. 30–31.
59. Conversely, the Congress considered it inadvisable on the part of the Sindh Congress to demand the resignation of its Sindh chief minister from the national defence council. *IAR*, 1941, vol. II, p. 15.
60. QAP, F. 113, p. 11.
61. File 770 of the QAP contains numerous telegrams and letters. Jinnah, in his address to the Aligarh Muslim University union on 2 November 1941, criticized the government action; he said, 'Muslim India from one end to another' stood behind the League to teach the British government 'a lesson'. Ibid., F. 1095, p. 138; AFM, vol. 164, no. 33; vol. 237; and *IAR*, 1941, vol. II, p. 12.
62. Jinnah to Sir Hasan Suhrawardy, 1 August 1941, QAP, F. 457, p. 18. He was so infuriated that, according to one source, he blamed the viceroy for 'double-crossing' him. Cited in Stanley Wolpert, *Jinnah of Pakistan*, OUP, 1984, p. 189.
63. Sikandar to Jinnah, 26 August 1941, QAP, F. 1092, p. 123; and Jinnah to Sikandar, 29 August and 13 September 1941; and Sikandar to Jinnah, 1 September 1941, ibid., F. 353, pp. 39 and 46; and for Sikandar's statement see the *Leader*, 28 August 1941.
64. For details, see Chapter 8.
65. Jinnah to Sir Sultan Ahmad, n.d., QAP, F. 874, pp. 170–71.
66. Jahan Ara to Jinnah, 4 September 1941, and Jinnah to Jahan Ara, 8 September, ibid., F. 441, pp. 5 and 9.
67. Resolution passed at the meeting of the working committee held on 24–26 August 1941, AFM, vol. 133, no. 30.
68. Ibid., vol. 277, p. 86. This resolution was not included in the officially printed resolutions.
69. *Dawn*, 16 November 1941; and *IAR*, 1941, vol. II, pp. 92 and 108.
70. For his address to the union on 2 November 1941, see AFM, vol. 237.
71. Resolution passed by the working committee in Delhi on 16 November 1941, ibid., vol. 136, no. 17.
72. When Jinnah was asked to suggest a person as Sir Akbar Hydari's successor in the Hyderabad state, he declined to do that because the government had taken the decision regarding the executive council and national defence council against the League's wishes. Jinnah to Firoz Khan Noon, 13 January 1941, QAP, F. 399, p. 20.
73. Initially, Churchill denied the application of these principles to India. Moore, *Churchill, Cripps and India*, p. 42.
74. Linlithgow to Amery, 16 February 1942, *TP*, vol. I, p. 181. Churchill tried to ward off the pressure by stressing the communal dimension of the issue. Churchill to Roosevelt, 4 March 1942, ibid., pp. 312–13.
75. Linlithgow to Churchill, 21 January 1942, and Amery to Attlee, 26 January 1942, ibid., vol. I, pp. 53–54.
76. Ibid., pp. 39–40 and 81–90.
77. *IAR*, vol. II, p. 40.
78. Sir R Lumley to Linlithgow, 1 January 1942, *TP*, vol. I, pp. 1–3; and *IAR*, vol. II, p. 33.
79. His statement to the *News Chronicle*, 20 December 1941, *IAR*, vol. II, p. 45; and Amery to Linlithgow, 13 January 1942, and Amery to Attlee, 26 January 1942, *TP*, vol. I, pp. 7 and 22.
80. Tej Bahadur Sapru to Sir Gilbert Laithwaite, 2 January 1942, *TP*, vol. I, pp. 3–5.

81. Linlithgow to Sir A. Clark Kerr, 26 January 1942, ibid., pp. 78–79.
82. Firoz Khan Noon to Generalissimo Chiang Kai-shek, 12 February 1942, Noon to Linlithgow, 12 February 1942, QAP, F. 399, pp. 21–24 and 25–27, respectively. On 14 February, Noon sent his correspondence with the Generalissimo to Jinnah through M.A.H. Ispahani [ibid., F. 399, p. 28]. Volume 1 of the *TP* has several documents about the Generalissimo's visit. See also Auriel Weigold, *Churchill, Roosevelt and India: Propaganda during World War II*, New Delhi, 2008, p. 48.
83. See Chapter 7.
84. Resolutions passed by the All-India Muslim League working committee in Nagpur on 27 December 1941, and in Delhi on 22 February 1942, AFM, vol. 136, no. 41; and Linlithgow to Amery, 21 January 1942, *TP*, vol. I, p. 45.
85. His statement to the *News Chronicle*, *IAR*, 1941, vol. II, p. 46.
86. Lumley to Jinnah, 15 January 1942, *TP*, vol. I, p. 26.
87. Lumley to Linlithgow, 15 January 1942, ibid., p. 29.
88. Churchill to Attlee, 7 January 1942, ibid., p. 14.
89. Amery to Churchill, 22 January 1942, ibid., pp. 54–55.
90. L.S. Amery, 'The Indian Political Situation: Memorandum by the Secretary of State for India', India Office, 28 January 1942, ibid., pp. 81–90.
91. Peter Clarke, *The Cripps Version: The Life of Sir Stafford Cripps, 1882–1952*, London, 2002, p. 390. Immediately on his return from Moscow, Cripps had urged a change in policy. *Dawn*, 22 February 1942. Ed.
92. Cripps is reported to have been advising the Congress leaders 'to stand firm as a rock' upon their demands. B.K. Mishra, *The Cripps Mission: A Reappraisal*, New Delhi, 1982, p. 41.
93. Clarke, *Cripps Version*, p. 279.
94. Linlithgow to Amery, 25 February 1942, *TP*, vol. I, pp. 243–46; and for Amery's opposition to change in policy, see Amery to Churchill, 15 February 1942, ibid., pp. 171–42.
95. Volume 1 of the *TP* contains the draft and the amendments.
96. For the text of the final draft declaration, see ibid., pp. 357–58.
97. Jinnah to Churchill, 25 February 1942, SHC, Misc.-I: 45.
98. *TP*, vol. I, p. 270.
99. Ibid., p. 279.
100. Waheed, *Nation's Voice*, vol. II, p. 393; SHC, Misc.-I: 47; and *IAR*, 1942, vol. I, p. 53.
101. Jinnah to Sir George Schuster (Liberal National), 25 February 1941, cited in Waheed, *Nation's Voice*, vol. II, p. 387; and also see Moore, *Churchill, Cripps and India*, p. 45.
102. For Jinnah's message, see Churchill to Roosevelt on 4 March 1942, *TP*, vol. I, p. 310.
103. Churchill to Roosevelt, 7 March 1942, Linlithgow to Amery, 7 and 8 March 1942, and note by Sir Geoffrey de Montmorency, *TP*, vol. I, pp. 363–64, 370–71 and 374. On 1 January 1941, Muslims were 37 per cent (155,000 out of 418,000) in the British Indian army, and Punjab contributed 48 per cent (96,000 Muslims and 51,000 Sikhs). Maj.-Gen. Rob M. Lockhart had warned that 'any concessions to the Congress would produce a violent reaction from the Muslim League. Should this happen and should Mr Jinnah and his party attempt to stir up serious trouble, the effect on the Army might be disastrous'. [Note by Maj.-Gen. Lockhart, 25 February 1942, ibid., pp. 238–89, which was circulated to the India committee.] Firoz Khan Noon, the defence member, in a 'secret' letter to Jinnah on 8 October

1942, gave totally different figures about the communal representation in the army. QAP, F. 399, pp. 69–70.

104. Amery to Linlithgow, 9 March 1942, *TP*, vol. I, pp. 386–87.

105. Ibid., p. 280.

106. As early as 24 January 1942, Attlee had proposed to send someone to India to bring the Indian political leaders together to satisfy the pressure from the British political parties. Attlee to Amery, ibid., p. 75; and a follow-up note by Attlee on 2 February, ibid., pp. 110–12.

107. Amery to Linlithgow, 10 March 1942, ibid., pp. 396–97.

108. For Jinnah waving a copy of the anti-League article, see Clarke, *Cripps Version*, p. 289; and also see *TP*, vol. I, p. 484.

109. Note by Sir S. Cripps, 25 March 1942; memorandum of conversation between Linlithgow and Cripps on the night of 25 March 1942; Cripps to Amery, 26 March 1942; and war cabinet, committee on India, 9th meeting, 26 March 1942, *TP*, vol. I, 484–85, 492 and 493.

110. Cook to Jinnah, 2 April 1942, in QAP, F. 19, p. 10; and Pirzada, *Foundations*, vol. II, pp. 387–88.

111. *TP*, vol. I, p. 566.

112. Ibid., p. 480; and QAP, F. 917, pp. 64–70; and 'War Cabinet Paper W.P. (43) 441', *TP*, vol. IV, p. 372.

113. *IAR*, 1942, vol. I, p. 66; and Waheed, *Nation's Voice*, vol. II, p. 421.

114. Note by Sir S. Cripps: Interview with Azad and Nehru, 2 April 1942, *TP*, vol. I, p. 609.

115. Churchill to Cripps, 10 April 1942, ibid., p. 722. In the event of an Indian defence member being appointed, the possible choice was Nehru. *Foreign Relation of the United States* 1942, Washington, p. 630, cited in Mishra, *Cripps Mission*, p. 142.

116. For details, see Menon, *Transfer of Power*, pp. 125–32; and Moore, *Churchill, Cripps and India*, pp. 77–113.

117. Churchill to Cripps, 9 April 1942, *TP*, vol. I, p. 704

118. Jinnah's press conference, 13 April 1942, *Dawn*, 19 April 1942.

119. Note by Cripps, 28 March 1942, *TP*, vol. I, p. 515. Jinnah raised the stakes high if the League was to come in without the Congress; in that case, the fifteen-member executive council was to have 8 of League, 2 of the All-India Hindu Mahasabha selected by the viceroy, and representatives of the depressed classes and Sikhs approved by Jinnah. Linlithgow to Amery, 12 April 1942, ibid., pp. 761–62.

120. For Cripps's refusal to accept Jinnah's proposal, see his letter, 9 April 1942, QAP, F. 490.

121. For the text of the resolution, see AFM, vol. 137, pp. 15–20; and Pirzada, *Foundations*, vol. III, pp. 377–80.

122. For the text, see *IAR*, 1942, vol. I, pp. 224–25.

123. *Dawn*, 19 April 1942.

124. The Congress decision, Rajagopalachari wrote in the annual number of the *Amrita Bazar Patrika* in 1943, 'betrayed a lamentable lack of foresight'. 'War Cabinet Paper W.P. (43) 441', *TP*, vol. IV, p. 370.

125. For his observations, see his press conference on 22 April 1942, ibid., vol. I, p. 815.

126. *Dawn*, 19 April 1942. Later on, Cripps denied that he had made those remarks.

127. Cited in Clarke, *Cripps Version*, p. 339.

128. Mishra, *Cripps Mission*, p. 86; Moore, *Churchill, Cripps and India*, p. 91; and *IAR*, 1942, vol. I, p. 73.

129. *IAR*, 1942, vol. I, p. 71; and Nehru's press conference, 12 April 1942, in Gopal (ed.), *Nehru: Selected Works*, vol. 12, pp. 219–21.

130. *IAR*, 1942, vol. I, p. 90. Mehr Chand Khanna and his friends also believed that the Congress had rejected the Cripps' proposals because these had 'the Pakistan element in them'. *TP*, vol. I, p. 832.

131. For Azad's remarks, see *IAR*, 1942, vol. I, p. 81; and the *Collected Works of Mahatma Gandhi*, vol. 76, pp. 274–77.

132. *IAR*, 1940, vol. I, p. 68.

133. Ibid., vol. II, p. 73; for Gandhi's immediate reaction to the resolution, see *Harijan*, 30 March, 6 and 13 April, and 4 May 1940; and for Jinnah's refutation of criticism, see his presidential address to the Punjab Muslim Students Federation conference on 2 March 1941, Waheed, *Nation's Voice*, vol. II, pp. 162–74.

134. *IAR*, 1940, vol. I, pp. 54 and 56; and vol. II, p.13.

135. Ibid., vol. I, p. 229.

136. *Star of India*, 28 December 1940; and Waheed, *Nation's Voice*, vol. II, p. 115; and Jinnah to Sir Hasan Suhrawardy, 11 July 1941, QAP, F. 457, p. 8.

137. *IAR*, 1940, vol. II, pp. 81–82; and for Jinnah's reaction, see his letter to Raghib Ahsan, 11 September 1940, Ahmad Saeed, *Quaid-i-Azam: Rare Letters*, p. 72.

138. Ahmad, *Some Recent Speeches and Writings*, p. 231.

139. Resolution passed by the All-India Muslim League council, 23 February 1941, AFM, vol. 263, pp. 74–76. Jinnah wrote to an Indian Christian that he 'would not negotiate with a man' who held a pistol at his head and that Gandhi should call off the individual Satyagraha before he could hold talks with him. Ramachandra Rao, president, All-India Council of Indian Christians to Jinnah, 24 May 1941, QAP, 487, pp. 160–62.

140. Nazimuddin to Jinnah, 25 February 1941; and Jinnah to Nazimuddin, 6 March 1941, QAP, F. 392, pp. 41 and 43.

141. Savarkar's observation in his address to the All-India Hindu Mahasabha meeting at the Ganga Prasad Memorial Hall meeting, *Civil & Military Gazette*, 3 March 1942. Dr Moonje considered it 'blasphemy' to talk of 'vivisection' of motherland. *Dawn*, 2 August 1942.

142. *IAR*, 1941, vol. I, pp. 47 and 288–91.

143. Ibid., vol. II, pp. 2, 3 and 5.

144. Jinnah to Liaquat, 15 July 1941, QAP, F. 335, p. 206; Waheed, *Nation's Voice*, vol. II, p. 226, and *IAR*, 1941, vol. II, p. 46.

145. Cited in Waheed, *Nation's Voice*, vol. II, pp. 344–45.

146. For his message, see the *Leader*, 15 April 1941; and Waheed, *Nation's Voice*, vol. II, p. 225.

147. For the proceedings of the conference, see *IAR*, 1941, vol. I, pp. 306–312. Jinnah felt that Sapru who 'was better than any other Hindu leader' was 'playing a deep game' and that his attitude and policy were 'far more dangerous towards the Muslim League than many realize. Also the tendency of Lord Linlithgow is pro-Hindu, because in these days the stronger is always feared and respected when it comes to choice'. Jinnah to A.M.K. Dehlavi, 3 December 1941, QAP, F. 256, p. 127.

148. For details, see Jinnah–Sapru correspondence, Pirzada, *Quaid's Correspondence*, pp. 347–51; *IAR*, 1941, vol. I, pp. 66–67; and Linlithgow to Amery, 8 January 1942, *TP*, vol. I, p. 18.

149. Mishra, *Cripps Mission*, p. 21; and AFM, vol. 334, no. 86.

150. Secretary of State for India Amery's speech in the parliament, 22 April 1941, as cited in the *Civil & Military Gazette*, 23 April 1941.

151. Waheed, *Nation's Voice*, vol. II, p. 226. For the Muslim Leaguers' response, see Haji Essak Sait to Jinnah, 6 May 1941, QAP, F. 447, p. 42; Jinnah to Nazimuddin, 12 May 1941, ibid., F. 392, p. 44; Abdullah Haroon to Jinnah, 27 May 1941, ibid., F. 274, p. 221; and statement by M.H. Gazdar, *Daily Gazette*, 29 April 1942; and Churchill to Roosevelt, 4 March 1942, *TP*, vol. I, p. 310. For Jinnah's perception that the conference had been sponsored by the Congress, see his statement, *Star of India*, 6 May 1941, and circular letter to the provincial Muslim Leagues, ibid., 24 May 1941.

152. Volume 334 of the AFM contains Liaquat's letter to honorary secretaries of the provincial Muslim Leagues and the resolutions passed by the branch Leagues in response that were sent to the viceroy.

153. Perhaps this strategy was in pursuance of Gandhi's initial comments on the passage of the Lahore Resolution that the Muslims like the rest of the Indians must have the right of self-determination. The Congress wanted to bring in its fold as many Muslims as it could to disprove the League's claim to be the sole representative Muslim party.

154. Jinnah to Liaquat, 18 July 1940, QAP, F. 335, pp. 91–92. Jinnah saw in Azad's 'innocent-looking' telegram 'a pre-meditated move to force the League to recognize him and negotiate with him the Hindu–Muslim question'.

155. Azad to Jinnah, 11 July 1940, and Jinnah to Azad, 12 July 1940, ibid., F. 281, p. 11. For some responses from the Muslim Leaguers and non-Leaguers, see honorary secretary, Madras presidency Muslim League to Jinnah, 14 August 1940, AFM, vol. 265, p. 45; Hakim Hafezul Haq to honorary secretary, All-India Muslim League, 30 July 1940, ibid., vol. 352, p. 66; and joint secretary, Chittagong district Muslim League to Jinnah, QAP, F. 37, pp. 37–38; and for views of the Peshawar Congress committee, Kerala Azad Muslim Association, A.R. Siddiqi, Karimbhai Ibrahim and Abdullah Haroon, see *IAR*, 1940, vol. II, pp. 6, 7, 8 and 10.

156. Pirzada, *Quaid's Correspondence*, p. 37.

157. AFM, vol. 422, p. 7.

158. The Muslim Leaguers believed that he was a puppet president who had no power in the Congress.

159. For a direct criticism of Azad, see Abdul Majid Jatoi, vice-president, Dadu Muslim League to Azad, 17 April 1942, AFM, vol. 248, pp. 44–45.

160. Its important gain in Sindh was Allah Bakhsh Soomro and his supporters. For the Congress campaign against the Punjab and Bengal ministries, see Sharif al Mujahid, 'Pakistan Resolution and the Indian National Congress', Dr (Miss) Kaniz F. Yusuf and others (ed.), *Pakistan Resolution Revisited*, Islamabad, 1990, pp. 305–6.

161. Azad to Abdur Rauf Shah, 24 June 1939, AFM, vol. 49, p. 60; and also see Chapter 8.

162. Waheed, *Nation's Voice*, vol. II, p. 17.

163. For instance, see Wasi Ahmad Khan to general secretary, All-India Muslim League, 16 June 1940, AFM, vol. 352, p. 64.

164. For the committee's resolution, see ibid., vol. 129, no. 28. Despite the ban, both the premiers met with Gandhi and Azad in Delhi without Jinnah's authorization. [*IAR*, 1940, vol. II, p. 4.] On 6 July, Jinnah formally refused Sikandar permission

to meet with Savarkar. Sikandar to Jinnah, 6 July 1940, and Jinnah to Sikandar, 6 July, QAP, F. 353, pp. 30–31.

165. Fazlul Haq to Jinnah, 8 December 1940, QAP, 107, p. 1; and also see Chapter 8. On that occasion, Jinnah wrote to Liaquat (12 December 1940), 'It is a pity that he [Fazlul Haq] allows himself to tumble into these pitfalls. You say "God help us from our friends". I say "organize our people. God is already with us."' Ibid, F. 335, p. 177.

166. For details, see Chapter 8.

167. *IAR*, 1940, vol. I, pp. 323–33; and *TP*, vol. I, p. 293.

168. *IAR*, 1940, vol. II, pp. 262–63.

169. For the All-India Momin Conference and the All-India Shia Conference, see ibid., 1942, vol. I, pp. 55, 56 and 57.

170. A. Haroon to Churchill, 9 March 1942, QAP, F. 274, pp. 233–34.

171. The Momins actually numbered about four million.

172. *IAR*, 1942, vol. I, pp. 9 and 52. The president of the All-India Momin Conference, Shaikh M. Zahiruddin, and its vice president, Abdul Qayyum, sent telegrams to Churchill, Cripps and Amery to this effect.

173. Recognizing the importance of the Momins, the pro-League Momins organized their own conference to support the League cause. Liaquat to Latifur Rahman, 29 June 1942, AFM, vol. 464, pp. 43–44.

174. Linlithgow to Amery, 2 and 7 March 1942, *TP*, vol. I, pp. 293–94 and 361–62; and *IAR*, 1942, vol. I, p. 52. Fazlul Haq and Mian Iftikharuddin were also present in the conference.

175. W.H.P. Gardiner Major's letter to Parker of 28 December 1940, [QAP, F. 939, pp. 36–40] whom Jinnah had shown cuttings of a number of articles from the Hindu press particularly from Madras to that effect.

176. *IAR*, 1942, vol. I, pp. 47–54 and 66.

177. *Dawn*, 26 April 1942.

178. The All-India Hindu Mahasabha observed 10 May as the 'Anti-Pakistan Day'. Savarkar to Linlithgow, 14 May 1942, *TP*, vol. II, pp. 85–7, enclosing a copy of the resolution passed on that Day.

179. *Tribune*, 21 May 1942; and *TP*, vol. II, p. 113; and for views of Savarkar, Moonje, Shyama Prasad Mukerjee, J.B. Kriplani and Nehru, see *IAR*, 1942, vol. I, pp. 82, 83, 85, 86, 88 and 92; and QAP, F. 1010, pp. 16–17.

180. *IAR*, 1942, I, p. 63.

181. Amery to Wavell, 30 December 1943, *TP*, vol. IV, p. 384; Frank Moraes, *Jawaharlal Nehru: A Biography*, Bombay, 1959, p. 288; and Abul Kalam Azad, *India Wins Freedom*, Calcutta, 1959, pp. 71 and 73.

182. Menon, *Transfer of Power*, pp. 142–43; and *Dawn*, 28 June 1942, ed.; *Harijan*, 3, 10, 17 and 24 May 1942, Mishra, *Cripps Mission*, p. 161; and *TP*, vol. II, p. 37.

183. Jinnah's interview with P. Grover of the Associated Press of America on 1 July, *Dawn*, 12 July 1942.

184. For details, see a two-page typed document, QAP, F. 909, pp. 43–44. Earlier, on 30 March 1942, Bose had called on Cripps to withdraw the British forces and 'recognize the complete independence of India.' *TP*, vol. I, p. 553.

185. Several documents in volume two of the *TP* reveal this fact.

186. Incidentally, on 1 October 1942, according to the home department, Government of India, the number of Hur prisoners whipped in Sindh was higher than the Satyagrahi prisoners of Madras, Bihar and Central Provinces put together. Telegram to the secretary of state for India, 5 October 1942, *TP*, vol. III, p. 95.

187. For full text of the resolution, see AFM, vol. 137, pp. 46–50.

188. *TP*, vol. II, pp. 699, 733, 956, 960 and 999; and vol. III, p. 223–24.

189. Ibid., vol. II, pp. 959–60.

190. AFM, vol. 137, no. 11.

191. For resolution of the All-India Muslim League working committee passed on 20 August 1942, see *IAR*, 1942, vol. II, p. 284; and for resolution passed at the Karachi annual session, see Waheed, *Nation's Voice*, vol. III, p. 673. For details, see Noon to Jinnah, 7 September 1942, QAP, F. 399, p. 63; and AFM, vol. 137, no. 25; vol. 311, pp. 50–51, 73 and 79, vol. 392, p. 1–4.

192. Jinnah was equally distrustful of the British who had ruled the subcontinent 'for 150 or 160 years' with the help of 'machine-guns and bayonets', and not with the consent of the people, and were still 'playing their own game'. See his speech at a meeting arranged by the Aligarh Muslim University students' union on 2 November 1942, in AFM, vol. 237.

193. Jinnah's address to the Aligarh Muslim University students' union, 2 November 1942, Ahmad, *Speeches and Writings of Mr. Jinnah*, vol. I, pp. 432–43; and speech at the All-India Muslim League council meeting on 9 November 1942, *IAR*, 1942, vol. II, pp. 286–87.

194. Linlithgow to Amery, 11 and 21 November 1942, *TP*, vol. III, pp. 230 and 289. Rajagopalachari told the viceroy that he was personally prepared to accept Pakistan as part of the post-war settlement.

195. Gandhi to Linlithgow, New Year's Eve 1942 and 19 January 1943, *TP*, pp. 439–40 and 517–19.

196. Menon, *Transfer of Power*, pp. 145–47.

197. Jinnah to Vijaya Anand, 20 February 1944, *JP*, vol. X, p. 165.

198. Menon, *Transfer of Power*, p. 147.

199. Jinnah's address to the Muslim Students Federation, Bombay, 24 January 1942, Waheed, *Nation's Voice*, vol. III, p. 146.

200. Rajagopalachari to Jinnah, 28 May 1942, QAP, F. 186, p. 7. The general impression about Jinnah's presidential address to the Delhi annual session was that he had now made 'Pakistan, total and complete, a *sine qua non* of any understanding with the Congress'. Sir J. Colville to Linlithgow, 6 May 1943, *TP*, vol. III, p. 947.

201. Waheed, *Nation's Voice*, vol. III, p. 196.

202. Secretary, home department, Government of India, to Jinnah (confidential), 24 May 1943, QAP, F. 1025, p. 67; and also see Jinnah to Sir Richard Tottenham, Home Department, Government of India, 15 August 1943, SHC, Misc.-I: 55.

203. According to Mashriqi, 0.25 million telegrams, letters, resolutions, petitions and memorials were sent to Jinnah and the viceroy during this period. For some telegrams, letters, etc., see QAP, Fs. 101, 521–24, 561, 763, 828, 925 and 966–68.

204. Jinnah's interview with Stewart Emeny of the *News Chronicle*, Waheed, *Nation's Voice*, vol. III, p. 391–92.

205. For his speech, see the *Leader*, 14 February 1944; and Waheed, *Nation's Voice*, vol. III, p. 392. At first, according to Khaliquzzaman, Rajagopalachari had agreed with Jinnah that the British government should make 'an unequivocal announcement of their unconditional acceptance of Pakistan' without a plebiscite but later, he changed his views. Francis Mudie to Sir E. Jenkins, 14 April 1944, *TP*, vol. IV, p. 879.

206. *Leader*, 12 July 1944; and Waheed, *Nation's Voice*, vol. III, pp. 520–21. For condemnation of the Formula by the All-India Hindu Mahasabha, see Savarkar to Amery, 26 July 1944, *TP*, vol. IV, p. 1123.

207. *Correspondence with Mr. Gandhi August 1942-April 1944*, New Delhi, 1944.
208. For Jinnah's analysis of the CR Formula, see his speech at the meeting of the All-India Muslim League council held in Lahore on 30 July 1944, *Jinnah–Gandhi Talks (September 1944): Text of Correspondence and Other Relevant Documents, etc.*, Foreword by Nawabzada Liaquat Ali Khan, Delhi, 1944, pp. v–xv. See also Wavell to Amery, 1 August 1944, *TP*, vol. IV, p. 1140.
209. Ahmad Saeed to Raghib Ahsan, 30 May 1944; and A.M. Khwaja to Jinnah, 27 July 1944, *Jinnah Papers* (hereafter *JP*), vol. X, pp. 466 and 606–7, respectively. For the text of the main resolution that the Muslim Majlis adopted, see QAP, F. 139, pp. 6–7.
210. For details about the scheduling of the meeting, see QAP, F. 98, pp. 28–39.
211. For Jinnah–Gandhi correspondence, see *Jinnah–Gandhi Talks*, pp. 2–52; and Pirzada, *Quaid's Correspondence*, pp. 107–41; Waheed, *Nation's Voice*, vol. III, pp. 613–43; and *Gandhi–Jinnah Talks: The Text of Correspondence and other relevant matters*, Preface by C. Rajagopalachari July-October 1944, New Delhi, 1944.
212. Gandhi made this statement to Rajagopalachari. For a slightly different version that Gandhi gave of his talks with Jinnah to Rajagopalachari, see the *Collected Works of Mahatma Gandhi*, vol. 78, pp. 87–90, 96–97 and 128.
213. It was argued that neither any plebiscite was held in Ireland when Ulster and Eire separated nor any plebiscite was organized at the time of separation of Burma and Sri Lanka from India. *Jinnah–Gandhi Talks*, foreword by Liaquat, pp. i–j.
214. Gandhi wrote: 'I understood from our talk that you were in no hurry for an answer. I was, therefore, taking the matter in a leisurely fashion, even hoping that as our talks proceeded and as cordiality increased mutual clarification would come of itself and that we would only have to record our final agreement.'
215. Later, Gandhi told Jinnah that 'absolute majority' meant those areas where the Muslims were more than 70 per cent of the entire population. *Dawn*, 7 October 1944.
216. *Pakistan or the Partition of India*, Bombay, 1941.
217. *Nationalism in Conflict in India*, Delhi, 1942.
218. Press interview, reported in the *Times of India*, 2 October 1942.
219. For the text of the resolution, see AFM, vol. 492, p. 4.
220. For resolutions passed by the branch Leagues, see AFM, vol. 336, pp. 40–49; vol. 492, pp. 7, 9–10, 13–14 and 17.
221. For memorandum, see *TP*, vol. IV, pp. 256–67; and for further details, see *TP*, pp. 227–30, 232–35, 274–77, 367–69 and 378–84.
222. *Legislative Assembly Debates*, vol. I, 17 February 1944, p. 342; and Wavell to Gandhi, 25 February 1944, *TP*, vol. IV, p. 757.
223. For his speech at the AMU on 9 March 1944, see the *Star of India*, 11 March 1944.
224. Shaikh Mohammad Ashraf published it in the 'Pakistan Literature Series', Lahore, 1945.
225. R.F. Mudie to Sir E. Jenkins, 14 April 1944, *TP*, vol. IV, p. 878.
226. Wavell, in a letter to Pethick-Lawrence on 27 August 1945, revealed: 'The object of the Simla proposals was to by-pass the Pakistan issue and to get the parties working together in the central government in the hope that after some inside experience they would take a more realistic view'. Ibid., vol. VI, p. 123.
227. For Wavell's memorandum, see enclosure to his letter to Amery, 20 September 1944, and note by Wavell, *TP*, vol. V, pp. 37–41 and 56–58.

228. Wavell to Amery, 5 October 1944, ibid., p. 85. Wavell did not accept Amery's alternative proposal to leave the existing executive council in office and call a representative conference to consider 'the constitutional future'. Amery to Churchill, 6 November 1944, ibid., p. 178.

229. War Cabinet Paper W.P. (44)684, 22 November 1944, ibid., p. 215.

230. Amery to Linlithgow, 10 October 1944, and note by Sir B. Glancy, 26 October 1944, ibid., pp. 98 and 141–43.

231. Wavell to Churchill, 24 October 1944, ibid., pp. 126–27.

232. Attlee disliked Wavell's undue insistence to visit London at an early date, and wrote to Amery (28 December 1944) that it was 'another example of the disadvantage of having a viceroy with no political experience'. Ibid., p. 342.

233. Ibid., p. 274.

234. Wavell to Amery, 15 November 1944, ibid., p. 206.

235. For his letter to Wavell, 30 December 1943, see *TP*, vol. IV, p. 584.

236. For memorandum supporting the resolution of the non-party conference held at Lucknow, April 1944, see ibid., pp. 29–33 and 990.

237. War Cabinet Paper W.P.(44)684, *TP*, V, p. 218; and statement by Tej Bahadur Sapru at a press conference on 19 November, *Dawn*, 20 November 1944.

238. Muslim members were: Wazir Hasan, Mohammad Yunus and Nabi Bakhsh Mohammad Husain. Wavell to Amery, *TP*, vol. V, pp. 272–73; and Sir H. Twynam to Wavell, 23 November 1944, ibid., p. 220.

239. Jinnah–Sapru correspondence, Pirzada, *Quaid's Correspondence*, pp. 351–52.

240. 'War Cabinet: India Committee. Paper I (44) 6', 20 December 1944, *TP*, vol. V, pp. 313–14.

241. *TP*, vol. V, pp. 334 and 340–42.

242. Ibid., pp. 860–61; and H.V. Hodson, *The Great Divide: Britain—India—Pakistan*, OUP, 1985, p. 218.

243. For his statement, see *TP*, vol. V, pp. 824–25.

244. For an account in defence of Liaquat's position in regard to the 'pact', see Muhammad Reza Kazimi, *Liaquat Ali Khan*, pp. 116–50.

245. 'Note on conversation with Mr Bhulabhai Desai', 15 November 1944, *TP*, vol. V, pp. 230–31.

246. Wavell to Amery, 29 November 1944, ibid., p. 252.

247. 'Note by Field Marshal Viscount Wavell', 6 December 1944, ibid., pp. 279–81; and also see Sir M. Hallet to Sir J. Colville, 27 March 1945, ibid., pp. 749–51.

248. *Dawn*, 15 December 1944; and Waheed, *Nation's Voice*, vol. IV, pp. 44–54.

249. *The Collected Works of Mahatma Gandhi*, vol. 79, p. 438.

250. The proportion agreed was 40 per cent each for Congress and League and 20 per cent for minorities.

251. For the text that Liaquat released to the press on 31 August 1945, see M. Rafique Afzal, *Speeches and Statements of Quaid-i-Millat Liaquat Ali Khan [1941–51]*, Lahore, 1967, pp. 28–29; and a slightly different version, see M.C. Setalwad, *Bhulabhai Desai*, Delhi, 1978, p. 367. For the versions of Liaquat and Desai about the talks, see *IAR*, 1945, vol. II, pp. 124–27.

252. Afzal, *Speeches and Statements of Liaquat Ali Khan*, pp. 30–32.

253. Earlier on 19 January, Mudie had learnt from the president of the Bombay presidency Muslim League, I.I. Chundrigar, that Jinnah knew nothing about the Liaquat–Desai talks and reported that information to the viceroy's private secretary, Evan Jenkins. *TP*, vol. V, p. 423.

254. Wavell to Amery, 29 January 1945, ibid., p. 478.

255. Ibid., pp. 400–403.

256. Wavell's response when Jinnah asked for a copy of Desai's scheme, Jenkins to Symington, 25 February 1945, ibid., 617.

257. Wavell to Amery, 21 January 1945, ibid., p. 425.

258. For the queries and objections, see ibid., pp. 444 and 454.

259. Wavell to Amery, 30 January 1945, and 11 February 1945, ibid., pp. 478–82 and 541.

260. 'War Cabinet: India Committee. Paper I (45) 21', 31 January 1945, ibid., pp. 487–88 and 494–96.

261. Wavell to Amery, 10 February 1945, ibid., p. 539.

262. For details, see Wavell to Colville, 22 February 1945, ibid., pp. 593–95.

263. Colville to Wavell, 24 February 1945, ibid., pp. 607–8.

264. Wavell to Amery, 12 and 13 March 1945, ibid., pp. 671 and 679.

265. Attlee to Amery, 13 March 1945, Amery to Wavell, 14 March 1945, Wavell to Amery, 15 March 1945, and Amery to Wavell, 15 March 1945, ibid., pp. 686, 691, 696 and 697.

266. Amery to Colville, 30 May 1945, ibid., vol. V, p. 1061.

267. Churchill agreed to the Wavell Plan because the India committee assured him that 'it was bound to fail!' Wavell: The Viceroy's Journal, p. 168.

268. For Wavell's invitation and Jinnah's response, see the correspondence, QAP, F. 1025, pp. 79–81.

269. Wavell to Amery, 25 June 1945, TP, vol. V, pp. 1153–54; and Wavell: The Viceroy's Journal, pp. 146–47.

270. Wavell to Amery, 25 June 1945, TP, vol. V, pp. 1154–57.

271. Wavell: the Viceroy's Journal, pp. 147–48; and Wavell to Amery, 26 June 1945, TP, vol. V, pp. 1162–63.

272. TP, vol. V, pp. 1165–66 and 1210. In retaliation, Azad began to mobilize minor anti-League Muslim parties on one platform.

273. Wavell to Amery, 28 June 1945, ibid., p. 1170.

274. TP, vol. V, p. 528; and Wavell: The Viceroy's Journal, p. 144.

275. Waheed, Nation's Voice, vol. IV, p. 162.

276. Ibid., p. 156.

277. Wavell to Amery, 29 June 1945, TP, vol. V, pp. 1173–74. On 1 July, Wavell wrote to Amery that 'Jinnah was entitled to a majority of Muslim representation in the new Council—say 3 seats out of 5—but his claim that the League represents all the Muslims of India is quite unacceptable'. Ibid., pp. 1182–85.

278. The Congress list had names of three Muslim Leaguers: Jinnah, Liaquat and Nawab Ismail.

279. Jinnah to Wavell, 7 July 1945, QAP, F. 505, 11–13; AFM, vol. 142, no. 29; and TP, vol. V, pp. 1205–6.

280. Wavell to Jinnah, 9 July 1945, QAP, F. 505, pp. 16–17.

281. Jinnah to Wavell, 9 July 1945, TP, vol. V, p. 1213.

282. For instance, see Cunningham to Wavell, 2 July 1945, ibid., p. 1190; K.H. Khurshid, Memories of Jinnah (edited by Khalid Hasan), Lahore, 1999, p. 109; and Wavell: The Viceroy's Journal, p. 153.

283. Dawn, 11 July 1945; and Waheed, Nation's Voice, vol. IV, p. 172.

284. For resolution no. 1 (c) of the working committee passed at its meeting on 6–14 July 1945, see Waheed, Nation's Voice, vol. IV, p. 684.

285. Amery to Wavell, 10 July 1945; TP, vol. V, p. 1224; Civil & Military Gazette, 4 July 1945; and Waheed, Nation's Voice, vol. IV, p. 160. For Jinnah's position on

this issue, see Jinnah to Hatim Alavi, 1 August 1945, SHC, Sindh-VI: 14. What passed on between Wavell and the Congress on this issue is not known because Wavell-Azad correspondence was not released despite repeated demands from the League. *Dawn*, 8 August 1945.

286. *TP*, vol. V, pp. 1221–24.
287. Wavell to Amery, 11 July 1945, and Wavell to King George VI, 19 July 1945, ibid., pp. 1224–45 and 1279.
288. Wavell to Azad, 13 July 1945, ibid., p. 1242.
289. Ibid., p. 1226.
290. *Wavell: The Viceroy's Journal*, p. 157.
291. For the minutes of final meeting of Simla conference on 14 July 1945, see *TP*, vol. V, pp. 1243–46; and for Jinnah's elaboration of this point, see his press conference on 14 July 1945, *Dawn*, 15 July 1945.
292. *TP*, vol. VI, p. 53.
293. AFM, vol. 180, no. 19.
294. *Dawn*, 8 August 1945.

10

The General Elections, 1945–1946

The central and provincial legislatures that functioned in India before the general elections of 1945–46 had a long life. The central legislative assembly with a normal life of three years was more than ten years old, and the council of state, with a normal life of five years, was eight years old.[1] Before the Second World War, the life of the central assembly was extended in the hope that the federal legislature under the 1935 Act consisting of British India and princely states would come into existence, but that did not happen due to opposition from the political parties and rulers of the states. The All-India Muslim League had not participated in the 1934 elections to the central assembly under the Act of 1919, although quite a few Muslim Leaguers had been elected as independent candidates or on the tickets of other political parties. But the League did participate in the provincial elections under the Act of 1935 but its performance was not noteworthy because the provincial Muslim Leagues had not yet been properly organized in the provinces. After the provincial elections, its growth and rise was phenomenal; and Muslim legislators began to join the League parties that were formed in the central and provincial legislatures. Its membership strength in the assemblies of some provinces soon rose to a level that enabled it to form League-led coalition ministries of different durations in Bengal, Sindh, Assam, NWFP and the Punjab as component part of the Punjab Unionist Party. From 1938 onward, it put up candidates in the bye-elections on Muslim seats of various legislatures and the results showed its enhanced strength in the Muslim electorates. During 1 January 1938–12 September 1942, the All-India Muslim League won 46 out of 56 bye-elections that were held on Muslim seats, Congress secured 3 and Independents 7.[2] Its success in the bye-elections after that and before the general elections was equally impressive.

The bye-elections were, however, no substitute for the general elections and did not show the influence that the All-India Muslim League had gained at the grassroots. The League demanded fresh elections so that its real strength was represented in various Legislatures, which would give a solid proof of Muslim support for the Pakistan scheme. When the general elections had to take place in early 1942, and a postponement was under consideration, the All-India Muslim League at its Madras session (April 1941) had urged upon the British government not to postpone the elections at least in those provinces where provincial autonomy was working under the Act of 1935, and also in the NWFP where the League confidently claimed that a stable government could be formed.[3] However, the governor-general in the case of central legislature and the British parliament in the case of provincial legislatures postponed the elections due to the war and the life of the existing legislatures was extended till the election of new ones.[4] Later on, the League at its Karachi session (December 1943) called upon the British Indian government to convey to the parliament to review the policy of 'staying' elections to the central and provincial legislatures during the war. This policy, it observed, had reduced the provincial Legislatures to a position where they were 'rapidly getting out of touch with public opinion' and were no longer representative of 'true views and sentiments of the people'. The excuse of war, it represented, was not reasonable because elections had been held all over the world including the USA and the British colonies such as Canada and South Africa.[5] The British government was not moved. Even in mid-1945, when the war was coming to an end and the process of general elections was under way in Britain, the British government was working on the Wavell plan that was to defer a long-term settlement of the constitutional problem and bring in office an interim government, which was to decide about the general elections. The League calculated that the Wavell plan was in fact a design to postpone the general elections and defer indefinitely the long-term settlement of the Hindu–Muslim problem in order to dilute the Pakistan scheme. Therefore, before the formal conclusion of the Simla conference on 14 July, its working committee demanded fresh elections to the central and provincial Legislatures to determine its representative character. Referring to the resolution passed at its Karachi session, it demanded 'immediate steps' to hold the general elections as important questions awaited solution which could 'only be properly dealt with by representatives in touch with public opinion'.[6] On 4 August, Liaquat followed up the League demand by a formal request to the viceroy for fresh elections.[7] The League leaders then built up popular pressure in support of holding fresh elections.[8] The Congress was, however, lukewarm about the general elections, as it wanted time to prepare its organization for the elections. Initially, its leaders after their release from jails were keen to assume power at the centre and in section 93 provinces but were pointlessly hesitant to make a request to that effect and their demand for elections came much later.[9]

After the Simla conference, Lord Wavell consulted the provincial governors who, except for Governor Glancy of the Punjab, advised for fresh elections; and, on 21 August, after consulting the government in London, he announced that elections to the assemblies would be held in the coming 'cold weather'.[10] The British government had to chalk out its own post-election policy and strategy; and for that, it invited Wavell for consultation who visited London along with Sir Evan Jenkins and V.P. Menon from 24 August, to 16 September. While the Congress and the Punjab Unionists wanted the British government to reject or bypass the Pakistan scheme, the All-India Muslim League considered 'Pakistan' as the only solution of the complex constitutional problems of India. The League was more interested in the holding of elections to prove its representative credentials than on putting pressure on the British government for the immediate acceptance of the Pakistan scheme. Besides, the League had neither any contact with the Labour Party and its government nor had it the resources in manpower and funds to lobby for its viewpoint in England or elsewhere. This was not the case with the Congress. The Labour Party leaders themselves were keen to mend fences with the Congress leadership after three years of bitter British–Congress hostility and to get a post-election Congress-dominated constitution-making body to sign a Britain–India post-independence treaty.[11] Krishna Menon, secretary of the London-based India League that was chaired by a Labour member of parliament, William Dobbie, was in charge of the Congress affairs in Britain, and he had developed close relations with the leaders of the British political parties, particularly the Labour Party. The idea of the parliamentary delegation that visited India in January–February 1946, originated in Krishna Menon's attempt to take Labour members of parliament to India to participate in the Congress election campaign; and subsequently, the British government included members of parliament of other parties in the delegation to negate any impression of partiality but Gandhi was the one who was consulted in the selection of its members.[12] When the Labour Party had secured a landslide victory, the Congress leaders were elated. Its president, Maulana Azad, was not the only one to congratulate Prime Minister Clement Attlee; its emissaries (Shiva Rao, G.D. Birla, Durga Das and others) swarmed London to put across the Congress viewpoint.[13] They brushed aside the Pakistan scheme or painted its bleak picture. Wavell, who was likewise opposed to the Pakistan scheme, simply put up Governor Glancy's pessimistic assessment of Pakistan.[14] The viceroy was himself eager to speak out his mind on the terrible effects of the Pakistan scheme in his address to the annual meeting of the associated chambers of commerce in Calcutta in December but Pethick-Lawrence (secretary of state for India) restrained him from doing that because the League was likely to exploit his comments in the elections as evidence of the British partiality.[15] The Labour cabinet had no other source to get an unbiased briefing on the Pakistan issue, even if it was open to persuasion. Whatever was fed to the cabinet on this issue was by those who were opposed to the Pakistan scheme. The cabinet discussed with Wavell during his London visit various possibilities. Instead of stating clearly that the British government would determine its policy on the Pakistan issue on the extent of Muslim support for the League in the elections, it decided not to go beyond the 1942 declaration, as the Congress emissaries had advised Stafford Cripps.[16] On 19 September 1945, Attlee, in his speech, focused on the Cripps offer and the British treaty with the Indian constitution-making body, as envisaged in that declaration, rather than on the Pakistan issue.[17] Simultaneously, Wavell, in a broadcast on that date, revealed that 'immediately after the elections', he would hold discussions with the representatives of the legislative assemblies in the provinces to ascertain whether the Cripps offer was 'acceptable or whether some alternative or modified scheme is preferable'. Discussions would also be conducted with the representatives of the Indian states to secure their participation in the constitution-making body.[18] Jinnah's comments on this policy simply were: 'no attempt will succeed except on the basis of Pakistan and that is the major issue to be decided by all those who are well-wishers of Pakistan . . . The division of India is the only solution of this most complex constitutional problem of India'.[19] Elections to the central assembly were scheduled in November–December 1945, and those of the provincial assemblies were spread over four months, starting in Assam on 9 January, and ending in Orissa on 20 April 1946. The elections in the 'Pakistan provinces' were scheduled in: Assam

9–22 January; Sindh 18–22 January; NWFP 1–14 February; Punjab 1–20 February; and Bengal 16–30 March.

(A) MECHANISM FOR SELECTION OF CANDIDATES

Two organs of the League, provincial parliamentary boards and central parliamentary board, were in principle responsible for the selection of candidates for the central and provincial assemblies and the organization of the election campaign. In July 1945, the central working committee revised the rules and regulations of these organs in regard to these responsibilities. The central parliamentary board, consisting of three members appointed by the working committee every year, had the authority: to ensure proper formation of the provincial parliamentary boards in every province; to select, in consultation with the provincial parliamentary boards, candidates for the central legislature with the right of appeal against its decisions vested in the central working committee; to supervise and control the activities of the provincial parliamentary boards; to hear and decide finally all appeals against the decisions of the provincial parliamentary boards; to set up a candidate for any Muslim constituency in a provincial legislature in case the provincial parliamentary board failed to select a candidate for that constituency within 'a reasonable period'; and to decide all the disputes between a provincial parliamentary board and a provincial Muslim League. The central parliamentary board was to elect its own chairman and could engage a paid secretary. These rules and regulations provided seven-member provincial parliamentary boards in case of unicameral provinces, composed of: (*i*) president of the provincial Muslim League (*ex-officio*);[20] (*ii*) leader of the provincial Muslim League assembly party (*ex-officio*); (*iii*) one member elected by the provincial Muslim League assembly party; and (*iv*) four members elected by the provincial Muslim League council. The provincial parliamentary board in case of bicameral provinces was to consist of nine members: two nominees of the provincial Muslim League assembly party and five nominees of its council, in addition to two *ex-officio* members. A provincial parliamentary board among other functions was to select candidates for the provincial legislature in the general elections and issue the party manifesto. A candidate whose application was rejected by a provincial parliamentary board had the right of appeal to the central parliamentary board within seven days from the date of announcement of the decision of the provincial parliamentary board. The decision of the central parliamentary board in appeal against the selection of any person by the provincial parliamentary board was final and binding on the provincial parliamentary board. The provincial Muslim Leagues were to support every candidate who had been finally selected by the provincial parliamentary board or the central parliamentary board. The provincial parliamentary boards were to function under the general supervision, control and direction of the central parliamentary board.[21]

The All-India Muslim League started the process of forming central parliamentary board and provincial parliamentary boards before the formal announcement of the general elections. On 8 July, its working committee constituted the central parliamentary board by simply re-appointing Husain Imam, Khaliquzzaman and Liaquat (convenor) as its members, and assigned Zafar Ahmad Ansari, one of the assistant secretaries of the All-India Muslim League, the duties of its secretary. The same month, the central committee of action decided that it would hold joint meetings with the central parliamentary board whenever policy matters relating to general elections were under consideration and decision.[22] On 13 August, Liaquat formally wrote to the presidents of the provincial Muslim Leagues that the prevailing political situation 'might bring about general elections much earlier' than was 'ordinarily expected' and impressed upon them the need to take 'immediate steps' to form the provincial parliamentary boards by 30 September, in accordance with the rules and regulations.[23] Zafar Ahmad Ansari followed up the matter till the boards were finally established. The provincial parliamentary boards were constituted without much controversy in all the provinces except in Sindh and NWFP. Factional tussle had re-appeared in the Sindh provincial Muslim League on the eve of the general elections that manifested itself in the struggle of the provincial leaders to control the process of selection of candidates. The provincial parliamentary board, which the provincial Muslim League formed, aggravated differences among the leaders. G.M. Sayed's opponents alleged that he had packed various League organs including the provincial parliamentary board with Sayyids and his favourites to control the selection process. Ghulam Ali Talpur who was a member of the provincial parliamentary board submitted his resignation in protest against this situation and demanded reconstitution of the provincial parliamentary board before applications were invited from the candidates.[24] Factional leaders represented their viewpoints before the central parliamentary board and requested Jinnah for intervention.

The central parliamentary board and central committee of action in response to these representations scheduled a joint meeting in Karachi to resolve the factional conflict and timed it with Jinnah's visit to that city.[25] Jinnah was to pass through Karachi on his way to Balochistan for his much needed rest on the advice of his doctors. He stayed in Karachi for a fortnight (28 August to 10 September) to assist the provincial Muslim League leaders to resolve their differences. After discussions with eleven top Sindh League leaders, it was decided by consensus to reconstitute the Sindh provincial parliamentary board; and at the conclusion of the talks, on 5 September, Jinnah himself made the announcement at a press conference.[26] The decision was that the provincial parliamentary board would be reconstituted to consist of: Ghulam Husain Hidayatullah, leader of the League assembly party, and G.M. Sayed, president of the provincial Muslim League, as *ex-officio* members, the League assembly party would recommend Ayub Khuhro as a member and the provincial Muslim League council would accept Ghulam Ali Talpur, Ilahi Bakhsh, Khair Shah, and Ghulam Nabi Pathan as members.[27] The League assembly party as well as the provincial Muslim League council endorsed these recommendations and the seven-member provincial parliamentary board was duly constituted.[28] But the tussle did not end with this decision and re-appeared in an acuter form during the process of selection of candidates and the election campaign.

Factionalism in the Frontier provincial Muslim League had resulted in the dissolution of its province-wide organization in April 1945, and the prolongation of its reorganization by the Qazi Isa-controlled *ad hoc* committee rendered it in complete disarray. The entry of several Congress–Khudai Khidmatgar and non-Congress Muslims particularly Abdul Qayyum Khan, deputy leader of the Congress party in the central Assembly, and Aminul Hasanat, Pir Sahib of Manki Sharif, into the League created an entirely new political environment.[29] Among others who joined the League included Arbab Abdul Ghafur, M. Abbas Khan, a former minister in the Congress ministry, Arbab Noor Mohammad, Ghulam Mohammad Lundkhwur and Mohammad Ali Hoti. A majority of the 'old' and 'new' Leaguers were against the *ad hoc* committee dealing with the election process.[30] Initially, three Leaguers, Nishtar, Pir of Manki Sharif and Qayyum united to sideline Aurangzeb and his supporters from the selection process. They did not have to do much canvassing for this venture because the anti-Aurangzeb feelings were widespread for the way he had handled the provincial Muslim League and run its ministry; even the Frontier students of his alma mater, the Aligarh Muslim University, wrote against him.[31] A direct consequence of factionalism was that no acceptable election machinery could be devised in the NWFP till the end of September. The committee of action and central parliamentary board then intervened and deputed two League leaders, Nawab Ismail and Khaliquzzaman, to make alternative arrangements for the elections.[32] On their recommendations, the central parliamentary board established three boards to look after the elections: (*i*) the selection board with Qayyum as its convenor to select candidates;[33] (*ii*) the election board with Nishtar as its convenor to organize the election campaign;[34] and (*iii*) the finance board with Ziauddin as its convenor to collect funds and maintain the accounts.[35] Qazi Isa did object to the composition of these boards especially the selection board and empowering new entrants like Qayyum and Pir of Manki Sharif in the selection process. When he pointed this out to Jinnah, he advised him to contact Liaquat but the repeated objections that he raised with the central parliamentary board carried little weight because of the general perception that Qazi Isa had messed up the reorganization process of the Frontier provincial Muslim League by his partisan, flippant and arrogant attitude.[36] The Frontier provincial Muslim League had this newly organized election machinery to participate in the general elections. Even this was soon replaced by a new one.

The provincial Muslim Leagues in other provinces faced difficulties in forming the provincial parliamentary boards but these were not similar to those that the Sindh and the Frontier provincial Muslim Leagues had to confront. The Bengal presidency Muslim League leaders demonstrated remarkable judiciousness in forming the provincial parliamentary board although there were alarming reports of Suhrawardy–Nazimuddin rift and left-right tensions in the party. The provincial Muslim League postponed the party elections with the approval of the central League to avoid any intensification of factionalism.[37] It set up the provincial parliamentary board and its ancillary bodies by a unanimous vote: Nazimuddin proposed Huseyn Shaheed Suhrawardy as secretary of the provincial parliamentary board; Suhrawardy proposed Nazimuddin as chairman of the election fund committee; and Maulvi Tamizuddin Khan as chairman of the propaganda committee.[38] Nazimuddin and his supporters had their reservations about the composition of the provincial parliamentary board, as they had four members on it as compared to five of the rival faction, but did not attempt to block its functioning and accepted the decisions of the statutory bodies without any overt protest.[39] In the Punjab, a hostile Unionist administration supported by an equally antagonistic British governor forced unity in the provincial Muslim League ranks and temporarily submerged all the intra-party conflicts. In Madras, there were complaints that Jamal Mohammad's family and supporters controlled the provincial Muslim League and that the Andhra region had been deprived of its due share on the provincial parliamentary board; but the central parliamentary board simply exhorted the Leaguers to constitute a provincial parliamentary board that would command the confidence of the Muslims of every region of the Madras presidency to avoid 'bickering and heartburning'.[40] Wherever there were differences in other provincial parliamentary boards regarding their composition, these were either easily resolved or were simply ignored. There were conflicts, however, during the distribution of party tickets; again, the most serious one arose in Sindh.

(B) SELECTION OF CANDIDATES

The provincial parliamentary boards and the central parliamentary board were empowered to select candidates. Every provincial parliamentary board determined its own procedure for their selection with the approval of the central parliamentary board. Jinnah kept himself aloof from this exercise. Except for the Sindh provincial parliamentary board, he was nowhere associated with the formation of the election machinery at the provincial level. Even in the case of Sindh, he had done that on the joint request of the central parliamentary board and central committee of action and appeals from members of the Sindh provincial parliamentary board. Otherwise, he repeatedly made it clear that the provincial parliamentary boards and the central parliamentary board had the final authority to award tickets, and he had no say in their decision-making process.[41] He himself applied for the party ticket and the central parliamentary board formally awarded him that from his traditional constituency in Bombay.[42] Still, several Leaguers approached him for the tickets or lodged appeals with him against the decisions of the boards. His response used to be typical: that the provincial parliamentary boards would initially select the official candidates of the League; the rejected candidates had the right of appeal to the central parliamentary board whose decision would be final; and that he could not 'interfere directly or indirectly with their functions'.[43] He did occasionally guide the aspiring candidates, advising them not to get tickets in return for a payment or a donation. His remarks on the donation made for a mosque by one candidate whom he otherwise liked were, 'the construction of the *masjid* [mosque] is one of the most laudable objects, any donation given for an object, however laudable, by persons who expect thereby to secure a League ticket is to my mind no charity at all in the true sense of the word and is otherwise most improper, and I can never be a party to any such arrangement'.[44] And his advice to the League voters and candidates, who were awarded or denied the party tickets, was:

> The vital issue is Pakistan. It is not a question of who gets the ticket and who does not, and who will be the chief minister or minister. All these matters are subsidiary. We have two Boards constituted in the best possible manner, Provincial and Central, and if the Provincial Board goes wrong, there is the Central Board, and after their decision, which of course must be final, the only course for every Muslim is to support the man who finally gets the League ticket, even though, to put it bluntly and emphatically, he be a lamppost.[45]

Subsequently, he made similar comments in his campaign speeches to forestall personal and factional rivalries.

The selection of candidates was an arduous process. The central parliamentary board and some provincial parliamentary boards faced problems but the Sindh provincial parliamentary board confronted the most serious ones. Factionalism and quest for power were the main reasons. Every faction in the provincial Muslim League—the Sayyids, the Baluchs, and the supporters of Khuhro and Hidayatullah—aspired to control the post-election Assembly to install its own, or at least a friendly, chief minister. Hidayatullah had at first suggested to G.M. Sayed that Sindh was the only Muslim majority province that had a League ministry whose members of the legislative assembly had stood by the party; therefore, the sitting members of the legislative assembly should be adopted as the League candidates in the elections and new candidates should be accommodated on the seats that had been occupied by non-Leaguers; but Sayed disagreed with his proposal because his favourites who happened to be Sayyids were candidates on seats of sitting members of the legislative assembly.[46] Sayed did not realize that he had lost a lot of influence by his performance as the provincial Muslim League president in the recent past. His opponents easily managed a majority in the provincial parliamentary board and united to outmanoeuvre him in the selection of candidates.[47] The provincial parliamentary board met for three days (29 September to 1 October), with Sayed in the chair, to decide about the tickets. On the third day, after the board had 'unanimously' distributed tickets for Larkana, Nawabshah and Jacobabad, differences arose over the award of tickets for Tharparkar and Hyderabad. Sayed who was anxious to give tickets in these constituencies to his favourite candidates was left with just one supporter on the provincial parliamentary board.[48] Therefore, he adjourned the meeting *sine die*. Instead of representing his case before the central parliamentary board, he scheduled a meeting of the provincial Muslim League council on 12 October, on the requisition of twenty-five councillors to express no-confidence in the council-nominated members of the provincial parliamentary board and to replace them with new members. Both sides wrote to Jinnah in Mastung, putting forward their respective viewpoints. Jinnah advised them to place their cases before the central parliamentary board, which again convened its meeting in Karachi.[49] From 20 to 30 October, Jinnah himself was available in Karachi for advice.[50] The central parliamentary board held discussions with the provincial parliamentary board members and awarded tickets on twenty-seven central assembly seats. On receipt of the list of candidates, all the members of the Sindh provincial parliamentary board gave an undertaking in writing that they would abide by the decision of the central parliamentary board, individually as well as collectively, and support every candidate that it would select, assuring that they would oppose any candidate rejected by the central parliamentary board if he stood in the elections.[51] In addition, every applicant for the League ticket had already signed a pledge that he would not stand in the elections if he was denied the party ticket. But such pledges failed to avert a conflict. The row started when one applicant, Ali Mohammad Rashidi, who was refused a party ticket, filed his nomination papers, and soon after Ali Ahmad Talpur was given the League ticket for the Tharparkar west rural Muslim (Mirpurkhas) constituency against a Sayyid candidate.[52] The League expelled Rashidi from the party for seven years for 'gross breach' of party discipline.[53]

Factional conflict in Sindh intensified after Sayed and his supporters began to campaign in support of Rashidi against the central parliamentary board-nominated candidate, Yusuf Haroon.[54] There was another development that weakened Sayed's position in the League. Nihchaldas Vazirani, the revenue minister, who was closely associated with Sayed, joined the Congress and united the Hindus under that banner; and his alleged campaign through revenue officials in support of Rashidi did not bring any credit to Sayed though it strengthened the electoral prospects of some of his candidates. When this campaign was reported in the press, Sayed was asked to contradict reports about his pro-Rashidi campaign.[55] On his silence, the central committee of action served Sayed with a show-cause notice for disciplinary action on the charge of canvassing against a League-nominated candidate. The conflict widened when more members of the Sayed group filed nominations papers against validly nominated League candidates and began to campaign for them, alleging that the central parliamentary board members did not know the conditions in Sindh.[56] Jinnah asked all those who represented to him for intervention to contact the central parliamentary board.[57] Allama I.I. Qazi who had some influence on Sayed could restrain him only temporarily from any extreme action.[58] The talks between the two sides lingered on till the central parliamentary board cancelled the tickets of four members of the Sayed group on the charge that they had been campaigning against a validly-nominated League candidate. On 26 December, Sayed resigned from his membership of the central working committee and central committee of action in protest against the way the 'League high command' had handled the situation in Sindh and surrendered the League ticket that had been issued to him; and he made this announcement from the residence of Seth Partabrai in Hyderabad.[59] His group, which he labelled as the genuine Progressive Muslim League, gave tickets to sixteen candidates for the Sindh assembly. Sayed complained that the central parliamentary board had taken the expulsion decision against the promise that Liaquat and Qazi Isa had made to him that no action would be taken against his supporters who were campaigning against the League candidates. Both, Liaquat and Isa, denied that they had made any such promise.[60] The All-India Muslim League expelled Sayed and seven others from the party for violating the party discipline.[61]

In the NWFP, the selection board exacerbated the anti-Aurangzeb atmosphere in the selection process, in which Qayyum gradually came to monopolize authority for the distribution of party tickets. Qayyum's opponents alleged that his criterion for selection was a candidate's loyalty to him rather than his services to the League or the possibility of his success. The result was an imbalanced distribution of tickets; not only Aurangzeb but several others like Sadullah, Samin Jan and Bakht Jamal were denied the League tickets.[62] When Jinnah visited NWFP in November, the Boards were replaced by a committee of action with

Ziauddin as its secretary to organize the election campaign.[63] The Punjab provincial parliamentary board did not face any serious difficulty in selecting the candidates although quite a few prominent Muslims had joined the League on the eve of the elections. Among them were Firoz Khan Noon, who resigned as defence member of the Viceroy's Executive Council with effect from 15 September 1945, Mian Iftikharuddin, a patron of the 'progressives' in the Punjab, who resigned as president of the Punjab Congress, and Begum Shahnawaz whose 'explanations and assurances' Jinnah accepted on 17 October, and removed the ban on her entry into the League.[64] Most of them had their own constituencies. The students of the Islamia college, Lahore, however, did protest against the refusal of ticket to Mian Bashir Ahmad, once president of the All-India Muslim Students Federation.[65] But differences on this and other issues did not develop into any serious conflict. In addition, the anti-League Glancy–Khizr administration kept the provincial Muslim League solidarity intact. The distribution of tickets in Bengal was a smooth affair although there was a tussle between two factions: one led by Suhrawardy and the other headed by Nazimuddin.[66] There were differences in the provincial parliamentary board on the award of tickets but neither of the factions took them to a breaking point.[67] Complaints against the allotment of tickets were settled through formal appeals to the central parliamentary board and no protests were lodged against its decisions. Factionalism in the Bengal presidency Muslim League might have worsened had Nazimuddin been a candidate for a provincial assembly seat or had Fazlul Haq rejoined the League before the elections.[68] Fazlul Haq had manoeuvred several indirect appeals to the League president for his re-entry into the League but he himself was reluctant to regret openly his actions that had resulted in his expulsion.[69] When Jinnah was directly questioned on this issue, his response was,

If Mr Fazlul Haq is really repentant he has only got to express his regret for what he has done and ask for the removal of the ban. But in the first instance he must leave the enemy camp [i.e. the Congress].[70] He cannot have it both ways. I believe in the saying "forgive and forget" and a great organization like the All India Muslim League . . . can never be vindictive or revengeful, but I am sure you will agree with me that certain fundamental principles have got to be observed in order to maintain the pledge, reputation and discipline of an organization.[71]

This is what Fazlul Haq did after the elections and rejoined the League but then he was not in a position to threaten internal cohesion of the party.[72]

The central parliamentary board selected candidates for the central Assembly on the recommendations of the provincial parliamentary boards, without any serious conflict except in Sindh, and made no nomination in any general constituency. There were six appeals against its selection: one (Pir Tajuddin) from the Punjab; two (N. Mohammad Anwar and A.K. Sharfuddin) from Madras; two (Abdul Majid Gheewala and Abdul Majid Tungekar) from Bombay; and one (Taqi Hadi) from the United Provinces. All the appeals were disallowed. The appeals in the first three cases were considered invalid because the candidates that the central parliamentary board had selected were from the list that had been recommended by the provincial parliamentary boards. The grounds that the fourth and the fifth appellants had mentioned against the selected candidate were not regarded sufficient enough to reverse the decision of the central parliamentary board. The appeal in the sixth case was rejected because it had not been received within the stipulated time. In the case of Yusuf Haroon, the central parliamentary board itself had selected him, as the provincial parliamentary board had made no recommendation for that constituency, and no appeal had been filed with the central board against his nomination.[73] The candidates for the provincial assemblies were selected by the provincial parliamentary boards and the appeals against their selection were dealt with by the central parliamentary board. The provincial parliamentary board in United Provinces, with Nawab Ismail Khan as its chairman, carefully selected candidates, overcoming sectarian claims and conflicts.[74] The Bombay provincial parliamentary board distributed the tickets without much controversy, while the Aga Khan silenced the dissenting claimants among his followers.[75] The dissenters in Madras criticised the award of all the tickets to members of the 'Jamal clan', but the central parliamentary board did not entertain any representations against the decisions of the provincial parliamentary board and the unopposed election of all the candidates proved the veracity of the selection.[76] In Orissa, five members of the seven-member provincial parliamentary board were themselves candidates for the tickets. Four of them were given the tickets, and the applicants from outside the list of board members were ignored, whatever had been their service to the Muslim community and the League.[77]

(C) ELECTION CAMPAIGN

No one doubted that the All-India Muslim League would perform in the general elections far better than it did in the provincial elections of 1937, but the scale of its success especially in some Muslim majority provinces was debated even in some friendly quarters.[78] They had reasons for such an assessment. It was partially due to the political developments immediately before the elections that had damaged the image and influence of the League. In mid-1944, the League–Unionist breakup had brought in an anti-League Governor Glancy-backed Khizr-headed civil administration that did not hide its desire to see the League routed in the elections; and its anti-League steps were not against the wishes of Punjabi non-Muslims, except the Indian Christians and a section of the Scheduled Castes. Besides, in March 1945, there were changes in the League ministries in the NWFP, Bengal, Assam and Sindh that, the League's opponents interpreted, would adversely affect its election prospects. In the NWFP, the Congress–Khudai Khidmatgars had weaned away five League members of the legislative assembly and, on 12 March, defeated with their support the faction-ridden Aurangzeb ministry. The new Dr Khan Sahib-headed ministry was not expected to provide a fair administration to the League in the elections. In Bengal, on 28 March, the Nazimuddin-headed League coalition ministry suffered a defeat in the Assembly. Although no unfriendly ministry succeeded it but the province came under the governor's rule. The change was a definite loss to the provincial Muslim League. In Assam, Chief Minister Sadullah under pressure from the opposition transformed the League coalition ministry into an all-party ministry with the key portfolio of revenue going to a Hindu minister as part of his agreement with the Congress and the Hindu Nationalist Party, which contributed to the weakening of its position in the province. In Sindh also, the changes that followed the Hidayatullah-Sayed conflict brought in the shrewd Nihchaldas Vazirani as the revenue minister. Vazirani after G.M. Sayed's exit from the League conducted tours along with him and influenced the voters in favour of Sayed-sponsored candidates.[79]

The Congress was the main all-India political party that opposed the League and its Pakistan scheme. When the general elections approached, it realized that it could not confront the League directly; therefore, it fielded an insignificant number of candidates against the League candidates in Muslim constituencies. Its strategy was to oppose the League indirectly by pooling its organizational, propaganda and

financial resources to prop up minor anti-League Muslim parties and
encourage them to put up common candidates against the League. A
few Muslim parties were opposed to the League and its leadership but
not the Pakistan demand. They naively hoped to establish Pakistan after
India had achieved independence.[80] The 'nationalist' Muslims painted
a rosy picture of the popularity of anti-League Muslim parties to keep
them within the Congress orbit.[81] Although the Congress confidence in
their 'loyalty' was severely shaken after the defection of several senior
'nationalist' Muslims like Mian Iftikharuddin and Abdul Qayyum Khan
and Maulana Azad's constitutional formula for Hindu–Muslim
settlement that Gandhi temporarily blocked from publication but still
it saw their utility.[82] It attempted to unite them—Jamiatul Ulama-i-
Hind, All India Muslim Majlis, Majlis-i-Ahrar-i-Islam, All India Shia
Political Conference, Sunni Board (United Provinces), Momin
Conference (Bihar), Khudai Khidmatgars (NWFP), Anjuman-i-Watan
(Balochistan) and Khaksars—on an anti-League common platform and
use them in the post-election constitutional negotiations. Azad guided
them to form an Azad (Independent) Muslim parliamentary board
which put up candidates against the League candidates. It was hard for
the pro-Congress Muslim parliamentary board to find trustworthy
candidates; soon after its formation, its secretary, Shamsuddin Ahmad,
defected to the League. The Congress and the anti-League Muslim
parties launched an aggressive provocative campaign against the
League, its leaders and the Pakistan scheme; Jinnah was their prime
target. Its intensity moved even some Hindus; one of them wrote to
Liaquat, 'It has pained me and it should pain every respectful man that
the Congress has come to such low tactics'.[83] Jinnah advised the
Leaguers to avoid attending, or walking out of, those meetings where
their leaders and their cause were 'attacked and abused'.[84] Normally he
disregarded vilification of his person, but once he did respond to the
vilification campaign in a statement from Quetta; he stated, 'It is
painful and regrettable that they [League's opponents] have stooped to
such a low depth of meanness in as much as they are directed to show
that I am not a Musalman, but the allegations made by them in their
speeches against me and my private life are tissues of falsehood'.[85]
Besides patronizing the Muslim parliamentary board, the Congress
extended financial and organizational support to candidates of other
anti-League parties: the Krishak Praja Samity in Bengal; the Unionists
in the Punjab; and G.M. Sayed's provincial Muslim League in Sindh.
But it was futile for the Congress to expect any reasonable volume of

Muslim support against the League; by March 1946, even Maulana Madni was thinking of reconciliation with Jinnah to support the League cause.[86]

The Muslim League organized its election campaign systematically within its limited resources. Jinnah had been its invaluable asset and, after its revival, the most active campaigner. In the provincial elections in 1937, he had untiringly campaigned for the League candidates, travelling without interruption from province to province. But now his health and multifarious engagements did not permit him to undertake any strenuous activity on that scale. From March 1945, onward, he had taken rest for three months on medical advice and after going through the gruelling fruitless talks at the Simla conference had followed it up by his five-week (14 September to 20 October 1945) rest in Balochistan. When the central parliamentary board and provincial parliamentary boards were devising the election machinery and selecting candidates, he was either in Karachi resolving intra-provincial Muslim League conflicts or in Mastung and Quetta as a guest of the Khan of Kalat. The only other province that he visited before the central Assembly elections was the NWFP. Otherwise, he stayed in Bombay, looking after his own election campaign, or in Delhi, from where he interacted with individual Leaguers and the party organs such as the central parliamentary board and provincial parliamentary boards, providing advice and guidance to those who were engaged in the election campaign. The central committee of action, central parliamentary board and other relevant party organs regularly sent him reports about their activities. He was relatively more active during the provincial elections but still his campaign was limited to visits of the remaining 'Pakistan' provinces: to the Punjab for one week (in January 1946) and to Bengal and Assam for three weeks (in February–March 1946).[87] He wanted the League leaders at all levels to take up the responsibility of the election campaign. Once, he wrote to a provincial Muslim League president, 'Now it is really for your provincial leaders to manage things in their own provinces. I have worked and put our people on a clear road. This has taken seven years of very hard work. I expect now that those, who are in charge of the provincial organizations and those who desire to lead our people, should work as a team in an organized manner and systematically carry on their work'.[88] He could not bear physically the strain of extensive campaign tours, which would involve receptions and lengthy processions. This can be gauged from his reply to invitations from Bengal. Such programmes, he wrote to Huseyn Shaheed

Suhrawardy, 'are entirely upset by our people . . . when they find me in their midst and there have been numerous instances, when I have been dangerously mobbed, no doubt, out of regard and affection for me'.[89] The provincial Muslim Leagues on their part wanted essentially his ceremonial presence in their midst for inspiration in order to draw popular support for their candidates. For instance, Suhrawardy wrote to him about his proposed tour of Bengal: 'It is not our purpose that you should visit Bengal or its cities as [part of] an electioneering programme. It will be a tour to give the people a chance to see you which they are most anxious to do'.[90] This was typical of similar requests from other provinces. Jinnah's few speeches that he made in these visits and his occasional press statements and interviews, which focused on basic campaign issues, more than compensated any formal campaigning on his part.

Every provincial Muslim League used essentially its own network and resources to campaign for the party candidates. Jinnah and the central League provided auxiliary support. The central committee of action and the central parliamentary board looked after the needs of the provincial Muslim Leagues and the candidates. The capacity of the central office was enhanced by hiring additional staff. A new department of publicity and information, with Qazi Isa as its head, was created in the central office to publish and distribute propaganda literature in the form of pamphlets, booklets, leaflets and posters.[91] In addition, the provincial Muslim Leagues and in some cases the district Muslim Leagues published literature locally and distributed that through its branch Leagues. Qazi Isa arranged publication of articles in the press that members of the committee of writers and other Leaguers wrote in support of the League.[92] The pro-League and the League press gave the election campaign maximum possible coverage.[93] The central committee of action arranged Muslim National Guards and volunteers to assist the League candidates. Funds were another important factor. Unlike the Congress, which was the richest political party of India and which provided liberally funds in the shape of grants to the anti-League Muslim parties, the All-India Muslim League had limited funds;[94] and Jinnah whom the All-India Muslim League had authorized to administer the central election fund prudently managed them under his direct supervision. The central League and the provincial Muslim Leagues had separately collected funds for the elections, but some provincial Leagues had either insufficient funds or did not manage them properly. Such provincial Muslim Leagues needed additional funds.[95] The central committee of action disbursed small amounts where needed out of the funds that had been placed at its disposal, but larger amounts were taken from the central election fund. Jinnah discreetly advanced the required funds to the provincial Muslim Leagues technically as loans, which they had to return 'as soon as possible' along with a statement of accounts with receipts and vouchers.[96] This mechanism was meant to forestall any mismanagement and misuse of funds. Jinnah provided the Bengal presidency Muslim League Rs 300,000, which a three-member committee (M.A.H. Ispahani, K.B. Moazamuddin Husain and A.W. Baakza) managed, and promised 'further help' after the provincial Muslim League had furnished him with 'the fullest account of the amount spent and the reasons for any further call on the Central Funds'. The Bengal presidency Muslim League on its part asked every candidate to whom it advanced money to submit a statement of expenditure along with receipts.[97] After the elections, the provincial Muslim League gave a duly audited statement of accounts and returned the balance of Rs 5,174 that it had in hand.[98] Jinnah gave Rs 300,000 as a subsidy to the Punjab provincial Muslim League, and obtained promissory notes from the provincial Muslim League general secretary for Rs 2 lakh; and from three Leaguers (Iftikhar Mamdot, Mumtaz Daultana and Iftikharuddin) for Rs 1 lakh that they would return the amount to the central election fund.[99] On 29 January, when Jinnah advanced an additional loan of Rs 50,000 'to be paid back as soon as possible', he reminded Mian Amiruddin, the finance secretary, that the Punjab provincial Muslim League 'ought to have taken steps long ago to raise sufficient funds to meet the requirements of your province'. On 3 April, he asked him to return the balance in the provincial account along with vouchers.[100] He gave Rs 50,000 to the Frontier provincial Muslim League for any 'legitimate' election expenses, which Qazi Isa and Mian Ziauddin operated; and subsequently, they provided Jinnah with a statement of accounts with receipts.[101] The Sindh provincial Muslim League was advanced Rs 51,105 and was reimbursed additional expenditure of Rs 27,228 that it incurred during the election campaign.[102]

The All-India Muslim League perceived that the general elections were part of a struggle for Muslim survival in the subcontinent. Therefore, it mobilized all the available Muslim resources for the election campaign. Besides its own extensive organizational network, the central committee of action and central parliamentary board formally sought the help of *ulama*, women and students in the campaign.[103] Muslim students had their own all-India organization, the All-India Muslim Students Federation, which had branches in all the provinces. A major portion of the work of training them for the elections was done at the Aligarh Muslim University, which supplemented the work that the provincial Muslim students federations did at the local level.[104] An election committee of seven teachers at the Aligarh Muslim University without any overt acknowledgement supervised the work of training students.[105] The central committee of action and central parliamentary board placed at the disposal of the Aligarh Muslim University chief accountant funds for this purpose, which could be drawn on the recommendations of the Aligarh Muslim University League president.[106] The trained students were sent to the Muslim constituencies, where needed, in batches to render assistance in the election campaign; and the League leadership formally recognized the invaluable work that they performed especially in the United Provinces, Bihar and NWFP.[107] The Pashto-speaking students at the Aligarh Muslim University from Peshawar, Hazara, Kohat, Bannu, Dera Ismail Khan and Mardan did useful election-related work in the NWFP.[108] In addition, the students of the Islamia colleges in Lahore and Peshawar, the Muslim college in Karachi and the Dhaka university did similar work locally in the Muslim constituencies, where the provincial Muslim Leagues needed their assistance.[109] Interestingly, the Muslim Students Federation in Balochistan, where no elections were held, collected funds for election purposes on their own and sent batches of students to some Baloch-dominated constituencies in Sindh and Pukhtun-dominated constituencies in the NWFP.[110] For Bengal, Jinnah placed at the disposal of Maulana Akram Khan and M.A.H. Ispahani Rs 20,000 that the students could incur during the elections and acknowledged 'the fine spirit' that the Bengali students demonstrated in the campaign.[111] Members of the all-India and provincial women's committees and female Muslim students federation did important work for the female League candidates.[112]

The Muslim League formally sought the assistance of *ulama* and *mashaikh* in the general elections. Some *ulama* of the Brelvi, Deobandi and other schools of thought had been active in its support independently or from its own platform since its revival in the mid-1930s.[113] Before the elections, they organized themselves into a pro-League party to counter the influence of the pro-Congress Maulana Husain Ahmad Madni-led Jamiatul Ulama-i-Hind after Madni, on

Azad's special invitation, attended meetings of the Congress working committee during the Simla conference in June–July 1945, and the Jamiatul Ulama-i-Hind *ulama* made provocative anti-League speeches at a conference in Saharanpur.[114] The pro-League *ulama* and the Bengal presidency Muslim League took the initiative; and at first, they set up a Jamiatul Ulama-i-Islam, Bengal in Calcutta on 21 July,[115] and then, at a conference of *ulama* and *mashaikh* from all over India in that city on 28–30 October, established the All India Jamiatul Ulama-i-Islam to mobilize the '*ulama* of *madrassas*, *imams* of mosques and *mashaikh* of the *khanqah*s' to counter the Congress–Jamiatul Ulama-i-Hind propaganda.[116] The conference passed several resolutions including two in which it supported the League and the Pakistan scheme.[117] Although the Leaguers welcomed the formation of a pro-League *ulama* party but its all-India leaders scrupulously kept themselves aloof from its proceedings and simply sent messages for its success.[118] Several personalities contributed to the formation of the new party; prominent among them were Maulana Raghib Ahsan (1904–1975), Maulana Tahir Qasimi, grandson of Maulana Qasim Nanotavi and younger brother of Maulana Mohammad Tayyab who was *Mohtamim* of the Darul Ulum,[119] Maulana Naimuddin and Zafar Ahmad Ansari. Maulana Shabbir Ahmad Usmani, the venerable Deobandi figure, who could not travel to Calcutta due to illness sent a lengthy message for the conference and agreed to his election as its first president.[120] Besides the establishment of the Jamiatul Ulama-i-Islam, quite a few Jamiatul Ulama-i-Hind and Majlis-i-Ahrar-i-Islam members came out to support the League in response to Jinnah's repeated appeals to them in September–October to join the League in the struggle for Pakistan.[121]

The Congress on its part used primarily the *ulama* and workers of the Maulana Madni-led Jamiatul Ulama-i-Hind and the Majlis-i-Ahrar-i-Islam against the League.[122] The League and the Jamiatul Ulama-i-Islam adopted a joint strategy to counterbalance their influence; and they sent pro-League *ulama* wherever pro-Congress *ulama* canvassed against the League candidates.[123] They rebutted the allegation that the League had broken the 1937 All-India Muslim League–Jamiatul Ulama-i-Hind 'agreement' as mere propaganda by those *ulama* who were at that time keen to join the Congress, and defended the League against the malicious propaganda that its leaders did not 'follow the tenets of Islam' in their daily life by countering that even if that was so, the Jamiatul Ulama-i-Hind's Muslim friends in the Congress could not be absolved of a similar charge.[124] They took the fight to the Darul

Ulum, Deoband, itself. On 7 December, Maulana Shabbir Ahmad Usmani led a delegation of Deobandi *ulama* to the Darul Ulum to convince Maulana Madni and his pro-Congress colleagues of the righteousness of the Jamiatul Ulama-i-Islam stance.[125] Although the two sides could not reach an agreement but Maulana Tahir Qasimi compiled the Usmani–Madni dialogue in the form of a booklet which the All-India Muslim League published under the title of *Mukalimatus Sadrain* (dialogue between the two presidents) and distributed it widely.[126] However, Usmani did succeed in convincing Madni that the Congress flag that had been hoisted on his house outside the Darul Ulum compound should be pulled down.[127] The Darul Ulum, Deoband was run by donations especially from rich Muslims who had representatives on its governing body, the Majlis-i-Shura; the Nizam of Hyderabad was the biggest donor and had three representatives on the Majlis. So far, the Darul Ulum had strictly followed 'a policy of neutrality' and Muslims of every persuasion—pro-League, pro-Congress, Ahrar and others—had been associated with this institution. The League approached the donors of the Darul Ulum to prevent the Jamiatul Ulama-i-Hind chief from using the Deoband resources—staff and students—for promoting just one viewpoint, that of the Congress.[128] On 26 December, this issue was raised in the governing body, which took an ambiguous decision by voting, allowing the staff and the students to take active part in politics.[129] The activities of the pro-League and pro-Congress *ulama* at Deoband following this decision once led to an open conflict and students' strike but normalcy was soon restored.[130] The Jamiatul Ulama-i-Islam organized religious conferences in major cities such as Peshawar, Meerut, Lahore, Dhaka, Karachi, Delhi, Patna and Bombay in which all-India and local *ulama* and *mashaikh* participated to campaign for the League candidates.[131] Maulana Usmani's speeches at some of these conferences were published separately and distributed in the Muslim constituencies.[132] The *mashaikh* effectively countered the Congress–Jamiatul Ulama-i-Hind propaganda in the rural areas where the League organization was relatively weak in some provinces. Other Muslim groups came out to support the League. Among them were the Jamiat-i-Ahle Hadith and its leader Maulana Mohammad Ibrahim Sialkoti (1874–1956) and the Mullaji of the Bohras who advised his followers to support the League candidates.[133] The Ahmadis also began to join the League before the elections. Maulana Usmani defended their presence on the League platform; however, their votes at Qadian could not be registered on time that deprived them from voting for the League candidates.

After the elections to the central assembly, the League faced organizational problems in Sindh and NWFP. In Sindh, G.M. Sayed's expulsion from the party left the provincial Muslim League with no president, no party office and no funds. The central committee of action hastily set up a six-member [Ayub Khuhro, Hashim Gazdar, Ghulam Nabi Pathan, Hatim Alavi, Ghulam Ali Talpur and Yusuf Haroon (convener)] committee to control the damage and look after the election-related work. G.M. Sayed who continued to claim that he was the president of a genuine provincial Muslim League refused to surrender the party funds amounting to Rs 10,000 to the newly formed League committee. The central League provided funds to the committee from the central election fund till the provincial Muslim League had made its own arrangements for a provincial fund.[134] Sayed's exit did not end factionalism. Now Khuhro and Hidayatullah competed for leadership. Hidayatullah, and his supporters, accused Khuhro of 'openly working' against him but this infighting did not develop into an open rift.[135] The provincial Muslim League's victory somewhat eased the situation. The party would have been in a more comfortable position in the Sindh assembly had G.M. Sayed not deserted its ranks or had he rejoined it after the elections. But that did not come about. Khuhro had rightly cautioned that Sindh would not have a stable ministry if G.M. Sayed was returned to the assembly.[136] This is what happened. Although Hidayatullah was skilful enough to form a ministry in March by a margin of one vote but within a few months Sayed destabilized it by manoeuvring the defection of two Leaguers (Noor Mohammad Shah and Yusuf Chandio). This time Hidayatullah, instead of staying in office by intrigue, advised the governor to dissolve the assembly and hold fresh elections.[137] Both in the December 1946 and earlier elections, Muslim election campaigners from outside Sindh augmented the local campaign resources. The Aligarh Muslim University League sent trained students for the campaign.[138] Similarly, the *ulama* and *mashaikh* from outside Sindh came in large number to canvass for the League candidates; Jinnah formally appreciated the services of one, Makhdum Murid Husain Qureshi of Multan, on the recommendation of the Sindh provincial Muslim League working committee.[139] On the League's request, Khan of Kalat asked Pir Ahmad Shah of Ranipur and Sardar Abdur Rahim Khan Khoso to help the League in constituencies where they had influence. Consequently, the provincial Muslim League improved upon its membership strength and formed a stable ministry. After both the elections in Sindh, Jinnah persuaded Khuhro to forego leadership of the League assembly party in favour of Hidayatullah.[140] More important factor for the stability of the ministry was the defeat of G.M. Sayed who filed a writ petition but the election tribunal did not give its verdict on the petition till after independence.

In NWFP, the rapid changes in the Frontier provincial Muslim League election campaign machinery confused the Leaguers which partially disabled the party to translate its support at the grassroots into election victory. Jinnah's visit particularly the warm welcome in a unique procession in his honour and his speeches restored the Leaguers' confidence and inspired the Muslim youth but even after his visit, factionalism persisted in the provincial Muslim League.[141] Those Leaguers who had been marginalized or denied the party tickets generally showed patience and sullenly accepted the changed situation without much protest. A few of them and their supporters might not have turned up for voting but none of them deserted the party. Now the Qayyum–Nishtar factional tussle dissipated the Leaguers' energies. Both the League leaders were candidates on the dual constituency of Peshawar. They campaigned against each other and Jinnah's intervention whom they met in New Delhi failed to bring about genuine harmony between them which cost the League one seat in Peshawar and hurt its campaign in other constituencies.[142] This infighting also prevented the provincial Muslim League from exploiting the corruption that prevailed in the NWFP under the Congress ministry for which the Aurangzeb ministry had been discredited.[143] Added to the League's own limitations was a hostile Congress-controlled civil administration which exercised complete control over items of daily use in that era of scarcities and manipulated their distribution for election purposes. It attempted to curb any organized pro-League groups; the teachers' association was one of them whose demands were not accepted and its president was removed from service.[144] It appointed J.V. Dhawan, 'a fanatic, inexperienced and junior' civil servant, son-in-law of Mehr Chand Khanna, as election officer. The resourceful Khanna was secretary of the Frontier Congress and revenue minister in its ministry. Most of the decisions that Dhawan took were allegedly against the League. The electoral roll was revised under his supervision, ignoring the provincial Muslim League's protests against irregularities and discrepancies. Polling date and in some cases polling stations were changed without informing the League candidates.[145] Ballot boxes were tampered with at some polling stations on the polling day; and one League candidate even withdrew from the contest in protest.[146] There were numerous other allegations of election malpractices.[147] Maulana Shakirullah, the Frontier Jamiatul Ulama-i-Islam leader, asserted that if 'the Congress had contested elections in the circumstances in which the Muslim League did, I am sure, the Congress would not have won a single seat', and countered the charge that the League had given tickets to the big khans by observing that the Congress–Khudai Khidmatgar nominees such as Sardar Asad Khan, Nawabzada Allah Nawaz (b. 1906) and Raja Manochehr were not commoners.[148] Surprisingly, despite the disarray in the provincial Muslim League leadership and gross election malpractices, the League still demonstrated the support that it enjoyed at the grassroots by securing more Muslim votes than the Congress–Khudai Khidmatgars.

The League faced the toughest opposition in the Punjab. Nowhere the British governor was so blatantly antagonistic to the League and the Pakistan scheme as in the Punjab. Khizr (chief minister) had his blessings in every action that he took against the League.[149] Khizr paid no heed to friendly counsel; he ignored to listen to Firoz Khan Noon's repeated appeals that he could 'bring about an understanding' between him and Jinnah and the provincial Muslim League.[150] But he rightly perceived that his stay as chief minister was dependent upon the extent of his hostility towards the League although he himself occasionally advocated the Pakistan scheme to assuage the sentiments of his Muslim constituents. With such a governor and chief minister in office, the League could not expect a fair atmosphere. The Khizr ministry used patronage, in the form of 'grants of land', and security laws to restrict the popularity of the League.[151] The comments of one British observer were that 'the services of the Unionist party in the elections' would 'now earn more land' to the Unionist supporters than did the 'services to Government in the War'.[152] Posting and transfer of civil servants were subject to their amenability to be used against the League. Of course, there were a few rare exceptions where officers resisted such orders and secretly kept the League informed about the official moves. But as the campaign progressed, complaints against official interference began to pour into the provincial Muslim League office from all over the province.[153] When the volume and seriousness of such cases mounted, prominent Leaguers sent telegrams to the governor, the viceroy and the secretary of state for India, asking them to restrain the

Punjab government from these actions.[154] Pethick-Lawrence did point out to Wavell the complaints that he had received about the partiality of Governor Glancy and the Punjab administration but the viceroy dismissed such complaints as routine matters in any Indian elections.[155] The Unionist party had more funds (Rs 2.1 million) for the elections as compared to the League (Rs 0.4 million). Besides the revenue officials including the zaildars and lambardars, it could use the *ulama* and Majlis-i-Ahrar-i-Islam leaders for its campaign, but it had completely lost influence among the Muslim students. The Congress also funded these elements but it could not be sure of their support. There was a regular trickle of defections from the anti-League Muslim parties into the League. As compared to its opponents, the provincial Muslim League organized a more sophisticated, effective and multi-faceted propaganda strategy within its limited resources. The Aligarh Muslim University students (270 in number) and the Punjab Muslim Students Federation members (in thousands) spread all over the province to campaign for the League candidates. The provincial Muslim League and Muslim Students Federation published booklets and pamphlets which supplemented the literature that they received from the central League for distribution; Mian Bashir Ahmad headed the publicity section as its secretary.[156] The pro-League *ulama* and *mashaikh* launched an intense province-wide election campaign that was more successful than that of the Unionists; for instance, one 80-year old man who was threatened by the zaildar to vote for a Unionist candidate refused to submit, saying that if he voted against the League, his *iman* (faith) would be in danger.[157] The Unionist government felt so agitated by the religious propaganda that it empowered the district magistrates under section 196 to prosecute any person under section 171 C (2) (b) who was engaged in such a propaganda, but excluded from their purview section 171 C (2) (a) that covered use of undue influence by the civil servants.[158] These tactics, however, failed to save the Unionists from an unexpectedly disastrous defeat.

The Bengal presidency Muslim League in a way enjoyed smoother atmosphere than any that its counterparts had to face in other 'Pakistan provinces'. It faced no hostility from the officials. Factionalism was there in the provincial Muslim League ranks but its manifestation was not as crude and acute as in some other provincial Muslim Leagues. The rival factions were willing to bury temporarily their factional differences; and they demonstrated remarkable unanimity in the election campaign. Jinnah's visit further softened factional tensions whose advice was: 'There should be only one thing—Elections! We may call it a "fortnight truce". Work wholeheartedly for one objective—Pakistan'.[159] The factional leaders supported one another's candidates.[160] The students League launched its own campaign in support of the League and coordinated its activities with the provincial Muslim League leaders. Muslim students in large number, about 20,000 according to one estimate, were engaged in the election campaign.[161] They brought out propaganda literature including a booklet, *Shaheed Nazir*, in memory of Nazir Ahmad, a fifth year student of the Dhaka university and founding editor of the magazine, *Pakisthan*, who was stabbed to death by a fellow Hindu student at the university gate.[162] The *ulama* and *mashaikh* made their contribution to the campaign. Interestingly, Suhrawardy moved the resolution in the provincial Muslim League council on 29–30 September 1945, that welcomed the Jamiatul Ulama-i-Islam support to the 'Muslim League's Pakistan movement for Islamic renaissance', and it was seconded by Maulana Abdur Rashid Tarkabagish, a well-known peasant leader.[163] Maulana Bhashani, who was then president of the Assam provincial Muslim League, came down from Assam to North Bengal to campaign actively for the League candidates and his services were formally acknowledged by the Bengal presidency Muslim League.[164] The financial assistance from the central election fund, according to party estimates, saved for the presidency Muslim League at least twenty seats which might have otherwise been lost in the elections.[165] Jinnah visited Sylhet, Shillong and Gauhati in Assam during his first ever official visit to that province. The enthusiasm that the masses displayed was remarkable; the Surma Mail equipped with loud speakers that carried him from Calcutta to Sylhet was delayed for about thirty-two hours.[166] The students played a commendable role in the election campaign. The line system and eviction of Bengali Muslim immigrants, of course, remained in focus.[167]

United Provinces and Bihar were among those provinces on which the Congress and the Maulana Madni-led Jamiatul Ulama-i-Hind leaders had focused their attention. The most heated contest was in the constituency in which Liaquat was a candidate. The Congress and the anti-League parties pooled in all their resources to defeat him and so did the League to ensure his victory. Liaquat won his seat by a wide margin.[168] In Bihar, the Muslim Students Federation with Jafar Imam as president and Zubair Malik as secretary did admirable work for the League candidates. The communists and Adibasis who supported the League demand for Pakistan also extended whatever support that they could muster for the League.[169] In Madras, it was a walkover for the League candidates, as there was not even a semblance of an opposition. So was the case for the League candidates in Bombay and Orissa; it easily managed to defeat the opposing candidates many of whom lost their security deposits.

The main election campaign issue was whether or not the Muslims of India wanted 'Pakistan'. All the other issues were woven around this single issue or were relegated into the background. The survival of the Muslims, it was emphasized, was dependent upon its achievement, and 'Akhand Bharat' or 'United India' with a unitary system, as the Congress visualized, would result in their elimination as a separate entity.[170] Focus of the campaign, therefore, was on those elements that united the Muslims and not on those that might possibly divide them. Jinnah and other League leaders urged them to concentrate on their Muslim identity that emanated from their belief in one God, one Book, and one Prophet. They should not think, Jinnah appealed, in terms of their geographic, ethnic, tribal and sectarian identities, and he discouraged every move that was directed to organize them on those lines.[171] 'Pakistan', termed as the 'avalanche of Muslim national renaissance', was perceived as panacea for all the ills in the Muslim society and a means of their salvation.[172] The League campaign was so intense and effective that it became extremely difficult for any Muslim organization to speak against the Pakistan demand, and radically changed the situation on the ground. There was no possibility of a Hindu or Hindu-dominated party finding acceptance among the Muslims. In fact, their anti-Pakistan campaign only strengthened Muslim attachment to the Pakistan demand. Consequently, the Congress with all its long self-perceived non-communal history and 'nationalistic' claims but with anti-Pakistan rhetoric did not put up any significant number of candidates against the League candidates; instead, it tried to prop up anti-League Muslim parties and promoted their candidates, hoping that they would be elected and oppose the Pakistan scheme. The anti-League Muslim parties were forced to abandon, or soften, their opposition to the Pakistan demand, whether it was the Krishak Praja Samity, the Unionist Party, G.M. Sayed's provincial Muslim League, Khaksar movement, or the Khudai Khidmatgar movement.[173] Now if they wanted acceptance in the Muslim community, the maximum that they did was to oppose 'Pakistan' of the League's conception which, they alleged, would be controlled by pro-British elements and Muslim 'vested interests'. The changed atmosphere left little chance of success for the anti-League candidates. Wherever the anti-League Muslim candidates won the elections, it was primarily due to their own merits or because of intra-League tussle in that province or in that constituency.

One less noticed issue that helped to create a favourable atmosphere for the League in the Punjab and NWFP was the Indian National Army trials. The public trial of the officers of the Indian National Army coincided with the general elections. Both the League and the Congress opposed these trials and appointed teams of lawyers to defend the accused.[174] The trials were held in the Red Fort, Delhi. The first group of three officers, Shahnawaz, G.S. Dhillon and Prem Sahgal, were found guilty and sentenced to death for treason and abetment to murder. General Claude Auchinleck, the commander-in-chief, set them free on appeal, following country-wide demonstrations. But the deposition of Captain Abdur Rashid of the 14th Punjab regiment who hailed from the NWFP at the trial of next group and his conviction gave a communal touch to the proceedings.[175] Abdur Rashid deposed during his trial, 'I was convinced that the non-Muslims who were the moving spirit in the Indian National Army were going to invade India with the help of the Japanese. I was also convinced that this would result in the domination of India by the non-Muslims with the help of the Japanese. In order to safeguard the interests of my community I decided like most of the other Muslims to join the Indian National Army in order to arm myself and thus be in a position to safeguard the interests of my community in India.'[176] He was found guilty of a 'lesser crime of grievous hurt' and sentenced to transportation for life. When he lodged an appeal against the sentence, General Auchinleck, contrary to what he had done in the case of three pro-Congress Indian National Army officers, refused to set him free and reduced the sentence to seven years rigorous imprisonment.[177] Jinnah considered the official policy as 'legally wrong, logically untenable and morally indefensible', terming the commander-in-chief's explanation in the council of state as unconvincing 'in the eyes of any thinking man', and appealed to the viceroy to abandon any further trial of Indian National Army men and remit Abdur Rashid's sentence.[178] The All-India Muslim League working committee and council formally called on the viceroy to intervene and, if no other course was open, to grant pardon to those convicted and remit their sentences.[179] The Frontier legislative assembly on the motion of a Leaguer, Sardar Bahadur Khan, called on the government to release all those Indian National Army men who had

been convicted.[180] The League propaganda campaign that Abdur
Rashid's sentence amounted to humiliation of 100 million Muslims
created an emotional atmosphere in its favour that helped its candidates
in the elections.[181] Shahnawaz who had pro-Congress leanings and
aspired to get himself elected unopposed from the Punjab on the
Congress ticket had to withdraw his candidature because Abdur
Rashid's deposition created a pro-League atmosphere. Later on, the
League helped in the rehabilitation of the Indian National Army men
and the demobilized military personnel.[182] Jinnah continued to press for
the release of Abdur Rashid and others; and under that pressure, on 12
April 1946, Wavell asked the chief justice of the federal court to peruse
their cases; and it was a few days before independence that the chief
justice and two other Judges gave their opinion that Abdur Rashid's
conviction was not 'justified' and that he should be 'released
forthwith'.[183]

(D) ELECTION RESULTS

The League secured 453 out of 524 Muslim seats in the central and
provincial assemblies, and polled about 75 per cent of the total vote.
The Congress in total put up 96 candidates, won 19 seats in the NWFP
and only 4 in other provinces, and polled about 4.4 per cent of the total
Muslim vote. The League won all the 30 seats reserved for the Muslims
in the central legislative assembly; quite a few of its candidates were
elected without a contest and it polled 86.6 per cent of the total votes
cast in the Muslim constituencies. Most of the candidates opposing the
League candidates forfeited their security deposits. Its success in the
provinces, except in the NWFP, was equally impressive [see Table 1].
In Bengal, it won 95 per cent of the total Muslim urban vote and 84.6
per cent of the rural vote and about 96 per cent Muslim seats. In Assam,

Table 10.1: Election results, 1945–46

Name of the Legislature[184]	Total number of Muslim seats	Strength of the PML	%
Assam	34	31	91
Bengal	122	116	95.8
Bihar	40	34	85
Bombay	30	30	100

Central Provinces and Berar	14	13	93
Madras	28	28	100
NWFP	38	17	45
Orissa	4	4	100
Punjab	88	79*	89.28
Sindh	34	28	82
United Provinces	66	54	82

*This figure includes four members who joined the League immediately after the elections.

the League won 91 per cent seats, or 31 out of 34 Muslim seats, the remaining seats went to the Jamiatul Ulama-i-Hind. In Sindh, it won 82 per cent seats, plus one Independent (Sardar Nabi Bakhsh Bhutto) who joined the League soon after the elections. In NWFP, the League won 17 seats (including two Zamindara seats), the Congress 19 Muslim seats and the Jamiatul Ulama-i-Hind 2. Although the League secured only 42 per cent of the Muslim seats, it polled 41.65 per cent votes as against 38.34 per cent votes polled by the Congress which secured 53 per cent of the Muslim seats. In Bihar, the League gained 34 (85 per cent) out of 40 seats, the pro-Congress Momins 5 and Congress Muslims 1. In United Provinces, where the Congress supported both the Sunni board and its rival, the Shia Political Conference, the League secured 54 (82 per cent) out of 66 seats, the Congress 2 out of 30 seats that it had contested, and the nationalist Muslims 7. Rafi Ahmad Kidwai, a former Congress minister, lost in all the three constituencies he had contested, and so did his brother. In the Central Provinces and Berar, it captured 13 (93 per cent) out of 14 seats and the Momins one; all the 3 Congress candidates lost their security deposits. In Orissa, Bombay and Madras, the results were cent per cent for the League. In Orissa, the League won all the four seats, with its opponents forfeiting securities in two of the three contested seats. In Bombay, the League captured all the 30 seats, with 7 uncontested; the League polled 93.2 per cent votes and its opponents in 19 constituencies forfeited their securities. In Madras, its candidates were elected unopposed on all the 4 seats in the legislative council and 13 in the legislative assembly. In the 16 contested constituencies, the League polled 93.04 per cent votes. Its unexpectedly resounding victory in the Punjab, where it secured 90 per cent seats, gave Jinnah 'the most pleasant shock' of his life and 'stunned its opponents'.[185]

NOTES

1. The life of the council of state was extended till 1 May 1946.
2. R. Coupland, *Indian Politics, 1936–1942*, p. 333.
3. Sir R. Lumley to Linlithgow, 15 January 1942, *TP*, I, pp. 27–28; and resolution passed at its Madras annual session on 12–15 April 1941, Pirzada, *Foundations*, vol. II, p. 373.
4. The British parliament passed the India and Burma (Postponement of Elections) Act, 1941 to extend the life of the provincial legislatures.
5. For the resolution moved by Qazi Isa and seconded by Yahya Bakhtiar, see Pirzada, *Foundations*, vol. II, pp. 277–79.
6. Resolution passed by the working committee at its meeting on 6–14 July 1945, AFM, vol. 180, no. 19.
7. Ibid., vol. 180, no. 18.
8. *TP*, vol. VI, p. 71.
9. Ibid., p. 2.
10. Glancy wanted the British government to declare the inviability of the Pakistan scheme before the general elections in view of its implications for the Punjab. For Glancy's views and his memorandum, see ibid., pp. 7 and 114–19.
11. *Wavell: The Viceroy's Journal*, p. 178.
12. *TP*, vol. VI, pp. 300, 313, 413 and 655.
13. Ibid., pp. 100–105; and Azad's message to Attlee, 2 July 1945, *Selected Works of Maulana Abul Kalam Azad*, vol. 2, p. 34.
14. Wavell to Pethick-Lawrence, 6 and 31 August 1945, *TP*, vol. VI, pp. 37 and 90; and *Wavell: The Viceroy's Journal*, p. 169.
15. Wavell to Pethick-Lawrence, 23 September 1945, and Pethick-Lawrence to Wavell, 12 October and 9 November 1945, *TP*, vol. VI, pp. 296, 336 and 466.
16. Wavell to Sir J. Colville, 29 August 1945, ibid., p. 180.
17. Waheed, *Nation's Voice*, vol. IV, pp 231–32.
18. *Wavell: The Viceroy's Journal*, p. 171.
19. *Dawn*, 21 September 1945.
20. In a province where the provincial Muslim League president was also leader of the assembly party, the deputy leader of the League assembly party was to be *ex-officio* member of the board.
21. For the text of rules and regulations of the central parliamentary board and provincial parliamentary boards, see Waheed, *Nation's Voice*, vol. IV, Appendix III, pp. 687–92.
22. For the resolution of the committee of action passed at its meeting in Simla on 13 July 1945, see AFM, vol. 193, p. 36.
23. Ibid., vol. 401, p. 49.
24. QAP, F. 462, pp. 10–11. The Muslim Leaguers also objected to fixation of Rs 500 as the application fee.
25. Liaquat to Quaid-i-Azam, 2 September 1945, SHC, OM-1: 79.
26. The eleven leaders were: G.M. Sayed, Mohammad Ali Shah, Ghulam Husain Hidayatullah, Ayub Khuhro, Ghulam Ali Talpur, Bande Ali Talpur, Ilahi Bakhsh, Hatim Alavi, Qazi Fazlullah, Yusuf Haroon and Mahmud Haroon.
27. AFM, vol. 180, nos. 51 and 54; and Waheed, *Nation's Voice*, vol. IV, p. 218.
28. QAP, F. 830, p. 1; F. 854, p. 21
29. For Qayyum's overtures to the League leaders for joining the League even in mid-1942, see Nawab Ismail to Jinnah, 14 July 1942, QAP, F. 761, pp. 68.

30. SHC, Pb-V: 85; and Sadullah Khan to Quaid-i-Azam, 1 September 1945, SHC, NWFP-I: 59.
31. For a representation of the Aligarh Muslim University students from different parts of the NWFP against Aurangzeb, see QAP, F. 962, pp. 41–44.
32. AFM, vol. 180, nos. 32, 40 and 41; and vol. 344, nos. 98 and 99.
33. Its members were: Nawab Iftikhar Mamdot, Arbab Noor Mohammad, M.R. Kiyani, Sohbat Khan, Jalaluddin Jalal Baba, Habibullah Khan, Pir Sahib of Zakori Sharif and Arbab Abdul Ghafur.
34. Its members were: Ziauddin (secretary), Qayyum Khan (Peshawar), Samin Jan (Mardan), Bakht Jamal (Mardan), Pir Mohammad Khan (Mardan), Niamatullah Khan (Bannu), Taj Ali Khan (Kohat), Fazal Karim (Kohat), Pir Jalal Shah, Asadul Haq (Hazara), Jalaluddin Jalal Baba (Hazara), Arbab Sher Ali Khalil (Peshawar), Mir Alam Khan (Tangi) and Nawab Nasrullah Khan (Bannu). AFM, vol. 366, p. 71.
35. Its members were: Ghulam Hyder Khan Sherpao, Ayub Khan, Mohammad Ali Khan Hoti, Karim Bakhsh and Yusuf Khattak. Jinnah who was in Mastung heard about the appointment of these Boards 'on the Radio and read from the Press reports'. Jinnah to Nawab Ismail, 14 October 1945, ibid., vol. 417, p. 46.
36. Qazi Isa to Quaid-i-Azam, 21 June 1948, QAP, F. 614, p. 9.
37. Nazimuddin to Liaquat, 25 August 1945, and Abdul Rahman to Liaquat, 6 October 1945, AFM, vol. 42.
38. Raghib Ahsan to Liaquat, 12 October 1945, ibid., vol. 393, p. 40.
39. For a detailed but slightly magnified picture of the factional tussle, see Haroon-or-Rashid, *Foreshadowing of Bangladesh*, pp. 199–224.
40. Zafar Ahmad Ansari to M. Ismail, 22 September 1945, AFM, vol. 338, p. 56.
41. Jinnah's press statement on 15 September 1945, Waheed, *Nation's Voice*, vol. IV, p. 230.
42. He applied for the ticket when he was in Karachi. Hamid Nizami reported this information for the *Nawa-i-Waqt* from there on 8 September 1945. QAP, F. 783, p. 10.
43. For instance, see his response to Major Mir Haider, 24 September 1945, in SHC, Pb-I: 55; Nawab Mohammad Zafar Khan of Bannu, 25 November 1945, QAP, F. 140, p. 17; Abdur Rauf, working president, Peshawar city Muslim League, ibid., F 1011, p 110; Abdul Haye, SHC, Assam-I: 72; and Maulana Shabbir Ahmad Usmani, 1 February 1946, Ahmad Saeed, *Quaid-i-Azam: Rare Letters*, p. 183. Jinnah took a similar position during the repeat elections in Sindh; for instance, see his letters to Mrs Sharfunnisa Shahban and Yusuf Chandio, 29 October 1946, SHC, Sindh-VIII: 34 and 38.
44. Jinnah to Dr A.A. Khan, 3 September 1945, SHC, Sindh-VI: 31.
45. Jinnah to Ahmad Ispahani, 11 November 1945, SHC, Bengal-III: 42.
46. Ghulam Husain Hidayatullah to G.M. Sayed, 17 August 1945, QAP, F. 830, p. 77; and SHC, Sindh-VI: 20.
47. For the decline in Sayed's popularity, see Mohammad Akbar Kazi to Sayed, 24 August 1945, SHC, Sindh-VI: 26.
48. Hidayatullah, Khuhro and three others to Quaid-i-Azam, 1 October 1945, and Sayed to Quaid-i-Azam, 1 October 1945, SHC, Sindh-VI: 52 and 54.
49. Liaquat to Hidayatullah, 2 October 1945, Liaquat to Quaid-i-Azam, 8 October 1945, Liaquat to Sayed and Ayub Khuhro, AFM, vol. 142, nos. 29, 35 and 43; Ayub Khuhro to Quaid-i-Azam, 3 and 7 October 1945, SHC, Sindh-VI: 69 and 71; Sayed to Quaid-i-Azam, 3 October 1945, and Jinnah to Sayed, SHC, ibid.: 66 and

67. See also the correspondence, AFM, vol. 180, nos. 46, 48, 53 and 56–62; and vol. 385, pp. 80, 81 and 82.

50. Jinnah to Ilahi Bakhsh, 15 December 1945, in SHC, Sindh-VII: 16; and Waheed, *Nation's Voice*, vol. IV, p. 264.

51. For the text, see SHC, Sindh-VI: 73.

52. Ali Ahmad Talpur to Yusuf Haroon, 12 November 1945, ibid., VIII: 69. For Rashidi's claim for the party ticket, see ibid.-VI: 32.

53. For Rashidi's expulsion and resolution of the central committee of action passed in its meeting on 8–9 November 1945, see AFM, vol. 385, pp. 74, 75 and 93; and for a subsequent expression of regret by Rashidi, see his letter to Quaid-i-Azam, 24 February 1947, SHC, Sindh-VIII: 89.

54. For Yusuf Haroon's letters to Sayed, Mohammad Ali Shah and Khair Shah with copies to Jinnah and Liaquat, see QAP, F. 274, pp. 283–85.

55. Yar Mohammad and Ahmad Tejani to Liaquat, 7 October 1945, AFM, vol. 385, pp. 77–79; Yusuf Haroon to Liaquat, 14 November 1945, QAP, F. 274, p. 287; and Ayub Khuhro to Sayed, 16 November 1945, SHC, Sindh-VII: 7.

56. Ghulam Mohammad Wassan, Imam Bux Talpur and Arbab Togchi to chairman, committee of action, AFM, vol. 385, pp. 103–6.

57. SHC, Sindh-VII: 23.

58. A.H. Siddiqi, principal, Muslim college, Karachi to Quaid-i-Azam, 30 October 1945, ibid.-VI: 74.

59. Abdur Rashid Arshad to Quaid-i-Azam, 26 December 1945, ibid.-VII: 28.

60. As late as 19 December, Sayed had assured Liaquat that he would support every candidate to the Sindh assembly who was nominated according to the rules. [For his letter, see AFM, vol. 294, p. 22] For Sayed's allegations, see his statement, *Dawn*, 27 December 1945; and for the response by Liaquat (28 December 1945) and Qazi Isa (1 January 1946), see ibid., 2 January 1946.

61. For the eight Muslim Leaguers expelled from the party, see AFM, vol. 386, p. 81.

62. For criticism on this point, see Maulana Zafar Ahmad Usmani to Zafar Ahmad Ansari, 14 February 1946, ibid., vol. 438, p. 55.

63. Ziauddin to Nawab Ismail, 6 June 1946, ibid., vol. 366, no. 25.

64. SHC, Pb-IV: 41.

65. AFM, vol. 230, Nos. 53 and 58.

66. One faction had Suhrawardy, Abul Hashim, Moazzam Husain, Lal Mian, Ahmad Husain and Raghib Ahsan, and the other faction had Nazimuddin, Akram Khan, Nurul Amin and Fazlur Rahman.

67. SHC, Bengal-1:68 and 69; and Abul Kasem and Abdur Razzaq to Quaid-i-Azam, 9 February 1946, QAP, F. 883, pp. 10–11.

68. On the eve of the elections, there was a proposal for general amnesty for those who had left, or had been expelled from, the Muslim League. Besides Fazlul Haq, several politicians such as Sir Sultan Ahmad, Hafiz Mohammad Ibrahim and Wazir Hasan were keen to rejoin the League. Mohammad Khalilullah to Quaid-i-Azam, 24 August 1945, SHC, Bengal-I: 55.

69. For appeals on his behalf by Maulana Akram Khan, M.A.H. Ispahani, Hasan Suhrawardy, Pir Sahib of Sarsina, Mohammad Shahjehan and M.A. Ghani of Aligarh and others, see ibid.: 62; and QAP, F. 962, pp. 45–50.

70. He was close to the Congress and accepted the chairmanship of the Congress-sponsored Bengal Muslim parliamentary board.

71. Jinnah to Aley Hasnain Ansari, University of Allahabad, 5 October 1945, SHC, Bengal-1: 58.

72. For Jinnah's statement on 8 September 1946, following Fazlul Haq's letters to him of 1 and 3 September, and a written statement, see QAP, F. 132, p. 49.
73. For Jinnah's statement of 24 October 1945, see Waheed, *Nation's Voice*, vol. IV, p. 269.
74. AFM, vol. 359, pp. 6, 9 and 48–50.
75. Fazalbhai to I.I. Chundrigar, 4 March 1946, QAP, 1042, p. 88.
76. AFM, vol. 536, 13 and 16.
77. Ibid., vol. 535, p. 44.
78. For instance, see the estimates about the Punjab given by Shaukat Hayat (his letter to Quaid-i-Azam, 18 July 1945, QAP, F. 350, p. 5), Mian Bashir Ahmad (his letter to Quaid-i-Azam, 14 November 1945, SHC, Pb-III: 21), and S. Sadiq Hasan (his letter to Quaid-i-Azam, 25 September 1945, QAP, F. 880, p. 209).
79. See Chapter 8.
80. For Allama Mashriqi's statement, see the *Tribune*, 19 September 1945; and *Dawn*, 21 February 1946.
81. AFM, vol. 294, p. 17.
82. For Azad's proposals sent to Gandhi on 2 August 1945, see *TP*, vol. VI, pp. 155–57; and for Gandhi's telegram asking him not to publish them, see ibid., p. 172. Azad confidentially wrote to Gandhi that to alley Muslim fears of Hindu domination, the future constitution should be federal with fully autonomous units in which the central subjects must be only of an all-India nature and agreed upon by the units; the units must have the right of secession; joint electorates with reservation of seats; Hindu–Muslim parity in the central executive and legislature; and by a convention the head of the Indian federation should be Hindu and Muslim by turn in the initial period.
83. Madan Lal to Liaquat, 25 September 1945, AFM, vol. 452, p. 50.
84. For his interview with the Associated Press of America, 1 November 1945, see Waheed, *Nation's Voice*, vol. IV, p. 287.
85. For his response to a question on 24 September 1945, see ibid., p. 238.
86. (Maulana) Tahir Ahmad to Jinnah, 10 March 1946, QAP, F. 1136, pp. 329–36.
87. His campaign in the Muslim-minority provinces was limited to a stop for a short while at the Allahabad railway station on his way to Calcutta where the E.I. Railway Muslim Employees Association, Allahabad, presented him an address and a purse, and he addressed the gathering.
88. Jinnah to Akram Khan, 27 August 1945, SHC, Bengal-IV: 6.
89. Jinnah to Suhrawardy 7 February 1946, QAP, F. 458, pp. 46–47.
90. Suhrawardy to Jinnah, 31 January 1946, ibid., F. 458, p. 44.
91. AFM, vol. 180, nos. 27, 31, 68 and 69; and vol. 556, pp. 22, 31, 51 and 55. In November 1945, the central committee of action allocated Rs 5,000 for engaging six persons on a salary up to Rs 150 per month each for conducting propaganda in the elections.
92. Qazi Isa to Jamiluddin, 19 November 1945, AFM, vol. 237.
93. For the press supportive of the Muslim League, see Chapter 7.
94. It was alleged that the Congress spent Rs 2 crore on the anti-League candidates. Note by Wavell, 18 March 1946, in *TP*, vol. VII, p. 17; and also Khalid, *Punjab Muslim League*, pp. 151–52.
95. Jinnah had occasionally reminded the provincial Muslim Leagues that the central election fund was not meant for distribution among the provinces. For instance, see Jinnah to Suhrawardy, 30 October 1945, SHC, Bengal-III: 14.

96. Jinnah did not give funds directly to individual Muslim Leaguers. For instance, see Ghulam Bhik Nairang to Jinnah, 28 August 1945 and Jinnah to Nairang, 19 September, SHC, Pb-III: 59 and 61.

97. For Jinnah's letters to members of the committee and Suhrawardy, 9 March 1946, see QAP, F. 57, pp. 8–9, 11–12 and 57; and Star of India, 18 March 1946.

98. Ispahani to Jinnah, 23 April 1946, QAP, F. 588, p. 578.

99. Jinnah-Daultana correspondence, and receipt signed by Mian Amiruddin, the provincial Muslim League finance secretary, all documents dated 17 January 1946, ibid., F. 68, pp. 7–8.

100. For a statement of expenditure submitted by the Punjab provincial Muslim League, see ibid., F. 224, pp. 4, 7 and 9; and F. 588, pp. 151–52 and 371–76.

101. Qayyum, Nishtar, Ziauddin, Jalal Baba and M.R. Kiyani had asked for this amount. Ibid., F. 588, pp. 139 and 140; and F. 574, p. 28.

102. For a statement of accounts that Yusuf Haroon sent to Jinnah, see ibid., F. 56, pp. 1–4. See also Ayub Khuhro to Quaid-i-Azam, 26 December 1945, SHC, Sindh-VII: 27.

103. AFM, vol. 193, no. 11.

104. For example, for their assistance in the selection of candidates, see ibid., vol. 229, nos. 6–19.

105. Ibid., vol. 180, no. 79; vol. 231, nos. 15 and 27; and vol. 237. The teachers were: Dr M.B. Mirza, Prof. A.B.A. Haleem, Prof. M.M. Shareef, Dr Aziz Ahmad, Dr Afzaal Husain Qadri, Dr S. Moinul Haq and Enayat Ali Khan.

106. Zafar Ahmad Ansari to chief accountant, Aligarh Muslim University, 20 November 1945, ibid., vol. 417, p. 47.

107. Qazi Isa to Manzar-i-Alam, 8 January 1946, AFM, vol. 237; and Inayat-i-Kibrya, general secretary, Sarhad Muslim Students Federation, to Quaid-i-Azam, 21 January 1946, QAP, F. 154, pp. 88–90.

108. AFM, vol. 238, no. 26. For the Aligarh Muslim University students' work in Bihar, see ibid., vol. 438, p. 48.

109. The administration of the Islamia college, Lahore, closed down the college for some time to enable the students to participate in the election campaign. For an account of the students' role, see Mirza, Muslim Students and Pakistan Movement and Punjab Muslim Students Federation; and Mukhtar Zaman, Students' Role in the Pakistan Movement.

110. AFM, vol. 371, p. 13.

111. Jinnah to Akram Khan and M.A.H. Ispahani, 8 March 1946, QAP, F. 68, p. 31.

112. Miss Ghiasuddin, secretary, girls students' federation to Khaliquzzaman, member, central parliamentary board, 8 December 1945, AFM, vol. 230, nos. 55 and 56.

113. See Chapter 7.

114. Raghib Ahsan to Nawab Ismail, 2 September 1945, and Raghib Ahsan to Liaquat, 11 October 1945, AFM, vol. 436.

115. On 31 July, Ahmadullah Khan, Medical Officer at Deoband, in a letter to Jinnah, had proposed the formation of an ulama party that could be headed by Maulana Shabbir Ahmad Usmani. Jinnah forwarded this letter to Nawab Ismail, chairman of the committee of action, who marked it to Zafar Ahmad Ansari, asking him to go to Deoband to ascertain Maulana Usmani's consent and also see Maulana Tahir. For details, see AFM, vol. 436.

116. Raghib Ahsan to Liaquat Ali Khan, 12 October 1945, ibid., vol. 393, pp. 40–41.

117. For the seven sections into which the Jamiatul Ulama-i-Islam divided its deliberations and for the themes and chairmen of these sections, see ibid., vol. 393, pp. 41–42; and vol. 437.

118. Raghib Ahsan to Zafar Ahmad Ansari, 18 October 1945, ibid., vol. 437, no. 5

119. He claimed that a majority of those educated at Deoband and spread all over India were with the Muslim League. Ibid., vol. 453, p. 29.

120. His message entitled *Maujuda Siyasi Kashmakash mein Musalman kia Karein?* ('What Should the Muslims do in the Present Conflict?') [Delhi, 1945] was separately published and circulated.

121. For a copy of Jinnah's appeal and the response, see AFM, vol. 436, p. 32; Waheed, *Nation's Voice*, vol. IV, pp. 236–37; Jinnah to Ahmad Saeed, 15 May 1944, *JP*, vol. X, p. 357; Raghib Ahsan to Zafar Ahmad Ansari, 11 November 1945, ibid., vol. 437, no. 19; and president of the Majlis-i-Ahrar-i-Islam, Tehsil Charsadda to general secretary, All-India Muslim League, ibid., vol. 464, p. 37.

122. For a report that the Congress put at the disposal of Maulana Madni Rs 50,000, see Maulana Tahir Qasimi to Zafar Ahmad Ansari, 17 October 1945, ibid., vol. 437, no. 2.

123. For instance, see the *ulama* sent to Liaquat's constituency, ibid., vol. 453, pp. 49, 66 and 81.

124. Statement by Zafar Ahmad Ansari, 22 April 1946, ibid., vol. 439, p. 11; and *Dawn*, 27 April 1946.

125. Numerous Deobandi *Ulama* were with the Congress because Maulana Madni, 'a sworn enemy of the British', who believed in the Congress slogan of complete independence, was with that party. QAP, F. 893, pp. 168–69.

126. The department of publicity and information, All-India Muslim League, published it in 1945.

127. For an interesting account of this incident by Shabbir Ahmad Usmani himself, see his letter to Zafar Ahmad Ansari, 19 October 1945, AFM, vol. 437, no. 4.

128. Liaquat to Nawab Ismail, 1 December 1945; and Nawab Ismail to Nawab of Chhatari, 10 December 1945, ibid., vol. 437, nos. 40 and 46.

129. For details, see ibid., vol. 437, nos. 53, 55, 57–60.

130. Abdul Haq to Zafar Ahmad Ansari, 4 April 1946, ibid., vol. 439.

131. S.A. Ashraf, secretary, Meerut city Muslim League to Liaquat Ali, 15 July 1946; and Husain Imam to Nawab Ismail, 7 November 1945, ibid., vol. 396, p. 92; Zafar Ahmad Ansari to Liaquat Ali Khan, ibid., vol. 437, no. 50; and for tours of *ulama* and conferences in major cities, see letters from such personalities as Khaliquzzaman, Tahir Ahmad Qasimi, Abdul Hamid Badauni, Sayyid Quraish, Raghib Ahsan, Zafar Ahmad Usmani, Sardar Nishtar, Ghulam Murshid, Abdul Qayyum Kanpuri, Yusuf Haroon, and S.A. Ashraf to Zafar Ahmad Ansari, ibid., vol. 438. The central committee of action supported these conferences; for instance, it deputed its secretary to organize the conference in Delhi and allocated Rs 3,000 for this purpose.

132. For instance, see ibid., vol. 350, p. 105. The All-India Muslim League and its branches published/republished numerous religious tracts and *fatawa* by such *ulama* as Ashraf Ali Thanvi, Shabbir Ahmad Usmani and Mufti Mohammad Shafi.

133. For instance, see SHC, Sindh-III: 13.

134. Ayub Khuhro to Quaid-to-Azam, 4 January 1946, QAP, F. 365, pp. 109–110.

135. Ilahi Bakhsh to Liaquat, 2 January 1946; and Ghulam Husain to Quaid-i-Azam, SHC, Sindh-VII: 33, 42, 43 and 49; and Ghulam Husain to Liaquat, 26 January and 1 February 1946, AFM, vol. 386, pp. 4–6.

136. Ayub Khuhro to Quaid-i-Azam, 26 December 1945, SHC, Sindh-VII: 27.
137. SHC, Sindh-VIII: 50.
138. QAP, F. 227, p. 18.
139. For resolution of the Sindh provincial Muslim League working committee, see Yusuf Haroon to Quaid-i-Azam, 26 December 1946, ibid., vol. 386, p. 87; and also see SHC, Sindh-VIII: 1.
140. Ayub Khuhro to Quaid-i-Azam, 25 December 1946, QAP, F. 627, pp. 1–3.
141. *Dawn*, 26 November 1945.
142. For representations made to Jinnah, see Abdul Qayyum to Quaid-i-Azam, 4 and 9 January 1946; and Inayat Kibrya to Quaid-i-Azam, 10 January 1946, SHC, NWFP-II.
143. Abdul Wajid to Liaquat, 1 December 1945, QAP, F. 882, pp. 169–70.
144. Secretary, Provincial Teachers' Association, Suba Sarhad to Quaid-i-Azam, QAP, F. 906, p. 123; and Abdul Wajid to Liaquat, 1 December 1945, ibid., F. 882, pp. 169–70.
145. For election malpractices, see the statements by Nishtar and Mian Ziauddin, *Deccan Times*, 10 March 1946, cited in Sharif al Mujahid, *Quaid-i-Azam Jinnah: Studies in Interpretation*, Karachi, 1981, p. 135; and Nishtar to Mountbatten, 22 April 1947, Nishtar Papers, vol. III.
146. Nawab Nasrullah Khan to Quaid-i-Azam, 6 February 1946, QAP, F. 342, p. 12; and Pir Zakori to Quaid-i-Azam/Liaquat, 17 February 1946, ibid., F. 407, p. 1.
147. Anwar Khan, *Role of N.W.F.P. in the Freedom Struggle*, pp. 208–9.
148. Joint statement by Maulana Shakirullah, Maulana Rahman Shah and Sayyid Sultan Mohammad on 20 February 1946, AFM, vol. 366, pp. 12–13.
149. Glancy to Wavell, 16 August 1945, *TP*, vol. VI, pp. 71–72. Denouncing Glancy for 'shameless' interference, Jinnah alleged that no Governor had brought 'such disgrace to British Administration as this one'. Waheed, *Nation's Voice*, vol. IV, p. 382–83.
150. Firoz Khan Noon to Khizr Hayat, 21 August 1945, SHC, Pb-IV: 15; and Khalid, *Punjab Muslim League*, pp. 143–44.
151. Wavell to Pethick-Lawrence, 9 October 1945, *TP*, vol. VI, p. 320.
152. QAP, F. 1042, p. 85.
153. For interference by the police and revenue officials in the districts of Shahpur, Faisalabad, Jhang, Multan and Sahiwal (Montgomery), see Firoz Khan Noon to Quaid-i-Azam, SHC, Pb-IV: 32–34; Vicky Noon to Jinnah, 10 October 1945, ibid.-IV: 19; (Mian) Abdul Bari to Quaid-i-Azam, 23 January 1946, ibid.-I: 33 and 34; Shaukat Hayat to Quaid-i-Azam, 27 December 1945, ibid.-III: 52; Fazal Haq Piracha to Quaid-i-Azam, 4 January 1946, QAP, F. 405, pp. 6–7; Abdul Haq to viceroy with copy endorsed to Liaquat, 6 January 1946, Abid Husain to Quaid-i-Azam, 10 January 1946, Abdul Halim to Quaid-i-Azam, 21 January 1946, ibid., F. 579, pp. 110–13; Nazir Ahmad Khan to Quaid-i-Azam, 20 November 1945, ibid., F. 331, pp. 10–11; and Daniyal Latifi to Quaid-i-Azam, 28 August 1945, ibid., 830, p. 86.
154. For copies endorsed to Jinnah, see QAP, F. 579, pp. 107–9; AFM, vol. 237, p. 78; and SHC, Pb-IV: 29. Wavell doesn't mention any action that he took on these complaints. *Wavell: The Viceroy's Journal*, p. 178.
155. Major Wyatt to Pethick-Lawrence, 8 October 1945, and Wavell to Pethick-Lawrence, 1, 12 and 16 October 1945, *TP*, vol. VI, pp. 304–5, 335 and 338.
156. Mian Bashir succeeded Raja Ghazanfar Ali who was not keeping good health. Besides circulating the Punjab provincial Muslim League manifesto that Mian

Bashir had himself translated into Urdu, the provincial Muslim League and Muslim Students Federation published and distributed such booklets as '*Quaid-i-Azam ka Islami Paigham*', '*Pakistan aur Islami Mumalik*', '*Congress aur Musalman*', '*Muslim League aur Khaksar*' and '*Tarique Tabligh*'.

157. Habib to K.H. Khurshid, 3 February 1946, QAP, F. 784, p. 171.
158. SHC, Pb-IV: 26 and 28. After the elections, most of the petitions filed against the League candidates alleged 'undue influence exercised by threats of divine displeasure'. *TP*, vol. VII, p. 274.
159. Jinnah to Suhrawardy, 11 January 1946, SHC, Bengal-III: 17; and *Star of India*, 28 February 1946.
160. Haroon-or-Rashid, *Foreshadowing of Bangladesh*, p. 205.
161. *Star of India*, 20 March 1946.
162. For letter by Qazi Najmul Haq, editor and compiler of the *Shaheed Nazir*, finance and joint secretary, All Bengal Muslim Students League, 3 November 1945, see QAP, F. 958, p. 178.
163. AFM, vol. 42.
164. For report signed by M.A.H. Ispahani, A.W. Baakza and one other, see QAP, F. 588, pp. 367–68.
165. Suhrawardy, secretary, Bengal provincial parliamentary board, to M.A.H. Ispahani, treasurer, provincial parliamentary board, 28 March 1946, and 'Report of the working committee of the All India Muslim League Central Fund', ibid., F. 57, pp. 62–66.
166. *Dawn*, 4 March 1946.
167. Ibid., 7 March 1946; and *Morning News*, 5 March 1946.
168. *Dawn*, 4 April 1946.
169. For details, see Taqi Rahim, *Tehrik-i-Azadi*, pp. 502–7.
170. For Jinnah's speeches in Ahmadabad on 27 October 1945, and in Bombay while inaugurating his election campaign on 31 October 1945, see Waheed, *Nation's Voice*, vol. IV, pp. 280 and 284.
171. For instance, see his speeches on 24 September and 22 October 1945, ibid., pp. 237 and 264; and his advice to the secretary of the All Party Shia Conference, Sajjad Ali, 1 October 1945, ibid., p. 240.
172. Speech in Bombay on 20 December 1945, ibid., pp. 353–57.
173. Wavell to Pethick-Lawrence, 22 November 1945, *TP*, VI, p. 521.
174. On 1 November 1945, the central committee of action appointed a three-member (Raza Ali, Qazi Isa and Qadiruddin Ahmad) committee for this purpose which was to report to the League president and general secretary. Earlier, the Punjab provincial Muslim League had also appointed a defence committee of lawyers. Nehru headed the Congress team of lawyers. For League–Congress cooperation on this issue in the central assembly, see Mountbatten to Pethick-Lawrence, 2 April 1947, ibid., vol. X, p. 97.
175. For his trial and conviction, see *Dawn* of January and February 1946.
176. *Dawn*, 23 January 1946; and The Indo-British Union, Poona, Circular No. 1, 1 March 1946, pp. 3–4, AFM, vol. 472, pp. 90–91; and for a statement of similar content by Shahzada Ataul Mulk of Chitral, son of Sir Shujaul Mulk, see his letter to Quaid-i-Azam, QAP, F. 974, pp. 2–3.
177. *Dawn*, 5 February 1946.
178. Wavell to Pethick-Lawrence, 13 February 1946, *TP*, vol. VI, p. 969; and for Jinnah's statements, see QAP, F. 505, p. 39; and AFM, vol. 294, No. 50.

179. For resolutions of the working committee and council, see AFM, vol. 142, p. 48; and vol. 278, p. 23.
180. Ibid., vol. 294, No. 94.
181. *Dawn*, 18 February 1946.
182. For instance, see resolution 5 of the All-India Muslim League council, 10 April 1946, AFM, vol. 278, p. 24; and Zafar Ahmad Ansari, secretary of the central committee of action, to presidents of the provincial Muslim Leagues (confidential letter), 20 April 1946, AFM, vol. 181, no. 15.
183. For the reduction of sentences of others, see G.E.B. Abell to Jinnah, 5 August 1947, QAP, F. 10, pp. 102–4.
184. Issued by the Publicity and Information Department, All India Muslim League, Delhi [1946].
185. Jinnah's address to the Punjab League assembly party, *Dawn*, 21 and 22 March 1946.

11

Bypassing the Pakistan Demand, 1945–1946

By 1945, the All-India Muslim League had gained so much support at the grassroots that its demand for Pakistan had to be addressed in any long-term settlement of the constitutional problem of India. Jinnah had disrupted the 'snare' that the Wavell plan had laid down to dilute the Pakistan demand.[1] Now even Sir Stafford Cripps, who soon took over as president of the board of trade in the Labour cabinet, realized that the constitutional problem could not be settled without solving the Pakistan issue.[2] Before the general elections, the Cabinet had decided in talks with Lord Wavell that if the Indian political parties failed to reach an agreement, the Cripps offer would be the basis of post-election negotiations; but as the League's unswerving faith in Pakistan gradually sank in, the British and Hindu politicians looked for strategies to bypass the League demand. The British policy was partially influenced by the provocative anti-British rhetoric of the Congress leaders. More influential were Pandit Jawaharlal Nehru and Sardar Vallabhbhai Patel who, besides raising other issues, denounced those British Indian administrators who had used brutal methods to suppress the Quit India movement and threatened to put them on trial. They were equally critical of the All-India Muslim League and vehemently opposed the Pakistan scheme. Both the Congress leaders vowed not to approach the League again for a Hindu–Muslim settlement.[3] The trial of the Indian National Army officers in the Red Fort, Delhi at this time fuelled the already inflamed public sentiments, provoking violent demonstrations that resulted in the death of thirty-three persons in Calcutta.[4] The British administrators were shaken by the Congress leaders' aggressive campaign. Soon added to these concerns was the 'revolt' of the Royal Indian Navy's personnel in Bombay, Calcutta and Karachi, which was controlled without much difficulty but the riots following the revolt left about 200 civilians dead.[5] The Labour government was so anxious to appease the Congress that it appeared, according to Wavell, 'bent on handing over India to their Congress friends as soon as possible'.[6] The sentences of three pro-Congress Indian National Army officers were converted from transportation for life to forfeiture of their pay and allowances.[7] Then, secretary of state for India, Pethick-Lawrence (1871–1961), in a statement in the house of lords on 4 December 1945, emphasized the importance of one constitution-making body after the elections, as visualized in Wavell's announcement of 19 September; and the Bengal governor, Richard Gardiner Casey, in his talks with Gandhi tried to divert the Congress anger from the British to the League, by suggesting that it was 'not "the British" but the Muslim League, who were suffering from "Hinduphobia". . . . The Congress was slanging the umpire instead of their opponent'.[8] These overtures softened the Congress attitude and the tone of its leaders, which was reflected in the resolution of its working committee on 7 December, and the Nehru–Cripps correspondence.[9] After the elections, Wavell had to hold negotiations with the political parties. V.P. Menon, the reforms commissioner, offered to draft a strategy paper; and Sir B.N. Rau, a constitutional lawyer, who had recently been removed from the prime ministership of the state of Jammu and Kashmir, assisted him in this task. The Congress leaders were privy to what Menon put up to Wavell who in turn forwarded it to London.

(A) THE CABINET MISSION

(i) *Breakdown Plan.* Lord Wavell was personally opposed to the Pakistan scheme. He was willing to go along with any move that would keep India united. V.P. Menon's note (of 6 December 1945) developed into what was referred to as Wavell's 'Reserve' or 'Breakdown Plan', which detailed the post-election strategy, if the parties failed to reach an agreement on framing a constitution. Menon and Rau prepared the draft note, which, on 27 December, Wavell forwarded to Pethick-Lawrence with his own comments.[10] The basic idea was to spell out the ill-effects of the Pakistan scheme to scare the League leadership. Jinnah was to be told that if he insisted 'on self-determination in genuinely Muslim majority areas', the non-Muslim majority areas would be detached from the 'Pakistan provinces'.[11] It was calculated that if he was threatened about the consequences, the 'attractiveness of Pakistan' for the Muslims would dwindle to a 'vanishing point'.[12] The plan, in the Menon–Rau paper entitled 'Appreciation of Political

Situation', listed various stages in the post-election political process: formation of the executive council with parity of representation to Muslims and Hindus other than Scheduled Castes and with representation to the Congress and the League proportionate to their success in the elections to run the administration for the interim period; preliminary conference with representation on similar lines to draft the agenda and create a constitution-making body to frame the constitution; and formation of governments in the provinces. All the states were to accede to the union; a provision that was subsequently deleted from the draft on Rau's request who was worried about his image of impartiality.[13] The British government, Wavell wrote to Pethick-Lawrence, had to choose between a deadlock and an 'award', in case all attempts to end the deadlock failed. A breakdown in the League–Congress talks, he wrote, could occur at any stage: at the time of forming the executive council due to 'excessive' demands of the League or at the stage of constituting the constitution-making body or the framing of a constitution. In case of the League's 'intransigence', Wavell wanted the Labour cabinet to empower him to 'send for Jinnah and press him not to persist in his attitude' and if he still persisted, he would threaten the League president with the 'award' that would deprive Pakistan of at least two divisions (Ambala and Jalandhar) of the Punjab and almost the whole of western Bengal including Calcutta. Thus, only the 'husk', in Jinnah's own words, would remain. These tactics, Wavell wrote, would force Jinnah 'to secure the best possible terms for the Muslims' within the Indian federation. The British government, he advised, should face any 'serious communal conflict' resulting from the League's 'refusal to accept such an award' by force.[14] Depriving the League to form its ministry in the Punjab was in line with this policy; as on 3 March 1946, Wavell had written to Pethick-Lawrence that it was 'essential to keep Punjab out of League's reach' to facilitate the 'formulation of British policy'.[15]

Jinnah had no means to know Wavell's plan. The Leaguers had thought that after the League's landslide victory in the elections to the central assembly, the British government would accept its mandate and concede the demand for Pakistan without any resistance. This is evident from Jinnah's interaction with various individuals and in his public statements. On 5 January 1946, Wavell in an interview with him indirectly and vaguely hinted at the idea behind his plan. He informed Jinnah that His Majesty's Government was 'determined to make a big effort to settle the constitutional problem this year' and that it would go 'to considerable lengths to avoid a breakdown'. Jinnah's response to this veiled threat was that His Majesty's Government should settle the 'fundamental issue' of Pakistan, and that the Muslims were prepared 'to face the consequences' of any action that it might take. Wavell saw in Jinnah 'no signs whatever of any spirit of compromise' on the Pakistan issue.[16] Three days later, Jinnah, in his meeting with Woodrow L. Wyatt, who had accompanied a parliamentary delegation from London to New Delhi, spelt out with clarity the League's position, that it would not participate in any interim or permanent government without (a) a prior declaration accepting the principle of Pakistan; (b) parity of the League with all other parties, i.e. it should have 7 out of 14 portfolios; (c) two constitution-making bodies, one for Pakistan and the other for Hindustan, which would also negotiate the frontiers between them with only 'predominantly non-Muslim areas like the Ambala Division' in the Punjab going to Hindustan; (d) Pakistan would remain within the Empire; and (e) relations with Hindustan would be purely diplomatic; there would be 'no common currency, transportation system, army, etc.'[17] Then, on 10 January, he told the ten-member Professor R. Richard-led parliamentary delegation when it visited his residence in Delhi that His Majesty's Government should immediately accept Pakistan, which was the only solution of India's constitutional problems; and the members of parliament reported back in London that Jinnah wanted two constitution-making bodies and recognition of 'Pakistan' as the 'real issue'.[18] Later in that month, in a lengthy conversation with Arthur Moore, editor of the *Statesman* (Delhi), on different aspects of Pakistan, he confidently expressed the view that if 'the British accepted the verdict of the Muslim electorate, the Congress would have to do the same'. Moore informed Attlee who circulated the 'notes' of his conversation with Jinnah among the members of the India committee.[19] When Wavell, in his seven-minute inaugural address to the Indian legislative assembly on 28 January, spoke about the formation of an executive council composed of political parties and convening of one constitution-making body to frame the constitution, Jinnah in his response the same day demanded that instead of forming the executive council, focus should be on a permanent solution of the constitutional problem by the creation of a Muslim state.[20] On 9 February, in separate letters of similar content to Pethick-Lawrence and Cripps, he opposed the formation of any interim government under the new phraseology of 'political' executive council and a single constitution-making body, pointing out the futility of forcing such measures on Muslim India, because these 'must result in disaster, not to say that it will be a breach of the solemn declaration of August 1940' and the repeated assurances given by responsible British leaders to the Indian Muslims.[21] And on 31 March, in an interview with Norman Cliff, foreign editor of the *News Chronicle* (London), and Fraser Wighton, special representative of Reuter, he emphasized that there was 'no room for us to compromise on the issue of Pakistan. It is a question of our very existence'. Three days later, in an interview with Donald Edwards of the BBC, he stated that 'Pakistan must be a fully sovereign state, with complete control of defence and foreign policy'.[22] But the Congress and the British Labour leaders were thinking on totally different but mutually almost similar lines.

The Congress leaders resented the League's celebration of 11 January 1946, as the 'Victory Day' on its success in the central assembly elections, and launched an aggressive anti-League campaign to prevent any softening of the British policy on the Pakistan issue. Sardar Patel held out a threat that the League 'may celebrate victory day and believe that Pakistan has been achieved in this manner. Pakistan is not in the hands of the British government. If Pakistan is to be achieved, Hindus and Muslims will have to fight. There will be civil war'.[23] Pandit Nehru threatened that the Indians were 'sitting on the edge of a volcano' that might 'erupt at any moment', warning the British with 'the biggest ever mass movement', and surprisingly, still viewed the League even after its landslide victory in the general elections as an 'organization of Nawabs and Taluqdars', which was raising the 'Pakistan slogan' 'to sidetrack' the Indians from the 'problems of poverty and starvation'.[24] At the same time, he kept the British on edge by denouncing Linlithgow and Wavell for strengthening the League by their policies. Forcing Pakistan of Jinnah's conception, which he regarded 'a fantasy', on India would 'lead to civil war'. Pakistan in real terms, he wrote in a long letter to Cripps on 27 January, should consist of only parts of Punjab and Bengal. 'Even if there were two separate States', he maintained, they should have 'a joint scheme of defence' that would include foreign affairs, communications, etc. He wanted the British government to declare the independence of India whose constitution should be framed by a constituent assembly elected on the basis of 'a wide franchise'. Free India, in his view, would be a federation of fully autonomous units with 'defence and allied subjects' as common subjects. All the provincial governments, he wrote, should jointly propose the formation of one Constituent Assembly and provisional central government without any interference from the viceroy or the British government.[25] Cripps wrote back to Nehru that he had stated 'exactly what I wanted'.[26] Azad had already apprised Wavell of similar views on behalf of the Congress; and Gandhi who regarded Pakistan a 'national suicide' advocated a federation of provinces and States with residuary powers vested in the units.[27] The ideas of the Congress leaders about the future constitution were nearer to the viewpoint of the British leaders, and the Cabinet prepared its policy and strategy in that light.

The British cabinet's confidence in Wavell's skills and capacity to handle the delicate post-election negotiations had been shaken after he had presented the 'Breakdown Plan'.[28] It was pointed out that he had relied on no 'expert help' other than that of Menon and Rau who were not 'qualified with first hand knowledge'.[29] The cabinet set aside his plan, directing him not to circulate it among the governors, and decided to send a mission of three ministers—consisting of Sir Stafford Cripps, Lord Pethick-Lawrence and Mr A.V. Alexander (first lord of the admiralty)—to India to conduct negotiations. Wavell who now suspected that he might be sidelined in the negotiations and called upon to implement the decisions afterwards raised objections; and he was then assured of his participation in the deliberations along with the mission.[30] Pethick-Lawrence prepared a detailed plan of action for the mission. On 24 February, six persons—Prime Minister Attlee, three ministers/members of the proposed mission (Cripps, Pethick-Lawrence and Alexander), Sir William D. Croft (under secretary of state in the India office), and Francis F. Turnbull (private secretary to the secretary of state for India and secretary of the mission)—discussed at Chequers in complete secrecy his plan dealing with 'fundamental issues'. They all agreed that the mission should cover 'the whole field simultaneously', and not focus first on the formation of the executive council, and hear the views of as many people as possible, without expressing its own opinion that might show 'a bias for or against' Pakistan. The India office was asked to prepare a scheme of a confederation of Pakistan, Hindustan and some of the larger states, in which the confederal units would be 'sovereign' with 'equal voice' in its decisions, and the confederal field would be determined by agreement. They also discussed a draft directive for the mission and sent its copy, but not the copies of other decisions, to Wavell for opinion.[31] Interestingly, Wavell was asked not to consult V.P. Menon on the draft directive.[32] The India office prepared a scheme of confederation that the mission was to put before the Indian leaders only after 'partition in some form' was 'seen inevitable'. However, there was a realization that 'a Confederation would be only a little better than the complete recognition of Pakistan as a sovereign and independent State'.[33] The India office also drafted 'Proposals for a Provisional Constitution' of a federation of united India that the British government was to enforce in case the mission failed to achieve its objective.[34] The Labour government, besides its desire to prolong its stay to preserve the unity of India and to protect the British commercial and strategic interests, was influenced by other factors. It felt that a united India would be in a better position to defend the subcontinent than a weak Pakistan with limited resources. A threat from the Soviet Union was already being foreshadowed and the perceived 'infiltration' of communists into the League was a cause for serious concern.[35] Another British anxiety that influential American circles shared was the impact of an independent and belligerent Islamic Pakistan on pan-Islamic sentiments and the planned partition of Palestine and creation of a Jewish state. Jinnah's statements on Palestine did not alleviate their concerns. In an interview with the *New York Times* correspondent on 13 February 1946, Jinnah had stated that 'he will go to any length to help' the Palestinians. When asked to define 'any length', he said, 'It means whatever we can do, violence, if necessary'.[36] The mission enjoyed virtually *carte blanche* in its negotiations with the Indian leaders and broadly followed a course of action that the Labour leaders chalked out at Chequers.

(*ii*) *Legislators' Convention*. The Leaguers were unaware of the exact nature of the Nehru–Cripps contacts or the strategy devised at Chequers. They got a vague inkling about the new British policy on 15 March 1946, when Prime Minister Attlee made the announcement in the House of Commons about the visit of a three-member Cabinet Mission to India and its mandate. The mission was to have 'as free a hand as possible' in setting up the machinery with the cooperation of the Indian leaders to decide the form of future government of a free India and establish an interim government. Attlee's emphasis was on 'the great work' that the British had accomplished in uniting India, which did not exist 'over previous centuries'. The British government was 'mindful of the rights of minorities' and would enable them to live without fear but it could not, he warned, 'allow a minority [meaning thereby the Muslims] to place a veto on the advance of the majority'.[37] Like the debate in the British parliament on the Lahore Resolution on

18 April 1940, none of the members of parliament who spoke on this occasion had a word of support for the Pakistan scheme.[38] Attlee's comments about the denial of 'veto' power to the Muslims enthralled the Congress leaders. Patel declared that once power came into their hands, they would 'surely bury Pakistan once for all' while Nehru threatened those who had not supported the 1942 movement that they would have 'to pay for it now'.[39] Jinnah deplored Attlee's 'vicious formula' that 'a minority cannot place a veto on the advance of the majority' and called on Britain and the US to make their position clear in regard to the Muslim Middle East, Indonesia and Muslim India. He reiterated that the Muslims in India were not a minority but 'a nation and self-determination was their birthright', and they were prepared to face 'any Anglo-Hindu alliance'.[40] He tried to highlight the gravity of the situation through his interviews with the British and American journalists, cautioning that Britain would face a 'Muslim revolt' if it did not concede Pakistan. To a query from a journalist, his response was, 'Revolt is a revolt'.[41] Emphasizing the Muslim resolve, he stated 'in unequivocal terms' that they were determined to establish Pakistan by negotiations, peacefully if possible, but, if necessary, by shedding 'our blood' if that was the test.[42]

The All-India Muslim League had not so far formally defined the exact territories of Pakistan. Jinnah in his interviews especially with foreign journalists including Beverley Nichols in late 1943, and in his talks with Gandhi in September 1944, had elucidated that Pakistan would consist of 'six provinces' or units, Punjab, Sindh, the NWFP, Balochistan in the west, and Bengal and Assam in the east, with minor territorial adjustments.[43] The minor adjustments that the All-India Muslim League had in view were the non-Muslim majority Ambala division in the Punjab and Burdwan division in Bengal. But the Leaguers were alarmed by rumours in political circles of plans to chop off vast areas of Pakistan, in an attempt to make it virtually an unviable state. Besides these rumours, Jinnah got a 'short report' from Nazimuddin who had gone to London with the Indian food delegation and who, after his meetings with Pethick-Lawrence, Stafford Cripps, John Henderson (parliamentary under-secretary), and John Woodhead, informed him that none of the British leaders liked 'the idea of Pakistan' although they thought it 'inevitable'. However, they could not visualize the inclusion of Ambala division, Calcutta, and Burdwan division in the Pakistan zones; Nazimuddin asked Jinnah 'to be ready to meet them [members of the Mission] on this point'.[44] The response that the All-India Muslim League decided to give to such an eventuality was to define the areas of Pakistan from its platform with clarity. The forum that it selected was a convention of the recently elected League legislators to the central and provincial legislatures. The convention met in Delhi on 7–9 April 1946. A meeting of the central council was also scheduled on 10 April, to consider the resolutions that might be passed by the convention. The council did meet on that date but this item was deleted from its circulated agenda, perhaps because the convention virtually constituted elected 'parliament of Muslim India'.[45] Meanwhile, Jinnah had some idea about the attitude and policy of the Cabinet Mission on Pakistan in his 'long talks' with Cripps unofficially (30 March) and with the Mission 'as a whole' officially (4 April).

The convention was a mega event in Delhi where more than 450 League legislators from all the provinces participated in its deliberations; and about 200 local and foreign journalists covered its proceedings. After Jinnah's address, a subjects committee consisting of 10 per cent legislators from every province, plus representatives of the central legislative assembly and the council of state drafted a lengthy resolution, which, on 9 April, the convention on Huseyn Shaheed Suhrawardy's motion adopted in the open session.[46] After recounting the incompatibility of social orders advocated by Islam and Hinduism, the Hindu caste system and the Congress 'misrule' during 1937–39, the convention's Pakistan Resolution declared that the 'Muslim nation' would not accept a single constitution-making body and any constitution for a united India. It demanded the establishment of 'a single sovereign independent State' in the Pakistan zones, where the Muslims were in 'a dominant majority', comprising Bengal and Assam in the east and Punjab, the NWFP, Sindh and Balochistan in the west of India; two separate constitution-making bodies for Pakistan and Hindustan to frame their constitutions; and safeguards for the minorities in both the countries on the lines suggested in the Lahore Resolution. After the convention had unanimously passed this resolution, Liaquat read out a pledge that the legislators had signed. Every legislator declared his belief in Pakistan and pledged to undergo any sacrifice for its achievement. Jinnah, in his concluding remarks, said:

> Is Britain going to decide the destiny of 100 million Muslims? No. Nobody can. They can obstruct, they can delay for a little while, but they cannot stop us from our goal. Let us, therefore, rise at the conclusion of this historic Convention full of hope, courage and faith. Insha' Allah we shall win.[47]

The resolution and the pledge inspired every segment of the Muslim society and region.[48] Even Muslim personnel of the British Indian army did not remain unaffected; and the district army commanders reported that if the League raised 'trouble' on the Pakistan issue, it would be more difficult to deal with than the Congress disturbances of 1942.[49] However, the fight was still at the negotiating front; and the League had to go a long way to reach its goal.

(*iii*) *Tripartite Negotiations*. The Cabinet Mission arrived in New Delhi on 24 March 1946. The mission along with the viceroy heard the views of every political segment that mattered in Indian politics, initially without showing any overt bias for or against the Pakistan scheme. They talked to, or interviewed, members of the Viceroy's Executive Council, governors, chief ministers, leaders of the Congress, Muslim League and other parties and interests, chancellor of the chamber of princes and a select number of princes on different aspects of the constitutional problem.[50] The talks gradually came down to Mission–League–Congress negotiations or bridging basically the League–Congress gulf by tackling the League leadership on the Pakistan issue. During these talks, the mission members especially Cripps worked closely with the Congress leaders—Gandhi and Nehru in particular—to settle the constitutional issues. Gandhi who assumed the role of its unofficial 'adviser', at Cripps' request, and whose spokesman was Nehru and not Azad or Patel was shown deference that 'horrified' Wavell.[51] Both Gandhi and Nehru operated essentially from behind the scene while Azad formally presented the official viewpoint of the Congress. Cripps looked to Gandhi who, he believed, had wrecked his mission in 1942, for advice whenever there was any serious hurdle. The main reason for the cordiality was the commonality of the British and Congress interests, i.e. to preserve the unity of India and secure its defence. The differences between them were at rare moments when the mission felt that the British Imperial interests were not receiving due consideration or they were squeezing the other side, the Muslim League, too harshly and unfairly or when the Congress suspected that the proposed constitutional framework was too loose and faulty that it might facilitate the emergence of Pakistan at a future date. During three-month-long talks, the mission frequently modified its formal stance to appease the Congress.

The League was on the receiving end throughout the tripartite talks. Jinnah and his colleagues had to strategize in a difficult and complex situation. On 17 March, Liaquat invited members of the central working committee to meet in New Delhi and asked them to arrange for their indefinite stay in the city. The working committee nominated Jinnah to represent the League before the mission, and he regularly consulted its members or the working committee as a whole on the emerging developments.[52] The Leaguers' optimism that their electoral victory had brought them nearer to their goal of fully sovereign Pakistan with control on defence gradually waned. On 30 March, Jinnah, in his one-hour-long informal meeting with Cripps, who wanted to judge the level of his commitment to Pakistan, was 'calm and reasonable' but 'completely firm on Pakistan'. He was willing to meet Gandhi, but not Azad, to arrive at a settlement, and was receptive to the suggestion for arbitration by the United Nations if the political parties failed to reach an agreement.[53] His first official interview with the mission was on 4 April that lasted for three hours. He tried to explain comprehensively the rationale behind the Pakistan demand, focussing on the divergences in Hindu and Muslim cultures and civilizations, citing the cow as a symbol which the Hindus worshipped but the Muslims sacrificed, and the killing of a cow in some Hindu-ruled Indian states could entail ten years in jail. He admitted that about 70 per cent Indian Muslims were converts who were ostracized once they embraced Islam and who had contributed to the enrichment of a distinct Indo-Muslim culture. He wanted two completely independent and sovereign states, Pakistan and Hindustan, with nothing in common between them at the centre, but which could have treaties and agreements like two independent sovereign states on any matter of common interest. He supported mutually agreed territorial adjustments but was unwilling to give up Calcutta because 'Pakistan without Calcutta would be like asking a man to live without his heart', or to agree to surrender the areas in which the Muslims were 50 per cent or more, because such a Pakistan would not be 'economically viable'. Even at that early stage, Jinnah's discerning mind could see through the thinly-veiled anti-Pakistan demand bias of the mission members; hence his remarks at the end of the long interview that 'if he had not convinced the [Cabinet] Delegation he could not do so'.[54] Even otherwise, the mission's partiality is quite visible from the line of questioning that it adopted with Jinnah and other interviewees.[55]

Jinnah's interview (4 April) and the Pakistan Resolution (9 April) of the legislators' convention disturbed the Cabinet Mission, which had not anticipated much resistance to its plan for a united India with limited subjects. The most upsetting element for the mission was Jinnah's inflexibility on complete sovereignty of Pakistan and control of defence, which in his view was 'the key pin of the problem'. On 28 March, when Jinnah had met with Lieutenant General Sir Arthur Francis Smith (chief of general staff, India), about the remission of the Indian National Army sentences, he had raised the issue of two 'entirely separate armies' for Pakistan and Hindustan but he did not receive a satisfactory response.[56] Subsequently, before Jinnah's interview with the mission, the chiefs of staff (India) in an assessment concluded that 'Pakistan even in the widest territorial form would not be viable in respect of external defence'.[57] But Jinnah resolutely resisted the idea of retaining anything in common at the centre between Pakistan and Hindustan. On 10 April, a day after the legislators' convention, the mission discussed Cripps-drafted proposals that suggested two alternative schemes to circumvent Pakistan of Jinnah's conception. Scheme A, visualized a three-part all-India union consisting of the Hindu majority provinces, the Muslim majority provinces and the states with three subjects — defence, foreign affairs and communications. Each part was to have an optional list of subjects, and the remaining subjects and residuary powers were to vest in the units. This scheme laid down the procedure for framing the constitutions of the various tiers. Any part of the union had the right to secede from the union after fifteen years. Scheme B, which bore similarities with Gandhi's proposals that he had made in the Jinnah–Gandhi talks, proposed two states, Pakistan and Hindustan, to either of which the princely states could join but during the interim period paramountcy would remain with the crown. Pakistan was to consist of Sindh, the NWFP, Balochistan and Muslim majority districts of west Punjab in the west and east Bengal along with the district of Sylhet but without Calcutta in the east. A treaty with Hindustan dealing with defence, foreign affairs and communications was 'a condition precedent' to establish a two-part Pakistan.[58] However, it was realized that such a treaty was unlikely to assure harmony between the two countries, as Pakistan would look to the Muslim states in the Middle East for friendship and Hindustan would tend to look to Russia, China and South-east Asia.[59] Pakistan in Scheme B was designed to pressurize Jinnah 'to try to make terms with the Congress'. The mission itself preferred Scheme A; and interestingly, Cripps reported that 'this might be acceptable to the Congress', as if he had its consent. Since these schemes went beyond what the cabinet had visualized, their approval was sought from London before presenting them first to Jinnah and then to Azad.[60] The British cabinet gave its approval subject to the advice from the chiefs of staff of the British army who advised that Scheme B should be accepted 'if the only alternative is complete failure to reach agreement' but even then a 'central defence council' should control defence as 'Pakistan lies across the two entrances to India from Peshawar to the sea in the west and from Himalayas to the sea in the east'.[61]

After the cabinet's approval of the two schemes, the mission prepared its strategy, which was primarily meant to dissuade Jinnah from his concept of Pakistan, and interviewed him on 16 April.[62] On that day, its members grilled him as if they were advocating the Congress case. Pethick-Lawrence informed Jinnah right at the outset that 'full and complete demand for Pakistan' had 'little chance of acceptance'. He then put before Jinnah the two schemes. Communal balance, it was promised, would be maintained at the centre in case of Scheme A even if the princely states came into the union. Jinnah doubted the efficacy of equality because, in his view, the dominance of the numerical majority ultimately could not be prevented in such a case. The principle of Pakistan, he insisted, should be accepted first before negotiations were held on the area of six provinces that he claimed for Pakistan. He refused to accept the exclusion of Calcutta in case of Scheme B because most of its population was 'imported labour' and comprised Depressed Classes who would in any case 'prefer' Pakistan. Even after conceding the whole of his Pakistan, he argued as he had done earlier on several occasions, the Congress would still have three-quarters of India. The mission could not pin him down to accept any of the two schemes. 'So far as the [All-India] Union was concerned', he told the mission, 'he could not accept the principle'; he had claimed 'six Provinces and if the Congress considered that that was too much they should say what they considered he ought to have'.[63] He expressed his readiness 'to do anything which would not prevent Pakistan from being, in the delegation's own words, a "viable" state economically, strategically and politically'. The Lahore Resolution, he said, 'contemplated a transitional period', and a 'peaceful transfer of power' would result if defence remained under British control in the transitional period but that did not mean that 'Britain must retain it for ever'; Cripps, however, ruled out that possibility. The mission asked Jinnah to think over the matter and let it know his response on its return from Kashmir where its members had planned to go for the Easter holidays.[64] Aware of the mission's views on Pakistan, the Congress working committee, on 15 April, after a four-day session, had called for complete independence, a united India, one federation with fully autonomous units vested with residuary powers; Azad represented the Congress viewpoint before the mission, one day after Jinnah's interview.[65] The mission gave Azad no information about its discussions with Jinnah. Cripps did not wait till the mission's return from Kashmir; he met with Jinnah the same evening but saw no change in his stand.[66] The next day, 18 April, he presented a memorandum before the mission, which ruled out Pakistan as a 'practicable scheme', and which proposed a three-tier system. The mission also discussed the pros and cons of an award if the negotiations ended in a deadlock.[67]

On 24 April, the mission returned from Kashmir. Instead of taking up the three-tier proposal, at first it discussed with Jinnah the Menon-drafted plan, which it considered as its 'last suggestion' to reach an agreement.[68] This plan proposed an interim government formed by the recently elected members of the central and provincial assemblies in proportion to the strength of various parties in those forums. Such a government that would have absolute Congress majority was to set up a constitution commission to decide within thirty days whether there should be one or two sovereign states, and to provide for the protection of minorities in the constitution(s). In case of disagreement, Muslim representatives of each Muslim majority province in the west and Bengal plus the district of Sylhet in the east would meet separately to decide whether that province desired to be excluded from the rest of India. If 75 per cent voted for exclusion, non-Muslim representatives of the district(s) contiguous to India could decide by a similar procedure to stay with India. Jinnah turned down the plan when Cripps discussed it with him that evening.[69] Then, on 25 April, there was a new development; the Anglo-American report on Palestine was published in London, allowing immigration of 100,000 more Jews into Palestine, contrary to the promises made to the Arabs and the Indian Muslims in 1939, which impacted upon the Pakistan demand.[70] There was a change in the mood of the mission. It ruled out both smaller as well as larger Pakistan, spelling out its reasons for the rejection, and pressed for the acceptance of a three-tier confederal system.[71] Jinnah was visibly upset by the renewed pressure. But he did not give up. He had two options: to launch a movement immediately to fight for the acceptance of a fully sovereign Pakistan, for which the League was perhaps ill-equipped and unprepared as it had never thought of such a strategy, and put the whole region into chaos by taking the Muslims on an unknown militant course or to struggle peacefully for a sovereign larger Pakistan within the given constraints. He went for the second option, and reluctantly agreed to place the three-tier proposal before the working committee provided the mission sent it to him in writing. On 27 April, Pethick-Lawrence, in identical letters to him and Azad, invited the Congress and the League to send four negotiators to meet the mission and the viceroy at a joint conference in Simla—the idea of a joint conference had emanated from the Congress—to discuss a three-tier system based on a union government dealing with foreign affairs, defence and communications; and the predominantly Muslim and predominantly Hindu provinces in two separate groups would deal with subjects that the provinces would desire to be dealt with in common. The provinces would manage all other subjects and have 'residuary sovereign rights'.[72] On 25 and 28 April, the working committee, after drawing attention to the League's standpoint from the Lahore Resolution to the Pakistan Resolution of the legislators' convention, authorized Jinnah to nominate four negotiators who were to raise its reservations about the three-tier proposal at the conference; four League nominees were Jinnah, Nawab Ismail, Liaquat and Abdur Rab Nishtar.[73] The Congress was also receptive, as it perceived in the League's acceptance the end of a sovereign Pakistan.[74] Two out of four Congress nominees—Nehru, Patel, Azad and Abdul Ghaffar Khan—were Muslims who could not interact without an interpreter, and it pointed out its reservations about the proposal.[75]

The negotiations at Simla lasted from 5 to 12 May. The League and the Congress put up diametrically opposite viewpoints on basic issues: all-India union, grouping of provinces, constitution-making body(s), interim government, and the time-frame of the union. After two days' intensive discussions, when there was a deadlock, Jinnah offered to suspend the Pakistan demand for five years and accept three-subject union in return for 'compulsory grouping of provinces' into two groups—Pakistan group and Hindustan group—with separate executives and legislatures; the two groups were to have their own constitution-making bodies dealing with all matters including the provincial constitutions, except the three subjects; the union was to stand dissolved, if it failed to work successfully.[76] Early in May, the League working committee had discussed and approved this offer although some Leaguers were staunchly opposed to any compromise on a fully sovereign Pakistan and defence.[77] Even after this offer, the

League–Congress differences could not be bridged. Cripps then wrote down 'Suggested Points of Agreement between the Representatives of Congress and the Muslim League', which had a pro-Congress bias. He 'showed' the document to Gandhi, and Wavell 'informed' Jinnah about its 'gist'.[78] On 8 May, when the mission gave the document to the party leaders, Jinnah argued that these points were fundamentally different even from the original formula that Pethick-Lawrence had sent to him on 27 April. The issue of grouping of provinces, he pointed out, had been left 'exactly as the Congress spokesmen desired in the course of discussions'. He felt that 'no useful purpose would be served' to discuss it.[79] Nevertheless, on 9 May, the mission and the party leaders did discuss this document but they failed to reach an agreement. After that, Nehru came up with the idea of an umpire—similar to the one that Gandhi had suggested in the Jinnah–Gandhi talks—to settle the points of difference but in the ensuing Jinnah–Nehru talks no acceptable solution could be agreed upon.[80] On 11 May, Nehru's proposal was further dissected in a meeting. Jinnah emphasized that 'the acceptance of a Union' was 'a great concession from his point of view' and that 'he was already the subject of criticism from his supporters for having yielded on this'. In case of arbitration, he argued, there had to be terms of reference; the League regarded 'the partition of India' as settled because of 'the verdict of the Muslims' in the general elections; and it was 'inconceivable that a matter of this sort should be the subject of arbitration'. The two groups of provinces, he stated, should constitute two separate federations 'which would confederate' at the centre. Each federation would have a constitution-making body, and a province could opt out of a federation only after the framing of the constitution. The League could not agree to give more than three subjects to the centre and their financing should be 'left open to the Constituent Assembly' that the two constitution-making bodies would constitute on the basis of parity. On the contrary, Nehru insisted on a strong centre with more than three subjects, with powers to raise its own revenues by direct taxation, and opposed grouping of provinces and parity at the centre.[81] At the end, the mission asked the League and the Congress to put down in writing their conditions for further negotiations 'to find common ground'.[82]

On 12 May, Jinnah gave a ten-point memorandum to Pethick-Lawrence embodying the minimum demands of the League 'as an offer to the Congress'. The demands were that: (*i*) the six Muslim provinces (Punjab, Sindh, NWFP, Balochistan, Bengal and Assam) should be grouped together as one group that would deal with all subjects except foreign affairs, defence and communications necessary for defence, which might be dealt with by the constitution-making bodies of the two groups of provinces—Muslim provinces (to be named as the Pakistan group) and Hindu provinces—sitting together; (*ii–iii*) a separate constitution-making body of the Pakistan group with proper representation to various communities in proportion to their population would frame the constitutions for the group and provinces vesting 'residuary sovereign powers' in the provinces; (*iv*) a province could opt out of its group after the framing of the constitutions, provided the wishes of the people had been ascertained by a referendum to opt out or not; (*v*) the joint meeting of the constitution-making bodies of the two groups would determine whether the union would have a legislature or not; and it would also decide the method of providing the union with finance but in no event should it be 'by means of taxation'; (*vi*) there should be parity of representation between the two groups in the union executive and legislature, if any; (*vii*) no major communal issue would be decided unless a majority of members of the two constitution-making bodies, present and voting, were separately in its favour; (*viii*) the union would not decide any matter of controversial nature, except by a three-fourth majority; (*ix*) the group and provincial constitutions would provide safeguards for fundamental rights and for religion, culture and other matters of different communities; and (*x*) the union constitution should provide that any province by a majority vote of its legislative assembly could secede from the Union at any time after an initial period of ten years.[83] The Congress countered the League's demands and called for one constitution-making body elected by the provincial assemblies through proportional representation by a single transferable vote; similarly, the representatives of the states were to be taken on the basis of population, in proportion to the representatives from British India. The constitution-making body would frame a constitution for the union with more than three subjects and with powers to raise taxes to finance them; and the remaining powers were to vest in the units. The provinces could form groups and the grouping was optional. Any point of disagreement could be referred to arbitration, and the constitution could be 'reconsidered' after ten years.[84] On 12 May, the conference collapsed, as it could not reconcile the conflicting positions of the two parties; however, no party was blamed for the failure and the mission promised to announce its own statement. Jinnah wanted to publish immediately all the documents relating to the conference, arguing that such documents were 'no longer confidential' but he was persuaded to refrain from doing that 'with great difficulty'.[85] A three-member (Cripps, Jinnah and Patel) committee was to prepare a list of documents for publication.[86] The next day, Jinnah gave an account of what had happened at the conference from 5–12 May to the working committee, which endorsed the stand taken by the party negotiators.[87] The working committee dispersed after that but Jinnah stayed in Simla to recuperate after three months of gruelling activity.

(B) CABINET MISSION PLAN AND THE RESPONSE

(i) *The Plan*. On 16 May, the mission issued a statement that contained its plan/scheme for a long-term arrangement and an interim government.[88] The statement, it was asserted, had kept a balance between the two main parties but the balance was conspicuously tilted towards the Congress rather than the League.[89] It reflected essentially Cripps' viewpoint who had written in his diary: 'we can get through I believe without the League if we have Congress with us but not without Congress even if we have the League.'[90] After a detailed unnecessarily provocative denunciation of the Pakistan scheme, which was obviously intended to please the Congress, the Cabinet Mission Plan recommended that the future constitution should be based on a union embracing British India and the states, dealing with foreign affairs, defence and communications with powers to raise finances to support them; all the other subjects and residuary powers should vest in the provinces; the union should have an executive and a legislature; any major communal issue in the legislature should be decided by a majority of the representatives of each of the two communities as well as a majority of all the members present and voting; provinces should be free to form groups with executives and legislatures and each group could determine common provincial subjects; the states would retain all subjects other than those ceded to the union; and the constitutions of the union and groups should provide that any province could by a majority vote of its legislature call for a reconsideration of the terms of the constitution after ten years and at ten yearly intervals thereafter. A constituent assembly, elected by the provincial assemblies, was to draft the new constitutional structure. Each province was allotted seats in the constituent assembly proportionate to its population, roughly in the ratio of one to a million, dividing these seats 'between the main communities—the 'General' community (including all persons who were not Muslims or Sikhs), Muslims and Sikhs—on the basis of their proportion in population. Each community in the provincial assemblies was to elect its own members.

After a preliminary meeting of the constituent assembly, in which it would elect its chairman and other officers and an advisory committee (to prepare a list of fundamental rights, the minority protection clauses and the proposals for the administration of tribal areas and excluded areas),[91] it was to split up into three sections: Section A comprising group of Hindu provinces (Madras, Bombay, United Provinces, Bihar, Central Provinces, Orissa, Delhi, Ajmer-Merwara and Coorg) with 20 Muslims out of 190 members; Section B consisting of north-western group of Muslim provinces (Punjab, the NWFP, Sindh and British Balochistan) with 23 Muslims out of 36 members; and Section C consisting of north-eastern group of Muslim provinces (Bengal and Assam) with 36 Muslims out of 70 members. The states were to have not more than 93 members; their mode of selection determined by consultation. Each group would settle the provincial constitutions and decide about any group constitution and its subjects. A province could opt out of the group, by a decision of its legislative assembly elected under the new constitution. After the framing of the group and provincial constitutions, the constituent assembly would settle the union constitution. A majority of the representatives, present and voting, of each of the two major communities could change the provisions of the plan or decide about a major communal issue; however, the chairman of the constituent assembly was to decide what constituted a 'major communal issue'. The viceroy was to instruct the provincial assemblies immediately to elect their representatives, and the states were to set up a negotiating committee. The constituent assembly and the UK were to sign a treaty to provide for 'certain matters arising out of the transfer of power'. Meanwhile, an interim government having the support of major political parties was to run the administration and attend to food shortages, post-war developments and participation in international conferences; and the Indians were to hold all its portfolios including that of war member. Two days later, Cripps at a press conference clarified that the British troops would stay in India for the interim period and constitution-making would proceed in accordance with the procedure laid down in the statement.[92]

The plan demonstrated that the mission and the Congress had successfully bypassed the Pakistan demand. Instead of showing a spirit of accommodation after the League's acceptance of a common centre, the Congress leaders impatiently sought 'immediate and unchecked control' of the central government to promote the party objectives.[93] The spirit needed for reconciliation was absent. After an initial positive response, Gandhi followed by Nehru and Azad (who communicated the Congress working committee's decision of 20 May) demanded, among other things, that the constituent assembly should be accepted as a sovereign body, empowered to amend the statement of 16 May, and its decisions should automatically take effect; there would be no grouping of provinces; a province would not be forced to stay in the assigned section; India would be independent from the moment that a 'national' provisional government responsible to the central legislature was installed; the advisory committee—where the Congress would have absolute majority—should determine the issue of representation of British Balochistan and look after the interests of the states if no agreed formula could be devised for their representation; paramountcy would cease immediately and henceforth it would be exercised in consultation with the 'national' provisional government; and the British troops would immediately withdraw whether the constituent assembly succeeded or failed to frame a constitution.[94] The Congress demands momentarily shocked even Cripps and Pethick-Lawrence; Wavell and A.V. Alexander had already registered dissenting voices.[95] The mission informed Gandhi and Azad that the Plan stood 'as a whole'; grouping of provinces was its essential feature that could be changed only by agreement between the two main parties; the parliament would take a decision on the new constitution taking into consideration two points— adequate provisions for the protection of minorities and signing of a treaty between the constituent assembly and UK to cover matters arising out of the transfer of power; and independence must follow and not precede the coming into operation of the new constitution.[96] Still, the Congress working committee re-emphasized its demands for: complete sovereignty of the constituent assembly with final authority to draft and implement a constitution; an interim government responsible to the central legislature; and withdrawal of British troops from India.[97] On 25 May, the mission issued an explanatory statement: after reiterating the points that it had already communicated to the Congress leaders, it stated that there would be no outside interference in the work of the constituent assembly; the provinces could opt out only after the elections under the new constitution; the interim government would not be responsible to the central Legislature; the British troops would stay in India during the interim period which it hoped would be short; and a joint meeting of the Shahi Jirga and non-official members of the Quetta municipality would elect the representative of British Balochistan.[98] The Congress leaders still pressed for 'absolute power' and did not listen to Wavell's not so unfriendly advice that 'We are giving you a chance of a united India, and I think it may be the last chance, and are prepared to give every possible help to you to obtain it. But we are not prepared simply to abdicate to one political party'.[99] The maximum that the Congress could extract from the mission was a vague assurance communicated by Wavell to Azad in his letter of 30 May, that His Majesty's Government 'would treat the new Interim Government with the same close consultation and consideration as a Dominion Government' but it was not prepared to give it 'the same powers as a Dominion Cabinet'.[100] The mission and the viceroy were apprehensive of the Congress reaction on a scale wider than the 1942 agitation, if it rejected the plan, and thought of even withdrawal of British forces in such an eventuality from the Hindu provinces to the Muslim provinces but the cabinet disagreed with this proposal because it would 'in effect' mean 'giving Jinnah the Pakistan which we have so far resisted'.[101] The Congress working committee dispersed without taking a decision, promising to meet again after a clearer picture had emerged following a response from the League on 6 June. If it was expecting that the League might reject the Plan and clear its way for complete control of the central government, it was seriously mistaken.[102]

(*ii*) *Response of the Parties*. The League faced a serious dilemma. Since 23 March 1940, it had consistently demanded a fully sovereign Pakistan. Muslims from every corner of India had rallied round its demand and given solid proof of their support in the general elections. The high point of its advocacy of Pakistan was the resolution of the Legislators' Convention and the Legislators' pledge of 9 April. Acceptance of the Cabinet Mission Plan would mean a climb down from that high pedestal. To that was added the incessant post-statement anti-Pakistan propaganda of the Congress press that came out with banner headlines 'Pakistan rejected'. Hindus felt jubilant by this propaganda but the Leaguers were disillusioned and depressed; Jinnah himself had 'sleepless nights' reflecting on the 16 May statement.[103]

Numerous Leaguers urged him to reject the Plan. Keeping this pressure in view, Jinnah was unwilling to comment on the plan till after he had consulted the working committee and council.[104] He expressed his views in a statement from Simla on 22 May. After censuring the mission's negative depiction of the Pakistan scheme, which he reiterated was 'the only solution of the constitutional problem of India', and after stating the League's ten-point offer of 12 May, he observed that the mission had divided the Pakistan provinces into two sections—B and C—instead of keeping them in one section; it had provided only one constitution-making body divided into three sections; the constitution-making body would have an overwhelming Hindu majority that would elect its chairman and other officers and the advisory committee by a simple majority; the chairman had wide powers in determining the communal nature of any issue that came before the assembly; the powers assigned to the advisory committee could result in adding more subjects to the union; communications had not been limited to what was necessary for defence; the union had been empowered to raise finances for the three subjects by taxation rather than by contribution from the groups; the Pakistan provinces had not been clearly given the right to secession after ten years; and the provision regarding the princely states was vague. The working committee and the council, he stated, would take the final decision on the plan.[105] Besides the explanatory statement of 25 May, the League representatives were assured that each section could frame the provincial and group constitutions even if some members boycotted the constitution-making process; the reference was obviously to the Congress members in the NWFP and Assam assemblies.[106]

Jinnah was prepared to accept the Cabinet Mission Plan. Besides a peaceful settlement of the constitutional problem, the League expected to consolidate its position in the Pakistan provinces in the transitional period and eventually secure a larger Pakistan, if the experiment of an all-India union failed. In fact, there were strong possibilities of consolidation of the Pakistan provinces. There had been a sharp swing to the League in the NWFP; and contrary to the Congress expectations, the non-League Frontier Muslims were all set to participate in the constitution-making process in Section B without any reservation.[107] Even Assam in Section C could emerge as a Muslim majority province or at least a province with the largest Muslim population if the Assam government simply implemented its own resolution of August 1943, or abolished the Line System and accepted the Bengali Muslim migrants as legal settlers.[108] Moreover, the League could easily win over the Tribal and Scheduled Castes leaders in Assam by providing their communities with separate electorates and weightage.[109] In addition, every section was empowered to frame the provincial and group constitutions even if some assembly members resorted to a boycott of its proceedings. Besides the demand for parity in the interim government, it was for this reason—the possibility of a larger Pakistan emerging out of such a union—that Gandhi had described the plan as 'really worse than Pakistan'.[110] Jinnah's concern at the time was that the Congress might reject the plan or press for its amendment; and the British government might succumb to that pressure. Therefore, he asked for a firm assurance that there would be no discrimination between the two main parties in the process of its implementation. The mission and the viceroy were reluctant to give him that assurance in writing. Wavell offered verbal assurance but Jinnah insisted on a written assurance. He discussed the issue with the mission members and secured a written note from Cripps to the effect that 'It is our intention to stick to the scheme as far as possible if either party are prepared to come in and work it'. He showed that note to Jinnah and gave him on behalf of the mission his personal assurance in writing on 4 June, that there would be no discrimination between the two parties in implementing the plan but surprisingly requested him not to make 'the existence of this assurance' public and simply use it for the satisfaction of the working committee.[111] On Wavell's direction, Cripps' note and his own letter to Jinnah were kept on the official file; and on 12 June, Pethick-Lawrence informed Attlee about this assurance.[112] The League had also a verbal statement from the viceroy that there would be parity in the executive of the union. With these assurances, Jinnah approached the working committee and the council for a decision.[113]

The working committee discussed the plan on 3–4 June, and decided after lengthy deliberations not to bind the council by a formal resolution and let it take a decision without any restrictions. On 5–6 June, the council held its session *in camera*, which 440 out of 475 councillors attended. Twenty-six councillors spoke for and against the plan.[114] Before the voting, Jinnah expressed his views for one and a half hours. He tried to assuage the Leaguers' sentiments by reiterating that fully sovereign Pakistan was still the League's ultimate goal and criticized the mission for advancing 'commonplace and exploded' arguments against it to please the Congress. Reminding the councillors that they had rejected the Cripps Proposals (1942) and Wavell Plan (1945) on his advice, now he advised them to accept the Cabinet Mission Plan as it 'conceded the substance of Pakistan' by 'compulsory grouping of the Muslim provinces' and provided 'a machinery for achieving fully sovereign Muslim State in ten years'; it was 'useless', he exhorted them, 'to shed blood when they could achieve their goal by peaceful methods'. He apprised the councillors about the assurances that he had received from the mission and the viceroy which influenced the council's final decision. The council accepted the plan by a large majority although a substantial number of councillors still voted against its acceptance.[115] Its resolution criticized the mission's 'injudicious' remarks about Pakistan, but 'prompted' by an 'earnest desire for a peaceful solution', it expressed its willingness to cooperate with the constitution-making body in the hope that it would eventually result in the establishment of a fully sovereign Pakistan. Its ultimate attitude, it resolved, would depend upon the final shape of the newly-framed provincial, group and union constitutions; and in the meantime, it reserved the right to modify its policy during the deliberations of the constitution-making body in the light of its fundamental ideals. It authorized Jinnah to negotiate with the viceroy regarding the interim government.[116]

The formation of interim government proved another hurdle in the tripartite negotiations. Wavell had started talks with the Congress and League leaders on this issue before the conference in Simla, visualizing an interim government of 12 members consisting of Congress (including one Scheduled Caste) 5; Muslim League 5; Sikh 1; and Indian Christian 1.[117] Although the talks were not finalized by the time of the League's acceptance of the plan yet this formula was their basis and no alternative proposal was seriously put forward from any quarter including the Congress. Jinnah got the impression in his talks with Wavell in Simla and then in Delhi on 3 June, that there would be Congress–League parity in the interim government. This was 'one of the most important considerations' for the League council's acceptance of the plan; and he informed Wavell to that effect.[118] After the council's acceptance, the Congress working committee did not meet to take a decision on the long-term plan on 7 June, as had been the understanding at the time of its dispersal on 25 May.[119] Instead, a systematic campaign was launched in the press against parity; G.D. Birla told Turnbull at a lunch that the Congress was opposed to an interim government based on a formula of 5:5:2 and desired one on the basis of 15 members with Congress 5; Muslim League 5; and others 5.[120] Azad and Nehru in their meeting with the mission and the viceroy divulged the Congress objective behind its opposition to parity. Nehru stated in so many words that the interim government would have 'its effect on the Constitution-making Body. The Congress . . . [was] . . . going to work for a strong Centre . . . to break the Group system. . . . They did not think that Mr Jinnah had any real place in the country'. A.V. Alexander's defence of Jinnah that he had swallowed 'a bitter pill' by accepting the long-term plan and that 'the best way' to solve India's problem was 'to work together' had little impact on them.[121]

Again, the pressure was on the League to appease the Congress. Jinnah was now 'pledged' to parity as he had secured the League council's approval on that basis.[122] He refused to meet Wavell and Nehru in a joint meeting unless he was assured that parity would be the basis of discussion. Besides parity he wanted a fair distribution of important portfolios—demanding defence, foreign affairs and planning for the League—and looked forward, on Wavell's insistence, to work himself in the interim government 'in a non-communal spirit for the good of India' as a defence member, but subsequently he abandoned the idea of joining the government when Wavell informed him that in that case he could not retain his seat in the constituent assembly.[123] Then, he asked for defence portfolio for a League member but his request was not conceded because, according to A.V. Alexander, if that was done, 'the Muslims might take the opportunity of redistributing the Indian army in a way which would facilitate the creation of Pakistan'.[124] Bypassing the issue of parity, Wavell started discussions with Jinnah and Nehru separately for the names of 'best individuals' who could hold different portfolios. But this line of talks could not lead to any agreement. Under pressure and persuasion from the viceroy and request from the Scheduled Castes leader, Jinnah agreed to place before the working committee the addition of one Scheduled Castes' member provided the Congress accepted Wavell's formula of Congress–League parity.[125] The Congress now insisted on a fifteen-member interim government consisting of Congress 5, Muslim League 4, 'independent' Muslim 1, Scheduled Castes (Congress) 1, Sikh 1, Indian Christian 1 and Congress woman 1.[126] When the talks were deadlocked, the mission decided to issue its own statement. Meanwhile Cripps got information through Rajagopalachari on the evening of 15 June, that the Congress would accept an interim government of fourteen members. At his suggestion, the mission devised a fourteen-member formula although William Croft and Wavell supported by A.V. Alexander disagreed with the increase in members because Jinnah, they argued, would regard it 'as a breach of faith and that it would in fact very nearly be one'.[127] On 16 June, Wavell announced: (*i*) a fourteen-member interim government with names that he planned to inaugurate on 26 June;[128] (*ii*) the viceroy would select another person after consultation if any of the announced persons was unable to accept the invitation; (*iii*) the selection had been made to obtain the best coalition government and was not to be taken as a precedent for the solution of any other communal question; and (*iv*) if the two major parties, or either of them, proved unwilling to join the interim government, the viceroy would proceed with the formation of government which would be as representative as possible of those willing to accept the statement of 16 May (Paragraph 8).[129]

Jinnah, in a meeting with Pethick-Lawrence and Alexander on 17 June, protested that the mission had 'all the time' yielded to the Congress pressure and 'pushed' him beyond 'endurance' to make concessions. Now he wanted a guarantee that the distribution of portfolios would be fair and no major communal issue would be decided without the concurrence of the two main parties.[130] On 19 June, the League working committee, in addition to these two demands and after raising objection to the nomination of five Leaguers without calling for a list from the League president,[131] sought assurance that: the proposals were now final and would not be changed at the instance of any party or person; the total number of fourteen and the community-wise proportion would remain unchanged during the interim period; and any substitution of a minority member including that of the Scheduled Castes would not be made without the consultation and consent of the League leader. The viceroy was informed that in view of the changes that had been made 'from time to time to satisfy the Congress', the League could not arrive at a decision on the statement of 16 June, until the Congress had conveyed its decision on the proposals.[132] While the Congress demanded the substitution of Hare Krishna Mahtab by Sarat Chandra Bose (1889–1950);[133] the replacement of the nominated Parsi, Sir Noshirwan Phirozsha Engineer, who was advocate-general to the Indian army, by another one; the removal of Abdur Rab Nishtar from the list who had lost in the recent elections; and the selection of a non-League Muslim in place of a Congress Hindu. On 20 June, Wavell assured Jinnah that a decision on the portfolios would be negotiated after the two main parties had accepted the statement of 16 June, and gave him assurance on all the

points that he and the working committee had raised.[134] Similarly, all
the points that the Congress had made were resolved including its
objection to the inclusion of Nishtar, after Ghaffar Khan took 'no
strong objection to it', except the nomination of a nationalist Muslim
in place of a Congress Hindu.[135]

The mission tried to persuade the Congress leaders not to press the
demand for the inclusion of a nationalist Muslim. Its argument was that
the Congress had not formally made such a demand before 16 June,
and if it did so now, it would 'jeopardize the whole future of India'.
Pethick-Lawrence reminded the Congress leaders that the mission had
supported them 'in their objective of a united India', opposed a
'sovereign Pakistan' and refused to accept 'the principle of parity,
either in their long-term proposals or in the interim period'.[136] But it
could not convince them. The Congress itself was divided on the issue.
A majority of its working committee members including two
Muslims — Azad and Asif Ali — were unwilling to support the
demand.[137] However, Gandhi was adamant and insisted on the inclusion
of a Congress Muslim to prove the 'national' non-communal character
of the Congress.[138] Besides, the Congress leaders were intrigued by the
League's attitude: it had accepted the statement of 16 May, without any
intra-party split and it was not unwilling to endorse the statement of
16 June.[139] They distrusted the genuineness of its acceptance. On 25
June, the Congress working committee rejected the proposal of an
interim government because of the assurances given to Jinnah and
refusal to include a Congress Muslim in place of a Congress Hindu;
and it accepted the long-term plan but with reservations and its own
interpretation. Its main reservation was about the system of grouping
of provinces.[140] It called upon the All India Congress Committee to
meet on 6–7 July, to ratify its decision.[141] It put the mission in a
quandary vis-à-vis Jinnah. Paragraph 8 required that in such an event
Wavell should form an interim government with the help of the League,
as it had accepted the statements of 16 May, and 16 June. But the
mission had never thought of acting without the Congress. It then
clumsily tried to wriggle out of its commitment under paragraph 8.

Sardar Patel suggested a way out to Cripps: he proposed that there
should be a temporary government of officials and negotiations for an
interim government should be restarted afresh after some time. Cripps
immediately embraced the idea, with which Wavell concurred, and the
mission approved it.[142] Its communication to Jinnah was, however, a
very unpleasant affair. In the mission's talks with Jinnah on 25 June,

636   A HISTORY OF THE ALL-INDIA MUSLIM LEAGUE

Pethick-Lawrence defended the Congress position regarding the 16 May statement, but Jinnah maintained that sections and groups were an essential feature of the plan for which the 'League had made one concession after another'. He requested the mission not to accept the Congress interpretation but could not convince its members. Then, Wavell drew Jinnah's attention to the new proposal of a caretaker government of officials and re-negotiations for an interim government after 'a short interval'. On this Jinnah reminded the mission members of their commitment under paragraph 8; but Cripps contended that that paragraph required fresh negotiations 'on a new basis'! Jinnah did not accept that interpretation and pleaded against any postponement of the interim government because that would be 'bad' for his and the mission's 'prestige'. When he expressed the opinion that it would be wrong to deviate from the statement of 16 June, Pethick-Lawrence retorted that the mission members were not asking his 'opinion of their conduct'. He was discourteous and insulting to Jinnah who then accused the mission of 'bad faith and of giving way to the Congress'.[143] Heated exchanges that followed marred the atmosphere. At the end, Jinnah told the mission that 'every move' that it 'had made had been at his cost'.[144] After the meeting, the mission realized the unfairness of its treatment of Jinnah and deputed A.V. Alexander the next day to see him at his residence to apologize on its behalf. Jinnah told Alexander 'frankly' that 'last night he had felt very hurt and [that] he had not felt [like] that [ever] before'.[145] He showed no interest in the caretaker government or the constituent assembly when Alexander asked him about his future course of action; the mission, Jinnah told him, could do as it chose to do and did not 'disclose his own attitude'.[146] He issued his version of the tripartite talks in a statement, in which he emphasized that Muslim India would regard any change in the statement of 16 June, or whittling down of assurances given to him as going back on the 'pledged word' given to him in writing, and 'as a breach of faith'.[147] He asked the viceroy to proceed in terms of paragraph 8, urging him to postpone the elections to the constituent assembly scheduled in July. The mission neither accepted his version of the tripartite talks nor did it agree to the postponement of elections.[148] Its decision, the daily *Statesman* (New Delhi), the only British-owned newspaper in India, commented editorially, 'seemed a descent from the high level of political ethics. . . . Politicians may do so, but it is not the business of statesmen to eat their words; they should not risk bold, sweeping, unequivocal public undertakings unless they mean them . . . During the long-drawn Delhi–Simla negotiations there have been already too many tactical shifts of ground and changes of front by others. It grieves us that a venerable and idealistic secretary of state, a fine viceroy, and their two eminent colleagues of Britain's new and good cabinet should at this last stage have descended—as we see matters—to similar swithery courses.'[149] On 29 June, a temporary caretaker government was announced, pending negotiations with the political parties, which the Congress and not the League was told could not start until 25 July. After the meeting with Jinnah, the mission reiterated to the Congress representatives its interpretation of the Statement of 16 May, as given in its statement of 25 May.[150] But such statements had little impact on the course of political developments.

Early in July, the League participated in the elections to the constituent assembly. On 9 June, its working committee had authorized the central parliamentary board to select candidates in consultation with the presidents of the provincial Muslim Leagues and leaders of the League parliamentary parties in the provincial legislatures. The president was empowered to make any modifications that he might consider proper, whose decision was final.[151] Jinnah qualified his powers of modification, by stating that he would modify only if there was (a) any serious objection to the selection of a particular individual; (b) any gross miscarriage of justice; and (c) any omission of an outstanding person whose selection might have been necessary in the interest of the League.[152] The central parliamentary board followed the same procedure that it had adopted in the selection of candidates for the central legislative assembly in the general elections. The provincial Muslim Leagues made the initial selection. The central parliamentary board did not interfere where the provincial Muslim Leagues unanimously selected the candidates without any controversy, and minor differences in the selections were settled without any conflict. Jinnah did not make any changes in the selections that were made by the provincial Muslim Leagues and central parliamentary board when individual aspirants made representations to him; and there were a few representations from Sindh, United Provinces, Bengal and Bihar.[153] The League did not put up any official candidate on the one seat in Balochistan where the Shahi Jirga and non-official members of the Quetta municipality were to cast their votes for his election.[154]

(C) RESUMPTION OF THE PAKISTAN DEMAND

(i) *Withdrawal of Acceptance*. On the mission's departure from India on 29 June, Wavell felt relieved that the 'danger of a Congress mass movement' had 'receded for the time being'.[155] Jinnah still hoped that the League would get a fair deal from His Majesty's Government in London. He wrote 'private, personal and confidential' letters of similar content to Prime Minister Attlee and Sir Winston Churchill (leader of the opposition), in which he expressed 'deep regret' that the mission and the viceroy had 'impaired' the British 'honour' and 'shaken the confidence of Muslim India' in handling the negotiations. They had played into 'the hands of the Congress', which had 'all along held out the threat of non-cooperation and civil disobedience' to establish 'Caste-Hindu domination over Muslim India and other communities'. The desire to dominate, he wrote, had become not only 'an obsession' but 'a disease' with the Congress. It had rejected the interim government and put interpretations on the long-term plan contrary to those embodied in the statements of 16 and 25 May, particularly the grouping of provinces, which amounted to its rejection. He hoped that His Majesty's Government would maintain 'the honour of the British nation for fair play'.[156] Meanwhile, Nehru took over the Congress presidency on 6 July, and the All India Congress Committee endorsed the working committee's decision of 25 June; speaking on that occasion and at a press conference in Bombay on 10 July, he declared that the Congress would enter the constituent assembly 'completely unfettered by agreements' and change the plan 'as it thought best'. Expressing his doubts about the grouping of provinces, he 'envisaged a stronger central government' than that proposed in the 16 May statement.[157] Still later, on 20 July, he declared that the Congress would kill the constituent assembly, if it failed to achieve its objective.[158] His observations and the debate on the mission's report in the parliament on 18 July, and Cripps' observations in that forum disillusioned Jinnah about any chance of getting a fair deal for the Muslims.[159] On top of it, Attlee and Churchill felt no urgency to respond to his letters. Attlee's letter of 23 July, was delivered to Jinnah on 30 July, and Churchill's reply first in the form of a short telegram reached him on 31 July, and then in a formal letter on 3 August.[160] The contents of their replies could not restore the Leaguers' confidence.

The Muslim Leaguers had felt depressed on 6 June, when the central council suspended the Pakistan demand and accepted the long-term plan. The interpretation that the mission and the Congress had put on the plan added to their frustration. Their disapproval of the plan and criticism of the League leadership within the party for accepting a common centre gradually mounted.[161] The ensuing situation left the League no option but to withdraw its acceptance of the plan. On 27–29 July, the council met to decide the party policy in view of the postponement of the interim government and the conditional acceptance of the long-term plan by the Congress. Jinnah in his opening address lasting two and a half hours gave a detailed account of the tripartite negotiations. The mission and the Congress, he reported, held a 'pistol' in their hands in these negotiations: the former of 'authority and arms' and the latter of 'mass struggle and non-cooperation'. The mission, he observed, had been 'intellectually paralyzed' and its report to the parliament, which was devoid of 'political ethics' and 'every manner of principle and morality', was not 'even honest to themselves'. The League had made concessions after concessions not because it was 'overawed' by them but for its 'extreme anxiety for an amicable and peaceful settlement' and to prevent the situation from deteriorating 'into bloodshed and civil war'. It had exhausted all avenues for a peaceful settlement; and now it looked to the only tribunal available, that of 'the Muslim nation', for guidance. In its whole history, it had never done anything 'except by constitutional methods' but now it had decided to 'bid goodbye' to these methods. In conclusion, he quoted Firdausi (940/41–1020), the Persian poet, 'If you seek peace, we do not want war, but if you want war, we will accept it unhesitatingly'. Twenty-three councillors who spoke on the occasion were divided in their views on the plan: some of them termed its acceptance 'a mistake' and others regarded it 'a great act of statesmanship' but they were united on one thing—that the plan must be rejected. The council adopted two resolutions. The first one stipulated that in view of the British and Congress attitude, Muslim participation in the constitution-making body was 'fraught with danger'; therefore, the council had decided to withdraw its acceptance of the plan and directed the working committee to organize the Muslims for direct action, as and when necessary, to achieve Pakistan and get rid of 'the present British slavery and the contemplated future Caste-Hindu domination'. The second resolution called upon the Muslims to renounce the titles that had been conferred on them by the 'alien government' as a mark of protest against its attitude. Several top-ranking League leaders attending the session renounced such titles. Those present in the session who renounced their titles were: Ghulam Husain Hidayatullah, Ayub

Khuhro, Nazimuddin, Firoz Khan Noon, Mehr Shah, Mohammad Saadulla (Assam), Ghazanfar Ali Khan, Jalaluddin (NWFP), Hasan Ali Ibrahim, Karamat Ali Khan, Alibhai Patel, Amjad Ali, Abdullah al Mahmud and Hasan Ispahani.[162] The renunciation of titles by the Leaguers continued after that.

The central working committee called on the Muslims to suspend all business on Friday, 16 August, and observe complete *hartal* (strike); and directed all the provincial Muslim Leagues, district Muslim Leagues and primary Leagues to hold public meetings on that day to explain the two resolutions passed by the council. It entrusted the task of organizing the Muslims and drawing up of a direct action programme to the central committee of action, which chalked out a schedule of activities for that day. Jinnah declared that the day was 'aimed at British imperialism which lies at the root of all the evils in India' and not 'against any Indian people or party'.[163] The day was observed peacefully everywhere, except in Calcutta. That city witnessed ugly scenes of communal violence; according to official estimates, during four days (16–19 August) of rioting 4,000 humans lost their lives and 10,000 were injured.[164] Muslims and Hindus accused each other for the riots and high causalities were exploited for propaganda. Muslims were just 26 per cent of the total population of the Calcutta city but their casualties were higher than those of the Hindus.[165] The killings inflamed Muslim sentiments in other cities of Bengal. The Congress blamed Suhrawardy's ministry for not taking preventive and prompt steps to stop the violence.[166] But it had its own plan for using the disturbances in Calcutta to remove the Suhrawardy ministry, which is evident from the intercepted telephonic conversation between Patel and Sudhir Ghosh who was in London as the Congress emissary; Patel asked Sudhir on the telephone, 'Cripps had promised if there was any disturbance in Calcutta, he will order for section 93 [i.e. governor's rule]. What is he doing?'[167] Sudhir especially travelled to Paris at government expense where Cripps was staying at the time but his visit did not produce the desired result.[168] The viceroy and the governor did repeatedly press Suhrawardy to form a League–Congress coalition ministry in Bengal but Jinnah ruled that out till an agreement had been reached for a coalition between the two parties at the centre.[169] The Calcutta tragedy influenced the formation of the interim government.

(*ii*) *Interim Government*. The process of forming the interim government had re-started in July 1946. By that time, Jinnah's condemnation of the Cabinet Mission had brought the cabinet members much closer to the Congress than before. The Congress leaders missed no opportunity to strengthen the Congress–Labour bonds.[170] Indirect contacts especially with Attlee and Cripps through Krishna Menon and Sudhir Ghosh were used to achieve that end. Wavell's 'personal and secret' letters of similar content to Jinnah and Nehru on 22 July, calling for an agreement on the interim government, reflected this development.[171] He asked the two leaders not to disclose its contents, which were almost in line with the Congress demands.[172] The letter proposed a fourteen-member interim government with Congress 6 (including one Scheduled Castes), Muslim League 5, and minorities (including one Sikh) 3 nominated by the viceroy; no party could object to the names submitted by the other party provided these were acceptable to the viceroy; the two main parties would have an equitable and not equal share of the important portfolios; the status of the interim government would be in accordance with the assurance conveyed to Azad in Wavell's letter of 30 May; and instead of a formal condition, the viceroy would welcome a convention, if 'freely offered by the Congress', that major communal issues should be decided by the assent of both the major parties.[173] Nehru replied to Wavell's invitation the very next day, 23 July, but Jinnah conveyed his response on 31 July. Meanwhile, the provocatively critical anti-British speeches by the Leaguers at the central council meeting further alienated the British leaders. To that was added Jinnah's strong denunciation of the British and US policies in Palestine on 30 July, calling for an end to their influence from there and urging not only the cessation of Jewish immigration into Palestine but also demanding the emigration of those Jews already there to Australia, Canada or elsewhere otherwise their fate would 'be worse than it was under Hitler'.[174] Jinnah's anti-British posture angered the British leaders. Churchill's reply to Jinnah amply demonstrated that feeling, and Attlee through Pethick-Lawrence directed the viceroy to proceed with the formation of the interim government and the constituent assembly without the League, if Jinnah did not cooperate.[175] Jinnah's response to Wavell's proposal of 22 July, was that most of its points were contrary to the assurances that had been given to the League and that the working committee was unlikely to accept it. Ignoring his objections, on 6 August, Wavell with the cabinet's approval invited Nehru to make proposals for an interim government on the basis of assurance given to the Congress in his letter to Azad of 30 May, leaving it to him to consult Jinnah or not. Two days later, Wavell simply informed Jinnah that in view of the League's resolutions of 29 July, he had decided to invite the Congress to make proposals for an interim government, hoping that he would accept a reasonable offer for a Congress–League coalition.[176] On that day, the Congress working committee accepted the invitation extended to Nehru and authorized him to negotiate with the viceroy.[177] The invitation to Nehru and his acceptance was issued in a communiqué on 12 August. The next day, Nehru approached Jinnah for cooperation in forming a coalition government. Jinnah responded that he knew nothing about what had transpired between him and the viceroy or as to the nature of any Nehru–Wavell agreement, but if it meant that the viceroy had commissioned him to form the executive council and agreed to accept his advice, that position was not acceptable to the League. However, he expressed his willingness to meet Nehru to settle the Hindu–Muslim question to resolve the deadlock. Nehru denied any agreement with Wavell, but nothing positive came out of the eighty-minute Jinnah–Nehru meeting in Bombay, in which he informed Jinnah that he was forming the 'provisional national government' which would be responsible to the central legislative assembly.[178] Then, there followed the Nehru–Wavell talks about the composition of the interim government and distribution of portfolios, and minor points of difference were resolved by 24 August, when Wavell announced its members who took oath of office on 2 September. The need to bring in the League was half-heartedly raised in these talks but no serious attempt was made to seek its cooperation.[179]

Soon after, several factors brought about a slight change in the British policy towards the League. Firstly, the British–Congress one-sided talks for the formation of an interim government tempted none of the League leaders to run after the interim government offices. Besides, the League did not suspend the observance of the Direct Action Day on 16 August, if that was the object of invitation to Nehru. It continued its preparations for 'direct action' even after the Calcutta riots; and there was realization in official circles that the League threat could make governance 'exceedingly difficult'.[180] On the announcement of the interim government, Liaquat under instructions from Jinnah asked the members of the League party in the central assembly not to attend meetings of any committees, including the standing committees of various departments and select committees on bills, or any Government of India-sponsored conference.[181] When Yamin Khan asked Jinnah's permission to attend a committee meeting as deputy president of the central assembly, on the analogy that Sardar Vithalbhai Patel (1873–1933) had attended committee meetings in that capacity during the Congress-organized Civil Disobedience Movement (1930), Jinnah advised him not to do that.[182] Similarly, he advised Raza Ali not to accept membership of an official delegation.[183] Both of them accepted his advice. Jinnah did not tone down the criticism of the British policies in his statements of 25 August—when he released his correspondence with Wavell from 22 July to 8 August—, and 26 August, while commenting on Wavell's announcement about the interim government, and in his Eid message on 28 August, in which he said: 'Today the horizon is dark for us. The doings of the British government and the Viceregal Lodge are shrouded in mystery; we are vilified, misrepresented and threatened. . . . The Viceroy and the British government have surrendered to the Congress'.[184] Then, speaking at a Jashn-i-Eid function on 30 August, he accused the British government of 'gross and wicked betrayal' for violating its own declaration of 8 August 1940. If the Indian Muslims, he observed, stood 'united under one flag', all the British and Congress 'diabolic conspiracies' would fail and they would achieve the 'sacred goal of Pakistan'.[185] Secondly, the League on Jinnah's advice postponed the party elections that had been scheduled in September; instead, its central committee of action organized committees of action at provincial and lower levels. It reorganized the Muslim League National Guards, accelerating their recruitment and training, and discussed with the All-India Muslim Students Federation and the All India Muslim Women's Subcommittee the role that their members could play in the coming struggle.[186] It mobilized the *ulama* and *mashaikh* who on its initiative held conferences in different provinces to mobilize the Muslim masses. An all-India conference of *ulama* and *mashaikh* from different provinces deliberated upon 'the future of the Millat-i-Islamia in India'.[187] The intensity of the All-India Muslim League's activities made the British Indian administrators nervous that the League struggle might not dangerously turn against them rather than the Hindus or the Sikhs; and when the League finally came into the interim government, the British intelligence chief heaved a sigh of relief.[188] Thirdly, the British intelligence also knew about the growing support for Jinnah and the Pakistan demand in the tribal areas of the North-West Frontier. Pir Aminul Hasanat of Manki Sharif was among those who played a significant role in mobilizing that support. There were reports of possible armed struggle with the support of the tribes; and the central committee of action and working committee formally condemned 'the so-called punitive' bombing in Waziristan and assured the tribesmen of their support 'to save them from these atrocities'.[189] The Fakir of Ipi and other religious leaders in the tribal areas declared themselves in favour of Pakistan.[190] The increased contacts between Jinnah and the tribesmen worried the British administrators.[191] In addition, Muslim personnel of the British Indian army were writing to, or meeting with, Jinnah secretly and promising him their support in the event of armed struggle.[192] Two young army officers, Major Irshad and Lieutenant Colonel Gulzar Ahmad, 7th Battalion, Baloch Regiment, submitted a plan to Jinnah for a coordinated multi-pronged simultaneous armed uprising of the Muslim masses, Muslim personnel of the Indian army and a striking force from the North-West Frontier, if the constitutional struggle to achieve Pakistan did not succeed.[193] Sir Claude Auchinleck was conscious of the pro-Pakistan feelings of the Muslims in the army and had told the chiefs of staff committee that in the event of any serious communal trouble it would be impossible to call upon Muslim troops to take action against the Muslims.[194] Lastly, the League had always supported the Muslims in the Middle East and elsewhere especially those in Palestine. Now it sought their support. It sent goodwill missions to Muslim countries. For instance, in July–August, two Leaguers, Mir Ghulam Ali Talpur and Firoz Khan Noon, separately visited the Middle Eastern countries and submitted their reports to Jinnah on return. The response from Iraq was positive and quite effective, which must have influenced the British policy. In August 1946, the British embassy in Baghdad had approached the government of Iraq with a request on behalf of the Government of India for permission to appoint a trade commissioner and a vice-consul at Basra. The prime minister of Iraq, who had 'great admiration' for Jinnah, refused to grant the requisite permission for these positions because, he accused, the Government of India was 'brutally suppressing' the Indian Muslims. The League had always supported Iraq, he pointed out, over Palestine and his government would support the League. The Iraq government, he told the British embassy representative, did not recognize the new Government of India because it had excluded the League from governance; and if the Government of India 'in revenge' for its refusal to grant permission 'asked for the removal of Iraqi consuls in India the Iraq government would withdraw them'.[195]

The British government realized that it could not move forward without some overture to the League. The change in its attitude was noticeable around the time of the Direct Action Day. Pethick-Lawrence's hand-written personal letter of apology to Jinnah of 16 August, indicated that change in which, referring to the unpleasant exchanges of 25 June, he wrote that 'there were pretty harsh things said on both sides. . . . If our political duel was exacerbated by any remarks of mine which could be construed as personally discourteous I should greatly regret it'. However, this did not mean that Pethick-Lawrence had changed his views on Pakistan. Jinnah wrote back that he had been 'hurt at the behaviour' of all the Cabinet Mission members—except A.V. Alexander—and the viceroy but the matter was closed as far as he was concerned after Alexander came to see him before leaving for London to apologise on behalf of his colleagues and that many things 'of much worse character' had taken place since 25 June, which had stabbed the Muslims 'in the back'.[196] It was after such gestures that on 31 August, Jinnah sent a brief reply to Attlee's letter of 23 July, enclosing copies of his own statements of 25 and 26 August, Eid message of 29 August, and speech at the Jashn-i-Eid, and asked the prime minister 'to do what you think proper'.[197] Within two weeks, Wavell approached Jinnah with the approval of Attlee and Pethick-Lawrence to bring the League into the interim government and did not find him 'as bitter about his treatment by the Cabinet Mission as' he expected him to be.[198] The Congress came to know of the change when Krishna Menon saw Pethick-Lawrence in London on 26 September, on Nehru's behalf about the governor's rule in Sindh in place of a Hidayatullah-headed caretaker government and about a similar action in Bengal following the Calcutta riots. From Pethick-Lawrence's response, Krishna Menon suspected that he and Wavell were 'acting together', and that when he pointed out that Wavell's move would not bring about 'a coalition which the Congress desired', Pethick-Lawrence remained 'silent and appeared very cold', and simply stated that 'the Constituent Assembly was no good without the Muslim League'.[199] Wavell approached Jinnah to bring the League into the interim government.[200] After intensive negotiations for nearly a month, Jinnah and Wavell reached an agreement within the knowledge of the Congress on the League's entry into the interim government, and a communiqué to that effect was issued on 15 October.[201] The League working committee in a resolution criticized the scheme of the interim government, considering it contrary to the August 1940 declaration, but did not want to leave 'the entire field of administration to the Congress' because that would be against the interests of the League and the minorities.[202] While Jinnah did not insist on the exclusion of a nationalist Muslim in the Congress quota, and Wavell after consultation with Nehru accepted Jinnah's proposal to include in the League quota a Scheduled Caste Hindu from Bengal who was a minister in the Suhrawardy ministry, a move which one Leaguer regarded in Punjabi terminology, *nehle pe dehla* (tit for tat). Nehru was to continue as leader of the house in the assembly and Nishtar would be Leader on behalf of the League in the council of state. Jinnah did not press for the rotation of the office of vice-president in the interim government between the League and the Congress; and the League got the vice-chairmanship of the coordination committee of the cabinet despite opposition from the Congress.[203] Wavell in his anxiety to bring the League into the interim government and the Congress in its ambition not to surrender any of the three important portfolios (defence, external affairs and home) did not wait till the League council had rescinded its July resolution. They accepted Jinnah's position on that issue, that this matter should 'stand over until a better and more conducive atmosphere' had been created after the interim government was 're-formed and finally set up', and the League had secured 'certain guarantees' from the Congress.[204] For the satisfaction of the viceroy and the Congress, Jinnah discussed with Sir B.N. Rau, constitutional adviser to the constituent assembly of India since July 1946, difficulties that stood in the way of the League's acceptance of the statement of 16 May, but without any conclusive outcome.[205] Immediately, Wavell was satisfied that the two main parties had joined the interim government and the Congress was happy that it had not surrendered any 'important' portfolio to the League and looked forward to working with the fourteen-member interim government as Nehru-headed cabinet that had only five Leaguers out of its fourteen members. But this satisfaction was very short-lived.

The League selected its members for the interim government without much controversy. There was a demand for the inclusion of a Sindhi in the list of League nominees and objection to the nomination of Sardar Nishtar because he had lost in the general elections but none pressed these points seriously or publicly.[206] The League was not given the portfolios that it demanded; and it accepted those that it was offered for which it faced some criticism within the party ranks.[207] Its members and their portfolios were: Liaquat Ali Khan—finance; I.I. Chundrigar—commerce; Abdur Rab Nishtar—ports and air; Ghazanfar Ali Khan—health; and Jogendra Nath Mandal—legislative.[208] If one keeps the background to the interim government-formation in view, there was hardly any possibility of its functioning successfully or smoothly. The League–Congress trust that was needed for its smooth working was totally absent. All the five League nominees had handed in to Jinnah undated signed letters of resignation addressed to the viceroy before they took oath of office.[209] They had no intention to let the interim government succeed; instead, they wanted to use its platform to press the demand for Pakistan. Even before the League members were sworn in, on 19 October, one member, Ghazanfar Ali, made it clear in an address to the Islamia College students in Lahore, 'We are going into the Interim Government to get a foothold to fight for our cherished goal of Pakistan and I assure you that we shall achieve Pakistan'.[210] The next day, Liaquat, speaking in Karachi, remarked that the League's entry into the interim government was not inconsistent with the 29 July resolution, and that the Muslims must prepare themselves for the ultimate fight 'for their goal — Pakistan'.[211] After that, Jinnah himself repeatedly observed that Pakistan was the only solution to the 'irreconcilable' Hindu–Muslim differences and that the League had entered the interim government as it had 'no other choice', and its members were there as 'the sentinels of the Muslims to protect their interests'. The League's entry in the interim government, he clarified, did not mean 'automatically acceptance of the 16 May Statement'.[212] The League members shattered Nehru's self-image as the leader of a 'cabinet'. They refused to accept the interim government as a cabinet or to acknowledge Nehru as its head, maintaining that the interim government had a Congress bloc and a League bloc, 'each functioning under separate leadership'. They rejected the idea of informal 'tea party' meetings of all the interim government members every day and were 'only prepared to meet individuals as individuals'.[213] On the other hand, Nehru, instead of staying in Delhi to welcome and placate his new colleagues, went on a high profile untimely one-week tour of the tribal areas of the North-West Frontier, a day after the communiqué was issued. He did that against the advice of Governor Olaf Caroe and members of the Congress high command including Azad and Patel.[214] Nehru and other Congress leaders could not assess correctly the pro-League sentiments that the Pakistan demand and its pro-Palestine stance had generated in the tribal areas. Jinnah did point out to Wavell the inadvisability of his tour at that inopportune time, and informed him that the central League had issued no instructions to the Frontier provincial Muslim League to stage demonstrations against Nehru.[215]

But Nehru's tour was focused on the tribal areas, and he faced hostile demonstrations wherever he went. The tribes in retaliation were heavily fined for organizing the demonstrations; and subsequently, the fine money on their request was transferred to Bihar for the relief of victims of the Bihar massacre that took place soon after Nehru's visit.[216]

(*iii*) *The Bihar Massacre*. The campaign for the general elections had embittered Hindu–Muslim relations which after its conclusion led to disturbances in several constituencies in the Muslim-minority provinces. More serious riots occurred in Ambetta, and the central committee of action deputed a two-member (Qazi Isa and Zafar Ahmad Ansari) committee to inquire into these riots.[217] However, communal tension subsided during the more than three-month-long tripartite British–League–Congress negotiations but the uncertainties around the time of withdrawal of League's acceptance of the Cabinet Mission Plan revived the animosities, which exploded on the Direct Action Day in Calcutta, resulting in immense loss of human lives. The Calcutta riots had repercussions in Bengal and elsewhere; Bombay witnessed 622 killed and 1,896 injured, United Provinces 445 killed and 66 injured, and Punjab 20 killed and 61 injured but the Calcutta killings overshadowed the killings elsewhere.[218] League's defence was that if it had wanted to foment communal trouble, Calcutta would have been the last place of its choice, because Bengal was one of the two provinces where it was in power, and Muslims constituted a minority in the Calcutta city.[219] The blame was ultimately put on the hooligans of the Calcutta underworld of the two communities. Higher Muslim casualties in Calcutta stirred up Muslim sentiments against the Hindus especially in the eastern districts of Bengal. After sporadic incidents of violence, serious riots broke out in Noakhali and other eastern districts on 10 October, and after that, which claimed 200–300 Hindu lives and turned thousands homeless within ten days. The severity of the violence provoked the Hindus who began to propagate, according to the Leaguers, exaggerated accounts of atrocities committed on their co-religionists and gave calls for avenging 'Noakhali'.[220]

The Congress and Hindu Mahasabha leaders organized a systematic anti-League propaganda particularly in Bihar, which had been the scene of some fierce communal riots in the past: in 1917, in 1937–39 during the Congress rule, and in April 1941. This propaganda comprised a series of provocative articles in the *Searchlight* (Patna), publication of handbills, posters and leaflets and their extensive distribution in the cities and villages, and public meetings addressed by prominent Hindu leaders who chided the Hindus for permitting 'the Muslims to plan for Pakistan in a land which was exclusively theirs to dominate and rule'.[221] 'Noakhali Day' was observed in Bihar on 25 October; and on that day, the Hindus brought out huge processions, chanting abusive slogans against Jinnah and the Pakistan scheme.[222] The Congress government in Bihar unwittingly allowed this propaganda to go unchecked. Riots started on 26 October, the day the League members joined the interim government, and the rioters had a free hand to do anything for fifteen days. Rioting started from Chapra, and flared up in the districts of Patna, Monghyr, Muzaffarpur, Bhagalpur and Gaya. The rapidity with which the riots spread on a vast area gave credence to the Leaguers' allegation that the massacre had been 'planned and directed by top-ranking Congress leaders, with the cooperation of high ranking Government officials'.[223] The general plan of attack was uniform everywhere; mobs in large numbers would gather at a prearranged place usually by the signal of whistling, completely surround an isolated village and set it on fire. Minimum death toll was estimated at 30,000 and half a million persons were displaced. Innumerable homes, mosques, libraries with rare books and cultural monuments were burnt and destroyed. The Bihar government took neither any preventive measure nor did it attempt to control the situation during the occurrence of violence. A force of about 800 armed men was stationed in Patna and elsewhere in the district but the Congress government, it was alleged, did not use it immediately; and when a part of it was belatedly employed the only officer killed was a Muslim who, while protecting a party of refugees, was done to death. A month later, Muslims of Garhmukteshwar were killed to the last person in another wave of riots.[224]

The brutality of the Bihar massacre shocked every one. It 'eclipsed Noakhali', and the conduct of the Congress ministry, according to Gandhi, was 'shameful and disgraceful'.[225] Moved by the enormity of human and material loss, the Bihar provincial Muslim League called for an exchange of population between Bengal and Bihar, a demand that Jinnah endorsed to Pethick-Lawrence (secretary of state for India) and Attlee (prime minister). The secretary of state for India with the concurrence of the prime minister deflected the demand, by suggesting that a proposal of this nature could be taken up only if a proposition was made out by the government of Bengal to the government of Bihar. The proposal was abandoned when the League did not press it seriously.[226] Then, Jinnah supported a proposal for the formation of pockets of Muslim settlements, wherever it was feasible.[227] No one took notice of the central committee of action's demand for the trial by special tribunals of the culprits responsible for the massacre; however, its demand for a judicial commission of inquiry was accepted but at the governor's instance its appointment was indefinitely delayed; and finally, on 9 July 1947, Mountbatten (1900–1979) asked Jinnah to drop the idea as it would cause further harm to the Muslims of Bihar.[228] The All-India Muslim League and the Bengal presidency Muslim League sent inquiry teams, which after visiting the riot-affected areas submitted reports to the party.[229] Jinnah instituted a Bihar Relief Fund and the central committee of action appointed a five-member (Nazimuddin, Firoz Khan Noon, Husain Imam, Jafar Imam and Muhammad Yunus) central Muslim League relief committee to help the affected Muslims; and the committee had a setup at the provincial and district level as well. Besides the fund, relief items in the form of medicines and clothes were sent to Bihar from all over India.[230] Muslim Leaguers from the Muslim majority provinces sent teams of medics and social workers in the riot-affected areas to do relief work.[231] When the riots had started, Muslims had fled from the affected and even the non-affected areas of Bihar in terror. They sought refuge at safe places within Bihar or in Bengal and Sindh, where the League was in power. The refugees in Bengal were initially accommodated in relief camps administered officially as well as privately. In Sindh, the provincial Muslim League welcomed them and when the provincial Muslim League formally assumed office after the elections in December, the responsibility for providing relief passed on to the Sindh government.[232] The emigration of Muslims from Bihar continued after the riots and at one time it was feared that the entire Muslim population might not evacuate the province.[233] But then due to security measures taken by the Bihar government and limited resources of Bengal and Sindh to accommodate the refugees on any large scale put a stop to the migration.[234] The Muslims who left Bihar declined to return to their homes. Their rehabilitation in Bengal and Sindh was an arduous, painful and unending process before and after independence.[235]

(iv) *Refusal to Re-accept the Plan*. The Bihar massacre did not help in the creation of the 'conducive' atmosphere that Jinnah had considered a pre-requisite for the withdrawal of the 29 July 1946 resolution; it rather reaffirmed the Leaguers' faith in a fully sovereign Pakistan.

Earlier, the Congress had shown no interest in bringing the League into the interim government; instead, it had concentrated on consolidating itself in power, believing that it could then deal with the Muslims 'by bribery, blackmail, propaganda and if necessary force'.[236] It wanted the interim government to function as a Nehru-controlled cabinet with the tacit support of the British, which would not be responsible to any other body, if not to the central legislature. Nehru and his Congress colleagues urged Wavell to convene the constituent assembly without delay and issued vague and general statements that they would meet the League's demands about grouping, and offered to refer any differences to the federal court for decision.[237] If the League did not come in on these terms, they were ready to proceed with governance and constitution-making without the League. Wavell and Pethick-Lawrence, who now realized that Jinnah had been unfairly treated in the tripartite negotiations, did not want to provide him another excuse to denounce them and the British policies.[238] However, Wavell tried to meet the Congress demands, wherever possible, but declined to go out of the way in doing that. He made an effort to meet its demand for the formation of coalition ministries in Bengal and Sindh—the two provinces where the League ministries were in office—as suggested by Pethick-Lawrence and Attlee, but refused to succumb to the pressure for arbitrary removal of the League ministries because, in his opinion, that would spoil the chances of conciliating Jinnah and result in serious law and order situation.[239] Similarly, he was not in favour of summoning the constituent assembly without a Congress–League agreement about grouping.[240] At first, he hesitated to contact Jinnah directly and tried to ascertain indirectly his conditions for the rescission of the July resolution. More credible are the conditions that Liaquat indicated to a member of his staff, I.D. Scott, that (i) the Congress must categorically state that the sectional assemblies as a whole and not the provinces would frame the provincial and group constitutions; (ii) the provinces would have the option to opt out only after the first elections under the new constitution; and (iii) the union assembly would not have the power to change the provincial or group constitutions except to prevent overlapping with the union constitution on the scope of which federal court might decide. These conditions, Wavell admitted, had been agreed to by the Cabinet Mission in its meeting with the League representatives on 16 May.[241] But the Congress was unwilling to forgo a province's right to frame a constitution to a majority vote of the sectional assembly.[242]

On 10 September, Jinnah himself revealed his mind in an interview with the representative of the *Daily Mail* (London). He was willing to hold talks afresh with a 'clean slate' and was ready to go to London to negotiate on an equal footing with other negotiators, provided he was invited by His Majesty's Government.[243] He did neither commit himself to a date when the council of the All-India Muslim League would rescind its July resolution nor did he specify exactly the guarantees that he needed for participation in the constituent assembly.[244] On 30 October, he told Wavell point-blank that the council would not rescind its July resolution unless the Congress accepted, what Wavell described, 'the literal interpretation of the Mission's plan', which perhaps meant the conditions mentioned by Liaquat to I.D. Scott.[245] When Wavell wrote to Jinnah on 5 November, asking him to hold a meeting of the council to accept the 16 May statement, the latter did not respond to him until 17 November.[246] Meanwhile, on 14 November, after the League committee's report on the Bihar massacre, he observed that the 'only solution' of India's present communal situation was 'Pakistan—anything else would be artificial and unnatural'.[247] The central committee of action discussed the report with all its horrific details on the next two days at a meeting which Jinnah and some members of the committee (Nazimuddin, Firoz Khan Noon, Mian Amiruddin and Mumtaz Daultana) attended. A day after this meeting, he replied to Wavell's letter of 5 November, maintaining that the Congress had not really accepted the 16 May statement, citing the Congress working committee's resolutions of 26 June, and 10 August, Nehru's letter to Gopinath Bardoloi of 30 September, and Gandhi's pronouncement of 23 October. Neither the 16 May statement itself, he wrote, had made any provision for reference to the federal court nor was its basic principle justiciable. The plan had made recommendations that could only be carried out when both the major parties 'agreed, in the clearest manner and unquestionably, upon the fundamentals'. Evading to mention the assurances that the League required, he pointed out, the real issue was to get the Congress to agree to the fundamentals in the clearest language and then devise a mechanism by which the proposals could be enforced by His Majesty's Government 'if the Congress broke its word'. He urged that in view of the Bihar massacre, all energies should be focused on restoring peace and order rather than on convening the constituent assembly; and in his interview with Wavell on 19 November, he reiterated that the convening of the constituent assembly in the prevailing situation would be 'the greatest possible mistake' and demanded its postponement *sine die*.[248] On the other hand, the Congress insisted that invitations for a meeting of the constituent assembly on 9 December, should be issued immediately and the League council should rescind its July resolution.

Wavell considered the League's stand as correct and was in favour of postponing the constituent assembly meeting till the two main parties had reached an agreement but Attlee and his cabinet colleagues overruled him and directed him to issue the invitations as demanded by the Congress, which he did on 20 November, and to ask the League to come into the constituent assembly; and if it was not satisfied with the procedure framed by the Assembly, it could come out of it at any stage.[249] Jinnah viewed the summoning of the constituent assembly 'one more blunder of very grave and serious character', which was meant to appease the Congress. No League member, he announced, would attend the constituent assembly meeting, and that the July resolution was still operative.[250] Nehru took up Jinnah's observation with Wavell as well as in the subjects committee of the Congress annual session at Meerut, demanding that the League should leave the interim government as it had not accepted the long-term plan. Besides, the League, he alleged, was endeavouring to enlist the British support to establish itself as the King's Party; and that since it had joined the interim government, there was neither a cabinet nor a coalition.[251] When Wavell in pursuance of Nehru's demand told Liaquat that the League could not stay in the interim government without accepting the long-term plan, the latter responded that the League members were prepared to resign whenever the viceroy required them to do so but maintained that the League's acceptance had been conditional, mentioning the conditions that he had earlier indicated to I.D. Scott. The only attraction in the long-term plan, Liaquat firmly told Wavell, which had induced the League to accept it was the possibility of forming groups and of framing group and provincial constitutions by a process of voting by majority in the sections.[252] On 26 November, Jinnah repudiated Nehru's assertions in much stronger terms, countering that Nehru had himself taken oath of allegiance to the king emperor as a member of the Viceroy's Executive Council, which could in no way be termed a cabinet. The interim government had been constituted, and was functioning, under the Act of 1919; and the League would not let the Congress 'torpedo the Pakistan demand' by the 'instrumentality of such powers' as were vested in the interim government. Nehru must understand, Jinnah stated, that he was neither the prime minister nor was the interim government a Nehru government; he was simply a member for external affairs and commonwealth relations.²⁵³ These conflicting positions of the two major parties created a deadlock that the viceroy could not resolve.

The British cabinet made a last-minute attempt to break the League–Congress deadlock. It decided to invite, what had been continuously suggested since August, two representatives of the Congress, two of the League and one of the Sikhs along with the viceroy to a conference in London for this purpose.²⁵⁴ But the move was a non-starter from the beginning. When Wavell extended the invitation to Nehru on 26 November, the Congress suspected that it might be a move to abandon the Cabinet Mission Plan and to reopen the whole process of constitutional negotiations. Therefore, Nehru communicated to Wavell his party's refusal to accept the invitation. On this, Prime Minister Attlee sent a personal message to Nehru assuring him that the object of the talks in London was to ensure a successful meeting of the constituent assembly on 9 December, and not to abandon or alter the Cabinet Mission Plan, and promised to arrange his return to India before that date. All the three members of the Cabinet Mission individually and collectively, Attlee informed Nehru, had asked him to insist upon Nehru the importance of these talks. Nehru then accepted the invitation, and the Congress decided to send him as its sole representative. Liaquat initially accepted the invitation but after the Attlee–Nehru contact, Jinnah who was in Karachi at the time for the Sindh elections wanted to know what had passed between Attlee and Nehru, and when he was provided with copies of the Attlee–Nehru correspondence, he telegraphed that he could not attend the talks unless 'the whole situation' was open for discussion. He agreed to go to the London conference only after Attlee without informing Nehru sent him a personal message, promising him full consideration of 'all points of view'.²⁵⁵ The talks were held from 3 to 6 December, in accordance with what Attlee had written to Nehru, i.e. to persuade the League to participate in the constituent assembly. From the British side, Prime Minister Attlee, three Cabinet Mission members—Pethick-Lawrence, Cripps and Alexander—and Wavell, participated in the talks, with Francis F. Turnbull and George E. Abell (1904–1989) as secretaries of the conference; and Jinnah and Liaquat represented the League, Nehru the Congress, and Baldev Singh (1902–1961) the Sikhs. Before the talks, the opinion of Lord Chancellor, Lord William Allen Jowitt, had been obtained on the disputed points in the 16 May statement, which was in accord with the League's standpoint, that 'it is for the majority of the representatives in each section taken as a whole to decide how provincial constitutions shall be framed and to what extent, if any, they shall be grouped'.[256]

The modus operandi for the London talks was such that the League–Congress differences could not be resolved. The participants as a whole met only once, at the end of the talks. Before that, the British participants individually or in batches held discussions separately with the representatives of the League, Congress and Sikhs. They had exclusive meetings of their own, presided over by Prime Minister Attlee or Secretary of State for India Pethick-Lawrence, in which they would evaluate their discussions with the Indian participants. The minutes of all the meetings are available, except of two important meetings, one of Attlee's meeting with Nehru and the other of his meeting with Jinnah and Liaquat.[257] During the talks, Nehru objected to the way the League had been inducted into the interim government, and complained that its members had refused to recognise his leadership. The constituent assembly should continue to function, he maintained, even if the League did not come in; and he confidently assured Cripps that the League members would come in sooner or later provided they knew that the assembly was 'going ahead in any case'.[258] He agreed that the members of the constituent assembly could meet in sections but refused to accept that the sections should frame the provincial constitutions by a majority of votes. He wanted any points of difference in the constituent assembly referred either to its chairman or to the federal court for decision. He also rejected the idea of adjourning the constituent assembly after its opening session to provide time for the settlement of the controversial issues.[259] Conversely, Jinnah affirmed that the Cabinet Mission Plan had been 'a fraud and a humbug'. All the recent communal riots 'with the possible exception of Noakhali', in his view, were of 'Hindu origin', which had been 'fomented and organized by the Congress leaders', and 'only the creation of Pakistan' could deal with the situation that had arisen from 'the deliberate butchery of Muslims by Hindus in Bihar'. When his attention was drawn to the concerns of the outside world, he responded that he realized the value of world opinion but his own supporters for him were more important who were 'determined not to be submerged in the Hindu nation'; and he felt it 'better to resist now than to be gradually overwhelmed'.[260] The interim government was functioning under the Act of 1935, Liaquat emphatically stated, and the League members had refused to attend the so-called 'cabinet meetings' over which Nehru 'purported to preside as premier, and the decisions of which were to go by majority'. He accused the British of 'surrendering in all directions to the Congress with the object of getting good terms by treaty in regard to trade and defence'.[261] When Jinnah was asked if the Congress accepted the League's interpretation of the Cabinet Mission Plan or if the decision of the federal court was favourable to the League, would the League then come in the constituent assembly? Jinnah opposed any reference to the federal court because the 16 May statement was not a legal document; and he was not willing, even if the interpretation of the statement was as desired by the League, to undertake that he would recommend to the League council the re-acceptance of the plan; he was prepared simply to place the matter before the council 'in whatever way he considered right and proper'.[262] The London talks failed to break the deadlock; and on 6 December, Attlee read out a statement at the concluding meeting that sent mixed signals; it accepted the League's interpretation as correct and called on the Congress to accept it to enable the League to re-accept the 16 May statement. But if the Congress still desired to refer this fundamental point to the federal court for decision, a reference should be made at an early date. The constituent assembly was allowed to proceed with the process of framing the constitution, and in case a large section of the Indian population did not participate in the process, it was clearly stated, His Majesty's Government's could not contemplate—as the Congress itself had stated—'forcing such a constitution upon any unwilling parts of the country'. Immediately after Attlee read out the statement, Jinnah made it clear that the decision of the federal court would not be binding on the League.[263] Four days later, Sir William Patrick Spens, the chief justice of the federal court, in a letter to the acting viceroy, Sir John Colville, remarked that the federal court was 'most unlikely to entertain such reference or express an opinion' unless given 'appropriate statutory powers to do so'.[264] The chief justice's opinion rendered any reference to the federal court meaningless.

After the London conference, Nehru and Baldev Singh immediately returned to India to attend the opening session of the constituent assembly on 9 December. But Jinnah and Liaquat stayed on in London till 15 December, and used the opportunity to explain to the British public, politicians and the press that Pakistan was the only solution of the constitutional impasse. On the way back, they stopped in Cairo to apprise the Egyptians of the Indian Muslims' urge for a separate homeland and acquainted themselves with the problems of Egypt and other Arab countries. On his return, Jinnah made it clear that he would not call a meeting of the council to revise its previous decision, as Cripps had suggested in the house of commons, until the Congress unequivocally accepted the statements of 16 May, and 6 December.[265] Political developments moved in a different direction. The constituent assembly on Nehru's motion took up consideration of an Objectives Resolution that declared India an independent sovereign republic which, after an adjournment of about a month, was passed at its six-day session that started on 20 January 1947. The Objectives Resolution settled the fundamentals on which the future constitution of India would be based; and the constituent assembly then proceeded to appoint important committees, which practically shut the door on the League and the Pakistan scheme. Meanwhile, on 5–6 January, the All India Congress Committee endorsed the working committee's resolution of 22 December 1946, that had invoked provincial autonomy to oppose the element of compulsion on a province or part of a province or on the Sikhs to stay in the assigned section till the framing of the constitution; and, on 16 December, Gandhi advised two Assam Congress leaders who approached him for advice not to go into Section C, if there was no clear guidance from the Congress.[266] Earlier, in July, the Assam assembly, on a directive from the Congress, had called on its newly elected members of the constituent assembly to have nothing to do with Group 'C', in spite of opposition from the Muslim and minorities' members.[267] On 29 January–2 February 1947, the League working committee reviewed the situation arising out of His Majesty's Government's statement of 6 December, and resolutions of the Congress working committee and All India Congress Committee, and passed a lengthy resolution, which in essence stipulated that since the Congress had not accepted the 16 May, and 6 December 1946, statements, no useful purpose would be served to convene a meeting of the council to reconsider its July resolution.[268]

After the League's resolution, Nehru and eight other non-League members of the interim government again demanded the resignation of the League members; and the League resisted any such demand, both sides using arguments similar to those that they had advanced earlier.[269] While the League and Congress were engaged in pressurizing Wavell to accept their respective positions vis-à-vis the interim government and the constituent assembly, the British government was planning to take decisions about the final phase of the *Raj* in India. The first decision was about the change of the viceroy. Before the London talks, the Congress leaders had begun to accuse Wavell of partiality, alleging that he had taken a pro-League stance on various issues including the formation of the interim government, removal of the Bengal and Sindh ministries, grouping of provinces and convening of the constituent assembly although he had in fact never even once spoken a word in support of the Pakistan scheme. Gandhi directly charged Wavell of pro-League leanings, and Sudhir Ghosh indirectly suggested to Attlee his replacement for the sake of Nehru–Viceroy smooth relations.[270] With Cripps' assistance, Attlee discovered Lord Louis Mountbatten—a member of the British royalty and a war hero whom Nehru had met in Singapore during his visit to South-east Asia and who had frequently visited India during the war—to succeed Wavell. His appointment was finalized in December 1946, while Wavell was still in London but he was kept completely in the dark till all the arrangements had been finalized. When he was informed about his 'termination', Wavell was shocked and refused to accept the explanation that Attlee gave about his replacement but digested the 'indignity' of 'so summary a dismissal' at 'such short notice' with grace.[271] Pethick-Lawrence was the next to go as desired by Mountbatten; and he was replaced by Lord William F.H. Listowel, a lot younger than his predecessor, who was unlikely to stand up to the new viceroy on any issue. Mountbatten was allowed to take his own staff members, an unprecedented privilege for a viceroy. The League could not have a more unfavourable set-up so close to the transfer of power. The second decision was about the new British policy that had been evolved after long deliberations following Wavell's pressure for the acceptance of his 'breakdown plan' and fixation of a date for the transfer of power in India not later than 31 March 1948. On 20 February 1947, Prime Minister Attlee announced that policy in the parliament along with the appointment of Mountbatten as the viceroy.[272]

NOTES

1. For Jinnah's comments, see his press statement in Simla issued on 14 July 1945, *Dawn*, 15 July 1945.
2. Sir Stafford Cripps made this observation on 15 July 1945, a day after the Simla conference.
3. Wavell to Pethick-Lawrence, 4 November 1945, *TP*, vol. VI, p. 440.
4. Shiva Rao to Cripps, 20 November 1945, ibid., p. 564.
5. Waheed, *Nation's Voice*, vol. IV, pp. 460–62.
6. *Wavell: The Viceroy's Journal*, pp. 169–70.

7. Sir Claude J. Auchinleck to Wavell, 22 January, *TP*, vol. VI, p. 835.
8. Ibid., pp. 481 and 590; and Menon, *Transfer of Power*, pp. 223–25.
9. Cabinet: India and Burma Committee. I.B. (45) 9th Meeting, Minutes, 1–3, 19 December 1945, *TP*, vol. VI, p. 663.
10. For the text, see ibid., pp. 686–99.
11. G.D. Birla and other Congress leaders had been urging the Labour cabinet to do that to prevent the League from advocating Pakistan. Ibid., pp. 613–15.
12. Ibid., pp. 649–50.
13. Ibid., pp. 890–908, 1209–10 and 1229.
14. 'Breakdown Plan', 27 December 1945, ibid., pp. 700–701. Later, in September, Wavell again sent a detailed 'breakdown plan', which Prime Minister Attlee ruled out as impractical. Ibid., vol. VIII, pp. 454–66, 550–55 and 571.
15. Ibid., p. 1112.
16. For Wavell's interview with Jinnah on 5 January 1946, and note on Wavell's interview, see ibid., vol. VI, pp. 737–38; and *Wavell: The Viceroy's Journal*, p. 202.
17. For Woodrow Wyatt's talk with Jinnah, 8 January 1946, see *TP*, vol. VI, pp. 798–99.
18. Ibid., pp. 886–7, 935 and 948.
19. On 22 January, Arthur Moore sent his notes to Prime Minister Attlee. Ibid., pp. 874–78.
20. For Jinnah's statement on 28 January 1946, see ibid., pp. 1015–16.
21. Jinnah to Pethick-Lawrence, 9 February 1946, ibid., pp. 1011–12; and Jinnah to Cripps, 9 February 1946, QAP, F. 490, pp. 16–17.
22. QAP, Fs. 810 and 1022; and Jamil-ud-Din Ahmad, *Speeches and Writings of Mr. Jinnah*, vol. II, pp. 278–84.
23. For Patel's remarks at a meeting in Ahmadabad, see *Hindustan Times*, 16 January 1946; and AFM, vol. 294, no. 31.
24. *Statesman*, 4 March 1946, *TP*, vol. VI, p. 1118; Nehru's comments in an interview with Woodrow Wyatt, Wavell to Pethick-Lawrence, 15 January 1946, ibid., p. 796; and Nehru to Cripps, 5 March 1946, ibid., pp. 1107–8. Nehru's remarks provoked Jinnah to repeat his July 1937 comments that Nehru was like 'Peter Pan' who 'never unlearns or learns anything and never grows old'.
25. Nehru to Cripps, 27 January 1946, ibid., pp. 851–59.
26. P. Clarke, *Cripps Version*, p. 402. The editors of the *TP* volumes could not trace Cripps' reply to Nehru's letter. *TP*, vol. VI, p. 1107, note 2.
27. For Azad's views, see *TP*, vol. VI, pp. 863–66 and 1026–30; and for Gandhi's views, see ibid., p. 1074.
28. The Cabinet members' views about Wavell changed when the three-member mission interacted with him during its visit. Ibid., p. 789; and vol. VII, p. 431.
29. Minutes by Mr Gibson, Mr Patrick and Sir D. Monteath, 12 March 1946, ibid., vol. VI, pp. 1158–59.
30. Ibid., pp. 1003–4 and 1025.
31. Record of discussions at Chequers on 24 February 1946, and Wavell to Pethick-Lawrence, 3 March 1946, ibid., pp. 1057–64 and 1101–2.
32. Wavell to Pethick-Lawrence, 3 March 1946, Pethick-Lawrence to Attlee, 4 March, and Pethick-Lawrence to Wavell, 5 March, ibid., pp. 1101–2, 1106 and 1107.
33. Note by Lord Pethick-Lawrence, 12 March 1946, ibid., pp. 1159–63.
34. Ibid., pp. 1213–28.

35. Cabinet: Defence Committee. Paper D.O. (46)68, 12 June 1946, ibid., vol. VII, pp. 891–92; and Habib I. Rahimatullah (after his meeting with A.V. Alexander) to Jinnah, 3 June 1946, QAP, F. 419, p. 12.
36. Waheed, *Nation's Voice*, vol. IV, pp. 439–40.
37. For a copy of his speech as circulated by the Press Information Bureau, Government of India, see QAP, F. 12, pp. 5–8.
38. For the text of speeches as circulated by the Press Information Bureau, Government of India, see ibid., pp. 3, 8–13, 30–32 and 38–39.
39. Mohammad Husain, general secretary, Shawl Merchants Association, Amritsar, to Wavell, ibid., F. 907, pp. 255–58.
40. *Dawn*, 16 and 25 March 1946.
41. For example, see his interview with Godfrey Nichols of the *New York Times* and Ernest Dharma, of the United Press of America, Waheed, *Nation's Voice*, vol. IV, pp. 439 and 455.
42. Jinnah's Pakistan Day message, *Dawn*, 23 March 1946.
43. Beverley Nichols to Jinnah, 11 January 1944, QAP, F. 785, pp. 98–104; and Beverley Nichols, *Verdict on India*, Lahore, 1943.
44. Nazimuddin to Jinnah, 24 February 1946, QAP, F. 392, pp. 83–84.
45. Notice issued by Liaquat on 24 March 1946, AFM, vol. 279, p. 18.
46. The quota of representatives decided was: Madras 4, Bombay 4, Bengal 14, United Provinces 8, Punjab 9, Bihar 4, Central Provinces and Berar 1, Assam 4, the NWFP 4, Orissa 1, Sindh 3, central assembly 10 and council of state 3.
47. For the text of the resolution, the pledge and Jinnah's concluding remarks, see Pirzada, *Foundations*, vol. II, pp. 512–13 and 522–23; and for a draft of the resolution with corrections by Jinnah, see QAP, F. 835, pp. 107–9.
48. For instance, see AFM, vol. 366, no. 17; and for reaction in the tribal areas, see QAP, F. 1133, pp. 144 and 174.
49. *TP*, vol. VII, pp. 23 and 325. For support of 400 Muslim NCOs (Indian National Congress [Organisations]) of Jhansi, see AFM, vol. 359; and for Muslim Royal Indian Air Force personnel, Royal Air Force stations, Jodhpur and Salawas to secretary of state for India, 24 April 1946, see QAP, F. 1025, p. 115.
50. Except for Sir Mohammad Usman and Dr Ambedkar, who wanted the issue of Pakistan to be settled first, the executive council members opposed the division of India. [Note of Meeting, 26 March 1946, *TP*, vol. VII, pp. 8–9.] The League leaders whom the mission interviewed expressed Muslim resolve to establish Pakistan; and even G.M. Sayed who had left the League deposed that his group agreed with Jinnah's aims but differed with him on economic issues. Ibid., 2 April 1946, pp. 92–93.
51. *Wavell: The Viceroy's Journal*, p. 236.
52. The League premiers of Bengal, Sindh and Assam were also invited to the meetings of the working committee by special invitation. QAP, F. 335, pp. 253–54; SHC, OM-I: 90; and AFM, vol. 142, nos. 46 and 49.
53. Note by Cripps, 30 March 1946, *TP*, vol. VII, pp. 59–60. Jinnah refused to shake hands with Azad or interact with him whenever there were joint meetings.
54. For a summarized version of the interview, see ibid., pp. 118–24 and 277.
55. For questions asked from the Sikh leaders, see ibid., pp. 138–41.
56. Note by Lieutenant General Sir Arthur Smith, 28 March 1946, ibid., pp. 20–22.
57. A.V. Alexander to Pethick-Lawrence, 9 April 1946, L/WS/I/1029: ff 96–128, cited in ibid., p. 181, footnote 2.
58. Memorandum by Sir S. Cripps, ibid., pp. 174–80.

59. For a note by Sir W. Croft and Turnbull, 9 April 1946, see ibid., pp. 196–98.
60. Record of Meeting of Cabinet Delegation and Field Marshal Viscount Wavell (henceforth Record of Meeting), 10 April 1946, ibid., pp. 209–213; and Cabinet Delegation to Attlee, 11 April, ibid., pp. 220–21.
61. Attlee to Cabinet Delegation, 13 April 1946, ibid., pp. 260–61.
62. For the strategy that was devised to deal with Jinnah, see note by Sir S. Cripps (case for Jinnah), ibid., pp. 233–34; brief prepared by Wavell (brief for interview with Mr Jinnah— 16 April); and Record of Meetings on 13 and 15 April 1946, ibid., pp. 251–52 and 265–67.
63. Later, on 19 November, he reminded Wavell that 'he had never rejected the smaller Pakistan suggested by the mission, though he had insisted on Calcutta'. Ibid., vol. IX, p. 109.
64. Record of Interview between Cabinet Delegation and Jinnah, 16 April 1946, ibid., vol. VII, pp. 280–85; and Cabinet Delegation to Attlee, 18 April 1946, ibid., p. 313.
65. Ibid., p. 285.
66. Record of Meeting, 18 April 1946, ibid., pp. 310–12; and RSC dairy, 18 April 1946, Clarke, *Cripps Version*, p. 415.
67. Memorandum by Cripps and Record of Meeting, 18 April 1946, *TP*, vol. VII, pp. 303–12.
68. Record of Meeting, 24 April 1964, ibid., p. 324.
69. Cabinet Delegation to Wavell, 22 April 1946, ibid., pp. 316–21; Record of Meeting, 24 April, pp. 324–24; and Menon, *Transfer of Power*, pp. 253–54.
70. Its summary appeared in India on 1 May. Jinnah termed it as 'the greatest betrayal' of the Arabs, and the AIML observed 10 May, as the Palestine Day. *TP*, vol. VII, p. 445; and also see Wavell to Henderson, 25 April 1946, ibid., pp. 341–42.
71. Record of Meeting, 25 April 1946, ibid., pp. 330–34; Wavell to Henderson, 25 April, ibid., pp. 341–42; and 1st Revise of Draft Statement of Cabinet Mission and Wavell, [27 April], ibid., pp. 361–67.
72. Ibid., p. 352.
73. Ibid., pp. 349–50; and for the text of the working committee's resolution, see AFM, vol. 142, no. 51.
74. Record of Meeting, 26 April 1946, *TP*, vol. VII, pp. 342–47.
75. For the reservations, see Azad to Pethick-Lawrence, 27 April 1946, ibid., p. 353.
76. For details, see ibid., pp. 440–42.
77. For instance, see Shabbir Ahmad Usmani to Liaquat, 8 May 1946, AFM, vol. 439; Hasrat Mohani to Quaid-i-Azam, 12 May 1946 (with copies to Liaquat, Nawab Ismail and Nishtar), QAP, F. 378, pp. 12 and 17; and Raghib Ahsan to Quaid-i-Azam, 24 July 1946, SHC, Bengal-IV: 53.
78. Record of Meeting, 7 May 1946, *TP*, vol. VII, p. 448; and text in Cabinet Delegation to Attlee, 7 May, ibid., pp. 452–53; and QAP, F. 12, p. 51–52.
79. Jinnah to Pethick-Lawrence, 8 May 1946, *TP*, vol. VII, pp. 465–65; and QAP, F. 12, pp. 52–53 and for his conditions, see note by Major Wyatt of conversation with Jinnah on 9 May 1946, *TP*, vol. VII, pp. 475–76.
80. QAP, F. 12, pp. 55–56.
81. The Congress was apprehensive that the principle of parity once accepted might be extended to the services and the army. Record of Meeting, 9 May 1946, *TP*, vol. VII, p. 480.
82. Record of the 6th Meeting of the second Simla conference, 11 May 1946, ibid., pp. 508–511.
83. Ibid., pp. 516–17; and QAP, F. 12, pp. 56–57.

84. Azad to Pethick-Lawrence, 12 May 1946, *TP*, vol. VII, pp. 518–19; and QAP, F. 12, pp. 57–59.

85. Record of seventh Meeting, 12 May 1946, *TP*, vol. VII, p. 525; and Cabinet Delegation to Attlee, 13 May 19 May 1946, ibid., p. 544.

86. For publication of the documents, see *Jinnah Papers*, Second Series, vol. XIII, p. 485.

87. For the working committee's resolution, see AFM, vol. 142, no. 52; and for statement issued by the League delegation from Simla on 12 May 1946, see QAP, F. 132, p. 25.

88. For text of the Statement, see *TP*, vol. VII, pp. 582–91.

89. For instance, see Sir Olaf Caroe to Wavell, 17 May 1946, ibid., p. 603–4.

90. Cited in Clarke, *Cripps Version*, p. 431.

91. For composition of the advisory committee, in which the Muslims were in a minority, see Record of Meeting, 8 and 21 June 1946, *TP*, vol. VII, pp. 842 and 998.

92. Pethick-Lawrence to Gandhi, 18 May 1946, ibid., p. 618.

93. Ibid., p. 600.

94. Gandhi to Pethick-Lawrence, 20 May 1946, ibid., pp 635–36; and Record of Meeting, 20 May, ibid., pp. 637–38; and Azad to Pethick-Lawrence, 20 May 1946, ibid., 639–41.

95. Clarke, *Cripps Version*, p. 434.

96. Pethick-Lawrence to Gandhi, 20 May 1946; and Pethick-Lawrence to Azad, 22 May 1946, *TP*, vol. VII, pp. 642 and 659–60. Writing as 'an old friend', Gandhi stuck to the position that he had taken in his letter of 20 May. Ibid., p. 660.

97. Resolution of the Congress working committee passed on 24 May 1946, ibid., pp. 679–82.

98. For the text of the Statement, see ibid., pp. 688–89.

99. Note for Wavell's talk with Nehru, 26 May 1946, ibid., vol. VII, pp. 698–700; and Pethick-Lawrence to Attlee, 26 May 1946, ibid., p. 705.

100. Wavell to Azad, 30 May 1946, ibid., p. 738.

101. Record of Meeting, 31 May 1946, ibid., pp. 744–54; Cabinet Delegation to Attlee, 31 May 1946, ibid., pp. 747–49; and Attlee to Cabinet Delegation and Wavell, 6 June 1946, ibid., p. 830. The League leaders did not know about this proposal. Later, in September, when Wavell made a similar proposal, it was shot down. Ibid., vol. VIII, p. 570.

102. For Abell's assessment, see Record of Meeting, 20 May 1946, ibid., vol. VII, p. 637.

103. Sir F. Mudie (Sindh) to Wavell, 24 May 1946, ibid., p. 678; Hatim Alavi to Quaid-i-Azam, 10 June 1946, SHC, Sindh-VII: 62; and ibid., Pb—V: 84.

104. For comments of a few Muslim Leaguers, see QAP, F. 12, pp. 67–107; and AFM, vol. 228, no. 46. See also Note by Abell, 18 May 1946, *TP*, vol. VII, p. 619; and Turnbull to Pethick-Lawrence, 18 May 1947, ibid., pp. 622–23.

105. For the text of his statement, see *TP*, vol. VII, pp. 663–69; note by Major Wyatt after his meeting with Jinnah, 25 May 1946, ibid., pp. 684–86; and Ahmad, *Speeches and Writings of Mr. Jinnah*, vol. II, pp. 287–98.

106. *TP*, vol. VII, pp. 577–80.

107. Sir Olaf Caroe to Wavell, 9 June 1946, ibid., vol. VII, p. 852.

108. For a rationale about Assam's inclusion in Pakistan, see Abdul Matin Choudhury, 'Assam in Pakistan Scheme', 25 April 1946, QAP, F. 1122, pp. 25–30.

109. Minutes by E.W.R. Lumby and Turnbull, 22–23 January 1947, *TP*, vol. IX, p. 532.

110. Gandhi to Cripps, 8 May 1946, ibid., vol. VII, p. 466.
111. Wavell to Jinnah, 4 June 1946, ibid., p. 799; and for other documents, see ibid., pp. 785–86.
112. Ibid., p. 887.
113. Jinnah to Wavell, 8 June 1946, ibid., p. 841; and I.D. Scott's talk with Liaquat on 1 June 1946, ibid., p. 763.
114. For views of some councillors, see incomplete handwritten minutes of the meeting, AFM, vol. 278, pp. 53–55.
115. For newspaper reports, see Waheed, *Nation's Voice*, vol. V, pp. 28–35 and 41–43.
116. For the text of the resolution, see AFM, vol. 278, pp. 56–58; and Pirzada, *Foundations*, vol. III, pp. 347–49.
117. For a note by Wavell, [28 April 1946], see *TP*, vol. VII, p. 360; Record of Meeting, 3 May 1946; and Cabinet Delegation to Attlee, 5 May 1946, ibid., pp. 360, 403 and 432.
118. Jinnah to Wavell, 8 and 19 June 1946, ibid., pp. 841–42; and Waheed, *Nation's Voice*, vol. V, pp. 81–82 and 94–96.
119. Pethick-Lawrence to Azad, 25 May 1946, *TP*, vol. VII, p. 627.
120. Turnbull to Abell, 6 June 1946, enclosing a note of interview with G.D. Birla, ibid., pp. 824–26.
121. Record of Meeting with Azad and Nehru, 10 June 1946, ibid., pp. 854–55; and for his views on the Congress attitude, see ibid., p. 1024.
122. Note by Wavell, 7 June 1946, note by Wyatt, 11 June 1946, and Jinnah to Wavell, 12 June 1946, ibid., pp. 839, 866–67 and 885.
123. Wavell to Jinnah, 11 June 1946, Record of Meeting, 12 June 1946, ibid., pp. 872 and 876; and Waheed, *Nation's Voice*, vol. V, p. 148.
124. A.V. Alexander's observation, *TP*, vol. VII, p. 974.
125. Ambedkar to Jinnah, 17 June 1946, and Ambedkar to Prime Minister Attlee, 17 June 1946, QAP, F. 175, pp. 6 and 7.
126. Cabinet Delegation to Attlee, 14 June 1946, *TP*, vol. VII, pp. 923–24. Another Congress demand was about the European members in the Bengal and Assam assemblies that they should neither put up any candidates nor vote for the candidates. Its demand was accepted, and they did not take part in the voting. Ibid., p. 946.
127. Record of Meeting, 16 June 1946, ibid., pp. 950–52.
128. Five Muslim Leaguers were: Jinnah, Liaquat, Nawab Ismail, Nazimuddin and Nishtar. Ayub Khuhro asked for the inclusion of representatives from Sindh. Ghulam Husain Hidayatullah to Jinnah, 20 June 1946, QAP, F. 365, p. 111; and F. 513, p. 1.
129. For the text of the Statement, *TP*, vol. VII, pp. 954–55.
130. Note of interview between Jinnah, Pethick-Lawrence and Alexander, 17 June 1946, note by Wavell of an interview with Jinnah on 18 June 1946, and Record of Meeting, 19 June 1946, ibid., pp. 960–61 and 971–77.
131. Liaquat, Nawab Ismail, Nazimuddin and Nishtar declined to accept the invitation, as the League president had not been asked to submit a list. QAP, Fs. 14–15, pp. 22–23; and *TP*, vol. VII, p. 977.
132. Jinnah to Wavell, 19 June 1946, *TP*, vol. VII, pp. 974–77; and Waheed, *Nation's Voice*, pp. 974–77.
133. The British objection to Sarat Bose's appointment was that he had been in touch with the Japanese during the war.
134. Wavell to Jinnah, 20 June 1946, *TP*, vol. VII, pp. 988–89.

135. Record of Meeting, 20 June 1946, ibid., pp. 986–88.

136. Record of Meeting, 23 June 1946, ibid., p. 1011; and Record of Meeting with Representatives of the Congress Party, 23 June 1946, ibid., pp. 1013 and 1017.

137. Sir W. Croft to Sir D. Montreath, 22 June 1946, ibid., 1007.

138. Azad and Dr Zakir Husain were possible candidates for this slot; and the former had declined to accept his nomination.

139. On 25 June, the League working committee formally accepted the statement of 16 June.

140. For Jinnah's allegation that the Congress accepted the long-term plan with its own interpretations and the mission abandoned the interim government scheme as a result of a Mission–Patel understanding and his challenge to the viceroy to disprove its authenticity, see Jinnah's statement of 27 July 1946, Waheed, *Nation's Voice*, vol. V, pp. 137–51.

141. *TP*, vol. VII, pp. 1032–38.

142. Record of Meeting, 25 June 1946, ibid., pp. 1043–44.

143. Minutes by Scott and Wavell, 1–2 August 1946, ibid., vol. VIII, pp. 174–75; and *Wavell: The Viceroy's Journal*, p. 306.

144. Record of Meeting with Jinnah, 25 June 1946, ibid., vol. VII, pp. 1044–48.

145. Record of Meetings, 26 June 1946, ibid., pp. 1050–52, 1053 and 1060–61.

146. Record of Meeting, 26 June 1946, ibid., pp. 1060.–61.

147. Jinnah's statement, 27 June 1946, ibid., pp. 1069–73; and *Dawn*, 28 June 1946.

148. Wavell to Jinnah, 28 June 1946, Waheed, *Nation's Voice*, vol. V, p. 91.

149. *Statesman*, 29 June and 1 July 1946. Editorial.

150. Record of Meeting with representatives of the Congress, 26 June 1946, *TP*, vol. VII, pp. 1050–52.

151. QAP, F. 31, p. 13.

152. Hatim Alavi to Jinnah, 10 July 1946, ibid., F. 884, p. 80.

153. Ibid., F. 368, pp. 3–7; F. 851, p. 45; and F. 884, pp. 1–7, 11–12 and 80–82.

154. For details, see 'Balochistan Provincial Muslim League' in Chapter 8; and Qazi Isa to Quaid-i-Azam, 28 May 1946, ibid., F. 1133, p. 208; Liaquat to Jinnah, 11 July 1946, ibid., 629, pp. 1–2; and Khan of Kalat to Jinnah, 28 May, 1946, and Jinnah to the Khan of Kalat, 31 May 1946, ibid., F. 1133, pp. 210–212.

155. Note by Wavell, 29 June 1946, *TP*, vol. VII, pp. 1084–85.

156. QAP, F. 14, pp. 72–73; and *TP*, vol. VIII, pp. 106–7.

157. *Selected Works of Jawaharlal Nehru*, New Delhi, 1982, vol. 15, pp. 236–39 and 241–48.

158. *Hindustan Times*, 21 July 1946.

159. Note by Wavell after discussions with Jinnah on 16 September 1946, *TP*, vol. VIII, p. 525.

160. QAP, F. 20, pp. 13–15 and 27–30; and *TP*, vol. VIII, pp. 110–11.

161. For a letter highly critical of the League's acceptance of the Mission's plan, see Raghib Ahsan to Quaid-i-Azam, 24 July 1946, SHC, Bengal-IV: 53–54.

162. For the text of the resolution, see QAP, F. 113, p. 39. For further details, see Pirzada, *Foundations*, vol. II, pp. 544–62.

163. *Star of India*, 15 August 1946.

164. For a secret report from Sir F. Burrows, governor of Bengal, to Pethick-Lawrence, 23 August 1946, see *TP*, vol. VIII, pp. 293–304. For the estimates of killed and injured, see ibid., p. 303, footnote 5.

165. Pethick-Lawrence to Wavell, 28 August 1946, ibid., p. 335; and Durga Das (ed.), *Sardar Patel's Correspondence*, Ahmadabad, vol. 3, p. 40. Wavell 'entirely refused

to accept' that the riots had been 'engineered by the Muslim League'. *TP*, vol. VIII, p. 494.

166. An inquiry commission with the chief justice of the federal court, Sir Patrick Spens, as its chairman was appointed but it had not completed its inquiry till independence.

167. Wavell to Attlee, 28 August 1946, *TP*, vol. VIII, pp. 328–30; and for Pethick-Lawrence's recognition of his services 'as a go-between', see his letter to Cripps on 23 September 1946, ibid., p. 575.

168. Abell to Wavell, 8 October 1946, ibid., p. 677.

169. Wavell to Pethick-Lawrence (Enclosure 1), and Sir F. Burrows to Wavell, 28 August 1946, ibid., pp. 316–17.

170. Pethick-Lawrence to Wavell, 19 July 1946, ibid., p. 91; and for priority passage for Sudhir Ghosh as Gandhi's emissary to facilitate his London visit and his stay there till the formation of Nehru-headed interim government, see ibid., p. 90.

171. Wavell personally gave Nehru the letter when the latter saw him that day. Note by Wavell, ibid., p. 106.

172. The embargo was removed when it was decided to invite Nehru to make proposals for an interim government. Ibid., p. 190.

173. Pirzada, *Quaid's Correspondence*, pp. 387–88; and ibid., pp. 156–57.

174. Ibid., p. 155; and *Dawn*, 31 July 1946. That day, an announcement was made in the parliament after the British and US representatives had examined the recommendations of the Anglo-American committee of enquiry on Palestine, that Palestine should be divided into four areas including a Jewish province and an Arab province, and that 100,000 European Jews be immediately accepted with continuing immigration thereafter. The League working committee passed a strongly worded resolution, condemning this policy.

175. Churchill's telegram and letter, QAP, F. 20, pp. 27–30; and also see Pethick-Lawrence to Wavell, 31 July 1946, *TP*, vol. VIII, pp. 162 and 165–66.

176. Wavell to Jinnah, 8 August 1946, *TP*, vol. VIII, p. 203; and Pirzada, *Quaid's Correspondence*, p. 390.

177. Menon, *Transfer of Power*, p. 290.

178. For the Jinnah–Nehru correspondence, see Pirzada, *Quaid's Correspondence*, pp. 298–301.

179. For details, see Menon, *Transfer of Power*, pp. 293–99.

180. Sir F. Wylie, governor of United Provinces, to Wavell, 31 August 1946, *TP*, vol. VIII, p. 369; and Burrows to Wavell, 10 September 1946, ibid., p. 487.

181. Secretary to Liaquat to Quaid-i-Azam, 24 August 1946, QAP, 335, p. 259; and Liaquat to members of the legislative assembly, 26 August 1946, SHC, OM-I: 82.

182. Yamin to Jinnah, 30 August 1946, and Jinnah to Yamin, 2 September 1946, QAP, F. 341, pp. 1–4.

183. Jinnah to Raza Ali, 2 September 1946, ibid., F. 559, p. 554.

184. *Dawn*, 26, 27 and 29 August 1946.

185. QAP, F. 1133, pp. 234–36.

186. AFM, vol. 182, nos. 26 and 35; and vol. 193, pp. 51–66.

187. For details, see ibid., vol. 439, pp. 17–25.

188. E.M. Jenkins to Wavell, 14 September 1946, QAP, F. 1024, p. 18; and Abell to Harris (enclosing note by N.P.A. Smith, the director of intelligence), 24 January 1947, *TP*, vol. IX, p. 542.

189. For resolutions of the central committee of action (27 September) and the working committee (13 October), see AFM, vol. 142, no. 57.

190. The *Daily Mail* (London, 28 September 1946) reported that in addition to the Fakir 'other holy men in the tribal areas who control the Afridis and Mahsuds are known to hold League sympathies. Against this combination Khan Abdul Ghaffar Khan would be helpless'. AFM, vol. 402, pp. 34–35.

191. For the pro-League stance of the Mahsud, Wazir and Afridi tribesmen and the Azad tribes of North Waziristan, see QAP, F. 559, pp. 582 and 584; and F. 884, pp. 71–72; also see Ghazi Mohammad Asmat Ali Khan, president, Junud-i-Rabbi (chief president, Saralim Ghazi Hajee Mustafa Mirza Ali Khan) to Jinnah, 20 October 1946, ibid., F. 588, p. 504; and SHC, D-71 and 72; for armed struggle, see F.H. Elkhairabadi to Quaid-i-Azam, QAP, F. 132, pp. 50–58; and F. 895, pp. 242–44; *TP*, vol. VIII, pp. 155 and 417; and for a meeting with Jinnah in New Delhi of a Shia–Sunni joint deputation of tribesmen from the Kurram Agency, see *Dawn*, 30 September 1946.

192. For offer of services by the Royal Indian Air Force Muslim Airmen, Royal Air Force, Station Ambala to Quaid-i-Azam, 16 August 1946, QAP, F. 257, p. 14; and *TP*, vol. VIII, p. 376.

193. QAP, F. 893, pp. 155–58.

194. *TP*, vol. VIII, pp. 225–26.

195. Douglas Laird Busk, British embassy, Baghdad to G.C.L. Crichton, secretary, external affairs department, Government of India, confidential by Bag 676/9/46, 27 September 1946, QAP, F. 884, pp. 381–82.

196. Pethick-Lawrence to Jinnah, 16 August 1946, and Jinnah to Pethick-Lawrence, 11 September, ibid., F. 20, pp. 34–36; and Pethick-Lawrence to Wavell, 19 August 1946, *TP*, vol. VIII, p. 263.

197. Waheed, *Nation's Voice*, vol. V, pp. 227–40, 242–45 and 933n 1.

198. Pethick-Lawrence to Wavell, 13 September 1946, *TP*, vol. VIII, p. 498; and Wavell to Jenkins, 18 September 1946, QAP, F. 1024, p. 24.

199. Krishna Menon to Nehru (personal), 26 September 1946, QAP, F. 183, pp. 11–14.

200. Attlee and Cripps wanted Wavell to proceed with the convening of the constituent assembly even if the League did not come in and similar was the thinking of a section of the Congress leaders including Gandhi. *TP*, vol. VIII, pp. 570–72, 581–82 and 634.

201. Meanwhile, Nawab Hamidullah of Bhopal, chancellor of the chamber of princes, made a move at Gandhi's instance for a Congress–League agreement but the proposal fizzled out before Jinnah could consider it because its terms were not acceptable to Nehru and Patel. Jinnah to Nehru, 7 and 12 October 1946, Nehru to Jinnah, 8 October 1946, and Wavell to Pethick-Lawrence, 9 and 11 October 1946, ibid., pp. 673–74, 676–77, 683, 694, 697, 701–3 and 737; Jinnah to Hamidullah, 5 October 1946, QAP, F 238, pp. 22 and 24; and *Dawn*, 17 October 1946.

202. Jinnah to Wavell, 13 October 1946, *TP*, vol. VIII, 709–710.

203. Ibid., pp. 654–58, 703–6, 735 and 826.

204. Jinnah to Wavell, 3 October 1946, QAP, F. 99, p. 5; and note by Wavell after his meeting with Jinnah and Liaquat, 14 October 1946, *TP*, vol. VIII, pp. 712–13.

205. For some points raised by Jinnah with Sir B.N. Rau (18 September 1946) and his replies (22 September 1946), see QAP, F. 21, pp. 14–15 and 21–23; and *TP*, vol. VIII, pp. 543–44, 556, 561 and 562–64. Wavell did not want Rau's response to be treated as the official viewpoint; and Rau was careful to mention that in his reply to Jinnah.

206. QAP, F. 294, p. 6; and F. 895, pp. 1–2 and 59–62. Nawab Ismail whose selection as a League member of the interim government was a possibility declined to be nominated.
207. Ibid., F. 990, p. 107.
208. Jinnah to Wavell, 25 October 1946, ibid., F. 20, p. 101.
209. Ibid., F. 20, p. 216.
210. *TP*, vol. VIII, p. 756.
211. *Hindustan Times*, 21 October 1946, cited in *TP*, vol. VIII, p. 779.
212. Interview with Walt Mason, 6 November 1946, QAP, F. 1012, pp. 141–42.
213. Nehru to Wavell, 30 October 1946, and Pethick-Lawrence to Wavell, *TP*, vol. VIII, pp. 835–36 and 841–42; and Menon, *Transfer of Power*, pp. 320–21.
214. Olaf Caroe to Wavell, 15 October 1946, *TP*, vol. VIII, p. 730; *Wavell: The Viceroy's Journal*, p. 361; and Abul Kalam Azad, *India Wins Freedom*, Calcutta, 1959, pp. 169–70.
215. Jinnah to Wavell, 15 October 1946, QAP, F. 20, pp. 88 and 89; and *TP*, vol. VIII, p. 737.
216. For one version of his visit, see Sir O. Caroe to Wavell, *TP*, vol. VIII, pp. 786–92; and for the transfer of fine money to Bihar, see Viceroy's Personal Report No. 7, 15 May 1947, ibid., vol. X, p. 837.
217. AFM, vol. 359, pp. 22–23; and vol. 515, pp. 1–4 and 8.
218. Sir A. Clow (Bombay) to Wavell, 4 November 1946, *TP*, vol. IX, p. 3; and see also ibid., p. 188.
219. At that time, Sindh had a caretaker government headed by Ghulam Husain Hidayatullah.
220. Sir F. Burrows to Pethick-Lawrence, 20 October 1946, *TP*, vol. VIII, pp. 753–54.
221. The Bihar massacre was extensively documented. For instance, see *The Bihar State Killing 1946: the Official Statement and Resolution of Bihar Provincial Muslim League on the Bihar Massacre of 1946*, Calcutta, 1947; 'Report submitted by Khwaja Nazimuddin, Iftikhar Husain Khan of Mamdot, Malik Firoz Khan Noon, Mian Amiruddin, Maulana Daud Ghaznavi and Mian Mumtaz Muhammad Daultana on the Bihar Massacres, October–November 1946', AFM, vol. 399, pp. 17–30; Syed Jafar Husain, *Whither Bihar*, Patna, 1947; Syed Abdul Aziz, *Reflections on the Bihar Tragedy, 25th Oct.–31st Dec. 1946*, Patna, 1946; Mujtaba Ahmad, *Divide Bihar*, Patna, 1947, AFM, vol. 399; report by a committee consisting of Abul Hashem, Fazlul Haq, Fazlur Rahman, and Dr A.M. Malek, in the *Morning News*, 10 November 1946; and *Report on Bihar Riots (October–November 1946)* by Ranjan Singh Gill, 20 February 1947, Majitha, Amritsar District, Punjab, QAP, F. 965, pp. 69–94.
222. Some slogans reported were: *Khun ka Badla Khun* (Blood for Blood), *Jinnah ko Goli Maro* (Shoot Jinnah) and *Pakistan ko Kabaristan Banado* (Make Pakistan a Graveyard).
223. Report on the Bihar Massacre by Nazimuddin and others, AFM, vol. 399, p. 17; and Sir Francis Tuker, *While Memory Serves: Last Two Years of British Rule in India*, London, 1950, pp. 181–82.
224. Tuker, *While Memory Serves*, p. 198.
225. *The Patna Times*, 29 January 1947; and the *Statesman*, 7 February 1947. Winston Churchill felt that 'Bihar had put into the shade the Armenian atrocities with which Gladstone once stirred the moral sense of Liberal Britain'. Cited in *The Bihar State Killing 1946*; and see also Sharif al Mujahid, 'Communal Riots', *A History of the Freedom Movement*, Karachi, 1970, vol. IV, Parts I & II, 151–58.

226. Secretary, Bihar Provincial Muslim League Relief Committee to Jinnah, 4 December 1946, Jinnah to Pethick Lawrence, 5 December and Pethick-Lawrence to Jinnah, 7 December, QAP, F. 21, pp. 61 and 63.

227. Ibid., F. 7–7A, pp. 2–6.

228. AFM, vol. 193, pp. 68–69; Wavell to Pethick-Lawrence, 12 February 1947, *TP*, vol. IX, p. 683; for Patel's opposition, see Record of Interview between Mountbatten and Patel, 1 April 1947, ibid., vol. X, p. 73; for the Congress ministry's opposition, see H. Dow to Mountbatten, 23 April 1947, ibid., pp. 387–88; and Mountbatten to Jinnah, 9 July 1947, QAP, vol. 1, p. 205.

229. For a resolution of the AIML working committee, see AFM, vol. 142, no. 60.

230. SHC, Bengal-III: 20; and QAP, F. 962, pp. 57–59.

231. The commendable work done by one, M.K. Mir of Lahore, who was designated director-general, Central Bihar Muslim League Relief Committee, Dilkusha, Patna, was widely recognized. Abdul Aziz, *Reflections on the Bihar Tragedy*, p. 13.

232. Statement by Yusuf Haroon, president, and Agha Ghulam Nabi Pathan, secretary, Sindh PML, QAP, F. 832, p. 48.

233. Ibid., F. 565, pp. 102–4.

234. Ibid., F. 296, pp. 56–59; F. 458, p. 57; F. 468, pp. 10–11; F. 565, pp. 120–34 and 151.

235. For Khuhro–Hidayatullah differences on availability of land for the Bihari refugees, and for related issues, see ibid., F. 561, pp. 68–69; and QAP, F. 286, p. 38.

236. Wavell to Pethick-Lawrence, 10 September 1946, *TP*, vol. VIII, pp. 474 and 482; and note by Wavell, 2 December 1946, ibid., vol. IX, p. 241.

237. Ibid., vol. VIII, pp. 355–56, 367.

238. On 31 August, Wavell wrote to Pethick-Lawrence that Jinnah was 'continuing his campaign of abuse against the Congress, [Cabinet] Mission and myself.' Ibid., p. 368.

239. For the Bengal ministry, see ibid., pp. 400, 469 and 485–86; and for the Sindh ministry, see ibid., pp. 418–19, 421–22, 429–30 and 445–47, 448–49, 454, 466, 468–69, 475, 483, 492, 561–62 and 741.

240. For Wavell's note of discussion with Nehru on 1 September 1946, see ibid., p. 384.

241. I., D. Scott to Abell, 2 September 1946; Wavell to Pethick-Lawrence, 4 and 9 September 1946, p. 416; and minute by Abell and Wavell, 6 September 1946, ibid., pp. 398–88, 416, 428 and 471; and for views of Suhrawardy and Nazimuddin and Sir Sultan Ahmad, see ibid., pp. 453, 518–19 and 548–49.

242. Ibid., pp. 628 and 668.

243. *Dawn*, 11 September 1946; and *TP*, vol. VIII, pp. 476–77 and 478.

244. *TP*, vol. VIII, pp. 588, 592

245. Note by Wavell of his interview with Jinnah on 30 October 1946, ibid., pp. 832–34.

246. QAP, F. 20, pp. 107–8.

247. Ahmad, *Speeches and Writings of Mr. Jinnah*, vol. II, pp. 361–66; and *TP*, vol. IX, pp. 73–76.

248. Jinnah to Wavell, 17 November 1946, and note by Wavell of his interview with Jinnah, on 19 November, *TP*, vol. IX, pp. 92–94 and 108–110; and QAP, F. 20, pp. 40, 42 and 104–6.

249. Wavell to Pethick-Lawrence, 17 November 1946, Pethick-Lawrence to Wavell, 18 November 1946; and note by Wavell after an interview with Jinnah, 19 November 1946, *TP*, IX, pp. 91–92, 103–5 and 108.

250. Ahmad, *Speeches and Writings of Mr. Jinnah*, vol. II, pp. 370–71.

251. Nehru to Wavell, 21 November 1946, *TP*, vol. IX, pp. 123–24; and *Hindustan Times*, 22 November 1946.

252. Wavell to Pethick-Lawrence, 23 November 1846, *TP*, vol. IX, pp. 153–54.

253. Ahmad, *Speeches and Writings of Mr. Jinnah*, vol. II, pp. 371–76; and for similar views expressed by Liaquat and Ghazanfar Ali, see *Hindustan Times*, 23 and 25 November 1946; and QAP, F. 1048, pp. 7–8 and 10–11.

254. For instance, see *TP*, vol. VIII, pp. 148, 265, 332 and 353.

255. Ibid., vol. IX, pp. 184–87, 215–17 and 226–27.

256. Jowitt to Pethick-Lawrence, 2 December 1946, ibid., pp. 239–40.

257. Ibid., pp. 240–300. The editors of the *TP* volumes could not trace these documents in the prime minister's archives. Ibid., pp. 253 and 261.

258. Ibid., p. 257. Sardar Patel was advising the acting viceroy, Sir Colville, that if a date was fixed for the transfer of power—he suggested 1 January 1948—Jinnah was 'bound to compromise'. Colville to Pethick-Lawrence, 10 December 1946, ibid., p. 323.

259. Ibid., p. 294.

260. Ibid., pp. 246–48.

261. Ibid., p. 254.

262. Ibid., pp. 265, 274, 280–81 and 291–92.

263. Ibid., pp. 297–300.

264. Sir P. Spens to Sir J. Colville, 10 December 1946, ibid., pp. 324–25.

265. *Dawn*, 22 December 1946.

266. Menon, *Transfer of Power*, pp. 332–33; *Hindustan Times*, 21 December 1946; Burrows to Wavell, 24 December 1946, *TP*, vol. IX, p. 418; and *Dawn*, 26 January 1947.

267. F.C. Bourne to Sir F. Burrows, 17 July 1946, *TP.*, vol. VIII, p. 77.

268. AFM, vol. 142, no. 60; and QAP, F.51, pp. 2–22 and 24–33. All attempts to secure a resolution supporting the League's entry into the constituent assembly by using the governors' pressure on members of the League working committee failed. *TP*, vol. IX, pp. 489, 497, 502 and 529.

269. Ibid., vol. IX, pp. 622, 626, 635, 647–51 and 688–89.

270. Joseph T.A. Burke, private secretary to Attlee, 6 September 1946, ibid., vol. VIII, p. 437; and for Gandhi's views, see ibid., p. 606.

271. Attlee to Wavell, 31 January 1946, and Wavell to Attlee, 5 February 1946, ibid., vol. IX, pp. 582–83 and 624–25.

272. Wavell to Attlee, 20 December 1946, ibid., p. 395.

12

Plans, Partition, and Pakistan, 1947

Even in 1947, the British government and the Congress leadership were unwilling to accept the Pakistan demand. The British policy was reflected in Prime Minister Clement Attlee's statement of 20 February 1947, in which he announced that the British would leave India by a date not later than June 1948, and, if an agreed constitution had not been framed by that date, he mentioned three options for the transfer of power: (*i*) as a whole to some form of central government for British India; or (*ii*) in some areas to the existing provincial governments; or (*iii*) in such other way as might seem most reasonable and 'in the best interest of the Indian people'. Paramountcy in the princely states was not to end earlier than the date for final transfer of power; and for the intervening period, the relations of the crown with the individual states would be adjusted by agreement. And the commercial relations between India and Britain would continue to their mutual advantage.[1] Attlee further elucidated this policy in his letter to Lord Louis Mountbatten on 18 March 1947, in which he instructed the viceroy-designate 'to avoid partition and obtain a unitary government' for British India and the states and 'keep the Indian army undivided and to retain India within the Commonwealth' and if he failed to achieve that, he was asked to make his own recommendations by 1 October 1947.[2] The Congress standpoint was that the All-India Muslim League should accept the Cabinet Mission Plan but with its interpretation and reservations; and if that was not acceptable to the League, the authority in British India should be immediately demitted to the existing interim government on the basis of a suitably modified Act of 1935. Consequently, Mountbatten and the Congress leaders were inflexibly committed to a united India and hardly concealed their intention that if they were pushed into a situation where they were left with no option, they would concede Pakistan in such a shape that it would be unacceptable to the All-India Muslim League. They mutually agreed that speedy transfer of power without the division of the armed forces would make the creation of Pakistan of the League's conception impossible and did not calculate or care for the consequences. Thus, the scales were clearly tilted against the League, which had to strategize in this uncongenial atmosphere to persuade the British and the Congress to accept its demand for Pakistan.

(A) THE LAST VICEROY

On 23 March 1947, Lord Mountbatten took over as the last viceroy of India. Although he had never held any official position in India, he had developed friendly relations with Nehru who had met him during his visit to Singapore during the war. In addition to his own ambitions, Nehru's confidence in him was an important factor in his selection by the British government and unreserved acceptance by the Congress. Attlee and Cripps manoeuvred Wavell's unceremonious 'dismissal' and Mountbatten's appointment as the viceroy.[3] It might be debated whether or not he had plenipotentiary powers but he came to exercise wide discretionary powers in that post-war era of confusion and turmoil by his own skilful handling of the situation. A close relative of the British royalty and commander of the allied forces in South-east Asia during the war, he never felt shy to project himself as a war hero to boost up his status and authority among the Indians. He had a freer hand than all his predecessors in dealing with the political situation in India: the secretary of state for India was changed to meet his wishes and he was allowed to take British staff of his choice. The staff that he selected was: Lord Hastings Lionel Ismay, a former Indian army officer and a close friend of Churchill, as chief of staff, Sir Eric Charles Mieville who had been private secretary to a former viceroy, Lord Willingdon (1866–1941), and assistant private secretary to King George VI, as principal secretary, Captain Ronald Vernon Brockman as personal secretary, Lieutenant Colonel V.F. Erskine Crum (1918–1971) as conference secretary and Alan Campbell-Johnson as press attaché. The British members who were already on the viceroy's staff like George E.B. Abell, private secretary, and Ian Dixon Scott, deputy private secretary, were retained and they easily adjusted themselves with the new staff. But V.P. Menon who was also part of the viceroy's secretariat took some time to gain acceptability; at first, on Abell's advice, he was not invited to the viceroy's staff meetings at which the plan for the transfer of power was discussed and finalized, and which Ismay took to London on 2 May; the reason for this discrimination was his 'genuinely' pro-Congress viewpoint.[4] The first Mountbatten-chaired staff meeting that he attended was the twenty-seventh that was held on 7 May, and from then onward he became a key figure in these meetings.[5]

Besides his own predilections, Mountbatten's 'mandate' required him to befriend the Congress rather than the League. Prime Minister Attlee had given him primarily three instructions: to secure a unitary government for India; to preserve the unity of the armed forces; and to keep India within the British Commonwealth. The first two points were important for both the British and the Congress for emotional and security reasons; and the Congress could use the third point as bait to extract concessions from the British government because the constituent assembly had already passed a resolution declaring India an 'independent sovereign Republic' and entry into the commonwealth required its reversal or suitable modification. The League's position was diametrically opposed to what Mountbatten had been mandated to achieve: it stood for the partition of India and creation of Pakistan and division of the armed forces. Mountbatten faithfully followed his mandate. While he showed cordiality in his interaction with the Congress leaders, he often used threats to coerce Jinnah to accept his viewpoint.[6] Endowed with remarkable personal qualities, he did his best to employ them to fulfil his responsibilities. He could be unbelievably flexible; and whenever any of his proposals was turned down, he would immediately come up with possible alternatives without any hesitation or embarrassment. He felt no qualm to hide, distort or falsify information to achieve his goal. He adopted a novel procedure to work out a plan. He held regular discussions on the constitutional issues with his staff; before 7 May, exclusively with his British staff, and after that, V.P. Menon was included in these discussions. The proceedings of these meetings were recorded as 'Minutes of Viceroy's Staff Meeting', and some of their parts were not meant for circulation, which were preserved as 'Uncirculated Record of Discussion'. The meetings or interviews that he along with one or more members of his British staff had with the Indian leaders were recorded as 'Miscellaneous Meetings' or as 'Record of Interview' between Mountbatten and a particular Indian leader(s). A two-day governors' conference on 15–16 April, discussed the constitutional proposals that had been evolved till that time. The documents relating to these meetings are an invaluable source for understanding the evolution of the plan and the issues involved in the transfer of power. His British staff prepared and finalized the plan that Ismay took to London on 2 May; V.P. Menon who had unmatched drafting skills assisted them in drafting some of its parts but he was not shown the whole text of the draft plan.[7] Mountbatten kept Nehru regularly informed at different stages of the plan but kept the League leaders in the dark about its exact details.

(B) THE CONGRESS AMBITIONS

The Congress was determined to preserve the unity of India and prevent the creation of Pakistan at all cost. Its leaders believed that if the British government speedily transferred power to the existing interim government, or under the Cabinet Mission Plan with the modifications suggested by them, without the division of the Armed forces, they could keep India united and control any adverse post-transfer situation. They seriously pursued this strategy. Gandhi was one of its ardent advocates. On 1 April 1947, he suggested a formula to Mountbatten based on this strategy that he should invite Jinnah to form the central government as prime minister, with power to select all his ministers and reiterated it on 8 May.[8] The Congress, he promised, would support all his policies by its majority in the Legislature if these were 'in the interest of the people as a whole' — the people's interest would be decided by Mountbatten who would stay on as the viceroy to act as 'an umpire' with 'veto power' until June 1948; and after that, power should be handed over to that central government. There would be no Muslim League National Guards or any private army. If Jinnah refused to accept this formula, which would definitely have been the case, similar offer should be made to the Congress.[9] Mountbatten told Gandhi that he could not propose such a formula to Jinnah without the 'unreserved acceptance' of the Cabinet Mission Plan by the Congress.[10] When Gandhi discussed his formula with that condition with Nehru and other members of the Congress working committee, none, except Abdul Ghaffar Khan, supported his formula. Even then, he advised Mountbatten to 'go ahead' with the formula on his own initiative and strengthen the interim government for the next fourteen months; after which he should transfer power to the central government. Still later, in May, foreseeing the partition of India, he reiterated his formula and asked Mountbatten to hand over power either to the League or the Congress on the basis of dominion status and to leave the Indians 'to their own devices'.[11] When the partition plan was near finalization in London, he urged the British at a prayer meeting, 'to withdraw and leave India, if possible . . . in an orderly manner but withdraw in any case on or before the promised date, maybe even in chaos'.[12] He was not alone in making such demands.

Quite a few Congress leaders and supporters came up with similar demands. Acharya J.B. Kripalani (1888–1982), then Congress president, asked the British government to demit power to the existing interim government on the basis of dominion status, with the viceroy as the constitutional head, and that government should decide the future of India after June 1948.[13] On 17 April, Krishna Menon, Nehru's close confidante, proposed to Mountbatten that if 'the British were to give us now [undivided India on] Dominion Status [basis] . . . we should be so grateful that not a voice would be heard in June 1948, suggesting any change'.[14] V.P Menon, the manifestly pro-Congress reform commissioner, even before Mountbatten's arrival as the viceroy, had sent with Patel's approval and Wavell's concurrence a plan for the demission of power to the existing interim government on the basis of full dominion status by a special messenger to the secretary of state for India, which, however, did not receive approval in London.[15] On 5 April, he presented a similar plan to Mountbatten's principal secretary, Sir Eric Mieville, in case Gandhi's formula was not acceptable to Jinnah; and a modified version of the same plan was attached as an appendix to the 'Dickie Bird Plan', the plan that Ismay took to London on 2 May.[16] So did Sir B.N. Rau, another pro-Congress constitutional expert attached to the viceroy's secretariat. Sardar Patel also made a similar proposal for the transfer of power in his meetings with the viceroy and then in a press statement on 9 May.[17] And the spirit behind the ambition of Brigadier K.K.M. Cariappa (1899–1993)—who after independence became the first Indian chief of army staff and was honoured with the title of field marshal—to establish 'military dictatorship' after the British withdrawal from India was meant to keep India united by force.[18] Cariappa propagated his views among the Indian army officers at the Staff College; and one Muslim student, Mr Naqvi, reported the matter to Liaquat. This propaganda and Cariappa's statement supported by senior Indian army officers and the commander-in-chief that it would take at least five years to make the Indian army 'stand on its legs' alarmed the League leaders who pointed out to Mountbatten the Congress ambition to seize power by a coup d'état and demanded division of the armed forces before the transfer of power.[19] When Cariappa mentioned his proposal of a military takeover to Lord Ismay, the latter warned him that it was 'impractical' and 'highly dangerous', counselling him that army rule had 'proved tyrannical and incompetent' throughout history and that the army 'must always be servant and not masters'. He asked him to put the idea 'out of his mind' and never mention it 'again even in the strictest secrecy'.[20]

The best bet for the Congress to keep India united was Nehru whose friendship with Mountbatten deepened after his assumption of viceroyalty of India. The Congress leaders were privy to this cordiality between him and Mountbatten; and for that reason, it appears, the party virtually assigned Nehru the task of negotiations with the viceroy. More importantly, in addition to this friendliness, Mountbatten's 'independent and impartial conclusions' and Nehru's views on basic constitutional issues were identical, i.e. both wanted 'a unified India with a strong centre'.[21] Before Mountbatten's arrival in India, Krishna Menon as Nehru's emissary had twice met the viceroy-designate in London; and, in the meeting on 13 March 1947, he had discussed with Mountbatten a strategy for the transfer of power, in which both agreed that if it was eventually impossible to keep India united and establishment of Pakistan became 'inevitable', the 'outer line of India must remain intact', i.e. Pakistan should be confined to Sindh and west Punjab, and it should be surrounded by India-controlled territories. On 14 June, after reminding Mountbatten about his discussions in London, he wrote, 'If Kashmir and N.W.F.P. go to Pakistan, all hopes of the (3rd June) plan being a settlement will prove fanciful'.[22] The Congress leadership had devised its 'outer line' strategy much before Mountbatten's assumption of viceroyalty. When did it actually do that? It is difficult to pinpoint its exact timing but the Congress began to implement it when it joined the interim government and the British transferred the authority over the tribal areas from the governor-general to member in charge of external affairs; and Nehru visited the tribal areas to demonstrate his authority. Mountbatten and Nehru exerted to follow the 'outer line' strategy before and after the 3 June Plan. The Congress adopted an ingenious strategy in the pursuit of its policies. Despite its leaders' own collusion with the Labour leaders and Mountbatten, they missed no opportunity to propagate that the British were supporting the League and its demand for Pakistan.[23]

(C) ALL-INDIA MUSLIM LEAGUE'S STRATEGY

The League on its part had little leeway to influence the decision-making process in New Delhi or in London. Jinnah's denunciation of the British policies vis-à-vis Muslim India and Muslim Middle East had alienated the British prime minister and members of his cabinet who were even otherwise opposed to the Pakistan scheme. The Leaguers hardly knew Mountbatten before his assumption of viceroyalty and were ignorant about his fascination for a united India and the level of his understanding with Nehru. They had no means to know directly the exact contents of the plan that he evolved. Their knowledge of its details was mostly indirect and limited to whatever they could glean by their interaction with Mountbatten and his staff or through the assertions of the Congress leaders or by press reports. What the League could do in these circumstances was that it could simply press the demand for a fully sovereign Pakistan with its own armed forces or invoke the British promises made to the Indian Muslims during the war. After its July 1946 resolutions, it had focused its energies on consolidating its position in the Pakistan provinces and the tribal areas. Besides, it had struggled to protect its ministries in Bengal and Sindh and blocked every move that was aimed at its removal from power in these provinces. Mounting communal tension following the riots in Bengal and Bihar and re-admission of Fazlul Haq and his group into the League in October 1946, provided it with a comfortable majority in the Bengal assembly that strengthened the position of its ministry; and fresh elections in Sindh on 9 December 1946, ensured its clear majority in the Sindh assembly and the stability of its ministry. Jinnah's long stay at Mastung and Quetta had contributed to broaden its influence among the people of Balochistan that included the non-official members of the Quetta municipality and the sardars of the Shahi Jirga, which functioned as a substitute for an elected legislature. By a prudent strategy, it had secured the victory of a pro-League sardar against the Congress-supported candidate by a wide margin on the only seat allocated for British Balochistan in the constituent assembly. There was no threat to its position here from any local or all-India political party. Then, it began to prepare itself overtly and in secrecy for civil disobedience in the three remaining 'Pakistan provinces'—Punjab, the NWFP and Assam.[24] The provincial Muslim League committees of action in these provinces were re-formed to organize and mobilize various elements of the Muslim society. The Khurshid Enver-organized Muslim League National Guards in the Punjab and NWFP and the volunteers of the Muslim Students Federation and women's committees served as the vanguard. These movements plus the diminished capacity of the British Indian administration to control the law and order situation, Liaquat's 'poor man's budget', the negative effects of the Mountbatten–Nehru/Congress collusion, the August 1940 Declaration and above all Jinnah's unrivalled skills at negotiations eventually resulted in the creation of Pakistan. Ultimately, the British government finalized the plan for the transfer of power that was initially prepared by Mountbatten and his British staff, and then revised by him in consultation with the Congress leaders.

(*i*) *Civil Disobedience Movement.* The civil disobedience movements consolidated the position of the League in the Punjab, the NWFP and Assam and served as a constant pressure on the British and Congress leadership to accept the Pakistan demand. The provincial Muslim League committees of action, which had been reorganized after the July 1946 resolutions, made the preparations for the civil disobedience movements without much overt display of their activities.[25] In November 1946, when the Punjab provincial Muslim League's preparatory activities especially those of the Muslim League National Guards worried Governor Jenkins, he promulgated the Punjab public safety ordinance without Chief Minister Khizr's active involvement.[26] Its use in the arrest of Muslim League National Guards who were returning from the campaign in the Dera Ghazi Khan bye-election triggered the civil disobedience movement in the Punjab. Jenkins fully backed the anti-civil disobedience movement actions of the Unionist–Congress–Akali coalition ministry. Despite all the restrictions, the civil disobedience movement gained momentum when on 24 January, the Unionist ministry under Jenkins' direction banned the Muslim League National Guards with a simultaneous ban on the Rashtriya Swayamsevak Sangh under the Criminal Law (Amendment) Act in a show of impartiality.[27] The real object was to contain the rapidly expanding influence of the League and the Muslim League National Guards. The Punjab committee of action brought in volunteers of the Muslim Students Federation and women's committees into the civil disobedience movement to raise its tempo. The Punjab police, in an attempt to find out its real strength, unwittingly launched a search operation. The provincial Muslim League leaders put up resistance when it came to search the Muslim League National Guard headquarters, and seven top leaders—Iftikhar Mamdot, Mumtaz

Daultana, Firoz Khan Noon, Shaukat Hayat, Iftikharuddin, Begum Shahnawaz, and Amir Husain Shah, head of the Punjab Muslim League National Guards—courted arrest.[28] These arrests inflamed Muslim sentiments, and the demonstrators clashed with the police in several cities, leading to further arrests. The League branches organized hartals and passed resolutions all over India, condemning the Punjab government's action; and some Leaguers from outside the Punjab pressured to join the protesters.[29] Khizr could not stand the pressure. He held talks with the Punjab provincial Muslim League that led to the release of its leaders and lifting of the ban on the Muslim League National Guards and Rashtriya Swayamsevak Sangh. The provincial Muslim League then transformed its movement into one for 'civil liberties'. Again, there were large-scale arrests including those of members of the provincial assembly and about thirteen thousand political workers. Punjab witnessed unprecedented unrest and it had to be practically cordoned off to block the entry of the League supporters from outside the province. The Military was called in Amritsar to control the situation. Amidst demonstrations in Lahore, a female student (Fatima Sughra) hoisted the League flag on the Punjab civil secretariat building. No mediation efforts including that of Nazimuddin could bring about reconciliation.[30] Faced with a popular Muslim upsurge, Khizr was no longer willing to withstand this renewed pressure and, on 2 March, resigned as chief minister, giving Governor Jenkins eight hours', and his non-Muslim colleagues four hours', notice of his resignation.[31]

The Leaguers were jubilant that they had successfully dislodged the Unionists from power and called off the movement for 'civil liberties' but frustration awaited them when they made moves to form a ministry.[32] The authority to form the ministry rested with the governor. The League could not do much about it. Communal riots that erupted in Rawalpindi, Multan, Amritsar and elsewhere—for which the Hindus and Sikhs gave ample provocation by denouncing Jinnah and the League demand in widely organized anti-Pakistan meetings and processions—and their possible escalation were used to oppose the installation of a League-led ministry.[33] Although the riots were controlled but the violence in the Rawalpindi division especially in the small town of Kahota was used against the League.[34] Muslims denied that they were the aggressors in these riots and, according to the communists, the Akalis backed by the Congress and the Rashtriya Swayamsevak Sangh were the real aggressors.[35] Besides, the 'preponderantly non-Muslim' special investigation staff appointed to inquire into these disturbances and the deputy inspector general, Rawalpindi division (James Alexander Scott), in particular, the League alleged, were 'hostile to the Muslims'.[36] The opposition to a League-controlled Punjab was even otherwise not unexpected because it could result in a larger Pakistan. Therefore, contrary to the spirit of the Act of 1935 and parliamentary norms, Jenkins assumed a partisan role and resisted the formation of a League ministry, though a day after Khizr's resignation he had on his advice invited Mamdot, the League assembly party leader, to form a ministry and gave him time till 8 March, for its formation.[37] Meanwhile, he manoeuvred the imposition of section 93 (governor's rule) in the province and then, along with the Congress and Sikh leaders, indulged in bizarre plans for the governance of the Punjab on a system based on two or three regional ministries with one governor but could implement none of these plans, leaving the situation fluid and fertile for the growth of communalism.[38] Jenkins and the Congress skilfully pushed the Sikhs to the forefront to oppose a League-led ministry transforming the conflict virtually into a Sikh–Muslim issue; the underlying object was to negate the Pakistan scheme. On 5 March, Jenkins took lightly Mamdot's claims of a majority and, instead of installing him in office, asked him to conciliate the Hindus and the Sikhs; and, two weeks later, he was himself threatening to resign along with all the British officers in the Punjab if the League was put in power; and Mountbatten on assuming the viceroyalty fully supported him.[39] On 23 and 28 April, Mamdot demanded in writing that he should be allowed to form the ministry, claiming the support of 91 members of the legislative assembly (Muslims 84, Scheduled Castes 4 and Christians 3) in a house 175 members and offering to face the assembly within twenty-four hours.[40] His contention was that in several Hindu majority provinces exclusively one-party or one-community ministries were in office and 'it would be illogical to impose an exception contrary to all primary democratic principles only in the case of the Punjab'.[41] Both Jenkins and Mountbatten used the pretext of possible Sikh reaction, and asked Mamdot to wait for the fate of the Punjab in the plan for the transfer of power.[42] When Jinnah and Liaquat jointly raised the issue with Mountbatten on 2 May, his response was quite interesting, that it would be 'a gross act of betrayal to the Muslim League' to install its ministry and that he (Mountbatten) might 'well have saved the Punjab for Mr Jinnah by not allowing Mamdot to form a ministry'![43] But now even Khizr's support to a League-led ministry made no difference; and when, on 14 May, Mamdot again wrote to Jenkins, repeating the demand, the latter with Mountbatten's approval formally asked him to wait for a review of the Punjab situation after the leaders' meeting on 2 June. The resistance to the formation of a League ministry was really meant to cover up the partition of the Punjab. Jinnah in his meetings with Mountbatten and public statements consistently opposed the partition of the Punjab, as the League's demand visualized Pakistan based on undivided provinces.

The NWFP was crucial for the Congress strategy to keep the 'outer line of India' under its control. The Frontier provincial Muslim League blunted that strategy and played a decisive role in the final phase of the Pakistan movement. Although due to the intra-provincial Muslim League conflicts, the Congress-controlled NWFP administration and its manipulation of resources in that era of scarcity of commodities of daily use and its influence on the election machinery, the Congress had secured a majority of seats in the general elections but even then the League had demonstrated more popular Muslim support at the grassroots than the Congress: it secured 147,940 Muslim votes as against 136,201 votes polled by the Congress–Khudai Khidmatgars. The provincial Muslim League's and Muslim League National Guards' post-election reorganization, denunciation of the Congress policies and exploitation of sensitive issues like the Bihar massacre of the Muslims with whom the Pathans had historical links radically changed the political scene in the NWFP. During November 1946–January 1947, a provincial Muslim League fact-finding deputation and half a dozen medical missions accompanied by dozens of volunteers went from the NWFP to Bihar and their members brought back horrific accounts of atrocities.[44] The Leaguers recounted the Bihar tragedy in meetings and processions organized in different cities and towns including a province-wide 'Bihar Day' on 8 November. It was easy for the provincial Muslim League committee of action, Muslim League National Guards, Frontier Muslim Students Federation, Women's Committee, and pro-League Jamiatul Ulama and Jamiatul Asfia to expand their network in such an emotionally charged atmosphere.[45] At first, in December 1946, there was unrest and violence in the Hazara district and raids of the 'Black Mountain' tribes. The army was used to control the situation. The Leaguers in Peshawar and other districts observed 17 January 1947, as the 'Hazara Day' to sympathize with those who suffered in these events. The League waited for the Kamalzai (Mardan) bye-election that was scheduled in mid-February 1947, which its candidate won by a significant margin, to launch a full-fledged civil disobedience movement in the province. Jinnah justified the movement, arguing that 'whereas in other countries there were many ways, for example bye-elections', to demonstrate 'the loss of confidence of the people' in governments, in India the only way to show that was 'by means of demonstrations'; and he called for fresh elections in view of the Congress defeat in the bye-election and the impending transfer of power.[46]

The Frontier League set up a provincial 'war council' headed by the young energetic Aminul Hasnat, Pir Sahib of Manki Sharif, who had considerable influence in the tribal areas as well, with some Leaguers put in charge of the movement in various districts, and kept contact with Jinnah through private emissaries. The quiet work that the Pir Manki-chaired committee of action, Khurshid Enver-organized Muslim League National Guards, Frontier Muslim Students Federation and Women's Committee had done since the adoption of the July 1946 resolutions now bore fruit. The male and female Leaguers from outside the province came to the NWFP to extend their support. The League devised novel techniques to counter the well-financed Congress propaganda that included distortion of news through the Mehr Chand Khanna-controlled All India Radio news bulletins about the NWFP and free distribution of copies of the weekly *Pakhtun*. Besides the daily demonstrations, the pro-League newspapers increased the number of their publications and some Leaguers established a secret radio station, *Sada-i-Pakistan*, to disseminate news about the civil disobedience movement.[47] The Congress ministry desperately tried to contain the civil disobedience movement by putting a ban on meetings and demonstrations and by arresting the League leaders, except Pir Manki, and workers.[48] Consequently, jails were soon full and overcrowded; and the use of troops and twenty-four hours' curfew in Peshawar and other cities could not stop the daily defiance of the ban.[49] Abdul Ghani-organized Zalme Pakhtun armed by 'some official rifles' could not scare the Leaguers.[50] When nothing worked, Pir Manki was also arrested on 28 March; after that, the Tribal areas could not remain unaffected, which added to the British concerns for security. Foreseeing the League's ascendancy in the NWFP, Mountbatten approached Jinnah to visit the Frontier to calm down the situation or to invite the Frontier Leaguers to come and see him in Delhi; but Jinnah refused to do that until everything was formalized and agreed to issue only an appeal to his supporters 'to refrain from violence'.[51] After the governors' conference and his discussions with Nehru, Caroe and Dr Khan Sahib, Mountbatten himself visited the NWFP to assess personally the prevailing situation after getting assurances from Jinnah that the Leaguers would hold merely a peaceful demonstration.[52] During the visit, he told the Congress ministry that he would have to go into Section 93 to ensure fairness of elections although Dr Khan Sahib disagreed with his estimation; on his return from the visit, he informed Nehru that only election could restore peace in the Frontier.[53] The Leaguers refused to leave the jails when the Congress ministry decided to release all political prisoners,[54] and the provincial Muslim League did not call off the movement even after the informal promise of fresh elections. When the League leaders who were released on parole met Jinnah in Delhi, it was decided to continue the movement peacefully. The League-led civil disobedience movement pressure produced positive result although Mountbatten shifted his stance from general elections under section 93 to referendum without any assurance about elections if the vote went in favour of Pakistan.

Before the Second World War, the three communities in Assam— Muslims, Hindus and tribals—were population-wise almost evenly balanced. But the large-scale Bengali Muslim migration into Assam following the Bengal famine and official 'Grow More Food' policy during the war radically altered the demographic balance; by 1947, the Muslims constituted the largest, if not the majority, community in Assam and actually had a majority in many parts other than Sylhet.[55] However, the Line System deprived them of their rightful status in Assam, and the Bardoloi-led Congress ministry supported by the Congress central leadership resolutely resisted any change in that System and strictly enforced the policy of eviction of 'illegal migrants'. The intra-provincial Muslim League conflicts in Assam had hurt the party's solidarity and its capacity to follow a unified policy. But Abdul Hamid Bhashani, the Assam League president, persistently demanded the abolition of the Line System and opposed the policy of eviction of migrants. In January 1947, the Assam provincial Muslim League under his leadership launched the civil disobedience movement while the Congress ministry used the security forces to preserve the line system. Heavy casualties could not end the eviction policy because a basic issue was involved in its continuance: if the Line System was abolished and evictions were stopped, the Muslims would definitely emerge as the dominant community in Assam, and then it would be impossible to obstruct the accession of the whole of Assam to Pakistan.[56] The fixation of 1941 census in the partition plan as the bench mark for exercising the option of accession to Pakistan or Hindustan was meant to prevent that possibility because Assam was the only region that had undergone radical demographic changes during the war. The Bardoloi Congress ministry opposed the surrender of any part of Assam to Pakistan, and the accession of only Sylhet district was largely the result of the Congress strategy and the pressure of the League's civil disobedience movement.

(*ii*) *Tribal Areas.* The tribal areas of the North-West Frontier, inhabited by *azad qabail* (independent tribes), known for their spirit of independence and love of Islam, was within the 'outer line of India'. Whatever were the reasons—whether it was British reluctance to pursue a forward policy, the difficulties of the terrain, or the human and material cost of keeping the tribal areas under direct control without any economic benefits in return—, the British had followed a policy that had vacillated between annexation of the tribal areas and keeping it under indirect control through the governor-general. Following the Khilafat movement and surfacing of the Palestine issue, the unrest in the tribal areas had frequently been marked by resistance to the British rule and tribal raids into the settled districts. The British had tried to maintain their hold by punitive military expeditions and aerial bombing. The League had condemned this 'inhuman and uncivilized' method of control as well as the tribal raids into the settled districts.[57] During the Second World War, the Khudai Khidmatgars tried to establish contacts in the tribal areas but their linkage with the Hindu-dominated Congress proved a hindrance; and because of that association, the tribes did not welcome them.[58] On the contrary, Jinnah's emissaries to the tribal elders and religious figures brought back positive response. For instance, in May–July 1944, Maulana Midrarullah of the pro-League Jamiatul Ulama toured the Mohmand, Charmung, Bajaur and Jandul areas to familiarize the people with the League and its Pakistan demand and conveyed Jinnah's message to Badshah Gul at Ghaziabad and Gul Sahib in Bajaur.[59] The League stepped up these contacts with the tribal religious and spiritual leaders in the tribal areas when the Cabinet Mission was discussing the future of India.[60] The League-tribes interaction deepened after the League's withdrawal of acceptance of the Cabinet Mission Plan and the observance of Direct Action Day; Pir of Manki and Abdul Qayyum Khan were among those who made a vital contribution in this connection.

Another factor that strengthened the League-tribes bond was the constitutional position of the tribal areas and the aspirations of the tribes. The League and the Congress held conflicting views on the future of the tribal areas: the League supported the tribes' struggle to preserve their 'distinctive culture' and 'internal independence' while the Congress wanted merger of the tribal areas into the NWFP.[61] According to the Act of 1935, the governor-general had jurisdiction over the tribal areas, which he exercised in his discretion and could direct the governor to act as his agent.[62] Surprisingly, when the Congress joined the interim government and Nehru took over the portfolio of external affairs, the authority over the tribal areas was transferred from the governor-general to external affairs.[63] Immediately on takeover as member, external affairs, Nehru decided to pay a one-week visit to the tribal areas to demonstrate his authority and to counter the pro-League and pro-Pakistan sentiments that prevailed in the tribal areas.[64] If the Congress had calculated to implement any strategy of controlling the 'outer line of India' by this visit, it was in for a rude shock. Nehru was confronted with hostile demonstrations of tribesmen wherever he went in the tribal areas, whether it was Miran Shah, Razmak, Wana, Tank, Landi Kotal, Malakand or Dargai.[65] Shaikh Mahbub Ali, the Political Agent, was wrongly accused of instigating the demonstrations at Malakand and a judicial inquiry instituted on Nehru's complaint exonerated him of the charge.[66] In fact, the tribes saw in Nehru's visit the advent of a Hindu-dominated government at the centre. Abdul Ghaffar Khan and Dr Khan Sahib who accompanied him on this tour damaged their own image in the tribal belt. Nehru's visit 'unwittingly' proved 'an effective instrument' of the League propaganda and, according to one Leaguer, the League achieved within one week what it could not have done 'in several years'.[67] Nevertheless, the Congress leadership did not give up easily. Before Nehru's visit, Abdul Ghaffar Khan had foreshadowed the tribal areas–NWFP merger; and after the visit, on 2 December 1946, Dr Khan Sahib at a press conference and, on 1 April 1947, Qazi Ataullah in Bannu boastfully hinted at a five-year merger plan.[68] The Congress moves in the constituent assembly added to the apprehensions of the tribes about the future of the tribal areas and brought them closer to the League.

The Cabinet Mission Plan had provided for a constituent assembly-appointed tribal advisory committee to determine the status of the tribal areas in the future constitution. In February 1947, the Congress-dominated constituent assembly, which had proceeded with the constitution-making process unilaterally, appointed an advisory committee with Sardar Patel as its chairman, which planned to visit the tribal areas. The tribes immediately reacted to this move; and on 6 March, a tribal Jirga of the Waziristan elders held out a warning that the reception of the Patel Committee in the tribal areas would be 'more disgraceful than that of Jawaharlal'.[69] The League encouraged and mobilized them in their pro-Pakistan and anti-Congress moves. On 15 March, a Jirga of the Afridi tribe asked Governor Caroe to convey it 'to the proper quarter' that they were not prepared to deal with the advisory committee of the present constituent assembly, which they regarded as 'purely a Hindu body'.[70] Then, on 20 March, the Waziristan tribes (Wazirs, Mahsuds and Bhitttanis) at a joint Jirga of prominent tribal figures in Spinkai Raghzai unanimously passed three resolutions. In the first resolution, the Jirga resolved that 'it is our birthright to have Pakistan. The very intention of the Hindus to dominate Muslim India would be crushed. If we don't get our goal by a political settlement, we would have it by bullet. We must have Pakistan whatever the consequences may be'. The second resolution called on Dr Khan Sahib to resign or else 'the situation in the province would be far worse' if he remained in office. In the third resolution, the Patel Committee was warned to stay in Delhi otherwise the 'consequences would be very grave'. Early in March 1947, a Waziristan Muslim League with its head office in Tank had been established. Sher Badshah Khan Mahsud, office secretary of the League, sent copies of the three resolutions to the viceroy, governor, Jinnah, Nehru, Patel, Dr Khan Sahib, political agent of South Waziristan and the press, along with a list of the prominent participants in the joint Jirga.[71] The tribes did not slacken their pressure.[72] The League with its limited resources extended them full support. When Mountbatten visited the NWFP, the representatives of the Afridis, Shinwaris, Salmanis and Kullaghoris at Landi Kotal and those of Waziristan tribes—Mahsuds, Wazirs and Daurs—at the Government House in Peshawar conveyed to him that 'in no circumstances will they come under Hindu domination—they would sooner make terms with Afghanistan than do that. The Mahsuds and Wazirs pressed hard for Pakistan and the dismissal of the Congress government'.[73] The pressure that the League built up in the NWFP and tribal areas critically influenced the decision of the British government and the Congress leadership to accept the Pakistan demand.[74]

(*iii*) *Liaquat as Finance Member*. When the League entered the interim government, it had demanded one of the three portfolios, defence, external affairs or home, but the Congress refused to surrender any of them. The only significant portfolio that it got was that of finance. Even that portfolio was given with the confidence that the League Member would not be able to get services of any senior financial expert and that it would have to depend on non-Muslim officers in the finance department. Even otherwise, the general impression in the subcontinent had been that Muslims had neither the liking for finance nor the requisite expertise in handling financial matters. The governance in the provinces under the Act of 1935 confirmed that belief. The portfolios of finance and revenue in the Muslim majority provinces had invariably been held by non-Muslims or when these portfolios were held by the chief ministers they were administered in effect with the help of non-Muslim finance officers. Liaquat as member of finance negated that impression by his skilful handling of this portfolio with the help of young Muslim bureaucrats. Through this portfolio, he came to exercise influence in departments other than finance by subjecting even the smallest expenditure to the minutest scrutiny and sought justification for every item requiring finances.

Hindu capitalists who controlled business and industry had amassed huge profits during the war. They were the main financiers of the Congress and its campaigns. Liaquat was determined to use the central budget for the year 1947–48 to erode that financial support-base of the Congress and push forward the League cause. His 'Poor Man's Budget', as it was popularly referred to for its 'social objectives', was meant to 'even out the glaring disparities' between the income levels of a small wealthy class and the poverty-stricken masses. Its taxation proposals (the business profits tax, the capital gains tax, the corporation tax and the lowering of the super tax levels) and measures against tax evasion hit the Congress financiers, the Hindu industrialists and businessmen. His proposals had the support of the Leaguers and 'a large proportion of the Congress backbenchers'.[75] He was determined to expose the 'socialist' credentials of the Congress and its leaders; on 13 March, he had written to Jinnah, 'I have got the Congress fellows in a tight corner and I am going to fight to the last ditch. . . . It means a great strain but the cause is too great to think of . . . little matters. One comes to this world only once and one must do his duty irrespective of what it costs him'.[76] His proposals imposed 25 per cent tax on business profits exceeding Rs 1 lakh. On Mountbatten's intervention, the business profits tax was brought down to 16.66 per cent with abatement of 6 per cent on capital, which the Congress still considered high but it accepted the *fait accompli* because it was sensitive to public impression that big business influenced its policies.[77] Liaquat's handling of the finance portfolio played a significant role in persuading the Congress leadership to accept the Pakistan demand.

(D) EVOLUTION OF THE PARTITION PLAN

(*i*) *'Dickie Bird' Plan.* Lord Mountbatten liked the Cabinet Mission Plan, which he regarded the 'ideal solution'; but that Plan in his view provided a weak centre and he looked for a strong centre.[78] Consequently, he drafted his own plan as a possible alternative by modifying the Cabinet Mission Plan; and, on 31 March, just eight days after his arrival and before his meetings with Jinnah, discussed it with his British staff. His plan presented 'a form of Partition', in which India was divided into three units: Hindustan, to include the predominantly Hindu provinces; Pakistan, to include predominantly Muslim provinces; and the states. Each unit was to have dominion status; and the number of units could be increased if larger states or groups of smaller states were accorded similar status. Punjab and Bengal were to be partitioned, as Nehru had advised him in his very first meeting. A central authority—called 'central government' or 'central council', consisting of representatives of the units—was to deal with reserved subjects of defence, foreign affairs, communications and food; and finance required to administer them, with veto power to the viceroy for these subjects. The central authority and the Hindustan government would be situated in Delhi, but difficulty was seen in forming and locating the Pakistan government. Three 'prototypes' were envisaged for the future constitution of India: those of the USA, USSR and the Australian Commonwealth. This plan was to be implemented in May 1947, and about three months before June 1948, it would be decided whether or not the central authority should remain after that date.[79] Mountbatten and, on his direction, his British staff deliberately created an impression that the Viceroy was working on more than one option, and if the Indian political parties did not accept the Cabinet Mission Plan, he would go for one of those options.[80] Such tactics were used to camouflage the actual contents of Mountbatten's plan. On Nehru's advice, Mountbatten held his talks with Jinnah on wrong assumptions, that he could 'frighten' the League president to accept a unitary government for India and abandon 'Pakistan' by simply suggesting limited time available for the transfer of power or by merely mentioning the possibility of partition of the Punjab and Bengal.[81] From 5 to 10 April, he held intensive talks with Jinnah on all constitutional issues including a unitary government for India based on the Cabinet Mission Plan or any similar plan, without mentioning his own plan, in six meetings — each meeting lasting 2–3 hours. But his position on crucial issues was poles apart from that of Jinnah. For the League, the Cabinet Mission Plan or for that matter any plan advocating a united India was a 'dead' issue, and Jinnah did not mince words in its rejection. He felt that the Cabinet Mission Plan could have worked 'in a spirit of cooperation and mutual trust', and there was 'some prospect' in May 1946, that such an atmosphere 'could be created', but after the lapse of one year that was not possible. The League was so disillusioned by the Congress attitude that it was ready to accept a separate Muslim state, figuratively, even in the Sindh desert than to live 'in bondage to the Congress with apparently more generous concessions'. Mountbatten considered the arguments in support of Pakistan unfeasible but Jinnah inflexibly stuck to the Pakistan demand and division of the armed forces, dismissing the counter arguments and giving the impression that 'the League would resort to arms' if its demands were not accepted.[82] Later on, Liaquat told Mountbatten that the League had 'a phobia' against the mere words 'Cabinet Mission' and that the Cabinet Mission Plan 'should not even be mentioned' at the leaders' conference that he had planned to hold in May.[83] Mountbatten's own hopes of its acceptance 'without any reservations' by the Congress were also 'killed' after he talked to Patel and received his letter of 26 April — then even for him the Cabinet Mission Plan was 'dead' — but he still often displayed ceremonial admiration for the Cabinet Mission Plan.[84]

Mountbatten was deeply offended by his six unfruitful meetings with Jinnah. He expressed his frustration and failure to persuade the League president to accept a unitary government for India and to change his inflexible stand on Pakistan and division of the armed forces — the issue of a common governor-general was added afterwards — in highly improper language at his staff meetings and in his reports to London.[85] However, he did not abandon the idea of a united India and devised a partition plan to make Pakistan unacceptable to the League. Ignoring the League's stand on Pakistan and the armed forces, he prepared two alternative plans: (i) 'Plan Union', which meant the Cabinet Mission Plan as modified by his own plan of 31 March, and in case of its rejection; (*ii*) 'Plan Balkan', for which he had input from Nehru and Patel and a major portion of which was drafted by V.P. Menon.[86] 'Plan Balkan', in which on Mountbatten's direction 'no mention of Pakistan' was made, contemplated leaving to each province the choice of its own future; partition of the Punjab, Bengal and Assam; general elections in the NWFP 'as soon as possible'; provinces to confederate; the states to join any of the confederations; determination of the status of the tribes on the north-western and north-eastern Frontier; and retention of a centre for some time to deal with the division of the armed forces, 'which would in no circumstances be split up before June 1948', and with some sort of a central organization 'even after the division for the coordination of defence'.[87] The 'choice' of one of the three options for the 'future'—Pakistan, Hindustan or Independence—was applicable only to the Pakistan units/provinces; and this exercise, it was hoped, would eventually result in a Pakistan consisting of only Sindh and west Punjab, which Sir Francis Mudie, then governor of Sindh, assured Mountbatten was quite viable; but the Hindu majority provinces were exempt from this exercise.[88] Such a Pakistan, surrounded by Hindustan-controlled territories, was acceptable even to Patel. 'Plan Balkan' was discussed and revised in the light of discussions at a two-day (15–16 April) governors' conference. The Pakistan provinces were the target and 'a quick decision', Mountbatten hoped, would give 'Pakistan a greater chance to fail on its demerits'.[89] As if to pacify his own conscience or his audience, Mountbatten made 'it quite clear' to the governors' conference that he was neither pro-Congress nor was he opposed to the League.[90] Mountbatten and the Congress leaders ignored the impact that their desperation to block 'Pakistan' and their fiddling with the Pakistan provinces would have on the political situation in the area.

Punjab was an important unit of the League's concept of Pakistan. Its governance after Khizr's exit remained the victim of indecision. Communal composition of its population (Muslims 57.1 per cent; Hindus 29.1 per cent; and Sikhs 13.2 per cent) was a constant source of tension.[91] The British authorities (governor and viceroy) and Nehru/ Sikh leaders discussed its governance by dividing it into two or three regions without taking the League into confidence but did not arrive at any decision. Despite their limited proportion in the population, the Sikhs came to wield more importance ostensibly for their representation in the army and sacrifices in the Second World War and because they along with the Hindus owned more than 50 per cent landed and financial assets of the Punjab.[92] In addition, the Sikhs had not forgotten that they had ruled the Punjab and the British had taken it over from them. But the problem was that they had majority in none of its districts or the Punjab states, except the small state of Malerkotla.[93] They disliked the prospect of Muslim domination if Punjab became part of Pakistan, a feeling that they shared with the Hindus who missed no opportunity to coax them to resist the Pakistan scheme.[94] Their leaders, Master Tara Singh in particular, used highly provocative language to express their views.[95] Besides, persons like V.P. Menon believed that the Hindus could not stand up to the Muslims without the support of 'a very virile community', the Sikhs, much less to a possible combination of Sikhs and Muslims.[96] When Cripps proposals had vaguely brought Pakistan to the realm of possibility, the Sikhs emotionally looked for a separate Sikh state; and, in 1942–44, their leaders held protracted unsuccessful talks with Jinnah who repeatedly advised them that they would be much better off in Pakistan than in India and offered them 'special autonomy'.[97] The Cabinet Mission gave them unusually sympathetic hearing, which raised their expectations, but the Cabinet Mission Plan ignored even to mention their case:[98] They denounced the Cabinet Mission Plan in protest and boycotted the elections to the constituent assembly. But, in August 1946, the Congress promised to support their 'legitimate' grievances and Nehru successfully persuaded them to join the constituent assembly and the interim government, and used them against the Pakistan scheme. It was generally perceived that a League-controlled Punjab could force the British and the Congress leaders to accept Pakistan. Khizr's resignation brought Jenkins, Nehru/Congress and the Sikhs 'face to face with the Pakistan issue'.[99] Besides preventing the League from forming its ministry, they began to advocate partition of the Punjab.

At that time, Punjab consisted of five divisions—Rawalpindi, Multan, Lahore, Jalandhar and Ambala (first three with Muslim majority and last two with non-Muslim majority)—and twenty-nine districts (seventeen with Muslim majority and twelve with non-Muslim majority). After his talks with the Sikh leaders, Governor Jenkins prepared a memorandum proposing partition of the Punjab up to the tehsil level but on Wavell's direction did not hand it over to them.[100] On 8 March, the day Mamdot was to form the ministry according to Jenkins' invitation, the Congress formally demanded partition of the Punjab.[101] The next day, Nehru wrote to Wavell that 'a proper and fair solution' of the Punjab 'problem' was its division into 'a predominantly

Muslim area and predominantly non-Muslim area' and that the Sikhs were 'agreeable' to it and indeed desired it.[102] Simultaneously, he urged Baldev Singh to write directly to the viceroy about the demand for partition.[103] The same day, the Sikh and Punjab Hindu leaders in a press statement opposed Pakistan 'in any shape or form' and asked for Ravi river as the boundary of the non-Muslim state, while some others suggested Chenab river as the boundary.[104] Again, on 2 April, eleven Hindu and Sikh leaders wrote to Nehru to send with his own endorsement to the viceroy and His Majesty's Government that Punjab should be immediately divided into two provinces by an order-in-council or by any other suitable way.[105] Non-Muslim plans for the partition of the Punjab did not reflect any uniformity of thought. For example, Kartar Singh considered Ravi as the most suitable boundary between the 'Sikh state' and the Muslim state with Sahiwal (Montgomery) as part of the former state and Nankana Sahib as a 'free city'.[106] Others demanded division on the basis of possession of immovable property, contribution to the revenue of the province by the communities and location of the Sikh religious shrines.[107] They asked for three divisions (Ambala, Jalandhar, and Lahore) for the non-Muslim state and as the total area of the three divisions fell short of 50 per cent of the total area of the Punjab, they demanded either the district of Sahiwal or Faisalabad (Lyallpur) to make up the balance![108] Similar was the demand of the three Sikh leaders (Kartar, Harnam and Ujjal Singh), who met the viceroy's principal secretary on 30 April.[109] Whimsical plans for partition continued to pour in partly because Jenkins and Mountbatten lent them receptive ears, which left the governance of the province in a state of complete uncertainty, bordering on anarchy.[110] The League leaders remained in the dark about the Jenkins–Congress/Sikh leaders' machinations. They simply opposed the division of the Punjab and continuously pressed for the installation of a League ministry.[111] When there were positive signals for the partition of India, the Hindus and Sikhs especially of west Punjab showed signs of some hesitation.[112] But by then the Sikh leaders had 'committed themselves so deeply' to the idea of partition that it was 'difficult, and perhaps impossible, for them to take a different line'.[113] The district-based partition was transformed into notional partition based on seventeen Muslim majority and twelve non-Muslim majority districts, and a Boundary Commission was to demarcate the limits of the partitioned provinces.[114] Then, at the viceroy's meetings, Nehru raised the issue of Gurdaspur which would provide Hindustan the land link with the state of Jammu and Kashmir and facilitate the encirclement of western Pakistan; after deliberating upon various proposals, it was decided to leave its future to the Boundary Commission that would take it into consideration among 'other factors'.[115] The League was ignorant about these Mountbatten–Nehru plans. The prolongation of section 93 in the Punjab and indecision to install a League-led ministry left the pot of communalism boiling. An unprecedented tragedy awaited the Punjabis due to Jenkins' machinations, Congress–Sikh ambitions and the League's persistence to have undivided Punjab. The aggressive posturing of some Sikh leaders, who were coaxed to assume such an attitude, and their preparations for post-transfer militant action with plans to seize 'the main irrigation centres in order to exercise physical control over the whole of Punjab' reflected a mindset of the eighteenth century Punjab; the British Indian government ignored, or were unable to control, such activities.[116]

The civil disobedience movement-generated pressure in the NWFP persuaded Mountbatten to accept Jinnah's demand for fresh elections under section 93 government. At first, Nehru went along with this suggestion, as there was still optimism in the Congress circles that its candidates could easily win the elections, an estimation that the provincial chief secretary endorsed in his interview with Mountbatten.[117] Therefore, the paper that was presented to the governors' conference on 15–16 April, recommended that general elections should be held in the NWFP 'as soon as possible', although Sir Olaf Caroe, the provincial governor, who was personally dealing with the deteriorating law and order situation, insisted that normalcy would return only if elections were announced immediately.[118] When Mountbatten held further discussions on the issue with Caroe and the Congress leaders, the two sides presented conflicting viewpoints. Caroe still stuck to his viewpoint for an immediate announcement of fresh elections, contending that 'the present administration' was near 'breaking point' and was surviving merely 'by the use of troops', but by then, the intensity of the League's civil disobedience movement had jolted the Congress leaders' confidence in all optimistic assessments of victory at the polls.[119] Now Nehru opposed Caroe's proposal for fresh elections, arguing that it had 'in effect been a proposal of the Muslim League' and its acceptance would mean succumbing to the League's pressure;[120] subsequently, the Congress leaders began to demand Caroe's removal from governorship, obviously for presenting his viewpoint so candidly.[121] Mountbatten then attempted to persuade the League leadership to give up the NWFP on its own accord because it was a deficit province, costing annually Rs 35 million! Liaquat flatly rejected the idea.[122] The situation took a serious turn when about 5,000 League prisoners refused to leave the jails after the Congress ministry on Mountbatten's instructions ordered their release. On this, Mountbatten told Nehru that only a promise of fresh elections would bring peace to the Frontier. Nehru agreed with him in principle that it was 'right and fair' to hold elections before the transfer of power but opposed the elections 'being held too hurriedly'.[123] During his Frontier visit (28–29 April), Mountbatten told Dr Khan Sahib and his colleagues that he would have to go into section 93 'to ensure fairness of elections',[124]— he had promised Jinnah to that effect before he went for the visit—but he soon changed his standpoint on elections.[125]

As for Bengal, the All-India Muslim League had visualized the whole as a unit of Pakistan. The moves for its partition or its formation as a united independent state were meant to 'torpedo' the Pakistan demand; and for Mountbatten anything that resulted in torpedoing Pakistan was of 'advantage' because it would lead to 'a more commonsense solution', i.e. united India.[126] The Hindu Mahasabha led by Dr Shyama Prasad Mukerji started the movement for the division of Bengal, which on 8 March, the Congress working committee formally endorsed.[127] However, the Sarat Chandra Bose-led forward bloc of the Bengal Congress and Gandhi opposed the partition movement.[128] Initially, Mountbatten embraced the idea of partition with Calcutta as part of west Bengal and used it in his talks with Jinnah to frighten him to give up Pakistan. Jinnah was 'horrified' at the suggestion and argued that it was not based on 'wisdom and foresight' but born of 'bitterness and spitefulness'; Mountbatten, however, countered that similar arguments could be used against the partition of India but the League leader was not convinced.[129] Sir Frederick John Burrows, the Bengal governor, felt that East Bengal without Calcutta would be transformed into a 'rural slum'; and in case of partition, he proposed that Calcutta should be made a 'free city', which both East and West Bengal could jointly administer and use, but none supported that proposal. Suhrawardy was keen to preserve the unity of Bengal, willing to accept even joint electorates to placate the Hindus without authorization from the central League or the provincial Muslim League. He began talks on that basis with those Hindus who held views similar to his own.[130] When Mountbatten came to know of his views about united independent Bengal through John Dawson Tyson, secretary to the governor of Bengal, who attended the governors' conference of 15–16 April on behalf of Governor Burrows because of his illness, he anxiously sought to meet him; and in that meeting, he encouraged Suhrawardy to pursue his ambition of a united independent Bengal. He promised to support him and gave him an erroneous impression that Jinnah had no objection to such a move.[131] Ismay was surprised when Suhrawardy told him about Mountbatten's statement and his promise of support 'to keep Bengal as a separate state'.[132] Mountbatten promoted the idea of united independent Bengal even after he had sent the 'Dickie Bird' Plan to London.

Another issue was of the Armed Forces. All-India Muslim League had all along envisaged Pakistan with its own armed forces but Mountbatten and the Congress leaders opposed the breakup of the forces. When Mountbatten asked the members of the interim government at a meeting about the division of the forces by June 1948, the Congress members 'unhesitatingly' responded that that was 'out of the question' while the League members thought that possible.[133] After Jinnah came to know of Mountbatten's views about the forces in the meetings with him, Liaquat wrote to Mountbatten on 7 April, that post-war reorganization and nationalization of the forces should be done in such a manner that these could be readily split into two forces at the proper time—one for Pakistan and the other for Hindustan; meanwhile, the two forces could be held together under a single command till the constitutional issue was settled. 'Unless that was done', he represented, the forces, which constituted 'the ultimate sanction and support for any state', would become 'predominantly Hindu in character' and come under 'the control of the Hindus'. He also pointed out that Muslim proportion in the officer ranks of the army was very low and that there was not a single unit composed of Muslims while there were a number of wholly Hindu units.[134] Mountbatten disagreed with Liaquat on the issue of division of the forces because, he maintained, the constitutional question had not yet been finally settled but promised to talk to the commander-in-chief about the inadequate number of Muslims in the forces.[135] His contention was that nationalization would 'greatly weaken the Forces' and they could not stand division on top of it. Conversely, Jinnah insisted that 'begin all and end all' of Pakistan was to have its own army and 'nothing short of this could possibly satisfy' the League.[136] On 13 April, Liaquat again wrote to Mountbatten to remind him that the Muslims should have adequate representation in the forces, and that reorganization should be done in such a way that the forces could be split up when a decision about partition of the country was taken, and the commander-in-chief should be directed to prepare a plan for the division of the forces.[137] On this, General Auchinleck, the commander-in-chief, acknowledged that the proportion of Muslims in the army which was 37 per cent before the war had come down to 29 per cent and that the Hindus dominated the forces from behind the scene as most of the senior officers were Hindus and the Muslim senior officers, for one reason or another, had faded out but maintained that Pakistan, if created, would not be able 'to afford a bigger Army' than the total 29 per cent represented.[138] Mountbatten added to this that 'if a form of Pakistan was eventually decided', he would 'in no circumstances agree to a split in the Indian armed forces before June 1948', and the plan that he sent to London had a provision to that effect.[139] On the contrary, Jinnah continued to insist that the defence forces should be 'completely divided' and, in his opinion, could be divided before June 1948, and that Pakistan and Hindustan should be made 'absolutely free, independent and sovereign'.[140]

By 1 May, Mountbatten had drafted a plan, known as the 'Dickie Bird Plan', which he sent to Listowel (secretary of state for India) and Ismay took it to London the next day. He intended to hold a leaders' conference on 17 May, for which he planned to issue a notice on 10 May. The 'Dickie Bird' Plan was a modified version of the 'Plan Balkan', which was meant to torpedo the Pakistan demand. It provided that without dividing the armed forces and keeping the governor-general (Mountbatten) as constitutional arbiter, members of the legislative assemblies of the Punjab and Bengal from the Muslim majority and non-Muslim majority districts, sitting separately (excluding European members), and members of the Sylhet district in Assam, sitting separately, would vote to decide whether or not their provinces should be divided. Before a vote about division, there might be demand from the members for joint meetings of the two halves of the Punjab and Bengal to consider whether their provinces should stay united. The provinces or half provinces of the Punjab and Bengal would decide whether to join the existing constituent assembly or to group together in one or more new constituent assemblies or stay independent and act as their own constituent assembly. If Bengal was divided Sylhet would exercise similar options. The 1941 census would be the basis to determine the proportion of population. In the NWFP, a general election would be held under section 93 government. The representatives of Assam (with or without Sylhet) and of Sindh and the NWFP would also exercise one of the three options. In British Balochistan, the members of the Shahi Jirga (other than Sardars of the Qalat State) and non-official members of the Quetta municipality would have similar options. If there were more than one constituent assembly, joint machinery would be devised for matters of common concern, particularly defence, and for negotiations in regard to these matters. Fresh agreements would be negotiated with the tribes of the North-West Frontier. The policy towards the states would remain unchanged, i.e. they would be free to negotiate with those parts to which power would be demitted.[141] Surprisingly, on Mountbatten's insistence, a note prepared by V.P. Menon was appended to the 'Dickie Bird' Plan papers that Ismay took to London, which called for 'immediate demission of power to Pakistan and Hindustan on the basis of dominion status', otherwise the Congress would threaten that when the time came the basis of transfer of power would be based on 'complete independence'. Except for immediate demission of power, the contents of V.P. Menon's note were almost similar to those of the 'Dickie Bird' Plan. His note provided for a joint council to deal with matters of common concern, particularly defence. The governor-general was its chairman who would have 'absolute discretion in all matters affecting British troops in India'. If the transitional 'dominion status' worked well, it was hoped, it might 'prove to be acceptable as a permanent arrangement'. Mountbatten informed Ismay, 'I take it VP can get Congress to put forward the request when the time comes'.[142] The draft of the 'Dickie Bird' Plan was shown to Jinnah and Nehru without providing them with its copies. They were asked to keep its contents secret. Jinnah did inform Mountbatten that he would discuss its contents with Liaquat. He opposed the partition of the Punjab and Bengal, demanding dissolution of the constituent assembly as the Cabinet Mission Plan had not been accepted, division of the armed forces as a *sine qua non* for the transfer of power, and a plebiscite in Bengal because the Scheduled Castes and the tribes had no representation in the existing Legislature.[143] While Nehru's primary objection was about the elections in the NWFP which he considered 'unnecessary and dangerous'.[144]

(*ii*) *Revision/Amendment of the 'Dickie Bird' Plan.* Before Ismay reached London with the 'Dickie Bird' Plan, the Congress leaders and Mountbatten had begun to have second thoughts about its contents; they were apprehensive that it might not prevent the emergence of Pakistan. They began a process of its revision that essentially moved around Bengal and the NWFP. Their object was to preserve the broader unity of India. Mountbatten tried to sever Bengal from the rest of Pakistan by extending support to the idea of a united independent Bengal despite Nehru's initial reluctance and subsequent strong opposition.[145] Strangely enough, he categorically recorded in his interview with Jinnah on 26 April, that the latter was agreeable to the idea of united independent Bengal, while he reported to the staff meeting on 7 May, that Suhrawardy had told him that Jinnah 'would agree to an independent Bengal'.[146] Jinnah denied that he ever authorized 'anyone to make any commitment on behalf of the Muslim League'; surprisingly, Suhrawardy concealed from Jinnah his meetings with Mountbatten.[147] Mountbatten on his part unrelentingly pursued the idea of united independent Bengal. When he met with Kiran Shankar Roy, leader of the Bengal Congress assembly party, he used a veiled threat of shifting of jute factories from west Bengal to east Bengal to persuade him to embrace that concept although Governor Burrows told Mountbatten about the impracticality of that suggestion.[148] Kiran was visibly shaken by the threat and readily expressed his willingness to support the idea provided Suhrawardy offered joint electorates to the Hindus; Mountbatten had already persuaded Suhrawardy to make that kind of offer.[149] Suhrawardy along with Sarat Chandra Bose and Kiran Shankar Roy with Mountbatten's blessings and under Burrows' umbrella worked out a formula of a united independent Bengal on the basis of joint electorates with reservation of seats to various communities in proportion to their population. On Mountbatten's advice, Roy and Bose agreed to name Bengal as a 'Free State' rather than a 'Socialist Republic', a name that they had at first proposed. Although he warned Suhrawardy that Nehru was against 'an independent Bengal unless closely linked to Hindustan' yet he advised him not 'to abandon his efforts for unity' and independence.[150] Suhrawardy's passionate advocacy of a united independent Bengal and unauthorized talks with the Hindu leaders threatened the unity of the Bengal presidency Muslim League but an open clash was averted. His opponents within the party opposed his possible surrender on the issue of electorates and any move to de-link Bengal from the rest of Pakistan.[151] His was a naïve and futile exercise because the Congress wanted united Bengal to go with Hindustan and the League visualized it as part of Pakistan; however, Mountbatten's blessings to the move continued till the end.[152]

The Congress leaders made frantic efforts to keep their hold on the NWFP. The rapidity with which they, and at their instance Mountbatten, changed their stance showed their desperation. The 'Dickie Bird' Plan had provided that general elections would be held in the NWFP under section 93 government but when Nehru discussed the issue with the Congress working committee, there was opposition to elections from its members. The Congress, Nehru communicated to Mountbatten after the working committee meeting, would accept only a referendum on the issue, 'whether the NWFP was to join Pakistan or Hindustan', and demanded the deletion of the option of independence only in the case of the NWFP and held out the threat of boycott if elections were held as a result of the League's civil disobedience movement.[153] Mountbatten readily accepted the Congress demand and embraced the idea of referendum under section 93 government as his own and, even before he mentioned it to Jinnah, he wrote to Ismay in London about possible alterations in the 'Dickie Bird' Plan in regard to this issue and also suggested the replacement of Caroe by Sir Robert Lockhart as governor.[154] When the Congress opposed the dissolution of the provincial assembly and the removal of its ministry, he defended its stand, arguing that there were 'no legal grounds for going into Section 93' or 'even to hold election in the face of violent opposition from the Congress'. He proposed referendum organized by himself and run by specially selected officers who would be 'independent of the government'.[155] But he must have felt embarrassed in defending his changed standpoint before the League leaders. On 2 May, when he met with Jinnah and Liaquat, he did not mention the proposal of a referendum but, referring to the provision of elections in the 'Dickie Bird' Plan, pressed Jinnah to call off the civil disobedience movement quietly 'without any announcement', fully knowing that a day earlier the Frontier Leaguers had decided to continue the movement and Jinnah had endorsed their decision after his meeting with six of them who had come to see him on parole in Delhi.[156] Two days later, on 4 May, when he raised the issue with Jinnah, the latter agreed to have referendum under section 93 government with only two options, Pakistan or Hindustan, but wanted elections to follow in the event of a pro-Pakistan vote in the referendum. Nehru's opposition to elections after a pro-Pakistan vote created difficulties for Mountbatten in his talks with Jinnah who continued to insist on elections under Section 93 government.[157] Finally, the 'Dickie Bird' Plan, as revised by the cabinet's India committee on 7 and 9 May, provided that the Hindu majority provinces (Bombay, Madras, United Provinces, Bihar, Central Provinces, Orissa, Delhi, Ajmer–Merwara and Coorg) were to simply confirm that they wished to remain in the existing constituent assembly but gave to the Pakistan units/provinces—Punjab, Bengal, Assam (and in case of division to the Muslim majority parts), the NWFP and Balochistan—three options, to join Pakistan or Hindustan or to stay independent; elections had to follow in the NWFP if the vote in the referendum was in favour of Pakistan, though Mountbatten did communicate to London Nehru's opposition to elections; and a boundary commission was to demarcate the boundaries of the partitioned provinces.[158] Before Mountbatten showed the revised 'Dickie Bird' Plan to Nehru on his so-called 'hunch', the Congress had made a tempting offer to him to achieve its objective, i.e. to keep India united.

After a heated debate within the party, the Congress leaders decided to accept dominion status for India—contrary to their long-time stand on dominion status which the Congress-dominated Constituent Assembly had recently endorsed by declaring that India would be an independent sovereign republic—and agreed to join the commonwealth, expecting in return immediate transfer of power to the interim government without the division of the armed forces.[159] Mountbatten was elated by this offer because it met the last point of Prime Minister Attlee's instructions to him, i.e. 'to retain India within the Commonwealth'; and he enumerated with great fervor its advantages: 'terrific world-wide enhancement of British prestige'; completion of the framework of 'world strategy from the point of view of Empire defence'; early termination of responsibility of law and order; and 'further strengthening of Indo-British relations'.[160] He was ready to meet any of the Congress demands.[161] In a show of cordiality, on 8 May, he invited Nehru and Krishna Menon to Simla—V.P. Menon had already gone with him a day earlier—to deliberate upon possible alternative options; concurrently, he decided not to take Jinnah into confidence about any changes in the plan until after its announcement. Now the Congress leaders came up with all kinds of fanciful proposals/ plans. After a meeting with the representatives of the Frontier ministry and the Congress leaders, Gandhi reiterated his proposal of immediate demission of power to either the League or the Congress, considered referendum in the NWFP as 'dangerous', calling for everything done according to Dr Khan Sahib's wishes, and wanted 'all innovations' to come after, and not before, the British withdrawal from India 'as a result of understanding between the parties or an armed conflict'![162] While Nehru now opposed even 'referendum vehemently' and demanded a modified version of the Cabinet Mission Plan, i.e. immediate demission of power to the central government responsible to either the constituent assembly or the central legislative assembly; rejection of the Pakistan demand 'straight away'; and option for the provinces to form groups with a provision to opt out after the framing of a constitution. Mountbatten agreed with him that the existing provinces should be referred to as the 'Union of India' and the others as 'provinces contracting out of the Union'.[163] Krishna Menon who claimed to have initiated the move in the Congress for the acceptance of dominion status for India told Mountbatten that if India was given early dominion status, the Congress would never agree 'to the splitting of the Army'; and in that case, Pakistan would have to build its own army 'from nothing', and informed about Nehru's 'belief' that Mountbatten would 'influence the States' in favour of the Congress.[164] Lastly, on 9 May, Patel asserted in an interview with the Associated Press of America that 'India's political impasse would be broken at once if power were transferred' to the existing interim government, with the viceroy 'standing out'. If that was done, he observed, it would bring peace in the Punjab and the NWFP 'within a week'. The Congress and the League, he went on, would settle their differences; and if there were 'conflicts in the Cabinet on any question, the majority would rule'.[165] When Jinnah's attention was drawn to this interview, he responded that the League would never agree to such 'a monstrous proposal' and that the Congress was making 'it more and more difficult' for those who wanted separation 'to separate in a friendly way' although, on 8 March, it had proclaimed not to 'coerce any group or area'. 'Transfer of power without division of the armed forces' in case of division of India, he said, was 'meaningless'.[166]

Keeping Jinnah in the dark about the whole process of the revision of the 'Dickie Bird' Plan made Mountbatten and the Congress leaders uneasy that he might reject the plan at the final stage.[167] Therefore, they devised two alternative plans to face that eventuality. According to the first plan, Mountbatten after consulting Nehru wanted to assume authority to threaten Jinnah that if he did not accept the plan, power would be demitted to a united India on dominion status basis with the understanding that the 'Congress would publicly announce safeguards' which would allow the League to form its Pakistan later! Nehru preferred this plan to any one else, and told Mountbatten that he gave 'due weight' to Gandhi's views but Patel's interview to the Associated Press of America gave 'a clear expression of the Congress viewpoint'.[168] But when Mountbatten wrote to Listowel (secretary of state for India) to have such an authority, the latter did not consider it 'desirable' to give him that authority but suggested that the viceroy could tell the League president that the plan could be implemented without his cooperation.[169] The second plan was the one that V.P. Menon on Mountbatten's instructions worked out in detail, and which he had already discussed first with Patel and then with Nehru.[170] This plan envisaged division of India into two parts with a suitably modified Act of 1935, each part having dominion status. A joint consultative council would deal with defence, foreign affairs and communications; and there would be a single governor-general. This council had defence ministers of the two parts as members with Mountbatten as chairman having authority 'equal to either of the others'; Nehru, however, insisted that even if India was partitioned the army should 'continue to function as a whole'. V.P. Menon supported by Mountbatten proposed that a common governor-general would be a constitutional governor-general of India but he would exercise 'special responsibilities' (or existing powers) for Pakistan for an interim period of 8–9 months till that state was able to set up its own 'executive'.[171] Mountbatten foresaw no problem in implementing this strategy and, on 10 May, invited Nehru, Patel, Jinnah, Liaquat and Baldev and the States Negotiating Committee to meet him on 17 May, 'to have a final talk about the conclusions that he had arrived at before an announcement'. He and the Congress leaders ignored the real snag that could come in their way, as hinted at earlier by the India committee, i.e. the plan had to be acceptable to both the parties—the Congress as well as the League—and defensible in the British parliament. That stage could come later. Even before that, Nehru conveyed his strong reservations about the plan when Mountbatten showed him its India committee-approved draft on a 'hunch'. Now he expressed his extreme dislike of its provisions especially those relating to the NWFP and the princely states although there was nothing new that Mountbatten had not discussed with him. Attlee, Mountbatten and others who had been associated with the evolution of the plan were 'rattled' by his *volte face* and his denunciation of the plan.[172] On 13 May 1947, Attlee almost apologetically wrote to Mountbatten, 'All that we have done is to try to clarify the presentation of the case. We have made no alteration in substance, except as regards the referendum in the NWFP, which was included at your suggestion to meet Nehru's objection to a General Election'.[173] Why did Nehru react the way he did? One explanation is that the Congress leaders, after their voluntary offer to accept dominion status and to join the Commonwealth and Mountbatten's enthusiastic response, had expected immediate demission of power to the interim government under a modified Act of 1935. Nehru reacted when that did not happen.

After Nehru's negative reaction, Mountbatten sat down with him to modify the plan to make it acceptable to the Congress. He postponed his meeting with the Indian leaders that he had scheduled on 17 May, and erroneously gave 'parliamentary recess' as the reason for the postponement; the new date fixed for the meeting was 2 June. Besides suggesting modifications in the plan, Nehru presented his own plan. Thus, two plans were in place: the Nehru/Congress plan or 'Plan THEY'; and the amended version of the Mountbatten plan or 'Plan WE'. Both plans were meant to disrupt the Pakistan demand. Plan THEY was similar to the one with which Mountbatten had 'previously decided to threaten Jinnah', if he did not accept the plan. On 11 May, Nehru in a meeting with Mountbatten maintained that the Congress could not abandon 'basic all-India Union', arguing that the Cabinet Mission Plan was not dead and the constituent assembly was functioning except for a few provinces which had not accepted it. These provinces, Punjab and Bengal, where there was demand for partition, and the district of Sylhet, had to choose what to do. As for NWFP, he reluctantly agreed to have referendum when Mountbatten told him that civil war would break out if that was not done and suggested possibly a plebiscite in Balochistan as its future for him raised 'many strategic problems' but wanted Sir B.N. Rau to make a definite proposal for that region. He proposed that the existing constituent assembly should frame a constitution and the League should frame its own constitution and then all the provinces should decide in a plebiscite about an acceptable constitution. Until then, the interim government must be transformed into 'a cabinet with joint responsibility based on full Dominion autonomy'. Later that evening, he proposed a plan to Mountbatten for the early demission of power on dominion status basis with 'full control of the Army except on very limited subjects, for which the Joint Defence [Consultative] Council would be in control', and assured that the Congress would provide 'safeguards' to the League if power was handed over to the existing interim government.[174] When Mountbatten sent Nehru's plan to Ismay, the latter wrote back that the

Congress leaders seemed to be under the impression that there was 'some alternative plan which would be substitute to partition', and that they would be given a free hand as advocated by Patel in his press statement of 9 May. 'This would', he wrote, 'be contrary to assurances given by H.M.G. and is not I imagine what you contemplate'.[175] Still, Mountbatten defended Nehru's plan and considered 'most convincingly genuine' his promises of post-transfer safeguards for the creation of Pakistan: to let those areas which wished to secede not only to go but also to set themselves up independently; to assist in the division of the armed forces and not to use them in the seceding areas; and to cooperate in the referendum in the NWFP and in setting up boundary commissions; and not to use the Congress majority in the interim government against the League.[176] The India committee, however, pointed out that the Cabinet Mission Plan could not be adopted unless all the political parties accepted it and that 'a plan for partition in India must precede decisions determining the status of India or parts of India'.[177] Simultaneously, Mountbatten had redrafted the plan in the light of Nehru's objections. He suggested, besides some 'small drafting points', three major amendments: the NWFP should not be given the option of independence and the promise of election after the referendum be withdrawn; the option of independence provided for Balochistan and Sylhet should also be withdrawn and they would exercise one of the two options, to join Pakistan or Hindustan; and Punjab and Bengal should have an alternative to partition also, if there was a joint demand to that effect. No provision was made for Bengal remaining independent but, Mountbatten wrote to Ismay, 'there was nothing in the plan to prevent the Bengal Legislative Assembly passing a resolution for independence'.[178] Strangely enough, as suggested earlier by V.P. Menon, there was a provision for an 'interim period' of 6–8 months to enable Pakistan to set up an 'executive'; and Mountbatten wrote to Ismay that 'the Union of India will be ready to receive power before Pakistan . . . and that I could be Constitutional Governor-General of the [Indian] Union and my existing powers could remain meanwhile for Pakistan' for the interim period.[179] This was in fact a mechanism to create a Congress-controlled Pakistan.

Jinnah did not have direct information about the Mountbatten-Nehru/Congress strategy. He could only guess their design against the Pakistan demand through his interaction with Mountbatten and his staff and press reports. His options to counteract that strategy were limited. In addition to keeping the League mobilized behind its demand, he firmly stated the party position with remarkable patience and confidence, reminding the British government and the opposition in the British parliament of promises made to the Muslims of India during the war.[180] On 16 May 1947, V.P. Menon on Mountbatten's instructions drafted an eight-point Heads of Agreement which, besides providing for 'early transfer of power on a Dominion Status basis as an interim arrangement' with a modified Act of 1935, and division of the armed forces after the new Act came into operation, had a provision: 'The Governor-General should be common to both the States. We suggest that the present Governor-General should be re-appointed'. The Heads of Agreement provided no option for separate governors-general of the two states.[181] Nehru and Patel readily accepted this agreement but Mountbatten was apprehensive that Jinnah might not sign the document that he had drafted for this purpose. Therefore, again, he asked the British Cabinet to empower him to threaten Jinnah that if he insisted on 'Province-wise Pakistan' and offered 'no alternative acceptable solution', His Majesty's Government would demit power to the interim government which would 'in all probability be the end of his Pakistan', and 'if these tactics fail', he urged, 'the threat must be put into effect as the only workable solution'.[182] Instead of waiting for a reply from London, he 'cautiously' threatened Jinnah that unless he signed the agreement, power would be demitted to the interim government on the basis of dominion status. Jinnah refused to sign the relevant document and took Mountbatten's threat 'very calmly', responding that he 'could not stop such a step in any event'. This 'abnormal reaction, which was typical of Mr Jinnah, was rather disturbing' for Mountbatten.[183] When the India committee discussed Mountbatten's request, the ministers disagreed with his strategy and expressed the view that such an action on his part would be 'breach of the pledges that they had given to parliament about safeguarding minorities'; the plan could 'only be put into effect if it was acceptable to the Muslim League' as well; and 'any Bill not based on Indian agreement would be fought in the Parliament at every stage'.[184] By 17 May, Jinnah and Nehru had handed in comments of their parties on the plan. Jinnah conveyed that the Cabinet Mission Plan was *ab initio* invalid and the constituent assembly should not be allowed to continue to function; India should be divided and Pakistan be established; all power including defence, foreign affairs, finance and communications and all other matters which were being dealt with by the central government or by His Majesty's Government should be transferred to the constituent assemblies of Pakistan and

Hindustan; argued at great length against the partition of the Punjab and Bengal, demanding referenda in these provinces,[185] and in case of division Calcutta should not be taken away from east Bengal; opposed any consultation with the NWFP ministry, which could not be allowed to carry on the administration if the vote in the referendum was in favour of NWFP joining the Pakistan constituent assembly; some truly representative democratic machinery be set up, if needed, to elect a new representative from British Balochistan;[186] Sylhet district and other Muslim majority areas of Assam contiguous to Bengal should join east Bengal; in case of partition of Bengal those areas of the Purnea district in Bihar which were contiguous to east Bengal and had a Muslim majority should be amalgamated with eastern Bengal; and the Pakistan constituent assembly must be the appropriate successor authority for the tribes of the North-West Frontier.[187] While Nehru communicated that the Congress regarded the plan as continuation of the Cabinet Mission Plan and accepted it with minor alterations subject to other parties accepting it as a final settlement with no further claims. He claimed the Chittagong Hill area and other territories like the Andaman Islands which had not been mentioned in the plan.[188]

On 14 May, Prime Minister Attlee had asked Mountbatten to visit London 'to reach final conclusions' because conflicting and confusing proposals had been coming from Delhi. Before Mountbatten visited London, he tried to wrap in Jinnah on three issues—'interim period', transfer of power to the executives rather than the constituent assemblies of the two states during the interim period and common governor-general—by a naïve move of deception. The object was to prevent the creation of a sovereign Pakistan or to control its shape if it was eventually conceded. On 17 May, V.P. Menon on his direction prepared two documents. The first document, six-point 'Proposals for Transfer of Power during the Interim Period', called for the transfer of power to the existing constituent assembly if there was one central government but to the executives of each part if there were two sovereign states on dominion status basis with a modified Act of 1935 (Point 1–3); the division of the armed forces should be done when the dominion constitution came into operation, and redistribution of the mixed units should be looked after by a council consisting of the governor-general and the two defence ministers, and the council should cease to function on the completion of its work (Point 5); the interim government at the centre should by convention be treated as a dominion government subject to the governor-general exercising over-riding powers to safeguard the legitimate interests of the minorities, pending necessary legislation by the parliament 'which should be enacted as soon as practicable' (Point 6); and the governor-general should 'be common to both the States' (Point 4).[189] The same day, Mountbatten obtained Nehru's comments on these proposals. Nehru accepted them, provided all parties took it as a final settlement, and agreed to have common governor-general for the two states and expressed his happiness if Mountbatten filled that position. Jinnah was neither given a copy of the six-point proposals nor was he asked to offer his comments. Instead, Mountbatten at a meeting with him on the evening of 17 May, 'read' out to him parts of Nehru's comments from his letter of the same date in which he had accepted the proposals and agreed to share a common governor-general with Pakistan; and then asked for Jinnah's reaction. Jinnah told him that he could not commit himself on that subject 'straight away' but felt that the two states should have separate governors-general but a representative of the crown could be appointed who would be responsible for the division of assets and that Mountbatten could fill that position—a position that the latter expressed his unwillingness to accept as the crown's representative because it would be junior in rank to the two governors-general. After some discussion, Mountbatten who was to leave for London the next morning asked Jinnah to send him a letter in London by 19 May, giving full description of his suggestion of 'a supreme Arbitrator' and two governors-general. He wanted Jinnah to indicate in that letter that if His Majesty's Government found his scheme 'impracticable, he would accept as a less desirable alternative and as an interim measure' a common governor-general for the two states. On Jinnah's insistence, Mountbatten agreed that Mieville would provide him with a copy of the proposals and Nehru's comments; and Jinnah would then write the required letter.[190]

Mountbatten did not want Jinnah to see the six-point proposals because their contents conflicted with what he and his staff had been telling the League president. Therefore, after his meeting with Jinnah on that evening, he asked V.P. Menon to draft a second document, three-point 'Proposals for Transfer of Power during the Interim Period on the basis of Two Independent States' with Alternatives 'A' and 'B'. Points 1 and 3 in both alternatives were similar in content: Point 1 provided that if there were two independent states, the 'executive' of each state should take over power in responsibility to its constituent assembly on a dominion status basis with a modified Act of 1935, and

Point 3 was similar in content to Point 5 of the first document. Point 2 in alternative 'A' provided that if the states desired, there could be one common governor-general for the two states who would act by agreement as arbitrator in matters of common concern and in alternative 'B' there was a simple provision that there would be a separate governor-general for each state.[191] There was no mention of 'interim period' in the three-point proposals. On 18 May, after Mountbatten's departure, Mieville gave Jinnah a copy of the three-point proposals but did not provide him with a copy of Nehru's letter. Jinnah wrote back that if he did not get a copy of Nehru's letter as agreed, he would not be in a position to give his comments.[192] After a reminder from Jinnah, Mieville sent to him very reluctantly 'only extracts' from Nehru's letter of 17 May; his worry was that Mountbatten would be 'extremely angry' of his action. After reading the extracts, Jinnah sent a note to Mieville for transmission to Mountbatten in London that he had been given three-point proposals while Nehru in his comments had referred to Point 5, which showed that Nehru's comments were on some other draft and 'not the draft on which my views are sought'. He was 'unhappy' to know the stress that Nehru had laid in his letter on the 'interim period'. He could not understand what was meant by the interim period, as there was no question of an interim period if 'Dominion Status was granted to both states'. Again, he could not understand what Nehru meant by 'immediate transfer by convention' while three-point proposals made no reference to such an arrangement. Furthermore, Nehru had stated that 'power to change' the Act of 1935 'during the interim period will rest with the authority in India'. Jinnah wanted to know the authority to which Nehru had referred to. In view of these contradictions, he expressed his inability to give the required letter to Mountbatten and wrote that the subject of the proposals could be taken up after 2 June, in the light of the announcement by the British government.[193] On 20 May, Mieville supplied Jinnah with copies of full texts of Nehru's letters of 17 and 19 May (containing his comments on 3-point proposals). But that did not change Jinnah's position.[194]

Jinnah's discovery of Nehru's comments killed any prospect of his acceptance of a Congress-proposed governor-general-controlled Pakistan for an 'interim period' or any possibility of transfer of power to the executives rather than the constituent assemblies of the two states or sharing of a common governor-general. Mountbatten hid his embarrassment caused by Jinnah's refusal to provide him the required letter by unfairly terming it his 'somersault' and by making incorrect statements before the India committee about Jinnah's acceptance of dominion status for Pakistan, speedy transfer of power and other issues.[195] Nevertheless, on 20 May, the India committee on the suggestion of Lord Chancellor, William Allen Jowitt, and with Mountbatten's concurrence approved the details of a plan based on the division of British India into two states, each having its own parliament and executive; this plan was developed into the 3 June Plan.[196] The same day, Mountbatten sent through Mieville its copies to Jinnah, Nehru, Liaquat, Baldev and Patel. He was unsure about Jinnah's response, which is indicated by the verbal 'message' that he obtained from Churchill (leader of the opposition), for Jinnah urging him to accept the plan and from his interview with Jinnah before its formal announcement.[197] If that was not the case, his concern was an expression of his wishful thinking that the League would give up Pakistan on seeing the provisions regarding the partition of the Punjab and Bengal.[198] The League leaders, however, gave clear signals that their party would accept Pakistan even with partitioned provinces. Sardar Nishtar told Alexander C.B. Symon (deputy high commissioner for the UK in India), at a 'predominantly Muslim party' on the evening of 22 May, that the League would continue to press for a Pakistan based on undivided provinces but accept 'a truncated Pakistan' if it was forced on the party.[199] And, on 26 May, John Colville, the acting viceroy, after his talks with Jinnah over lunch, formed the opinion that he was 'absolutely determined on the principle of Pakistan' but willing to negotiate on details and was unlikely to throw away 'a limited Pakistan in an attempt to get the whole'.[200] Jinnah's interview with the Reuter soon after he had received the India committee-revised plan also confirms that his observations were based on his acceptance of the partition of provinces and discussed the policies of the Pakistan state and called for complete division of the armed forces although he still vehemently opposed the partition of the Punjab and Bengal—in the event of partition, he maintained, the Sikhs would be the 'greatest sufferers' and Caste Hindus would suffer the most in West Bengal and East Punjab but did not foresee mass killings and migration in the partitioned Punjab.[201] In that interview, he reiterated the demand for a corridor between the two parts of Pakistan, a demand that he did not seriously pursue. Mountbatten had this information about Jinnah which makes his dramatic account of forcing Jinnah to give a nod in the meeting of the Indian leaders as a mark of his acceptance of the plan look childish and questionable; the official minutes of that meeting also negate his version.

(E) CREATION OF PAKISTAN

(i) *3 June Plan.* On 3 June, after a meeting with the leaders of the Indian political parties a day earlier, Mountbatten issued along with his own broadcast speech the statement that incorporated the plan; Attlee made an introductory broadcast from London. None of the three documents mentioned even once the word 'Pakistan'; and Patel was 'deeply distressed' at Jinnah's 'misuse' of his broadcast on the All India Radio for his appeal to the Frontier voters to vote in the referendum for Pakistan and his declaration at the end, 'Pakistan *Zindabad*'.[202] The sentence in the statement that there was nothing in 'this Plan to preclude negotiations between communities for a united India' was expression of a wish to see India united. While the Congress leaders had all along emphasized speedy transfer of power, Jinnah had urged Mountbatten not to go 'too fast'.[203] Accepting the Congress viewpoint, Mountbatten at his press conference on 4 June, announced 15 August, as the date for the transfer of power. Was this on his part the 'quick decision' that was meant to give 'Pakistan a greater chance to fail on its demerits'? If that was his desire, the League disproved that by its response. The 3 June Plan allowed the existing constituent assembly to continue its work and laid down a procedure for those parts which had not accepted it to determine their future. The Punjab and Bengal assemblies were to decide separately whether the two provinces should be divided or stay united and which constituent assembly should the divided or united provinces join, and Boundary Commissions were to demarcate the boundaries of the partitioned provinces on the basis of 'contiguous majority areas of Muslims and non-Muslims' and 'other factors'. In case of partition of Bengal, the Muslim majority district of Sylhet would decide in a referendum whether it should be merged into East Bengal or form part of Assam, and a Boundary Commission would demarcate the boundary. The Sindh assembly at a special meeting would take its decision. The voters of the NWFP assembly would decide in a referendum held under the aegis of the governor-general and in consultation with the provincial government about one of the two options. Similarly, British Balochistan would choose one of the options and the governor-general was authorized to determine the mechanism. Appropriate successor authority would negotiate agreements with the tribes of the North-West Frontier. The policy towards the states was to remain the same as was contained in the Cabinet Mission's memorandum (of 12 May 1946).

Mountbatten, in a meeting with the Indian leaders on 2 June 1947, had desired that the working committees of the League and the Congress should accept the plan before its announcement. But for the League, acceptance of the plan that visualized partition of the Punjab, Bengal and Assam was a major decision that Jinnah wanted its council rather than himself or the working committee to take; he had adopted a similar procedure for the approval of the Cabinet Mission Plan on 6 June 1946. Despite pressure from Mountbatten, he refused to give anything in writing. While Nehru accepted to communicate the decision of the working committee in writing before the All India Congress Committee's endorsement, Jinnah agreed to convey the reaction of the League working committee to Mountbatten only verbally, maintaining that the council would take the final decision.[204] The League council met in Delhi on 9–10 June. Some Khaksars who were for a larger Pakistan tried to disrupt the meeting by capturing the stage but the Muslim League National Guards foiled their attempt and evicted the intruders. After lengthy deliberations, the council recorded its satisfaction that the Cabinet Mission Plan had finally been abandoned and expressed the opinion that the division of India into Pakistan and Hindustan was the only solution of India's problem. It neither agreed with the partition of the Punjab and Bengal nor did it give its consent to such partition but authorized Jinnah to accept the fundamental principles of the plan as a compromise. He was given full authority to work out complete division of India including that of defence, finance, communications, etc. Four hundred councillors voted for, and eight against, the resolution. On 14–15 June, the All India Congress Committee while opposing the two-nation theory accepted the plan; 157 members voted for the relevant resolution, 21 opposed it and 32 abstained.[205] Any change or amendment in the plan required agreement of both the main political parties. Thus, the plan finished the Bose–Roy–Suhrawardy proposal for a united independent Bengal because of the opposition of the Congress and the League.

(*ii*) *Implementation of the Plan.* Mountbatten did not wait or hesitate to restart his move to become the common governor-general of Pakistan and Hindustan. On 2 June, in his talks with Jinnah, and on 4 June, at his press conference, he upheld that the governors-general would be appointed 'on the recommendations of the Heads of the two Governments' but advised Jinnah to avoid any 'commitment on the subject' for two months. On the other hand, he tried to manoeuvre that the draft India bill should have a provision 'for the two Dominions to have the same person' as the governor-general and simultaneously told his staff that it would be 'quite fatal' if Jinnah came to know of this move.[206] As he desired, the draft Bill had a clause to that effect but the secretary of state for India wrote to him that letters from the League and the Congress requesting the same person as the governor-general would be required to keep this clause in the bill. Now his strategy was that two members of his staff, Ismay and Mieville, should approach Liaquat to ask him to convince Jinnah about the usefulness of a common governor-general. Ismay and Mieville raised the issue with Liaquat; and on 20 June, when they inquired from him about the progress, Liaquat told them that he had not yet had an opportunity to talk it over with Jinnah but cautioned them that the League had resolved not to take over government 'unless they had an army on the spot and under their control'.[207] On Liaquat's response, Mountbatten's patience ran out; and on 23 June, he himself raised the issue with Jinnah. He asked Jinnah whom he wanted to be the first governor-general of Pakistan and stressed the advantages of a common governor-general, making it 'abundantly clear' that he was not seeking the appointment for himself. He explained that he wanted the name because it affected a clause in the India bill that was shortly to be placed before parliament. When he informed Jinnah that the Indian leaders would be shown the draft bill, Jinnah immediately responded that he would give the name for the office of governor-general after he had seen the bill. He told Mountbatten that it had been 'the rule of his life' to keep in mind 'the interests of his people' and that at 'various times of his career he had to pass over those nearest and dearest to him.' On 1 July, the draft bill was shown to the leaders. After a full evaluation of the pros and cons of the issue of governor-general, the League working committee decided to have Jinnah as the first governor-general of Pakistan; and on 4 July, Liaquat formally communicated the decision to Mountbatten.[208] Why was Mountbatten so keen to become the common governor-general of both the successor states? It is not easy to answer that question. One explanation is that he wanted to preserve the unity of the Armed Forces, secure the smooth accession of the states to India and create a Congress-approved Pakistan. Pakistan did suffer for the League's decision not to have

Mountbatten as the common governor-general but, if one keeps in mind the Mountbatten–Nehru/Congress understanding before the 3 June Plan, the idea of sovereign Pakistan might have been fatally damaged if he had become common governor-general of Pakistan and India.

The implementation of the plan began on 20 June, when the Bengal legislative assembly met and decided to join the Pakistan constituent assembly by 126 to 90 votes. Then, the members of the non-Muslim majority areas of West Bengal met and decided by 58 to 21 votes that Bengal should be partitioned and West Bengal should join the existing constituent assembly. This was followed by a meeting of the members from Muslim majority areas of East Bengal who decided by 106 to 35 votes that Bengal should not be partitioned and East Bengal should join the Pakistan constituent assembly. While the proceedings in Bengal were conducted in a relatively peaceful atmosphere, those in the Punjab were held amidst demonstrations and under police guard. The Punjab legislative assembly met on 23 June, and decided by 91 to 77 votes to join the Pakistan constituent assembly. After that, members from the Muslim majority areas of West Punjab decided by 69 to 27 votes that Punjab should not be partitioned while the members from the non-Muslim majority areas of East Punjab decided by 50 to 22 votes that the Punjab should be partitioned and East Punjab should join the existing constituent assembly. On 26 June, the Sindh legislative assembly passed a resolution to join the Pakistan constituent assembly by 33 votes; 2 Muslim members were absent for health reasons and 20 Congress members voted against the resolution. On 12 June, the Assam provincial Muslim League had called off the civil disobedience movement; and after the release of its leaders and workers including Bhashani, it organized a systematic campaign for the referendum in Sylhet, and a three-member (M.A.H. Ispahani, Moazzam Husain and A.W. Baakza) committee, which the All-India Muslim League appointed, extended it necessary assistance.[209] On 6–7 July, the voters in the referendum decided to merge Sylhet into East Bengal; 239,619 voted for and 184,041 against the merger.[210]

The League-led civil disobedience movement (mid-February–5 June) in the NWFP had eroded the support-base of the Congress in the frontier region and shook its leaders' confidence that they could win in any reference to the voters. Therefore, they avoided a referendum with just two options, Pakistan or Hindustan, and began to demand a third option of 'Pakhtunistan', a proposition that Caroe had 'advised them to take up some months ago' but they had refused to do that at that time.[211] When Acharya Kripalani, the Congress president, raised the issue of a third option with Mountbatten, the latter simply informed him that the British cabinet had withdrawn that option from the plan at Nehru's request, and when Abdul Ghaffar Khan himself raised it in the Congress working committee on 2 June, he could hardly elicit any support from its members. After 3 June, Gandhi backed by Mountbatten asked Jinnah to go to the NWFP and explain the Pakistan demand to its people. Jinnah was willing to do that provided the Congress promised not to interfere in the affairs of the NWFP people; but Gandhi declined to give such an undertaking. Then, at his and Mountbatten's initiative, a Jinnah–Ghaffar meeting was arranged in which Ghaffar Khan offered to accept Pakistan if Jinnah gave a prior three-point commitment on behalf of the state of Pakistan that: the NWFP would have complete provincial autonomy; it would have the right to secede from Pakistan, if it so desired; and any contiguous Pakhtun-inhabited territories would have the right to join the NWFP. Jinnah responded that he had no authority to bind the state of Pakistan to any pre-conditions. On this, Ghaffar Khan promised to place 'everything before his colleagues' in the NWFP and communicate their decision to him. On 21–22 June, the Frontier Congress–Khudai Khidmatgars at a meeting in Bannu decided to boycott the referendum unless it had a third option of Pakhtunistan, but he forgot to communicate that decision to Jinnah, as promised. Soon thereafter, under pressure from the Congress, Lieutenant General Sir Robert Lockhart replaced Caroe as governor, and the army personnel were assigned to supervise the referendum. Brigadier J.B. Booth was appointed referendum commissioner and military personnel, who were selected in consultation with Dr Khan Sahib, were put at his disposal to conduct the referendum; in addition, 50,000 troops were posted to assist the police to maintain peace. The Congress made an unsuccessful bid to manoeuvre intervention of the Afghan government on the issue.[212] Referendum was organized from 6 to 17 July. The Congress campaigned to persuade the voters not to cast their votes. When the League protested that the boycott campaign was a violation of the 3 June Plan, which the Congress had accepted, it promised to desist from the campaign. But notwithstanding its promises, it relentlessly campaigned for a boycott and the climax was the observance of a 'Pakhtunistan Day' on 7 July. On that day, Dr Khan Sahib in his exuberance declared that if a little over 31 per cent of the electorate voted for Pakistan, his ministry would resign; this percentage was about 50 per cent of about 62 per cent of the votes cast in the general elections. But that did not happen when the vote went in favour of Pakistan. A League-appointed four-member [I.I. Chundrigar, Raja Ghazanfar Ali, Pir Manki and Sayyid Wajid Ali (1911–2008)] committee supervised the party campaign. In addition to mobilizing local resources, the Sindh provincial Muslim League provided transport, microphone and other facilities.[213] Support came from other sources as well.[214] The vote for Pakistan was 289,244 (i.e. 50.99 per cent of the total electorate entitled to vote) and for Hindustan 2,874. After the referendum, neither Dr Khan Sahib honoured his promise to resign from his office nor did Mountbatten and the British government thought it proper to remove the ministry before independence.[215]

The British had direct treaties with the tribes of the North-West Frontier. After the referendum, these tribes in popularly organized *jirgas* and meetings declared their allegiance to Pakistan. The Pakistan government continued the treaties with the tribes; and subsequently, Jinnah withdrew the army from North and South Waziristan. As for British Balochistan, the 3 June Plan had authorized Mountbatten to determine the mechanism for its decision. Jinnah proposed that an electoral college of either the holders of ration cards (about 2000 persons), or all *maliks* and *motabars* (about 500 persons), or all members of the district *jirgas* (about 400 persons) should take a decision. But Mountbatten accepted none of these proposals because that would have delayed the process of partition; and finally, he assigned the task with Nehru's consent to an electoral college consisting of the Baloch and Pakhtun *sardars* of the Shahi Jirga and non-official members of the Quetta municipality.[216] Jinnah appealed to the voters to vote for Pakistan.[217] There was no doubt at any stage about the final outcome. Still, besides the provincial Muslim League's formal campaign, several individuals did some hectic canvassing before the voting; Mir Jafar Khan Jamali, Nawab Jogezai and his son, Jahangir Shah, were the most active and enthusiastic campaigners among them. Nasim Hijazi, a novelist and editor of the daily *Tanzeem*, and M. Masud, an Indian civil service officer, used their influence in the pro-Pakistan campaign. On 29 June, 49 members of the Shahi Jirga and 5 members of the Quetta municipality voted for joining the Pakistan constituent assembly; the remaining 8, including non-Muslim members (three of Shahi Jirga and five of Quetta Municipality) absented themselves on that day.[218]

The Congress inherited a functional state apparatus in India but the League had not only to find a capital for Pakistan but also to organize a new administrative structure of the state. The League initially thought of making Rawalpindi as the capital but besides communal strife in that district as well as in the whole of the Punjab, various other factors including its distance from East Bengal persuaded it to abandon that idea.[219] East Bengal could not afford to make an offer of a capital city as it had to establish its own capital, which it did in Dhaka. The NWFP even after the pro-Pakistan vote in the referendum had remained with a Congress ministry till a week after independence. Balochistan was too distant and underdeveloped to extend an invitation. Sindh was the only province which had a League ministry, enjoying a relatively peaceful atmosphere and could provide the requisite facilities. The Sindh provincial Muslim League offered to make Karachi as the capital of the state and the All-India Muslim League accepted that generous offer.[220] After the adoption of the independence bill on 19 July, the interim government was replaced by two provisional cabinets, one for Pakistan and the other for India, which assumed charge of portfolios of the two states. The two cabinets with Mountbatten as chairman dealt with common matters. After 3 June, Mountbatten had set up a four-member Partition Committee with equal representation to the League and the Congress to give effect to partition; and on 27 June, the committee was replaced by a Partition Council with Mountbatten as chairman and Patel and Rajendra Prasad with Rajagopalachari as alternate, representing the Congress, and Jinnah and Liaquat with Nishtar as alternate, representing the League, as members. The Partition Council worked through a steering committee consisting of two civil servants, Chaudhri Mohammad Ali (1905–1980) and H.M. Patel (1904–1993). Ten expert committees assisted the steering committee in its task, and in turn, several departmental committees supported each expert committee. Similar bodies were created for the three partitioned provinces of the Punjab, Bengal and Assam. The process of division had not been completed by 15 August; and after that, a reconstituted committee consisting of two representatives each of Pakistan and India continued to look after the work of the Partition Council. Any unresolved issue could be referred to an arbitral tribunal, which was chaired by Sir Patrick Spens (1885–1973), former chief justice of India, and which functioned till 31 March 1948. The employees were given the option to opt for either of the two states.[221] This exercise glaringly brought out Muslim underrepresentation in the services especially in the senior positions. Muslim officers were 101 out of 1,157 in the Indian civil service and police service, out of whom 95 opted for Pakistan. Almost similar was the proportion of Muslims in the higher cadres of other services.[222] Most of the optees were stationed in the Indian areas and their transfer to Pakistan presented a serious problem. On 8 August, when a train carrying personnel of the Pakistan government from Delhi to Karachi was derailed by a bomb explosion, killing four and injuring twenty persons, transportation of employees had to be done by air and sea. The 'Operation Pakistan', as it was called, which began on 4 September, and was completed in December 1947, transported some 7,000 employees by air and more than 17,000 employees and their families by sea via Bombay.[223]

Despite the inadequacy of administrative staff, inexperience of the League leaders in administration, unfriendly top British representatives and hostile Congress leadership, the League under Jinnah's guidance made the miraculous survival of Pakistan possible. The Leaguers proved wrong the expectations of the Congress leaders that Pakistan 'Provinces would ultimately have to seek re-union with the remainder of India'.[224] Of course, the odds were heavily tilted against Pakistan. Its areas were industrially backward: 14 out of the 394 textile mills, all the 106 jute mills and only 1414 out of 14,677 registered factories — even those comprising mostly small-scale establishments — were located here. Almost all the financial institutions in the Pakistan areas such as banks, insurance and credit facilities were in the hands of non-Muslims who migrated *en bloc* to India. Pakistan received unfair treatment in the division of cash balances, and it managed its affairs with great difficulty.[225] Similar was the case with the division of the armed forces. Early in July, an armed forces reconstitution committee with General Claude Auchinleck as the supreme commander and four subcommittees that dealt with army, navy, air force and financial assets was established to bring about the division. Auchinleck worked under a joint defence council consisting of Mountbatten (chairman), Liaquat (representing Pakistan) and Baldev Singh (representing Hindustan) but the defence council had no operational control over the armed forces of the two dominions, except the Punjab Boundary Force. The last date for the division of the forces was 1 April 1948, but due to the dispute over the accession of the state of Jammu and Kashmir, communal violence in the Punjab and winding up of the headquarters of the supreme commander, Pakistan assumed control of its armed forces on 1 December 1947, four months ahead of the scheduled date. The defence council allocated one-third of the military stores and other materials to Pakistan but India withheld major part of its share on the plea of its possible use in the Kashmir conflict. Similar was the fate of Rs 60 million that India had agreed to pay in place of Pakistan's share in the sixteen ordnance factories that were located in the Indian territories. More serious was the distribution of waters of the Punjab rivers. As a result of the boundary award, the control of the major canal headworks that controlled the waters flowing into West Punjab and the Bahawalpur state passed on to East Punjab. The League members of the Punjab Partition Committee naively accepted the Indian members' verbal promises that there was 'no question of varying the authorized share to which the two zones [East and West Punjab] and various canals are entitled' and did not press for reference of the matter to the arbitral tribunal for a clear verdict. Sir Cyril Radcliffe's observations that the existing share of waters would be respected lulled their possible suspicions. But on 1 April 1948, the day the arbitral tribunal stood dissolved, India cut off the water supplies to every canal crossing into (West) Pakistan; thus began the waters' dispute between Pakistan and India.[226]

Immediately, Pakistan had to deal with the carnage following the partition of the Punjab, resulting from unattended communal tensions and official policies of the preceding months. Sporadic communal riots had started in the Punjab cities in March 1947. Then, the Sikhs, joined by the Rashtriya Swayamsevak Sangh, began to plan extermination of the Muslim population in east Punjab and east Punjab states. They did not observe much secrecy about their designs. Jinnah and Liaquat urged Mountbatten to take preventive steps. Their information was corroborated by reports from the Punjab governor who gave evidence of the plans and the leaders involved but no arrests were made. The Radcliffe Award further aggravated the deteriorating situation. Mountbatten, after rejecting a proposal to entrust the task of demarcation of boundaries either to a UN commission or to a three-member committee of the law lords from the UK, had appointed Sir Cyril Radcliffe, a British lawyer, to chair the boundary commissions that were to demarcate the boundaries of the partitioned provinces of the Punjab, Bengal and Assam on the basis of contiguous Muslim and non-Muslim majority areas, taking 'into account other factors'.[227] In case of a deadlock, Radcliffe was empowered to give his own award(s), and the parties gave prior commitments to accept such awards. Since the commissions failed to reach agreements, Radcliffe gave his own awards. Mountbatten under pressure from the Congress and Sikh leaders manoeuvred changes in the award in regard to the Punjab after its submission, which resulted in the transfer of two Muslim majority tehsils of Ferozepur and Zira to India; thus, India gained control of the canal headworks that directed flow of water into West Punjab and the Bahawalpur state. Governor Jenkins, whom the League suspected of partiality, and the Punjab League assembly party on 21 June, had demanded his removal from office, left in haste on his departure a sketch-map in the governor's house, which showed these two tehsils as part of Pakistan. Any doubts about the authenticity of this sketch-map were removed in 1992, when Herbert C. Beaumont, private secretary to Radcliffe, confirmed this act of extreme injustice in a detailed statement.[228] Jinnah must have known Jenkins' role in the process of partition, and he expressed his displeasure by refusing to extend him the courtesy of staying at the governor-general's house in Karachi on his way to London when he made a request to that effect.[229] Even before the tampering of the award, Radcliffe, using 'other factors' of his instructions and in accordance with Mountbatten's promise to Nehru on 12 May, had drawn a boundary line that transferred to India without any justification two Muslim majority tehsils (Gurdaspur and Batala) in the Gurdaspur district, which provided India with a physical link to the state of Jammu and Kashmir.[230] Similarly, Radcliffe assigned Calcutta to India, and drew a boundary line that deprived Pakistan of Murshidabad district, major part of the Nadia district and other Muslim majority areas contiguous to East Bengal and Sylhet.[231]

On 1 August, a 55,000-strong Punjab Boundary Force, headed by Major General T.W. Rees under the control of the supreme commander, had been set up to enforce law and order in the disturbed areas of the Punjab but after exactly one month, on 31 August, it was disbanded amidst controversy as it failed to control the situation. It was replaced by area headquarters in east and west Punjab, answerable to the commanders-in-chief of Pakistan and India. However, communal violence persisted especially after the announcement of the Radcliffe Award and spread to Delhi and the surrounding areas. The object was obviously to overwhelm Pakistan with riots and refugees. Neither appeals from the top leaders of the two parties nor tours of the affected areas by the prime ministers of Pakistan and India could stop the bloodbath. Finally, it was decided to arrange organized evacuation of Muslims from East Punjab and Hindus and Sikhs from West Punjab. A joint military evacuation organization was established that provided mixed guards for the refugee camps and armed escorts for foot, railway and motor convoys. Jinnah proved a source of inspiration and confidence for the Pakistanis in this hour of national crisis. He stayed in Lahore, capital of (West) Punjab, for thirty-five days, returning to Karachi on 1 December, and Prime Minister Liaquat on his instructions shifted the cabinet secretariat to Lahore from September to December to supervise the evacuation process and look after the relief work for the refugees. No authentic estimates are available of the number of persons killed and displaced; the figures of all surveys on this subject are tentative. About one million Muslims lost their lives; 50,000 Muslim and 10,000 non-Muslim women were recovered, the League's women's committee led by Fatima Begum played a remarkable role in the recovery of Muslim women from East Punjab; and over 7 million Muslim refugees arrived in (West) Pakistan and about 4.5 million non-Muslims went over to India. The rehabilitation of refugees, to which were soon added over 0.4 million refugees from the state of Jammu and Kashmir was a job of colossal dimensions for the new state. The League workers and Muslim League National Guards did selfless and admirable work for the immediate relief of the refugees. By 14 August 1947, Sindh, West Punjab, East Bengal and Sylhet, NWFP, tribal areas and British Balochistan had joined Pakistan.

(*iii*) *The States*. Negotiations for the accession of states to Pakistan began after the passage of the Indian Independence Act. The delay was the result of the British policies, Congress manoeuvres and the League's policy in regard to the states. The 1937 constitution of the All-India Muslim League was silent about the states; therefore, its activities had been confined to British India. It had practically no plan for the all-India federation that the Act of 1935 visualized for British India and the states. While the Congress leaders demonstrated hostility towards those states whose rulers were unlikely to nominate its supporters to the federal legislature, Jinnah cultivated some of them to counterbalance the Congress moves and to demolish the whole scheme of federation. When the war virtually buried the proposed federation, the Congress tried to secure for India the status of successor authority to the British power on the lapse of paramountcy, but the League remained ambivalent and did not devise any pro-active policy about the states. The post-war British policy was laid down in the Cabinet Mission's memorandum of 12 May 1946, and the statement of 16 May. It provided categorically for the lapse of paramountcy, which could 'neither be retained by the British Crown nor transferred to the new government', and recognized the consequential freedom of the states to decide their own future.[232] The Congress leaders considered it 'wicked of Cripps' not to have recommended the transfer of paramountcy to India while the focus of the League struggle was on the acceptance of Pakistan in British India.[233] On 9 December 1946, the viceroy on the direction of the British cabinet convened the constituent assembly to appease the Congress and allowed it to function without the League's participation. A Patel-chaired States Negotiating Committee of the constituent assembly did the groundwork by pressurizing the rulers to join the constituent assembly. Nehru as president of the All India States Peoples' Congress made his contribution to facilitate its task. His statements foreshadowed the Congress policy towards the states. On 18 April 1947, in his presidential address to the States Peoples' Congress in Gwalior, he threatened those states which had not come into the constituent assembly that they would be regarded as 'hostile' states and would have 'to bear the consequences' of their action.[234] His subsequent explanation that he had been 'misquoted' or that he had made the statement 'purely' as president of the States Peoples' Congress did not mitigate the impact of his threat.[235] Then, his famous comments about the 'balkanization' of India related to the provisions of the India committee-approved plan about the states and the NWFP. By the time the League came into the picture, the Congress strategy had secured the entry of most of the States into the Congress-controlled constituent assembly.

The All-India Muslim League knew nothing about the negotiations between the Patel-chaired States Negotiating Committee and the representatives of the chamber of princes or about Mountbatten's talks with the Congress leaders on the issue of states, after their acceptance of dominion status and their concurrence to join the Commonwealth. The 3 June Plan had simply stated that the British policy towards the states would remain the same as laid down in the Cabinet Mission's memorandum of 12 May. Explaining the 3 June Plan on 4 June, Mountbatten observed that with the lapse of paramountcy, the states would be 'absolutely free' to choose one constituent assembly or the other, or make some other arrangement.[236] The League and the Congress leaders put conflicting interpretation on the options available to the states: while the Congress leaders regarded any declaration of independence by the states as a declaration of war, Jinnah categorically stated that constitutionally and legally, on the lapse of paramountcy, the states would be free to choose any course they liked.[237] The Indian Independence Act snapped all connections between the British crown and the states with effect from 15 August, and provided that nothing prevented their accession 'to either of the new Dominions'.[238] Two documents were drawn up: one, an Instrument of Accession for three subjects—defence, external affairs and communications; and two, a Standstill Agreement to cover existing arrangements for customs, currency and other similar matters. Mountbatten who was still the crown representative convened a meeting of the chamber of princes on 25 July, and advised the rulers of the states contiguous to India to accede to that country, and at the reception that he gave to the princes on 28 July, he pressurized them individually to do so. He did nothing of the kind in the case of the states contiguous to Pakistan; in fact, he did quite the opposite. He pressurized the rulers of the Hindu majority states of Jodhpur and Jaisalmer, who wanted to join Pakistan, to accede to India, on the plea that any other action on their part would be against the principle underlying the partition of India and result in communal strife. But he forgot this principle in the case of Kapurthala, a state contiguous to (West) Punjab with 64 per cent Muslim majority and ruled by a Sikh, which resulted in the extermination and exodus of Muslims from that state.

The All-India Muslim League remained too absorbed in the struggle for Pakistan in British India to formulate any clear policy in regard to the states. It could have demanded the accession of Muslim majority states to Pakistan but it did not do that, although that was the principle that Mountbatten and the Congress used to justify the forcible accession of Hindu majority states to India. Jinnah was too busy in the fight for the acceptance of the Pakistan demand to attend to the states and none else in the League had the authority or initiative in such matters.[239] Another plausible explanation is that the Muslims could not think of abandoning Muslim-ruled Hindu majority states like Hyderabad, Bhopal and Rampur which had historically been custodians of Indo-Muslim culture. Conversely, the Congress had a clear stand and its leaders felt no qualm to use pressure tactics and even violence against those states whose rulers were reluctant, or declined, to accede to India at its bidding. Travancore, a Hindu majority State, wanted to stay independent, but when the *diwan* (prime minister), Sir Ramaswamy Aiyer (1879–1966), resisted accession to India, the Congress workers assaulted him; and the maharaja saw his safety in acceding to India. The resistance to accession to India in Rampur and Bhopal, whose ruler aspired to align his state with Pakistan, was suppressed by the use of force.[240] Similar fate awaited the Hyderabad state. The Nizam, its ruler, had planned to see his state independent and considered Pakistan an 'impracticable' proposition and 'a shadow without substance'.[241] He tried in vain to persuade the British government either to cede the port of Masulipatam to his state or to help her buy Goa from the Portuguese to have direct access to the sea and took no step that would annoy the Hindu community in the state.[242] His ambition to keep communal balance had often spoiled his relations with the Majlis-i-Ittehadul Muslimin, the most influential party of the Hyderabad Muslims. His unfair treatment of Nawab Bahadur Yar Jung after the latter's election as the Majlis-i-Ittehadul Muslimin president hurt popular Muslim sentiments in and outside the State.[243] His cordial relations with Jinnah who had influence with every section of the Hyderabad society facilitated his moves to conciliate Bahadur Yar Jung. During 1939–46, he appointed two League leaders, Sayyid Abdul Aziz of Bihar and Nawab Ahmad Saeed Khan Chattari (1889–1982), successively as prime ministers on Jinnah's advice, and the British government raised no objections. But in the middle of 1946, there was a change in that practice. Sir Mirza M. Ismail, a pro-Congress Muslim, who believed in the unity of India and on whose advice Bahadur Yar Jung was clumsily thrown out of Kashmir in September 1943, was appointed prime minister amidst Jinnah's frantic opposition.[244] That was the beginning of the end of the Hyderabad state. The Nizam's calculation that he could win over the Congress by such gestures proved wrong. He belatedly realized his mistake and appointed Mir Laiq Ali, a Muslim industrialist, as the prime minister but by then it was too late.[245] The Congress government forcibly suppressed Nizam's attempt to maintain the independent status of the Hyderabad state, and the ill-equipped Majlis-i-Ittehadul Muslimin volunteers who put up resistance were no match to the well-organized and well-equipped Indian armed forces. Hyderabad's appeal to the UN against the Indian aggression could not draw any immediate and effective response.

Pakistan secured the accession of states by constitutional and peaceful means. The accession of four states in the North-West Frontier—Swat, Dir, Amb and Chitral—was without any complication.[246] So was the case with the Khairpur state, which was contiguous to Sindh. The accession of the Bahawalpur state that was contiguous to West Punjab was delayed till 3 October, although it had decided to send its representative to the Pakistan constituent assembly on 15 August.

The delay was partly because Mushtaq Ahmad Gurmani (1905–1981), its prime minister, had been negotiating with the rulers of the states contiguous to West Punjab for their accession to Pakistan. There were four states in Balochistan: Qalat, Kharan, Las Bela and Makran. Qalat was a landlocked state: Kharan separated it from Iran and Makran and Las Bela blocked its access to the sea. Ahmad Yar Khan, its ruler, claimed overlordship over the other states and the areas leased to the British—Quetta, Nushki and Nasirabad—but his authority outside Qalat was neither recognized by the British nor accepted by the rulers of these states.[247] The British government had rejected his claims but Mountbatten tried to complicate his relations with Pakistan by suppressing facts and by giving him wrong advice.[248] Qalat signed a Standstill Agreement with Pakistan and the Khan agreed to negotiate an accession agreement at Karachi. The Khan, on his own authority, declared Qalat's independence making provision for a bicameral legislature. Instead of deciding the issue of accession himself, he brought it before a newly elected legislature: the lower house opposed accession while the upper house took no decision. After the Sibi durbar in February 1948, Jinnah who had been negotiating with the khan the accession of the state dissociated himself from the talks; and the Pakistan government then assigned this responsibility to the ministry of foreign affairs.[249] A stalemate continued till 17 March 1948, when Pakistan accepted the accession of Kharan, Makran and Las Bela whose rulers had been pressing for it since July 1947.[250] Still, the khan took ten days to accede to Pakistan. Immediate cause was V.P. Menon's assertion on the All India Radio that India had refused to accept the khan's offer of accession to India. On listening to the radio, the khan refuted the allegation and announced the accession of his state to Pakistan. Military action was taken five months after the accession when khan's brother, Prince Abdul Karim, who had gone over to Afghanistan returned with 200 armed men and refused to submit despite appeals from his brother. Subsequent turmoil in Balochistan was the by-product of the merger of the provinces and states of West Pakistan into one unit rather than Qalat's accession to Pakistan. Eleven years after independence, in September 1958, Gwadar, with an area of about 300 square miles, became part of Pakistan, when Pakistan purchased it from the Sultan of Muscat for £3,000,000. The Northern Areas, consisting of Gilgit, Chilas, Hunza, Nagar, Punyial and Baltistan, were the only areas that joined Pakistan after an armed struggle.[251]

In July 1947, Junagarh, a small state about 300 miles from Karachi by sea, and the Manavadar state, requested for accession to Pakistan; and on 3 September, Pakistan accepted the request.[252] Two feudatories of Junagarh, the ruler of Mangrol and landlords of the Babriawad taluka, who had no independent constitutional status, joined India. Junagarh with a Muslim ruler had 20 per cent Muslims in a total population of 700,000. The Government of India protested against Junagarh's accession to Pakistan, arguing that the accession had ignored 'ties of geographical contiguity' and the 'wishes of the people'. It encouraged Shamlal Nehru, Gandhi's nephew, to raise a 'liberation' army and set up a provisional government. Pakistan offered to hold a plebiscite in the Junagarh state under the joint auspices of Pakistan and India, but the Government of India did not accept that offer and resorted to force. Economic blockade of Junagarh was followed by invasion of the State with regular Indian army units which led to its conquest on 10 November. The nawab and his family had already left for Karachi. Pakistan watched the situation helplessly as it had no military resources to resist the Indian aggression. It raised this issue of blatant violation of international law at the UN but without any positive result. India arranged a plebiscite in Junagarh under its own auspices, which obviously went in its favour. Pakistan refused to accept this farce.

The accession of the state of Jammu and Kashmir, which had borders with China, created an unending Pakistan–India conflict. The state had cultural and strategic importance for Pakistan; K in Pa$k$istan represented Kashmir. It had absolute Muslim majority: 77 per cent of its population was Muslim and Muslim proportion was more than 90 per cent in the Kashmir valley. Muslims had experienced the worst oppression under the Dogra Hindu chief who had purchased it from the British for a sum of Rs 7.5 million under the treaty of Amritsar (1946). In 1931, Muslims started a movement for reforms and established the All Jammu and Kashmir Muslim Conference with Shaikh Abdullah as president and Chaudhri Ghulam Abbas as general secretary.[253] Consequently, moderate reforms were introduced that were based on the Glancy Commission Report. In the first elections of the legislative assembly that these reforms created, Muslim Conference secured 16 out of 21 seats, but the repression of the Muslims did not stop. In 1939–40, the All Jammu and Kashmir Muslim Conference suffered a split: Shaikh Abdullah set up the non-communal All Jammu and Kashmir National Conference, which aligned itself with the Congress;

and Ghulam Abbas and Mir Waiz Mohammad Yusuf subsequently led the All Jammu and Kashmir Muslim Conference, which subscribed to the League viewpoint. The divergence in viewpoints caused bitterness between the two parties which facilitated the continuance of the oppressive regime of Sir Gopalswami Iyengar. Jinnah's efforts brought about the end of Iyengar's rule (1937–1943) but his mediation failed to bridge the gulf between the Muslim conference and the National Conference.[254] Instead, Shaikh Abdullah moved away from the League and the Pakistan demand. The state authorities showed partiality towards the National Conference and against the Muslim Conference. While they banned the conference that the All Jammu and Kashmir Muslim Conference planned to hold in Srinagar in September 1943, they allowed the National Conference to organize a conference in the city in August 1945, which several British Indian leaders including Nehru, Azad, Ghaffar Khan and Abdus Samad Achakzai attended.[255]

The Congress desire to encircle Pakistan, the British strategic interests, the League's ambiguous policy towards the states and the maharaja's desire for exclusive control landed Kashmir into a state of confusion and uncertainty. The National Conference-organized quit Kashmir movement that was launched after the Cabinet Mission led to the arrest and conviction of Shaikh Abdullah for three years, and the incarceration of Ghulam Abbas followed soon after that, following protest demonstrations for not allowing the Muslim Conference to hold its annual session. Although the Muslim Conference won a majority of the Muslim seats in the 1946 elections, the conference itself was divided, not without the involvement of the Congress; one faction was led by Hamidullah and the other by Mir Waiz Yusuf.[256] Ghulam Abbas who could have brought about unity in the party ranks remained in jail. The issue of accession came up in such an atmosphere of turmoil. Mountbatten who had a 25-year long friendship with the maharaja came to the Congress assistance.[257] While, on 19 July, the Muslim Conference called for the accession of the state to Pakistan, Mountbatten in his visit to Srinagar advised the maharaja not to accede to either of the two states before independence perhaps because Gurdaspur district as part of the Muslim majority districts in the notional division of the Punjab under the 3 June Plan had voted for accession to Pakistan, and that had deprived India geographical contiguity with the state. The Leaguers' possible doubts about the accession of Kashmir to Pakistan were lulled by the absolute majority of the Muslims in the state, its contiguity only with (West) Punjab and the NWFP, its cultural and economic ties with these areas and the signing of the Standstill Agreement only with Pakistan. After the Radcliffe Award, the state troops and police, assisted by the Sikh and Rashtriya Swayamsevak Sangh zealots, started a systematic campaign of extermination of Muslims. The Kashmiris of the western part of the state including the recently demobilized personnel of the Indian army rose in revolt; and on 24 September, they established a provisional government of Azad Jammu and Kashmir. A tribal *lashkar* from the tribal areas joined the Kashmiri resistance. Now it was easy for India to manipulate the terrified maharaja. On 27 October, the papers relating to the state's accession to India were flown into Kashmir along with the Indian army units. Dubious accession of the state and fierce resistance in Kashmir persuaded India to appeal to the UN for intervention, promising a plebiscite after the restoration of normal conditions. The UN appointed a commission for India and Pakistan, which took almost a year to arrange a ceasefire. Meanwhile, India launched an offensive in April 1948, and Pakistan sent its own regular army into Kashmir the following month to block the Indian progress towards certain strategic points. The Pakistan army succeeded in holding the Indian offensive. A stalemate in fighting and negotiations for a ceasefire continued till the end of the year. On 5 January 1949, the UN commission arranged a ceasefire and Pakistan and India agreed to the appointment of a plebiscite commissioner who was to hold a plebiscite in the Jammu and Kashmir state after the withdrawal of armed personnel of the two countries. But the promised plebiscite could not be organized in the state, and the Kashmir dispute has lingered on unresolved between Pakistan and India.

NOTES

1. For the text of his statement, see *TP*, vol. IX, pp. 773–75.
2. Attlee to Mountbatten, 18 March 1947, ibid., pp. 972–74.
3. P. Clarke, *Cripps Version*, pp. 469–70; and Ghosh, *Gandhi's Emissary*, pp. 44–48.
4. Note by George Abell, 26 March 1947, *TP*, vol. X, pp. 26–27.
5. For Minutes of the Staff Meetings till 7 May, see ibid.
6. For instance, see *TP*, vol. XI, p. 5.
7. H.V. Hodson, *The Great Divide: Britain—India—Pakistan*, Karachi, 1984, p. 300.
8. After the Lahore Resolution, Rajagopalachari and Gandhi had repeatedly made similar proposals. On 11 May 1947, Jinnah responded that in such a case he would be a 'prisoner' in the hands of the Hindu majority. QAP, F. 487, pp. 41–42.
9. Record of Interview between Mountbatten and Gandhi, 1 and 2 April 1947, *TP*, vol. X, pp. 69 and 84; Ismay to Gandhi and Gandhi to Ismay, 6 April 1947, ibid., pp. 140–42.

10. Viceroy's Staff Meetings: Uncirculated Record of Discussion No. 7, 12 April 1947, ibid., p. 208.
11. Record of Interview between Mountbatten and Gandhi, 12 April and 4 May 1947, ibid., p. 611; and also see pp. 548–49 and 667–68.
12. Gandhi's views, 27 May 1947, ibid., p. 1037.
13. Ibid., p. 1038.
14. Record of Interviews between Mountbatten and Krishna Menon, 17 and 22 April 1947, ibid., pp. 312–13 and 373–74.
15. Pethick-Lawrence to Wavell, 14 March 1947, ibid., vol. IX, p. 956; and Menon, *Transfer of Power*, p. 359. See Section (*d*) Evolution of the Partition Plan of this Chapter.
16. Menon to Mieville, 5 April 1947, *TP*, vol. X, pp. 129–31; Ismay to Menon, 11 April 1947, ibid., pp. 193–94; Viceroy's Staff Meetings: Uncirculated Record of Discussion No. 7, 12 April 1947, ibid., p. 209; and Menon to Ismay, 28 April 1947, ibid., pp. 437–40.
17. Record of Interview between Mountbatten and Patel, 24 April 1947, ibid., p. 398.
18. The second Field Marshal was General Sam Manekshaw. Both were given this honour for leading wars against Pakistan.
19. According to Auchinleck, it would take 5–10 years to divide the Indian army satisfactorily. Minutes of Viceroy's 4th Staff Meeting, 28 March 1947, *TP*, vol. X, p. 35.
20. Mountbatten to Ismay, 4 May 1947, and Ismay to Mountbatten, 10 May 1947, and Minutes of Viceroy's Seventh Miscellaneous Meeting, 23 April 1947, ibid., pp. 381, 755 and 603.
21. Record of Interview between Mountbatten and Nehru, 11 April 1947, ibid., p. 199.
22. Record of Interview between Mountbatten and Krishna Menon, 5 April 1947, ibid., p. 133; and for the Congress–Mountbatten strategy, see Krishna Menon to Mountbatten, 14 June 1947, ibid., vol. XI, pp. 390–91. Krishna Menon asked him to destroy the letter after reading it.
23. For instance, see 'Question and Draft Answer for Mr Jalal Husseini of the Egyptian Trade Delegation', QAP, F. 10, p. 83.
24. For the effects of these movements even on leaders like Patel, see Patel to Henderson, 16 April 1947, *TP*, vol. X, pp. 268–69.
25. Almas Daultana to Quaid-i-Azam, 2 June 1947, QAP, F. 156, pp. 136–38, for funds provided for the Punjab civil disobedience movement. For the preparation of the movement, see the minutes of the central committee of action in QAP, F. 831.
26. Talbot, *Khizr Tiwana*, pp. 154–55.
27. Jenkins to Pethick-Lawrence, 26 January 1947, *TP*, vol. IX, pp. 556–57; and *Police Abstract of Intelligence, Punjab*, 26 January 1947, p. 39.
28. For Noon's negotiations with the police without consulting his colleagues, see Iftikhar Husain to Quaid-i-Azam, 22 February 1947, QAP, F. 372, pp. 22–23.
29. For reports about meetings and *hartals*, see AFM, vol. 346, nos. 3–33.
30. Wavell to Pethick-Lawrence, 26 February 1947, *TP*, vol. IX, p. 819.
31. Jinnah encouraged them to keep up the pressure; he wrote to Mamdot on 23 February, 'Honourable defeat, if it is to be, is better than a compromise which is discreditable and contrary to accepted constitutional principles and precedents and the rules of democracy for which we are fighting'. QAP, F. 372, pp. 24–27.
32. Liaquat to Nawab Mamdot, Express telegram, AFM, vol. 346, no. 58.

33. Jenkins to Mamdot, 5 March 1947, *TP*, vol. IX, pp. 867–69; note by Auchinleck to Abell, 22 March 1947 (communicating a note by Messervy), ibid., 1005; and note by E. Jenkins, 16 April 1947, ibid., Vol. X, pp. 282–83.

34. For Mountbatten's impressions after his visit to Kahota, then a small town of 1,500 Muslims and 2,000 Hindus and Sikhs, see Viceroy's Personal Report No. 5, 1 May 1947, ibid., p. 537; and for two Gurmukhi pamphlets, giving 'grossly exaggerated account' of the events in the Rawalpindi division, and establishment of a war fund of Rs 50 lakh, on an appeal signed by eighteen Sikh leaders, with Baldev Singh and Bhag Singh as treasurers, see Jenkins to Mountbatten, 9 April 1947, ibid., pp. 172–75.

35. For Muslim denial, see Jenkins to Mountbatten, 31 March 1947, ibid., p. 59; and for the communists, see Mrs Rallia Ram to Jinnah, 27 March 1947, QAP, F. 487, p. 31.

36. Out of 29 district magistrates only 9 were Muslim and there was not a single Muslim commissioner or deputy inspector general of police in the Punjab. In Rawalpindi, only 5 out of 26 officials of the special investigation staff were Muslims and 'this at a time when justice by any except a mixed staff is out of the question'. Liaquat to Mountbatten, 15 April 1947, *TP*, vol. X, p. 257; and also see ibid., p 283.

37. For the League's allegations against Jenkins and his partisan role, see Liaquat to Mountbatten, 15 April 1947, ibid., pp. 256–57; and Note by E. Jenkins, 20 March 1947, ibid., 997; and for Khizr's advice to Jenkins to invite Mamdot to form the ministry, see ibid., vol. IX, pp. 565–66.

38. For Jenkins' advocacy of Section 93 and his manoeuvrings even before the outbreak of riots, see his letters to Wavell (3 and 5 March) and Pethick-Lawrence (4 March), ibid., pp. 829, 851 and 869; and Wavell to Pethick-Lawrence, 5 March 1947, ibid., p. 854; and for the advocacy of two or more ministries in the Punjab by Jenkins, Nehru, Sir B. N. Rau, and the Sikh and Hindu leaders, see ibid., pp. 39, 925, 504–5 and 927.

39. Note by E. Jenkins, 20 March 1947, ibid., pp. 996–97; and record of interview between Mountbatten and Liaquat, [19] April 1947, ibid., p 331.

40. Jenkins to Mountbatten, 28 April 1947, ibid., vol. X, p. 477; and Mamdot to Jenkins, 28 April 1947, QAP, F. 126, pp. 3–4.

41. *TP*, vol. X, pp. 500–503.

42. Viceroy's Personal Report No. 5, 1 May 1947, ibid., p. 538.

43. Record of Interview between Mountbatten and Jinnah and Liaquat, 2 May 1947, ibid., p. 568.

44. A provincial Muslim League-appointed 'Muslim Minority Provinces Protection Board' sent a three-member (Arbab Abdul Ghafur, Fida Mohammad Khan and Mian Burhanuddin) deputation to Bihar to apprise itself about the riots and plight of the Muslims.

45. Caroe to Wavell, 22 February 1947, *TP*, vol. IX, pp. 787–89; and Wavell to Pethick-Lawrence, 26 February 1947, ibid., p. 819. In December 1946-January 1947, the events surrounding the conversion of a Sikh woman who took refuge at the chief minister house and her return to her community fuelled the emotional atmosphere. For details, see Erland Jansson, *India, Pakistan or Pakhtunistan*, Stockholm, 1981, pp. 190–91; and Syed Waqar Ali Shah, *Muslim League in N.W.F.P.*, Karachi, 1992, pp. 131–32.

46. Minutes of the Viceroy's Seventh Meeting, 23 April 1947, *TP*, vol. X, p. 379.

47. For instance, see Atta Hasan Ali Khan, Mohammad Aminul Hasanat, Pir Zakori, Sardar Bahadur Khan and a few others to Quaid-i-Azam, 20 November 1946, AFM, vol. 366, p. 42; and for Mountbatten's request to Jinnah for stopping advertisements in the *Dawn* regarding 'a secret broadcasting station', see Viceroy's Seventh Misc. Meeting, 23 April 1947, *TP*, vol. X, p. 379.

48. With 'the aid of troops' and the 'opposition in jail', the ministry carried through the budget session; and the governor shortened its duration. Caroe to Mountbatten, 22 March 1947, *TP*, vol. X, p. 1.

49. Caroe to Mountbatten, 31 March 1947, ibid., pp. 60–61; and Mountbatten to Pethick-Lawrence, 9 April 1947, ibid., p. 166; and for details of the movement, see Sayed Wiqar Ali Shah, *Ethnicity, Islam, and Nationalism: Muslim Politics in the North-West Frontier Province, 1937–1947*, OUP, 2000, pp. 201–210.

50. Caroe to Mountbatten, 17 May 1947, *TP*, vol. X, pp. 874–75.

51. Mountbatten to Pethick-Lawrence, 9 April 1947, ibid., p. 167; and Minutes of the Viceroy's Seventh Meeting, 23 April 1947, ibid., p. 379.

52. Mountbatten to Jinnah, 27 April 1947, ibid., p. 465.

53. Mountbatten's meeting with the governor and four ministers, 28 April 1947, ibid., p. 494; Note by Mountbatten, 29 April 1947, ibid., p. 480; Mountbatten to Nehru, 30 April 1947, ibid., pp. 491–92; and for the basis of his impression, see Viceroy's Personal Report No. 5, 1 May 1947, ibid., p. 535. Earlier, Ismay had communicated similar conclusions after a visit to the NWFP. Viceroy's Personal Report No. 2, 9 April 1947, p. 168; and Record of Meeting, 14 April 1947, ibid., p. 233.

54. Viceroy's Personal Report No. 7, 15 May 1947, ibid., p. 837.

55. Till 1878, Sylhet had been part of Bengal.

56. For details, see Chapter 8.

57. For instance, see the resolution of the All-India Muslim League council passed on 25 February 1940, AFM, vol. 284, p. 60.

58. Wiqar Ali Shah, *Ethnicity, Islam, and Nationalism*, pp. 134–35.

59. Midrarullah to Jinnah, 1 July 1944, *Jinnah Papers*, Second Series, vol. X, pp. 514–16; and Jinnah to Midrarullah, Daily *Shahbaz* (Lahore), 15 July 1944.

60. Abdul Qayyum to Jinnah, 28 June 1946, QAP, F. 324, pp. 3–4.

61. AFM, vol. 142, no. 57; and Pirzada, *Foundations*, vol. II, p. 323.

62. Clauses 11 (1) and 123 (1) of the Government of India Act 1935.

63. For the transfer, see Mountbatten's statement in Minutes of Viceroy's Twenty-fifth Staff Meeting, Item No. 3, 3 May 1947, *TP*, vol. X, p. 581.

64. *Daily Mail* (London), 28 September 1946; AFM, vol. 402, pp. 34–35.

65. For expression of support for Pakistan in Jirgas and by individuals, see QAP F. 891, pp. 114–20; and for hostile demonstrations, see Wiqar Ali Shah, *Ethnicity, Islam, and Nationalism*, pp. 175–83. See also Chapter 11.

66. Wavell to Pethick Lawrence, 19 March 1947, *TP*, vol. IX, p. 991.

67. Abdul Qayyum to Jinnah, 25 October 1946, SHC, NWFP-II: 113; and *Khyber Mail*, 25 October 1947.

68. AFM, vol. 366, pp. 57–58.

69. President, Waziristan Tribal Jirga to Quaid-i-Azam, 6 March 1947, QAP, F. 560, p. 22.

70. Caroe to Weightman, 17 March 1947, *TP*, vol. X, pp. 205–6.

71. QAP, F. 574, pp. 30–31. For a League in the Kurram Agency, see Jinnah to general secretary, All Kurram Agency Muslim League, 18 April 1947, ibid., p. 34.

72. For the activities and plans for armed struggle of the tribes, see Report Nos. 1–3, ibid., F. 917, pp. 149–51; F. 918; and F. 892, p. 112.

73. Viceroy's Personal Report No. 5, 1 May 1947, *TP*, vol. p. 537.
74. AFM, vol. 366, pp. 39–40, 52–54, 62 and 64–65; and QAP, F. 560, p. 27; F. 886, pp. 232–33; F. 896, pp. 69–71; and F. 908, p. 107.
75. Viceroy's Personal Report No. 1, 2 April 1947, and Sir T. Shone to Sir N. Brook, 23 April 1945, ibid., pp. 92 and 382–83, respectively.
76. QAP, F. 335, pp. 280–81.
77. Cabinet: India and Burma Committee, I B. (47) 16th Meeting, 28 March 1947, *TP*, vol. X, pp. 40–41; and Chaudhri Muhammad Ali, *The Emergence of Pakistan*, New York, 1967, pp. 104–111.
78. Minutes of the Viceroy's Sixth Staff Meeting, 31 March 1947 (Uncirculated Record of Discussion No. 2: Alternative to the Cabinet Mission Plan, *TP*, vol. X, pp. 48–51.
79. For the text of the plan, see Minutes of the Viceroy's Sixth Staff Meeting: Addendum to No. 34/Uncirculated Record of Discussion No. 2/Mountbatten Papers, 31 March 1947, ibid., pp. 49–51. See also Minutes of the Viceroy's Fifth Meeting/Addendum No. 33/Uncirculated Record of Discussion No. 1, 29 March 1947, ibid., p. 47.
80. For example, see Enclosure No. 120: 'One of Possible Plans for the Transfer of Power, which are Receiving Examination', in Ismay to Menon, 11 April 1947, ibid., pp. 193–94.
81. Record of Interview between Mountbatten and Nehru, 24 March 1947, ibid., pp. 11–12. Patel, Azad and Baldev Singh held similar views and advised Mountbatten to the same effect. For their interviews with Mountbatten, see ibid., pp. 214, 216 and 370.
82. Record of Interview between Mountbatten and Jinnah, 7 April 1947, ibid., pp. 149–50; Uncirculated Record of Discussion No. 6, 11 April 1947, ibid., p. 190; and for his refusal to accept the Cabinet Mission Plan 'under any conditions whatsoever', see Mieville to Mountbatten, undated, ibid., p. 631.
83. Record of Interview between Mountbatten and Liaquat, 3 and 19 April 1947, ibid., pp. 102 and 332; Record of Interview between Mountbatten and Jinnah, 7 April 1947, ibid., 149–50; and Minutes of Viceroy's Fifth Misc. Meeting, 21 April 1947, ibid., pp. 357–58.
84. Ibid., pp. 445–48 and 540–41; and for Mountbatten's views, Minutes of First Day of First Governors' Conference, 15 May 1947, and Minutes of Viceroy's Ninth Misc. Meeting, 1 May 1947, ibid., pp. 251 and 507.
85. Viceroy's Personal Report No. 3, n.d. ibid., pp. 298–300.
86. For Nehru's advice, see Record of Interview between Mountbatten and Nehru, 8 April 1947, ibid., p. 154; and for its drafting, see Ismay to Menon, 11 April 1947, ibid., pp. 193–94.
87. Uncirculated Record of Discussion No. 5 and 7, 10 and 12 April 1947; and Viceroy's Conference Paper (VCP) 28, 14 April 1947, ibid., pp. 176–77, 207–8 and 227–31.
88. Record of Interview between Mountbatten and Mudie, 15 April 1947, ibid., pp. 259–60; and also see Mountbatten's observations in Minutes of Second Day of First Governors' Conference, 16 April 1947, ibid., pp. 270–71.
89. Minutes of First Day of First Governors' Conference, 15 April 1947, ibid., p. 251.
90. Ibid., p. 255.
91. This proportion in population was according to the 1941 census.
92. On 7 May, Baldev's letter in which he claimed that non-Muslims owned more than 50 per cent of immovable property (and over 80 per cent of urban property)

of the Punjab was circulated among the members of the India committee. Ibid., pp. 652–55.

93. Glancy to Linlithgow, 1 May 1942, ibid., vol. II, pp. 7–8.
94. Jenkins to Wavell, 31 August 1946, ibid., vol. VIII, p. 372.
95. *IAR*, 1940, vol. I, p. 61.
96. Menon to Abell, 29 March 1947, *TP*, vol. X, p. 44.
97. For instance, see 'The Sikh Problem', QAP, F. 930, p. 6; Jinnah to Baldev Singh, 16 December 1942, ibid., F. 189, p. 25; Teja Singh Swatantra and Sohan Singh Josh to Jinnah, 29 July 1944, ibid., F. 187, pp. 33; Wavell to Amery, 15 August 1944, *TP*, vol. IV, p. 1199; for the creation of a separate province comprising area between Delhi and Jhelum river, see QAP, F. 189, pp. 6–12; and *TP*, vol. I, pp. 582–88; for comments on the Sikh demands by E.P. Moon, 11 January 1946, see ibid., vol. VI, pp. 773–74; and Listowel to Mountbatten, 9 May 1947, ibid., vol. X, pp. 711–12.
98. Record of Meeting between Cabinet Delegation and Sardar Baldev Singh, 5 April 1946, *TP*, vol. VII, p. 143; Glancy to Linlithgow, 27 August 1942, and Linlithgow to Glancy 28 August 1942, ibid., vol. II, pp. 834–35 and 841.
99. Wavell to Pethick-Lawrence, 5 March 1947, ibid., vol. IX, p. 870.
100. Jenkins to Wavell, 7 March 1947, ibid., pp. 878–84; and Wavell to Jenkins, 8 March 1947, ibid., p. 893.
101. For text of the Congress resolution, see ibid., 8 March 1947, ibid., pp. 900–901.
102. Nehru to Wavell, 9 March 1947, ibid., vol. IX, pp. 906–7; and also see Minutes of Viceroy's First Staff Meeting. 25 March 1947, ibid., vol. X, p. 15.
103. Earlier, on 6 March, Baldev Singh had talked to Abell about the partition of the Punjab on communal lines. Wavell to Jenkins, 6 March 1947, ibid., p. 877.
104. Jenkins to Wavell, 9 March 1947, ibid., p. 903.
105. Record of Interview between Mountbatten and Nehru, 1 April 1947, ibid., vol. X, p. 88.
106. Note by Jenkins, 10 April 1947, ibid., pp. 183–84.
107. For Baldev Singh's letter to the India Committee and for a telegram from Tara Singh, Baldev Singh and Swaran Singh on this subject, see ibid., pp. 652–55 and 660; and for Maharaja of Patiala's proposal, see ibid., 915.
108. Baldev Singh to Mountbatten, 27 April and 1 May 1947, ibid., pp. 468 and 520–21.
109. Mieville to Mountbatten, 30 April 1947, ibid., p. 490.
110. For a proposal of the Hindu and Sikh conventions, see the discussion between Jenkins and Swaran Singh, Harnam Singh and Bhem Sen Sachar, in Jenkins to Mountbatten, 3 May 1947, ibid., pp. pp. 593–98; and for those by Ujjal Singh, Kartar Singh, Baldev Singh and others, see ibid., pp. 632, 643–46 and 649–51.
111. Ibid., pp. 646–48.
112. For Kartar Singh's views, see ibid., vol. XI, p. 163. As late as 5 August 1947, some Sikh leaders including Baldev Singh indirectly approached the League for some sort of arrangement with Pakistan on the basis of a Sikh province and fixed share for the Sikhs in the army. I.H. Qureshi to Qaed-e-Azam, 5 and 6 August 1947, QAP, F. 416, pp. 6–8.
113. Jenkins to Mountbatten, 30 April 1947, *TP*, vol. X, p. 506.
114. Minutes of Viceroy's Thirteenth Misc. Meeting, 11 May 1947, ibid., pp. 759–60. Ismay had told Harnam Singh that partition of the Punjab was 'inevitable' and that it 'would be by Muslim majority districts and non-Muslim majority districts'. Jenkins to Mountbatten, 3 May 1947, [Enclosure to 296] ibid., pp. 594–95.

115. Minutes of Viceroy's Thirteenth Misc. Meeting, 11 May 1947, ibid., pp. 759–60; and Minutes of Viceroy's Thirty First Staff Meeting, 12 May 1947, ibid., p. 781.

116. Ibid.; Viceroy's Personal Report No. 1, 2 April 1947, and No. 2, 9 April 1947, ibid., pp. 90 and 167–68; and Liaquat to Mountbatten, 15 April 1947, ibid., pp. 255–58.

117. Record of Interview between Mountbatten and Lt. Col. de la Fargue, 11 April 1947, ibid., pp. 196–97; and see also Record of Interview between Mountbatten and Azad, 12 April 1947, ibid., p. 217; and Viceroy's Staff Meetings: Uncirculated Record of Discussion No. 3, ibid., p. 255.

118. Minutes of First Day of First Governors' Conference, 15 April 1947, ibid., pp. 252–53.

119. Minutes of Viceroy's Third and Fourth Misc. Meetings, 16 and 18 April 1947, ibid., pp. 290–91 and 317.

120. For chief secretary's views, see Record of Interview between him and Mountbatten, 11 April 1947, ibid., p. 196; and for Azad's and Nehru's views, see Record of Interview between Mountbatten and Azad, 12 April 1947, ibid., 217.

121. Nehru to Mountbatten, 17 April 1947, ibid., pp. 305–7.

122. Minutes of Viceroy's Fifth Misc. Meeting, 21 April 1947, ibid., p. 355.

123. Minutes of Viceroy's Sixth Misc. Meeting, 22 April 1947, ibid., p. 364.

124. Mountbatten's meeting with the governor and four ministers, 28 April 1947, ibid., p. 494.

125. Mountbatten to Listowel, 1 May 1947, ibid., p. 531. Mountbatten obtained Jinnah's views about Pakistan joining the British Commonwealth through the Nawab of Bhopal (1894–1960) who had emphasized that Jinnah should not know that he had conveyed that information. Ibid., p. 444.

126. Minutes of First Day of First Governors' Conference, 15 April 1947, ibid., pp. 254–55.

127. The Hindu Mahasabha at a conference at Tarakeswar (Hoogly district) made the demand for a separate homeland for the Hindus of Bengal. Burrows to Mountbatten, 11 April 1947, ibid., p. 203.

128. Burrows to Wavell, 19 March 1947, ibid., vol. IX, pp. 985–86.

129. Minutes of Viceroy's Seventh Misc. Meeting, 23 April 1947, ibid., vol. X, pp. 379–80.

130. Star of India, 28 April 1947; Haroon-or-Rashid, Foreshadowing of Bangladesh, pp. 330–31; and Viceroy's Personal Report No. 5, 1 May 1947, TP, vol. X, p. 539.

131. Note by Sir T. Shone, 17 April 1947, TP, vol. X, p. 293; J.D. Tyson to Abell, 24 April 1947, ibid., pp. 389–90; Record of Interview between Mountbatten and Jinnah, 26 April 1947, ibid., p. 452; and Minutes by Ismay and Mountbatten, 26 April 1947, ibid., pp. 450–51.

132. For details, see ibid., pp. 448–51. Similarly, Ismay's impression about a Jinnah–Mountbatten meeting on the issue of Bengal was that Jinnah was 'so keen to get the principle of Pakistan settled once for all, that he will acquiesce in what has come to be known as truncated Pakistan, which excludes Calcutta'. Ismay to Burrows, 28 April 1947, ibid., pp. 472–73.

133. Viceroy's Personal Report No. 1, 2 April 1947, ibid., p. 92.

134. Liaquat to Mountbatten, 7 April 1947, ibid., pp. 151–52.

135. Mountbatten to Liaquat, 9 April 1947, ibid., p. 165.

136. Record of Interview between Mountbatten and Jinnah, 8 and 9 April 1947, ibid., pp. 159 and 163–64.

137. Liaquat to Mountbatten, 13 April 1947, ibid., pp. 220–21.

138. Record of Interview between Mountbatten and Auchinleck, 14 April 1947, ibid., pp. 223–24. Before the separation of Burma from India, Muslim proportion in the population had been about 25 per cent but after its separation the proportion had gone up to more than 30 per cent.

139. Minutes of the Second Day of First Governors' Conference, 16 April 1947, ibid., pp. 269–70; and Viceroy's Personal Report No. 5, 1 May 1947, ibid., pp. 545–47.

140. Viceroy's Personal Report no. 5, 1 May 1947, ibid., p. 545; and *Dawn*, 1 May 1947.

141. Mountbatten to Listowel, 1 May 1947, *TP*, vol. X, pp. 550–53.

142. Mountbatten to Ismay, 28 April 1947, ibid., pp. 437–40; and Viceroy's Conference Paper (VCP) 40, 1 May 1947, ibid., pp. 525–25. Mieville also informed that, according to Menon, Patel might accept 'an offer of Dominion Status for the time being'. Minutes of Viceroy's Twenty-Fourth Staff Meeting, 1 May 1947, ibid., p. 524.

143. Jinnah continued to demand a referendum in Bengal, or at least in Calcutta, to give the Scheduled Castes a chance to express their views but Mountbatten did not accept the demand. Viceroy's Personal Report No. 8, 5 June 1947, ibid., vol. XI, p. 158.

144. For details, see Mieville to Mountbatten, 30 April 1947, ibid., vol. X, pp. 487–89.

145. For Nehru's views, see Minutes of the Viceroy's Fourteenth Misc. Meeting, 11 May 1947, ibid., p. 764. Dr Shyama Prasad Mukerji had told Mountbatten on 2 May,' that 'whether division of India takes place or not, it is essential that the Punjab and Bengal should be partitioned'. Ibid., p. 555.

146. Ibid., pp. 539, 554–55 and 657.

147. On 31 May 1947, Suhrawardy told Mieville, 'I have had an interview with Mr Jinnah. He asked me if I had seen H.E. and, may the Lord forgive me, I told him "no" as I did not want him to think H.E. had seen me. (Please show this to H.E.).' [Ibid., vol. XI, p. 20]. For Jinnah not having authorized anyone, see the statement by Habibullah Bahar, member of a Bengal presidency Muslim League delegation that met Jinnah in Delhi, in *Star of India*, 20 May 1947; and for Suhrawardy's correspondence with Liaquat rather than Jinnah on the subject of united independent Bengal, see Suhrawardy to Liaquat, 19 May 1947, AFM, vol. 394; and Suhrawardy to Liaquat, 21 and 23 May 1947, QAP, F. 458, pp. 74–80.

148. Burrows to Mountbatten, 4 May 1947, *TP*, vol. X, p. 614.

149. Record of Interview between Mountbatten and Kiran Shankar Roy, 3 May 1947, ibid., pp. 585–86.

150. Mountbatten to Burrows, 16 and 18 May 1947, ibid., pp. 849–50 and 889; and Burrows to Listowel and Mountbatten, 19 May 1947, ibid., pp. 903–6.

151. Statement by Maulana Akram Khan, 4 May 1947, *Star of India*, 5 May 1947; Statement by Habibullah Bahar, ibid., 21 May 1947, and Suhrawardy to Liaquat, 5 May 1947, SHC, Bengal-III: 21.

152. Minutes of Viceroy's Thirty Fourth Staff Meeting, Items 1–7, 31 May 1947, *TP*, vol. XI, pp. 1–3; and Mieville to Mountbatten, 18 June 1947, ibid., p. 495.

153. Nehru to Mountbatten, 1 May 1947, ibid., vol. X, pp. 517–19; and Mountbatten to Listowel, 1 May 1947, ibid., p. 530. Two other demands were: partition of the Punjab and Bengal; and a broader forum to ascertain the will of the people of British Balochistan than leaving it to a few Sardars of the Shahi Jirga and non-official members of the Quetta municipality.

154. Minutes of Viceroy's Twenty-fifth Staff Meeting, 3 May 1947, ibid., pp. 579–82; and Mountbatten to Ismay, 3 and 7 May 1947, ibid., pp. 599–600 and 662–63. The

Hindu-controlled press started a campaign for Caroe's removal and the Congress observed an anti-Caroe Day in Delhi.

155. Mountbatten to Ismay, 4 May 1947, ibid., pp. 608 and 616.

156. Record of Interview between Mountbatten and Jinnah and Liaquat, 2 May 1947, ibid., pp. 566–68.

157. Record of Interview between Mountbatten and Jinnah and Liaquat, 4 May 1947, ibid., pp. 612–13; Mountbatten to Ismay, 4 and 6 May 1947, ibid., pp. 616 and 634–35; Viceroy's Personal Report No. 6, 8 May 1947, ibid., p. 684; and for Jinnah's statement, see ibid., pp. 689–91 and also see p. 630.

158. Ismay to Mountbatten, 6 May 1947, ibid., pp. 636–37, and three telegrams sent on 9 May, ibid., pp. 700–701; and Cabinet: India and Burma Committee. Paper I.B. (47) 56, 6 May 1947, ibid., 637–42; and 2nd Meeting, 7 May 1947, pp. 661–62. Mountbatten assured Nehru that he was 'no longer of the view that it is necessary to go into Section 93 in the Frontier Province, or that fresh elections should be held now. . . . Instead I had recommended to H.M.G. that there should be, at a suitable date, when the partition of India was clearer, a referendum on the electoral roll.' Ibid., pp. 739 and 753–54.

159. Alan Campbell-Johnson, *Mission with Mountbatten*, London, 1953, p. 81; and Mountbatten to Ismay, 8 May 1947, *TP*, vol. X, p. 699.

160. Mountbatten to Ismay (via IO), Simla, 11 May 1947, *TP*, vol. X, p. 774.

161. After this offer, Mountbatten gave Nehru a free hand to make appointments of ambassadors, etc. 'without consulting the Muslim League'. Viceroy's Staff Meetings, Uncirculated Record of Discussion No. 12, Mountbatten Papers, ibid., p. 714.

162. Gandhi to Mountbatten, 8 May 1947, ibid., pp. 667–68.

163. Minutes of Viceroy's Tenth Miscellaneous Meeting, 8 May 1947, ibid., pp. 871–74; and Mountbatten to Ismay, 8 May 1947, ibid., pp. 69–98. V.P. Menon came up with a note 'dictated to him by Nehru' which provided that 'referendum [in the NWFP] will be with the concurrence of the Provincial Government and under the supervision of the Governor General'.

164. Minutes of Viceroy's Twenty Ninth Staff Meeting, Item 5, and Thirtieth Staff Meeting, Item 1, 9 and 10 May 1947, ibid., pp. 703 and 729.

165. Remarks by Sardar Patel, ibid., pp. 716–17.

166. For his statement on 11 May 1947, see ibid., pp. 778–79.

167. Record of Interview between Mountbatten and Nehru, 5 May 1947, ibid., p. 623. Before the Congress leaders made their proposals, Mountbatten tried to revive the Cabinet Mission Plan but abandoned it because of Jinnah's resistance and Nehru's qualified support who told him that the Congress could not 'force' Assam and the Sikhs to accept it.

168. Mountbatten to Ismay, 8 May 1947, ibid., pp. 665 and 675–76; and Minutes of Viceroy's Thirteenth Misc. Meeting, 11 May 1947, ibid., p. 761; and for the text of Nehru's letter to Mountbatten, see ibid., p. 739–40.

169. Cabinet: India and Burma Committee. Paper I. B.(47)65, 10 May 1947, ibid., pp. 743–44.

170. Earlier, V.P. Menon at Patel's instance and with Wavell's approval had sent a version of this plan through Sudhir Ghosh to the secretary of state for India. Hodson, *Great Divide*, p. 302.

171. Minutes of Viceroy's Eleventh Misc. Meeting, 10 May 1947, *TP*, vol. X, pp. 731–32 and 735–36; and Minutes of Viceroy's Thirty First Staff Meeting, 12 May 1947, ibid., pp. 781–82.

172. Mieville to Ismay, Ismay to Mieville, 12 May 1947, ibid., pp. 780, 798.
173. Ibid., p. 806.
174. Note by Nehru, 11 May 1947, ibid., pp. 767–71; and Minutes of Viceroy's Fourteenth Misc. Meeting, 11 May 1947, ibid., pp. 764–65.
175. Ismay to Mountbatten and Ismay to Mieville, 12 May 1947, ibid., pp. 798–99.
176. Mountbatten to Ismay, 13 May 1947, ibid., pp. 800–801.
177. Cabinet: India and Burma Committee. I.B.(47), 14 May 1947, ibid., pp. 821–22.
178. Ibid., I.B.(47)66, 'Viceroy's Suggested Amendments to Draft Statement', and Minutes of Viceroy's Thirty First Staff Meeting, 12 May 1947, ibid., pp. 780–85; and Mountbatten to Ismay, 13 May 1947, ibid., pp. 806–8.
179. Mountbatten to Ismay (via IO), 11 May 1947 at 9 pm, ibid., pp. 774–76.
180. For instance, see Jinnah-Churchill correspondence, 2 May–17 October 1947, Waheed, *Nation's Voice*, vol. VI, pp. 512–17.
181. For full text of the eight-point Heads of Agreement, see *TP*, vol. X., pp. 842–43.
182. Mountbatten to Ismay, 13 May 1947, ibid., pp. 814–15.
183. Minutes of Viceroy's Thirty Third Staff Meeting, Item 7, 16 May 1947, ibid., p. 841.
184. Ismay to Mountbatten, 15 May 1947, ibid., p. 834; Turnbull to Harris, 14 May 1947, ibid., p. 817; and Cabinet: India and Burma Committee. I.B.(47) 24th Meeting, 14 May 1947, ibid., p. 821.
185. For views of the Governors of Bengal and the Punjab against referenda in these provinces, see ibid., p. 914.
186. Earlier, Liaquat had supported a plebiscite but due to 'vast distances and complete lack of local government officials' agreed to 'any form of democratic vote' as the League was confident of winning Balochistan. Note by Scott, 15 May 1947, ibid., pp. 826–27.
187. Viceroy's Conference Paper (VCP) 49, Muslim League Comments on the Draft Announcement, 17 May 1947, ibid., pp. 851–55.
188. Viceroy's Conference Paper (VCP) 50, Congress Comments on the Draft Announcement, 17 May 1947, ibid., pp. 855–57. Nehru raised the issue of transfer of Hindu majority area in Sindh to the Jodhpur state but Mountbatten advised him not to do that 'since it would open the way for the Muslim League in other parts, which they [Jinnah and Liaquat] have hinted at'. Ibid., p. 847.
189. For its text, see ibid., pp. 861–62.
190. Record of Interview between Mountbatten and Jinnah and Liaquat, 17 May 1947, ibid., pp. 872–73.
191. For its text, see ibid., pp. 888–89.
192. Jinnah to Mieville, 18 May 1947, QAP, F. 21, p. 63.
193. Jinnah to Mieville, 21 May 1947, ibid., p. 82; and Mieville to Mountbatten, 19 and 20 May 1947, *TP*, vol. X, pp. 906 and 907–8.
194. Mieville to Mountbatten, 20 May 1947, *TP*, vol. X, p. 916; and for Jinnah's note to Mieville after reading Nehru's two letters, see Mieville to Abell (via India Office), 22 May 1947, ibid., pp. 946–48.
195. Cabinet: India and Burma Committee. I.B.(47) 26th Meeting, 20 May 1947, ibid., vol. X, pp. 917–18; and Mountbatten to Mieville, 21 May 1947, ibid., p. 923.
196. For details, see Cabinet: India and Burma Committee. I.B.(47) 26th Meeting, 20 May 1947, ibid., pp. 916–22.
197. Record of Interview between Mountbatten and Churchill, 22 May 1947, ibid., p. 946.

198. Earlier, he had sent the Maharaja of Patiala to Jinnah with similar objective. Mieville to Mountbatten, 20 May 1947, ibid., p. 915.
199. Note by Mr Symon, 23 May 1947, ibid., p. 961.
200. Mieville to Mountbatten, 26 May 1947, ibid., p. 991.
201. On 20 May, he had asked Mieville to communicate his views to Mountbatten in London; he wrote: 'At the end of our talk he [Jinnah] took my arm and said, "I am not speaking as a partisan, and I beg you to tell Lord Mountbatten once again that he will be making a grave mistake if he agrees to the partition of Bengal and the Punjab." [Ibid., p. 916.] For Jinnah's views on the policies of the Pakistan State, see ibid., pp. 929–30.
202. Patel to Mountbatten, 3 June 1947, ibid., vol. XI, pp. 102–3.
203. Mieville to Mountbatten, 20 May 1947, ibid., vol. X, p. 916.
204. For Jinnah's contention, see ibid., vol. XI, pp. 39–47.
205. IAR, vol. I, pp. 137 and 268–70.
206. Minutes of Viceroy's Fortieth Meeting, 9 June 1947, TP, vol. XI, p. 199.
207. Ismay to Mountbatten, 20 June 1947, ibid., p. 534.
208. For a discussion of the issue, see M. Rafique Afzal, 'The Common Governor Generalship Issue and the Quaid-i-Azam: Mountbatten's Version and the Real Story', South Asian Studies, Lahore, vol. 3, no. 1, January 1986, pp. 29–42.
209. For funds provided by Jinnah to the Assam referendum committee, see Jinnah to Ispahani, 1 July 1947, QAP, F. 683, pp. 344 and 392.
210. For details, see Shibly, Abdul Matin Chaudhury, pp. 135–39; and also see Menon, Transfer of Power, pp 387–89.
211. Caroe to Colville, 22 May 1947, TP, vol. X, p 944
212. QAP, F. 324, pp. 18–21.
213. Ibid., pp. 15–16; and ibid., F. 286, p. 48.
214. For instance, see Syedna Taher Saifuddin to Jinnah, 24 June 1947, ibid., pp. 2–3.
215. For details, see M. Rafique Afzal, 'Dismissal of the NWFP Congress Ministry, August 22, 1947', Pakistan Journal of History & Culture, Islamabad, vol. XXIV/2 (2003), pp. 1–22.
216. M. Rafique Afzal, Pakistan: History and Politics, 1947–1971, OUP, 2001, pp. 14–15.
217. Dawn, 26 June 1947.
218. For details, see Nawab Jahangir Shah Jogezai, Muqaddima Sadiq British Balochistan, Islamabad, 1996.
219. Sardar Nishtar's statement in the 'Note by Mr Symon', 23 May 1947, TP, vol. X, p. 961.
220. Yusuf Haroon to Jinnah, 1 May 1947, QAP, F. 274, p. 308.
221. Those seeking jobs in Pakistan were asked to send their particulars to Dr Ishtiaq Husain Qureshi, Professor of History, University of Delhi. [Statement by Liaquat, ibid., F. 162, p. 210.] File nos. 162 and 163 of the QAP contain particulars of some of those candidates.
222. Ralph Braibanti, 'The Higher Bureaucracy of Pakistan', in Ralph Braibanti, Asian Bureaucratic Systems Emergent from the British Imperial Tradition, Durham, 1966, pp. 209–354; and Afzal, Pakistan: History and Politics, pp. 14–15.
223. Ibid.; Constituent Assembly (Legislature) of Pakistan, Debates, Official Report, vol. 1, no. 9, 21 March 1951, pp. 596–70; and Richard Symonds, The Making of Pakistan, Lahore, 1976, p. 96.
224. Cabinet: India and Burma Committee. I.B.(47) 25th Meeting, 19 May 1947, TP, vol. X, p. 896.

225. Afzal, *Pakistan: History and Politics*, pp. 16–17.
226. Ibid., pp. 18–19 and 29; and 'Pakistan: End of the Water Dispute', *Round Table* (London) no. 201, September 1960, p. 72.
227. Campbell-Johnson, *Mission with Mountbatten*, p. 124. The members of the Punjab Boundary Commission were Justices Din Mohammad, Mohammad Munir, Mehr Chand Mahajan and Teja Singh, and those of the Bengal Boundary Commission were Abu Saleh Mohammad Akram, S.A. Rahman, C.C. Biswas and B.K. Mukerji.
228. Beaumont's statement appeared in the Daily Telegraph of 24 February 1992.
229. QAP, F. 921, p. 185.
230. Minutes of Viceroy's Thirteenth Misc. Meeting, 11 May 1947, *TP*, vol. X, pp. 759–60; and Minutes of Viceroy's Thirty First Staff Meeting, 12 May 1947, ibid., p. 781; and Ali, *Emergence of Pakistan*, pp. 215–20.
231. For a detailed letter on this issue from Suhrawardy to Jinnah on 4 August 1947, see QAP, F. 458, pp. 83–89.
232. Para 14, Cabinet Mission's statement of 16 May 1946. The comments are from Cripps' observations on the statement.
233. Record of Interview between Mountbatten and Gandhi and Abdul Ghaffar Khan, 4 April 1947, *TP*, vol. X, p. 121; and *Dawn*, 18 July 1947.
234. *TP*, vol. X, p. 337, footnote 2.
235. Ibid., pp. 353–54, 362 and 376.
236. For his clarification about the independence of the states, see ibid., vol. XI, p: 420.
237. For Nehru's and Jinnah's views, see Minutes of Viceroy's Eighteenth Misc. Meeting, 13 June 1947, ibid., pp. 320–23; Jinnah's press statement on 17 June 1947, ibid., p. 438; Ali, *Emergence of Pakistan*, pp. 228–29; E.W.R. Lumby, *The Transfer of Power in India, 1945.1947*, London, 1954, p. 233; and Note of Discussion on Retraction of Paramountcy with Sir C. Corfield at the India Office, 9 May 1947, *TP*, vol. X, p. 718.
238. Clause 2 (4) and Clause 7 of the Indian Independence Act, 18 July 1947.
239. QAP, F. 227, pp. 23–24; and SHC, Pb-III: 68–69. For instance, Jinnah told B.N. Rau, 'Let us first put our own house in order in British India and then it will be time enough to bother about the States.' B.N. Rau to Abell, 1 June 1946, *TP*, vol. VII, pp. 762–63.
240. His Highness' Notes (Dictated to Mr H.M. Hayat, private secretary to be conveyed to Qaid-e-Azam Mr M.A. Jinnah in Delhi), Bhopal, 6 June 1947, QAP, F. 1120, pp. 68–72. For his resignation as chancellor of the chamber of princes, see *TP*, vol. XI, p. 133.
241. Nizam of Hyderabad (Mir Osman Ali Khan) to Wavell, *TP*, vol. VIII, p. 473.
242. Wavell to Pethick-Lawrence, 9 October 1945, ibid., vol. VI, p. 323; and *Wavell: The Viceroy's Journal*, p. 175.
243. For the Nizam–Bahadur Yar Jung relations and Jinnah's intervention, see SHC, Hd-II: 1, 3 and 8; and QAP, F. 29, pp. 45–50.
244. For Jinnah's attempt to block Mirza Ismail's appointment, see QAP, F. 31, p 10–12, 16–22, 26–28, 31, 33–35 and 46; F. 505, p. 27; F. 1107, pp. 16–17; and SHC, Hd-II: 15–17; the *Hindu* (Madras), 3 and 4 July 1946; and *Dawn*, 5 July 1946.
245. For the Hyderabad state's accession or independence, see QAP, F. 696, pp. 114–15, 117 and 124; and Fs. 1264–66; and for its possible relations with Pakistan, see Osman Ali (the Nizam) to Jinnah (confidential), 28 July 1947, QAP, F. 696 (Enclosure: Note for the consideration of Mr Jinnah).
246. For instance, see Ruler of Swat to Qaid-e-Azam, 19 July 1947, QAP, F. 36, p. 1; and Jinnah to the Ruler of Amb State, 16 July 1947, ibid., F. 35, p. 1.

247. QAP, F. 703, p. 3.
248. Ibid., F. 34, pp. 13–18 and 20–30; and F. 978, p. 1.
249. Ahmad Yar Khan claimed that his relations with Jinnah had 'not only been of friends but rather those of a father and son'. Ahmad Yar to Qaid-e-Azam, 9 June and 30 July 1947 and Jinnah to the Khan of Qalat, 14 June 1947, QAP, F. 699.
250. Ghulam Husain Hidayatullah to Jinnah, 16 July 1947, ibid., F. 286, p. 48.
251. Afzal, *Pakistan: History and Politics*, pp. 4–8.
252. QAP, F. 705, p. 1; and F. 706, pp. 1–2.
253. For a League resolution on the situation in Kashmir, see AFM, vol. 197, no. 15.
254. QAP, F. 701, pp. 35, 73–88; F. 498, pp. 36–39, 40 and 42; F. 505, pp. 9–19; F. 1117, p. 183; SHC, K-43, 44 and 447; and *TP*, vol. IV, 186, 210–11, 312, and 255–56.
255. SHC, K-15–17; and *Hamdard*, 4 August 1945.
256. SHC, K-50, 59–61 and 64–69; and *The Kashmir Times*, 2 November 1946.
257. Record of Interview between Mountbatten and Gandhi, 4 June 1947, *TP*, vo. XI, p. 131; and Mountbatten to Listowel, 12 June 1947, ibid., vol. XI, p. 300.

Glossary

alim (pl. ulama):	scholar
anjuman:	an association
anna	one-sixteenth of a rupee
Biri	rolled betel leaf with shredded tobacco for smoking
Crore	ten million
Darul Ulum	religious school
fatwa (pl. *fatawa*)	ruling according to Islamic law
gurdwara	a Sikh temple
haram	unlawful, or forbidden by religion
hari	cultivator
Hukumat-i-Ilahiya	Kingdom of God
Jagirdar	holder of *jagir* (fief)
Jagirdari	feudalism
jamaat	a party or an association
jamiat	an association
Jatha	group
Lakh	one hundred thousand
Madrassa	seminary/school
mashaikh (pl. of shaikh)	a venerable person (Sufi) or a Pir
Mutawalli	custodian
nazim	an administrator
Paisa	unit of money
Pandal	marquee
Sajadanashin	successor to a Muslim saint
salar-i-azam	supreme commander
salar-i-suba	provincial commander
satyagraha	'soul-force'; Gandhian civil disobedience
sawad-i-azam	grand majority
Shaikhul Hadith	one who is well-versed in the Traditions of the Holy Prophet (PBUH)/Head of the Hadith Department
Shariat	Islamic law
Tabligh	missionary work/preaching
Taluka	a revenue subdivision of a district
Taluqdar	holder of a taluqa
Tanzeem	an organization
Tanzimul Muslimin	organization of the Muslims
Rupee	unit of money
waqf/wakf	trust
wuzu	ablution

Bibliography

(a) Documents, Collections, etc.

Ahmad, Waheed (ed.), *Quaid-i-Azam Mohammad Ali Jinnah: Speeches, Indian Legislative Assembly, 1935–1947*, Karachi, 1991.

Ahmad, Waheed (ed.), *Quaid-i-Azam Mohammad Ali Jinnah: The Nation's Voice*. 7 vols., Karachi, 1992–2003.

– Vol. I: Towards Consolidation, March 1935–March 1940.
– Vol. II: United We Win, April 1940–April 1942.
– Vol. III: Unity, Faith and Discipline, May 1942–October 1944.
– Vol. IV: Towards the Popular Verdict, November 1944–April 1946.
– Vol. V: Deadlock, Frustration and Riots, May 1946–February 1947.
– Vol. VI: Achieving the Goal, March 1947–August 1947.
– Vol. VII: Launching the State and the End of the Journey, August 1947–September 1948.

All-Parties Conference, Report of the Committee, Allahabad, 1928.

Archives of the Freedom Movement, National Archives, Government of Pakistan, Islamabad.

Collected Works of Mahatma Gandhi, vols. 78 and 79.

Gopal, S. (ed.), *Selected Works of Jawaharlal Nehru*, vol. 3, New Delhi, 1985.

It Shall Never Happen Again, with a foreword by Qazi Isa, Delhi, 1946.

Jinnah, M.A., *History of the Origin of "Fourteen Points"*, Bombay, 1929.

Kumar, Ravindra (ed.), *Selected Works of Maulana Azad*, New Delhi, 1991–1992.

Letters of Iqbal to Jinnah, (Preface by M.A. Jinnah), Lahore, 1968.

Mansergh, N. and Lumby, E.W.R., eds. *Constitutional Relations between Britain and India: The Transfer of Power*. 12 Vols. London: Her Majesty's Stationery Office, 1970–82.

– Vol. I: *Cripps Mission, January–April 1942* (1970).
– Vol. II: *Quit India, 30 April–21 September 1942* (1971).
– Vol. III: *Reassertion of Authority, Gandhi's Fast and the Succession to the Viceroyalty, 21 September 1942–12* (1971).
– Vol. IV: *The Bengal Famine and New Viceroyalty, 15 June–31 August 1944* (1973).
– Vol. V: *The Simla Conference, Background and Proceedings, 1 September 1944–28 July 1945*(1974).
– Vol. VI: *The Post-War Phase: New Moves by the Labour Government, 1 August 1945–22 March 1946* (1974).
– Vol. VII: *The Cabinet Mission, 23 March–29 June 1946* (1977).
– Vol. VIII: *The Interim Government, 3 July–1 November 1946* (1979).
– Vol. IX: *The Fixing of a Time Limit, 4 November–22 March 1947* (1980).
– Vol. X: *The Mountbatten Viceroyalty, Formulation of Plan, 22 March–23 May 1947* (1981).
– Vol. XI: *The Mountbatten Viceroyalty Announcement and reception of the 3 June Plan, 31 May–7 July 1947* (1982).

Memorial of Grievances of Muslims presented by the Ahmadabad District Muslim League, Ahmadabad, 22 December 1939.

Muslim Sufferings under Congress Rule, issued by the Bengal Provincial Muslim League, December 1939.

Punjab Police Abstract of Intelligence, Lahore.

Quaid-i-Azam Papers, National Archives, Government of Pakistan, Islamabad.

Report of the Bihar Muslim Grievances Enquiry Committee, prepared and written by S.M. Shareef, Patna, 2 December 1938.

Report of the Inquiry Committee appointed by the All-India Muslim League to inquire into Muslim Grievances in Congress Provinces, President, Raja Syed Mohammad Mehdi of Pirpur, [and] published by the Secretary, All India Muslim League, Lucknow, 1939.

Report of the North-West Frontier Enquiry Committee and the Minutes of Dissent, Delhi, 1924.

Sedition Committee Report, Calcutta, 1918.

Shamsul Hasan Collection, National Documentation Centre, Government of Pakistan, Islamabad.

The Proceedings of the All-Parties National Convention, Calcutta, 1928, Allahabad, 1929.

Vidyarthi, Mohammad Abbas, *Dastan-i-Bihar*, Patna, [1939].

What Muslims Suffered When Congress Ruled—The Tragic Story of 1937–39 [Delhi?], 1946.

(b) Books, Monographs, and Articles

Abbasi, M.Y., *London Muslim League (1908–1928)*, Islamabad, 1981.

Abbasi, M.Y., *Muslim Politics and Leadership in South Asia, 1876–92*, Islamabad, 1981.

Abbasi, M.Y., *The Political Biography of Syed Amir Ali*, Lahore, 1989.

Abbasi, Professor Mohammad Sarwar, *Kashmiri Mussalmanon ki Jiddo Juhd-i Azadi, 1892–1947*, Muzaffarabad, 1992.

Abdul Aziz, *Fatawa-i-Azizi*, Delhi, 1906.

Abdul Hamid, *Muslim Separatism in India: A Brief Survey, 1857–1957*, London, 1967.

Abdul Karim, Maulvi, *Letter on Hindu-Muslim Pact*, Calcutta, 1924

Abdurrub, A.S.M, *A. K. Fazlul Haq: Life and Achievement*, Lahore, n.d.

Afzal, M. Rafique (ed.), *The Case for Pakistan*, Islamabad, 1988.

Afzal, M. Rafique, 'Dismissal of the NWFP Congress Ministry, August 22, 1947', *Pakistan Journal of History & Culture*, Islamabad, vol. XXIV/2 (2003).

Afzal, M. Rafique, 'The Common Governor Generalship Issue and the Quaid-i-Azam: Mountbatten's Version and the Real Story', *South Asian Studies*, Lahore, vol. 3, no. 1, January 1986.

Afzal, M. Rafique, *Malik Barkat Ali: His Life and Writings*, Lahore, 1969.

Ahmad, Aziz, *Islamic Modernism in India and Pakistan, 1857–1964*, London, 1967.

Ahmad, Jamil-ud-Din (ed.), *Some Recent Speeches and Writings of Mr. Jinnah*, 2 volumes, Lahore, 1964.

Ahmad, Muhammad Saleem, *The All India Muslim League: A History of the Growth and Consolidation of Political Organisation*, Bahawalpur, 1988.

Ahmad, Mujeeb, *Jam'iyyat Ulema-i-Pakistan, 1948–1979*, Islamabad, 1993.

Ahmad, Riaz, *Quaid-i-Azam Mohammad Ali Jinnah: The Formative Years, 1892–1920*, Islamabad, 1986.

Ahmad, Sayyid Noor, *Marshal La se Marshal La tak*, Lahore, 1965.

Ahmad, Waheed, (ed.), *Quaid-i-Azam Mohammad Ali Jinnah: Speeches, Indian Legislative Assembly, 1935–1947*, Karachi, 1991.

Ahmad, Waheed, *Road to Indian Freedom: The Formation of the Government of India Act 1935*, Lahore, 1979.

Aibak, Zafar Hasan, *Aap Biti*, Lahore, 1964.

Ali, Imran, *Punjab Politics in the Decade before Partition*, Lahore, 1975.

Ambedkar, B.R., *Pakistan or the Partition of India*, Lahore, 1976.

Ashraf, Mujeeb, *Muslim Attitudes Towards the British Rule and Western Culture in India*, Delhi, 1982.

Azad, Abul Kalam, *India Wins Freedom*, Calcutta, 1959.

Aziz, K.K., (comp.), *Modern Muslim India in British Periodical Literature*, Islamabad, 1998.

Aziz, K.K., *A History of the Idea of Pakistan*, Lahore, 1987, 4 volumes.

Aziz, K.K., *Muslims under Congress Rule, 1937–1939: A Documentary Record*, Islamabad, 1978–9.

Baha, Lal, *N.W.F.P. Administration under British Rule, 1901–1919*, Islamabad, 1978.

Bahadur, Lal, *The Muslim League History*, Agra, 1954.

Baloch, Dr Nabi Bakhsh, *Maulana Azad Subhani: Tehrik-i-Azadi key aik Muqtadar Rahnuma*, Lahore, 1989.

Bamford, P.C., *The Histories of the Non-co-operation and Khilafat Movements*, Delhi, 1925.

Batalvi, Ashiq Husain, *Hamari Qaumi Jiddo Jud*, Lahore, 1968.

Batalvi, Ashiq Husain, *Iqbal ke Akhiri do Saal*, Lahore, 1978.

Bolitho, Hector, *Jinnah: Creator of Pakistan*, London, 1954.

Braibanti, Ralph, *Asian Bureaucratic Systems Emergent from the British Imperial Tradition*, Durham, 1966.

Burke, S.M., and Salim al Din Qureshi, *The British Raj in India*, Karachi, 1997.

Campbell-Johnson, Alan, *Mission with Mountbatten*, London, 1953.

Casey, Lord, *Personal Experience, 1939–1946*, London, 1962.

Chand, Duni, *The Ulster of India*, Lahore, 1936.

Chaudhri, Mehnaz Ata, *Muslim League ki Tarikh, 1906–47*, Lahore, 2011.

Cheragh Ali, *A Critical Exposition of the Popular Jihad*, Calcutta, 1885.

Clarke, Peter, *The Cripps Version: The Life of Sir Stafford Cripps, 1882–1952*, London, 2002.

Clymer, Kenton I., *Quest for Freedom: The US and India's Independence*, New York, 1995.

Collins, Larry and Dominique Lapierre, *Freedom at Midnight*, New York, 1975.

Coupland, Reginald, *The Indian Problem, 1833–1935*, Oxford, 1968.

Duni Chand, *The Ulster of India*, Lahore, 1936.

Dwarkadas, Kanji, *India's Fight for Freedom, 1913–1945*, Bombay, 1966.

French, Patrick, *Liberty or Death: India's Journey to Independence and Division*, London, 1997.

Garewal, Sher Muhammad (ed.), *Jinnah-Wavell Correspondence (1943–47)*, Lahore, 1986.

Ghosh, Sudhir, *Gandhi's Emissary*, New Delhi, 1981.

Gilmartin, David, *Empire and Islam: Punjab and the Making of Pakistan*, London, 1988.

Gopal, Ram, *Indian Muslims: A Political History (1857–1947)*, Bombay, 1949.

Haq, Noorul, *Making of Pakistan: The Military Perspective*, Islamabad, 1993

Hardy, P., *The Muslims of British India*, Cambridge, 1972.

Harun-or-Rashid, *The Foreshadowing of Bangladesh: Bengal Muslim League and Muslim Politics, 1936–1947*, Dhaka, 1987.

Hasan, Tariq, *The Aligarh Movement and the Making of the Indian Muslim Mind, 1857–2002*, New Delhi, 2006.

Hayat, Sikandar, 'Syed Ahmad Khan and the Foundation of Muslim Separatist Political Movement in India', *Pakistan Journal of Social Sciences*, vol. VIII, no. I–II, January-July-December 1982.

Hayat, Sikandar, *The Charismatic Leader: Quaid-i-Azam Mohammad Ali Jinnah and the Creation of Pakistan*, Karachi, 2008.

Hodson, H.V., *The Great Divide: Britain–India–Pakistan*, Karachi, 1984.

Husain, Azim, *Fazl-i-Husain: A Political Biography*, London, 1946.

Ikram, S.M., *Mauj-i-Kausar*, Lahore, 1968.

Ikram, S.M., *Modern Muslim India and the Birth of Pakistan (1858–1951)*, Lahore, 1970.

Iqbal, Afzal, *Life and Times of Mohamed Ali*, Lahore, 1979.

Isa, Qazi Mohammad, *Balochistan: Case and Demand*, Karachi, 1944.

Ispahani, M.A.H., *Quaid-e-Azam Jinnah As I Knew Him*, Karachi, 1967.

Iyer, C.S. Ranga, *India: Peace or War*, London, 1930.

Jalal, Ayesha, *The Sole Spokesman: Jinnah, the Muslim League and the Demand for Pakistan*, Cambridge, 1985.

Jansson, Erland, *India, Pakistan or Pakhtunistan*, Stockholm, 1981.

Jayakar, M.R., *The Story of my Life*, vol. I, Bombay, 1958.

Jogezai, Nawab Jahangir Shah, *Muqaddima Sadiq British Balochistan*, Islamabad, 1996.

Jones, Allen Keith, *Politics in Sindh, 1907–1940: Muslim Identity and the Demand for Pakistan*, Karachi, 2002.

Josh, S.S., *Hindustani Gadar Party: A Short History*, New Delhi, 1977.

Kaura, Uma, *Muslims and Indian Nationalism: The Emergence of the Demand for India's Partition, 1928–40*, New Delhi, 1977.

Kausar, Inamul Haq, *Pakistan Movement and Balochistan*, Quetta, 1999.

Kausar, Inamul Haq, *Tehrik-i-Pakistan aur Sahafat*, Quetta, 1997.

Kazimi, Muhammad Reza, *Liaquat Ali Khan and the Freedom Movement*, Karachi, 1997.

Khalik bin Sayeed, *Pakistan: The Formative Phase*, Karachi, 1960.

Khaliquzzaman, Choudhry, *Pathway to Pakistan*, Longmans, Lahore, 1961.

Khan, Abdul Rashid, *The All India Muslim Educational Conference: Its Contribution to the Cultural Development of Indian Muslims, 1886–1947*, OUP, Karachi, 2001.

Khan, Dr Muhammad Anwar, *The Role of N. W. F. P. in the Freedom Struggle*, Lahore, 2000.

Khan, M. Khalil, *Judgment of the Judicial Committee of the Privy Council*, Ajmer, 1946.

Khan, Mohammed Reza, *What Price Freedom?* Karachi, 1977.

Khan, Sayyid Ahmad, *Akhiri Mazamin*, Lahore, n.d.

Khuhro, Hamida, *Mohammed Ayub Khuhro: A Life of Courage in Politics*, Lahore, 1998.

Khurshid, K.H., *Memories of Jinnah*, (ed. Khalid Hasan), Lahore, 1999.

Lateef, S.A., *The Great Leader*, Lahore, 1947.

Latif, Dr Abdul, *The Muslim Problem in India*, Karachi, 1939.

Leigh, M.S., *The Punjab and the War*, Lahore, 1922.

Long, Roger D. (ed.), *Dear Mr. Jinnah: Selected Correspondence and Speeches of Liaquat Ali Khan*, Karachi, 2004.

Low, D.A., *The Indian National Congress: Centenary Hindsight*, Delhi, 1988.

Lumby, E.W.R., *The Transfer of Power in India, 1945–1947*, London, 1954.

M.R.T. [Mohammad Sharif Toosy], *Nationalism in Conflict in India*, Delhi, 1942.

M.R.T. [Mohammad Sharif Toosy], *Pakistan and Muslim India*, Delhi, 1942.

Madni, Husain Ahmad, *Naqsh-i-Hayat,* Deoband, 1953.

Malik, Aslam, *The Making of the Pakistan Resolution,* Karachi, 2001.

Malik, Aziz, *Sahafat aur Tehrik-i-Azadi,* Lahore, 1984.

Malik, Iftikhar Haider, *Sikandar Hayat Khan: A Political Biography,* Islamabad, 1985.

Malik, Ikram Ali (comp.), *Muslim League Session 1940 & the Lahore Resolution (Documents),* Islamabad, 1990.

Malik, Ikram Ali, *Truth is Truth: A Rejoinder to Abdul Wali Khan,* Lahore, 1990.

Menon, V.P., *The Transfer of Power in India,* New Delhi, 1981.

Metcalf, Barbara D., *Islamic Revival in British India: Deoband, 1869–1900,* New Jersey, 1982.

Mirza, Akhtar Husain, *Tarikh-i-Muslim League,* Bombay, 1940.

Mirza, Janbaz, *Tehrik-i-Masjid-i-Shahidganj* (Urdu), Lahore, 1988.

Mirza, Sarfaraz Husain (comp.), *Tehrik-i-Pakistan aur Majlis-i-Kabir-i-Pakistan ka Qalmi Jihad,* Islamabad, 1998.

Mirza, Sarfaraz Husain, *Muslim Students and Pakistan Movement Selected Documents (1937–1947),* Lahore, 1988–89.

Mirza, Sarfaraz Husain, *Muslim Women's Role in the Pakistan Movement,* Lahore, 1969.

Mirza, Sarfaraz Husain, *The Punjab Muslim Students Federation (1937–1947),* Islamabad, 1991.

Mishra, B.K., *The Cripps Mission: A Reappraisal,* New Delhi, 1982.

Moore, R.J., *Churchill, Cripps and India, 1939–1945,* Oxford, 1979.

Moore, R.J., *The Crisis of Indian Unity, 1917–1940,* Oxford, 1974.

Moraes, Frank, *Jawaharlal Nehru: A Biography,* Bombay, 1959.

Muhammad Ali, Chaudhri, *The Emergence of Pakistan,* New York, 1967.

Mujahid, Sharif al, 'Communal Riots', *A History of the Freedom Movement,* Karachi, 1970, vol. IV, Parts I & II.

Mujahid, Sharif al, *Muslim League Documents, 1900–1947, Volume I (1900–1908),* Karachi, 1990.

Mujahid, Sharif al, *Quaid-i-Azam Jinnah: Studies in Interpretation,* Karachi, 1981.

Nair, C.G., *The Moplah Rebellion, 1921,* Calicut, 1923.

Nehru, Jawaharlal, *A Bunch of Old Letters,* Bombay, 1960.

Nichols, Beverly, *Verdict on India,* London, 1944.

Noman, Muhammad, *Muslim India: Rise and Growth of the All India Muslim League,* Allahabad, 1942.

Noon, Firoz Khan, *From Memory,* Lahore, 1966.

Obhrai, Diwan Chand, *The Evolution of the North West Frontier Province,* Peshawar, 1938.

Page, David, *Prelude to Partition: The Indian Muslims and the Imperial System of Control, 1920–32,* Karachi, 1987.

Phadnis, U., *Towards the Integration of the Indian States, 1919–47,* London, 1968.

Philips, C.H., and Mary Doreen Wainwright (eds.), *The Partition of India: Policies and Perspectives, 1935–1947,* London, 1970.

Pirzada, D.A., *Growth of Muslim Nationalism in Sind,* Karachi, 1995.

Pirzada, Sharifuddin, *Evolution of Pakistan,* Karachi, 1963.

Pirzada, Sharifuddin, *Foundations of Pakistan: All India Muslim League Documents, 1906–1947,* Karachi, 1989, 2 volumes.

Pirzada, Sharifuddin, *Pakistan Resolution and the Historic Lahore Session,* Karachi, 1968

Pirzada, Sharifuddin, *Quaid's Correspondence,* Rawalpindi, 1987.

Qalb-i-Abid, S., *Muslim Politics in the Punjab, 1921–47,* Lahore, 1992.

Qureshi, I.H., *The Muslim Community of the Indo-Pakistan Subcontinent,* The Hague, 1962.

Qureshi, I.H., *The Struggle for Pakistan*, Karachi, 1969.

Qureshi, I.H., *Ulema in Politics*, Karachi, 1972.

Qureshi, M. Naeem, *Mahomed Ali's Khilafat Delegation to Europe (February-October 1920)*, Karachi, 1980.

Qureshi, M. Naeem, *Pan-Islam in British India: The Politics of the Khilafat Movement, 1918–1924*, Karachi, 2008 (Rev. ed.).

Qureshi, M. Naeem, *Pan-Islam in British Indian Politics: A Study of the Khilafat Movement, 1918–1924*, Leiden, 1999.

Rahim, Taqi, *Tehrik-i-Azadi mein Bihar ke Mussalmanon ka Hissa*, Patna, 1998.

Rahman, Matiur, *From Consultation to Confrontation: A Study of the Muslims in British Indian Politics, 1906–1912*, London, 1970.

Rajput, A. B., *Muslim League: Yesterday and Today*, Lahore, 1948.

Rizvi, Gawhar, *Linlithgow and India*, London, 1978.

Roberts, Andrew, *Eminent Churchillians*, London 1994.

Robinson, Francis, *Separatism among Indian Muslims: The Politics of the United Provinces' Muslims, 1860–1923*, London, 1974.

Rozina, Parvin, *Jamiatul Ulama-i-Hind: Dastawezat-i-Markazi Ijlas hai Aam 1919–1945*, Islamabad, 1980.

Saeed, Ahmad, *Muslim India (1857–1947): A Biographical Dictionary*, Lahore, 1977.

Saeed, Ahmad, *Quaid-i-Azam Mohammad Ali Jinnah: A Bunch of Rare Letters*, Lahore, 1999.

Saeed, Ahmad, *Writings of the Quaid-i-Azam*, Lahore, 1976.

Saiyid, Dushka H., *Muslim Women of the British Punjab: From Seclusion to Politics*, London, 1998.

Saiyid, Matlubul Hasan, *Mohammad Ali Jinnah (A Political Study)*, Lahore, 1945 and 1962 editions.

Sanyal, Usha, *Devotional Islam and Politics in British India: Ahmad Riza Khan Barelwi and his Movement, 1870–1920*, New York, 1996.

Sareen, T.R., *Indian Revolutionary Movement Abroad, 1905–1921*, New Delhi, 1979.

Sayed, G.M., *Struggle for New Sind: A Brief Narrative of the Working of Provincial Autonomy in Sind during the Decade of 1937–47*, Karachi, 1949.

Seervai, H.M., *Partition of India: Legend and Reality*, OUP, 2005, pp. 118–19.

Shah, Sayed Wiqar Ali, *Ethnicity, Islam, and Nationalism: Muslim Politics in the North-West Frontier Province, 1937–1947*, Oxford, 1999.

Shah, Sayed Wiqar Ali, *Muslim League in N.W.F.P.*, Karachi, 1992.

Shamsul Hasan, Khalid, *The Punjab Muslim League and the Unionists: An Account Based on the Documents in the Shamsul Hasan Collection*, Karachi, 2005.

Shamsul Hasan, Syed (comp.), *Plain Mr. Jinnah*, Karachi, 1976.

Shan Muhammad, *The All-India Muslim Educational Conference (Select Presidential Addresses), 1886–1947*, New Delhi, 2003.

Shan Muhammad, *The Indian Mussalmans: A Documentary Record*, Delhi, 1985.

Sherwani, Latif Ahmad (ed.), *Speeches, Writings and Statements of Iqbal*, Lahore, 1977, p. 28.

Singh, Anita Inder, *The Origins of the Partition of India, 1936–47*, Delhi, 1987.

Sitaramayya, B. Pattabhi, *The History of the Indian National Congress (1885–1935)*, Allahabad, 1935.

Smith, Wilfred Cantwell, *The Muslim League, 1942–45*, Lahore, 1945.

Suleri, Z.A., *My Leader*, Lahore, 1973.

Symonds, Richard, *The Making of Pakistan*, Lahore, 1976.

Talbot, Ian, *Khizr Tiwana, Punjab Unionist Party and the Partition of India*, Surrey, 1996.

Talbot, Ian, *Provincial Politics and the Pakistan Movement*, Karachi, 1990.

Talbot, Ian, *Punjab and the Raj, 1849–1947*, New Delhi, 1988.

Thadani, R.V. (ed.), *The Historical State Trial of the Ali Brothers and Five Others*, Karachi, 1921.

Tuker, Sir Francis *While Memory Serves: Last Two Years of British Rule in India*, London. 1950.

Waheed-uz-Zaman, *Towards Pakistan*, Lahore, 1964.

Waseem, Mohammad, *Politics and the State in Pakistan*, Lahore, 1989.

Wasti, Syed Razi, *Lord Minto and the Indian Nationalist Movement, 1905 to 1910*, Oxford, 1964.

Wavell, *The Viceroy's Journal*, ed. Penderel Moon, London, 1973.

Weigold, Auriol, *Churchill, Roosevelt and India: Propaganda during World War II*, New Delhi, 2008.

Wolpert, Stanley, *Jinnah of Pakistan*, New York, 1984.

Wolpert, Stanley, *Shameful Flight: The Last Days of the British Empire in India*, Karachi, 2006.

Yajnik, Indulal K., *Gandhi as I knew him*, Bombay, 1933.

Yusuf, Kaniz F., et al., *Pakistan Resolution Revisited*, Islamabad, 1990.

Yusufi, Allah Bakhsh, *Maulana Mohamed Ali: the Khilafat Movement*, Karachi, 1980.

Yusufi, Allah Bakhsh, *Sarhad aur Jiddo Juhd-i-Azadi*, Lahore, 1968.

Zafrul Hasan, Syed, and Muhammad Afzaal Husain Qadri, *The Problem of Indian Muslims and its Solution*, Aligarh, 1939.

Zafrullah Khan, Mohammad, *Tahdis-i-Ni'mat*, Lahore, 1971.

Zaidi, A.M., and S.G. Zaidi (eds.), *The Encyclopedia of the Indian National Congress*, New Delhi, 1981.

Zaidi, Nasir and Mahmudur Rahman (comp.), *Woh Rahbar Hamara woh Quaid Hamara*, Karachi, 1976.

Zaidi, Z.H. (ed.), *Jinnah–Ispahani Correspondence, 1936–1948*, Karachi, 1976.

Zaman, Mukhtar, *Students' Role in the Pakistan Movement*, Karachi, 1978.

(c) Newspapers

Civil & Military Gazette (Lahore)

Daily Mail (London)

Dawn (Delhi)

Deccan Times (Hyderabad)

Eastern Times (Lahore)

Evening News (Bombay)

Hindustan Times (Delhi)

Inqilab (Lahore)

Leader (Allahabad)

Muslim Outlook (Lahore)

Nawa-i-Waqt (Lahore)

Observer (Lahore)

Pakistan Times (Lahore)

Star of India (Calcutta)

Statesman (Delhi)

Times of India (Delhi)

Zamindar (Lahore)

Index